THE CAMBRIDGE ECONOMIC HISTORY
OF THE UNITED STATES

VOLUME II

The Long Nineteenth Century

In the past several decades there has been a significant increase in our knowledge of the economic history of the United States. This has come about in part because of the developments in economic history, most particularly with the emergence of the statistical and analytical contributions of the "new economic history," and in part because of related developments in social, labor, and political history that have important implications for the understanding of economic change. *The Cambridge Economic History of the United States* has been designed to take full account of new knowledge in the subject, while at the same time offering a comprehensive survey of the history of economic activity and economic change in the United States, and in those regions whose economies have at certain times been closely allied to that of the United States: Canada and the Caribbean.

Volume II surveys the economic history of the United States, Canada, and the Caribbean during the long nineteenth century, a period of massive international and intercontinental movements of labor, capital, and commodities. The United States and Canada began the period as small but vigorous societies; the United States ended the period as the world's premier economic power. Five main themes frame the economic changes described in the volume: the migration of labor and capital from Europe, Asia, and Africa to the Americas; westward expansion; slavery and its aftermath; the process of industrialization; and the social consequences of economic growth that led to fundamental changes in the role of government. Other topics include: inequality, population, labor, agriculture, entrepreneurship, transportation, banking and finance, business law, and international trade.

Volume I covers the economic history of British North America and the early United States, and Volume III surveys U.S. economic history during the twentieth century.

Stanley L. Engerman is John H. Munro Professor of Economics and Professor of History at the University of Rochester.
The late Robert E. Gallman was Kenan Professor of Economics and History at the University of North Carolina at Chapel Hill.

THE CAMBRIDGE
ECONOMIC HISTORY
OF THE UNITED STATES

VOLUME II

The Long Nineteenth Century

Edited by

STANLEY L. ENGERMAN

ROBERT E. GALLMAN

CAMBRIDGE
UNIVERSITY PRESS

PUBLISHED BY THE PRESS SYNDICATE OF THE UNIVERSITY OF CAMBRIDGE
The Pitt Building, Trumpington Street, Cambridge, United Kingdom

CAMBRIDGE UNIVERSITY PRESS
The Edinburgh Building, Cambridge CB2 2RU, UK   http://www.cup.cam.ac.uk
40 West 20th Street, New York, NY 10011-4211, USA   http://www.cup.org
10 Stamford Road, Oakleigh, Melbourne 3166, Australia
Ruiz de Alarcón 13, 28014 Madrid, Spain

First published 2000

Printed in the United States of America

Typeface Garamond 11/13 pt.   *System* QuarkXPress [BTS]

A catalog record for this book is available from the British Library.

Library of Congress Cataloging in Publication Data is available
ISBN   0 521 55307 5   hardback

CONTENTS

v

PREFACE TO VOLUME II OF THE CAMBRIDGE ECONOMIC HISTORY OF THE UNITED STATES

Volume II of the *Cambridge Economic History of the United States* covers what we term the "long nineteenth century," from the passage of the Constitution until the start of World War I. In the context of world history this period begins with a global war and ends with another global war. Between these two events the world was relatively peaceful; but there were exceptions. Most important was the American Civil War, an exceptionally destructive event in terms of loss of life and property, leading to fundamental changes in political and institutional arrangements, most importantly the ending of legal slavery in the South. With the world otherwise relatively peaceful, the long nineteenth century was a period of massive international and intercontinental movements of labor, capital, and commodities. The United States and Canada began the period as small but vigorous societies. The United States ended the period as the world's premier economic power.

The long nineteenth century was a period of rapid economic expansion for both Canada and the United States. Five big themes frame the economic changes described in this volume. The first is the migration of labor and capital from Europe, Asia, and Africa to the Americas. A second, related theme lies in the North American frontier, a magnet for westward expansion, a source of opportunities and problems (including conflicts with Indians, described in Volume I). Third, for the United States, unlike Canada, the adjustment to slave emancipation was extensive and was not easily accomplished. Fourth, the process of industrialization was an important component of the structural changes that the American and Canadian economies underwent. And, fifth, the nature of the social consequences of economic growth led to fundamental changes in the role of the government.

There were, of course, major contrasts between Canada and the United States. At the end of the colonial experience, the U.S. economy was much larger. Thus, even though Canadian growth rates of population and income were high during the long nineteenth century, Canada did not catch up in either total income or total population. Geographic conditions and historical developments varied sufficiently to produce differences in the growth patterns of the two nations, but the fundamental forces at work – the opportunities presented by the continent's land, industrial opportunities, and factor inflows – were the same in the two cases and yielded similar trends.

Two of the chapters were not easily organized on a nineteenth-century basis. Business law had to be treated for the much longer period of the eighteenth to the twentieth century, and transportation, the nineteenth and twentieth. Note also that some parts of the nineteenth-century story are told in Volume I, for the American Indians and the British West Indies, for similar reasons.

Volume I had one chapter (by David Galenson) that dealt with economic growth in general. Volume II has expanded that theme into four chapters: a quantitative account of U.S. economic growth; a general account of Canadian economic growth (the only chapter devoted to Canada in this volume); a description of the effects of economic growth on the distribution of income and wealth; and a discussion of the social consequences of economic growth.

In several other respects the organization of Volume II is somewhat different from Volume I (and is more similar to Volume III). In Volume I the fundamental units of study tended to be geographical entities: the northern colonies, the southern colonies, the West Indies. Volume II adopts a more conventional framework. The big themes mentioned above are treated, directly or indirectly, in many of the chapters, but receive special treatment in the four listed in the previous paragraph as well as in chapters dealing with: population and labor, wage changes, agriculture, westward movement, slavery and its aftermath, industrialization, entrepreneurship, government tax and expenditure policy, transport, banking and financial institutions, international trade, international capital flows, and business law.

This volume, like all Cambridge histories, consists of essays that are intended to be syntheses of the existing state of knowledge, analysis, and debate. By their nature, they cannot be fully comprehensive. Their purpose is to introduce the reader to the subject and to provide her or him with a bibliographical essay that identifies directions for additional study. The audience sought is not one of deeply experienced specialists but of undergraduates, graduate students, and the general reader with an interest in pursuing the subjects of the essays.

The title of Peter Mathias's inaugural lecture (November 24, 1970) when he took the chair in economic history at Oxford was "Living with the Neighbors." The neighbors alluded to are economists and historians. In the United States economic history is not a separate discipline as it is in England; economic historians find places in departments of economics and history — most often, economics, these days. The problem of living with the neighbors nonetheless exists, since economic historians, whatever their academic affiliations, must live the intellectual life together, and historians and economists come at things from somewhat different directions. Another way to look at the matter is to regard living with the neighbors not as a problem but as a grand opportunity, since economists and historians have much to teach one another. Nonetheless, there is a persisting intellectual tension in the field between the interests of history and economics. The authors of the essays in these volumes are well aware of this tension and take it into account. The editors, in selecting authors, have tried to make room for the work of both disciplines.

Volume I was published according to schedule. That is not true of Volume II. Despite the editors' strong resolve to be ruthless in defense of our deadlines, we were obliged to delay publication to assure a comprehensive volume. On behalf of those whose dilatory ways slowed the publication of the volume, we apologize to those who conscientiously met their obligations and whose contributions saw the light of publication later than should have been the case. The slow sailors apologize to the fast sailors for slowing the convoy.

During the preparation of this volume we have been helped by the Department of Economics, University of North Carolina, the Department of Economics, University of Rochester, and the Faculty of Economics and Politics, University of Cambridge. From the very beginning we have benefited from the help, guidance, and general expertise of our editor, Frank Smith. In the final stages of production we have had the expert management of Camilla Knapp. The copyediting was done by John Kane and the indexing by Kathryn Torgeson.

An expanded version of Chapter 16, by Lance E. Davis and Robert J. Cull, was published under the title, *International Capital Markets and American Economic Growth, 1820–1914* (Cambridge: Cambridge University Press, 1994). An earlier version of Chapter 13, by Albert Fishlow, was published in Lance E. Davis, Richard A. Easterlin, William N. Parker, et al., *American Economic Growth: An Economist's History of the United States* (New York: Harper & Row, 1972).

Robert E. Gallman and I worked as co-editors of the three volumes of *The Cambridge Economic History of the United States* from their conception through to the publication of Volume I and the submission of final versions of the chapters for volumes II and III, prior to his death in November 1998. The contributors, as well as myself, greatly benefited from his knowledge, insights, and good nature in the preparation of these volumes.

Stanley L. Engerman

1

ECONOMIC GROWTH AND STRUCTURAL CHANGE IN THE LONG NINETEENTH CENTURY

ROBERT E. GALLMAN

INTRODUCTION

This chapter is concerned with quantitative features of the development of the American economy in the period between the late eighteenth century and World War I – the long nineteenth century. A reasonable place to begin is with measurements of the size of the economy. Since a central feature of any economy is production, size is appropriately measured by aggregate output. Other indicators, such as population and geographic extent, are considered below.

The conventional measures of aggregate output are the national product – that is, output produced by factors of production owned by Americans – and the domestic product – output produced by factors of production domiciled in the United States. The proper index to select depends upon whether one thinks of the United States as the sum of all Americans or as a geographic entity. We are interested in the history of the people of the United States, and therefore the national product is the more appropriate concept. It underlies most of the measurements treated in this chapter; in practice the choice matters little, however, since in the years under examination the national product and the domestic product were virtually identical. A more important question is the extent to which these conventional measures properly describe levels of output and changes in output over time, a question set aside for the moment but treated later in this essay.

SIZE AND GROWTH OF
THE AMERICAN ECONOMY

Size

The American gross national product probably ran around $144 million just before the Revolution (Table 1.3). (A wide margin for error must be allowed.) By modern standards, that is a small value, considerably less than half as great as Helene Curtis's sales in the quarter ending August 31, 1995. If we allow for price changes, gross national product in 1774, expressed in prices of 1995, would run roughly $2.8 billion. That is less than four-tenths of the current annual output of the state with the smallest total output, Wyoming, and less than one-third greater than A&P's sales in the twelve weeks ending September 9, 1995.

By the standards of the world of 1774, however, the American economy was not small. It yielded a gross national product that was probably more than one-third that of Great Britain (excluding Ireland) (see Table 1.1). Great Britain was then undergoing an agricultural revolution and was in the early stages of the Industrial Revolution; it was one of the most powerful nations in the world, economically and politically. The American economy was smaller than the British – and, no doubt, smaller than the Spanish or French, in Europe, and the Chinese or Indian, in Asia – but it was by no means tiny. It may very well have been as large as the well-developed Dutch and Belgian economies, taken together.

Growth

Between 1774 and 1909 the American real gross national product increased about 175-fold, or at an average rate of 3.9 percent per year (Table 1.3). Higher rates have been recorded in recent times, but only for much shorter periods. In the nineteenth century, the frontier economies of Australia and Canada grew about as fast as the American, and the Argentine economy, considerably faster. (See Table 1.2.) Again, the periods these records cover are substantially shorter than the 135 years encompassed by the American record. Although it is possible that higher rates of growth were recorded by one or more of these three economies over the extended period 1774–1909, the rates would be computed on very small bases: for example, in 1774 the entire population of Australia consisted of a small number of aborigines – Captain Cook had arrived only four years before –

Table 1.1. *Aggregate product in various countries, compared with aggregate American product, various dates*

	Current prices		1990 Geary-Khamis dollars			
	1774	1840	1850	1870	1890	1913
1. *Western Europe*						
a. United Kingdom	2.7	1.3–1.5	1.42	0.97	0.67	0.41
b. France		1.7	1.43	0.73	0.44	0.28
c. Germany			0.69	0.45	0.33	0.28
d. Belgium			0.19	0.14	0.10	0.06
e. Netherlands			0.14	0.10	0.07	0.05
f. Ireland			N.A.	0.07	0.03	0.02
g. Denmark			0.06	0.04	0.03	0.02
h. Norway			0.04	0.02	0.02	0.01
i. Sweden			0.11	0.07	0.05	0.03
j. Finland			N.A.	0.02	0.01	0.01
k. Italy			N.A.	0.42	0.24	0.18
l. Switzerland			N.A.	0.06	N.A.	0.03
m. Portugal			0.10	0.05	0.04	0.02
n. Spain			0.40	0.23	0.15	0.09
o. Czechoslovakia			0.22	0.12	0.08	0.05
p. Hungary			N.A.	0.07	N.A.	0.03
q. Austria			0.15	0.09	0.06	0.05
r. Totals (excl. Switzerland and Hungary)			N.A.	3.52	2.32	1.56
2. *Eastern Europe*						
a. USSR			N.A.	0.85	0.47	0.45
3. *Australia, New Zealand, and the Americas*						
a. Australia			0.03	0.06	0.07	0.05
b. New Zealand			N.A.	0.02	0.01	0.01
c. Canada			0.07	0.06	0.05	0.06
d. Argentina			N.A.	0.02	0.03	0.06
e. Brazil			0.12	0.07	0.05	0.04
f. Mexico			0.12	0.07	0.05	0.04
g. Chile			N.A.	N.A.	N.A.	0.02
h. Colombia			N.A.	N.A.	N.A.	0.01
i. Peru			N.A.	N.A.	N.A.	0.01
j. Venezuela			N.A.	N.A.	N.A.	0.01
k. Totals (excl. Chile, Colombia, Peru, Venezuela				0.30	0.26	0.26

Table 1.1 *(cont.)*

	Current prices		1990 Geary-Khamis dollars			
	1774	1840	1850	1870	1890	1913
4. *Asia*						
a. China			N.A.	1.90	1.09	0.58
b. India			2.42	1.20	0.66	0.32
c. Indonesia			0.36	0.19	0.12	0.09
d. Thailand			N.A.	0.04	0.02	0.01
e. Japan			N.A.	0.26	0.18	0.13
f. Totals				3.59	2.07	1.13
Grand Totals (Σ of 1r, 2a, 3k, 4f)				8.26	5.12	3.40

Note: The table should be read in the following way: in 1774 the aggregate product of Great Britain (excl. Ireland) was roughly 2.7 times as large as the aggregate product of the Thirteen Colonies, when both aggregate products are expressed in prices of 1774; in 1913, aggregate product in the United Kingdom was roughly 41 percent as large as the aggregate product of the United States, when both aggregate products are expressed in Geary-Khamis dollars of 1990. Aggregate products refer to GNP, in 1774 and 1840, and to GDP, in 1850–1913.

Source: 1774: The estimate is based on Alice Hanson Jones, *Wealth of a Nation To Be* (New York, 1980), 39, 68. The American per capita income level is the higher of Jones's two estimates, on the authority of Weiss. Thomas Weiss, "U.S. Labor Force Estimates and Economic Growth, 1800–1860," in Robert E. Gallman and John Joseph Wallis (eds.), *American Economic Growth and Standards of Living before the Civil War* (Chicago, 1992), 32. See also, Lance E. Davis, Richard A. Easterlin, William N. Parker, et al., *American Economic Growth, An Economist's History of the United States* (New York, 1972), 24; 1840: Derived from Gallman, "Gross National Product in the United States 1834–1909," in Dorothy S. Brady (ed.), *Output, Employment, and Productivity in the United States After 1800*, Studies in Income and Wealth, Volume 30 (New York, 1966), 5, 26; 1850–1913: Angus Maddison, *Monitoring the World Economy, 1820–1992* (Paris, 1995), 180, 182, 184, 186, 188, 190. The Geary-Khamis procedure yields multilateral comparisons. See Maddison, 162–63.

and the total European population of Argentina in the same year was probably no more than 160,000. Canada was larger, but not much larger. The U.S. economy remained much bigger than the other three, down to World War I: American real Gross Domestic Product in 1913 was almost six times as large as the sum of the real GDPs of Argentina, Australia, and Canada (Table 1.1).

These four countries shared several characteristics. They were colonized by Europeans (and Africans, in the case of the United States), their native

Table 1.2. *Average annual rates of change of real GDP (1990 Geary-Khamis dollars), nineteen countries, 1820–1913*

Argentina	[6.0%]
U.S.A.	4.1
Canada	(3.8)
Australia	[3.5]
Netherlands	2.4
Germany	2.4
Denmark	2.3
Belgium	2.1
Finland	2.1
Brazil	2.0
U.K.	2.0
Austria	1.9
Norway	1.9
Sweden	1.9
Italy	1.6
Mexico	1.6
Spain	1.4
Japan	1.2
Ireland	0.6

Note: ( ) = 1850–1913; [ ] = 1870–1913
Source: Derived from Maddison, *Monitoring the World Economy*, 180, 182, 184, 188.

populations were small and easy to brush aside, and having done so, the colonizers were left with abundant, rich natural resources. All four countries then experienced rapid population and economic growth. Rapid growth simply began earliest in the colonies that ultimately became the United States.

No European economy grew so fast for so long as did that of the United States before World War I. For example, the British growth rate ran only about 2.2 percent per year from circa 1770 to 1913. The difference between Britain and the United States with respect to the pace of growth had important consequences. In 1774 the British current price GNP was almost three times the American; in 1840 it was only about one and a half times as great, while in 1913, the entire United Kingdom had a real GDP only about 41 percent as large as the American real GDP. As time passed, the relative standing of the two economies had reversed.

By the beginning of World War I the United States was by far the largest producer of goods and services in the world. Aggregate annual output was greater in the United States than in the three main World War I belligerents – the United Kingdom, Germany, and France – combined. In fact, at that time it was roughly two-thirds as large as the total GDP of *all* of the leading Western European economies (Table 1.1).

The Price Level

Most of the preceding remarks refer to measures of real output. Over the long term, U.S. real and nominal output grew at approximately the same rates (Table 1.3). That is, prices seem to have been at roughly the same level just before the Revolution as just before World War I. This statement is subject to well-known qualifications, arising from the changing composition of aggregate output as time passed. Many items produced in large amounts before the Revolution (e.g., oil lamps) were either not produced at all in the early twentieth century, or in very small quantities. Similarly, important products of the years just before World War I (e.g., electric lamps) were completely unknown in 1774. Price indices that cover many years thus pose serious problems of construction and interpretation. Nonetheless, there can be little doubt that American experience with the long-term drift of the price level was very different in the long nineteenth century from what it has been since. In the first period there was little trend (prices rose about 0.05 percent per year); in the second, the trend has been strongly upward, the index rising at a rate of about 3.4 percent per year. In 1991 the price level was about 13.5 times as high as it had been on the eve of World War I.

Although the trend in nineteenth-century prices was approximately zero, there were periods of marked inflation and periods of marked deflation. Table 1.3 is not ideally suited to deal with this issue. Nonetheless, the inflations associated with the French-British wars, the boom following the War of 1812, and the inflation of the Civil War all make their imprints on the record in the table. So do the periods of price decline after the collapse of the 1819 boom and after the Civil War. The reflation of the world economy after the gold discoveries of the 1890s also appears. (See Rockoff, Chap. 14, this volume for a more comprehensive treatment of this subject.)

Table 1.3. *U.S. gross national product, current prices and prices of 1860, 1774–1909, and rates of change*

	Panel A: GNP (Mil. $)		
Years	Current prices	Price index (1860 = 100)	1860 prices
1774	144	(97)	149
1793	(317)	(119)	266
1800	(544)	(151)	360
1807	(680)	(139)	489
1810	(765)	(148)	517
1820	(1,079)	(141)	765
1830	(1,229)	(111)	1,107
1834/43	(1,803)	(112)	1,610
1839/48	1,951	97.4	2,003
1844/53	2,649	100.8	2,628
1849/58	3,474	102.3	3,397
1859			4,226
1869			5,547
1869/78	8,009	120.7	6,633
1874/83	9,736	111.8	8,711
1879/88	11,467	104.4	10,987
1884/93	12,536	97.1	12,915
1889/98	13,464	91.9	14,655
1894/03	16,335	93.1	17,546
1899/08	22,588	103.1	21,903
1909			25,968

Panel B: Average annual short-term rates of change, GNP in prices of 1860	
1774–1793	3.1%
1793–1800	4.4
1800–1807	4.5
1807–1810	1.9
1810–1820	4.0
1820–1830	3.8
1830–1834/43	4.2
1834/43–1839/48	4.5
1839/48–1844/53	5.6
1844/53–1849/58	5.3
1849/58–1859	4.1
1859–1869	2.9
1869–1869/78	4.1
1869/78–1874/83	5.6
1874/83–1879/88	4.8
1879/88–1884/93	3.3

Table 1.3. *(cont.)*

Panel B: Average annual short-term rates of change, GNP in prices of 1860	
1884/93–1889/98	2.6
1889/98–1894/1903	3.7
1894/03–1899/1908	4.5
1899/08–1909	3.1

Panel C: Average annual long-term rates of change, GNP in prices of 1860	
1774–1800	3.5%
1800–1834/43	3.9
1834/43–1869	4.2
1869–1909	3.9
1774–1909	3.9

Note: The estimates for the later years are more reliable than those for the earlier years. See the bibliographic essay. Bracketed price index numbers refer to the cost of living, not to the GNP deflator; parenthetical GNP figures were derived by use of a cost of living index, rather than by the more appropriate GNP deflator.

Source: *GNP, 1834/43–1909, 1860 prices, and 1839/48–1909, current prices*: Taken from Robert E. Gallman, "Gross National Product in the United States, 1834–1909," in Dorothy S. Brady (ed.), *Output, Employment, and Productivity in the United States After 1800*, Studies in Income and Wealth, Vol. 30 (New York, 1966) 26 (and underlying worksheets), adjusted to incorporate inventory changes, the latter computed from Robert E. Gallman, "The United States Capital Stock in the Nineteenth Century," in Stanley L. Engerman and Robert E. Gallman (eds.), *Long-Term Factors in American Economic Growth*, Studies in Income and Wealth, vol. 51 (Chicago, 1986), 204 and Robert E. Gallman, "American Economic Growth Before the Civil War: The Testimony of the Capital Stock Estimates," in Robert E. Gallman and John Joseph Wallis (eds.), *American Economic Growth and Standards of Living Before the Civil War* (Chicago, 1992), 94 (and underlying worksheets). The years 1834/43 through 1859 are census years. For example, the year 1859 refers to the 12 months from June 1, 1859, to May 31, 1860. The current price figures for 1839/48, 1844/53, and 1849/58 are actually 3-year averages, rather than decade averages: 1839, 1844, 1849; 1844, 1849, 1854; 1849, 1854, 1859. *Price Index, 1839/48–1909*: Computed by dividing current price GNP by GNP in prices of 1860. *GNP, 1774–1830, prices of 1860*: The figure for 1834/43 was extrapolated to the earlier years on real GDP estimates (1840 prices) drawn from Thomas Weiss, "U.S. Labor Force Estimates and Economic Growth, 1800–1860," in Gallman and Wallis (eds.), *American Economic Growth*, 27, 31, 32. The resulting estimates are treated as calendar year estimates. *Price Index, 1774–1834/43*: David and Solar cost of living index, base 1860 (Paul A. David and Peter Solar," A Bicentenary Contribution to the History of the Cost of Living in America," *Research in Economic History*, 2 (1977). *Current Price GNP, 1793–1834/43*: GNP in 1860 prices multiplied by the price index. *Current Price GNP, 1774*: See source note to Table 1.1.

Variations in the Rate of Growth

Although there was virtually no trend in the rate of change of aggregate output between the Revolution and World War I (Panel C of Table 1.3), there were important short-term changes, many of an episodic character (Panel B of Table 1.3). The data in Table 1.3 are not well devised to show short-term movements in the economy – for example, the estimates for the years before 1834 (except for those for 1793 and 1807) make no allowance for variations in the level of employment of inputs, nor do they take into account differences in the level of crop production from one year to the next occasioned by variations in weather, the ravages of insects, crop diseases, etc. The estimates were devised for the study of long-term trends, not for short-term changes. Nonetheless, some of the short-term variations exhibited by this series for the early period probably do reflect real phenomena. For example, the rate of growth shown for the period 1774 to 1793 is relatively low, no doubt due to the effects of the Revolutionary War and the troubles of the Confederation years. It is a little surprising that it is not lower. The years of prosperity for American merchants, shippers, and ship-builders during the hostilities between France and England show up clearly in the table (1793–1800 and 1800–1807) as a time during which the growth rate was high. The rate drops off sharply in the period 1807–1810, likely a consequence of events leading up to the War of 1812.

More reliance can be placed on the series beginning in 1834. The data show clearly the surge of growth during the 20 to 30 years before the Civil War, a surge usually associated with the beginning of industrialization, the westward movement, and the first great nineteenth-century inflow of European migrants. The impact of the Civil War is registered in the low rate of growth for the interval 1859–1869, 2.9 percent per year (a rate that would undoubtedly have been lower still, if the period had been limited to the war years), and the Great Depression of the 1890s made its mark in an even lower rate for the period 1884/93 through 1889/98, 2.6 percent per year. The so-called Great Depression of 1873–1879 does not show up in the aggregate statistics, partly because the decade averages in Table 1.3 are not well designed to catch its effects, but partly also because the quantitative record for the 1870s does indeed suggest that there was a strong upward movement of output in that period. The seeming conflict between the evidence on vigorous output growth and persistent, deep unemployment has received much scholarly attention, without being resolved.

Several of the fluctuations in output described above are the economic consequences of political or military events. Others are due to economic processes that can be regarded as systematic. Every market economy experiences undulations in economic activity. Some – seasonal variations – do not influence annual data; others – business cycles – are difficult to trace in annual data, and even more so in decade-average data of the type contained in Table 1.3, since nineteenth-century business cycles were typically short – three to five years, peak to peak or trough to trough. Important collapses, such as the Great Depression of the 1890s, affect annual series, and even decade-average series, but less cataclysmic events are difficult to date and to measure.

There is a third form of economic fluctuation – the long swing, or Kuznets cycle, of an amplitude of fifteen to twenty-five years, peak to peak or trough to trough – that occurred during this period. It is observable in annual data and in decade averages of the sort figuring in Table 1.3. It has been subject to analysis by Simon Kuznets, Moses Abramovitz, Richard Easterlin, Brinley Thomas, and Douglass North, among many others. All five see these fluctuations as central to the story of American nineteenth-century economic growth.

North's account relates exclusively to the period before the Civil War. To North, the impetus to American antebellum growth from 1815 onward was British demand for American cotton, a demand that arose out of the Industrial Revolution. In the two decades immediately preceding the Civil War, cotton accounted for almost one-half of the value of American exports. The cycling of the Southern economy was a consequence of the process by which planters responded to the British demands. The expansion of the British economy gradually raised the price of raw cotton and eventually encouraged planters to move westward onto new, fertile land, to clear the land, and to begin to produce. There were also investments in social overhead capital, such as railroads, that went along with the westward expansion. When such investments matured, cotton hit the market in unusually large amounts, prices fell, and investment by planters ceased, not to begin again until the expansion of British demand caught up with the ability of Americans to produce, and cotton prices again began to rise.

According to North, the cycle influenced the rest of the American economy through Southern expenditure of cotton earnings. Planters bought manufactures from the Northeast and food supplies from the Northwest. During the expansion phase of the cycle, these demands were pronounced, and they stimulated growth in the North; during the contraction phase, they fell, both because planters' incomes fell and because planters diverted labor from the production of low-priced cotton to the production of food to feed their slave labor forces, and therefore did not need to buy as much from the Northwest. North's transmission mechanism – particularly the posited links between the West and the South – has been subject to a variety of serious criticisms, as have aspects of the fit of his model to the data, but his account of the impact of cotton demand on the Southern economy remains compelling.

Kuznets, Abramovitz, Easterlin, and Thomas focus chiefly on the migration of European labor and capital to the United States, and, thus, their stories are particularly relevant to the period from the second half of the 1820s onward. Thomas's view is that the long swing was generated by British activities. British labor and capital were induced to migrate overseas during periods of deep and enduring depression in Britain. In turn, British investment of capital and labor stimulated booms in the recipient countries, of which the United States was the chief. These booms involved investment in social overhead capital with long gestation periods. Thus the booms were extended, running roughly 8 to 12 years, rather than the 1.5 to 2.5 years of the standard business cycle.

Kuznets believed that the impetus for these developments came not from England but from the United States. In a very influential paper, Easterlin built and tested a model that was intended to describe both long-term and trend-cycle influences on international migration. In brief, his argument is that the long-term forces at work were essentially European demographic forces, which in turn reflected the diffusion of modernization across Europe. Modernization stimulated population swarming, which, with a substantial lag, led to clogged European labor markets, which in turn stimulated internal and overseas migration. The specific timing of the long swings, however, depended upon developments in the United States. Easterlin's paper represents a test of Kuznets's hypothesis, a test that the hypothesis survived. The debate, however, is by no means closed. Papers continue to appear, setting out a variety of explanations of the long swing, and some denying that the long swing, as a systematic phenomenon, existed.

The manner in which domestic and international factors figured in the American long swings was developed in particularly persuasive form by Kuznets, Abramovitz, and Easterlin. Although their accounts differ in detail, in each a recovery from a severe depression in the United States (e.g., the depression of 1839–1843) eventually led to tightening labor markets, which drew in workers from abroad, easing the American labor constraint and encouraging further investment, particularly in housing for the new workers. The boom also called for investment in social-overhead capital such as railways. Railways, in turn, were attractive projects for British investors, and the foreign capital thus called in to the United States solved at least temporarily the balance of payments problems that would otherwise have developed from the pronounced increase in imports arising from the boom. Expansion periodically slowed, in response to inventory adjustments, but these adjustments were relatively mild. Ultimately, there was a major collapse, leading to a deep and long depression, and to a slowing of immigration.

The long swing as an interaction between domestic and international phenomena seems to have been confined to the period before World War I, which ended the phase of mass migration for several decades. According to Easterlin, however, there has remained a modified domestic element, in the form of the Baby Boom, the Baby Bust, and further echo effects. (See Easterlin, Chap. 9, Volume III of this series.)

Factor Inputs and Productivity

The general phenomenon of rapid growth of output during the long nineteenth century was chiefly a consequence of the expansion of the supplies of factors of production. As part of the settlement with Great Britain after the Revolutionary War, the United States received enormous tracts of western land that the people of lower Canada had regarded as their own and that they had been exploiting in pursuit of the fur trade (see McInnis, Chap. 2, this volume). This cession represented a very large gain for the new country, and a very large loss for its northern neighbor. In 1803 the Louisiana territory was purchased, which almost doubled the area of the United Sates. Another 72,003 square miles – consisting chiefly of Florida – were obtained in 1819 from Spain, while in the 1840s the acquisition of Texas, Oregon, and the Mexican Cession added another 1,204,740 square miles, a territory almost half again as large as was gained with the Louisiana Purchase. The Gadsden Purchase (1853), Alaska (1867), and Hawaii (1898) rounded out American acquisitions of the eighteenth and nineteenth centuries. By 1900 the United States encompassed 3,002,387 square miles of land and water, almost three and a half times as much territory as it held after the post-Revolutionary agreement with Britain.[1]

Population grew even faster, from about 2.354 million in 1774 to about 5.297 million in 1799, despite the losses of the war and the emigration of large numbers of loyalists (roughly 100,000). By the beginning of the Civil War population was almost six times as large as it had been in 1799, and by 1909, three times as large again. All told, then, population expanded almost fortyfold between 1774 and 1909.

The labor force increased even more strikingly – by a factor of over 48 in the same period. The rise in the labor force participation rate thus implied was due partly to the employment of women and children in the industrial factories built during the nineteenth century.[2] It was also partly due to a change in the structure of the population, arising from the effects of immigration and, to a lesser degree, to the effects of a decline in the birth rate. As a consequence of these two developments, the average age of the population increased, and the fraction in the age groups that had high labor force participation rates went up. The labor force, then, grew a good deal faster than the population. (See, also, Haines and Margo, Chaps. 4 and 5, this volume.)

Finally, the capital stock increased at even higher rates. Capital more than tripled between 1774 and 1799, increased more than 16-fold between then and the Civil War, and a bit more than another eightfold, between 1860 and 1909. In toto, the capital stock increased all of 388-fold between 1774 and 1909.

Supplies of inputs, then, grew very rapidly. The question arises as to what part of the growth of output was due to the growth of inputs, and what part arose out of improvements in input productivity. The conventional way to answer such a question is to weight the rate of growth of each factor by the factor's percentage share in aggregate income, sum up the results for the three factors, and subtract the sum from the rate of growth of aggregate output. Productivity change is taken as a residual.

The theoretical warrant for this approach may be found in the literature on production functions, a literature filled with qualifications and doubts. A commonsense interpretation of the procedure is to say that if the rates of growth of the three factors are to be averaged, for purposes of determining

---

[1] Including various occupied territories outside the United States – Puerto Rico, the Phillipines, Guam, American Samoa, the Canal Zone, and the Corn Islands – the United States held 3,735,002 square miles at the outbreak of World War I.

[2] The rise due to this factor was more apparent than real, since it was a consequence of a definition of laboring that leaves out household work.

the contribution of inputs to the growth of aggregate output, then the average employed must be weighted average, and the weights should reflect the relative importance of the three factors. In the context of production, importance may be taken to be the fraction of output paid to each factor, since the payment represents a judgment as to the contribution of each factor to production. (At least this is true in competitive equilibrium.)

Since not all laborers are equally important to production – and the same may be said of individual pieces of capital or of land – one can make a case that more than three inputs should be recognized, and that more than three weights should be established. The point is a good one and will come up for subsequent discussion. For the present, however, three factors will be all that will be considered. Furthermore, since the output and input series for 1774 are particularly chancy, the analysis will be confined to the years subsequent to 1774. Finally, the input series represent supplies of inputs available, rather than supplies of inputs actually employed. The measurements of productivity change – at least for the period from 1834 onward (see above) – therefore include shifts arising out of changes in levels of employment as well as changes in the intensity of use of factors. Whether intensity went up or down over the long run is not perfectly clear. The end of slavery tended to reduce labor intensity, as did the modest downward movements in the industrial work week, but the shift in the structure of the economy, which increased the relative importance of industrial activity, must have raised it (as it did the intensity of use of capital.) The estimates of productivity change must, therefore, be interpreted with caution. It seems doubtful, however, that changes in employment levels or the intensity of factor use are responsible for a large part of measured trends in productivity in the long nineteenth century.

In the nineteenth century, growth of U.S. output was apparently dominated by the increase of supplies of factor inputs. The rates of change of these inputs, taken together, accounted for between about 82 and 85 percent of the growth rate of output (see Table 1.4); productivity change, of course, accounted for the residual, 15 to 18 percent. Productivity seems to have contributed more to the expansion of the economy after 1840 than before, but the contrast between the two periods is not great. It is certain that in the years after World War I productivity had a larger relative significance. (See Abramovitz and David, Chap. 1, Volume III of this series.) It should be said, however, that the increase in *relative* importance is only partly due to improvements in productivity growth as time passed; it is also partly a consequence of the lower factor input rates of growth after World War I: the same productivity gain in each of the two periods

Table 1.4. *Rates of growth of real GNP , labor, capital, land, and total factor productivity, 1800–1900*

Panel A: Rates of growth			
(1) Real GNP	(2) Labor	(3) Capital	(4) Land
1800–1840 3.92	3.09	3.98	2.80
1840–1900 4.10	2.72	4.96	2.17

Panel B: Computation of rates of change of total factor productivity				
Weighted rates of growth			(4)	(5) Rates of growth of total factor productivity
(1) Labor	(2) Capital	(3) Land	Sum, Col (1)–(3)	
1880–1840 2.10	1.15	0.08	3.33	0.59
1840–1900 1.85	1.44	0.07	3.36	0.74

Panel C: Contributions (%) to output growth			
Growth of			
(1) Labor	(2) Capital	(3) Land	(4) Productivity
1800–1840 54%	29%	2%	15%
1840–1900 45	35	2	18

Note: The real GNP estimates refer to the calendar year 1800, the average real GNP for census years 1834 through 1843 (centered on calendar 1839), and the average real GNP for calendar years 1894 through 1903 (centered on 1898.5). The capital and land estimates refer to 1799, 1840, and 1900.
Source: Panel A: GNP: See the notes to Table 1.3; Capital: Gallman, "American Economic Growth," 88 [Table 2.4, Panel A, Column (3)]; Labor and Land: Ibid, 97; Panel B: Weights: Ibid; Rates of Growth of Total Factor Productivity: Panel A, Col. (1) minus Panel B, Col. (4); Panel C: Panel B, Col. (1), (2), (3), and (5) divided by Panel A, Col. (1). The results multiplied by 100.

would account for a larger share of output growth in the period in which inputs were expanding the more slowly – the later period.

Productivity is taken as a residual and therefore its measurement is affected by many factors, including the precise definitions of inputs and outputs adopted (discussed above), and errors of estimate with respect to the rates of growth of inputs and output. Given the definitions used in this chapter, the forces that are likely to have been most important in the nineteenth century (other than errors) are four: improvements in technology (that is, improvements in production processes and the development of new products), improvements in efficiency (that is, improvements in the allocation of factors of production), improvements in human capital, and economies of scale. Individual chapters in this series (see Margo, Chap. 5, and Engerman and Sokoloff, Chap. 9, this volume) are devoted to the first, the third, and the fourth forces; the second will be treated further, below.

Changes in the relative importance of the three factors of production also have some interest. Land supply, because of the small weight assigned to it, but particularly because of its relatively slow rate of growth (compared with the other factors), contributes little. But that statement surely understates the true importance of the land factor and exhibits the severe limitations of this style of analysis. It was, after all, the enormous potential of the continent that encouraged the high rates of fertility and immigration by which the population grew so rapidly, the high rates of internal migration, by which it was more efficiently distributed, the enormous recorded investment, and the technical change that contributed to the improvement in productivity. The land estimates, which describe only the physical volume of land in production, bear on the direct effects of the expansion of the land supply, but leave out of account these indirect effects.

The shifts in the relative importance of the other two factors, labor and capital, speak to an important development, the extraordinary rate at which capital was formed in the nineteenth century. The share of capital in the responsibility for the expansion of output is shown to grow rapidly, relative to the share of labor. At the same time, the increases in the supply of capital per worker must have had favorable consequences for labor productivity and, thus, labor income – there was almost ten times as much capital per worker at the end of the long nineteenth century as at its beginning. Furthermore, the capital was new and therefore near the frontier of best practice techniques – between 1870 and World War I roughly two-thirds of the capital stock was ten years old or younger.[3] Finally, the great

---

[3] In part the rapid growth represented recovery from a decade – the 1860s – during which the increase of the capital stock was unusually low. But the rate of growth before the war was even higher than it became after 1870, and the average age of capital in 1860 must have been even lower than it was to become toward the end of the century.

speed with which the capital stock grew meant that the redeployment of capital to meet new and unexpected opportunities could be made quickly, so that the distribution of capital among alternative uses should have been remarkably efficient.

THE PERFORMANCE OF THE AMERICAN ECONOMY

Concepts

The scale of the economy is an important phenomenon, but most students of growth focus more attention on the level of output generated per member of the population. The reason is clear enough. Economics is concerned centrally with the allocation of scarce resources among alternative uses to produce output to meet human wants. In the per capita real product measure, the output of the economy is compared with the number of people to be supported, and the size of the ratio is a crude index of the success of the economy – its performance. Many criticisms of the per capita output (income) measure have been made, and they will be entertained shortly. But it is useful to begin with the per capita measure and to see how far it can take us toward understanding American economic growth in the long nineteenth century. We can then consider the shortcomings of the concept.

During a substantial part of the long nineteenth century a fraction of the population was enslaved, and during a shorter part of this period another fraction was in indentured servitude. A case has been made that these exploited workers – at least the slaves – should not be counted in the denominator of per capita national product. Rather, their consumption should be treated as intermediate production – like the coal used to run the industrial steam engines – and subtracted from the aggregate output. The remainder should then be divided by the number of free persons to get the measure of per capita output in the economy.

Such a choice represents a decision to evaluate the economy in terms of the views of the slaveholders, for whom the slaves represented a means to the end of planter well-being. But if we look at the economy from the standpoint of the late twentieth century, and if we are interested in economic performance, clearly we must see slaves and servants as part of the population being supported by the economy, and the performance of the economy must be judged not by how much output there was to divide among free persons, but how much there was to divide among all. That is, appraisal must be in terms of modern standards. The fact that the incomes of slaves and servants were low is irrelevant; the incomes of some free persons were also low – some as low as or lower than that of the slaves and servants. The way to deal with this issue is not by dropping the poor from the population for whom per capita income measures are to be made, but by analyzing the income distribution of the population and changes thereto (for which, see Pope, Chap. 3, this volume).

More relevant is an aspect of the qualitative differences among the lives of the free, the servants, and the slaves. The free may have been imperfectly free, but they were freer than indentured servants, and indentured servants in turn were better off in this respect than slaves since, if they only managed to live through servitude – a matter of four to seven years – they would become free, while the prospects for freedom faced by most slaves were negligible for most of the period in which slavery existed. The way to deal with this issue is to put a consumption value on freedom and to assign this consumption value to all free persons. Then when indentured servitude died out, the measure of output would record a gain, and when the slaves were emancipated, the output index would record a bigger gain. With such an adjustment the big drop in the rate of growth of recorded output between 1859 and 1869, referred to above, would be moderated and, perhaps, turned into an increase.[4] What is not so obvious is how one could make an index of the consumption value of freedom. (For more on these issues, see Engerman, Chap. 8, this volume.)

Per Capita Income (Output)

In August of 1793 Thomas Cooper traveled from England to the United States, with the object of considering the virtues of resettling there with his family. He returned to Great Britain in 1794 to collect his family and to settle up his accounts before emigrating, and while there he published a little book on America in the form of letters to an English friend. The first of these letters begins:

---

[4] The issue is more complex than these comments suggest. There are also distributional considerations. The gains achieved by slaves with emancipation were paired with losses to slaveholders. See Engerman, Chap. 8, this volume.

While land is so cheap, and labor is so dear, it will be too hazardous a speculation to embark a capital in any branch of manufacture which has not hitherto
been actually pursued with success in this country. Even though these obstacles
did not present themselves, I should fear the common lot of inventors and first
improvers; they usually enrich the country and impoverish themselves . . .[5]

In expressing these sentiments, Cooper ran none of the risks he believed
innovators bore; it would be hard to find a written work by a visitor that
did not make the identical points. Americans, too, spoke of the extent of
the land and the impact it had on American economy and society. Benjamin
Franklin believed the abundance of land led to universal and early marriage
and large families. Tench Coxe stressed American comparative advantage
and the structure of the American economy. (Franklin's ideas are taken up
in Haines, Chap. 4; Coxe's, in Lipsey, Chap. 15, both in this volume.) For
present purposes the point that needs to be drawn from Cooper's little book
is that in the late eighteenth century American land was abundant and labor
scarce; land was cheap and labor dear. Wages were relatively high, the
distribution of income among free families was relatively egalitarian, as
compared with the distribution in England, and income per capita – the
variable of central interest here – was also high.

How high is not perfectly clear, but Alice Jones estimated that before
the Revolution American per capita income was perhaps "on a par" with
that of England and Wales, but more likely somewhat below the English-
Welsh level.[6] The data for the nineteenth century indicate that the gap
between the two economies – the comparison now being drawn between
the United States and the United Kingdom – was roughly 30 percent, at
least down to 1870, with the advantage on the side of the British. Thereafter, American performance improved the faster, and by 1913 the United
States probably had a GDP per capita slightly higher than the one achieved
by the United Kingdom (see Table 1.5).

As to the rest of Europe for which estimates are available, income
levels were generally below the American level (exceptions: Belgium
and the Netherlands) throughout, and sometimes very much below. For
example, late in the nineteenth century, average income in Russia was
roughly one-fourth the American level, and in Italy and Finland, less than
half. Furthermore, almost without exception the European countries were

[5] Thomas Cooper, *Some Information Respecting America, Collected by Thomas Cooper, Late of Manchester*
(Dublin, 1794, Reprinted New York, 1969), 1, 2.
[6] Alice Hanson Jones, *Wealth of a Nation to Be: The American Colonies on the Eve of the Revolution* (New
York, 1980), 68–69.

Table 1.5. *Aggregate product per capita in various countries, compared with agrregate American product per capita, various dates*

	Current prices		1990 Geary-Khamis dollars			
	1774	1840	1850	1870	1890	1913
1. *Western Europe*						
a. United Kingdom	1.25	1.20–1.40	1.30	1.33	1.21	0.95
b. France		0.78	0.92	0.76	0.69	0.65
c. Germany			0.81	0.78	0.75	0.72
d. Belgium			0.99	1.07	0.99	0.78
e. Netherlands			1.04	1.07	0.92	0.74
f. Ireland			N.A.	0.72	0.66	0.51
g. Denmark			0.93	0.78	0.71	0.71
h. Norway			0.59	0.53	0.48	0.43
i. Sweden			0.71	0.68	0.61	0.58
j. Finland			N.A.	0.45	0.39	0.39
k. Italy			N.A.	0.60	0.48	0.47
l. Switzerland			N.A.	0.88	N.A.	0.79
m. Portugal			0.60	0.44	0.36	0.26
n. Spain			0.63	0.56	0.54	0.42
o. Czechoslovakia			0.59	0.47	0.44	0.39
p. Hungary			N.A.	0.52	N.A.	0.40
q. Austria			0.91	0.76	0.72	0.66
2. *Eastern Europe*						
a. USSR			N.A.	0.56	0.27	0.28
3. *Australia, New Zealand, and the Americas*						
a. Australia			1.69	1.55	1.41	1.04
b. New Zealand			N.A.	1.27	1.11	0.98
c. Canada			0.70	0.66	0.66	0.79
d. Argentina			N.A.	0.53	0.63	0.72
e. Brazil			0.39	0.30	0.23	0.16
f. Mexico			0.37	0.29	0.29	0.28
g. Chile			N.A.	N.A.	N.A.	0.50
h. Colombia			N.A.	N.A.	N.A.	0.23
i. Peru			N.A.	N.A.	N.A.	0.20
j. Venezuela			N.A.	N.A.	N.A.	0.21
4. *Asia*						
a. China			N.A.	0.21	0.18	0.13
b. India			0.30	0.23	0.18	0.12
c. Indonesia			0.36	0.27	0.20	0.17
d. Thailand			N.A.	0.29	0.23	0.16
e. Japan			N.A.	0.30	0.29	0.25

Source: See Table 1.1 and text.

falling behind the United States as time passed; that is, per capita real incomes in these countries were growing more slowly than per capita real incomes in the United States.

For the rest of the world, the contrasts are even more striking, with certain exceptions. On the whole, American per capita income levels were much higher than those observed in Asia and Latin America, and they were growing much faster. For example, according to Maddison, Indian GDP per capita was about three-tenths of the U.S. level, in 1850, but only 12 percent, in 1913 (Table 1.5). There are two classes of exceptions. Australia and New Zealand had unusually high levels of per capita GDP in the nineteenth century, but as time passed both lost ground to the United States, ending in 1913 with per capita incomes similar to that of the U.S. (Table 1.5). In the other class, the performances of Argentina and Canada were well below that of the United States, but both countries experienced higher rates of growth – between 1890 and 1913 for Canada, and from 1870 to 1913 for Argentina. All of the nineteenth-century high-income, and/or fast-growing economies, with the exception of the United Kingdom were settler economies, with abundant natural resources, all of which received very large infusions of European capital and labor.

The performance of the American economy between 1774 and 1913 was unusually strong, then. Indeed, although comparisons across long reaches of time and across widely different cultures are problematical, it is likely that American late-nineteenth-century income levels were higher than those in most parts of the world today.[7]

The short-term variations in U.S. per capita product roughly match the movements of aggregate product (see Table 1.6), previously discussed. For example, the small gain recorded by real GNP between 1774 and 1793 is converted into a small loss, for per capita real GNP, and the success of the period 1793–1807 comes through clearly, as does the unfavorable economic impact of the Civil War – the rate of growth between 1859 and 1869 amounts to 0.5 percent per year.

The major new result obtained from the per capita series has to do with long-term rates of growth. The rate of change of real GNP, as we have seen, exhibits no pronounced long-term trend. The pace of change of real GNP per capita, on the other hand, does shift over time. From 1774 until the 1830s, the average rate of growth of this variable is less than 1 percent

[7] Angus Maddison, *Dynamic Factors in Capitalist Development: A Long-Run Comparative View* (Oxford, 1991), 198–206.

Table 1.6. *U.S. gross national product per capita, prices of 1860,* *1774–1909, and rates of change*

Panel A: Real GNP per capita (prices of 1860)			
1774	63.3	1859	135.9
1793	61.4	1869	142.0
1800	68.0	1869/78	152.4
1807	73.6	1874/83	178.9
1810	71.6	1879/88	200.7
1820	79.5	1884/93	211.3
1830	85.8	1889/98	216.7
1834/43	96.5	1894/1903	236.6
1839/48	102.4	1899/1908	269.1
1844/53	116.1	1909	287.0
1849/58	127.9		

Panel B: Average annual short-term rates of change, GNP per capita in prices of 1860			
1774–1793	−0.2%	1849/58–1859	1.2%
1793/1800	1.5	1859–1869	0.5
1800–1807	1.1	1869–1869/78	1.6
1807–1810	−0.9	1869/78–1874/83	3.3
1810–1820	1.1	1874/83–1879/88	2.3
1820–1830	0.8	1879/88–1884/93	1.0
1830–1834/43	1.3	1884/93–1889/98	0.5
1834/43–1839/48	1.2	1889/98–1894/1903	1.8
1839/48–1844/53	2.5	1894/1903–1899/1908	2.6
1844/53–1849/58	2.0	1899/08–1909	1.2

Panel C: Average Annual long-term rates of change, GNP per capita in prices of 1860	
1774–1800	0.3%
1800–1834/43	0.9
1834/43–1869	1.3 (1.7)ª
1869–1909	2.4
1774–1909	1.1

Note: 1774–1830, 1869, 1909: Both the GNP and population data refer to calendar years. 1834/43–1859: The GNP data refer to census years, centered roughly on calendar years 1839,1844,1849,1854 and 1859.5. The population data refer to the calendar years on which the GNP estimates are centered $\left(1859.5 = \dfrac{1859+1860}{2}\right)$. 1869/78–1899/08: The GNP data refer to calendar years. The averages are centered on calendar years 1873.5, 1878.5, 1883.5, 1888.5, 1893.5, 1898.5, 1903.5, and the population data refer to these calendar years (e.g., 1873.5 = the mean of 1873 and 1874, etc.) ª1834/43–1859. *Source*: Table 1.3 and U.S. Bureau of the Census, *Historical Statistics of the United States, Colonial Times to 1970* (Washington, DC, 1975), Series A-7.

per year. It then rises to an average of well over 1.5 percent per year between 1834/43 and 1859, and between 1869 and 1909, to the still higher rate of almost 2.5 percent per year. The timing of the increase is suggestive. The process of industrialization advanced in important respects in the 1820s, and the industrial sector began to assume significant weight in the 1830s and 1840s, as we will see. There is the strong suggestion that the acceleration of the rate of growth of per capita GNP was associated with the process of modernization.

A second new result has to do with the sources of economic growth. When economic growth is measured in terms of aggregate real output, the responsibility of productivity improvements for growth is modest (see Table 1.4). But when growth is measured in terms of real GNP per capita, the story is quite otherwise – productivity improvements now account for a substantial fraction of total growth (see Table 1.7). The growth of factor

Table 1.7. *Rates of growth of per capita real GNP, labor, capital, land, and total factor productivity, 1800–1900*

Panel A: Per capita rates of growth				
	(1) Real GDP	(2) Labor	(3) Capital	(4) Land
1800–1840	0.90	0.10	0.99	−0.19
1840–1900	1.52	0.18	2.42	−0.37

Panel B: Computation of rates of change of per capita total factor productivity					
	Weighted rates of growth			(4) Sum, Col (1)–(3)	(5) Rates of growth of total factor productivity
	(1) Labor	(2) Capital	(3) Land		
1800–1840	0.07	0.29	−0.01	0.35	0.55
1840–1900	0.12	0.70	−0.01	0.81	0.71

Panel C: Contributions (%) to per capita output growth				
	(1) Labor	(2) Capital	(3) Land	(4) Productivity
1800–1840	8%	32%	−1%	61%
1840–1900	8	46	−1	47

Source: Tables 1.4 and 1.6 and the sources cited therein.

inputs was thus sufficient to increase aggregate output as fast as population, and somewhat faster, but the pronounced increase in output per capita depended importantly on the rising productivity of inputs, a matter of some importance.

Qualifications

CAPITAL CONSUMPTION AND
NET NATIONAL PRODUCT

Real GNP per capita is a reasonable first approximation to an index of material well-being, for reasons previously given, but it is not in every respect ideal. First, the GNP may measure the aggregate output of the society, but if the entire GNP is consumed each year, the level of output will not long persist. A better index of well-being, then, would be a measure of the Net National Product – that is, the GNP minus the investment that must be made to sustain output at its current level. The actual measurements of NNP are only rough approximations of the desired measure, but they are better than nothing.

Table 1.8 contains rates of growth computed from NNP per capita measurements, and the table shows that real NNP per capita increased more slowly than real GNP per capita. There are two reasons for this development. First, the process of modernization called for more and more capital per unit of output, so that a larger and larger fraction of real GNP was required just to replace capital that was being worn out or discarded because it was obsolete – that is, a larger fraction of output had to be witheld from consumption just to assure that the level of output would not decline in future. Second, modernization called for new forms of capital. Traditional agriculture depended heavily on long-lived capital, such as improvements to land of one sort or another, and non-depreciable capital – inventories of animals and crops; artisanal industry also used long-lived capital, such as tools that changed little as time passed. The modern industry that was growing up after 1820, and particularly, after 1840, made heavy use of machines, which had relatively short lives, both because machines wore out faster than buildings, and, more important, because they were subject to particularly high rates of obsolesence. The modernization of the American economy in the nineteenth century, then, called for a much larger annual consumption of capital goods than had been true formerly. Consequently,

Table 1.8. *Average annual rates of growth of per capita real GNP and real NNP (1860 prices), 1834/43–1894/03*

	GNP	NNP
1834/43–1844/53	1.87%	1.85%
1844/53–1859	1.51	1.38
1859–1869	0.46	0.45
1869–1874/83	2.46	2.45
1874/83–1884/93	1.68	1.34
1884/93–1894/1903	1.11	1.00
1834/43–1894/1903	1.52	1.41

Source: Rates of growth of GNP per capita computed from data in Table 1.6. Rates of growth of NNP per capita: NNP was computed by subtracting capital consumption from GNP. Capital consumption was derived from capital stock data – equipment and improvements (Variant B) – in Gallman, "United States Capital Stock," 204, table 4.A.1, constant price data. I assumed a life span of 15 years for equipment and 50 years for improvements, and average ages of 5 and 10 years for equipment and improvements, respectively. The depreciation method adopted was straight line. For population data, see the notes to Table 1.6.

a smaller and smaller fraction of GNP was left over for consumption and new investment.[8]

HOME MANUFACTURING AND FARM CREATION

A second respect in which GNP per capita falls short of the ideal measurement is that it does not include all elements of output. It does include all agricultural output and all of the shelter value of houses, but it excludes other elements of output that fail to pass through markets. For many periods of history, the omission leads to a downward bias in the measured *level* of aggregate output, but does not inordinately influence the *rate of change* of that variable. Since the rate of change is usually the measure that attracts analytical attention, the omissions are of little importance.

[8] This is not strictly correct. All of gross investment is always employed in new investment, sometimes to replace capital that is being retired, and sometimes to open up new avenues of investment. Capital consumption allowances are as readily used for the second purpose as for the first.

That is not the case, however, when one considers the United States in the nineteenth century. This was a period of industrialization, and many economic activities were being shifted from the home to the shop or factory. Since the standard GNP concept ignores home production but counts the output of shops and factories, the rate of growth computed from the real GNP during this period will be biased in an upward direction.[9] Table 1.9 contains estimates intended to deal with this problem, at least in part. It incorporates in GNP both major elements of home manufacturing – baking, the production of textiles and clothing, the slaughter and butchering of animals – and the clearing and first breaking of farm land, and farm construction from farm materials. It is incomplete, because it leaves some elements of home production out of account, but it is a useful addition to the list of measurements. It will be observed that the incorporation of these elements of output leads to lower, but still high, rates of growth of real GNP per capita.

It will be obvious that the same problem treated here in the context of changes across time reappears when one makes international comparisons among nations at very different levels of development. For example, in a previous paragraph I pointed out that the conventional measurements show that in 1913 per capita income in India was 12 percent of the level in the United States. Without much doubt, in 1913 the fraction of output passing through markets was much larger in the United States than in India. Thus, although India was surely much poorer than the United States, the conventional GNP measures overstate the extent of the difference between these two countries.

EXTERNALITIES

There are yet other ways in which the standard measures of real GNP probably exaggerate true economic growth during the process of modernization. One way arises from the fact that modern industry produces costs that are not incorporated in the costs of the goods sold, and therefore are not taken into account when the GNP is measured. Pollution is a good example. An ideal measure of GNP would deduct the cost of pollution.[10] Modernization also leads to a reorganiza-

---

[9] See Simon Kuznets, *Economic Change* (New York: 1953), Chapter 6.

[10] "Externalities may be positive or negative . . . From a practical point of view the most significant are negative pollution activities." J. J. Laffont, "Externalities," in John Eatwell, Murray Milgate, and Peter Newman (eds.), *The New Palgrave: A Dictionary of Economics*, Volume 2, *E to J* (New York: 1987), 263. See also the conceptual works cited in the bibliographic essay.

Table 1.9. *Average annual rates of growth of real GNP, real GNP per capita, and real NNP per capita, conventional and unconventional concepts, 1834/43–1894/03*

Panel A: GNP		
	Conventional	Unconventional
1834/43–1844/53	5.02	4.28
1844/53–1874/83	4.15	3.93
1874/83–1884/93	4.02	3.91
1884/93–1894/03	3.11	3.02
1834/43–1894/03	4.10	3.83

Panel B: GNP per capita		
1834/43–1844/53	1.92	1.18
1844/53–1874/83	1.52	1.30
1874/83–1884/93	1.72	1.61
1884/93–1894/03	1.16	1.07
1834/43–1894/03	1.56	1.29

Panel C: NNP per capita		
1834/43–1844/53	1.85	1.12
1844/53–1874/83	1.42	1.21
1874/83–1884/93	1.34	1.24
1884/93–1894/03	1.00	0.90
1834/43–1894/03	1.41	1.15

Source: See Tables 1.3 and 1.6. The unconventional estimates are based on Gallman, "Gross National Product," 35. It was assumed that the ratios of home manufacturing to the value of perishables and semi-durables in current and constant prices were the same.

tion of life that generates additional costs ignored by the standard concept – for example, costs of commuting and the increased costs of policing, which arise with the geographic concentrations of population. There is no good way to allow for these costs in the measurement of nineteenth-century U.S. growth, but it seems improbable that proper adjustments would have major impacts on the measurement of growth, in any case.

THE WORK YEAR

The well-being of a population depends not exclusively on output per capita but also on how much must be given up to obtain the output. Modern economic growth has led to shorter work weeks, and some scholars have argued that the free time thus generated should be valued as leisure and treated as a gain stemming from economic growth. Whether or not life in the twentieth century has become more leisured, it is certainly true that the lengths of the work week and work year have declined. In the nineteenth century the probable changes in these measures are more problematical. We know that with emancipation a substantial fraction of the work force was able to work shorter hours and engage in less intense labor. The work year in industry also probably did decline somewhat, but the shift in the structure of the economy no doubt increased the weight of those sectors – mining and manufacturing – that had long work years, and reduced the weight of agriculture, a sector – outside the plantation South – with a relatively short work year. (See Margo, Chap. 5, this volume.) In all likelihood, the average, overall work year at first lengthened, and then possibly shortened. Part of the gains achieved in per capita income in the early and middle decades of the nineteenth century were bought with more intense work routines, but in the later decades these developments may have been reversed.

How should this matter be taken into account? One way would be to attach to non-work time a value, perhaps the opportunity cost of the leisure. To the extent that work time was not chosen – for example, to the extent that farm workers worked short work years only because there was inadequate employment for them and would have chosen to work longer hours for more income, given the choice – this procedure would overestimate the gains from "leisure."

Similarly, when factory work became available to young women, the opportunities may have importantly improved their lot. Surely at home they had work around the house to do. There they were at the bottom of a work pecking order. In the factory, they not only were able to earn money, but were also thrown in with young women of their own age. The transition from home to factory, then, may not have been just a transition from leisure to work, but from one kind of life to a preferred kind.

These questions identify the tip of an iceberg. How did people judge the changing life styles in which they participated? Were cities places of loneliness for young people, places of limited social support? Or were they welcome resorts from the gossiping and lack of privacy of small villages, from the sure knowledge that some piece of idiocy one once performed will never be forgotten by the village? Were cities places of bright lights, or were they dark and Satanic? How far would the standard per capita income levels have to be altered to take into account changes in welfare arising out of changes in work routines?

HUMAN CAPITAL

One item that can be measured and added to the GNP consists of the value of schooling. Of course some elements of that value appear in the standard GNP – for example, the incomes of teachers. But we typically ignore the time spent by students in school. In a century in which child labor was common and time in school may have reduced time at work, there is not only a clear connection between schooling and value, but a simple way to estimate the value of the time of children: opportunity cost. Albert Fishlow's estimates show that opportunity cost of the time of school children amounted to:[11]

$24.8 million, in 1860
$72.1 million, in 1880
$213.9 million, in 1900

That is, there was a substantial increase over time, an increase greater than that exhibited by GNP (see Table 1.3). In 1860, the opportunity cost of schoolchildrens' time came to a value equal to a little more than 0.5 percent of GNP; the figure rose to 0.7 percent in 1880 and about 1.2 percent in 1900. These are small values, in one sense, certainly not great enough to influence importantly the rate of growth of GNP, were they incorporated into the measurements of GNP. Compared with aggregate savings and investment, however, they are more impressive, as will appear.[12]

Another source of human capital, and one requiring no investment by Americans – although it involved other costs – was immigration. Immigrants consisted disproportionately of young adults, people raised, educated, and trained abroad but with a long work life before them. The

---

[11] These values came to roughly 40 percent of total school costs, direct costs plus opportunity costs. There was very little variation in the proportion from one year to the next.

[12] Albert Fishlow, "Levels of Nineteenth-Century American Investment in Education," *Journal of Economic History* 26 (1966), 418–36.

numbers of immigrants increased dramatically in the two decades before
the Civil War, and returned to the previous high level once the Civil War
was over. (See Haines, Chap. 4, this volume.) Paul Uselding argues per-
suasively that human capital acquired by the United States from immigration was probably almost as large as the volume of conventional
investment made in the United States in the twenty-odd years before the
Civil War.[13] Similar calculations for the postwar period would probably
show a more limited relative importance for this source of human capital,
but it would surely remain large.[14]

CONSUMPTION

Finally, the previous comments refer to income and income per capita,
defined in various ways. These measures include output consumed by final
consumers and output saved and invested. The second component –
savings and investment – bears on the prospects of the society more
than on its current circumstances. If we are interested in current
well-being, a case can be made that we should concentrate on the first
component, consumption, and that consumption should be expressed in
per capita terms. Table 1.10 contains data concerning various aspects of
consumption.[15]

Between 1834/43 and 1899/08 real per capita consumption rose by
about 1.26 percent per year (computed from data in Table 1.10), a lower
rate than the one describing the growth of per capita real GNP. The explanation is that the fraction of national product saved *increased* over time.
Necessarily, then, the fraction consumed *declined*, and per capita consumption increased more slowly than did per capita income. Nonetheless,
the data suggest that it did increase, and that the rate of increase was by
no means negligible: per capita consumption more than doubled, between
1834/44 and 1899/1903.

---

[13] Paul Uselding, "Conjectural Estimates of Gross Human Capital Inflows to the American Economy,
1790–1860," *Explorations in Economic History* 9 (1971), 49–61.

[14] The gains to society as a whole were not without their associated costs. The flood of immigrants
spoiled the labor market for native workers, reducing employment opportunities and wage rates
for native workers. On the other hand, those new Americans, the immigrants, presumably realized
very substantial gains – including Irish immigrants who would probably have died in Ireland but
survived in America. For a treatment of immigrant gains, see Joseph P. Ferrie, *Yankeys Now: Immigrants in the Antebellum United States, 1840–1860* (New York, 1999). See also, Margo, Chap. 5 in
this volume.

[15] The figures refer not literally to consumption, but to output minus exports plus imports; they do
not allow for inventory changes. For convenience I use the term consumption.

Table 1.10. *Goods flowing to consumers, 1834/43–1899/08*

Panel A: Percentage distributions among classes of goods and classes of commodities, constant prices

	Goods				Commodities		
	Perishables	Semi-durables	Durables	Services	Perishables	Semi-durables	Durables
1834/43	57%	9%	2%	32%	84%	13%	3%
1839/48	57	11	3	29	80	15	4
1844/53	53	16	4	27	73	22	5
1849/58	51	17	6	26	69	23	8
1869/78	51	17	8	24	67	22	11
1874/83	51	17	8	24	67	22	11
1879/88	51	17	10	22	65	22	13
1884/93	50	18	11	20	63	23	14
1889/98	51	18	11	20	64	23	14
1894/1903	52	18	10	20	65	23	13
1899/1908	50	18	10	22	64	23	13

Panel B: Percentage distribution among classes of goods, excluding and including home manufacturing; current prices

	Excluding			Including		
	Perishables	Semi-durables	Durables	Perishables	Semi-durables	Durables
1839	79%	16%	5%	75%	21%	4%
1849	68	24	8	67	27	7
1859	69	23	8	68	24	7

Panel C: Flows of consumer goods, per capita ($ of 1860)

	All Goods	All commodities	Perishables	Semi-durables	Durables	Services
1834/43	85%	58%	49%	8%	2%	27%
1839/48	89	63	50	10	3	26
1844/53	99	73	53	15	5	26
1849/58	107	79	55	18	6	28
1859	115	85	59	20	6	30
1869	108	82	56	17	10	26
1869/78	115	88	59	20	10	27
1874/83	137	105	70	23	11	32
1879/88	151	118	77	26	15	33
1884/93	152	121	77	27	17	31
1889/98	153	123	78	27	17	30
1894/1903	170	135	87	30	18	35
1899/1908	192	150	96	34	20	42

Table 1.10. *(cont.)*

Panel D: Ratios of the cost of distribution to the value of commodities flowing to consumers, current prices	
1839	20%
1849	23
1859	24
1874/83	22
1884/93	28
1894/03	29

Note: The estimates make no allowances for changes in inventories, and, therefore, only roughly correspond with the value of goods actually moving into the hands of consumers.
Source: Gallman, "Gross National Product," 27, 35; Robert E. Gallman and Thomas J. Weiss, "The Service Industries in the Nineteenth Century," in Victor R. Fuchs (ed.), *Production and Productivity in the Service Industries,* Studies in Income and Wealth, vol. 34 (New York, 1969), 306.

The rate of increase was substantially greater – 1.47 percent per year – for the somewhat more reliable series "flows of commodities to consumers." Rates of gain varied widely from decade to decade. There was a slight decline between 1859 and 1869, the legacy of the Civil War, and relatively small gains between 1834/43 and 1839/48 – surely the result of the Great Depression of the early 1840s – and between 1879/88 and 1889/98 – perhaps at least in part due to the Great Depression of the 1890s. (Table 1.10, Panel C). There are marked gains in the antebellum years after 1839/48, in the period 1869–1879/88 – partly recovery from the war – and in the period 1889/98 to 1899/08 – recovery from the Great Depression.

Increases in the per capita real value of commodities flowing to consumers, shown by the data in Table 1.10, should not be regarded as exclusively due to increased quantities of goods flowing to consumers. Remember that the data are unadjusted for changes in inventories; were they so adjusted the short-term fluctuations in consumer commodities per capita would surely be moderated. So far as the trend is concerned, it is no doubt affected by increases over time in the extent to which consumer commodities were processed outside the home and by the growing importance of distribution. Some data that support these views appear in Table 1.10, Panel B. When adjusted to incorporate home manufacturing, the long-term rate of growth of consumer commodities is reduced. Table 1.10

also shows that the cost of distribution rose, relative to the value of consumer commodities, as time passed.

The structure of consumption also changed, particularly in the antebellum years. In general, the consumption of semi-durables (e.g., textiles and clothing) and durables (stoves, cookware, carriages) increased faster than the consumption of perishables. Nonetheless, per capita consumption of perishables, in real terms, increased in every interval in the table but two; across one of these intervals there was no change, and across the other – an interval during which the Civil War was fought – there was a slight decline. Overall, the increase was almost 100 percent between 1834/43 and 1899/08.

In the cases of both durables and semi-durables, the antebellum gains described in the table represent in part a shift of production out of the home and into the factory. For example, the estimates of semi-durables produced in the home that underlie Table 1.9 sum to a value almost half as large as the reported commercial production of semi-durables. By the end of the century these goods were almost exclusively a matter of commercial production.

The relative prices of both semi-durables and (particularly) durables fell quite dramatically, in the antebellum years, reflecting important technical improvements in production. Some of these improvements contributed to the quality of life in ways not fully captured in the output data. For example, in the antebellum years the production and sale of stoves increased dramatically. Stoves vastly improved the quality of the heating of homes and of cooking. Several improvements in construction were introduced. The balloon frame made it possible for a man and a boy to frame a house on their own, with great advantages for farm families. It also meant that buildings could be constructed quicker and cheaper than before, but just as strongly: the boom towns of Chicago and San Francisco were balloon frame towns. Improvements in iron production contributed to the construction of buildings and to the decorative grillwork that became popular in the period. Central heating and inside plumbing began to diffuse.

OTHER MEASURES OF WELL-BEING

There are indexes of material well-being other than measures of real income or consumption. Two have received much attention recently – measurements of height and of expectation of life. Clayne Pope has found

that over the period 1760/69 and 1880/89 there was almost no improvement in the life expectation of native white adults, despite the marked
gains in per capita income achieved during this period. (In the twentieth
century, rising income and improvements in life expectation seem to have
gone hand in hand.) Even more striking, the life expectation of adults
fluctuated over time, and Pope finds that forces making for decline were
concentrated in the decades 1840/49, 1850/59, and 1860/69.[16] Why there
should be this apparent disengagement of mortality from economic growth
is still under investigation. The role of the Civil War on mortality in the
1860s cannot be ignored, of course. As to the 1840s and 1850s, these were
years of heavy immigration, which apparently put pressure on labor
markets, to the detriment of native workers. Immigrants also brought with
them diseases that were obviously very destructive (such as cholera in
1849, yellow fever in 1853, and, later in the century, typhoid fever), and
others less striking in their immediate impact that were, nonetheless,
eventually causes of worsening mortality experience. It has also been
argued that the movement of population – to the west, in the 1840s and
1850s, and in various directions, by the armies of the Civil War – led to
an effloresence of malaria, which did not kill on the scale and with the
speed of cholera or yellow fever or typhoid fever, but that could and did
shorten lives. Anthony Trollope's description of the westerners he visited
in 1861 is telling:

Visit him and you will find him . . . too often bearing on his lantern jaw the signs
of ague and sickness . . . their thin faces, their pale skins, their unenergetic tem-
perament. . . . He will sit for hours over a stove . . . chewing the cud of reflection
. . . [Western women] are generally hard, dry, and melancholy. . . . In the West I
found men gloomy and silent.[17]

The growth of cities and urban industry, in the absence of a full
understanding of the causes of the spread of disease, could also have had
unfavorable consequences – Floud, Wachter, and Gregory find that it did
in Great Britain.[18] These are issues that call for much more study, but at
this stage the differences between trends in mortality and in per capita
income seem, in principle, not surprising, even if we do not understand

---

[16] Clayne Pope, "Adult Mortality in America before 1860: A View from Family Histories," in Claudia
Goldior and Hugh Rockoff, eds., *Strategic Factors in Nineteenth-Century American Economic Growth: A
Volume to Honor Robert W. Fogel* (Chicago, 1992), 267–96.

[17] Anthony Trollope, *North America* (New York, 1862), 128, 133, 135.

[18] Roderick Floud, Kenneth Wachter, and Annabel Gregory, *Height, Health, and History* (Cambridge,
1990), chaps. 7, 8.

precisely which factors influencing mortality were the crucial ones and exactly how they operated. (See also Haines, Chap. 4, this volume.)

Students of anthropometric measurements tell us that two factors determine the heights at given ages (either sex) in populations, such as that of the United States in the nineteenth century, drawn chiefly from European and African backrounds: genetics and net nutrition. The genetic influence shows itself in the distribution of a population (one sex) by height at a given age, a roughly normal distribution. The level of this distribution – and sometimes its shape – is affected by the net nutrition absorbed by the population during the crucial growth periods. Good net nutrition in the womb, during infancy, and during the adolescent growth spurt will lead to a tall adult population, and bad nutrition will lead to a short one, *ceteris paribus*.

Net nutrition depends both upon the volume and quality of food intake and upon the claims on nutrition exerted by work and by illness. Two groups with identical food intake may, nonetheless, ultimately exhibit different average heights, if one of the two has a more demanding work schedule or more trying health conditions during the growth spurt years.

Measurements of height can, then, serve as indexes of certain elements of well-being. These measurements have two clear advantages: (1) Since evidence on heights is more readily available in early times than are income or output data, height indexes can be used to push the quantitative exploration of human material well-being backward in time to historical periods otherwise beyond out reach; (2) Evidence on heights bears on specific elements of well-being and can be used to identify problems that may not – indeed, probably will not – emerge from a study of incomes or outputs alone. Anthropometric measures and income data, then, are complementary approaches to the study of human well-being. While in the very long run these two types of measures typically run in parallel, in the short run that need not be the case. This does not mean that the two measures are inconsistent; they simply refer to different parts of the human experience.

The principal disadvantages of the height-by-age data are also two in number. Since adult height is affected by events occurring over a period of, say, twenty years in the life of a cohort, an increase or a decrease in adult height between one cohort and the next may not be easy to explain: the insult that resulted in a decline in height could have come when the cohort was in the womb, or when it was in infancy, or when it was in its late teens.[19] Since cohorts can gain back early losses by exceptionally good net nutrition in the teen years, however, it is reasonable to suppose that these years tend often to be the crucial ones. Since height can be affected by food intake, work efforts, and illness, a decline (or rise) in height between one cohort and the next has three possible causes, and the relevant cause(s) are not revealed by the height measurements themselves. These two points come down to the single one that height is an index of net nutrition, but that the interpretation of the index – with respect to the timing and causes of changes – calls for additional study, employing other forms of evidence.

The existing evidence on heights indicates that American white males were already very tall in the late eighteenth century and early nineteenth century, by the standards of the day – around 173 centimeters (see Table 1.11). This figure compares with the late-twentieth-century standard for men of 178 centimeters.[20]

Between the cohorts of 1830 and 1840, average height declined to about 172.2 centimeters. It continued to fall to the cohort of 1860 – 170.6 centimeters – rose slightly (to 171.2 centimeters) in the 1870 birth cohort, and then cycled mildly, achieving a nadir at 168.9 centimeters in the cohort of the early 1880s. It then rose slowly, finally reachieveing the late colonial level in the cohort of 1921.

It should be said that all of these heights quality as "tall" in the world history of heights, but the decline is by no means small, and it suggests problems in American society in the mid- to late nineteenth century. The sources of these problems are only now beginning to be explored, and no compelling conclusions have yet been reached. The topics discussed above, in connection with adult life expectation – the Civil War,[21] changes in the disease environment,[22] the various impacts

---

[19] This problem could be minimized by focusing on the heights of young children. Unfortunately there are few such nineteenth-century data, other than those for slaves, and, of course, slave life experiences differed substantially from those of free persons.

[20] Personal communication from Richard Steckel. Another way to put it is that 173 centimeters is at the 28th percentile of modern standards.

[21] The Civil War could easily have affected the height of members of the birth cohorts of the 1850s and 1860s, and even the 1840s, since growth spurt periods of all of these cohorts were located in the 1860s.

[22] Cholera and yellow fever were killers. Survivors probably did not suffer long-term effects in their heights. Malaria, on the other hand, was a debilitating disease that was likely to have led to stunting. And while cholera and yellow fever probably did not have important direct impacts on the heights of those who were afflicted, they probably *did* influence the average heights of the whole community, since the deaths caused by these diseases were probably not randomly distributed among height groups: the shorter and weaker people were probably over-represented

Table 1.11. *Adult stature of birth cohorts of native-born white American males, 1780–1931*

Year on which observation is centered	Height (centimeters)
1780	173.2
1785	173.2
1790	172.9
1795	172.8
1800	
1805	
1810	
1815	173.0
1820	172.9
1825	173.1
1830	173.5
1835	173.1
1840	172.2
1845	171.6
1850	171.1
1855	170.8
1860	170.6
1865	171.1
1870	171.2
1875	170.7
1882.5	168.9
1887.5	169.2
1892.5	169.0
1897.5	170.0
1902.5	170.0
1906.5	171.6
1911	172.2
1916	172.9
1921	173.2
1931	175.5

Source: Richard H. Steckel, "Stature and Living Standards in the U.S.," in Gallman and Wallis (eds.), *American Economic Growth*, 288.

of immigration, industrial pollution, urban crowding, problems of public health, water supply, and sewage disposal – anything that increased illness – are all probably relevant.[23] Increases in the intensity of child labor – especially labor in factories – may also have figured in the result, although the numbers of children subject to factory discipline must have been quite small.[24] It has been suggested that the structural shifts of the economy were sufficiently pronounced that the agricultural sector was unable to maintain an adequate level of nutrition, especially in the face of increased exports of food late in the century. But the quantitative evidence shows that the level of nutrients available per capita for consumption (output minus waste, minus exports, plus imports) was high by all relevant standards throughout the entire period 1834/43 through 1899/08.

Notice that several of these possible causes of the reductions in heights are endogenous to the economy, and some are exogenous, although it is not always easy to identify the proper location of the line between these two types of causes. Are cholera and yellow fever exogenous, or are they endogenous, since they spread by human contacts associated with international trade and migration? Much work needs to be done on these issues. A particularly promising avenue of exploration has to do with the disease environment.[25]

---

among those killed. Oddly enough, then, a bout of cholera or yellow fever might raise the average heights of surviving members of the community, whereas success in dealing with these diseases could, by saving the weak from death, lower the average heights of members of the community.

[23] Two other factors are relevant. The rise of the public schools in the antebellum years brought children together and led to the diffusion of disease. Improvements in transportation increased human contacts, which also spread diseases – to populations particularly vulnerable, because they had previously been relatively isolated.

[24] According to Weiss, in the antebellum years roughly 21 percent of white males and 6.6 percent of white females 10 through 15 years of age were in the work force. For blacks, most of whom were slaves, the figure would be much closer to 100 percent. Thomas Weiss, "U.S. Labor Force Estimates and Economic Growth, 1800–1860," in Robert E. Gallman and John Joseph Wallis (eds.), *American Economic Growth and Standards of Living before the Civil War* (Chicago, 1992), 49.

[25] Easterlin has suggested yet another measure of wellbeing: self-reported indexes of happiness. Such measurements are not available, however, for the nineteenth century. Easterlin's most recent conclusion, based on his work on these topics, is worth reporting, since it bears on the ultimate meaning of measurements of growth: Of this world he writes: "It is a world founded on belief in science and the power of rational inquiry and in the ultimate capacity of humanity to shape its own destiny. The irony is that in this last respect the lesson of history appears to be otherwise: that there is no choice. In the end, the triumph of economic growth is not a triumph of humanity over material wants; rather, it is a triumph of material wants over humanity." Easterlin, *Growth Triumphant: The Twenty-first Century in Historical Perspective* (Ann Arbor, 1996), 154.

CHANGES IN THE STRUCTURE OF THE ECONOMY

Savings and Investment

PATTERNS

In the decade 1839 through 1848 Americans saved about 14 percent of the gross national product (see Table 1.12, Panel A, column 1), a large savings rate by recent standards. From there on it rose – by three percentage points in the antebellum years, by another two between the decades 1849/58 and 1869/78, by another two by 1879/88, and by yet another two by 1884/93, when it was 23 percent. From the first -mentioned decade to the last the savings rate advanced by almost two-thirds. The first decade, 1839/48, spans a long and deep depression, which may have depressed the savings rate. But even if one measures from the economically prosperous decade 1844/53 to 1889/98, a decade of

Table 1.12. *U.S. investment, 1834/43–1909*

	Panel A: Gross investment as a percentage of GNP		
	Conventional measure		Unconventional measure
	Current prices	Constant prices	Constant prices
1834/43		12	19
1839/48	14	14	17
1844/53	16	16	18
1849/58	17	17	20
1859		16	
1869		24	
1869/78	19	24	26
1874/83	19	24	25
1879/88	21	25	26
1884/93	23	27	28
1889/98	23	29	30
1894/03	21	28	29
1899/08	22	29	29
1909		27	

Table 1.12 *(cont.)*

Panel B: Net investment as a percentage of NNP, constant prices		
	Conventional measure	Unconventional measure
1774/1800	5	8
1800/40	7	8
1834/43	9	15
1844/53	13	15
1874/83	19	20
1884/93	19	20
1894/03	18	19

Panel C: Composition of gross investment (%)								
	Conventional measure							Unconventional Measure
	Current prices				Constant prices			Constant prices
	MD	C	Δ INV	Δ CF	MD	C	Δ INV	Δ CF	CL + B
1834/43					17	63	26	−5	41
1839/48	19	57	23	+1	16	58	23	+4	22
1844/53	20	60	23	−3	18	62	22	−2	15
1849/58	20	59	23	−2	20	66	17	−3	17
1859					20	60	19	+1	
1869					27	69	15	−10	
1869/78	26	71	9	−6	28	62	15	−4	8
1874/83	26	63	11	−*	33	52	15	−ᵃ	6
1879/88	25	66	11	−2	39	48	14	−2	4
1884/93	21	73	8	−3	42	55	6	−2	3
1889/98	20	71	8	+1	42	52	6	+1	2
1894/03	25	66	4	+5	46	45	5	+4	2
1899/08	27	65	4	+5	54	41	2	+3	1
1909					54	46	3	−2	

Note: MD = Manufactured durables; C = Construction; ΔINV = Changes in the value of inventories; ΔCF = changes in claims on foreigners; CL + B = Farm land improvements: first clearing and breaking of farm land
ᵃ Less than 0.5%
Source: See the notes to Tables 1.3, 1.8, and 1.9. The unconventional measure here excludes income generated by home manufacturing. Were this income included, the figures in the last column of Panel A would exhibit a more pronounced upward trend. The net investment estimates for 1774/1800 and 1800/40 (Panel B) were made by differencing the capital stock estimates and dividing by the number of years separating them. For example:

$$I_{1800-1840} = \frac{K_{1840} - K_{1800}}{40}$$

depression, the savings rate is found to have risen by four-tenths. The observed trend in the savings rate, then, is clearly a true phenomenon.

The trend is even more pronounced when savings and GNP are expressed in constant prices. The antebellum savings rates are similar to the current price figures (Table 1.12, Panel A, column 2), except that there is now an observation for the decade 1834/43, a value two percentage points below that for 1839/48. More striking is the fact that the rates for the postwar period are much higher than they were when expressed in current prices. The peak savings rate is now 29 percent, almost two and a half times as high as the value for 1834/43. Clearly, the prices of capital goods *fell* very sharply, relative to the prices of the goods that make up the rest of the GNP. Panel C of Table 1.12 plus Table 1.13 indicate, furthermore, that the price decline was especially pronounced among manufactured producers' durables – machines and tools. Three sources of this improvement in the prices of durables have been suggested: developments in the machine tools industry; innovations in iron and, in particular, steel; and changes in the structure of tariffs. All should have redounded favorably on the prices of machinery, but it should be said that the topic awaits its historian.

The significance of the falling relative prices of capital goods should be evident: a savings rate of 23 percent of current price GNP in 1889/98 would buy 29 percent of the real value of the GNP.

When the GNP is amplified by the addition of the value of home manufactures and investments in farm formation, the picture changes only modestly (Table 1.12, Panel A, column 3). Savings rates become higher, and their increase across time slightly less pronounced. Nonetheless, the figures continue to show a small rise in the antebellum period, a larger one (six percentage points) between the ante- and postbellum periods, and a further rise of three percentage points to 1889/98. The increase across the full period, 1834/43 to 1889/98, is a substantial eleven points, or almost six-tenths of the original value. Once again, Panel C of Table 1.12 and Panel D of Table 1.13 show why the rise in rates, in this version, is smaller than in the conventional version. Land clearing and fencing represented a larger investment, per acre, in the 1830s and early 1840s, when much land being brought under cultivation was still forest land, than it did in later decades, when first prairie land, and then the plains, came under the plow. Furthermore, the number of acres being cleared increased much more slowly than did the other elements of investment. Consequently, land clearing and fencing became much less

Table 1.13. *Constituents of the domestic capital stock, expressed as percentage shares in the domestic capital stock, 1774–1900*

Panel A: Current price data (percentages, excluding farmland clearing, breaking, and fencing)

	Structures	Equipment	Inventories	Animals
1774	39%	13%	23%	25%
1799	33	14	35	18
1805	35	15	34	16
1815	41	13	26	21
1840	45	14	24	17
1850	47	13	26	13
1860	54	12	22	12
1870	54	11	24	11
1880	55	11	24	9
1890	61	13	19	8
1900	60	14	19	7

Panel B: Prices of 1860 (percentages, excluding farmland clearing, breaking, and fencing)

1774	40	8	28	25
1799	34	9	35	23
1805	40	9	32	19
1815	41	7	29	22
1840	43	8	26	23
1850	46	9	27	17
1860	54	12	22	12
1870	55	13	22	10
1880	50	16	25	9
1890	49	25	21	6
1900	46	30	19	4

Panel C: Current price data (percentages, including farmland clearing, breaking, and fencing)

	Structures	Equipment	Inventories	Animals	Land Clearing, etc.
1774	24	8	14	15	40
1799	21	9	23	11	36
1805	26	11	24	12	28
1815	33	10	21	17	19
1840	33	10	18	12	28
1850	35	10	20	10	25

Table 1.13. *(cont.)*

Panel C: Current price data (percentages, including farmland clearing, breaking, and fencing)

	Structures	Equipment	Inventories	Animals	Land Clearing, etc.
1860	42	9	17	9	22
1870	44	9	20	9	17
1880	47	10	21	8	14
1890	55	11	17	7	10
1900	55	13	18	6	8

Panel D: Prices of 1860 (percentages, including farmland clearing, breaking, and fencing)

1774	17	4	12	11	56
1799	19	5	20	13	44
1805	25	5	20	12	39
1815	27	5	19	14	36
1840	29	6	17	15	32
1850	33	7	19	12	28
1860	42	9	17	9	22
1870	44	11	18	8	19
1880	41	13	21	7	17
1890	44	22	19	5	11
1900	42	28	18	4	8

Source: Gallman, "American Economic Growth," table 2.8.

important, relative to other forms of investment, as the nineteenth century wore on.

Finally, Panel B of Table 1.12 shows net savings rates in place of the gross figures so far dealt with. The data have the advantage of extending backwards into the eighteenth century, but they must be regarded as less reliable than the gross figures.

The new series suggest that the increase in the savings rate began much earlier than 1834/43, and this point holds for both the conventional and unconventional measurements. As to the former, the suggestion is that Americans had been saving an increasing share of net national product since at least the eighteenth century; as to the latter, the increase seems to have been under way since at least the beginning of the nineteenth century. The increases also are very large: almost a fourfold rise, in the conventional series, and a two-and-a-half-fold gain, in the unconventional series, from the beginning to 1884/93.

All of the data discussed so far have related to savings (and investment) by Americans – it excludes investment in the United States by foreigners. Panel C of Table 1.12 indicates that the omission is relatively unimportant, in a quantitative sense – foreign investment typically accounted for only a very small part of investment in the United States. It should be said, however, that foreign investment tended to be concentrated in certain sectors, especially in railways and banks, and that for those elements of the economy it could be important. Furthermore, American investment banks grew up under the tutelage of British merchant banks, acting as agents in the British finance of American railways. Their lessons learned, the American bankers began financing American railroads on their own, and a second and third generation of such organizations served as financiers for the industrial mergers at the end of the century. Thus British interest in American investment opportunities helped to promote a system of American intermediaries that became important in industrial finance. (See Davis and Cull, Chap. 16, this volume.) Finally, as we have seen, foreign investment figured in the long swings of American economic growth, alleviating balance of payments problems during booms and therefore helping to extend these booms.

Three periods of foreign investment can be distinguished: the antebellum period, the immediate postbellum period, and the decades beginning with 1889/98. In the antebellum period Americans were sometimes borrowers abroad, and sometimes lenders. On average, the amount borrowed or loaned was always small, compared with total savings, never running over 5 percent. The decade averages, of course, smooth out investment flows that fluctuated widely, and were sometimes important. For present purposes, however, we need to know about average performance, and that is what the table reports.

The second period is one in which Americans were typically borrowers – 1869 to 1884/93. The values are substantial – 6 to 10 percent of total investment – in 1869 and 1869/78, but they then become again, on average, modest.

In the third period Americans become net foreign lenders. Again, the values are not large, but they do reach 5 percent of total American investment before the end of the period.

WHY DID THE SAVINGS/INVESTMENT RATE RISE?

Many explanations for the rise in the savings/investment rate have been offered. Most are complementary, although there is pronounced disagreement as to the relative weights to be assigned to the different causes. The explanations may be usefully grouped around four potential sources of a change in the savings/investment rate:

(a) financial changes arising out of the Civil War;
(b) the development of financial intermediation;
(c) a rightward shift of the savings function (and an associated movement along the investment function);
(d) a rightward shift of the investment function (and an associated movement along the savings function).[26]

The first explanation is that domestically held federal debt (which was built up during the War) was liquidated in the postwar years and the resources thus reclaimed were invested in the U.S. economy, thereby raising the measured private investment rate. This explanation, of course, accounts at best for the rise in the rate between the pre- and postwar periods, but does not show why the rate increased in the decades before the war or why it continued to rise in the postwar years.

Intermediaries help to bring potential savers and investors together, thereby realizing savings and investment plans that otherwise would be unrealized. They reduce search costs, so that the net returns to savers are increased and the net borrowing costs of investors are reduced. These activities tend to raise savings/investment rates. That intermediation improved dramatically during the long nineteenth century is evident (see Davis and Cull, Chap. 16, this volume), and that this development had important consequences seems to be demonstrated by the convergence of regional interest rates, at least since the Civil War, and perhaps for longer than that.[27] Econometric efforts to sort out the factors accounting for the upward movement in the savings/investment rate also seem to leave a role for the effects of intermediation.

Several reasons have been given for believing that the savings function shifted to the right and dominated the forces making for higher

---

[26] A fifth set of explanations, concerning the relative decline in the prices of investment goods, have been previously set out.

[27] There is disagreement with respect to convergence before the war. See the bibliographic essay at the end of this volume.

savings/investment rates. Econometric evidence has been marshaled to
support some of these explanations. For example, one study has shown that
a decline in the dependency rate is likely to have increased the savings rate
by as much as one-fifth or one-quarter. A second study supports this
finding, holding that a little more than six-tenths of the rise was accounted
for a change in the occupational structure of the work force. The same
study concludes that the remaining 16 percent was due to improvements
in intermediation.

Still other suggestions have been offered: the distribution of income
became more concentrated as time passed, and since the rich save at higher
rates than do the poor, the shift in distribution led to rising overall savings
rates; the fraction of total income composed of property income rose as
time passed, and since property holders probably saved at higher rates than
did nonproperty holders (as David Ricardo argued, long ago), the change
in distribution led to higher overall savings rates; emancipation meant the
loss of property by the former slaveholders, who attempted to recover their
former positions by saving at higher rates than before – thus the overall
savings rate rose.

None of these explanations can be regarded at present as very powerful.
There are very few direct measures of the size distribution of income or
wealth; of those that permit comparisons over long reaches of time, the
data sources and methods of computation are sufficiently different so that
the change over time that they describe must be taken with a grain of salt.
Indirect measures have been interpreted by some analysts to imply that
the distribution did, indeed, become less egalitarian as time passed; other
analysts deny it.

Evidence on the functional distribution of income is a little more
direct, and it does suggest that property holders received a growing share
of total income. But the data on which these results rest are quite heavily
processed.

The argument concerning the savings activities of former slaveholders
can help to explain only the rise in the rate between the pre- and postwar
periods, not the earlier or later developments. Given the small fraction
of total income earned in the South after the war, even pronounced efforts
on the part of former slaveholders to replace their slaves with other forms
of capital would be unlikely to have a major impact on national savings
rates.

Finally, the strongest efforts by this group of analysts have been devoted to explaining developments between the 1830s and the 1890s, and in particular, the period between the ante- and postbellum years. Much less attention has been devoted to the years before the 1830s, although the arguments developed by those who stress the rise of intermediaries and those who believe that changes in the distribution of income were important are relevant to this period.

Those who believe that the savings/investment rate rose because the investment demand schedule shifted to the right argue for technological change of a capital-using, labor-saving nature, and see the rise of the savings and investment shares as part of a Solow-style neoclassical traverse. Evidence presented to support this view includes the observed stability of the share of income flowing to capital. If the experience is analyzed in terms of an aggregate production function, a result of this type, given the relative rates of growth of capital and labor and the likely elasticity of substitution between the factors, indicates that technical change was labor saving and capital using. The demand for capital, then, it is argued, must have been shifting to the right.

It is certainly true that the capital/output ratio rose as time passed, and that could be interpreted as a result of capital-using technical changes; but it could equally be (and has been) interpreted to mean that a rise in the savings rate flooded capital markets and permitted capital deepening. The factors making for the change in the capital/output ratio are therefore worth exploring.

The increase in the capital/output ratio was virtually universal in the United States – that is, the individual sectoral ratios rose, as did the ratios for individual manufacturing industries. The most obvious shift in the structure of the economy – the rise of manufacturing and the relative decline of agriculture – interestingly enough worked to lower the aggregate, overall ratio, not to raise it – the average ratio was lower in manufacturing than in agriculture. The main force at work to increase the aggregate ratio was the rise of the transportation sector. The capital/output ratio of this sector was high both because it is a capital-intensive sector, and because transportation firms are "faced with indivisibilities [such that] the size of the capital stock is not a good proxy for the annual flow of services it delivers."[28] That is, it took time for the economy to grow up to

---

[28] Albert Fishlow, "Productivity and Technological Change in the Railroad Sector, 1840–1910," in Dorothy S. Brady (ed.), *Output, Employment, and Productivity in the United States After 1800*, Studies in Income and Wealth, vol. 30 (New York, 1966), 630.

the transportation network put in place during this period. There is a question, then, as to whether the increase in the aggregate, national ratio should be regarded as a result of technical change, or as due to a shift in the structure of the economy, consequent on the westward movement, urbanization, and industrialization – a set of structural shifts accommodated by a rightward movement of the savings function.

It has been suggested that the way to sort out the relative importance of the movements in the savings and investment functions is to look at the real interest rate: if it rose, then the predominant force at work is likely to have been the movement of the investment function, and if it fell, one must grant the importance of a change in the savings function. That position has been criticized on the ground that international capital markets were working very well, and that therefore the interest rate reflected international, not domestic, forces. This argument would be compelling if foreign capital had been flowing into the United States at rates very large compared with total U.S. investment. As we have seen, this was not characteristically true: investment sometimes flowed in, on balance, and sometimes flowed out, and the fraction of domestic investment it typically accounted for when it flowed in was small. The suggestion is that the impact of foreign influences on the American capital markets – at least trends in capital markets – was not likely to have been typically strong – was not likely to have deflected the risk-free interest rate from the course that would have been determined by domestic forces alone. That argument is weakest, of course, in regard to the period spanning and following the Civil War, when capital inflows were unusually large and the investment rate rose especially far.

A second difficulty with studying the real interest rate for a clue as to the relative importance of savings and investment phenomena is that changes in the interest rate will depend both on the relative movements of supply and demand schedules, and on the elasticities of these schedules. For example, assume that the supply schedule (the savings function) is highly elastic. Then the interest rate would fall if the demand for capital expanded dramatically, while the savings function moved only slightly to the right. As it happens, the disputants in this field have not yet agreed as to the likely elasticity of the savings schedule – one group arguing that it was probably very large, another group holding that, on the basis of modern evidence, it must have been very small.

Finally, there are different ways to measure the real rate of interest, and different nominal rates from which the calculations can be made.

Naturally, then, there are disagreements as to the probable course of the real interest rate. (The bibliographical essay at the end of this volume provides some guidance for the reader who would like to delve more deeply into these questions.)

THE STRUCTURE OF INVESTMENT AND THE CAPITAL STOCK

By the end of the century, the structure of investment and the capital stock – conventionally measured – had changed quite dramatically, especially if one concentrates on real magnitudes. The biggest shifts involved manufactured producers' durables and inventories (including animal inventories): the former became more important, relative to other components of investment, particularly if measurements are made in constant prices, while the latter became markedly less important. The decline in the relative scale of inventories reflects the fate of the agricultural sector, a sector that held large amounts of inventories – animals and crops.

The Industrial Distribution of Income

Industrialization began for the United States perhaps as early as the 1820s (see Engerman and Sokoloff, Chap. 9, this volume). The next twenty or so years involved a reorganization of industry, with associated productivity improvements, but without heavy reliance on mechanization. Mechanization began in earnest in the last fifteen to twenty years before the Civil War. In the late 1830s and early 1840s, there was a marked increase in the number of new industrial products produced in America, some entirely new, others invented abroad and innovated in the United States during this period.

As Table 1.14 shows, as late as 1840, mining, manufacturing, and the hand trades accounted for only 17 percent of aggregated U.S. output. Were the artisanal hand trades dropped from the industrial total, and were the product of non-market activities more fully represented in aggregate output, the share would be substantially smaller, and this smaller share would represent the contribution of modern industry to the American economy of that time. By 1900, however, industry accounted for almost one-third of aggregate output, a fraction that was close to the maximum share that industry was ever to contribute to total U.S. output. Since industrial prices fell relative to the GNP price index between 1840 and 1900,

Table 1.14. *The sectoral distribution of GNP 1840–1900 (percentages)*

	1840	1850	1860	1870	1880	1890	1900
Agriculture	41	35	35	33	28	19	18
Manufacturing, mining, and hand trades	17	22	22	24	25	30	31
Transportation and public utilities	7	4	6	6	8	9	9
Commerce and all other private business	23	26	26	26	29	32	32
Government and education	2	2	2	2	2	3	3
Shelter	10	11	9	9	8	7	7

Note: The agricultural estimates include land clearing, breaking, and fencing as well as home manufacturing. The estimates, however, are understatements. If they were corrected, the share of agriculture in GNP would decline more pronouncedly over time than do the figures in this table. Mining excludes the important precious metals mining industries. *Source*: Gallman "United States Capital Stock," table 4.8. These are estimates of sectoral value added. "Commerce" includes only the trade in final goods.

the rise in the share of industry in GNP across time, shown in the table, would be even greater if all values were expressed in constant prices. This period of industrial growth – which made the United States by World War I the leading industrial economy in the world – took place in the presence of extraordinary opportunities in agriculture, which might have been expected to distract the United States from industrial concerns. The agricultural sector did, indeed, expand, of course, but at a much lower rate than the remaining sectors of the economy. By 1900 it accounted for less than half as large a fraction of total U.S. output as it had in the antebellum years. Meanwhile, other features of the extraordinary U.S. environment were being exploited; enormous reserves of minerals of all sorts were discovered and technologies innovated to put them to use.

These are the main shifts in the relative importance of the industrial sectors of the economy in the long nineteenth century. The share of shelter in the total declined a little – an Engels curve phenomenon? – and that of transportation, government, and education increased. Commerce and "all other private businesses" – a hodge-podge of construction, finance, professional services, and personal services – show a more marked relative advance, the share in output moving from about a quarter, before the War, to almost a third at the end of the century. Commerce, construction, and professional services were chiefly responsible for this result. The rapid growth of construction is tied up with the increase in the investment rate; commerce, with the expanding scope of the market; and professional services, with the modernization of the economy and the increasing scale of economic units.

The shift in the structure of the economy affected the *level* as well as the *structure* of output. Output per worker was higher in the secondary and tertiary sectors than in the primary sector.[29] Consequently, the shift in the composition of the economy tended to raise output per worker, on average.[30] Since the participation rate was rising, output per member of the population, measured in a conventional way, also rose, partly as a consequence of the altered structure of the economy, and partly due to the higher participation rate.

The Regional Distribution of Economic Activity

One of the great themes in American history is the westward movement. The march of population and economic activity to the west followed a sequence of land acquisitions (discussed previously) and was coterminous with the construction of transportation, communications, and financial networks that tied the expanding economy together. The scale of the westward movement is broadly captured in Panels A and B of Table 1.15, which show a persistent decline in the fraction of total income and population claimed by the Northeastern regions, the South Atlantic, and the East South Central. The gainers were the two North Central regions, the West South Central, the Mountain, and the Pacific. The shift was substantial. In 1840, the western regions generated less than one-fifth of total income – 17 percent – whereas in 1920 this figure had risen to 54 percent.

What were the forces driving this redistribution of population and income? Economic opportunity is a frequently cited cause; the west clearly

---

[29] The tertiary sector includes housing and the transportation industries. Thus the high level of per worker income in this sector is at least in part due to a high capital/labor ratio. Also, a large part of the total income of these industries flows to property, rather than labor. Thus, the table overstates the relative level of well-being of workers in the tertiary sector. Finally, workers in the tertiary and secondary sectors had longer work years than workers in the primary sector, so that differences in sectoral output per worker levels reflect, in part, different amounts of labor time committed per worker in the three sectors.

[30] The shift to the secondary sector also meant a heavier weight for the sector experiencing the highest rate of labor productivity growth.

Table 1.15. *Personal income and personal income per capita, 1840–1920*

Panel A: Percentage distribution of personal income, by region					
	1840	1860	1880	1900	1920
U.S.	100	100	100	100	100
Northeast	58	50	44	41	32
New England	17	14	11	10	7
Middle Atlantic	41	36	33	31	25
North Central	13	20	34	36	32
East North Central	12	15	23	22	23
West North Central	2	4	11	13	9
South	29	26	15	15	21
South Atlantic	14	9	6	5	9
East South Central	11	9	6	5	5
West South Central	4	8	4	5	8
West	—	4	7	8	15
Mountain			2	3	3
Pacific			4	5	12

Panel B: Percentage distribution of population by region					
	1840	1860	1880	1900	1920
United States	100	100	100	100	100
Northeast	43	36	31	30	30
New England	13	10	8	7	7
Middle Atlantic	30	20	23	22	22
North Central	20	29	35	35	32
East North Central	17	22	22	21	21
West North Central	2	7	12	14	12
Sourth	37	33	31	30	29
South Atlantic	20	14	13	12	11
East South Central	15	13	11	10	8
West South Central	3	6	7	9	10
West	—	2	4	5	9
Mountain	—	—	1	2	3
Pacific	—	—	2	3	5

Table 1.15. *(cont.)*

Panel C: Personal income per capita as percentage of the U.S. average					
	1840	1860	1880	1900	1920
United States	100	100	100	100	100
Northeast	135	139	141	137	132
New England	132	143	141	134	124
Middle Atlantic	136	137	141	139	134
North Central	68	68	98	103	100
East North Central	67	69	102	106	108
West North Central	75	66	90	97	87
South	76	72	51	51	62
South Atlantic	70	65	45	45	59
East South Central	73	68	51	49	52
West South Central	144	115	60	61	72
West	—	—	190	163	122
Mountain	—	—	168	139	100
Pacific	—	—	204	163	135

Source: Richard A. Easterlin, "Regional Income Trends, 1840–1950," in Seymour E. Harris (ed.), *American Economic History* (New York, 1961), tables 1, 2, and 3.

had superior agricultural resources, and as time passed, new resources were discovered in this treasure house – coal, iron, lead, zinc, copper, petroleum, silver, mercury, gold. Each discovery led to a boom, some modest, some enormous, as was the California gold rush.

Static theory would suggest that the redistribution of labor and capital in response to this emerging series of opportunities would tend to produce a convergence of per capita income levels, a convergence that might be upset by exogenous events – such as the Civil War – and by the persistent discovery of new opportunities in new areas. Panel C of Table 1.15 assembles some information that is germane.

First, in very broad terms the data show convergences: relative per capita income levels in the Northeast and the West decline over time, approaching the national average (100), although in the cases of three of the four sub-regions the levels of per capita income are well above average in 1920, the end of the period.

The picture in the South is more complex. Before the Civil War the West

South Central converges toward the average, whereas the South Atlantic and East South Central show a modest divergence. All three of these regions, it should be said, enjoyed increases in per capita income; the increases were simply not as rapid as that of the country as a whole. Between 1860 and 1880, all three Southern regions suffered marked declines in relative per capita income – indeed, all were, in 1880, at an absolute level not much different from that achieved twenty years before, in 1860. The explanation for this set of changes is the Civil War and the destruction of the plantation form of agricultural organization. The recovery was long. By 1920 convergence is observable, but per capita income in the South remained well below the average for the rest of the country.

Income per capita levels in the West were substantially above average, so that the attractiveness of the West to migrants is clear. The same could be said for the West South Central before the Civil War. How does one account for the attractiveness of the North Central, in view of the fact that per capita income levels were below average throughout the pre–Civil War years, and only roughly at the average level thereafter? One possibility is that the measures are biased against the North Central. Specifically, they exclude income from home manufacturing and farm making (clearing, breaking, and fencing farm land), elements of income that must have been far more important in the North Central than in the Northeast. Furthermore, the income measures do not allow for differences in the cost of living. Since the cost of living was almost certainly higher in the Northeast and the West than in the North Central, the measures in the table overstate the differences in regional real incomes. Nonetheless, even allowing for these two sources of bias, the per capita income levels were probably lower in the North Central than in the Northeast and the West.

The explanation for the movement into the North Central – especially in the antebellum years – despite the relatively low levels of per capita income is that migrants must have been disproportionately farmers and farm workers, and whereas the average level of income per capita was higher in the Northeast than in the North Central, there is not much doubt that farming opportunities in the North Central – particularly if one takes into account the prospect of capital gains from the appreciation of land values – were much better than they were in the Northeast. That is, for farmers, income prospects were much better in the North Central than in the Northeast.

Finally, the relatively rapid growth of population in the North Central was not exclusively due to migration. The favorable circumstances –

especially for farmers – led to higher birth rates in the North Central than in the Northeast.

CONCLUSIONS

At the beginning of the long nineteenth century the United States had a seaboard economy, largely agricultural and mercantile, smaller than the leading powers in Europe, but by no means tiny; the economy generated a level of living high by the standards of the day. The economy grew rapidly and spread across a continent. Despite the attractions of its rich agricultural resources, by the beginning of World War I it had the largest industrial sector in the world. Of course it also had one of the largest agricultural sectors in the world. The economy in toto produced more than the economies of the three chief belligerents in World War I taken together.

The level of per capita income also grew, not at an extraorindarily high rate, by the standards of other modernizing countries, but for an exceptionally long period, so that by World War I it was among the highest in the world – perhaps the highest. These several features of the American economy gave to the United States in its international dealings a power that had political and military dimensions and that came to shape a substantial part of the history of the United States in the twentieth century, for good or for ill.

2

THE ECONOMY OF CANADA IN THE NINETEENTH CENTURY

MARVIN MCINNIS

FOUNDATIONS OF THE NINETEENTH-CENTURY CANADIAN ECONOMY

For the economy of Canada it can be said that the nineteenth century came to an end in the mid-1890s. There is wide agreement among observers that a fundamental break occurred at about that time and that in the years thereafter Canadian economic development, industrialization, population growth, and territorial expansion quickened markedly. This has led economic historians to put a special emphasis on the particularly rapid economic expansion that occurred in the years after about 1896. That emphasis has been deceptive and has generated a perception that little of consequence was happening before 1896. W. W. Rostow was only reflecting a reasonable reading of what had been written about Canadian economic history when he declared the "take-off" in Canada to have occurred in the years between 1896 and 1913. That was undoubtedly a period of rapid growth and great transformation in the Canadian economy and is best considered as part of the twentieth-century experience. The break is usually thought to have occurred in the mid-1890s, but the most indicative data concerning the end of this period are drawn from the 1891 decennial census. By the time of the next census in 1901, major changes had begun to occur. It fits the available evidence best, then, to think of an early 1890s end to the nineteenth century.

Some guidance to our reconsideration of Canadian economic development prior to the big discontinuity of the 1890s may be given by a brief review of what had been accomplished by the early years of that decade. Rostow and others were quite wrong in thinking that the Canadian economy was not progressing before the 1890s and that the transition to modern economic growth had not by then taken place. The economic history of Canada over the course of the nineteenth century is predominantly a story of achievement and success. By the early 1890s Canada was among the most prosperous of the world's economies. Its level of national income per head was about on a par with that of Belgium and Switzerland, and only three nations – Australia, Great Britain, and the United States – were decidedly more prosperous. Furthermore, Canadian prosperity was to a considerable extent based on successful industrialization. By 1891 the value of per capita manufacturing output in Canada was higher than in Germany or France and surpassed only by Great Britain, Belgium, and the United States. Canada was a large and prominent player in the world trading economy and had for some years operated one of the world's largest merchant fleets. A lot had been achieved.

Still, in the interest of gaining overall perspective on the development and performance of the Canadian economy, we should offer a more balanced assessment. There is more than one way to gauge industrialization, and from a different viewpoint late-nineteenth-century Canada does not look so prominently industrialized. At 25 percent, the share of national income contributed by the manufacturing sector was not particularly high, nor was the 22 percent of the labor force engaged in that sector. This reflects the large size of the extractive sectors; fishing and forestry were relatively prominent, but it is mainly the consequence of the fact that Canada was still a largely agricultural economy. In that sense Canada was a somewhat heightened reflection of the United States at the time. In contrast with the latter country, though, the other outstanding feature of the Canadian economy was its small absolute size. Canada encompassed a vast territory, of course, but the greater part of it was unsettled and made no contribution to the economy. With only 4.8 million people in 1891, Canada was about the same size as Sweden or the Netherlands and smaller than Belgium. Canada had only one-tenth the population of Germany and barely 7 percent of its American neighbor to the south. Not only was by far the greater part of Canadian territory uninhabited, but even the main settled area was rather thinly populated. Matters of economies of scale and social overhead costs were worrisome features of this small economy. Canada had few cities of any appreciable size and only two, Montreal and Toronto, with populations above 100,000. At the time the United States had twenty-five cities larger than that and three with populations in excess of 1 million. Finally, the last three decades of the nineteenth century had been years of considerable pessimism about the state of the economy and of large-scale emigration to the United States.

For Canada the nineteenth century was a period of substantial accomplishment. Its economy had been one of the world's most successful. At the same time, there were limitations to the record. In the late years of the nineteenth century Canadian economic growth had slowed. Success was tempered by some economic shortcomings that Canada still had not surmounted.

European settlement and the initiation of economic activity in Canada began at the same time as in the area to the south that was to become the United States. The French first established on the Bay of Fundy in 1605, then made a permanent settlement at Quebec in 1608 – the year after the Jamestown colony began in Virginia. The very early histories of the Canadian and American settlements differed markedly, and that had a strong bearing on the subsequent development of the two countries. For many years New France was little more than a trading post, whereas both Virginia and Massachussetts received large influxes of settlers from Britain within a few years of their initial settlement. Those large migrations of the early 1630s were especially telling in establishing the sizes of the respective colonies. By 1650 the pattern was already well established. At that early date the British settlements in America were far more populous than the French settlements. The long-continued circumstance of the United States being about ten times as populous as Canada was thus ingrained by the earliest historical experiences of the two areas. It was not until after 1663, when the French colony was tranferred to direct royal administration, that it received any sizeable amount of immigration, and over the entire course of the French regime up to 1759, it is unlikely that any more than 10,000 immigrants came to New France. Although beginning with so few people, the French settlement in Canada grew about as rapidly as a human population can reproduce. The extraordinarily high birth rate of the French-Canadians has been widely commented upon. By the end of the French regime about 70,000 people resided in Quebec. In addition, there was a much smaller French colony in what is now Nova Scotia. That had been the site of the very first French settlement, prior to the establishment of Quebec, and a small community continued in Acadia, as it was called. Part of its territory was ceded to British rule in 1713, and in 1755, out of concern for possible disloyalty on the part of their French Acadian subjects, the British had forcibly removed those whom they were able to round up. Many ended up in Louisiana, where they were able to

give the world Cajun cooking and inspire maudlin poetry. Indeed, like
Evangeline, many of the transported Acadians made their way back to
their homeland. Others had fled to the woods and escaped expulsion, so
there remained a small French community in Acadia. It was more dispersed than it had previously been – some had crossed to the west side of
the Bay of Fundy and others had moved to Île St-Jean, renamed Prince
Edward Island by the British captors. The island of Cape Breton remained
a French possession after 1713, and there, at Louisbourg, the French
established a military stronghold. When that fell in 1758, and when the
peace settlement was arrived at in 1763, the whole of Canada came under
British rule.

New France had begun, like Virginia and Massachussetts, as a commercial venture – the outpost of a trading company. In the case of Quebec,
the central objective was to trade in furs, especially beaver pelts to be used
for felting. Control of the colony eventually passed to the crown, but the
main business continued to be the fur trade. To expand the supply of furs,
the French were impelled to explore the interior of the continent and to
establish a chain of trading posts far inland. Disaffected French traders
sought English support, resulting in the founding of the Hudson's Bay
Company and the establishment of English trading posts in the far north.
This introduced a British presence to the northern interior of Canada and
offered serious competition to the French in the fur trade. Economically,
New France consisted essentially of the fur trading center at Quebec and
a subsidiary center at Montreal, along with ever expanding agricultural
settlements in the vicinity of those two centers. Increasingly it became a
self-sufficient agricultural community, but markets for farm products were
very limited. Apart from furs, no significant export trade to France or to
the French West Indian colonies was ever established. The fur trading
enterprise represented only a small market for farm products. For some
years in the eighteenth century, the garrison at Louisbourg provided more
substantial market opportunities. Quebec, though, continued to be mainly
a self-sufficient agricultural community. Tobacco could be grown, but
unlike Virginia and Maryland, no large export trade in tobacco with the
mother country was ever established. Hemp was tried but did not catch
on. New France had a decidedly limited economy.

In the mid-eighteenth century New France was swept up in the larger
conflict between England and France, and in 1759 Quebec fell to the
British. With some hesitation – the Caribbean sugar island of Guadeloupe
looked like a possibly more attractive prize – the British took control of

Quebec in 1763. This event, widely referred to by French-Canadians as "The Conquest," has continued to have profound political consequences for Canada. Initially, however, it meant little change for most of the French inhabitants of Quebec, especially after 1774, when the Quebec Act assured legal recognition of the French language, civil law, and religion.

In the Atlantic region, settlement under British rule proceeded slowly. Capitalizing on the splendid natural harbor at the site, the British established a military center at Halifax in 1749. Four years later they actively promoted settlement by situating a colony of Germans at Lunenburg, to the south of Halifax. After the expulsion of the Acadians, settlers from New England, and a few directly from Britain, began to trickle in. Some of these settlers were able to make an advantageous start by taking over land cleared by the Acadians. That included diked hay marshes on the Bay of Fundy that represented a significant capital investment. The large herds of cattle maintained by these settlers at an early date suggest that they may also have benefited by taking possession of cattle left behind by the Acadians. On the island of Newfoundland there had long been continuing settlements, even though these were actively discouraged by the British authorities. Throughout the Maritime settlements under British rule it was not until near the beginning of the nineteenth century that substantial economic expansion got underway.

One could argue that from a strictly economic point of view the British "Conquest" turned out to be a boon to the French inhabitants of Quebec. The rapidly growing population was able to extend its settlement into areas of good land that previously were unsafe for habitation. Neither the English nor the Indians allied with them were any longer a threat. In 1763 French settlement was still a thin band along the St. Lawrence. Thereafter it pushed south along tributaries of the great river, especially the Richelieu. As part of the British empire, Quebec gained access to markets both in Britain and in other British colonies. Oak staves cut by new settlers on the Richelieu were shipped to the West Indies. More importantly for this essentially agricultural community, wheat and flour could be exported to Britain, where prices were moving toward an all-time high. In a small way, Quebec had established itself as a regular supplier of wheat flour to Britain by the early 1780s, and it continued exporting for almost thirty years. That is a longer period of continuous export than enjoyed by Upper Canada in the nineteenth century, yet no one has written of a Lower Canada "wheat staple." Be that as it may, wheat and flour exports helped to generate a

level of prosperity not before experienced in Quebec. They also served to
accelerate the commercialization of the rural economy.

The urban centers, Quebec and Montreal but especially the latter, also
got a considerable boost. British merchants with established ties to
markets and established sources of finance moved into Canada to take
advantage of economic opportunities. To some extent they moved into
positions that, under different circumstances, might have been occupied
by the French. While in the long term this may have had political consequences, the immediate effect was to facilitate the functioning of the
economy. A resurgent fur trade invigorated the urban economy of Montreal and stimulated opportunities for artisans. All sectors of the economy
showed a quickening. The urban side of things was limited, though, and
became increasingly so. At the time of the "Conquest," Quebec had a
somewhat higher proportion of its population living in urban centers
than was the case in the American colonies. That shortly changed because
the countryside was the more rapidly growing sector of the Canadian
economy.

It was the rupture between Britain and those of her American colonies
that gained independence by force of arms that brought about the
real foundation of Canada as a nation. Attempts were made to draw
Canada into the War of Independence on the American side, but the
French-Canadians remained loyal to Britain. So did some American
colonists, and many of these Empire Loyalists sought refuge in the
northern colonies of British North America. By far the largest group
landed in Nova Scotia. Of the almost 40,000 who arrived there, possibly
one-fifth moved on elsewhere. About 32,000 Loyalists remained in Nova
Scotia, suddenly more than doubling the population of that colony. These
people were granted land in scattered locations throughout the colony,
in part because Nova Scotia has only a small area of usable farm land
and little of that in any single district. Just under half of the Loyalists
who remained in the Nova Scotia colony settled across the Bay of Fundy
in the valley of the Saint John river. They were shortly organized into
the separate colony of New Brunswick. Very few of the Loyalists put
down roots in Prince Edward Island. The land of that island had
previously been alienated by the British Crown into the hands of a
small number of absentee landowners. At the time the island had a small
population of Acadian French, and it soon began to receive settlers from
Britain.

These Maritime colonies were primarily agricultural settlements, but the close proximity to the sea meant that the fishery was from the outset an available supplement to farming. There were markets for fish, lumber, and staves in the British West Indian colonies from which the now politically independent New Englanders were nominally excluded. The Maritimers, however, were able to make only a limited response. Their production was small relative to the needs of the West Indian colonies. The need to provide shipping to the West Indies under the umbrella of the British Navigation Acts offered another opportunity for profitable enterprise. Nova Scotia's capabilities were still limited, however, and that led the planters in the Indies to be more than willing to seek out illicit supplies from the United States. One area where the Maritimes had more success in taking the place of New England was in the provision of masts and spars for the British navy. With a mix of farming, fishing, shipping, and commerce, the basic structure of the economy of the Maritime colonies was slowly being worked out.

The Loyalist influx into Quebec was smaller, but its political and economic ramifications were nevertheless profound. About 6,000 Loyalists were established in the western part of Quebec, along the St. Lawrence River, at the eastern end of Lake Ontario, and also along the Niagara River. A smaller group settled in the old province of Quebec itself, mostly near the mouth of the Richelieu River. The western Loyalist settlement was small but influential enough to lead to a division in 1791 of the Quebec colony into two separate parts – Upper and Lower Canada. Following closely in the steps of the Loyalists, additional settlers continued to move in from the United States. Until 1794 it was not entirely certain where the boundary with the United States was actually going to be. Good agricultural land was being freely granted in Canada, and settlement extended along the riverfront and lakeshore. German-Americans from Pennsylvania established communities at several locations – north of York (now Toronto) and to the west of there at Waterloo. A number of Quaker settlements were also founded. In Lower Canada, settlers came north from New York and Vermont to take up land south and east of Montreal in what came to be referred to as the Eastern Townships. That area was outside of the seigneuries of old Quebec. It was surveyed along British lines and settled in block fashion whereby whole townships of land were granted out to township leaders on the understanding that they would bring in additional settlers. In Upper Canada, land was granted lavishly to prominent individuals in a conscious effort to create a society headed by a prosperous landowning class – a reproduction of something resembling the British squirearchy. A trickle of immigrants began also to come from Britain. Especially prominent were Scots Highlanders who settled in the easternmost townships of Upper Canada and other Scots in Lower Canada, in the district southwest of Montreal. There were even settlements of French nobles fleeing the Terror of the Revolution. By far the most substantial inflow, however, came from the United States.

In this period, around the beginning of the nineteenth century, both Upper and Lower Canada were overwhelmingly agricultural economies, consisting of newly established, expanding, largely subsistence farms. Lower Canada was at the peak of its period of exports of wheat and flour to Britain. Upper Canada was still essentially struggling with the problem of basic subsistence and the general make-up of an economic system. The seaport city of Quebec was the center of administration and the key point of contact with Britain. Montreal was rapidly gaining on Quebec in size and was the center of a much more productive agricultural area. It was not at this time an important port for overseas trade, since shipping could not easily ascend the shallow passages of the St. Lawrence between Quebec and Montreal. The orientation of Montreal was landward, westward towards the interior of the continent. It was the commercial center of the still vigorous fur trade, in which the upstart North West Company of Montreal – an association of mainly Scottish traders – was locked in serious competition with the much older Hudson's Bay Company. Some of those Scottish traders were to become the commercial elite of Montreal.

Upper Canada was, if anything, even more of a rural community than Lower Canada. Nascent urban centers were established at Kingston, the transshipment point at the foot of Lake Ontario, at Newark (later to be named Niagara), which was the earliest administrative center, and at York, which eventually became the capital. York had a sheltered harbor on Lake Ontario and was the lake terminus of an old portage route to the north. An early British administrator, John Graves Simcoe, contemplated a capital established far from American influence, at a location in the western part of the province, on a river appropriately named the Thames. He called the place London, but for many years it struggled along as a mere village, and York retained its status as the capital.

Jay's Treaty in 1794 finally settled the division of territory between Canada and the United States. The American colonists had been ambitious in their claims; they were willing to take everything. The British were resistant but not very eager to strike a tough bargain; hence they were not inclined to be very possessive about the extensive territory they had earlier assigned to Quebec. The big issue concerned whether much of what is now the states of Michigan, Minnesota, and Wisconsin would be in the United States or in Canada. From an early stage the British negotiators seemed to be quite willing to trade away nominal control of territory for economic advantage. An early draft of the settlement would have ceded much of the territory to the United States but retained a right of commercial access. By that scheme, written into the initial draft of the Peace of Paris, the United States would have acquired the territory conditional upon unimpeded transport access and no tariff barriers to trade in the Great Lakes and Mississippi Valley area. It was a blueprint for a very different Canada than what actually resulted. Protectionist sentiment in Britain began to worry about precedent, and the free commerce provision was dropped from the final text of the Peace of Paris. The intention was to make it the topic of a subsequent treaty conference, but that was never acted upon. Canada was forever consigned to more limited boundaries than Canadians had contemplated, and it failed to obtain unimpeded access to the larger economy to the south.

In the early nineteenth century, relations between the United States and Britain became increasingly strained, and Canada was caught in the middle. Tensions escalated to the Embargo and Non-Intercourse Acts of the United States, but these did not prove enough to keep the United States out of war with Britain. Eventually, Canada became the focus of the hostilities between the two nations. The United States attacked Britain by launching an invasion of Britain's remaining colony on mainland North America. The war was fought to a stalemate, but its ending brought a cooling of relations between Canada and the United States. Settlers no longer came to Canada in large numbers from the United States, and the authorities in Canada were no longer willing to make free grants of land to those American immigrants who did come. Concern for Americanization became a continuing Canadian worry. The British authorities in Canada turned their attention to schemes for attracting settlers from Britain to fill up the unsettled lands in Canada that might otherwise have a dangerous appeal to the Americans. Economic contacts between Canada and the United States were not extensive. Canada's farm products faced tariffs in addition to transport barriers in any attempt to gain access to markets in the United States. Commercial ties were with Britain, and manufactured goods were imported mainly from Britain. In hammering out a structure for its economic existence, Canada faced a number of disadvantages. It was a long distance from the British motherland. Little capital had been accumulated, and social overhead was primitive. Skilled labor was especially scarce, and only the rudiments of an education system had been put in place. The climate was harsh and the growing season short; an especially serious implication of that was that in all but a few districts of Canada Indian corn could not reliably be ripened. Indian corn was the backbone of American agriculture, an especially productive crop, well suited to hand planting and picking, and a cheap, abundant food for both man and beast. Growing conditions unsuitable to maize may have been the single most serious drawback to agricultural development in Canada.

At the same time it is important to recognize some of the advantages that Canada possessed. There was an abundance of good agricultural land still to be cleared and settled. There was open and easy access to the knowledge and technology of the most advanced economies in the world at the time. The entire economy was closely tied together by an outstandingly good natural transport system – the St. Lawrence–Great Lakes waterway. It has been common in historical writing to emphasize the difficulties and shortcomings of early-nineteenth-century transport. Many authors describe the horrific conditions on the few roads that did exist without noting that scarcely anyone but unwise British visitors would even think of traveling on the roads. The waterway was an excellent one, complicated only by the great falls at Niagara and a few stretches of rapids on the St. Lawrence. The economy of Canada consisted of a thin band of agricultural settlement stretched out along this magnificent waterway. For the purposes of transport, the long, harsh winters were an added benefit. Overland travel by horse-drawn vehicles was cheaper on firmly frozen ground, especially if covered by snow. With winter transport and excellent waterways, Canadians in the early nineteenth century had transport costs as low as anywhere in the world.

Some merchants and visionaries had ambitions to use the great St. Lawrence waterway to capture the commerce of the interior of North America. The idea presumed a vast export trade with Britain. Such a plan confronted three major impediments – first, the high costs of transatlantic travel via the St. Lawrence; second, the British Corn Laws that after 1820 frequently barred access of North American breadstuffs to the British market; and, third, the ingenuity of the Americans in building their own low-cost transport route in the form of the Erie Canal. Thus the Commercial Empire of the St. Lawrence never came into existence.

Only the simplest and crudest indicators of the dimensions of the early Canadian economy are known to us. In 1815, when war with the United States was over and the real story of nineteenth-century Canadian development was to begin, the population of the colony of Canada amounted to about 400,000, while another 200,000 may have resided in the Maritime colonies (including Newfoundland). Fully three-quarters of Canadians resided in the Lower province (Quebec); Upper Canada still did not have quite a hundred thousand people. Fewer than 20 percent lived in urban centers. Canada was essentially an agricultural community but already, because of the abundance of land, one of the more prosperous agricultural communities in the world.

THE AGRICULTURAL ECONOMY OF EARLY-NINETEENTH-CENTURY CANADA

The colonies of Upper and Lower Canada in the early nineteenth century, in the years around 1815–1820 when the world was groping towards a new, post-Napoleonic order, were essentially pioneer agricultural communities. Land was still available in abundance. The small populations of the colonies were growing about as rapidly as is possible through the natural increase of population while being further augmented by immigrants. Albeit with a lot of hard work and some early privation, farms could be made that returned the ordinary person considerably more material output than might be expected in Britain. These were, however, farms in a remote and severe land, farms that had to be laboriously carved out of a forested wilderness. Settlement of the territory was forefront in the minds of the British colonial administrators. It was in their interest to have an established functioning economy. Furthermore, a settled territory could not so readily be claimed by the Americans.

Experiments were made with fostering immigrant settlements both by private and public endeavor. The authorities were very receptive to encouraging any private individuals or organizations willing to facilitate migration and settlement and they were more than willing to bestow great advantage on anyone who could make a credible claim to bring in a substantial number of settlers. Large grants of land were made to individuals who committed to bring in settlers. Numerous schemes were launched, and they varied greatly in the degree of their success. Highland Scots, in overabundance in their homeland and being pushed out by the economic and social transition of the Highlands, were especially encouraged to move to British North America. The Irish, particularly Protestant Irish from the North, were drawn in large numbers. Experiments were made with publicly organized and supported settlements of migrants from Britain. In that way settlements of Irish were made at Peterborough and of Scots at Perth, both in areas well away from existing settlements. Private individuals were also relied upon to manage the settlement process. The Irish promoter Thomas Talbot was granted extensive lands in western Upper Canada to establish new farmers. For many years the paternalistic Talbot ran a tightly managed settlement program that is generally considered to have been very successful. The bold Highland chieftain McNab imperiously tried to do the same thing in the Ottawa Valley in a more limited area and produced only a community of resistant, protesting settlers who complained that they had come to Canada to escape petty local feudalism. Lord Selkirk, with a particular concern for the condition of peasant farmers in Scotland, made several attempts to establish settlements. He tried, without success, to establish a colony on Prince Edward Island. Then he deposited a few settlers in a very remote and unhealthy area of Upper Canada. Finally he established a settlement in the Red River Valley that would eventually become the nucleus of the province of Manitoba.

The publicly supported settlements were soon judged to be more costly than the authorities in Britain were willing to accept. By the mid-1820s the era of state planned settlements was over, but the pace of settlement slackened only temporarily. By the end of the decade of the 1820s a rising tide of British settlers was moving into Canada. Increasingly, individuals saw an advantage in migrating to farms in Canada. In this period, the late 1820s and early 1830s, Canada was receiving as many or more immigrants from Britain as was the United States. Australia was beginning to be recognized as an opportunity for settlement, at least when passages were subsidized, and the United States was always there, welcoming immigrants, but in the period between 1816 and 1835, Canada was the preferred destination of British emigrants.

Land in Canada was freely granted. "Official" settlers – those who had a claim based in some way upon service to Britain – received relatively large grants, in some cases up to several thousand acres. Ordinary immigrants, though, could claim 200 acres, conditional upon actually settling and establishing a farm. That was not so easily done, however, unless the immigrant brought substantial funds. Many settlers found it advantageous to take up smaller tracts of land already claimed by settlement organizers.

A tension existed between the desire to settle the land quickly and the use of generous free grants to establish a landed class. With the many large private grants that were speculatively held, and the reservation of a substantial fraction of the land to finance the colonial government and the Established Church, one consequence was a more dispersed settlement than might otherwise have occurred. The spreading-out of settlement raised transport costs generally and may have retarded the commercialization of the colony. There were many complaints about unsettled land taking up so large a segment of the established districts, and many fingers pointed accusingly at absentee landlordism. The costs of basic local services – roads and schools – were high when settlement was less dense than might otherwise have been the case.

In the mid 1820s there was a major shift in policy. It was decided that publicly assisted immigration could not be economically justified. Under the influence of Edward Gibbon Wakefield, the British authorities became convinced that land should be sold and not just given away. A private concern representing British investors, the Canada Land Company, offered to purchase the unsettled Crown and Clergy Reserves. The colonial government declined to relinquish the lands set aside to provide for the Established Church but agreed to sell off the lots designated as Crown Reserves plus 1 million acres of unsurveyed land – referred to as the Huron Tract – to the company. This massive land transfer was intended at one and the same time to foster settlement and to generate revenue for the colonial administrators. There has been controversy over the assessment of the Canada Company transaction, but at least in some districts the company appears to have successfully accelerated settlement. It built mills, established market centers, and invested in improved transport, all as ways of raising the returns on its investment. It also was prepared to rent as well as sell land. In Lower Canada a counterpart of the Canada Company in the form of the British American Land Company in a similar way acquired almost 850,000 acres in the Eastern Townships. Its land was relatively remote, much of it hilly, and not in as strong demand, so the British American Land Company was much less of a financial success than the Canada Company. Eventually, though, it supplied land to French-Canadian habitant farmers as they moved away from the overcrowded seigneurial area of Quebec.

The first concern of Canadian pioneer farms was to provide for the subsistence of members of the farm household. It would be wrong to

describe this as merely self-sufficient farming. From the outset there was
market contact, and credit played a central role in the system. The farms,
though, produced a mix of output prescribed mainly by local consumption needs. In addition, we must not lose sight of the fact that farm land
itself was a major product. Farm making was a long, slow process of transforming human labor into a valuable item of capital-improved land. The
mostly regular, rectangular survey of Upper Canada and the township area
of Lower Canada laid out farms of 100 acres, although some pioneers began
with only 50 acres. Completed farms eventually would have 75 to 80 acres
improved, the remainder being left as rough pasture and woodlot. It was
possible for a farmer, with some assistance, to clear 4 or 5 acres of forest a
year, but the overall experience was an average of just less than 2 acres.
Making a farm was evidently a lifetime occupation. The felled trees were
mostly burned. The best farm land was covered in great abundance by
deciduous trees that seldom had value as lumber. The ashes of the burned
trees were gathered up and leached for potash. The trade in potash was
well organized, as there was a ready export market for potash, and that
product soon emerged as one of the Canadian colony's principal exports.
The tree stumps on cleared land took many years to rot to a condition
where they could be pulled. In the meantime the land was tilled, and crops
grown among the stumps.

The leading crop was wheat. Wheat bread was a large element in the
diet of Canadians, both British and French, so wheat was grown foremostly
for the consumption of farm families, but it was also widely marketed.
There was little off-farm demand for other grains, and crops other than
wheat mostly had to be fed to livestock to be converted into meat, eggs,
and dairy products. That required investment in a stock of animals,
another aspect of farm making that typically proceeded slowly. Most of
Canada was at a disadvantage in comparison with the United States in that
Indian corn, the cheapest and most efficient animal feed, could not reliably be ripened. Only in the westernmost district of Upper Canada was
corn extensively grown. Wheat had the additional advantage of requiring
relatively little capital. It was more land intensive than livestock products
and did not necessitate the investment in stocks of animals. That was an
appealing characteristic of wheat that made it a prominent crop of pioneer
districts in both the United States and Canada. Spring wheat was the only
variety that could be grown in Lower Canada and the eastern districts of
Upper Canada. That was also somewhat of a disadvantage, since spring
wheat was harder to mill into good-quality flour and sold at a lower price

than winter wheat. From about the mid-northshore of Lake Ontario westward and for just a few miles inland, it was possible to grow winter wheat. That area developed as the principal wheat farming district of Upper Canada. It was there that the greatest concentration of settlement occurred before the 1840s. Throughout Canada farmers limited their wheat acreage to the 10 to 12 acres a family could harvest in the short time available in the fall. That was sufficient to provide a surplus well above the consumption needs of the average family. Where winter wheat could be grown, an additional 10 to 12 acres would be planted to that crop, since it ripened enough earlier to have a separate harvest season.

Most writers on Canadian economic history have emphasized the central place of wheat in pioneer farming, and they have mainly stressed its marketability. They have generalized from the winter wheat district; many parts of Upper Canada were not nearly so devoted to wheat but engaged more in mixed farming. There were reasons other than market demand, though, why wheat played such a prominent role in pioneer farming. Wheat was more labor intensive than most other forms of farm production, and what the pioneer farmer had most of, apart from uncleared land, was labor. Growing wheat was a way of getting by with limited capital. Moreover, we should not lose sight of the fact that bread from wheat flour was the leading item of food consumption. Farmers also grew potatoes and garden vegetables, and oats for both human and animal consumption. Oats was the most favored feed crop, but as numbers of livestock increased, greater amounts of hay and field peas were also produced. In most areas farm-raised food was supplemented by fish and game. The former especially were widely and abundantly available.

The most widely held interpretation of Canadian economic history emphasizes the role of wheat as an export staple. By this approach, the economic success of newly settled lands is seen to be tied to their ability to exploit a natural resource-intensive "staple" product for export to established metropolitan markets. Wheat is claimed to be the staple of Upper Canada in the first half of the nineteenth century, with prosperity linked to the export of wheat and wheat flour to Britain. Thus, the production of wheat for export is commonly claimed to be the *raison d'être* of the agricultural economy of Upper Canada. It is doubtful, though, whether in fact it was commonly the case that in the years before 1850 wheat could be profitably grown in Upper Canada for export to Britain. The greatest obstacle to wheat exports from Upper Canada was the "tyranny of distance." The British market was far away, and the freight costs on such bulky commodities as wheat and flour were onerous. Before 1815 the exceptionally high wheat prices in Britain had allowed profitable exports of wheat despite those high transport costs. In the post-Napoleonic period the British market was much less favorable. Furthermore, the British Corn Law tariff applied to its North American colonies. British North America received preferential treatment relative to non-British countries such as the United States, and that preference has been played up by many writers. The main fact, though, was that in addition to heavy transport costs Canadian suppliers of wheat flour frequently faced a substantial tariff and in some years complete prohibition. Consequently, it was more often than not the case that in the years between 1820 and 1850 Canadians found it unprofitable to export wheat or wheat flour to Britain.

The situation in the market can be considered at a representative location in Upper Canada – say Dundas, at the head of Lake Ontario. The important features are that, first, the demand for wheat at Dundas would be perfectly elastic at the price in Britian less costs of supplying that market from Dundas. There are three important components of those costs. There was the cost of shipping wheat or wheat flour from Quebec to Liverpool. Before that the flour had to be transported by lake schooner and then by river boat on the St. Lawrence to Quebec. Finally, there was the tariff. The upshot was that more often than not the price at which Canadian wheat could be sold in Britain, less tariff and transport costs, was lower than the price prevailing in Canada. Exporting was just not profitable, and in most years before 1850 there were either no actual exports or else small shipments were made to be held in bond in Great Britain until market conditions there improved. Exceptions were in 1826 and 1827 and again in 1830–32, when hopes were raised by successful exports, but those years were only a small part of the period that is claimed by many writers to have encompassed the first Canadian "wheat staple."

The situation points up the lines of action along which Canadian economic development proceeded in the first half of the nineteenth century. Amelioration could be sought in each of the components of the gap between the Upper Canadian and the British price of breadstuff. Not much could be done actively to reduce transatlantic freight costs. Largely for exogenous reasons, though, they were coming down, and that was a help. In addition, by shipping flour rather than wheat, a saving in transport costs could be obtained, and Canada's abundant waterpower provided many cheap milling sites. Internal transport costs could be reduced by investment in waterway improvement, and Canada embarked upon an ambitious program of canal building and dredged the St. Lawrence between Quebec and Montreal to permit ocean ships to take on freight further inland. Finally, the course of action most readily available was to press for removal of the onerous Corn Law duties as applied to grain from Canada, and in that the Canadians were eventually successful.

The farmers of Upper Canada did, however, find a market for their wheat in Lower Canada. After about 1820, wheat from Upper Canada increasingly displaced locally grown supplies in Lower Canada. That was especially so in the 1830s, when crops in the lower province were ravaged by the wheat midge. Wheat could be grown more cheaply in Upper Canada, and that province gained from an increasing specialization in wheat. Two questions arise. First, where did that leave the farmers of Lower Canada? That will be taken up below. The second major question is how was Lower Canada able to balance payments with Upper Canada if it abandoned growing its own breadstuff and imported from Upper Canada instead? The answer lies in the success of Lower Canada's timber exports, which were probably more important for the whole economy of the colony of Canada than has usually been claimed.

The forest had from the beginning been an outstanding feature of British North America. There was so much of it, and for the most part it was just an impediment to settlement, although farmers typically avoided the poorer, sandier land on which the great pine forest stood. If high transport costs were an impediment to wheat exports, they were even more inhibiting to bulky wood. In the earliest years only rarer, high-valued products, such as masts and spars, could be exported. Circumstances changed dramatically in the early nineteenth century when, embroiled in the Napoleonic Wars, Britain sought a secure source of timber by imposing exceptionally heavy tariffs on foreign timber and encouraging the import of pine timber from its North American colony. Under this heavily protective arrangement the timber industry of British North America boomed. Pine was the desired product, and British North America had vast amounts of pine. New Brunswick was the timber colony *par excellence*, but Canada also had a vast area of pine forest to exploit. The valley of the Ottawa river became the principal locus of the pine timber industry. A simple hand technology was all that was required. Trees were felled in the winter months, cut into manageable lengths, and squared on the site. In the spring the "sticks" were floated downstream. On the Ottawa River the squared timber was formed into rafts and directed on down to the St. Lawrence and on to the port of Quebec. There the timber was loaded onto ships for export to Britain. A substantial fraction of world shipping became involved in this trade in a very bulky product.

The British timber duties were lowered in 1821 but still remained formidable, and by then Britain's former suppliers in northern Europe had largely been displaced in the market by British North America. Squared pine timber was by a considerable margin the leading export of British North America, although it was complemented by squared oak, staves, shingles, lathwood, and as time went on, a growing amount of sawn lumber. If there were truly a staple export of British North America, it was wood. In the early 1830s per capita exports of wood from British North America were triple the value of per capita exports of cotton from the United States. The trade was sustained over the entire course of the nineteenth century, even though British North America lost its preferred status. The differential duty was reduced by Britain in 1842 and effectively eliminated in 1851, yet Canadian exports of wood to Britain continued to grow long after that, while Canada also found a growing market for its wood in the United States. Wood was the veritable backbone of the Canadian economy in the nineteenth century. In addition to being exported directly, it supplied a large shipbuilding industry both in the Maritime colonies and at the city of Quebec. Many of the ships were also exported, but a large fraction went to supply the merchant marine of British North America, which by the latter half of the nineteenth century was second in the world in tonnage only to Britain. The immediate and most important market for Canadian shipping services was the timber trade. The whole fit together into an integrated economy, an economy that was ultimately based on the exploitation of the forest. Wood exports were, in a direct sense, the driving force behind the development of the Canadian economy, but they also contributed importantly, in an indirect way, by facilitating agricultural specialization.

Most often in Canadian historical writing the tenor of appraisal of the timber industry has been negative. "Hewers of wood and drawers of water" has come to represent economic backwardness and failure to industrialize. By this view the timber trade is looked upon as a mere passing phase and not very consequential for Canadian economic development. Assertions are frequently made that the trade was artificially created by British policy, that it led to a rapid dissipation of Canada's forest wealth, and that the benefits accrued mostly to British merchants. It is claimed to have diverted labor resources away from agriculture, where they might have better been used for farm improvement. The fluctuating nature of the trade is emphasized as well, although instability has been a charge commonly laid against primary product exports of all sorts, and the evidence is that timber was no more subject to fluctuation than other primary product exports.

In general the criticisms that have been levied against the timber trade have been asserted but not shown to have a clear foundation in fact. Mainly they have been based on a characterization of the trade in hewn timber. That, however, was the predominant product only in the early years of the trade. The more rapidly growing and long sustained sector of the industry was the manufacture of planks and boards. Mills sawing deals, the thick planks demanded in the British market, appear on the scene relatively early and rapidly expand their output to overtake hewn timber as the leading product. The all-time peak export of squared timber occurred in 1845, and by 1851 manufactured wood exports surpassed those of unmanufactured wood. By that time Canadian sawmills had successfully penetrated the U.S. market as well, and exports there grew considerably faster than the trade to Britain. By the late 1860s the United States took more Canadian wood than did Britain. The sawn lumber business was much less volatile than hewn timber had been. For most of the nineteenth century, saw milling was Canada's leading manufacturing industry. Typically it has been portrayed as an industry with hundreds of small plants, yet the bulk of sawn lumber exports was produced in a small number of very large, capital-intensive mills that were the high-tech establishments of their day. Water power predominated, but that was because Canada had such an abundance of great hydraulic power sites. The technology was a continuous process whereby the logs were hauled mechanically from the storage ponds and fed through twenty-five or more frames of gang saws. This was no mere "hewing of wood."

The agricultural economy of Lower Canada proceeded in the first half of the century along lines quite similar to those already described for Upper Canada. Land clearing and farm making to provide for largely subsistence agriculture prevailed. For a long time it was widely believed that the French-Canadian farmers of Lower Canada remained backward and inefficient in comparison with their English-Canadian counterparts, and much has been written about an early-nineteenth-century crisis in Quebec agriculture. A new and more factually based interpretation of early-nineteenth-century Quebec has emerged that is more favorably disposed towards the habitant farmers of French Canada. There is little foundation for arguments of culturally based deficiencies in farm practice. French farmers performed much like their anglophone neighbors in Lower Canada and not much differently from farmers in Upper Canada. By the 1820s there was a vigorous development of villages and rural industry. The countryside was becoming commercialized. There is no evidence of a decline in prosperity. Indeed, per capita real output may have been slowly edging upward.

The main agricultural difference between Lower Canada and Upper Canada is that in the lower province farmers were abandoning wheat to concentrate on the production of meat and dairy products while increasingly coming to rely on Upper Canada for breadstuffs. In the harsher climate of Lower Canada, farmers could not produce wheat as cheaply as in the winter wheat district of Upper Canada. Then, infestations of wheat midge ravaged Lower Canada in the 1830s and forced at least a temporary abandonment of wheat growing as they did in Upper Canada twenty-five years later. Lower Canada, however, set aside wheat permanently and catered to the other food demands of a growing local non-farm population, yet this was a limited form of agriculture. As many observers noted, there was little sign of improvement, of progressive husbandry; but it is important to remember that until about the middle of the nineteenth century that could be said generally of all but a few small districts of North America. There is no indication that before mid-century farm practice in Upper Canada was on the whole superior to that in Lower Canada. The entire difference lay in the more favorable growing conditions for winter wheat in a few districts of Upper Canada. With more limited opportunities in agriculture, many farmers in Lower Canada turned to seasonal, off-farm work, cutting the forests, building ships, and working on the transport system.

What Canadian farmers and merchants who dealt in farm products wanted most was better access to remunerative markets. As has already been pointed out, faraway Britain was more often than not an unprofitable place to sell wheat flour, the only farm product that offered much prospect of an external market. Transport costs were not so much of a barrier to access to the U.S. market, but a hefty tariff that averaged 20 to 25 percent was. From time to time, shipments were made across Lake Ontario, but it was a very intermittent thing. Canadians could address their fundamental problem in part by making improvements to the transport system. That point will be dealt with in more detail below. Initially, they made the

British Corn Law tariff their chief target. As loyal British subjects, the Canadians could see no justification for the tariff to be imposed on them, even if it was at a lower rate than imposed on Americans and other foreign suppliers of grain to Britain. The Canadians repeatedly pressed their case and in 1842 won agreement that Canadian wheat would be admitted to Britain at a fixed, virtually nominal tariff of one shilling per quarter of grain. That concession was made conditional upon Canada imposing a tariff on wheat from the United States so that American wheat could not flood into Britain, laundered by the St. Lawrence. Canadian merchants anticipated a boom in wheat exports and rapidly expanded milling capacity. Flour could be milled cheaply in Canada, and the reduction in bulk provided some saving in transport costs. The limited supply of Canadian wheat, however, kept prices above the levels at which it was profitable to ship wheat and flour to Britain until 1846, by which year Britain gave up the Corn Laws altogether and opened its market to Americans and other foreign suppliers. Canadians panicked, especially the merchants. They felt totally abandoned.

At the farm level the change in British policy was felt hardly at all, and production continued to increase. Prices in Britain strengthened, and after 1848 Canada began regularly to export wheat and flour to Britain. Wheat finally got firmly established as an export staple, and for a decade a crescendo of wheat export provided a foundation for a booming Canadian economy. Wheat surpassed wood, exports of which were also booming, as the leading export of the country. The decade of the 1850s was a period of notably accelerated economic change. The economy both expanded rapidly and became more complex in structure. We do not have reliable estimates, but real per capita income was almost certainly rising. By mid-century the process of continuously rising per capita income that is the hallmark of modern growing economies was underway in Canada.

Worried about the loss of preferred status in the British market, Canadians looked desperately for alternatives. As a British colony, although having achieved a large measure of domestic independence in 1848 in the form of responsible parliamentary government, Canada still had no independent foreign policy. On behalf of all its North American colonies, Britain negotiated a treaty with the United States providing for reciprocal free trade in natural products that came into effect in 1854. This arrangement helped to placate the colonials, and it resolved long-standing friction between the United States and Britain over rights to fishing grounds in the North Atlantic. Coming as it did in a period of pronounced economic prosperity, the Reciprocity Treaty of 1854 was long hailed as an important contributor to Canadian economic development. Recent research has tended to cast doubt on the extent of the independent contribution made by the Reciprocity Treaty. Many other growth-promoting factors were operating at the same time, and reduced U.S. tariffs may have played only a modest role in the boom of the 1850s.

Reciprocity contributed little to the growth of the country's two leading exports. The market for wheat flour was in Britain, although free trade generated some advantages in rationalizing Canada–U.S. supplies in border areas. Exports of lumber from Canada to the United States had already begun to increase rapidly prior to the removal of the tariff, but by 1854 the British market was strongly booming, and so the main effect of Reciprocity was merely to divert to the United States wood that might otherwise have been shipped to Britain. The main contribution of Reciprocity was to foster a widening of trade by encouraging the development of exports to the United States of commodities that previously had not been viably traded. Examples are malting barley to supply the newly established lager beer industry in the United States, butter, and horses. The sturdy and economical French-Canadian breed of horse found particular favor in the U.S. market. Free trade combined with improvements in the transport system to make it profitable to ship even such bulky goods as firewood, oats, and hay from Canada to urban markets in the United States. By the late 1850s Canada had developed a substantial export trade in steers to be fattened in the United States. What was important about this broadening of the spectrum of goods exportable to the United States is that those goods could be produced in districts where wheat could not profitably be grown. It widened the base of economic development and prosperity. These developments were valuable and important, yet they were small in impact in comparison with the great exports of wheat and wood that were the main propellants of the Canadian economy.

The United States anticipated that it would increase exports of manufactured goods to Canada. It did, but the gains were far from dramatic. Then in 1859 Canada introduced a new tariff schedule that was clearly designed to protect its manufacturing industries. The United States complained that Canada had acted against the spirit of the treaty. Political pressures were mounting from the usual alignment of competitors with imports from Canada and, overall, there was not much in the treaty to benefit the United States. It abrogated the treaty in 1866. The period of the Reciprocity Treaty went down in Canadian annals as one of notable prosperity, and that alone cast the treaty in a favorable light from the Canadian point of view. For a long time thereafter Canadians looked upon some form of free trade arrangement with the United States as a first-best policy.

At mid-century Canada was still essentially a farming economy, with an important forestry sector, but the settlement period was almost over. The agricultural community was well established. Frontier expansion was limited to a few fringe areas, and by the late 1850s Canada had run out of land suitable for new settlement. The problem was critical. Population was growing rapidly. Natural increase was running about as high as attainable by human populations, and immigrants were still arriving in large numbers, although by the late 1850s the influx had begun to diminish. The arising problem was what to do with the large, new generation coming to adulthood. There were three alternatives, and resort was had to all three: an intensification of agriculture, industrialization, and emigration. By 1860 the flow of emigration to the United States had become large, and the 1861–71 decade saw net emigration from Canada, something that would continue until almost the end of the century.

Agricultural development with diversification, intensification, and productivity advance was the outstanding characteristic of the Canadian economy between the late 1840s and the late 1860s. That was especially so of Upper Canada, designated as Canada West in the years after political union with Lower Canada in 1842. The period began with an export boom in wheat. That was relatively short-lived, and by the late 1850s limitations on the supply side were evident. All the good wheat land had been taken up, and wheat production could no longer be increased just by moving onto new land. The loss of forest shelter exposed more of the fall wheat crop to winter-kill, and the wheat midge had arrived. There was a great need to shift to other agricultural products. Rapidly growing urban markets in Canada and the access to the U.S. market gained under the Reciprocity Treaty to some degree facilitated that. Mixed farming required a substantial investment in herds of animals. A pioneer economy in which labor was applied to land, with little capital, to grow marketable cereals was being supplanted by mixed farming, which was much more capital intensive. Meat and dairy products were becoming the predominant items of agricultural output. The whole range of agricultural improvement was underway – mechanization, more sophisticated crop rotations, better animals, better knowledge of animal feeding, and more careful handling of products. These required both capital and improved technique.

Economic historians have given their greatest attention to farm mechanization and, especially, to the adoption of the mechanical reaper. That certainly occurred, especially after the mid-1850s, but reapers were far from the whole story. Threshing had become mechanized even before reaping and, even where the flail was still used in the 1850s, winnowing was done by mechanical fanning mills. Hay was mechanically mowed and raked, stumps were pulled by machine, animal-powered mechanization of the farm was proceeding apace. At the same time herds of animals were being built up in quantity and improved in quality. Superior breeds of animals were introduced. The ability to market products well beyond just what the farm family could produce for its own consumption was a powerful incentive to improve agricultural practice.

In most respects agricultural improvement in Canada in this period was a close reflection of what was happening in the northern United States. Canadian farmers shared most of the same knowledge. They drew extensively upon what was being developed south of the border, but they also made some valuable contributions of their own. They were closely involved in the development of improved livestock herds, especially cattle, and they developed a superior strain of hard spring wheat, Red Fyfe, that would be critical to American agricultural expansion into Minnesota and the Dakotas. In this period after mid-century, agricultural progress in anglophone Upper Canada moved decidedly ahead of francophone Lower Canada. It was after 1850, not in the earlier period, that the productivity gap widened. Upper Canada made especially notable strides in dairying. Exports of butter to Britain increased, although there was a long struggle to upgrade quality. Butter that was palatable enough if consumed fresh would deteriorate on the long journey to Britain if the quickly deteriorating buttermilk was not thoroughly pressed and washed out. A few districts of Upper Canada were able to establish a reputation for good quality. In the 1860s auspicious beginnings were made in copying the American system of factory production of cheese. Canadians were not cheese eaters, but a huge market existed in Britain if only a suitable product could be made. The first factories were established in Canada in the late 1860s. Exports increased rapidly over the ensuing three decades.

Lumber, the other leading industry of Canada, made great strides in the years immediately following mid-century. In 1850 almost one-half of the exports of sawn lumber was produced by a handful of large deal mills. The 1850s saw a sharp increase in the number of large mills, especially in the Ottawa valley. Bytown, later to be renamed Ottawa, became the leading sawmill center of the world. A massive hydraulic power site existed right on the main transport route. By 1860 Ottawa had a large collection of big commercial mills, including the single largest sawmill in the world. Industrially the Canadian economy began to diversify in these years. Factories were established to produce agricultural machinery. Other factories made milling equipment for both sawmills and flour mills. Small woolen mills catering to the local market for blankets and other simple woolen goods sprung up in locations across the province. General-purpose iron foundries and shops building steam engines and other capital goods likewise appeared. In the 1850s Canada made some clear and definite beginnings in industrialization.

TRANSPORT IMPROVEMENT AND EARLY INDUSTRIAL DEVELOPMENT

In the nineteenth century transport improvement was a central element of economic development everywhere in the world, and this was very much the case in Canada as well. As has already been pointed out, Canada had been greatly favored with about the most favorable natural internal transport to be found anywhere in the world. Being an ocean away from Britain meant that transatlantic transport was a costly burden, but within Canada goods could be moved relatively cheaply by the standards of the day. Almost everything could, and did, move by water. Overland travel, which nowhere needed to involve long distances since the settlements were all close to the waterway, was further benefited by the severe winters. Horse-drawn wagons could haul over firm, frozen surfaces or, as was more commonly the case, drawn by sleigh over snow. Sleighing was about one-third cheaper than wagon haulage. Consequently, rather than focus on the difficulties of early transport we should appreciate the important advantages that Canada enjoyed. There were, nevertheless, some impediments to the transport system. The great waterfall at Niagara barred connection between Lake Ontario and the upper lakes. On the main river routes, both the St. Lawrence and the Ottawa, there were stretches of rapids that mainly impeded the upstream movement of goods. Canals with locks around the rapids were an evident answer, and as early as the late eighteenth century a modest attempt had been made at Montreal to build a small canal around the rapids that lay just upstream of the city.

The canal as a solution to improvement in transport got a great boost from the construction of the Erie Canal in New York State. The Erie dramatically reduced costs of transport, and it effectively put to rest Canadian hopes to use the St. Lawrence waterway to draw on the export grain trade of the U.S. midwest. Canadians too could build canals, but they would be of a different sort than the long trunk canals constructed in the United States. The first two Canadian canals to draw attention were the Lachine, built to avoid rapids in the St. Lawrence just above Montreal, and the Welland, built to bypass Niagara Falls. The Lachine canal was built contemporaneously with the Erie, and the first Welland was completed only five years later. Canada was thus an early participant in the North American canal boom. In the 1840s three short canals were constructed to bypass rapids on the St. Lawrence, and the Lachine and Welland canals were enlarged. By 1848 Canada possessed a first-class canal system that made the St. Lawrence–Great Lakes waterway indeed the finest inland system in the world. These were ship canals, not the narrow barge canals commonly built in the United States. They were short, but owing to the large dimensions of their locks, cost many times more per mile than the canals in the United States. Lake schooners of considerable size could pass directly between Lake Erie and Lake Ontario via the Welland Canal. Sailing large vessels on the upper St. Lawrence River was problematic, so it was typical for cargoes to be transshipped at Kingston or Prescott onto smaller vessels or barges hauled by steam tugs. It would not be until after the middle of the twentieth century that large oceangoing ships would have full access to the Great Lakes.

A long canal from Kingston on the St. Lawrence to Bytown on the Ottawa River was built between 1826 and 1834 by the British military. Its large, solidly constructed locks and absence of a towpath make clear that it was intended from the outset to carry steamboats. It had limited commercial significance and was justified from the outset as a means of moving military material between Montreal and Upper Canada without having to pass within artillery range of the U.S. shore. A few other small canals were built: around the rapids on the Richelieu River at St. Jean (that one tied into Lake Champlain and the New York state system), a couple of sets of locks around rapids on the Ottawa River, and a canal on the lower reaches of the Grand River.

Canada had invested in a vast capacity for canal traffic – far more than the needs of its economy might reasonably justify. In part this huge investment was required by the need to accommodate large vessels in short canals, in part it was the outcome of a long-standing ambition to use the St. Lawrence system to transport the production of the U.S. midwest. The Erie Canal had demonstrated that human ingenuity and capital investment could overcome natural disadvantage. The real disadvantage of the St. Lawrence route, however, lay in the passage from Quebec across the Atlantic. That route had a shorter season and was considerably more dangerous than the routes from the east coast ports of the United States. Much of the Canadian canal investment may also have been premature. It was pointed out above that only after 1848, when the canals had been completed, did it start to be profitable to export Canadian wheat to Britain. It has been common in Canadian historical writing to fault the canal investments for coming too late, since by 1848 railroads were already a feasible alternative. Contrary to the common view, though, many of the key pieces of the Canadian canal system may have been built earlier than demand would have warranted. In particular, the Welland Canal was opened in 1829, six years before any substantial cargoes were being received at Buffalo from the west and before there was much development of the district of Upper Canada north of Lake Erie. The first Welland Canal was a private venture, financed to a large extent by American investors, but it was not profitable and it soon became a public enterprise, as were the other canal ventures in Canada. The large growth of bulk shipping on the Canadian lake and river system came after mid-century, after the economy had grown to a more substantial size, when exports of flour and lumber from the interior had become firmly established, and contemporaneously with the development of railroads. The canals were extensively utilized then.

Canada showed neither technical nor entrepreneurial backwardness in introducing both canals and steam navigation. Railroads were slow to be developed in Canada, however, and that was a source of concern to both contemporary and later commentators. A lot of traffic was needed to justify the large capital investment required by railroads, and Canada was a small economy with a very good and cheap system of water transport. By 1850 only 54 miles of railroad were in operation. The following decade saw major railroad development on three principal themes. There was a project to make a year-round, all-weather link between Montreal and ice-free ports on the Atlantic, there were rail lines built inland from the ports on the lake and riverfront, and there was the Grand Trunk Railway of Canada – an ambitious project to lay rails paralleling the great waterway that formed the spine of the economy. By 1867, the year of Canadian Confederation, the new nation had 2,600 miles of railroad in operation.

Montreal merchants were especially concerned about the short shipping season on the St. Lawrence. The steam railroad offered to them a possibility of overcoming that natural constraint. In 1845 the St. Lawrence and Atlantic was chartered to connect Montreal with a year-round port at Portland, Maine. The struggle to finance the line delayed it, but construction was underway by 1849 and completed in 1853. The Great Western Railway of Canada, a line to run from Niagara to Windsor and connect there with the Michigan Central, thus providing a short-cut route for U.S. railroads from New York to the American midwest while at the same time offering valuable transport services to the western area of Upper Canada, was completed in 1855. The previous year saw the completion of the Northern, a line from Toronto to Collingwood on Georgian Bay. Several other lines from the lake or riverfront back into the interior were built in the 1850s. The Prescott and Bytown ran from the St. Lawrence port opposite the U.S. rail terminus at Ogdensburg, New York, to the great sawmill center on the Ottawa River. A second line roughly paralleling it was completed in 1859. Farther west, the Buffalo and Lake Huron was built from the Niagara frontier to Goderich, on Lake Huron, the Canada Company's town in the Huron Tract. There was even the St. Lawrence and Industry, privately built by Barthelemy Joliette from the St. Lawrence river, running on wooden rails the 15 miles back to his mills in the village of Industry. These were all railroads providing modern transport service that complemented the waterway system.

The Grand Trunk Railway of Canada was a venture that overshadowed all of the others. This was a line planned to run from Quebec City, directly paralleling Canada's outstanding waterway system, to reach the United States at Sarnia at the southern tip of Lake Huron. It was financed in the British capital market by the most reputable of firms and presented as the de facto state railway of Canada. As planned, it was the longest railroad in the world and was to be built all at once rather than in segments that might start raising revenue, and at the very outset it acquired the St. Lawrence and Atlantic, which had just been completed but had not yet carried any freight. Right from the beginning the Grand Trunk was a financial fiasco, and in such difficulties that the government had to step in to bail it out. Some of the most renowned British financiers and railroad contractors almost collapsed under the weight of the Grand Trunk. Eventually it would get on its feet and become a great railway, but its inception was extremely clouded. It was much too ambitious a venture and was not even socially justified, let alone privately profitable. Later writers have stressed the short-run benefits of the Grand Trunk in terms of job creation and injection of investment expenditures into the local economy. The ebullient economic times of the mid-1850s have even been characterized as the "Grand Trunk Era," even though this railroad, as planned, was a mistake. It is too often overlooked that the original project had little hope of success. It has also been overlooked that for a decade or more the financial problems of the Grand Trunk impaired the ability of Canadian ventures, both private and public, to raise capital in the London market. Without the Grand Trunk, Canada would undoubtedly have built railroads, but perhaps a little later, more gradually, and more wisely. Canada's first romance with the steam railroad in the 1850s led to a large investment in railroad construction and resulted in a substantial network of railroad services by the end of the decade. Canada had entered the railroad age, but in a decidedly wasteful way. It quickly acquired a lot of unprofitable miles of track. If Canada had overinvested in canals, it overinvested to a much greater extent in railroads.

The first railroad era in Canada coincided with many other major developments in the economy. Economic development was clearly under way. The traditional export sectors — wheat flour and forest products — were propelling the economy in a vigorous way, but at the same time the economy was diversifying. A range of industrial products was emerging. Closely associated with the timber and lumber industries was shipbuilding. The 1850s and 1860s were the heydays of the shipbuilding industry. Canada had been early to put steamships on the rivers and lakes, and as early as the 1820s steam engines were being built in Canada. In the 1850s foundries and machine shops that custom built engines, boilers, and other capital equipment proliferated. By the latter half of the 1850s, steam locomotives were also being manufactured in Canada, as was the railroad rolling stock.

The hallmark of the Industrial Revolution was factory production of textiles. This was a sector where Canada lagged. Small woolen factories were first to be established in numbers. From an early date there were many local carding and fulling mills. Some of these expanded into spinning and weaving. By the 1840s a boom in the development of woolen mills was underway. These mainly produced blankets and wool flannel. Finer grades of woolens and worsteds were still imported from Britain. A factory cotton textile industry emerged slowly and haltingly. New England was expanding its cotton textile industry with the aid of immigrant French-Canadian labor, but in Canada not much was happening. The promoters of the British American Land Company in Lower Canada attempted to establish the town of Sherbrooke as a center for their operations and in 1844 opened Canada's first cotton mill. Then in the early 1860s several additional cotton mills were established. These were small mills, rather experimental, and not grandly successful.

A much more vigorous line of industrial development was the manufacture of agricultural implements. In the 1840s small plants emerged, producing fanning mills, threshing machines, improved plows, and patented stump pullers. The following two decades saw much more vigorous development. There was little indigenous innovation. The Canadian factories produced American mowers and reapers either under license or simply by pirating the technology. By the 1860s several of the agricultural implement builders had emerged as relatively large-scale, nationally marketing producers. Canada was almost self-sufficient in manufactured agricultural implements.

Canadian manufacturers relied on the technical advances being made in the United States and closely copied American developments. Machine fabrication of wood to produce furniture, shoe lasts, and a great range of other products became commonplace. Sewing machines were being manufactured in Canada by the 1860s, and boots and shoes were being machine sewn at about the same time. There are two points to be made. One is that Canadian manufacturing development was vigorous and based largely on similar development going on in the United States. The second point is that Canada's manufacturing development lacked an internal, technically innovative drive. One cannot find sectors in which Canadians were exhibiting technical leadership and were spawning the innovations on which sustained manufacturing development was based. Canadians were for the most part competent imitators but not keen innovators. The situation is complicated by the tendency of innovative Canadians to realize that the larger U.S. market, where there was also easier access to venture capital, was the place to launch innovations. Thus, for example, Abram Gesner moved to New York to establish a refinery to produce his newly developed "kerosene" – a superior illuminant derived from petroleum – and thereby to lay the foundation of the world petroleum industry.

Historically, industrialization has been associated with urbanization, and Canada's industrialization in the pre-Confederation period brought rapid urban development, but that was built upon a preponderantly rural base. Furthermore, urban development followed a different pattern in the two provinces of Canada. In Lower Canada industrial development was heavily concentrated in the city of Montreal. By 1850 it was Canada's largest city, and its subsequent growth was in part attributable to its becoming a major and diversified industrial center. Montreal had the foundries and engine works, the locomotive factory, and the rolling mill. It had the tailoring and apparel shops and the shoe factories. At the same time traditional industries were important in Montreal as well. It was the country's leading center of flour milling and was prominent for its breweries and its sugar refinery. The Lachine Canal provided an extremely valuable water-power site. Indeed, the canal may have been as valuable for its water power as for its transport benefits. Urban development is not just industrially based; cities are important as market centers. Montreal was the focus of many of the important markets of Canada. It was the principal distribution point for imported goods. After the dredging of the St. Lawrence was completed in 1853, Montreal increasingly came to displace Quebec as the main port of export. It was also the center of insurance and finance. Canada's first bank, and for a long time its largest, was the Bank of Montreal. While Montreal was indisputably Canada's foremost urban center in the nineteenth century, it never held as dominant a position as did New York in the United States. Early in the century the city of Quebec was the country's port for overseas trade. The city of Quebec was as large a center as Montreal until about 1825, and remained a close contender until the middle of the century. Quebec was always a more specialized city than Montreal. It was a trade and maritime center, not an industrial city. It was the focus of the timber trade, the place where the vast amounts of wood were assembled and loaded onto ships. One of the world's great centers of shipbuilding, it was also a seat of government, a military and administrative center. In later years it became a prominent location for shoe and tobacco manufacturing, but it was never primarily an industrial city, and by mid-century it was a city that was losing its dynamic.

What Lower Canada most notably lacked was a collection of smaller, growing urban centers. It had few manufacturing towns. In that respect it contrasted conspicuously with the upper province. In 1850, outside of Montreal and Quebec, there were in Lower Canada only five towns of more than 2,500 people. Trois-Rivieres was an old market center located on the St. Lawrence halfway between Quebec and Montreal, but it had a population of less than 5,000. It had played a prominent role in the fur trade, and just north of it the St. Maurice forges was the country's principal iron smelting establishment. On the south bank of the St. Lawrence, a short distance upstream from Trois-Rivieres was Sorel, at the mouth of the Richelieu River, a trade and transport center of 3,500 persons. St. Jean, further up the Richelieu, St. Hyacinthe in the same district, and Sherbrooke, the modest urban center of the Eastern Townships, rounded out what comprised urban Lower Canada. In general, though, the outstanding feature of urban Lower Canada was the dominance of Montreal and Quebec and the paucity of larger market and manufacturing towns.

Upper Canada offers a sharp contrast. The primary city, Toronto, was still considerably smaller than either Montreal or Quebec. With about 33,000 people at mid-century, it was more than double the size of any other city of Upper Canada. Initially, Kingston had been the primary urban center of Upper Canada, but by the early 1830s Toronto had surpassed it in size and importance. Toronto was essentially a transport node and commercial center but had begun by the 1840s to develop an industrial base. It was a center for domestic manufacturing that catered essentially to the local market. In the years before 1850 Toronto was the leading market center of Upper Canada, but it was foremost among a substantial collection of subsidiary cities and sizeable towns.

Hamilton was not quite half the size of Toronto. Although well situated, it had lost out to Toronto in the struggle to become the metropolis of Upper Canada. In 1851 Hamilton was still more of a commercial center than the industrial city it would become over the next couple of decades. Kingston had been the earliest urban center to emerge in Upper Canada but had soon been surpassed by Toronto and did not grow rapidly after mid-century. Bytown, the fourth-ranked city of Upper Canada in 1851, was the most rapidly growing. Renamed Ottawa, it became the national capital in 1867, but its growth was mostly a consequence of its emergence between 1851 and 1871 as a great center of lumber manufacturing. The striking difference between Upper and Lower Canada in urban development, though, was the paucity of towns in the lower province. At mid-century there were only five towns with more than 2,500 people. By contrast Upper Canada had a dozen such towns and five cities compared with two. Overriding all that was the very low level of urbanization generally in Canada. In 1851 less than 15 percent of the population lived in centers of 2,500 or more, and in Upper Canada the fraction barely exceeded 10 percent.

Between 1851 and 1871 the population of the old province of Canada grew by a little more than 50 percent. The growth was twice as rapid in Upper Canada as in Lower Canada. At least in the first half of the period immigrants were still coming to Upper Canada in large numbers. Urban population growth was rapid and, overall, quite similar in the two provinces. In Lower Canada urban growth was concentrated heavily in the two largest cities. The towns of more than 2,500 people in 1851 grew by only a little more than their natural increase, and the number of them rose only from five to eight. In Upper Canada the number of towns outside the five main urban centers proliferated so that by 1871 more than thirty-one of them had more than 2,500 people. Population in all urban places increased by 150 percent; the population in towns of 2,500 to 10,000 people almost tripled, although that was more a result of additional towns than of growth of population in places already in that category in 1851. It was this emergence of a layer of small but significant urban centers that set Upper Canada apart from the lower province. The towns were both commercial and manufacturing centers. They included the significant points on the transport system – early-established lake ports such as Goderich, Whitby, and Port Hope, and junctions on the more newly built railway system such as Barrie and Stratford. Many of the new towns were manufacturing centers. At Galt and Owen Sound steam boilers and milling machinery were built, at Bowmanville and Napanee, furniture; Brantford and Guelph were centers of agricultural implement production. In this respect Upper Canada was similar to adjacent regions of the United States – western New York and Ohio especially.

Canada was making the transition from an agricultural to an industrial economy in the years before 1871. The transition to Modern Economic Growth had been accomplished. Yet Canada was still predominantly a rural society with an agricultural economy. By a fairly generous definition of urban, less than 20 percent of the population lived in cities and towns as late as 1871. Farming continued to be the occupation of more than half the work force. But good land for new settlement had run out well before 1871. By 1860 British North America had reached the extent of settlement in its then existing territory. Extensive agricultural settlement was no longer providing the dynamic of the economy. The British adoption of free trade had deprived British North America of its privileged relationship with Britain, and the experiment in reciprocal free trade with the United States had been brought to an end by the Americans. To the Canadians of the 1860s a prosperous present belied a troubled and uncertain

future. The solution sought after was territorial aggrandizement and union
of all the British North American colonies.

THE ECONOMICS OF CANADIAN
CONFEDERATION

In 1867 the three British North American colonies of Nova Scotia, New
Brunswick, and the United Canadas came together to form a new federal
state under the name of the Dominion of Canada. Two other British North
American colonies, Newfoundland and Prince Edward Island, declined to
join at that time. The plan had been under consideration and debated since
1864 and was finally brought into effect by an act of the British Parliament. The British North America Act of 1867 was to serve as a constitution for the new nation. For the purposes of this chapter, two questions
are of interest. First, what economic influences were at work in bringing
this union about? Secondly, what were the consequences of Confederation
for the economy of the new Dominion of Canada?

It is widely believed that economic influences played at least a partial
role in Canadian Confederation, although we should be careful not to
overemphasize them. There was also a political agenda, and there were
significant matters of national security. Serious discussions about Confederation began in the later years of the American Civil War. Relations
between the United States and Britain were tense, and it had not been forgotten that in the past, when U.S.-British relations had boiled over, the
reaction of the United States had been to invade Canada. In a longer-term
setting, it was becoming evident that the British were increasingly concerned to reduce the costs of empire and to push dependencies such as
those in British North America into more independent positions. That
would mean that the colonies would have to be concerned about the possibly very expensive matter of providing themselves with effective defense
at a time when the United States was heavily armed and, from time to
time, making expressions of its Manifest Destiny to control the whole of
North America. One should perhaps not read too much into the tenor of
the times, but matters of national security comprised a substantial element
of the Confederation debates.

The immediate impetus to the Confederation plan, though, was the
political stalemate in the colony of Canada where largely French Lower
Canada had been welded together in a legislative union with British

Upper Canada in an arrangement that was almost guaranteed not to work. Politicians in Canada were seeking desperately to break the stalemate between French and English. The Maritime colonies had begun to contemplate a legislative union and to that end had organized a convention at Charlottetown in Prince Edward Island in 1864. Representatives of the larger colony of Canada moved in on it with more pretentious ambitions; they had in mind a plan that might offer a solution to everyone's problems.

One of the foremost economic problems was the need for more extensive markets. Each of the British North American colonies was small. An attempt had been made to solve the problem of market size through reciprocity with the United States, but the Americans had decided to back out of that arrangement, and they abrogated the treaty in 1866. As a minimal, second-best solution, the British North American colonies might amalgamate into a single market. It would still be relatively small and a weak substitute for open acccess to the United States, but it might at least be feasible. There was more than that, however, to the economic drive behind Confederation. In the colony of Canada some believed that continuing economic prosperity might be linked to a major increase in size achieved by acquiring the vast territory owned and managed under British rule by the Hudson's Bay Company. That land included, admittedly, thousands of miles of uninhabitable rock and bush, but it also included vast areas of western plains that might be transformed into a new agricultural frontier. The continuous movement of agricultural settlement onto a western frontier was widely seen as important for the economic prosperity of the United States. Canada too might have its western frontier. Hence, visionaries in Canada had begun to think of dramatic spatial aggrandizement as a solution for Canada's economic problems. A new frontier of settlement would provide a place to accomodate the all-too-numerous sons of farmers in Canada who could not otherwise be provided with livelihoods. It should attract immigrants as well. Newly populated territories would expand the Canadian domestic market. Canada might seek its economic future by emulating the United States.

The people of the Maritime colonies did not wholeheartedly buy into the scheme of grand territorial expansion. They were, at best, only lukewarm to the Confederation idea. With their commercial and shipping interests, their orientation was to the Atlantic. Some in the Maritimes, however, had visions of transforming the region into an industrial economy along the lines of New England. In that way the Maritimers might find a new prosperity as cotton textile and metal product manufacturers in a federated Canada. That would involve a reorientation of the Maritime economy away from the Atlantic and its prospering shipping and ship-building industries, towards the interior of North America and toward the industries most characteristic of the Industrial Revolution. Attention would thus be shifted from ships to railways, but railways seemed more "modern."

Newfoundland and Prince Edward Island declined to join Canadian Confederation in 1867. The other Maritime colonies merged with Canada, which in turn was split into the two provinces of Ontario and Quebec, corresponding to the upper and lower provinces of the former colony of Canada. The Hudson's Bay Company lands and the remainder of British territory in North America were absorbed into the new Dominion of Canada. In 1871 a new province, Manitoba, was established in the new territory, with the remainder of the unsettled plains administered as Territories, and in that same year the small British colonies on Vancouver Island and on the mainland of British Columbia were consolidated into a single province of that name. In 1874 Prince Edward Island reversed its stand and came into the Dominion in 1874. Thus was made up the Canadian "Dominion from sea to sea" in the form it remained for the rest of the nineteenth century. Newfoundland would eventually join in the middle of the twentieth century.

The intention was to form a strong federation in which the central government played the dominant role. At the outset it was an economic union with no tariff impediments permitted between provinces. Only the federal government was empowered to impose indirect taxes such as import tariffs and excise duties. The provinces were permitted to levy only direct taxes. In this federation the provinces were allocated only powers over matters which at the time were thought to be of essentially local concern – the family, welfare, education, laws governing property and what in those days were called civil rights. Joint authority was awarded on agriculture and immigration. The federal government, though, was granted the power of disallowance of provincial legislation and direct control of the natural resources in the new territories acquired in the west. This was intended to be a centralized federation, with only such powers granted to the provinces as seemed absolutely necessary at the time. Right from the outset, however, constitutional interpretation shifted power away from the center to the provinces. This is not the place to review the long and complicated history of Canadian constitutional development. The important point to explore here is the economic implications of the new federal arrangements. The intention was to leave to the provinces the administration of relatively mundane, local affairs but to place in the hands of the central government the powers to promote the development of the new nation as, at one and the same time, an expanding agricultural economy and a developing industrial one.

The economic plan imbedded in Canadian Confederation was to form an economic union of the existing British North American colonies but at the same time to establish a new settlement frontier on the western plains that would be integrally linked to the older regions of the country and would provide a needed economic dynamic. It was a two-pronged plan of increasing in size through new agricultural settlement while at the same time fostering industrial development in the older regions. Federal control of natural resources, especially the land, of the newly acquired territory was central to the development plan. Transportation was a key feature of the Canadian plan of federation, and railroads were the prized mode of transport. To draw the Maritime provinces into Confederation a railroad link was promised – imbedded right in the constitution. That was a costly promise. In 1871, to cement the arrangements with British Columbia, a transcontinental railroad to the Pacific was also promised. That would be costlier still. The Canadian federation was literally to be bound together by iron rails. To assuage the low-tariff Maritimes, an initial commitment was made to set the Canadian tariff at a relatively low level. That, as we shall see, was not to last. The new union began on an optimistic note. The Articles of Confederation themselves, and the broader conception that gave rise to them, reflected an ambitious economic plan for the development of a new Canadian nation.

A NATIONAL POLICY FOR NATIONAL DEVELOPMENT

Railways were looked upon as the sinews of the new Canadian nation. A terse answer to the question of what the Canadian economy did for the remainder of the nineteenth century might be "it built railways." A rail link between the lines in Quebec and the short line that ran across the middle of Nova Scotia to the port of Halifax was a condition of the new constitution. Geography was cruel. The Intercolonial Railway was to be built entirely on Canadian soil and, for security reasons, as far from the

U.S. border as feasible. That meant that it would be much longer and pass through largely unsettled and unproductive territory than a line built on strictly economic considerations. Furthermore, it was built to high quality standards. The result was 500 very expensive miles of railway (completed by 1876) that had no real hope of ever repaying the investment made in it. At a cost of almost $35 million, the Intercolonial was entirely financed by and operated by the federal government. Coming as it did after the financial fiasco of the Grand Trunk, the building of the Intercolonial serves to reinforce an image of Canada as a chronic builder of too many, not very useful railway lines.

The purpose of the Intercolonial was to promote the economic integration of the Maritime provinces with the rest of Canada so as to reinforce the political union. Integration came very slowly. Before Confederation there had been little movement of labor, capital, or goods between the colonies. Confederation did not change the situation much. The Maritimes had little to sell to Quebec and Ontario and, for that matter, the reverse was largely true as well. The Maritimes had long imported flour, mostly from the United States but some from Canada; however, by 1867 Ontario was scarcely able to generate enough surplus over the needs of central Canada to be able to supply the Maritimes. Nova Scotian coal was too costly to transport to Montreal and compete with fuel from the United States. Mainly, the Maritimers went on doing what they had before Confederation – building ships and providing shipping services to the world, catching and drying codfish for the European and West Indian markets and, to an increasing extent, supplying themselves with a variety of manufactured goods. Some Maritimers, though, had gone into Confederation with ambitions to emulate New England and to become manufacturers to the new Canadian nation. A few promising steps were taken in that direction. Shoe factories, a few cotton textile mills, and a variety of metal manufactures were expanded to produce for the "Upper Canadian" market.

The economy of the Maritimes still prospered, mainly on the basis of its earlier shipbuilding and shipping activities. Increasingly, however, a problem it shared with the rest of Canada was becoming pressing. Employment opportunities were not expanding enough to engage fully the growing population of the countryside. There was little new land onto which to expand and little scope for transition to a more labor-intensive agriculture. The agricultural base of the Maritimes was very limited. The non-agricultural sectors, especially manufacturing, were not growing rapidly enough to absorb the outpouring of population from the rural districts. Prince Edward Island, which had finally thrown in its lot with the Canadian union in 1874, reached a plateau in absolute population size in 1881, where it remained for several decades. The other two Maritime provinces also were feeling the severe pressure of numbers, and that resulted in emigration on a large scale. What is especially significant, though, is that it was not emigration to other parts of Canada, but to the United States, very largely to New England. An indication that Confederation did not quickly bring about an integrated national economy is that seven decades passed before any substantial part of the excess population of the Maritimes began to move to other provinces of Canada.

There is an unresolved issue of whether the Maritime provinces came into Canadian Confederation with productivity levels below those of central Canada. For the first few years after 1867 the economy of the Maritime region continued to be relatively strong, but it became increasingly evident that the region was not going to become the industrial New England of Canada, and to a growing extent the Maritimes became the economically lagging region of the nation – a problem area. That was already apparent by the 1880s, when people left the region in large numbers. Development in the rest of Canada was not redounding to the benefit of the Maritimes. As Canada's orientation became westward and continental, the Maritimes became more and more a left-over and left-out part of the nation.

One of the foremost elements of the economic developmental plan associated with Confederation was the acquisition for agricultural settlement of the vast area of land to the west that had been owned by the venerable Hudson's Bay Company. Canada brought this land into its sovereign domain and immediately made plans to settle it. The intention was to promote a U.S. model of extensive settlement. The land was surveyed in square-mile sections, subdivided into quarters; a Homestead Act was proclaimed so that settlers might be attracted to freely granted quarter sections; and a large area of land was reserved to be granted out to railway developers as an inducement to providing the needed transport system.

The Northwest Territory was not wholly unoccupied land. In addition to an uncertain number of aboriginal residents there was the small remnant of the colony of Scots established early in the nineteenth century by Lord Selkirk. About 6,000 descendants of those colonists remained in an

agricultural settlement around Fort Garry on the Red River. That provided a nucleus for the new province of Manitoba. These farmers engaged
in a largely subsistence agriculture, but had some limited market opportunities in provisioning the fur trade. Loosely associated with the same
community was a population of Metis – mixed-bloods of either Scottish
or French combination with aboriginal peoples. The Metis ranged across
the plains, commercially hunting buffalo and providing transport services
for the Hudson's Bay Company.

Manitoba began to be augmented by newcomers from Ontario just as
it was absorbed into Canada as a new province. Winnipeg, just to the south
of Fort Garry, was founded as a kind of inland port – the eastern gateway
to the Canadian plains. Access to Manitoba was easier via the United
States, down the Red River from points in Minnesota. That state was
undergoing rapid settlement at the time and was about to witness
experiments with very large scale wheat farming on the "bonanza" farms
of the Red River valley. Manitoba also seemed destined to be a wheat-
producing province. By the mid-1870s river boats were taking the first
small shipments of Manitoba wheat south to St. Paul. The Canadian
port on Lake Superior was 400 miles away over difficult terrain. A
first need was for railroad linkage between Winnipeg and the head of
the lake at Fort William. It was a costly proposition but an integral
part of the Pacific Railway of Canada. There was some urgency to getting
on with that whole project, especially as the commercial interchange
with Minnesota increased. A railway from St. Paul to Winnipeg was in
operation by 1880.

The Pacific Railway had been promised to British Columbia as a condition of Confederation and was to have been built by 1881. The project
stalled partly because of a corruption scandal, but mostly because of the
sheer magnitude of the task. For political reasons several daunting conditions were attached. The business was to be Canadian owned and the route
was to lie entirely within Canada; it would not be acceptable just to tie
into lines that went through the United States south of the Great Lakes.
Consequently, the railway would have to push west through more than a
thousand miles of rock and bush to the north of Lake Superior, over unsta-
ble muskeg, through a territory that offered no promise of generating *en
route* traffic. Then it would cross another thousand or more miles of as yet
unsettled plains, parts of which were dubiously fit for agricultural settlement. It would truly be a railroad built in advance of demand. Finally

a route had to be found through the difficult terrain of the Cordillera, down the steep Fraser Canyon to a western terminus. It was an extremely expensive undertaking with a prospect of private profitability only in a distant and highly uncertain future. Such a railway would require massive subsidization. An impatient government began work on two segments of the line as public undertakings – the route from the Lakehead to Winnipeg and the especially costly route from the western terminus up the tortuous Fraser Canyon.

Finally, in 1880, a deal was struck with the Canadian Pacific Railway Company (CPR). Remarkably, the line was completed only five years later. The subsidy granted was massive indeed. The most important provisions were (1) a cash subsidy of $25 million, (2) a grant of 25 million acres of land "fairly fit for settlement" in a band 24 miles wide on either side of right of way, (3) the segments already completed (valued by later writers at about $40 million) to be handed over to the company, (4) an exemption from taxes (later thought to be worth a little over $20 million), and (5) a guarantee that no other railway lines would be chartered south of the CPR to the border with the United States. Eventually, by the end of the nineteenth century, the CPR became a profitable enterprise and remains today one of the leading business concerns of the nation. It has been greatly lauded as a stupendous, nation-building venture, a symbol of national might and capability.

Economic historians have questioned the wisdom of the magnitude of subsidy granted to this railway. There is little doubt that the project, as set out in conditions laid down by the government, had to be subsidized if it were to be carried through. It could not have been privately profitable. Nevertheless, especially in light of the earlier Canadian experience of sinking vast amounts of resources into unprofitable railway lines, the wisdom of doing the same thing again with the CPR, on an even grander scale, has to be questioned. A prior, if narrower, question has been addressed by Peter George and by Lloyd Mercer, who have made alternative estimates of the amount of subsidy needed to render the CPR profitable and thereby get the railway built. Both writers conclude that much more was paid than needed, although Mercer calculated the excess subsidy at between $20 and $40 million, about $20 million less than George. Either way, Canadians gave up a lot to get the CPR. One way of putting it is that the *excess* subsidy, as a percentage of 1885 Canadian GNP is of the same order of magnitude as Robert Fogel's estimate of the social saving attributable to the entire U.S. railway network. A broader question has not been so concretely addressed; it focuses on the costliness of the conditions imposed on the CPR. How much subsidy, and real resources for that matter, might have been saved had Canada been content with a less ambitious, more slowly evolving project that avoided or postponed the more costly features? Was a single integral, transcontinental railway firm really needed? To promote the settlement of the western plains of Canada what was essentially required was public subsidy for a trunk line from the Lakehead to Winnipeg – the line the government itself had begun to build. Lines out into the settlement areas from Winnipeg might have been anticipated as private ventures as the progress of settlement justified them. That might have spread out the process through time but, as it turned out, rapid settlement did not immediately follow completion of the CPR in 1885. It was another ten years before the pace of settlement turned up. Pushing across the prairies quickly, in a heavily subsidized way, was premature. Most questionable was the rail line north of Lake Superior. The grain eventually produced in the Canadian west went out not by rail but by lake steamer. Many passengers also went by water. What would have been given up had that segment of the rail line not been built would only have been quicker, all-season movement. For the few for whom that mattered, it could have been obtained, for the time being at least, through the United States. The political symbolism of the all-Canadian rail route can only be judged to have been very expensive. There remains the segment through the mountains to the Pacific coast. Was it necessary to promise British Columbia a railway connection? That is ultimately a political judgment that many writers have thought to have been worthwhile, but economic historians may be justified in questioning whether creative nation building really needed to be so costly.

The completion of rail connections to Manitoba brought a pronounced but brief settlement boom in the early 1880s. In a few years farmers filled up the fertile, sub-humid lands that extended west from the Red River for 70 miles or so. A greater density of settlement might have been achieved had not so much of the land been handed over to the railways. By the late 1880s, however, there was frustration that the Canadian development plan based on western settlement was not proceeding anywhere as quickly as had been hoped. Canadians, mostly from Ontario, were moving west only to turn their backs on their country and settle in northern Minnesota and North Dakota. Few French-Canadians showed any interest in western settlement, and farming in the west hardly got the attention of Maritimers at all. Canada looked eagerly to the wider world for prospective settlers. In the mid-1870s it found discontented German-speaking Mennonites in Russia and distressed Icelanders who were willing to seek refuge in Manitoba. On the whole, though, the expected flood of settlers failed to materialize.

In eastern Canada as well there was a perception that the Confederation plan was not working out as well economically as might have been hoped. Things had begun well enough, but the economy foundered seriously after 1873 in a depression that was worldwide. It was little consolation that other countries also were seeing their aspirations of economic prosperity frustrated. Traditional accounts of late-nineteenth-century Canadian economic development place heavy emphasis on the slowdown that came in 1873 and ushered in an extended period of reduced economic expansion. Most of the recent writing on this topic suggests that the problems, both in the short run and the long run, may not have been so severe as usually painted. The depression may have been more financial than real. Prices fell sharply, but the changes in production varied considerably across sectors. Forest products were still the leading export, and those exports exhibited contrasting experiences in the two principal markets. Exports to the United States fell sharply in 1874 and continued at depressed levels for several years. By contrast, while prices fell in the British market, the volume of exports continued to rise sharply until 1877, tapered off a bit in the following year, and plummeted sharply only in 1879. The strength of the British market meant that in 1877 the value of Canadian wood exports to all destinations was still as much as 84 percent of the 1873 peak that was not reattained for the rest of the century. Some of the Canadian sawmill industry's best years were in the depths of the Great Depression of the 1870s.

The message driven home by the depression, however, was how fragile was the industrialization that had been going on in Canada. In the years immediately following, the chronic outflow of population to the United States was greatly accentuated. Canada had a high rate of natural increase of population – a carryover from the past – that posed a very pressing problem of how the younger generation could be provided for. The fact is that for Canada to have absorbed all of the surplus population from its countryside would have required higher rates of growth in industrial employment than experienced by any other country in the years before 1860. Rapid economic development, high industrial wages, and free homestead land in good locations in the United States were a compelling attraction for many Canadians. The massive exodus was viewed by spokes-men of the day as an affront to Canadian nationhood.

Canada's response to its dimmed economic prospects was a turn to pro-tectionism. Some would trace the roots of protectionist policy to 1859 and argue that inherent from the beginning in Canadian Confederation was a plan to foster industrial development through the tariff. Only temporary political concessions to the Maritime provinces delayed implementation of this part of the plan. Others would portray the policy of tariff protection as less deliberate and more pragmatic – more a consequence of circum-stance. Whatever the ultimate explanation, the Conservative party swept back into power in 1879, after five years of severe depression in the economy, on a platform of industrial development through a National Policy of tariff protection. It was in tune with protectionist sentiment in the United States at the time and could be seen as part of a movement sweeping across all of the industrializing nations. In the Canadian case one might note that an earlier protectionist step had already been taken in 1871 when the first Canadian patent legislation offered protection only to those who shortly set up production facilities in the country. In 1879 high levels of tariff protection were offered indiscriminately to manufac-turers of all kinds. It was a desperate policy to increase industrial employ-ment at almost any cost. However one might judge its consequences, it would be the foundation of Canadian economic policy for the next one hundred years.

THE CANADIAN ECONOMY IN THE LATE NINETEENTH CENTURY

The late years of the nineteenth century – from Confederation in 1867 to the end of the century – have traditionally been seen in Canada as years of little economic progress, even of stagnation. The years immediately fol-lowing Confederation were good ones for the economy but the worldwide depression that began in 1873 is viewed as having ushered in a long period of sluggishness in the Canadian economy. This interpretation was not based on extensive quantitative evidence but more on impressions and con-temporary comment. Political and business leaders in late-nineteenth-century Canada were certainly discontented with what they saw as a failure of the economy to progress satisfactorily.

The lumber industry, which had long been the leading export sector of the economy, appeared to have saturated its markets and was no longer expanding so rapidly. Wheat exports, which had propelled the Canadian economy in the two decades leading up to Confederation, had diminished to the point where by 1868 Canada had ceased to be a net exporter of wheat and flour. No new major export staple had arisen to take the place of these two mainstays. The development plan of settling the vast territory acquired in the west to produce wheat for the world market was not working out. Perhaps more seriously, Canada was viewed, by the common standards of the day, as having failed to industrialize; that is, it did not have a modern coke-fueled iron industry, it had made limited progress in the development of a factory cotton textile industry, and it had taken only modest steps in the adoption of steam power. In short, it was not undergoing an Industrial Revolution along British lines. The upshot of this weak performance of the Canadian economy, and a problem that especially irked the country's political leadership, was that large numbers of Canadians were abandoning their country to emigrate to the United States.

More recently, with the advent of pioneer attempts to measure Canadian historical national income, and as economic historians came to pay more attention to statistical evidence, this period of Canadian economic development has been cast in a more optimistic light. The first historical GNP estimates, introduced by O. J. Firestone, indicated that the average rate of growth of real per capita income over the period 1870 to 1900 was not notably slower than the average for the longest period for which measurement could be made (1867–1955). These early GNP estimates were essentially based on decennial census data for 1870, 1880, 1890, and 1900. Moreover, their reliability was in some doubt. Nevertheless, they indicated that in the first two intercensal decades after Confederation, 1870–1880 and 1880–1890, the rate of income growth was commensurate with the experience of growing industrial countries generally. Only the last decade of the century showed a real slowdown in the rate of economic progress. At the very least, real per capita income was growing over the whole period at an average rate of just a little over 1 percent per annum. That may not be rapid growth by international historical standards, but neither can it be characterized as "stagnation." Within the period there was at least one decade, 1880–1890, when growth appeared to have been relatively rapid.

Other quantitatively oriented economic historians picked up this revisionist theme and questioned the proposition that Canada was failing to industrialize in the late nineteenth century. Focusing on the growth of manufacturing industry, they have shown that there was substantial expansion for two decades and that only in the 1890s did the pace of industrialization slow down. Moreover, they have emphasized that Canadian industrialization in this period was broadly based. It was not simply an expansion of a few natural resource–processing industries. Since an alleged failure to industrialize lay at the heart of the older, traditional complaints about the economy in the post-Confederation period, statistical evidence of relatively rapid industrial growth has served to cast the performance of the whole economy in a more optimistic light.

Recently a greatly improved set of historical national income statistics for Canada has been produced by M. C. Urquhart and his associates. These are more solidly based than were the pioneer estimates of Firestone and provide reliable annual figures for the period from 1870 onward. That arbitrary starting date, dictated by the first national census as a benchmark, is still a serious limitation. Nevertheless, we are able to make a fresh re-examination of the performance of the Canadian economy in the last three decades of the nineteenth century. The new data give a quite different portrayal of the economy than has been offered in recent, "optimistic" writing, a portrayal that is rather more attuned to the earlier, "pessimistic" interpretation.

It is widely accepted that the growth rate of the Canadian economy accelerated sharply around the end of the nineteenth century. Growth of GNP was substantial in 1897, after a notably depressed year in 1896, and continued rapidly for many years thereafter. The average rate of increase of real GNP over the period 1870–1896 was 2.36 percent per annum. That is relatively modest by the standards of developing industrial economies and well below the 4.59 percent rate experienced from 1896 to 1926. It is also well below the rate of 4.17 percent posted by the U.S. economy in the period 1870–1910.

Any division of the late-nineteenth-century years into sub-periods runs afoul of the sticky problem of separating longer-term trends from short-run business fluctuations. The traditional division of the period into inter-censal decades is especially plagued by that problem, since 1880 lay below the long-term trend, while 1870 and 1890 were slightly above it. Examination of the new annual GNP series suggests that the late-nineteenth-century years might tentatively be examined in five sub-periods. The first sub-period, from 1870 to the average of 1876/77, is somewhat artificial – the consequence of having an arbitrary initial date in 1870. It might be regarded as little other than a broadening of that arbitrary beginning. It combines the early years of the decade of the 1870s, prosperous years at the end of an extended boom that may have begun as early as the middle of the preceding decade, with the early years of the Great Depression that began in 1873 or 1874. It does serve to point up that the depressed years of the late 1870s did not experience an output decline below the prosperous years of the beginning of the decade. Actually, real per capita income in 1876/77 was just slightly lower than in 1870 and aggregate output was almost 10 percent higher. What is most notable is that the stagnation of the economy was largely located in agriculture, a sector that still comprised almost 40 percent of Canadian national income. Agricultural output failed to grow at all over the 1870–1876/77 period. By contrast, output originating in manufacturing and in trade and services increased 16 percent. That is not strong growth but it is hardly stagnation. All sectors of manufacturing, with the exception of an especially depressed leather products industry, experienced increased output. Food and beverage manufacturing and transport equipment had notably strong growth. Value added in construction did not decline but rose over this period. Total exports also increased. It was already pointed out in the preceding section that lumber, Canada's leading export, held up through most of the depression period and collapsed only with a big drop in sales to Britain in 1879. By that time the U.S. and Canadian economies were in recovery. Over all, the Canadian economy made no gain over the years from 1870 through 1878.

The depressed condition of Canadian agriculture centered mainly on the large and important livestock sector. During the Civil War and the postwar Reconstruction periods Canada had built up a strong export trade in feeder cattle and horses to the United States. That trade collapsed with the arrival in the American midwest of cattle from the Texas plains. Livestock production in Canada dropped sharply. Other areas of agriculture continued to grow but not by enough to provide an offset. Dairy output grew strongly, but it was still too small a sector to have much overall impact. The stagnation in the Canadian economy in this period was an agricultural, not an industrial stagnation, and concentrated heavily in one large sector of agriculture at that.

By 1879 Canadian real GNP had finally risen above the level of any previous year. The depression was over and was followed by three years of especially rapid growth. This was the most vigorous period of growth in the last three decades of the nineteenth century. Real GNP went up at a rate of more than 6 percent per annum. The expansion was broadly based; output was up substantially in all sectors of the economy. Lumber and grain exports rose sharply and, in proportional terms, dairy exports went up especially strongly. Total agricultural output was up in all sub-sectors, with wheat and other small grains leading the way. Manufacturing output also increased substantially in this period – partly the reflection of a strong resurgence of the lumber industry, but there were large expansions as well in iron and steel products, in clothing and factory textiles, and food and beverages. The leather products industry made a good recovery from its depressed condition of the previous period. One can only speculate about the expansionary influences of two features of this period. There was a burst of rapid settlement in Manitoba – a first hint of fulfillment of the grand Canadian plan of nation building. Second, the National Policy tariff had been introduced in 1879, and much of the manufacturing expansion may have represented the initial effects of the tariff in putting to work other-wise idle resources, especially older plant capacity, and also inducing the construction of much new, up-to-date plant capacity. The strong expan-sions in clothing and textile manufacturing may reflect something like that, but the in-depth studies needed to reach firm conclusions have not been carried out. Whatever the ultimate causes, this expansion was the strongest of the entire late-nineteenth-century period. Fifty-nine percent of all the increase in per capita income that occurred over the 1870–1897 period came in this short 1879–1882/83 sub-period.

Rather surprisingly, the remainder of the decade of the 1880s was a period of little change. From 1882/83 to 1887/88 GNP went up less than 10 percent overall; per capita GNP, only 4 percent. Earlier writers have depicted the decade of the 1880s as a period of growth, the most success-ful decade of the late nineteenth century. Most of the development, however, came at the very beginning and then at the very end of the decade. Another very slow growth period spans the middle years of the decade – interestingly enough, the period in which the Canadian Pacific Railway was constructed. The main weakness of the economy once again lay in agriculture. Total agricultural output went down, and there was decline in all sectors of agriculture except dairying, which experienced a small increase in output. Prices of good agricultural land in Ontario fell. The value of agricultural exports declined, especially those of grains. That export decline reflected mainly a fall in prices on world markets. Manu-facturing output increased by a small amount, but only for iron and steel products and clothing was the increase anything more than trivial.

The very slow growth of the 1880s was broken by a sharp upturn between 1887/88 and 1891/92. In that short period Canadian output again grew fairly rapidly, although not so rapidly as in the growth period ten years earlier. The average annual rate of growth almost doubled. This time agriculture did not lead; manufacturing and other primary sectors such as mining and fishing were the main growth sectors. Exports experienced a healthy increase, with dairy products and fish leading the gains. All sectors of manufacturing industry showed prominent gains in output, although the increases were especially strong in clothing and food and beverage manufacturing. Agricultural output did not increase much, but at least did not decline. Dairying was again the strong sector, but wheat production also increased as Manitoba wheat began to have an impact. Overall, though, the increase in agricultural output was less than 10 percent.

From 1891/92 until late in the decade there was virtually no further growth in the Canadian economy. GNP per capita actually declined to 1896, which was a depressed year, and over a period ending in 1894/95 showed no growth at all. Total output increased by less than 5 percent. This was a period of very pronounced decline in prices, and that showed up in a weak performance of exports. The value of all agricultural output fell, even though dairy production went up strongly. Manufacturing output also declined, and there was a collapse of construction. Lumber production declined despite a modest increase in exports of lumber over the period. The output of the iron and steel industries went down substantially. Only clothing manufacturing and non-metallic mineral products showed any increase.

An overall impression of the last three decades of the nineteenth century, as revealed in the newly available historical national income statistics for Canada, is one of a slowly growing economy – one that was almost marking time, with a couple of short, fairly strong bursts of economic growth. Four-fifths of all the increase in per capita income that occurred between 1870 and 1896 came in fewer than one-third of the years of the period. The economy was able to make progress, especially in the industrial sector, but seemed to have difficulty sustaining growth. It would be hard to attribute the causes to external influences. There was no general collapse of export markets, although the loss of live-animal markets in the United States in the 1870s and of the malting barley market after the U.S. tariff hike in 1891 were serious blows. Canada's leading export, lumber, which had provided a strong base for economic growth through much of the nineteenth century, was losing its dynamic. The settlement of the prairie west still had little impact, and the established agriculture of the older regions of the country was unable to provide a substantial enough foundation for large scale exports. Dairy production, to supply the factory cheese industry, grew rapidly, but at best it provided only a partial offset for losses of export markets for other agricultural products. The domestic urban market was expanding, but not rapidly enough to invigorate agriculture across the country.

Manufacturing industries showed some impressive bursts of growth over this three-decade period, but developments were not sustained. Apart from sawmills and cheese factories, manufacturing was not for export but was essentially import-competing catering to the domestic market. That market, in turn, was weakened by heavy emigration and by a faltering agricultural base. The latter problem has not received much attention in past writing on Canadian economic history but would appear to stand out as the source of much of the difficulty. One might argue, in contrast to the earlier pessimistic writers, that Canada's shortcoming in this period was not so much industrial as agricultural. Total agricultural output failed to grow after about 1882, and farm output per worker in 1896/97 was no higher than it had been in 1870/71. Admittedly, there were some promising areas of agricultural development, but too much of the large farm sector remained stagnant. Had agriculture grown more vigorously, the manifest successes in manufacturing for the domestic market might have been considerably more extensive and have had greater aggregate impact.

It is not easy to come to a satisfactory net appraisal of the experience of the Canadian economy in the last three decades of the nineteenth century. All national economies exhibit variations by region, and it is not at all clear that the lagging, rural regions of Canada were any more substantial a part of the Canadian economy than, for example, the rural south of the United States. It may be more pertinent that the progressive sectors of the Canadian economy were not as strong or as vigorous in their growth as those of its southern neighbor. Both economies benefited greatly from the important changes in technology that came at the end of the nineteenth century – electricity, chemicals, and the internal combustion engine. It is also the case that the greatest impact of those developments came in the years after 1896. The late-nineteenth-century Canadian economy lacked size at a time when economies of large-scale production were coming into prominence. Partly because of that, the development of a modern steel industry in Canada lagged about twenty years behind the

United States. At the same time Canada was gaining in the extent and breadth of manufacturing, but not to the degree that could be seen in the United States. Canada was slow in replacing its older industries with new, modern industries in a really substantial way. Steel was not displacing iron; steam-powered iron ships were not being built in place of wooden sailing ships, and Canada did not yet have the mineral resource base that was so important to the United States at the time.

With due recognition of the slower growth of the Canadian economy toward the end of the century, we should not lose sight of the substantial accomplishments of that economy. Those seem largely to be attainments of the third quarter of the century. Canadians had settled an extensive part of the North American continent and transformed it into a prosperous agricultural economy. They had made effective use of their abundant forest resources to become the world's foremost exporter of wood. They had initiated a successful industrialization. All this had created a nation that was well on its way to joining the list of world leaders in economic prosperity. By the last decade of the nineteenth century Canada was not only a nation with high income but in per capita terms ranked among the highest in manufacturing production as well. That was accomplished in the shadow of a much larger and even more prosperous economy with which Canada shared the continent. All too often that placed Canada in a diminished light. It is important, then, to appreciate the attainments of the nineteenth-century Canadian economy. At the same time we have to recognize that Canadian development was not moving forward with as much vitality in the last quarter of the century. It appears to have depleted its opportunities for development and to have been awaiting the shift in circumstances that would permit it to enter the next century in a greatly invigorated way.

INEQUALITY IN THE NINETEENTH CENTURY

CLAYNE POPE

THE THREE GREAT QUESTIONS

Alexis de Tocqueville, Frederick Jackson Turner, and Simon Kuznets have set out the fundamental questions that dominate consideration of inequality in the nineteenth century. Their questions, posed in 1835, 1893, and 1955 respectively, have not yet been definitively answered. Nor are answers close at hand, for these questions pose difficult methodological issues, relate to changing values concerning inequality and economic opportunity, and require quantitative evidence on poorly measured distributions of income and wealth as well as information about economic opportunity. Yet each of the questions retains its interest and relevance to judgments today about economic equality in the nineteenth century.

From May 1831 to February 1832 Alexis de Tocqueville, in the company of Gustave de Beaumont, made his epic journey through North America, traveling west across New York to the frontier in Michigan, then northeast into Canada, down to Boston, Baltimore, and Philadelphia, west to Cincinnati, Nashville, and Memphis, down the Mississippi to New Orleans, overland to Washington, and back to New York City. Tocqueville and Beaumont were entertained by various levels of society, which they interviewed extensively, and observed with dispassion and insight the structure of this strange new democracy.

Tocqueville saw the relative equality of condition compared to Europe and the strong egalitarian ethic of the United States as the foundation of American democracy. He recognized that economic inequality assumed increased importance in the United States because of the absence of privilege through birth.

Money makes a real privileged class in society, which keeps itself apart and
rudely makes the rest conscious of its pre-eminence. . . . In America, in
the absence of all material and external distinctions, wealth appeared as the
natural test to measure men's feeling for the pleasures of the mind. Exclusively
occupied in making their fortunes they must naturally have a sort of venera-
tion for wealth. It arouses their envy, but tacitly they recognize it as the chief
advantage.[1]

Thus, wealth could be the basis in the United States for important class
distinctions, but they never appeared. Why not? Tocqueville's answer
emphasized economic opportunity or mobility.

This pre-eminence of wealth in society has less fatal consequences for equality
than those which spring from prejudices of birth and profession. It is not at all
permanent;

It is not that in the United States, as everywhere, there are no rich; indeed I know
no other country where love of money has such a grip on men's hearts or where
stronger scorn is expressed for the theory of permanent equality of property. But
wealth circulates there with incredible rapidity, and experience shows that two
successive generations seldom enjoy its favors.[2]

Tocqueville clearly posed a primary question about nineteenth-century
inequality. Was this a society of economic mobility and opportunity? The
question may be posed in several different forms. Were the poor households consigned to be poor always, or was there upward (and downward)
mobility? Were the economic positions of individuals determined by the
economic positions of their parents? Did immigrants from different ethnic
backgrounds really enjoy the economic opportunity they anticipated in
America?

   In July of 1893 Frederick Jackson Turner read a paper at the meetings
of the American Historical Association that would turn out to be one
of the most influential papers in American historiography. The Turner
thesis first outlined in "The Significance of the Frontier in American
History" has since generated a stream of scholarship of definition, reinterpretation, and testing of this provocative hypothesis. The economic
aspects of Turner's thesis were more explicitly stated in his article in the
Atlantic Monthly in 1903 entitled "Contributions of the West to American Democracy." Here, he stated the egalitarian effect of the frontier in
explicit terms.

---

[1] Alexis de Tocqueville, *Journey to America*, ed. J. P. Mayer (New Haven, 1960), 260.
[2] Alexis de Tocqueville, *Journey to America*, 260; Alexis de Tocqueville, *Democracy in America*, ed. J. P.
   Mayer (Garden City, N.Y., 1969), 54.

If now in the way of recapitulation, we try to pick out from the influences that have gone to the making of Western Democracy the factors which constitute the net result of this movement, we shall have to mention at least the following:

Most important of all has been the fact that an area of free land has continually lain on the western border of the settled area of the United States. Whenever social conditions tended to crystallize in the East, whenever capital tended to press upon labor or political restraints to impede the freedom of the mass, there was this gate of escape to the free conditions of the frontier. These free lands promoted individualism, economic equality, freedom to rise, democracy. . . . In a word, then, free lands meant free opportunities.[3]

Some of the economic dimensions of the Turner thesis appear doubtful. Land in the sense of land ready to farm was never free, since considerable capital and labor were required to make a farm. Direct migration of discontented or unemployed urban workers migrating to the frontier to farm was never a significant force in the nineteenth-century migrations westward. But the proposition that the frontier and greater land availability increased economic opportunity, created more egalitarian communities, and reduced overall inequality in the United States is still worth consideration.

The third question, associated most closely with Simon Kuznets, concerns the relationship between the process of economic development and the extent of economic inequality. In his presidential address before the American Economic Association in December of 1954, Simon Kuznets posed a fundamental question: "Does inequality in the distribution of income increase or decrease in the course of a country's economic growth?" Kuznets identified forces that he thought would increase inequality over time. For example, savings, which are concentrated among the upper-income groups, could have the effect of increasing the relative income of the richest segment of the population. Further, the shift of households from the relatively egalitarian rural sector to the more unequal urban sector could also increase inequality with time. But he also identified forces, such as government intervention and the rise in importance of high-wage service jobs, that might offset the tendency toward more inequality. After an extended discussion of the effects on the rural–urban shift, Kuznets hypothesized that there would be a long swing in distribution of income accompanying the process of development. In the early stages of industrialization, inequality would rise because of the quick gains being made in new industries; then inequality would stabilize and

[3] Frederick Jackson Turner, *The Frontier in American History* (New York, 1920), 259–60.

eventually fall as the transitions to a mature industrialized economy were completed.

One might assume a long swing in the inequality characterizing the secular income structure: widening in the early phases of economic growth when the transition from the pre-industrial to the industrial civilization was most rapid; becoming stabilized for a while; and then narrowing in the later phases.[4]

For the United States, he suggested that inequality might have risen in the nineteenth century "particularly from 1870 on" and begun to fall with the First World War in the twentieth century. It is important to note that for Kuznets this inverted U-shaped trend in the distribution of income was a theoretical conjecture, not based on substantive empirical evidence available to him. But the question of the relationship between inequality and the process of economic growth is an intriguing one. Would the poor gain doubly from growth because of an increase in the average standard of living and a narrowing in the distribution of income, or would there be a trade-off, with the increase in the average accompanied by more inequality?

Tocqueville, Turner, and Kuznets posed the fundamental and still largely unanswered questions about inequality in nineteenth-century America. Was the industrialization of the nineteenth century accompanied by a rise or fall in inequality? What role did the frontier play in fostering either more equality at a point in time or more economic opportunity over time? Was the United States an egalitarian land of opportunity where the poor could look forward to improvements in their own standard of living or that of their children?

Any serious consideration of these three major distributional questions quickly leads to a set of perplexing and largely irresolvable measurement issues. A few of these measurement issues are discussed in the appendix at the end of this chapter. While these measurement issues are often technical and complex, they must be kept in mind as data and results from various flawed sources are brought together in the examination of nineteenth-century inequality.

Before reviewing what is known and not known about answers to the three major questions, it will be useful to consider the covariates of wealth and income. These covariates tell us much about the forces that create inequality. That is, knowledge of the distribution of a characteristic that influences the distribution of wealth and the influence that characteristic

---

[4] Simon Kuznets, "Economic Growth and Inequality," *American Economic Review*, 45 (1955), 18.

has on wealth gives us an idea as to the effect of that characteristic on the inequality that is observed. A number of studies of nineteenth-century wealthholding by individual households have isolated a set of variables that have systematic relationships with wealth. Knowledge of the effects of these variables shed light on the tentative answers that can be given to the questions posed by Tocqueville, Turner, and Kuznets.

CHARACTERISTICS THAT INFLUENCE WEALTH ACCUMULATION

Distributions of income and wealth represent the aggregation of the economic benefits or costs of characteristics and decisions of millions of individuals or households. Understanding of the underlying forces that create wealth or income adds to our understanding of these distributions. Since data on the income of households are virtually nonexistent in the United States before the institution of the income tax in the twentieth century, research on nineteenth-century inequality has relied heavily on wealth data. In particular, the manuscripts of the federal censuses of 1850, 1860, and 1870, each of which report some measure of wealth as well as age and some other relevant variables, have been used to examine the correlates with wealth. Not all variables that theory would suggest influence wealth accumulation are recorded in these nineteenth-century sources. In particular, there have not been studies measuring the effect of education on wealth accumulation. But the effects of other variables having a systematic relationship to wealth, including location (and thus migration), age, sex of the household head, occupation, duration in a local economy, family background, literacy, and ethnicity have been measured and systematic patterns are fairly well established.

AGE AND WEALTH

Wealth accumulation has several motives, including desires to make bequests to children, concerns over possible hard times in the future, and what economists refer to as "life-cycle" motives. The life-cycle hypothesis is based on the conjecture that individuals will wish to smooth consumption over a life cycle characterized by variable income. Labor earnings grow during early adulthood as an individual acquires skill and experience, but they eventually decline as a person ages. Households thus will save in early years in order to increase consumption in later years. In its most basic form, the life-cycle view of wealth accumulation would suggest that wealth will, at first, grow with age, but will peak well before expected age of death and then decline as consumption exceeds income.

All studies of nineteenth-century wealth accumulation have found a positive relationship between age and wealth through young ages. For example, Soltow found that average real estate holdings in 1850 for males in their thirties was a little more than a third of the holdings of males in their sixties. He found similar increases with age for total wealth in 1860 and 1870. Atack and Bateman also found substantial increases in wealth with age in their study of rural townships in the antebellum North. The increases in wealth per year usually decrease with age, imparting a concave shape to the age–wealth profile. The age–wealth profiles appear to have been flatter for frontier households, for immigrants, and for African-Americans.

Not only have most studies of age–wealth profiles found positive age–wealth relationships, but they have also found peaks in wealth with modest declines in wealth in old age. For example, Galenson found that wealthholdings peaked at age 50 in Chicago in 1860; Schaefer found a peak at age 48 in real estate holdings for Texas slaveowners; and Kearl and Pope conclude that wealth peaked between ages 53 and 60 for Utah in samples drawn from 1860 to 1900. Soltow does not find an age-peak in wealth for his U.S. sample, but he does find a peak for sub-groups such as farmers and immigrants. A peak in the age–wealth profile is consistent with a life-cycle view of wealth accumulation.

It should be noted that these studies all involve cross-sectional estimates of the relationship between age and wealth. Cross-sectional data confound the effects of age and cohort, while longitudinal studies confound age and economic growth. The pattern of wealth accumulation of a cohort of individuals as they age might well give a much different pattern than the more typical cross-sectional pattern reported in most studies. The differences between the actual patterns of wealth accumulation for households through time and the cross-sectional pattern will be a reflection of differences in behavior among cohorts and, perhaps most important, the positive effect of economic growth on wealth accumulation. Actual wealth accumulation of households may be followed in Utah between 1850 and 1900. These households still had peaks in their wealth accumulation, giving support to the life-cycle hypothesis.

The consistent age–wealth pattern described above creates wealth inequality. That is, a narrow age distribution would produce a more equal wealth distribution than a more disperse distribution of ages, other factors being equal. Differences in the age distribution could also create differences in the distributions of wealth in an indirect way. If inequality declines with age, as Soltow suggests that it does in the nineteenth century, then a shift toward an older age distribution could reduce inequality. Some researchers, believing income inequality produced by age differences is unimportant, adjust measures such as the Gini coefficient (see appendix and note to Table 3.7 for an explanation of the Gini coefficient) for the age distribution. Of course, whether or not inequality in wealth or income due to age differences matters ethically is a value judgment. Nevertheless, much of the observed wealth inequality is age related.

RACIAL AND ETHNIC DIFFERENCES IN WEALTH

Foreign-born households owned substantially less wealth than native-born throughout the nineteenth century. This unsurprising result is borne out by all of the micro-level studies of wealth in the nineteenth century, some of which are listed in Table 3.1. Soltow found the foreign-born men owned less than half of the real estate of native-born men in 1850 and 1860 and less than half of the total wealth in 1860. The wealth disadvantage of immigrants declined between 1860 and 1870, largely because of the lack of growth of the wealth of natives in the Civil War decade with the freeing of slaves, which reduced the wealth of slaveowners, most of whom were native-born.

Immigrants accumulated wealth at rapid rates in the mid-nineteenth century. Joseph Ferrie, using a sample of immigrants linked from ship lists to the censuses of 1850 and 1860, estimated that the wealth of immigrant households was growing at 10 percent per year. As immigrants participated in the economy, they gathered information that allowed them to better match their skills to occupations and locations within the United States. Immigrants appeared to do better in the frontier West than in the more settled East. Whereas Galenson found that mean wealth of English and Irish immigrants in Chicago was 32 percent and 18 percent of the mean wealth of U.S.-born men in Chicago, Herscovici estimated the wealth of English and Irish of Boston to be 9 percent and 4 percent respectively of the wealth of the native-born.

Table 3.1. *Wealth of natives and immigrants*

Coverage	Year	Type of wealth	Wealth of natives	Wealth of foreign born	Ratio
U.S. (Soltow)	1850	Real estate	$1,103	$535	2.06
U.S. (Soltow)	1860	Real estate	1,722	833	2.07
U.S. (Soltow)	1870	Real estate	2,001	1,204	1.66
U.S. (Soltow)	1860	Total estate	3,027	1,297	2.33
U.S. (Soltow)	1870	Total estate	3,035	1,798	1.69
Trempealeau County Wis. Farmers (Curti)	1870	Total estate	2,532	1,644	1.54
Utah (Kearl/Pope/Wimmer)	1860	Total estate	1,320	726	1.82
Utah (Kearl/Pope/Wimmer)	1870	Total estate	1,310	873	1.50
Chicago (Galenson)	1860	Total estate	6,040	1,166	5.18
Texas (Campbell/Lowe)	1860	Total estate	7,019	2,811	2.50

Source: Lee Soltow, *Men and Wealth in the United States, 1850–1870* (New Haven, 1975); Merle Curti, et al., *The Making of An American Community* (Stanford, 1959); J. R. Kearl, Clayne L. Pope, and Larry T. Wimmer, "The Distribution of Wealth in a Settlement Economy: Utah 1850–1870," *Journal of Economic History*, 40 (1980); David W. Galenson, "Economic Opportunity on the Urban Frontier," *Journal of Economic History*, 15 (1991); Randolph B. Campbell and Richard G. Lowe, *Wealth and Power in Antebellum Texas* (College Station, TX, 1977).

Controlling for age, location, occupation, and duration in the economy eliminates much of the wealth differential between the foreign-born and native-born. For example, the differential of $1,730 between natives and immigrants in Soltow's 1860 sample is reduced to $1,211 in a regression controlling for age, occupation, and region. Atack and Bateman find similar results for their large sample of the rural North. In Chicago, Galenson found that wealth differences among German-, Irish-, British-, and U.S.-born were largely captured by occupational differences. In Utah, the interplay between duration and nativity could be clearly seen. Table 3.1

shows the foreign-born of Utah with only two-thirds of the wealth of the native-born in 1870. But a comparison of households that had been in Utah in 1860 reduces the disadvantage of the foreign-born to only 12 percent. A significant part of the foreign-born disadvantage in wealth was due to their shorter duration in the economy. As the foreign-born gained time and experience in the economy, they were able to reduce any disadvantage they had in wealthholdings.

It is likely that the migration of more than twenty million immigrants to the United States in the nineteenth century increased overall inequality in the United States, though it probably reduced inequality in Western Europe and the United States taken together. The international migration brought individuals who on average had less wealth than natives. The waves of immigration may also have created changes to the returns to labor, land, and capital by lowering wages paid to labor and increasing the rent on land and the return to capital – increasing inequality.

Non-white households owned very little wealth in the mid-nineteenth century. Non-whites in Soltow's sample had mean wealth of $74 in 1870, compared to $2,691 for whites. Less than 20 percent of the non-white households in the sample reported any wealth. In the sample of the 1860 census manuscripts for the rural North, white households had on average more than thirteen times the wealth of black households holding age, literacy, and occupation constant. Wealth had obviously not accompanied freedom from slavery.

OCCUPATION AND WEALTH

The relationship between wealth and occupation is consistent across a number of studies. Soltow's national samples reported in Table 3.2 for 1850, 1860, and 1870 indicate that farmers held more wealth than non-farmers. Farmers owned 100 percent more real estate in 1850, 72 percent more in 1860, and 43 percent more in 1870. The decline in the advantage of farmers from 1860 to 1870 is due, in part, in part to the effect of the Civil War on the agricultural South. An increasing tendency to classify farm laborers as farmers rather than non-farmers may also have contributed to the trend. But the changes in the proportion of farmers and non-farmers with property were not large enough to account for all of the decline in the ratio of farmers' wealth to that of non-farmers. It must also have been the case that non-farm property was enjoying more rapid capital gains as cities and towns gained importance in the economy.

Table 3.2. *Wealth of farmers and non-farmers in mid-nineteenth century*

	1850	1860	1870
Proportion owning real estate			
Farmers	0.61	0.57	0.58
Non-farmers	0.26	0.30	0.31
Mean value of real estate			
Farmers	$1,385	$1,894	$2,121
Non-farmers	694	1,099	1,480
Ratio of farmers to non-farmers	2.00	1.72	1.43
Proportion owning total estate > $100			
Farmers		0.72	0.74
Non-farmers		0.52	0.51
Mean value of total estate			
Farmers	NA	$3,166	$2,948
Non-farmers	NA	2,006	2,475
Ratio of farmers to non-farmers	NA	1.58	1.19

Notes: "NA" is not available. Data for 1850 and 1860 is for free adult males over 19 years of age. Data for 1870 is for white males over age 19.
Source: Soltow, *Men and Wealth*, ch. 3.

The wealth differential for farmers in terms of total wealth was not as large. The proportion of farmers and non-farmers holding either some real estate or some personal wealth in excess of $100 did not change materially between 1860 and 1870. Between 1860 and 1870 the wealth of non-farmers increased, while that of farmers actually declined. Most Northern farmers of 1860 experienced a gain in their wealth over the Civil War decade, but new farmers who entered farming after the Civil War lowered the mean value of farmers' wealth.

Wealthholdings for the non-farm occupations follow anticipated patterns. For example, high white-collar occupations of Chicago were much wealthier than other groups with wealth of $15,448 on average in 1860; low white-collar, $966; skilled, $617; semiskilled, $325, and the unskilled, $238. Most urban dwellers were less wealthy than farm households, though their incomes may well have been higher. In Salt Lake County, with an 1870 population of 18,035 and a good mixture of occupations, mean wealth by the occupation of the household head was as shown in Table 3.3. Farmers

Table 3.3. *Wealth by occupations, Salt Lake County, 1870*

Occupation	Percentage of all workers	Average Wealth
Merchants	2.7%	$14,145
Professional	3.1	4,018
Clerks	3.9	1,744
Farmers	16.1	1,445
Craftsmen	25.6	1,388
Semi-skilled	15.5	962
Laborers	17.3	530
Not in the labor force	15.7	585

Source: Kearl, Pope, and Wimmer, "Distribution of Wealth."

were, on average, in the middle of the occupational hierarchy with merchants, professionals, and clerks or aspiring professionals ahead of them. Skilled craftsmen owned a little less than farmers, while the less-skilled blue-collar workers were considerably less wealthy.

Occupational differences added to inequality. Our view of inequality connected with occupations probably depends, in part, on the mobility of individuals across occupations. If individuals moved up the occupational ladder with regularity, the view of occupational inequality might be similar to the view of age inequality. If a person's occupation remained the same over time, then occupational inequality takes on a different meaning.

URBAN–RURAL DIFFERENCES

It has already been noted that farmers were somewhat wealthier than non-farmers, although control for regional differences and nativity eliminate that difference for whites in 1870. Comparisons of rural areas with nearby urban areas often show an advantage for the urban area. Mean wealth in Milwaukee in 1870 was $2,434 for males age 20 and over and only $1,478 for Wisconsin as a whole. Average wealth in Salt Lake, the "urban" part of Utah, was 70 percent above the Utah average. The U.S.-born living in Chicago in 1860 held more than twice the national average wealth. Urban areas appeared to have higher mean wealth, though the evidence is not pervasive. What is clear is that urban distributions of wealth were more unequal. The Gini coefficient for non-farmers was 0.89 in 1870 and only

0.77 for farmers in Soltow's national sample. The distribution of wealth for rural townships in the North produced a Gini coefficient of 0.63, which is considerably below the national Gini coefficient of 0.83 in 1860. In Boston, Herscovici calculated a Gini coefficient of 0.95 with the richest decile owning 95 percent of all wealth. In contrast, Gregson calculated a Gini coefficient of 0.63 for six Missouri townships in 1870, with the richest quartile owning 71 percent of all wealth. Thus, the shift from a rural area to an urban area usually put the household in a less egalitarian environment. The greater inequality in the cities does not necessarily imply that inequality was increased by the increased urbanization through-out the nineteenth century, but such a result is likely, given the levels of wealth and the differences in the distribution of wealth.

MIGRATION AND WEALTH

The regional differences in per capita income in the nineteenth century have been well documented. Per capita income was highest in the North-east and the West, with lower but rapidly growing incomes in the North Central region and lower rates of income growth in the South. In the North, migrants moved from high-income areas to lower-income areas, creating a lower rate of growth for the North as whole than the rates for its sub-regions. In the South, migrants moved from low-income regions to high income areas, creating a higher rate of income growth for the South than the rates of its sub-regions.

There were also significant differences in average regional wealth-holding by household in the mid-nineteenth century. Soltow estimates that wealthholding of free adult males was 95 percent higher in the South than the North prior to the Civil War. Of course, most of this difference was due to wealth in slaves. Within the North, wealthholdings in the Northwest increased to a position of equality with the Northeast. The ratio of mean real estate per household in the Northwest to mean real estate per household in the Northeast moved from 0.77 in 1850 to 0.88 in 1860 to 1.07 by 1870. The same ratios for total estate were 0.81 in 1860 and 0.99 in 1870. People migrating westward could reasonably have expected to accumulate a little wealth in the form of a farm or small business. They could also expect their wealth to benefit from high rates of capital gains. This higher rate of wealth accumulation in the Northwest was the moti-vation for the migration from the high-income region, the Northeast, to the lower-income region, the Northwest. Similar westward migratory flows occurred in the South, with the added element of Southern wealth migrating westward in the form of slaves.

The migration westward throughout the nineteenth century was an investment. It cost wealth to move, but households could expect to make a return on their moves to better locations. Studies have consistently found that new arrivals have less wealth than others. This finding suggests that the costs of migration were significant. It could also have been the case that migrants were poorer than non-migrants – that poverty induced their migration. Schaefer found that migrants between 1850 and 1860 to Arkansas and Texas in the antebellum period were less wealthy than those who came earlier (controlling for other characteristics, including wealth in 1850). Steckel found that movers from the Northeast to the Northwest before 1860 had relatively less wealth than did non-migrants.

DURATION AND WEALTH ACCUMULATION

There was a positive relationship between duration in a local economy and the level of wealth of a household for most locations in the nineteenth century. Along the frontier, early arrivers tended to be more wealthy. Gregson estimates that the annual rate of wealth accumulation was 1.7 percentage points higher for early arrivers to Missouri. Galenson found that those who were in Chicago in 1850 owned more wealth, controlling for other characteristics, than those who came to the city between 1850 and 1860. Schaefer found the same result for the migrants to Texas and Arkansas. Steckel found that stayers in a place did, on average, better than movers. Ferrie found that early immigrants had much higher levels of wealth than those with similar characteristics who came later. Households that had been in Utah since 1850 had over four times as much wealth in 1870 as households that had arrived after 1860.

The relationship between duration and wealth accumulation was not constant. Faster population growth and a larger population increased the return to duration. Duration in eastern rural counties with stagnant populations did little to increase wealth.

The costs of migration and the return to duration in the local economy increased inequality in areas with heavy in-migration. Recent migrants were considerably poorer than early migrants. Thus, the migration of households within the country created inequality within a local economy, but probably ameliorated national inequality. Similarly, international immigration increased inequality within the United States while reducing overall inequality in North American and Western Europe.

Few studies, either historical or contemporary, have been able to isolate the effect of family background on the level of wealth or income of a household. Data that link family members (e.g., fathers and sons, brothers) and contain observations on income or wealth are quite rare even in contemporary sources. Nineteenth-century data that allow the measurement of family background are very rare.

The results from the one dataset – the Kearl-Pope dataset for Utah – that permits measurement of family background on wealth and income clearly indicate that family background played an important role in the determination of income and wealth. Unobserved family background accounted for at least as much of the variation in wealth among a nineteenth-century sample of brothers as did the combined effects of commonly observed characteristics. Age, occupation, county of residence, birthplace, and duration in the local economy taken together accounted for 21 percent of the variance in the logarithm of wealth, while the common family background of the brothers accounted for 29 percent of the variance. When father and sons were considered, family background was less important than the observed characteristics. (Observed characteristics accounted for 24 percent of the variance and family background only 18 percent of the variance.) Similar patterns were found for income, with family background accounting for more of the variance in the incomes of brothers than the observed characteristics and slightly less of the variance in the incomes of fathers and sons. This study, if it is representative of the effects of family background in other areas, would lead to the conclusion that family background is a strong source of the inequality observed in nineteenth-century distributions of income and wealth. However, there is no reason to believe that changes in the effect of family background produced any trend in inequality.

These studies of the correlates of wealth provide a framework for the consideration of the questions of economic opportunity, the role of the frontier, and the trend in inequality. For example, migration created some inequality, but it enhanced economic opportunity. Other characteristics such as race or family background were strong barriers to equality, but they probably did not affect the trend. Other factors such as urban inequality raise the possibility that inequality may have increased in the nineteenth century.

WAS NINETEENTH-CENTURY AMERICA A LAND OF ECONOMIC OPPORTUNITY?

We now turn back to the three great questions posed by Tocqueville, Turner, and Kuznets. The first of these questions concerns the extent of economic opportunity. Opportunity can be measured in a variety of ways. Did individuals move up the economic ladder to higher occupational status over the course of their lives? Alternatively, did individuals accumulate wealth over the life cycle, regardless of their occupational status, so that they moved higher in the distribution of wealth? Or, did the children of the poor make progress as measured by higher occupational status or wealth accumulation? Finally, were there discernible barriers to either good occupations or wealth accumulation?

Distributions of income and wealth change slowly if at all. But the constancy or slight trend of the distributions of income and wealth in the nineteenth century mask constant and substantial movement of households within those distributions. It would be an error to view inequality as fixed through time, with households frozen into poverty, wealth, or the much larger middle class. Instead, there was a movement of households upward or downward within distributions that changed slowly. In other words, the stability of the distributions of income and wealth did not translate into a stability in the economic fortunes of households.

OCCUPATIONAL MOBILITY

Occupational mobility, both intergenerationally and through time for the same person, has been the most common approach to the study of economic opportunity because occupations are recorded quite often and occupations may be readily related to notions of class. Studies of occupational mobility are most useful in urban areas, where real estate is less widely held and occupations relate more closely to earnings. In rural areas, the occupation of farmer covers the majority of the population, so occupation and occupational change yield relatively little information about the economic position of the household or individual.

Table 3.4 summarizes the results of a number of studies that report occupational mobility of individuals over time. Table 3.5 clearly shows that between 1860 and 1870, occupational mobility among quintiles, both upward and downward, is quite common. Upward mobility should, in principle, be more common than downward movement because the occupational distribution slowly shifted toward more skilled and white-collar jobs over time. Hence, there could be some upward occupational mobility without any offsetting downward mobility.

Studies of occupational mobility for the nineteenth century indicate that there was substantial mobility into higher occupational categories. In cities such as Boston, Omaha, and Atlanta, between one in ten and one in five blue-collar workers moved into white-collar occupations. Comparisons of first and last occupations for men of Poughkeepsie (born 1820–1850) and Boston (born 1850–1859) reinforce the impression of mobility. Of men starting in low manual occupations, 41 percent in Boston and 32 percent in Poughkeepsie moved to higher occupations. Over a quarter of skilled laborers in both cities moved into white-collar occupations.

Occupational mobility in rural areas is harder to gauge because so much of the movement is from laborer to farmer, which covers a broad range of socio-economic groups. But, again, there was substantial upward mobil-

Table 3.4. *Occupational mobility*

Place	Time period	Percentage of blue-collar workers moving upward
Boston	1840–50	10%
	1850–60	18
	1880–90	12
Poughkeepsie	1850–60	17
	1860–70	18
	1870–80	13
Atlanta	1870–80	19
	1880–90	22
Omaha	1880–90	21
	1880–1900	25
San Francisco	1850–80	35
Salt Lake City	1860–70	48

Source: Adapted from Stephan Thernstrom, *The Other Bostonians* (Cambridge, MA, 1973) 234.

ity. In nineteenth-century Utah, half or more of unskilled laborers including farm laborers moved into the category of farmers from one census to
the next. An additional 13 to 17 percent became craftsmen. Similar results
were found for rural Wisconsin, where most farm laborers and tenant
farmers were able to become farm owners over a decade or two.

WEALTH MOBILITY

Wealth and income mobility through time add an important dimension
to the picture of economic opportunity, especially in rural areas, where the
occupation of farmer covers the full range of economic success or failure.
Even in cities, there may be important economic movement even though
there is no change in occupation. For example, in Newburyport, Massachusetts, there was relatively little occupational change because the
economy was quite stagnant with considerable out-migration, especially
of the more ambitious and able. Only 11 percent of laboring families found
in the 1860 Newburyport census owned property. But 48 percent of those
still in Newburyport in 1870 owned property, even though few had moved
out of the laboring class.

In rural areas wealth change is the best gauge of economic mobility. Farm
operators in rural Wisconsin almost tripled the value of their property
between 1860 and 1870. Moreover, absolute gains were not closely correlated with initial wealth. Consequently, there was both upward and downward mobility as well as some increased equality within the group of farmers
observed in both years. Similar results were obtained for Utah farmers.

Table 3.5 represents an illustration of one way of examining economic
mobility – a transition matrix between two different distributions of
wealth. This particular matrix represents data for Utah in 1860 and 1870.
The values of the matrix represent the proportion of households in a particular quintile of the initial year (1860) who end up in a particular quintile of the distribution of the terminal year (1870). If there were absolutely
no mobility within a wealth distribution, then off-diagonal values of the
matrix would be 0 and the diagonal values would all equal 1, implying
no movement whatsoever. On the other hand, there could be so much
mobility that wealth in the initial year would have no effect on wealth
position in the terminal year. In such a case, the expectation would be that
all values of the matrix would be 0.20.

Few of these transition matrices have been constructed for any historical distributions, but the ones that have been constructed generally show

Table 3.5. *Utah wealth mobility, 1860 to 1870*

		Distribution of wealth in the terminal year (1870)				
Distribution of Wealth in the Initial Year (1860)		Poorest quintile	2nd quintile	3rd quintile	4th quintile	Richest quintile
	Poorest quintile	0.35	0.27	0.17	0.12	0.09
	2nd quintile	0.25	0.27	0.25	0.16	0.07
	3rd quintile	0.19	0.21	0.26	0.24	0.10
	4th quintile	0.16	0.18	0.23	0.25	0.18
	Richest quintile	0.00	0.06	0.11	0.23	0.53

Source: J. R. Kearl and Clayne Pope, "Choices, Rents and Luck: Economic Mobility of Utah Households," in Stanley L. Engerman and Robert E. Gallman (eds.), *Long-Term Factors in American Economic Growth*, Studies in Income and Wealth, vol. 5 (Chicago, 1986), 221.

immobility in the poorest and richest tails of the wealth distribution and mobility in most other parts of the distribution. For example, Table 3.5 indicates that 35 percent of the poorest quintile in Utah in 1860 remained in the poorest quintile in 1870, while 53 percent of the richest quintile of 1860 stayed in the richest quintile in 1870. (Note that the quintile boundaries are determined by the distribution of wealth in this particular sample, not by the distribution of wealth for the population. If the distribution of wealth for the population were used, most of a sample that necessarily must have been in the economy for ten years will end up in the richer part of the wealth distribution of the population.) But the middle part of the distribution displayed considerable mobility. Of the middle quintile in 1860, 19 percent fell to the poorest quintile, 21 percent fell to the 2nd quintile, 26 percent stayed in the third quintile, 24 percent rose to the fourth quintile, and 10 percent rose to the top quintile.

Steckel found similar results for a national sample of households linked for the censuses of 1850 and 1860. Both tails exhibited some immobility, but there was substantial mobility within the middle parts of the wealth distribution. Only 20 percent of the households with no real estate in 1850 still had none in 1860. More than 60 percent of the sample moved at least one decile in the wealth distribution, and about 40 percent moved at least two deciles. Still, there was a high propensity for the wealthy in 1850 to also be wealthy in 1860, with 46 percent of the richest decile of 1850 still in the richest decile of 1860.

INTERGENERATIONAL MOBILITY

There was also substantial mobility across generations. Table 3.6 shows the occupational attainment of the sons with blue-collar fathers. Clearly, the extent of upward mobility of sons of blue-collar fathers in these local samples depends on the occupational opportunities. In Boston the opportunities to move into white-collar occupations were substantial, and the sons of blue-collar families moved into those occupations. Fewer opportunities were available in Newburyport. In spite of the limitations of local samples, the intergenerational samples available indicate that there was no substantial barrier to intergenerational mobility – at least for whites. Blacks were not able to move up the occupational ladder to white-collar occupations with any frequency.

An alternative way to look at intergenerational mobility is to consider the relationship of the wealth of fathers and sons. Complete mobility, obviously not observed, would exist if a son's wealth or income was independent of the wealth or income of his father. There would be some mobility if there were regression toward the mean. That is, rich fathers would have sons who were, on average, rich, but not as rich as their fathers. Similarly, poor fathers would have sons who were not as poor as their fathers. Studies

Table 3.6. *Intergenerational mobility as measured by occupations, blue-collar fathers*

City or state	Year	Occupational level of son				Number of obs.
		White-collar	Skilled	Farmers	Unskilled	
Newburyport	1880	10%	19%	na	71%	245
Poughkeepsie	1880	22	35	na	43	121
Boston	1890	43	14	na	43	63

Source: Adapted from Thernstrom, *The Other Bostonians*, 246.

of twentieth-century data and the available studies of the nineteenth century indicate that there is substantial regression toward the mean. On average, fathers 10 percent wealthier than the average had sons who were between 2 percent and 4 percent wealthier than the average.

Consideration of occupational and wealth mobility, both within an individual's lifetime and between generations, leads to the conclusion that there was substantial economic mobility in the nineteenth century. Clearly, there was immobility within the extreme tails of the economic distribution. Clearly, black families did not have opportunity on any level resembling that of whites or immigrants. Households headed by women were usually poor and unlikely to improve their economic position significantly. Yet, many poor Americans could anticipate movement upward through the distribution either for themselves or their children. Studies of economic mobility always lead to the question of how much is a lot. Scholars are free to interpret the same data as evidence of either mobility or immobility, since there is no accepted standard of reference. Comparisons of American mobility with European mobility show considerable, but variable, mobility on both sides of the Atlantic. There is less downward mobility in the United States because of its economic growth and abundance of opportunity, but Europeans did move out of the unskilled labor classes with some frequency.

DID THE FRONTIER PROMOTE ECONOMIC EQUALITY AND ECONOMIC OPPORTUNITY?

Turner's frontier thesis has many dimensions and interpretive themes. Here we concentrate on the two dimensions that are the most economic and leave aside those that are more political, such as the relationship between the frontier and the development of democracy. The first question centers on the effect of the frontier on economic equality. Did the frontier create a more equal distribution of income and wealth than would otherwise have occurred? The second question focuses on the relationship between the frontier and upward economic mobility. Did the frontier provide significant opportunities for the poor, unskilled, or landless to move up the economic ladder? Clearly, these questions are related.

Turner's frontier thesis has been approached on both micro or macro levels. That is, one may consider whether or not frontier communities had more equal distributions of economic rewards than more settled communities to the east. But there is also the possibility that the frontier created a more equal national distribution of income or wealth. The macro questions are intrinsically more difficult, and definitive answers are not yet available. More is known about equality and opportunity in frontier communities.

Table 3.7 reports inequality measures for frontier and more settled agricultural areas. The evidence suggests that there is relatively little difference between the distribution of wealth in frontier and in more settled areas. In 1860 frontier states such as Iowa, Kansas, Missouri, and Minnesota, Gini coefficients were 0.60, 0.59, 0.62 and 0.68, respectively, while Gini coefficients in the rural areas in more settled states such

Table 3.7. *The distribution of wealth in rural areas*

State or community	Time period	% held by the richest 1%	Gini coefficient
Frontier or newly settled areas:			
Kansas	1860	10	0.59
Wisconsin	1860	17	0.59
Iowa	1860	10	0.60
Minnesota	1860	23	0.68
Missouri	1860	10	0.62
Utah	1860	20	0.62
Utah	1870	22	0.73
Texas	1860		0.74
More settled areas:			
Ohio	1860	11	0.59
Pennsylvania	1860	12	0.67
Vermont	1860	21	0.67
Northeast	1860	12	0.65

Note: The Gini coefficient, a traditional summary measure of inequality, is based on ordering observations of wealth from highest to lowest, computing the percentage of wealth held by each percentage of the population (e.g. the percentage of wealth held by the richest 5 percent of the population), and computing these with the hypothetical shares if there was total quality. The Gini coefficient will be zero when there is complete equality and one when there is complete inequality.

Source: All data but that for Utah were taken from Jeremy Atack and Fred Bateman, "The 'Egalitarian Ideal' and the Distribution of Wealth in the Northern Agricultural Community: A Backward Look," *Review of Economics and Statistics* 63 (1981), 124–29; Utah data was taken from Kearl, Pope, and Wimmer, "Distribution of Wealth."

as Ohio, Pennsylvania, and Vermont in 1860 were 0.59, 0.67, and 0.67, respectively. The Gini coefficient in 1860 for the western region was 0.62 and 0.65 for the eastern region. Whatever increased equality that existed on the frontier appears to have been slight. Urban areas consistently exhibited more inequality than rural areas in the nineteenth century.

The trend of inequality in Utah during its initial settlement illustrates a plausible pattern for inequality on the frontier. Even in the earliest days of settlement, Utah did not have a particularly egalitarian distribution of wealth. The Gini coefficient of total wealth in 1860, thirteen years after initial settlement, was 0.62, and the richest 10 percent of the population owned 49 percent of aggregate wealth. In 1870, as settlement increased, the Gini coefficient for the distribution of total wealth increased to 0.73, and the richest 10 percent increased their share to 59 percent. The most newly settled areas tended to have the highest levels of equality, and inequality increased as settlement continued. Income inequality also increased with settlement. The Gini coefficient for income was 0.32 in 1855 and had risen to 0.44 by 1880.

The reason for the temporary nature of frontier equality may be found in the correlates with wealth. Duration in the local economy increased wealth, especially in newly settled areas. The process of settlement brought new households with very little wealth, while those who had arrived early increased their wealth significantly. Many nineteenth-century frontier areas attracted immigrants who arrived with little wealth, adding to the inequality. Thus, the process of settlement seemed to contain its own dynamic toward more inequality.

Though the frontier did not deliver the promised equality in frontier communities, it did provide substantial opportunity. Farm laborers systematically moved into farm ownership, and poor farmers usually increased their wealth. The study by Merle Curti, et al. of Trempealeau County, Wisconsin, found that farmers arriving there between 1850 and 1860 were able to acquire substantial acreages, with virtually no differences between ethnic groups. Galenson and Pope found that opportunity was also the norm in Appanoose County, Iowa, where the majority of farmers below the national average in wealth in 1850 had risen above the national average by 1860, with an annual increase of more than 20 percent per year. Turner conjectured that the frontier produced equality and opportunity. Apparently, it only produced opportunity.

DID NINETEENTH-CENTURY ECONOMIC DEVELOPMENT CREATE INEQUALITY?

Since Kuznets posited an inverted U-shape relationship between economic development and inequality, scholars have attempted to give that intriguing hypothesis both theoretical and empirical foundations. The Kuznets hypothesis is more directly concerned with income inequality than wealth inequality. In general, distributions of income and non-human wealth move together, though the two distributions do not have a fixed relationship. Cross-sectional data on incomes from the post–World War II period and declines in inequality in the twentieth century have given some support to the possibility that there is a systematic relationship between development and inequality. However, the historical dimension of the Kuznets hypothesis – inequality trends for particular economies over the full span of development – have been more difficult to document.

There are strong *a priori* reasons to believe, as Kuznets pointed out, that inequality should increase with development. First of all, savings tend to be concentrated within the richest households of the distribution. If the return on investment increases as the process of development goes forward, then inequality would increase. Second, a most fundamental aspect of the process of development is the shift of households from the agricultural to the urban or industrialized sector. The agricultural sector tends to be characterized by low wages and equality when compared with the urban sector. So that it might be expected that the rural–urban shift would create increased inequality. Consequently, it is somewhat surprising, on first thought, that development is not accompanied by increased inequality. Twentieth-century trends in inequality and the high levels of inequality in developing countries compared to more advanced countries contradict these initial conjectures.

But, of course, once we are aware that inequality does not increase with economic development, we can imagine countervailing forces that reduce inequality, such as the increasing importance of human capital, changes in the levels of inequality in each sector as the rural–urban shift takes place, demographic changes, and the increased economic mobility that accompanies economic development. Clearly, theoretical conjectures about the relationship between economic development and inequality could plausibly go in many directions, producing no strong theoretical justification for any particular pattern between growth and inequality.

Most empirical evidence on the relationship between inequality and development before the twentieth century has been based on either the trend in the distribution of wealth or the trend in the skill differentials for wages. Unfortunately, the distribution of income, the distribution of most interest for this issue, is not available prior to the twentieth century for the United States.

TREND IN THE DISTRIBUTION OF WEALTH

Estimates of the national distribution of wealth for three benchmark time periods have often been compared in order to provide a picture of the trend in the wealth distribution – the distribution of 1774 based on probate inventories, the distribution of 1798 based on the data collected for the dwelling census, the distributions of 1860 and 1870 based on a sample of manuscript census responses, and the survey of financial characteristics of households conducted by the Federal Reserve in 1962. Table 3.8 summarizes the findings for some well-known cross-sections.

Table 3.8. *Trends in wealth inequality*

Period, type of wealth, and wealth-holding unit	Percentage of wealth held by the richest 1%	Percentage of wealth held by the richest 10%	Gini coefficient
Gross wealth			
1774 Free wealthholders	12.9%	50.7%	0.66
1860 Free adult males	29	73	0.832
1870 Adult males	27	70	0.833
1870 White adult males	24	68	0.814
1890	26	72	
1962 All households	26	61.6	0.76
Real estate			
1798	13	45	0.59
1860	19	53	0.66

Source: Alice Hanson Jones, *Wealth of a Nation to Be* (New York, 1980), 289; Lee Soltow, *Distribution of Wealth and Income in the United States in 1798* (Pittsburgh, 1989); Lee Soltow, *Men and Wealth*.

At first glance, these data support the Kuznets hypothesis that inequality would initially increase with development and then decline. The distributions of 1774 and of 1798 appear to be more equal than the distributions of mid-nineteenth-century wealth. However, caution is in order, since the data are drawn from three disparate sources, making comparability a problem.

The 1774 estimates are based on a sample of probate inventories that give quite detailed appraisals of the wealth of the estates inventoried. To move from the wealth of probated estates of those who died to a wealth distribution of the living of 1774 requires two important adjustments. The age distribution of the living was younger than the age distribution of decedents who had probated estates. So adjustment must be made for these differences in age distribution. The more difficult problem involves a necessary assumption about the level and distribution of wealth of non-probated estates relative to the probated estates. Certainly, non-probated estates had lower wealth on average than probated estates, but probably not always zero wealth. It is difficult to estimate the average wealth of these non-probated households. It is even more difficult to estimate the distribution of wealth for the non-probated, but that distribution significantly affects the estimated distribution of wealth for 1774 and, hence, the inferred trend.

Wealth estimates for 1798 are based on a census of dwellings taken in 1798. Consequently, the 1798 wealth estimates omit personal property, including slaves, which were such an important part of wealth within the South. Since the data were collected locally, the value of property for the very wealthy who had holdings in different locales may be understated, which would, in turn, lead to an overstatement of the increase in inequality between 1798 and 1860.

The wealth estimates from 1860 and 1870 are drawn from a sample of the census manuscripts in which individuals were asked to estimate the value of their real estate and personal estate. Consequently, there may be more measurement error in the reported wealth of 1860 or 1870 essentially based on a population survey relative to the wealth estimate for 1774 based on detailed inventories. If measurement error were uncorrelated with the level of wealth, it would add spurious inequality, biasing the measured levels of inequality upward.

The samples of 1860 and 1870 include over 30 percent in each year who report no wealth while, the techniques used for the 1774 sample would include far fewer with zero wealth. There are a number of reasons for this difference. The national samples for 1860 and 1870 included all men age 20 and over. Single men and sons over age 20 in their fathers' households usually held little or no wealth and, therefore, add to the level of inequality when they are included. In 1870, personal wealth below $100 was not normally reported and few real estate values below $100 were reported in either 1860 or 1870. Thus, low wealth values may be included in the zero category.

These differences between the 1774 and 1798 sources and procedures and the source and procedures for the mid-nineteenth century estimates suggest that the comparison of the summary measures of inequality such as the Gini coefficients should be done with reservations and caution. The percentage of total wealth held by the richest 1 percent or 10 percent of the population being considered is also affected by the differences in the two data sources. If households with low but not zero wealth in 1870 are reported with zero wealth, then the total wealth of the sample would be underestimated, and the proportion of total wealth held by the richest groups would be overestimated. Similarly, if the average level of the wealth of the non-probated households in 1774 was overestimated, then total wealth of the 1774 sample would be overestimated and the share of the richest households underestimated. This discussion simply illustrates how difficult it is to determine the trend in the distribution of wealth when such different sources of wealth estimates have been used.

Other approaches to the trend in inequality also suggest that there may have been some increase in wealth inequality in the nineteenth century. For example, an approach utilizing the mid-nineteenth-century samples in conjunction with the demographic changes and urban–rural shifts of the nineteenth century leads to the conclusion that inequality increased over the nineteenth century. This approach produced an estimate that the richest 1 percent owned 21 percent of the wealth in 1810, 24 percent in 1860 and 26–31 percent in 1900, while the richest 10 percent owned 69 percent of the wealth in 1810, 71–72 percent in 1860 and 73–74 percent in 1900. The upward increase in inequality in this approach is generated by the population shifts toward the cities.

Another approach is to look at trends in wealth inequality for particular locales. Most local trends point to an increase in inequality in the nineteenth century. For example, there was an increase in wealth inequality in frontier Utah between 1850 and 1870. The distribution of wealth of probated estates in Butler County, Ohio, a county that moved from a frontier area to more economic maturity, generally became more unequal through the antebellum period, with the share held by the richest 10 percent of families rising from 72 percent in 1830 to 82 percent in 1860. The share of the top decile of taxable wealth in samples from Boston and Hingham, Massachusetts, increased in the antebellum period. A few samples do not sustain the picture of upward local trends. The distribution of wealthholding in Wisconsin does not appear to have changed substantially between 1850 and 1900, although the sources for different time periods are not easily compared. Of course, it is possible to have upward trends in inequality in all locales and still not generate an upward national trend because of shifting weights and different levels of wealth for different areas.

All of the fragments of unsatisfactory evidence taken together may justify a conclusion that wealth inequality increased somewhat during the nineteenth century, at least in the antebellum period. Such a conclusion is not based on strong quantitative evidence, but the evidence that does exist points in that direction. Certainly, the evidence for the increasing inequality of wealth in the nineteenth century consistent with Kuznets's inverted U hypothesis is not as strong as the evidence for an increasing equality in the twentieth century.

Comparisons of wealth distributions between the United States and Europe are also of interest, although such comparisons to not bear directly on Kuznets's conjecture. For the nineteenth century, the distribution of wealth in the United States appears to have been more equal than wealth distributions in Europe. Soltow found that England and Wales, Sweden, Scotland, Denmark, and Norway all had more unequal distributions of wealth than the United States at the beginning of the nineteenth century. Lindert puts the wealthholding shares of the richest 1 percent, 5 percent, and 10 percent of England and Wales at 61 percent, 74 percent, and 84 percent respectively, compared to 27 percent, 54 percent, and 70 percent for the United States. While the nineteenth-century distribution of wealth for the United States was certainly unequal, it was more equal than the distributions of European countries that sent so many immigrants to North America in search of economic opportunity.

EVIDENCE ON CHANGES IN WAGE DIFFERENTIALS

Kuznets's hypothesis about the relationship between growth and distribution is really focused more on the trends in the distribution of incomes than on trends in wealth distribution. Unfortunately, income distributions are extremely rare before the twentieth century. (Income inequality for Milwaukee County appeared to decrease from 1864 to 1913 but remained fairly constant for the rest of Wisconsin. Income inequality in Utah appeared to increase from 1855 to 1900.) Because of the scarcity of income data for the pre–income tax era, research has been directed toward wage differentials, with the assumption that increases in the returns to skilled labor would increase inequality.

There is no consensus on the movement of wage differentials in the nineteenth century. Various economic historians have argued that there was a significant increase in the relative wage of skilled labor in the antebellum period followed by little change in the period between the Civil War and World War I and then a decline in the skill differential after World War I. Others find no increase in skill differentials for the antebellum period. A conclusion awaits more definitive data on wages and prices for this crucial period. Even if the trend in skill differentials was clear, the move from skill differentials to incomes is difficult because of changing employment practices as well as changes in hours or days worked. Hence, the historical record has little to say about the historical trend in the distribution of income in the nineteenth century as it relates to the increasing inequality phase of the Kuznets's hypothesis.

SUMMING UP

While only tentative answers exist for the three major questions that have been posed here, there are a set of conclusions that may be made about inequality in the nineteenth century.

The nineteenth-century U.S. economy, like most other economies, was one of considerable inequality. Whenever the richest 1 percent of adult males owns 27 percent of the wealth, as it did in 1870, or when a Gini coefficient is 0.83, as it was then, or when the poorest half of the wealth distribution own virtually no wealth beyond housewares and furniture, the distribution of economic rewards can properly be described as unequal. With considerably less evidence, the distribution of incomes also appears to have been very unequal. This inequality is not surprising, since most economies in most times and places have had very unequal distributions of economic rewards. But America had, to some degree, promised more. It was at the very least portrayed as a land of opportunity and at the very best a land where an egalitarian dream could become a reality. Sadly, the reality of the nineteenth-century economic distribution reminds us of how difficult, even impossible, any dramatic change in the distribution of wealth or income really is.

Not only was the nineteenth-century distribution of economic rewards unequal, there appears to have been a trend toward more inequality throughout the century. This trend, discernible with some doubt in changes in the distribution of wealth, was probably generated by the forces of urbanization and immigration that marked this century. Thus, the nineteenth-century wealth experience appears to confirm tentatively the increasing inequality phase of Kuznets' inverted U-hypothesis. There is really no evidence on the trend in the distribution of income.

More is known about the variables that affect the distribution of wealth than is known about the trend in the distribution. There was a systematic relationship between wealth and age. For most of the life cycle, wealth increased with age. But wealth appears to have peaked about ages 60 to 65, as wealth was either consumed or conveyed to children.

There were in the nineteenth as in the twentieth century a set of barriers to equality. Those barriers included, race, foreign birth, sex, and family background. Households who were foreign-born or headed by a woman or a black or individuals with a disadvantaged family background were much more likely to be poor. All of these characteristics created significant disadvantages for an individual or family to overcome, though the disadvantage of foreign birth was ameliorated with time in the United States. All of these characteristics are notable because, unlike occupation or location, they cannot be changed through choice or effort, but are instead characteristics that stay with the individual throughout their lifetime.

Though the nineteenth century may have been a period of inequality or even increasing inequality, it was also a period of considerable opportunity. Blue-collar workers and farm laborers were not frozen in those occupations throughout their lifetimes. Many were able to move into skilled occupations or become farmers owning land. Some were even able to move into white-collar positions or become merchants or entreprenuers.

The frontier was a source of opportunity and most likely equality. But the equality was very short-lived. As the process of settlement continued, inequality increased as early arrivers accumulated wealth and exploited the gains from early arrival. Thus, Turner appears to have been half right in his description of the economic benefits of the frontier. The frontier was not a place of "economic equality," but it did provide the "freedom to rise" or "free opportunity."

While family background was an important determinant of economic success, the children of poorer parents were not destined to poverty. There was considerable intergenerational mobility and regression toward the mean in the distributions of income and wealth.

There was also considerable wealth mobility. Households with low wealth quite often improved their economic position. The rich were not guaranteed to stay in the richest tail of the wealth distribution.

These last four conclusions – considerable upward occupational mobility, wealth mobility over time, the beneficial effect of the frontier on opportunity, and significant intergenerational mobility – suggest that Tocqueville's observation about the "fluidity" of the American wealth distribution was generally correct. To be sure, there was a segment of the very poor and the very wealthy who maintained their economic position, but most of the wealth distribution of nineteenth century could properly be characterized as mobile or fluid.

To capsulize, Kuznets was probably right, although the evidence in favor of increasing equality with later development is much stronger than the evidence in favor of increasing inequality with the early stages of development. Turner was probably correct in seeing the frontier as a generator of opportunity, but wrong in seeing it as a creator of an egalitarian economy even at the local or regional level. Tocqueville was probably right to see American as a society filled with opportunity for both the poor to advance and wealthy to fall.

Whatever the answers to these fundamental questions about inequality, the political relevance the distributions of income and wealth is not in doubt. The nineteenth century was filled with political struggles that reflected the omnipresent battle over the division of the economic pie. In addition to the great regional battles over economic effects of tariff policy and slavery, the conflicts over land distribution, immigration policy, the plight of farmers, and the threat of big business developed from underlying discontent with the distributions of income and wealth.

Federal land policy illustrates the struggle between equity and other goals of public policy. This tension was reflected in United States land policy from the first sale of Northwest lands. Jefferson's memorandum of 1784 expressed his ideal of a yeomanry on small, but adequate, farms. On the other hand, Congress's first sale of public lands in 1787 was one million acres to the Ohio Company, and subsequent sales were often to other large landholding companies. Congress also established minimum prices in order to raise money from public land sales for the public treasury. But Congress bowed to the forces for more equality by instituting the principle of pre-emption (giving squatters the right to buy their claim at the minimum price) and the policy of graduation (lowering the minimum price according to the amount of time the land had been available). The egalitarian pressures eventually dominated culminating in the passage of the Homestead Act of 1862, giving free land, subject to time settled and to improvements by the claimant. Distributional struggles played an equally strong role in immigration policy, control of monopoly, concern over agrarian discontent, tariff policy, slavery, and struggles over the gold standard. The nineteenth century produced no consensus about what the distribution of wealth or income should be. Indeed the distributional struggles of nineteenth century foreshadowed those of twentieth century.

The dynamics of the U.S. economy in the nineteenth century created a vigorous growing economy that attracted millions of immigrants. A high standard of living and rapid growth in that standard did not create an egalitarian society. Equality may be a more feasible outcome, though not a necessary outcome, of a stagnant or less dynamic economy. An economy that attracts because of the opportunities it presents is most likely to create inequality as new participants enter, relocate, change occupations, and take risks to capture the opportunities before them. Such was the case in the United States in the nineteenth century. It gave attractive opportunities and created inequality at the same time.

APPENDIX: ISSUES OF MEASUREMENT

There are a set of measurement problems that confront any attempt to measure distributions of income or wealth or their trend over time. These measurement issues, like most others in economics, are never completely resolved, but they must be kept in mind in any discussion of inequality, its trend over time, or the factors that influence inequality.

HOUSEHOLDS, FAMILIES OR INDIVIDUALS

Is inequality to be measured among households, families, or individuals? One would like the recipient unit, the unit for which we are measuring income or wealth, to include all individuals likely to be affected significantly by any change in the economic position of the unit and no one else. On this basis, we would combine children with parents because the children share significantly any change in income of their parents. In addition, it would seem prudent to require that the units be mutually exclusive, so that no individual is in two recipient units. A college student away from home should not be counted as a single-person household at school and part of his family at home. It is also necessary that we be able to assign all income to particular units. Unfortunately, these criterion cannot usually be easily met. The income or asset value of small enterprises and farms cannot always be parceled out to the various family members involved.

Intergenerational transfers, especially the informal transfers while both generations are living, create significant measurement difficulties. Contrast the situation of a widow living in a separate household with a small income supplemented by transfers from a well-to-do child with the situation where the widow lives with the child. In the first instance, one poor household and one rich household will be recorded, while only one rich household with one additional member will be recorded in the second instance. Consumption of the individuals involved may not vary significantly across the two situations. If there were an adequate way to account for these transfers, then treating each household as a separate entity would be satisfactory. However, there is no evident way to measure the extent of inter-household transfers. Consequently, changes in household structure will change our measurement of inequality in ways that are not consistent with the changes in actual economic conditions of households.

There is also a question of whether we wish to consider all households, which include both families and unrelated individuals, or only families. The transfers between families and unrelated individuals are likely to be quite extensive. In the twentieth century the percentage of households composed of unrelated individuals has risen. Further, the mean income of unrelated individuals is much lower than that of families, with more inequality among unrelated individuals than among families. Consequently, the distribution of income among both families and unrelated individuals is likely to be more unequal than the distribution among families alone. There are fewer unrelated individuals in the nineteenth-century households. But there are significant numbers of boarders and others living alone, especially in cities and towns in the nineteenth century. The trend throughout the nineteenth century is toward somewhat smaller households, a trend that accelerates in the twentieth century.

DEFINITIONS OF INCOME

In an ideal world, we would want to measure the full income of the recipient unit, including imputed income, income from home production, and income in kind. We would also want to know the effect of taxes and transfers to measure income available for consumption or saving. Obviously such a measure of income does not exist for the twentieth century, and even poor measures of income are rare in earlier times. Given some imperfect measure of income, does one want to measure and analyze income per family or income per family member? Typically family income rises somewhat irregularly with the size of the family, while the income per family member falls significantly with an increase in family size. For example, income per household and income per person in 1980 is shown in Table 3.9.

However, we do not know if this pattern of a rise in household income and a fall in income per person with size is a consistent historical pattern or if it is a pattern that has developed in the twentieth century. If one does wish to move to income per person, there is the immediate problem of the treatment of children. Should they be considered as full persons, or should household size be translated into some sort of adult equivalent units? There are no easy answers to these measurement problems, and most historical work has been constrained by the data at hand. But these measurement problems should be kept in mind, especially at the points of interpretation.

Table 3.9. *Income per household and income per person, 1980*

Household size	Mean income per household	Mean income per person
One person	$10,981	$10,981
Two people	20,943	10,472
Three people	24,387	8,129
Four people	26,921	6,730
Five people	28,126	5,625
Six people	27,880	4,647
Seven or more people	27,280	3,897

Source: *Current Population Reports* Series P-60, 1983, 7.

SOURCES AND DEFINITIONS OF WEALTH

Wealth data are more readily available than income data and are found in nineteenth-century data sources such as census manuscripts in 1850, 1860, and 1870 as well as probate inventories and tax records. Each is beset by its own particular problems as a source for the estimate of the distribution of wealth. Household or individual wealthholdings are never fully given. At best, the calculation is net worth, with both assets and liabilities given in some probate inventories. In census manuscripts and tax rolls, wealth will be given as gross wealth and may include all physical wealth sources or only real estate. Of course, none of the sources give an estimate of human capital. While probate inventories give a more detailed picture of an individual's wealth, the coverage is more limited than census manuscripts or tax rolls. Alice Hanson Jones suggests that in 1774 between one-third and two-thirds (depending on the region of the country) of decedents did not probate their estates. To complicate further, the age distribution of those who die is skewed, fortunately, toward the elderly. Consequently, assumptions must be made in moving from the distribution of wealth for probated estates to the distribution for all decedents to the distribution of interest – the distribution of wealth of the living.

Census manuscripts and tax rolls cover all households in principle, although there were omissions in the census manuscripts, and households were sometimes excused from the tax rolls. In no source is the coverage complete. In the census manuscripts, wealth below $100 is rarely recorded, making it difficult to distinguish between households with virtually no wealth and households with a small amount of wealth.

MEASURES OF INEQUALITY

There is always a strong impulse to reduce the information about inequality given by a complete distribution to a single number so that comparisons are made easier. There is no unambiguous clear way to do this. Any single number, such as a Gini coefficient or the Theil index of the variance of the logs, discards substantial information. The Gini coefficient is used here because it is still the most common summary measure of inequality. The Gini coefficient takes a value of 0 when complete equality has been attained and a value of 1 for complete inequality.

4

THE POPULATION OF THE UNITED STATES, 1790–1920

MICHAEL R. HAINES

In the late eighteenth century, Benjamin Franklin commented on the remarkably high fertility and large family size in what was British North America, which he attributed to the ease of acquiring good farm land. His comments were reiterated by Thomas Robert Malthus in his famous *Essay on the Principle of Population*:

> But the English North American colonies, now the powerful people of the United States of America, made by far the most rapid progress. To the plenty of good land which they possessed in common with the Spanish and Portuguese settlements, they added a greater degree of liberty and equality. . . . The political institutions that prevailed were favorable to the alienation and division of property. . . . There were no tithes in any of the States and scarcely any taxes. And on account of the extreme cheapness of good land a capital could not be more advantageously employed than in agriculture, which at the same time that it supplies the greatest quantity of healthy work affords the most valuable produce of society.
>
> The consequence of these favorable circumstances united was a rapidity of increase probably without parallel in history. Throughout all of the northern colonies, the population was found to double in twenty-five years.[1]

Although Malthus guessed at the rate of natural increase (implying a 2.8 percent per year rate of growth), he was not far off. During the period 1790 to 1810, population growth in the new nation (including migration) exceeded 3 percent per annum (see Table 4.2). In addition to notably high fertility, areas of North America, especially the New England and north-

The author wishes to thank Richard Easterlin, Henry Gemery, and Richard Steckel for helpful comments.

[1] Thomas Robert Malthus, *An Essay Concerning the Principle of Population* (1798), ch. VI. Reproduced in Thomas Robert Malthus, *An Essay on the Principle of Population* and *A Summary View of the Principle of Population*, edited with and introduction by Antony Flew (Baltimore, 1970), 105.

ern Middle Atlantic regions, also had a reputation as having more benign mortality conditions than those prevailing in much of Europe. These factors, combined with significant net in-migration in the early seventeenth century and after about 1720, led to the relatively high rates of population increase.[2]

Every modern, economically developed nation has undergone a demographic transition from high to low levels of fertility and mortality.[3] This was certainly true for the United States, which experienced a sustained fertility decline from at least about 1800. Around that time, the typical American woman had about 7 or 8 livebirths during her reproductive years, and the average person probably lived about 35–40 years. But the American pattern was distinctive. First, the American fertility transition was underway from at least the beginning of the nineteenth century, and some evidence indicates that family size was declining in older settled areas from the late eighteenth century (see Table 4.3). All other Western, developed nations, with the exception of France, began their sustained, irreversible decline in birth rates only in the late nineteenth or early twentieth centuries.[4] It is perhaps not coincidental that both France and the United States experienced important political revolutions in the late eighteenth century and were then characterized by small-scale, owner-occupier agriculture. Second, it appears that fertility in America was in sustained decline long before mortality. This is in contrast to the stylized view of the demographic transition, in which the mortality decline precedes or occurs simultaneously with the fertility decline. Mortality in the United States did not stabilize and begin a consistent decline until about the 1870s. Third, these demographic processes were both influenced by the large volume of international net in-migration and also the significant internal population redistribution to frontier areas and to cities, towns, and (later) suburbs.

While the American case may be, in many respects, *sui generis*, it furnishes a long-term view of a completed demographic transition with accompanying urbanization. The new United States was a demographic

[2] See chapter 5 of Volume I, by David Galenson, "Population, Labor, and General Economic Development" for a treatment of the demography of colonial British North America in the seventeenth and eighteenth centuries.

[3] For a survey of various theories of the fertility transition, see George Alter, "Theories of Fertility Decline: A Non-Specialist's Guide to the Current Debate on European Fertility Decline," in John R. Gillis, Louise A. Tilly, and David Levine, eds., *The European Experience of Declining Fertility, 1850–1970* (Oxford, 1992), 13–27.

[4] See Ansley J. Coale and Susan Cotts Watkins, eds., *The Decline of Fertility in Europe* (Princeton, 1986).

laboratory in which natives and migrants, different racial and ethnic groups, and varying occupational and socioeconomic strata experienced these significant behavioral changes in a fertile, land-abundant, resource-rich land.

SOURCES

A difficulty for the study of American historical demography is a lack of some types of data for the calculation of standard demographic measures. For the colonial period, regular census enumerations or vital registration were not in effect. A number of scholars have, nonetheless, conducted family reconstitutions and other demographic reconstructions using a variety of sources, including parish registers, genealogies, biographical data, wills and probates, and other local records.[5]

For the period prior to the first federal census in 1790, we thus have some ideas about vital rates and population characteristics. We know more about population size than other matters, especially because British colonial authorities carried out some enumerations.[6] The non-Amerindian population of British North America had increased to about 2.5 million (with about 2 million whites and about half a million blacks) in 1780.

As commented above, birth rates were high, with crude rates ranging from over 40 livebirths per 1,000 population per annum to well over 50. The crude birth rate for the United States as a whole has been estimated at over 50 around 1800 (see Table 4.3 below). It is unlikely that there had been a substantial rise of fertility in the late eighteenth century. Evidence for three western Massachusetts towns (Deerfield, Greenfield, and Shelburne) points to crude birth rates in the range 43–52 around 1790 and at 51 for Deerfield in 1765. Completed family sizes in Sturbridge, Massachusetts, for cohorts of married women born in the decades 1730/1759 and 1760/1779 were 8.83 and 7.32 respectively, consistent with relatively high crude birth rates (given the high propensity to marry). Even Quakers in the Middle Colonies, who began controlling fertility relatively early, had completed family sizes of 6.7 and 5.7 children for women born

---

[5] See examples in Maris Vinovskis, ed., *Studies in American Historical Demography* (New York, 1979), passim. See also Robert V. Wells, *Uncle Sam's Family: Issues in and Perspectives on American Demographic History* (Albany, 1985).

[6] Robert V. Wells, *The Population of the British Colonies in America before 1776* (Princeton, 1975).

before 1730 and between 1731 and 1755, respectively. New Jersey likely had a crude birth rate of 45–50 in 1772. Data on the proportions of children aged 0 to 15 in the population from colonial censuses imply crude birth rates in the range 45–55 and total fertility rates between 6 and 7 for most colonies in the New England and Middle Atlantic areas. The one southern colony with appropriate census age data, Maryland, showed crude birth rates in the range 44 to 54 for the white population between 1712 and 1755. In general, data by age and sex in censuses in the eighteenth century imply crude birth rates in the range 45 to 60 and total fertility rates between 6 and 7.[7]

Mortality was moderate for the era. Crude death rates varied from about 20 per 1,000 population per year to over 40 (and even higher in crisis periods). Lower mortality was found, as a rule, in the colonies and states from Pennsylvania and New Jersey northward, and high mortality characterized the South. In the North, expectations of life at birth ranged all the way from the mid- to early 20s to about 40 years. For example, Dedham, Massachusetts, is estimated to have had a crude death rate of about 24 per 1,000 population in the seventeenth century. This was probably typical of New England in this period. Death rates likely rose in Massachusetts in the eighteenth century from the comparatively healthy levels of the seventeenth century. Male expectation of life at age 20 in Andover, Massachusetts, fell from an average of 44.6 years for those born in the seventeenth century to 39.7 years for those born in the eighteenth century. For Ipswich, Massachusetts, there was a similar decline from 45 years for males married prior to 1700 to 39.9 years for those married 1700–1750. The increase in mortality for Salem was less severe, with a decline of expectation of life at age 20 for males from 36.1 years for those born in the seventeenth century to 35.5 years for those born after 1700. The expectation of life at age 20 for males in Salem was reported as about

---

[7] H. Temkin-Greener and A. C. Swedlund, "Fertility Transition in the Connecticut Valley: 1740–1850," *Population Studies*, 32 (1978), 27–41; Nancy Osterud and John Fulton, "Family Limitation and Age at Marriage: Fertility Decline in Sturbridge, Massachusetts, 1730–1850," *Population Studies*, 30 (1976), 481–94; Robert V. Wells, "Family Size and Fertility Control in Eighteenth-Century America: A Study of Quaker Families," *Population Studies*, 25 (1971), 73–82. Wells *The Population of the British Colonies*, 141–42. The relationship between the proportion of children aged 0–15 in the total population and a crude child-woman ratio (children aged 0–15 per 1,000 women aged 16 and over) was calculated for the white population of the United States for 1800, 1810, and 1820. The average relationship to crude birth rates and total fertility rates in Table 4.3 was calculated and applied to proportions of children and the child-woman ratios in the available colonial censuses from the U.S. Bureau of the Census, *Historical Statistics of the United States, Colonial Times to 1970* (Washington, DC, 1975), 1169–71. The resulting crude birth rates were in the range 45–60 and the total fertility rates in the range 6–7.

33 years in 1818–1822 (based on registered deaths), indicating a moderate worsening of mortality into the early nineteenth century as well. Overall, both infant and adult mortality was equal to or above that for Europe in the same era. Further south, New Jersey is believed to have had a crude death rate of at least 15–20 and likely higher in the early 1770s. The colonies still further south in the Chesapeake region, had considerably higher mortality. Males expectations of life at age 20 in the Chesapeake area of Maryland ranged from 22.7 to 30.5 in the seventeenth and early eighteenth centuries, while they ranged from 21 to 34 on the Virginia side in the same period. Expectations of life at birth covered the range from 19.7 to 28.6 years, implying probable crude death rates above 30 and possibly as high as 40.[8] Based on available records and analysis done to date, we know a good deal about New England, somewhat less about the Middle Colonies and states, and least about the South (with the notable exception of the Chesapeake area).

A milestone in American demographic history was the institution of the federal decennial census in 1790.[9] Originally intended to provide the basis for allocating seats in the U.S. House of Representatives, the published census grew from a modest one-volume compilation of spare, aggregated statistics in 1790 to multiple-volume descriptions of the population, economy, and society by the late nineteenth and early twentieth centuries. Original manuscript returns exist for all dates except 1890, opening great analytical opportunities.[10] The census has been *the* major source for the

[8] Kenneth Lockridge, "The Population of Dedham, Massachusetts, 1636–1736," *Economic History Review*, second series 19 (1966), 324–39; Vinovskis, *Studies in American Historical Demography*, 185–202. Wells, *The Population of the British Colonies*, 141–42; Lois Green Carr, "Emigration and the Standard of Living: The Seventeenth Century Chesapeake," *Journal of Economic History*, 52 (1992), Table 1.

[9] For a recent history of the American census, see Margo J. Anderson, *The American Census: A Social History* (New Haven, 1988).

[10] The original enumerators' manuscripts exist for all the population censuses except 1890 and for many of the states for the censuses of manufacturing and agriculture for 1850–1880. The 1890 census returns were destroyed in a fire in 1921. The population schedules are now available on microfilm from the National Archives through 1920. Some of the manufacturing and agriculture schedules have been microfilmed for the 1850–1880 period, but only a few escaped destruction for the period 1900–1950. This has permitted machine-readable public use micro-data samples to be constructed for 1900, 1910, and 1940–1980. National public use samples are currently being constructed for 1850, 1880, and 1920 by Steven Ruggles and his colleagues at the University of Minnesota. National samples of the agriculture schedules matched to population schedules have been done for 1860. See Jeremy Atack and Fred Bateman, *To their Own Soil: Agriculture in the Antebellum North* (Ames, IA, 1987); William N. Parker and Robert E. Gallman, "Southern Farms Study, 1860," Inter-University Consortium for Political and Social Research, *Guide to Resources and Services, 1992–1993* (Ann Arbor, MI, 1992), 116. National samples of the manufacturing schedules have been made for 1850, 1860, and 1880. See Fred Bateman and Thomas Weiss, *A Deplorable Scarcity: The Failure of Industrialization in the Slave Economy* (Chapel Hill, 1981); Jeremy Atack, "Returns to

study of population growth, structure, and redistribution as well as fertility prior to the twentieth century. Some states also took censuses, usually in years between the federal censuses. A number have been published and some also exist in manuscript form.[11]

Vital registration was left, however, to state and local governments and, in consequence, it was instituted unevenly. A variety of churches kept parish records of baptisms, burials, and marriages, and these have been used to construct demographic estimates for the colonial period, especially for New England and the Middle Atlantic regions.[12] Although some cities (e.g., New York, Philadelphia) began vital registration earlier in the nineteenth century, the first state to do so was Massachusetts, in 1842. An official Death Registration Area consisting of ten states and the District of Columbia was only successfully established in 1900, and data collection from all states was not completed until 1933. A parallel Birth Registration Area was only instituted in 1915, and all-state collection was also achieved in 1933.[13] The federal census did collect mortality information with the censuses of 1850 to 1900, but there were significant problems with completeness. The data do improve over time, and, after 1880, census information was merged with state registration data.[14] Nothing similar, unfortunately, was undertaken for birth data. One consequence of the lack of vital registration data before the early twentieth century has been a resort to special estimation techniques and indirect measures of fertility and mortality to gain insight into the demographic transition of the nineteenth century.

International migration statistics are better than the vital data, although there are also serious shortcomings. No official statistics exist prior to 1819, return migration was not counted until 1908, only immigrants through major ports were enumerated, and those crossing land borders

---

Scale in Antebellum United States Manufacturing," *Explorations in Economic History*, 14 (1977), 337–59; Fred Bateman and Jeremy Atack, "Did the United States Industrialize Too Slowly?" paper presented at meetings of the Development of the American Economy Program, National Bureau of Economic Research (March, 1992).

[11] Henry J. Dubester, *State Censuses: An Annotated Bibliography of Censuses of Population Taken after the Year 1790 by States and Territories of the United States* (Washington, DC, 1948).

[12] See Wells, *Uncle Sam's Family*; Vinovskis, *Studies in American Historical Demography*, 2–11.

[13] The ten states in the Death Registration Area of 1900 were Maine, New Hampshire, Vermont, Massachusetts, Rhode Island, Connecticut, New York, New Jersey, Michigan, and Indiana, as well as the District of Columbia. The original states in the Birth Registration Area of 1915 were Maine, New Hampshire, Vermont, Massachusetts, Rhode Island, Connecticut, New York, Michigan, and Minnesota, and also the District of Columbia.

[14] Gretchen A. Condran and Eileen Crimmins, "A Description and Evaluation of Mortality Data in the Federal Census: 1850–1900," *Historical Methods*, 12 (1979), 1–23.

were counted only for the period 1855–85 and again after 1904. Some of these deficiencies have been remedied by new estimates, but Table 4.5 reports only the official data.[15] Despite deficiencies, these provide a reasonable overview of this important source of population growth over the period 1790–1920.

The census also provides, from 1850, information on a person's place of birth and, after 1870, on the nativity of each person's parents. This was either state of birth for the native born or country of birth for the foreign born. These data permit study of international migration (e.g., the geographic distribution of the foreign born) and also analysis of internal migration by providing cross-classification of the native born by birth and current residence (from 1860 onward). Internal migration is a rather difficult issue because of lack of evidence on date of change of residence between birth and current residence. For the foreign born, questions on duration of residence in the United States were asked in the censuses of 1890 to 1930, but a question was not asked of all inhabitants about duration of current residence until 1940 (when a question was asked concerning a person's place of residence five years prior to the census).

The census cannot be assumed to have been entirely accurate. A number of studies have been done on the federal census and on various systems that collected vital data in the nineteenth and twentieth centuries.[16] Overall, it seems that censuses in the mid-nineteenth century missed anywhere from 5 percent to 25 percent of the population. A careful analysis of the white population from 1880 to 1960 indicates overall underenumeration of 6.1 percent in 1880, declining to 5.7 percent by 1920 and 2.1 percent by 1960.[17] Results varied by age and sex, with the very young and the elderly being least well enumerated. Blacks were more likely to be missed than whites. A summary of recent work on the mid-

[15] Henry A. Gemery, "European Emigration to North America, 1700–1820: Numbers and Quasi-Numbers," *Perspectives in American History*, New Series I (New York, 1984), 283–342; Peter D. McClelland and Richard J. Zeckhauser, *Demographic Dimensions of the New Republic: American Interregional Migration, Vital Statistics, and Manumissions, 1800–1860* (New York, 1982); Simon Kuznets, "Long Swings in the Growth of Population and in Related Economic Variables," *Proceedings of the American Philosophical Society*, 102 (1958), 25–52.

[16] Ansley J. Coale and Melvin Zelnik, *New Estimates of Fertility and Population in the United States: A Study of Annual White Births from 1855 to 1960 and of Completeness of Enumeration in the Censuses from 1880 to 1960* (Princeton, 1963); Condran and Crimmins, "A Description and Evaluation of Mortality Data in the Federal Census"; and *Social Science History*, 15 (1991), especially papers by Donald Parkerson and Richard Steckel.

[17] Henry S. Shryock, Jacob S. Siegel, and associates, *The Methods and Materials of Demography* (Washington, DC, 1971), Vol. 1, 109, based partly on the estimates of Coale and Zelnik, *New Estimates*.

nineteenth-century federal census notes that those more likely to be counted were older, native-born, heads of more complex households, with moderate wealth and better-paying occupations, in the political mainstream, and living in smaller communities or rural areas having slow economic and population growth. Those less likely to be enumerated were younger, male, native-born sons or foreign-born boarders, living in smaller households, working in low-wage occupations in large, rapidly growing urban areas, and not in the political mainstream.[18]

Similarly, collection of vital data also had deficiencies. A criterion for admission to the official federal Death Registration Area after 1900 and the Birth Registration Area after 1915 was only that registration be 90 percent complete. As late as 1935, it was estimated that birth registration was about 91 percent complete and only 80 percent complete for the nonwhite population.[19] No comprehensive study of death registration completeness has been done, but it appears to have been less than fully complete even in the best states of the Death Registration Area in 1900.[20]

Nonetheless, many of these deficiencies do not affect overall results too dramatically. Calculation of rates involves canceling errors. The extent of the errors usually did not change too much from census to census or year to year. In addition, demographic estimates often involve some corrections to the data. Many of the tabular results presented here use uncorrected data, but some of the estimates do make adjustments.

A number of other sources can be used to provide basic demographic measures and some sophisticated analyses. Genealogies have been utilized to provide estimates of fertility, mortality, and migration for particular populations in the nineteenth century.[21] Parish registers, tax rolls, military muster rolls, pension records, wills, probates, and hospital and other

---

[18] Donald H. Parkerson, "Comments on the Underenumeration of the U.S. Census, 1850–1880," *Social Science History*, 15 (1991), 514.

[19] Shryock and Siegel, *Methods and Materials of Demography*, 404.

[20] Condran and Crimmins, "A Description and Evaluation of Mortality Data in the Federal Census"; Eileen M. Crimmins, "The Completeness of 1900 Mortality Data Collected by Registration and Enumeration for Rural and Urban Parts of States: Estimates Using the Chandra Sekar-Deming Technique," *Historical Methods*, 13 (1980), 163–69; Shryock and Siegel, *Methods and Materials of Demography*, chs. 14 and 16.

[21] Examples include Lee L. Bean, Geraldine P. Mineau, and Douglas Anderton, *Fertility Change on the American Frontier: Adaptation and Innovation* (Berkeley, 1990); Jenny Bourne Wahl, "New Results on the Decline in Household Fertility in the United States from 1750 to 1900," in Stanley L. Engerman and Robert E. Gallman, eds., *Long Term Factors in American Economic Growth*, Studies in Income and Wealth, vol. 51 (Chicago, 1986), 391–425; Clayne L. Pope, "Adult Mortality in America before 1900: A View from Family Histories," in Claudia Goldin and Hugh Rockoff, eds., *Strategic Factors in Nineteenth Century American Economic History: A Volume to Honor Robert W. Fogel* (Chicago, 1992), 267–96; John W. Adams and Alice Bee Kasakoff, "Migration and the Family in Colonial New England: The View from Genealogies," *Journal of Family History*, 9 (1984), 24–42.

institutional records are examples of other sources employed to reconstruct American demographic history.[22]

MEASUREMENT AND ESTIMATION

Demography, the study of human populations, depends heavily on measurement and estimation techniques. Most of the results presented here are simple tabulations or standard demographic rates. But a number of the newer findings arise from rather sophisticated techniques.[23] Estimation of better demographic information is of importance for research in economic history. Basic demographic structures and events, reflected in birth and death rates, population size and structure, growth rates, the composition and growth of the labor force, marriage rates and patterns, household composition, the levels and nature of migration flows, causes of death, urbanization and spatial population distribution, and so forth determine the human capital of society as producers and consumers and also how that human capital reproduces, relocates, and depreciates. Demographic events are important both as indicators of social and economic change and as integral components of modern economic growth.

Most of the measures presented here are relatively straightforward, such as crude birth and death rates, rates of total and natural increase, and rates of net migration. These are presented in Tables 4.1 and 4.3 and are given as rates per 1,000 mid-period population per year. In addition, however, some of the results discussed in this essay arise (at least in theory) from age-specific measures, but such data must usually be summarized to be useful and intuitively interpretable. One technique of summarizing them is the life table. It takes age-specific death rates either for cross-sections of a population at various ages at a point in time, which generates period life tables, or for an actual group of people born in the same time period (a cohort), which provides cohort life tables, and converts them into other measures. These other measures would include the expectation of life at any age: that is, the average number of years of life remaining if that group experienced the age-specific mortality rates embodied in the life table.

---

[22] For examples, see Wells, *Uncle Sam's Family*; J. Dennis Willigan and Katherine A. Lynch, *Sources and Methods of Historical Demography* (New York, 1982); Michael R. Haines, "Economic History and Historical Demography," in Alexander J. Field, ed., *The Future of Economic History* (Boston, 1987), 185–253.

[23] See Haines, "Economic History and Historical Demography"; Michael R. Haines and Barbara A. Anderson, "New Demographic History of the Late 19th-Century United States," *Explorations in Economic History*, 25 (1988), 341–65.

Table 4.3 (below) presents the expectation of life at birth for the white and black populations from 1850 onward. Another life table measure is the probability of an infant surviving from birth to the first birthday (exact age 1), which is presented here as the infant mortality rate (infant deaths per 1,000 livebirths per annum).

Similarly, age-specific fertility rates can be summarized. One instance provided in Table 4.3 is the total fertility rate (TFR), which is the sum of age-specific births for all women aged 15 to 49.[24] This can be interpreted as the average number of births a woman would have if she survived her whole reproductive life and if she experienced rates of childbearing given by the age-specific data. It is akin to completed family size for all women of childbearing age (not just married women). This is calculated here for cross-sectional (or period) data and would apply to a synthetic cohort. It can be estimated for true cohorts, however.[25]

Table 4.3 also provides a measure of fertility known as the child-woman ratio, which is the number of surviving children aged 0–4 per 1,000 women aged 20–44. It is a wholly census-based fertility rate, requiring no vital statistics. It is, in fact, the main direct source of information on fertility in the United States in the nineteenth century and is the basis for the early estimates of the crude birth rate and the total fertility rate also given in Table 4.3. The child-woman ratio does have some serious drawbacks, since it deals with surviving children at the census and not actual births in the preceding five years. It also suffers from relative differences in underenumeration of young children and adult women.[26]

POPULATION GROWTH IN THE UNITED STATES, 1790–1920

As mentioned above, the United States began its demographic transition from high to low levels of fertility and mortality from at least the beginning of the nineteenth century, if not earlier. Table 4.1 provides summary

[24] In fact, the total fertility rates before 1940 in Table 4.3 were estimated indirectly without first obtaining the age-specific rates, though estimates of age-specific overall and martial fertility rates now exist for the period back to the late nineteenth century. See Michael R. Haines, "American Fertility in Transition: New Estimates of Birth Rates in the United States, 1900–1910," *Demography*, 26 (1989), 137–48.

[25] For an example, see Bean, Mineau, and Anderton, *Fertility Change on the American Frontier*, ch. 4.

[26] Discussion of alternative measures of fertility, mortality, marriage, and migration, in addition to estimation procedures, may be found in Shryock and Siegel, *Methods and Materials of Demography* and Haines, "Economic History and Historical Demography."

Table 4.1. *Components of population growth, United States, 1800–1980 (rates per 1,000 mid-period population per year)*

PERIOD	Average population (000s)	RTI	CBR	CDR	RNI[a]	RNM[a]	RNM as % of RTI
1790–1800	4,520	30.08			26.49	3.59	11.9%
1800–1810	6,132	31.04			26.85	4.19	13.5
1810–1820	8,276	28.62			24.70	3.92	13.7
1820–1830	11,031	28.88			26.93	1.95	6.8
1830–1840	14,685	28.27			23.67	4.60	16.3
1840–1850	19,686	30.65			22.88	7.77	25.3
1850–1860	26,721	30.44			20.35	10.09	33.2
1860–1870	35,156	23.62			17.64	5.98	25.3
1870–1880	44,414	23.08	41.16	23.66	17.50	5.58	24.2
1880–1890	55,853	22.72	37.03	21.34	15.69	7.03	30.9
1890–1900	68,876	18.83	32.22	19.44	12.78	6.06	32.2
1900–1910	83,245	19.08	30.10	17.27	12.83	6.25	32.8
1910–1920	98,807	14.86	27.15	15.70	11.45	3.41	23.0
1920–1930	114,184	14.01	23.40	11.08	12.32	1.68	12.0
1930–1940	127,058	7.01	18.39	11.18	7.21	−0.20	−2.9
1940–1950	140,555	13.50	22.48	10.39	12.09	1.41	10.4
1950–1960	164,011	17.67	24.81	9.47	15.34	2.33	13.2
1960–1970	190,857	12.27	20.26	9.55	10.71	1.56	12.7
1970–1980	214,306	10.83	15.49	9.00	6.49	4.34	40.1
1980–1990	238,466	9.34	15.91	8.70	7.21	2.13	22.8

Note: RTI = rate of total increase. CBR = crude birth rate (livebirths per 1,000 population per year. CDR = crude death rate (deaths per 1,000 population per year). RNI = rate of natural increase (CBR-CDR). RNM = rate of net international migration.

[a] Rate of net migration calculated directly from net migrants 1790–1860. Gross migrants used for 1860–1870. For 1870–1990, RNM = RTI-RNI and thus is a residual. Prior to 1870, RNI is calculated as a residual (RTI-RNM).

Source: (1) Unadjusted populations. U.S. Bureau of the Census, *Historical Statistics of the United States* (Washington, DC, 1975). U.S. Bureau of the Census, *Statistical Abstract of the United States, 1990* (Washington, DC, 1990).

(2) Births & Deaths. 1870–1940: Simon Kuznets, "Long Swings in the Growth of Population and Related Economic Variables," *Proceedings of the American Philosophical Society*, 102 (1958), 25–52. 1940–1990: Same as in (1).

(3) Net Migrants. 1790–1820: Henry A. Gemery, "European Emigration to North America: Numbers and Quasi-Nubers," *Perspectives in American History*, 1 (1984), supplemented by estimates of slave imports from Philip Curtin, *The Atlantic Slave Trade: A Census* (Madison, WI, 1969.) 1820–1860: Peter D. McClelland and Richard J. Zeckhauser, *Demographic Dimensions of the New Republic: American Interregional Migration, Vital Statistics and Manumissions, 1800–1860* (New York, 1982) and also supplemented by estimates of slave imports from Curtin.

measures of population growth and its components by decades from 1790 to 1980. The table is organized around the demographic balancing equation, which states that the decade rate of total population growth (RTI) equals the birth rate (CBR) minus the death rate (CDR) plus the rate of net migration (RNM). The difference between the birth rate and the death rate is the rate of natural increase (RNI).[27] For the period 1790 to 1870, the crude birth and death rates are not given because independent estimates of the crude death rate are too uncertain (see Table 4.1). For 1790–1870 the rate of natural increase is calculated as the difference between the rate of total increase and the rate of net migration. The rate of net migration is based on new direct calculations of white net migration supplemented by estimates of slave importation (smuggling after 1808, when slave imports were made illegal). For the decade of the 1860s, official estimates of gross in-migration were used. After 1870, estimates of births and deaths are available from the work of Simon Kuznets for the period 1870–1940. Official vital statistics data are used thereafter to 1980. In addition, after 1870 the rate of net migration is calculated as the difference between the rates of total increase and natural increase (i.e., a residual).[28]

Several features of the American demographic transition can be discerned from Table 4.1. The United States experienced a truly remarkable population increase during its transition in the "long" nineteenth century (1790–1920). From a modest 4.5 million inhabitants in 1790, the population grew to over 114 million persons in 1920, an average annual growth rate of 2.5 percent per year. In the early years of the republic, population growth rates were even higher, above 3 percent per annum for the period 1790–1810 and again in the 1840s and 1850s. Such rapid growth is historically rather unusual and is comparable to the recent experience of some developing nations. Growth rates of that magnitude would lead to a doubling of the population in slightly over two decades (approximately 23 years). The surge of growth in the 1840s and 1850s was particularly due to a significant increase in migration from abroad – the now familiar story of Irish, Germans, and others from western and northern Europe fleeing the great potato famine, the "Hungry Forties," and political upheaval and seeking better farming, business, and employment opportunities in the New World. Natural increase had been declining from the

---

[27] That is, RTI = CBR - CDR + RNM, and CBR - CDR = RNI.
[28] See sources to Table 4.1.

early 1800s, largely from decline in birth rates for both the white and black populations. Some of the decline in natural increase in the 1840s and 1850s was also likely due to *rising* mortality in those decades. Table 4.1 indicates, however, that mortality did decline steadily from the 1870s onward.

Another feature notable in Table 4.1 is the dominant role played by natural increase in overall population growth. In the decades before 1840, less than a sixth or a seventh of total growth originated in net migration. With the surge in overseas migration after 1840, however, the share of net migration in total increase rose to a quarter or a third. Notably, the share of *labor force* growth accounted for by migration was higher, since migration was selective of persons in the labor force ages. Nonetheless, despite declining birth rates, the American population grew rapidly in the nineteenth century principally from an excess of births over deaths, although it must be recognized that the births to the foreign born and their descendants contributed importantly. If it could be assumed that no immigration occurred after 1790 and that the natural increase of the colonial stock population had been what it actually was (with no effect of immigration on the natural increase of the native born), then the white population would have been about 52 million in 1920, or about 55 percent of what it actually was.[29] The surge in migration after 1840 can also be recognized in Table 4.2 in the rise in the proportion of the population foreign born from less than 10 percent in 1850 (the first census for which such data were available) to nearly 15 percent in 1890 and 1910.

Although beyond the temporal scope of the present essay, a few comments on the post-1920 demographic evolution are in order. The effects of immigration restriction after World War I may be seen in the reduced rate of net migration after 1920. The Great Depression had a dramatic damping effect on both fertility and migration from abroad. The post–World War II "baby boom" is apparent in the higher crude birth rates in the 1940s and 1950s. More recent changes in immigration regulations clearly affected the surge in net immigrants in the 1970s, when over 40 percent of population growth was due to this source. This was unprecedented in our history, even considering the decades preceding both the Civil War and World War I.

The effects of regional differences in population growth are apparent in

---

[29] Richard A. Easterlin, "Population Issues in American Economic History: A Survey and Critique," in Robert Gallman, ed., *Recent Developments in the Study of Business and Economic History: Essays in Honor of Herman E. Krooss* (Greenwich, 1977), 149.

Table 4.2. *Population by race, residence, nativity, age, and sex, United States,*
1800–1990 (population in ooos)

Census Date	Total	% p.a. Growth	White	Black	Other	Urban	%	Foreign-Born	%	Median Age	Sex Ratio[b]
1790	3,929	—	3,172	757	(NA)	202	5.1	(NA)	—	(NA)	103.8
1800	5,308	3.01	4,306	1,002	(NA)	322	6.1	(NA)	—	16.0[a]	104.0
1810	7,240	3.10	5,862	1,378	(NA)	525	7.3	(NA)	—	16.0[a]	104.0
1820	9,639	2.86	7,867	1,772	(NA)	693	7.2	(NA)	—	16.7	103.3
1830	12,866	2.89	10,537	2,329	(NA)	1,127	8.8	(NA)	—	17.2	103.1
1840	17,070	2.83	14,196	2,874	(NA)	1,845	10.8	(NA)	—	17.8	103.7
1850	23,192	3.06	19,553	3,639	(NA)	3,544	15.3	2,245	9.7	18.9	104.3
1860	31,443	3.04	26,923	4,442	79	6,217	19.8	4,104	13.1	19.4	104.7
1870	39,819	2.36	33,589	4,880	89	9,902	24.9	5,567	14.0	20.2	102.2
1880	50,156	2.31	43,403	6,581	172	14,130	28.2	6,680	13.3	20.9	103.6
1890	62,948	2.27	55,101	7,489	358	22,106	35.1	9,250	14.7	22.0	105.0
1900	75,994	1.88	66,809	8,834	351	30,160	39.7	10,341	13.6	22.9	104.4
1910	91,972	1.91	81,732	9,828	413	41,999	45.7	13,516	14.7	24.1	106.0
1920	106,711	1.49	94,821	10,463	427	54,158	50.8	14,020	13.1	25.3	104.0
1930	122,755	1.40	110,287	11,891	597	68,955	56.2	14,283	11.6	26.5	102.5
1940	131,669	0.70	118,215	12,866	589	74,424	56.5	11,657	8.9	29.0	100.7
1950	150,697	1.35	134,942	15,042	713	96,468	64.0	10,431	6.9	30.2	98.6
1960	179,823	1.77	158,832	18,872	1,620	125,269	69.7	9,738	5.4	29.5	97.1
1970	203,302	1.23	178,098	22,580	2,883	149,325	73.4	9,619	4.7	28.1	94.8
1980	226,546	1.08	194,713	26,683	5,150	167,051	73.7	14,080	6.2	30.0	94.5
1990	248,710	0.93	208,704	30,483	9,523	187,053	75.2	21,632	8.7	32.8	95.1

[a] White population.
[b] Males per 100 females.
Source: Bureau of the Census, *Historical Statistics*. U.S. Bureau of the Census, *Statistical Abstract of the United States,*
1992 (Washington, DC, 1992).

the population distribution figures in Table 4.4. The 4.5 million inhabitants in 1790 were clustered along the Atlantic coast, about evenly divided between North (New England and Middle Atlantic regions) and South (South Atlantic region). By 1860 only 51 percent of the 31 million Americans were still in these regions, and this had fallen to 41 percent in 1920. Regions of early settlement grew at average rate of 1.9 percent per annum over the whole period, while the whole United States was growing at 2.5 percent. This regional disparity was driven, of course, by the relentless westward movement of population, agriculture, and industry. Much of the growth that did occur on the Atlantic coast was in yet another "frontier" – urban areas. In the regions of original European settlement cities and towns grew from just 5 percent of the population in 1790 to 28 percent in 1860 to 61 percent in 1920, an annual growth rate of 3.8 percent per annum while that of the rural population was merely 1.2 percent per annum. This led to an increase in the share of national urban population over the century from 5 percent in 1790 to over half of the population in 1920.[30]

FERTILITY AND NUPTIALITY

The young republic was notable for its large families and early marriage. The total fertility rate in Table 4.3 indicates an average number of births per woman of approximately seven in 1800, and the TFR was still over five on the eve of the Civil War. While we know relatively little about marriage early in the nineteenth century, female age at first marriage was probably rather young, perhaps below 20. Males married on average several years older, and all but a relatively small proportion of both sexes eventually married. The federal census did not ask a question on marital status until 1880 and did not begin reporting results on this until 1890. Several state censuses did, however, ask these questions earlier. A sample of seven New York state counties from the manuscripts of the census of 1865, for example, reveals an estimated age at first marriage of 23.8 years for females and 26.6 years for males. Percentages never married by the ages 45–54 were 7.4 percent for females and 5.9 percent for males, pointing to quite low levels of lifetime non-marriage.[31] Although marriage age was probably higher in New York than in the nation as a whole and although marriage age had very likely risen by 1865, nuptiality was still rather extensive by European standards. The average age at first marriage for females was 25.4 years in England and Wales in 1861 and 26.3 years in Germany in 1871 (with German males having had an average age at marriage as late as 28.8 years).[32]

In 1880, when the U.S. census first asked a question on marital status, the average female age at first marriage was 23.0 years, while that for males was 26.5 years. The proportions never marrying by middle age were still

---

[30] Urban areas are as defined by the U.S. Bureau of the Census as places (incorporated or not) of 2,500 or more inhabitants. See Bureau of the Census, *Historical Statistics*, 2–3.

[31] The counties are Allegany, Dutchess, Montgomery, Rensselaer, Steuben, Tompkins, and Warren.

[32] Data for England and Wales are from Michael S. Teitelbaum, *The British Fertility Decline: Demographic Transition in the Crucible of the Industrial Revolution* (Princeton, 1984), 100. For Germany, John E. Knodel, *The Decline of Fertility in Germany, 1871–1939* (Princeton, 1974), 70.

Table 4.3. *Fertility and mortality in the United States, 1800–1990*

Approx. Date	Birthrate[a] White	Birthrate[a] Black[f]	Child-Woman ratio[b] White	Child-Woman ratio[b] Black	Total fertility rate[c] White	Total fertility rate[c] Black[f]	Expectation of life[d] White	Expectation of life[d] Black[f]	Infant mortality rate[e] White	Infant mortality rate[e] Black[f]
1800	55.0		1,342		7.04					
1810	54.3		1,358		6.92					
1820	52.8		1,295	1,191	6.73					
1830	51.4		1,145	1,220	6.55					
1840	48.3		1,085	1,154	6.14					
1850	43.3	58.6[g]	892	1,087	5.42	7.90[g]	39.5	23.0	216.8	340.0
1860	41.4	55.0[h]	905	1,072	5.21	7.58[h]	43.6		181.3	
1870	38.3	55.4[i]	814	997	4.55	7.69[i]	45.2		175.5	
1880	35.2	51.9[j]	780	1,090	4.24	7.26[j]	40.5		214.8	
1890	31.5	48.1	685	930	3.87	6.56	46.8		150.7	
1900	30.1	44.4	666	845	3.56	5.61	51.8[k]	41.8[k]	110.8[k]	170.3[k]
1910	29.2	38.5	631	736	3.42	4.61	54.6[l]	46.8[l]	96.5[l]	142.6[l]
1920	26.9	35.0	604	608	3.17	3.64	57.4	47.0	82.1	131.7
1930	20.6	27.5	506	554	2.45	2.98	60.9	48.5	60.1	99.9
1940	18.6	26.7	419	513	2.22	2.87	64.9	53.9	43.2	73.8
1950	23.0	33.3	580	663	2.98	3.93	69.0	60.7	26.8	44.5
1960	22.7	32.1	717	895	3.53	4.52	70.7	63.9	22.9	43.2
1970	17.4	25.1	507	689	2.39	3.07	71.6	64.1	17.8	30.9
1980	15.1	21.3	300	367	1.77	2.18	74.5	68.5	10.9	22.2
1990	15.8	22.4	298	359	2.00	2.48	76.1	69.1	7.6	18.0

Note:

[a] Births per 1,000 population per annum.

[b] Children aged 0–4 per 1,000 women aged 15–44. Taken from W. S. Thompson and P. K. Whelpton, *Population Trends in the United States* (New York, 1933), table 74. Adjusted upward 5 percent for relative under-enumeration of white children aged 0–4 and 13 percent for black children for the censuses of 1800–1950. Based on corrections made in W. H. Grabill, C. V. Kiser, and P. K. Whelpton, *The Fertility of American Women* (New York, 1958), table 6.

[c] Total number of births per woman if she experienced the current period age-specific fertility rates throughout her life.

[d] Expectation of life at birth for both sexes combined.

[e] Infant deaths per 1,000 live births per annum.

[f] Black and other population for CBR (1920–1970), TFR (1940–1990); e[o] (1950–1960), IMR (1920–1970).

[g] Average for 1850–59. [h] Average for 1860–69. [i] Average for 1870–79. [j] Average for 1880–84. [k] Approximately 1895. [l] Approximately 1904.

Source: Bureau of the Census, *Historical Statistics U.S.* Bureau of the Census, *Statistical Abstract of the United States, 1986* (Washington, DC, 1986) and *Statistical Abstract of the United States, 1993* (Washington, DC, 1993). Ansley J. Coale and Melvin Zelnik, *New Estimates of Fertility and Population in the United States* (Princeton, 1963). Ansley J. Coale and Norfleet W. Rives, "A Statistical Reconstruction of the Black Population of the United States, 1880–1970: Estimates of True Numbers by Age and Sex, Birth Rates, and Total Fertility," *Population Index*, 39 (1973), 3–36. Michael R. Haines, "The Use of Model Life Tables to Estimate Mortality for the United States in the Late Nineteenth Century," *Demography*, 16, (1979), 289–312. Samuel H. Preston and Michael R. Haines, *Fatal Years: Child Mortality in Late Nineteenth-Century America* (Princeton, 1991), table 2.5. Richard H. Steckel, "A Dreadful Childhood: The Excess Mortality of American Slaves," *Social Science History*, 10 (1986), 427–65.

relatively low, at 7 percent for both males and females. Age at marriage rose a bit up until 1890 and 1900 and thereafter began a longer term decline up to the 1950s. By 1920, age at marriage had fallen to 22.5 years for women and 25.9 years for men, although this was now accompanied by a gradual increase in the proportion of those never marrying.[33]

Overall, marriage in the U.S. was pervasive and early compared to the western and northern European countries in which many of the migrants to North America originated. This was more so early in the nineteenth century, as the marriage age rose in the United States up until roughly 1900. Americans were also very unlikely *not* to have been married at some time during their adult lives.

Similarly, in 1800 the United States was a nation of high fertility, but it then experienced a sustained decline in birth rates up until the 1940s, when the "baby boom" interrupted this pattern. The unusual aspect of the American experience is that the reduction began before the nation was substantially urban or industrial. Both rural *and* urban birth rates declined in parallel, although rural fertility remained higher throughout the period considered here. Fertility decreased across regions, but the South lagged behind the Northeast and Midwest in the timing and speed of the reduction. A decomposition of the fertility transition into the contributions of nuptiality and marital fertility found that, up to approximately 1850, half of the decline could be attributed to adjustments in marriage age and marriage incidence. Thereafter most of the decline originated in reductions of fertility within marriage.[34] Even the fertility of the antebellum slave population showed signs of decline just prior to 1860, though family sizes for

---

[33] Calculations of the singulate mean age at marriage (SMAM) and of the proportion never marrying for the period 1890 to 1910 are based on published federal census data. SMAM is calculated by Hajnal's method (see Shryock and Siegel, *Methods and Materials of Demography*, 294–95). The results for 1880 are based on a preliminary sample of the 1880 census made available by Steven Ruggles of the University of Minnesota. The overall results for this period are:

	SMAM		% Single at 45–54	
	Male	Female	Male	Female
1880	26.5	23.0	6.9	7.3
1890	27.6	23.6	9.1	7.0
1900	27.4	23.6	10.4	7.8
1910	26.7	23.1	11.1	8.5
1920	25.9	22.5	12.0	9.6

[34] Warren C. Sanderson, "Quantitative Aspects of Marriage, Fertility and Family Limitation in Nineteenth Century America: Another Application of the Coale Specifications," *Demography*, 16 (1979), 339–58. Sanderson treats all fertility as marital fertility. Illegitimate fertility was not too important in nineteenth-century America, and it was, in any event, difficult to measure. Sanderson uses an application of both the Coale-McNeil marriage models and the Coale-Trussell model fertility schedules to estimate the extent of fertility control within marriage.

blacks were, on average, significantly larger than those for whites (see Table 4.3).[35]

Such evidence as we have concerning fertility differentials by nativity (native versus foreign born) points to relatively small differences at mid-century but generally higher fertility for the foreign born thereafter. The fertility of native white women continued to decline, while large families continued among the successive cohorts of incoming migrants. Birth rates of native-born women of foreign-born parentage was intermediate between those of native white women of native parentage and foreign-born white women, suggesting a form of assimilation to native white demographic patterns. Data on children ever born (parity) from a sample of seven New York counties in 1865 revealed few differences between native- and foreign-born women born near the beginning of the nineteenth century. But published data from the Massachusetts census of 1885 showed substantially more births per ever-married foreign-born woman relative to the native born for those born 1826/35. Such differentials also appeared in the parity data from the federal censuses of 1900 and 1910. Much of the difference was due to the lower age at marriage and lower percentages remaining single among the foreign born. But fertility within marriage was also greater for foreign-born women in the late nineteenth and early twentieth centuries. Relatively few of them, for instance, remained permanently childless. Published results from the federal census of 1910 reported that native white women aged 55–64 (i.e., born in the years 1846/55) had an average number of children ever born of 4.4 (4.8 for ever-married women). Over 17 percent of all native white women (and 9 percent of those who married) remained childless. Among the foreign born enumerated at the same census, average number of children was 5.5 for all women and 5.8 for ever-married women, with only 12 percent of all women, and 7 percent of ever-married women, remaining childless. Such differentials between native- and foreign-born women had largely disappeared for those born at the end of the nineteenth century and enumerated in 1940.[36]

[35] See Table 4.3 and evidence presented in Richard Steckel, "The Fertility of American Slaves," *Research in Economic History*, 7 (1982), 239–86.

[36] A problem for the analysis of the fertility of the native born versus the foreign born is that most of the children of the foreign born were native born. Hence census tabulations by age, sex, race, and nativity cannot provide the appropriate child-woman ratios. One solution is reported in the text, namely asking women questions in censuses on their fertility history. This was first done in New York in 1865, in Massachusetts in 1885, and in the federal censuses of 1890–1910 and again from 1940 onward. No results were published for the federal censuses of 1890 and 1900, although the public use sample of the 1900 manuscripts (as well as those of 1910) permits analysis. Another solution is to use the micro-data from the census manuscripts to estimate own-children birth rates

The inexorable decline of American birth rates continued apace after the Civil War. By now most of the decline originated in adjustments in fertility within marriage. Recent work with parity data from the 1900, 1910, and 1940 federal censuses shows rapid reductions in marital fertility, especially among white urban women. In 1910, for example, over half of native white urban women aged 45–49 were estimated to have been effectively controlling fertility within marriage, and about a quarter rural farm and nonfarm women were doing the same. Among younger women (aged 15–34) the proportions were much higher, rising to over 70 percent for native white urban women and over half for native white farm women. It could certainly be said that the "two-child norm" was being established in the United States in this era. Some fascinating supporting evidence is furnished by the Mosher survey of several dozen wives of professional and white-collar men over the period 1892 to 1920. Mosher found extensive use of a wide variety of contraceptives and contraceptive practices and very active strategies of family limitation. This was a preview of the rapid adoption of such behaviors in the twentieth century.[37]

One of the conclusions from this detailed study of fertility has been that the spacing of births from early in childbearing was, by the late nineteenth century, as important as the more conventional behavior of stopping before the biological end of the female reproductive span. Results from a different source, the genealogical data base of the Mormon Historical Demography Project, have shown the importance of spacing behavior, which had formerly been considered a relatively modern development, prevalent only in very low-fertility populations. New estimates of age-specific fertility rates for the United States around the turn of the century point to low

by nativity of mother. For examples, see Tamara K. Hareven and Maris A. Vinovskis, "Marital Fertility, Ethnicity, and Occupation in Urban Families: An Analysis of South Boston and the South End in 1880," *Journal of Social History*, 8 (1975), 69–93; Michael R. Haines, *Fertility and Occupation: Population Patterns in Industrialization* (New York, 1979), ch. IV and "American Fertility in Transition". Finally, there are some nineteenth- and early-twentieth-century birth registration data reported by mother's nativity. These reveal substantially higher birth rates for the foreign born for Massachusetts and other states from the late nineteenth century. Much was due to higher marriage incidence for foreign women. See J. J. Spengler, "The Fecundity of Native and Foreign-Born Women in New England," *Brookings Institution Pamphlet Series*, II (1930).

[37] See Paul David and Warren Sanderson, "Rudimentary Contraceptive Methods and the American Transition to Marital Fertility Control, 1855–1915," in Engerman and Gallman, eds., *Long-Term Factors in American Economic Growth*, 307–79; "The Emergence of a Two-Child Norm among American Birth Controllers," *Population and Development Review*, 13 (1987), 1–41. Their results derive from a new technique known as cohort-parity analysis, which compares actual parity distributions for age or marriage-duration cohorts of women to a known "natural fertility" distribution. The survey referred to was conducted by Clelia Mosher.

marital fertility at young ages, quite unlike Europe at the time and further suggesting spacing early in childbearing in American families. The one exception was France, which shared with the United States an early fertility decline preceding significant urbanization and industrialization.[38]

The period after 1865 was further marked by reductions in fertility by residence and by race. For the rural and urban populations, relative differences in child-woman ratios did not disappear. Rural fertility remained above urban fertility, but absolute differences diminished as both types of residents progressively limited family size. The rural child-woman ratio was 56 percent higher than the urban in 1800, 62 percent higher in 1840, and 58 percent greater in 1920. But the absolute gap had dropped from 474 more children aged 0–4 per 1,000 women of childbearing age in rural areas in 1800 to 273 in 1920. A standardization and decomposition of the rural–urban differential and its connection to the fertility transition found that over 50 percent of the overall decline in child-woman ratios from 1800 to 1940 originated in the decline in rural birth rates, with over one-quarter due to urban fertility decline, and only about 20 percent stemming from the shift from higher-fertility rural to lower-fertility urban areas.[39]

As Table 4.3 shows, fertility differences by race tended to converge after the middle of the nineteenth century. Whereas the black total fertility rate was 48 percent higher than that for whites in the 1850s, it was only 15 percent higher in 1920. The end of slavery, difficult conditions in the agrarian South, and increased urbanization of the black population all played roles in this. Differentials in birth rates by race have persisted up to the present and have actually widened somewhat after 1920, but decline has continued for both blacks and whites after the peak of the "baby boom" around 1960.

Birth rates also varied across regions after the Civil War, with the South and West having been higher-fertility areas relative to the Northeast and Midwest. Variation across space narrowed from 1800 onward, but the convergence was not smooth. The coefficient of variation (the standard deviation divided by the mean) of child-woman ratios across the nine census regions was 0.57 in 1810 but declined to 0.16 in 1860.[40] It rose there-

---

[38] See Bean, Mineau, and Anderton, *Fertility Change on the American Frontier*, ch. 7; Michael R. Haines, "Western Fertility in Mid-Transition: A Comparison of the United States and Selected Nations at the Turn of the Century," *Journal of Family History*, 15 (1990), 21–46.

[39] Wilson H. Grabill, Clyde Kiser, and Pascal K. Whelpton, *The Fertility of American Women* (New York, 1958), 16–19.

[40] The nine census regions are: New England, Middle Atlantic, East North Central, West North Central, South Atlantic, East South Central, West South Central, Mountain, and Pacific.

after to 0.22 before falling again to 0.15 in 1920. In 1810 the South had fertility ratios over 30 percent higher than in New England (the lowest-fertility region). This differential had increased to about 60 percent in 1860, and the relative difference was nearly the same in 1910 before modern convergence began. The Midwest moved from being a region of quite large families to, by 1920, one with fertility close to the "leaders" in the transition, New England and the Middle Atlantic states.

Finally, although we know rather less about the fertility of different socioeconomic status groups, the evidence points to smaller families among higher socioeconomic status groups, such as professionals, proprietors, clerks, and other white-collar workers. This was true, at least, from the middle of the nineteenth century onward. Among proprietors, however, an exception was owner-occupier farmers, who, throughout the century, typically had larger families than other groups. Unskilled workers (often characterized simply as laborers or farm laborers) tended to have fertility closer to that of farmers, while skilled and semiskilled manual workers and craftsmen occupied an intermediate position. These socioeconomic fertility differences may have widened over the course of the nineteenth century before they eventually narrowed.[41]

One consequence of declining fertility has been an aging of the population. As Table 4.2 shows, the median age of the American people rose from 16 years in 1800 to over 20 in 1870 and over 25 in 1920. Today it stands above 30. The reason is that the age structure of the population, particularly the proportion of children, is most affected by fertility, which adds only to the base of the age pyramid. Mortality, in contrast, affects all ages. As fertility declines, so does the proportion of children, and teenagers. The population ages. The implications of this are great, changing the society from one oriented towards children to one centered on adults and eventually the elderly. This process was underway at the end of our period (1920), but its effects are more dramatic today.

THEORIES OF FERTILITY DECLINE

Explaining the American demographic transition poses a series of difficult issues. Conventional demographic transition theory has placed great

---

[41] For a summary of evidence on this, see Michael R. Haines, "Occupation and Social Class during Fertility Decline: Historical Perspectives," in Gillis, Tilly, and Levine, eds., *The European Experience of Declining Fertility*, 193–226.

reliance on the changes in child costs and benefits associated with structural changes accompanying modern economic growth, such as urbanization, industrialization, the rise in literacy and education, and increased employment of women outside the home. A classic statement of the theory was made by Frank Notestein in 1953:

> The new ideal of the small family arose typically in the urban industrial society. It is impossible to be precise about the various causal factors, but apparently many were important. Urban life stripped the family of many functions in production, consumption, recreation, and education. In factory employment the individual stood on his own accomplishments. The new mobility of young people and the anonymity of city life reduced the pressure toward traditional behavior exerted by the family and community. In a period of rapidly developing technology, new skills were needed, and new opportunities for individual advancement arose. Education and a rational point of view became increasingly important. As a consequence the cost of child-rearing grew and the possibilities for economic contributions by children declined. Falling death-rates at once increased the size of the family to be supported and lowered the inducements to have many births. Women, moreover, found new independence from household obligations and new economic roles less compatible with childbearing.[42]

But, of course, the fertility transition began in the United States well before many of these structural changes became important.

The leading theory of the American fertility decline for the antebellum period has been the land availability hypothesis. It is a special case of a child cost theory and was first proposed by Yasuba in 1962, when he discovered, for the period 1800–1860, a strong inverse relationship between population density and child-woman ratios. He interpreted density as measuring the availability of cheap potential agricultural land. High population density would raise the price of land and increase the cost to farm families of endowing their children with adequate farmsteads, that is, a suitable means of earning a living. This is, in reality, a rather sophisticated concept involving bequest motives and intergenerational transfers. More refined fertility and land availability measures and statistical analysis were subsequently employed by Forster and Tucker, but, if anything, the results were strengthened. Research on colonial New England suggests that this was taking place there prior to 1800. Further tests using county-

---

[42] Frank W. Notestein, "The Economics of Population and Food Supplies. I. The Economic Problems of Population Change," *Proceedings of the Eighth International Conference of Agricultural Economists* (London, 1953).

level data within states, micro-data from the 1860 census, and data for the analogous case of Canada have provided support.[43]

The decline in American fertility did not take place evenly across regions. Much of the interest in the historical fertility patterns arose because of spatial differences in the timing and pace of the fertility transition. A prominent feature of regional fertility differentials of whites in the nineteenth century has been a consistent east–west gradient, with higher fertility in the Midwest and the South Central regions than in the Northeast and South Atlantic areas. The gradient was prominent up to about 1900 but had largely disappeared by 1920. To a lesser extent there was a north–south gradient, with higher fertility among Southern whites. This became more prominent over the nineteenth century.[44]

Competing views look to more conventional economic and demographic variables to explain the phenomenon. One possibility is that sex ratios were biased toward males on the frontier because of sex-selective migration. Since the child-woman ratios measure total and not marital fertility, the observed differences might have been largely due to more complete and earlier marriage for the frontier female population. This was true, but data from census micro samples still reveal strong differences in marital child-woman ratios by density and settlement date. In another study, Vinovskis found for 1850 and 1860 much stronger associations of state-level fertility ratios with the extent of urbanization, industrialization, and literacy. Yasuba had seen the weakening of the density effect on fertility for censuses closer to the Civil War, but Vinovskis also noted that urban child-woman ratios fell in parallel with rural ones. This is unlikely to be explained by land availability. Finally, it is clear for the period after 1860 that such structural variables as urbanization, industri-

[43] Yasukichi Yasuba, *Birth Rates of the White Population of the United States, 1800–1860: An Economic Analysis* (Baltimore, 1962); Colin Forster and G. S. L. Tucker *Economic Opportunity and White American Fertility Ratios, 1800–1860* (New Haven, 1972). A county-level analysis of Ohio was provided by Donald R. Leet, "The Determinants of Fertility Transition in Antebellum Ohio," *Journal of Economic History*, 36 (1976), 359–78, and the 1860 census micro-data for the North have been used by Richard A. Easterlin, George Alter, and Gretchen Condran, "Farms and Farm Families in Old and New Areas: The Northern States in 1860," in Tamara K. Hareven and Maris A. Vinovskis, eds., *Family and Population in Nineteenth-Century America* (Princeton, 1978), 22–84 and in Richard A. Easterlin, "Population Change and Farm Settlement in the Northern United States," *Journal of Economic History*, 36 (1976), 45–75. Marvin McInnis, "Childbearing and Land Availability: Some Evidence from Individual Household Data," in Ronald Demos Lee, ed., *Population Patterns in the Past* (New York, 1977), 201–27 provides results for Canada. For the colonial period, see John J. McCusker and Russell R. Menard, *The Economy of British America: 1607–1789* (Chapel Hill, 1985), ch. 5.

[44] Conrad Taeuber and Irene B. Taeuber, *The Changing Population of the United States* (New York, 1958), 250–53.

alization, labor force composition, literacy, etc. dominated the statistical relationship.[45]

An intriguing alternative to the land availability–child bequest hypothesis has been proposed by Sundstrom and David. They suggest a model of life cycle fertility, savings, parental demand for old age support, and bargaining within the family. They argue that the development of nearby non-agricultural labor market opportunities had much more to do with smaller families than the march of the frontier and the disappearance of inexpensive bequests. Larger material inducements were then necessary to keep children "down on the farm" once jobs were readily available within easy distance. Urban growth and increased education behind the frontier would have been part of this process. This hypothesis can also explain the decline in rural birth rates after the Civil War and is relevant to the urban fertility transition. A related model, that of Ransom and Sutch, emphasizes the westward migration of children who then "defaulted" on their implicit contracts to care for their parents in old age. In response, parents began accumulating real and financial assets as a substitute for offspring as retirement insurance, leading to smaller families.[46]

Still other hypotheses, or at least provocative findings, have appeared in the search for explanations for the unusual American fertility transition. Steckel, using micro-data from the 1850 and 1860 federal censuses, ran some tests on competing hypotheses. While finding some modest support for the land availability view, the strongest predictors of marital fertility differentials just prior to the Civil War were the presence of financial intermediaries (banks) and labor force structure (i.e., the ratio of non-agricultural to agricultural labor force). This is more supportive of the bargaining and/or old age/savings theories. An inquiry by Jenny Bourne Wahl following a more theoretical line finds that parents progressively traded off quantity (number of children) for quality (education, health care, etc.

[45] Maris A. Vinovskis, "Socioeconomic Determinants of Interstate Fertility Differentials in the United States in 1850 and 1860," *Journal of Interdisciplinary History*, 6 (1976), 375–96; "Recent Trends in American Historical Demography," in Vinovskis, ed., *Studies in American Historical Demography*, 614–20. The post-1870 situation was analyzed by Bernard Okun, *Trends in Birth Rates in the United States since 1870* (Baltimore, 1958). The urban/industrial explanations were found to dominate in 1900 by Avery M. Guest, "Social Structure and U.S. Inter-state Fertility Differentials in 1900," *Demography*, 18 (1981), 465–86.

[46] William A. Sundstrom and Paul A. David, "Old-Age Security Motives, Labor Markets, and Farm Family Fertility in Antebellum America," *Explorations in Economic History*, 25 (1988), 164–97; Roger L. Ransom and Richard Sutch, "Two Strategies for a More Secure Old Age: Life-cycle Saving by Late-Nineteenth Century American Workers," paper presented at the NBER Summer Institute on the Development of the American Economy (July, 1989).

per child) as the nineteenth century progressed. As the price (cost) of quality declined (via public education, more effective public health and medicine), parents opted for greater human capital per child.[47]

Wahl used the extensive and rich Mormon genealogical data base. This was also the basis for the study of fertility decline in Utah from the mid-nineteenth century to the early twentieth century by Bean, Mineau, and Anderton. In the latter work, the emphasis is on distinguishing between family limitation as an adaptation to changing environmental, economic, and social circumstances versus a behavioral innovation that simply spread across groups. These distinctions are related to Ansley Coale's statement of the three preconditions for family limitation: (1) fertility control must be within the calculus of conscious choice; (2) effective means of fertility regulation must be available at reasonable cost; and (3) it must be economically and socially advantageous to limit family size. These preconditions are more likely true with adaptive behavior, that is, when family limitation is understood and accepted and occurs when socioeconomic conditions favor it. The Utah study of the Mormon Demographic History Project looks at detailed age-specific cohort and period fertility data and concludes that adaptive behavior is the most consistent explanation. It provides some support to a number of the hypotheses attempting to explain fertility decline, since the changing circumstances to which behavior adapted included not just land costs and availability but also improved socioeconomic opportunities in non-agrarian sectors (e.g., higher urban wages) as well as changes in the institutional and cultural environment. While not entirely satisfactory on grounds of parsimonious explanation, the case is made for a rather more complex explanatory framework.[48]

Most of the hypotheses about the American fertility transition can also be fit into the more general model offered by Caldwell.[49] He proposes that family limitation sets in when the net flow of resources over the life course shifts from children to parents over to parents to children. This signifies a rise in the net cost of children (i.e., benefits minus costs) and is acceler-

[47] Richard H. Steckel, "The Fertility Transition in the United States: Tests of Alternative Hypotheses," in Goldin and Rockoff, eds., *Strategic Factors in Nineteenth Century American Economic History*, 351–74; Jenny Bourne Wahl, "Trading Quantity for Quality: Explaining the Decline in American Fertility in the Nineteenth Century," in Goldin and Rockoff, eds., *Strategic Factors in Nineteenth Century American Economic History*, 375–97.

[48] Bean, Mineau and Anderton, *Fertility Change on the American Frontier*; Ansley J. Coale, "The Demographic Transition," International Union for the Scientific Study of Population, *International Population Conference: Liege, 1973* (Liege, 1974), I 53–72.

[49] John C. Caldwell, *Theory of Fertility Decline*, (New York, 1982).

ated by such things as the introduction of mass education (implying more years in school and greater enrollment rates), child labor laws, compulsory education laws, and more pervasive views on the positive value of transmitting improved human capital across generations. This intergenerational wealth transfer view is consistent with both the land availability and the socioeconomic and cultural structural adjustment hypotheses. It can also fit the quantity–quality tradeoff explanation.

Fertility of the black population is also described in Table 4.3 by child-woman ratios from 1820 and by the crude birth rate and the total fertility rate from the 1850s. Interestingly, from 1830, fertility decline also occurred for the black population, largely in the context of slavery, since 86 percent of the black population were slaves at that date. Also, despite the higher infant and child mortality among blacks (see Table 4.3 and below), black child-woman ratios were higher than those for whites, pointing to even larger differential fertility for blacks. Further, the regional pattern was the opposite of that for the white population, with higher black child-woman ratios in the east and lower ratios in the west. This, of course, was mostly in the South, where the overwhelming proportion of the black population lived prior to the twentieth century. (The proportion of the black population in the South was 87 percent in 1800 and 85 percent in 1920.) The fertility decline prior to the Civil War is puzzling. Lower slave fertility was associated with larger plantation size and a movement away from tobacco cultivation and the mixed farming characteristics of the South Atlantic region (the "Old South"). Selective movement of adult unmarried slaves to the West and the emphasis on slave reproduction in the Old South likely played a role, as did the quite harsh work regime on the newer larger plantations of the New South specializing in cotton and sugar. For the antebellum period, correlations of white and slave child-woman ratios by county were quite low, emphasizing a difference in causal factors. After the Civil War, the decline in black fertility was more similar in nature to the white fertility transition, influenced by urbanization, industrial development, growing shortage of good farmland, and changes in family norms.[50]

In sum, the fertility transition in the United States was unusual. It began in a largely rural and agrarian nation long before most of the

---

[50] Richard H. Steckel, "The Fertility of American Slaves," Stanley Engerman, "Changes in Black Fertility, 1880–1940," in Hareven and Vinovskis, eds., *Family and Population in Nineteenth-Century America*, 126–53, 239–86.

presently developed nations began their fertility transitions in the late nineteenth century. Prior to 1860 it seems that the disappearance of good, cheap land for bequests to offspring provides a reasonable model for declining family size across states, at least for rural areas. As the nineteenth century progressed, however, the more conventional socioeconomic variables seem have more explanatory power. These variables would include rising literacy and education, increased urbanization (with more expensive housing and crowding), more work by women and children outside the home, the spread of institutional restrictions such as child labor laws and compulsory education statutes, the rising value of time as real wages and incomes increased, less reliance on children for support in old age, and less available familial child care as smaller, urban nuclear families became dominant. There is also likely a role for declining infant and child mortality, at least after about 1880, which reduced the number of births necessary to achieve a desired number of children surviving to adulthood (see Table 4.3 and below). The land availability hypothesis contributes little to explaining the nineteenth century urban fertility decline. Several other models have been discussed, but many reduce to a rise in net child costs and an increased desire of parents to trade off numbers of children for greater human capital per child. It is not unreasonable to conclude that a range of changing circumstances – including increased resource scarcity (including land), the rise of mass education, greater accessibility to urban labor markets, rising real incomes and value of time – all contributed to the transition. But the fact remains that the United States was unusual, although similar to France. As noted above, it is perhaps not coincidental that both nations had democratic political revolutions late in the eighteenth century and were characterized, in the nineteenth century, mostly by smallholder agriculture.

MORTALITY

We know less about the American mortality transition of the nineteenth century than we do about that for fertility. There are no ready census-based mortality measures like the child-woman ratio, and vital statistics were absent or incomplete for most areas up until the early twentieth century. We know the most about Massachusetts, which began statewide civil vital registration in 1842, but Massachusetts was not typical of the nation in the nineteenth century. It was more urban and industrial, had more immigrants, and had lower fertility.[51] The federal census collected mortality information from 1850 to 1900, but the data were seriously flawed by incompleteness, biases, and uneven coverage. In consequence, there has been disagreement about trends, levels, and differentials in American mortality over the nineteenth century.

As mentioned, the official Death Registration Area was not formed until 1900, although there had been earlier attempts. In 1900, the Death Registration Area comprised 10 states and the District of Columbia, covering 26 percent of the population. It was significantly more urban (63 percent) than the nation as a whole (40 percent) and had a higher fraction of foreign born (22 percent) in contrast the overall average (14 percent). In addition, the nation had 11.6 percent of its population black, while the Death Registration Area had only 2 percent of its population black. Most blacks (80 percent) lived in rural areas in 1900, but those in the Death Registration Areas were 82 percent urban. Since we know that important mortality differentials existed by rural-urban residence, size of place of residence, and race around the turn of the century, these are significant considerations. Coverage of the Death Registration Area had increased to 34 states and the District of Columbia by 1920, representing 81 percent of the population. It covered the entire United States from 1933 onward.

Prior to 1900, official mortality data are limited to selected states and cities and to the imperfect mortality data of the census. Massachusetts is a widely cited source for nineteenth-century mortality information. Its data were of reasonable quality by about 1860, but before that time evidence must be sought in other sources, such as genealogies, family reconstitutions, and bills of mortality. Some analysts, such as Coale and Zelnik, have assumed that Massachusetts mortality was typical of the nation, but the representativeness, particularly of the Massachusetts-Maryland life table of Jacobson for 1850, has been questioned. Even earlier, for the colonial period, local studies dominate, with evidence of reasonable levels of expectation of life in New England but few signs of improvement in the eighteenth century. Research on the Chesapeake does point to some improvement from very unfavorable mortality levels in the seventeenth

---

[51] For example, in 1880 Massachusetts was 75 percent urban, with 25 percent of the population foreign born and a crude birth rate of 24.8. For the United States as a whole, the proportions were 28 percent urban and 13 percent foreign born with an estimated crude birth rate of 39.8.

century. But we know discouragingly little about mortality in colonial America.[52]

Some previous work has involved strong assumptions and considerable *a priori* reasoning. Thompson and Whelpton assumed a decline in mortality throughout the nineteenth century, with an acceleration after about 1880. Taeuber and Taeuber posited little improvement prior to about 1850, but considerable gains in expectation of life thereafter. Coale and Zelnik assumed a linear trend in improvement from 1850 to 1900 and used the Jacobson Massachusetts-Maryland life table of 1850 to anchor their estimates as well as a model life table system based on the experience of six European nations. Easterlin, assuming an inverse association between mortality and income per capita and between mortality and public health and a positive association between mortality and urbanization, suggested that rising income per capita after about 1840 dominated these effects and outweighed the negative effect of urban growth, with public health playing only a small role in the nineteenth century. This led him to believe that expectation of life was rising from about 1840. Vinovskis, on the other hand, believes that little change in Massachusetts mortality levels took place between the 1790s and 1860. More recent work with the Mormon genealogical data by Fogel and Pope has concluded that adult mortality (on a period basis) was relatively stable after about 1800 and then rose in the 1840s and 1850s before commencing improvement after the Civil War. This finding is quite unusual, since we have evidence of rising real income per capita and of significant economic growth during the 1840–1860 period. But income distribution may have worsened, and urbanization and immigration may have had more deleterious effects than hitherto believed. (The share of population living in areas of 2,500 persons and over grew from 11 percent in 1840 to 20 percent in 1860.) Further, the disease environment may have shifted in an unfavorable direction.[53]

---

[52] Ansley J. Coale and Melvin Zelnik, *New Estimates of Fertility and Population in the United States: A Study of Annual White Births from 1855 to 1960 and of Completeness of Enumeration in the Censuses from 1880 to 1960* (Princeton, 1963). Questions on the representativeness of the Massachusetts data, especially the 1850 Massachusetts-Maryland life table have been raised by Maris A. Vinovskis, "The Jacobson Life Table of 1850: A Critical Re-examination from a Massachusetts Perspective," *Journal of Interdisciplinary History*, 8 (1978), 703–24. On the colonial period, see Wells, *Uncle Sam's Family*, ch. 3; McCusker and Menard, *The Economy of British America*, Section II; Vinovskis, *Studies in American Historical Demography*, passim.

[53] Warren S. Thompson and P. K. Whelpton, *Population Trends in the United States* (New York, 1933), p. 230; Conrad Taeuber and Irene B. Taeuber, *Changing Population of the United States*, p. 269; Coale and Zelnik, *New Estimates of Fertility and Population in the United States*; Paul H. Jacobson, "An Esti-

For the postbellum period, we have better information. Higgs has argued, based partly on the death rate data from Kuznets presented in Table 4.1, that rural mortality began its decline in the 1870s and that this occurred mostly because of improvements in diet, nutrition, housing, and other aspects of standard of living. He saw little role for public health before the twentieth century, at least for rural areas. As for urban places, Meeker believes that there was little improvement prior to about 1880 and that thereafter urban public health measures, especially construction of pure central water distribution systems and sanitary sewers, were important. Some work by Condran and Crimmins-Gardner with the census mortality data for larger American cities in 1890 and 1900 found that mortality seemed to be improving and that the improvements were partly related to public health, although the precise relationships were difficult to measure. After about 1900, on the other hand, there is no doubt that mortality improved dramatically in both rural and urban areas and across groups.[54]

Table 4.3 provides data on the expectation of life at birth and the infant mortality rate (deaths in the first year of life per 1,000 livebirths) for the white population from 1850 onward. No information is given prior to 1850 because of the difficulty of finding comprehensive, comparable, and reliable mortality estimates. The mortality estimates in Table 4.3 for the 1850–1890 period are based on estimates made by the author using a collection of actual nineteenth- and early twentieth-century American life tables (for various states and cities, as well as for the Death Registration

mate of the Expectation of Life in the United States in 1850," *Milbank Memorial Fund Quarterly*, 35 (1957), 197–201; Richard A. Easterlin, "Population Issues in American Economic History"; Maris Vinovskis, "Mortality Rates and Trends in Massachusetts before 1860," in Vinovskis, ed., *Studies in American Historical Demography*, 225–54 (article reprinted from 1972 original); Robert W. Fogel, "Nutrition and the Decline in Mortality since 1700: Some Preliminary Findings," in Engerman and Gallman, eds., *Long-Term Factors in American Economic Growth*, pp. 439–555, esp. Figure 9.1; Robert W. Fogel, "Nutrition and the Decline in Mortality since 1700: Some Additional Preliminary Findings," National Bureau of Economic Research, Working Paper No. 1802 (January, 1986); Robert W. Fogel, "Nutrition and the Decline in Mortality since 1700: Some Additional Preliminary Findings," Clayne L. Pope, "Adult Mortality in America before 1900: A View from Family Histories," in Goldin and Rockoff, eds., *Strategic Factors in Nineteenth Century American Economic History*, 267–96.

[54] Robert Higgs, "Mortality in Rural America, 1870–1920: Estimates and Conjectures," *Explorations in Economic History*, 10 (1973), 177–95; Edward Meeker, "The Improving Health of the United States, 1850–1915," *Explorations in Economic History*, 9 (1972), 353–73; Gretchen Condran and Eileen Crimmins-Gardner, "Public Health Measures and Mortality in U.S. Cities in the Late Nineteenth Century," *Human Ecology*, 6 (1978), 27–54. The census mortality data for many cities at the end of the nineteenth century were rather reasonable for the reason that they often reported registered vital statistics. For an overview, see Samuel H. Preston and Michael R. Haines, *Fatal Years: Child Mortality in Late Nineteenth Century America* (Princeton, 1991), chs. 1 and 2.

Area) to construct a model American life table system. Census mortality data for older children and young adults were then fitted to this model system to produce the estimates presented here. For 1920 and thereafter, official Death Registration Area data are used. Indirect estimates of overall child mortality made using the data on children ever born and children surviving from the public use samples of the 1900 and 1910 censuses are presented for 1900 and 1910. After 1900 the Death Registration Area grew rapidly and became quite representative by 1920 (and complete by 1933).[55]

The evidence in Table 4.3 is quite consistent with the interpretations given. Both the expectation of life at birth and the infant mortality rate (and the crude death rate estimates in Table 4.1) show sustained improvement in mortality (i.e., rising expectation of life or falling infant mortality or crude death rates) only from about the 1870s onward. It does not appear that the 1880 census year (June 1879 to May 1880) was especially unusual in terms of high mortality, but the 1850 census year was marked by a cholera epidemic. What is apparent is that serious fluctuations in mortality were less likely after the 1870s and that this was integral in the process of the mortality transition. This also confirms one unusual aspect of the American demographic transition – fertility commenced its decline substantially before mortality. Although levels of mortality in the United States in the middle nineteenth century were comparable with those in western and northern Europe, significant mortality fluctuations were still occurring right up to the twentieth century. Consistent control of mortality in terms of a sustained decline and a damping of mortality peaks only comes after the 1870s. This was also true in England and Wales.[56] The new findings of rising mortality in the 1840s and 1850s support this contention that mortality in the United States was not substantially under control until after the Civil War.

What were the origins of the "epidemiologic transition" in the United States? A variety of factors affect mortality. They may conveniently be grouped into ecobiological, public health, medical, and socioeconomic. These categories are not mutually exclusive, since, for example, economic growth can make resources available for public health projects and

[55] Michael R. Haines, "The Use of Model Life Tables to Estimate Mortality for the United States in the Late Nineteenth Century," *Demography*, 16 (1979), 289–312; Preston and Haines, *Fatal Years*, ch. 2.

[56] B. R. Mitchell, *European Historical Statistics, 1750–1975*, second revised edition (New York, 1981), Table B6.

advances in medical science can inform the effectiveness of public health. Ecobiological factors were not likely significant. While there may have been favorable changes in the etiology of a few specific diseases or conditions in the nineteenth century (notably scarlet fever and possibly diphtheria), reduced disease virulence or changes in transmission mechanisms were not apparent.[57]

The remaining factors, socioeconomic, medical, and public health, are often difficult to disentangle. For example, if the germ theory of disease (a medical/scientific advance of the later nineteenth century) contributed to better techniques of water filtration and purification in public health projects, then how should the roles of medicine versus public health be apportioned? Thomas McKeown has proposed that, prior to the twentieth century, medical science contributed little to reduced mortality in Europe and elsewhere.[58] His argument was basically one of elimination of alternatives: if ecobiological and medical factors are eliminated, the mortality decline before the early twentieth century must have been due to socioeconomic factors, especially better diet and nutrition, as well as improved clothing and shelter (i.e., standard of living). Indeed, the trend in standard of living itself is subject to considerable debate. Some room was left for public health, albeit a rather empirical (as opposed to scientific) one. These results were based particularly on the experience of England and Wales, where much of the mortality decline between the 1840s and the 1930s was due to reductions in deaths from respiratory tuberculosis, other respiratory infections (e.g., bronchitis), and non-specific gastrointestinal diseases (e.g., diarrhea, gastroenteritis). No effective medical therapies were available for these infections until well into the twentieth century.

It is true that medical science did have a rather limited direct role before the twentieth century. In terms of specific therapies, smallpox vaccination was known by the late eighteenth century and diphtheria and tetanus antitoxin and rabies therapy by the 1890s. Many other treatments were symptomatic. The germ theory of disease, advanced by Pasteur in the 1860s and greatly advanced by the work of Koch and others in the 1870s and 1880s, was only slowly accepted by what was a very conservative medical

---

[57] The term "epidemiologic transition" and a similar causal categorization were advanced by Abdel Omran, "The Epidemiologic Transition: A Theory of the Epidemiology of Population Change," *Milbank Memorial Fund Quarterly*, 49 (1973), 509–38.

[58] Thomas McKeown, *The Modern Rise of Population* (New York, 1976).

profession. Even after Robert Koch conclusively identified the tuberculosis bacillus and the cholera vibrio in 1882 and 1883, various theories of
miasmas and anticontagionists views were common among physicians
in the United States and elsewhere. Hospitals, having originated as pest
houses and alms houses, were (correctly) perceived as generally unhealthy
places to be. In 1894 in Milwaukee, for example, an angry crowd prevented the removal of a child to a hospital during a smallpox outbreak on
the grounds that the child would die there (as another child had previously). Surgery was also very dangerous before the advances of William
Halsted at Johns Hopkins in the 1880s and 1890s. Major thoracic surgery
was rarely risked and, if attempted, patients had a high probability of
dying from infection or shock or both. The best practice in amputations
was to do them quickly to minimize risks. Although anesthesia had been
introduced in America in the 1840s and the use of antisepsis in the operating theater had been advocated by the British surgeon Joseph Lister in
the 1860s, surgery was not considered even reasonably safe until the twentieth century.[59]

Although the direct impact of medicine on mortality in the United
States over this period is questionable, public health did play an important role and thereby indirectly allowed medicine a part. After John Snow
had identified a polluted water source as the origin of a cholera outbreak
on London in 1854, pure water and sewage disposal became important
issues for municipal authorities. New York City constructed its 40-mile-
long Croton Aqueduct in 1844, and Boston was also tapping various
outside water sources by aqueduct before the Civil War. Chicago, which
drew on Lake Michigan for its water, also had to cope with sewage disposal directly into its water supply from the Chicago River. Water intakes
were moved further offshore in the 1860s, requiring tunnels several miles
long driven through solid rock. But this was only a temporary solution.
Finally, the city had to reverse the flow of the Chicago River, using locks
and the Illinois Sanitary and Ship Canal, and send the effluent down to
the Illinois River. The project took eight years (1892–1900) and was called
one of the "engineering wonders of the modern world." The bond issue
to fund it and create the Chicago Sanitary District was overwhelmingly

[59] John Duffy, *The Healers: A History of American Medicine* (Urbana, 1976), chs. 10, 16–17; Paul Starr,
    The Social Transformation of American Medicine (New York, 1982), chs. 4–5; Judith W. Leavitt, "Pol-
    itics and Public Health: Smallpox in Milwaukee, 1894–95," in Susan Reverby and David Rosner,
    eds., *Health Care in America: Essays in Social History* (Philadelphia, 1979), 84–101.

approved in 1889 by a vote of 70,958 to 242. This does not take into account that, at an early date, the entire downtown area had to raised by one story to facilitate gravity sewage flow.[60]

A pattern was emerging in the late nineteenth century – massive public works projects in larger metropolitan areas to provide clean water and proper sewage disposal. But progress was uneven. Baltimore and New Orleans, for example, were rather late in constructing adequate sanitary sewage systems. As time went along, filtration and chlorination were added to remove or neutralize particulate matter and microorganisms. This was a consequence of the acceptance of the findings of the new science of bacteriology. According to Charles Chapin in his compendious 1901 study of urban sanitation in the United States, public health officials were often much more cognizant of the need to use bacteriology than were physicians, who sometimes saw public health officials as a professional threat. There was also the issue of marshaling resources to pay for many of these public works and public health projects. Much of it was locally funded, with the consequence of uneven and intermittent progress toward water and sewer systems, public health departments, and so forth. Indeed, one reason for the better mortality showing of the ten largest cities in 1900 as compared with remaining cities over 25,000 population was the capacity of the largest cities to secure the necessary resources for public health reform and improvement.[61]

By 1900 public water supplies were available to 42 percent of the American population and sewers to 29 percent, although many households were not connected to the pipes running under the streets and roads in front of their houses. It took longer for filtered water to reach many families. In 1870 almost no water was filtered in the United States. By 1880 about 30,000 persons in urban areas (places over 2,500 persons) were receiving it. The number had grown to 1.86 million in 1900, 10.8 million in 1910, and over 20 million in 1920, about 37 percent of the whole urban population and a much higher proportion of those living in large cities. In a study of the mortality decline in Philadelphia 1870–1930, Condran and Cheney showed the drastic reduction in typhoid mortality on a ward-by-

---

[60] Louis P. Cain, "An Economic History of Urban Location and Sanitation," *Research in Economic History*, 2 (1977), 337–89; Stuart Galishoff, "Triumph and Failure: The American Response to the Urban Water Supply Problem, 1860–1923," in Martin V. Melosi, ed., *Pollution and Reform in American Cities, 1870–1930* (Austin, 1980), 35–57.

[61] Charles V. Chapin, *Municipal Sanitation in the United States* (Providence, RI, 1901); Cain, "An Economic History of Urban Sanitation and Location"; John Duffy, *The Sanitarians: A History of American Public Health* (Urbana, 1990), chs. 12–16; Preston and Haines, *Fatal Years*, ch. 3.

ward basis as water filtration was progressively introduced after the turn of the century.[62]

Progress in public health was not confined to water and sewer systems, though they were among the most effective weapons in the fight to prolong and enhance human life. Simply by reducing the incidence and exposure to disease in any way, overall health, net nutritional status, and resistance to disease was improved. Other areas of public health activity from the late nineteenth century onward included vaccination against smallpox; use of diphtheria and tetanus antitoxins (from the 1890s); more extensive use of quarantine (as more diseases were identified as contagious); cleaning urban streets and public areas to reduce disease foci; physical examinations for school children; health education; improved child labor and workplace health and safety laws; legislation and enforcement efforts to reduce food adulteration and especially to obtain pure milk; measures to eliminate ineffective or dangerous medications (e.g., the Pure Food and Drug Act of 1906); increased knowledge of and education concerning nutrition; stricter licensing of physicians, nurses, and midwives; more rigorous medical education; building codes to improve heat, plumbing, and ventilation in housing; measures to alleviate air pollution in urban settings; and the creation of state and local boards of health to oversee and administer these programs.

Public health proceeded on a broad front, but not without delays and considerable unevenness in enforcement and effectiveness. Regarding the case of pure milk, it became apparent that pasteurization (heating the milk to a temperature below boiling for a period of time), known since the 1860s, was the only effective means of insuring a bacteria-free product. Certification or inspection of dairy herds was insufficient. This was, however, resisted by milk sellers, and it only came into practice quite late. In 1911, only 15 percent of the milk in New York City, one of the more advanced urban areas in public health, was pasteurized. In 1908 only 20 percent of Chicago's milk was so treated. Pasteurization did not become compulsory in Chicago until 1908, and in New York City until 1912. Boston began required medical examinations of school children in 1894, and mandatory vaccination of school children in New

---

[62] S. W. Abbott, *The Past and Present Condition of Public Hygiene and State Medicine in the United States* (Boston, 1900); George E. Whipple, "Fifty Years of Water Purification," in M. P. Ravenel, ed., *A Half Century of Public Health* (New York, 1921), 161–80; Gretchen A. Condran and Rose A. Cheney, "Mortality Trends in Philadelphia: Age- and Cause-Specific Death Rates, 1870–1930," *Demography*, 19 (1982), 97–123.

York City was started in 1897. The federal government instituted the Children's Bureau in 1912, and a 1914 pamphlet on infant care became the best selling publication ever issued by the Government Printing Office. Examples of success but with rather uneven progress can easily be multiplied.[63]

Public health can thus be seen as having played a significant part in the mortality transition. But there were interactions between reduced incidence of infectious and parasitic disease and improvements in general health. An indicator of health status is final adult stature. A population may have reasonable levels of food intake, but a virulent disease environment will impair net nutritional status; that is, the amount of nutrients available for replacement and augmentation of tissue. Repeated bouts of infectious disease, especially gastrointestinal infections, impair the body's ability to absorb nutrients and divert calories, proteins, vitamins, and minerals in the diet to fighting the infection rather than to tissue construction or reconstruction. Recent research by Robert Fogel and his colleagues indicates cycles in stature in the nineteenth century. The stature estimates are based largely on military records. There was a downturn in these heights dating from those born about 1830, which also coincides with the rise in mortality seen in the genealogical data in the 1840s and 1850s, the period of child and adolescent growth of these age cohorts. There is some evidence that food availability or distribution (by region or socioeconomic status) deteriorated in the 1820s and 1830s and possibly later. But the case is far from clear as a sole cause. More likely was nutrition interacting with a changing disease environment which was, in turn, affected by urbanization, rapid population turnover, settling of new areas, migration waves from abroad, and the apparent spread of malaria, fevers, and gastrointestinal disease. Something close to modern stature had been achieved in the United States by the late eighteenth century, but these new factors, the reduced food availability, and the worsening disease environment led both to a deterioration of mortality and stature in the mid-nineteenth century before a recovery after the Civil War.[64]

---

[63] John Duffy, *The Sanitarians: A History of American Public Health* (Urbana, 1990), chs. 12–16; Preston and Haines, *Fatal Years*, ch. 1.

[64] Fogel, "Nutrition and Decline of Mortality since 1700"; Pope, "Adult Mortality in America before 1900"; Richard Steckel, "Stature and Living Standards in the United States," in Robert E. Gallman and John Joseph Wallis, eds., *American Economic Growth and Standards of Living before the Civil War* (Chicago, 1992), 265–308; John Komlos, "The Height and Weight of West Point Cadets: Dietary Change in Antebellum America," *Journal of Economic History*, 47 (1987), 897–927.

CAUSE OF DEATH

By the late nineteenth century we begin to have reasonable data on cause of death. Much of the mortality decline since the Civil War originated in reductions in death from infectious and parasitic diseases, both of the respiratory (usually air-borne) and gastrointestinal (usually water-borne) types. In a study of Philadelphia over the period 1870–1930, about two-thirds of the drop in age-standardized death rates came from various infectious diseases, including 22 percent from respiratory tuberculosis alone. Among children (who accounted for much of the decline), significant contributions were made by reductions in mortality from diphtheria and croup, scarlet fever, smallpox, and respiratory tuberculosis. Diphtheria antitoxin, water filtration, and quarantine helped, but an improved standard of living was also important, especially for tuberculosis. Over half of the mortality decline for those aged 20–39 came from that of respiratory tuberculosis, for which no specific therapy was available until the 1940s.[65]

Reliable cause of death information for larger areas of the nation become available in 1900 with the initiation of the Death Registration Area. Calculated from these data, the crude death rate declined (for the Death Registration Area, at least) by 25 percent between 1900 and 1920. Of this decline, 70 percent was accounted for by that in all infectious and parasitic diseases. And of that reduction in infectious disease, 24 percent came from reductions in mortality from respiratory tuberculosis. Over the longer period 1900–1960, the crude death rate declined by 45 percent, while mortality from all infectious and parasitic diseases was reduced by 90 percent. The decline in mortality from infectious disease actually exceeded that from all causes combined because mortality from chronic, degenerative diseases (cancer, cardiovascular disease) increased.[66]

One of the great events in human history has been the prolongation of life and reduction in mortality in the modern era, chiefly due to great declines in death from epidemic and endemic infectious disease. Americans and most in the developed world no longer live with the kind of fear and fatalism that characterized a world in which sudden and pervasive

---

[65] Condran and Cheney, "Mortality Trends in Philadelphia."
[66] Samuel H. Preston, Nathan Keyfitz, and Robert Schoen, *Causes of Death: Life Tables for National Populations* (New York, 1972).

death from disease was a fact of life. For the United States, most of this improvement took place since the late nineteenth century.

MORTALITY DIFFERENTIALS

During our period, both prior to and during the mortality transition commencing in the 1870s, significant differentials in mortality existed – by sex, rural–urban residence, race, region, nativity (native versus foreign born), and socioeconomic status. Male mortality usually exceeds female mortality at all ages. This was generally true in the United States in the nineteenth century. The relative differences were often smaller than in the mid- to late twentieth century, as a consequence of the hazards of childbearing and pervasive exposure to disease-causing organisms.[67]

It is clear that, before about 1920, urban mortality was much in excess of rural mortality. In general, the larger the city, the higher the death rate. A variety of circumstances contributed to the excess mortality of cities: greater density and crowding, leading to the more rapid spread of infection; a higher degree of contaminated water and food; garbage and carrion in streets and elsewhere not properly disposed of; larger inflows of foreign migrants, both new foci of infection and new victims; and also migrants from the countryside who had not been exposed to the harsher urban disease environment. Writing at the turn of the century, Adna Ferrin Weber noted the positive relationship between city size and mortality levels, both in the United States and Europe:

It is almost everywhere true that people die more rapidly in cities than in rural districts. . . . There is no inherent or eternal reason why men should die faster in large communities than in small hamlets. . . . Leaving aside accidental causes, it may be affirmed that the excessive urban mortality is due to lack of pure air, water and sunlight, together with uncleanly habits of life induced thereby. Part cause, part effect, poverty, overcrowding, high rates of mortality, are found together in city tenements.[68]

According to the Death Registration Area life tables for 1900/02, the expectation of life at birth was 48.2 years for white males overall – 44

---

[67] Pope, "Adult Mortality in America before 1900," notes that adult female mortality often did exceed adult male mortality between ages 20 and 50, but this was associated with the hazards of frontier life and migration.

[68] Adna F. Weber, *The Growth of Cities in the Nineteenth Century: A Study in Statistics* (New York, 1899), 343, 348.

years in urban areas and 54 years in rural places. The comparable results for females were similar (51.1 years overall, 48 years urban, 55 years rural). For the seven states with reasonable registration data in both 1890 and 1900, the ratio of urban to rural crude death rates reported in the 1890 census was 1.27, and 1.18 in 1900. For young children (aged 1–4) the ratios were much higher, with urban mortality being 107 percent higher in 1890 and 97 percent higher in 1900. For infants the excess urban mortality was 63 percent in 1890 and 49 percent in 1900. Residence in cities with poorer water quality, lack of refrigeration to keep food and milk fresh, and close proximity to a variety of pathogens was very hazardous to the youngest inhabitants. The rural–urban differential seems to have been true earlier as well. For seven New York counties in 1865, the probability of dying before reaching age five was 0.229 in urban areas but 0.192 in rural locations. A study of Massachusetts by Vinovskis found a rough direct relationship between city size and mortality for 1859–61, but he believed that the differences had been larger in the seventeenth and eighteenth centuries.[69]

The excess urban mortality was diminishing from the late nineteenth century onward, especially as public health measures and improved diet, shelter, and general living standards took effect. The excess in expectation of life at birth for rural white males over those in urban areas was 10 years in 1900. This fell to 7.7 years in 1910, 5.4 years in 1930, and 2.6 years by 1940. The original cause of the rural advantage was unlikely superior knowledge of disease, hygiene, and prevention in rural areas, since farmers were not known to be particularly careful about disease and cleanliness: "There are few occupations [other than farming] in which hygiene is more neglected."[70] The rural advantage seems simply to have been that rural residents were farther from each other, reducing chances of contagion and contamination of water supplies. Rural–urban mortality differentials likely played a role in the deterioration of mortality in the middle of the nineteenth century, as the population shifted to cities and towns. Also, the twentieth-century mortality decline was partly propelled by the elimination of excess urban deaths.[71]

---

[69] Preston and Haines, *Fatal Years*, 36–39; Maris A. Vinovskis, *Fertility in Massachusetts from the Revolution to the Civil War* (New York, 1981), ch. 2; Gretchen A. Condran and Eileen Crimmins, "Mortality Differentials between Rural and Urban Areas of States in the Northeastern United States, 1890–1900," *Journal of Historical Geography*, 6 (1980), 179–202.

[70] Abbott, *The Past and Present Condition of Public Hygiene*, 71.

[71] Preston and Haines, *Fatal Years*, 36–39; Taeuber and Taeuber, *The Changing Population of the United States*, 274–75.

The black population of the United States certainly experienced higher death rates, both as slaves and then as a free population in the postbellum period than did whites. Table 4.3 provides a breakdown of the expectation of life at birth and the infant mortality rate by race. As of 1920, when reasonably representative data are available for the black population in the official registration states, it is apparent that the mortality of blacks was substantially higher, despite their living in predominantly rural areas. For the 1890s, based on estimates using the 1900 census public use sample, the infant mortality rate was 111 infant deaths per 1,000 live-births for the white population and 170 for the black population. The implied expectations of life at birth were 51.8 years for whites and 41.8 years for blacks.[72] The differential clearly had not disappeared by 1920, when the absolute difference in expectation of life at birth by race was 10.4 years and the black infant mortality rate was 60 percent higher than that for whites. Even in 1990, although some convergence had occurred, the difference in life expectancy was still 7 years and black infant mortality was 237 percent higher than white. The absolute difference had narrowed, but the relative difference in infant survival had actually worsened. Mortality is a sensitive indicator of socioeconomic well-being, and, by that standard, the absolute improvement for the black population had been considerable, although relative progress had been mixed. The historical disadvantaged status of the black population is apparent, since, despite a greater proportion living in comparatively healthier rural areas, blacks still had substantially higher death rates than whites.

The mortality and health of the antebellum slave population has more recently been studied using plantation records and coastal shipping manifests (giving heights of transported slaves). It has revealed very high mortality and very stunted stature among slave infants and young children, pointing to poor health conditions. For example, the infant mortality rate for slaves is estimated to have been as high as 340 infant deaths per 1,000 livebirths in comparison with 197 for the whole American population in

---

[72] Preston and Haines, *Fatal Years*, ch. 2 and Table 2.5. The estimates given are from the surviving children method. They differ from the results in Table 4.3 for whites because the numbers in Table 4.3 apply only to the Death Registration Area (DRA), while those given here apply to the entire nation. Since the black population in the DRA was predominantly urban (82 percent), black mortality was higher there than for United States as a whole. Compare the DRA infant mortality rate of 234 and an expectation of life at birth of 33.8 years for blacks with the national estimates of 170 and 41.8, respectively. On the other hand, the results for the white population are virtually identical between the DRA official data and the census-based estimates (DRA: infant mortality rate 121 and expectation of life at birth 49.6 years; census-based estimates: 124 and 49.5 years).

1860 (see Table 4.3). Death rates among slave children aged 1–4 were also very high, although they began to move closer to those for whites for older ages. An hypothesis for the high mortality and short stature of slave children is that they were not given much animal protein in their diets until about age 10. In addition, pregnant and lactating women were often kept hard at field work, leading to lower birthweights and to less breastfeeding and earlier weaning. The better diets of adolescent and adult slaves brought their mortality rates and stature closer to those for the white population.[73]

Information on mortality differences between the native and the foreign-born populations is ambiguous. In Massachusetts, for example, the crude death rate for the native population was higher (20.4 per 1,000 population) than that for the foreign born (17.4) for the period 1888 to 1895.[74] This difference disappears, however, once the results are adjusted for the younger age structure of the immigrant population. Using census samples to estimate the mortality of children of native- and foreign-born parents reveals the opposite: for seven New York counties in 1865, the probability of dying before age 5 was 0.189 for children of native-born parents but 0.234 for children of foreign-born parents. The same calculation using the national sample of the 1900 census gives a probability of death before age 5 of 0.166 when both parents were native born and 0.217 when both parents were immigrants. For the Death Registration Area life tables of 1900/02, life expectancies at age 10 were rather similar by nativity: 51.6 years for native white males and 49.1 years for foreign white males. The results for 1909/11 were 51.9 and 50.3 years, respectively. Differentials by nativity were converging and had largely disappeared by the 1930s, since the higher mortality of the foreign born was largely due to lower socioeconomic status and a greater proportion living in large cities. As socioeconomic attainment narrowed between the groups and as the rural–urban mortality difference disappeared, the mortality penalty paid by the foreign born also diminished. There had been in the late nineteenth century an effect on mortality cycles in large cities that coincided with waves of immigrants. Surges in immigration produced increased death rates. They likely were affected by changes in disease environments for both the immi-

---

[73] Richard H. Steckel, "A Peculiar Population: The Nutrition, Health, and Mortality of American Slaves from Childhood to Maturity," *Journal of Economic History*, 46 (1986), 721–41; "A Dreadful Childhood: Excess Mortality of American Slaves," *Social Science History*, 10 (1986), 427–65.

[74] Samuel W. Abbott, "The Vital Statistics of Massachusetts: A Forty Years' Summary, 1856–1895," Massachusetts, State Board of Health, *Twenty-Eighth Annual Report of the Massachusetts State Board of Health*, Public Document No. 34 (Boston, 1897), Table 35.

grants and the natives. These cycles too had largely disappeared in the early 20th century.[75]

Regional differences in mortality before the twentieth century are rather difficult to establish because of the incompleteness of geographic coverage of both vital statistics and of local studies. In colonial times, New England was the area of lowest mortality, while the region from the Chesapeake to the south had higher mortality. This pattern continued into the first half of the nineteenth century, as is confirmed by estimates of adult mortality from genealogies for cohorts born in the late eighteenth and early nineteenth centuries. The Midwest also appeared as a relatively healthy region. For cohorts born in the middle of the century, however, these regional differences had dissipated. Indeed, the highest life expectation at age 20 for white females born in the 1850s and 1860s was in the South Atlantic states. Regional differences, such as they were, converged into the twentieth century, but as late at 1950 the region of lowest mortality was still the western Midwest, while the highest death rates were found in the Mountain states. Regional areas of poverty (e.g., West Virginia, New Mexico) have led to significant variation across states.[76]

Differences in survival probabilities also existed across socioeconomic groups, although here too the information is sketchy. Using census mortality data for adult males reported by occupation in 1890 and 1900 and vital registration for 1908/10, Paul Uselding found a rough gradient, with the lowest death rates among proprietors, clerical, and other white-collar workers and the highest death rates among laborers and servants. Interestingly, professionals did only about average. Farmers and clerks did well, as, surprisingly, did workers in forestry and fisheries. The more rural environment for those in agriculture and extractive industries undoubtedly helped.

These results are echoed in estimates of child mortality according to occupation of father from the 1900 census sample. Children of white-collar workers, professionals, proprietors, and farmers did better than average, while children of laborers (including agricultural laborers) had worse than average survival chances. Again, the advantage to professionals, such as

---

[75] Preston and Haines, *Fatal Years*, chs. 2 and 3; Michael R. Haines, "Mortality in Nineteenth Century America: Estimates from New York and Pennsylvania Census Data, 1865 and 1900," *Demography*, 14 (1977), 311–31; James W. Glover, *United States Life Tables, 1890, 1901, 1910, and 1901–1910* (Washington, DC, 1921); Robert Higgs, "Cycles and Trends of Mortality in 18 Large American Cities, 1871–1900," *Explorations in Economic History*, 16 (1979), 381–408.

[76] Preston and Haines, *Fatal Years*, chs. 3 and 4; Pope, "Adult Mortality before 1900," 284–90; Taeuber and Taeuber, *Changing Population of the United States*, 282–86.

physicians, teachers, clergy, was not great. These results stand in contrast to similar calculations from published data from the 1911 Census of Marriage and Fertility of England and Wales. In England the differences in child mortality across socioeconomic group lines were steep. There was a strong, consistent gradient from the low-mortality professional, proprietary, and white-collar groups through moderate mortality among skilled and semi-skilled manual workers and finally to the highest mortality among the children of unskilled manual workers. Social class clearly had much more salience in the sense of an outcome (child mortality in this case) in England in 1911 than in the United States in 1900. Social class did not have as fundamental an importance in this sense in the United States as in Britain. Greater geographic and possibly socioeconomic mobility likely played a role in the smaller American socioeconomic differences. Also, the eleven-year difference in census dates may well have been important, since this was the period in which the impact of public health advance was greatly accelerating. In the United States at the turn of the century, rural or urban residence was more important than father's occupation (or estimated father's income) for child survival. An exception was race, where the black population was at a disadvantage both within occupations and within rural–urban categories. Indeed, it is important to note that race in the United States took the place of class in Britain in terms of differential child mortality.

There is some evidence from earlier in the nineteenth century that socioeconomic variables, such as wealth or income, occupation, and literacy, were less important in predicting mortality differentials. For the 1850s, for instance, survival probabilities differed little between the children of the poor and the wealthy. Rural or urban residence and region made more difference.[77]

This had begun to change in the early twentieth century, however. Analysis of the 1910 census public use sample and published vital statistics from the Birth Registration Area in the 1920s has revealed, however, that the socioeconomic differentials widened in the United States as the new century progressed. Higher-income and better-educated groups more easily assimilated advice and improvements in child care, hygiene, and health practices and so were "leaders" in the mortality decline of the early twentieth century, much as the upper British socioeconomic status groups

[77] Richard H. Steckel, "The Health and Mortality of Women and Children, 1850–1860," *Journal of Economic History*, 48 (1988), 333–45.

had been. Public health improvements led to a reduction in the *level* of mortality but did not lead to a reduction in relative differentials across class and occupation groups. Rural–urban differences did converge into the early twentieth century, but both relative and absolute mortality differences by race did not. The role of personal and household health behavior has been inadequately emphasized in the debate on the origins of the mortality transition. It was very likely central, although the precise contribution to differential child mortality is not easy to assess. For adults, the mortality gradient observed at the turn of the century from high mortality among laborers to intermediate levels among skilled manual workers to the most favorable mortality among white-collar workers persisted up to the middle of the twentieth century.[78]

Overall, the mortality transition in the United States was a delayed event. Instead of a decline of death rates across the nineteenth century in parallel with the decline in birth rates, mortality exhibited an increase prior to the Civil War. The sustained decline only commenced nationally in the 1870s. A damping of year-to-year mortality fluctuations also took place after mid-century. In the nineteenth century, cities were definitely less healthy environments – the larger the city, the higher the mortality risk. The rural advantage was slowly eroded from late in the century, particularly due to the advance of urban public health, broadly defined. The mortality disadvantage of the black population persisted throughout the period considered here, although mortality levels improved for both whites and blacks. It is not easy to assign credit to various causal factors in the mortality transition, but the principal proximate cause was the control of both epidemic and endemic infectious diseases. By the later nineteenth century, public health certainly contributed much, with improvements in diet, housing, and standard of living also significant. The direct role of medical intervention was rather limited before the twentieth century but then increased as the germ theory of disease was accepted and better diagnosis and effective therapies were developed. Though difficult to assess,

---

[78] Paul Uselding, "In Dispraise of Muckrakers: United States Occupational Mortality, 1890–1910," *Research in Economic History*, 1 (1976), 334–71; Preston and Haines, *Fatal Years*, ch. 5; Douglas C. Ewbank and Samuel H. Preston, "Personal Health Behavior and the Decline of Infant and Child Mortality: the United States, 1900–1930," in John Caldwell, et al., *What We Know About Health Transition: The Cultural, Social and Behavioral Determinants of Health*, Vol. I (Canberra: Health Transition Centre, Australian National University, 1990), 116–49; Aaron Antonovsky, "Social Class, Life Expectancy and Overall Mortality," *Milbank Memorial Fund Quarterly*, 45 (1967), 31–73.

changes in personal health behavior must be assigned importance, particularly after the turn of the twentieth century.

MIGRATION: SOURCES

The United States was, and to a great extent remains, a nation of migrants. As seen in Table 4.1, a large share of total population growth (approximately 25 percent) of total population growth over the period 1790–1920 was due to migration from abroad. Between 1819 and 1920, according to official statistics, over 33.7 million migrants entered the United States from abroad. But, once here, both immigrants and the native born continued to move – westward to the frontier, from rural to urban areas, and, more recently, to suburbia and to the "sun belt."

In terms of sources of quantitative information, there exist, for international migration, ship manifests after 1819. They recorded landing in major ports, though omitting first-class passengers. Entrance at other points, especially land borders with Canada, were not recorded. Efforts to remedy these deficiencies were made intermittently after 1855, but coverage was not complete on this until 1908. Similarly, return migration was not counted until 1908 (and discontinued in 1957). In addition to the border counts, the federal census, of course, asked questions on place of birth of each individual from 1850 onward and on the nativity of the respondents parents from 1870 onward. Between 1890 and 1930 questions were asked of immigrants concerning their duration of residence in the United States or year of immigration.[79] Some of the basic official international migration statistics by country of origin are reported in Table 4.5.

For internal migration, reliance must be placed on census data by place of birth and current residence (which begins in 1850), "surviving" age cohorts forward or backward from census to census, direct linkage of individuals from census to census, and the census questions on residence at a previous date. Some additional help can be found in genealogical data and such things as military pension records. The census-survival technique requires estimates of mortality (and sometimes fertility), which, as is apparent, are not available at the state or local level for many places in the

[79] Bureau of the Census, *Historical Statistics*, 97–98.

nineteenth and early twentieth centuries. The question on residence five years prior to the census was not instituted until 1940, though the New York State census of 1855 asked a similar question.

INTERNAL MIGRATION

Table 4.4 provides a glimpse of regional population growth at selected censuses between 1790 and 1920. Not surprisingly, the demographic "center" of the nation was moving from the Atlantic coastal states (New England, Middle Atlantic, South Atlantic regions) to the Midwest (East North Central and West North Central) and western South (East South Central and West South Central). By 1920, the Mountain and Pacific states were still relatively small demographically, comprising less than 10 percent of the total population (as opposed to 21 percent in 1990). Two migrations were driving the numbers in Table 4.4 – the movement from east to west and the movement from rural to urban areas. As Table 4.2 demonstrates, urban population grew from about 5 percent of the total population in 1790 to 51 percent in 1920. The average annual growth rate was 4.3 percent for the urban population in contrast to only 2.0 percent per annum for rural dwellers. Since we have every indication the birth rates were lower and death rates higher in urban relative to rural areas, the more rapid growth of urban areas originated in population redistribution and not differences in natural increase. This rural to urban shift reflects, of course, labor market conditions as the economy changed its structure of opportunities from a rural, smallholder agriculture to an urban, industrial and service-based economy made up predominantly of employees. This is certainly exemplified by the increase in the non-farm share of the labor force from 25.6 percent in 1800 to 44.2 percent in 1860 to 74.1 percent in 1920.[80] A primary motive for migration in ordinary times is to take advantage of wage and income differences across space, which substitutes factor mobility for interregional trade in goods and services.

Table 4.4 also reveals that urbanization did spread across regions, albeit

[80] Thomas Weiss, "U.S. Labor Force Estimates and Economic Growth, 1800–1860," in Gallman and Wallis, eds., *American Economic Growth and Standards of Living before the Civil War*, Table 1.1; Stanley Lebergott, "Labor Force and Employment, 1800–1960," in Dorothy S. Brady, ed., *Output, Employment, and Productivity in the United States after 1800*, National Bureau of Economic Research, Studies in Income and Wealth, vol. 30 (New York, 1966), p. 117.

Table 4.4. *Population by region and residence, United States, 1790–1920 (000s)*

Region	1790	%	1830	%	1860	%	1890	%	1920	%
Total Population										
New England	1,009	25.7%	1,955	15.2%	3,135	10.0%	4,701	7.5%	7,401	7.0%
Middle Atlantic	959	24.4%	3,588	27.9%	7,459	23.7%	12,706	20.2%	22,261	21.0%
East North Central	—	—	1,470	11.4%	6,927	22.0%	13,478	21.4%	21,476	20.3%
West North Central	—	—	140	1.1%	2,170	6.9%	8,932	14.2%	12,544	11.8%
South Atlantic	1,852	47.1%	3,646	28.3%	5,365	17.1%	8,858	14.1%	13,990	13.2%
East South Central	109	2.8%	1,816	14.1%	4,021	12.8%	6,429	10.2%	8,893	8.4%
West South Central	—	—	246	1.9%	1,748	5.6%	4,741	7.5%	10,242	9.7%
Mountain	—	—	—	—	175	0.6%	1,214	1.9%	3,336	3.1%
Pacific	—	—	—	—	444	1.4%	1,920	3.0%	5,878	5.5%
Total	3,929	100.0%	12,861	100.0%	31,444	100.0%	62,979	100.0%	106,021	100.0%
Urban Population										
New England	76	37.8%	274	24.3%	1,148	18.5%	2,894	13.1%	5,620	10.4%
Middle Atlantic	83	41.3%	511	45.3%	2,639	42.4%	7,372	33.3%	16,784	30.9%
East North Central	—	—	37	3.3%	974	15.7%	5,112	23.1%	13,050	24.1%
West North Central	—	—	5	0.4%	290	4.7%	2,306	10.4%	4,726	8.7%
South Atlantic	42	20.9%	227	20.1%	615	9.9%	1,728	7.8%	4,336	8.0%
East South Central	—	—	28	2.5%	237	3.8%	817	3.7%	1,994	3.7%
West South Central	—	—	46	4.1%	215	3.5%	716	3.2%	2,969	5.5%
Mountain	—	—	—	—	18	0.3%	356	1.6%	1,218	2.2%
Pacific	—	—	—	—	82	1.3%	805	3.6%	3,555	6.6%
Total	201	100.0%	1,128	100.0%	6,218	100.0%	22,106	100.0%	54,252	100.0%

Table 4.4. (cont.)

Region	1790	%	1830	%	1860	%	1890	%	1920	%
Rural Population										
New England	933	25.0%	1,681	14.3%	1,987	7.9%	1,807	4.4%	1,780	3.4%
Middle Atlantic	875	23.5%	3,077	26.2%	4,820	19.1%	5,334	13.1%	5,478	10.6%
East North Central	—	—	1,433	12.2%	5,953	23.6%	8,366	20.5%	8,425	16.3%
West North Central	—	—	136	1.2%	1,880	7.5%	6,626	16.2%	7,818	15.1%
South Atlantic	1,810	48.6%	3,419	29.1%	4,750	18.8%	7,130	17.4%	9,654	18.6%
East South Central	109	2.9%	1,788	15.2%	3,784	15.0%	5,612	13.7%	6,899	13.3%
West South Central	—	—	200	1.7%	1,532	6.1%	4,025	9.8%	7,273	14.0%
Mountain	—	—	—	—	157	0.6%	858	2.1%	2,118	4.1%
Pacific	—	—	—	—	363	1.4%	1,115	2.7%	2,322	4.5%
Total	3,727	100.0%	11,734	100.0%	25,226	100.0%	40,873	100.0%	51,767	100.0%

Source: U.S. Bureau of the Census, *U.S. Census of Population, 1970* (Washington DC, 1972), Vol. I, Part 1, Section 1, tables 8, 18. Totals have been adjusted for rounding errors.

unevenly. The Northeast was the urban-industrial center of the nation in the nineteenth century. Table 4.4 confirms this view. By 1860, New England the Middle Atlantic regions had 61 percent of the nation's urban inhabitants but only 33 percent of the overall population. Conversely, the South had 17 percent of the urban population but 36 percent of the overall total. Even in 1920, the Northeast still had 41 percent of urban dwellers with the Midwest close behind at 33 percent. The South still had but 17 percent.

From 1850 onward we are able to examine migration by place of birth and current residence. The proportion of the native-born population resid-ing outside the state of birth ("lifetime" migrants) was relatively stable from the middle of the nineteenth century – 23.3 percent of the white population in 1850, 23.5 percent in 1890, and 23.9 percent in 1920. The non-white population had lower rates of lifetime mobility in this period, about 15–20 percent until after 1920.[81] Much of this interstate movement was on an east-west axis until the closing of the frontier at the end of the nineteenth century. For instance, in 1850, of those born in Pennsylvania but residing elsewhere, 67 percent could be found in Ohio, Indiana, or Illinois, while 77 percent of those born in South Carolina but residing outside that state were in Georgia, Alabama, Mississippi, and Tennessee. A variety of explanations has been advanced for the migration along lati-tudes, but recently it has been shown that real and human capital invested in seed, livestock, implements, and farming techniques made movement along climatic bands much more rational. This also provides a partial explanation for the greater preference of the bulk of the nineteenth-century immigrants from northern and western Europe for the Northeast and the Midwest – their human capital matched that climatic band better.[82] That was true for those going to rural areas, at least. The remainder of the explanation was largely the greater opportunities in the more rapidly urbanizing and industrializing North, as well as the tendency of migra-tion streams, once established, to grow along familiar paths.

Agrarian motives for migration diminished as the frontier closed in the late nineteenth century and as rural population growth slowed dramati-cally (to only 0.8 percent per year over the period 1890 to 1920). For most

[81] Bureau of the Census, *Historical Statistics*, Series C1–3.
[82] Richard Steckel, "The Economic Foundations of East-West Migration during the Nineteenth Century," *Explorations in Economic History*, 20 (1983), 14–36. This does not explain *why* the ante-bellum South failed to urbanize and industrialize more rapidly. See Bateman and Weiss, *A Deplorable Scarcity*.

of the nineteenth century, migration flows westward were consistent with the land availability hypothesis discussed in connection with the fertility transition. Rural migrants moved west to secure cheaper, good-quality land. Frederick Jackson Turner's thesis that the frontier was a demographic "safety valve" in nineteenth-century America remains a durable view. Nevertheless, by late in the century, rural to urban flow assumed the dominant role. But much of the rural–urban migration was within regions or along an east–west axis, since the bulk of urban and industrial growth from the Civil War to 1920 was in the Northeast and Midwest. Notably, the South failed to increase its share of urban population over this period. The major shift to a south-to-north movement only began on a large scale with the radical shifts in demand for labor accompanying World War I and the restriction, after 1921, of cheap immigrant labor. The shift to the "sun belt" came even later, largely after World War II. Changes in transportation technology, particularly the electric street and underground railways and later the automobile and motorized bus, led to a movement out of central cities and into suburban communities. This process was underway in parts of the Northeast by the end of the nineteenth century, but really accelerated after World War I, and again after 1945. So, for instance, during the 1920s the rural part of metropolitan districts (as defined by the Bureau of the Census) increased by 55 percent, faster than any part of the metropolitan population except for small cities. This development was suburbanization.[83]

The urbanization process was accompanied by a filling out in the city size hierarchy. Large cities did tend to grow most rapidly. In 1810 there were only two cities with more than 50,000 population (New York and Philadelphia), and together they made up 29 percent of the total urban population. By 1860 there were 16 places of over 50,000 population, containing 50 percent of urban inhabitants. In 1920, the first census when more than half of the American population was urban, 144 cities exceeded 50,000 persons (with 25 over 250,000 inhabitants), and they now had 60 percent of city dwellers. The three largest cities of over one million each (New York, Chicago, Philadelphia) alone had 19 percent of America's urbanites. But the urban size hierarchy did not become distorted, as it has

[83] Morton Owen Schapiro, *Filling Up America: An Economic-Demographic Model of Population Growth and Distribution in the Nineteenth-Century United States* (Greenwich, CT, 1986); Frederick Jackson Turner, "The Significance of the Frontier in American History," paper read at the meeting of the American Historical Association, Chicago, July 12, 1893 and reprinted many times; John R. Stilgoe, *Borderland: Origins of the American Suburb, 1820–1939* (New Haven, 1988).

in some developing nations. That is, large cities did not grow such that medium and smaller urban places became unimportant. There were 213 places of 5,000 to 50,000 population in 1860, holding 41 percent of the urban inhabitants. In 1920 this number had risen to a total of 1,323 places, with 32 percent of the urban population.[84]

And this urban growth had powerful economic linkages. Considerable industrial output of the period 1865–1920 was devoted to providing infrastructure and materials to house, transport, and deliver public services for this massive population shift to towns and cities. Iron and steel for sewer and water pipe, bridges, rails, structural pieces, and nails; concrete, stone, brick, and asphalt for roads and structures; cut timber; transport equipment; glass, etc. were demanded in huge quantities to build the cities.

Migration patterns, both internal and international, did affect regional population growth rates and shares. In 1790, the North and South each had about 50 percent of total population. But differential migration and not differential natural increase began to drive the share in the North upward as slower population growth in New England was balanced by more rapid growth in New York, Pennsylvania, and later the Midwest. The Northeast and Midwest together accounted for 56 percent of the nation's inhabitants in 1830 and 62 percent in 1860, compared to 35 percent for the South at the latter date. This demographic shift alone was instrumental in the political crisis leading up to the Civil War, as southern representation in the Congress slowly ebbed.[85]

The regional preference of migrants from abroad, once they had landed in the United States, was strongly in favor of the Northeast and Midwest and not for the South. For instance, in 1860 a mere 5.6 percent of the South's white population was foreign born, while the proportion was 19.3 percent in the Northeast and 17.4 percent in the Midwest. For 1910, the proportion of foreign born living in the Northeast had risen to 26.2 percent. It had fallen to 3.5 percent in the South and held at 17.4 percent in the Midwest. Further, at the latter date, only 6.1 percent of Southern whites had a foreign-born parent or parents, whereas 30.1 percent of white residents of the Northeast were first-generation native born. This had pro-

---

[84] Bureau of the Census, *Historical Statistics*, Series A 43–72.

[85] The relative decline of the South took place despite the high natural increase of the black population, which raised the share of blacks from 35 percent of the population in 1790 to 37 percent in 1860. Legal importation of slaves was permitted up to 1808, but the real factor in black population growth was excess of births over deaths.

found political implications in terms of regional growth both before and after the Civil War. Not only did it change the Congressional balance of power, but it limited the labor supply in the South for industrial and agricultural development throughout the nineteenth and early twentieth centuries.[86] The southern share slipped even further, to 31 percent, in 1920, while the Northeast and Midwest held about steady at 60 percent. These population realignments were both cause and effect of rapid industrial growth in the postbellum era, as many of the rural migrants and most of the later immigrants were destined for northern cities.

INTERNATIONAL MIGRATION

In discussions of migration to the United States over the long nineteenth century, the flood of immigrants from Europe usually takes center stage. It was dramatic and colorful, as new arrivals added an ethnic flavor which pervades our culture today.[87] Like internal migrants, the immigrants were most often motivated by economic concerns. Labor market models of migration provide sufficient explanations for the phenomenon in circumstances other than war or serious political or environmental upheaval. Individuals and families move to maximize the present discounted net benefits of shifting to a location with better wages, incomes, and opportunities. They must factor in the costs, including direct transportation and moving expenses as well as lost earnings and psychological costs. The comparisons of these factors helps explain why migration is selective: movers tend to be younger and single and have less wealth than non-movers.[88]

The selectivity of migration is partly the cause of the sex ratio above 100 seen for the total population in the last column of Table 4.2. The sex ratio of the population (males per 100 females) was well above 100 in 1790 and increased in decades of highest immigration (the 1840s, 1850s, 1880s, and 1900s). Migration was selective of males in this case, as they were first

---

[86] Bureau of the Census, *Historical Statistics*, Series A 172–94.

[87] John Bodnar, *The Transplanted: A History of Immigrants in Urban America* (Bloomington, 1985); Malwyn Allen Jones, *American Immigration*, 2nd edition (Chicago, 1992); J. D. Gould, "European Inter-Continental Emigration, 1815–1914: Patterns and Causes," *Journal of European Economic History*, 8 (1979), 593–679; "European Inter-Continental Emigration. The Road Home: Return Migration from the U.S.A.," *Journal of European Economic History*, 9, (1980), 41–112; "European Inter-Continental Emigration: The Role of 'Diffusion' and 'Feedback'," *Journal of European Economic History*, 9 (1980), 267–315.

[88] Larry Sjaastad, "The Costs and Returns of Human Migration," *Journal of Political Economy*, 70 (1962), Supplement, 80–93.

to seek the opportunities. The sex ratio of the foreign-born white population in 1850 was 124. It was 129 in 1910. They clearly were raising the
national average.[89] The general decline of the sex ratio over time was,
however, due to the aging of the population. In a normal closed population the sex ratio at birth is about 105 male births per 100 female births.
Higher male than female mortality (at most, if not all, ages) then leads to
a slow decline in the ratio to below 100 for older age groups. Early in the
nineteenth century, the sex ratio was well above 100, since a young population (median age 16) was weighted towards groups with higher sex
ratios. With an aging population caused by declining fertility, the overall
sex ratio would fall as the population was weighted towards older age
groups with lower sex ratios. This process was offset to a degree by inflows
of migrants heavily selective of males (with the exception of the years of
the Great Depression of the 1930s).

Push and pull factors operate in the migration arena, although it is often
difficult to disentangle the simultaneous effects of push and pull.[90] From
this perspective one could ask whether it was poor conditions in nineteenth
century Europe (push) or the expanding opportunities in the United States
(pull) that propelled millions of souls to make the long and difficult
journey? A clue lies in the waves of migration that characterized the
period. While not easily apparent from Table 4.5, there were decades in
which migration surged: the 1840s, 1850s, 1880s, and the period
1900/14. These surges can be seen clearly in Figure 4.1, which plots the
annual numbers of officially recorded migrants from 1820 to 1940.
Upswings in in-migration corresponded to periods of relative prosperity
in the American economy: the boom beginning in 1843 and lasting until
the panic of 1857; the post–Civil War economic upsurge (1865–1873);
the economic peaks of the 1880s; and the prolonged prosperity from the
end of the 1890s until the end of World War I. The fall off in the 1920s
reflects the new restrictive legislation. Similarly, migration troughs corresponded to the panics of 1837, 1857, 1873, and the sustained economic
dislocations of the 1890s. It is not surprising that the uncertain prospects
of the American Civil War should have led to a fall off in migration,
though recovery in the flows commenced before the end of the war. In
sum, waves of immigration were roughly synchronous with long swings

---

[89] One exception was the 1930s, when the Great Depression reduced demand for labor and, consequently, reduced the flow of migrants from abroad. The sex ratio changed in favor of females in
that decade as opportunities for new employment for males fell drastically.

[90] J. D. Gould, "European Inter-Continental Emigration, 1815–1914: Patterns and Causes."

Table 4.5. *Recorded immigration to the United States by origin, 1819–1920 (in 000s)*

Period	Total	Origins: All Europe	North & West	East & Central	South	Other	America	Asia	Australia New Zealand	Pacific Islands	Africa
1819–20	8	8	8	—	—	—	—	—	—	—	—
1821–30	143	99	96	—	3	—	12	—	—	—	—
1831–40	599	496	490	—	5	—	33	—	—	—	—
1841–50	1,713	1,598	1,592	1	5	—	62	—	—	—	—
1851–60	2,598	2,453	2,431	2	20	—	75	41	—	—	—
1861–70	2,315	2,065	2,032	12	21	—	167	65	—	—	—
1871–80	2,812	2,272	2,070	126	75	1	404	124	10	1	1
1881–90	5,247	4,737	3,779	627	331	1	427	68	7	6	—
1891–1900	3,688	3,559	1,643	1,211	704	—	39	71	3	1	7
1901–10	8,795	8,136	1,910	3,915	2,310	1	362	244	12	1	7
1911–20	5,736	4,377	998	1,918	1,452	8	1,144	193	12	1	8

Percentage Shares

Period	Total	Origins: All Europe	North & West	East & Central	South	Other	America	Asia	Australia New Zealand	Pacific Islands	Africa
1819–20	100.0%	100.0%	100.0%	—	—	—	—	—	—	—	—
1821–30	100.0%	69.2%	67.1%	—	2.1%	—	8.4%	—	—	—	—
1831–40	100.0%	82.8%	81.8%	—	0.8%	—	5.5%	—	—	—	—
1841–50	100.0%	93.3%	92.9%	0.1%	0.3%	—	3.6%	—	—	—	—
1851–60	100.0%	94.4%	93.6%	0.1%	0.8%	—	2.9%	1.6%	—	—	—
1861–70	100.0%	89.2%	87.8%	0.5%	0.9%	—	7.2%	2.8%	—	—	—
1871–80	100.0%	80.8%	73.6%	4.5%	2.7%	0.0%	14.4%	4.4%	0.4%	0.0%	0.0%
1881–90	100.0%	90.3%	72.0%	11.9%	6.3%	0.0%	8.1%	1.3%	0.1%	0.1%	—
1891–1900	100.0%	96.5%	44.5%	32.8%	19.1%	—	1.1%	1.9%	0.1%	0.0%	0.1%
1901–10	100.0%	92.5%	21.7%	44.5%	26.3%	0.0%	4.1%	2.8%	0.1%	0.0%	0.1%
1911–20	100.0%	76.3%	17.4%	33.4%	25.3%	0.1%	19.9%	3.4%	0.2%	0.0%	0.1%

Source: Conrad Taeuber and Irene B. Taeuber, *The Changing Population of the United States* (New York, 1958), 53, 57. Prior to 1871, totals are not always for calendar years.

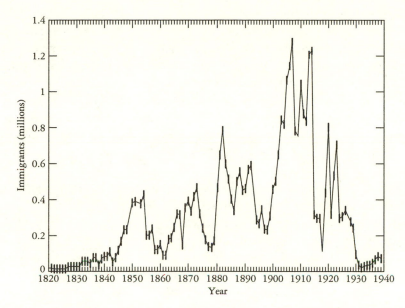

Figure 4.1. Immigrants to the United States, 1820–1940. Source: U.S. Bureau of the Census, *Historical Statistics of the United States from Colonial Times to 1970* (Washington, DC, 1975), Series C89.

in economic activity in the United States. It is also of importance to consider migration to the United States as one part of a global labor market that emerged in the second half of the nineteenth century.[91]

Long swings (of about fifteen to twenty-five years in duration) were historically associated with construction cycles and need to be distinguished from the shorter business cycle (of about eight to ten years in duration) or even shorter inventory cycles. The roughly synchronous cyclical movements in the economies of the United States and the European countries of migrant origin point to the dominance of pull factors in the United States rather than push factors from Europe since favorable conditions generally existed on both sides of the Atlantic during upswings in migrant flows to the United States. If, in times of relative prosperity in Europe, migrants left in increased numbers, then American labor market conditions were the dominant factor. An important exception was the great

[91] See, for example, Timothy J. Hatton and Jeffrey G. Williamson, *The Age of Mass Migration: Causes and Economic Impact* (New York, 1998).

potato famine of the later 1840s. It was not just confined to Ireland, but also affected the continent of Europe, particularly Germany, Scandinavia, and the Netherlands, where the potato had become an important part of the diet. Here push factors were more clearly at work. Analysis of the cycles in migration to the United States in the nineteenth century has found that migration had a close correlation with such sensitive cyclical indicators as miles of railroad constructed in the United States and railroad rails consumed.[92] There is also evidence, albeit more sketchy, that long swings in economic activity and demand for labor also affected interstate migration flows.

Figure 4.1 also points to a long-term upward trend in gross migration across the Atlantic. Average migration increased from about 14,000 persons per year in the 1820s to almost 260,000 per year in the 1850s to approximately one million annually in the peak years 1911/14, an average growth of 4.9 percent per annum between the 1820s and 1911/14 – very rapid indeed. Over one million migrants entered the United States in six of the fourteen years before the First World War erupted in Europe in 1914. These magnitudes have not been exceeded for recorded, legal migration until very recently.

This substantial secular increase was assisted by technological improvements in transportation. In the early to mid-nineteenth century, the transatlantic passage on sailing vessels could take up to several weeks and cost a substantial fraction of the annual income of a peasant or manual worker. The replacement of wooden square-riggers by larger iron- or steel-hulled vessels with steam power and screw propellers reduced the passage to about ten days in the 1870s and about a week in 1900. Transatlantic passenger fares became cheaper over the century, as did those on railroads and vessels on the inland waterways of both the United States and Europe.

This reduction in the barriers of time and cost also led to increases in return migration. For the five-year period 1908/12, when information about return migration first became available, there were 4.75 alien arrivals and 2.36 million departures of non-citizens, giving a return rate

---

[92] Richard A. Easterlin, "Influences in European Overseas Emigration before World War I," *Economic Development and Cultural Change*, 9 (1961), 331–53; ". . . typically, the swings in migration were a response to corresponding swings in the demand for labor in the United States," Richard A. Easterlin, *Population, Labor Force, and Long Swings in Economic Growth: The American Experience* (New York, 1968), 30–31 and ch. 2; Larry Neal, "Cross-spectral Analysis of Long Swings in Atlantic Migration," *Research in Economic History*, 1 (1976), 260–97; J. D. Gould, "European Inter-Continental Emigration, 1815–1914: Patterns and Causes."

of about 50 percent. This is a somewhat neglected feature of immigration history, but it was quite important. For Italy, one of the best documented and quantitatively significant cases, over 43 percent of all migrants who left for the United States in the 1880s returned to Italy. This "repatriation ratio" rose to 53 percent in the first decade of the twentieth century and to 63 percent during 1910/1920. Overall, it seems that, by the late nineteenth century, one Italian migrant returned home for every two who left for the United States. This proportion was even higher for non-Jewish migrants from Greece, Hungary, Russia, and the Balkans. Jewish migrants tended to stay, largely because of the greater freedom and lesser fear of persecution. The reasons for return were varied. A large number of migrants planned to return after having earned a "nest egg." Others became unsatisfied with their lot in the New World or longed for friends, family, and familiar landscapes.[93]

Another salient feature of immigration to America apparent in Table 4.5 is the changing composition of the flows across the long nineteenth century. For the decades between 1821 and 1890, 82 percent of all immigrants originated in northern and western Europe and only 8 percent in central, eastern, and southern Europe.[94] For the three decades 1891 to 1920, the situation had altered dramatically: only 25 percent of the migrants came from northern and western Europe and 64 percent from central, eastern, and southern Europe. This was termed by contemporaries as the shift from the "old" to the "new" immigration. This shift in composition, along with the strong upward trend in migration, spurred the formation of the U.S. Immigration Commission of 1907/10 and probably to immigration restriction. Thompson and whelpton estimate that, at the time of the first federal census in 1790, 90 percent of the white population was ultimately of northern and western European origin, with 77 percent from Great Britain and Ireland alone. Their definition excluded Germany, which was the origin of 7.4 percent of the 1790 population. By 1920, northern and western Europe (excluding Germany) was the origin of only about 63 percent of the American population (41 percent from Britain and Northern Ireland) with 27 percent having their ancestry in

[93] J. D. Gould, "European Inter-Continental Emigration. The Road Home: Return Migration from the U.S.A."; "European Inter-Continental Emigration: The Role of 'Diffusion' and 'Feedback'."

[94] Northern and western Europe are defined here as Great Britain (England, Wales, Scotland); Ireland; the German states and, after 1871, the German Empire; Sweden; Norway; Denmark; Belgium, the Netherlands; France; and Switzerland. Central, eastern, and southern Europe would include Austria-Hungary; Russia; Italy; Greece; the Balkan states; European parts of the Ottoman Empire; Spain; and Portugal.

central and eastern Europe (16.3 percent from Germany) and 4.5 percent in southern Europe.[95]

Why did this shift to the "new" immigration occur? As modern economic growth progressed in many of the original sending nations of northern and western Europe, growth in demand for labor in their domestic economies improved and absorbed many of those who would have migrated abroad. The decline of the size and share of the agrarian sectors in these economies also contributed, since many of the migrants came from rural areas. Germany is an excellent case in point. In the 1880s, 1,342,000 Germans emigrated. This number dropped to 527,000 in the 1890s and to 274,000 in the 1900s.[96] The decline coincided with Germany's rapid emergence as an urbanized industrial power. The increase in outflows from central, eastern, and southern Europe began as these nations (Austria-Hungary, Russia, the Balkan states, Italy) began to experience the dislocations associated with modern economic growth and structural change. There is, however, also the persuasive argument that only late in the nineteenth century did the feedback of information about migration opportunities diffuse widely in southern and eastern Europe. This, combined with cheaper fares and shorter and less hazardous journeys by railway and steamship, led to an upsurge in "migration fever." Legal and institutional barrier to out-migration were also reduced or eliminated in many of these nations from the late nineteenth century onward.[97]

There was considerable nativist opposition to these migrants. The "Know Nothing" or American Party, which flourished in the 1840s and 1850s, proposed anti-alien and anti-Catholic legislation, particularly directed at the Irish. Similar groups arose in the 1870s and 1880s, including in California, where hostility to Chinese immigration was strong. As the labor movement grew, there were calls for immigration restriction from that quarter, which is understandable, since the more rapid expansion in the supply of labor provided by immigrants restricted the growth of real wages, raised unemployment, and made labor organizing more difficult. The short-lived National Labor Union (1866–1872) advocated limits to immigration as well as repeal of the Contract Labor Law (1864). The latter allowed employers to advance the costs of passage to prospective immigrant workers. The American Federation of Labor (founded

---

[95] Thompson and Whelpton, *Population Trends in the United States*, p. 91.

[96] Brian R. Mitchell, *European Historical Statistics, 1750–1975*, second revised edition (New York, 1981), Table B8.

[97] J. D. Gould, "European Inter-Continental Emigration: The Role of 'Diffusion' and 'Feedback'."

1886) long campaigned for quotas on immigration. Nonetheless, between the Alien Act of 1798 (only briefly in force) and the Immigration Act of 1917, which imposed a literacy test, virtually nothing was done to restrict European immigration to the United States. Although migrants had to register with ships' masters (after 1819) and had to be screened for diseases, criminal records, or the possibility of becoming a public charge (after 1891), there was basically an "open door." A notable exception was the Chinese Exclusion Act of 1882 (renewed 1892 and made indefinite in 1902), directly aimed at cutting off the flow of East Asian migrants to the west coast. The literacy test imposed in 1917 over Woodrow Wilson's veto was merely a forerunner of the much more restrictive Emergency Immigration Act of 1921, which imposed quotas based on national origins. Immigration was limited annually to 3 percent of each nation's share of the American population in 1910. An even more narrow law was enacted in 1924, which reduced the annual quota per country to 2 percent of a nation's share of the U.S. population in 1890, clearly favoring the nations of northern and western Europe at the expense of the areas of the "new" immigration. All immigration from East Asia was terminated. In 1929, the quotas were ultimately to be based on the census of 1920 but for a total not to exceed 150,000 per year, in contrast to the levels in excess of a million a year in the years just prior to World War I.[98]

It is interesting to speculate why, after such a long period of open immigration and of strong business and employer opposition to immigration restriction, that there would have been such a rapid change in direction around 1920. The cumulative reaction to the new immigration and the increase in immigration flows since 1900 likely played a role. Labor unions were gaining some legislative influence, as the instance of the Clayton Act of 1914 (exempting them from the Sherman Antitrust Act) shows. But union influence waned after the war, as the failure of the large steel strike of 1919 and the decline in union membership in the 1920s attest. More important, the war itself, the postwar "red scare," and especially the discovery by employers that they had a large pool of lower-skilled workers in the rural South were more significant. Further, the rationalization of manufacturing production was underway, reducing the need for additional labor as organizational change, further mechanization, and other technological change greatly improved productivity. For example, manufacturing output subsequently grew by 53 percent between 1919 and 1929,

---

[98] E. P. Hutchinson, *Legislative History of American Immigration Policy, 1798–1965* (Philadelphia, 1981).

while the manufacturing labor force was virtually stationary over the same period.[99]

It is true that immigrants did tend to be disproportionately in lower-skill occupational groups. In 1910, the foreign-born white population was 21 percent of the labor force, but they were 37 percent of all laborers. Only 20 percent of them were white-collar workers, as opposed to 41 percent of the native whites of native parentage. Relatively few of them were proprietors, especially since only a small number went into agriculture. But the foreign born and their second-generation offspring did make up 44 percent of all white-collar workers and 54 percent of all craftsmen and operatives.[100] Even though they did occupy a disproportionate share of the lower-skill and lower-status positions, they made possible, in some sense, the better-paid, higher-status occupations of the native white population.

Things did improve as the foreign-born white population and their children assimilated to the patterns of labor force activity, occupations, and residence of the native whites of native parentage. A series of mobility studies has been done since the 1960s on the geographic and occupation mobility of Americans. Beginning with the pioneering work of Thernstrom on Newburyport and Boston, Massachusetts, these mobility studies have used a variety of nominal record sources (census manuscripts, city directories, voter lists, tax and property rolls) to link individual records. Although fraught with difficulties, such studies have found a high degree of geographic mobility, particularly for urban areas, in the nineteenth and early twentieth centuries. For Newburyport, almost the entire population of 1850 had gone by 1880, both through natural attrition and through migration (as well as linkage failure). For Boston in the period 1880–1920, net migration made up two thirds of the population growth. There was less occupational mobility, both within the lifetimes of individuals and also across generations, but the results have indicated significant rates of upward occupational mobility, both among the native and the foreign born. Overall, about 10–30 percent of sons of working-class fathers were able to advance to higher-income and/or higher-status positions over the period 1830–1920. Over time this would have a telling effect, and the foreign born, even the relatively unskilled, did have some

[99] Bureau of the Census, *Historical Statistics*, Series D130 (employees on manufacturing payrolls) and P13 (the Federal Reserve Board index of manufacturing production).

[100] Easterlin, "The American Population," in Lance Davis, Richard A. Easterlin, William N. Parker, et al., *American Economic Growth: An Economist's History of the United States* (New York, 1972), Tables 5.7 and 5.8.

real prospects of upward socioeconomic progress. More recent studies, using censuses, immigrant ship lists, property rolls, pension records, and genealogies, are exploring mobility further. A national mobility study has linked about 40 percent of approximately 10,000 men from the 1880 to the 1900 manuscript censuses. Considerable geographic mobility was confirmed, and the rate of occupational mobility among the non-farm population was considerable, not differing greatly from those found in the middle of the twentieth century.[101]

SUMMARY AND CONCLUSIONS

This chapter has focused on the evolution of the American population over the "long" nineteenth century, 1790–1920. The discussion has perforce covered fertility, marriage, mortality, and both internal and international migration. The relatively rapid population growth over this period (averaging 2.5 percent per year) was driven largely by high (though declining) birth rates and moderate levels of mortality, but immigration was also significant. About three quarters of the growth was due to natural increase and about a quarter to net in-migration. Over 34 million persons entered the United States between the 1790s and the end of World War I.

Family sizes were large in the early days of the republic, being about seven children per woman for the white population and between seven and eight children per black slave mother in the 1850s. There was a sustained decline in white birth rates from at least 1800 and for black birth rates from at least mid-century. The fertility decline proceeded in both rural and urban areas. Conventional explanations for the fertility transition have

---

[101] A summary of these mobility studies (up to 1977) may be found in Hartmut Kaelble, *Historical Research on Social Mobility: Western Europe and the USA in the Nineteenth and Twentieth Centuries* (New York, 1981). The results for Massachusetts refer to Stephan Thernstrom, *Poverty and Progress: Social Mobility in a Nineteenth Century City* (Cambridge, MA, 1964) and *The Other Bostonians: Poverty and Progress in the American Metropolis, 1880–1970* (Cambridge, MA, 1973). For a recent study using genealogies, see Adams and Kasakoff, "Migration and the Family in Colonial New England." For more recent census linkage studies, see Richard Steckel, "Household Migration and Rural Settlement in the United States, 1850–1860," *Explorations in Economic History*, 26 (1989), 190–218, and David W. Galenson and Clayne L. Pope, "Economic and Geographic Mobility on the Farming Frontier: Evidence from Appanoose County, Iowa, 1850–1870," *Journal of Economic History*, 49 (1989), 635–56 and "Precedence and Wealth: Evidence from Nineteenth-Century Utah," in Goldin and Rockoff, eds., *Strategic Factors in Nineteenth Century American Economic History*, 225–42. The 1880–1900 national panel study is discussed in Avery M. Guest, "Notes from the National Panel Study: Linkage and Migration in the Late Nineteenth Century," *Historical Methods*, 20 (1987), 63–77 and Avery M. Guest, Nancy S. Landale, and James McCann, "Intergenerational Occupational Mobility in the Late Nineteenth Century United States" (unpublished paper).

involved such factors as the rising cost of children because of urbanization, growth of incomes and non-agricultural employment, increased value of education, rising female employment, child labor laws and compulsory education, and declining infant and child mortality. In addition, changing attitudes towards large families and towards contraception, as well as better contraceptive technologies, are also cited. Such structural explanations do well for the American experience since the late nineteenth century, but they are less appropriate for the fertility decline in rural, agrarian areas prior to about 1870. The increased scarcity and higher cost of good agricultural land has been proposed as a prime factor, although the explanation remains controversial. The standard explanations are also not adequate to explain the post–World War II "baby boom" and subsequent "baby bust." One fruitful alternative has been to examine the increase of non-agricultural opportunities in farming areas, and the effect of these opportunities on parent-child bargaining over bequests and old age support for the parents.

Mortality did not begin its *sustained* decline until the 1870s. Prior to that, death rates fluctuated in response to periodic epidemics and changes in the disease environment. There is even evidence of rising death rates during the 1840s and 1850s. Expectation of life at age 20 may have fallen by 10 percent between the 1830s and the 1850s.[102] The demographic transition in the United States was thus characterized by the fertility decline prior to the mortality decline, unlike the standard model. The mortality decline since the late nineteenth century was particularly promoted by improvements in public health and sanitation, especially better water supplies and sewage disposal. The improving diet, clothing, and shelter of the American population over the period since about 1870 also played a role. Specific medical interventions beyond more general environmental public health were not as important until well into the twentieth century. While it is difficult to disentangle the precise effects of these different causal factors, much of the mortality decline was due to rapid reductions in specific infectious and parasitic diseases, including tuberculosis, pneumonia, bronchitis, and gastrointestinal infections, as well as such well-known conditions as cholera, smallpox, diphtheria, and typhoid fever. In the nineteenth century, urban areas were especially unhealthy places, especially the largest cities. Rural areas and small towns had the most salubrious environment. These circumstances began to change by about the 1890s,

---

[102] Pope, "Adult Mortality in America before 1900," Table 9.4.

when the largest cities instituted effective large public works sanitation projects and public health administration. The largest cities then experienced the most rapid improvements in death rates. Rural–urban mortality differentials have converged and largely disappeared, unlike those between whites and blacks.

Migration has been a fact of life for Americans. Within the nation's boundaries, there has been significant movement east to west, following the frontier (until the late nineteenth century); from rural to urban areas; and, later, from central cities to suburbs, from South to North, and ultimately to the "sun belt." These developments have been responsible for changing the United States from a rural to an urban nation: from only 5 percent urban in 1790 to over half urban in 1920 and over three-quarters urban today. The population shifted from the original areas of settlement on the Atlantic coast to the center of the nation and later to the Pacific and Mountain states. Migration from abroad, first from western and northern Europe and then, after about 1890, from central, eastern, and southern Europe, came in waves in response to upswings in business cycles and the expansion of economic opportunities in the United States. This flood of immigrants both directly augmented population growth rates and indirectly acted to raise birth rates, before it was severely restricted in the 1920s by legislation and subsequently by the Great Depression. But it left an indelible stamp on the American economy, society, and culture.

5

THE LABOR FORCE IN THE NINETEENTH CENTURY

ROBERT A. MARGO

American economic growth in the nineteenth century was the wonder of the Western world. Over the course of the century the growth rate of national product averaged 3.5 to 4.0 percent per year, far higher than in England or other European countries. Compared with the twentieth century, nineteenth-century American growth owed much more to increases in factor supplies than technological change. Of the three major productive inputs – labor, natural resources, and capital – increases in the supply of labor account for the largest fraction of aggregate growth in the nineteenth century: twice as important as capital accumulation, five times as important as additions to the stock of natural resources. If it is true that labor makes a nation's wealth, few better examples could be found than the American economy of the nineteenth century.

This chapter surveys the major developments in the American labor force in the nineteenth century: its size and composition; rewards to labor; and labor relations, within firms and with the government. The scope of the chapter is deliberately wide, with an underlying emphasis on aspects of change important in the subsequent development of the labor force in the twentieth century. For example, I give considerable attention to trends in nonfarm wages because a majority of American workers in the late twentieth century are employed in nonfarm industries. In keeping with this theme,

I am grateful to T. Aldrich Finegan, Gerald Friedman, Bruce Laurie, Stanley Lebergott, Joshua Rosenbloom, and seminar participants at the National Bureau of Economic Research for helpful comments, and to Gerald Friedman, Joshua Rosenbloom, and Thomas Weiss for providing me with unpublished research materials. This paper was written in the early 1990s but has not appeared until now due to delays in publication beyond my control. I have attempted to update the bibliography and text, where appropriate, to take account of more recent research, but the bulk of the discussion reflects my interpretation of the literature at the time the paper was originally written.

the chapter concludes with a snapshot view of labor markets at the turn of the twentieth century compared with labor markets today.

THE LABOR FORCE, 1800–1900

This part of the chapter discusses the size, composition, and structure of the nineteenth-century labor force. Before turning to this task, it is useful to review how the nineteenth-century labor force is measured. For the census years 1870 to 1900 measurement is based on the "gainful worker": persons reporting an occupation to census enumerators. Various studies suggest that the gainful worker concept probably gives a larger estimate of the size of the labor force at any point in time than the measurement concept used today (the "labor force week").[1]

Before 1870 the occupation detail in the decennial censuses is not sufficient to apply the gainful worker concept rigorously for all census years. Procedures have been developed to infer labor force participation rates for specific population groups before 1870. Estimates of the size of the labor force are then built up piece by piece, by applying these group-specific participation rates to population figures.

Trends in Size

Table 5.1 gives the best current estimates of the aggregate labor force, population, and the aggregate labor force participation rate for the census years 1800 to 1900. In 1800 about 1.7 million persons were in the labor force, or 32 percent of the population. By 1900 the labor force had swollen to 29.1 million, fully 38 percent of the population. Over the century the labor force grew at an average annual rate of 2.8 percent. Growth was faster before the Civil War (3.1 percent per annum from 1800 to 1860) than after (2.4 percent per annum from 1860 to 1900). Growth also varied across decades. The labor force jumped during the 1840s but grew slowly during the 1860s.

Despite the long-term slowdown in the growth rate of the labor force, the aggregate labor force participation rate (the ratio of labor force to population) increased by 6 percentage points over the century. All of the

---

[1] The "labor force week" concept measures the size of labor force according to whether an individual was employed or actively looking for work during a specified period of time, usually the week of the survey.

Table 5.1. *Labor force and population in the United States, 1800–1900*

	Labor force	Population	LFPR × 100 (percent)
1800	1,712	5,308	32.3%
1810	2,337	7,240	32.3
1820	3,150	9,638	33.7
1830	4,272	12,866	33.2
1840	5,778	17,069	33.9
1850	8,192	23,192	35.3
1860	11,290	31,443	35.9
1870	12,809	38,558	33.2
1880	17,392	50,156	34.7
1890	23,547	62,948	37.4
1900	29,073	75,995	38.3

Source: Labor Force: unpublished estimates of Thomas Weiss; Population: Total population, U.S. Bureau of the Census, *Historical Statistics of the United States, Colonial Times to 1970* (Washington, DC, 1975), series A-2, 8; LFPR (labor force participation rate): Labor Force/Population.

increase before the Civil War occurred in the 1840s. The postbellum increase commenced in 1870, with most occurring after 1880. The economic significance of the postbellum increase in the aggregate participation rate can be judged by its impact on per capita income growth. If the aggregate participation rate in 1900 had equaled its value in 1870, the rate of growth of per capita income between 1870 and 1900 would have been lower by 20 percent.

The timing of the decadal changes in aggregate participation suggests that cycles in immigration affected the growth of the nineteenth-century labor force, a conclusion that is documented in the next section of the chapter. The 1840s witnessed a sharp jump in immigrant arrivals compared with the 1830s, while immigration was curtailed in the 1860s because of the Civil War. Huge waves of immigrants, primarily from southern and eastern Europe, arrived after 1880. On an annual basis, immigration was closely tied to business cycle conditions in the United States and the sending country, so that bad times in the United States (compared with Europe) slowed the rate of immigration. During expansionary phases of the American business cycle, immigration to the United States surged.

Variations in Labor Force Participation

Information on variations in labor force participation across population groups is more abundant for the late nineteenth century, particularly from census data. Sufficient evidence exists, however, to sketch out various patterns for the antebellum period.

For free males ages 15 and over, participation in the labor force (in the gainful worker sense) was near universal: the participation rate was close to 90 percent. For free males between the ages of 10 and 14, the participation rate was sharply lower, around 18 percent. The lower participation rate among children was a consequence of school attendance, and the fact that relatively few children were engaged in a gainful occupation according to the census definition, although many, perhaps most, worked on the family farm or in family businesses.

For free females ages 16 and over, a rough estimate suggests a participation rate of about 8 percent at the start of the nineteenth century.[2] By mid-century the participation rate had climbed to about 11 percent, reflecting economic developments that created job opportunities in the market economy for young, single women. Chief among these opportunities was the emergence of factory employment. Others found work as domestic servants or teachers. North–South differences were pronounced: few young women in the South worked in factories, and relatively fewer than in the North were employed as teachers. Participation rates for married women were very low throughout the first half of the century (5 percent or less), although research suggests they may have been somewhat higher in the late 1700s.

For slaves over age 10, the labor force participation rate was around 90 percent, with virtually none of the age or gender differences evident among the free population. The absence of age and gender differences in participation among slaves meant that their aggregate participation rate was markedly higher than that of free labor. The abolition of slavery at the end of the Civil War brought a sharp decline in the measured labor force participation rate of former slaves, as black women and children reduced their labor force activity once they were free to do so.

The public use sample of the 1880 census enables a detailed look at labor force participation at approximately the midpoint of the second half of the nineteenth century. Table 5.2 gives participation rates derived from

[2] Recall that "participation" means market work in the gainful worker sense; there is no question that free women labored at home or on family farms, among other activities.

Table 5.2. *Labor force participation in 1880*

Adults (ages 20 and over)

Age	Men N	Men LFPR	Women N	Women LFPR
20–24	2,568	90.5%	2,382	24.0%
25–34	3,708	96.3	3,430	14.5
35–44	2,670	96.8	2,712	11.2
45–54	1,969	96.6	1,850	11.6
55–59	659	95.6	1,594	11.1
60–64	564	90.3	474	8.7
65–74	645	82.6	595	5.5
>=75	263	58.2	282	4.6
White	11,360	93.2	10,685	10.5
Black	1,686	96.1	1,639	37.8
Native	10,058	93.5	9,891	14.2
Foreign	2,998	93.9	2,433	14.0
Unmarried	4,579	88.6	4,141	31.2
Married	8,467	96.2	8,183	5.5
Rural	8,990	93.7	8,230	10.9
Urban	4,056	93.3	4,094	20.7
Total	13,046	93.6	12,324	14.1

Children and young adults (ages 10 to 19)

Age	N	LFPR	N	LFPR
10	670	14.5%	566	7.2%
11	525	20.0	529	5.7
12	593	30.2	576	9.6
13	547	33.6	504	10.3
14	542	43.4	510	14.3
15–19	2,391	68.7	2,486	26.6
White	4,503	43.1	4,400	13.1
Black	765	65.5	771	43.7
Native	4,949	45.9	4,877	16.7
Foreign	319	53.6	294	32.7
Unmarried	5,246	46.2	4,896	18.1
Married	22	95.5	275	10.2
At School	2,830	24.7	2,606	5.2
Rural	3,956	48.5	3,749	15.4
Urban	1,312	39.9	1,422	23.5
Total	5,268	46.4	5,171	17.7

Note: LFPR: percent reporting a gainful occupation. At school: attended school during the census year.
Source: Steven Ruggles and Russell Menard, 1880 Public Use Sample.

the sample for various population groups. Labor force participation among adult men (ages 20 and over) remained close to universal, declining only after age 65. By modern standards, however, participation rates among the elderly were very high; "retirement," in other words, was far less common than today. Among adult women, participation was more a function of age than among adult men, and also of race, marital status, and urban-rural status. Black women were much more likely to be in the labor force than white women. A study drawing upon the census manuscripts for 1870 and 1880 shows that the racial difference was partly due to the lower economic status of adult black men, and that some of the difference was a legacy of slavery. The participation rate of married women remained low, around 5 percent, or 26 percentage points below the participation rate of unmarried women. Women in urban areas were much more likely to report a gainful occupation than were rural women.

Among children and young adults (ages 10 to 19), labor force participation was a function of age, gender, race, and ethnicity. Labor force participation among children under age 15 was much higher than today, reflecting the absence of effective child labor legislation and much lower levels of formal schooling.[3] Males entered the labor force in large numbers around age 15, and were more than twice as likely as females in the age group to participate in the labor force. Black children had higher participation rates than white children. The same contrast is evident among foreign and native-born children: because the foreign-born population was older, the gap in participation between the foreign- and native-born was even greater in the aggregate than among children. Urban males had lower participation rates than rural males, but the opposite was true among females; the gender difference was such that, in the aggregate, urban-rural status had no effect on the participation rate.

Thus labor force participation in the nineteenth century was sharply delineated by age, ethnic, racial, and gender differences. These differences suggest three factors behind the long-term upward trend in aggregate participation noted in the previous section. First, because fertility fell throughout the nineteenth century, the composition of the population shifted toward adults of working age. Second, immigration raised the aggregate participation rate, in two ways: foreign-born children had higher participation rates than native-born children, and the foreign-born were

---

[3] The extent of child labor is understated by the gainful occupation rate, since many children who labored on the family farm or in family-run enterprises without pay probably did not report a gainful occupation.

more likely to be adults. Third, urbanization raised the aggregate participation rate by increasing the fraction of women who held gainful occupations.

Structure

The structure of the labor force refers to the distribution of workers across industries or occupations. By far the most important change affecting the structure of the labor force in the nineteenth century was the shift of labor out of agriculture. Table 5.3 shows the percent in agriculture at census years intervals. In 1800 approximately three-quarters of the labor force was engaged in agriculture. Agriculture's share of the labor force fell by 14 percentage points between 1800 and 1850. The shift out of agriculture accelerated in the second half of the century. By 1900 only 36 percent of the workforce was employed in farming. The shift out of agriculture varied across regions. New England led the way, with less than 40 percent of its workers in farming on the eve of the Civil War. The South was the only region to have a majority of workers in farming at century's end.

Economic historians have explained the shift of labor out of agriculture by appealing to technological change and the nature of demand for agricultural goods. Technological change increased the productivity of labor

Table 5.3. *Agriculture's share of the labor force*

	U.S.	NE	MA	MW	SA	SC	WS
1800	0.744	0.680	0.707	0.865	0.786	0.823	na
1810	0.723	0.631	0.663	0.838	0.784	0.792	na
1820	0.714	0.631	0.616	0.786	0.784	0.803	na
1830	0.698	0.591	0.582	0.803	0.777	0.782	na
1840	0.672	0.538	0.545	0.763	0.743	0.768	na
1850	0.597	0.386	0.423	0.669	0.739	0.749	0.228
1860	0.558	0.313	0.348	0.621	0.721	0.739	0.306
1870	0.498	0.246	0.276	0.547	0.716	0.725	0.337
1880	0.477	0.205	0.231	0.525	0.711	0.737	0.324
1890	0.401	0.154	0.172	0.429	0.625	0.668	0.294
1900	0.361	0.120	0.133	0.369	0.587	0.640	0.275

Note: NE: New England; MA: Mid-Atlantic; MW: Midwest; SA: South Atlantic; SC: South Central; WS: West; na: estimate not available.
Source: Unpublished estimates of Thomas Weiss.

in agricultural and nonagricultural occupations. However, the demand for agricultural goods was relatively inelastic with respect to price and to income; conversely, the demand for nonagricultural goods was relatively elastic. Increases in agricultural productivity reduced the value of the marginal product of labor in agriculture relative to other sectors. To restore equilibrium, labor migrated out of agriculture.

Where did the labor go? In terms of numbers, manufacturing was by far the most important sector on the receiving end. Essentially nonexistent before 1820, manufacturing employed slightly less than a third of all nonfarm workers by 1840. The proportion in manufacturing reached 37 percent in 1860, where it more or less remained for the rest of the century. Employment in mining, wholesale and retail trade, and construction also grew rapidly. Between 1840 and 1900 employment in mining increased at an average annual rate of 5.0 percent; growth in trade and construction employment over the same period was a bit slower but still brisk (4.0 and 2.9 percent per year, respectively).[4]

Table 5.4 shows the distribution of employment across industries in 1900. After manufacturing, trade and transportation claimed the most workers, about 32 percent. Services, including government employed another 20 percent, followed by mining and construction (12 percent).

The distribution of employment by occupation classifies the labor force in a manner more closely related to worker skills than the distribution by industry. Although some information on occupations was collected in the 1820 and 1840 censuses, the data were very crude and not readily comparable to later census years. A glimpse at the structure of occupations at mid-century can be gleaned from the published volumes of the 1850 census. The figures pertain to free males, ages 15 and over; similar data for females, unfortunately, cannot be extracted from the published census volumes.[5]

Table 5.5 lists the ten principal occupations in 1850. Approximately half of the census respondents declared themselves to be farmers. Laborers were the next most common workers, making up nearly 17 percent of all

---

[4] Growth rates of employment in mining, trade, and construction were calculated from Stanley Lebergott, *Manpower in Economic Growth* (New York, 1964), 510, figures on the structure of the labor force. If Lebergott's estimates of the total nonfarm labor force are adjusted on the basis of Weiss' revisions, the growth rates reported in the text would be slightly higher.

[5] The census did not collect occupational information on slaves. Other records suggest that between 20 and 30 percent of adult male slaves held semi-skilled or skilled occupations; the majority, however, were field hands. For evidence on slave occupations, see Robert W. Fogel, *Without Consent or Contract: The Rise and Fall of American Slavery*, Vol. I (New York, 1989), 6.

Table 5.4. *Distribution of nonfarm employment by industry, 1900*

Mining	4.2%
Construction	7.6
Manufacturing	36.0
Transportation, Communications, and Public Utilities	15.0
Wholesale and Retail Trade	16.5
Finance, Insurance, and Real Estate	2.0
Business Services	11.5
Government	7.2

Source: Calculated from Bureau of the Census *Historical Statistics*, Series D-127 to D-141, 137.

Table 5.5. *The ten principal occupations in 1850: free males ages 15 and over*

	Number	Percent of Total
Blacksmiths	99,703	1.9%
Carpenters	184,671	3.4
Clerks	101,325	1.9
Cordwainers	130,473	2.4
Farmers	2,363,958	44.0
Laborers	909,786	16.9
Mariners	103,473	2.0
Masons	63,342	1.2
Miners	77,410	1.4
Merchants	100,752	1.9

Source: Computed from J. D. B. DeBow, *Compendium of the Seventh Census* (Washington, DC, 1854), 126–27.

occupations reported. Blacksmiths, carpenters, masons, and plasterers made up 6.5 percent of free male workers. Clerks and merchants, the biggest white-collar occupations, comprised another 3.8 percent. The remainder of workers labored at the several hundred additional trades listed in the 1850 volumes.

Table 5.6 shows the distribution of occupations in 1900. Approximately 40 percent of males were in agriculture. Among males in nonfarm occupations, 30 percent held white-collar occupations, primarily as managers

Table 5.6. *Distribution of occupations in 1900*

	Male		Female		Total
White-Collar					
Professional-					
Technical	3.4%	[5.8]	8.2%	[10.1]	4.3%
Managers	6.8	[11.7]	1.4	[1.7]	5.8
Clerical-Sales	7.4	[12.7]	8.3	[10.2]	7.5
Blue-Collar					
Skilled	12.6	[21.6]	1.4	[1.7]	10.5
Semi-skilled	10.4	[17.8]	23.8	[29.3]	12.8
Unskilled	14.7	[25.2]	2.6	[3.2]	12.5
Service occupations	3.1	[5.3]	28.7	[35.4]	9.0
Farmers	23.0		5.8		19.8
Farm Laborers	18.7		13.1		17.6

Note: [ ]as a percent of nonagricultural employment.
Source: Calculated from on Bureau of the Census, *Historical Statistics*, Series D-182 to D-215, 139.

or proprietors, while 39 percent labored as skilled tradesmen or in semi-skilled blue collar jobs. Unskilled labor and various low-skilled service occupations employed another 30 percent. Compared with men, women reporting an occupation were much less likely to work in agriculture (19 percent compared with 40 percent) and, off the farm, were less likely to hold a white-collar or skilled blue-collar job. Approximately two-thirds of female workers were employed as semi-skilled operatives, unskilled laborers, or in the service sector, primarily in domestic service.[6]

Some additional insights into the determinants of occupations in 1900 are provided by Table 5.7, which reports regressions of occupations for adult men, ages 20 to 59. Race and ethnicity strongly influenced the occupational distribution among males. Blacks were concentrated in unskilled occupations, farm and nonfarm. The foreign-born were less likely than native-born whites to be white-collar workers or farm operators, but were more successful than blacks at obtaining semi-skilled and skilled blue-collar jobs. Various studies suggest that controlling for language skills, work experience, and time in the United States explains most of ethnic

---

[6] The higher proportion of women employed in professional and technical occupations than men reflects the fact that teaching is classified as a professional occupation and that most teachers were women in 1900.

Table 5.7. *Occupation regressions: Adult males in 1900*

A. *White-Collar*

	Prof./Tech.		Managerial		Clerical/Sales	
	ß	t-stat	ß	t-stat	ß	t-stat
Constant	0.046	6.263	0.041	4.287	0.138	13.571
Black	−0.014	−2.870	−0.041	−6.669	−0.061	−9.321
Age						
20–24	−0.021	−4.423	−0.042	−6.940	0.017	2.596
25–29	0.002	0.415	−0.028	−4.757	0.008	1.337
30–34	−0.001	−0.151	−0.010	−1.653	0.002	0.374
40–44	−0.003	−0.725	0.014	2.320	−0.009	−1.310
45–49	−0.003	−0.511	0.009	1.306	−0.009	−1.269
50–54	0.008	1.446	0.025	3.544	−0.005	−0.654
55–59	0.066	0.988	0.005	0.616	−0.001	−0.176
Married	−0.007	−2.436	0.016	4.398	−0.022	−5.544
Foreign	−0.026	−8.233	−0.014	−3.545	−0.056	−12.822
Literate	0.027	6.135	0.045	7.980	0.033	5.437
Urban location						
Urb2	−0.016	−2.928	−0.020	−2.972	−0.064	−8.756
Urb3	−0.023	−4.464	−0.041	−6.009	−0.104	−14.423
Urb4	−0.014	−3.092	−0.019	−3.323	−0.072	−11.985
Urb5	−0.022	−6.321	−0.052	−11.291	−0.125	−25.614
Region of residence						
MA	−0.007	−1.338	0.007	1.079	0.001	0.150
ENC	−0.003	−0.562	0.014	2.092	0.015	1.970
WNC	−0.002	−0.387	0.022	2.972	0.014	1.683
SA	−0.006	−1.011	0.030	3.665	0.023	2.686
ESC	−0.011	−1.602	0.028	3.263	0.013	1.430
WSC	−0.005	−0.755	0.023	2.623	0.033	3.542
MN	0.011	1.195	0.011	0.888	−0.002	−0.140
PAC	−0.001	−0.151	0.030	3.041	0.045	4.163
Dep.var.-Mean	0.037		0.063		0.075	
R^2	0.009		0.024		0.052	

B. *Blue-Collar*

	Skilled		Semi-skilled		Unskilled	
	ß	t-stat	ß	t-stat	ß	t-stat
Constant	0.183	13.407	0.176	14.582	0.301	20.629
Black	−0.047	−5.359	−0.009	−1.167	0.140	14.820

Table 5.7. *(Cont.)*

B. Blue-Collar

	Skilled		Semi-skilled		Unskilled	
	ß	t-stat	ß	t-stat	ß	t-stat
Age						
20–24	−0.027	−3.074	0.019	2.461	0.009	0.983
25–29	−0.016	−1.890	0.015	2.067	0.010	1.094
30–34	−0.006	−0.770	−0.002	−0.233	0.007	0.755
40–44	−0.003	−0.393	−0.017	−2.172	−0.015	−1.549
45–49	−0.021	−2.208	−0.034	−4.040	−0.015	−1.478
50–54	−0.005	−0.468	−0.048	−5.332	−0.033	−3.008
55–59	−0.013	−1.149	−0.059	−5.888	−0.049	−4.035
Married	0.022	4.097	0.013	2.635	−0.052	−9.063
Foreign	0.016	2.721	0.056	10.824	0.089	14.157
Literate	0.068	8.440	−0.0005	−0.070	−0.110	−12.784
Urban Location						
Urb2	−0.054	−5.494	0.002	0.249	0.020	1.890
Urb3	−0.109	−11.321	−0.045	−5.243	−0.021	−2.044
Urb4	−0.064	−7.983	0.004	0.520	0.028	3.254
Urb5	−0.127	−19.399	−0.049	−8.507	−0.023	−3.314
Region of Residence						
MA	−0.001	−0.071	−0.024	−2.814	0.014	1.382
ENC	−0.014	−1.392	−0.064	−7.353	−0.005	−0.495
WNC	−0.048	−4.420	−0.095	−9.914	−0.023	−1.948
SA	−0.022	−1.942	−0.066	−6.495	−0.044	−3.549
ESC	−0.050	−4.094	−0.077	−7.116	−0.090	−6.881
WSC	−0.057	−4.575	−0.119	−10.719	−0.068	−5.037
MN	−0.014	−0.825	0.067	4.451	−0.020	−1.125
PAC	−0.046	−3.240	−0.037	−2.892	−0.016	−1.057
Dep.var.-Mean	0.146		0.109		0.172	
R^2	0.052		0.044		0.046	

C. Service and Farm

	Service		Farm Operator		Farm Laborer	
	ß	t-stat	ß	t-stat	ß	t-stat
Constant	0.023	3.296	−0.047	−3.153	0.138	12.078
Black	0.071	15.515	−0.078	−8.082	0.039	5.332
Age						
20–24	0.013	2.897	−0.088	−9.318	0.120	16.526
25–29	0.010	2.341	−0.033	−3.597	0.031	4.421
30–34	0.018	4.207	−0.021	−2.302	0.012	1.737

Table 5.7. *(Cont.)*

C. Service and Farm

	Service		Farm Operator		Farm Laborer	
	ß	t-stat	ß	t-stat	ß	t-stat
40–44	0.017	3.709	0.021	2.148	−0.005	−0.657
45–49	0.015	2.962	0.065	6.227	−0.006	−0.798
50–54	0.007	1.291	0.063	5.719	−0.013	−1.537
55–59	0.011	1.807	0.122	9.788	−0.020	−2.145
Married	−0.009	−3.351	0.172	29.400	−0.133	−29.534
Foreign	−0.001	−0.462	−0.058	−9.101	−0.004	−0.887
Literate	0.026	6.197	−0.025	−2.828	−0.062	−9.300
Urban Location						
Urb2	−0.036	−7.159	0.104	9.687	0.064	7.870
Urb3	−0.051	−10.139	0.244	23.114	0.150	18.572
Urb4	−0.034	−8.107	0.108	12.278	0.063	9.298
Urb5	−0.050	−14.591	0.316	44.259	0.132	24.044
Region of residence						
MA	0.016	3.232	0.003	0.306	−0.010	−1.281
ENC	0.013	2.513	0.042	3.840	0.003	0.355
WNC	0.006	1.052	0.115	9.720	0.011	1.177
SA	−0.002	−0.309	0.077	6.130	0.011	1.116
ESC	−0.009	−1.409	0.192	14.364	0.004	0.378
WSC	0.001	0.156	0.174	12.653	0.019	1.762
MN	0.010	1.163	−0.043	−2.343	−0.019	−1.333
PAC	0.020	2.733	−0.011	−0.712	0.016	1.360
Dep.var.-Mean	0.034		0.256		0.108	
R^2	0.027		0.258		0.142	

Note: Prof./Tech.: professional or technical occupation; URB2 = 1 if resident of county with a city of population 10,000 or more and adjacent to an "urbanized" county (an urbanized county contains a city of population 50,000 or more), 0 otherwise; URB3 = 1 if resident of a county with no city of population 10,000 and adjacent to an urbanized county, 0 otherwise; URB4 = 1 if resident of a nonadjacent county (not adjacent to an urbanized county) with a city of 10,000 or more, 0 otherwise; URB5 = 1 if resident of nonadjacent county with no city of population 10,000 or more, 0 otherwise; MA: MidAtlantic; ENC: East North Central; WNC: West North Central; SA: South Atlantic; ESC: East South Central; WSC: West South Central; MN: Mountain; PAC: Pacific. Left-out age dummy is 35–39; left-out urban dummy is URB1 (= 1 if resident of an urbanized county, 0 otherwise); left-out region is New England.

Source: Public use sample of 1900 census.

differences in occupational (more generally, economic) status. Racial differences, however, were far more a consequence of employment and other forms of discrimination that hindered the efforts of black men to improve their occupational status.

The structure of occupations varied by age and literacy status, two indicators of human capital. Younger men were more likely to be employed as unskilled laborers or semi-skilled operatives than as skilled blue-collar workers, as farm laborers than as farm operatives, and in clerical or sales work rather than in higher-income managerial or professional occupations. Basic literacy clearly raised the odds of holding a white-collar or skilled blue-collar occupation.

Reflecting geographic differences in the structure of industries, the distribution of occupations varied across regions and, within regions, with proximity to an urban area. Residents of the South Central states, for example, were less likely to be skilled blue collar workers than residents of the Midwest or New England. Urban residents were more likely to be white-collar workers or employed in a skilled trade, but urban proximity mattered much less in determining the chances of being a factory operative.

WAGES IN NINETEENTH-CENTURY AMERICA

The return to labor is a fundamental statistic in the economic history of any country. The growth of nominal wages in the long run, adjusted for the cost of living, is a conventional yardstick of improvement in living standards. Because no national surveys of income were taken in nineteenth-century America, wage differentials between occupations have been used to gauge the extent of income inequality. Changes in real wages over the short or medium run are central to the labor history of the period. Geographic differences in wages provide insights into regional migration patterns and the evolution of national labor markets.

This part of the chapter reviews the available evidence on wages in nineteenth-century America. Although it is not possible to construct a single, aggregate index of real wages over the century, there is abundant evidence that real wages were substantially higher at the end of the century than at the beginning, and that long-run growth in real wages was experienced by all the various groups making up the working class. Equally central to that experience, however, was short- and medium-run variability in real wages around the upward trend. At various times real wages declined or remained constant. Although there is some evidence that, in the aggregate, hours of work increased on average with the shift of labor out of agriculture into manufacturing, weekly hours of work in manufacturing appear to have declined over the century.

Long-Run Trends in Real Wages

1800–1860

Except for a few years (1832, 1850, and 1860) no national surveys of wages were taken before the Civil War. As a substitute, economic historians have turned to government surveys conducted retrospectively in the late nineteenth century and scattered archival records: manuscript censuses, account books, and firm payrolls.

The most famous compilations of nineteenth-century wages for the United States are contained in two federal government documents, the *Weeks* report, published as part of the 1880 federal census; and the *Aldrich* report, published by the Senate in the early 1890s as part of a lengthy investigation of wages and prices in different industries and countries. Both reports are useful for the post–Civil War period, but for the antebellum era, gaps in temporal and geographic coverage have led economic historians to search for alternative sources.

Perhaps the most famous such source consists of the payroll records of the Erie Canal. Estimates of the trend in real wages between 1828 (the first year data are available) to 1860 for two of the principal canal occupations, common labor and carpenters, are 1.4 percent per year for common labor and 1.6 percent for carpenters.[7] For the pre-1830 period the Erie Canal data can be supplemented by information on daily wages of common laborers and artisans in the building trades in Philadelphia. Common laborers' pay rose by 1.6 percent per year between 1800 and 1830, while the growth rate for artisans was 1.8 percent per year.[8]

---

[7] The estimates are the coefficients of a time trend from regressions of real wages of canal workers. Real wages were computed by dividing the nominal daily rate by a price index made up of wholesale prices in New York. Jeffrey G. Williamson and Peter H. Lindert, *American Inequality: A Macroeconomic History* (New York, 1980), 319.

[8] The Philadelphia growth rates were computed in the same manner as for the Erie Canal date. The price deflator, which pertains to Philadelphia, was taken from the U.S. Bureau of the Census, *Historical Statistics of the United States, Colonial Times to 1970* (Washington, DC, 1975), series E-97, 205.

Data on wages paid to manufacturing operatives and agricultural labor
have also been compiled. One study found that real wages of manufacturing workers in the Northeast increased by 1.2 to 1.6 percent per year
between 1820 and 1860, depending on the price index used to deflate
nominal wages.

Evidence on agricultural wages yields a somewhat mixed picture.
Analysis of evidence for the South Atlantic states suggests very little or
no real wage growth in agriculture from 1800 to 1850. Data on monthly
wages of farm labor in the Midwest and Middle Atlantic states, however,
suggest a rate of growth similar to that of nonfarm labor, as do farm wages
in Massachusetts and Vermont. Further, other studies indicate little or no
systematic gap in wages between agricultural and nonagricultural work,
for workers at comparable levels of skill.

Table 5.8 shows estimates of long-run growth rates of real wages computed from another source examined in recent work, wages paid to civilian employees of the United States Army. For common laborers the growth
rates range from 0.71 percent per year in the Midwest states to 1.28
percent in the Northeast. Growth rates of real wages of artisans were lower,
particularly in the Midwest and the South Atlantic states. Clerks, a major
white-collar occupation of the period, experienced greater real wage gains
than either common laborers or artisans. It is also clear that real wage
growth differed across regions. Occupational and spatial differentials are
discussed in greater detail later in the chapter.

1860 TO 1900

For the years during and after the American Civil War the measurement of
trends in real wages is on a reasonably firm footing. The *Weeks* and *Aldrich*

Table 5.8. *Real wage growth, 1821 to 1860*

	Common labor/Teamsters	Artisans	Clerks
Northeast	1.28%	1.18%	1.57%
Midwest	0.71	0.07	0.87
South Atlantic	0.97	0.24	1.12
South Central	0.85	0.66	1.44

Note: Growth rate is coefficient (β) of regression of log of daily wage; In $W = \alpha + \beta t + \mu$, where t is time.
Source: Robert A. Margo, *Wages and Labor Markets in the United States, 1820 to 1860* (Chicago, 2000), table 3.3.

reports, previously described, provide the evidential basis for the construction of real wage series. Combined with census and other data, on occupations and hours worked, an economy-wide real wage series for nonfarm labor can be constructed. This series is graphed in Figure 5.1.

Real wages plunged during the American Civil War, falling by 28 percent between 1860 and 1865, then recovered from 1866 to 1872. The worldwide depression of the early 1870s left its imprint on the American working class in the form of falling real wages throughout the 1870s. As of 1880, real annual earnings of nonfarm workers were no higher, on average, than they had been on the eve of the war. The remainder of the century, however, witnessed a pronounced increase in real wages, punctuated by stagnation (and brief decline) between 1892 and 1898.

Thus, despite episodes of stagnation and decline, the trend in real earnings for nonfarm workers from 1860 to 1900 was upward. A regression of real wages on a time trend produces an estimated average annual rate of growth of 1.1 percent. Although the available evidence is not as abundant,

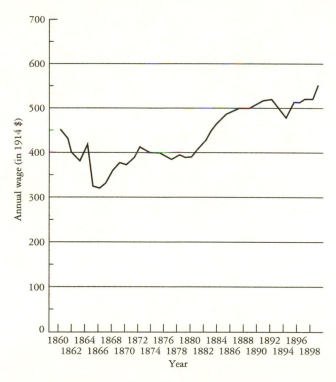

Figure 5.1. Real wages, 1860–1900. Source: U.S. Bureau of the Census, *Historical Statistics of the United States from Colonial Times to 1970* (Washington, DC, 1975), Series A-736.

data on daily wages of agricultural workers without board suggests a slightly lower growth rate, about 0.9 percent per year.

SUMMARY

Because there are no comprehensive sources of wage data that cover the entire nineteenth century, we cannot be certain of how much higher real wages were at the end of the century than at the beginning. An economy-wide average increase of 1.0 to 1.2 percent per year for daily wages is a plausible guess, based on the available evidence. If these growth rates are taken seriously, real daily wages were about 270 to 330 percent higher in 1900 than in 1800. Current estimates place the rate of growth of per capita income between 1800 to 1900 at 1.1 to 1.2 percent per annum. Given the uncertainty over these estimates, a fair conclusion is that real wages grew at approximately the same rate as, or just slightly below, per capita income. A small gap in favor of per capita income can be explained by the long-term increase in the aggregate labor force participation rate, and by the possibility that annual hours of work increased on an economy-wide basis over the century.[9]

Upon demonstrating that real wages rose, it is customary (for economists) to infer that the increase made workers "better off." Whether American workers in 1900 really were better off than in 1800 rests on several implicit assumptions. Work in a large, impersonal factory in Chicago at the turn of the century was fundamentally different from work in a small Massachusetts town in 1810. In principle, real wage series can be adjusted to take account of changes in the nature of work, but in practice, such adjustments have not been made for the nineteenth-century United States.

Some work has been done recently to produce international comparisons. Before the Civil War real wages for common labor were much higher in the United States than in Europe. From the 1840s to the end of the century, however, real wage gaps between the United States and Europe tended to diminish, as a consequence of factor migration (labor and capital) and increased international trade.

Wage Differentials

While aggregate wage developments are important, American economic historians have also been interested in wage differentials. In the late

---

[9] See the discussion of hours of work later in the chapter.

twentieth century, the availability of large-scale social surveys has permitted labor economists to study wage differentials in great detail. Because of a lack of similar evidence, much less is known for the nineteenth century.

Geographic wage differentials have been studied in some depth. Economic historians are interested in geographic wage differentials for two reasons. First, such wage gaps indicate the spatial extent of labor markets. The erosion of geographic differentials over time is taken as evidence of the formation of national markets for labor of different skills. Second, geographic wage differentials provide evidence of regional differences in living standards that supplement other evidence, such as per capita incomes.

Studies of geographic price differentials in wholesale markets for similar goods suggest the emergence of national markets over the course of the nineteenth century as the outcome of improvements in transportation and communications. Recent research suggests that regional labor markets also shared in this process.

To measure the extent of labor market integration it is customary to compare estimates of real wages at different locations for narrowly defined occupational categories. One study of farm wages in Massachusetts, for example, revealed that spatial differentials widened in the late eighteenth and early nineteenth centuries, as economic development progressed at different rates across rural locations in the state. Analysis of interregional differences in real wages in the North using the army payrolls described earlier in the chapter, suggests that real wages were significantly higher in the Midwest early in the century, particularly for skilled artisans. However, the real wage advantage of the Midwest diminished over time, consistent with the direction of inter-regional migration. Beginning in the 1830s, real wages of unskilled labor in the South appear to have been below real wages in the North. The North–South wage gap declined somewhat in the 1850s but grew substantially by the end of the nineteenth century.

Economic historians have also been interested in occupational wage differentials, primarily as a way of gauging the relationship between economic growth and inequality. Does modern economic development produce rising inequality during its early phases? This important hypothesis, long associated with the economist Simon Kuznets, has been examined using contemporary and historical data. Investigating the relationship between growth and inequality in nineteenth-century America is compli-

cated, however, by the fact that no systematic surveys of the size distribution of income were conducted. In their place, economic historians
have assembled evidence on occupational wage differentials. The working
hypothesis is that, if such differentials widened over time, so did income
inequality.

Attempts to identify a positive relationship between growth and
inequality in America appeared to be successful initially. A time series
composed of ratios of daily wages of skilled artisans to wages of common
laborers in urban areas showed a steady increase after 1830 to about 1860,
and then a plateau from 1860 to 1900. Another body of wage evidence,
from Massachusetts, suggests increases in the wages of skilled artisans relative to common labor before 1860.

Rising inequality has been linked to early industrialization through the
economic notion of capital–skill complementarity. The price of capital
goods fell between 1830 and 1860, resulting in increased capital accumulation. Capital is said to have been a complement to skilled labor; thus
the falling price of capital goods leads to an increase in the demand for
skilled labor, relative to unskilled labor. The relative supply of skilled labor
is assumed to have been inelastic over the period in question. The increase
in relative demand led to a rise in the skill differential, the ratio of skilled
to unskilled wages.

Both the evidence and explanation have proven controversial. It is not
clear that capital–skill complementarity was a characteristic of early manufacturing technology. The opposite is more widely believed: the factory
system led to a substitution of less-skilled labor, predominantly children
and young women, for skilled artisans. The growing demand for the labor
of children and young women in factories, initially in the Northeast, led
to an increase in their wages relative to adult men. Econometric analyses
of data from the 1850 Census of Manufactures suggest that capital was a
substitute for skilled labor, and a complement to natural resources.

The empirical evidence cited above for an antebellum widening in wage
differentials is also questionable. The linked urban series combined wages
from disparate locations, and the differentials implied by the series for the
1820s are much smaller than those suggested by other sources. The
increase in the skill differentials evident in Massachusetts is not robust to
the method used to analyze the data.

The U.S. Army data mentioned earlier in the chapter yield the most
comprehensive antebellum evidence on wage differentials. Table 5.9 shows
estimates of the ratios of wages of skilled artisans to unskilled labor from

Table 5.9. *Occupational wage ratios, 1821–1856*

	Northeast	Midwest	South Atlantic	South Central
1821–30	1.47	2.28	2.38	2.31
1831–40	1.68	1.97	2.63	2.13
1841–50	1.51	1.66	2.39	2.36
1851–56	1.44	1.82	2.05	2.14

Note: Figures are decadal averages; they are ratios of average wages of skilled artisans to common laborers and teamsters.
Source: Margo, *Wages and Labor Markets*, Appendix table, 3A.5, 3A.6, 3A.7.

this source. Separate estimates are shown for each census region. Clearly, there is no indication of a rise in the relative wage of skilled artisans. Wages of white-collar workers, however, did increase relative to common labor (and artisanal pay) before the Civil War.[10]

The level of the occupational wage differentials has also been of interest. According to the economic historian H. J. Habakkuk, wage differentials between skilled and unskilled labor during the antebellum period were smaller in the United States than in England, which led to a higher capital–labor ratio in various American industries compared with their British counterparts. The differentials shown in Table 5.9, however, are uniformly larger than the contemporaneous estimates of British differentials, contradicting Habakkuk's thesis.

Data on skill differentials in the late nineteenth century have not been subjected to the same critical scrutiny as the antebellum evidence. The best available evidence suggests slight upward trends in the wages of skilled artisans and white-collar workers relative to common labor from 1860 to 1900.

In regard to other sources of wage differentials before the Civil War, workers hired on a daily basis (as opposed to monthly or yearly) commanded a wage premium, partly to compensate them for the costs of regularly searching for work but also because longer-term workers frequently received non-wage compensation (for example, board or housing). Except in agriculture during the harvest, seasonal wage variation appears to have

[10] Claudia Goldin and Robert Margo, "Wages, Prices, and Labor Markets before the Civil War," in Claudia Goldin and Hugh Rockoff, eds., *Strategic Factors in Nineteenth Century American Economic Growth: Essays to Honor Robert W. Fogel* (Chicago, 1992), 77, and Robert A. Margo, *Wages and Labor Markets in the United States, 1820 to 1860* (Chicago, 2000), ch. 3.

been small; nor is there evidence of a substantial farm-nonfarm wage gap in daily wages, if perquisites such as board are carefully accounted for. Female workers received lower wages than male workers, although the relative importance of gender differences in productivity versus discrimination is not known.

The availability of a number of surveys conducted by various state bureaus of labor statistics provides a somewhat richer picture for the late nineteenth century. An age–earnings profile is apparent, one which apparently peaked at earlier ages than today. Although the magnitude of the effect is uncertain, there is some evidence that formal schooling raised earnings. Differences in wages between immigrants and natives were substantial although, as with women, the extent of pure wage discrimination is unclear.

Cyclical Instability in Wages

In the long run, real wages increased during the nineteenth century. In the short run, macroeconomic fluctuations caused significant variation in real wage growth. The causes of these fluctuations are in dispute. Some scholars argue that nominal wages lagged behind changes in the price level. Others point to the effects of real shocks such as unexpectedly high rates of immigration in the late 1840s and early 1850s, which are thought to have slowed the growth of real wages in manufacturing. Research suggests that, regardless of the source, the effects of nominal and real shocks were surprisingly persistent, causing real wages to deviate for substantial periods from their long-run path. With respect to purely nominal shocks, it appears that long-run "neutrality" held: in the long run, increases in the price level led to approximately one-for-one increases in the level of nominal wages. In the short run, real wages fell during periods of rising prices (for example, the mid-1830s) and rose during periods of falling prices (the early 1840s). Because prices tended to be procyclical during the antebellum period, real wages were countercyclical.

That real wages were countercyclical before the Civil War does not mean that workers were uniformly better off during a recession than during a boom. Real wages rose during deflations for *employed* workers, not for those out of work. The available real wage indices for the antebellum period pertain to daily, not monthly or annual wages. The gains from a higher daily wage while employed were offset by greater unemployment during the year.

The persistence of shocks to real wages before the Civil War clarifies certain aspects of the financing of the Union war effort. It has long been known that real wages fell during the war years. Wesley Clair Mitchell's exhaustive study concluded that nominal wages lagged behind prices, so that a portion of the war effort was financed by an inflation tax. Other scholars have disputed Mitchell's conclusion, claiming that real factors, such as a deterioration in the skill composition of the northern workforce between 1861 and 1864, and changes in the terms of trade, explain falling real wages during the war. An econometric study has shown that both nominal and real factors contributed to the wage lag; the fact that sluggish adjustment in wages can be dated to the antebellum period gives credence to the study's conclusion.

Economic development during the postbellum period contributed to further changes in the relationship between macroeconomic events and wage dynamics. The growth of large-scale enterprises, coupled with the increasing likelihood of collective action, may have lowered the aggregate likelihood that firms would resort to wage cuts during a period of declining demand. Other scholars point to the interruption of persistent deflation by rising prices in the late 1890s, which, like similar inflations earlier in the century, produced a wage lag. By 1900 the responsiveness of wages to nominal and real shocks was sluggish both absolutely and relative to the antebellum period. Compared with today, however, wages were more flexible at the turn of the century.

HOURS OF WORK

The phrase "hours of work" refers to the amount of work per day, week, or year. Most of what is known about hours of work in the nineteenth century pertains to manufacturing. A time series of weekly hours in manufacturing is shown in Figure 5.2. The general trend in manufacturing hours was downward. In the early 1830s the average work week was 69 hours. By the eve of the Civil War the work week had fallen to 62 hours, with the greatest reductions occurring during the 1850s. Further declines occurred during the postbellum period, but the pace of change was slow. At the end of the century the average work week was still quite long by modern standards, about 59 hours.

The proximate cause of the decline in weekly hours was a decline in daily hours. The earliest available estimate, from the McLane Report for 1832, puts manufacturing hours at 11 hours 20 minutes per day. Daily

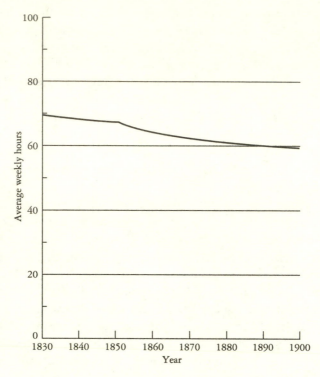

Figure 5.2. Average weekly hours in manufacturing. Note: The points in the figure are as follows:

1830	69.1 hrs	1870	62.1
1840	67.8	1880	61.3
1850	67.3	1890	60.0
1860	64.0	1900	59.1

Source: Computed from Robert Whaples, "The Shortening of the American Work Week," (doctoral dissertation, Department of Economics, University of Pennsylvania, 1990), 33. The figures for 1840–1880 are unweighted averages combining the *Weeks* and *Aldrich* reports, as computed by Whaples.

hours fell to around 10.5 by the eve of the Civil War and to just over 10 hours in 1880. Daily hours in 1880 were longest in the food, paper making, and chemical industries, and shortest in construction. Although hours were generally longer in southerly latitudes and during the summer, geographic and seasonal differences were small because of widespread use of artificial lighting by firms in the Northeast, particularly in urban areas.

On an economy-wide basis, it is probable that annual hours of work rose over the century, by around 10 percent. The increase in annual hours had three sources. First, annual hours were greater for indoor work, such as manufacturing, than for outdoor work, such as agriculture. Thus the shift of labor out of agriculture, by itself, raised annual hours. Second, factory owners had an incentive to keep fixed capital in operation, and this incentive became more pressing as firms grew in size and production became more capital intensive. The result was a decline in the seasonality of labor demand, meaning that employment was more evenly distributed throughout the year. Third, improvements in the spatial mobility of labor between industries reduced the seasonal component of labor supply, and arguably the amount of annual "downtime" (nonemployment) for the average worker.

The true increase in annual labor supply over the nineteenth century is arguably understated by the change in annual hours. Although it is difficult to be precise about magnitudes, it is clear that the pace of work was more intense at century's end. In the archetypal factory of 1900, labor was much more closely supervised than had been the case on the family farm on in the family business earlier in the century. Breaks in daily routine were less frequent, and the labor was more routinized.

In explaining the decline in weekly hours, historians have traditionally emphasized the twin roles of organized labor and the state. According to this view, employers steadfastly resisted a decline in weekly hours, and they could only be convinced by strike or government edict. The union push for shorter hours essentially began in the late 1820s and early 1830s, as workers in Philadelphia, Boston, and New York clamored for a ten-hour day. Agitation for shorter hours diminished during the Panic of 1837 and its immediate aftermath but picked up in the 1840s, leading to the passage of the first "maximum hours" laws in New Hampshire (1847) and Pennsylvania (1848). The federal government, at the direction of President Martin Van Buren, established a ten-hour day for its manual laborers in 1840.

After the Civil War the cry of organized labor changed from the ten-hour to the eight-hour day. Legislatures in eight states and the federal government responded by passing laws limiting employment to eight hours a day. By 1896, thirteen states had passed maximum hours laws. Although the provisions of the laws were aimed at women, ostensibly as protection for their health, a careful study of their origins reveals that organized labor had a different goal: the reduction of hours for all. Because of occupational segregation, men and women were complementary factors in most nineteenth-century manufacturing industries – reducing the use of one entailed reducing the use of the other. At the same time, strikes for shorter hours became more common.

Although there is no doubt that unions and the state played some role in generating the decline in hours, the traditional emphasis on both factors is probably misplaced. Except in a few states, such as Massachusetts, direct enforcement of maximum hours legislation was nonexistent, although some employers may have been prompted to obey the law out of civic duty. The length of the workday was not the major issue in the vast majority of strikes, even in the 1880s. For the most part, reductions in weekly hours in the nineteenth century appear to have been the outcome of bargains struck between workers and employers, in the context of a competitive labor market.

LABOR RELATIONS

Hidden beneath the statistics of the labor force in the nineteenth century are fundamental alterations in the nature of work. The American economy in 1800 was an agricultural economy. Work for wages as a way of life was uncommon, and families sought economic independence in ownership of land or physical capital. Although there are no reliable statistics on self-employment early in the nineteenth century, there is no doubt that the economy-wide fraction of workers who were self-employed was higher circa 1820 than in 1900. As more and more Americans worked for someone other than themselves, there were important changes in informal and formal relations among employer, employee and, to a far lesser extent, the government. In the twentieth century these changes have continued as economic development has further diminished the share of the labor force that is self-employed.

From Artisanal Shop to Factory

Some of the most profound changes in labor relations took place in manufacturing, as the factory mode of production eventually displaced the "artisanal shop." In an artisanal shop, journeymen and apprentices labored under the supervision of a master craftsman, producing goods on custom order. Each worker labored from start to finish on a product, using his own tools. Over time, an apprentice might become a journeyman, and a journeyman might master his craft. With luck and sufficient foresight to accumulate capital and managerial skills, a journeyman could achieve economic independence and high social status through ownership of an artisanal shop.

In terms of labor organization, factories differed from their artisanal counterparts in numerous ways. Tasks in the factory were much more specialized and work more routinized, as the goal was the production of a standardized good for a national or international market. As Adam Smith first recognized, division of labor brought economies of scale. Workers were allocated to those tasks at which they had a comparative advantage, and efficiency could also be enhanced through learning-by-doing. From the perspective of the factory worker, the price of specialization was the boredom and alienation induced by the repetitive nature of factory jobs. The pace and intensity of factory work were also far greater than in artisanal shops. Because the skills embodied in the average artisan were superior to those embodied in the average factory worker, it is not surprising that many journeymen viewed the factory system with concern. Some, as described later, sought refuge in labor organizations or political action, hoping to stem the tide. Others embraced the new system, seeking to become factory owners themselves.

The efficiency gains from division of labor did not happen overnight. Workers had to become accustomed to the discipline of factory life. Factory owners used a variety of means of supervision to realize productivity gains: direct monitoring of employees on the shop floor; piece rates and various other payment schemes to induce and reward effort; company towns, in which personal behavior was closely watched. Workers unable to fit in were fired, and in many cases found themselves blacklisted, unable to find similar work elsewhere. The difficulties of molding a factory workforce out of a pre-industrial population occurred wherever manufacturing spread in nineteenth-century America.

Factories offered an employment package of wages and working conditions different from that offered to wage labor in agriculture and certainly different from artisanal shops. It is not surprising, therefore, that factories initially drew upon rather different sources of labor. As noted earlier, the growth of manufacturing in the Northeast before the Civil War was fueled by the ready availability of children and young, single women whose productivity in agriculture (relative to adult males) was comparatively low. By mid-century another type of cheap labor, immigrants, emerged as a dominant source. The foreign-born filled a large share of manufacturing jobs throughout the second half of the nineteenth century, particularly in

urban areas in the Northeast and Midwest, which received a disproportionate share of new immigrants.[11]

Although the factory method was in place before the Civil War, it should
not be inferred that the artisanal shop was dead. Most manufacturing
workers, in fact, still labored in small, nonmechanized establishments in
1860 – hardly factories in the modern sense, in the eyes of many historians.[12] There were also intermediate organizational forms between the artisanal shop and the true factory. In the putting-out or domestic system,
workers (who were mostly women) labored at home producing intermediate goods that would later be turned into finished products by specialized
workers. The putting-out system first emerged in textile production but
soon spread to other industries in a closely related form, the "sweating"
system. In the sweating system, "outworkers" performed finely subdivided
tasks for which they were almost always paid by the piece. Outworkers
escaped the constant supervision of the factory foreman and, because they
were paid by the piece, had some control over their work pace. This does
not mean, however, that outwork was especially desirable. Outworkers
whose product did not meet acceptable quality or quantity standards might
be fined, have their piece rates reduced, or be fired. Piece rates appear to
have declined and the pace and intensity of outwork increased in the late
1840s and early 1850s, as immigrants glutted labor markets in large cities,
such as New York, where outwork was common.

After the Civil War factory workforces grew substantially in size. The
growth of large-scale manufacturing was a consequence of technological
progress in production, distribution, and transportation networks. Capital
per worker rose, and the use of inanimate sources of power become the
norm, not the exception (as was true before the Civil War). The larger scale
of production, coupled with the increase in capital intensity, created new
problems of organization and supervision of factory labor. The rules
describing acceptable behavior in the workplace increased in number and
complexity. Shop foremen were vested with authority over hiring, firing,
and promotion. Manufacturing workers might comfort themselves with

[11] Recall that, controlling for other factors, foreign birth raised the probability of employment as a
semi-skilled operative in 1900 (see Table 5.7). By World War I, approximately one of every three
manufacturing workers was foreign-born.
[12] Many historian prefer to use the term "factory" in reference to the large-scale mechanized firms,
which emerged after the Civil War. Describing an antebellum manufacturing establishment, even
a relatively large one, as a factory amounts to reading "Gilded Age developments into the antebellum years", Bruce Laurie, *Artisans into Workers: Labor in Nineteenth Century America* (New York,
1989), 42.

the knowledge that their real wages had increased since the Civil War, but the social gap between themselves and the managers and owners of the firms for whom they worked was vastly larger than it had been in the days of the artisanal shop.

The Growth of Unions, 1800 to 1900

Although craft unions existed during the colonial period, the first recognizable attempt at a labor movement in the United States occurred in the 1820s. The stirring of the factory system alarmed journeymen who foresaw the devaluation of their hard-won skills, social standing, and way of life. The ideology that fueled this early labor movement has been called "radicalism" by the labor historian Bruce Laurie. Radicalism was not against private property, nor did it seek widespread involvement of the state in labor relations and in regulating economic activity. Radicals embraced bread-and-butter causes such as shorter hours, higher wages, and better working conditions. In keeping with the spirit of the times (the Jacksonian era), radical labor also inveighed against imprisonment of debtors and favorable legislative treatment of the "unproductive" classes, such as bankers and lawyers. The intellectual underpinnings of radicalism were provided by eighteenth-century English political economists such as Thomas Spence, William Thompson, and John Gray, who advocated worker control of the means of production; and Americans like Langston Byllesby, whose 1826 book *Observations on the Sources of and Effects of Unequal Wealth* studied the impact of technology on class differences, and Philadelphian William Heighton, who founded the *Mechanics' Free Press* in 1827.

Concrete manifestations of radicalism from the late 1820s to late 1830s took the form of union organizing, political action, and greater frequency of strikes. Perhaps the most colorful attempt at politics was the establishment of the Working Men's Party in Philadelphia in 1828. A New York branch of the party followed within a year, as did a Massachusetts branch. Although the Working Men did relatively well in garnering votes in Philadelphia and New York in the late 1820s, the party disintegrated in the early 1830s, a victim of internal squabbles, poor organization, and co-option by established parties.

Like the Working Men, the great majority of antebellum labor organizations were short-lived and ill-fated. In retrospect, it could hardly have been otherwise. Radicalism found favor among white male journeymen in large, urban areas who were a minuscule fraction of the aggregate labor force at the time. Since one of the appeals of radicalism involved the preservation of the economic and social status of journeymen, the movement outside of New England stood in uneasy alliance with (indeed, largely ignored) factory hands, putting-out labor, and outworkers.

Given such shaky foundations, the fortunes of the antebellum labor movement were closely tied to the business cycle. Strikes before the Civil War were procyclical, rising in booms and falling in recessions. Journeymen cabinetmakers in New York City struck in 1835 because the "price book [for journeymen's wages] used by their masters was more than a quarter of a century old . . . [t]he old book failed to keep up with the cost of living."[13] But, when the Panic of 1837 turned into a depression in the early 1840s, unionism all but ceased.

If macroeconomic blows were not enough, the legal system sometimes stood in waiting to strip labor of its growing power. In an 1830s case involving journeymen shoemakers in Geneva, New York, Chief Justice Savage of the New York Supreme Court ruled that union members who refused to work for employers who also hired non-union labor were guilty of criminal conspiracy. Not all decisions were as anti-labor as the one in Geneva, however. In *Commonwealth v. Hunt* (1842), Justice Lemuel Shaw of the Massachusetts Supreme Court held that mere formation of a union was not evidence of criminal conspiracy, and that the union members did have the right to press for a closed shop.

The boom-and-bust cycle continued for the final two decades of the antebellum period. Except for a slight flowering in the mid-1840s, labor activism remained dormant until the early 1850s, when new concerns over immigration and expansion of slavery were added to the older causes embraced by radicalism. Once again, however, the nascent labor movement was severely curtailed in 1854 and 1857, both years of economic downturn.

Despite their limited penetration into the labor force, antebellum labor organizations were far from total failures. Many strikes did raise wages, forestall wage cuts, reduce hours, and improve working conditions, if only for a while. Today, while some of the political causes taken up by radical laborism may seem quaint, others such as extension of the suffrage, public education, the right to union activity, and an end to unjust imprisonment of debtors were matters of the utmost urgency to early labor advocates until success was won.

The early years of the Civil War witnessed a short-run decline in the

[13] Sean Wilentz, *Chants Democratic: New York City and the Rise of the American Working Class* (New York, 1986).

labor movement. Unionism increased markedly after 1862, however, in response to rapid price inflation and declining real wages. Most of the increase in membership occurred in local crafts unions. In the three industrial states of New York, Massachusetts, and Pennsylvania, approximately 200,000 workers were members of 300 local unions in 1864. With the end of the war came a temporary lull, as returning soldiers glutted local labor markets, thereby straining labor's bargaining power. Still, by 1872, several hundred thousand workers were members of craft unions.

Over time, labor leaders recognized that national organizations had more clout at the polls and more bargaining power in local disputes. Advances in transportation and communications had made both capital and labor more mobile. Strikes and other labor disputes were more likely to be resolved in the favor of workers in one area if employers were unable to attract strikebreakers from another locality. At least eleven national unions had been organized by 1865. One of the most prominent was the National Labor Union (NLU), a loose confederation of trade unions that sought working-class solidarity in its struggle against capitalists. Unfortunately, the NLU was unable to hold together its diverse political coalition of agrarians, conservative craft unions, and social reformers, and it was essentially dead by 1868.

The Knights of Labor were another organization that attempted to establish a national power base. Formed in 1869, the Knights grew haltingly until 1885. Membership in the Knights then exploded in 1886, reaching over 750,000 in the summer of that year. The Knights' success, however, was as short-lived as its meteoric rise. Contributing in no small measure to the Knights' decline was a bombing incident at a rally in Haymarket Square in Chicago on May 4, 1886, during which several people were killed. The public recoiled in horror at the carnage, and subsequent rallies in other cities met with a repressive police and militia presence. The Knights' membership fell precipitously shortly afterwards.

Data collected by the U.S. Commissioner of Labor provide the basis for an econometric analysis of the outcomes of the strikes during the ascendancy of the Knights. Today it is uncommon for a strike to end in total victory for the union or the employer, but strikes in the early to mid-1880s were much more likely to be "winner-take-all." About half ended in victory for the workers; only about 10 percent were compromise settlements. Benefits to victorious workers, in the form of higher wages, shorter hours, or the forestalling of wage cuts, were often substantial (if only temporary). Strikes were more likely to be successful if initiated or sanctioned by a union, and if the duration of the strike were brief. Strikes were more likely to fail if the employer hired strikebreakers, and employers' bargaining power was higher after the Haymarket affair.

Although less auspicious in the beginning than the Knights, the American Federation of Labor (AFL) had more staying power. Membership in the AFL grew slowly but surely in the late 1880s and throughout the 1890s, reaching half a million by 1900. Growth in membership then accelerated, to about 4 million workers by the end of World War I. The AFL, under the leadership of its first president, Samuel Gompers, became the dominant player in the American labor movement for many years.

Like the Knights, the AFL leadership did not shun strikes it felt were necessary and winnable. Unlike the Knights, the AFL adhered to the belief that unions should be organized predominately by craft. Mixing together workers of different skills, the AFL believed, would weaken solidarity. And, unlike the Knights who focused their organizing efforts on large corporations, the AFL concentrated (with few exceptions) on relatively small employers who lacked the clout to bust unions. An important legacy of the AFL was its ability to obtain written contracts with some employers. Uncommon before the 1890s, written contracts were to become the mainstay of collective bargaining in the twentieth century.

By 1914, the eve of World War I, approximately 16 percent of the American industrial labor force was unionized, up from roughly 3 percent in 1880. In absolute terms, the extent of unionization was low, but in this respect the United States was not unusual compared with other industrialized countries. France and Germany, for example, had unionization rates around 14 percent. Unionization rates were considerably higher in the United Kingdom (23 percent) and the Scandinavian countries (34 percent in Denmark), but they were lower in Italy, Spain, and Belgium.[14]

In one respect, the American labor movement of the early twentieth century appeared to differ from its European counterpart – American union members seemed less eager to embrace socialist causes. The transatlantic difference prompted the German sociologist Werner Sombart in 1906 to pose the question "Why is there No Socialism in the United States?" The classic answer, associated with the labor economist John R. Commons and his student Selig Perlman, is that there was nothing inherent in American capitalism that would lead workers to socialism. Capitalism might lead workers to develop "job consciousness" and thus support

---

[14] The figures in this paragraph are derived from Gerald Friedman, *State-Making and the Labor Movements: France and the United States, 1876–1914* (Ithaca, 1998).

trade unions, but support of socialist causes was another matter. Perlman noted that the franchise had been extended to American (white male) labor far earlier than it had in Europe, that (most) Americans believed in the right to private property, that high rates of internal migration mitigated against the formation of stable working-class communities, and that high rates of immigration made it easier for employers to divide and conquer the working class.[15]

The "new labor history" has sought to distance itself, not always successfully, from Commons and his disciples. New labor historians argue that class consciousness, if not socialism, was quite strong. Antebellum radicalism lingered on well into the late nineteenth century, and radicalism, unlike socialism, was skeptical of an active state. And sometimes for good reason: violent repression of unionism frequently occurred with the tacit or explicit approval of state or federal authorities.[16] Nor could labor organizations seek refuge in the courts. Although the legality of unions was not in doubt, late-nineteenth-century employers had the right to insist that workers leave the union as a condition of hiring. Labor historians also point to class conflicts within the labor movement that stifled solidarity. When other, more radical unions were threatened with repressive state tactics, big-city construction unions stood idly by, anxious to preserve their high wages.

In the end, the postbellum labor movement could claim partial success. Unions were sometimes able to mitigate the arbitrariness and harshness of workplace rules in some firms. Union members were generally paid higher wages than their non-union counterparts, although the gap was small except in a few industries. And their very existence was much less at the mercy of the business cycle than it had been during the antebellum period.

Government Regulation of Labor Markets: Protection by Legislation

Contemporary labor markets are subject to an enormous array of government regulations. The vast majority of these regulations have their origins in the Progressive era of the early twentieth century or the New Deal of

---

[15] Perlman's argument about internal migration has received support in the work of Stephan Thernstrom, *The Other Bostonians* (Cambridge, MA, 1973), and other historians who have discovered extraordinarily low "persistence" rates in various cities in the late nineteenth century. A persistence rate refers to the fraction of individuals living in a location in one year (for example, 1870) still living in the location at a later date (for example, 1880).

[16] Employers, of course, did not have a monopoly on labor violence. The point is simply that the state-sponsored repression was not rare, and this limited labor activism.

the 1930s. By comparison, government played a more limited role in regulating labor market behavior in the nineteenth century.

Aside from the court cases directed at union activity, the only notable attempts at direct government interference involved legislation directed at "protecting" various population groups: compulsory schooling laws, child labor legislation, and maximum hours laws. Compulsory schooling laws sought to require children to remain in school until particular ages or to require a certain amount of days attended within the year. Child labor laws regulated the employment of children at certain ages. Maximum hours, discussed earlier in the chapter, set upper limits on the number of hours persons could work per week. Massachusetts and other states in the Northeast were leaders in the passage of such legislation. Southern states, with very few exceptions, lagged behind.

Among economic historians, the general view is that such laws were not very effective because, with few exceptions, they were not rigorously enforced; where they seemed to work they mostly ratified behavior that was not due to the law. Compulsory schooling laws, for example, did lead to higher rates of school attendance, but the effects were quantitatively small. Opposition to compulsory schooling laws was greatest where child labor was relatively important, and where parental demands for schooling were comparatively low. As economic development led to higher real incomes of parents and lowered the relative wage of child labor, the demand for schooling increased, reducing the supply of child labor to the market. Schooling laws, in other words, were more a consequence than a cause of increased school attendance over time.

Maximum hours laws, mentioned earlier, exemplify the importance of enforcement. An analysis of the effect of maximum hours laws on manufacturing hours in 1880 reveals that only the Massachusetts law had its intended impact because there the state government attempted to enforce the law. Some firms, of course, tried to evade prosecution, but the legality of the Massachusetts law was upheld by the State Supreme Court.

The relative dearth of government regulation reflected a "strict constructionist" interpretation of Article 1, section 10 of the U.S. Constitution, which declared that states could not pass laws abrogating contracts. The maximum hours laws, among others, contained loopholes that permitted employees to evade the law, rendering them ineffective.[17] In the

---

[17] Compulsory schooling laws did not face the same legal challenges as maximum hours laws; see Jeremy Atack and Fred Bateman, "Whom Did Protective Legislation Protect? Evidence from 1880," National Bureau of Economic Research Working Paper Series on Historical Factors in Long Run Growth, Working Paper No. 33 (Cambridge, MA, 1991).

late nineteenth century legal opinion began to shift as monopoly and other undesirable elements of unfettered market capitalism appeared. While protectionist legislation may not have had much effect at the time, it was part of a broader ideological movement that set the stage for a vastly larger government role in the economy, which came to fruition in the twentieth century.

THE LABOR MARKET AT CENTURY'S END: A SNAPSHOT

Textbook accounts of labor markets are built on simple notions of demand and supply. The demand for labor depends on the demand for the firm's product and its technology. Aggregation to the industry level determines the industry demand for labor. Labor supply is the outcome of a decision process at the individual or household level. The intersection of demand and supply determines the equilibrium wage at any point in time. In this formulation the market for labor does not differ conceptually from the market for, say, apples. Economists refer to such a formulation, speaking loosely, as a spot market.

But labor markets today differ from the spot market conception. It is doubtful that wages alone play the allocative role of equating labor demand and supply. Much allocation of labor takes place within structured frameworks specific to firms, dubbed "internal labor markets" by economists. The timing of the switch from spot to internal labor markets is uncertain, but is usually dated to the 1920s and 1930s. In the 1920s large-scale enterprises adopted the various modern personnel practices associated today with internal labor markets. The trend towards bureaucratic methods accelerated in the 1930s, as mass unemployment permitted firms to more carefully screen workers, and unionism fostered the growth of seniority-based wage scales and layoff rules.

Exactly how one distinguishes one type of market from the other is unclear, but most economists believe that a spot labor market is characterized by greater labor turnover than an internal labor market. In this sense, labor markets at the turn of the century were somewhere on a continuum, probably closer to the spot market than the internal labor market model. Job tenure with a firm was generally shorter than today, but a nontrivial fraction of workers did remain with one employer for lengthy periods of time (for example, a decade or longer). The device of the promotion ladder, one aspect of an internal labor market, was present in some large enterprises before the 1920s. Wages at the turn of the century did not automatically adjust to equate labor supply and demand, as the spot market model implies.

Evidence on unemployment provides the sharpest contrast between labor markets in 1900 and today. The long-term decline in self-employment, coupled with the emergence of regular business cycles, caused unemployment to be a social and economic phenomenon worthy of attention in the late nineteenth century. Information on unemployment was first collected by the federal census in 1880, but the data were judged to be so poor at the time that they were never compiled in published form. Not until the 1900 and 1910 censuses was a reasonably clear definition in use. Unemployment data, similar to those collected by the federal census, were also compiled as part of various state censuses (for example, Massachusetts) and by state bureaus of labor statistics.

Analyses of these data have provided an overall picture of turn-of-the-century unemployment. The probability of becoming unemployed was less a function of personal characteristics, such as age, work experience, education, marital status, than in the post-World War II period. By modern standards, the duration of a spell of unemployment was also relatively brief. Unemployment was, however, ubiquitous among the working class, because the probability that an individual would spend some time unemployed during a given year was higher than after World War II. Except among the infirm or elderly workers at the margin of leaving the labor force, long-term unemployment (of six months or longer duration) was uncommon.

Some scholars attribute the egalitarian nature of turn-of-the-century unemployment and the short duration of unemployment spells to frequent and widespread use of "industrial suspensions" by firms – short periods of time in which plants would shut down entirely, throwing everyone out of work. Others argue that the technology in many industries resulted in sharp, seasonal fluctuations in labor demand, and thus widespread unemployment at specific times of the year. Economic historians believe that the risk of layoff was widespread because most workers, regardless of their skill or seniority, were not protected by an explicit contract, union or otherwise, or an implicit contract within the context of an internal labor market.

There being no unemployment insurance system in the late nineteenth century, how did the unemployed survive? In occupations or locations in which unemployment was predictable, wages were higher: unemployment risk commanded a wage premium. By saving during periods of employment, the unemployed could finance their consumption when out of work. Others relied on odd jobs or the earnings of other family members, some of whom would enter the labor market when the head of the household was unemployed (called the "added-worker" effect). Still others depended on the kindness of relatives and friends, churches, benevolent societies formed for the purpose of providing support to the unemployed, or unions.

CONCLUSION

This chapter has surveyed the major trends and changes in the labor force in the nineteenth-century United States. In the aggregate the labor force grew faster than the population. Economic development led to a pronounced shift of labor out of agriculture. Although there were significant short-run fluctuations in wages due to macroeconomic events, real wages grew for all classes of workers during the century, and there is little evidence that the rates of growth of wages differed across occupations. Geographic differences in wages diminished, but were still substantial at century's end.

The nature of employment relations also changed over the century. Workers in the late nineteenth century labored in manufacturing establishments vastly larger and more structured than their antebellum counterparts. Although the majority of workers were non-unionized in 1900, labor activism had made substantial progress. With the long-term move away from self-employment, unemployment became a much more prominent social and economic problem, affecting a widespread portion of the working class. Except for certain types of protectionist legislation, government regulation of labor markets was minimal.

6

THE FARM, THE FARMER, AND THE MARKET

JEREMY ATACK, FRED BATEMAN, AND WILLIAM N. PARKER

INTRODUCTION

The relationship between the farmer and the market in the nineteenth century was frequently ambiguous and fraught with contradictions. Agriculture's champion, Thomas Jefferson, the philosopher and politician, urged farmers to avoid "the casualties and caprice of customers" through self-sufficiency.[1] But Jefferson the farmer lamented the "total want of demand except for our family table" and wished for nothing more than "a rich spot of earth, well watered, *and near a good market* for the productions of the garden [emphasis added]."[2] While Jefferson exalted the self-sufficient farmer, he was among the first to admit that Americans had a "decided taste for navigation & commerce."[3] Indeed, the debt-free farmer with the means of sustenance at his back door was free to choose his level of market involvement in a way open to few, if any, others. For most, self-sufficiency and barter were indicators of market absence, not market avoidance. The "moral economy" where community values dominated individual self-interest, where prices were set by custom, and where reciprocity governed exchanges may have existed, but only temporarily and hardly ever by choice.[4] Settlements on the frontier had little choice

---

[1] Thomas Jefferson, "Query XIX" *Notes on the State of Virginia* (Baltimore, 1800), 165.
[2] Thomas Jefferson to Charles W. Peale, August 20, 1811.
[3] Thomas Jefferson to Count van Hogendorp, October 13, 1785.
[4] See James Henretta, "Families and Farms: *Mentalité* in Pre-Industrial America," *William and Mary Quarterly*, 35 (1978), 3–32; Michael Merrill, "Cash is Good to Eat: Self-Sufficiency and Exchange in the Rural Economy of the United States," *Radical History Review* 3 (1977), 42–71; Robert Mutch, "Yeoman and Merchant in Pre-Industrial America," *Societas* 7 (1977), 279–302; Christopher Clark, "Household Economy, Market Exchange and the Rise of Capitalism in the Connecticut Valley,

but to be self-sufficient. With low population densities, great distances, and high transport costs, few crops could be profitably marketed by the frontier farmer. Under such circumstances, the successful farmer – one who best provided for his family – was indeed the one "who did everything within himself."[5] Such a person survived and prospered only on the fringes of Von Thünen's Isolated State, but his isolation did not last long.[6]

In the frontier countryside, a settler's neighbors were his market – a potential outlet for his time and labor, for any natural surpluses from his lands or woods. They were also the focus of his social energies, a relief from loneliness, and a source of marriage partners for his children. Denser settlement enlarged this market beyond the household, introducing the direct exchanges of labor and produce as well as the sharing of surpluses, even of tools and capital items. A sense of neighborliness is often attributed to the frontier, coexisting with the extreme isolation and the mistrust of every cohesive group for strangers. But below a community spirit – awareness of common destiny and interdependence – in all the giving and sharing, people expected to receive a counter-gift. As in all primitive gift-giving, the willing return of a service or a commodity, or repayment by its equivalent in kind, was rewarded by friendship, respect, and a readiness to continue the relationship.

In thinly settled new regions, a crust of suspicion sometimes greeted an intruder, but this was broken very quickly as the frontier moved west and an eagerness for news, variety, and social life made itself felt, along with the readiness to accept more hands to share the burdens of defense and help provide insurance in catastrophe. Rural neighborhoods began to grow: separate parcels of land were taken up, new trails and roads worn, and new structures raised, creating communities grouped around a crossroads, a portage point on a canal and, finally, at last a rail-junction. Each farm family found itself entangled in a thickening web of social and economic relationships. Then specialization developed. Special qualities of the land and the individual could be exchanged through services and produce.

1800–1860," *Journal of Social History* 13 (1979), 169–89; Philip Greven, *Four Generations: Population, Land, and Family in Colonial Andover, Massachusetts* (Ithaca, 1970); Kenneth Lockridge, *A New England Town: The First Hundred Years: Dedham, Massachusetts, 1636–1736* (New York, 1970); John Demos, *A Little Commonwealth: Family Life in Plymouth Colony* (New York, 1970); Michael Zuckerman, *Peaceable Kingdoms: New England Towns in the Eighteenth Century* (New York, 1970); Winifred B. Rothenberg, *From Market-Places to a Market Economy* (Chicago, 1992); and Rothenberg, "The Market and Massachusetts Farmers, 1750–1855," *Journal of Economic History* 41 (1981), 283–314.
[5] New York State Agricultural Society, *Transactions* (1852), 29.
[6] Johann Heinrich von Thünen, *Isolated State* (Oxford, 1966).

This richer and safer material life – the "gains from trade" – grew along with the developing social life, contributing to the "booster" spirit of the American countryside, villages, and towns. Given the peculiar mixture of an individualism centered on self and immediate family with an awareness of the strengths of sociability, it is not surprising that money and credit, and the willingness to calculate in money terms – these devices of the merchant – entered so thirstily into this agrarian setting. The magic of money – like language – is that it acts as a means of communication for specific, limited, and temporary purposes. Nearly every frontier from New England to California experienced a phase of exchange where primitive gift-giving, based on anticipations of reciprocity, shaded imperceptibly into payments in kind – the harvest hand for his board, the minister for supplies and lodging – and from that, into the demand for specific forms of credit, banks, and coin (or paper) of the realm. Country banks then grew up, supplying a reasonably reliable medium of exchange and serving as essential middlemen between farmers, their energies, resources, and aspirations, and markets both near and far.

On the East Coast, these changes were apparent even in the colonial period. Winifred Rothenberg has shown that Massachusetts farmers were active in market exchanges, seeking out those buyers offering the best prices for their products, even those at considerable distance, with the result that price differentials between markets narrowed sharply.[7] Connecticut farmers were likewise concerned with market opportunities, and the vast majority of farmers in Chester County, Pennsylvania, produced surpluses averaging some 40 percent beyond personal and farm consumption needs.[8] That astute observer of American life, Alexis de Tocqueville, remarked in the 1830s that "almost all farmers of the United States combine some trade with agriculture; most of them make agriculture itself a trade."[9] By the early 1850s, Horatio Seymour, president of the New York State Agricultural Society, reminded the farmer that

it is in his interest to buy for money every article that he cannot produce cheaper than he can buy. He cannot afford to make at home his clothing, the furniture or

---

[7] Rothenberg, "The Market and Massachusetts Farmers," and *From Market-Places*.

[8] Charles S. Grant, *Democracy in the Connecticut Frontier Town of Kent* (New York, 1961); Richard L. Bushman, *From Puritan to Yankee: Character and Social Order in Connecticut, 1690–1765* (Cambridge, MA, 1967); James T. Lemon, "Household Consumption in Eighteenth Century America and its Relationship to Production and Trade: The Situation Among Farmers in Southeastern Pennsylvania," *Agricultural History* 41 (1967), 59–70; James T. Lemon, *The Best Poor Man's Country* (Baltimore, 1972).

[9] Alexis de Tocqueville, *Democracy in America* (New York, 1948), volume 2, 136.

his farming utensils; he buys many articles for consumption for his table. He produces that which he can raise and sell to the best advantage, and he is in a situation to buy all that he can purchase, cheaper than he can produce. *Time and labor have become cash articles, and he neither lends nor barters them.* His farm does not merely afford him a subsistence; it produces capital and therefore demands the expenditure of capital for its improvement [emphasis added].[10]

Farming was becoming more of a business than a way of life. *The Prairie Farmer* reminded its readers that "Agriculture, like all other business, is better for its subdivisions, each one growing that which is best suited to his soil, skill, climate and market, and with its proceeds purchase his other needs."[11]

As western grain and livestock began to compete for eastern markets, established northeastern farmers found themselves at a disadvantage, cultivating less productive, higher-priced land. Thus, land-extensive eastern grain production declined, first on the thin rocky soils of upland New England and in New York where land productivity was especially low, and then in the grain-specializing regions of the mid-Atlantic. Those who stayed in eastern farming were forced to choose a new crop mix, one both suited to soil conditions and demand patterns, yet capable of competing against agricultural commodities from the interior. This generally meant specializing in dairy farming, vegetables, fruits, or other similar products for nearby cities. Thousands made this switch, particularly in the years before refrigerated shipping. Because these products were much more land- and labor-intensive than those produced on farms further west, they were adopted only reluctantly, because labor had to work harder and longer for the same return. Alternately, one could become a part-time farmer, growing crops such as hay. Beyond these choices, one could only move west or exit farming completely.

The dairy became a primary focus for farmers in the New England and Middle Atlantic states. Early in the century, milk and dairy products had been produced in very limited quantities on most farms for home consumption. Gradually surplus cheese and butter were sold or bartered in nearby villages and towns. The butter and cheese marketed in this way were not anonymous, homogeneous products but rather closely identified with the farm that produced them. Individual reputations were important and jealously guarded. Substandard or marginal products, rather than being consumed in the local area, were instead collected, blended and

---

[10] New York State Agricultural Society, *Transactions* (1852), 29–30.
[11] *Prairie Farmer*, XXI (1868), 17.

shipped to the larger cities as "Orange County butter" or "Herkimer cheese."[12]

The first serious dairying specialization emerged within the reach of urban milksheds around Boston, New York, Philadelphia, and Washington, where fluid milk was the primary product. Farther from the cities, butter and cheese production flourished, making New York and Vermont early commercial centers for these products. Just as the railroad played a key role in the development and commercialization of western agriculture, it was vital to the growth and extension of the dairy industry beyond the urban fringes. By 1860, the milkshed for cities such as Boston, New York, and Philadelphia encompassed farms within perhaps a 60- to 70-mile radius, with more distant farms specializing in butter and cheeses.[13]

Fluid milk and other dairy products became profitable mainstays for northern farmers. Urban demand for these products was strong, but long-distance shipping was impossible before refrigerated rail cars. Production typically employed family members who might not otherwise be fully employed: grandparents, children, and women performed major roles in dairy production. The techniques, especially butter churning, were well known. And as production advanced, silage methods facilitated both expanded winter production and reduced land usage. Dairying consequently became a primary source of farm profit, especially in the northeastern region.

Alternatives to – or perhaps more accurately, supplements to – dairying included producing either other perishables such as vegetables, or products that could be farmed on a small acreage using intensive farming techniques. Ideally an eastern farm combined livestock, perishable products, silage, and intensive techniques that helped sustain that region's agriculture even after the productive West was opened.

Along with the switch to crops that retained a locational advantage, eastern farmers gravitated toward capital- and labor-intensive and high-revenue-per-acre farming. Some experimented with fertilizer and crop rotation schemes as a means of saving land with declining fertility. One should not make too much of this movement, though. Relatively little was

[12] Percy Bidwell and John Falconer, *History of Agriculture in the Northern United States, 1620–1860* (Washington, DC, 1925), 421–34.
[13] See U.S. Patent Office, *Annual Report, 1861, Part II, Agriculture*; New Hampshire Agricultural Experiment *Bulletin 120* (Durham, 1905); Edward G. Ward, "Milk Transportation: Freight Rates to the Fifteen Largest Cities in the United States," United States Department of Agriculture, Division of Statistics, *Bulletin, 25* (1903).

known before the Civil War about capital-intensive, scientific farming, and we have no strong basis for believing that it was profitable to use "land-saving" technology anyway, as long as it was relatively easy and inexpensive to open virgin lands in the West. Instead, eastern adaptation to western agricultural expansion was largely based on shifts to crops in which the East had a comparative advantage.

Although the Civil War appears to have interrupted the process of geographic market integration, there is considerable evidence that, over time, price differentials between markets decreased and fluctuations were increasingly synchronous. Markets became increasingly integrated, whether for capital, labor, or products, both domestically and internationally. With the spreading rail network supplementing and eventually displacing much of the river and canal traffic, midwestern framers were brought closer to East Coast and overseas consumers. The East Coast had long had a deficit in grain production relative to consumption that was met by midwestern farms, but beginning in the 1850s, Europe increasingly turned to American farmers for its supply of wheat. Initially, as during the Crimean War, this drove grain prices higher, but eventually supply expanded in America, as in the rest of the world. These changes had a profound impact upon the midwestern economy.

The Midwest and West quickly came to dominate wheat, and especially corn production, though farms, unlike those today, continued to produce a diverse mix of crops and kept a variety of livestock beyond the workstock (see Figures 6.1 and 6.2). According to C. Knick Harley's estimates, by 1875–79 the East Coast was producing barely half of the wheat it consumed; by 1910–1913, its production relative to consumption had slipped to only 23 percent. The East North Central states, on the other hand, produced more than twice what they consumed, and the West North Central states, two and a half times as much. By the early twentieth century, increasing wheat specialization in the West North Central states increased their wheat surplus to more than three times what they consumed.[14] As a result, there was an expanding wheat export trade from the Midwest that not only supplied East Coast demands but also helped meet the growing needs of countries such as Great Britain. Midwestern wheat exports grew fourfold between 1870 and 1892, joining a growing flood of wheat onto world markets from Canada, Australia, India, and Argentina.[15]

[14] C. Knick Harley, "Western Settlement and the Price of Wheat, 1872–1913," *Journal of Economic History* 38 (1978), 865–78.
[15] Harley, "Western Settlement."

Wheat production, 1859

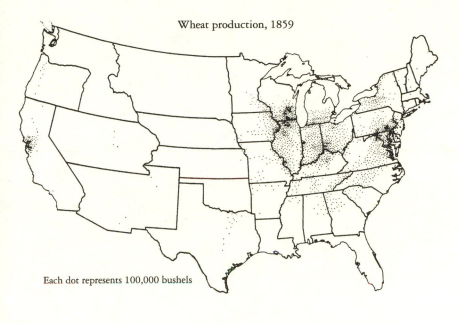

Each dot represents 100,000 bushels

Wheat production, 1889

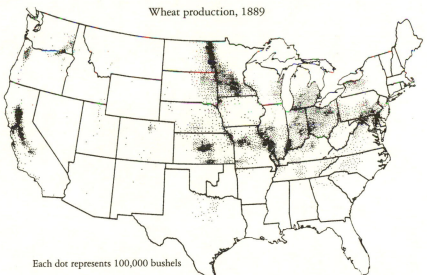

Each dot represents 100,000 bushels

Figure 6.1. The wheat belt. Source: Charles O. Paullin, *Atlas of Historical Geography* (Washington, DC, 1932), Plate 143.

Corn production, 1859

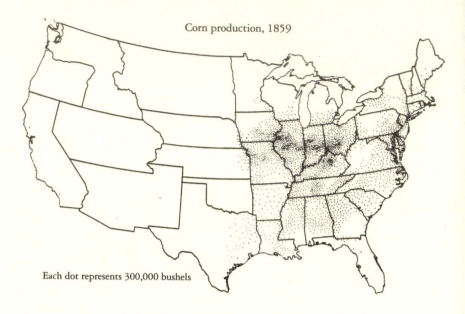

Each dot represents 300,000 bushels

Corn production, 1889

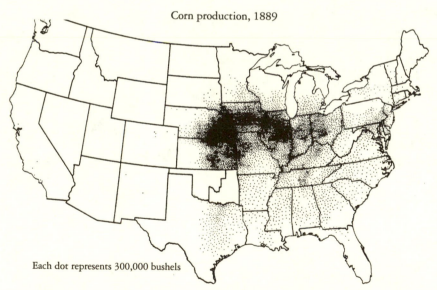

Each dot represents 300,000 bushels

Figure 6.2. The corn belt. Source: Charles O. Paullin, *Atlas of Historical Geography* (Washington, DC, 1932), Plate 143.

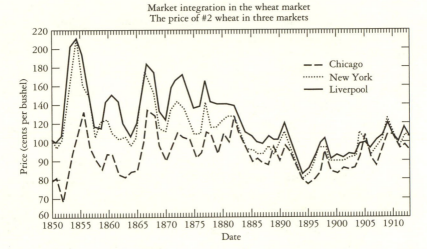

Figure 6.3. Market integration in the wheat market: The price of #2 wheat in three markets. Source: C. Knick Harley, "Transportation, the World Wheat Trade, and the Kuznets Cycle," *Explorations in Economic History* 17 (1980), 246–47.

As transport costs fell, farmers could supply markets at ever greater distances from the farm. In 1852/56, for example, the freight cost on a bushel of wheat from Chicago to New York was 20.8 cents; by the early 1880s it had fallen to 8.6 cents and by 1910/13 to only 5.4 cents. Moreover, the substitution of steam and iron for sail and wood reduced the transatlantic shipping costs from 14.3 cents per bushel to 4.9 cents by World War I. Consequently, the gap between the price received by the producer and the price paid by the consumer narrowed sharply. In the early 1850s, for example, the price of No. 2 wheat in Chicago was just 46 percent that in Liverpool, but by 1880–85, the price in Chicago was 84 percent of the British price, and on the eve of World War I, the prices were virtually the same (see Figure 6.3).[16] Cheaper transportation chipped away at the margin of protection that had isolated markets one from another. Farmgate prices may have risen, but farmers lost a degree of income assurance that they had enjoyed when markets were more isolated. At earlier dates, a poor harvest in an area had meant proportionately higher prices, but local harvest conditions no longer had any impact upon market prices once markets became integrated. Instead, prices were

[16] C. Knick Harley, "Transportation, the World Wheat Trade, and the Kuznets Cycle, 1850–1913," *Explorations in Economic History* 17 (1980), 218–50, especially Table 3.

determined in markets that the farmer could not see or influenced by people whom he did not know. He became dependent upon economic conditions in Buenos Aires or Melbourne as much as those in Chicago or Kansas City.

In areas with higher prices and greater railroad density, farmers quickly planted more acres in wheat. Harley estimates that within six years, farmers expanded settlement and increased the area under cultivation sufficiently to eliminate about half of any differential between actual and desired production of wheat.[17] Jeffrey G. Williamson argues that during the late 1860s and early 1870s it was lagging export demand rather than this increasing supply that caused the western terms of trade to deteriorate, giving rise to the first phase of farm protest across the Midwest.[18]

The American producers had certain advantages in European markets after 1870, one of which was shared with the farms, ranches, and estates of the world's other great plains and prairies in Russia, Argentina, Australia, and Canada. In all these areas, the terrain was favorable to horse-drawn mechanical equipment. Horses could pull plows, cultivators, and harvesters, including the giant combine, and could be fed on both grain and hay, which, again, did not need hand harvesting or cultivation. The capital structure of these vast areas was deep, in that they produced their own power by the same instruments which they used to produce their export products. This technical advantage was increased by the possibility of combining grasslands for a portion of the feed in a livestock cycle.

By 1850, the Middle West, and even the border states, had passed the stage where hogs were turned out to root and graze in the forest for a major portion of their feed. A corn-hog belt established itself from central Ohio westward to the edge of the Nebraskan Plains. But the comparative advantage of the open plains lay in wheat and, further west on the grasslands, in beef cattle. Eastern markets, linked by the railroad through great milling and slaughtering centers by the railroad in midwestern cities, drew on these lands to form the areas of intense specialization: the wheat belt, as always on the edge of settled mixed farming, and the area of range cattle and sheep. Cattle brought to feed on the nearly free food on the range could then be moved east to fatten on grain farms in the central states, and thence to urban markets for slaughter.

---

[17] Harley, "Western Settlement."

[18] Jeffrey G. Williamson, "Greasing the Wheels of Sputtering Export Engines: Midwestern Grains and American Export Growth," *Explorations in Economic History* 17 (1980), 189–217.

Demand from growing European industrial areas and urban capitals began to make itself felt in the 1860s, overlaid atop the home market. It was less steady and reliable, since it depended not only on demand fluctuations in the aggregate but on supply conditions in the world's competing areas and the often freakish incidence of European protective restrictions. Yet between 1900 and 1914, the international system worked well. The peasant populations of Southern and Central Europe sent their migrants into the farm markets of European and American industrial areas. The American Middle and Far West joined the world's other food-exporting regions. And British capital movements in abundance continued to lubricate the trade under a rather thoroughly internationalized gold standard.

A distinction, however, remained for the American farmers between the domestic and the foreign market, as shown in the persistence of American tariffs against European manufacturers and the appearance of American industrial exports in competition to American farm products for foreign purchasing power. During World War I the interruption of the internal European grain shipments intensified the export demand for U.S. products despite German efforts to enforce a submarine blockade. This was reflected at once in an expansion in wheat lands on the margin, that is, on the plains.

Although the geographic distribution and volume of crops imply a growing regional specialization, symbolized, for example, by the emergence of the "Corn Belt" (but also to be found in dairying, beef production, or wheat cultivation), northern agriculture during the nineteenth century remained remarkably diversified at the farm level. While regions were increasing their share of national production of particular crops, farmers were growing a greater diversity of crops. Improved acreage increased throughout the Midwest and West, although in some parts of the East land once in crops was abandoned and returned to nature (see Figure 6.4). Moreover, the proportion of improved acreage in farms increased. These changes, as well as marginal increases in land productivity, increased total output.

Declining transport costs allowed farmers the luxury of growing those crops best suited to the often diverse mix of soils on their farms. From the outset, pressure for "internal improvements" derived from the quest to sell the natural surpluses which farmers could earn – or thought they could earn – if only transport were near enough and cheap enough to cart away their produce. Once the prairies and Plains were reached, the railroad, with

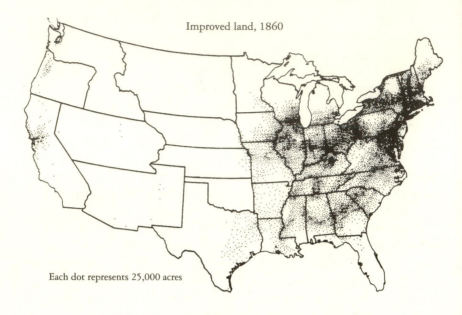

Improved land, 1860

Each dot represents 25,000 acres

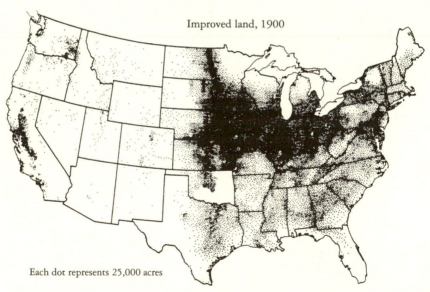

Improved land, 1900

Each dot represents 25,000 acres

Figure 6.4. The distribution of improved acres. Source: Charles O. Paullin, *Atlas of Historical Geography* (Washington, DC, 1932), Plate 144.

its flexibility of routing, promised to make this possible everywhere. Thus crops such as hay or oats, which had had little economic market beyond the farm gate because of their bulk and low value, could now profitably be shipped and sold far from the farm.[19]

As markets widened, trade became increasingly impersonal. The producer no longer personally delivered his product to market, exchanging words with the buyer as well as title to the product and thus no longer conveyed an individualized identity to his farm's output. Instead, grains were delivered to an elevator to be graded and mixed with the similar product of tens or hundreds of other farmers, losing forever any unique identity, becoming instead a part of an impersonal, homogeneous supply to be traded to unknown, anonymous, distant consumers who cared nothing for its source. Farming had become a business.

This transition of American farming from way of life to a business enterprise is nowhere clearer than in the concerns of farmers at the end of the nineteenth century. Consider, for example, the platform of the American Society of Equity, organized by midwestern farmers in 1902:

No. 1. To obtain profitable prices for all farm products, including grain, fruit, vegetables, stock and their equivalents. No. 2. To buy advantageously. No. 3. To secure equitable rates for transportation, storage in warehouses, etc. No. 4. Various insurance features. No. 5. To secure legislation in the interests of agriculture, open new markets and enlarge old ones. No. 6. To establish institutions for educating farmers, their sons and daughters, and the general advancement of agriculture. No. 7. Crop reports and securing new seeds, grains, fruits, vegetables, etc. No. 8. To improve our highways. No. 9. To irrigate our land. No. 10. To establish similar societies in foreign countries, as the Russian Society of Equity, etc., but societies only in surplus-producing countries. No. 11. To prevent adulteration of food and the marketing of the same. No. 12. To promote social intercourse. No. 13. To settle disputes without recourse to the courts.[20]

Excepting goal No. 12, it is hard to conceive of a broader commercial agenda for agriculture than this.

However, the transition from production for self-consumption – from the introspection and insularity of the family economy – to satisfying increasingly distant and impersonal demands registered through the price

[19] See Mary Eschelbach Gregson, "Rural Response to Increased Demand: Crop Choice in the Midwest, 1860–1880," *Journal of Economic History* 53 (1993), 332–45; Gregson, "Strategies for Commercialization: Missouri Agriculture, 1860–1880," unpublished Ph.D. diss., University of Illinois at Urbana-Champaign, 1993); Theodor Brinkmann (trans. M. R. Benedict), *Theodor Brinkmann's Economics of the Farm Business* (Berkeley, 1935).

[20] *The Plan of the American Society of Equity* (Indianapolis, 1903), quoted by Carl C. Taylor, *The Farmers' Movement, 1620–1920,* (New York, 1953), 369–70.

mechanism was hardly smooth and uncomplicated. Farmers found it virtually impossible to separate hearth and home from the business enterprise. The market brought new challenges and new opportunities but also new disappointments.

PRODUCTIVITY GROWTH

Markets generated powerful incentives to increase agricultural productivity. Total factor productivity is estimated to have grown at about 0.5 percent per year or by approximately two-thirds over the course of the nineteenth century. That is to say, the same quantity of land, labor, and capital produced about two-thirds more agricultural output in 1900 than it had produced, on average, in 1800.[21] The pace of total factor productivity growth, however, was not constant throughout the century. Thomas Weiss estimates that the rate of growth was fastest in the two decades after 1860, growing by 1.38 percent during the Civil War decade and averaging 0.91 percent per year between 1860 and 1880, and slowest during the first twenty years of the century (see Table 6.1).[22] Although agriculture was expanding onto the more fertile midwestern soils during the 1820s and 1830s, these years do not seem to have been ones of marked change in agricultural practice or technique, whereas in the Civil War years and immediately thereafter, mechanization was proceeding rapidly and there were more organized and systematic efforts to diffuse knowledge about best-practice farming methods. Total factor productivity growth in the North was probably even more rapid than shown by these figures, since it was not forced to confront the fundamental change in factor relationships resulting from Emancipation. The rate

---

[21] Thomas Weiss, "Long Term Changes in U.S. Agricultural Output per Worker, 1800 to 1900," NBER Working Paper Series on Historical Factors in Long Run Growth, No. 23 (1991), Table 4B.

[22] These new estimates based upon revisions to the Towne and Rasmussen farm gross product series and the Lebergott labor force estimates resolve the paradox noted by Gallman that the original data imply that productivity growth was most rapid in the 1820s and 1830s. Marvin Towne and Wayne Rasmussen, "Farm Gross Product and Gross Investment During the Nineteenth Century," in William N. Parker (ed.), *Trends in the American Economy in the Nineteenth Century*, Studies on Income and Wealth vol. 24 (Princeton, 1960); Stanley Lebergott, "Labor Force and Employment, 1800–1960" in Dorothy S. Brady (ed.), *Output, Employment and Productivity in the United States after 1900* Studies on Income and Wealth vol. 30 (New York, 1966); Robert Gallman, "Changes in Total U.S. Agricultural Factor Productivity in the Nineteenth Century," *Agricultural History* 46 (1972), 191–210; Robert Gallman, "The Agricultural Sector and the Pace of Economic Growth: U.S. Experience in the Nineteenth Century," in David Klingaman and Richard K. Vedder, eds., *Essays in Nineteenth Century Economic History* (Athens, OH, 1975).

Table 6.1. *Average annual rates of total factor productivity growth in U.S. agriculture, 1800–1900 (beginning to terminal year)*

Terminal year	Beginning Year									
	1800	1810	1820	1830	1840	1850	1860	1870	1880	1890
1810	0.29									
1820	0.14	0.00								
1830	0.16	0.09	0.19							
1840	0.21	0.18	0.28	0.36						
1850	0.20	0.18	0.24	0.27	0.18					
1860	0.30	0.30	0.37	0.43	0.47	0.76				
1870	0.45	0.48	0.57	0.67	0.77	1.07	1.38			
1880	0.45	0.47	0.55	0.63	0.69	0.86	0.91	0.45		
1890	0.47	0.49	0.56	0.63	0.68	0.80	0.82	0.54	0.63	
1900	0.49	0.51	0.57	0.63	0.67	0.77	0.77	0.58	0.64	0.51

Source: Computed from Thomas Weiss, "Long Term Changes in U.S. Agricultural Output per Worker, 1800 to 1900," NBER Working Paper Series on Historical Factors in Long Run Growth, No. 23 (1991), table 4B.

of productivity growth slowed again during the 1870s before accelerating in the 1880s.

Weiss's revised productivity growth estimates are consistent with those of Loomis and Barton, who estimate that productivity increased by 32 percent between 1870 and 1910. They are also consistent with those made by John Kendrick, who estimated the average annual improvement for the farm sector at about 0.7 percent per year compared with 1.7 percent for the nonfarm sector between 1889 and 1899. Agriculture's overall rate of productivity growth might not have been as impressive as that achieved by the industrial sector, but it was sustained over a long period of time. Moreover, it was achieved at a time dominated by capital widening in the form of farm creation rather than capital deepening through farm improvement as well as when agriculture continually faced new challenges from unfamiliar soils, terrain, and climate.

Land productivity, measured by the yield per acre, changed relatively little for most crops during the nineteenth century, in large part because land, particularly in the western states, was not the resource on which most farmers needed most to economize. Indeed, initial yields following land clearing were often higher than those realized later as soil nutrients depleted by repeated cropping were not replaced. The better farmers made some use of animal dung and the more progressive farmers plowed under nitrogen-fixing crops such as cow peas and beans, but most did little to maintain, let alone improve, the quality of their soil. The great improvement in yields lay almost a century into the future when chemical fertilizers, hybrid seeds, irrigation, and various scientific developments came into widespread use.

At mid-century, wheat yields probably averaged about 10–13 bushels an acre, while the better farmers working the best soils might realize twice as much. Corn yields averaged about 30 bushels per acre, with a range from 25 to 60 bushels.[23] These were low compared with yields in Europe, where land was more scarce.[24] Some small gains were made in these over the course of the century through careful seed selection, but so long as land was abundant and labor scarce, farmers had little incentive to invest much time and effort to raise the productivity of land.

Modest gains were made also in animal yields, primarily through the replacement of livestock of uncertain parentage with livestock carefully bred for specific characteristics. Yields also rose because of improvements in care and feeding. The impetus for these changes was economic, but the changes were not the dramatic ones observed in mechanization. Instead they were much less spectacular, involving cumulative minor changes. Fred Bateman estimates that nationwide the average milk yield per cow increased from 2,371 pounds per year in 1850 to 3,352 pounds in 1900 – an increase of about 40 percent or (approximately 0.75 percent per year).[25] However, this growth exaggerates the improvement in the North, where dairy yields in 1850 were much higher than in the South. In Louisiana, for example, the average yield per cow increased about eightfold during the second half of the nineteenth century but even then averaged less than 2,100 pounds per cow by 1910. Among the northern states, Oregon and Missouri had the lowest yields in 1850 (1,011 pounds and 1,480 pounds per year, respectively); New York and Vermont, the highest (4,511 pounds and 4,498 pounds). By 1910 Missouri had improved to

---

[23] See, for example, the various annual reports on agriculture issued by the Commissioner of Patents between the late 1830s and the 1850s and the yield reports of the USDA post-1866. U.S. Patent Office, *Annual Report, Agriculture* (1839–1852).

[24] M. M. Postan, *The Medieval Economy and Society* (London, 1972); Gregory Clark, "The Economics of Exhaustion, the Postan Thesis, and the Agricultural Revolution," *Journal of Economic History* 52 (1992), 61–84.

[25] Fred Bateman, "Improvement in American Dairy Farming, 1850–1910: A Quantitative Analysis," *Journal of Economic History* 28 (1968), 255–73, especially 257.

about 2,400 pounds while yields in the other northern states generally averaged well over 3,000 pounds and were as high as 4,849 pounds per cow in Washington state.[26]

While land was not scarce, labor was, and great efforts were expended to conserve on labor effort in American agriculture. As a result, agricultural labor productivity grew sharply, particularly when agriculture began to be mechanized. Rothenberg's Massachusetts farm wage data deflated by her Massachusetts price index, for example, suggest a rise of perhaps 40 percent in real wages during the first half of the nineteenth century in an area not noted for its advanced agriculture.[27] For the entire North after 1840, data assembled by Parker and Klein show a much faster pace of labor productivity growth for specific crops, ranging from a more than fourfold increase in wheat production to a threefold one for workers in corn production (see Table 6.2). Man-hours to produce a bushel of wheat, for example, are estimated to have fallen from 2.96 hours in 1840–60 to 0.71 hours in 1900–10. These rates are somewhat lower than Parker and Klein estimate for the country as a whole, since they exclude the South, where productivity lagged behind the national average in 1840. Following the procedure of Parker and Klein, we have also estimated how many man-hours it would have taken to produce a bushel of grain in 1900–10 if yields had remained unchanged from their 1840–60 levels (index i_2), if regional shares had remained unchanged (index i_4), and if mechanization had not changed the time involved in pre-harvest, harvest and post-harvest activities (index i_3), as well as combinations of any two of these changes. Mechanization – more complete tillage from improved plows, better seed distribution with seed drills, a speedier and more gently handled harvest with a reaper, and a more complete threshing with a steam-powered thresher – accounts for between one-half and two-thirds of the estimated increase in labor productivity between 1840 and 1910. Such devices not only eased the burden of back-breaking labor but also reduced the number of workers and the period of employment for each task. By contrast, the individual contributions of the westward movement and improvements in yields were minimal, accounting, at most, for a 26 percent increase in labor productivity. The combination of mechanization and the westward movement, however, accounts for virtually all of the growth in labor productivity.

---

[26] Bateman, "Improvement in American Dairy Farming," 258.

[27] Rothenberg, "The Emergence of Farm Labor Markets and the Transformation of the Rural Economy: Massachusetts, 1750–1855," *Journal of Economic History* 48 (1988), 537–66; Rothenberg, *From Market-Places*, Chapter 6, especially 172 and Appendix C, 177–9.

Table 6.2. *Labor requirements as affected by inter-regional shifts, regional yields, and regional labor inputs per acre in the northeast, midwest, and west*

Index (i_n)	Period for values of			Labor requirement (hours) per bushel			Productivity index $\left(\dfrac{\text{Index}_1}{\text{Index}_n} \bullet 100 \right)$		
	Regional share	Yield	Preharvest, Harvest & postharvest labor	Wheat	Oats	Corn	Wheat	Oats	Corn
i_1	1840	1840	1840	2.96	1.27	2.51	100	100	100
i_2	1840	1910	1840	2.68	1.28	2.36	110	100	106
i_3	1840	1840	1910	0.97	0.55	1.30	307	233	193
i_4	1910	1840	1840	2.85	1.16	1.99	104	110	126
i_5	1840	1910	1910	0.86	0.54	1.21	344	234	207
i_6	1910	1840	1910	0.75	0.35	0.83	394	359	303
i_7	1910	1910	1840	2.69	1.22	2.03	110	104	124
i_8	1910	1910	1910	0.71	0.37	0.83	419	340	302

Source: Calculated from William N. Parker and Judith Klein, "Productivity Growth in Grain Production in the United States 1840–60 and 1900–10" in Dorothy S. Brady (ed.), *Output, Employment and Productivity in the United States after 1800*, Studies in Income and Wealth, vol. 30 (New York, 1966), 532.

Labor productivity in dairying, on the other hand, actually declined during the late nineteenth century in the Northeast and Midwest, though it more than doubled in the West. According to estimates by Bateman, milk output per man-hour declined from 43 pounds in 1850 to only 29 pounds in 1910 in the Northeast, and from less than 32 pounds per man-hour to less than 24 pounds per man-hour in the Midwest. But in the West, output per man-hour in dairying increased from just over 15 pounds per hour to more than 30 pounds by 1910. This unusual pattern of labor productivity change in dairying is explained by an alteration in technique towards a much more intensive feeding and care regimen, particularly in cold climates, that demanded far greater labor inputs for relatively modest increases in milk yield, and by the increasingly stringent sanitation requirements imposed by law.[28]

Although labor productivity in dairying did not improve, the aggre-

[28] Fred Bateman, "Labor Inputs and Productivity in American Dairy Agriculture, 1850–1910," *Journal of Economic History* 29 (1969), 206–29.

gate effects were not necessarily bad. Working the dairy was generally considered women's or children's tasks. Thus as the market for milk and dairy products grew, farmers could increase output by tapping this underutilized labor pool. The opportunity cost of older women and younger children in heavy field work was probably near zero, but they could make a significant contribution to farm income through milking and butter and cheese making. The farm – and the economy – could therefore expand food production without a commensurate rise in real labor costs.[29] The cost, of course, was the foregone leisure among underemployed family members.

LABOR

Land abundance that encouraged extensive rather than intensive agriculture contributed to the general lack of interest in land productivity by nineteenth-century American farmers, while stimulating their interest in mechanization to substitute for labor that was particularly scarce at planting and harvest time. Hired labor was hard to find and even harder to retain, given the opportunities for geographic or upward economic mobility on the agricultural ladder. This labor supply constraint limited farm size while encouraging both large families and the search for labor-saving farm machinery. So long as it took two full days of hard labor to harvest an acre of small grains, farmers were limited in how much they could plant. With a harvest-time opportunity of only about two weeks before the heads of grain shattered and the grain was lost upon the ground, a farmer could not risk planting more than 7 to 10 acres per available worker in any particular small grain.

One solution to the problem was to have a large family. The tendency for families to be bigger in the West has been remarked upon repeatedly by contemporaries as well as by historians and demographers. Large families have been linked to the availability of land. For example, a French consular official, Chevalier Felix de Beaujour, noted that

In the United States, more children are necessarily born than among us, because the inhabitants, in such an extent of country, finding the means of subsistence more abundant, marry at an earlier age. No human consideration there operates

[29] Ibid.

as a hindrance to reproduction, and the children swarm on the rich land in the same manner as do insects.[30]

This East–West fertility differential was particularly pronounced among farm families. Estimates by Atack and Bateman suggest that fertility rates among midwestern rural non-farm families at mid-century were much like those among the same group in the East, whereas fertility rates among farm families differed by more than a third between the East Coast and Midwest.[31] Richard Easterlin explains this difference in terms of a bequest motive: farm families wished to give each of their children a start in life at least equal to that which the parents had received. In the East, the high price of land made this an impossible goal for those with large families. Even where the expense was not prohibitive, the absence of available land in the immediate vicinity required that the family be scattered or the homestead subdivided, possibly into uneconomically small parcels. As a result eastern farm families limited their family size. In the Midwest on the other hand, and especially on the frontier, good land was readily and cheaply available in the neighborhood as a result of initial overbuying. Because land was cheaper and readily available within the immediate vicinity there was little incentive to check fertility.[32] The strength of the hold over children through a promised bequest was, however, less in the West, where land was less valuable.

Others, notably David and Sundstrom, and Ransom and Sutch, have explained the difference in fertility in terms of old-age security. Families had children to look after the parents in old age. However, as urban employment opportunities increased, fewer children stayed around to provide for their parents' old age. The relative price of having children rose as a result of this so-called "child default," and parents had fewer children in the East than the West.[33]

The strategy of having larger families to ease the farm labor constraint on the frontier seems to make sense, given the wide range of employment

---

[30] Chevalier Felix de Beaujour, *Sketch of the United States of North America* (London, 1814).

[31] Jeremy Atack and Fred Bateman, *To Their Own Soil* (Ames, IA 1987), 65.

[32] See Richard A. Easterlin, "Population Change and Farm Settlement in the Northern United States," *Journal of Economic History* 37 (1976), 45–75; Richard Easterlin, George Alter and Gretchen Condran, "Farms and Farm Families in Old and New Areas: The Northern States in 1860," in Tamara Hareven and Maris Vinoviskis (eds.) *Family and Population in Nineteenth Century America* (Princeton, 1978), 22–84.

[33] Roger Ransom and Richard Sutch, "Did Rising Out-Migration Cause Fertility to Decline in Antebellum New England? A Life-Cycle Perspective on Old-Age Security Motives, Child Default, and Farm Family Fertility," University of California Working Papers on the History of Saving, No. 5 (April 1986).

opportunities that were available in land clearing, farm formation, crop cultivation, and livestock tending. Moreover, this labor could create value through capital, through improvements to the land, and increases in livestock populations even when markets for crops were absent or limited. Work by Lee Craig, however, reveals that children were of only marginal economic benefit in a newly settled region.[34] They lacked the physical strength to do many of the arduous tasks of clearing land, digging wells, and erecting buildings and fences. Once an area had passed through this phase – a decade or so after settlement – children became economic assets, able to help feed and tend the livestock as well as weed and harvest the crops. In the East, where agriculture was much more labor intensive from necessity rather than choice, women and children, even quite young children, were particularly valuable.[35]

Alternative stategies offered more immediate solutions to the labor constraint: mechanization and the diversification of the crop mix to spread the peak labor demand. Corn with hay and small grains, for example, spread the work load between April and November with the hay typically ready for harvest before the small grains, which in turn were ready before the corn could be harvested (see Figures 6.5 and 6.6). Mechanization, while it dampened peak labor demand and differentially affected the labor required for particular tasks, did not alter the fundamental nature of seasonal labor demand. Only one farm activity, the care and feeding of livestock, was a year-round activity. The dairy, in particular, imposed a constant and high level of demand upon labor, averaging perhaps as much as 45 minutes per cow per day in the nineteenth century, effectively limiting herd size to 12 or 13 cows per dedicated dairy worker. Herd size on a less specialized farm had to be much smaller, since milking would not wait upon the spring plowing or the summer and fall harvest.

MECHANIZATION

Mechanization generated the most dramatic changes in nineteenth-century agricultural productivity. Abundant land in America encouraged extensive rather than intensive farming. But hired labor could be hard to find, even

[34] Lee Craig, "The Value of Household Labor in Antebellum Northern Agriculture," *Journal of Economic History* 51 (1991), 67–82, and "Farm Output, Productivity, and Fertility Decline in the Antebellum Northern United States," Ph.D. dissertation, Indiana University, 1989.
[35] Ibid.

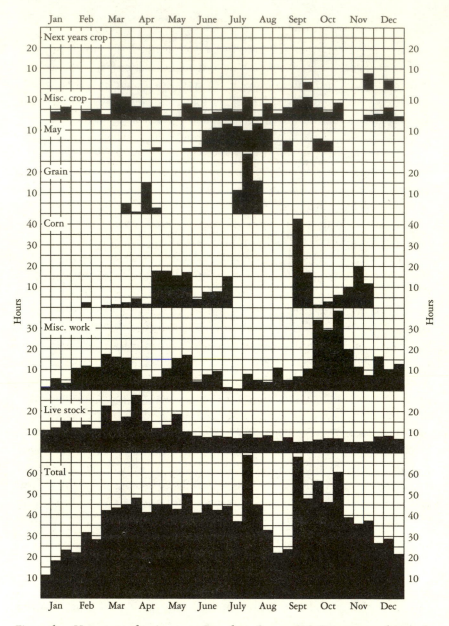

Figure 6.5. Hours spent farming on an Iowa farm. Source: U.S. Department of Agriculture, "Labor and Material Requirements of Field Crops," *Bulletin* 1000 (Washington, DC, 1921), 55. Note: This farm had the following crop and livestock organization: silage corn, 28.4 acres; ear corn, 69 ac.; corn hogged down, 5.75 ac.; oats, 6.1 ac.; barley, 15.88 ac.; spring wheat, 4.7 ac.; winter wheat, 17 ac.; clover, 13.2 ac.; timothy hay, 19.3 ac.; timothy seed, 17.5 ac.; alfalfa, 9.3 ac.; potatoes, 3.5 ac. Total group acreage, 227.63. Horses, 14.1; cows, 6; steers, 24.2; breed cattle (breeding herd), 28.1; hogs, 15.1; making a total of 88.5 animal units. Black bars indicate hours per day for each 10-day period.

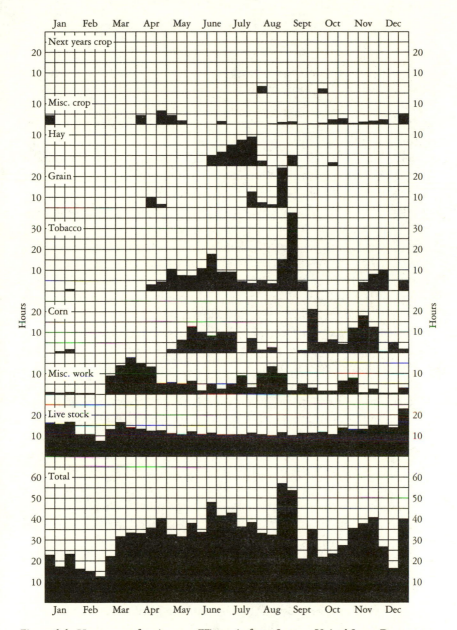

Figure 6.6. Hours spent farming on a Wisconsin farm. Source: United States Department of Agriculture, "Labor and Material Requirements of Field Crops, "*Bulletin* 1000 (Washington, DC, 1921), 56. Note: On this farm the following crops were grown: silage corn, 10 ac.; husked corn, 39.8 ac.; tobacco, 10.6 ac.; barley, 12.5 ac.; oats, 39.8 ac.; clover hay, 38.8 ac.; alfalfa, 3.4 ac.; potatoes, 1 acre. Total crop area, 143.7. The live stock organization was as follows: horses, 5; dairy cow, 19; hogs 0.8. Total 24.8 animal units. Black bars indicate average hours per day for each 10-day period.

at relatively high wages, particularly at planting and harvest time. This labor supply constraint encouraged both large families and the demand for labor-saving farm implements that the emerging manufacturers, such as John Deere and Cyrus McCormick, were eager to satisfy.

The machinery and techniques typically employed by northern farmers in the first third of the nineteenth century were remarkably crude by modern standards. The process of growing wheat and other small grains – the most important antebellum crops – is illustrative. First the soil had to be loosened sufficiently to bury the seed and provide adequate drainage and space for root development. This was done with a simple wooden or metal-sheathed wooden plow pulled by horse or oxen – a job taking perhaps 6 or 7 hours for an acre. Then seeds were scattered by hand (about an hour and a quarter) and buried under a shallow cover of earth by a light, animal-drawn plow or harrow (2.5 hours). When the plants matured, they were cut using a hand-swung scythe and bound together in shocks (20 man-hours per acre), which were then stored in a barn (4 hours per acre) until the farmer had time to separate the grain from the straw and remove the remaining chaff and dirt by screening (anywhere from 25 to 50 hours for the product of an acre of land).[36]

Technical improvements to the basic farm implements came fairly easily as mechanics adapted techniques used in the construction of industrial machinery. The first implements to be improved were plows. Wooden plows gave way to cast-iron plows of superior durability and, more importantly, of superior design requiring less animal power. Steel plows gradually replaced cast iron, particularly in the West, where they were better suited for turning heavy prairie soil while cutting a deeper furrow. By the 1860s, sulky and gang plows were introduced, reducing the drudgery even further. No longer did the farmer have to walk behind the plow; he could now ride atop it while cutting more than one furrow at a time. Mechanical threshers, introduced in the 1830s and 1840s, greatly reduced the labor of removing the grain from the stalk. These machines, however, were very expensive and had the capacity to thresh much more than the average farm with thirty or forty acres in small grains could turn out. But the marketplace adapted easily to this economic "indivisibility." Entrepreneurs rented out threshing services to neighboring farmers as their needs required. Prior to mechanization, it took about an hour to hand-thresh a bushel of wheat. Mechanical threshing could cut the time to perhaps

---

[36] U.S. Commissioner of Labor, *Thirteenth Annual Report* (1898): *Hand and Machine Labor* (Washington, DC, 1899), II, 470–73.

Table 6.3. *Hours of work involved in specific farm tasks when relying on hand labor alone versus mechanized labor*

	Man-hours of work	
	by hand	with machines
An acre of corn (hand: 1855; Machine: 1894)		
Plowing	7.50	2.00
Harrowing	2.50	0.88
Planting	4.25	0.67
Cultivating	10.00	5.00
Cutting and shocking	5.00	3.75
Husking	13.33	5.00
Shelling	66.67	0.60
An acre of wheat (hand: 1829; Machine: 1895)		
Plowing	6.67	1.00
Sowing	1.25	0.25
Harrowing	2.50	0.20
Reaping, thrashing and winnowing	43.33	1.00

Source: U.S. Commissioner of Labor, *Thirteenth Annual Report (1898): Hand and Machine Labor* (Washington, DC, 1899), II, 438–41, 470–73.

10–12 minutes and the cost of the operation to 3 or 4 cents per bushel, a saving of half over hand threshing. Seed drills were also introduced about the same time.[37] Successful mechanical milkers, however, were not introduced until the twentieth century.

The single most demanding task in the grain production cycle was harvesting (see Table 6.3). Until the 1830s harvesting placed a clear constraint on overall labor productivity. Hand harvesting took a great deal of time, yet the task had to be started and completed in a very limited season. Temporary harvest labor might be used to break the constraint for an individual farmer, but because everyone's wheat in the area needed to be harvested at about the same time, there was a real risk that outside help would be unavailable, or only available at very high wages. Hence the importance of the mechanical, horse-drawn harvester. The first harvesters were patented by Obed Hussey in 1833 and Cyrus McCormick in 1834. At first, the machines sold poorly – only 3,400 were

---

[37] For a summary of the principal mechanical improvements and their impact upon labor requirements, see Leo Rogin, *The Introduction of Farm Machinery in its Relation to the Productivity of Labor* (Berkeley, 1931).

manufactured in the years through 1850. But in the early 1850s sales took off: over 70,000 of the labor-saving devices were purchased between 1850 and 1858 and by 1862 perhaps a quarter of a million reapers were in use nationwide.

Farmers planting relatively few acres in wheat harvested by hand. But when wheat prices rose, particularly in the 1850s, farmers planted more land in wheat and some achieved a threshold of operation at which the cost of harvesting by machine was less than the cost by hand.[38] These producers then adopted mechanical harvesting. The threshold becomes irrelevant, however, if farmers purchased shares in a reaper, rather than opting for individual ownership. Did they do this? The answer seems to be yes; Alan Olmstead has evidence of such cooperative purchases from the McCormick archives.

Farm mechanization, particularly of the harvest, was seductive. Once the farmer had become accustomed to the reaper, he was reluctant to return to the brutally hard physical toil of hand harvesting. The early reapers cut from twelve to fifteen acres a day; McCormick, for example, warranted his for fifteen acres in 1843 and by 1849 was promising 2 acres per hour from Indiana westward and an acre and a half on lands to the east. The reaper was thus equivalent to four or five cradles.[39]

THE DIFFUSION OF KNOWLEDGE

Although mechanization dominated productivity growth, other sources of growth included learning-by-doing, adaptation of European and Native American techniques, and copying from one's more successful neighbors. By closing the gap between the average and best available practices, these activities shifted farming closer to the production possibilities boundary. Evolutionary rather than revolutionary, these changes nevertheless were an important force underlying improvement in agriculture. Institutional

---

[38] See Paul A. David, "The Mechanization of Reaping in the Antebellum Midwest," in H. Rosovsky (ed.), *Industrialization in Two Systems* (New York, 1966), 3–28. David estimates that the threshold was 46.5 acres in the early 1850s – far above the typical Illinois farmer's acreage in small grains, based on estimated yields, that at the time of the 1850 census averaged just 15–16 acres statewide and 37 acres in the northern Illinois wheat belt – but by the mid- 1850s, the threshold had fallen to about 35 acres as wages rose faster than reaper prices. For a critique of David's estimate of the threshold, see Alan Olmstead, "The Mechanization of Reaping and Mowing in American Agriculture," *Journal of Economic History* 35 (1975), 327–52. Olmstead estimates that the threshold was 89.4 acres around 1850 and 67.6 acres later in the decade.

[39] Rogin, *Farm Machinery*, 133–35.

changes, notably the agricultural experiment stations, the county agent system, the land-grant colleges, the Department of Agriculture, land banks and various farm credit agencies and, of course, land disposal policies, helped develop and diffuse knowledge that raised national farm productivity. Millions of immigrants arriving on these shores from every corner of the world brought new seeds and knowledge with them. Conditions in the American Plains were similar to those in eastern Europe, which supplied a growing number of immigrants. Moreover, nature itself provided additional bounty through natural adaptations and selection. The devasting ravages of pests and diseases, such as the Hessian Fly and rust (a fungus) helped to identify those varieties with greater natural immunity, while simultaneously impelling westward movement onto virgin land. Hogs and cattle turned out to survive in the virgin forests either adapted or died. Those that adapted best survived to breed. While the results might not win prizes for appearance or productivity, they could survive neglect and the frequently harsh conditions before agriculture in a region was fully developed.

Knowledge was often diffused by farmers themselves. The wealthier ones, though hardly rich landowners by European standards, were the most prominent innovators, partly because any given small innovation involved them in less proportionate risk. But much innovation may have been tried by farmers whose fortunes suffered when experimentation failed. A high degree of venturesomeness was often looked upon, in America as elsewhere, as a form of insanity. But in the rural areas clustered around the county seats were men whose opinions counted and whose example might be followed. And the motives for talking about one's practices, as the literature reveals them, are interesting to examine. The simple love of talk and of boasting, by hard-working, half-educated men, was an important source of conversations over farming.

Since local demonstration was important, it was important also that high risk-takers be widely scattered and that their activities should be readily communicated. Here the structure of rural society must have played an important part. To introduce a practice and to benefit financially from it was only half the game; the rest was to show one's neighbors that one was right. Given the purely competitive organization of the industry, there was no advantage to keeping an invention secret unless it could be patented and sold to other producers. To talk about a successful innovation added pleasure and prestige to the profit. It is no wonder then that in such an atmosphere, patent rights were so little respected. If a farmer could not patent a new feed for cattle, why should he, or the local black-smith, respect a patented modification on the plow?

Singly or in agricultural societies and clubs, farmers worked to develop new implements, produce new varieties, and adapt to new soils and climate. These local and state agricultural societies, established by oppor-tunistic local merchants, politicians, or reforming farmers, but eventually embracing a broad cross-section of the nation's farmers, provided a forum for exchanging experiences and diffusing information.[40] By 1858, there were 912 boards or societies nationwide dealing wholly or in part with agriculture, all but 137 of them in the North. New York had 97 societies, Illinois, 94, and Indiana, Iowa, and Ohio had over 70 each.[41] The county fairs which they sponsored, the first in 1807, were the occasion to display crops and animals, award prizes, and show local manufactures – including the products of the home food-processing industry.[42] At state fairs, where displays of farm machinery by regional and national producers were a prominent feature, blue-ribbon standards for crops or stock were high. State agricultural societies also published broadsheets, pamphlets and books, collected statistics and sometimes sponsored research. Such activi-ties transferred farming from folk arrangements to the formal institutions of organized agricultural science and education.

An emerging agricultural press also helped to disseminate this growing body of folk wisdom and scientific knowledge. The pioneer, *The American Farmer*, begun in 1819, was discontinued in 1834 but others such as *The Plough Boy* (1819), *The New England Farmer* (1822), *The Western Farmer* (1839) and *The Prairie Farmer* (1840) carried on the tradition.[43] The gov-ernment was also involved in this effort from an early date. Members of the increasingly far-flung American diplomatic corps, for example, were charged with sending interesting samples back to the Smithsonian. In 1839 Congress appropriated $1,000 for the "collection of agricultural sta-tistics, investigations for promoting agriculture and rural economy, and the procurement of cuttings and seeds for gratuitous distribution among the farmers by the U.S. Patent Office."[44] The success (and sometimes, failure) of these seeds and cuttings was reported in letters from corre-spondents around the country published in a separate volume of the *Annual*

---

[40] According to Bidwell and Falconer, the first such society was the Philadelphia Society for Promoting Agriculture, established in 1785. See Bidwell and Falconer, *History of Agriculture*, 184.
[41] U.S. Patent Office, *Annual Report* (1858), *Agriculture*, 91.
[42] Bidwell and Falconer, *History of Agriculture*, 187.
[43] Bidwell and Falconer, *History of Agriculture*, 316–17.
[44] U.S. Patent Office, *Annual Report* (1857), *Agriculture*, 24.

Report of the Commissioner of Patents, along with full-length feature articles about the latest and best in husbandry. This agricultural report for 1845, the largest issued, totaled 1,376 pages, while over a quarter of a million copies of the 1855 report were printed.[45]

The activities of the Patent Office and the privately sponsored U.S. Agricultural Society in the 1850s culminated in 1862 in the establishment of the U.S. Department of Agriculture and provision of federal grants for colleges devoted to the agricultural and mechanical arts. These state agricultural colleges educated the next generation of farmers' sons, and sponsored laboratory research, sometimes of a rather "pure" and academic character. In the USDA, research bureaus had proliferated by 1900 to most branches of agricultural science. In 1887 agricultural experiment stations on the German model were added. Like the colleges, these stations were set up, one in each state, with federal funds and the expectation that state governments would provide physical facilities and supplemental funding. With the Act of 1914 establishing the Extension Service, with agents in every county, the formal structure of agricultural research and development was complete.

From the outset, the agricultural experiment stations were acutely aware of the practical problems facing farmers and the market potential of agriculture. As a result, their research had a strong practical bent and their results commanded respect. The positioning of these stations in conjunction with the state agricultural colleges, however, was a mixed blessing. It gave them some underpinning in agricultural chemistry and put a theoretical basis, at least in statistics, under some of the work. On the other hand it made for an all-too-plausible division of labor between the scientific and theory-based experiment and applied, trial-and-error research. The station farm was sometimes looked on as a demonstration farm, and farmers even expected it to show a profit in its operations. Equally distracting was the tendency to load the stations with regulatory and policing functions. Of these the testing of fertilizers was the most widespread. Given the rather simple soil science of the 1880s, the analysis of a farmer's soil, a prescription for supplements, and a testing of the commercial fertilizer used seemed to many farmers to be the sum of agricultural research. But milk testing, seed testing, and even forestry work were added to some stations' duties by state legislatures, often without supplemental appropriations.

---

[45] U.S. Patent Office, *Annual Report* (1845), *Agriculture*; U.S. Patent Office, *Annual Report* (1857), *Agriculture*, 25.

The Granger and Populist agitation after the Civil War made agricultural research appear to progressives as a welcome and intelligent alternative: to do something, not just in Washington but at the state level where it could be visible, became a political necessity. The demand came not just from Populist agitators who often paid little attention to production problems but also from the larger, more enlightened farmers who were aware that science had something to do with farming.

FARM FINANCE

Title to the farm did not leave the farmer to relax in self-satisfaction and the self-sufficiency of a securely-titled peasantry. Farming became increasingly expensive in the late nineteenth century. The real price of land was rising throughout the period until after World War I.[46] Moreover, mechanization, a growing imperative for the successful farmer, further strained the financial resources of farmers. For many, tenancy was the only way to farm, but others chose to borrow. The most obvious and immediate consequence was mortgage debt – a phenomenon about whose extent and terms much is suspected and little has been reliably measured.

American farmers – North and West – in the nineteenth century certainly do not appear unusually debt-ridden, relative to farmers elsewhere. For some, however, indebtedness was a fatal mistake resulting in foreclosure and loss of the family farm. Others were successful but had to pay close attention to agricultural product markets and farm cash flow to generate the cash to meet their periodic financial obligations and avoid default. Even for the successful farmer, however, a mortgage in the nineteenth century must have been cause for worry. The only available mortgages were short-term, balloon mortgages. Such loans are unamortized. Periodic payments meet the interest but contribute nothing to the principal, which is payable in full at maturity. Mortgages typically lasted three years or less and might be renewed, though renewal terms were never certain. The long-term, amortized mortgages so familiar today did not begin to appear until the 1920s.

Farmers at the time complained that monopoly power allowed the representatives of banks and insurance companies to charge interest above purely competitive rates. However, Allan Bogue's evidence suggests that

---

[46] Peter H. Lindert, "Long-Run Trends in American Farmland Values," *Agricultural History* 62 (1988), 45–85.

the western mortgage industry was immensely competitive – thanks, ironically, to the entry of eastern moneylenders into the western market. Rates
in the 1850s in Iowa averaged 10 percent (which was the usury limit in
Iowa and many other states – true interest rates after fees, commission and
other expenses were probably much higher) and had declined to 6.5–7.5
percent by the 1890s. These interest rates were higher than rates on gilt-
edged securities, but they probably only reflected the risks of farming on
the Great Plains in the 1880s. They were far lower (in nominal terms, at
least) than rates had been in earlier years on the agricultural frontier.[47]

Mortgages, however, committed farmers to fixed nominal payments. As
a result, while they gained in periods of rising prices, repaying their creditors in increasingly less valuable dollars, they lost in periods of deflation
such as the first three post–Civil War decades. To the extent that debtors
failed to anticipate declining prices they were caught short, but it is
hard to believe that price expectations could have failed to adjust to a
trend that lasted thirty years. Farmers were simply unlikely to borrow at
interest rates that they believed could not be supported by future crop
revenues. Moreover, with a short time to maturity, any losses due to
unanticipated price changes should have quickly worked through the
system. As a result, Robert Fogel and Jack Rutner calculate that the
overall wealth loss to farmers could not have been large, especially since
the average mortgage debt was small.[48] Still, some losers were vocal,
engaging in a wide range of political activities and, sometimes, in civil
disobedience.

Nationwide in 1890, only 29 percent of farmers were encumbered
by mortgages, and among those that were, the debt averaged only 35
percent of their worth. Debt rates, however, were higher in the troubled
Plains states (60 percent in Kansas, 54 percent in Nebraska).[49] Average
mortgage debt relative to equity fell between 1890 and 1910, but more
and more farmers became encumbered.[50] Such encumbrances were a source

---

[47] Allan G. Bogue, *From Prairie to Cornbelt* (Chicago, 1963); Barry Eichengreen, "Mortgage Interest
Rates in the Populist Era," *American Economic Review* 74 (1984), 995–1015; Kenneth Snowden,
"Mortgage Rates and American Capital Market Development in the Late Nineteenth Century,"
Journal of Economic History 47 (1987), 671–91.

[48] Robert W. Fogel and Jack Rutner, "The Efficiency Effect of Federal Land Policy, 1850–1890," in
William O. Aydelotte et al. (eds.), *The Dimensions of Quantitative Research in History* (Princeton,
1972), 390–418.

[49] U.S. Census Bureau, *1890 Census,* Vol. 13.

[50] 13th Census (1910), Vol. V, *Agriculture,* 159–60; 14th Census (1920), Vol. V. *Agriculture,* 484–86;
Gavin Wright, "American Agriculture and the Labor Market: What Happened to Proletarianization?" *Agricultural History* 63 (1988), 182–209.

of risk, particularly given the particular nature of late-nineteenth-century mortgages. James Stock has argued that, although the risk of individual foreclosure was quite small – the 1890 census, for example, quotes foreclosure rates of 0.61 percent in Illinois in 1880 and 1.55 percent in Minnesota in 1891 – or between 2.4 percent and 6.1 percent of all mortgages assuming an average life of four years – it was quite likely that a farmer had a neighbor who had been foreclosed.[51] As a result farmers had a genuine, personal, and palpable fear of foreclosure particularly during some of the longer-lasting periods of low farm prices or repeated harvest failures.

FARM PROFITABILITY

Farmers generally seem to have earned positive, but not particularly high, rates of return on their capital investments. This should not be surprising, given the relative ease of entry arising from such factors as federal land policy, widespread familiarity with the industry, the diffusion of knowledge about new opportunities, productivity-raising techniques, and access to capital markets (albeit for relatively short-term credit). In 1845, for example, the secretary of the Treasury reported that "the profit of agriculture varies from 1 to 8 percent."[52] These returns depended not just upon harvests, prices, and the costs of getting surplus products to market but upon capital gains on land arising from local community development and other externalities such as road, canal, or railroad construction. In 1836, for example, an Albany, New York, farmer wrote in his local farm magazine, the Albany *Cultivator*, "That percentage [rate of capital gain] is sometimes very high, but in almost all cases, it adds materially to the profits of the investment . . . a tract of land, under judicious culture must be enhanced in value at least five percent per annum."[53] This has been a commonly expressed idea among historians. Lewis Stilwell argued that "Vermonters' profits in the past [before 1860] were derived as much from increasing land values as they were from agriculture."[54] Similarly, Paul Gates has asserted, "The pioneer farmer was well aware that in the end his profits would come

[51] James Stock, "Real Estate Mortgages, Foreclosures, and Midwestern Agrarian Unrest, 1865–1920," *Journal of Economic History* 44 (1984), 89–106.
[52] U.S. Congress. 29 Cong, 1st. sess., Senate Document 2.
[53] Quoted by Paul W. Gates, *The Farmer's Age: Agriculture 1815–1860* (New York, 1960), 403.
[54] Lewis D. Stilwell, "Migration from Vermont 1776–1860," *Proceedings of the Vermont Historical Society* 5 (1937), 63–245 especially 232.

largely from rising land values."[55] Between 1850 and 1860, for example, the cash value per acre of eastern farmland rose annually by 2.8 percent; western, by 7.3 percent. However, after the Civil War the current return on farm output dominated the return to capital, and formal or informal land speculation was no longer a leading source of farm profits.

On the eve of the Civil War, the average farmer in Illinois earned a return of 19 percent. Profits were lower in the other states, generally declining north, east, and west. Farmers in Kansas, for instance, averaged 10 percent, while those in Ohio earned 13 percent and in Michigan, 5.8 percent. Returns earned by New York farmers, about 17 percent, were also generally higher than those earned by farmers in states immediately to the north, south, or west. Returns were somewhat higher in 1880, though their pattern was broadly similar. Farmers in Illinois were then averaging almost 20 percent, while farmers in Ohio averaged 13.8 percent and farmers in New York were making 15.8 percent, although farmers in many of the northeastern states were averaging higher returns than farmers in New York (see Table 6.4).

Despite vocal protests to the contrary, American farmers were not doing badly. They averaged a return of 6 to 10 percent on current production, a usually realized capital gain of 3 to 7 percent. They enjoyed some margin of income security against market vicissitudes because of their ability to store surplus labor value in land improvements. The owner-occupier further had the satisfaction of being his own boss. True, these profits were sensitive to market prices, local vicissitudes of weather, and the ravages of disease as well as the scale of farming – smaller farms earned lower rates of return – but prospects looked fairly rosy. If commercial markets soured badly, they could still feed and otherwise maintain themselves in a secure way unavailable to nonfarm workers.

During the next 20 years, however, farmers seem to have been disappointed. Fogel and Rutner estimate that returns fell far short of earlier levels in the Northeast and Midwest, though farmers in the West did very well, earning a return of almost 22 percent (see Table 6.5). Indeed, as the agricultural historian Theodore Saloutos remarked, "Perhaps no development of the nineteenth century brought greater disppointment to the American farmers than did their failure to realize the prosperity that they had expected from industrialization."[56] And they made known their unhappiness.

[55] Gates, *Farmer's Age*, 399.
[56] Theodore Saloutos, "The Agricultural Problem and Nineteenth-Century Industrialism," *Agricultural History* 22 (1948), 156.

Table 6.4. *The rate of return to farming by state, 1860 and 1880*

	Return in 1860		Return in 1880	
	without capital gains	with capital gains	without capital gains	with capital gains
Northeast				
Connecticut	8.7	10.6	9.8	13.9
Delaware	n.a.	n.a.	10.2	15.7
Maine	n.a.	n.a.	13.2	16.5
Massachusetts	n.a.	n.a.	10.8	14.2
New Hampshire	5.3	6.8	11.4	14.7
New Jersey	6.8	10.0	9.8	15.6
New York	14.5	17.3	10.8	15.8
Pennsylvania	6.7	10.1	8.4	15.1
Vermont	8.9	12.2	12.7	19.0
Northeast average	9.5	12.6	10.1	15.1
Midwest				
Illinois	10.8	19.1	11.2	19.9
Indiana	3.8	10.4	10.1	17.3
Iowa	4.5	11.1	11.9	18.4
Kansas	1.0	10.0	10.0	18.8
Michigan	−0.5	5.8	10.0	17.4
Minnesota	3.1	8.8	13.0	19.2
Missouri	−2.8	1.9	12.2	18.0
Nebraska	n.a.	n.a.	13.3	21.9
Ohio	8.3	13.3	7.9	13.8
Wisconsin	6.6	11.4	10.8	16.6
Midwestern average	5.8	11.9	10.5	17.6
Average for North	*7.6*	*12.1*	*10.3*	*16.9*

Source: 1860: Jeremy Atack and Fred Bateman, *To Their Own Soil: Agriculture in the Antebellum North* (Ames, IA, 1987), 255; 1880: calculated from the 1880 census of agriculture.

Table 6.5. *Real return to agricultural capital by region, 1880–99 (average annual rate)*

Source:	Northeast	Midwest	West
Current production	6.4	5.8	20.3
Capital gains on land	−0.3	1.7	0.3
Capital gains on livestock	1.6	4.6	6.3
Overall Return	6.4	7.6	21.9

Source: Robert W. Fogel and Jack Rutner, "The Efficiency Effects of Federal Land Policy 1850–1900," in William O. Aydelotte et al. (eds.), *The Dimensions of Quantitative Research in History* (Princeton, 1972), 398.

FARM PROTEST

By elevating expectations, the Civil War prosperity, with its positive impact on mechanization and profits, may account for some of the disillusionment and the pessimism of American farmers afterwards. Certainly productivity growth can become a curse to producers in a purely competitive industry when either demand or input quantities do not adjust. American agriculture periodically found itself caught in this bind. Productivity growth was sometimes not accompanied by sufficient exit. Neither acreage in farms nor the labor force shrank. As a result, prices fell sharply. Immigration, particularly to urban areas, and foreign demand helped American farmers, but heavy reliance upon these sources of demand made farmers vulnerable when international markets for American products diminished or immigration slowed. Indeed, agricultural supply did not begin serious adjustment until the 1920s, when new farm creation finally ceased and farm population began to shrink as farm children abandoned the farm to seek their fortune elsewhere.

In the interim, from the late 1860s through the mid-1890s, farmers felt at the mercy of forces beyond their control. Expecting an arcadia where small farmers would be the central players and where the common man would be kind, they found themselves being shunted aside by the powerful forces of industrialization and financial capitalism. Their day was passing. Farmers considered themselves to be what Jeffersonian democracy described: fundamental to America's success economically, socially, and politically. But manufacturing, transportation, and finance increasingly intruded upon their lives. Ironically, their own acquisitiveness for nonfarm products had contributed to this turn of events. Their quest for commercial sales drove them toward greater production, which induced acreage expansion, mechanization, and the march westward onto new soils. To achieve their goal, they went into debt and plunged into the competitive and uncertain world of market sales. Once in debt, they became enmeshed in a capitalistic system from which withdrawal was virtually impossible.

Jefferson had warned them against indebtedness and against subjecting themselves to "the caprice of customers." But they did not listen. And they wanted more. The sought a standard of material consumption beyond self-sufficiency. Once in the system, they could not insulate themselves from what happened in the system. Farmers apparently overestimated their gains from industrialization – or perhaps underestimated manufacturing's swift ascendency – and underestimated the competitive effects of their actions. As consumers they cherished industrial expansion; as producers they viewed it as competitive economically and destructive of their way of life. Refusing to abandon farming, they chose to seek political solutions, eventually creating Populism and in the process laying the foundation for twentieth-century American public policy.

On December 4, 1867, Oliver Kelley organized a secret fraternal society for farmers known as the "National Grange of the Patrons of Husbandry." By 1875, it had over 850,000 members and was a potent political force, particularly in the American Midwest. In Kansas, for example, there was one Grange for every 66 farm families in 1875. This was just the first of a number of protest movements organized around disaffected farmers – the Greenbackers, the Alliance, and eventually the Populist campaigns of the 1890's followed – that challenged established political parties and offered a prescription for the economic woes of farmers.

These farmers were distinctly unhappy with falling commodity prices, increased entry costs to farming, rising tenancy, farm foreclosure, and uncertainties generated by harvests in another hemisphere and reliance upon markets an ocean away. They demanded regulation of their enemies: the railroads, the banks, and big corporations. From this upheaval emerged the foundations for regulation and public policy toward business and agriculture in the United States.

The facts, however, are not so clear cut. True, farm prices fell during most of the post–Civil War period. Corn that had sold for about 70 cents a bushel in the early 1870s fetched only 30 to 40 cents in the late 1880s and wheat prices slipped from about $1 to 70 cents, but these figures are not very useful as a measure of farm purchasing power. The prices of nonagricultural commodities sometimes fell even faster and farm terms of trade, defined as the ratio of farm prices to all prices, generally improved.[57]

Unable to do anything about market prices for their products, farmers often blamed the nearest railroad as the messenger that brought the bad news and as a monopolist deriving excess profits from the storage and transporation of undervalued commodities. As a result, farmers agitated for the regulation of railroad freight rates and the prices and services offered by terminal facilities, securing such legislation in four midwestern states, Illinois, Iowa, Minnesota, and Wisconsin. However, the fall in average freight rates per ton-mile roughly paralleled the fall in farm prices

[57] See John D. Bowman and Richard H. Keehn, "Agricultural Terms of Trade in Four Midwestern States, 1870–1900," *Journal of Economic History* 34 (1974), 592–609.

through 1890 and fell more rapidly thereafter.[58] Moreover, railroads were just the first link in the distribution chain. A good portion of American wheat was exported and, over the 1870–1900 period, Atlantic freight rates fell by two-thirds. Increased competition and organizational efficiencies guaranteed that reduced international distribution costs narrowed the gap between what consumers paid and what farmers got.

Discontented, debt-ridden farmers found it easy to believe that interest rates on farm mortgages were excessive, that the principal goal of lenders was foreclosure, and that land speculators "over-priced" land thereby capturing gains which rightfully belonged to the farmer. True, barely 40 percent of homestead entries were completed, and failure rates among western farms were relatively high, but the evidence suggests that mortgage lending was competitive, so interest rates must have approached the market rate of interest subject only to a risk premium. Certainly, lenders faced a potentially serious default risk in times of falling land values. While it was not in the lender's interest to incur foreclosure costs and potential capital losses, there was the question of moral hazard: if delinquent borrowers were rewarded, further delinquency would be encouraged.[59] Farmers had an incentive to use the bargaining power from threat of default to secure preferential terms, a strategy limited by the short term of mortgages, making the system one of repeated games.

Western farm failures, however, may simply reflect that many farmers were unprepared for the risks of prairie farming, particularly in the West North Central states. Personal bankruptcy, due largely to individual inability to outlast the vagaries of the weather, does not mean that resources were misallocated or that the government should have prevented individuals from voluntarily taking big risks. Finally, by definition, capital gains are unearned rents accruing as a result of the secure property rights in this country. They do not affect current resource use. The only economic question is therefore one of distribution, and late-nineteenth-century speculators seem to have fared much worse than their prewar land counterparts.

Why, then, did farmers complain? Possibly the system produced large numbers of losers who had much to complain about. Farmers took little comfort in the news that there were others further down the line who

---

[58] Robert Higgs, "Railroad Rates and the Populist Uprising," *Agricultural History* 43 (1970), 291–97.

[59] Kenneth Snowden, "The Evolution of Interregional Mortgage Lending Channels, 1870–1940: The Life Insurance–Mortgage Company Connection," in Naomi R. Lamoreaux and Daniel M.G. Raff (eds.), *Coordination and Information: Historical Perspectives on the Organization of Enterprise* (Chicago, 1995), 209–55.

gained where the railroad faced cut-throat competition. Increasing capital market integration did not help the farmer foolish or unlucky enough to be caught between an expensive mortgage and declining grain prices. Indeed, the very impersonal nature of the market was likely to spur even greater anger and frustration. In a democratic system, just a few vocal losers can win the support of the majority if the majority perceives itself just one step away from joining the losers.

Institutional changes also exposed post–Civil War farmers to greater risks. Before the war, most farmers did not depend upon the market even though they actively participated in it. They grew much of their own feed and food. Market purchases were luxuries, not necessities, and certainly not necessary for their farm activities. The postwar grain farmer, however, was compelled by growing competition to lower costs and raise productivity. For many this meant mechanization and farming more extensively than before. But this strategy brought with it fixed debt obligations that had to be serviced. Farm incomes thus became subject to much greater price leverage. Moreover, instead of serving customers just beyond the farm gate in isolated markets, farmers supplied consumers thousands of miles distant whose wants, tastes, and habits were transmitted by an impersonal market signal – price. But this price also reflected global supply conditions. Farmers could no longer count on a higher price to offset their poor crop.

Geographic expansion and transportation improvements had opened up vast new agricultural areas capable of delivering grain to market at constant real resource cost. Farm goods prices consequently did not rise sharply as demand expanded, denying established farmers the high profits they might otherwise have received by entering the business on the "ground floor."

In a competitive labor market, the wage is determined by the minimum price necessary to retain the marginal worker. Farmers were often unhappy with their wages because others were willing to work the land for very little return. When farm prices went up, raising the total return to farm enterprise, either other farmers moved onto virgin land, driving down land and produce prices and farmers' incomes or, if more good land was unavailable, the price of existing acreage was bid up to the point where the return was back at the competitive rate. Those fortunate enough to own property received the capital gains from land, but the returns to current productive activity were depressed to the competitive margin. Entry for the next generation of aspiring yeoman farmers was made that much more difficult.

CONCLUDING REMARKS

Commercialization beyond some critical point is a one-way street; once family self-sufficiency began to unravel, skills were lost, equipment abandoned, values altered, and tastes changed. The dividing line between demand patterns among farm families and those of town dwellers became obscured or obliterated. Prestige was inherent in what money would buy or had bought. The road back, when hard times came in the 1870s and thereafter, was doubly difficult. By 1914 three of the most destructive agents of rural culture still lay on the horizon: the gasoline engine, the telephone, and the radio. These affected farm social life in obvious ways. But the commercialization of farm power resulting from substituting tractor for horse directly influenced the structure of farming as a productive sector.

Farm families, having embarked on the road of money and markets, often came to find that they – like small capitalists everywhere – had little control over the rate or evenness of their economic journey. Farmers differed from contemporaries in industry and commerce in other ways, notably the dual nature of their product and factor markets. Farm demand embraced family as well as the outside world. Agriculturalists' labor market included "captive" family members plus hired hands. Their capital market divided between farm-produced physical capital (such as fencing or buildings) and commercially purchased goods (mechanized implements). Even their land could be divided between improved acreage and unimproved. To a large degree the ability to spend idle time creating capital investment or clearing land distinguished the farmer's economic life from that of the industrial or commercial worker. And the capacity to continue feeding one's family even when external market opportunities went bad gave farmers an economic security unavailable to most people. Compared to others in the world, they lived well materially, particularly in the settled northern regions.

Within the bounds of their constraints, American farmers behaved consistently with rational choice: they settled the best soils first, their mobility patterns maximized their human capital, they diversified against risk, they responded to prices, they tried to smooth out seasonal labor usage, and they capitalized on knowledge of markets and production techniques. The farm press prodded them to become better managers and better market forecasters. While individual performance varied enormously, northern farmers as a group proved to be economically responsive actors in a capitalist system. This rationality, however, was bounded. By concentrating so hard on agriculture, farmers may have ignored emerging opportunities elsewhere, but within those bounds their entrepreneurial and managerial skills are evident. As the long nineteenth century progressed, they usually commercialized as quickly as demand and transport availability allowed. No longer guided by Jefferson's narrow vision, they acted according to a broader American ideal: farming became a business.

7

NORTHERN AGRICULTURE AND THE WESTWARD MOVEMENT

JEREMY ATACK, FRED BATEMAN, AND
WILLIAM N. PARKER

INTRODUCTION

Thomas Jefferson envisioned the United States as an experiment in political democracy founded upon an economy of small farms. This essay examines the geographic expansion and economic development of agriculture during the nineteenth century across the northern region, where Jefferson hoped his vision would materialize most clearly. Central to realizing this goal was transferring land in the public domain into the hands of aspiring farm families. Our theme in this chapter is the heightening tension between the political vision of a nation inhabited by self-sufficient, landowning farmers and the economic reality of increasing agricultural commercialization, tenancy, wealth inequality, and industrialization.

The century opened with an agricultural-commercial economy in which farming played the central role. It closed, however, with agriculture as a relatively diminished sector encroached upon by a rapidly advancing industrial system and by corporate business. In between, farming evolved from a simple, traditional activity into a highly productive commercial enterprise that not only fed the domestic population but exported worldwide and supplied the raw materials that fueled American industrialization. The outcome, ironically, was an increasingly productive farm sector populated by increasingly discontented farmers. These individuals, who believed that the national economy was developing at their expense, ultimately sought governmental solutions when markets did not meet their personal expectations. Nevertheless, the structural transformation progressed, becoming a driving force behind the national population's dramatically improving economic well-being over the nineteenth century.

TERRITORIAL EXPANSION

In 1800 the Atlantic Coast economies that formed the newly created United States of America looked outward. Foreign suppliers met many of their consumer needs; Americans in turn sought to satisfy the demands of distant buyers. Of their agricultural crops, only tobacco – collected from the Tidewater farms and plantations in upper Virginia and eastern Maryland – had any substantial international significance, although supplies of Carolina rice, northern grains, and barreled meat had found small but steady markets in the Caribbean sugar islands. Together, these agricultural crops accounted for almost two-thirds of export value in the early 1790s. The balance was largely timber, fish, and other resource-based manufactured products.[1] A Yankee merchant marine carried this trade across the Atlantic and, with the opening of the former Spanish empire, around Cape Horn and across the Pacific. The chief sources of colonial wealth were either tobacco or mercantile trade and shipping. However, the vast unsettled western lands of the new nation represented an untapped bounty.

By the Treaty of Paris, signed in 1783, Great Britain had ceded all the lands south of Canada, east of the Mississippi, and north of Florida to the United States. However, except for a few isolated settlements – primarily remnants of French exploration and fur trading such as Kaskaskia – in what is now Illinois, only the eastern third of this land was occupied by European settlers and their descendants. Agricultural expansion onto these lands depended upon the commercial and political policies of the East Coast merchants and southern planters, but their commercial exploitation also relied upon the goodwill of other nations, since the easiest and cheapest means of transportation and communication from the region to the rest of the country was down the Mississippi River and into the Gulf of Mexico through territory controlled first by Spain and then by France. Barely forty years later, farmers in search of new homesteads were spilling over these original borders into new lands even farther west.

Next in this territorial expansion was the Louisiana Purchase in 1803, by which the United States acquired from France the central and northern Plains of the continent up to the eastern slope of the Rocky Mountains. In a single stroke, President Thomas Jefferson freed navigation of the Mississippi through New Orleans from foreign control while almost

---

[1] See James F. Shepherd and Gary M. Walton, "Economic Change after the American Revolution," *Explorations in Economic History* 13 (1976), 408–9.

doubling the territory of the United States. Thirty years later, revolutions by American settlers overturned Mexico's government in Texas and California. The Mexican War of 1845–48, together with the Oregon cession in 1846, moved the boundary to the Pacific.

Thus, within little more than sixty years, the United States had expanded its control by purchase, treaty, and conquest from the 864,000 square miles between the Mississippi River and the East Coast to almost three million square miles (excluding Alaska) stretching from the Atlantic to the Pacific. These political boundaries guaranteed the property rights and provided the physical protection for a settled society, and across these 2,000 miles of rich and varied terrain, tens of thousands of hunters, trappers, miners, ranchers, and farmers took up occupancy. They carried with them tangible expressions of the two main cultural impulses that created American civilization in the nineteenth century: democracy and capitalism. Capitalism was the more powerful and apparent force in forming the agricultural industry, but there appeared no serious conflict between these two ideas until later in the century.

Both forces were at work in this settlement. Capitalism motivated land purchase and speculation, the annually burgeoning trade, and expansion of the money economy. Democracy conditioned the settlement pattern and governance in these newly settled lands and played an increasing role in the original land transfer form the federal government to the people.

FEDERAL LAND POLICY

Under the Articles of Confederation, the various states had ceded their claims over the tens of millions of acres west of the Appalachians to the United States, simultaneously passing to the weak central government the politically thorny issue of how, and how quickly, this land should be settled. The Federalists viewed the public lands as a potential revenue source for the government – an important consideration for an authority with no power to tax.

To maximize the gain to the public treasury, Alexander Hamilton urged that these lands be sold by public auction, subject to a high reservation price.[2] Assuming competitive bidding, this plan assured that the govern-

---

[2] For a complete summary of Hamilton's views on land policy, see his 1790 report: *American State Papers, Public Lands* (Washington, DC, 1832).

ment would capture the economic rents associated with each lot, while the high reservation price assured that these rents would not be dissipated. Such a plan also guaranteed that the land be transferred to those who placed the highest economic value upon it and who thus, presumably, had the highest valued use for it. This plan offered one further advantage so far as Hamilton was concerned: high prices would discourage rapid settlement. This, he apparently assumed, would limit agricultural expansion and indirectly encourage manufactures.

Thomas Jefferson and his supporters, on the other hand, saw the public lands as offering an opportunity to create a nation of small landed farmers. To him, these settlers would be the bulwark of a sustainable democracy and a protection against the arbitrary exercise of government power. To achieve this goal, he argued that the land should be sold at low prices on credit in small lots, or even given away. His argument is succinctly set forth in a letter that he wrote to the father of James Madison while Jefferson was Ambassador to France:

Whenever there are in any country uncultivated lands and unemployed poor, it is clear that the laws of property have been so far extended as to violate natural right. The earth is given as a common stock for man to labor and live on. If for the encouragement of industry we allow it to be appropriated, we must take care that other employment be provided to those excluded from the appropriation. If we do not, the fundamental right to labor the earth returns to the unemployed. It is too soon yet in our country to say that every man who cannot find employment, but who can find uncultivated land, shall be at liberty to cultivate it, paying a moderate rent. But it is not too soon to provide by every possible means that as few as possible shall be without a little portion of land. The small landholders are the most precious part of a state.[3]

Indeed, Jefferson cautioned that "by selling land you will disgust them [the frontiersmen] and cause an avulsion of them from the common union. They will settle the lands in spite of everybody."

Such idealism aside, the debate over the transfer of public land into private hands was dominated by self-interested rent-seekers. The propertyless stood to gain a saleable asset from Jefferson's policy, while cheap land was a threat to all existing property owners, limiting, if not actually diminishing their property's value. Keeping land prices high benefited existing land owners; setting them low benefited the poor, especially if credit were available, and increased the opportunities for profitable speculation.

---

[3] Thomas Jefferson to the Reverend James Madison, October 28, 1785.

In New England, colonial settlement had proceeded in an orderly manner through the process of "township planting." Promoters received permission to establish new townships at the boundaries of existing township settlements. These tracts were commonly six miles square, subdivided into smaller plots for sale at public auction. The resulting settlement was compact. Township lands often were reserved for schools and churches. Title to unsurveyed land could not be secured. The system imposed order upon the land.

In the South, the practice had been one of prior settlement. Settlers simply took up unclaimed land, seeking to acquire the most desirable properties first. This land was then marked off by the county surveyor – usually the deputy sheriff – who had little or no professional training. With haphazard surveys and carelessly kept records, there resulted a patchwork quilt of land claims, some overlapping, interspersed with publicly owned tracts of less desirable land.

To deal with these issues, Congress appointed a committee chaired by Jefferson, with representatives from Rhode Island, Massachusetts, and North and South Carolina. The committee recommended preserving the key features of the New England system: survey prior to sale and careful recording of titles with the land divided by rectangular survey in "hundreds" of 10 square miles and "lots" of 1 mile square. No lands, however, were reserved for public purposes; no minimum price was fixed, and no system for land sale was specified, although warrants could be used for land purchases.

After its second reading (by which time Jefferson was in Europe as ambassador to France), Congress referred the report back to a new committee with one member from each state. This group submitted a report reducing townships to seven miles square, divided into sections of 1 square mile, with sections reserved for schools and for religious purposes. Four were reserved to the federal government. These lands were to be sold, after survey, by public auction for a minimum of $1 per acre. After a series of compromises, Congress finally passed the Land Ordinance on May 20, 1785, which preserved the principle of orderly systematic settlement on the New England model. The land was to be surveyed prior to sale, establishing a rectangular grid with respect to east–west baselines and north–south principal meridians divided into townships 6 miles square.[4] Each township in turn was to be subdivided into 36 sections 1 mile square

---

[4] See *Journals of the American Congress*, 4, Ordinance of May 20, 1785, 5207; J. C. Fitzpatrick (ed.), *Journal of the Continental Congress*, 28, 375ff.

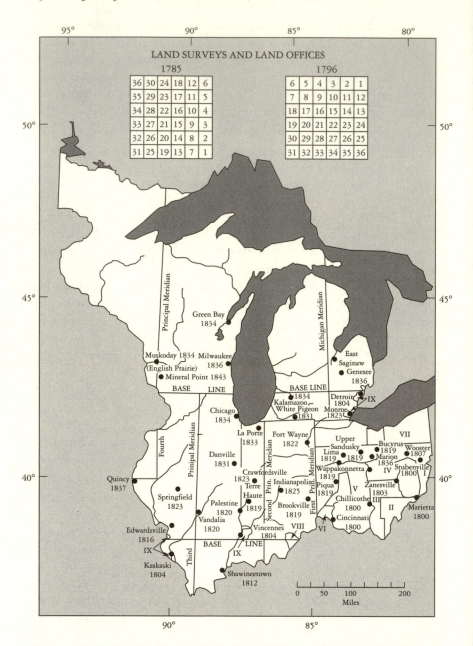

Figure 7.1A. The Land Ordinance of 1785. Key: I. The Seven Ranges. II. Ohio Company Purchase. III. Congress Lands by Greenville Treaty. IV. United States Military District. V. Virginia Miliary District. VI. Symmes Purchase. VII. Connecticut Western Reserve. VIII. Clark's Grant. IX. Old French Grants. Source: R. Carlyle Buley, *The Old Northwest* (Bloomington, IN, 1951), vol. I, 117.

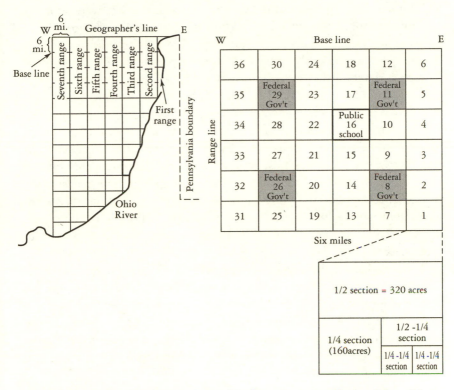

Figure 7.1B. The Land Ordinance of 1785: The first seven ranges. Source: Adapted from Ray A. Billington, *Westward Expansion* (New York, 1949), 208.

(see Figures 7.1A and 7.1B), imposing a lasting and visible pattern upon the landscape.[5]

Two years later, Congress adopted the Northwest Ordinances, establishing the terms under which the newly settled land would be incorporated into the political system. The ordinances provided that the area be administered by a governor appointed by Congress until such time as the population exceeded 5,000 males of voting age. A territorial legislature was then to be elected. When population exceeded 60,000 the territory was to be accepted as a state on the basis of complete equality with the existing states, ensuring the continuation of the democratic tradition.[6]

[5] For a detailed treatment of early federal land policy, see Payson J. Treat, *The National Land System, 1785–1820* (New York, 1910). See also Hildegard B. Johnson, *Order Upon the Land* (New York, 1976).
[6] See Jay A. Barrett, *Evolution of the Ordinance of 1787* (New York, 1901).

These initial terms represented a Federalist victory. Prices were set high, and minimum acreages were large. Alternating townships were to be sold as units; the others, by section – 640 acres. Tenure was allodial – that is granted by the state to the purchaser in fee simple for the annual payment of property taxes. All sales were to be by public auction, subject to a reservation price of $1 per acre, in gold, silver, or public debt certificates. Section 16 in each township was reserved to underwrite public education. Congress retained sections 8, 11, 26, and 29 in each township plus one-third of the mineral rights. In 1796, the Federalists triumphed again when the reservation price was raised to $2 per acre. Although this further reduced direct access to the land by the common man, one year's credit was extended on half the purchase price (see Table 7.1).[7] Land sales were disappointing (see Figure 7.2), and the anticipated bounty to the public treasury failed to materialize. Thereafter, sales terms were progressively liberalized.

Congress halved the acreage requirement in 1800, and again in 1804. In 1820, the minimum price was slashed to $1.25; in 1832 the acreage requirement was cut to forty. It thus became possible to buy land for a 40-acre farm from the federal government for as little as $50 – about half the annual per capita income in the 1830s – whereas in the late 1790s, when per capita income was perhaps $75, it had cost at least $1,280 to purchase land at public auction.

The credit provisions in the 1796 law eased the burden of purchase, but the fortunate buyer still had to come up with $640 within 30 days and the balance within a year. By the same token, abolition of credit provisions in 1820 undoubtedly reduced the chances for the poorest potential buyers to become owners. Even so, it seems clear that access to public land became much more open and less exclusive with the passage of time, more in the spirit of Jefferson than of Hamilton. Land cost itself no longer represented a real barrier to entry into the business of farming.

Despite public land sales, purchase, conquest, and treaty continued to expand the public domain, adding new lands on the western frontier. Consequently, by 1850 the federal government found itself holding 1.2 billion acres, and by 1880, despite almost twenty years of free land under the Homestead Act, the government still held over 900 million acres (excluding Alaska).

[7] See Benjamin H. Hibbard, *A History of the Public Land Policies* (New York, 1924), for a summary of the various public land laws.

Original land entries, 1800-1934

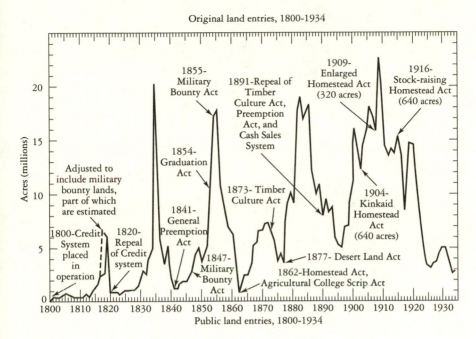

Figure 7.2. Public land entries, 1800–1934. Source: Roy M. Robbins, *Our Landed Heritage* (Princeton, 1942), 344.

The orderly transfer of secure land titles from public to private hands was frequently disrupted by overly eager settlers who occupied some of the best lands shead of the survey teams. These squatters presented a challenge to the government. They contributed to national development and to the value of the land by converting it to farmland, but they took up the best acreage, potentially making it unavailable to those who played by the rules. Public sale of these lands was often frustrated by the appearance of a well-armed settler, with friends, determined to protect his investment. Moreover, they often encroached on Native American rights that had not yet been extinguished.

The solution was to recognize the squatter's contribution by allowing the settler the exclusive right to purchase some of the land illegally taken. Various temporary preemption laws were passed, beginning in 1830 and culminating in the General Preemption Law of 1841, which granted squatters rights to up to 160 acres at the minimum price of $1.25 per acre. This law was repealed in 1891.

Table 7.1. *Significant public land laws, 1785–1916*

Year	Legislative initiative	Minimum price/acre	Minimum acreage	Maximum acreage	Conditions and terms of sale
1785	Land Ordinance of 1785	$1	640	none	Cash
1787	Northwest Ordinance of 1787	$1	640	none	½ cash; balance in 3 months.
1796	Land Act of 1796	$2	640	none	½ in 30 days; balance within a year. First land offices established at Cincinnati and Pittsburgh.
1800	Harrison Land Act (Land Act of 1800)	$2	320	none	¼ in 30 days; balance in 3 years at 6 percent interest
1804	Land Act of 1804	$2	160	none	$1.64/acre for cash. Credit terms as per Land Act of 1800
1812	General Land Office established.				
1820	Land Act of 1820	$1.25	80	none	Credit system abolished. Cash only.
1830	Preemption Act of 1830	$1.25		160	Permitted unauthorized settlers – squatters – to purchase up to 160 acres
1832	Land Act of 1832	$1.25	40	none	Cash only.
1841	General Preemption Act of 1841	$1.25	40	160	Pre-emption only. Cash.
1854	Graduation Act	12½¢	40	none	Price progressively reduced on unsold lands to as little as 12.5 cents per acre after 30 years

1862	Homestead Act	Free	40	160	$10 registration fee. Five years' continuous residence on land for full title. Commutation available after 6 months for $1.25/acre.
1873	Timber Culture Act	Free	160	160	Cultivation of trees on one quarter of the lot for title. Amended in 1878 to require trees on only one sixteenth of a lot.
1877	Desert Land Act	$1.25		640	Irrigation within three years. $0.25/acre on entry, balance due upon proof of compliance.
1878	Timber and Stone Act	$2.50	40	160	Stipulation that timber and stone for personal use only and not for speculation or other parties.
1909	Enlarged Homestead Act	Free		320	Five years residence with continuous cultivation. Law for semi-arid areas.
1912	Three-Year Homestead Act	Free		160	Seven months residence a year for three years with extension for bad weather, etc.
1916	Stock Raising Homestead Act	Free		640	On land suitable only for grazing.

Source: Benjamin Hibbard, *A History of Public Land Policies* (New York, 1924).

Table 7.2. *Bounty land warrants issued to June 30, 1907*

Bounty Land Act	Number of warrants	Acreage
Revolutionary Wars (acts prior to 1800)	16,663	2,165,000
War of 1812	29,186	4,845,920
Act of 1847	88,274	13,213,640
Act of 1850	189,145	13,168,480
Act of 1852	11,992	694,400
Act of 1855	263,100	34,151,590
		68,239,030

Source: Hibbard, *Public Land Polices*, 132.

Although successive land acts had specified a minimum reservation price on federal lands, not all sold for a price equal to or greater than this minimum. Some lands, worth much less than the government's reservation price, were not taken when at auction. For example, about 70,000 acres of public domain remained in Ohio in the early 1850s, and as the frontier pushed westward, these small pockets of unsold public land surrounded by private holdings were a nuisance to the federal government (see Figure 7.3).[8] Congress determined to dispose of them through a Dutch auction under the terms of the Graduation Act of 1854: the price on unsold public land in areas already settled was gradually reduced to a minimum of 12½ cents per acre for land unsold more than thirty years and these small parcels were eventually moved into private hands. Some twenty-seven million acres in the Midwest were transferred under the terms of the Graduation Act; for example, 1.3 million acres in Illinois realized 33 cents an acre, while the almost 14 million acres sold in Missouri drew an average of 77 cents (see Figure 7.4).[9]

The government also made other uses of the public lands. Potential enlistees were induced to join the military by the promise of land warrants – rights to settle specific acreages of unoccupied land – and veterans received land warrants for their military service in the Revolutionary Wars, the War of 1812–14, and the Mexican War (see Table 7.2). Many of these warrants were transferable and actively traded at prices of 60 to 85 cents per acre. Indeed, warrants were quoted in stock exchange reports alongside stocks and bonds.

[8] See Hibbard, *Public Land Policies*, 302.   [9] Ibid.

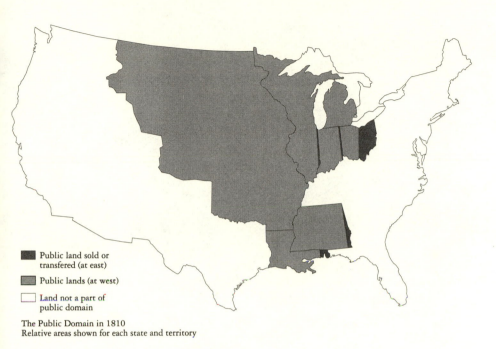

Public land sold or transfered (at east)

Public lands (at west)

Land not a part of public domain

The Public Domain in 1810
Relative areas shown for each state and territory

Figure 7.3. The public domain in 1810. Source: After Charles O. Paullin, *Atlas of Historical Geography* (Washington, DC, 1932), Plate 57.

The increasingly liberal terms and the sociology of the auctions eventually gave smallholders the upper hand, even though information was not always perfect. Surveyors, for example, had superior and potentially valuable information about the physical characteristics of particular tracts. But this could not keep land off the market for very long or out of the hands of those eager to exploit it. Alexis de Tocqueville credited this land policy, where the "lands of the New World belong to the first occupant; they are the natural reward of the swiftest pioneer" with founding American democracy and equality.[10]

Public land sales, however, were sluggish until they exploded in the 1830s influenced by high crop prices, resulting from a series of poor grain harvests and government-sponsored internal improvements that

[10] Alexis de Tocqueville, *Democracy in America* (first published, Paris, 1835). The quote is from the Henry Reeve text as revised by Francis Bowen with corrections by Phillips Bradley (New York, 1946), v. 1, 431.

Public lands (at the westward)

Land sold or disposed of (at the eastward)

Lands not a part of the public domain

The Public Domain in 1850
Relative areas are shown graphically for each state and territory

Figure 7.4. The public domain in 1850. Source: After Charles O. Paullin, *Atlas of Historical Geography* (Washington, DC, 1932), Plate 58.

expanded supply on areas newly opened to profitable commercial agriculture (see Figure 7.5). In 1836, for example, at the height of this land boom, 20 million acres of public land were sold. Sales boomed once again during the 1850s when the federal government sold almost 50 million acres – an area approximately one and a half times the size of New York state.[11]

Under these land laws, tens of millions of acres of land were conveyed by the General Land Office from the public domain to private ownership. The bulk of it, as well as undeveloped land in settled areas, was turned into farms. During the 1850s, for example, farmland increased by over 100 million acres, of which about half was cultivable, and almost 600,000 new farms were created as farmers worked to clear land they had already purchased. The most rapid expansion took place on the fron-

---

[11] Hibbard, *Public Land Policies*, 103, 106, 113.

Public lands sold or transfered (at east)

Public domain (at west)

Not in public domain

The Public Domain in 1910
Relative areas are shown graphically for each state and territory

Figure 7.5. The public domain in 1910. Source: After Charles O. Paullin, *Atlas of Historical Geography* (Washington, DC, 1932), Plate 59.

tier. Farmland in Illinois increased by 9 million acres between 1850 and 1860; in Iowa farmland increased by over 7 million acres. In Massachusetts and Rhode Island, by contrast, the land in farms was beginning to decrease.[12]

The passage of the Homestead Act of 1862 ushered in a new era: 160 acres of "free" land for the cultivator. Although free land did not make for a free farm, as we show below, tens of thousands took advantage of the offer. Almost 2.5 million homestead claims had been filed by 1913. Homestead entries in the 1870s averaged well over 20,000 a year; they were more than double that in the 1880s and over 98,000 in 1910 (see Figure 7.6).[13]

[12] U.S. Census Office. Eighth Census, *Agriculture of the United States in 1860* (Washington, DC, 1864), 222.
[13] Hibbard, *Public Land Policies*, 396. U.S. Bureau of the Census, *Historical Statistics of the United States, Colonial Times to 1970* (Washington, DC, 1975), I, 428–9, Series J8-15.

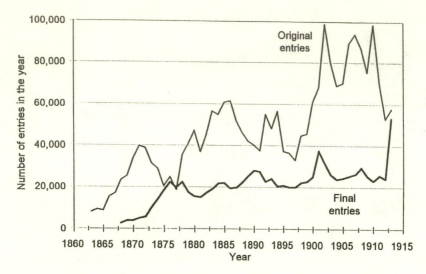

Figure 7.6. Original homestead entries and final entries. Source: U.S. Bureau of the Census, *Historical Statistic of the United States, Colonial Times to 1970* (Washington, DC, 1975), Series J13, and Benjamin H. Hibbard, *A History of Public Land Policies* (New York, 1924), Table 27.

The original Homestead Act required five years' residency on the land to prove the claim, but settlers could commute this requirement after six months by paying the government's reservation price on the land. According to Benjamin H. Hibbard, in the period down to 1880, about 4 percent of the settlers availed themselves of this privilege, but thereafter commutation was much more common since it permitted immediate resale.[14] Between 1881 and 1904, about 23 percent of the homesteaded land went through commutation.

Despite these low entry costs, thousands of entries failed. Only about 40 percent of the original entries were finalized.[15] Drought, insect plagues, low prices, and isolation caused thousands of farm sites to be abandoned. Moreover, fraud and deceit further circumvented the intent of the law – the permanent settlement of the land by small-scale owner-operators. Oaths were sworn that the land had a house of "12 by 14" that was, in

[14] Hibbard, *Public Land Policies*, 386.   [15] *Historical Statistics*, Series J15.

reality, a doll's house, a dry-goods box, or a house on wheels.[16] Such fraudulent devices helped establish claim after claim, which might then be consolidated into bonanza farms of many thousands of acres.

The switch in land sales policy from high prices for large tracts to low or zero ones for small tracts increased sales. Scholars such as Theodore Saloutos have argued that sales increased too rapidly, however, inducing too much labor and capital into agriculture while starving manufacturing of resources despite its relatively much higher rate of return.[17] Conversion costs form virgin woodland or prairie to tillable farm also meant that there was an optimal (output-maximizing) date for the transformation of each plot from unsettled territory to settled farmland. Federal land policy, by offering the land for sale at public auction with competition between buyers paying cash, should have ensured that conversion took place at the "right" time. The donation of land under the Homestead Act, however, led to settlement of the land further west "too early."[18] Paul Gates has argued that by establishing minimum rather than maximum acreages, public land policy promoted speculation, concentration of ownership, and tenancy rather than individual smallholdings as Jefferson had hoped.[19] In short, federal land policy has been criticized as inefficient and growth inhibiting.[20]

Besides selling land or giving it directly to the settlers, the federal government also granted vast acreages to states and private businesses for various worthy purposes. For example, states received federal land grants to help underwrite education. The Ordinance of 1787 had reserved section 16 in each township for public education, but states received a variety of other grants for education, such as 23,000 acres or so of land around salt springs in Ohio, Indiana, and Missouri.[21] However, the most famous edu-

---

[16] See, for example, Roy M. Robbins, *Our Landed Heritage* (Princeton, 1942), especially 236–54. Also A. M. Sakolski, *The Great American Land Bubble* (New York, 1932).

[17] Theodore Saloutos, "The Agricultural Problem and Nineteenth-Century Industrialism," *Agricultural History* 22 (1948), 156–74.

[18] See R. Taylor Dennen, "Some Efficiency Effects of Nineteenth Century Land Policy: A Dynamic Analysis," *Agricultural History* 51 (1977), 718–36. See also Theodore Saloutos, "Land Policy and its Relation to Agricultural Production and Distribution, 1862 to 1933," *Journal of Economic History* 22 (1962), 445–60; Thomas LeDuc, "Public Policy, Private Investment, and Land Use in American Agriculture, 1825–1875," *Agricultural History* 37 (1963), 3–9.

[19] Paul W. Gates, "The Homestead Law in an Incongruous Land System," *American Historical Review* 41 (1936), 652–81.

[20] Robert W. Fogel and Jack Rutner, "The Efficiency Effects of Federal Land Policy, 1850–1900: A Report on Some Provisional Findings," in William O. Aydelotte et al. (eds.), *The Dimensions of Quantitative Research in History* (Princeton, 1972), 390–418 and Dennen, "Some Efficiency Effects," This view is disputed by Fogel and Rutner but is consistent with Dennen's dynamic analysis of the Homestead Act's effects.

[21] Hibbard, *Public Land Policies*, 319.

cational grants were made under the terms of the 1862 Morrill Act, which granted each state public land equal to 30,000 acres for each senator and representative to which it was entitled under the 1860 census enumeration. All revenues from the sale of these lands were to be invested in safe stocks paying at least 5 percent per year, creating a perpetual fund to underwrite "such branches of learning as are related to agriculture and mechanic arts," leading to the founding of the land-grant public universities.[22] Subsequent extensions of the time limit for establishing such institutions extended the benefit to those states that were in rebellion when the act was originally passed.[23] The 1890 Morrill Act further extended this system, thereby creating a network of predominantly African-American technical colleges in the South and public colleges in the West. These institutions, which played a key role in advancing American agriculture, transferred knowledge to a new generation of farmers. States also received other land grants from the federal government to help underwrite internal improvements such as canal construction or river improvement.

More controversial were the millions of acres granted to the railroads to help finance construction of the nation's rail system, particularly the transcontinentals. This policy began with a grant of about 2.5 million acres to the Illinois Central Railroad in 1850, but was vastly expanded during and after the Civil War. For example, the Atlantic and Pacific Railroad was granted over 49 million acres, the Northern Pacific got 42 million acres, the Union Pacific received almost 20 million acres; the Central Pacific had claims to about 12 million acres.[24] Much of this land lay within areas covered by this study.

FARM SIZE DISTRIBUTION AND FEDERAL LAND POLICY

The immediate short-term impact of land sales and homestead donations is seen in the contemporaneous size distributions of farms. The midwestern distribution in 1860 differs markedly from that in the East. A broad

---

[22] Cornell University received the largest grant – 990,000 acres – while Ohio and Pennsylvania each received well over half a million acres. In the more settled eastern states (and especially in those states that were never a part of the public land policy, that is all the states in existence in 1785), the grants were given in western land. Thus, for example, Cornell received a large area in Wisconsin. See Hibbard, *Public Land Policies*, 328–37.

[23] For example, South Carolina (1872), Arkansas (1872), Florida (1884), and Georgia (1872).

[24] See Thomas Donaldson, *The Public Domain* (Washington, DC, 1884), especially 782–83.

dispersion of farm sizes characterized the Northeast, as might be expected from the resale or division of land among heirs. Nevertheless, there were clusters of farms with specific sizes – 50, 100, 150, and 200 acres – within this broad dispersion. In New York, for example, in 1860 the modal farm had 100 acres. About 8 percent of that state's farms were this size (see Figures 7.7A and 7.7B). Over 6 percent of its farms were 50-acre units. In the Midwest there were proportionately fewer farms of "odd" sizes plus much greater concentrations that were multiples of 40, sizes that are fractions of the land survey section of 640 acres. Indeed, midwestern farms in 1860 were being frequently sized at the minimum lot sold at public auction when the state was being settled, suggesting that they might have been originally purchased at a public land sale auction. Much of Illinois was settled under the 1820 land act that set a minimum of 80 acres for purchase at public auction, and 80-acre farms were the modal farm in both 1860 and 1880 in the state, making up over 16 percent of all farms in 1860 and 1880 (see Figures 7.8A and 7.8B). Michigan, on the other hand, was largely settled after passage of the 1832 revision that cut the minimum acreage to 40 acres, and 40-acre farms were much more common there than in states settled either earlier or after general preemption and homesteading. In 1860 about 20 percent of farms were 40-acre farms, while in 1880 25 percent of farms in that state had just 40 acres (see Figures 7.9A and 7.9B). In contrast, settlement in Kansas began after the adoption of general preemption in 1841 which allowed settlers to preempt up to 160 acres of land at the minimum price. Such sized holdings constituted about 45 percent of Kansas farms in 1860. Twenty years later, 80-acre units had become the modal size (see Figures 7.10A and 7.10B).

LAND SPECULATION

By setting the price of land "too low," by failing to establish maximum holdings while setting minimum purchase requirements and by granting millions of additional acres from the public domain to states and private companies, the federal government created an extremely active market in land. This market, however, was not restricted to those who had a productive use for the land. Nor could it be. Rather, speculators, attracted by low entry costs and the potential for capital gains, played an important but often misunderstood role in the market for land and in western settlement. Speculators fell into three groups: (1) those who remained in the Northeast, taking shares in land companies or buying up the land war-

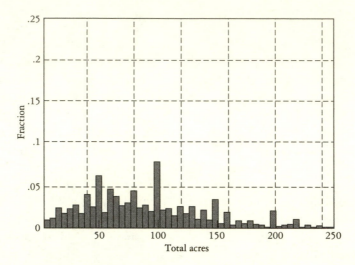

Figure 7.7A. The size distribution of farms in New York in 1860. Source: Jeremy Atack, Fred Bateman, and James Foust, Manuscript Census Samples.

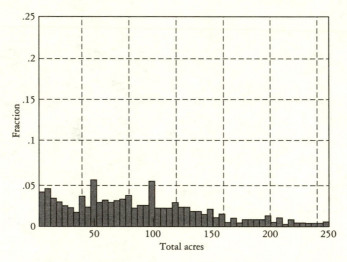

Figure 7.7B. The size distribution of farms in New York in 1880. Source: Jeremy Atack and Fred Bateman, Manuscript Census Samples.

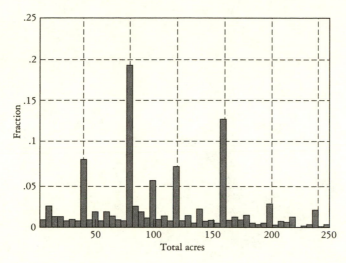

Figure 7.8A. The size distribution of farms in Illinois in 1860. Source: Jeremy Atack, Fred Bateman, and James Foust, Manuscript Census Samples.

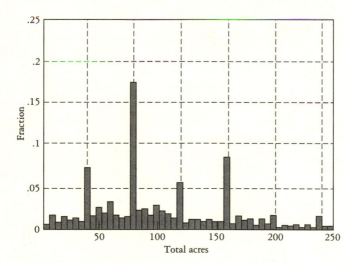

Figure 7.8B. The size distribution of farms in Illinois in 1880. Source: Jeremy Atack and Fred Bateman, Manuscript Census Samples.

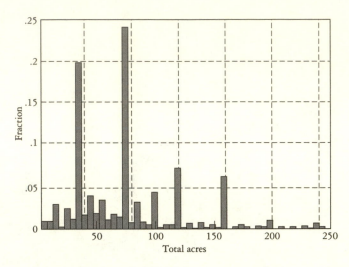

Figure 7.9A. The size distribution of farms in Michigan in 1860. Source: Jeremy Atack, Fred Bateman, and James Foust, Manuscript Census Samples.

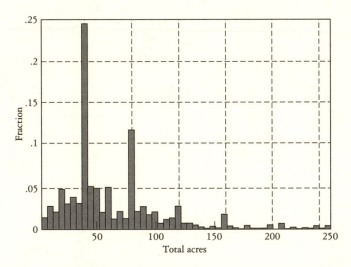

Figure 7.9B. The size distribution of farms in Michigan in 1880. Source: Jeremy Atack and Fred Bateman, Manuscript Census Samples.

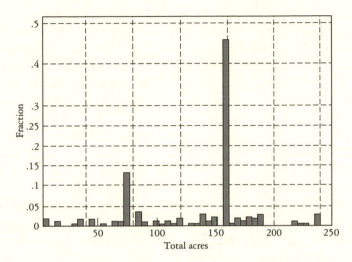

Figure 7.10A. The size distribution of farms in Kansas in 1860. Source: Jeremy Atack, Fred Bateman, and James Foust, Manuscript Census Samples.

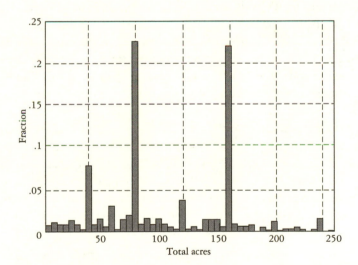

Figure 7.10B. The size distribution of farms in Kansas in 1880. Source: Jeremy Atack and Fred Bateman, Manuscript Census Samples.

rants that governments had given to soldiers in lieu of pay before 1783; (2) those who bought tracts for eventual subdivision and resale; and (3) bona fide settlers who bought more land than they had the means to farm as a result of overoptimism or to "bank" for later use, sale, or bequest.

Investors in land company stock and land warrants helped make the market and transferred eastern capital to midwestern development but, since these investors did not assume ownership of the underlying asset – midwestern land – they have attracted relatively little attention. Those who settled the new country – the "pioneers" – are accorded a special place in American folklore, while the pioneers of capital – speculators who bought up tracts of land for subdivision and resale – have been reviled as parasites whose activities are regarded with opprobrium. Speculators might have bought – and in some notable cases *did* buy – large tracts of land. For example, some large livestock enterprises on the extensive, flat grasslands from central Ohio across to the edge of the Great Plains anticipated the large-scale ranching to the west later in the century.[25] More importantly, the activities of men such as John Grigg (who had 124,000 acres in Illinois), Isaac Funk (27,000 acres), Matthew Scott (47,600 acres in Illinois and Iowa), William Scully (220,000 acres in Illinois, Missouri, Kansas, and Nebraska) and Matthew Sullivant (80,000 acres) were often quite visible.[26] Indeed, the farm "Broadlands" carved out of the Illinois prairie by Matthew Sullivant and financed by $500,000 in debt, was widely reported by the contemporary press.[27] William Scully, however, as an absentee, foreign landlord, was singled out by the press for special abusive attention.[28]

When these and other land speculators were successful in identifying particularly desirable parcels of land that others had ignored, or by buying good land earlier than others, they earned high rates of return and became rich. Iowa speculators studied by Robert Swierenga, for example, averaged 73.1 percent return per year on their investement between the 1840s and the 1880s – and the annual rates of return were generally well above those

[25] See, for example, Paul W. Gates, "Frontier Landlords and Pioneer Tenants," *Journal of the Illinois Historical Society* 38 (1945), 143–206.

[26] Ibid. and Paul W. Gates, "Land Policy and Tenancy in the Prairie States," *Journal of Economic History* 1 (1941), 60–82. See also Paul W. Gates, "The Role of the Land Speculator in Western Development," *Pennsylvania Magazine of History and Biography* 66 (1942), 314–33.

[27] Gates, "Frontier Landlords," 15–20.

[28] See, for example, Homer E. Socolofsky, "William Scully: Ireland and America, 1840–1900," *Agricultural History* 48 (1974), 155–75.

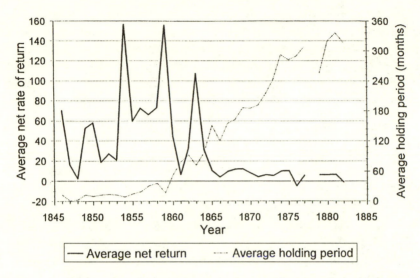

Figure 7.11. Returns to land speculation and average holding periods for land. Source: Robert Swierenga, "Land Speculator 'Profits' Reconsidered: Central Iowa as a Test Case," *Journal of Economic History* 26 (1966), Table 6.

paid by alternate investments until the 1870s.[29] Such profits created envy, and speculators were reviled for reaping where they did not sow and robbing the yeomanry of capital gains that were "rightfully" theirs. But not all land speculation was a sure path to riches. Speculator profits suffered wild gyrations in the uncertain land market. Returns to speculation in Iowa, for example, were high during the land boom of the 1850s and very high in 1859, but just two years after that, the return was only 6.9 percent, or about the same as on government bonds (see Figure 7.11). Sometimes speculators even lost. The decline in average returns was associated with a reduction in turnover and a marked lengthening of the holding period before speculators disposed of their land. To the extent that speculators bought land much earlier than farmers would have purchased it for more immediate productive use, their activities imposed a negligi-

---

[29] Robert P. Swierenga, "Land Speculator 'Profits' Reconsidered: Central Iowa as a Test Case," *Journal of Economic History* 26 (1966). Also Robert P. Swierenga, *Pioneers and Profits: Land Speculation on the Iowa Frontier* (Ames, IA, 1968).

ble burden upon the economy. Indeed, where speculators succeeded in quickly reselling the land to someone who would use it productively, their activities may have been socially beneficial. One such speculator, Nathan Parker, a principal in the Iowa and Minnesota Land Agency, alluded to this in his guidebook for would-be migrants when he defended speculators:

So far from speculators being a drawback to the settlement of a new country, they are the very men who contribute most to the rapidity of its settlement. Lands would be idle and unimproved for years, were it not for this class of men. They come out here and purchase wild lands in vast bodies, and then make a business of inducing farmers and others in the East to emigrate higher and cultivate them.[30]

Between 1846 and 1860, speculators in Iowa held an acre of land for about 16 months before reselling it. After 1865, the average holding period for an acre of land was 179 months – almost 15 years. This drastic lengthening of the average holding period increases the probability that land speculation reduced net national product by withholding productive resources from use.

As prominent as some land speculators were and despite all that has been written about their activities, the principal speculators ultimately were the farmers themselves, who knowingly or in a burst of boundless optimism bought more land than they could farm with family labor and the available technology. According to Paul Gates:

American farmers regarded their land as a means of quickly making a fortune through rising land values which the progress of the community and their own individual improvements would give it. Meanwhile they mined the land by cropping it continually to its most promising staple. They did not look upon it as a lifetime investment, a precious possession whose resources were to be carefully husbanded . . . To them land was not an enduring investment but a speculation.[31]

The pattern of public land sales ebbed and flowed with fluctuations in the price of grains. When grain prices were high, as in the late teens, mid-thirties, and mid-fifties, so too were land sales, suggesting that farmers purchased land to meet short-term production goals.

Farmers were willing to invest not only their cash or credit, but their life's labors and those of their family in the family farm. At this level, cap-

---

[30] Nathan H. Parker, *The Iowa Handbook for 1856* (Boston, 1856), 149.
[31] Paul W. Gates, *The Farmer's Age: Agriculture 1815–1860* (New York, 1960), 399–400.

italism and democracy worked cooperatively to create rural communities that combined individual ownership with a fierce sense of the community interest in local economic development. Within this class of cultivators, a structure of prestige based on priority in settlement, "reputation," Protestant sobriety and behavior, knowledge of farming, and most of all on canniness, enterprise, hard work, and modest financial success, held the whole structure in place. The farms multiplied holdings not as self-sufficient peasants, but in close symbiosis with the area's bankers, lawyers, merchants, artisans – the businessmen, the speculators, the "developers" – who with the farmers' support, controlled state government and the congressional delegations.

THE TENANT FARMER AND THE YEOMAN

While farmers themselves frequently profited from personal land speculation, they reviled the "pure" land speculator for robbing them of capital gains from land value appreciation that otherwise would have accrued to the cultivator-owner. Land speculators were accused of pricing land out of reach of the common man, thereby forcing would-be land-owning yeoman farmers to settle for tenancy. In other instances, speculators were blamed for persuading, or forcing, the yeomen to take on such large debt that farm profits were drastically reduced and then foreclosing upon the cash-strapped, debt-ridden farmer, particularly later in the century.

Regardless of the speculators' marginal impact on the price of a specific lot of unimproved land, purchasing virgin land for a new farm was often one of the smaller expenses facing the pioneer farmer-settler. After 1820, land in 80-acre bundles could be bought for as little as $100 from the federal government, and in 40-acre lots for $50 after 1832. Publicly traded land warrants offered even lower prices per acre on larger lots: in 1852 warrants were selling for between $110 and $115 for a 160-acre tract, that is 69 to 72 cents for an acre. Even plots sold by large speculators in Iowa between the 1840s and the 1880s were relatively cheap, bringing an average price of less than $4 per acre.[32] However, settlers who wanted to be close to water or rail transport or within proximity to a market town paid much more. Locational advantage was everything. The

---

[32] Swierenga, "Land Speculator 'Profits' ", particularly his tables 2, 3, 4, and 5.

Illinois Central Railroad offered land (obtained by government land grant) along its right-of-way in Illinois for $8 to $12 per acre.[33] But even then, land costs represented only a small portion of the costs of setting up a farm.

The major expenses for farm formation lay not in acquiring virgin farmland, but in complementary necessary investments in clearing, livestock, tools, machinery, structures, fences, and roads. Farm-making involved much more than acquiring title to 40, 80, or 160 acres of arable land. The land had to be cleared, and in the forests of Ohio, Michigan, Wisconsin, and Minnesota, clearing was an extremely arduous task. First, huge, original-growth trees had to be cut down by two-man saw – or more likely, axe – and burned or hauled away. Then the stumps and any large rocks had to be removed by brute animal force or blasting powder. Martin Primack estimates that about a month's labor, plus the services of a team of oxen, was required to clear an acre.[34] Although a farmer might do this work during his or her own free time, a month of farm labor devoted to land clearing was a month in which the family still had to be fed, sheltered, and clothed. Nor did settlement on the treeless prairies avoid these costs. Rather, hired help with specialized equipment was all the more necessary. Breaking the prairie sod – an almost impenetrable tangle of roots from millenia of grasses – required a special "sod-busting" plow and a team of four to eight oxen, although the job had to be done only once, taking but a day and a half.[35] At a cost of $10 to $12 per acre for clearing woodland and $2 to $5 for prairie,[36] land clearing represented a vast economic investment for the United States of $13–16 million per year in the 1850s for the forested areas of the Midwest alone.[37] It also diverted perhaps one-sixth of the total midwestern agricultural labor force from current production, although the investment eventually paid off in greater output and higher land prices after the Civil War. Substantial additional labor was needed to fence the land to keep the livestock out of the crops.

One saving grace, however, was that land could be cleared, ditches dug, hedges planted, and fences built over a period of years, especially in idle times during the crop year, by farm family labor, or by the cooperative

---

[33] Paul W. Gates, *The Illinois Central Railroad and Its Colonizing Work* (Cambridge, MA, 1941).

[34] Martin Primack, "Land Clearing Under Nineteenth-Century Techniques: Some Preliminary Calculations," *Journal of Economic History* 22 (1962), 484–97, especially 491.

[35] Ibid.

[36] Clarence H. Danhof, "Farm-Making Costs and the Safety Valve: 1850–1860," *Journal of Political Economy* 49 (1941), 317–59.

[37] Primack, "Land Clearing."

exchanges of time among families in a rural neighborhood. This approach avoided much of the cash outlay but still involved a substantial opportunity cost (except to the extent that the labor so used was truly "surplus" labor without alternative gainful employment) and might take five or ten years to build a complete farm, time during which the farmer would be forced to draw down savings in order to survive.

The Minnesota Commissioner of Statistics offered would-be settlers the following advice on what they would need to establish a farm in that state:

Counting at government price, one hundred and sixty acres is two hundred dollars. The cheapest and best fence, where lumber is cheap . . . is made of boards one inch by six and fourteen feet long, and two posts for every length of boards . . . the cost of fence complete, forty cents per rod. One mile of fence, inclosing forty acres, would cost $3.20 × 40 = $128; though most have neighbors who help build line fences. . . . A man may build a comfortable house of logs by paying, say fifty dollars for lumber, nails, shingles, windows, &c., and he may make comfortable quarters for stock with poles and straw only, and men seldom put grain in barns when they have them. Horses are worth at present $50 to $100 each; oxen $40 to $50 per yoke; cows $20 each. . . . [It] is highly desirable that all emigrants should have [excluding fencing]

The price of their land,	$200.00
Team and wagon,	150.00
Two cows,	40.00
For building house,	100.00
Breaking twenty acres,	60.00
One steel plow, for crossing,	14.00
One harrow,	6.00
Axes, shovels, spade, forks, scythe, & c.,	25.00
House furniture and provisions for family, which must be bought till they can raise them,	200.00
	$795.00

Some men have started with nothing, and by working out or hiring farms have soon secured homes of comfort, and others will do the same; but to do this requires peculiar material in the man and his wife, and usually families with $500 to $1,000 on their arrival find they have need of the strictest economy.[38]

Even assuming that the land could be mortgaged, typically on a short-term (3–5 year) "balloon" (i.e. unamortized) mortgage with no down payment required, the balance of $595 – more than a year and a half's wage for the average worker in 1860 and four times per capita income in

---

[38] Minnesota Commissioner of Statistics, *Minnesota: Its Place Among the States, Being the First Annual Report of the Commissioner of Statistics* (Hartford, 1860), 88.

the North at that time – would have to be paid in cash. Thus the prospective farm family would have to save a large sum of money and then endure a long period of backbreaking work and subsistence living in order to own a frontier farm that would barely be self-sustaining for many years to come.

Examining a wide range of similar estimates, Clarence Danhof concluded that "the farm-maker's wealth could not fall much short of $1,000" for a 40-acre farm. The average 80-acre farm – the most common size – averaged $1,364 for the land, improvements, and buildings plus $285 for livestock and $67 for implements – a total of $1,716. In a less settled area, such as Iowa, Minnesota, or Wisconsin, it would cost less, perhaps $800–1,300, while further east such as in Ohio costs would typically be much more, perhaps $2,000 or more.[39] A comparable farm in the Northeast would require between two-thirds more and twice as much. For example, the land and buildings for an 80-acre farm in the Northeast averaged $2,657, plus $109 in implements and $377 in livestock. Owner-occupancy, thus, was not for the impecunious, and farm makers had either large precautionary savings, powerful motivations, or some combination thereof.

Farmland prices rose over time, reflecting myriad influences, including improvements made to the land, increased demand, and changes in locational advantage as well as decreased supply. According to estimates by Peter Lindert, between 1850 and 1915, the real value of land in the United States rose at an average annual rate of 2.08 percent, increasing more than fourfold over the period (see Figure 7.12).[40] It would have risen even faster, 2.18 percent a year, had not the drift to poorer-quality land in the West more than offset the 0.29 percent per year quality gain through improvements to fixed sites. Whatever the reason for higher land prices, though, if demand was inelastic, prospective farmers would be compelled to spend more of their income on land. Those who could not afford the higher prices and could not borrow were faced with either farming a smaller area or becoming tenants. Some may have been excluded from the market altogether, unless they were willing to move to more distant western land.

If these capital costs represented a barrier to entry into farming as an

---

[39] Jeremy Atack, "Farm and Farm-Making Costs Revisited," *Agricultural History* 56 (1982), 663–76; Atack and Bateman, *To Their Own Soil*, Chapter 8.

[40] Peter H. Lindert, "Long-Run Trends in American Farmland Values," *Agricultural History* 62 (1988), 45–85.

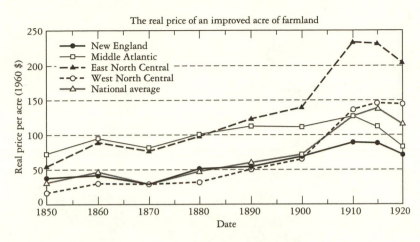

Figure 7.12. The real price of an improved acre of farmland. Source: Peter Lindert, "Long-Run Trends in American Farmland Values," *Agricultural History* 62 (1988), 58–59.

Table 7.3. *Average farm and farm-making costs for owner-occupied farms in the American Midwest in 1860*

Size of farm	Farm and farm buildings, fences, etc. ($)	Implements ($)	Livestock ($)	Total cost ($)
40-acre farms	738	46	197	981
80-acre farms	1,364	67	285	1,716
160-acre farms	2,491	96	426	3,013

Source: Calculated from Jeremy Atack and Fred Bateman, *To Their Own Soil: Agriculture in the Antebellum North* (Ames, IA, 1987). 135.

owner, there remained the alternative of tenant farming for cash or shares. Tenancy avoided the substantial cash outlay in the farmland, improvements, and buildings but still required some minimum, not insignificant, investment. According to estimates by Atack and Bateman, in 1860 the average midwestern tenant farmer of 80 acres had about $325 tied up in the venture, compared with $1,716 for the average owner (see Table 7.3). Although these costs were substantially lower than for owner-occupiers, they were still out of range for perhaps a third of the population.

Northern tenant farming has often been ignored on the grounds that "with so much land yet unoccupied, the cultivated portions could

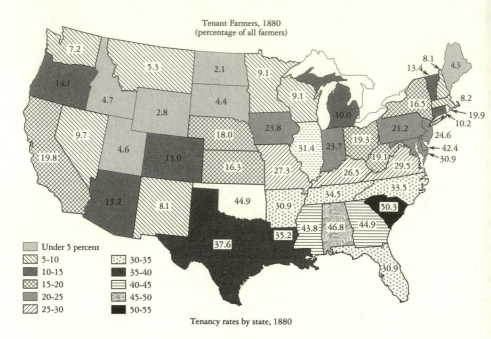

Figure 7.13. Tenancy rates by state, 1880. Source: Charles O. Paullin, *Atlas of Historical Geography* (Washington, DC, 1932), Plate 146.

command but little rent and tenancy was not common."[41] Bidwell and Falconer in their classic study of northern agriculture virtually ignore tenancy, not regarding it as an issue in American agriculture before the Civil War.[42] Nevertheless, the first official tenancy statistics, collected in 1880, revealed that over 20 percent of the farmers in the Old Northwest were tenants, while along the Pacific Coast almost 17 percent of farmers were so categorized, despite almost twenty years of homesteading. In contrast, in New England, where good farmland was scarcer and considerably more expensive, tenancy rates were much lower (see Figure 7.13.)[43]

[41] Russell H. Anderson, "Agriculture in Illinois During the Civil War Period, 1850–1870," unpublished Ph.D diss., University of Illinois, 1929, 63.

[42] Percy W. Bidwell, "Rural Economy in New England at the Beginning of the Nineteenth Century," *Transactions of the Connecticut Academy of Arts and Sciences* 20 (1916), 241–399. The quotation is from 371. Percy W. Bidwell and John I. Falconer, *History of Agriculture in the Northern United States, 1620–1860* (Washington, DC, 1925), 242.

[43] US Census Office, *Report upon the Statistics of Agriculture* (Washington, DC, 1883), Volume 3, xiii–xiv.

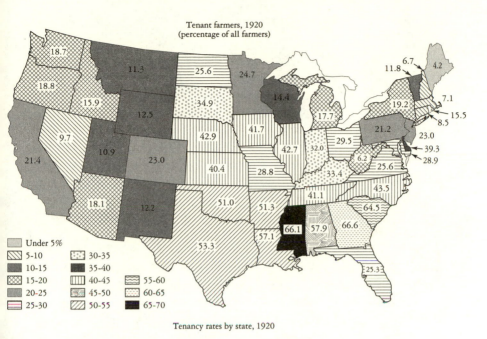

Figure 7.14. Tenancy rates by state, 1920. Source: Charles O. Paullin, *Atlas of Historical Geography* (Washington, DC, 1932), Plate 146.

These rates increased almost everywhere in subsequent years (see Figure 7.14).

Much less is know about tenancy earlier in the century. Most thought that tenancy must have been far less prevalent – indeed, nonexistent – earlier when land was relatively more abundant and unsettled land existed on the frontier. Paul W. Gates, however, disagreed. He argued that the very institutions that were supposed to promote owner-occupancy – the land acts, low prices, and public auction – had, in fact, promoted land speculation, monopolization, and tenancy:

The Land Ordinance of 1785 and subsequent laws had placed no restrictions upon the amount of pubic land that individuals or groups could acquire . . . The policy of unlimited sales and unrestricted transfer of titles made possible land monopolization by speculators, who acquired most of the choice lands in certain areas

. . . This resulted in the early disappearance of cheap or free land and the emergence of tenancy.[44]

The evidence is mixed. On the eve of the Revolution there were an estimated six to seven thousand tenant farmers in New York.[45] James Lemon estimated that in Chester and Lancaster counties, Pennsylvania, perhaps 30 percent of the married taxpayers were landless in the late colonial period.[46] These rates suggest that tenancy at the time of the Revolution was as high as it was a century later. In the first half of the nineteenth century, tenancy rates were much lower than those both earlier and later but still far from negligible. Allan Bogue has estimated that tenancy rates in 1860 in three Iowa townships ranging from 6.6 to 11.2 percent.[47] Seddie Cogswell concluded that in eastern Iowa tenancy rates increased irregularly from 17.6 percent in 1850 to 27.3 percent in 1880.[48] Across the entire Midwest, Jeremy Atack estimates that the overall tenancy rate in 1860 was about 17 percent, though it was much lower in Michigan (7 percent) and higher on the frontier (over 30 percent).[49]

Given the substantial advantages to land ownership, particularly receipt of unearned capital gains arising from local development and the extension of the transportation network, it is unlikely that many tenants voluntarily chose their status. Apologists blamed the rising tenancy rate in the late nineteenth century on "the fact that free land was practically exhausted by 1900, and . . . to the hard times that prevailed in the nineties and caused a large number of mortgages to be foreclosed, making it necessary for many farm operators to rent farms in order to continue farming,"[50] while the 1923 *USDA Yearbook* attributed long-term tenancy

[44] Paul W. Gates, "Land Policy and Tenancy in the Prairie Counties of Indiana," *Indiana Magazine of History* 35 (1939), 3.

[45] John Watt, *Pennsylvania Ledger: or the Weekly Advertiser*, Oct. 29, 1777, quoted by Sung Bok Kim, *Landlord and Tenant in Colonial New York: Manorial Society, 1664–1775* (Chapel Hill, NC, 1978), vii. Unfortunately, the lack of data on the number of farms precludes expressing this as a tenancy rate. Based on the enumeration at the first census in 1790, however, it seems unlikely that there would have been more than about 80,000 families in New York at the time of the Revolution and that more than 70,000 could have been engaged in farming. On this basis, no more than 10 percent of farmers were tenants.

[46] James T. Lemon, *The Best Poor Man's County* (Baltimore, 1972), 94.

[47] These are the recalculated tenancy rates from Allan G. Bogue, *From Prairie to Corn Belt: Farming on the Illinois and Iowa Praries in the Nineteenth Century* (Chicago, 1963), Table 9, 65, if "farmers without farms" are excluded from both the denominator and numerator.

[48] Seddie Cogswell Jr., *Tenure, Nativity and Age as Factors in Iowa Agriculture, 1850–1880* (Ames, IA, 1975), 23.

[49] Jeremy Atack, "Tenants and Yeomen in the Nineteenth Century," *Agricultural History* 62 (1988), 6–32, especially 19. Also Atack and Bateman, *To Their Own Soil*.

[50] E. A. Goldenweisser and Leon E. Truesdell, *Farm Tenancy in the United States* (Washington, DC, 1924), 21.

to the below-average capabilities of the tenant farmer.[51] Atack explains cross-sectional variations in tenancy in terms of the barrier to entry posed by the cash investment necessary to be a yeoman farmer.[52] Donald Winters, on the other hand, describes it as "an integral part of an evolving, maturing agricultural system," that placed more emphasis upon cash grain farming; that is, tenancy was an artifact of increasing commercialization in agriculture.[53]

Rising tenancy rates, however, were clearly contrary to Jefferson's aspirations for a nation of small landowners arising from the transfer of the public domain into private hands. As Thomas Hart Benton expressed it:

Tenantry is unfavorable to freedom. It lays the foundation for separate orders of society, annihilates the love of country, and weakens the spirit of independence. The farming tenant has, in fact, no country, no hearth, no domestic altar, no household god. The freeholder, on the contrary, is the natural supporter of free government; and it should be the policy of republics to multiply their freeholders . . . pass the public lands cheaply and easily into the hands of the people; sell, for a reasonable price, to those who are able to pay; and give, without price, to those who are not able to pay.[54]

Land tenure plays a key role in the metaphor of the "agricultural ladder" used by generations of agricultural historians to describe social and economic mobility within the farm economy. This metaphor likens the hierarchical status of agriculturalists to the rungs of a ladder on which the landless agricultural laborer stands lowest, with various stages and degrees of tenancy occupying intermediate rungs, and the mortgage-free owner-occupier farmer standing on top. Crucial to the interpretation of the agricultural ladder is whether tenants were upwardly mobile farm laborers on their way to independent status as owner-occupiers or yeomen fallen upon hard times and slipping back towards landless wage labor. For a long time, the former interpretation had dominated the literature. Goldenweisser and Truesdell argued that tenancy was but "one step in the process whereby a man starting in life with a limited capital, or with nothing but his own

---

[51] L. C. Gray et al., "Farm Ownership and Tenancy," in United States Department of Agriculture, *Agricultural Yearbook* (Washington, DC, 1924), 507–600.

[52] Atack, "Tenants and Yeomen," 26–28.

[53] Donald L. Winters, "Tenancy as an Economic Institution: The Growth and Distribution of Agricultural Tenancy in Iowa, 1850–1900," *Journal of Economic History* 37 (1977), 382–408. Quote is from 406.

[54] See Thomas Hart Benton, *Thirty Years' View* (New York, 1854), Vol. 1, 103–4.

energy and enterprise, may after a time acquire the ownership of a farm."[55]
A more pessimistic view prevailed in the 1930s and 1940s, reflecting the depressed state of the farm economy and the persuasive arguments of Paul W. Gates.[56] Lawanda Cox, for example, claimed that "historical studies of the economic conditions of the western farmer suggest that back-sliding may have been a major factor in many localities."[57] More recently, there has been a resurgence of the more traditional view describing a process of upward mobility.[58] Bogue, for example, describes tenancy as a "step up the tenure ladder, which carried them from their original status as hired men to positions where they not only owned their farm homes but often rental property as well."[59]

Movement up and down the agricultural ladder is hard to trace. Most evidence is indirect. Perhaps the best was collected by the 1920 census. This shows that in the Middle Atlantic and midwestern states at least 30 percent of persons who became yeoman farmers between 1915 and 1920 had, at one time, been tenants.[60] On average, farm laborers had become tenants by their late twenties or early thirties and moved onward and upward from there. In Illinois, for example, the truly upwardly mobile — those who had been both laborer and tenant before becoming owners — had spent an average of 6.2 years as laborers and 11.1 years as tenants. However, there was also some downward mobility. Across the northern

[55] Goldenweisser and Truesdell, *Farm Tenancy*, 83–104. See also Gray, et al., "Farm Ownership and Tenancy," especially 547–63 and Twelfth Census, *Agriculture, Part I*, lxxvii.

[56] See especially Paul Wallace Gates, "The Homestead Law" plus his essays reprinted in *Landlord and Tenants on the Prairie Frontier* (Ithaca, 1973), especially "Frontier Landlords and Pioneer Tenants."

[57] Lawanda Cox, "Tenancy in the United States; 1865–1900: A Consideration of the Validity of the Agricultural Ladder Hypothesis," *Agricultural History* 18 (1944), 97–105.

[58] Thomas LeDuc, "The Disposal of the Public Domain on the Trans-Mississippi Plains: Some Opportunities for Investigation," *Agricultural History* 24 (1950), 199–204, especially 201 and 203. Merle Curti et al., *The Making of An American Community: A Case Study of Democracy in a Frontier County* (Stanford University Press, 1959). Theodore Saloutos, "Land Policy and its Relation to Agricultural Production and Distribution, 1862 to 1933," *Journal of Economic History* 22 (1962), 445–60. Most recently, Margaret B. Bogue, *Patterns from the Sod: Land Use and Tenure in the Grand Prairie, 1850–1900* (Springfield, 1959); A. Bogue, *From Prairie to Corn Belt*; Robert Swierenga, *Pioneers and Profits*; Seddie Cogswell Jr., *Tenure, Nativity and Age*; Clarence Danhof, *Change in Agriculture* (Cambridge, MA, 1969), 87–94; Donald L. Winters, *Farmers Without Farms: Agricultural Tenancy in Nineteenth-Century Iowa* (Ames, IA, 1978); Donald L. Winters, "Agricultural Tenancy in the Nineteenth Century Middle West: The Historiographical Debate," *Indiana Magazine of History* 78 (1982), 128–53, and Jeremy Atack, "The Agricultural Ladder Revisited: A New Look at an Old Question with Some Data for 1860," *Agricultural History* 63 (1988), 1–25.

[59] A. Bogue, *From Prairie to Cornbelt*, 56.

[60] Gray et al., "Farm Ownership," 553–61, especially Figure 52, 556. See also Goldenweisser and Truesdell, *Farm Tenancy*, 102–14.

Table 7.4. *Changes in the proportion of farmers who were tenants by age group,*
1860–1930

Age Group	1860 (North)	1870	1880	1890	1900	1910	1920	1930
Under 25	234			562	718	756	758	865
25–34	162			421	543	550	565	670
35–44	108			301	353	373	397	463
45–54	74			230	290	268	302	346
55–64	54			167	207	211	207	247
65 and over	46			118	149	151	165	164

Notes: The data for the period 1890–1920 were originally from E. A. Goldenweisser and Leon E. Truesdell, *Farm Tenancy in the United States*, (Washington, DC, 1924), table 32, 90. The data for farmers age 55–64 and farmers age 65 and over in 1890 were combined in the original but distributed between the two age groups by Black and Allen in their retabulation of the data. There are currently no estimates for 1870 and 1880.
Source: 1860 North: Computed from the Bateman-Foust sample; 1890–1930: John D. Black and R. H. Allen, "The Growth of Farm Tenancy in the United States," *Quarterly Journal of Economics*, 51 (1937), table 6, 409.

states (except Maine), perhaps 20 percent of tenants farmed land that they once had owned.[61]

Some indirect evidence, however, can be inferred from information about tenure status by age from the various censuses (see Table 7.4 and Figure 7.15). Assuming that the experiences of different age cohorts at a single point in time provide information about the life cycle of a *particular* cohort over time, we can infer from the entries along the diagonal of the table whether more people entered tenancy than left it since each age cohort at successive censuses is composed primarily of survivors from younger age cohorts at earlier censuses. The data indicate that while over time, more young farmers started out as tenants and more remained tenants in each age group, the proportion of tenants in successive age cohorts generally declined, suggesting that upward mobility dominated. Moreover, although proportionately more of the same age cohort at successive decades started out as tenants, they moved out of tenancy into owner-occupancy at a faster rate later in the nineteenth and in the early twentieth centuries. This pattern is consistent with the view that rising

[61] Gray et al., "Farm Ownership," especially figures 48–53. Also Goldenweisser and Truesdell, *Farm Tenancy*, 102–14.

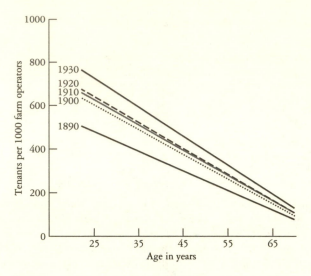

Figure 7.15. Tenancy rates by age. Source: Gavin Wright, "American Agriculture and the Labor Market: What Happened to Proletarianization?" *Agricultural History* 62 (1988), 192, Figure 3.

capital costs, driven largely by rising land values, posed an increasing barrier to entry to the ranks of the yeomanry for the young.

WESTERN SETTLEMENT

After 1800 settlers from the northeastern states poured across the formidable barrier imposed by the Appalachians into the Midwest. Ohio was the first to be settled. Between 1800 and 1820 its population rose thirteen fold, mostly due to in-migration[62] but reinforced by relatively higher birth rates among midwestern farm families than among those back East or among the non-farm population.[63] Later migrants flooded into the other states bordering the Great Lakes. From there, the tidal wave of population

---

[62] Estimates by Gallaway and Vedder, for example, suggest that net migration into the Old Northwest probably exceeded the natural increase each decade before the 1840s. See Lowell E. Gallaway and Richard K. Vedder, "Migration and the Old Northwest," in D. Klingaman and Richard K. Vedder (eds.), *Essays in Nineteenth Century Economic History* (Athens, OH, 1975).

[63] See Atack and Bateman, *To Their Own Soil*.

quickly pushed further westward into Iowa, Minnesota, and Kansas before bypassing much of the high Plains and Rocky Mountains in the rush to lay claim to the gold of the Golden State. Whereas in 1810 less than 4 percent of Americans lived in what became the Midwest, by 1840, 3 million people – 17 percent of the population lived there – and by 1860, 25 percent of America's population lived in the Midwest. In addition, there were more than 100,000 new settlers in Kansas thanks to the activities of agencies such as the abolitionist New England Immigrant Aid Society. Thousands more were settling in Nebraska. The West Coast population was rapidly approaching half a million and by 1900, the population of the North Central states and the West exceeded 30 million – about 40 percent of the total population.

Opening western land to settlement was to have a profound impact upon the distribution of population and national economic activities. As people settled the West, with its more fertile soils and generally salubrious agricultural environment, those remained in the old farm areas in the Northeast had to make some hard choices: Did they wish to go or stay? If they stayed, how were they to compete with western agriculture? Those who migrated westward could continue growing corn and wheat, becoming settlers and small farmers in Ohio, Indiana, and Illinois. Those who stayed behind were forced to choose between a new crop mix or joining the growing pool of eastern industrial and commercial labor.

Settlers moved north and west of Chicago without much difficulty into the upper Great Lakes states. But the grasslands of western Kansas, Nebraska, and the Dakotas imposed on pioneers a technical and psychological barrier that required a new settlement technology. The treeless plains offered no shelter from sun and wind or protection from attack. Worse still, they offered no fencing or building materials, fuel, or woodland pasturage for hogs, and they seemed at first sight to be seriously deficient in water supplies (indeed, they arguably have remained so). The pioneers doubted the fertility of soils where trees would not grow and where the familiar thick carpeting of forest humus accumulated over the centuries was replaced by a dense tangle of grasses, so thick as to resist the settlers' plow. Indeed the open lands appeared to offer only one advantage over forest cover: clearing them did not require an axe.

American migration in the nineteenth century was a mixture of short movements from adjoining states, and occasional settlement by a religious or community group from the East and from the great grain-growing plains of central Europe. Settlers rarely stayed in one place very long before pushing on to new lands and new opportunities further west. Having braved the uncertainties of one move, they seemed more inclined to risk additional ones. Although farmers had greater attachment to place than the landless, presumably because of the value of their human capital in the form of knowledge of their land and the local micro-climate, even they were often quick to move on.[64] In Trempeleau County, Wisconsin, for example, only 32 percent of the farm operators in 1860 were still there in 1870. Fewer than 20 percent were still there in 1880.[65] Farmers in Blooming Grove, Wisconsin (near Madison), and in Chelsea, Vermont, were more persistent but even in these communities more than 60 percent of the farm operators could not be traced between 1860 and 1880.[66]

Those who moved, particularly across states, overwhelmingly moved westward. Indeed, they typically went due west. Richard Steckel explains this very specific migration path in terms of the desire by farmers to maximize the value of their human and physical capital.[67] This human capital was their knowledge of particular soils, seasonal rhythms, specific crops, and so forth, all of which are strongly influenced by latitude. Such movement also made the best use of the farmer's physical capital – the seed and the milch cows – that went with him on the move since these were phototropic, that is, adapted to specific durations of sunlight and seasonal variations. Deviations north or south of the latitude for which the crops or livestock were adapted could have a serious impact upon productivity.

The incentives to maximize the economic return from migration were reinforced by ties of kinship, friendship, or common cultural or ethnic heritage. Families gravitated towards those areas about which they had some information. This often came through personal, albeit sometimes remote, relationships. Letters home from migrants and immigrants were generally upbeat and optimistic. On the frontier, people clustered around others with similar backgrounds. Thus, for example, David Davenport,

---

[64] In Chelsea, Vermont, for example, fewer than 30 percent of men were traceable between censuses twenty years apart, whereas almost 40 percent of farm operators could be traced during the same periods. See Hal S. Barron, *Those Who Stayed Behind* (Cambridge, 1984), 79.

[65] Curti et al., *The Making of an American Community*, 70. See also James C. Malin, "The Turnover of Farm Population in Kansas," *Kansas Historical Quarterly* 4 (1935), 365–66; A. Bogue, *From Prairie to Cornbelt*, 26.

[66] Michael Conzen, *Frontier Farming in an Urban Shadow* (Madison, 1971), 127; Barron, *Those Who Stayed Behind*, 79.

[67] Richard Steckel, "The Economic Foundations of East-West Migration During the Nineteenth Century," *Exploration in Economic History* 20 (1983), 14–36.

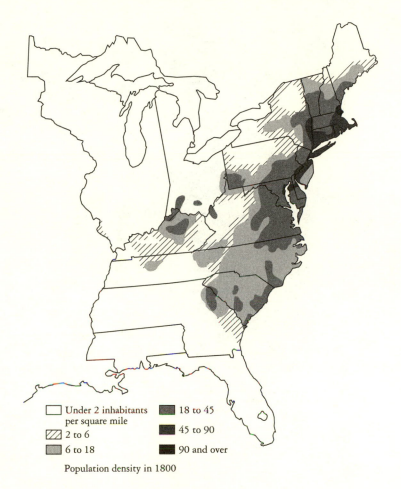

Figure 7.16. Population density in 1800. Source: Charles O. Paullin, *Atlas of Historical Geography* (Washington, DC, 1932), Plate 76.

traced out-migrants from Schoharie County, New York through letters back home to local newspapers.[68] Moreover, extraordinary clusterings of specific ethnic groups were to be found in particular communities such as the Dutch immigrants in Holland township, Ottawa County, Michigan.

[68] David Davenport, "Population Persistence and Migration in Rural New York, 1853–1860," Ph.D. diss., University of Illinois, 1982; Atack and Bateman, *To Their Own Soil*, 78.

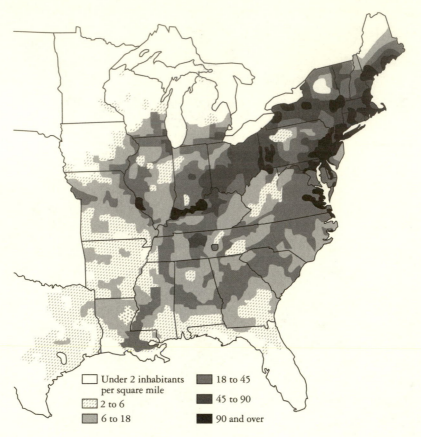

Figure 7.17. Population density in 1850. Source: Charles O. Paullin, *Atlas of Historical Geography* (Washington, DC, 1932), Plate 77.

Legend:
- Under 2 inhabitants per square mile
- 2 to 6
- 6 to 18
- 18 to 45
- 45 to 90
- 90 and over

Despite the influx of migrants and a relatively high birth rate, population density throughout much of the Midwest and West remained low. In 1800 virtually all of Ohio except for a few isolated pockets, such as in the first seven ranges and around Cincinnati, lay beyond the frontier, defined as the margin of settlement with between two and six persons per square mile (less than one family farm per square mile) (see Figure 7.16). In 1850, the frontier had pushed westward across the Mississippi River but there

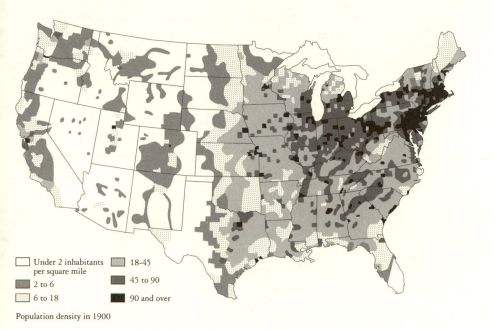

Population density in 1900

Figure 7.18. Population density in 1900. Source: Charles O. Paullin, *Atlas of Historical Geography* (Washington, DC, 1932), Plate 77.

remained isolated pockets, as in the prairie lands of east central Illinois, where density was still under six persons per square mile (see Figure 7.17). Even as late as 1900 much of the Plains and Mountain states remained on or beyond the frontier (see Figure 7.18).

Facing such low population densities, farmers in these areas had to choose between individual self-sufficiency, with its attendant lack of variety and poor-quality consumption goods, or satisfying the impersonal market's demands from distant consumers. Most chose the latter course. Settlement patterns still resembled those of the isolated farm houses and small commercial towns in the forested areas of the East, but the scale was different. Land holdings were larger, settlements less populous, and distances greater. While the drift of the land laws in the direction of free settler access was completed by the Homestead Act in 1862, the market and the power of bourgeois capital broke through and around the democratic equalitarian constraint. Much of the western soil was obtained from land or mortgage companies, or from the sales offices of the land-grant railroads. Despite "treaties," Native American claims to prior land use were disregarded in the rush to give settlers speedy access. The Plains Indians posed a different and more difficult problem than the agriculturists and forest-dwellers east of the Mississippi. But the U.S. Army, from the Mexican War onward, held the native population at bay. In less than half a century, wilderness was converted into one of the world's great agricultural regions – one more than able to keep pace with the food requirements of an emerging urban-industrial power.

8

SLAVERY AND ITS CONSEQUENCES FOR THE SOUTH IN THE NINETEENTH CENTURY

STANLEY L. ENGERMAN

INTRODUCTION

Slavery had long existed in many parts of the world prior to the settlement of the Americas. While the basic legal provisions and the conditions in which slave labor was used differed, few, if any, periods in world history had not had some form of enslavement of individuals. These individuals were frequently, but not always, from other societies. While sociologists might point to the distinguishing features of slavery in most societies as including "social death" and alienation – the slave as an outsider – in order to understand the economic implications, we wish to regard the slave as property. Slaves could be bought and sold (as well as freed), the rights to their labor belonged to their owners, and the offspring of a slave mother was regarded as slave property of her owner. To function effectively, slavery must be accepted by members in the potential slaveowning class and, to those societies with a code of legal controls, defended by the law.

ORIGIN OF SLAVERY IN THE AMERICAS, OUTSIDE THE UNITED STATES

Although slavery has been widespread throughout history, the distinguished classicist Moses Finley has argued that "there have been only five genuine slave societies," societies whose social and economic institutions were dominated by the existence of slavery. Two were in the ancient world, Greece and Rome, and three in the Americas between the sixteenth and nineteenth centuries, Brazil, the Caribbean, and the U.S. South. Except

329

for the British, French, Dutch, and Danish areas of the Caribbean, where the slave populations were about 90 percent of the overall population, the shares of slaves in the populations were generally between 30 and 40 percent (as in the Spanish areas of the Caribbean), but the impacts on the society and economy were sufficiently extensive to become the focus of attention of contemporaries as well as of subsequent scholars. Slavery in the Americas differed from slavery elsewhere in that it came to be based upon racial considerations. Whites could be indentured servants or convict laborers, and made to suffer other forms of coercion, but they were not slaves. In the Americas, after some initial experiments with the enslavement of Native Americans, slavery was restricted to Africans, brought across in the transatlantic slave trade, and to their descendants. The transatlantic slave trade, lasting over three centuries, entailed the purchase and transportation of Africans, originally captured within Africa, to various parts of the Americas. Mainland North America received only a relatively small share (about 7 percent) of slaves brought over in the transatlantic slave trade. The high rate of natural increase of the slave population led to relatively minor contributions of the new slave imports from Africa to total population. The trade to North America began relatively late compared to that to Brazil and the Caribbean, and the United States was among the first to end the slave trade by legislation.

The slave trade from Africa to the New World represented one of the major trans-oceanic movements of population during the more than three centuries of traffic before the last Africans came, in the 1860s, to Cuba. The numbers imported down to the first decades of the nineteenth century exceeded the number of white immigrants, and as late as the start of the nineteenth century, about four times the number of slaves as whites had come to the Americas. The estimates of the slave trade range from 10 to 12 million slaves imported, with Brazil being the largest receiver of slaves, having both an early start of importation and a late date of ending the slave trade. The British were long a major carrier of slaves, particularly to the Caribbean and to mainland North America. Most slaves in this period came from areas along the western coast of Africa, the trade to the Americas from the east coast being minor until the early nineteenth century. While there were variations by time and by place of export and arrival, there were certain overriding demographic characteristics of the slave trade, as there were also for voluntary immigrations. In regard to sex composition, the enslaved were about two-thirds male, one-third female; in regard to age, most were probably young adults, although adolescents and children were often overrepresented compared with their shares in the African populations from which they came.

Slaves played important economic roles in many parts of the Americas. The gains to slaveowners can be considered to be of two categories. First, ownership of slaves meant that slaves could be forced to work in places and under working conditions that would not voluntarily be selected by workers free to choose, unless at a considerable wage premium. Second, ownership, with its ability to determine the consumption of slave workers, meant that owners would be able to gain the income represented by the difference between what the worker produced and the consumption allowed the worker. Indeed, it was this excess that was being purchased by owners when they bought slaves, and the excess represented one measurable aspect of the exploitation of the enslaved. The coercion involved in the assignment of slaves to the production of specific crops and locations helps explain why the incidence of slavery varied throughout the Americas. For, while slaves could perform all occupations that free labor could (and vice versa), slaves tended to be most numerous in tropical areas, and they were used in the production of plantation-type crops – or, at the least, crops grown on units where the optimum size for production was larger than the family farm. Thus slavery was most important in the sugar-producing areas of Brazil and the Caribbean from the start of settlement and was also important in the production of other plantation crops, such as rice, tobacco, indigo, cotton, and coffee. Drawing a line from the British Caribbean to British Canada we find a distinct relation between climate (and crop) and the proportion of the population enslaved, with the highest proportions being in the sugar areas of the British Caribbean, and with the ratio falling in the rice, cotton, and tobacco regions of the U.S. South. The percentage of slaves was relatively unimportant, even before the late-eighteenth-century legal emancipations, in the U.S. North, and was relatively inconsequential in Canada. While slavery long persisted in the northern climates, such as in the U.S. North, the role of slave labor was different, and its quantitative importance was considerably less than in the southern states in which plantation crops were grown. It is perhaps not unexpected that the ending of slavery by law occurred in the northern states before it took place in the South, and was attained with relatively little controversy in the North.

Slave labor dominated the economies of the British West Indies from their settlement to the legislated ending of slavery in 1834 and the ending of apprenticeship in 1838. Although some slaves lived and worked in urban areas, and slaves were also involved in the production of foodstuffs and other crops on small farms, most lived on relatively large plantations (often with 200 or more slaves), and most slaves were involved primarily in the production of sugar for export to the British and European markets. The image of slavery as a demographic disaster accurately characterized this region, since the death rates of the enslaved exceeded their birth rates, so that slave imports were required to maintain the slave population. Thus, at any time there were large numbers of African-born in the Caribbean slave population.

The first island of settlement was Barbados, and at first it was based upon white British labor, mainly indentured servants, producing tobacco. Sugar was soon introduced, and the nature of production and the racial mix of the population shifted. Later settlements, such as that on the large island of Jamaica, were more generally based from the beginning on the production of sugar by slave labor, a pattern persisting with the later acquisitions of Trinidad and British Guiana at the end of the eighteenth century and start of the nineteenth century. Based on the share of slaves in the population and the importance of sugar production, the British West Indies were almost completely slave areas.

SLAVERY ON THE MAINLAND

The situation on the mainland was rather different, both before and after the American Revolution. While slavery was legal and had existed in all parts of the colonies, the share of slaves in the population, their patterns of fertility and mortality, and the principal uses of slave labor were different from those in the British West Indies. The share of slaves in the northern populations was generally less than 5 percent, particularly in rural areas. Higher shares were recorded in cities, such as New York and Philadelphia, particularly early in the eighteenth century. The number of slaves in New England was less than in the middle states, New York, New Jersey, and Pennsylvania. Throughout the North slaves performed a large range of occupations, and generally lived, except for small pockets of larger farms in rural areas of New York and Rhode Island, on relatively small farms or in towns and cities.

It is in the southern states that slavery was economically more important, with major increases in the share of slaves in the population starting about three-quarters of a century to one century after the initial settlement of the colonies. In the late eighteenth century, slaves were about 40 percent of the overall southern population, and about 20 percent of the total national population, but slavery's significance in shaping social and political life in the South was most dramatic. Although slaves had been brought to the southern states earlier in the seventeenth century, it was only in the last decade of the century, in the tobacco-growing Chesapeake states, that slavery began its first large-scale expansion. Tobacco had become an important crop in coastal Virginia and Maryland on the basis of a labor force consisting primarily of indentured English males. In the 1690s, however, a decline in the availability of such workers, due to a reduction in English population growth and to improved opportunities for workers in England, combined with the increased availability of slaves in the transatlantic market, due to a slump in the Caribbean and Brazilian sugar markets, led to a substitution of slave labor for indentured labor. In the subsequent decades this shift persisted. Plantations of ten to twenty slaves dominated the tobacco-producing sector, and the share of slaves rose to over one-third of the population of the Chesapeake colonies by the middle of the eighteenth century.

The climate and soil of North Carolina and its lack of adequate coastal port facilities were not conducive to a considerable plantation sector, but there was some expansion of the slave population, and the share of slaves in its population rose to about one-third before the Civil War. South Carolina, however, became a major plantation slave colony, starting with the expansion of the rice economy after 1700. Slave imports grew rapidly for work on the large rice plantations of coastal South Carolina and (after 1751) Georgia, and slave labor was also used to produce sea island cotton, indigo, and, after the invention of the cotton gin in 1793, short-staple cotton in the upland areas of the state. Mortality on the coastal plantations was high, and the demographic experience for slaves in South Carolina was less favorable than for those in the tobacco areas of the Chesapeake. Georgia was settled under the auspices of the Oglethorpes, and settlement was initially expected to be based upon white labor. Due to difficulties in the settlement process, however, there was agitation for change, and after 1751 slave importation began, primarily for production of rice and sea island cotton along the coastal strip. Georgia rapidly became one of the major slaveowning colonies in the second half of the eighteenth century.

The mainland colonies received fewer slaves than they did free whites in the colonial period, unusual for a New World settlement. The demographic experience of slaves, predominantly in the South, was less favorable than that of whites. The exceptional rates of white natural increase in New England, the Middle Atlantic states, and Canada provided for rapid population growth with limited numbers of migrants. Even in areas where the migration of slaves exceeded that of whites, the differential rates of natural increase meant that whites exceeded blacks in the total population. Nevertheless, in some areas the numbers of slaves increased absolutely, even in the South. More striking, however, was the comparison of the population change of slaves in the mainland colonies with that of slaves elsewhere in the Americas. Starting very early in the settlement process, the size of the mainland slave population expanded by an excess of fertility over mortality, although in some areas it took a generation or so for this positive increase to occur. Elsewhere in the Americas there was a substantial net decrease in the slave population, with mortality (due in part to the environment in which sugar and other tropical crops were produced) exceeding fertility. Thus, by the early nineteenth century, although the United States received only a relatively small number of those slaves coming to the New World, the high rate of natural increase there resulted in a growth of population sufficient for the United States to account for about one-quarter of the New World black population. The colonies that were to become the United States constituted the one major slaveowning area to experience such a high rate of natural increase, and it had done so early in the settlement process, while the transatlantic slave trade was still open. This positive rate of increase continued until the Civil War emancipation of the slaves. Thus, while most parts of the Americas retained their slave numbers by a process of importation to compensate for the natural decrease, the growth of the U.S. slave population reflected the high rate of natural increase, slave imports being important only early in the settlement of the United States.

Slave fertility in mainland North America was unusually high, at levels achieved by U.S. free whites in the eighteenth century, and above those of slaves elsewhere. Mortality rates in the U.S. South were higher than in the North, but below those of the tropical areas of the Caribbean and South America. The early achievement of high population increase, and the lesser dependence on new slave arrivals, meant that the proportion of native-born slaves (creoles) was greater on the mainland than elsewhere. In this sense, the U.S. slaves were more "American" than slaves elsewhere, and, particularly after the closing of the slave trade, they were also more "American" than were the whites, in that their ancestors had been longer in the Americas.

Although slavery lasted in the United States for about two-and-one-half centuries, most of the current historiography covers only the last fifty years of that period, which has meant that certain significant characteristics of slavery have been downplayed. For nearly two centuries, including one century as a dominant institution in the South, slavery was confined to the coastal states along the eastern, Atlantic seaboard. While there was some small westward movement, particularly in the Chesapeake, few slaves by 1790 had been moved beyond the boundaries of the initial set of colonies. Whereas the nineteenth-century South could be aptly described as the "Cotton Kingdom," in 1790 little of the upland cotton that later characterized the South was being grown, due to its economic impracticality prior to the invention of the cotton gin. Slave labor was mainly involved in the production of tobacco (and after the Revolution, wheat) in the Chesapeake, and rice and indigo in coastal South Carolina and Georgia. Production of these crops, dependent on export markets in England and elsewhere in Europe, were influenced by the Revolutionary War and the changing trading arrangements that were the result of the war. The declining exports of these crops in the immediate post-Revolutionary period meant some shifts to mixed agriculture and general farming by slave laborers. And, given the technology of the crops produced by slave labor, there were some differences in the sizes of the units on which slaves worked before and after the start of the nineteenth century. Rice units tended to be larger than cotton plantations, while those producing tobacco tended to be smaller. The nineteenth century, in contrast, would see the emergence of a "Cotton Kingdom" to account for the heaviest use of slave labor, a sharp southward and westward movement of the slave population, and a relative movement to larger units than a century earlier. It is not that the eighteenth century did not have a dynamic, adaptive slave economy, but that the changes at this time were smaller than those that were to occur in the next three-quarters of a century.

SLAVERY AFTER THE REVOLUTIONARY WAR

The Revolutionary War created major difficulties for the American slave-owners. In addition to the weakening of control that resulted from the warfare on the mainland, the British policy of encouraging runaways had some success in Virginia. Yet despite these unsettled conditions and the economic impact of the changing trade relations with England on

American production patterns, the slave society of the southern United States did not appear threatened nor was its continuation in serious doubt. The economic importance of slavery was less in the states of the North than in those further south. Many northern states did introduce measures to end slavery in the post-Revolutionary period. Generally the measures called for gradual emancipation. They entailed continued enslavement for those born prior to a certain date, and a legally free status, subject to apprenticeship to the mother's owner, until the late teens or into the twenties, for those born after a specified date, the specific ages depending upon each state's legislation. Pennsylvania (1780), Connecticut (1784), Rhode Island (1784), New York (1799), and New Jersey (1804) all passed gradual emancipation laws. The Vermont (1777) and Massachusetts (1780) constitutions provided for immediate emancipation (in two states where there totaled only about 5,000 blacks, not all of whom were enslaved). As a result of the dying off of the slave populations, and a legal acceleration of emancipation in several of the states with gradual emancipation schemes, by 1850 the census recorded, in all of the North, only a few hundred slaves, all in New Jersey. While some of this slave population decline was attributed to sales of slaves from North to South, the major explanation for the disappearance of northern slavery was the death of those enslaved prior to, and the free legal status of those born subsequent to, the legislation.

There had been some increase in slave manumissions in the South, particularly in Virginia, reflecting the initial aftermath of the Revolutionary War's rhetoric of rights and liberties. The rate of manumission soon slowed and, in the nineteenth century, slave manumissions in the United States remained low relative to their frequency elsewhere, particularly in the Spanish colonies and in Brazil. Even before the demands of the international market made cotton the primary user of slave labor, slaves yielded a sufficient return to maintain the demand for slave labor. The high value of slaves in the United States, as well as specific social reasons, limited manumission, whether by deed or by sale. This resulted in a higher ratio of slave blacks to free blacks in the southern states than among the other major slave powers of the American continents.

The Constitutional debates indicated the power of the southern bloc in maintaining the institution of slavery. Attempts to restrict the international slave trade were deferred to 1808, twenty years after the debates, at which time the United States did end its role in the transatlantic slave trade, in the same year as did the British. This twenty-year period, however, saw more slaves imported than in any other twenty-year period in the era of the slave trade. Nevertheless, the main source of growth of the slave population throughout this period remained natural increase. The legal ending of the slave trade was successful, the numbers of slaves smuggled into the United States in the nineteenth century being quite limited. Although the terms of the Constitution did nothing to limit slavery in those states where it still existed – indeed the word *slave* was nowhere mentioned in the Constitution – the existence of slaves was recognized in the assignment of seats for the House of Representatives and in votes in the electoral college. Slaves, termed by the Constitution "other persons," were included as three-fifths of a free person. This practice increased southern representation, but not by as much as it would have if slaves were counted as equals. The care of slaves, and matters relating to the their legal personality, was left as primarily a state issue. The ensuing debates that were to affect the nation's politics concerned not the existence of slavery in those states where it was legal, but rather the question of the possible existence of slavery in the territories which were to enter the union as new states. Also significant for slavery and the emerging sectional disagreements were the provisions of the Northwest Ordinance, effectively precluding the expansion of slavery into the Northwest Territory. While some ambiguities in interpretation continued to be debated, the ordinance served to limit slavery's area of possible expansion to the southern states. In that region, however, slavery was about to undergo a major expansion – economically, demographically, and, geographically – as a result of the invention of the cotton gin and the ability of short staple cotton to be grown in most parts of the South.

THE GROWTH OF THE
"COTTON KINGDOM"

The first half of the nineteenth century saw dramatic changes in the nature of southern slavery. After the development of the cotton gin, slavery within the South moved southward and westward, and by the start of the Civil War more slaves lived in the newer areas of the South than resided in the original colonies of settlement. With this geographic expansion of the slave population there was also a movement of southern whites – planters, yeomen, and others. The major crop grown by slave labor was now short-staple cotton, and it is estimated that in 1850 nearly three-quarters of all agricultural slaves worked where cotton was the principal crop. Cotton plantations thus accounted for more than half of all southern slaves. The optimum size for a cotton plantation was between sixteen and fifty slaves, and this size range came to account for the largest proportion of the slave population. In general these farms consisted of the family of the owner and, depending on size, an overseer, but relatively few other white laborers. Thus as the plantation size increased, so did the ratio of black slave to free white. Some cotton (in 1850 less than 10 percent) was grown on farms without slaves. This share rose in the cotton boom of the 1850s. The reasons for the continued low level of cotton production by free white labor in the antebellum period relative to the amounts after the Civil War, remains one of the debated issues of southern economic development, but their increased output during the cotton booms, and then after the disappearance of the plantation with emancipation, suggests the impact of competition between the different forms of production.

Slave labor dominated cotton production, and U.S. cotton production dominated the world cotton market, accounting for over three-quarters of the input into British cotton textile production. Yet there remained many other uses for slave labor within the South. In 1850 in the states of Virginia, Maryland, and Kentucky, slaves were used on tobacco units, and these accounted for about 14 percent of all agricultural slaves. There was some use of slave labor in the Virginia wheat economy, while hemp production in Kentucky took about 2 percent of agricultural slaves. Rice, grown in coastal South Carolina and Georgia, accounted for about 5 percent of agricultural slaves in 1850, while sugar, grown in Louisiana, utilized about 6 percent of agricultural slaves. The average size of producing units in rice and sugar exceeded that of the average cotton unit, as well as those in tobacco, wheat, and hemp. About 10 percent of the slaves resided in urban areas, where their functions included skilled crafts as well as domestic service, and several hundred thousand were also considered to be doing domestic work on agricultural units.

The expansion of cotton production, and the increased concentration of slave labor, represented a dramatic shift in a period of about one-half century. Those few slaves producing cotton before the start of the nineteenth century were primarily involved in the growing of sea island, not short-staple, cotton. Clearly this transition reflected the great expansion in demand in the textile mills of England and New England for raw cotton, leading to an increase in cotton production averaging almost 7 percent per annum between 1800 and 1860. Export growth in tobacco and rice was more limited, as was the growth in the production of sugar, produced mainly for sale in internal markets, behind tariff barriers. Thus, as suggested by the nature of the geographic movements, the cotton kingdom expanded by drawing labor away from use in producing other crops, a pattern seen both in secular movements as well as in the response to cyclical fluctuations in cotton demand. Cotton accounted for about one-fifth of overall southern output, as well as for about 50 percent of total U.S. exports during much of the second quarter of the nineteenth century. The slave plantation was an integral aspect of the U.S. economy, solidly linked to the world market, and entailing a wide range of distribution services to market this production.

The westward and southward movement of the southern economy was influenced by the new crop technology that permitted the expansion of short-staple cotton production, as well as the innovations in transportation – steamboats, canals, railroads – that increased accessibility to markets at lowered cost. The westward movement was persistent throughout the period, but greatly accelerated in the cotton booms of the 1830s and the 1850s. These periods were years of sharply rising slave prices. While these relocations provided a dramatic shift in the residence of the southern population, Virginia remained the state with the largest number of slaves even at the start of the Civil War. The nature and impact on the older parts of the South of the interstate movement of slaves remains somewhat controversial. One issue concerns the proportion of the nearly one million slaves who left the older areas of the South for newer regions who went with relocating owners or family members of slaveowners in the Old South, in contrast with the proportion of slaves who were sold by owners from one part of the South to another without other members of their families. No scholarly consensus with respect to the relative magnitudes of movements by sale or with owners has been achieved, but both factors clearly played a role in interstate migrations and both, being involuntary, had disruptive effects on marriage and family patterns. A related debate concerns the extent to which the economies of the older parts of the South were dependent on the slave sales to maintain their economic viability. On this the answer seems more straightforward, both because the contribution of slave sales to incomes in older areas of the South could not have been large, and because there were clearly other causes of the continuing economic prosperity of most of these areas. And, to the extent that these older areas did experience some economic problems, they often were the consequence of, and not the cause of, the interregional competition generated by the geographic expansion of production of cotton and other crops into new areas of high productivity.

The westward movement had a relatively limited impact on the percentages of whites owning slaves, at least until the 1850s. About one-third of the southern white population owned slaves up to 1850, falling to 25 percent in the cotton boom of the next decade. Many owners owned only one or two slaves; only about 10 percent of slaveowners in 1850 had the twenty or more slaves necessary to be considered members of the planter class. Yet these plantations had more than one-half of southern slaves. Plantations in the Lower South were larger than those in the other states, so that the geographic movement led to increases in the concentration of slaves and of slave ownership.

Given the different optimum size of units for different crops, and the differences in extent of slave ownership by whites (and the small number of free blacks), the distribution of wealth as well as of slave ownership differed within the regions of the South. Overall, there was a small increase in wealth inequality over time. The distribution of wealth for the free population of the South differed little from that in the North in the first half of the nineteenth century. While the rural South, because of the presence of large slaveowners, had more inequality than did the rural North, with its family-sized farms, the frequency of nonwealthholders in urban areas and the greater number of urban dwellers in the North made for a roughly similar distribution of wealth for the free population in both regions. In both North and South wealth inequality led to disproportionate political representation. For the South this meant, at state and national levels, a high degree of representation by larger slaveowners, although this was not always sufficient for them to obtain all their political demands.

While there remains debate between scholars of different political and methodological persuasions as to the pre-, non-, or a-capitalist nature of the overall southern economy (as well as debates as to whether such distinctions are meaningful for many political and economic issues), it seems agreed that the plantation itself had many of the characteristics of modern industrial firms, being described as "a factory in the field." Indeed slave plantations, even in the U.S. South, were often among the most heavily capitalized firms anywhere in the early nineteenth century. The planter, as entrepreneur, made production decisions based upon the profits expected from producing crops for sale in local or export markets, and for consumption on the plantation. Increased foreign and northern demands for export crops, initially tobacco and rice and then cotton, led to increased use of slave labor, and the shifts in the relative prices of different crops influenced the relative amounts of crops produced. Within the plantation there was an extensive division of labor and an effective use of labor of different ages and sexes. Even on cotton plantations there was extensive production of other crops, including foodstuffs; indeed plantations were more frequently self-sufficient than were yeoman farms. Slaves were engaged in skilled, artisan-like functions, such as blacksmithing, carpentering, coopering, as well as performing as nurses and domestic servants. Slave children after about age 7 or 8 often found themselves doing odd jobs, before joining the field gangs when they reached the prime ages, after about 16. Some then did other work, but gang labor continued for most until they were in their 40s or early 50s, when those older workers performed other functions, such as being watchmen and doing other less physically demanding work. The ability to assign functions in this manner led to an (involuntary) increased labor force participation rate among the slave population, and an ability by the slaveowner to extract a higher measured output from slave children and females than was obtained from members of free populations, where measured labor force participation tended to be lower.

In addition to the higher labor force participation rate, what made the plantations so productive and profitable was the ability to force slave workers into large-scale gangs to produce primarily export commodities. The efficiency of production of southern farms rose dramatically with the numbers of slaves actually used in production. Slave labor only became highly productive on farms of over 15 slaves, where gang labor was possible. Farms of this size could be efficiently maintained only for the production of certain crops, particularly cotton, sugar, and rice. The ability to force slaves into units of this size in a manner that free workers would not accept did not, however, eliminate all problems for slaveowners. Measures were necessary to provide incentives, positive as well as negative, for slaves, so that they would be made willing to do the work and to be sufficiently productive to yield high incomes to their owners. In addition to whippings and the threat of sale, incentives included rewards of time off, occupational change, and enhanced material consumption. The highly seasonal nature of agricultural work in the South meant that planning and decisions on labor allocation were necessary. Thus, while the profitability of the slave plantation rested on the ability to legally coerce labor onto plantations producing export crops, a location that free workers avoided wherever possible, the ability to benefit from this coercion still required considerable planning and management in coordinating and controlling labor and in making effective production choices.

The expansion of the cotton kingdom of the nineteenth century flowed from the growth of demand for raw cotton, mainly from Great Britain, which took over two-thirds of U.S. exports (the share of the cotton crop exported was over three-quarters in the last three antebellum decades), and New England, for use in producing cotton textiles. British cotton textile production expanded dramatically at the end of the eighteenth century, with a shift from woolens, and the increase continued at high rates through at least the first half of the nineteenth century. There had been, and continued to be, other sources of raw cotton, some based on slave labor (e.g., the West Indies), others not (e.g., Turkey, India, and Egypt), and the initial expansion of British textiles preceded large-scale cotton imports from the United States. Once cotton supplies from the United States began to enter Britain, however, with the exception of the American Civil War and its immediate aftermath, the South dominated the world cotton trade into the twentieth century. The South was the world's major exporter of tobacco in the first half of the nineteenth century, but the value and importance of the crop to the southern economy was considerably less than that of cotton.

Given the importance of foreign demand in influencing cotton production, the southern economy participated in the major international business cycles in the early decades of the nineteenth century as well as those of the 1830s and 1850s. The impact of these cycles was felt throughout the nation, moreover, due to the linking of the sectional economies via finance, services, and manufactured commodities. The one antebellum cyclical depression that was not so widely diffused was that of 1857, which was more severe in the Northeast and Midwest than in the South, an aspect widely commented on in the late antebellum debates comparing the sectional economies. It has been argued that cotton, which accounted for about one-half of U.S. exports throughout the antebellum period, was the "leading sector" of the early-nineteenth-century U.S. economy, at least through the 1840s. While such a claim might overstate its role, clearly the cotton economy was a large and conspicuous part of the overall economy drawing, directly and indirectly, upon resources, commerce, and manufacturing throughout the nation (particularly the Northeast) and tied in with the important cotton textile–producing sector of the world's most advanced economies.

The other primary export crops also increased in production throughout the antebellum years, although at rates below that of cotton. Tobacco production moved westward into Kentucky but remained important in Virginia and, to a lesser extent, North Carolina. Rice and sugar remained concentrated in South Carolina and Louisiana, respectively, but they expanded their output and used larger numbers of slaves than at the start of the century. And slave labor produced other crops, including foodstuffs, on smaller units as well as on the large farms producing staples. Cotton was the most noted and important use of southern slave labor, but not its only use, and the dominating importance of cotton came only with the last decades of southern slavery.

There had been a long debate, among both contemporaries and historians, concerning whether slavery was profitable to slaveowners, in the sense of earning a market return from ownership sufficient to justify the costs of purchasing and/or raising of slaves. While this is not the same question as whether the South could have been better off with free than with slave labor, given the different effects upon southern society and institutions, it is a question with important implications for understanding the southern planting class and southern economic structure. It has come to be generally held that the slaveowners who raised and purchased slaves tended to make a competitive return on their investments, and that all indications are that, prior to the political events leading to the Civil War, they expected to continue to do so for a long period into the future. The fact that southern planters were disproportionately among the wealthiest Americans in 1850 and 1860, with an average wealth that had risen throughout the antebellum period, suggests the profitability to planters of slave ownership.

The South had developed modern transportation and banking sectors, generally with the same types of state and local government aids that were used in the North, and southern urban centers provided financial and other services, including slave markets. New Orleans was one of the major export centers for the United States, and until the 1840s had served as a major outlet for midwestern, as well as southern, commodities. The level of industry was limited compared to the North, but there had developed some iron manufacturing, mainly in Virginia, and several textile mills, in addition to a broader range of industries, many of which were based on the use of slave labor.

An excellent indication of the behavior of the slave economy and of the expectations of the planters was in the prices of slaves. These prices were observed at times when slaves were sold in the market or evaluated for transfers at the time of owner death or for other commercial purposes. The prices of slaves were determined by expectations concerning physical output of goods produced by the slaves, the prices at which these goods could be sold, the amount of consumption allowed slaves, the other costs (e.g., overseers) of slave ownership, the expected period over which returns and costs would be realized (that is, time to death, individual emancipation, or the legal abolition of the slave system), and the rate of interest. Slave productivity was influenced by a number of factors, including age, sex, skill, and health. Slave prices were influenced by changes in the demand for slaves, based upon changes in the demand for the crops they produced and their productivity in crop production, and the supply of slaves. Within the antebellum South slave prices rose with the cyclical increases in the demand for cotton and fell in periods, such as the 1840s, when the cotton market was in recession. Prices in the late 1850s were two to three times those of the 1820s and 1840s. The influence of slave price changes upon the southern economy can be seen in the shifts in the mix of crops produced and in the variations in the rate of geographic mobility when prices varied. The fact that slave prices were high in the 1850s, and that, earlier, the decline in prices the 1840s did not lead to a belief in any imminent ending of the system, suggests that southern planters had anticipated that the slave economy would survive for many more decades.

There were dramatic differences in the demography of the slave population in the United States in comparison with slave populations elsewhere in the Americas, as well as those of earlier slave societies. The U.S. slave population grew at a natural rate of over 2 percent per annum after the closing of the slave trade. This natural increase started sometime in the eighteenth century, although at first growth was probably at a lower rate than it was in the nineteenth century. In contrast, the slave population of the British and French West Indies experienced continued natural decrease, from settlement to the ending of slavery in the first half of the nineteenth century, a pattern of decline that was not reversed by the ending of the transatlantic slave trade. No other major slave society had so large a rate of natural increase as did the United States; indeed few free white societies, the U.S. North and South being major exceptions, had as high a rate of natural increase as did southern slaves. When compared to Caribbean slaves, what was most striking demographically about U.S. slaves was their higher rate of fertility, even more than any differences in their death rates. The southern slave fertility rates were roughly equivalent to those of southern whites, about the world's highest at that time.

This fertility pattern has become central to a number of important debates about the nature of U.S. slavery. To those who argued, as did many in the nineteenth and twentieth centuries, that slaves would not wish to have children or that slaveowners did not provide adequate subsistence to permit high rates of reproduction, a pattern of low fertility and natural decrease was the obvious expectation, buttressed by the examples of slave societies elsewhere and at earlier times. The finding of high fertility for U.S. slaves thus posed a major challenge for understanding the condition of slaves in the United States. To those who believed slaves were otherwise unwilling to have children, the pattern reflected something called slave-breeding: a deliberate interference with slave reproduction to encourage more children for sale. The evidence that children had a positive value at birth and early ages, and the considerable westward movement of younger slaves, were seen to be consistent with the argument of deliberate encouragement of reproduction for purposes of sale. Those arguing a relation between owner mistreatment and low fertility found that the U.S. slave population increase raised important questions concerning the depiction of the treatment and material conditions of life for U.S. slaves. This evidence suggested more favorable circumstances on the mainland, whether due to different natural resources, different crops grown, or different owner attitudes.

Recent research has introduced alternative explanations for the high fertility of U.S. slaves. Breakdowns of the characteristics of slave fertility have pointed to the fact that the slaves had an earlier start of childbearing, a higher percentage of childbearing women, and somewhat shorter spacing between births, than did Caribbean slaves. The first was the result of the better diet of U.S. slaves, and thus the earlier onset of menarche and the potential for childbearing; the second was influenced by what has come to be seen as the greater marital stability of the U.S. slave population, with a greater frequency of continued two-adult households, and the impact of the lower adult mortality rate on the continuity of these family relationships; and the third was attributed to differences in childnursing patterns, reflecting differences in diet and in cultural adjustments after arrival from Africa. These factors, in conjunction with the relative magnitude of sales in the westward movement, as well as consideration of the costs of bearing and raising offspring, have shifted attention from the hypothesized existence of "slave-breeding" to explanations dealing with slave family patterns and material living standards in accounting for the high U.S. slave fertility.

It is now clear that the somewhat lower mortality of U.S. slaves than those in the Caribbean, although their rates were above those of U.S. whites, even those in the South, reflected the better living standards found on U.S. plantations, and the more favorable working conditions on the mainland than in the sugar-producing areas of the Caribbean. Estimates suggest a high rate of food consumption in general, although there were cyclical variations over the antebellum era, depending on weather and on the allocation of labor between staples and foodstuffs. There was geographic variation in mortality within the South, e.g., higher in the coastal lowlands growing rice in wet fields in South Carolina, lower in the upland areas where cotton and other crops could be grown. Tropical diseases, such as malaria, were not as frequent a cause of death as in the Caribbean, although U.S. slaves were hit by epidemics of yellow fever and cholera (as were southern whites). It is probable that mortality rates for slaves fell over time, even after adjusting for the measured impact of the ending of the international slave trade with its higher age-specific mortality during the period known, euphemistically, as "seasoning."

Recent work on slave height-by-age in the antebellum South has reinforced some of the recent interpretations of slave health, while raising some new (as well as old) issues. Heights of adult slaves in the U.S. tended to be quite close to those of adult whites, above those of Caribbean slaves and, by several inches, greater than those of Africans. These data suggest that factors influencing height, such as nutritional input and work intensity, were more favorable for U.S. slaves than for Caribbean slaves. An important issue raised, however, is the apparent shortfall of U.S. slave heights for children of younger ages prior to entry into the labor force. The reasons for this shortfall and the subsequent recovery at older ages is currently under examination, with attempts to understand possible factors causing differing treatment of slaves by their masters at different times in the slave's life-cycle, including their responses to cost considerations or their imperfect knowledge of food requirements. Little is yet known about whether such a pattern characterized slaves elsewhere, as well as the southern white population.

In addition to the economic questions, there have long been many related debates about the nature of southern society and culture. There have been recent reinterpretations of the nature of slave life, and of slave and southern culture, with important implications for the understanding of the southern economy. This work is difficult to summarize, in part since many patterns varied with the size and location of the slave units. The complex psychological issues concerning the balance of slave autonomy and owner control, as well as the precise degree of flexibility and of cruelty within the South, all remain open for more analysis. Resistance to enslavement by individuals and groups, by running away and by malingering, persisted. Rebellions were planned and undertaken. Revolts, although they failed to become widespread or great in number, influenced white reactions (and overreactions). The major U.S. slave rebellions were those in New York City in 1712, the Stono Rebellion (1739), Gabriel Prosser's Revolt (1800), the Point Coupee Uprising (1811, in Louisiana, the largest in the United States), Denmark Vesey's Revolt (1822), and Nat Turner's Rebellion (1831), but there were numerous others. The important role of African-Christianity in the slave population, the depth of the two-parent pattern of slave families, and the importance of slave production on their own plots (for sale or consumption by the slave), have been studied, and this research has yielded rather different interpretations of the operations of the slave system than had been presented in earlier generations, interpretations pointing to greater accomplishments by the slaves, with more space allowed to them on a day-to-day basis.

Relative both to slaves and to whites, little is known of the less than 10 percent of the black population who lived in the South as free blacks. Some, particularly in the Upper South, were from families who had been free for several generations, while others were newly manumitted, whether by grant or by self-purchase. About one-half of the southern free blacks were described in the census as mulattos, not blacks; they were more frequently female than male; and they more frequently lived in urban areas than did slaves. There were important communities of free black families of propertyholders in Charleston and New Orleans. While several states had passed laws that would have required manumitted blacks to migrate out of state, these laws were seldom enforced, and there were free black owners of slaves, land, and other forms of property throughout the South. Nevertheless, the social, if not legal, controls over free blacks persisted, and their status was frequently under attack.

To a great extent, the economic and social role of Native Americans within the nineteenth-century South was quite limited. Their numbers were relatively small, and particularly after the 1820s, with governmental removal policies, many lived in areas isolated from the rest of the southern population. Some, such as the Cherokees, were owners of slaves, and there were often schisms within tribes based upon relative degrees of acculturation to white society. With the initial declines in population with the white settlement, however, the numbers and direct economic impact of Native Americans upon southern society declined.

There has recently been considerable re-examination of the behavior of the planter class, including their commercial behavior and responsiveness to market incentives. To the extent they responded to price incentives and acquired relatively large amounts of wealth, clearly they fit into a market-based economy, albeit one based upon the use of unfree rather than free labor. More complex is the nature of their dealings with the slave labor force. At issue is the extent to which paternalism played a role in mitigating commercial influences and moderating behavior and whether it is meaningful to regard these as separate influences upon the control of the enslaved. In trying to account for the origins of planter culture under slavery, as well as its absence in non-slave areas, it still remains an issue whether slavery was initially created by individuals with a different culture than among those in non-slave societies or if the prior existence of slavery, however generated, led to the emergence of individuals and a society with different beliefs than what is considered to be characteristic of capitalist societies. That the planters were often wealthy and behaved like rich men is clear, as is the fact that they regarded the continuation of the slave-based economy as central to their existence.

There has also been debate about the characteristics of the many non-slaveholding whites within the South, both those groups residing within the plantation belts and those residing in upland areas that had relatively few plantations. Some of these yeomen were relatively well-off by the standards of rural agriculture in the North, some were poor and considered relatively backward by the standards even of those times. The former group contained many farmers who were productive and earned returns from family labor, even if generally producing few of the agricultural staples in most normal years. They did gain from, and were involved in, the emergence of the transportation improvements necessary to increase access to markets. Some also became slaveowners, if not moving immediately into the plantation-owning class, and clearly increased their wealth. The extent to which their limited (compared to planters) involvement with the market economy was due to limitations resulting from the competition of the large-scale staple-producing plantation or, rather, indifference (for whatever cultural reasons) to the market, is still debated, and is an issue to which we shall return when examining the yeomen's postbellum adjustment to the ending of the plantation system. Yeomen produced cotton and tobacco, among the staples, their production varying with the levels of market demand. They also produced corn and other foodstuffs, livestock, and other agricultural commodities. They differed from planters not in what they produced, but in the mix and amount of what was produced. Traditionally described as being in a lower economic condition than yeomen were the so-called poor whites, who were, however, relatively few in number. They lived in low-income conditions, either as owners of small farms on poor soil or as migrants and vagrants doing seasonal labor, and were not upwardly mobile in wealth or status. Their numbers, their cultural backgrounds, their beliefs, and their differences from other members of southern society are still the basis of disagreement.

Most political issues of antebellum America had some connections to the South and slavery, if only because they often involved the differing economic concerns of the North and the South. Even while disagreements were not immediately threatening to slavery, they often provided the potential for dramatic shifts in the geographically based political balance, and thus for debates about the future course of slavery. Slavery had been ended in several northern states by the start of the nineteenth century. More dramatically, it had been ended by a slave revolution in the French colony that was to become Haiti in 1804. Slavery had also ended in the first half of the nineteenth century in several of the South American countries where slavery had been of lesser importance, after their successful revolts against Spain. The first legislated American ending of slavery by a major nation with an extensive and productive slave economy came with British emancipation, to start in 1834. The British scheme entailed a payment to slaveowners in the West Indies (and other colonies), as well as a projected period of some four to six years of compelled labor under a system called apprenticeship. An antislavery movement had begun in the northern states of the United States in the first decades of the century, but it was only after the 1830s that it began to become a major force, with both white and black, free and ex-slave, speakers and advocates, and not until the 1850s that it become a major political force with the emergence of the Republican Party. It was this link of antislavery sentiment and political concern that ultimately was to play a role in the secession of the southern states and onset of the Civil War.

The antislavery ideology consisted of a number of strands, religious and secular. It was most prevalent among the Methodists and other dissenting groups, who placed a heavy value on the individual. It was influenced by the "free labor" ideology, advocating the benefits of free labor in contrast with the argued-for limited productivity of slave labor and the evils of the slave-based society for whites as well as blacks. The free labor ideology, with its call for "free labor, free land, free men," was most closely identified with the small artisan, independent farmer, segment of northern society, concerned with the continued availability of land for further expansion, and it was often nativist, anti-immigrant in belief.

The emergence of a significant antislavery movement in the North led to the more explicit statement of proslavery defense in the South in the 1830s. While many strands of the proslavery argument had been presented previously, it was this first major questioning of the nature of slavery that led to the drawing together of a full-scale defense. This defense was generally one of conservatism, befitting an institution that had existed for thousands of years, and thus was reflected in southern religion, politics, and social organization. The economic defense often drew upon comparisons of U.S. southern economic expansion with the reduction in export production in Haiti and in the British West Indies after emancipation. The proslavery advocates also provided a strong critique of the disarray and hardships of wage-earners in capitalist society. In addition, the southern proslavery argument contained a strong component of racism – stronger than earlier – arguing for the limited abilities and civilizing potential of the black population. These sets of views influenced whites at all wealth levels, and the southern interest in maintaining slavery was widely diffused throughout the population in the antebellum era. Indeed, the major political attack on slavery by a southern white, Hinton Helper, was based on the deleterious effects of slavery upon the non-slaveowning whites of the South, not its impact on blacks.

The closing of the international slave trade in 1808, after the ending of the twenty-year period allowed it by the Constitution, was not a very controversial action, since it did not bear on the continued existence of slavery, and may have aided some slaveowners in the Old South by raising slave prices as a result of restricting the number of new slaves imported from Africa. It was with the opening of the debate on the Missouri Territory in 1819 that slavery became a central political issue. The major focus was on the expansion of slavery and the limits set originally by the Northwest Ordinance. The compromise resolution of 1820 left the sections politically balanced, and while there were a number of actions relating to slavery in the next quarter-century that had Congressional implications, it was the Wilmot Proviso of 1846 that began the legislative process that led to the Civil War and the ending of slavery. The controversy was based on problems created by geographic expansion into new territories, and the effects of geographic expansion upon political representation. While both sections anticipated some economic benefits from expansion, these benefits did not become central to the discussion.

Compounding the geographic problems, requiring the Congressional action taken in the Compromise of 1850 and in the Kansas-Nebraska Act, were the economic and social aspects of the economic expansion of the 1850s and the great burst of immigration in that decade. Antislavery and anti-immigration forces came together, with the demand for "free land" for settlement by northerners, with the formation of the Republican Party. Abraham Lincoln's election in 1860 led to secession, disunion, and Civil War. There seemed no direct economic cause of this southern action – indeed the pre–Civil War decade was one of unusual southern prosperity. There seemed, to those at the time as well as later scholars, no economic need for southern expansion in the immediate future, and southern prosperity could be maintained without movement into areas basically unsuited for the production of staples. Nor, for the North, was there an explicit goal of freeing and benefiting the black. Many states in the North had laws discriminating against the black in matters such as voting, education, and other issues, and the various forms of discrimination and limits imposed on blacks in practice suggest that ending slavery was not intended to lead to black equality. Thus, while it seems that in the absence of slavery the Civil War might not have occurred, there was no economic need for the South to fight nor was the cause of the war northern humanitarianism and a concern for the black slave. Whatever prevented a political settlement in 1861, it was the outcome of complex political conditions and concerns, including the symbolic and political value of expansion and its impact on representation. As seen in the prices of land and slaves, as late as 1861 the southern planter did not believe the institution of slavery to be threatened, and its demise was seen only in a distant future – a view shared by most northerners at the time. Slave prices were near all-time highs, reflecting slaveowner optimism as to the future course of the cotton market and economy, and the expected continuation of the institution.

THE CIVIL WAR AND THE END OF SLAVERY

The outbreak of the Civil War forced a number of key decisions upon the southern economic decision-makers. Mobilization for a war that required many troops and much manufactured equipment drew heavily upon the white yeomanry and, until laws accepting the need for planter control of slaves and thus exemptions from military service based on slave owner-ship, the planter class. It is estimated that most southern whites of mili-tary ages served some time in the war, and that they died at high rates. The conflict between the need for military manpower and the control of slaves, which had led to exemptions for the slaveowning class, generated a split between planters and yeomen, a split that become quite sharp later in the war when southern defeats mounted and food and other resources became scarce. The South needed to choose the mix of agricultural output to pursue during the war. A shift away from cotton would both permit more foodstuffs to be produced and, by reducing the amount of cotton available to foreign countries, perhaps lead to their political support of the southern cause. This shift to foodstuffs production was also influenced by the blockade imposed by the North on southern exports, limiting access to export markets. There was a weakening of the controls over the slave population when prime-aged white males left for military duty, placing heavier reliance upon women and younger and older men for plantation control. Southern agricultural production fell during the war, due to mil-itary factors and also other causes, such as poor harvests, and not only did cotton output fall, but, over time, so did the production of foodstuffs. And, with the military actions of the North in the last years of the war, trans-portation and distribution were greatly affected, limiting the southern economy's adaptability.

During the war the problem of control of slaves became a critical issue. While in areas removed from military action the numbers of runaways — including men who enlisted in the Union Army black regiments — remained relatively small, in the Upper South and in those areas where the Union army undertook operations and gained control, the slave system was severely weakened and, after several years, effectively destroyed. Although initially those slaves captured by the Union army were regarded as legally still enslaved, the northern movement to regard them as free and no longer slaves succeeded. Many ex-slaves, over one hundred thousand, enrolled in and fought with the northern army against the South, while others were involved in northern-controlled agriculture within the wartime economy after their freedom was attained. There was a rather mixed pattern of ex-slave mobility after emancipation, some ex-slaves using the freedom to move elsewhere in the South, while others preferred remaining in those places where they had long resided. Whatever the adaptation, the Civil War period itself saw the de facto ending of the slave system, and freedom was brought directly to many of the slaves by the army's operations. During the war the South used slaves for various purposes in the military, although their possible use as soldiers was discussed only in the war's last stages, too late to be implemented.

The northern triumph meant the ending of slavery in the South. The Emancipation Proclamation declared the ending of slavery in those states at war with the North, but its enforcement required northern military success. With the ending of the war the passage of the thirteenth, fourteenth, and fifteenth amendments marked the ending of slavery in the United States and the provision of voting and other civil rights to the black population. During the later stages of the war, concern emerged about the implications of slave emancipation and the perceived need to control the black population and its labor input. Control was thought necessary to avoid the chaos expected to occur when the black population was free to choose their living and working conditions without the controls of slavery. There was fear throughout the nation that the southern economy would be destroyed and that, with the blacks unwilling to enter into productive activities, the white southerners would suffer even more severe hardships than those created by the physical destruction of wartime. Thus, some limits on the ex-slaves' ability to freely choose the types of work performed and on their ability to withdraw from the white-dominated economy were sought, by those in the Union army and by those northerners involved in southern control after peace was achieved. The southerners, to the extent politically able, clearly desired to restrict those black opportunities that permitted them to avoid wage work in agriculture, and they introduced so-called Black Codes to coerce blacks into wage labor by provisions relating to vagrancy, mobility, and loss of work time. While these codes were soon reversed, the basic spirit of this set of provisions remained to influence the postbellum adjustments. "Free labor" to many at this time mean non-slave wage labor working for whites, not freedom to choose the nature and amount of work by blacks.

To provide for change in the southern economy and for the adjustment of the ex-slaves into a "free" economy, Congress created the Freedmen's Bureau. Its purposes, as initially defined, were to regulate the contractual and other arrangements between planters and the freedmen, to ensure that appropriate contracts were made, and to see that both parties lived up to the terms of their agreement. These arrangements generally included contracts for one year of labor at specified wages, with subsidiary provisions relating to hours of work, types of crops to be grown, and payments for other chores. The Bureau was to enforce the work of ex-slaves and to prevent adult male ex-slaves from avoiding work, while enforcing the agreement to and payment of an acceptable wage by the hiring planters. The role of the Freedmen's Bureau has long been debated. It was attacked by the planters, as well as by the ex-slaves (and their advocates) who argued that the Bureau influenced the economic adjustments in a manner unfavorable to the ex-slave. It is possible that over its few years of existence, the Bureau's actions became more sympathetic to the planter class, but its role as a mediator between planter and ex-slave did influence the adjustment to emancipation in a manner that was, at times, advantageous to the ex-slaves.

While the southern and northern desire to control, for whatever professed reasons, the opportunities of freedmen was clear, less thought was given to what were the expected outcomes of emancipation. Planters wished to maintain plantations but were forced to accept the ending of slavery. They sought to control black labor with other institutional arrangements. The economic desires of ex-slaves, beyond freedom and independence, remained uncertain. While there was an unfulfilled desire for land by many, whether this was to produce mainly for subsistence or for markets to yield higher incomes, is difficult to determine. Wage labor was not desired by ex-slaves, however, as the controls permitted while under contract were considered to resemble too much those of the previous system, slavery. This would indicate that a movement to smaller farms was desired by the ex-slaves, freedom leading to the end of the plantation system, unless a system of greater compulsion to achieve white economic aims was introduced in the postbellum South than was seen to have been possible. The mobility of ex-slaves was not halted, even if attempts were made to do so; some decline in hours worked and labor force withdrawal, particularly of children, took place; but the wages necessary to get ex-slaves to work on wage-based plantations were not offered. All of these developments played a role in influencing the economic meaning of freedom to the ex-slaves. The decline of the plantation, and thus the loss of its scale economies, had an effect upon southern output not fully anticipated, while the impact of labor force reductions also meant output declines.

In some critical ways the impact of the ending of slavery in the South followed a pattern similar to that elsewhere in the Americas, indicating that the basic patterns of the economic adjustments to emancipation were not unique to the United States. The first large-scale emancipation, Haiti, generated, after a period of adjustment, politically and militarily as well as economically, a fall-off of sugar production for export to effectively zero, a very sharp reduction in coffee production (with a movement to much smaller farms), and a complete disappearance of the plantation sector, which was replaced by an economy of small-scale, owner-operated farms producing mainly foodstuffs for subsistence and for local sales. It was the decline in export production from what was once the most profitable slave plantation colony that became the frequently commented upon example of the economic effects of emancipation, and that influenced the debates upon the policies for emancipation in the South. The British West Indian emancipation after 1838 provided several scenarios of possible outcomes, based on resource endowments and political forces. On those islands of high population density the limited availability of land led to the maintenance of the plantations and the expansion of sugar output. In the areas where output was expanding rapidly in the last years of slavery, with low levels of population density, many ex-slaves left the plantation sector for small farms, and sugar exports fell sharply. It was only after several decades that plantation production grew rapidly, based primarily not on the labor of ex-slaves but on contract labor imported from Asia and Africa. In other areas of relatively low population density, the plantation sector contracted, sugar production fell, and exports declined for long periods, with a shift to small farms, often in areas outside the old plantation belt. Thus, throughout the Caribbean, except in areas of high population density, emancipation had meant a shift in production away from sugar, which at that time had required large-scale plantations for effective production, a decline in the plantation sector, and a withdrawal of ex-slave labor from production for export markets. The avoidance of the plantation was a general characteristic of emancipation, and in most areas the ex-slaves were able to acquire some, albeit limited, amounts of land via purchase. Whether the shift in crop-mix led to an overall increase or decline in agricultural output is unclear, but that component most easily measured and examined by observers, exports, did decline, leading to the belief that emancipation, whatever else it achieved, was not an economic success and that emancipation without controls could be disastrous to all both in the short run and the long run. It was these beliefs that came to influence the postbellum attitudes to emancipation in the United States.

THE POSTBELLUM SOUTH

The initial economic adjustments in the U.S. South to the end of slavery after the Civil War were in many ways similar to the economic changes that accompanied emancipation elsewhere. There were declines in the production of export staples, varying in extent of initial decline and time to recover antebellum levels of output with the degree of economies of scale in production under slavery; the overall measured output of southern agricultural, as well as total southern, output per capita fell; the plantation sector declined; and there were apparent reductions in overall black labor input. Cotton output declined sharply in the aftermath of the war and after emancipation, and the plantation system was replaced by a system combining small, black family farms, often sharecropped, and white family farms (some hiring labor, black and white). White farmers entered into cotton production to a greater extent than before the war. By the mid-1870s total cotton output levels reached antebellum magnitudes, and they then continued to expand rapidly, so that by the 1880s the United States had regained its dominant share in the world cotton markets, a dominance that continued into the first decades of the twentieth century. Tobacco, the slave-grown crop with the most limited economies of scale, initially declined little in output level, and total output then continued to expand, based on production from black and white farms, while the westward movement of tobacco production from Virginia to Kentucky continued. Those crops that had the largest scale effects and largest sizes before the war, however, experienced the longest declines in output and the slowest recoveries. Rice, indeed, never recovered antebellum levels in coastal South Carolina and Georgia, and when, decades later, the national level of rice output increased it was based on new locations, primarily in Louisiana. The initial decline in Louisiana sugar exceeded that in sugar production elsewhere in the Americas – a combination of war disruption and slave emancipation – but recovery over the next several decades restored earlier levels, with a combination of plantations based on black labor and small cane farms operated by whites selling to central mills. Overall, southern output in 1870 was estimated to be at about two-thirds that of 1860, and, despite a relatively rapid growth rate, it was not until about 1890 that the level of per capita income returned to antebellum levels. By this time southern per capita incomes had fallen from three-quarters to one-half of the national level.

Where there were some differences from emancipation elsewhere was in the nature of the labor force that led to the post-emancipation growth. Areas in the British West Indies drew upon contract labor from China, India, and elsewhere to obtain a plantation labor force, leaving ex-slaves outside the export sector, while, after 1888, Brazil drew upon subsidized immigrants from Italy and southern Europe to provide labor in coffee farming. The South, however, did not depend upon immigrants for its labor. There were some early attempts to recruit labor – from the North, from among the Chinese, from Italy, and from elsewhere in Europe – but these attempts were rather limited in magnitude and effect. In the South, the labor producing for export markets came from the resident whites who, in large numbers, increased their shares of cotton output when the slave-based plantation was legally ended and the plantation as producing unit could not be reintroduced. There was some southward and westward movement of both black and white populations, but these were not initially large, and movement northward did not accelerate until the twentieth century. These population movements do indicate, however, the extent to which black labor could be mobile even under the coercive restraints attempted at the time.

While the plantation as a producing unit became less important in the postbellum era, this did not imply a decline in the concentration of southern landholding. The pattern of landholding changed relatively little after the war, concentrated postbellum landholdings being consistent with operations by small, family-sized units renting or sharecropping from large landowners. In the continued concentration of economic power the South resembled ex-slave societies elsewhere, although it remains uncertain how much of the land remained concentrated among families that had had similar wealth in antebellum years and how much represented newly emerging wealthholders. In either event, however, the shift to smaller producing units meant that production became less efficient for most staples, and thus levels of production per worker fell. There was some decline in labor force participation on all farms, explaining some, but not the most dramatic aspects of, the decline in production of southern agricultural staples. These changes, moreover, had significant implications for southern black health, mortality, and credit arrangements in the postbellum decades.

The debate continues, in the United States and elsewhere, as to the timing and causes of the decline of the plantation sector. This debate relates to discussions concerning the freedmen's initial response to emancipation and

how this influenced decisions as to residence. Obviously many different patterns occurred, but two were most frequently discussed by contemporaries.
One is that freedom led to a desire to escape from the place of enslavement,
and we thus have descriptions of considerable movement of ex-slaves within
the South. Second is the desire of those ex-slaves, who had had limited voluntary mobility under slavery, to remain within the geographic and social
circumstances with which they were most familiar. If this were the initial
reaction, however, it need not preclude mobility to avoid a plantation-like
situation as the nature of the postbellum economy fully emerged. The
planters, it appears, initially had a desire to reimpose, in the production
of staples, the plantation sector on the basis of some modified form of
coercion-based wage labor. Despite these attempts, even though planters
were supported by various legal and extralegal (and illegal) measures, the
ex-slaves resisted the plantation, preferring smaller producing units. The
systems of sharecropping, share-wages, hired wage labor, and small owner-
operated farms that emerged in the next quarter-century reflected the compromises in southern society. The planters did not fight to maintain slavery
after the war, but they had attempted to maintain the plantations as the
basis of the new labor order.

There are also debates about the nature of the adjustment of white
owner-operated farms in the postbellum era. This group, which tended to
produce relatively less cotton than was produced on plantations in the
antebellum years, expanded their cotton output in the postbellum era.
Soon more cotton was produced on white-operated farms than on black.
White production of cotton had varied in the antebellum era, rising
sharply in the boom of the 1850s. The question is whether white attitudes
toward producing cotton for the market changed as a result of Civil War
circumstances, or if earlier attitudes remained but yeoman behavior differed in the postbellum period due to the changing circumstances in the
cotton sector with the decline of the plantation.

Based on aggregate measures, the rate of growth of output in the South
from about 1870 to 1890 was at a rate approximately equal to that in
the northern states, then experiencing substantial large-scale industrialization. While the South was left poor as a result of the Civil War and
the subsequent adjustments, the ensuing postbellum decades were not
ones of southern stagnation and an absence of economic adjustment.
Rather, the South's relative economic position changed little, although, of
course, the absolute differences in per capita income between the sections
increased.

In tracing the conditions of the postbellum South from the Civil War to the start of the twentieth century, it is useful to distinguish several sub-periods. The war and its immediate adjustments led to a sharp once-for-all decline in output, due to a combination of wartime dislocation and the ending of slavery, with its effect on the work location and worktime of the ex-slaves. There were, however, significant differences within the subregions of the South in the nature of the postbellum adjustments and patterns of growth, reflecting differences in the proportion of the black population and the nature of the major crops produced in the antebellum era. The declines in income were most severe and prolonged in those states of the Deep South that had produced the major antebellum staples – rice, sugar, cotton – and shorter and less severe in the Upper South, as well as in the Southwest, in which population expansion was occurring. After some adjustment, there was a period of sustained growth, reflecting a boom in cotton demand and a movement into more productive areas such as Texas. This growth occurred with only limited movement of southern labor out of the agricultural sector. The decade from 1890 to 1900, however, saw major problems in the cotton market and in the growth of southern income, and led to major political and social changes within the South.

There were some unexpected changes in the southern crop-mix after the war. While sugar and rice tended to become less important with the ending of the plantation system (sugar regaining antebellum output levels only with the aid of higher tariffs and, later, with a new technology), and tobacco remained of roughly similar importance, the share of cotton in overall southern agricultural output rose in the postbellum period relative to what it had been before the war. With this increase in the share of cotton, there occurred a decrease in the share of corn and other foodstuffs in output, leading to a decline in southern self-sufficiency. This shift, with white farmers increasing cotton production while many black farmers still worked on cotton farms, reflected the changed credit system and transportation networks within the postbellum South. Since midwest foodstuffs were more readily available, the shift within the South, to increase cotton production relative to that of corn, was to be expected.

A significant change within the postbellum South was in the organizational structure of black farms. By 1890 nearly one-quarter of black farmers owned the land they operated on, although their farms tended to be smaller and less valuable than the farms of the nearly two-thirds of white owner-operators. Many blacks were still farm laborers. Most dramatic, however, had been the rise of sharecropping by blacks on white-owned land. This represented a compromise between the planter's desire to maintain a wage-based plantation and the ex-slaves' desire to have their own smaller family farms (whether for subsistence or to earn incomes by producing for the market). The choice between share-arrangement and renting was influenced by the availability of currency and credit within the South. The customary discussions of sharecropping suggest that it was a form of rental contract with tenant-operator decision-making. What is called share-cropping, however, was, based upon the legal arrangements, generally a form of a share-wages (a system of wages based on value of output, not set nominally by prior agreement) with control by the landowner. The legal distinctions are important both for determining the claims to revenues received and for understanding the priority of liens in dealings with merchants and other sources of credit. There were some differences in productivity based upon location, crop-mix, and in part, race, although, within race, neither crop-mix nor productivity varied by form of organization. In general, white farmers worked on larger holdings, with more capital in livestock and equipment, and tended to earn higher incomes than did blacks. With the weakening of the cotton market in the 1890s, both blacks and whites suffered. The whites who owned land were seriously affected, as were those blacks who owned land or were working as tenants or on shares. Land ownership did not preclude economic hardship for southerners, and the 1890s became a period of serious political unrest, with the emergence of pronounced racism and racial legislation.

Within the southern economy, there was some expansion of industrialization and urbanization, as well as shifts in the geographic location of population and of economic activity, but these changes were not as dramatic as the movements occurring elsewhere in the nation. The chief changes in industrial development were in the expansion of the lumber industry in the Old South, the initial stages of the movement of cotton textiles to North and South Carolina, and the growth of an iron and steel complex in central Alabama. Some of these plants were northern-owned, and there was a continuation of the debate from antebellum times as to whether the South was to be regarded as a colonial economy. The banking and financial sector became more restrictive compared with the antebellum period, in part because of the postbellum structural adjustments in the economy, but also because of the limits imposed on bank development by the National Bank Act, which had been passed by the northern Congress in the Civil War. Credit was scarce within the South in the postbellum period, and the changing characteristics of borrowers helps to explain the high cost of credit charged by southern rural storekeepers and merchants. If the southern economy was not colonial in the sense of northern-owned or dominated, the still heavy reliance on the agricultural sector provided an appearance consistent with what contemporaries could regard as a colonial economy.

There were significant demographic changes within the South in the postbellum era, and these were particularly marked for blacks. The white fertility rate generally fell throughout the period, continuing its antebellum decline, although it remained somewhat above that elsewhere in the nation. White mortality fell also, but still remained above that of whites elsewhere in the nation. For whites, and for blacks, while there was some migration to the southwest, and northward migration had not yet started on a large scale, the cyclical demands for labor in the North being met by the migration of white Europeans rather than southerners. For blacks, mortality and fertility trends were somewhat more dramatic than they were for whites. Black fertility rates remained high, perhaps increasing slightly between 1860 and 1880, and remained above those of southern whites. After 1880 black fertility declined, roughly in parallel with that of whites, albeit perhaps influenced by different factors – disease, particularly venereal disease and tuberculosis, for blacks, choice for whites. Black fertility remained above that of whites, and fertility rates for both blacks and whites were quite different in rural compared with urban areas. It appears that, at this time, rates of illegitimate birth and childraising in one-parent households were less frequent for southern blacks than they would be for blacks in the next century, although probably greater within the southern black than the southern white community. The black mortality pattern differed from that of whites. The available estimates suggest that black mortality rates were greater in 1880 than in 1860, and it may not have been until the twentieth century that its 1860 level was regained. This was at a time when white mortality was decreasing, so that the difference between black and white mortality became greater after the Civil War than it had been before. The difficulties in receiving medical and health care in the South, the lower black incomes, and the problems in obtaining adequate food and nutrition meant higher mortality and poorer health for black southerners than for white southerners, while both suffered relative to the populations of the North.

There was black migration within the South, where about 90 percent of all U.S. blacks lived until the twentieth century. This migration was in the same directions, but of lesser amounts, than had been the involuntary movements in the antebellum period. There is some indication of an intra-South mobility of blacks, based on information in the 1910 census on the tenure of farmers. These data indicate that less than half of all black farmers had lived on their current place of residence for over five years, with one-quarter having been there for one year or less. Where blacks moved to when they moved off the farm, and how far they went, remains unknown, but this extent of mobility, even within the agricultural sector, may be suggestive of the economic alternatives open to blacks (although mobility did reduce the opportunities to benefit from increased experience in one location). Migration northward did occur, particularly during the downturn of the business cycle, when European immigration to the North was relatively small and did not "crowd out" black migration. The northward movement of blacks, however, was relatively limited until the World War I period, due primarily to the major role played by European migration in meeting the great demands for labor in the North in the late nineteenth and early twentieth centuries.

The social and cultural adjustments to emancipation by blacks and whites within the South, and by blacks and whites at the national level, have become among the most studied set of issues in American history. To the black ex-slaves emancipation meant freedom from ownership by another individual and, also, freedom from certain varieties of restrictive legislation initially imposed by southern state governments. With emancipation came freedom to move and migrate in search of better living and working conditions, and the right to receive more of the revenues earned from production. There was the ability to choose between work and leisure and to select (and implicitly to pay for) more desirable working conditions. Moreover, unlike ex-slaves elsewhere, ex-slaves in the United Sates had a right to vote and participate politically, and this right was not to be restricted for several decades. There did exist legal constraints on blacks throughout the South, but clearly plantation slavery was not re-introduced, and the patterns of migration and of black voting and political representation in the first decades after the Civil War indicate that there were dramatic, albeit ultimately limited, changes within the South.

After emancipation and with the initial northern concerns with the black population, came a large expansion in the schooling of blacks, with a combination of federal and state funding, as well as some self-financing and teaching by the black community itself. Rates of literacy for black children rose dramatically, although they did not approach those for southern whites. School expenditures per pupil for blacks were only about one-third those for whites, and by 1890 considerable ground had been gained, with the southern black literacy rate rising from approximately 10 percent at the end of the slave period to, for black teenagers, over 50 percent. Literacy and attendance rates for blacks continued to rise after 1890. There were quite dramatic changes in that decade in the relative expenditures on black and on white students. Black per pupil expenditures dropped to about one-tenth to one-fifth those of whites by the early twentieth century. Schools remained segregated.

The decade of the 1890s saw other dramatic changes in white relations with blacks in the South, reflecting some of the changes in race relations that had emerged in earlier years. In addition to the dramatic reduction in expenditures upon black students compared to whites, it was in the 1890s that most southern states changed voting laws to limit black political participation. There was expanded violence, with an increase in the number of black lynchings, and more legislated controls upon black behavior. At the national level, the Supreme Court accepted the doctrine of "separate, but equal" in transport facilities, and this was extended to include many other aspects of black-white interactions, including education.

By the first decade of the twentieth century the southern scene in regard to white racial control and the importance given to race in society seemed quite different from what it had been earlier in the postbellum period. While some changes meant the legalization of de facto patterns of behavior, there was an expansion of control by whites and a weakening of the rights of blacks in political, economic, and social life. Influencing these developments was the greater attention paid to racial factors within both the South and the North, and the diffusion of racism throughout the white population, with an intensity at least as great, if not greater, than previously. It is obviously not possible to describe the South before the 1890s as not concerned with the race issue, but some distinction should be made between the earlier period of greater black voting and political participation and what was to come over the next several decades as new forms of racial control emerged.

In explaining the increase and nature of the development of this virulent racism several questions remain in respect to timing. First, did the timing reflect the economic reaction to the cotton crisis of the 1890s, which had a marked impact upon southern agriculturalists and led to some political demands that seemed to threaten the ruling elites? Some see this political uprising as raising the possibility of an interracial coalition of poor whites and poor blacks to seek political and economic change, posing a threat to the established political powers. This argument points to the importance of the elite response to the threat of interracial politics, with the heightened attention to racial factors used as a means of destroying any possible coalition. This line of argument implies racism was introduced by the elite, who convinced the lower-class whites to accept the attack on blacks and to refrain from dealings with them. Others, however, argue the economic difficulties of poor whites led them to see blacks as competitors, particularly in cotton production, and to adopt the belief that it was in their economic interests to limit black rivalry. For whatever cause, however, the southern lower (and upper) class whites were receptive to legal and other changes that severely restricted the power of blacks.

The bases for these interpretations of changing race relations rest on different views concerning the beliefs of whites, and the overall prospects for any successful black-white coalitions after the Civil War. There are indications that, at least right after the Civil War, some blacks were able to acquire more wealth than they had in antebellum years, to serve in state and local political offices, and to benefit from greater expenditures by municipalities for desired services (even if this meant separate services). In early postbellum South Carolina, for example, free blacks were important members of the state legislature, although fissures developed between those who had been free persons of color in the antebellum period and those who had been black slaves. Reversals on all these fronts of black opportunity began relatively quickly, with the early postbellum successes of blacks in the South triggering the strong white reaction to reverse, or at least to prevent any further, gains made by blacks.

Supporting the changes in the southern states in this period were the attitudes of the North and the northern role in the redemption of the South after 1877. Congressional legislation and Supreme Court decisions eroded black rights, in part by returning more of the decision-making power to white-dominated southern political elites. By the end of the century virulent racism had also emerged in the North. Whether a different politics in the North would have meant a different response in the South is a moot question. In both sections, the status of the black was reduced, with black political rights more limited than in the preceding period, and with blacks subject to extensive controls by violence and by law. The North had either forgotten about the blacks or had joined in their control – but the impact of all this remained confined primarily to the southern states, where most blacks still resided.

The first decades of the twentieth century saw some continuities in the pattern of black economic conditions but also the beginnings of some changes that were to have rather dramatic effects later in the twentieth century. Most blacks remained within the southern states in 1900, most were still in agriculture, and many were still involved in cotton production on small, sharecropped, farms. As earlier, there were some shifts in location – to the Southwest and to urban areas – and the limited movement into industry and services continued. Except for the importance of domestic services among the black female population, many of these general labor force patterns were seen in the white population as well. The relative incomes of the southern states varied cyclically, but were generally about one-half of the national average. While southern poverty, compared to the North, remained, the overall growth rate for southern per capita income was still at about the national average. The South was, however, the poorest region of the country, and within the South it was the blacks who were poorest.

Starting with World War I, however, there were many large shocks to the old southern system, with a large shift in the location (and problems) of the black population. The major breakthrough began with the spread of the boll weevil in the cotton South, causing heavy economic losses for both blacks and whites within the southern cotton economy. Soon the cessation of large-scale European immigration into the United States, as a result of World War I and the ensuing immigration restrictions, provided the opportunities for southern blacks and whites to migrate northward. Blacks, in particular, migrated to work as unskilled labor in defense plants and in other manufacturing establishments. Unlike in the South, those blacks who went North went primarily into urban areas, particularly into the large cities of the Northeast and Midwest. This movement to the urban North accelerated in the 1920s, weakened in the 1930s, and then continued apace as a result of the New Deal agricultural policy (that some refer to as the second enclosure movement) and the needs of defense plants in World War II. By the 1980s almost one-half of the nation's blacks resided in the North, most in urban areas, and these cities had become the locale of major problems. Even those blacks who remained in the South tended to have become more urban and industrial than in the past. Overall, by

1980, fewer than 10 percent of the black labor force was in agriculture. Thus when the Civil Rights movement put pressure on government policies, and began to achieve major successes in the 1950s and 1960s, it was on the basis of a black population whose location and occupational status, as well as legal position, had changed dramatically from its conditions one century earlier.

9

TECHNOLOGY AND
INDUSTRIALIZATION, 1790–1914

STANLEY L. ENGERMAN AND KENNETH L. SOKOLOFF

During the long nineteenth century, the United States progressed from being a colonial economy relative to Britain to become the leading industrial nation in the world. This transformation in status came largely from a rapid expansion of the economy, which was both unexpected and unprecedented, beginning with the Northeast and then spreading to the other areas of the country. In 1789 the future of the young and still modestly populated republic of the United States, a successor to a failed confederation of former English colonies on the North American mainland, was uncertain. Victory in the Revolutionary War had garnered attention for the new country, and it enjoyed a reputation as a good place for a poor man to settle, but few observers thought the United States likely to become a major power – economic or otherwise. By 1914, of course, the situation had changed dramatically. The economy had grown to become the largest in the world, supported by a rich resource base, rates of investment and population growth that were exceptional for their time, and substantial productivity advance. Not only was the United States recognized throughout the world as the technological leader, but its institutions were widely admired and not infrequently imitated.

The study of American economic growth in the nineteenth century has been influenced by controversies concerning the sources and potential for manufacturing development during early industrialization. One group of scholars has long been skeptical about the attainment of progress before 1840. They typically hold that advances in manufacturing were crucial for the onset of sustained growth, but that only very limited increases in productivity in that sector were feasible prior to major capital deepening and the introduction of new technologies such as the steam engine and machinery driven by inanimate sources of power. Since the diffusion of such radically capital-intensive techniques didn't become widespread until the 1840s and 1850s, adherents of this position regard the possibility of substantial productivity growth before then as quite unlikely.

Another intellectual tradition views preindustrial economies as generally characterized by high transport costs, low incomes, and limited commercial development. Accordingly, decreases in transportation costs, as well as other sources of improved opportunities to trade, have the potential in such economies to generate substantial productivity and income growth through the return to greater specialization by factors of production, even without dramatic alterations in technology. In this conception, early economic growth in the United States was associated with rather balanced productivity growth, in which the expansion of markets spurred advances that were realized and diffused gradually across a broad range of industries. Moreover, with major changes in the transportation network and in institutions involved in commerce during the first few decades of the nineteenth century, this perspective suggests that there might well have been substantial productivity and income growth before 1840, especially in the Northeast, where these developments were most evident.

This framework for thinking about the sources and processes of early growth traces back to Adam Smith. Adherents to this perspective hold that major gains in productivity and income can be realized even without substantial changes in technology or in the stock of physical capital. The central idea is that change in the environment can yield important advances through inducing alterations in behavior by many agents, whose responses, though each individually have a small effect, have a large cumulative impact. Although the logic of his view encompasses many types of adjustments to new economic incentives or opportunities, Smith especially extolled the returns to the division of labor that arise from an expansion of the market. The expansion of markets leads to greater specialization by factors of production, firms, and geographic regions in producing those products in which they have a comparative advantage. The resulting changes in economic organization raise productivity through intensification or fuller utilization of resources, a better allocation or matching of factors to those activities in which they are relatively productive (encompassing the division of labor within firms as well as a social division of labor), and economies of scale. Smith's analysis seems particularly relevant for early industrial economies such as the United States in the colonial and early national periods, because they typically experience extraordinary growth in markets as transportation costs fall, institutional supports for trade develop, and income and expenditures rise. With these types of changes in the economic environment reverberating throughout the economy, the implication is that productivity growth will be induced across a broad spectrum of activities and industries.

1790 TO 1860

Recent work on the development of U.S. manufacturing before the Civil War has led to significant changes in the interpretation of the growth process. While generally characterized by small-scale industry, due in part to the limits on the markets caused by the high costs of overland transport and to the constraints imposed by seasonality in production due to the complications of water power and the timing of the needs for labor in a primarily agricultural economy, the economy was capable of relatively rapid growth in productivity. Even with initially limited capital and technological developments, important changes in firm organization, the intensity of labor input, and a lowered cost of transportation permitted productivity change across a broad scale of industries. Manufacturing growth was widely diffused, suggesting a pattern more of balanced than of unbalanced growth. This pattern is indicated by the estimates of labor productivity (output per laborer) and total factor productivity (output per weighted unit of labor and capital input), presented in Table 9.1. The overall productivity growth rates were similar for mechanized and non-mechanized industries, and for labor-intensive and capital-intensive industries in the American Northeast. The similarities were greater between 1820 and 1850 than between 1850 and 1860. In the latter decade there was an acceleration of productivity growth, consistent with the increased rate of patenting at that time (see Appendix).

The Colonial Era

The colonial period was one of relatively rapid economic growth in what was to become the United States. As with most economies at this time, the labor force remained predominantly in agriculture. There was some increase in manufacturing activities, but growth was for the most part based on developments in the agricultural sector. Manufacturing often

Table 9.1. *Per annum growth rates of labor and total factor productivity, by classes of manufacturing firms, 1820–1860, northeastern states*

	1820–1850	1850–1860	1820–1860
Mechanized industries			
Labor productivity			
Rural	1.2%	3.5%	1.8%
Urban	2.8	2.0	2.6
All	2.1	2.4	2.2
Total factor productivity			
Rural	1.2	4.2	1.9
Urban	2.2	2.2	2.2
All	1.8	2.7	2.1
Less- or non-mechanized industries			
Labor productivity			
Rural	1.8%	4.3%	2.4%
Urban	0.5	3.7	1.3
All	1.5	3.9	2.1
Total factor productivity			
Rural	1.8	2.0	1.9
Urban	0.8	2.0	1.1
All	1.5	1.9	1.6
Capital-intensive industries			
Labor productivity			
Rural	1.4%	2.8%	1.8
Urban	2.3	1.8	2.2
All	1.9	2.3	2.0
Total factor productivity			
Rural	1.2	3.3	1.8
Urban	1.8	1.9	1.8
All	1.6	2.5	1.8
Labor-intensive industries			
Labor productivity			
Rural	1.6%	5.6%	2.6%
Urban	0.7	4.4	1.7
All	1.7	4.5	2.4
Total factor productivity			
Rural	1.9	2.8	2.1
Urban	1.0	2.5	1.4
All	1.8	2.1	1.9

Source: Kenneth L. Sokoloff, "Invention, Innovation, and Manufacturing Productivity Growth in the Antebellum Northeast," in Robert E. Gallman and John Joseph Wallis (eds.), *American Economic Growth and Standards of Living before the Civil War* (Chicago, 1992), 360–61. See the source for more details on definitions and concepts.

involved the processing of raw materials in producing foodstuffs and textiles within farm households, dovetailing with the seasonal pattern of agricultural production. There were some exceptions to this agriculturally
based industry, such as the small blast furnaces and forges producing iron
in Pennsylvania, and the various artisan-type activities in urban areas. In
general, most of the urban manufacturing took place in the Northeastern
states, the South's manufacturing production being primarily on farms and
plantations.

Although the limited size of the manufacturing sector prior to the Revolutionary War was not unique, two different explanations have been provided. First, the British Navigation Acts were introduced in the interests
of encouraging British manufacturing and restricting that of its colonies.
Limitations were placed on the production and/or export of various manufactured commodities, such as iron, hats, and woolens, although the
British encouraged colonial production of some goods that were not made
in Britain, such as naval stores. Second, it has been argued both by contemporaries and by subsequent scholars that these Acts were not necessary. The land and resource abundance and the scarcity of labor would have
meant concentration on agricultural production no matter what the legislation. This latter point is buttressed by the approximately half-century
after independence it took before the United States manufacturing labor
force began its sharp rise.

With independence, and after much debate, the United States government followed various of the economic policies of the British. Mercan-
tilistic provisions to encourage manufacturing expansion and economic
growth were introduced. Secretary of the Treasury Alexander Hamilton
issued a formal *Report on Manufactures*, pointing to the great benefits to be
gained from their growth and development. Among the policies proposed
were tariffs on specific imports to increase their relative prices to favor
domestic producers; open immigration to allow for increases in the labor
force; the greater use of underemployed women and children in the labor
force: and the introduction of a patent system to encourage invention and
innovation. In addition to these direct encouragements of industry, the
concerns of manufacturers were often considered when dealing with other
of governmental policies, such as those affecting human capital (education,
immigration), land policy, controls over money and banking, laws regulating property rights, and government encouragement of invention and
technological development. Such policies influenced economic growth in
general, with significant impacts on the relative development of the manufacturing sector.

The development of manufacturing down to the start of the War of 1812 was, however, rather limited. The United States still depended upon imports from Britain for much of its manufactured goods, as had been predicted by Lord Sheffield after the Revolutionary War. The growth of some manufacturing industries, mainly in the Northeast, reflected major political events, which led to significant interruptions in foreign trade, such as the Embargo and the War of 1812, rather than the specifics of tariff rate protection.[1] Despite the U.S. onset of growth, at the start of the nineteenth century Britain was clearly the world's leading manufacturing nation (as it would be until almost the end of the nineteenth century).

The Years from the War of 1812 to the Civil War

Increases in income from the reexport trade and gains in agricultural productivity stimulated expenditures on manufactures through the 1790s and the early 1800s. A significant growth of domestic production did not take place until just prior to the War of 1812, however. Domestic manufacturers had found it difficult to compete with British goods, but the interruption of foreign trade via the Embargo enhanced opportunities. Due to the small scale of manufacturing enterprise and the relatively limited capital needs, particularly for fixed capital, entry was relatively free, and firms could be quickly established. Production was initially concentrated in the Northeast. The lure of material benefit was reinforced by patriotic appeals and public sentiment in favor of national autonomy in manufacturing. Also important were the extensive investments in transportation infrastructure, most frequently undertaken privately but encouraged by governments at all levels. As an increasing number of workers became specialized in nonagricultural products, and as household incomes rose, the markets for farm produce in the Northeast expanded as well. The volume of intraregional trade grew rapidly, and areas that had previously been isolated economically were gradually drawn into a broad northeastern, if not national, market.

This growth in manufacturing production began from a modest base. At the beginning of the nineteenth century, most urban areas still relied on foreign sources for many high-value manufactured items. Rural resi-

---

[1] Some place responsibility for these changes on the Embargos of the first decade of the nineteenth century, since closing foreign trade meant that, in effect, there was an infinite tariff. On the Embargo period, see Donald R. Adams, "American Neutrality and Prosperity, 1793–1808: A Reconsideration," *Journal of Economic History* 40 (1980), 713–738.

dents produced many manufactured goods at home and also obtained them from traveling artisans, traders, or peddlers who toured the countryside. Because both the 1810 and 1820 censuses of manufactures are complicated by irregular enumeration, it is difficult to precisely identify how the number and organization of northeastern manufacturing establishments evolved over the first two decades of the nineteenth century. What is clear, however, is that manufacturing output expanded during the Embargo and war years, and this was reflected in the decreased household production as well as the increased factory production. Though many of the new enterprises did not survive the severe economic contraction that followed the peace after the War of 1812, the buildings and equipment often helped to support the resumption of the industrial expansion during the 1820s. Similarly, while some agricultural workers left to enter agricultural production in the west, many stayed behind to become the basis of the eastern manufacturing labor force.

An important breakthrough in United States manufacturing came with the development of the first cotton textile mills in Lowell, during the War of 1812, and their subsequent expansion based primarily upon the use of female labor from rural New England. Massachusetts cotton textiles represented the first modern industry in the United States, based upon large factories, a labor force consisting primarily of women, and sophisticated transmission of water power.

Two systems of organization were used in the new cotton textile industry, the dominant Lowell system employing female labor, and the smaller segment of the industry based on the so-called Rhode Island system, which relied on family labor. In addition, a cotton textile industry developed in Philadelphia, based on relatively small, but flexible, firms. Cotton textile output growth was rapid and relatively continuous after the start of the factory system. The contribution of tariffs to this expansion remains a source of debate. What is clear, however, is the tremendous importance of growing consumer demand and the responsibility of factory production for the ultimate disappearance of home manufactures and the "putting-out" system. With expansion of output came, as predicted by Adam Smith, vertical disintegration of textile firms, first separating the production of textile machinery from the production of textiles, and then the process of sales and distribution from work within the factory. Expansion of the industry was also aided by the declining costs of key raw materials, particularly cotton, and the development of an effective system of financing industry within New England.

While the early-nineteenth-century development of industry in New England was based upon an atypical organization (in terms of size and employment levels and the use of the female labor) in the cotton textile sector, there was also considerable expansion of a more diverse set of industries relying for the most part on relatively traditional production technologies. Some of these, such a boots and shoes, were also concentrated in New England, but many others, including grist-milling and various metal-working and woodworking industries, were better represented in the Middle Atlantic states. They together with the presence of coal and iron, were to lead to more extensive manufacturing development in the Middle Atlantic region later in the nineteenth century.

There was a widespread shift in manufacturing power in the late antebellum period, when the geographic expansion of the economy took it into the coal fields of western Pennsylvania. Steam power came increasingly to displace water power or even hand power in many industries, and in most regions. New England remained more dependent on waterpower than did other sections, with water accounting for more than half of the region's power as late as the 1870s. The use of steam permitted the movement of industry into the Midwest, where sources of waterpower were limited. These developments were a major factor in leading to the increased production of coal in Pennsylvania and the Midwest. Given the greater ability to transport coal than waterpower, there was now a somewhat greater flexibility in location than previously, leading to more urban locations. This, however, also meant the generation of a greater degree of urban disamenities.

Changes in the sources of industrial power also had a significant impact on the production potential of industrial firms. Factories using water for power often had seasonal difficulties, with drought in summer and ice in winter. The shift to sources that permitted all-year production served to raise output, as the work-year could now be longer. The reduced impact of seasonality also meant that there was no longer a need for dovetailing production, by industry or by region, to keep labor fully occupied.

Also dramatic was a shift from rural to more urbanized locations for industries. In rural areas, firms in labor-intensive industries were quite small, generally with fewer than five adult males and perhaps an apprentice. It was typical in such "artisanal shops" for all workers to be skilled and involved in carrying out all steps in the production process. Firms in or near urban counties were generally larger and orgaized differently. Although operating with essentially the same capital-to-labor ratios as those of the small shops, these manufactories, or so-called non-mechanized factories, which included large numbers of workers under supervision working with a limited amount of machinery, were distinguished by work forces disproportionately composed of women and children, an extensive division of labor, a more intense pace of work, and greater standardization of output. Production was sometimes quite seasonal, due either to climate or the need to dovetail with the needs for agricultural labor at harvest time, a pattern that was to change over the century with the declining seasonality of production.

Recent examinations of manufacturing-firm data have found evidence that these manufactories were significantly more productive than were artisanal shops. There are significant differences in total factor productivity between the two modes of organization, with economies of scale being exhausted in labor-intensive industries at a size of about twenty employees. Average firm size in these industries increased steadily over the antebellum period, and growth was related to proximity to markets. As their shares in output fell over time, the artisanal shops that survived the competition were increasingly located in small towns, insulated by high transportation costs, or were focused on satisfying narrow market niches such as the demand for custom-made goods.

Nevertheless, based on the information contained in the manuscripts of the 1820 census, and in the 1832 Treasury Department survey known as the McLane Report, it is apparent that the great majority of establishments continued to operate at a small scale and to rely on traditional production processes and limited amounts of fixed capital. Textile mills were, of course, the prominent exception to this pattern and were the cutting-edge of the new era. Both cotton and wool manufacture were being transformed by major leaps in the design of machinery and other equipment, and production took place in large establishments. Most industries, however, remained dependent on hand tools or simple water-powered devices, with which manufacturers had long been acquainted. Inventories absorbed nearly all of the capital invested in these enterprises. In general, capital needs were low, the need being for short-term capital. As indicated in Table 9.2, industries using agricultural raw materials were still among the largest industries in 1860. Boots and shoes, for example, had the largest number of employees.

Detailed studies of the evolution of technology in industries such as boots and shoes, clocks, coaches and harnesses, furniture, glass, iron and steel, meat packing, paper tanning, and cotton and wool textiles suggest

Table 9.2. *Ten largest industries, by value added, 1860 and 1910*

	1860			1910	
	Value Added ($ million)	Employment (000)		Value Added ($ million)	Employment (000)
Cotton goods	$55	115	Machinery	$690	530
Lumber	54	76	Lumber	650	700
Boots and shoes	49	123	Printing and Publishing	540	260
Flour and meal	40	28	Iron and steel	330	240
Men's clothing	37	115	Malt liquors	280	55
Iron	36	50	Men's clothing	270	240
Machinery	33	41	Cotton goods	260	380
Woolen goods	25	61	Tobacco	240	170
Carriages and wagons	24	37	Railroad cars	210	280
Leather	23	23	Boots and shoes	180	200
All manufacturing	815	1,474	All manufacturing	8,529	6,615

Source: Peter Temin, "Manufacturing," in Lance E. Davis, Richard A. Easterlin, William N. Parker, et al., *American Economic Growth: An Economist's History of the United States* (New York, 1972), 433, 447. See also Jeremy Atack and Peter Passell, *A New Economic View of American History from Colonial Times to 1940*, 2nd ed. (New York, 1994), 461, 467, for rankings based on value-added in 1914 prices. There are a few differences from Temin's rankings but nothing substantial.

several steps in antebellum productivity growth. First was the rise of manufactories. Increases in technical efficiency stemmed from a series of improvements or refinements in the organization of production and from relatively subtle modifications in traditional capital equipment and in the nature of products. The data from the manufacturing censuses indicate a modest increase in the capital intensity of most industries until the 1850s. There was a gradual development of a more extensive division of labor, with also intensification of labor input and the substitution of less-skilled workers for more-skilled. There were also improvements in traditional tools and instruments, such as drills, lathes, and planes, as well as alterations in existing products and the development of new products aimed at differentiation or at facilitating standardized production under the new organization of labor. As important as some of these changes proved to be, few industries outside of textiles seemed to have undergone a fundamental breakthrough in technical knowledge.

A second phase of technical change was marked by an increasing reliance on machinery driven by inanimate sources of power, as well as the development of new machines. There were also modifications in organization to permit the exploitation of the full potential of the new, more sophisticated, capital stock. Precisely where one draws the line in classifying a particular invention is not always clear, but those scholars who attribute a revolutionary character to mechanization perceive a qualitative difference between the introduction of a new type of equipment and an alteration of a familiar tool. The textile industries are clearly the first to have entered into this new stage of technical change with an increased size of firms, but other industries had followed by 1860. In particular, with the discovery of first anthracite and then bituminous coal, firms in the iron industry grew in size, utilized larger furnaces, and employed steam power on a greater scale than did the charcoal using furnaces.

Estimates of the growth of labor and total factor productivity between 1820 and 1860 have been computed from the manufacturing census manuscripts by class of industry for rural and urban counties in the Northeast. Perhaps the most important point in Table 9.1 is the rapid rates of productivity growth in most industries. Total factor productivity and labor productivity grew between 1820 and 1860 at a rate in excess of that between 1869 and 1909.[2] Comparisons of the rates of labor productivity growth with that of total factor productivity growth raise other questions. In the growth accounting framework, capital deepening explains little of the substantial growth of labor productivity over the antebellum period, even in the most capital-intensive and mechanized industries.

In early industrial America it appears that substantial increases in productivity were realized through incremental changes in the organization of production and in the design of tools and products. These are the sorts of technical changes that could well have been realized continuously in response to investments in inventive activity, and with the participation of a broad cross-section of the population in their discovery and implementation. Indeed, the growth of manufacturing productivity (especially in less capital-intensive industries) and of patenting appear to have spread out together from urban districts after 1820, along with the extension of transportation networks and extensive involvement in inventive activity by individuals with rather ordinary skills and backgrounds. The record of productivity growth is, therefore, quite consistent with the hypothesis that during the initial phase of industrialization investments in inventive activ-

---

[2] See Table 9.3.

ity that followed the pattern of demand yielded technological advances across a wide range of industries.

Evidence demonstrates the positive relationship between firm productivity and local patenting rates. Because the expansion of markets during the first stage of industrialization was a powerful stimulus to patenting, studies further support the view that this era was one of "demand-induced" technical change in manufacturing. They also indicate the importance of "supply-side" factors, however, and suggest that the latter had become more influential by the 1850s, when a "second stage" of progress associated with capital-intensive technologies spread across the sector. The significance of these unidentified "supply-side" factors is revealed in the sustained leadership by the same various southern New England counties and urban centers in patenting and productivity throughout the period from 1820 to 1860. This continuity in leadership is a sign that the series of incremental improvements in production methods associated with Smithian growth did not simply exhaust themselves in a one-time increase in productivity, but rather prepared the ground for the next phase of technically more complex advances.

An "American System of Manufactures" was frequently discussed in the first half of the nineteenth century. While there were several different aspects of manufacturing structure that this term was applied to, in general they referred to differences between manufacturing in Britain and the United States, based on variations in factor endowments and in the distribution of income and patterns of demand. Most broadly, the nature of American factor proportions and technology, due to a relatively greater abundance of available land and a scarcity of labor, meant more capital-and-land intensity in American manufactures as well as, it was argued, a greater search for labor-saving innovations in the United States than in Britain. Moreover, these differences in factor availabilities meant that there was less rural cottage industry in the United States than in Britain and Europe. More specifically, the "American System" referred to the system of standardized production with interchangeable parts or assembly line production utilized in some United States industries, particularly arms production. Important to permitting this form of production was the scale of the demand for products and the impact of a relatively equal distribution of income upon the structure of demand, generating a demand for more standardized commodities than in Britain, which had greater inequality and more individualized demands among the rich. Also important in the United States was the development of an effective machine tool industry, which permitted the precision needed to produce interchangeable parts with applications possible in a large number of other industries. The combination of response to labor scarcity and the production of standardized commodities meant that labor productivity in United States manufacturing in the antebellum era was above that even of Britain.

THE CIVIL WAR AND ITS AFTERMATH

It had long been argued that the Civil War and its outcome were the starting point of American economic and manufacturing growth. This argument was based both on the presumed effects of wartime military needs, particularly in the North, as well as on the longer-term effects of the political changes that came with the war's outcome. Clearly the late-nineteenth-century manufacturing sector differed quite dramatically from that in the earlier part of the century, but the question is the extent to which these changes reflected the specifics of the Civil War rather than there being a general pattern of economic growth, one observed in other countries as well.

More recently, however, new data have led to changed interpretations of the pre–Civil War years. It has been established that in the antebellum period agricultural productivity grew rapidly, making it possible for that sector to use far less land, labor, and capital per unit of output. And because of the inelastic demand for agricultural products, a lowered share of agriculture in total inputs and output resulted. Thus, the political shifts of the Civil War era were no longer seen as necessary for an expansion in the manufacturing sector. Nor were the wartime demands in most sectors seen to be sufficient alone to generate such large-scale economic change. The antebellum period had seen rapid productivity growth in many manufacturing industries, which in most cases reflected more changes in the organization of production than in the magnitude and structure of capital, as well as increased regional specialization.

Moreover, a similar pattern of growth in scale and capital-intensity in Europe suggests that the American patterns of change were not based on unique forces. Thus, while the Civil War may have had some particular effects on individual industries, such as armaments and food preparation, it is not to be regarded as the cause of economic growth across a broad spectrum. While political forces could always limit and restrict economic growth, the basic pattern generating American manufacturing growth was apparently in place before the start of the Civil War. The war period itself, rather than being a period of accelerated growth, meant mainly a slowing down of manufacturing growth and limited transition within manufacturing.

THE CIVIL WAR TO WORLD WAR I

While the growth of the manufacturing sector had been rapid prior to the Civil War, in the half-century after the war ended growth and structural changes within manufacturing became more dramatic. This was the period in which the United States overtook Britain in terms of per capita income and industrial output, becoming the world's leading manufacturing economy. The nature of U.S. exports shifted from predominantly agricultural to mainly manufacturing, and these exports played a dominant role in forcing changes in the economies in Europe and other nations. Within manufacturing, the size of producing units increased (the number of employees per establishment doubled between 1870 and 1890), the sources of power changed, and there was a dramatic rise in the importance of durable goods-producing industries. The share of the labor force in manufacturing rose from 13.8 percent in 1860 to 22.1 percent in 1910. The share of manufacturing in GNP rose from about 24 percent in 1869 to 33 percent in 1899. After growing at a rate of 1.4 percent per annum between 1869 and 1899, the rate of growth of total factor productivity in manufacturing was at a rate of about 0.5 percent between 1899 and 1919. This was below that of the overall economy in those two decades, which was at an average of 1.2 percent, as well as below the rate of growth of total factor productivity in the antebellum period. Reflecting the great expansion of capital stock in manufacturing, particularly in the 1880s, manufacturing output per worker grew more rapidly than did national income per worker between 1869 and 1909. Despite the growth in total factor productivity, however, in this period a considerably larger proportion of measured output growth was due to growth in factor inputs.

The shift of labor and capital into manufacturing was generally at the expense of agriculture. The expansion in the manufacturing sector meant also that there were some increases in the output of manufacturing-related services that were instrumental in aiding production and in providing for more effective distribution of manufactured goods. The postbellum growth of manufacturing entailed a dramatic relocation of industry, with a shift from concentration in the Northeast to concentration in the Midwest. The South, however, still accounted for only a small fraction of the nation's industry.[3]

The growth of manufacturing was, of course, not at a constant rate over time, but occurred with a series of cyclical fluctuations that reflected those of the national economy. Cyclical downturns gave rise to major social and economic problems, but placing too much attention on the difficulties of the downturns provides a misleading picture of the economic growth in the period. There were two periods of unusually rapid growth in manufacturing during this period, 1884–1889, which experienced an even more rapid growth in capital than in output, and 1899–1909, a decade with extensive combinations and mergers of manufacturing firms, and which followed closely after an unusually severe macroeconomic contraction.

For growth to occur in the industrial sector, given the importance of technological and other supply changes, there must have been sufficient expansion in the demand for the products. The sources of demand depended on the nature of the product – some was for sale directly to consumers, others were sold to firms as intermediate products for further use in production. Consumer demands were particularly important in food-producing sectors, where factory production grew rapidly with the growth in population and the size of the market. Steel became an important intermediate product used in many manufacturing industries. Market-size for both consumer and producer goods was influenced by the characteristics of the product (size, weight, etc.) and by the costs of transporting the good. Although foreign trade had some impact in meeting demands, there was considerable import-substitution, substituting domestic production for foreign produced goods. Producers in the purchasing nations and others in the world economy paid attention to the effects of the substantial growth of U.S. manufacturing and manufacturing exports. The increased ability of U.S. manufactures to penetrate foreign markets was dramatic, and manufacturing exports as a share of total exports rose from 28 percent in 1860 to 60 percent in 1910.

Tariff rates for manufactured imports were increased several times. Despite the increased importance of exports, most manufacturing output

---

[3] For a recent summary of these geographic patterns, see Sukkoo Kim, "Expansion of Markets and the Geographic Distribution of Economic Activities: The Trends in United States Regional Manufacturing Structure, 1860–1987," *Quarterly Journal of Economics* 110 (1995), 881–908.

was still for domestic markets. The importance of domestic markets reflected the tremendous growth of population in the United States, with its high fertility and its ability to attract immigrants from Europe. Population increase was accompanied by growth in per capita income, further raising purchasing power and market size within the United States. Increasing urbanization made for more concentrated markets, while reductions in the costs of transportation and communication made for more extended markets. With the large increase in the size of the domestic consumer markets, many of the first large firms, if not necessarily large plants, were in consumer goods-producing industries, serving national markets. The prime motive for these larger firms was often the need for more efficient distribution networks to permit marketing of the increased production, which meant use of brand names, advertising, and the providing of various services and repair aids to consumers.

Crucial to the expansion of manufacturing at this time was the growth in the size of individual firms. In explaining this phenomenon, it is important to remember that there are several different dimensions to economies of scale. The benefit of larger-scale producing units (plants), based upon increased capital intensity, provides a basic image of industrial change. Yet most large firms were not based on the production of only one large plant, but rather consisted of several plants, with the benefits of scale coming in other functions, such as product distribution, financing, or the purchasing of material inputs. Some of these benefits of scale provided social as well as private gains, but often they yielded only benefits to the firm. Important to the ability of the multi-plant firm to grow were improvements in communication and in the internal controls coming from a central office, making geographically dispersed production and distribution possible.[4]

The expansion in the size of markets and in the size of firms often meant that many of the smaller firms, which had been able to compete when high transport costs provided local monopolies, were now driven out of business. But although the larger size of firms made it appear that market concentration had increased relative to the previous situation, it is possible that this apparent increase in market concentration did not mean a decrease in consumer welfare. Measured welfare changes depended upon the relative differences in the ratio of price to marginal cost in local as opposed to national markets. The alternative sources of supply that resulted from the lowered transport costs and increased competition in many markets

---

[4] For a useful discussion of these changes, see JoAnne Yates, *Control Through Communication: The Rise of System in American Management* (Baltimore, 1989).

may thus have meant a gain to consumers relative to the earlier situation of local monopolies.

From 1865 to about 1895 there were sharp declines in the relative prices of most manufactured goods, particularly in those periods when output was growing rapidly. This is indicative of the rapid shift downward in the supply curve for manufactured goods relative to the rapid (but not as rapid) growth in demand for manufacturing production, and the high elasticity of demand that meant that lower prices led to large increases in output. Those industries with the most rapid rate of productivity improvement tended to have the larger price declines and the greater growth in output. It has been further argued that the increased growth of an industry led to the demand for more inventive activity, so that there were even more extended gains in supply. Accompanying the growth in manufacturing output were significant shifts in industrial and regional distributions of firms and industries. As seen in Table 9.2, several of the largest antebellum industries lost their relative positions by 1910. These changes, with the differential growth of old industries and the development of new industries, were similar to the patterns in other countries when they experienced manufacturing growth.

The geographic redistribution of manufacturing continued the westward movement that had characterized the antebellum period. The movement from New England and the northeastern states to the Midwest persisted. In the Midwest, growth was most rapid in Illinois and Indiana, states whose shares of overall population were also increasing. It was in the South that the postbellum pattern differed most dramatically, the southern share of manufacturing declining from the antebellum period. This was due both to a Civil War decline in output and then to a relatively slow recovery. The South had expanded its manufacturing base during the Civil War, aided by substantial government funding and purchasing, but these activities did not provide the basis for a sustained postbellum expansion. And while southern manufacturing did not decline as dramatically as did southern agriculture, it continued to be a relatively small part of the regional economy. There were some major interregional movements of particular industries, due to technological changes and changes in the availability of labor and other supplies. Most commented upon were the expansion of cotton textile manufacturing in the southern states, particularly North Carolina, the declines in the importance of that industry in New England, and the movement of iron and steel production from Pennsylvania into the midwestern states.

The nature of the manufacturing sector in the midwestern states changed in the later part of the nineteenth century. In the antebellum period the largest industries were those producing consumer goods, often using agriculturally produced raw materials. In the postbellum period, however, midwestern expansion was more frequently on the basis of heavy industry, such as iron and steel, producing capital goods for sale outside the region. At the start of the twentieth century, the Midwest was poised for an even more rapid expansion of its metal-using industries, particularly with the development of two major new transportation means, the automobile and the airplane. The use of steam power, based upon coal, and the increasing use of minerals and metals as inputs into production, permitted the shifts in the location of many industries to the Midwest, industries in which the United States was to have particular advantages in world production that persisted into the twentieth century. Within each region there was some increase in the extent to which factories were located within urban areas. While in some industries factories and smaller producing units remained located in rural or suburban areas, particularly where company towns were able to develop, the nature of the larger labor pool and higher local demand made it advantageous for many firms to locate in large cities. In very large cities, such as New York, there were generally considerable numbers of industries with relatively small firms who were able to benefit from the availability of a larger pool of labor.

As indicated by the accounting for output growth, much of the increase in manufacturing output was due to an increased use of factor inputs (labor, capital, and raw materials), rather than to total factor productivity (see Table 9.3). As the discussion of the residual demonstrates, however, some proportion of growth was attributable to forces such as the effects of productivity changes, new technologies, new forms of organization, and various other changes that served to raise the level of output per unit of input.

Estimates of total factor productivity for individual manufacturing industries (see Table 9.4) indicate the continuation of several antebellum patterns. In addition to the positive growth in overall productivity, there was a relatively broad diffusion of productivity gains across industries. Growth in manufacturing productivity was not based only on developments in one or two key sectors, but rather it took place across a broad spectrum of industries. While the specific pattern of productivity gain by industry differed from that of the pre–Civil War era, the fact that gains were occurring in most industries suggests that there was some persistence

Table 9.3. *Growth rates of output, inputs, and total factor productivity, manufacturing, 1869–1919*

Years	Growth of output	Growth of man-hours of labor	Growth of capital input	Growth of total inputs	Growth of total factor production
1869–79	3.7%	2.7%	5.6%	2.9%	0.9%
1879–89	6.0	3.5	8.8	4.0	2.0
1889–99	4.2	2.7	5.2	3.0	1.1
1899–1909	4.7	3.3	6.4	3.9	0.7
1909–1919	3.5	2.3	5.5	3.2	0.3
1869–1919	4.4	2.9	6.3	3.4	1.0

Source: John W. Kendrick, *Productivity Trends in the United States* (Princeton, 1961), 464.

Table 9.4. *Average annual rates of change in total factor productivity, manufacturing, 1869–1919*

	1869–1899	1899–1909	1909–1919
Manufacturing	1.4%	0.7%	0.3%
Foods		0.3	−0.4
Beverages		0.9	−5.6
Tobacco		1.2	4.9
Textiles		1.1	0.9
Apparel		0.7	2.7
Lumber products		−0.4	−1.2
Furniture		−0.8	−0.5
Paper		2.4	0.3
Printing, publishing		3.9	3.0
Chemicals		0.7	−0.7
Petroleum, coal products		0.7	−1.0
Rubber products		2.3	7.4
Leather products		0.1	0.5
Stone, clay, glass		2.2	0.7
Primary metals		2.7	−0.5
Fabricated metals		2.3	1.8
Machinery, nonelectric		1.0	0.7
Electric machinery		0.6	0.3
Transportation equipment		1.1	7.0
Miscellaneous		0.8	−0.6

Source: Kendrick, *Productivity Trends*, 136.

of the underlying causes of growth. Gains in labor productivity in most industries were rapid, given the substantial increases in capital investment throughout this period. The increased capital in manufacturing went more for new machinery and equipment than for plant. This shift was made possible by the changing sources of power, particularly at the end of the nineteenth century, with the development of centrally generated electricity. Increases in capital intensity and the development of new, more productive machinery were characteristic of most industries, again indicative of a widespread ability to take advantage of economic changes. Increases in the capital–labor ratio were significant in the measured growth of labor productivity, as was the increased use of mineral resources in production. The wide availability, and low cost, of many important minerals, agricultural products, and other raw materials, provided a major base for the success of American industry. Recent studies have pointed to the importance of the greater U.S. availability of many minerals throughout most of this period as a determinant of U.S. manufacturing dominance. The United States was well endowed with the key resources and was able to extract them where located and use them in production.

While changes in technology embodied in machinery and other capital goods were central to the growth process, there were also important changes in organization, with better flows of information permitting more rational internal decision-making. Developments in accounting procedures, more rapid communication across long distances via the telegraph, telephone, and railroad, and more detailed paper work to record transactions, all permitted increases in firm size and efficiency. While these adjustments were not as dramatic as were the changes in physical equipment, their contributions affected most industries, and played a significant role in the successful emergence of the "managerial firm."

The rapid growth in manufacturing output and labor in this period was accompanied by an even more rapid growth in the capital stock, leading to increases in the capital–labor and capital–output ratios, trends that characterized almost all of the manufacturing industries. Since real interest rates did not continue their sharp decline after the 1870s, the surge in investment might be argued to have represented an increased demand for capital. The increased demand was influenced by new technologies, and it drew upon new varieties, and new designs, of machinery and equipment. Also important in meeting this increased demand for funds were key changes in the nature of the financing process that influenced rates of capital formation, particularly for larger firms. Rather than relying on internal financing out of profits, the changing structure of the banking sector after the Civil War, and then, during the 1890s, the development of stock markets and other related financial institutions trading in industrial securities, increased the importance of external financing. These new sources of financing provided more opportunities for growth in the size of firms.

Changes in the postbellum labor force similarly reflected many of the same patterns as those in the antebellum period. In particular, there was a more frequent use of female and child labor in manufacturing than in most other sectors, and the frequency of use of women and children varied with the size of the establishment.[5] Women and children formed a larger, and more noticeable, presence in certain sectors, such as cotton textiles. While the numbers of children in the manufacturing labor force at no time represented a large share of the population of children, their employment was regarded as a major social concern and therefore to be eliminated. There was legislation at the state level to limit child labor and/or to control their working conditions. This legislation was often tied in with legislation concerning required schooling and education for the young. Thus, by the early twentieth century, a sharp decline in the use of child labor had taken place. On the other hand, the magnitude of female labor increased over time, in manufacturing and in other sectors, with much of this employment being of non-married women who participated in the labor force for only a limited time. For this, and other reasons, the number of women with skilled occupations tended to be fewer than was true for men. There was some legislation at the state level to regulate female labor and working conditions, but even if successful legislatively, such restrictions did not always do well at the judicial level, state or national.

Immigrants were also disproportionately represented in the manufacturing labor force, particularly after the substantial inflow beginning in the 1890s. This reflected, in part, the immigrant's disproportionate location in urban areas, which frequently became major manufacturing centers. This migration was almost entirely voluntary and paid for by the migrants, since the attempts at contract labor introduced during the Civil War did not attract many workers, and they were mainly used to bring over strikebreakers.[6] The foreign-born, with their procyclical pattern of arrival, meant that it was probable that fewer native-born workers were in the manufacturing sector. This became the basis of an increased anti-

---

[5] See Claudia Dale Goldin, *Understanding the Gender Gap: An Economic History of American Women* (New York, 1990).

[6] This is discussed in Charlotte Erickson, *American Industry and the European Immigrant, 1860–1885* (Cambridge, MA, 1957).

immigration movement, a movement that, however, did not achieve major success until and after World War I.

There were a number of changes in the structure of the labor force, which influenced the level of skills and the amount of human capital embodied in workers. In particular, the increase in immigration meant some initial shift to relatively less skilled workers, because of the immigrants's lower levels of education and more limited knowledge of English upon arrival. This led to an occupational pattern for immigrants different from that of the native-born. Some debate persists as to the pattern and relative wages of native-born and immigrants. The wages of immigrants were generally lower, whether due to skill differentials or to wage or occupational discrimination. It has also been argued that the influx of immigrants led to a demand for technical changes in manufacturing aimed at taking advantage of the lower costs. In regard to the native-born laborers, it is probable that their skill levels increased, given the increased amount of education received, as well as their accrual of increases in on-the-job experience. Moreover, the increased life expectation toward the end of the period probably meant better health for workers, and thus a more productive labor force.

Among the most significant, and conspicuous, changes in this period were in the nature of power utilized in manufacturing production. Changing sources of power had significant effects on location, organization, and productivity. After earlier reliance on wind, animal, and human power, the early stage of industrialization in the Northeast, particularly New England, was based on the effective application of waterpower. In the mid-nineteenth century, steam power, based upon coal, became an important source of power. At the end of the century both steam and water were frequently used for the generation of electricity. The use of electricity made possible greater flexibility of location, and, also important, greater flexibility of interior design of operations in the factory. Electricity also made possible smaller optimum-sized firms in many industries, since the divisibility of electricity permitted cost-savings and capital-savings in power use as well as a greater degree of continuity in production.

A most favorable circumstance for U.S. manufacturing was the abundance of those raw materials that were used in production. This permitted successful development on the basis of industries, particularly foodstuffs and metal-based industries that were heavily dependent on raw material inputs and had low ratios of value added to gross output. Industries in which the United States was early favored by its supply of raw materials, mineral, vegetable, or animal, include the production of food-stuffs (such as meat packing, flour, canning, and baking), leather, including boots and shoes, and fibers for textile production. Timber was the basis for the production of wood and lumber products, and it also served as an important source of heat in much of this period. Coal was important for power and heat, and iron, copper, and related metals were used for the production of metalwares, machines, and related products. The raw material requirements did have an impact upon industrial location, depending upon where minerals were located, how transportable they were, and the need to balance the costs of several different factors and resources when determining optimum location. There was, therefore, some movement of industry to be closer to the sources of raw materials.

The role of technology in the production of output was central to earlier discussions of manufacturing growth. The development of measures of total factor productivity has meant that it is conceptually possible to estimate the importance of technological change in explaining manufacturing growth. While conceptually possible, it is often empirically difficult to separate out those enhancements to productivity that are due to new technologies and machinery, requiring tangible capital investment, and those due to organizational changes, which alter the manner in which businesses operate. Alfred Chandler's discussion of the growth of firms and industries has emphaized the role of organizational changes, allowing for improved flows of information within the firm, and thus permitting larger firms. These scale effects were generally not as visible, nor as costly, as improvements requiring expenditures on machinery and equipment.

Developments in technology in the late nineteenth century reflected changes in the process and organization of invention. While antebellum invention had been carried out largely by individuals who were actively involved in both invention and commercial development of their discoveries, the growing complexity of technology and the evolution of institutions supporting trade in patent rights encouraged a trend toward greater specialization by inventors – over the second half of the century particularly. These conditions made for a "golden age of independent inventors," who were highly entrepreneurial and organizationally mobile in how they extracted the returns to their efforts. By the early twentieth century, however, such individuals were increasingly inclined to develop long-term attachments with firms, perhaps because "independents" found it increasingly difficult to finance their activities as invention grew more and more capital-intensive. Industrial firms, in turn, set up research laboratories staffed by college-educated labor with technical skills. Science-based research became more important, especially in industries like electronics and communication, automobiles, chemicals, and metals. These changes were also found in the economically expanding areas of Western Europe. This new pattern of invention and innovation has been referred to as a second industrial revolution, one which has led to a greater international diffusion of means of production and of innovations than had occurred during the first industrial revolution. Similarly, innovations in organizations were based on increased educational levels, the expansion of business education, and the diffusion of administrative measures developed in certain industries, particularly the railroads, to other industries that shared problems of multi-plant locations requiring coordination. Trade journals often discussed solutions to organizational problems, and this greater flow of information meant a more rapid adjustment by firms.

Rates of invention, innovation, and diffusion were influenced by profit opportunities of domestic firms, by government measures providing incentives to invent, and by government regulation of international trade via tariffs and other measures. Yet, given these opportunities, it was critical that there be entrepreneurs willing to take advantage of them and not be content with their existing profit levels. These entrepreneurs include the major industrial figures that some call the Robber Barons (and others call Industrial Statesmen), such as Rockefeller, Carnegie, and Frick, as well as many small entrepreneurs. Monopoly may encourage innovation, but if monopoly benefits are taken in the form of profit "satisficing" by a monopolist enjoying a "lazy" life or concerned only with maintaining a dominant position, the extent of technical progress and its economic impact would be limited. Clearly, toward the end of the nineteenth century in the United States there were enough entrepreneurs who wished to obtain profits and economic power, that competition between them was intense and the rate of technical change rapid. Most innovations were the outcome of domestic research, invention, and innovation within the nation. The ability to adopt new technologies, which increased the size of the firm, was aided also by greater accessibility of capital markets, the expansion of corporations with their rights to limited liability, and, also, the overall advantages of higher incomes and wealth in the American economy.

The development of the manufacturing industry took place almost entirely within the private sector. Although the United States was probably more laissez-faire than were most other developed nations, the different levels of government – federal, state, and local – often had a significant impact in encouraging, as well as restricting, industrial activity. There were important policies and influences at the state and local level of governments, but most important for the growth of manufacturing was the role of the federal government, directly in terms of legislation, including those controls regarding trade across state lines, and also by the Supreme Court in interpreting (or redefining) state, local, and federal legislation.

Among the governmental activities accounting for overall economic growth are the many laws and actions regarding the existence and security of property rights by individuals, and their extension to corporate entities, provisions which were important for increasing certainty and security in transactions. It was often necessary for the courts to determine the meaning of new legislation, as well as to examine how past legislation was affected by the changing nature of the economy. The net outcome was that throughout the nineteenth century the government played a rather limited role in restricting individual rights – or at least those rights of the wealthy that permitted them to invest and make more money. Aiding invention and innovation were the tight legal enforcement of patent rights, a basic continuation from the antebellum period. Regulations restricting imports, permitting immigration, and limiting the establishment of labor unions did not protect the rights of all individuals but provided circumstances of more direct benefit to business than to consumers or laborers.

The government's regulation of non-manufacturing sectors also had major impacts on development within manufacturing, even if such impacts were not central to the introduction of such policies. Controls over banking and over the money supply and the national establishment of the gold standard influenced prices, borrowing terms, and the availability of funds. Prior to specie resumption in 1879, the pro-greenback group included numerous eastern manufacturers who claimed that remaining off the gold standard would encourage exports. Regulations such as those introduced by the Interstate Commerce Commission (1887), which influenced transportation costs and conditions, had an impact on relative regional freight patterns and influenced railroad costs and profitability.

The most direct aids to manufacturing industries, and ones that long attracted major political interest, were the tariffs legislated by Congress. The accepted limitations on tariff rates and structure meant that, despite

charges made by contemporaries, tariffs were not the key to U.S. manufacturing development. They were, however a significant nineteenth-
century political issue, and they probably did have impacts on specific
industries. Controls over foreign trade in this period differed dramatically
from those of the present day, there being little in the way of quotas or
outright restrictions, except for some restrictions on food imports for
public health reasons. Tariff rates fluctuated, as legislation changed, and
they were a constant source of contention, as they had been in the antebellum period. In general, however, the degree of interference with trade
was less than it was to be in the post–World War II era.

Throughout most of the nineteenth century the government played a
role in influencing industrial growth, to a great extent by providing positive incentives. It was only at the end of the century that the government
added widespread regulation to promotion. Supreme Court decisions, such
as *Munn v. Illinois* (1877), pointed the way to government regulation. The
Sherman Antitrust Act of 1890, following the Interstate Commerce
Act of 1887, was intended to reduce the extent of monopolization in
the economy, by making illegal certain business practices. Primarily
in response to agrarian concerns seeking to limit the ability of manufacturing firms to set monopoly prices, the Sherman Act made illegal
certain forms of business behavior, including active collusion among individuals and firms. This presumably meant that separate firms could not
reach agreements to restrict trade, making cartels illegal. However important this legislation was in indicating a new direction in government
policy, it did leave some loopholes. Businesses were able to take advantage
of such loopholes to increase their degree of market control, since the
Sherman Act effectively covered only a part of business's monopolization
activities.

Some loopholes were further opened by Supreme Court decisions that
redefined the terms of the law. In *U.S. v. E.C. Knight Co.* (1895), for
example, the Court decided that manufacturing was different from interstate commerce, so that the actions of the Sugar Trust were not considered
to be covered under the Sherman Act. Legislation by New Jersey permitting holding companies (1888–89) led to legalized acquisition of firms by
other firms via the purchase of securities. The desire for market control
within an industry led to increased horizontal mergers, replacing prospective cartels of several firms with one large firm, and this culminated in the
great Merger Wave of the years 1897–1903.[7] Mergers in the 1880s had

---

[7] Horizontal mergers are of firms producing the same output. Vertical mergers are of firms in successive stages in the production and distribution of output.

tended to be of the vertical type, based upon the desire to link the production and distribution of output, the advantages in obtaining supplies
from within a merged firm, and also to deal more effectively with technological complexity. Horizontal mergers led to increased concentration
in many industries, and to increases in the stock market evaluation of the
newly formed firm. These mergers were often unsuccessful, however, and
they did not persist for long periods of time unless there were some efficiency or scale gains. While most mergers did increase the size of firms,
and vertical mergers were generally seen as favoring efficiency, it should
be noted that the rate of growth of total factor productivity in the two
decades after the merger movement was about one-half that of the preceding two decades.

After 1903 the number of mergers declined and remained small until
the reemergence of a new merger movement in the 1920s. The Clayton
Anti-Trust Act (1914) attempted to restrict mergers by limiting the formation of combinations by stock acquisition. Before its passage, however,
there had been a significant court decision that served to redirect the thrust
of antitrust activity. The decision in *Standard Oil Company of New Jersey v.
United States* (1911) proposed a "rule of reason" in regard to monopoly
behavior, making the court's decision depend upon whether the trust was
"unreasonable," as Standard Oil had been, or if the outcome of pricing and
innovating policies were "reasonable" and in the presumed interests of
society. Thus, by World War I, despite the many attempts at limiting
manufacturing concentration, legislation and court decisions seem to have
lagged behind actual business practice, and the growth of big business and
industrial concentration continued.

The second half of the twentieth century has seen a great increase in
policies intended to lower the social costs of industrialization, such as those
aimed at reducing its effects on the environment. Numerous such policies,
however, had their beginnings in the nineteenth century. Dirty, unhealthy
cities were caused, in part, by industrial pollution, leading to urban regulation of sanitation, the development of clean water supplies, and some
limited restriction on the use of coal in industry and elsewhere. More frequently, the source of concern, particularly at the federal level, was policies effecting the depletion of natural resources. Timber policy was a major
source of debate in the late nineteenth century, although the specific extent
to which there had been large-scale depletion of timber was, and remains,
unclear. Other policies, including land policy, were used to limit the
amounts of coal, minerals, land, and other resources used, and to reduce
what was perceived as the destruction of nature. The limits to the use of

natural resources influenced the manufacturing industries by imposing constraints on the amount and price of their inputs. There were also constraints introduced in the early twentieth century, based on health and safety standards, including regulation of foods and drugs. Thus by the start of World War I there had occurred major changes in both the manufacturing sector and in manufacturing–government relations, changes that were to accelerate in subsequent years.

CONCLUSION

The long nineteenth century was a period of exceptional growth and development for American manufacturing. Growth of output was high, new products and new technologies were continuously introduced, and firms grew larger, used more capital per worker, and utilized steam power and electricity rather than waterpower. From a concentration in the Northeast, manufacturing spread westward and by the end of the period the Midwest became the largest manufacturing region.

The growth was accomplished with substantial increases in labor and capital inputs. Yet it was also greatly influenced by the development of appropriate institutions to encourage investment and innovation. A primary role was played by technological change and productivity growth. There were key institutional elements that provided important encouragements to invention and innovation, including a broad educational system and the patent system, and these served to make at least some parts of technological change endogenously determined. The opportunities to benefit from property rights in new processes and new products permitted a broad participation of the population in the inventive process. This was essential to development since, given the complexity of the economy, no single innovation would be able to do much to promote growth.

There were a number of characteristics of the economy and society that helped to spur manufacturing development. The importance of markets, and the responsiveness to market signals, enhanced the flexibility and resilience of the economy. Factors of production were mobile in response to opportunities, and the relatively wide distribution of income had some significant effects on product demands and on work incentives. This apparent interest in economic development led to the emergence of a set of policies that encouraged technological and organizational changes, as well as increased capital formation. Without these institutions manufacturing development would have been more limited, but the formation of these appropriate institutions themselves reflected a broad contemporary consensus on the economic aims of society.

APPENDIX: TWO GOVERNMENTAL CONTRIBUTORS TO THE GROWTH OF THE MANUFACTURING SECTOR

In describing the changing nature of institutional changes, it is useful to distinguish those that evolve within the private sector from those that require some governmental action. Some institutions will provide general benefits to the overall economy, while others may be more highly specific to the manufacturing sector. Laws and regulations influencing capital market developments can impact upon all groups and sectors of the economy, as would the allowing of specific privileges to the corporation as an organizational form. More directly concerned with the manufacturing sector, particularly in the nineteenth century, have been the provisions of the U.S. patent system and its influence on technological developments, and the role of tariffs on particular imports, most frequently of those manufactured goods produced elsewhere.

Patents

The United States patent system, the first modern patent institution in the world, was self-consciously designed to promote economic growth. It was created in accordance with the Commerce clause of the Constitution "to promote the progress of science and useful arts by securing for limited times to . . . inventors the exclusive right to their respective . . . discoveries," and these aids were improved quickly in laws of 1790 and 1793. Although the framers of the U.S. system were certainly familiar with, and influenced by, the British patent system, they chose to make important departures in the ways in which property rights in technology were defined and awarded. In Britain patent rights had evolved out of the practice of awarding royal privileges, and were still regarded as monopolies that restricted community rights and they were to be narrowly construed and carefully monitored. The debates in the United States over the early patent system reflected an appreciation of the long-term social benefits of stimulating inventive activity through granting inventors property rights in their inventions, if not giving them a sense that patents were the natural right of the inventor. It was taken for granted that would-be inventors were influenced by the prospects of material gain, and that providing inventors with an exclusive property right to their discoveries for a fixed term of years would indeed lead to higher rates of domestic ingenuity, technological change, and economic growth. Enforcing these rights was, especially at first, not easy or certain, as Eli Whitney's difficulties with enforcing the patent on the cotton gin illustrate. But responsibility was left to the judiciary, and within a few decades the courts had evolved a set of principles and procedures that provided rather effective protection of the property rights of both patentees and those to whom they sold or licensed their technologies.

Although the main purpose of the patent system was to stimulate invention, it was also designed to promote the diffusion of technological knowledge. The law required all patentees to provide the Patent Office with detailed specifications for their inventions (including, where appropriate, working models), which were to be made immediately available to all who wished to exploit the information. In addition, the establishment of secure property rights in invention itself encouraged the diffusion of technological knowledge. With the protection offered by the patent system, inventors had an incentive to promote their discoveries as widely as possible so as to maximize the returns from their ideas, whether they exploited them directly in commercial application or sold or traded the rights to others. Because infringers were subject to severe penalties, firms were at risk when they invested in a new technology without finding out whether others already controlled the property rights to related techniques. It is likely that new knowledge diffused more rapidly because of this stimulus to keeping well informed about technological developments elsewhere (including other sectors and geographic areas) in the economy, and that the resulting cross-fertilization was a potent stimulus to technological change overall.

The U.S. patent system of the early nineteenth century had several distinctive features and came to serve as a standard toward which other countries tended to converge over time. First, the patent application process entailed involved impersonal routine administrative procedures, meritocratic criteria, and relatively low costs. This provided much broader access to the patent system and incentives for invention than elsewhere. Second, the rights to a patent were reserved for the first, or true, inventor. This more democratic approach was suited for an age in which, due to education and on-the-job training, a relatively large fraction of the population had some basic knowledge of technology. And when, for a rather large fraction of the patents, there were inventors seeking partners with capital to invest, patent holders hoping to sell or license rights to their technologies, and producers of patented products trying to increase their sales. In industry after industry, specialized trade journals appeared that kept producers informed about patents of interest.

Another important channel of intermediation in the evolving market for technological information was through patent agents and solicitors. Their numbers began to grow rapidly during the late 1830s and 1840s, first in the vicinity of Washington and then in other urban centers. Although they were originally focused on shepherding applications for patents through the official review process and defending previously issued patents during interference and infringement proceedings, they soon began to act as agents for patentees, finding firms or individuals who would buy or lease the rights to their patented technologies. Not surprisingly, they tended initially to be concentrated in locations with high levels of patenting, but spread across the country through branch offices or chains of correspondent relations, not unlike those that characterized the banking system.

With the emergence of these types of intermediaries, and with a solid framework for enforcing property rights in place, trade in patented technologies grew to substantial levels as early as the second third of the nineteenth century. Many inventors responded to the opportunities for gain offered by the enhanced ability to sell off their rights by beginning to specialize more in the conduct of inventive activity. The greater complexity of technology and the rising fixed costs of inventive activity made such specialization increasingly desirable, but inventors required some assurance that they would be able to extract a return from their efforts by selling the products of their creativity before they could comfortably concentrate their resources and energies on invention. The relative ease of obtaining and enforcing patents, coupled with other institutional supports for trade in patents, provided that assurance.

The rate of patenting of inventions grew rapidly from 1790 through 1914. Occurring in virtually all industries and geographic districts, especially those where markets were expanding, the increase was conspicuous in scope as well as magnitude. There were some variations in the measured rates of growth, some reflecting changes in administrative procedures and definitions, but mainly due to changes in inventive activity. The numbers of patents filed were quite sensitive to macroeconomic conditions, as seen in the sharp rise in activity before the War of 1812, when interruptions in the supply of foreign manufactures due to the Embargo sparked a burgeoning of interregional trade within the Northeast. This was perhaps an unusual cause of boom times for domestic producers, but the remainder of the antebellum patent records were more conventionally procyclical. Patent growth in the antebellum years was particularly high between 1820 and 1835, and 1850 and 1860, both periods of rapid growth in economic activity. Growth was also high prior to 1810, starting from a quite low base point. In the postbellum period, after a sharp burst concentrated in 1867, growth was rapid in the 1880s and at the start of the twentieth century, again coincidental with periods of high manufacturing growth.

It has been emphasized that the early rise in patenting was associated with a growing proportion of the population being involved in inventive activity, but there are also indications of the increasing importance over time of investment influencing new inventions. Trends toward greater specialization and increases in the number of lifetime patents by patentees were evident by the middle of the nineteenth century. The sales of patents increased in this period, making for a broader accessibility to new inventions. These findings appear to reflect a rise in the return to, and investment in, invention-generating capital, such as the increased knowledge of the operations of the patent system, and the beginning of the modern pattern in which the bulk of invention is carried out by factors specialized in that activity. There was also an increase in the sale of patents between individuals and firms so that the sector of invention was not necessarily the sector of use. Individuals with such investments would be expected to cluster in cities, where there were greater incentives to specialize as well as a relative abundance of resources to support inventive activity or innovation. Indeed, patentees in urban areas were more specialized and filed more patents over their lifetimes. Although the first phase of growth in patenting was marked by the democratization of invention, the later stages of development were characterized by the growing importance of technical expertise for effective invention.

Tariffs

Perhaps the most highly debated issue relating to manufacturing development in the nineteenth century was the tariff, described by the end of the century as "the mother of trusts." Tariffs were the dominant means of raising revenue for the federal government, but they had also figured prominently in Hamilton's original proposals to stimulate industry. Except for several brief periods of heavy land sales tariffs generally accounted for 80–90 percent of all federal government revenues before the income tax was introduced. There was little controversy about the importance of tariffs for revenue, but the setting of rates for specific commodities to protect domestic industry from foreign competition was the subject of intense and long-running Congressional debate. Not all manufacturing industries were protected. In some cases, when U.S. commodities were being exported, any tariff protection would have been irrelevant. In other cases the industry was not considered of sufficient importance, or the entrepreneurs in that industry were unable to convince Congress of their importance so that they were not given protection. Thus only a few industries became the focus of major tariff debates. These were the textile industries, particularly cotton textiles, and the iron and steel industries. Both of these have attracted considerable attention from contemporaries and subsequent analysts, the textiles mainly discussed for the antebellum period, iron and steel for the late nineteenth century.

The first tariff was implemented in 1789, and statutory nominal rates generally increased through 1832, with the support of the Treasury Department, manufacturing interests, and a general public that had developed protectionist sentiments during the War of 1812. A backlash to the 1828 "tariff of abominations," led by southerners, triggered a reversal of this rising trend, beginning with the Compromise Tariff of 1833 and continuing with few interruptions until the outbreak of the Civil War. The revenue needs generated by that war induced a sharp increase in tariffs in 1861, and although they fluctuated, their levels remained high through World War I. Indeed, the passage of the McKinley Tariff in 1890 gave the United States the highest tariff rates in the industrialized world.

Despite long-standing concern with the impact of tariffs on industrial development, the fundamental issues of the direction and magnitude of their effects have not been fully resolved. In part the limited progress reflects the theoretical complexity of the problem as well as the difficulties of obtaining appropriate empirical measurement. Another factor, however, has been that scholars have differed as to how to gauge the contribution of tariff protection. Those who are more skeptical of tariffs having on net a beneficial effect on economic growth have tended to frame the question in terms of the overall impact of tariffs on the manufacturing sector, if not on the entire economy. Those who have a more favorable interpretation of tariffs seem to prefer a narrower criterion, and have concentrated their efforts on identifying whether there were periods during which particular industries were helped by protection.

Not all manufacturing industries received tariff protection, and although the breadth of the imports subjected to tariffs rose over the course of the nineteenth century, it is the antebellum period of early industrialization that is typically highlighted by those scholars who contend that trade protection had positive effects. This follows from the usual presumption that the context in which tariffs are most likely to have a socially beneficial effect is in the case of an infant industry that required protection to evolve to a stage in which it could compete effectively. A number of industries received protection during the early years of the nineteenth century, including glass, paper, hemp products, and earthenware, but textiles (especially cotton textiles) and iron and steel were the focus of the major tariff debates and have attracted the most attention from scholars. The traditional view, associated with the classic work of Frank W. Taussig, was that tariffs had played only a minor role in the growth of manufacturing overall, and even in cotton textiles and iron and steel. The central argument is that for both products, domestic producers may have been sufficiently insulated by other factors to survive and grow in producing for the American market, despite foreign competition. These other factors include a relative abundance of raw materials, lower costs of transportation to market, and, especially, differences in the product characteristics demanded in the United States. Recent studies focusing on cotton textiles have challenged the argument of minor, if any, effects of the tariff, and suggested that American producers would not have been competitive in some segments of the market but for the tariff. They argue that tariff protection may have made a broader contribution to industrial development in the United States, in providing key industries with a window of opportunity to develop the technological capability to compete against foreign producers.

There is room to question just how much more slowly the cotton textile industry would have developed if not for tariffs. How important tariffs were to overall industrial development is less clear. To begin with, the protective effects of the antebellum tariffs are generally acknowledged to have been concentrated among a few prominent industries in which Britain enjoyed technological leadership, such as cotton textiles and iron and steel. These industries may have been crucial for early British industrialization, as implied by the extremely unbalanced productivity growth in that country's manufacturing sector, but there is no reason that they should necessarily be so for all early industrializing nations. The United States had much different factor endowments and domestic markets than did Britain, and it would hardly be surprising if its path of industrial development was quite different as well. Indeed, given the manifest success at both productivity and output growth of a wide range of manufacturing industries operating without effective protection, including substantial ones such as boots and shoes, as well as the praise for American technological innovation received at international venues such as the exhibition at Crystal Palace, the United States seems to have been quite capable of building industrial capacity in a competitive environment. While it may be plausible that tariffs aided particular industries, their impacts, such as diverting resources from other industries, probably limited their contributions to overall economic growth. Tariffs can in principle be socially beneficial, if provided to infant industries, but these are difficult to demonstrate. Moreover, with tariff rates actually being higher after the Civil War, they seem to have been maintained long past the stages of infancy and adolescence.

10

ENTREPRENEURSHIP, BUSINESS ORGANIZATION, AND ECONOMIC CONCENTRATION

NAOMI R. LAMOREAUX

By the outbreak of World War I, the United States economy had acquired (to use Robert T. Averitt's phrase) a "dual" structure, consisting of a "center" of large, managerially directed firms surrounded by a "periphery" of much smaller concerns, often run by their owners.[1] In the center parts of the economy, large firms operated in tight oligopolistic markets, where price competition had been all but eliminated. Firms in these sectors were primarily interested in preserving their market shares and insuring their long-term growth. To this end, they integrated backward into raw-material acquisition and forward into distribution and worked to promote consumers' loyalty to their brands. In the peripheral sectors of the economy, by contrast, enterprises were small and markets competitive. Few firms had the resources to pursue vertical integration or advertise their brands nationally. Time horizons were typically short, and survival depended more than anything else on keeping production costs low.

This division of the economy into center and peripheral sectors was a relatively recent development. Outside the railroad industry, large firms did not appear until the last quarter of the nineteenth century. By then, however, technological change had raised the scale of enterprise in a number of important industries, and as firms increased in size their behavior changed. Once firms grew large enough relative to the market to affect the prices at which they (and others) could sell their output, the rivalry among them became more intense. Each firm stood to benefit by undercutting its competitors' prices and increasing its share of the market at its rivals' expense. At the same time, because firms were now large relative to

---

[1] Robert T. Averitt, *The Dual Economy: The Dynamics of American Industry Structure* (New York, 1968), 1–21.

the market, price competition had become something that could potentially be controlled. Firms attempted to band together in a variety of collusive arrangements to restrict price cutting, but for the most part success eluded them. Finally, they tried joining together in formal mergers. Although many of these combines also failed, in the most capital-intensive industries the resulting giants not only succeeded but often dominated their markets for decades to come.

This chapter begins by discussing the small-firm world of the early nineteenth century – its structure and dynamics. It analyzes the ways in which small firms organized their businesses during this period and the relationship between this kind of business structure and the process of technological change. The chapter then moves on to describe the early development of big-business forms in the railroad industry, and to detail the process by which similar large-scale enterprises emerged in other parts of the economy during the last quarter of the century. Wherever large firms appeared, managerial coordination replaced the market in directing the allocation of resources, and the chapter concludes by pointing out the significance of this change.

EARLY INDUSTRIAL DEVELOPMENT

Before the American Revolution, the industrial production of Britain's North American colonies was negligible. The only industry able to compete with British producers in British home markets was shipbuilding, and the only other industries whose products entered the stream of intercolonial and overseas commerce were those that processed raw materials: for example, rum distilling in New England and flour milling and crude-iron production in Pennsylvania. Most manufacturing activity during the colonial period was the work of small-scale craftsmen who produced goods on order for local consumers. Farm families also engaged in household production, furnishing most of their own clothing, for example.

One should not, however, minimize the extent of economic development that occurred during the colonial period. Northern port cities were home to growing numbers of merchants who developed commercial connections with traders in Canada, Europe, the West Indies, and Africa. Through their mercantile activities these men acquired important reservoirs of business knowledge and capital. Moreover, the constant pressure to find new sources of supply and new markets for their goods honed their entrepreneurial skills. The port cities were also home to growing numbers of craftsmen who possessed basic workbench skills and technological knowledge. It was the coming together of these two groups during the early part of the next century that would fuel the nation's industrial development.

Even in the colonial period merchants had invested to some degree in manufacturing activity. Timber and crude iron served as ballast on the vessels they shipped to England to pick up supplies, and merchants often helped to finance local iron works to assure themselves an adequate source. Merchants also invested in manufacturing in order to capture profits from the production of goods they were already handling. Thus merchants involved in the molasses and rum trade, such as the Browns of Providence, Rhode Island, sometimes built their own distilleries. The Browns also constructed a spermaceti candle works to process the products of the local whaling industry.

During the half century that followed the American Revolution, merchants' involvement in manufacturing increased dramatically. The restructuring of international trade that followed independence made overseas commerce a more risky and difficult endeavor than it had been during the colonial period. Deprived of the established trade routes and protected markets that membership in the British empire had afforded, merchants after the war also faced discrimination at the hands of former allies such as France and Spain. With access to European and West Indian markets limited, success depended on pioneering new trade routes in the Orient, where as a result of distance and cultural difference the risks were high. Only during the French Revolution and the Napoleonic Wars, when American merchants benefited from their position as neutral carriers, did commerce regain its prewar profitability.

As they expanded their involvement in manufacturing to compensate for declining earnings in commerce, some merchants invested in industries whose products they were already distributing. Thus the Whitaker Iron Company of Maryland was able to secure investment capital from iron commission merchants in the port of Baltimore, and the Mount Hope Iron Company of Massachusetts obtained comparable assistance from Boston traders. Similarly, the Jones and Laughlin Company of Pittsburgh had its origins in a partnership between two capital-starved iron masters (Benjamin and Francis Lauth) and two merchants (Benjamin Jones and Samuel Kier), who had recently entered the iron trade.

In other cases, merchants played a more entrepreneurial role. In the shoe industry, for example, traders in Lynn, Massachusetts began during the early nineteenth century to hire local craftsmen to produce for them in central shops. They quickly learned that they could reduce costs and increase output by subdividing the labor process, and by the 1830s they had developed a system whereby leather cut in central shops was "put out" to households throughout the region for "binding" and "bottoming."

In the textile industry, merchants not only reorganized production but played an important role in transferring key technological innovations from Great Britain to the United States. The first breakthrough occurred in 1789, when Rhode Island merchant Moses Brown convinced Samuel Slater, a former factory superintendent from England, to build a set of spinning machines for him. The two men negotiated an arrangement whereby Brown agreed that his family would finance construction of the mill and market its product, whereas Slater contracted to build the machinery and supervise operations.

Although Brown played an entrepreneurial role in introducing mechanized spinning to the United States, he and his family initially confined their participation to the mercantile end of the business. By 1815, however, when Francis C. Lowell and the Boston Associates built the first textile mill to integrate both spinning and weaving operations, merchants were involving themselves in the manufacturing end of the business as well. Lowell himself traveled to Britain to tour textile factories, taking special notice of the power looms that had not yet been successfully introduced into the United States. When Lowell returned to New England, he worked with machinists to develop his own version of the loom. Moreover, he and his merchant associates not only financed the enterprise but planned its construction, developing the system of boarding houses, churches, and schools that would attract a female labor force to staff their factories.

Although merchants played an important role in promoting early industrial development, craftsmen played an equally critical part. Neither the Browns nor the Boston Associates would have gotten very far without the assistance of local machinists. Moreover, in other cases craftsmen were the key entrepreneurs. The Berkshire paper industry, for example, was inaugurated by Zenas Crane, a journeyman paper maker who migrated westward to find a suitable location for a mill. Similarly, the three most important iron firms in Pittsburgh during the early nineteenth century were founded by craftsmen/mill owners who had migrated to the city from the Juniata region of Pennsylvania.

These early industrialists financed their factories by drawing upon their own resources and those of members of their families, plowing back their profits into the business. But merchants often played an important role in financing these enterprises as well. In addition to funds for plant and equipment, manufacturers needed working capital to cover the costs of purchasing raw materials, hiring workers, transporting goods to market, and storing inventories. These were not minor expenses – working capital requirements often exceeded the amount needed for plant and equipment – and merchants were an important source of such funds. Traders who sold raw materials to manufacturers often accepted IOUs in lieu of cash. Moreover, in exchange for the right to market a manufacturer's products, they sometimes provided loans to finance production. Thus a Philadelphia brokerage house dealing in pig iron provided Robeson, Brooke and Co., blast-furnace owners, with a loan of $30,000. In return for the loan, the furnace owners promised to supply the merchants with 5,000 tons of iron per year for two years. Such credit from merchants could be as important for technological progress as direct investments in plant and equipment. For example, Eli Terry's development of a process for mass-producing wooden clocks was made possible by a contract with merchants Levi and Edward Porter. Terry promised to deliver 4,000 wooden-movement clocks within three years, in exchange for which the Porters provided Terry with working capital and a guaranteed market.

EARLY METHODS OF BUSINESS ORGANIZATION

Given the important role that merchants played in financing early industrial ventures, it is not surprising that manufacturers borrowed heavily from mercantile practice in running their concerns. For bookkeeping models, for example, manufacturers turned to the double-entry methods that merchants had employed since the late middle ages. Because this type of accounting system was devised to record exchanges with the external world, it was not well suited for monitoring the flow of goods through the production process. Over time, manufacturers thus found it necessary to modify their accounts in order to keep tabs on raw-material and labor costs. At the Lowell textile mills, for example, managers developed the capacity to calculate labor efficiency and raw-material costs on a monthly basis. Similarly, Berkshire paper makers devised a system of time books that enabled them to track labor costs over comparable intervals.

Notwithstanding these innovations, manufacturers retained the mercantile practice of balancing accounts only once or twice a year. As a consequence, they had no way of determining the actual extent of their profits during the intervening period. Moreover, because this type of accounting system treated expenditures to improve or replace equipment as an operating cost, manufacturers also had no way of determining the true magnitude of their investment or, for that matter, their rate of return. These deficiencies would not be corrected until the rise of large-scale, managerially run businesses at the end of the century. In the meantime, the lack of information about capital investments was not perceived as a serious problem. Many businesses were family affairs whose accounts intermingled personal expenditures with business charges. Manufacturers drew out as much of the company's income as they needed for household expenses and reinvested the rest. So long as they were earning a comfortable living and their business was growing, they did not worry about their rate of return.

The mercantile influence was also evident in the organizational forms adopted by early industrialists. Most manufacturing ventures, like most mercantile firms, took the form of single proprietorships or partnerships. The members of a partnership were bound together by contracts that specified such details as the amount of capital each partner would contribute to the firm, the functions each would perform, the earnings that could be taken out of the business, and the procedures for terminating the agreement. For example, the partnership agreement between iron makers Benjamin and Francis Lauth and merchants Benjamin Jones and Samuel Kier specified that Jones and the Lauths were to receive salaries of $1,500 per year, in exchange for which they promised not to take any profits out of the business. The Lauths were to take charge of the rolling mill, while Jones had responsibility for keeping the accounts and running the commercial end of the enterprise. Kier was an inactive partner.

Partnerships had important advantages over single proprietorships. On the most obvious level, partners usually brought additional capital to the firm. But partners might also bring with them specialized knowledge and experience as well as business connections that could enhance the firm's access to markets or credit. In her study of the Berkshire paper industry, Judith McGaw found that the advantage to be derived from well-chosen partners was significant. Partnerships that included a trained paper maker were 167 percent more likely to succeed than those without, while those that included someone with commercial experience were 140 percent more likely to succeed. Relatives who owned paper mills were a valuable source of information and business contacts, and firms whose members had such relatives were 153 percent more likely to succeed than those that did not. Firms whose partners utilized all three sources of information were 47 percent more likely to succeed than firms that tapped only two, 62 percent more likely to succeed than those that tapped only one, and 320 percent more likely to succeed than those with none of these sources.[2]

The advantages of partnerships could be obtained, moreover, without much loss of flexibility. Partners could dissolve alliances that did not work well or that failed to serve their business interests. Conversely, new partners could be added to a firm if additional capital or expertise was required. When, for example, the Lauth, Jones, and Kier partnership still found itself short of funds, its members turned to a Pittsburgh commission merchant named James Laughlin, who invested $40,000 in the mill and joined the firm. Wheeling, West Virginia, nail producers organized and reorganized firms to suit their interests. In 1847, for example, John Hunter, William Fleming, Robert Morrison, E. W. Stephens, and Edward Norton joined together under the name of Hunter, Morrison & Company to build a nail mill. Two years later Norton withdrew to join with his brother and eight other craftsmen to found a new concern, Norton, Bailey & Company. Two years later Bailey and six of the partners withdrew to found yet another mill.

In addition, although individuals usually formed partnerships with the intention of engaging in a particular line of business, as new opportunities waxed and old opportunities waned, the business interests of the firms could easily shift. For example, the Brown and Ives partnership in Rhode Island mainly invested in overseas commerce until the Embargo that preceded the War of 1812, when the firm transferred some of its capital to cotton manufacturing. Over the next thirty years the partners increased their investments in the textile industry and decreased their involvement in trade, finally selling their last ship in 1838. Similarly, the partnership of Matthew Baldwin and David Mason added stationary steam engines to its line of bookbinders' tools and calico printers' rolls, after Baldwin designed an efficient engine for the firm's own use.

---

[2] Judith A. McGaw, *Most Wonderful Machine: Mechanization and Social Change in Berkshire Paper Making, 1801–1885* (Princeton, 1987), 127–47.

Directly related to this advantage of flexibility was the greatest draw-back of the partnership form of organization – its impermanence. Indus-trial investments required long time horizons, yet partnerships typically lasted only so long as their members and, in fact, only so long as the members wished to remain in business together. The dissolution of a part-nership, whether from the unexpected death of one of the partners or simply from one partner's desire to quit the business, often required the liquidation and division of assets, making it difficult for the remaining partners to continue the business. When, for example, disagreements between the Brooke and Bulkley families, who in partnership owned the Hopewell Furnace in Pennsylvania, culminated in a court suit in 1818, the firm was dissolved and its assets divided.

Another serious drawback was the unlimited liability that went along with membership in a firm. Each partner in the firm was personally liable for its debts, once the business's property was exhausted. Each partner, moreover, could incur debts in the course of prosecuting the firm's busi-ness that were binding on the other partners, whether they had agreed to them or not. Thus Samuel Slater's various textile-mill partnerships were all endangered in 1829, when David Wilkinson failed. Wilkinson was a partner in several of the mills, and Slater had also endorsed a considerable amount of his business paper. To meet Wilkinson's obligations, Slater was actually forced to sell his Pawtucket and Slatersville operations.

Manufacturers could, at least in theory, avoid these problems by incor-porating their enterprises. In the late eighteenth and early nineteenth centuries, however, incorporation required a special act of the legislature. At that time, the grant of a corporate charter conferred quasi-governmen-tal powers on the organizers, and hence was restricted to groups that undertook to perform vital public services – for example, building a bridge or a road to improve transportation routes, or organizing a bank to provide the community with a circulating medium and source of credit. In exchange for providing such services, the incorporators received certain privileges that ranged from the right to issue currency in the form of banknotes to monopoly franchises.

As other entrepreneurs clamored for the right to provide similar ser-vices to the public, these grants of privilege came under increasing attack. The opposition to special charters grew more powerful over time, more-over, because it was joined by members of the public who felt that they had been victimized by the economic power of the corporations. Shippers complained that incorporated transportation companies were able to extract monopoly rents. Similarly, small businessmen and farmers worried that legislatures had granted incorporated banks the power to contract or expand the money supply at will. These fears about monopolistic privileges swelled into a general attack on the corporate form of organization. Critics asserted that provisions such as limited liability provided incorporated firms with an edge in raising capital that would give them an unfair competitive advantage over partnerships. They also worried (somewhat contradictorily) that because the owners (stockholders) of a corporation often played a passive role in management, that corporations would not be run as efficiently as firms that adopted the partnership form.

The outcome of all this opposition was not the abolition of the corporation, but rather a tendency to reduce the element of privilege that inhered in the grants by making it easier to obtain charters. Legislatures first responded to political pressure by increasing the number of special charters they granted, but especially in the 1830s, they began to pass general incorporation laws that enabled any group of individuals to organize a corporation by filing an application and paying a fee. These moves to expand access to the corporate form were ratified by the U.S. Supreme Court in 1837 in the *Charles River Bridge* decision, wherein the Court declared that a corporate charter did not carry with it the implication of monopoly.

One enduring consequence of this early opposition to corporations, however, was a continued regulatory role for the states, which sought to insure that corporations did not enjoy unfair advantages over other firms and that their managements behaved responsibly. In order to accomplish these goals, state legislatures inserted regulatory provisions in corporate charters, and after the Supreme Court's decision (in the *Dartmouth College* case in 1819) that a corporate charter was an inviolable contract, also routinely added clauses that allowed the state to alter unilaterally a charter's terms. Regulatory provisions ranged from requiring banking corporations to submit semi-annual financial reports to restrictions on the amount of capital that firms could raise and the lines of business in which they could engage. Legislatures also imposed particular structures of governance on corporate enterprises, specifying, for example, the size and composition of the boards of directors, the frequency of elections for corporate officers, and the number of votes that large shareholders could exercise.

In the early nineteenth century, adoption of the corporate form of organization thus involved a considerable loss of flexibility compared to the partnership form. Members of corporations lost the freedom to write contracts specifying their governance structures. Instead, they had to accept the form of organization imposed by the state. They also lost the ability to add to their capital stock at will or to shift into new lines of business as opportunities arose. In extreme cases, the laws could be so restrictive as to limit opportunities for vertical integration. In late-nineteenth-century Texas, for example, the combination of a general incorporation law, which confined firms chartered in the state to one particular line of business, and an antitrust law prohibiting holding companies so effectively precluded vertical integration that it kept Standard Oil from entering the Texas petroleum industry.

The main benefit of the corporate form was the alienability of shares and the provision of limited liability, which made it easier for firms to raise funds in the capital markets. For example, the Boston Associates chose to organize their textile mills as corporations in large part because it enabled them to raise capital from friends and relatives who were primarily interested in other types of businesses and might not have been willing to participate in a partnership. As an added bonus, the Associates were able to sell off some of their own shares and profit from the appreciation in the value of the stock.

This advantage in raising capital, however, was not very important during the early years of the century. In the first place, the market for shares in manufacturing firms was shallow. With the exception of a few well-established companies such as those of the Boston Associates (whose shares were so coveted that they rarely appeared on the market), manufacturing firms had difficulty selling their stock to the general public because their ventures were perceived as risky. As a result, most of the stock issued by manufacturing corporations was closely held by people who were personally connected to the firm's promoters – precisely the same sources of funds that partnerships typically tapped. Moreover, so far as the credit markets were concerned, limited liability could be a definite disadvantage. Banks and other lenders typically required major stockholders to provide personal guarantees before they would discount a corporation's notes.

There were, moreover, other available vehicles for tapping the savings of the community. During the early nineteenth century many manufacturers banded together with small numbers of associates and relatives to secure charters and organize banks. These institutions then became engines of capital for the incorporators' enterprises, which typically included a variety of other ventures besides factories. In Rhode Island, for example, the Rhodes brothers joined together with a number of relatives to organize the Pawtuxet Bank, which by the early 1840s was pouring more than 50 percent of its resources into loans that supported the brothers' diversified investments in textile manufacturing, transportation, commerce, and real estate speculation. Investors eagerly purchased stock in banks like the Pawtuxet, because it enabled them to buy shares in the diversified portfolios of the region's most active entrepreneurs. Banks in the early nineteenth century functioned much like investment clubs – they were a means for ordinary savers to participate in the gains from industrialization without exposing themselves to serious risk.

Once manufacturers associated themselves with banks, moreover, they were able to reduce some of the drawbacks of the partnership form of organization. When firms dissolved, for example, banks could discount notes from partners who wished to continue in business, thus eliminating the need to liquidate assets in order to pay off claimants. Impermanence, moreover, was not an unremediable condition of the partnership form of organization. Contracts could be written in ways that would protect the firm's assets in the event of the decease of one of its partners. The most famous of such contracts was the so-called iron-clad agreement that Andrew Carnegie negotiated with his partners in 1887. The contract specified that if a partner died, the remaining members of the firm had the right to buy his share at book value. Not only were the remaining partners given a considerable period of time to pay off the heirs, but the firm's book value was held below its market value. There are plenty of other examples of agreements that aimed to protect the interests of existing members. For instance, the partnership contract signed by members of the firm Bailey, Woodward & Company, nail makers, specified that if any member of the firm wished to sell its interest, he had to offer it to all existing members of the firm (in ascending order of the value of their shares) before it could be sold to an outsider. These, however, were cumbersome arrangements, whose rigidities could scare potential partners away. The corporate form of organization provided a much simpler solution to the problem of succession, and its popularity would grow over time as a result.

The initial lack of advantage of the corporate form of organization for manufacturing firms is apparent in the statistics on charters. George Herberton Evans, Jr. collected information on corporations chartered in four states: Maryland, New Jersey, New York, and Ohio. During the first four decades of the century only about one-quarter of the corporations

organized in these states were manufacturing concerns, with the proportions rising from a mere 9 percent during the first decade to about 28
percent during the 1830s. The case of New York is particularly instructive. During the second decade the number of corporations formed for
manufacturing purposes suddenly soared, totaling 161 (41 percent of the
charters) as opposed to 24 (11 percent of the charters) during the previous decade. Apparently, however, promoters had been overly optimistic
about the advantages of the corporate form, because the number of manufacturing charters subsequently declined. During the next decade, only
93 manufacturing corporations were chartered (25 percent of the total
granted). Even during the expansion of the 1830s, the number of manufacturing corporations chartered in New York was still lower than it had
been during the earlier surge.[3]

The vast majority of corporations chartered during the first four decades
of the century were either banks, whose diversified portfolios attracted
investors looking for a safe way to participate in the gains from economic
development, or transportation companies, who could attract capital from
those who stood to benefit from the service as well as those who thought
the investment would be profitable. Not until the end of the century would
manufacturing corporations enjoy similar access to the capital markets. As
time went on, however, the corporate form became increasingly attractive
as a way of insuring the continued existence of the firm.

ENTREPRENEURSHIP AND TECHNICAL PROGRESS

According to Joseph A. Schumpeter's definition, entrepreneurs were
extraordinarily creative individuals who perceived new ways of combining
existing resources so as to increase productive efficiency or create new products. Entrepreneurs, in Schumpeter's view, had heroic stature. They were
not merely inventors – indeed, they were often not inventors at all. Rather
they were individuals who perceived the potential utility of an invention
and, through sheer perseverance and force of character, overcame all the
technical and institutional obstacles to making their ideas work.[4]

---

[3] George Herberton Evans, Jr., *Business Incorporation in the United States, 1800–1943* (New York, 1948), 10–30.

[4] Joseph A. Schumpeter, *The Theory of Economic Development: An Inquiry into Profits, Capital, Credit, Interest, and the Business Cycle* (Cambridge, MA, 1934), especially Chapter II.

Entrepreneurs who fit Schumpeter's definition certainly existed in the early-nineteenth-century United States. Robert Fulton is an excellent example. He did not invent the steamboat. John Fitch and James Rumsey had both secured patents on steamboats in 1791, though neither was able to develop his innovation successfully. Fulton succeeded in 1807 where others had failed because he turned his entrepreneurial energies toward securing adequate financial backing and market control. Robert Livingston provided him with sufficient capital to weather problems with boat design, and a twenty-year monopoly of steamboat navigation in New York waters guaranteed a market for his packet service.

In the case of most early-nineteenth-century industries, however, it is difficult to name a single individual whose innovations figured so prominently in its development. Fulton's monopoly of commerce allowed him to capture the gains from his innovation for a considerable period of time, but most innovators did not receive such protection. True, patent rights were well enforced by the courts, and the growing numbers of assignments (sales) of patents suggests that these temporary monopolies were perceived to have economic value. But the low level of investment in both human and physical capital required for successful invention during this period meant that most inventions were soon surpassed by others. As a result, though we can often name the individuals who were first to introduce a new technology into an industry, the achievements of these first movers were often swamped by followers who imitated and improved on their innovations. Once Francis C. Lowell demonstrated in 1815 the viability of power-loom weaving in the United States, for example, other textile manufacturers adopted similar devices. William Gilmore quickly introduced a cheaper machine; Dexter Wheeler improved on Gilmore's version; and the machine spread throughout southern New England. As early as 1820, there already were fifteen factories in Rhode Island that integrated machine spinning and weaving, fifteen in Connecticut, and eleven in Massachusetts.

Nor was Eli Terry able to maintain his lead in clock manufacture. After Terry demonstrated that it was possible to use machine tools to mass produce wooden movement clocks, he set to work designing a thirty-hour shelf clock, which he patented in 1816. Almost immediately, his patent was successfully challenged by other clock makers who had developed similar models, and new competitors flocked into the industry. By the mid-1820s there were twenty-two manufacturers producing wooden-movement clocks. By the mid-1830s there were as many as sixteen factories in Bristol,

Connecticut alone (Bristol was the home base of a merchant who financed the manufacture of clocks for his network of Yankee peddlers), and factories were clustered in other Connecticut towns as well.

Given the rapidity with which innovations were copied and improved by other manufacturers, it makes more sense when discussing the early-nineteenth-century United States to talk about an entrepreneurial culture rather than individual entrepreneurs. In this period, basic workbench skills were more important for technological innovation than scientific knowledge, and these skills were broadly diffused through the population. Kenneth L. Sokoloff and B. Zorina Khan found that as the numbers of patents began to soar during the period of the Embargo, there was a shift in the sources of invention: artisans of all types were accounting for a growing proportion of patents, and the share of merchants and professionals – that is, of gentlemen – was decreasing. Most (between 50 and 70 percent) of the patents granted over the next few decades were awarded to individuals who patented only one invention. Moreover, patenting activity clustered during periods of economic expansion. What seemed to be going on, in other words, was that skilled craftsmen throughout the economy were responding to opportunities for advancement by developing new productivity-enhancing ideas and attempting to capitalize on them.[5]

Inventive activity tended to concentrate in urban areas, where the exchange of technical information occurred on a routine basis. Some of this exchange was involuntary, as, for example, when craftsmen examined a competitor's product and tried to copy it, or when skilled workers from one shop went into business for themselves, bringing to the new firm the knowledge they had accumulated in the old one. Many transfers of information occurred voluntarily, however. Craftsmen visited each other's shops and met in coffee houses and taverns to discuss technical matters. They also formed organizations such as the Franklin Institute in Philadelphia, which appointed committees to assess the merits of important inventions or to discuss perplexing technical problems, and which published journals that disseminated information about inventions. Moreover, competitors often deliberately shared technical information with each other – a phenomenon that Robert Allen has called "collective invention."[6] During the

---

[5] Kenneth L. Sokoloff and B. Zorina Khan, "The Democratization of Invention During Early Industrialization: Evidence from the United States, 1790–1846," *Journal of Economic History* 50 (1990), 363–78.

[6] Robert C. Allen, "Collective Invention," *Journal of Economic Behavior and Organization* 4 (1983), 1–24.

early part of the century, for example, textile manufacturers visited each other's factories to view new types of machinery and obtain information about production costs. Later on, they presented papers describing recent technical advances at meetings of trade organizations, such as the New England Cotton Manufacturer's Association.

Such cooperative relations were particularly likely to develop in industries where the gains from invention were not easily appropriated and where firms were small relative to the market for their products — that is, where no one firm could dramatically affect the prices at which neighboring manufacturers could sell their goods. In such industries, assisting one's neighbor did not in any clearly perceivable way have a negative effect on one's own business prospects, yet cooperation could significantly increase everyone's profitability, especially in times of rapid technological change. Farming has typically had this kind of structure, and farmers have always understood the benefits to be derived from mutual assistance. So too did many manufacturers. When, for instance, Berkshire paper makers began to mechanize their operations in the late 1820s, there was a confusing variety of paper machines on the market, many of which required special modification to perform particular tasks. Manufacturers who were plugged into the community of paper makers had access to information that could reduce their risk in buying new machines. For example, when Byron Weston could not decide which paper cutter to select, he wrote to his colleague, R. W. Wilson. Wilson explained which machines he favored and recommended that Weston visit several local mills that had them installed: "I think I would see the different cutters and you could then tell better what to do." In another case, one manufacturer asked another to send him a badly needed machine: "I want too to have you send us *as soon as possible* that machine for turning rolls in the calender. Tom Carson says it worked well. . . . Tom told me he would lend me the turning tool he had made." Manufacturers not only shared information about technology, they sometimes even shared the machines themselves. Thus Byron Weston joined forces with a neighboring firm, Bartlett and Cutting, to purchase a calender lathe, which the two firms subsequently operated in common.[7]

This exchange of information, whether voluntary or not, sped the diffusion of new technologies. Because entrepreneurs were unable to control the spread of ideas, industries rapidly acquired a competitive market structure, insuring that productivity advances would be passed on to consumers

[7] McGaw, *Most Wonderful Machine*, 138, 171.

in the form of lower prices. Moreover, the rapid diffusion of technological information insured that innovations developed in one industry would be quickly applied to related problems in other industries, so that productivity advances occurred in many parts of the economy at about the same time.

Transportation improvements furthered the process of technological diffusion. Kenneth Sokoloff found that patenting activity tended to follow the course of navigable rivers and canals. As canals brought new areas within the domain of the commercial economy, local producers lost the monopoly protection that the expense of shipping to their communities had provided and were forced to compete in broader regional markets. The same improvements that opened local markets to outside competition also created opportunities for gain for local producers, and they responded by increasing their rate of invention.[8]

Most significant during this period in bringing new areas within reach of the commercial economy was the canal building craze that began with the completion of the Erie Canal in 1825 and lasted until the onset of depression in 1839. During this period, some 3,000 miles of canal were constructed, and by the mid-1840s transportation costs had fallen from an average of 20 cents per ton-mile using wagon haulage to less than 1 cent per ton-mile using canals. Most canals were either built or funded by state governments, and the financial problems that afflicted these projects after 1839 brought the era of canal building to an end. By the 1850s railroads had replaced canals as the favored form of transportation innovation. Although ton-mile charges were usually higher on railroads than on canals, the greater speed and efficiency of railroad travel, as well as the possibility for year-round shipments of goods, gave the former an advantage, and railroads garnered an increasing share of the tonnage wherever the two forms of transportation competed. Unlike canals, most railroads were built and operated by private corporations, though they too often benefited from government largess.

THE RAILROADS

The railroads were the first corporations to break out of the small-firm environment of the early nineteenth century and distinguish themselves

---

[8] Kenneth L. Sokoloff, "Inventive Activity in Early Industrial America: Evidence from Patent Records, 1790–1846," *Journal of Economic History* 48 (1988), 813–50.

in important ways from concerns that still used the partnership form of organization. As Alfred D. Chandler, Jr., has argued, railroads were the nation's first big businesses. They were the first private enterprises to raise substantial sums of money from the capital markets in New York and abroad. As a result, they stimulated the development of new types of financial intermediaries and instruments that would play an important role in the economy's subsequent growth. The railroads were also the first businesses to confront technical problems that were sufficiently complex to force them to articulate a managerial hierarchy. By the 1850s managers such as Daniel C. McCallum of the New York and Erie, Benjamin Latrobe of the Baltimore and Ohio, and J. Edgar Thomson of the Pennsylvania Railroad had realized that it was imperative to improve coordination of the rapidly increasing volume of traffic that was flowing over their lines. They set to work devising new accounting techniques that would enable them to measure the performance of all the operating units in their domain. They also devised organizational charts and manuals that arranged employees according to a hierarchy of responsibility and clearly specified the duties of each. The line and staff organizations they created would serve as models for the large-scale enterprises that emerged throughout the manufacturing sector later in the century.[9]

Despite their large size and more formal organizational structure, railroads continued the tradition of technological cooperation that had characterized so many early nineteenth-century industries. Representatives of the railroads met together and standardized gauges and railroad equipment so as to facilitate the movement of traffic from road to road. They also developed accounting systems that insured that each enterprise would be properly credited for the services it provided, and agreed on a basic structure of rates, classifying hundreds of different types of freight into four basic categories.

Unlike the small-firm industries of the early nineteenth century, however, where owners were responsible for most exchanges of information, in the case of the railroad cooperation was largely the work of managers. It was they who met frequently with their counterparts on other roads to work out the details of rate structures or discuss the merits of one type of equipment over another. Moreover, their cooperative activities were reinforced by their growing consciousness of themselves as professionals. In the post–Civil War period managers began to flock into national asso-

---

[9] This section is based largely on Alfred D. Chandler, Jr., *The Visible Hand: The Managerial Revolution in American Business* (Cambridge, MA, 1977), 79–187.

ciations such as the American Society of Railroad Superintendents, to present papers at professional meetings on technical details involving railroad administration, and to subscribe to publications such as the *Railroad and Engineering Journal*.

All this cooperative activity had a very different effect on competitive behavior in the railroad industry than it had in the case of small-firm industries such as textiles or paper. Because each individual railroad was much larger relative to the market than firms in those industries had been, its pricing and output decisions had immediate consequences for its market share. Although railroads had their own routes, they competed with each other in interregional shipping. If one road cut prices below the going rate, it could increase its volume of traffic at its rivals' expense. Moreover, because fixed costs were a high proportion of total expenses, earnings were directly related to volume. As a consequence, each railroad could operate more profitably if it could steal traffic away from its competitors. This rivalry had not been so important when roads had operated on different gauges or when transshipment from one road to another was difficult. But the cooperative activities of the managers gradually removed these impediments, and the competitive structure of the industry was laid bare. As each railroad sought to undercut its rivals' rates in order to gain an advantage in trade, earnings for the industry as a whole began to plummet.

Managers responded to these new competitive pressures by expanding their cooperative efforts to include price fixing. At first they tried to band together in informal alliances, but when this device proved too weak, they organized formal pools. One of the most elaborate was the Joint Executive Committee, organized in 1879 to control rates on shipments of grain and related products from Chicago to eastern markets. In contrast to European practice, however, such cartel agreements were not enforceable in court – a serious problem because the industry's cost structure created a substantial incentive to cheat. Nor, in the anti–big business, anti-railroad political climate of the late nineteenth century were the roads able to secure legislation that would provide government backing for their efforts to restrain competition. The Interstate Commerce Act of 1887 contained no provisions to support pooling. In addition, the rate-making powers it granted to the Interstate Commerce Commission were weak and operated mainly to prevent increases.

As a result, cartels had to rely on their own devices to prevent cheating. The Joint Executive Committee, for example, was headed by Albert Fink, a respected railroad administrator, who was given important enforcement powers. Cartel members were required to post bonds to guarantee their adherence to the pool's rate structure, and Fink could declare these bonds forfeit if members were convicted of cheating. Fink could also order the cartel to match immediately any rate cuts by its members, thus making violations unprofitable. Violators could only be punished, however, if their cheating was actually detected. Hence to aid in enforcement, the Committee collected and disseminated weekly statistics on freight shipments by each of its members. Such statistics, however, were an imperfect measure of cartel discipline, for members' shipments could fluctuate dramatically for reasons that had nothing whatsoever to do with cheating. As a result, periods of economic turbulence tended to cause breakdowns in cartel pricing, because members could not distinguish cheating from other causes of shifts in the demand for their services.[10] The long depression that followed the Panic of 1893 was a particularly disruptive period for the cartel, and members had pretty much given up on the organization's effectiveness when the Supreme Court, in the *Trans-Missouri Freight* and *Joint Traffic* decisions of 1897, declared such organizations illegal restraints of trade in violation of the Sherman Antitrust Act of 1890.

After the cartel movement collapsed, railroad leaders turned to mergers and "communities of interest" to relieve the competitive pressure on rates. The massive numbers of railroad bankruptcies that occurred during the rate wars of the 1890s facilitated reorganization (approximately one fifth of the nation's railroad mileage went into receivership over the course of the depression), and by the early twentieth century, thirty-two roads controlled nearly 80 percent of the nation's railroad mileage. The number of companies was still too high to make competition easy to control, so managers began to create formal communities of interest by exchanging stock in each other's roads. Such exchanges solved the information problems that had fueled cheating during the cartel period, and rate cutting disappeared as a problem. Over the next decade, the industry's main problem became to secure permission from the Interstate Commerce Commission for rate increases that would cover rising costs and attract the capital needed to improve track beds and rolling stock.

[10] Paul W. MacAvoy has argued that regulation by the Interstate Commerce Commission temporarily helped to promote cartel stability from 1888 until 1892, but Thomas S. Ulen vigorously disagrees, arguing that the cartel's success during these years owed to its sophisticated enforcement mechanisms and to generally favorable economic conditions. See MacAvoy, *The Economic Effects of Regulation: The Trunk-Line Cartels and the Interstate Commerce Commission Before 1900* (Cambridge, MA, 1965); and Ulen, "The Market for Regulation: The ICC from 1887 to 1920," *American Economic Review, Papers and Proceedings*, 70 (1980), 306–10.

MASS DISTRIBUTION

The sharp drop in transportation costs that resulted from the construction of canals and railroads stimulated the rise of large-scale business units in other sectors of the economy by making it possible to tap larger and larger segments of the domestic market. In distribution, for example, as Chandler has shown, the commission merchants of the early nineteenth century gave way to giant wholesalers, who purchased goods directly from a whole host of manufacturers and built marketing organizations capable of supplying retailers throughout the country. As in the case of the railroads, the far-flung operations of these wholesalers required the development of managerial structures to coordinate the movement of goods from supplier to purchaser and to monitor the activities of the firm's numerous employees.[11]

Wholesalers handled distribution for most manufacturing industries during the last third of the nineteenth century, but in a few instances they were unable (or unwilling) to do an adequate job. A good example was the case Swift & Company, meatpackers. Before the 1870s cattle were usually shipped live on railroad cars to eastern cities, where they were slaughtered and sold in the form of fresh beef. Gustavus Swift, the firm's founder, realized that the speed of railroad transportation presented new opportunities to effect tremendous savings in cost. If he could slaughter cattle in the Midwest and arrange to ship the beef to eastern markets in refrigerated cars, he could avoid paying freight on the inedible parts of the animal (more than half the weight of the carcass), obviate having to feed and water cattle in transit, and escape losses from animals losing weight and even dying en route to markets. Finally, by concentrating the slaughtering business in one midwestern location, he could capture economies of scale.

Swift faced a lot of opposition to his plan – not only from the butchers and wholesalers whose business he threatened, but also from the railroads, who already had extensive investments in cattle cars and feeding stations. As a result, he was forced to build his entire distribution system from scratch. He sunk all the capital he could raise into the construction of a small fleet of cars, managed to get one railroad to carry them, and plunged into the business. His initial successes gave him the wherewithal to expand into sales. He quickly built a network of wholesale offices that housed

---

[11] See Chandler, *The Visible Hand*, 215–24.

refrigerated storage space and a sales staff to market the meat to local stores. In addition, by buying rights to harvest ice from the Great Lakes and setting up ice houses along his routes, he protected himself against costly bottlenecks that could have damaged both his product and his business. As a consequence of his skill in system building, Swift's enterprise grew rapidly. Swift made his first shipments of dressed beef in 1877. By 1881 he owned nearly 200 refrigerator cars and shipped something on the order of 3,000 carcasses per week.

Swift's creation of a vertically integrated empire changed the nature of competition in the industry. Before Swift built his system, the meatpacking industry had consisted of hundreds of small local slaughterhouses. Afterward, the only firms that could meet his low prices were the few that could muster the financial resources to copy his strategy and build their own networks of refrigerated cars, ice houses, and distribution outlets. As a result, the industry was transformed into an oligopoly dominated by a very small number of large firms. By 1888 Swift and the three firms that built similar systems (Armour, Morris, and Hammond) together accounted for about two-thirds of the nation's supply of dressed beef.

Similar developments occurred in industries that produced technologically complex products such as sewing machines or mechanical reapers. Manufacturers could not tap the large potential market for these products unless they could teach customers how to use them and reassure purchasers that broken machines would be swiftly repaired. Independent wholesalers lacked the expertise and incentive to provide such instructional and repair services, so manufacturers had to provide them themselves. Firms such as Singer in sewing machines and McCormick in reapers took the lead. Thereafter the only firms that could successfully compete were those that completely duplicated their distribution systems, investing in retail outlets as well as production facilities. The tremendous amount of capital needed for such an effort kept the number of competitors small, and just as in the case of meatpacking, these industries too acquired tight oligopolistic structures.

THE GREAT MERGER MOVEMENT

As the nineteenth century progressed, technological change gradually increased the scale of industry. Between 1850 and 1870, for example, the average amount of capital invested per manufacturing establishment rose from $4,300 to $8,400. By 1890 it had increased to $18,400.[12] In some industries, of course, the increase was much more pronounced. In most of these cases, however, the road to oligopoly was more circuitous than it had been in meatpacking and complex machinery. Goods could still be effectively distributed through existing independent wholesalers, so there was no advantage to be gained from integrating forward into distribution, particularly because most manufacturing firms were as yet not large enough to be able to capture the wholesalers' economies of scale. So long as firms confined their operations to production, however, it was difficult for any one of them to secure the kind of competitive advantage that Swift had achieved.

In most industries no single entrepreneur was able to secure a long-term advantage. Although there were exceptions (the crude-steel industry, which Andrew Carnegie dominated, is a case in point), most industries came to be populated by ten to twenty firms that were quite evenly matched. Where technological change raised the minimum efficient scale of enterprise, the number of these firms tended to decline over time. But the reductions were usually not sufficient to reduce competitive pressures. Quite the contrary, once firms grew large enough relative to the market to affect the prices at which others could sell their products, they became direct rivals. Moreover, in those industries where technological change was embodied in expensive capital equipment, the proportion of fixed in total costs tended to rise. As a result, just as in the case of the railroad industry, firms had an incentive to try to increase their market share at their rivals' expense, and price wars were the inevitable result.

During the late 1880s and early 1890s, for example, a dozen or so newsprint manufacturers built mills that integrated new wood-pulp technology with paper manufacture on a scale large enough to capture available economies. None of the firms controlled patents that could give it an advantage over his rivals. Nor was there any way for one firm to differentiate its product from competitors'. Manufacturers in fact were so evenly matched that a long period of downward spiraling price competition, which lasted throughout the depression of the nineties, failed to divide the industry into winners and losers. Profits in the industry fell sharply, but no group of firms outperformed the rest.

During the same period, the development of cheap steel and a process for making steel wire into nails stimulated an influx of firms into the wire-

---

[12] U.S. Census Office, *Twelfth Census: Manufactures*, pt. I (Washington, DC, 1902), xlvii.

nail industry. Again, there were no patents to restrict entry, and by the early 1890s the industry was dominated by about ten large firms that combined nail manufacture with rolling mills. As in the case of the newsprint industry, wire-nail firms were plagued by severe price competition during the 1890s, but no firm or group of firms was able to secure an advantage. Instead the competition inflicted damage on them all.

In the face of such unrelieved competition, firms attempted to negotiate collusive arrangements to halt price cutting. These agreements, however, were rarely successful for several reasons. In the first place, as already noted, the contracts that resulted from these agreements were not enforceable in court. In addition, the temptation to violate such agreements was tremendous, for by slightly undercutting the agreed-upon market price, a firm could (at still remunerative prices) greatly increase its share of the market. As a result, some agreements barely lasted an hour. One association of wire producers collapsed when a member left the meeting to telegraph the details of the settlement to his sales force and discovered a competitor already ordering his agents to undercut the pool's price.

Manufacturers could and did form more tightly structured organizations with built-in enforcement mechanisms and information collection policies designed to prevent violations. As in the case of the railroad cartels, however, members found it difficult to distinguish shifts in demand from cheating, and the organizations tended to break down during periods of market turbulence. One of the most effective cartels was the Rail Association, formed in 1887 to control the price of steel rails. The pool operated successfully for almost a decade, but collapsed in 1896 when the demand for rails fell disastrously below projections.

In many manufacturing industries, moreover, barriers to entry were low, and hence successful cartels tended to attract new competition. During the mid-1890s, for example, wire manufacturers organized a formal pool that maintained good discipline among its members for over a year. But the high prices charged by the pool stimulated an influx of new competitors. When the pool inevitably collapsed, the firms were worse off than before. Ultimately, in industry after industry of this type, manufacturers turned to consolidation for relief.

The first giant merger, Standard Oil, had been organized in 1882 to enable the leaders of the Standard Oil alliance, an association of oil refiners, to make common managerial decisions. The alliance had already succeeded in eliminating competition among its members by means of

exchanges of stock. Now, however, the alliance needed to devise a governance structure that would enable it to make decisions that would reduce
costs, for example by concentrating production in the most efficient
refineries and shutting down others. With the help of a clever lawyer
named S. C. T. Dodd, an alternative form of organization was devised –
the trust company. Members of the alliance formed a new entity, the Standard Oil Trust, to hold the stock of firms in the group. This device gave
the trust's officers managerial authority to reallocate production among the
constituent firms.

In several other industries – most notably sugar, lead, whiskey, linseed
oil, cottonseed oil, and cordage – firms joined together in the 1880s and
adopted Standard Oil's trust form of organization. After the passage of the
Sherman Antitrust Act in 1890, this type of organization became vulnerable to prosecution. But the New Jersey legislature had enacted a general
incorporation law for holding companies during its 1888–89 session, so
an alternative form of organization was available. Most of the trusts were
subsequently reorganized as New Jersey corporations, and a number of new
consolidations were formed – also as holding companies chartered in New
Jersey or other states. However, the big wave of mergers came during the
late 1890s and involved industries that had experienced unrelenting price
competition during the depression of that decade. In these industries prices
did not rebound with the return of prosperity to the economy as a whole.
The upturn did, however, stimulate a rise in activity on the stock market
that made it possible to finance mergers. The result was a flurry of consolidations. Only thirteen multi-firm consolidations were formed during
the depression years 1895–97, but in 1898 the number suddenly rose to
sixteen and in 1899 to sixty-three. Thereafter the numbers began to tail
off again – to twenty-one in 1900, nineteen in 1901, seventeen in 1902,
five in 1903, and three in 1904.

Brief as the merger movement was, it had enormous implications for
the size distribution of firms in the manufacturing sector. Between 1895
and 1904 more than 1,800 manufacturing firms disappeared into consolidations, many of which acquired substantial shares (at least initially) of
the markets in which they operated. Of the ninety-three consolidations
whose market shares it is possible to estimate, seventy-two controlled at
least 40 percent of their industries and forty-two at least 70 percent. Even
assuming that none of the remaining mergers achieved significant market
power, this meant that nearly half the consolidations absorbed over 40
percent of their industries, and over a quarter absorbed in excess of 70

percent. G. Warren Nutter calculated that in 1899, at the peak of the merger movement, more than 17 percent of all national income derived from industries that were "effectively monopolistic," that is where the four largest firms accounted for at least half of industry output.[13]

CONSEQUENCES OF THE MERGER MOVEMENT

Despite their initially impressive market shares, many of the new consolidations were no more successful over the long run than the collusive agreements they had replaced. The high prices they charged after their formation stimulated an influx of competition, causing virtually all of them to lose ground and many even to fail. The most favorable assessment of the success rate of the turn-of-the-century consolidations, Shaw Livermore's 1935 study, showed that about half of the combinations were unsuccessful. Livermore collected information on 136 mergers that were powerful enough at the time of their formation "to influence markedly conditions in the industry." After examining their earnings records over the period 1901 to 1932, he categorized 37 percent as failures, 7 percent as failures that were subsequently rejuvenated, 12 percent as marginal or "limping" concerns, and only 44 percent as successes.[14]

There is no question, however, that the consolidations that survived transformed the business environment in important ways. Consolidations were usually financed by the issue of securities, and the profitability of the most successful ones paved the way for other industrial securities to be marketed on the national exchanges. As a result of the merger movement, then, large manufacturing corporations gained the same access to national capital markets that railroads had achieved by the middle of the nineteenth century.

At the same time, the process of consolidation typically brought about a sharp separation of ownership from control, comparable to that which

---

[13] Naomi R. Lamoreaux, *The Great Merger Movement in American Business, 1895–1904* (New York, 1985), 2–5; G. Warren Nutter and Henry Adler Einhorn, *Enterprise Monopoly in the United States, 1899–1958* (New York, 1969), 47.

[14] Shaw Livermore, "The Success of Industrial Mergers," *Quarterly Journal of Economics* 50 (1935), 68–96. These totals differ from the ones in Livermore's article because I restricted the focus to the manufacturing sector and eliminated double counting of reorganizations. The criteria Livermore used to measure success are not altogether clear, but he seems to have considered a firm successful if its profit rate (net earnings after deduction of fixed charges divided by total stockholders' equity) equaled or exceeded that for manufacturing firms in general.

had already occurred on the railroad. In those cases where owners sold their enterprises to the consolidation for cash and/or bonds (as Andrew Carnegie did at the time of the formation of the United States Steel Corporation), their connection with the firm usually ended abruptly. Even where owners accepted stock in the new corporation as payment, their holdings were usually too small relative to the total for them to be able to exert much influence. In some cases they stayed on as managers, but typically they found it difficult to accommodate themselves to their now restricted responsibilities and resigned after a couple of years, often to form new firms in competition with the consolidation. Thus Garrett Schenck resigned from the board of the International Paper Company to organize its major rival, the Great Northern Paper Company; Joseph Banigan quit the presidency of United States Rubber to form his own firm; and Charles Schwab left U.S. Steel to turn his talents toward building up the Bethlehem Steel Company.

The consolidations thus developed very different governance structures from those of the firms they acquired. Most decisions were now made by salaried managers who owned little or no stock in the enterprises they served. Such power as owners continued to wield was exercised by the board of directors, the most important of whose members were often the same salaried managers whose activities the board was supposed to regulate. For the first couple of decades, the interests of the owners were often represented on the boards by members of banking concerns that had financed the consolidations. Although the bankers did not meddle in the day-to-day operations of the corporations, their presence operated as a check on management, and sometimes the bankers even moved to replace managers who pursued policies that were contrary to their interests. J. Bradford DeLong has shown statistically that this kind of supervision by J. P. Morgan and his partners improved the performance of companies in a measurable way. By the 1920s, however, the influence of bankers on the boards of major corporations had waned, and managers were left to run their companies largely unchecked.[15]

In the industries where they proved successful, consolidations also had a major impact on competitive behavior. Just as in the case of the railroad industry, where mergers and exchanges of stock had made it easier to prevent rate cutting, so too did mergers in manufacturing make price

---

[15] J. Bradford DeLong, "Did J. P. Morgan's Men Add Value: A Historical Perspective on Financial Capitalism," in Peter Temin, (ed.) *Inside the Business Enterprise: Historical Perspectives on the Use of Information* (Chicago, 1991), 205–36.

competition easier to control. The consolidation of virtually all the firms in an industry into a single combination created a natural "dominant firm," whose pricing decisions could affect the behavior of the new competitors that quickly emerged. Consolidations had this power because by setting a price, allowing smaller firms to sell as much output at that price as they wished, and satisfying the rest of the market themselves, they could effectively transform their competitors into price takers – that is, into firms that could gain no advantage by cutting prices. This strategy did have a significant drawback, however. If competitors earned positive profits at the set price, they might expand their operations or new firms might enter the industry, and the dominant firm's share of the market would fall. If any one competitor acquired a significant share of the market, moreover, it was no longer likely to behave as a price taker.

At some point, the independents' market share would grow so large that it was too costly to continue dominant-firm pricing. Consolidations responded to this development by attempting to convince their competitors voluntarily to restrict output, but this strategy typically met with little success and eventually consolidations had to retaliate by cutting prices themselves. For example, after the International Paper Company saw its share of the market drop from about 80 to 90 percent at the time of its formation in 1898 to under 50 percent during the downturn of 1905, it slashed prices on its output and began aggressively to compete for business. The result was a price war reminiscent of the 1890s, but with one crucial difference – the price competition was easily ended. When the demand for paper began to rise again in 1907, International Paper reverted to its dominant-firm posture, raised prices substantially, and the independent manufacturers, with deep sighs of relief, followed suit.

As a result, then, of the emergence of corporations large enough relative to their competitors to play the role of dominant firms, price competition had become something that could be turned on and off. This change was enormously significant because it meant that, whenever a drop in market share indicated that discipline in their industries was breaking down, dominant firms could use the threat of price warfare to enforce cartel-like behavior. In other words, the existence of a dominant firm – a single entity that could detect and punish cheating – largely solved the information problems that had plagued cartels during the latter decades of the nineteenth century. Thus when demand turned down again after the Panic of 1907, the independent newsprint manufacturers had learned their lessons. With only an informal agreement to bind them, they cooperated with International Paper to divide up the market, maintain prices, and share the burden of curtailment of output. The famous Gary dinners in the steel industry were successful for precisely the same reason. Over the preceding half decade the United States Steel Corporation had periodically departed from its dominant-firm pricing strategy to cut prices and discipline rivals who were taking too large a share of the market. The threat behind Gary's soothing dinner conversation – that U.S. Steel would slash prices and take business away from the independents – was what made the meetings so successful. It also explains how such a loose and informal association could be so successful in maintaining prices, where much more tightly structured pools had failed in the past.

Dominant firms could only succeed in supporting prices for an extended period of time, however, if there were barriers to entry into the industry. Otherwise, the high prices a consolidation set would stimulate an influx of new competition, and its market share would erode until it no longer had the power to set prices for the industry. Federal court decisions during the late nineteenth and early twentieth centuries put limits on the kinds of barriers that dominant firms could construct. Tying contracts that bound suppliers or customers not to deal with competitors were early ruled illegal, as were railroad rebates that gave one firm an advantage over others that used the same service. More generally, the courts tended to outlaw barriers that derived from collusive behavior by two or more firms, forcing consolidations instead to develop wholly internal strategies to cope with the threat of potential competition.

The most successful were those that moved resources out of production and integrated vertically, either backward into raw materials or forward into distribution. Just as the system-building of Swift and Singer forced competitors to follow suit, the vertical integration pursued by the consolidations meant that new entrants had to invest in distribution and supply networks to be competitive. The large amount of capital vertical integration required kept the number of effective competitors small, and these industries too acquired tight oligopolistic structures.

Sometimes, moreover, vertical integration erected barriers to new competition besides those attributable to the high cost of entry. The United States Steel Corporation, for example, embarked on a strategy of acquiring the best of the nation's ore resources. At the time of its formation, U.S. Steel acquired, along with its constituent firms, massive iron-ore deposits in the Lake Superior region – the source of most of the ore used by the country's steel mills. Over the next few years U.S. Steel added greatly to its holdings, both through the purchase or lease of individual mining properties and the acquisition of steel firms with extensive ore resources. Other major steel producers were forced to follow suit, and by mid-decade most of the then commercially exploitable ore lands had been taken up. U.S. Steel held more than 50 percent of the ore in the ground; another 20 percent or so was in the possession of other big steel firms; most of the rest was controlled by James J. Hill, a railroad magnate, who had acquired the property in order to guarantee his Lake Superior district railroad an adequate tonnage. In 1906, U.S. Steel capped its string of purchases by leasing the Hill properties. The monopolistic intent of the corporation's action was clear, for the terms Hill extracted were onerous. Hill obligated U.S. Steel to mine a certain minimum tonnage annually (the amount increasing yearly over the next ten years), to ship this over his Great Northern Railroad, and to pay a royalty on the ore substantially in excess of the usual rate.

The Hill agreement gave U.S. Steel control of 70–75 percent of the iron ore in the Lake Superior region. There were still other (less desirable) ore deposits elsewhere in the nation. But in 1907 U.S. Steel gained control of vast ore fields in the southern United States when it acquired the Tennessee Coal, Iron and Railroad Company during the financial panic of that year. Competitors could still obtain iron ore from outside the United States, but only at a significant cost disadvantage. Not surprising, there was little new entry into the industry after the first decade of the twentieth century. Virtually all the firms that rose to prominence in the next fifty years were mergers or reorganizations of existing concerns – concerns that already had acquired ore resources.

The consolidation movement also made forward integration possible by creating firms that were large enough to take charge of their own marketing and still benefit from the economies of scale that independent wholesalers had effected. This shift in the locus of distribution was important because it afforded the firms new opportunities for product differentiation. Independent wholesalers had typically sold their wares as homogeneous products or sometimes, where it was necessary to signal differences in quality, under their own private brands. Before the formation of the National Biscuit Company, for example, crackers were distributed in bulk to retailers who dumped them unbranded into their store barrels. After consolidation, however, National Biscuit began to distribute its product in individual packages under the "Uneeda Biscuit" brand, building its own marketing organization to handle and promote the product.

Once consolidations began to market their own brands, they developed a new concern for protecting them from the encroachments of rival manufacturers. Although brands and trademarks had been a familiar aspect of business activity from time immemorial, protecting these product symbols did not engage the energies of most businessmen until the rise of large-scale organizations in the late nineteenth and early twentieth centuries. Before Congress passed the first national trademark law in 1870, the courts had handled only sixty-two cases involving trademarks, and most of these involved foreign firms seeking to protect their brands in American markets. The 1870 law treated trademarks just like patents and was declared unconstitutional by the Supreme Court. Subsequent legislation in 1881 provided only for the registration of trademarks used by firms in foreign trade or commerce with Indian tribes. Not until 1905 did Congress pass a law that protected trademarks in domestic commerce. As Mira Wilkins has argued, the timing of the legislation reflected the new needs of large firms competing in oligopolistic markets to preserve and expand their market shares.[16]

Another strategy that consolidations pursued to protect their market positions was to gain proprietary control over technological developments. In those industries where scientific knowledge was crucial for the development of new products and processes, consolidations began very quickly to invest large sums of money in research and development. One of the primary purposes of the new research labs that firms such as General Electric, RCA, and AT&T established in the early twentieth century was to insure that their products were adequately protected by patents. As Leonard S. Reich has shown, large firms often used patents for purposes other than product development, employing them to prevent competition by monopolizing crucial elements of a technology or suppressing innovations that might challenge their product lines. Thus AT&T's accumulation of (to use the president of the company's own words) "a thousand and one little patents" on the district exchange system kept competitors at bay by giving the company control of patents that were vital to all alternative varieties of exchanges – not just the versions the firm was employing in its own operations. Similarly, RCA protected itself against the develop-

---

[16] Mira Wilkins, "The Neglected Intangible Asset: The Influence of the Trade Mark on the Rise of the Modern Corporation," *Business History* 34 (1992), 66–95.

ment of strong rivals by securing patents that were crucial for radio manufacture and requiring firms that licensed its technology to give RCA the option to buy any radio-related patents they developed.[17]

A DUAL ECONOMY

Not all manufacturing industries went through the change in competitive structure just described. Large firms emerged in the late nineteenth and early twentieth centuries in two main types of industries. The first were industries such as meatpacking and sewing machines, where distribution problems forced firms to build national marketing systems. The second included industries such as steel and newsprint paper, where technical change raised the scale and capital intensity of enterprise, leading to repeated bouts of price competition. Most other manufacturing industries remained pretty much as they had during the early part of the century – competitively structured, populated by large numbers of small firms. In this manner, then, the economy acquired a "dual" structure, with a "center" of large oligopolistic industries surrounded by a "periphery" of small, competitively structure industries.

The center portions of the economy differed from the peripheral sectors in a crucial way: much of the activity that in the latter case occurred in the market, in the former case transpired inside firms. To use Chandler's evocative phrase, the visible hand of management had replaced the invisible hand of the market. Chandler has put a positive spin on this development, arguing that managerial coordination of economic activity was responsible for the tremendous achievements of the American economy in the twentieth century. A host of other eminent scholars have echoed his claim. Oliver Williamson, for example, has argued that, because large firms economized on transactions costs, they were a more efficient way of organizing economic activity than small firms contracting in the market to perform precisely the same functions. Richard Nelson and Sidney Winter have hypothesized that large firms developed special organizational capabilities that in themselves constituted valuable economic resources. William Lazonick has argued that progress has resulted from progressively greater levels of economic organization, as businesses have evolved from

---

[17] Leonard S. Reich, "Research, Patents, and the Struggle to Control Radio: A Study of Big Business and the Uses of Industrial Research," *Business History Review* 51 (1977), 208–35.

small proprietary firms into large-scale enterprises and (in the present period) into industrial groups.[18]

The price of greater levels of organization has been a loss of flexibility, however. In the early nineteenth century, firms could be formed, restructured, and dissolved as opportunities in their sectors waxed and waned. Capital flowed easily to promising new areas, and barriers to the diffusion of technological information were low. In the center portions of the early twentieth century economy, however, large firms acquired both extraordinary longevity and the ability to control new technological developments. In the most important sectors of the economy, therefore, the pace and direction of economic activity had become a matter for managerial decision-making, and thus the health of the economy had come to depend, as it never had before, on the organizational capabilities of a small number of very large firms.

---

[18] See Oliver Williamson, "The Modern Corporation: Origins, Evolution, Attributes," *Journal of Economic Literature* 19 (1981), 1537–68; Williamson, *The Economic Institutions of Capitalism: Firms, Markets, Relational Contracting* (New York, 1985); Richard R. Nelson and Sidney G. Winter, *An Evolutional Theory of Economic Change* (Cambridge, MA, 1982); and William Lazonick, *Business Organization and the Myth of the Market Economy* (New York, 1991).

11

BUSINESS LAW AND AMERICAN ECONOMIC HISTORY

TONY A. FREYER

Within broad limits business law always has been instrumental to American economic development. J. Willard Hurst's classic formulation characterized nineteenth-century law and the conditions of freedom as permitting a release of middle-class entrepreneurial energy. Elaborations of this idea stressed that law encouraged dynamic rather than traditional uses of property, often favoring capitalist exploitation of weaker groups. Emphasizing the importance of incentives in the operation of economic markets or political and legal systems, Douglass C. North recognized, by contrast, that imperfect information, transaction costs, and other factors brought about outcomes that often were neither optimal nor even beneficial to those who purportedly sought such results through manipulation of the rules of the game. Thus according to North, the institutional framework underlying the impressive economic growth of the nineteenth-century United States provided incentives for individual and group action that resulted in a mix of economically productive and adverse outcomes. Groups pursued contrary views of self-interest in part because ideological conflicts fostered opposing perceptions of property rights. Perhaps the most significant instance in which interest-group and ideological struggle followed an unpredictable course was the clash between Democrats and Republicans that culminated in the Civil War. Yet to a certain extent, in the nineteenth-century American economy such clashes were endemic.

Clifford Shearing, a sociologist at the University of Toronto, explored further the influence of institutional multiplicity. He argued that markets and other forms of social interaction can never exist outside of or separate

For support Professor Freyer thanks the Earhart Foundation, the University of Alabama Law School Foundation, and the Edward Brett Randolph Fund.

from an institutional order. At the same time, institutions incorporate private and public (i.e., governmental) forms of ordering, which taken together constitute social interaction, including markets. Thus according to Shearing's constitutive theory of institutional multiplicity, the market exists within "a space in which different regulatory schemes operate simultaneously. The occupants of this space may change but it is never empty." In the space constituting private market action, moreover, "regulatory schemes often compete with each other for control of the ordering process."[1] This constitutive theory places in useful perspective the institutional significance of the U.S. Constitution. Commentators from Hurst to North have assumed that the Constitution of 1787 created a national market for free trade. Yet this formulation should acknowledge that at least until the New Deal, the peacetime operation of the Constitution's federal system ensured that the rules governing property and contract rights varied from state to state. Moreover, different rules governing identical property or contract claims frequently existed side by side in the same place, making conflicted outcomes virtually inevitable. Following Shearing's theory, then, the Constitution formally constituted wide-ranging public and private interests whose legitimacy multiple lawmakers sanctioned, which in turn resulted in differing or even contradictory economic outcomes.

Between Independence and World War I business law influenced four periods of American economic development. The Constitution framed by the Philadelphia Convention of 1787 was the consummation of interest-group struggles over who would control the institutions that fashioned and enforced mercantilist policy inherited from British colonialism and the Revolution. From Ratification to 1860, the new federal system constituted a fragmented public space in which contract, property, and constitutional rules provided incentives for both the promotion of laissez-faire entrepreneurialism and the protection of a producer majority – people who were self-employed in small, generally unincorporated enterprises or who were principally agrarians – based on the republican fear of concentrated power, monopoly, and corruption. The struggle between larger entrepreneurial investors and producers reflected a dominant producer ideology in which the independence and opportunity of a middling sort of self-employed people or small firm was threatened from above by the corrup-

---

[1] Clifford D. Shearing, "A Constitutive Conception of Regulation," in Peter Grabosky and John Braithwaite, eds., *Business Regulation and Australia's Future* (Canberra, 1993), 67–79, at 72, 74.

tion and avarice of corporate and mercantile capitalists associated with banking, lawyers, and big firms and from below by dispossessed paupers whom capitalists manipulated to undermine republican institutions. During the Civil War era, lawmakers widened the private sphere of property and contract rights. As a result, by the end of the century large-scale corporations and consumer interests emerged which undermined the producer way of life and brought about a reformation of republican values. The triumph of Progressivism after 1900 indicated that the corporate economy had grown beyond the means of the new regulatory order to maintain constitutional and legal accountability, ensuring perpetual clashes between public interests and private rights.

MERCANTILISM AND THE ORIGINS OF THE CONSTITUTION

Before Independence and the Constitution created an independent and more united nation, British mercantilism governed the American economy. At least until the sequence of crises that between 1764 and 1776 culminated in the Revolution, the British Navigation Acts provided the American colonists with a protected international market within which each colony was relatively free to develop its own domestic economy. Under the system of mercantilism Americans had known for over a century, the prices of goods and services, market entry, the number of participants, and quality control were subject to oversight from small numbers of public authorities. In addition, according to mercantile theory, wealth was fixed. A nation's or state's share of wealth could and should be increased, however, through the promotion of exports and the protection of home enterprise from foreign competition in order to attain a favorable balance of trade.

The Revolution thus instituted a distinctive pattern of multi-state mercantilism shaped by a fragmented institutional regime. The American mercantilist order was distinctive primarily because it required formulating a new constitutional principle of sovereignty. In order for a rule or policy to be legitimate it had to rest upon a sovereign authority. Starting with the Greeks, classical political theory assumed that sovereignty was unitary. Thus in Europe sovereignty resisted either in a central government, as in England's King and Parliament, or in the separate states belonging to a confederation or empire. As a result of the struggle for Independence, however, Americans began thinking about the possibility of dividing sovereignty *between* national and state governments and *among* separate state governments. As a republic, sovereignty in the new American nation resided ultimately with the people; accordingly, the people theoretically possessed the authority to divide sovereign power between and among two levels of government. But since such a regime of dual sovereignty had never existed before, conflicts over the character and limits of each government's lawmaking authority were inevitable. The first phase of struggle culminated in the Constitution of 1787.

Following Independence the mix of each state's promotional and protectionist mercantilist policies varied. Massachusetts's brand of mercantilism gave bounties to producers of lumber, fish, and potash while it facilitated small-scale manufacturing through a combination of import duties, grants of monopoly to individuals, and public aid to private enterprise. The New York legislature empowered a Chamber of Commerce to impose quality controls upon the production of wheat and flour and the promotion of a wide range of manufactures. The state employed protective tariffs and bounties to encourage the production of hemp and iron. It also granted John Fitch the steamboat monopoly and supported the survey for what became one of the nation's foremost publicly funded transportation projects, the Erie Canal. The leading staple-producing regions enacted elaborate systems for quality control and protection from competition. Through an inspection and branding system Pennsylvania regulated the production of flour and other manufactured goods for domestic use and foreign export. Southern tobacco-growing states instituted a system of public warehouses, controls governing product quality and exports, inspection laws, subsidies of preferred crops, container-size regulation, and prohibitions against certain exports. During the 1780s these states also provided inducements for the construction of their own fleet of ships to overcome dependence upon the foreign carrying trade. In the Carolinas and Georgia similar regulatory regimes applied to the production of rice, indigo, and naval stores. In all states private enterprise owned roads, ferries, bridges, and grist mills. Not unlike later-day public utilities, these were subject to community control by local authorities.

The outcome of this state-based mercantilism was mixed. In 1786 there were 2,397 small factories operating in Massachusetts, producing a value of goods which was three times the total annual production of all the New

England states prior to 1776.[2] The tobacco growers' attempt to end the post-war price decline by constructing their own ships failed, however. The mercantile regulations nonetheless stimulated each state's productive enterprise sufficiently that local rather than national economic development prevailed. Americans enacted protectionist programs in part to retaliate against market restrictions the British imposed following peace. Interstate rivalry also encouraged protectionism. Tariff wars were not a problem, since most states formally exempted the products of neighboring states. Still, states did promote their own citizens' economic activity by using preferential enforcement of regulatory regimes to increase the costs of doing business for foreign traders and producers.

A particularly significant form of protectionism involved debtor–creditor relations. At the time the Constitution was conceived British merchants had extensive claims against American staple producers, particularly tobacco planters; these claims extended to the American mercantile interests and property holders serving as the merchants' credit intermediaries. Various states including Virginia and North Carolina enacted confiscation and sequester laws to protect debtors; at the same time state courts and juries generally decided against foreign creditors. In addition, state and local governments defended their debtors from American creditors residing in other states. Under the Articles of Confederation, Congress established a tribunal to adjudicate commercial and admiralty cases, but it did not offset the states' protectionism. At the county level local courts and juries were sufficiently independent that they too performed a protectionist role. In Virginia, Patrick Henry and a gentry-debtor faction dominating the local system successfully resisted James Madison's efforts to institute a less preferential judicial order. Similarly, Shays' Rebellion in 1786 may be seen as an attempt by western Massachusetts farmers to keep Boston merchants from using the local courts against them.

Debtor–creditor disputes reflected diverse property-rights claims. State legislatures enacted a variety of stay and moratoria measures that enabled debtors to postpone (sometimes indefinitely) payment of debts. States also enacted legal tender and paper money laws, which both fostered an inflationary currency and disrupted property rights generally by devaluing the

---

[2] According to John J. McCusker, the U.S. price index in 1776 was 105 and in 1786 was 114, indicating relatively modest change in the "real" value of money. I am grateful to Professor McCusker for this point. The source for the change in the value of goods between 1776 and 1786 is Forrest McDonald, *Novus Ordo Seclorum: The Intellectual Origins of the Constitution* (Lawrence, 1985), 102–3.

currency in which the law required contracts to be paid. In New York, Rhode Island, North Carolina, and other states, legislatures defeated judicial attempts to defend creditor rights. In some cases legislatures removed the judges and passed measures that directly or indirectly overruled the courts' decisions. Similarly, conflicts among debtors and creditors working through legislatures and courts influenced the demise of the Bank of North America. James Wilson and Alexander Hamilton attempted to defend the Bank and its stockholders when the Pennsylvania legislature repealed its charter and the shaky authorization from Congress proved ineffectual. Despite each man's efforts, the state's authority ultimately triumphed over contract and property rights.

The diverse legal rules protectionism facilitated reflected innovation and American singularity. During the time the Constitution came into being, the law governing contractual relations was in some manner more advanced, but in others more backward than that of Britain. The pervasive debtor–creditor struggles that characterized America indicated a more tolerant view toward indebtedness and business failure than that which prevailed in Britain. The British social class system, combined with less representative legal institutions dominated by large land holders, subjected debtors to stricter rules that reflected the assumption that debt default was a form of moral degeneracy. In America by contrast, representative government was sufficiently democratic that most debtors were also voters. As result, although debtor–creditor law incorporated some of the stricter English doctrines, the general policy embodied the assumption that most debtors were merely unlucky, and therefore, should be treated leniently. Similarly, the American law governing debt default was more egalitarian than its English counterpart, which often worked to the advantage of smaller, property-holding producers.

Yet even in routine, less contentious, contractual obligations the rules that applied to sales of goods were distinctive in America. In the forms of commercial paper such as bills and notes that were transferable from party to party under the principle of negotiability, American law was generally more creative in that, compared to Britain, assignment laws were more liberal. Americans also developed new forms of negotiable paper such as the chattel note; the defenses of bona fide holders were also stronger, and the dependence upon credit paper was correspondingly much greater. Also in contrast to Britain, the specific doctrines determining how extensive assignment should be, or the status of claims raised by other parties against bona fide holders involving fraud, not only varied *among* states but also were often conflicted *within* a given state.

American law governing contracts that were not negotiable, by contrast, lagged behind Britain. Under the old common law of medieval England numerous encumbrances existed upon contractual transactions, including the provision that a contract could be voided on the ground simply that it was unfair. The underlying concern about fairness grew out of the ancient doctrine of just price. Similarly, the civil law that dominated continental Europe protected the buyer from the predations, ignorance, or incompetence of the seller by following the principle that all sales contracts carried implied warranties ensuring the quality of traded goods. By the mid-eighteenth century Lord Mansfield was moving British law toward a new intentionalist theory, which required only that the parties arrive at a "meeting of minds." Mansfield's theory favored *caveat emptor* – "let the buyer beware" – over the impled warranties doctrine and rejected the moral values implicit in just price. American law, however, resisted the new contract theory generally and Mansfield's innovations in particular. Just as most Americans deferred to Montesquieu on broad issues of constitutionalism, they agreed with him that it was "absolutely necessary there should be some regulation in respect to . . . all . . . forms of contracting. For were we once allowed to dispose of our property to whom and how we pleased, the will of each individual would disturb the order of the fundamental law."[3]

American innovativeness was perhaps most evident in the area of property law. In the lives of Americans no corpus of legal rules was more important than that regulating the possession, transfer, and descent of real and personal property. Most of this corpus involved the status of land. The fundamental working principle governing all property, but most importantly land, was that ownership was *not* absolute. The classic treatment of property rights in English common law by William Blackstone significantly influenced the Framers of the Constitution. Blackstone began by proclaiming that as an abstract principle individuals exercised dominion over property. He then spent nearly 500 pages setting out all of the exceptions to the principle.

From the start, then, Americans understood property rights in terms of a bundle of shared claims among debtors and creditors, producers and

---

[3] Charles Louis de Secondat, Baron de Montesquieu, *The Spirit of the Laws*, translated by Thomas Nugent (New York, 1949), 43.

capitalists, and comparatively more egalitarian social-class groups generally. In Britain these claims involved a relatively small group of landlords of high social class ruling masses of tenants. Not only was land much more abundant in America, but it was also comparatively much more widely distributed among middling sorts of people, and tenancy was not dominant. As a result, by the time of the Constitution state legislatures and courts gradually had eradicated forms of title associated with elite families holding many large estates. Thus in America, partible inheritance of smaller claims among family members displaced the English rule of primogeniture (descent through the oldest son) and entail, which limited inheritance to only the owner's lineal descendants. Despite the dominance of the husband in marriage through coverture, moreover, it was comparatively easier in America for wives to hold property title through trusts and pre-nuptial agreements. Under *feme sole* trader laws American women also had greater rights in the conduct of commerce. Other innovations included the invention of the mechanic's lien, which protected small suppliers and artisans, the homestead exemption, which benefited most small property holders, and the triumph of the tenancy in common, which liberalized the transfer of land.

Innovation and state intervention also had contradictory consequences. English law did not sanction slavery. The "peculiar institution's" existence in America thus depended entirely upon the legislation and common law of each state. As a result, by the time of the Philadelphia constitutional convention Pennsylvania and other northern states, influenced by evangelical Protestant doctrines, free labor values, and Enlightenment teachings began a gradual movement for abolition. At the same time, slaveholders in most southern states remained sufficiently unaffected by foreign religious, philosophical, or free labor tendencies that they linked their support for constitutional reform to the defense of slavery. This divergence in the systems of property law governing labor fostered sectional tensions. Congress prohibited slavery in the Northwest Territory in 1787. In the unorganized territory south of the Ohio river, however, the law sanctioned the institution despite tangled land titles resulting from the old claims of Virginia, North Carolina, and Georgia. Meanwhile, throughout the rest of the country government strengthened the stability of land claims through another American innovation, the registry of titles, through means of a local recording system. Similarly, more so than was the case in Britain, state and local governments made taking property through eminent domain contingent upon a locally controlled assessment process.

The legal institutions with which the Framers were most familiar were also rooted in the local community. Despite sporadic resistance to English forms following Independence, and persistent suspicion of lawyers, Americans adopted the fundamentals of English procedure: the jury, the grand jury, writ, summons, written pleadings, and oral testimony. Yet because widespread property ownership corresponded to a broader distribution of political power among merchants, artisans, and agricultural groups, American legal process was speedier and cheaper, if more haphazard, than that of Britain. Especially in leading towns the bar was well trained and professional, though entry was much easier in America than it was in Britain. Laymen, too, exercised considerable influence throughout the American judicial system, and arbitration remained a meaningful alternative to the adversarial process.

The American judicial system was also less autonomous and more integrated into the community. Contrary to Lord Mansfield's displacement of the jury by the judge, American juries remained central to popular control of the legal order, deciding questions of both law and fact. County courts were the basic governing agency of day-to-day American life, responsible not only for administering justice but also the general enforcement of the mercantilist system. A pyramid of trial and appellate courts existed in each state, as did such specialized tribunals as admiralty and, outside New England, equity courts. An appeal meant, however, that essentially the whole case was tried again. In addition, ever since the Privy Council periodically had disallowed legislative and judicial decisions during the colonial era, Americans had had experience with some sort of judicial review. But because state legislatures freely intervened in the judicial process from Independence on, neither judicial review nor the principle of an independent judiciary upon which it depended was clearly defined.

The ideologies of the founding generation generally assumed that property rights were subject to considerable popular control. Americans knew that the teachings of John Locke made government interference with property the primary justification for the right of revolution. Still, the goal of the Lockean revolution was the restoration of a "neutral" judge, which in turn made preservation of property rights contingent upon the sort of government intervention that was consistent with enforcing the regulatory values of the just price. Americans also adhered fundamentally to various strains of civic humanism associated with republicanism. Each strain of republicanism sanctioned extensive government intervention to maintain a broad distribution among middling property holders against a perceived conspiracy perpetuated by mercantile and corporate capitalists, their "bloodsucking" lawyer allies, and dispossessed paupers they manipulated to corrupt civic virtue and republican liberty. In addition, some framers were acquainted with new theories of political economy identified with Adam Smith, Sir James Steuart, and others. These theories rejected mercantilist assumptions in favor of the belief in growth attainable through an exchange economy. Proponents of the new theories disagreed, however, as to how far government should intervene to foster economic growth. Thus while Steuart's reliance upon government intervention in the economy through the Bank of England ranked him among mercantilist theorists, he also departed from that tradition in his recognition that economic growth was the ultimate goal of such intervention. Steuart shared with Adam Smith this new awareness of the importance of economic growth. Even Adam Smith countenanced limited forms of mercantilist regulation where it fostered the dominance of agricultural producers over merchants and manufacturers, as had been the case in America under the Navigation Acts.

Incompatible ingredients thus characterized the institutional and ideological experience the Framers carried to the Philadelphia and Ratification conventions. In order to enact and enforce rules governing property and contract rights within an institutional order in which separate state and national governments coexisted, Americans following Independence struggled to develop a new constitutional principle of dual sovereignty. The conflict was exacerbated, not only by the subordination of a national regime to thirteen sovereign states pursuing their own mercantilist policies, but also because within each state local authorities were the agents of community control. The relatively widespread distribution of property, upon which rested a comparatively broad franchise, encouraged interest-group conflicts that limited the autonomy of both state and local officials. New theories of political economy, Lockean contractarian values linking the right of revolution to the maintenance of fair property relations, and the republican belief that a conspiracy of corrupt, exploitive capitalists and dispossessed paupers threatened the civic virtue and commonwealth liberty of middling, property-holding producers from above and below, further influenced the course of struggle. One outcome was that property and contract claims were always contingent and fluctuating. Another result was that compared to Britain, American legal rules were distinctive, often either more innovative or backward. Yet another consequence was that American courts and lawyers did not adhere strongly to the

British common law doctrine of *stare decisis*, according to which precedent controlled like cases.

At Philadelphia the Framers resolved these incompatibilities through two conceptual breakthroughs resulting in a new federalism. As noted above, from the ancient Greeks to the Enlightenment, political theorists assumed that sovereignty upon which any government rested was unitary. In the British empire the King in Parliament was sovereign, and under the Articles of Confederation sovereignty resided in the states. The Framers transformed federalism by giving the people the authority to divide sovereignty between national and state spheres coexisting within the same public space. The first conceptual breakthrough making possible this new federalism was that through a bicameral legislature the national government would at once rest upon individuals and incorporate the states without altering the basic structure of the states themselves. Accordingly, the Constitution was not a Lockean contract between the people and their sovereign. Nor was it a league of distinct, sovereign states. Rather the Constitution was a compact among indigenous political societies composed of numerous local communities exercising popular authority through such local institutions as the jury or specially called constitutional ratifying conventions.

The second conceptual breakthrough was a single executive, which also influenced the constitution of the judiciary. Selection of this single executive was dependent upon electors in the states, while the office's power was separated from and yet shared with the Congress. Thus the states as sovereign entities had a role in checking federal power through the selection process, while within the federal sphere itself the executive and legislature checked each other. The interaction of these checks and balances influenced the nature of the judicial branch. The formation of the judiciary and the scope of its jurisdiction were left largely to Congress, while the president appointed judicial officials. Consistent with the weak distinction between trial and appellate jurisdiction prevailing in the states, judicial review was implied but not explicitly stated. The clause making federal laws and treaties supreme in the state courts suggested that state decisions regarding national or constitutional issues were subject to review by the federal judiciary. But the Framers' failure to enumerate a specific power of judicial review meant that whether or not the judiciary would establish the authority was left to the future.

The Framers attempted to further check and balance power through the principle of enumeration. Following Independence, the central problem mercantilist regulation of property and contract rights raised was that of keeping government intervention accountable. Multiple rules applied to the various levels of lawmaking institutions constituting the American polity. The legitimacy of those rules in large part depended upon whether public officials were accountable to community interests and private rights. The republican fear of corruption and the Lockean search for a neutral adjudicator of fair property rights, as well as the selective reception of the diverse market goals of the new political economists, indicated, however, that the substantive standards defining the scope and limits of formal accountability were indeterminate and generally contingent upon shifting interests. In the Constitution the Framers addressed the interrelated issues of legitimacy and accountability primarily by enumerating or listing powers one by one, such as the taxing and commerce powers. The limits of this authority were nonetheless ambiguous because of the general grant contained in the necessary and proper clause.

Particular proscriptions also defined the scope of federal power. Congress could not interfere with the slave trade before 1808, prefer one port over another in commercial regulations, enact ex post facto laws or prevent jury trials in criminal cases, nor impose duties on interstate shipping. Congress was, however, given the power to impose taxes and to regulate domestic and international trade, including by implication the imposition of protective tariffs. The precise limits of the tax and commerce powers, particularly as they related to foreign trade, were nonetheless unclear. Although Hamilton argued that under the two powers Congress was authorized to enact tariffs, most Framers rejected Hamilton's contention on the ground that such policies were not specifically provided for in the powers enumerated in Article 1, section 8. Adhering to the same enumeration principle, the Framers also denied to Congress the power to tax exports. Specific provisions making possible federal payment of the national debt and constituting a slave three-fifths of a person for purposes of taxation and representation further prescribed the boundary of the federal sphere.

The Framers also used the enumeration principle to define the reach of state power. The federal authorities were involved in the enforcement of the states' slave codes under the fugitive slave clause. The states' role in the electoral college and their representation in the senate also influenced the growth of slave and free labor systems resulting from congressional control of the territories. The states formally were prohibited from taxing or restraining interstate or foreign commerce; their coining money, emitting bills of credit, making anything but gold or silver coin legal tender, or enacting ex post facto laws were also forbidden. The meaning and limits of these prohibitions were unclear, however, as the contract clause suggested. Article 1, section 10 stated that states should not impair the obligation of contract, but it was an open question whether the clause applied to ordinary private agreements between individuals only or also included those involving states as parties to land grants, state control over corporate charters as a form of contract, and legal tender laws as they affected the rights of debtors and creditors. During and after the Constitution's ratification the Framers kept an oath not to discuss their actions at Philadelphia. This silence, along with the incompatible ingredients underlying the Framers' compromises, ensured that conflict more than consensus would influence the Constitution's impact on the future course of the nation's business law and economy.

LAW AND THE PRODUCER'S ECONOMIC ORDER

Between 1789 and 1860 the governmental institutions shaping the American economy remained small, but their influence upon the economy was significant. In 1790 expenditures of state and local government were approximately only 3 percent and expenditures of the federal government less than 2 percent of the national income. As a percentage of the national civilian work force public employees did not exceed 2 percent, while the number of civilian federal employees averaged only about 50,000 – the vast majority being in the postal service. Throughout the next 70 years these figures changed little, maintaining a size that was considerably smaller than the governmental establishments of either Britain or continental Europe. The leading American lawmakers, moreover, were courts and legislatures subject to the world's most extensive democracy. Meanwhile, as the new American brand of federalism evolved, state and local governments established wider direct influence over the economic order than did the national government.

The "new" federal system of dual sovereignty provided conflicting incentives for individual and group action. On the formal institutional level, the largest policy issues involved the scope and limits of federalism. Political parties, the federal and state governments generally, and the Supreme Court in particular were the primary institutional channels through which ideological and social conflicts shaped economic policy-making. Throughout the period before the Civil War, the role and authority of these constituent institutions changed. Especially after 1815, the states displaced the federal government as the primary stimulators of economic development. The Supreme Court gradually acquired significant authority as the umpire of the federal system, but its rise to leadership ultimately accommodated and sustained the states' policymaking dominance. Political parties were the principal articulators of group interests and values. Even so, especially in the states local control was such a strong force that usually politicians could implement policies only by compromising their party's principles.

Institutional conflict reflected a producer ideology that favored both the promotion and protection of economic opportunity. Both the labor theory of value and the Old Republican commitment to personal independence were vulnerable to the aggressive and exploitative individualism identified with corporate and mercantile capitalism. In addition, corporate and large mercantile capitalist enterprise tied principally to the national market threatened the locally oriented market relations of unincorporated, producer enterprisers. True, the specter of business failure and the corresponding loss of independence haunted producers and capitalist groups alike. Yet merchant and corporate capitalists possessed financial advantages attained through risk, economies of scale, and political and legal influence that smaller-scale producers generally lacked. The threat to producer independence that these market and political advantages represented, more-over, seemed very great. So great that it was understandably difficult for average producers to conceive that they had the same economic opportunity as the corporate or mercantile capitalists. It was this abiding fear that politicians articulated in their public discourse.

Offsetting the producer's market weakness was his political influence. The central place that producers occupied in the public discourse of the period suggests the priority they were given as voters in the minds of elected public officials. At least insofar as this franchise democracy was an accurate measure of political clout, moreover, producers actually controlled juries and other local governmental institutions. None of this denies the obvious power that corporate and big mercantile capitalists possessed in American politics. On the contrary, the convergence of these large-scale capitalists' market and their political dominance compelled producers to employ a discourse that proclaimed the need to check both public and private power. As a result, producers appealed to the values of legitimacy and accountability inherent in the constitutional ideal. The practical form that this appeal took may have been simply attacks upon aristocracy, monopoly, and corporations. But the ideological force of such attacks derived from a popular faith that to be legitimate, power had to be accountable to external authority.

Prevailing constitutional and legal interpretations fostered a new mix of national and local rule-making authority. As the sectional struggle between the advocates of free and slave labor ideologies suggested, prior to 1860 state-based policymaking dominated the economic order. The resulting pressures facilitated the gradual emergence of an independent judiciary as the primary arbiter of constitutional and legal interpretation. Several factors suggested why American judges possessed so much more authority than their counterparts in other nations, including Great Britain. First, state and federal constitutions established the judiciary as coequal with the legislature and the executive, giving judges new legitimacy as law makers. Thus, American judges were not only independent like English judges; they were agents of the Constitution itself. Second, unlike the other branches of government that expressly represented groups, the courts were the only constitutional authorities formally responsible for articulating the interests of individuals. Third, constitutions were written documents that, like contracts, not only invited but often required judicial interpretation. Fourth, judges belonged to a legal profession that, despite recurring public criticism, possessed considerable social status and market power. Indeed, Alexis de Tocqueville intimated, judges and lawyers held more power in America than in any other nation. Taken together, these factors constituted a distinctive market for legal services that empowered individual litigants to assert particularistic demands, not only against the routine policies formulated by larger groups through legislatures and other representative bodies, but also to challenge the very constitutional foundation upon which that policymaking authority rested.

Nevertheless, American judicial supremacy emerged unevenly. In the states election of judges gradually became the norm: in 1850 alone seven states altered their laws to make the judiciary responsive to popular majorities. The federal judiciary often worked against these popular tensions. But political pressures arising from congressional control of jurisdiction and (at least under the Jeffersonian Republicans) the threat of impeachment meant that, as Tocqueville observed, the federal judiciary's general impact on the states was indirect. The democratized social basis of state and local legal institutions also provided repeated opportunities for lawyers to defend the constitutional ideal of legitimacy and accountability. Even so, notwithstanding the claim of Tocqueville and others that antebellum lawyers constituted a bulwark of conservatism, there was a growing diversity in the market for legal services.

The decentralization and constitutionally circumscribed autonomy of American lawmaking institutions facilitated lawmakers' discretion. Despite the persistence of legislative reform efforts identified with codification, such procedural basics as the law of evidence became intricate, balkanized, and more complex than the English counterpart, largely because Americans had a greater anxiety about centralized power. Thus in civil cases antebellum American courts eventually followed the policy pioneered by the eighteenth-century British judge Lord Mansfield of making the jury responsible for the facts while the judge controlled the law. Yet unlike the more flexible hearsay rules existing in England, the American business entry rule gave juries more access to records made in the regular course of business, even though technically they were hearsay. As a practical matter, the American rule opened to the public view of jurors the private affairs of business people. Similarly, American judges continued to have less regard for *stare decisis* than did English courts, even though such laxity compounded the diversity of legal rules within each state and throughout the federal system as a whole. One way to read these changes was that juries gradually lost their role as agents of local communities, increasingly becoming subject to judicial direction. Such a view, however, insufficiently takes into account the institutional linkages between local popular democracy and an indigenous courtroom culture that emerged before the Civil War, reflecting and expressing a multiplicity of community values and interests.

Before 1860 these rule-making institutions shaped a course of American economic development that was singular. The entire Atlantic world was undergoing the general process known as industrialization, and in Britain, other European nations, and the United States the agricultural sector persistently diminished in importance, as the relative number of farm workers declined. In the antebellum United States, however, despite this relative decline the amount of cultivated land, the number of workers, and the agricultural sector's output remained sufficiently strong that producers continued to think of themselves as the leading sector. During the decade of the 1840s the growth of the manufacturing sector's output was also impressive, rising by more than 150 percent. A source of conflict was a local and national market structure coexisting within sectional specialization. Thus although the rough profile of a capitalist industrial order was gradually emerging, involvement in the market existed along a continuum ranging from those engaged more in local activity to those whose enterprise was nationally and even internationally oriented.

The interaction between diverse market relations and rule-making institutions engendered ideological conflict. While they acknowledged the value of laissez-faire individualism and natural rights in the abstract, most political leaders and lawmakers contended that the producing classes were most important to American prosperity. This ideological separation of producers and capitalists assumed a tripartite social-class struggle. Capitalists were above and dispossessed paupers occupied a place below the middling classes, who more or less corresponded to the producers. This "middling sort" valued modest economic independence based on honest individual labor over the extremes of capitalist wealth or desperate pauperism. Eventually these producer values were amalgamated with evangelical Protestant moralism, providing a basis for the free-labor ideology that prevailed by the Civil War.

These institutional and ideological pressures shaped the federal government's distribution of public lands. Beginning with the Northwest Ordinance, despite persistent corruption and exploitive speculation producers identified with capitalist avarice, federal authorities gradually evolved a land distribution policy that progressively increased the access of small holders to more land at declining prices. The government also allocated land to promote education and, intermittently, the construction of roads, canals, and railroads. Meanwhile, an ongoing controversy involving squatters who asserted claims under the doctrine of adverse possession contributed to what Lawrence Friedman has called the "traumatic weakness of land titles."[4] Compounding the problem were legislative majorities in states such as Kentucky and Tennessee that successfully defied Supreme Court decisions favoring nonresident claimants. The Preemption Act of 1841 aided further the instability of land titles by indirectly authorizing multiple title claims in adverse possession cases and by encouraging "claim clubs," which were cartel-like organizations protecting the first arrivals from later arrivals. Miners adopted customary codes enforced by community sanction to achieve similar ends. Ironically, even the federal sanction of local registration of property titles fostered disputes because it provided lawyers the means to determine claims

---

[4] Lawrence M. Friedman, *A History of American Law* (New York, 1985), 432.

through litigation in courts which, like legislatures, often were influenced
by local bias.

Federal policy toward property rights had special significance concerning slavery. The Supreme Court sanctioned the expansion of slavery into
the territories in *Dred Scott v. Sanford* (1857). But antislavery defenders
and abolitionists resorted to defiance justified by a contrary constitutional
interpretation grounded upon personal liberty laws and the supremacy of
states' rights. Finally, the opposing theories regarding slave property highlighted the consequences of the South's losing its sectional advantage
within the national government to the Republicans in the election of
1860, bringing on a tragic civil war.

The law of private property reflected a similar tension between promotion and protection. Throughout the period leading to the Civil War
the American facility for creating distinctive rules by simplifying English
forms continued. The reverse side of disputed land titles was the ease
with which title was transferable, something American lawmakers fostered
by reducing the complex English law of conveyancing to two basic forms:
the warranty deed and quitclaim deed. Americans further reformed
property rules that tested title to land by replacing the maze of technical
English land actions with the single action of ejectment. Lawmakers
throughout the Union also adopted the mechanic's lien, an American
device invented in 1791 giving small-scale artisans a claim against the
land and improvements a land owner contracted for if he or she failed to
pay. As a technical legal matter mechanic's lien laws gave artisan bills
first claim against the estate of a debtor. Yet because business failure was
so pervasive in antebellum America, the right claim represented significant interest-group empowerment consistent with the protectionist values
of the producer ideology. The homestead exemption, a Texas innovation
that removed from the claims of creditors various kinds of property
involving basic necessities for productive labor, also spread. Boston merchants pioneered the dynastic trust; on the basis of the "prudent investor"
rule it gave trustees long-term discretionary authority to change portfolio
investments on a scale unmatched in Britain and in most of the United
States. Lawmakers also strengthened family property and at least partially
weakened the husband's control under coverture by enacting laws that
insulated married women's property from the claims of her husband's
creditors. Other innovations that broadened family property rights were
adoption (an American invention), secular forms of marriage, and easier
divorce laws. In the area of intellectual property Congress and the federal

courts strengthened the patent holder's monopoly by liberalizing licensing rules.

The law of mortgages suggested how readily American property law shifted between promotion and protection. Throughout American history land security was tied primarily to mortgages. Especially before the Civil War America's pervasive dependence upon credit, the widely believed chronic scarcity of specie currency frequently commented upon in commercial journals, at least until the Gold Rush, and the recurring cycle of boom and bust placed rules governing mortgages at the center of struggles between debtors and creditors. Since the colonial era American legislatures and courts had attempted to balance debtor–creditor rights. In the case of *Bronson v. Kinzie* (1843) the Supreme Court overturned as contrary to the contract clause an Illinois law that virtually prevented creditors from foreclosing on existing or future mortgages. Yet in less extreme cases the Court also generally sanctioned reducing the liability and vulnerability of debtors.

Similarly in the South, the property claims of landowners yielded to herdsmen. By the early nineteenth century the herding of livestock was not a primary economic activity in the North; but it remained so in the South. Thus under the common law adopted by many northern states stock owners were obligated to fence *in* their animals, whereas the law of most southern states required farmers to construct fences around their fields to keep wandering stock *out*. As a result of this divergence in property rights a sort of public domain existed in which landless stockmen could maintain large herds of animals at little direct cost. Mississippi, Georgia, and Alabama courts required even the railroads to recognize the herdsmen's rights.

There was also a significant protectionist dimension to the law of eminent domain. The delegation to private developers of the right to take private property for public use was undoubtedly important to the process of industrialization and the rise of capitalism. Yet at least during the initial stages of railroad and canal construction before 1860, federal and state constitutional provisions required that neither the government nor private corporations could take property without paying "fair compensation." Accordingly, the exercise of eminent domain was contingent upon the mode of assessing property values. The Marshall and Taney Courts sanctioned state constitutional rules legitimating the competing market interests of both property owners and developers. The constitutionally imposed trade-off between corporate privilege and obligation often enabled the

majority of small property holders to use the process to their advantage in
the name of local control.

During the antebellum period the law governing contracts also acquired
greater significance. Gradually, the moral strictures identified with just
price gave way to Lord Mansfield's intentionalist theory, embodying the
principle of *caveat emptor*. Still, the transition was slow and selective. Until
the Civil War the rules governing such areas as credit instruments, bankruptcy and insolvency, corporate charters, and leases developed more fully
than those including labor relations or common sales agreements between
two parties. Suggestive of the general trend was the change in the lease
from a document of property tenure to a basic commercial contract in
which the tenant's rights eclipsed those of an English-style landlord.
American contract law retained distinctive qualities in part because
federalism perpetuated rule diversity between and within states. Similarly,
the federal judiciary strengthened constitutional protections and, at least
within the federal sphere, uniformity of contract rights; simultaneously,
however, the Supreme Court extended the states' regulatory authority
under the police power.

As was the case in property law, recurring clashes between debtors
and creditors shaped the course of change. British social-class and moral
presumptions categorized bankruptcy as pernicious, sustaining clear and
strictly enforced rules favoring creditors. In the credit-based American
economy, where failure was common, and where debtors not only far outnumbered creditors but also possessed considerable clout within democratic politics, however, contract rules were more flexible and supportive
of debtors. State legislatures regularly considered and granted private
petitions exempting from debts small enterprisers and large mercantile
capitalists alike. Most states also enacted laws that, unlike Britain, gave
debtors the right to initiate insolvency proceedings. The intricacy, multiplicity, and diversity of rules facilitated sharp dealing and pressures for
federal action. Particularly controversial was the practice whereby insol-
vent or bankrupt debtors could prefer certain creditors, while others
received nothing. Such problems led to repeated appeals from big-city
mercantile capitalists for national laws, but except for two temporary measures in 1800 and 1841, Congress did not act. Taken together, the Supreme
Court's *Sturges* and *Saunders* contract clause decisions of 1819 and 1827
restricted the state legislature's regulatory authority over commercial contracts to those agreements made *after* a debtor–creditor law was passed. As

a result, American contract law was more than its British counterpart protective of debtors generally and bankrupts in particular.

The intentionalist principles underlying *caveat emptor* were bent in other ways, particularly concerning negotiable commercial contracts. The widely perceived scarcity of specie and the fact that most bank notes significantly depreciated beyond local limits meant that the economy depended principally upon commercial credit paper. Moreover, credit reporting agencies were underdeveloped. For practical purposes, then, credit exchanges represented by innumerable negotiable bills of exchange and promissory notes constituted the nation's medium of exchange, nationally and locally. Although Britain relied upon such forms of commercial paper, the social-class system and narrower elite control of banking institutions made the credit structure there less vulnerable to political pressures than in America, where credit was central to many of the leading struggles of democratic politics. Unlike Britain, too, the rules governing negotiable paper were more variable because of federalism. American law also enlarged this medium of credit exchange by extending the principle of negotiability beyond British doctrinal limits to include new forms of commercial paper such as municipal and corporate bonds, the bank certificate of deposit, bills of lading, the check, chattel notes, and even negotiable instruments payable in such valuables as "good merchantable whiskey."

American dependence upon credit also resulted in the steadily growing use of accommodation paper. Among the most important uses of credit that negotiability made possible were long-term loans known as accommodations. Commercial credit extended through the medium of negotiable paper by a lender to a borrower purely to raise money or to obtain a further extension of credit was an accommodation loan. Such loans involved no actual exchange of any valuable consideration; they represented merely the borrower's use of the lender's name to bolster his or her credit standing so that he or she could borrow more from third parties than otherwise would have been possible. Many accommodations were exchanges between family members or longtime associates who knew each other well. In such cases the motivations for extending credit often were rooted in social relationships. But it was also not uncommon for merchants and banks to make accommodation loans to strangers based solely on the word of others; here the motivation was more explicitly capitalistic since the borrower received credit only because the lender expected at some point to make a profit. *Hunt's Merchants' Magazine* described the distinction between the two forms of accommodation: one was "a matter of honor, of personal favor," whereas the other represented "a matter of business in a technical sense."[5]

As with other credit transactions, accommodation loans were the object of controversy. Many enterprisers, including producers, favored this form of credit because it enabled the individual holding accommodation paper to borrow more than was otherwise possible. But such uses of credit were also potentially objectionable because they were often employed for fraudulent purposes. Of course, what was in fact a fraud was not always clear. In either case, because of distance and the underdeveloped nature of credit reporting, nonresidents involved in accommodation loans were often least capable of judging the validity or worth of such transactions. This was especially true of large urban merchants who had extended accommodation loans to numerous debtors in smaller communities.

Federalism inhibited standardization of rules governing the rights and obligations of parties to negotiable contracts. State courts generally enforced commercial contract law leniently, especially where nonresident merchants or corporations challenged local business. The emergence of the federal judiciary's general commercial law culminating in *Swift v. Tyson* (1842) did not destroy local control of negotiable credit paper. On the contrary, it created a dual credit market: the federal courts aided interstate credit transactions while the state legal institutions protected locally oriented market relations. Similarly, in the famous decision of *McCulloch v. Maryland* (1819), the Court upheld the Second Bank of the United States (BUS) over the state's defense of local credit controlled by local banks.

Andrew Jackson's veto of the "monster" Bank did not diminish the Court's defense of congressional authority over the national credit market. The end of the BUS, however, strengthened the competitive advantage of state banks within local as well as national markets, which in turn facilitated the protectionist credit policies favorable to small as well as large debtors and enterprisers involved in both markets. Thus in the *Alabama Bank* case of 1839 the Court attempted to curb state protection of local banks from foreign competitors. The Court's regard for federalism and states' rights was sufficiently strong, nonetheless, that the principle of comity that the decision established limited states only if they consented to follow it. Accordingly, states continued to defend local banks. More broadly, there were powerful strands within Jacksonian ideology that

---

[5] "Ought Certain Creditors to Be Preferred in Making Assignments?" *Hunt's Merchants' Magazine* 7 (1842), 274.

assumed the dominant social and market importance of "independence" and the producer values it represented. Indeed, the opportunistic accommodation of state banks that Jacksonian economic theorists William M. Gouge and Condy Raguet made after Andrew Jackson vetoed the charter renewal of the Second Bank of the United States should not obscure the degree to which even on the bank issue the antimonopoly crusade epitomized the antebellum political culture's preference for protecting small-scale producers over corporate and mercantile capitalists.

That banks were often condemned as villains obscured the offsetting benefits even opponents recognized. Debate in the Pennsylvania constitutional convention of 1837–38 suggests the terms of the controversy. Few described the threat more pungently than C. J. Ingersoll, who condemned state-incorporated banks as "a vast fungus grown upon government, upon property, upon liberty, and equality, by which the common welfare is thoroughly affected." Yet there were undeniable benefits arising from state-incorporated banks. These institutions, observed one delegate, "assisted much in developing the wealth and resources of this great state." Banks were "essentially instrumental in establishing and sustaining our useful manufactures. They have contributed largely by their loans to build our towns, to construct the turnpike roads and other public improvements which now distinguish our commonwealth." Such defenders of incorporation recognized the need for banks to serve the many groups that constituted society. "The man of small means, as well as the capitalist, may vest their money in . . . a corporation, so as to afford credit to a community. . . . The business and transactions of banks are for the accommodation of *all*."[6]

These ideological constitutional and political considerations converged on the issue of taxation. As the controversy over banks grew following the proliferation of bank charters during the early nineteenth century, the call for taxation also increased. Most citizens, especially farmers and the modest mercantile and industrial proprietors who comprised the bulk of the region's property holders, resisted taxes. The absence of any general tax levy between the end of the Revolution and the War of 1812 encouraged the belief that revenue needs could be met through special taxes. At the same time, there was growing popular demand for a public school system. Lawmakers responded to these pressures with a special tax on banks. Although the precise terms varied from state to state, even from charter

---

[6] As quoted in J. Alton Burdine, "Government Regulation of Industry in Pennsylvania, 1776–1860" (Ph.D. diss., Harvard University, 1939), 45–46.

to charter, there were continuities among the school tax provisions. During the period for which the charters were granted, the banks were required to pay an annual tax, usually based on a percentage of paid-in capital. Placed in a distinct and separate fund in the state treasury, the revenue was invested and credited to the counties for the purpose of establishing free schools. Banks paying the tax were often exempt from other kinds of taxation, and in addition their charters were extended for as long as twenty years.

The most distinctive dimension of American contract law was the protection granted corporations under the contract clause. As the *Sturges, Saunders,* and *Bronson* decisions of 1819, 1827, and 1843 indicated, the Court used the Constitution's contract clause to circumscribe state authority over *private* contracts. The Court's more controversial strand of contract clause decisions involved *public* contracts, such as Marshall's overturning of the Georgia legislature's massive invalidation of corrupt Yazoo lands sales to innocent third parties in *Fletcher v. Peck* (1810). Subsequent litigation resulted in the *Dartmouth College* case of 1819, in which the Marshall Court interpreted the contract clause to include corporate charters as well as private contractual agreements. Although this extension of the contract clause was probably contrary to the original intention of the Constitution's Framers, it had enormous significance for the power that states exercised over the corporations they chartered. Potentially, corporations gained the same rights that individuals possessed under private contracts.

The Court, however, mitigated the pro-corporate potential of its public contract clause decisions. In *Dartmouth College* and other cases the Marshall Court held that states could formally reserve regulatory powers in the corporate charters they granted. This dual sanction of rights and regulatory authority established the constitutional boundary for political and legal clashes involving the trade-off between corporate privileges and obligations. Accordingly, from early in the nineteenth century, states included in bank, railroad, and canal charters the requirement that they pay taxes or tolls to support education, the operational expenses of government, and other social services. True to the Jacksonian Democrats' antimonopoly tradition, the Taney Court enlarged the states' regulatory authority. Beginning with the *Charles River Bridge* decision of 1837, it expanded the limits of the "reserve" power, thereby enlarging the states' ability to both promote new technologies such as railroads while also protecting local producer interests. By the 1850s the Court attempted to strike a balance similar to that worked out with regard to private contracts under the contract clause. States were empowered to include wide-ranging taxes and other requirements at the time they granted corporate charters. But subsequent lawmakers, including state constitutional conventions, generally could not then alter or enlarge upon those obligations except at the point of charter extension. The process the Court sanctioned gave constitutional legitimacy to interests who demanded alteration of the charter; accordingly, this course of decisionmaking politicized the states' process of incorporation, particularly at the point when a charter was originally granted or came up for renewal.

As a result, the traditional image of legislatures giving capitalist developers overflowing privileges was confirmed but incomplete. Less conspicuous yet no less important was the likelihood that the intensity of the bargaining process not only ensured that offsetting obligations were written into charters but also that those provisions would be enforced. Interest-group pressures exerted within legislatures and through the courts ensured that banks complied with provisions that required that they underwrite economic development in marginal as well as main market areas by purchasing stock in manufacturing and transportation companies. Banks also complied with charters stipulating that a percentage of bank loans must provide farm mortgages at low interest for producers or generous terms of credit for small as well as large contractors constructing canals, railroads, and related improvements.

Similar trade-offs between protection and promotion applied to transportation firms. Until the Civil War canals, railroads, turnpikes, and bridges – including such powerful incorporated capitalist enterprises as the Baltimore and Ohio Railroad and the Pennsylvania Railroad – developed routes through not only prosperous market areas, but also marginal ones as well. Transportation companies also paid toll taxes, which funded much of the public education in certain states and underwrote the operation of government. As a result, states significantly reduced reliance upon property taxes. New Jersey's notorious Camden and Amboy monopoly was a case in point: in return for the lucrative monopoly of the trade between New York City and Philadelphia the corporation paid about 10 percent of its profits as a toll tax, which funded between 60 and 90 percent of the state government's costs. The mix of trade-off policies varied from state to state, but virtually everywhere the farmers and other modest-sized producers constituting the majority of voters had good reason to condone and support the enforcement of the taxation of corporations.

The Supreme Court's commerce clause decisions affirmed the states' primary control of this trade-off making authority. In spite of his ringing defense of the federal commerce power in the Court's first decision involving the clause, *Gibbons v. Ogden* (1824), for instance, Chief Justice John Marshall formally recognized that a state's police power could reach interstate trade. Thus even though the Court defeated New York's steamboat monopoly in *Gibbons*, through the doctrine of selective exclusiveness the Court gradually formalized the dormant commerce power principle, upholding a state's regulatory power over markets touching interstate or international trade. Similarly, the long-term consequences of the tug and pull between the Court and Congress in the lengthy *Wheeling Bridge* litigation of the 1850s ultimately balanced the interstate interests of steamboats and railroads, protecting the steamboat's competitive opportunities.

Ultimately the Court sanctioned a state police power sufficiently wide to sustain the popular faith that producer and capitalist values were compatible. Until the 1860s state or local governments controlled large blocks of stock in transportation and other corporations, limiting the board of directors' decisionmaking authority. In addition, most private investors bought shares to avoid rather than assert investment and operational control over the corporation. Thus, although the law permitted a single stockholder to block any major financial decision, usually public rather than private stockholders were most active. Corporate directors challenged the public stockholder's influence, but state courts usually decided for the public. Similarly, early in the nineteenth century state and federal courts evolved the business interest rule, which provided that directors acting in good faith and with due care were not liable for losses caused by their errors in judgment. As originally formulated the rule meant that under special charters directors were insulated from dissident shareholder claims that they had gone beyond the powers formally granted by the charter. Nevertheless, the rule did not protect directors from the *ultra vires* doctrine and *quo warranto* proceedings, which largely determined what constituted an unlawful act.

Other state and federal rules limited corporate autonomy. State courts held that principles of fiduciary duty applied to corporate directors, requiring that they pursue the stockholders' interests according to stricter morals than those of the market. According to this moralistic reasoning, fiduciaries should possess values of honor, religion, and paternalistic duty transcending the narrowest pecuniary interest. As such, judges reflected the influence of people such as Stephen Colwell, an iron and steel manufacturer with close ties to the Presbyterian Church and Princeton Theological Seminary, who, like political economist Henry Carey, attacked "selfish, non-Christian individualism and competition under a socially irresponsible form of 'capitalism.'"[7] In addition, the Supreme Court's decision of *Dodge v. Woolsey* (1856) established the derivative lawsuit, encouraging shareholder litigiousness. The *Swift* doctrine established the basis for a uniform commercial law that could reduce the costs that the states' multiplicity of legal rules created for corporations doing interstate business. Yet, because the Court did not extend to corporations the full scope of federal jurisdiction, corporations were only beginning to benefit from the *Swift* doctrine before the Civil War.

During the antebellum era an increase in personal injuries identified with industrialization made tort law more important. Negligence doctrines developed unevenly among the various states, but the moral cause of injury or damage resulting from some fault was central to the negligence approach to liability. Coincident with the emergence of negligence a dual legal market for lawyers' services arose. Some plaintiff's lawyers represented victims before sympathetic local courts and judges, while corporate attorneys defended the enterprises causing injury and death. Encouraging the suits of victims was the contingent fee, which in England was illegal. In America, however, the practice meant that an injured plaintiff's attorney got nothing if he lost; but if he won, the fee amounted to a large percentage of the settlement. As early as the 1850s railroad managers noted that in order to avoid contingent fees in accident cases, they agreed to out-of-court settlements. Before the Civil War a minority of accident cases involved injured workers, but most litigants were members of the general public. Even so, most courts applied negligence doctrines in favor of injured plaintiffs while those same courts usually also decided against workers. Thus non-worker victims usually won recovery. Ultimately, attaining morally responsible and accountable conduct was of greater importance to most courts than shifting the costs of development from capitalists to weaker groups. In keeping with the prevailing producer and republican ideology, legal rules struck a balance between the promotion and protection of economic opportunity within a divided institutional order.

---

[7] Paul Conkin, *Prophets of Prosperity: America's First Political Economists* (Bloomington, IN, 1980), 281.

EXPANDING THE SPHERE OF
PRIVATE RIGHTS

Between 1860 and 1900 small businesses, farmers, and the growing class of consumers feared increased market vulnerability. The diffuse and predominantly agrarian market of the antebellum period gave way to a new, more integrated urban industrial order characterized by large corporations. Rural population increased by nearly five million during the 1880s, but urban population jumped by eight million, resulting in a drop of the proportion of rural Americans from 72 percent in 1880 to less than 65 percent in 1890. This decrease was greater than in any other ten-year census period in the nation's history. At the same time the frontier, at least in terms of the U.S. census, closed, limiting a vital possibility of improved opportunity, though, of course, much open land remained. By the 1870s the construction of 114,000 miles of new railroad track facilitated the nationwide distribution of goods. Yet farm and mercantile groups in localities on the margin of the expanding interstate rail network felt threatened by high rates resulting from underdeveloped service and competition with cheaper long-haul traffic. Similarly, the appearance of numerous technological advances facilitated the spread of the factory and of mass production, enabling a single firm to increase its potential rate of production greatly, and thereby supply the needs of the rapidly growing urban market.

As a result, the role of government slowly grew. As a fraction of GNP total local, state, and federal expenditures increased to about 7 percent by 1900. Pressures for expansion were felt largely at the local and state level, though the proportion of federal spending also increased in important sectors. By 1900 the localities' proportion of the total was about 55 percent and the states just 10 percent, while the federal government was 35 percent. New York suggested the degree of change in expenditures for regulatory agencies (as distinct from laws as separate means to enforce policy) from $50,000 in 1860 to $900,000 in 1900; during the same period the state's expenditures for social welfare and health rose from $263,000 to $6,500,000.

The Civil War and Reconstruction established the basis for the initial stage of transition at the state level. Decentralization of power remained pervasive. States continued to be relatively free from federal interference in their control of local government, family and criminal law, and (to a degree) commercial credit. Enforcement of Reconstruction measures that allowed for federal supervision of national elections in the South persisted, but declined precipitously after 1880. A vigorous mercantile rivalry continued after 1861 as manifested in discriminatory license fees and tax measures as well as in railroad promotion, aid, and regulation. Moreover, state governments struggled to contain the steady growth of large-scale, nationally operating corporate enterprises and developed their own antitrust policies and, beginning in 1869, commissions to regulate railroads.

After 1861 there was a slow but steady enlargement of federal authority. Early in the war the Republicans implemented the first significant centralization of banking policy since the 1830s, which initiated a nationalization of credit mechanisms and currency that continued unabated into the twentieth century. Similarly, the Homestead Act represented a new approach to the rapid, though guided, settlement of the West. Since the 1790s the federal government's chief sources of revenue had been tariff duties and land-sale receipts; the Civil War years saw, however, the creation of a new fiscal basis with the enactment of a temporary income tax and other new internal revenue measures. As the war progressed there was also a marked increase in civilian federal employees, many of whom staffed such new federal agencies as the Department of Agriculture. Federal charter of, and land grant and bond support for, transcontinental railroad corporations were other major centralizing measures.

The Radical Republicans' efforts to protect the freedmen also ultimately had a centralizing impact. Passage of the Thirteenth, Fourteenth, and Fifteenth Amendments, implementaion of civil rights legislation, and significant extension of the jurisdiction of federal courts fundamentally transformed the federal system. Briefly it seemed that this revolution might at least make possible attainment of legal and political equality for blacks. Political exigencies involving the nation's major parties, the Supreme Court's reactionary treatment of civil rights, and the rise of such brutal groups as the Ku Klux Klan killed such hopes. But the death of one promise opened up the possibility of fulfilling another. By the 1870s, equipped with their enlarged authority, federal judges were more than ever before able to promote economic liberty, based particularly on the Fourteenth Amendment's due process clause. Perhaps no one gained more from the federal court's promotional zeal than national businessmen, particularly corporations. A representative of the Boston and Maine Railroad suggested one reason why this was so: "Passengers who broke a leg would have their damage suits transferred to the United States courts . . . and if exceptions were once taken and the cause carried to the Supreme Court you die before your case is decided."[8]

But the transition from state to national control was gradual. The Supreme Court sanctioned decentralization in such famous cases as *Munn v. Illinois* (1877), which upheld the use of the state's police powers to control businesses "affected with a public interest." Through the police power, and application of the selective exclusiveness doctrine under the commerce power, or doctrinal derivatives of these, the Court also santioned state authority over out-of-state corporations. The supreme tribunal also persisted in allowing states wide discretion over eminent domain, although it strengthened the right of just compensation in such cases. Simultaneously, however, the Court and Congress enlarged national authority. In *Pensacola Telegraph Co. v. Western Union* (1877) the Supreme Court upheld congressional power over such new technologies as the telegraph. The justices also affirmed as constitutional the use of the federal taxing power for regulatory purposes. On the whole, especially after the mid-1880s, the Court construed the commerce clause in favor of increased federal power.

Social and economic dislocation transformed the ideology and economic theory legitimating law and government action. The producer ideology identified with "middling" small property interests and republican values that had reconciled protectionist and promotional policies under the vague rubric of laissez-faire before 1860 gradually declined by the 1890s. Natural law assumptions underlying legal and economic theories persisted, but were being displaced by the more pragmatic and instrumentalist thinking encapsulated in Oliver Wendell Holmes Jr.'s famous epigram that experience rather than logic was the "life of the law." Adam Smith's moralistic, natural law assumptions sustaining classical economics were increasingly challenged by neoclassical theories of marginal utility proposed initially by certain theories of Alfred Marshall and developed further by A. C. Pigou and others, according to which the desire of consumers rather than the cost to producers determined value. Unlike their British counterparts, American economic theorists embraced at the same time both neoclassical and moralistic assumptions. The emphasis on utility provided a new basis for government policies and legal rules favoring the interests of consumers and market efficiency, facilitating a re-working of republican values that linked faith in active government to the fear that corruption threatened the individual independence and community

---

[8] As quoted in Edward Chase Kirkland, *Men, Cities, and Transportation: A Study in New England History 1820–1900*, 2 vols. (Cambridge, MA, 1948), II, 19.

accountability upon which democracy depended. Increasingly, only farmers identified with the older producerism that the Populists advocated. Indeed, as the defeat of the Populists' platform in the election of 1896 indicated, an agrarian-based program had little resonance for the growing ranks of urban consumers, including industrial and white-collar workers. Similarly, although the supporters of laissez-faire defined in terms of Social Darwinism were sometimes conspicuous, their practical impact on formal policymaking was, according to Herbert Hovenkamp, little more than an "exaggerated vogue."

Conflicting pressures also influenced the uneven development of formal lawmaking institutions at all levels of government. Relying upon the ubiquitous police power the Court initially broadened the public interest doctrine of *Munn v. Illinois* (1877); accordingly, state legislatures responded to particularistic interest-group demands by delegating new authority to public utility commissions. As a result, railroads and other interstate businesses confronted increasingly diverse administrative policies. In addition, protectionist influences often continued to dominate local government, elected judges, and juries within the states. These and other institutional conflicts stimulated the gradual expansion of federal administrative authority, including funding of the transcontinental railroads, the Interstate Commerce Act of 1887, the Sherman Antitrust Act of 1890, and the Bankruptcy Act of 1898. Congress also extended the right of those engaged in interstate business to remove cases from state to federal courts, fostering tension between state contract and tort rules and the federal common law built up around the *Swift* doctrine.

Multiplicity of rules and institutional fragmentation persisted in the regulatory order that had emerged by 1900. The Supreme Court's uneven restriction of railroad commissions' efforts to determine rates was perhaps the most conspicuous instance of conflicted regulatory policymaking. But other sectors, ranging from banking and insurance to occupational licensing and the regulations governing railroad workers, also came under contested and correspondingly restricted bureaucratic control. Legislatures also assigned public regulatory power to private voluntary associations such as the commodity exchanges governed by the Chicago Board of Trade. The interest group demands and ideological appeals stimulating the expansion of state and federal regulation thus fostered successful countervailing pressures for its limitation.

Property law reflected local diversity, even as it became more routinized and the public lands decreased. In the west the distribution of free land under the Morrill Act, the Homestead Act, and the allocational policies of land grant railroads were the last major federal programs implementing land distribution as the nation's open land declined and the frontier gradually came to an end. Federal law continued to govern water, grazing, lumbering, and mineral rights in the region. Federal conservation and similar policies adopted by the states perpetuated public land. Generally, however, state common law and statutes evolved along an uneven course toward rules in which private market relations rather than government interests governed property possession and transfer. State courts sanctioned new tools of land-use control leading to the preservation of exclusive neighborhoods. Similarly, local diversity meant that English doctrines fell before such innovations as the "spendthrift trust" doctrine, which greatly extended a beneficiary's protection from creditors. The use of charitable trusts increased, while the rules involving landlord and tenant, as well as those ameliorating the tangle of land titles, became more standardized. Despite the enactment of federal bankruptcy legislation, the rise and fall of the business cycle encouraged vacillating policies toward debtor–creditor rights under mortgages. Virtually all states attempted to protect small property holders through various exemptions. As the social independence of women slowly increased, the use of dower and protective trusts declined. Even so, within each state there was enough predictability that, at least regarding its possession and transfer, stability more than conflict determined basic property rights.

By 1860 the idea of contract had generally defined property rights, but the substance of disputes was changing. The intentionalist theory prevailing during the middle of the nineteenth century had given individuals considerable freedom to make choices. As industrialization advanced during the second half of the nineteenth century the content of contractual disputes gradually changed. Fifty-four of the contract cases the Wisconsin Supreme Court decided during the decade before 1861, for example, involved land. Thirty-one others dealt with the sale of domestic animals or the wheat crop, rather than manufactured goods. The status of sureties who signed bills and notes gave rise to thirty-one cases concerning credit and finance. Relatively uncomplicated labor disputes were at issue in thirty other cases. By the turn of the century industrialization transformed the court's docket. Specialized businesses such as real estate brokers suing for their commissions represented the largest proportion of suits, while individuals and small firms identified with agriculture hardly appeared at all on the docket. Large-scale corporations litigated only the exceptional contract issue.

Similarly, prior to the Civil War negotiable bills and notes were the types of contracts at once most central to the economy as a medium of exchange and most bedeviled by diverse rules. From the 1860s on the federal government's banking and currency policies steadily diminished the reliance upon negotiable paper as a medium of exchange. By contrast, the regular contractual uses of bills and notes remained vital and subject to considerable litigation. America continued to innovate beyond British practice, creating new forms of negotiable paper, including municipal bonds, which as a result of *Gelpke v. Dubuque* (1864) pitted pro-debtor local governments against national and international creditors whose rights the Supreme Court ultimately vindicated in some 300 cases between 1860 and 1900. Meanwhile more than any other area of contract law by the end of the nineteenth century, negotiable paper law was becoming uniform as states began adopting a standardized Negotiable Instruments Law prepared by the Conference of Commissioners on Uniformity of Law.

Other innovations in contract law facilitated standardization and rationalized business practice. The old common law did not allow a third party to a contract to sue and collect from a buyer on a claim established by the original seller. Under the third-party beneficiary rule adopted by the new Field Codes of many states, however, the right to sue and collect was transferable, greatly extending the right to buy and sell within the market. A new law of damages also emerged in many states by the 1860s. Rules governing breach of contract permitted recovery of only economic damages, unlike tortious wrongs for which punitive damages were recoverable. Judges left the determination of those economic damages to the jury. But gradually courts began systemizing the rules for calculating damages by taking into account such factors as "natural consequences," damages that contracting parties may have been expected to foresee and thereby should have reasonably attempted to avoid. As a theoretical matter, the doctrine made contracting parties liable only for foreseeable or natural consequences. In actual practice, many exceptions weakened the doctrine because what amounted to a judge's measure of foreseeable harm was often quite variable and dependent upon the jury's perception of specific facts. Nevertheless, the policy drift was toward greater predictability of contract doctrine within most states.

The tension between predictability and exception was perhaps most evident regarding the venerable doctrine of *caveat emptor*. By the Civil War era the rule making the "buyer beware" had given the American law of sales contracts distinctiveness as a separate field of commercial jurisprudence. English cases determining who bore the risk as a matter of title favored the seller, particularly manufacturers and merchants. In America the nation-wide distribution of mass-produced durable goods such as machinery created new pressures requiring courts to adjust the balance between buyers and sellers. As a result, an American treatise on sales published in 1888 recognized various independent rules and doctrines which in practice limited *caveat emptor* and favored the concept of *implied warranty*. Marketing goods by sample "implied" a warranty that the sample was representative of the whole. If the reasonable presumption of conformity proved false, the buyer possessed a right to sue because the implied warranty was breached. Initially the market factors facilitating the growth of the doctrine influenced primarily the sale contracts for manufactured goods. But gradually the doctrines circumscribing *caveat emptor* facilitated the emergence of various standardized installment contracts throughout the distribution system. The law of sales slowly and unevenly accommodated the era's dominant consumer groups – small traders and farmers.

In other areas of market relations the law worked to balance the interests of new producer and consumer groups. Throughout the states there was persistent demand for repeal of regulated interest rates maintained through usury laws. Despite sporadic short-term successes, however, debtor interests usually prevailed and the free trade argument against laws prohibiting usury failed. Meanwhile, insurance companies attained enormous control over credit as financial intermediaries, and corporate lawyers drafted standardized contracts to protect the industry from consumer interests. But ultimately state legislatures and courts developed a complex body of regulations that broadly shifted the balance in favor of policy-holders. The right to remove cases to friendlier federal courts, according to Edward A. Purcell, Jr., initially gave the companies an advantage they used to force policyholders to accept "ruinously" discounted settlements: policyholders received less than was their due under the policy itself, and the settlements were smaller than those a state court would have awarded. By 1900 plaintiffs' lawyers nonetheless had learned to use state regulations and friendlier U.S. Supreme Court decisions to counter this advantage. Similarly, the passage of federal bankruptcy in 1898 did not displace state laws that at least in the long run tended to benefit debtors. The federal law excluded corporations, extended the right of voluntary bankruptcy, gave special priority to protecting wages due workmen, clerks, or servants, and did not end the most important state exemptions. Creditors could not force the law on a "wage earner or a person engaged chiefly in farming or the tillage of the soil." Unlike national bankruptcy regulation in Britain, American debtors and creditors generally used bankruptcy as a standard business device.

Thus the rules defining property rights possessed a contractual content partially consistent with laissez-faire values. The core common-law rules pertaining to damages, offer and acceptance, parol evidence, and contractual interpretation were either standardized by statute or eroded by exceptions. Accordingly, contract law prescribed a market place for individual choice that only the exceptional case meaningfully tested. The standardization of property rights enforced through the Fourteenth Amendment's due process clause and based on laissez-faire "freedom of contract" theories undoubtedly increased the exploitation of ever growing numbers of vulnerable workers because the law's underlying premise was that employers and employees stood on equal footing when in fact they did not. Yet, the great mass of middle-class property holders, consumers, and smaller enterprises benefited from this same predictability, creating a legal order in which more groups gained market opportunity than often was true in other nations. At the same time, formulation of property rights under contract doctrines enlarged individual dependence upon private enforcement through the courts and an adversarial process controlled by lawyers.

The regularization of ordinary property and contract rules contrasted starkly with the conflicted transformation of corporation law. As long as the rights pertaining to corporations depended on the special charters of each state, smaller unincorporated enterprises had leverage over legislatures and courts to enforce regulatory policies. The Supreme Court's contract and commerce clause opinions and other police power decisions directly or indirectly sanctioned such policies before the Civil War. The significant organizational pressures arising from the Civil War era, however, encouraged states more than ever before to replace special charters with general incorporation laws. By the 1870s these laws existed throughout the nation. The Supreme Court held, moreover, that corporations possessed a constitutional status that for jurisdictional and litigation purposes was like real persons, a position strengthened by the decision of *Santa Clara County v. Southern Pacific Railroad* (1886). As a result, corporations gained increased access to the enlarged jurisdiction of the federal courts and the laissez-faire "freedom of contract" theories enforced through the Fourteenth Amendment's due process clause, the *Swift* doctrine, the commerce power, the contract clause, and other doctrines. In addition, except for such enterprises as certain transcontinental railroads and national banking, there was no federal incorporation. In Britain and most other industrializing nations only national incorporation existed. Dependence upon the states rather than Congress for the formation of corporations thus inhibited regulatory uniformity and fragmented interest-group pressures pushing for regulation. At the same time the independence of the Supreme Court and the federal judiciary encouraged corporations to challenge state regulatory policies on the basis of constitutional provisions or – as occurred in the bond and insurance contract cases – the general commercial law identified with the *Swift* doctrine.

Legal and constitutional changes in corporation law fostered the emergence of managerial capitalism. As Alfred Chandler has shown, market demand and technological innovation promoted the rise of large-scale corporations, in which by the 1880s and 1890s salaried managers gradually exercised greater control than individual entrepreneurs or stockholders. An uneven mix of state laws generally outlawed looser organizational structures maintained through cartel practices, but, beginning with the New Jersey law of 1889, permitted mergers in the form of holding companies. The Supreme Court's initial interpretation of the Sherman Antitrust Act during the mid-1890s sanctioned a similar policy result. This interplay of state and federal rules thus facilitated managerial centralization in the great turn of the century merger wave. From the 1870s on, moreover, the Supreme Court interpreted the commerce power and the due process clause of the Fourteenth Amendment to establish boundaries around the state's use of the police power to regulate corporate enterprise. The Court affirmed more police power regulations than it invalidated, upholding especially laws aimed at hazardous industries such as mining. But the Court's restrictive interpretation of the Interstate Commerce Act of 1887, like that of the antitrust law, suggested a larger policy outcome in which the scale of corporate enterprise exceeded the ability of the emerging regulatory state to maintain legal and constitutional accountability consistent with popular perceptions of community welfare or the public interest.

Enlarged constitutional protections and general incorporation laws that weakened regulation coincided with doctrines favoring managerial autonomy. States enacted laws aimed at insider managers and promoters who cheated, requiring payment for all capital stock to be in "nothing but

money" or at "par value." The policy intent was to outlaw the sale to innocent investors of watered stock, stocks sold on the market which insiders
took in exchange for fictitious values. Ultimately, however, the law held
corporate managers to only a "good faith" standard that, along with the
proliferation of speculative investors in the open market, eroded the mean-
ingfulness of a fixed or par value. Encouraging the looser standard was the
practical reality that if investors, speculative or not, regarded a certain
stock as being worth, say $40 a share, it made no market sense to enter it
on the corporate books at the $100 par. Similarly, state lawmakers increas-
ingly held corporate managers to a standard of fiduciary duty defined under
the business interest doctrine as "reasonable." Most state courts interpreted
reasonableness to sanction expanded managerial autonomy. The overall
outcome was to raise the threshold of provable culpability, one consequence of which was to insulate managers from stockholders' suits. In
Britain, by contrast, a stricter fiduciary duty prevailed, and stockholder
class actions remained as they had been in antebellum America, a more
effective regulatory tool.

Other doctrines enhanced managerial control. When corporations
failed, especially during the two depression eras of the late nineteenth
century, the Supreme Court interpreted the "trust fund" doctrine to benefit
the authority of managers over stockholders. Often, managers could negotiate settlements that often were more beneficial to larger stockholders
than the more numerous small stockholders. The federal judiciary's
increased use of the equity receivership, particularly in railroad cases,
further increased managerial control. Federal judges held managers to the
flexible reasonableness standard of the business interest. The growth of
managerial autonomy also undercut the venerable doctrine of *ultra vires*,
the English principle that voided corporate transactions found to be
"beyond the powers" of the charter. In the long run most American legislatures and courts construed the powers permitted under general incorporation laws so broadly that *ultra vires* became irrelevant.

The new corporate economy brought gains and loses. Fiscal policies
remained favorable to the majority of voters in the sense that even the
states friendliest to corporations such as New Jersey and Delaware gained
profit from the volume of taxes. In tougher states progressive tax programs
achieved public profit also. In either case corporate tax policies reduced
reliance upon property taxes, benefiting the middle class. In addition,
despite the incentives for corruption, the rules fostering managerial autonomy often facilitated organizational efficiencies such as economies of scale,

which in turn benefited consumers. The federal judiciary's adoption of the labor injunction in 1895 as a result of the Pullman strike, by contrast, extended corporate managers' power over organized labor. Also, the Court's *Plessy* doctrine of 1896 broadened railroad managers' authority by allowing them to impose upon African American travelers in the South the separate but equal doctrine.

Tort law further suggested how diverse rules fostered a divergent pattern of winners and losers. During the antebellum period, the negligence system gradually displaced the English common-law emphasis upon procedure, which had left the determination of tort liability to the jury. By 1860 objective rules such as contributory negligence and assumption of risk gave the judge authority over the law, while the jury remained responsible for establishing facts. The shift from jury to judge was especially damaging to workers under the fellow servant rule, which sanctioned tort actions in accidental suits against negligent coworkers, but in such cases did not hold employers accountable. These and other negligence doctrines potentially permitted corporate defendants to transfer the costs of death and injury to plaintiffs, who tended to be employees or members of the public such as railroad passengers. Despite the formal simplicity and harshness of negligence doctrines, however, the general policy results were mixed. Quantitative studies of trial outcomes and decisions by appellate courts revealed consistently that in tort litigation plaintiffs more often than not won. The exception were plaintiff workers suffering from the fellow servant rule. But even here, by the end of the century treatise writers and scholarly empirical studies showed that courts were limiting the doctrine.

Tort rules also differed within states as patterns of pro-plaintiff or pro-defendant counties often existed. In addition, there was persistent disagreement among the federal courts, reflected in a shifting majority on the Supreme Court concerning what negligence rules federal judges should apply under the *Swift* doctrine. As was characteristic of insurance contracts, defendants initially used the threat of removal to force smaller settlements upon plaintiffs. Yet by the 1890s plaintiffs' lawyers won decisions from the Supreme Court that were more favorable. On the whole, then, the negligence system facilitated diverse enough results that a plaintiff's market for legal services existed in which personal injury lawyers relying on contingent fees succeeded more than they failed against corporate defendants.

By 1900 the legal rules governing the new corporate economy continued to define a fragmented regulatory order. Constitutional limitations the courts imposed upon state and federal administrative agencies, and the changing doctrines enhancing managerial autonomy, constituted an uneven, often contradictory, mix of lax and restrictive policies. Managers and their lawyers regarded some states as tough and others as friendly. The federal government developed increased regulatory potential as well as opportunities for countervailing interest-group pressures and federal court litigation. Workers, racial minorities, and women were generally losers. In addition the sheer multiplicity of channels by which interest groups articulated demands encouraged the pervasive corruption identified with the Gilded Age. Nevertheless, rules fostering the growth of managerial capitalism also benefited middle-class groups in the form of lower consumer prices and new entrepreneurial opportunities under more regularized contract and property law. Accordingly, a coincidence of altered republican values and new marginal utility theories sustained the popular faith that increased regulation and more stringent law enforcement was not part of America's problem but necessary for the solution.

PROGRESSIVISM AND THE CORPORATE ECONOMY

From 1900 to 1917 the Progressives narrowed the gap between regulator and regulated. The great turn of the century merger wave resulted in an economic order dominated by large-scale corporations. The Progressives nonetheless established the course of bureaucratic institutional development that resulted in consumers displacing producers, thereby enlarging the boundaries of the institutional order governing private market relations. The Supreme Court in turn balanced the limitations imposed by late-nineteenth-century laissez-faire constitutionalism against the growth of the regulatory state; but despite important exceptions, the drift of decisionmaking favored the latter. Meanwhile, elite professional legal groups broadly associated with Progressivism pushed for increased rationalization of judicial and regulatory institutions, increasing the systemization and uniformity of contract, tort, and property rules. By World War I the scale of the corporate economy still exceeded that of big government, but the path of institutional change that during the 1930s would culminate in New Deal Liberalism clearly was emerging.

The growth in government expenditures as a proportion of GNP involved relative expansion of federal authority. The growth of government expenditures as a proportion of GNP rose from about 7 percent in 1900 to about 40 percent in 1990. This involved a relative expansion of federal expenditures, from 35 percent of all government expenditures in 1900 to 45 percent in 1940, and 60 percent by 1990. Most of the peacetime change in the magnitude of the share of federal expenditures occurred after the Progressive era. Still, the Progressives' expansion of the federal bureaucracy established the future pattern. Between 1901 and 1917 Theodore Roosevelt, William H. Taft, and Woodrow Wilson proposed differing Progressive agendas. As a result, Congress enlarged federal control over antitrust (with the Federal Trade Commission and Clayton Act), food and drugs, seamen's working conditions, labor–management relations and rate setting in the railroad industry, child labor, farm credit, and perhaps most significantly through the new Federal Reserve System, currency and credit. New policies required a concomitant expansion of federal bureaucracy, emphasis upon civil-service merit systems, and reliance upon experts and technical expertise. The influence of policymaking technocrats cut across formal divisions of federal, state, and local authority. The bureaucratic process thus transcended formal political boundaries, facilitating a new cooperation between state and federal agencies, highlighted by the national highways law of 1916.

The Progressive brand of big government was consistent with the triumph of pro-consumer ideology. Following 1900, pragmatic and instrumentalist conceptions of law and society triumphed over natural-law and individualistic modes of thinking and classical economic theories that had sustained producer values. In accordance with marginal utility economics, Progressives placed the consumer, and to a lesser extent such technical experts as the engineers Thorstein Veblen thought were best suited to manage American social and regulatory institutions, rather than the producer at the center of the American economic order. Among agrarian and radical-labor groups traditional producer values persisted. These values were clearly marginal, however, to the growing urban economy in which Progressive political leaders represented white- and blue-collar workers against ethnic machine politics and big corporations. Progressives reworked traditional republican values opposing monopolies and corruption to argue that unregulated corporate giants gained vast profits at the expense of consumers. Simultaneously, they said, corrupt machines exploited taxpaying consumers by funding wasteful expenditures that benefited favored individuals and groups. The exploited consumer was the urban or rural middle- and working-class user of goods and services.

Many Progressives, however, like the Populists and their predecessors, favored small-scale units of production. The Progressives' faith in consumer efficiency attained through technicians nonetheless also meant that they recognized a moral distinction between good and bad big firms that could be maintained through regulation. This faith in moral conditions prescribing efficiency standards created contradictory tensions within Progressivism. On the one hand they liked the independence identified with small business; but on the other hand they yearned for the consumer advantages resulting from the efficiencies large-scale, managerially centralized large corporations made possible. Similarly, elite legal professionals supported various programs to rationalize law and to improve the organizational effectiveness and professionalization of government agencies, including the courts. Yet these efforts did not challenge nationwide anti-democratic restrictions of ethnic groups and the perpetuation of Jim Crow segregation in the South. These institutional and ideological tensions inhibited the growth of official authority to match the size of the corporate economy.

The Supreme Court sanctioned increased, if decentralized, state and federal regulatory activism. States protected competing local interests through control over public utilities, bus and truck transportation, and pricing in the retail-store industry. Similarly, after Congress gave the Interstate Commerce Commission the power to set railroad rates, the Court's decisions upholding that power enabled federal and state railroad commissions between 1910 and 1917 to subsidize the rates of small roads at the expense of larger ones. In the field of antitrust the Court adopted the rule of reason the Roosevelt administration advocated. Under the rule of reason federal and state prosecutors attacked corporate concentration generally where it could be proven that morally pernicious practices affected market effectiveness. Bigness in and of itself was not, therefore, bad. This policy blend of moralism and market efficiency broke up true monopoly but encouraged increased managerial centralization identified with oligopoly. At the same time federal and state prosecutors used the Court's per se rule – making most anticompetitive behavior in and of itself unlawful – to prevent cartelization, which often helped small business. Prior to World War I the Federal Trade Commission (FTC), created in 1914, also attempted to use its new investigative authority to aid smaller enterprises. Thus antitrust did not prevent the triumph of big business. But the strict prohibition against cartels and the FTC's policy benefited smaller firms; antitrust also served the interests of consumers by facilitating managerial centralization and economies of scale, which in turn made possible the high-volume production of goods at lower prices.

More so than Britain's, America's regulatory structure encouraged the adoption of incorporation. Britain possessed liberal incorporation laws; its business order also underwent the turn-of-the-century merger wave, though on a smaller scale than that which occurred in America. Nevertheless, unincorporated enterprise, partnership, and looser organizational forms identified with cartelized self-regulation dominated the British economy. Even the largest incorporated British companies were often "confederations" of smaller firms. By contrast, in the United States the number of incorporated companies rose from 341,000 in 1916 to 455,000 in 1926. More significantly, non-corporate proprietorships and partnerships produced just one-third of the nation's manufactured goods in 1904; by the 1920s the total produced by 93,415 corporations was 97.6 percent.

Ironically, antitrust facilitated the triumph of managerial capitalism and large-scale corporations. The Court's formulation of the rule of reason in 1911 – as well as the federal and state courts' consistent enforcement of a per se rule against cartel practices and the liberal merger laws of New Jersey, Delaware, and other states – encouraged firms to adopt tighter organizational structures. During the 1890s the Court's initial interpretation of the Sherman Act sanctioned wide adoption of holding companies as the corporate structure best suited to managerial centralization. The Court's implementation of the rule of reason in 1911, however, demonstrated that a cause of action existed against such merged firms if a link between its internal operational character and pernicious conduct could be proven. Admittedly, establishing such a link was difficult because under the business interest doctrine and other rules, state corporate law gave management considerable legal freedom over the firm's operation. Still, as Neil Fligstein suggested, the weaker organizational unity of the holding company often permitted insufficient coordination of multi-plant production, leading in some cases to predatory pricing practices and divisions of market territories that aroused opposition from middlemen, and ultimately competitors, which in turn led to government or other third-party antitrust prosecution.

After 1911 corporate lawyers increasingly realized that holding companies employing pernicious practices were vulnerable to antitrust suits. As a result, firms were encouraged to acquire greater managerial control over the process of production through tighter merger. By 1917, Chandler observed, most of the nation's largest corporations abandoned the holding company for more concentrated, managerially centralized corporate structures. As in the case of U.S. Steel, one result was increased scale, but these firms also developed market and pricing strategies that were less vulnerable to antitrust challenge. Of course, the formation of a tighter merger required the consent of stockholders. In Britain as well as America, groups of stockholders formed a powerful interest capable of blocking increased managerial control through such mergers. American antitrust law, however, indirectly weakened stockholder influence. Unlike those in Britain, American corporate directors operated within a legal environment in which the tighter the corporate structure the greater was the possibility of avoiding an antitrust suit. Accordingly, directors could use the threat or reality of legal prosecution to justify the need to choose the tighter merger and the increased managerial centralization it required. Such a strategy made it difficult to attain enough votes (usually one-third) to block the merger.

The antitrust prohibition against cartels influenced the movement toward tighter corporate forms in another way as well. In Britain the law governing cartels and the holding company permitted small firms to survive and even thrive. Louis Brandeis and others predicted that the American judiciary's refusal to apply the rule of reason to cartel practices would foster corporate consolidation and the demise of small firms. If the Court reversed this policy and followed British doctrine allowing the enforcement of loose agreements – including vertical restraints such as resale price maintenance (RPM) – Brandeis argued, small business might enjoy scale and organizational economies and still preserve their independence. Accordingly, Brandeis supported the FTC's making information available to small business that aided efficient cooperation and as a Supreme Court justice he dissented from the Court's invalidation of RPM and other vertical restraints. If the British example was any indication, this policy reversal would also have reduced the incentive for government and other third-party suits in cases involving managerially centralized firms because it would have limited the sort of conduct that was held to be unreasonable and therefore illegal. In either case, enforcement of Brandeis's idea would generally have depoliticized small business and reduced the political and symbolic significance of antitrust.

Managerial corporate autonomy further weakened investor ownership in conjunction with the Progressives' enlarged regulatory state. By the end of the great merger wave in 1904 the American middle class more than ever before was investing in corporate securities. Between 1900 and 1922 stock purchasers in corporate securities grew from 4.4 millon to 14 million. The trend toward liberalization of corporate law that facilitated mergers nonetheless also resulted in no-par rules that cut off claims that stockholders were liable for corporate malfeasance or failure. These rules also diluted the shareholder's right to dividends. Yet at the same time, no-par rules got rid of the necessity of an honest corporation's keeping its books dishonestly. On the whole, shareholders enjoyed greater protection in Britain. As a result, by World War I American corporation law sanctioned the growing separation between owners and management. At the same time antitrust law enforced countervailing rules governing managerial accountability that reduced incentives for the more conspicuous forms of culpable conduct prevailing during the Gilded Age.

Second in importance to incorporation was the legislative and judicial monitoring of trade and professional licensing. Generally controlled by state and local authorities, occupational licensing sought to protect consumers, while the trades and professions used it to police practitioners and restrict entry. Despite claims that the policy sanctioned special privilege and monopoly, occupational licensing grew in significance after 1900 in part because it provided formal channels of opportunity for all classes, from barbers to medical doctors. Lawmakers permitted a wide range of private self-governance, though the Supreme Court used the public interest doctrine to determine what occupational categories were constitutional. In addition various public boards provided general oversight within a broad framework of self-regulation. Meanwhile, the Supreme Court upheld congressional use of license taxes to regulate or prohibit wide-ranging endeavors, including oleomargarine, phosphorous matches, and drugs. In certain instances practitioners discriminated, limiting, for example, the entry of African American barbers. Yet like the more conspicuous state licensing of new technologies such as gas, electric, and telephone services, or trucks, buses, radios, and aviation, setting the boundary of private responsibility ultimately was left to judges rather than bureaucrats.

As commercial law underwent increased rationalization, federalism nonetheless enmeshed it in contentiousness. Following British precedent, the National Conference of Commissioners on Uniform State Laws attempted to further the success gained in the field of negotiable paper, drafting between 1905 and 1909 model laws for bills of lading, warehouses receipts, sales, and stock transfers. But while every state had enacted the Uniform Negotiable Instruments Law by 1916, few legislatures adopted the other measures. Similarly, by World War I at least two-thirds of the states had no laws against commercial bribery. Proposed federal commercial legislation failed to pass; meanwhile, the federal judiciary's general commercial law that had grown out of the *Swift* doctrine was the object of repeated, if unsuccessful, attack. After 1900 there was a revival of commercial arbitration; as many as 12,000 disputes were administered in 1910 alone. In 1917 Congress created an arbitration system for maritime and interstate commerce disputes. Still, the arbitration movement made only modest headway against the prevailing reliance upon litigation. Despite the efforts of the Commercial Law League and other groups seeking to reduce fraud, moreover, the administration of federal bankruptcy remained caught in the distinctive American tension between the need to compensate creditors and the willingness to provide debtors a chance to begin again.

Similar tensions limited the rationalization of contract law. Harvard Law School's Roscoe Pound and others identified with Progressive law reform stressed the conflict between consumer and individual interests that American contract law reflected. Since the mid-nineteenth century rules favoring warranty of contract gradually displaced *caveat emptor* in the innumerable business transactions to which middle-class people were party. New York judge Benjamin Cardozo's opinion in *McPherson v. Buick Motor Co.* (1916) indicated the accelerated direction of change during the Progressive era. A defective automobile wheel caused the plaintiff's injury. Under the old privity of contract rule the manufacturer was not liable to a third party, in this case the consumer who had purchased the manufacture's product from a retailer. Employing a creative warranty theory, however, Cardozo established the principle that in modern consumer dealings such as the present case there was no privity of contract, making the manufacturer liable to the consumer for harm resulting from a defective product.

Commentators noted, however, that the adoption of doctrines such as Cardozo's was gradual. Legal scholars discussed beginning a massive campaign to restate the whole law of contracts. But as was the case with the model uniform commercial laws, the states showed little interest in such efforts. Similarly, in the realm of constitutional law the record was mixed. In notorious cases the Court struck down legislative attempts to restrict New York bakers' freedom of contract (in *Lochner v. New York*, 1905) and Congress's efforts to prohibit the contacting of child labor (in *Hammer v. Dagenhart*, 1918). Yet during the same period, the Court upheld state limitation on contract terms employers could offer women working in the laundry industry (in *Muller v. Oregon*, 1908) or men employed in certain hazardous jobs. Despite the freedom of contract doctrine associated with economic due process, the Court also applied warranty theories to allow diverse state regulation of insurance contracts. Thus the *Harvard Law Review*'s summary of development to 1914 stated: "The law ... seems everywhere to be that the legislature may, to some extent, at least, restrict liberty of contract in the supposed interest of the persons restrained ... Complete freedom of contract is inconsistent with the necessity in a highly organized community for legislation to safeguard the public health, morals, safety, and general welfare."[9]

In less conspicuous areas of business the liberty associated with freedom of contract was still more problematic. Southern lawmakers sanctioned the development of contract rules that through the collusion of local law enforcement officials and planters entrapped poor white and African American laborers in an endless cycle of debt. Progressives condemned the practices as modern slavery, the federal government prosecuted it under laws outlawing peonage, and the Supreme Court overturned the state rules in *Bailey v. Alabama* (1911). Nevertheless, the evil continued under the auspices of customary contract relationships. Legitimate market practices arising from national product brands raised other complex contract issues. As growing numbers of nationally advertised brands reached the market, manufacturers attempted to impose tying price agreements on wholesalers, distributors, and retailers. Firms whose products depended on patents employed the same pricing strategy. British courts not only permitted such vertical price agreements, but by 1914 also often enforced them to the point of requiring damages if the contracts were not followed. Despite the support Brandeis and such groups as the Fair Trade League gave the British policy, however, the Supreme Court and various states declared most such pricing agreements to be illegal. The major exception the Court permitted was price fixing associated with the licensing of patented goods.

During the Progressive era tort law also underwent a transformation. The warranty rule of Cardozo's *McPherson v. Buick* opinion weakened the fault principle underlying the negligence system. As courts extended the liability of manufacturers for harm caused to third parties, they moved toward rules favoring strict liability in tort. The biggest change was the weakening of negligence doctrines by the principle of workers' compensation. The federal government adopted the bureaucratically managed

[9] "Extent of the Legislative Power to Limit Freedom of Contract," *Harvard Law Review* 27 (1913–14), 374.

limitation of negligence principles in the Federal Employers' Liability Act of 1908. The Court struck down the first law on the ground that it was too broad under the commerce clause; the Court, however, upheld a more narrowly written statute. Beginning in 1910 states began enacting broader legislation abolishing the fellow servant and assumption of risk rules. Despite some initial judicial attacks and opposition from the labor leader Samuel Gompers, boards or commissions increasingly handled most cases involving worker accidents. They were successful enough that the jurisdiction of the system eventually grew to include white-collar and service workers.

New conflicts involving property law also arose. The standardization of rules governing the possession and transfer of property, begun during the late nineteenth century, continued. Under the Progressives there were nonetheless important innovations that enlarged the rights of elite groups and sanctioned discrimination against minorities. In 1916 New York City enacted the first comprehensive residential zoning plan. Based on the states' police power, the policy reflected the emergence of Progressive urban planning experts within city governments. Progressives throughout the nation followed New York's lead. In part the new zoning rules insulated wealthier property owners from residential growth they disliked. Southern and border states also passed laws authorizing municipal governments to impose plans that formally discriminated on the basis of race. The Court struck down these laws as a violation of economic liberty and property rights protected under the Fourteenth Amendment's due process clause. Ironically, the defeat encouraged a nationwide planning movement to employ private restrictive contracts to prohibit the sale of residential property to Jews and African Americans. These restrictive covenants were symbolic of the distinctive regulatory order constituting American economic development since Independence.

CONCLUSION

Although Progressives trusted bigger government more than did their nineteenth-century predecessors, significant constraints circumscribed that trust. Population and occupational shifts favoring consumers over agrarian and labor producers fostered within Progressivism an ideological tension between rule incentives sanctioning efficiencies derived from large corporations and those enforcing republican values that favored smaller economic enterprise and opposition to concentrated power, corruption, and monopoly. Despite the Progressives' enlarged reliance upon federal bureaucracy, this ideological tension reflected the persistent decentralization of American lawmaking institutions created by the Constitution. As the ongoing existence of Jim Crow suggested, the Supreme Court's general sanction of a more extensive national and state regulatory order did not prevent considerable local autonomy. These decentralist institutional pressures prevented adoption of some but not other rationalizing measures that elite legal professionals proposed. Accordingly, American tort, property, and contract law remained, as it had since the nation's founding, less uniform and more distinctive than its British counterpart. The resulting diversity provided incentives for individual opportunity and group control that kept the scale of government smaller than that of the corporate economy itself, ensuring ongoing conflicts over the character of the American regulatory state.

12

EXPERIMENTAL FEDERALISM: THE ECONOMICS OF AMERICAN GOVERNMENT, 1789–1914

RICHARD SYLLA

The United States has such a complex system of government that a chapter can only begin to describe its nature and relationship to the American economy. Fortunately, the system itself was stable, holding throughout the 125 years from 1789 to 1914 to an essentially republican form at the federal, state, and local levels, a form that continues. Even the Civil War, great as it was on the scale of wars and bound up as it was with the moral issue of slavery, was waged to decide what history might regard as a minor issue – whether there would be two republics of American states or one. Larger issues of monarchy versus republic or of dictatorship versus democracy did not arise. These were settled by 1789, perhaps even earlier. Such stability, provided it is purchased at not too high a cost in money or freedom, may well be one of the greatest services any government can render its economy and its people. If so, Americans during their "long" nineteenth century were, with the exception of 1861–1865, indeed fortunate.

Because this long-term stability of governmental arrangements in the United States had favorable implications for economic activity, some attention ought to be given to how those arrangements came to be in place by 1789. This is done in the following section. Next is a section contending that, besides providing stability in governmental and political institutions, the federal system from its inception operated to promote a high rate of economic growth by augmenting the economic resources – the land, labor, and capital – available to the economy. In any full accounting of the unprecedented economic expansion of the United States, it is important to recognize government's role in establishing propitious initial conditions.

The third major section of the essay deals with long-term trends in the overall size of the governmental sector and its federal, state, and local components; the ways in which these component governments divided the responsibilities of government; and how each component financed its activities. A fourth section describes how the components of the federal system worked together through time to sustain the momentum of economic development, a theme that has not received the attention it deserves.

The fifth and final section treats the Civil War and the postbellum decades. The war's outcome established at last the supremacy of the federal government promised in the Constitution but resisted throughout the antebellum era. It also brought a host of financial and other public-sector initiatives with varying degrees of staying power. The war without doubt and in many ways changed the country. Its impact on the federal system, however, was less than might have been expected, which itself is a tribute to the stability of the governmental arrangements put in place seven decades earlier. Changes in, and greater centralization of, the economic functions of government would have occurred even if the southern confederacy's rebellion had not broken out after Lincoln's election in 1860. Many of them were responses to long-term economic developments unrelated to the war, such as urbanization and increases in the scale of enterprise.

By the late nineteenth century, government's developmental efforts were less needed, in part because of the successes they had achieved. American government therefore turned more toward regulating by legislative and judicial actions the huge economy it had helped build, and it began to expand governmental responsibilities in new directions increasingly demanded by members of an increasingly wealthy, urban, industrial society. The scale of American government in relation to the economy would increase greatly after 1914. But most of its modern functions that are often thought to have been the result of the increase in government's scale were already present in one form or another by that time.

AMERICAN GOVERNMENT BEFORE 1789

Tocqueville, the noble and wise French visitor to the United States in the 1830s, wrote a classic book based upon his experiences, *Democracy in America*. In it he made an important point about the new nation that so fascinated him. It is worth recalling. "The political existence of the majority of the nations of Europe," he wrote, "commenced in the superior ranks of society and was gradually and imperfectly communicated to the different members of the social body. In America, on the contrary, it may be said that the township was organized before the county, the county before the state, the state before the union."[1] Tocqueville was thinking about New England in this passage, which would not be strictly accurate if applied to all the regions of the early United States. But he was substantially correct.

The system of American government – the federal system – was built from the bottom up, and one cannot understand the way the system functioned since its inception in 1789, in economic or other areas of activity, without remembering the tradition of local self-government established far back in the colonial period. Not long after Jamestown and Plymouth were founded, communities in America would meet, organize a local government, levy taxes – typically property and poll taxes – on themselves, choose officers to carry out the community will, and get on with the business of life and government. Colonial assemblies grew out of this system before they transformed themselves into state legislatures in 1776. Members of the Continental Congress were thoroughly familiar with it when they drew up the Articles of Confederation and later put out the call for the Philadelphia convention of 1787. After two more centuries, Americans are still reminded of it when they pay their local property taxes. The tradition of local self-government dating far back into the colonial period gave the United States an element of stability and continuity after 1789 that underpinned the nation's endless experiments in federalism.

So strong was the tradition of self-government that it proved a relatively simple matter to establish state governments after the Declaration of Independence. Colonial assemblies with representatives from counties and towns had been in place for decades. All that was necessary to transform a colony into a state was, first, to clear out the loyalists and send the crown-appointed colonial governor packing, and then to write a state constitution defining and limiting the powers of government in ways that colonial charters and the unwritten British constitution did not. Next, elect a state governor and legislators in a republican fashion already well established in America. Finally, draft and implement state laws protecting life, liberty, and property.

---

[1] Alexis de Tocqueville, *Democracy in America* (New York, 1946; 1st French ed. 1835), vol. 1, 40.

As the states began to form themselves, elements of a larger union also appeared. In response to what were regarded as transgressions of the rights of British subjects, committees of correspondence of the various colonial assemblies called for a Continental Congress to meet at Philadelphia in September 1774. Delegates were elected (illegally, since British governors had dissolved colonial assemblies) by revolutionary conventions and committees. This First Continental Congress agreed to stop trade with Britain unless Parliament responded to American grievances. The British government responded instead with a military expedition to seize patriot munitions, resulting in bloodshed at Lexington and Concord in April 1775. A Second Continental Congress gathered a few weeks later, declared the Massachusetts militiamen to be a part of the "Army of the United Colonies," and appointed one of its members, Col. George Washington of Virginia, to be commander in chief. Positions hardened on both sides of the Atlantic, leading a year later to the Declaration of Independence of an entity called for the first time the United States of America.

The ease of forming a national government was again a tribute to the deep roots of self-government. After assuming powers of war and over foreign affairs, the Continental Congress in 1777 drafted and adopted a framework of national government, the Articles of Confederation. Twelve states approved the Articles by 1779, but they did not officially take effect until 1781 when, the war nearing an end, Maryland at last accepted them. The sticking point delaying full ratification was the problem of state claims to lands beyond their borders, of which only Maryland had none. It was resolved in one of the Confederation's greatest achievements, getting states with such claims to cede them to the new national government.

The intent of the Articles was to preserve and protect the sovereignty of the thirteen states, each of which had one vote in the Confederation Congress. Important national decisions required the assent of nine states, and – what proved to be the confederation's fatal flaw – amendments to the Articles had to be unanimous. The Articles gave to Congress the war and foreign affairs authorities it already exercised, but they granted the national government no powers of taxation. Instead, Congress could requisition funding for national purposes from the states in proportion to real property values within each. States themselves had to levy taxes to meet such requisitions. The fatal flaw was quickly exposed. Saddled with large domestic and foreign debts and without revenue, national leaders proposed several times during the early 1780s that a modest national impost – a

5 percent duty on imports – be enacted. Each time the measure, which required amending the Articles, failed when one or two states would not go along with it.

Although forming a national government was not difficult, making it work was another matter under the Articles. As the sovereign states printed their own fiat moneys and placed tariffs and other trade impediments on each other's goods as well as those of other countries, the Confederation Congress made requisitions for funds that usually were not forthcoming from the states. Indeed, one might argue that Dutch financiers had more confidence in the Confederation than did the states, for they lent more to it from 1784 to 1789 ($2.3 million, specie value) than the states paid in requisitions ($1.9 million). These sums, however, only tided over the national government. The Revolution's common debts were not paid, and arrears of interest added year by year to the total, although individual states began to meet their own debt obligations. A weak national government was in no position, try as it might, to challenge either state interferences with internal trade or mercantilist restrictions that European governments placed on America's foreign commerce. Moreover, signs of domestic unrest – notably Shays' Rebellion of 1786–1787, protesting the high taxes levied by a Massachusetts legislature trying to pay its own war debts – were everywhere.

It was in these trying circumstances that the long-nurtured American talent for self-government made its greatest achievement. The Confederation Congress, in response to the recommendation of the 1786 Annapolis convention of five states that met to consider interstate trade problems, called for a national constitutional convention. The Philadelphia convention of 1787 scrapped the Articles and replaced them with a new constitution. That document called for establishing a federal system of government preserving the sovereignty of the states within state spheres of authority, but at the same time inventing a new federal government with its own spheres of authority. Since the states had far more authority under the Confederation, the new Constitution effectively, and quite literally, reduced the scope of state authority. Some proponents of states' rights at the convention were induced to go along with this reduction by the so-called Great Compromise giving each state equal representation – two senators – in the Senate of the new bicameral Congress, and allowing state legislatures to choose the senators. Even that was not enough for Anti-Federalist delegates, who refused to sign the new Constitution. In the other chamber of Congress, the House of Representatives, representation was proportioned to population; a census would be taken every ten years for purposes of reapportionment. The new federal government was not a government of the states as the Confederation had been, any more than a state was the government of local counties and towns. The federal and state governments instead were governments of "the people," as American local governments had been from the first colonial settlements. In the new federal system, each level of government – local, state, and federal – operated directly on individual citizens in its particular sphere of authority.

Economic spheres of authority for the federal government were set forth in Article 1, section 8 of the Constitution dealing with powers of Congress. They included taxation, borrowing, regulation of interstate and foreign commerce, authority over naturalization of foreigners, bankruptcy law, coinage and monetary regulation, postal services, and patents and copyrights. War powers and the military establishment could also be included, for they were to have important economic consequences. In phrasing that long would haunt proponents of states' rights, Congress had the power "To make all laws which shall be necessary and proper for carrying into execution the foregoing powers, and all other powers vested by this Constitution in the government of the United States."

Next, Article 1, section 9, in a sop to slaveholding interests, said that the federal Congress could not prohibit slave imports before 1808, which it promptly did when that date was reached. It specified also that any federal direct taxes had to apportioned among the states according to population. And it forbade the federal government from imposing export taxes.

State authority was explicitly truncated in Article 1, section 10. The states were not to "coin money; emit bills of credit; make anything but gold and silver a tender in payment of debts," or "pass any law impairing the obligation of contracts." States were not to tax imports, exports, or ship tonnage. And they were not to maintain peacetime military establishments or make treaties with other states or foreign powers.

Succeeding articles vested executive authority in a president of the United States and judicial authority in a Supreme Court and such other federal courts as Congress might establish. Together, the first three articles established a system of checks and balances among the three branches of the federal government. Two more articles dealt with interstate relations, the admission of new states, and amendment procedures.

The Constitution further declared, in Article 6, that all debts of the prior Confederation were to be honored by the new federal government, and that the Constitution was "the supreme Law of the Land . . . any Thing in the Constitution or Laws of any State to the Contrary notwithstanding." The latter was another passage that grated on minds of Anti-Federalist defenders of states' rights, and so they made sure that the Tenth Amendment, a part of the cherished Bill of Rights adopted in 1791, read, "The powers not delegated to the United States by the Constitution, nor prohibited by it to the States, are reserved to the States respectively, or to the people."

Thus was established the federal system of U.S. government that persisted and is now into its third century of operation. But in 1789, when the new federal government with George Washington as president gathered in New York City, it was not clear how the Constitution's mandates would be implemented, much less how the unique federal system it called for would work. The implementation issue was settled, but not without spawning the Hamilton–Jefferson controversy during the first administration of the new government that ever after would mark out contending political positions in America. The issue of how the federal system would work was settled over ensuing decades. In each case, the result contributed greatly to the nation's economic expansion.

ECONOMIC GROWTH: GOVERNMENT AND THE FACTORS OF PRODUCTION

Two remarkable characteristics of U.S. development between 1789 and 1914 were its extensive economic expansion across a continent and its transformation from a small agricultural country on the periphery of a Euro-centered world to the world's largest industrial economy and one of its leading political powers. The territory of the country increased by a factor of four. The original thirteen states became forty eight. The population grew by a factor of twenty five, from nearly 4 million to 100 million people. The locus of economic life changed, geographically as a continent was settled, but also functionally as America became urban. One American in twenty lived in an urban area in 1790. By 1914 it was nearly one in two. And the economy increased its total output by a factor of approximately 100. "The old nations of the earth creep on at a snail's pace," wrote Andrew Carnegie in 1886, while "the Republic thunders past with the rush of the express."[2] History had not witnessed such an economic expansion in one nation. And since the conditions in which the expansion took place cannot be duplicated, history probably will not see anything like it again.

What was the role of government in the remarkable U.S. expansion? Views on this vary, as they always have since politics and ideology easily become involved. The ink on the documents ratifying the Constitution was barely dry when a great debate broke out among the leaders of the new federal administration. It brought about the formation of the nation's first political parties and staked out the basic positions they and their successors would take for two centuries. Led by Alexander Hamilton, the Federalist party in power championed centralized governmental initiatives that would build an energetic, creditworthy federal government capable of maintaining internal unity and looking after the international economic and political interests of the United States. In Hamilton's conception, the federal government would promote a diversified nationwide economy based on agriculture, commerce, and manufacturing by overcoming what he and his followers viewed as state and local parochialism in economic matters. Quickly aligning themselves against Hamilton and the Federalists were the Democratic-Republicans led by Thomas Jefferson. They were the ideological successors of the Anti-Federalists who had opposed the Constitution in the ratification debates. Jefferson and his followers wanted a federal government with powers strictly limited to what the Constitution had explicitly authorized. They favored relatively greater authority for state and local governments, and an egalitarian growth program based on expanding the nation's dominant economic activity, agriculture, westward to lands that then were, or later would become, part of the United States.

Two centuries of subsequent American history relating to government and the economy could be written along lines of the waxing and waning of the respective political philosophies and practical goals of Hamilton and Jefferson. Some have traced the origins of the two contending views to English eighteenth-century divisions, to Walpole and the "Court" party versus Bolingbroke and the "Country" party. And it may be that a similar division has existed in most countries at most times in modern history. Whatever the origins of the Hamilton–Jefferson division, it became more complicated in the United States than elsewhere because of the unique

---

[2] Andrew Carnegie, *Triumphant Democracy, or Fifty Years' March of the Republic* (Garden City, NY, 1933; 1st ed. 1886), 1.

federal structure of government, and it persisted long after the two charismatic leaders left the scene, indeed long after the period covered in this chapter. New Deal Democrats of the 1930s, who built a grand marble memorial to Jefferson even as they were centralizing the role of government in the economy, were fond of saying that they pursued Jeffersonian ends (for example, equality) through Hamiltonian means (centralization of power in an energetic federal government). Still later, in the 1980s and 1990s, Republicans, who opposed much of what the New Deal and its like-minded successors wrought, did not quite say that they pursued Hamiltonian ends (national power, economic growth) through Jeffersonian means (tax cuts, decentralized government), though they could have done so without a stretch of the political imagination.

Such twentieth-century intermixings of the two traditions do not undercut the validity of Hamilton versus Jefferson as an organizing principle for surveying the impact of government in American economic history. In the federal system it was always that way, and it became a part the system's strength and flexibility. Hamilton himself had no problem with state initiatives in bank chartering, even participating in several of them. But he might have been more wary if he had foreseen the role state-chartered banks later would play in destroying his federal bank. And Jefferson was to realize with regret that Americans would never be able to get rid of Hamilton's financial system, which he nonetheless took advantage of to accomplish the greatest achievement of his administration, the Louisiana Purchase.

By its very nature, the federal system would not allow either a pure Hamiltonian or a pure Jeffersonian approach to government to prevail. Checks and balances pervaded the entire system, not just its federal component. Complex from the start, and given to opposed Hamiltonian and Jeffersonian interpretations as to how it was to work, the system became even more so over time as more states and many more local governments were added to those of 1789. But judging by its results in the economic sphere, the system did work. The question is, why?

In searching for answers, a model to keep in mind is the economists' old favorite: competition. The layers of the federal system to some extent competed with each other in the work of development. Equally significant were the ways in which they complemented, and at times substituted for, each other. The more important competition was within federalism's layers, as state competed against state, city against city, town against town, to see which could grow the most, have the best banking and transportation systems, the best schools, and so on. The spirit of boosterism has always pervaded the federal system's three layers of government. While prone at times to excesses, on the whole the booster spirit seemed to serve the interests of rapid economic development. Intergovernmental competition in a federal system may have been one of the key elements of American development through space and time. For among other things it created an environment of experimentation that provided good examples for others to adopt as well as bad examples to be avoided.

Competition among governments, however, is only part of the story. Several national initiatives of the earliest years persisted in providing the basis for economic expansion through continual augmentation of available resources. In the tradition of classical economics, they can be discussed under the headings of land, labor, and capital. British interferences with resource augmentation were, it may be recalled, among the reasons Americans declared independence. George III's "repeated injuries and usurpations" listed in the Declaration included, "He has endeavoured to prevent the population of these States; for that purpose obstructing the Law for Naturalization of Foreigners; refusing to pass others to encourage their migrations hither, and raising the conditions of new Appropriations of Lands." Jefferson's words gave focus to Americans' expansive attitudes toward labor and land. But capital was not mentioned. In 1776, there was not much of a capital market in America to attract the King's interference, although parliament had restrained colonial monetary experiments. But the costs of achieving independence would soon provide the groundwork in Hamilton's financial program for a thriving U.S. capital market.

Land

Government's involvement with land falls under two heads, acquisition and privatization. Acquisition of the continental United States by Americans came in a few bold strokes. The first of these was the Revolution, which ended with Britain's recognition of American independence in the Treaty of Paris of 1783. By that treaty the United States consisted of essentially of the thirteen original states along the Atlantic and all the lands to the west extending to the Mississippi River. Florida, the Gulf Coast, and the mouth of the Mississippi, the last a matter of especially great concern to Americans, were excluded because they were in Spanish hands. Then, from 1803 to 1853, the rest of what is now the continental United States was acquired in additional bold strokes. The first was President Jefferson's purchase, for $15 million in cash and claims assumptions, of the Louisiana territory from Napoleon's France. The territory, which France had acquired from Spain in 1800, included the mouth of the Mississippi, the American's real objective. France needed money to finance its wars with Britain and other European countries more than land in America. Thanks to the strong U.S. credit established under Hamilton, Jefferson's ministers, in conjunction with their French counterparts, were able easily to raise the money required from European lenders. The Louisiana Purchase nearly doubled the size of the United States.

Florida and the rest of the Gulf Coast were gained by treaty from Spain in 1819. Texas, settled by Americans who won independence from Mexico in 1836 and then set up their own republic, became a U.S. state by annexation in 1845. Having pulled off this deal, President Polk then provoked a war with Mexico (or so Congressman Abraham Lincoln was convinced, and evidence supports his conviction) during 1846–1848, which resulted in nearly all of the southwestern territory from Texas to California being ceded to the United States by Mexico. At the same time, the rambunctious Americans rattled the British with talk of "Fifty-four, Forty or Fight," meaning they intended to grab the Pacific Northwest far into what is now Canada. The matter was settled by treaty when Britain recognized American sovereignty over the Oregon Territory up to the forty-ninth, not the fifty-fourth, parallel. The land area that became the forty eight contiguous states was rounded out in 1853 with the small Gadsden Purchase of what is now southern Arizona and New Mexico from old Mexico; it was thought desirable as offering fairly level terrain for a future transcontinental railroad.

Territories that eventually became the forty-ninth and fiftieth states were acquired later in the nineteenth century. Alaska was purchased in 1868 from czarist Russia, which like Napoleon's France needed money more than territory in the New World, for $7.2 million in gold. Although called "Seward's Folly" by opponents of the Secretary of State who negotiated the treaty, after thirty years the Americans would discover more gold in Alaska than their country had paid for it, and after a century Alaska would furnish even more valuable petroleum, the black gold of the twentieth century. In 1898 the Hawaiian Islands were annexed by the United States at the instigation of American investors who had developed extensive sugar production there. The timing of the annexation, which had been requested by the sugar interests several years earlier, was helped when the naval base at Pearl Harbor proved strategically important during the Spanish-American War of 1898.

Under the Constitution, the federal government was responsible for foreign affairs, for external matters. So it took the lead in adding new territory to the country, although in every case lesser American interests had moved in before Washington, D.C., acted. This was all a part of what nineteenth-century Americans termed "Manifest Destiny." A more modern perspective on the business of government under the federal system might say that the federal government was the division responsible for mergers and acquisitions, and that some of the takeovers were friendly while others were hostile. Buyouts were, of course, leveraged; debt was incurred to consummate the deals, and later a portion of the assets acquired were sold to raise revenue and discharge the debt.

With western territories ceded from the original states between 1781 and 1802, and with later territorial acquisitions, the federal government became one of the great landlords of world history. The key policy decisions concerning what to do with this vast public domain, like so many key decisions in U.S. history, were made at the start, under the Confederation and under the Federalist administrations up to 1801. Based on a wealth of colonial and state precedents, these decisions were not especially controversial. They set the pattern for all subsequent legislation, which can be considered as amendments to the initial understanding. That understanding can be summarized in one word, *privatization*.

Two pieces of legislation enacted by the Confederation Congress established the essential economic and political framework of U.S. land policy. The Land Ordinance of 1785 called for a rectangular survey of the public domain, with its basic unit being the 6-square-mile township, a term that showed the New England colonial influence. The first surveys, which commenced almost immediately in what became the state of Ohio, further subdivided the township into thirty six sections, each of 1 square mile or 640 acres, and offered them for sale at auction with a minimum price of $1 per acre. Two years later, as the Constitution was being hammered out, the Congress passed the Northwest Ordinance covering the lands north of the Ohio and east of the Mississippi Rivers. The region was to be divided into several territories under administrators appointed by the Congress. Upon reaching a certain population, the territory could elect a territorial legislature and send a nonvoting member to Congress. Upon reaching a higher population level, the territory became eligible for statehood on equal terms with existing states. Slavery was excluded from the Northwest, and a section of every township was dedicated to the support of education.

After the Constitution took effect, the new federal government continued the key policies of the Confederation. Its Land Act of 1796 raised the minimum price to $2 per acre (to discourage speculation, which had caused it some embarrassments), but it encouraged privatization by instituting sales on credit at 6 percent interest, and by formalizing the auction system. The last land act under the Federalists, that of 1800, reduced the minimum tract to 320 acres, liberalized credit terms to spread payments over four years, and located land offices and auctions in the vicinities of the lands being offered for sale.

Liberalization of land-sale policies continued after 1800. In 1804, the minimum tract was reduced to 160 acres and a discount was offered for cash sales. In 1820, the minimum price fell to $1.25, although credit sales were suspended. In 1832, the minimum tract was cut to 40 acres, so from then until 1862, when the Homestead Act made land "free," a settler could buy a farm from the federal government for $50. This assumes what was essentially fact, namely, so much land was offered for sale that the minimum price was close to the price realized at auction. Preemption acts were passed to recognize the rights of squatters, persons who had settled on public land in advance of its survey and sale. The Graduation Act of 1854 gradually reduced the prices of unsold, lesser-quality lands according to the time they had been on the market.

Land was not only sold; it was also spent. Veterans of military service received grants, often in the form of rights or warrants that traded in active secondary markets. States also received federal land grants to dispose of for worthy causes such as education, internal-improvement aid, and land reclamation. From the 1850s to the 1870s, the federal government directly granted millions of acres to railroads to encourage their construction through relatively unsettled territories.

In these ways, hundreds of millions of acres of public land passed into private hands during the century or so after independence. A geographically defined frontier of western settlement disappeared by 1890. The federal system operated to acquire and privatize a continent in record time. As a consequence, a wealth of natural resources quickly became economic resources.

Labor

America has always been, even during the slow development (by modern standards) of the colonial era, a nation of land abundance and labor scarcity compared to most of the world's countries. These conditions fostered the peculiar institutions of slavery and indentured servitude. After independence, further land acquisitions and liberal policies of privatization served to increase the relative scarcity of labor. The unfortunate entrenching of slavery in the South and the early resistance of northeastern manufacturing interests to the liberalization of western land distribution policies testify to this. More land made slave labor more valuable, which was good for slaveowners. More land, by giving free workers the option to take up farming in the west, also made labor more valuable, which was bad for manufacturers seeking to hire workers. Additions to the slave population were limited by law to natural increase after 1808. But there was a solution to the free labor problem: Welcome any and all who arrived from foreign shores to settle and live in the United States and, if they chose, to become citizens. After independence, king and parliament no longer could interfere with such a policy.

Free immigration was the unofficial policy of the nation for more than a century after it came into being. The Constitution was essentially silent on it, speaking only of "naturalization" and "the migration or importation of such persons as any of the States now existing shall think proper to admit," a euphemism for slaves. Until late in the nineteenth century, immigration was left in the hands of the states, which effectively meant free immigration. For what purpose would be served if one state, for whatever reasons, tried to exclude immigrants? They would merely go to a friendlier entry point in another state and, if they so wished, go over land to the state that had tried to exclude them. Within the country movement was free.

Despite periodic outbursts of nativism – for example, the Alien and Sedition Acts of 1798, Protestant anti-Catholicism after Irish and German Catholics began to arrive in numbers, and the Know-Nothing movement of the 1840s and 1850s – states most of the time welcomed and competed for immigrants. They alleviated labor scarcities and thereby made land and capital more valuable. Not until the 1880s, at the behest of racists and organized labor, did the federal government begin to restrict immigration. Compared to the total inflow, these first restrictions, which excluded Chinese (1882) and forbade the import of contract labor (1885), were relatively minor. Japan was persuaded to limit outmigration to the United States in 1908, in response to West Coast fears of a "yellow peril." These, along with the 1808 ban on slave imports, were essentially the only national actions conflicting with free immigration in the country's history to 1914. As policy, free immigration neatly complemented land acquisition and settlement policies. It also made the United States a country of great cultural diversity.

Capital

Land policies and immigration are staples of nineteenth-century historiography. Each represented a continuation of trends established in the colonial era. The capital market (or, one could as well say, the financial system) in contrast was new, different, and very much a creature of government policies. Its separate elements – monetary and banking arrangements, securities markets, public finance – have long been studied, but the intricacies of its structural interconnections and the flexibility it gave to the federal system have been less appreciated. For government not only created the system, but was also among its prime beneficiaries. State governments drew substantial tax revenues from the financial institutions they chartered. And all governments – federal, state, and local – drew on securities markets for borrowings that quickened the pace of U.S. development. A modern market for capital complemented the expanding markets for land and labor, and as a nation, the United States was fortunate to have all three from its earliest years.

In what ways did the capital market, unlike the land and labor markets, represent a change rather than a continuation of colonial trends? As late as 1780, there were no American coins (in the narrow, U.S., sense of America; coins from Spanish America were in common use), no commercial banks, no organized securities markets, and there were few business corporations operating in the country. The Confederation Congress borrowed domestic and foreign funds to wage war, but its ability to raise a revenue and service its debt was virtually nonexistent. Following established colonial precedents, the Congress during the Revolution printed up and spent more than $200 million of Continental currency that by 1780 had so depreciated that "not worth a Continental" would ever after be an American expression to indicate worthlessness. The states also borrowed and printed their own currencies, with results not quite so disastrous in terms of depreciation; states at least had the power to levy taxes, which could be paid with the paper money they issued.

After the Revolution was won, how to deal with its monetary and debt legacies at national and state levels was one of the most vexing problems of the Confederation period. Another was the continued propensity of the states to issue, and overissue, state paper money. These problems, as noted earlier, were addressed explicitly in the Constitution. Implementing financial change was among the new federal government's first agenda items when it formed in New York City in 1789.

Remarkably, the knotty financial problems were solved in the first few years of Washington's administration, largely as a result of the efforts of Alexander Hamilton. A leading proponent of the movement for a new constitution even before the Articles had been ratified, Hamilton was a New York delegate at the Philadelphia convention and served on the drafting committee for the Constitution. Then he recruited James Madison and John Jay to join him in explaining the purposes of the new Constitution to the ratification conventions and to posterity in what became known as *The Federalist*. Hamilton himself wrote a majority of the eighty five *Federalist* essays. Hamilton's expertise in finance led Washington to appoint his former aide de camp to the cabinet as Secretary of the Treasury, the key post in the new government. When Hamilton took office in September 1789, a tariff had already been enacted to implement the Constitution's revenue provisions, but it remained for him to set up the machinery of enforcement and collection. Consequently, he had to fund the new government with loans from two of the three state commercial banks that then existed, one of which – the still-operating Bank of New York – he had helped found in 1784.

Hamilton's first major task, as directed by Congress, was to come up with a plan for dealing with the nation's unpaid debts. Inclusive of domestic and foreign debts of the Confederation, state debts dating from the Revolution, and arrears of interest, the debt came to nearly $80 million. For perspective, this was about 40 percent of a roughly estimated GNP for the United States in 1790, compared to a British national debt that was about the same as British national income in that year. The United States, however, was less of a commercial society than Britain, and the U.S. debt loomed far larger than 40 percent of the monetized market sector in an economy composed for the most part of fairly self-sufficient agriculturalists. Hamilton's *Report on Public Credit* of January 1790 called for fully funding the entire debt into several issues of new federal bonds that would have interest immediately and principal eventually payable in specie or specie equivalents such as convertible banknotes. The federal government would collect the specie required from customs duties and from domestic excise taxes that Hamilton would soon propose.

Acceptance of the plan ran into difficulties when congressmen from some states, particularly Virginia, objected to the assumption of state debts. Their states had smaller debts per capita than others, and these debts had been partly paid, so they balked at having to pay a share of the larger unpaid debts of other states. Jefferson, the secretary of state, later recounted that Hamilton stopped him in a Manhattan street near the president's house and bent his ear for a time on the assumption problem, which Jefferson, not long back from France, claimed not to understand. But Jefferson agreed to arrange a dinner at his house, inviting Hamilton and Virginia congressman James Madison to discuss the matter. In an early and classic example of politics American style, the three leaders struck a deal later termed the Dinner Table Bargain of 1790. Several Virginia congressmen (but not Madison!) would change their previous votes and support Hamilton's assumption plan in return for moving the capital from New York to Philadelphia for ten years, and then to a new federal city to be constructed on the Potomac River bordering Virginia and Maryland. Deal done, the funding act passed in August 1790. Later, after political positions had hardened, Jefferson said he regretted his role in the bargain and claimed that he had been duped by Hamilton into facilitating a larger national debt and the evils that went with it.

The impact of debt funding and other Hamiltonian measures of the time can be measured by the behavior of the markets in which the old debt instruments were being traded. Continental loan office certificates, which could be exchanged for the most attractive of the new federal bonds authorized, were trading at 23 cents on the dollar when the new government gathered in the spring of 1789. They rose to 40 cents on the dollar early in 1790, when Hamilton's report came out, and to 60 cents after the funding act was passed. A year later, August 1791, they were at par; in another year they were 10 to 20 percent above par. They had thus risen fivefold in a little over two years. Since many congressmen were known to have owned government debt, one of the secrets of Alexander Hamilton's popularity and remarkable success as treasury secretary is apparent. Four decades later, Daniel Webster, another member of Congress known to appreciate, even solicit, a gift, recalled in biblical and classical phrasing what Hamilton had done:

He smote the rock of the natural resources, and abundant streams of revenue gushed forth. He touched the dead corpse of Public Credit, and it sprang upon its feet. The fabled birth of Minerva from the brain of Jove was hardly more sudden or more perfect than the financial system of the United States as it burst forth from the conception of Alexander Hamilton.

But what Hamilton considered high statecraft, cementing support for the new and untried federal government while at the same time laying the groundwork of a modern capital market, Jefferson took to be a corruption of republican virtue because it encouraged speculation, stock-jobbing, and political logrolling.

Relations between the two leaders did not improve when, a few months after the funding act, in December 1790, Hamilton proposed a national bank, the Bank of the United States, which Congress promptly enacted. Or when Washington, after due deliberation that included studying Jefferson's argument that the Bank was unconstitutional, in February 1791 signed the Bank bill into law. As designed by Hamilton, the Bank, in giving the government another source of loans and a dividend revenue from its holding 20 percent of Bank stock, would further support the federal debt. And the debt supported the Bank, since three-fourths of the remaining 80 percent of its stock could be purchased by private investors tendering federal debt at par. In mid-1791, when rights to purchase stock of the new Bank went on sale, they sold out immediately, and speculation ran up their price severalfold. The speculation Jefferson witnessed confirmed his worst fears about the direction his country was taking. By that time the rift with Hamilton was complete, and soon there would be Federalist and Democratic-Republican parties to debate and plan America's future.

From a later perspective, what was happening in 1789–1791 was the creation of key elements of a capital market. Hamilton's financial program, which also included monetary and banking arrangements discussed in greater detail elsewhere in this volume (see Rockoff, Chap. 14), created some $80 million of high-grade securities in the form of federal bonds and Bank stock. Trading markets for these securities, even elements of organized stock exchanges, quickly appeared in the larger cities such as New York, Philadelphia, Boston, and Baltimore. Much more important, the new securities that had replaced the "junk" debt of the 1780s appealed, as Hamilton had predicted they would, to foreign investors. By 1795 some $20 million of the $70 million or so of federal debt was held abroad. Foreign holdings of U.S. securities rose to $33 million in 1801, and to $50 million in 1803, when Jefferson as president offered more federal bonds to European investors, via the French government, in return for the Louisiana territory. Sixty percent of the stock of the Bank – which was capitalized at $10 million at a time when the few state banks in existence were each capitalized at several hundred thousand – was in foreign hands by 1803. These securities purchases, together with lesser amounts of American corporate securities, represented an inflow of foreign capital to the United States, the beginnings of portfolio investment in the new nation that would grow to far greater levels over the course of the nineteenth century. In modern terminology, the United States of the 1790s provides an example of a highly successful "emerging capital market."

Rounding out this precocious financial development, the Bank of the United States established branches in the cities of several states, providing the nucleus of a banking system. At the same time, state governments – at the behest of eager entrepreneurs – added to it by chartering more and more banks. The 3 state-chartered banks of 1790, none a decade old, became 28 by 1800, and 102 by 1810. That was just the beginning; there would be 327 state banks by 1820, 729 by 1837, more than 800 by 1850, and nearly 1,600 by 1860. Unchartered private bankers and brokers also flourished in these decades, as the states could not always keep up with the demand for charters, and sometimes for various reasons did not want to. The state-chartered banks, of course, added their equity shares to the securities markets, as did insurance companies and non-financial corporations chartered by the states.

By the turn of the nineteenth century, then, the federal and state governments, encouraging and working in conjunction with private entrepreneurs and investors, put in place an articulated, distinctly modern financial system. At its center was the system of public finance implemented by the Federalists, which directly increased financial capital by creating credible drafts on the future and pointed the way for others to do the same. Later discussions of the U.S. financial system, as they observed its development during subsequent decades, often dwelt on its defects and problems – banking panics and failures, stock market crashes, speculative bubbles, interest-rate and price-level fluctuations, state debt defaults, business cycles, and the like. In doing so, these discussions missed the more important point, namely that such a system existed at all, and so early in the nation's history. Nearly two centuries of colonial development had produced nothing like it, and then all of a sudden it appeared in barely a decade. "The fabled birth of Minerva from the brain of Jove," wrote Daniel Webster, as mentioned earlier, "was hardly more sudden or more perfect than the financial system of the United States as it burst forth from the conception of Alexander Hamilton."

A financial system – institutions such as banks and insurance companies, instruments such as coins, convertible banknotes, bonds and stocks, and securities markets – thus was present from the birth of the U.S. federal system. It would complement a land system that steadily would privatize millions of acres, as well as a labor market that would employ a rapidly growing native population and draw millions of immigrants to the United States. Neither labor shortages nor a lack of capital and credit would much constrain U.S. economic growth, although, as history often instructs us, either or both might have done so with less effective public policies. Together the land, labor, and capital market decisions of the 1780s and 1790s set the stage for the great economic and geographic expansion of the United States over the course of the nineteenth century. It is evident that government, with some credit to the Confederation Congress but a good deal more to the new federal system as it developed in the 1790s, had done much to set that stage.

THE FEDERAL SYSTEM: LONG-TERM TRENDS

All societies have to decide in some way what economic activities are to be carried out by government and which ones are better left to the private sector. Once that is decided, the next steps are to determine what levels of governmental activity are appropriate, and by what means they are to be financed. A federal system, especially one with the complexity and scope of that of the United States, raises further issue of what activities are to be carried out by each of the system's component governments. Here we deal with long-term trends in the size of the government sector, the division of responsibilities among federalism's components, and the methods of financing that each employed. The following section will examine how the components of the federal system meshed and how they interacted with one another and the economy during the nineteenth century.

Economic Share of Government and Its Distribution by Components of the Federal System

Measured by levels of public revenue and spending in relation to the size of the economy, government was far smaller a factor before 1914 than it later became. Census studies for 1902 and 1913, the first comprehensive quantitative accounts of the entire U.S. governmental sector, indicate that government collected and spent on the order of 8 cents of every dollar of

Table 12.1. *Government expenditures by functions as percentage of GNP (all levels of government)*

	Total	Defense	Public debt	Law, order, and administration	Economic and environmental services	Social services	Total civilian
					Civilian		
United States							
1890	7.1	1.4	0.7	1.2	2.0	1.8	5.0
1902	7.9	1.5	0.5	1.1	2.1	1.9	5.1
1913	8.5	1.1	0.4	0.9	2.6	2.1	5.6
United Kingdom							
1890	8.9	2.4	1.6	1.7	1.3	1.9	4.9
1900	14.4	6.9	1.0	1.4	2.5	2.6	6.5
1913	12.4	3.7	0.8	1.6	2.2	2.2	7.9
Germany							
1891	13.2	2.5		n.a.	n.a.	n.a.	9.9
1901	14.9	3.3		n.a.	n.a.	n.a.	11.5
1913	14.8	3.3	0.7	2.4	2.2	5.1	9.7

Source: Richard A. Musgrave, *Fiscal Systems* (New Haven, 1969), table 4-1. Components may not add to total because of omitted categories and rounding.

income generated by the economy in those years. Nearly a century later, the comparable figure is more like 33 or 34 cents of every dollar, implying a substantial relative growth of the public sector. The federal system of government was not less complex before 1914 than after, but from a later perspective its share of the economic pie was not nearly as large as it became during the twentieth century.

Another type of comparison is with other countries. In the late nineteenth and early twentieth centuries, the end of the period surveyed here, total governmental expenditures in the United States were smaller in relation to the size of the economy than was the case in two other large countries, the United Kingdom and Germany (see Table 12.1). Germany's government was nearly twice as large in relation to GNP as that of the United States, in part because it spent a substantially larger proportion on defense (including public debt payments) and social services. Germany, like other European powers, including the United Kingdom, but unlike the United States, had more to pay for past and future wars, and it had already instituted a welfare state that would come later to other countries. Also Germany, unlike either the United States or the United Kingdom, had state-owned railways; that added to its governmental share. The United Kingdom fell in between the United States and Germany in its ratio of government spending to GNP, again because of substantially greater defense spending and somewhat higher relative spending on civilian services. (Comparatively high U.K. defense spending in 1900 was related to the Boer War of that time.) The U.S. GNP was sustantially larger than those of the United Kingdom and Germany, implying that in absolute terms, its overall level of government spending was more on a par with those of the two European powers.

In the twentieth century, the distribution of public activity among the federal system's components changed, toward an increased concentration of revenue raising and spending at the federal level especially, but also at the state level, and away from the local level. Today's federal government accounts for about two-thirds of all government spending, with state and local governments accounting for roughly equal shares of the remainder. Rendering exact accounts is complicated because of the modern era's extensive intergovernmental transfers within the federal system; considerable state spending is financed with federal funds, and local governments draw on both state and federal funding sources. In contrast, of the 8 cents of every dollar spent by governments early in the century, the federal government spent about two cents, the states 1 cent, and local governments 5 cents (intergovernmental transfers, while not unknown before 1914, were typically minimal). Local government, the progenitor of American republicanism, thus went from first place to last in the twentieth century's era of big government.

Did government in the aggregate also increase its share of the nation's economic pie between 1789 and 1914? An informed guess, based on less complete information, is that it did, but not as markedly as in this century. Records are fairly complete only for the federal government. Relating the data to rough measures of total income or product, it appears that the federal government typically raised and disposed of 2 to 3 percent of total product over the entire 125-year period, with the percentage being considerably higher in the relatively few years of war and somewhat higher than usual after wars, when interest payments on war debts rose as a share of the federal budget. In Jefferson's era at the start of the nineteenth century, and during the age of Jackson after 1829, the

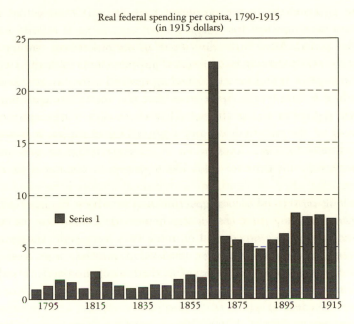

Figure 12.1. Real federal spending per capita, 1790–1915 (in 1915 dollars). Source: Derived from U.S. Bureau of the Census, *Historical Statistics of the United States, Colonial Times to 1970* (Washington, DC, 1975), Series A-7 and Y-336. Nominal data are put into real terms using an unpublished consumer price index compiled and kindly furnished by Professor Jack W. Wilson of North Carolina State University.

federal share of the economy's output dipped somewhat under 2 percent as a result of conscious policy actions to limit the scope of the government in Washington, D.C.

Federal fiscal records can provide many perspectives. Figure 12.1, showing federal spending per person in real (that is, in dollars of 1915 purchasing power, adjusting for price-level changes over the decades) terms at five-year intervals from 1790 to 1915, offers one such perspective. Federal spending increased roughly from $1.50–2.00 per person in the early decades to $7–8 per person toward the end of the period. This represents a rate of increase somewhat higher than that of the economy's growth in output per person, but not a lot. The pattern is more interesting. The peaks in 1815 and 1865 are war-related. And real federal spending per person was relatively constant or flat for extended periods, although at substantially higher levels after 1865 than before 1860.

State governments in the aggregate, even at their most active, never appear to have matched the federal government in fiscal activity for any extended period. Their high-water mark of the nineteenth century came during the era of state-financed internal improvements from the 1820s to the 1840s, when aggregate state spending reached some two-thirds of corresponding federal levels. Apart from that era, total state spending was typically a third or less of the federal level, though it rose again at the beginning of the twentieth century when, as noted earlier, it was about a half. Again the main impetus for rising state spending was internal improvements, this time for roads and highways to accommodate motor vehicles.

The long-term trend of local governmental activity is the most difficult to discern with any great confidence. Before 1914 there was, of course, only one federal government and no more than forty-eight state governments; local government, however, consisted of counties, cities, towns, and special districts numbering together in the tens of thousands. Fiscally as well as numerically, the local sector was by far the largest of the three components of the federal system at the start of this century, when it accounted for 60 percent or more of all government spending. Some have seized upon this established fact to contend that the local component was always the largest before 1914. Their reasoning is that the federal government was held strictly in check by Jeffersonians and Jacksonians between the Federalist era and the Republican era that arrived with the Civil War, while the states had but one burst of activity in the improvement era of the 1820s and 1830s, and then placed limits on themselves. Since the federal and state governments were limited in their activities, much of the work of government was left to counties, cities, and towns, and since these local governments in the aggregate were the largest component at the end of period, they must therefore always have been the largest.

There are grounds for doubting this reasoning. Examination of early local governmental records indicates that these governments were engaged, as in the colonial era, in important but relatively routine and not costly activities. Large increases in local activity did not occur until the 1840s, when the localities moved to continue improvement activities that were being abandoned by states chastened in the wake of the state debt defaults of the early 1840s, and when, at roughly the same time, the pace of U.S. urbanization quickened. City governments, of which there were few in 1789, typically spent far more per person than did federal, state, or county and town local governments. When, therefore, the numbers and sizes of cities began to grow rapidly after 1840, and cities invested in urban overhead projects and provided new and higher levels of urban services, the local governmental component in the federal system gained relative to the federal and state components. Chicago – no more than a small village at the start of the 1830s and one of the world's great cities by the 1890s – is the classic example.

What then can be said about the relative share of government overall and by component in the early years of the federal system? The federal government raised and spent from $1 to $2 per American during the 1790s. This was on the order of 2 to 3 percent of gross economic product at the time. Various state budgets of the time indicate annual per capita revenues and spending ranging from 37 cents (Massachusetts) to 13 cents (North Carolina), or an average of perhaps 25 cents for all states. This was likely no more than half of one percent of per capita product. Early state government in the U.S. federal system did not cost much, and it did not do much that required substantial funding. The federal government under the Constitution had assumed those public responsibilities that did cost a lot, mainly defense and debt service. The federal and state governments together thus absorbed about 3 percent of the economy's product, with by far the larger portion going to the federal government.

That leaves local government. Its variations were wide, even in the 1790s. Philadelphia, the largest city, spent about $2 per resident in 1797, on the order of what the federal government was spending per American at the time. But there were few such cities; the entire urban population, those residing in cities and towns of 2,500 or more, was only 5 to 6 percent of the population. Most town and county governments, like most states, stuck to basics. A 1796 report of Treasury Secretary Oliver Wolcott, the first federal survey of state and local revenue systems (made in connection with a proposed federal direct tax), found indications that local taxation varied from levels well in excess of what states collected in New England to a rough parity with state levels in the South.[3] North Carolina's counties, the main local governments then, collected more per person than did the state, but together in 1801, North Carolina's state and local spending per person was only 23 percent of the federal level per person. Even if all local governments, from Philadelphia to a county in North Carolina, spent twice on average what state governments did in the 1790s, local spending would have come to no more than 1 percent of total economic product.

[3] "Report of the Secretary of the Treasury on the Subject of a Direct Tax," [Oliver Wolcott, 1796] *American State Papers, Finance*, vol. I (Washington, DC, 1832–1861).

This means that total government spending in the 1790s, the first years of federalism, came to about 4 percent of total product. It means also that by the standards of the day Hamilton and his Federalist party really did believe, as their Jeffersonian opponents charged, in big government. For the federal share of all American government was about three-fifths, rather like today when once again the opposition to big government is strong. Finally, it means that the share of government in the economy roughly doubled from the 1790s to the early 1900s, from some 4 percent to around 8 percent. The percentages seem small by later twentieth-century norms, but because total product itself rose 100-fold over the period, aggregate government spending rose some 200 times. Government in the United States even in the nineteenth century was a growth sector.

Division of Governmental Responsibilities Under the Federal System

In another major event of 1776, Adam Smith's *Wealth of Nations*, the Scottish economist outlined the responsibilities of a government dedicated to liberty: first, protection against the violence and invasion of other societies; second, the administration of justice within the society; and third, building and maintaining public works and institutions that individuals and private associations of individuals would not find in the economic interest to carry out even though, from society's point of view, they were worthwhile. Adam Smith's duties of government, with which America's founding fathers were familiar and found appealing, included much, perhaps most, of what American government did before 1914. But Adam Smith did not indicate how a government should be structured to discharge its duties, or how a federal system should divide and allocate them among its components. Americans relied on both tradition and experimentation to provide answers.

1. *Local governments* were the basic American governments of the colonial era and the ones out of which higher levels of government developed. Local militias, from which colonial and state militias grew, were the first lines of collective defense against hostile Native Americans and Europeans. Towns elected selectmen, who then appointed, if they were not also elected, magistrates, tax listers, assessors, and collectors, as well as constables, clerks, and other petty officers. They levied taxes to pay for government itself, and for public buildings, roads, bridges, schools, and poor relief. And they sent representatives to colonial assemblies, which

formed counties having their own officers – commissioners, justices of the peace, sheriffs, and recorders of deeds – as well as their own public works and welfare programs. Patterns of local governmental organization varied regionally, with towns more important in the North and counties in the South, where there were few towns compared to the North. Despite the differences, an immersion in the surviving public records of the colonial and early national periods indicates that they were differences only of degree, not kind.

After independence, local governments continued doing most of the things they had always done. There were a few changes. Protective measures against external threats became less necessary, except perhaps on frontiers of settlement, with the advent of a militarily powerful federal government. For the slave South, the rise of abolitionist thinking and a growing consciousness among slaves that their condition of servitude was rather anomalous if indeed all men were created equal, resulted in tax rates for slave patrols being added to the long-standing lists of local assessments.

In the North and West, basic educational activities increased. Sometimes these were stimulated by state and federal initiatives such as land donations or matching cash grants. From the earliest days, however, basic education in the United States was financed mainly by local governmental funds. Since education forms human capital, these educational efforts were of significance for economic growth, and so they merit a further look. They may have been the most important long-term contribution of local governments to economic growth.

In New York, an influential state not only because of its size but also because it furnished migrants to the West who took institutional memories of New York with them, the state government established a school fund as early as 1795. It was to aid the regents of the state's university, private academies that catered to the well-to-do, and the local common schools that already existed. By 1840, the state's superintendent of common schools, as reported in a book by his deputy, could contrast

the present situation of the schools with their condition in 1815, the number of organized and reporting districts having increased from 2,631 to 10,397; the number of children instructed from 140,706 to 572,995; and the amount paid from the treasury towards defraying the compensation of teachers from $45,398 to $220,000; and after referring to the fact that $275,000 were annually contributed in taxes and nearly $500,000 in rate-bills, for the support of schools,

[he] observes, "A people who have thus freely expended their money and appropriated their private means for the education of their children, to an amount nearly double the expense of administering the [state] government cannot with any truth or justice be said to be indifferent to the subject. . . . Its fruits are seen in the education of one-fourth of an entire population, and of nearly every child of a proper age for the primary schools; in the advance of the wages paid to teachers."[4]

The school districts, taxes, and rate bills (assessments on families with children in schools) were local in nature; the state provided only an umbrella organization and supplemental financing. States such as New York, primarily by means of local governmental financing, were educating substantially all of their school-age children well before the so-called common school revival of the 1840s and 1850s. The revival was more about making education compulsory and increasing state-level involvement than about providing public schools where none had previously existed. Before the revival, local governments long had been active in providing basic education, even during the colonial period. As a result, the U.S. population from the first days of the nation's history was one of the most literate and educated of any country.

Providing education, along with laying out roads, building bridges, and improving waterways, was among the first developmental activities of local governments. Later, local governments extended their developmental initiatives, for example, by actively aiding large-scale transportation improvements – particularly railroads from the 1840s to the 1870s – and by making the large infrastructural investments of cities as America urbanized from the 1840s into the twentieth century. These later and larger-scale investments were financed, as discussed in more detail below, mainly by borrowing from the capital market, not by tax revenues.

2. *State governments* in a strictly fiscal sense were almost always the smallest component of the federal system before 1914. Yet as Woodrow Wilson, then a professor but later a state governor and U.S. president, noted late in the nineteenth century,

The states properly come first in a description of the government of this country, not only because it was in conformity with state models and precedents that the federal government was constructed, but also and more particularly because the great bulk of the business of government still rests with the state authorities . . . . [T]hey determine the power of masters over servants and the whole law of principal and agent, which is so vital a matter in business transactions; they

---

[4] S. S. Randall, *A Digest of the Common School System of the State of New York* (Albany, 1844), 74.

regulate partnership, debt and credit, and insurance; they constitute all corporations, both private and municipal, except such as specially fulfill the financial or other specific functions of the federal government; they control possession, distribution, and use of property, the exercise of trades, and all contract administration. . . . Space would fail in which to enumerate the particular items of this vast range of power; to detail its parts would be to catalogue all social and business relationships, to set forth all foundations of law and order.[5]

The influence of states on economic life, for reasons such as Wilson noted, was disproportionate to their taxing and spending. If the Constitution and the federal government provided a broad framework of law and dealt with foreign and interstate matters, state laws and regulations provided the specific frameworks that impacted most Americans in their everyday life and work. As the number of states increased from thirteen to forty-eight, there was ample room for state experimentation and imitation of what seemed to work in other states. A state or two would institute free banking in the 1830s, for example, and then, over the next quarter century many other states and even the federal government would get on board. Something similar happened in basic education. Such state initiatives illustrate the vitality of the federal system. Overall, the system proved stable (apart from 1861–1865), but not because it discouraged experimentation and diffusion of experiments that worked.

State governments could also become heavily involved in overhead investments. Two episodes stand out in the period covered here. One was the internal improvement era that began in a big way after the War of 1812 and extended into the 1850s. In it state planning, subsidies, and direct investment in banks, improved roads, canals, and railways were extensive. Since most of the financing was debt, the capital market was crucial to the whole enterprise. The other episode began toward the end of the period: the extensive state road building activity of the early twentieth century, called forth by the automobile. Once again states incurred large debts to finance infrastructure investment.

3. *The federal government* as originally envisioned had a role more circumscribed than those of either local or state governments. Hamilton in *Federalist* No. 23 described it this way: "The principal purposes to be answered by union are these – the common defense of the members; the preservation of the public peace . . . ; the regulation of commerce with other nations and between the States; the superintendence of our

[5] Woodrow Wilson, *The State: Elements of Historical and Practical Politics* (rev. ed. Boston, 1900; 1st ed. 1889), 469, 473.

intercourse, political and commercial, with foreign countries." That was it. Adam Smith's defense and justice (public peace) are mentioned, but public works and institutions are not, unless one would include them in a broad construction of "the regulation of commerce" that included promotional activities. Hamilton's Federalists after the Constitution was ratified, and later their Whig and Republican successors, subscribed to just such an expansive construction of federal purposes. The Jeffersonians and Jacksonians, who controlled the federal government most of the time between 1800 and 1860, did not.

Despite these differing interpretations, during the century and a quarter after 1789, the federal government in general did stick to the purposes stated in the original understanding. In virtually every year, the greater part of federal spending went to fund the army, the navy, to veterans of the army and navy, and to service the debts incurred in wars that engaged the United States. What later would be called domestic spending was relatively unimportant in a fiscal sense, and the federal government itself was far smaller in its absorption and distribution of economic resources than it would become in the twentieth century. The bureaucracy in Washington, for example, was minuscule, so small even at the end of the nineteenth century that it amounted to only a fifth of the employees of one large corporation, the Pennsylvania Railroad. Of the federal government's civilian employees, before 1914 most of them worked for the post office and rarely if ever set eyes upon the federal capital city.

Finances of the Federal System

Tocqueville, continuing his observations about the temporal primacy of local government that were quoted at the start of this essay, noted that

In New England, townships were completely and definitely constituted as early as 1650. . . . It [the township] gave scope to the activity of a real political life, thoroughly democratic and republican. The colonies still recognized the supremacy of the mother country; monarchy was still the law of the state; but the republic was already established in every township. The towns named their own magistrates of every kind, assessed themselves, and levied their own taxes.[6]

The local taxes to which he referred were, in New England and elsewhere, a combination of levies on real and personal property and on polls, that is, capitation taxes. The poll tax lasted into the twentieth

---

[6] Tocqueville, *Democracy in America*, 40.

century, but seldom was it as important as the property tax, and its relative decline as a revenue source was steady. The property tax, however, still is, as it always has been, the mainstay of local governmental finance in the United States. In the 1990s, direct taxes on property bring in about three-fourths of all local tax revenue and account for almost all of the tax revenues of the ubiquitous townships (93 percent) and school districts (97 percent). These modern township and school district percentages were typical of all local governments – town, city, county, school district, other special districts – during the nineteenth century. Americans have never enjoyed paying taxes, and the property tax has come in for much criticism over the centuries. But its staying power argues that in principle it is the optimal local tax, or close to it, for financing essential local governmental services.

An established property tax system could also underwrite borrowing from the capital market for public investment. To the extent that such investments raised property values, increased revenues would flow almost automatically into local public coffers to service the debts incurred. Local and state governments were well aware of this during the nineteenth century. They used it, usually but not always to good effect, to expand public investment far beyond what the tax system by itself would have financed.

After independence, while property and poll taxes continued to fund local government, the states did not have such a smooth adjustment. The Constitution took away two important state revenue sources, import and export duties and money printing (sometimes termed "currency finance"), and claims to western lands that several states later might have sold were ceded to the federal government. In Hamilton's view, this hardly mattered because the states would not require much revenue in the centralized federal system he envisioned. He wrote in *Federalist* No. 36, "A small land tax will answer the purposes of the States, and will be their most simple and most fit resource." Jefferson, Jackson, and others would delay for a long time the realization of Hamilton's vision of centralized federalism, and in the interim the property tax would become a mainstay of state finance, just as it was at the local level. But not in the early decades, for then the states often were reluctant to use it.

If the states lost revenue sources as a result of the Constitution, that document and Hamilton's financial program implementing it also relieved them of some of their important former obligations – defense and old debts incurred in the cause of independence – and also brought the states new revenue sources. In the settlement of the Revolution's accounts, creditor states – those that had contributed more than their share of the war's costs – were rewarded with the federal government's new, high-grade bonds, giving them steady interest income. The corresponding debtor states effectively had their settlement obligations forgiven. Moreover, loss of the power to print money hardly impacted state finances or, for that matter, the economy, because states retained the right to charter more and more banks, and they did so. These banks issued their own paper money, at times collateralized (as in the so-called free banking era after 1838) by required bank purchases of state bonds which, of course, made it easier for states to borrow. The banks also became important direct revenue sources for states, in such forms as charter fees, dividends on bank stock held by state treasuries, and a variety of taxes levied on banks. States sometimes even owned and operated banks. Finally, Hamilton's program gave the states access to the capital market it had created, and they would tap into this resource in rather bold fashion during the era of state-financed internal improvements after 1815.

With reduced obligations and the new revenue sources, the older states found that in the first decades after the Constitution they often could dispense altogether with property taxes. New states, as they entered the Union, did not have investment income or many banks and other businesses to tax, so they had to rely to a far greater extent than the old states on property taxes. Only in the 1840s, after nine states defaulted on their internal improvement debts and several others came close, did property taxes come to dominate the revenue raising of all states, old and new. Up to that time, business revenues (for example, income from portfolio investments and bank taxes), excise taxes, and activity revenues (canal fees, land sales) together vastly exceeded state property taxes as revenue sources. Most of these continued as lesser state revenue sources after property taxes vaulted to the forefront in the 1840s.

Federal revenues over the whole period 1789–1914 were derived almost entirely from three sources: import duties, excise taxes on alcoholic beverages and tobacco products, and land sales. Import duties were the most important federal source by a considerable margin, seldom accounting for less than half of annual revenues and more often for a much larger portion, especially before the Civil War. The explanation for this, which might seem odd to later generations more sympathetic to free trade, is straightforward. The duties were relatively easy to collect at the limited number of cities with good port facilities, they proved to be a reliable and growing revenue source as the growth of the economy drew in ever more imports, and they were popular with the increasingly influential business interests whose domestic markets they offered some protection.

Internal excise taxes were controversial from the start, when Congress enacted Hamilton's whiskey tax in 1791. After 1801 the Jeffersonians virtually abandoned excise taxation. Excise taxes did not supply significant revenues until the Civil War era and after, when the alcohol and tobacco excises proved to be abundant yielders of revenue while at the same time giving some satisfaction to the ever-present Puritan influence in American life. From the 1870s to 1914, the two excise taxes together ran a close second to import duties as a revenue source for the government in Washington.

Land sales were a steady but nearly always minor source of federal revenue. It seems likely that land revenues, when all is said and done, did little more than cover the full governmental costs of privatizing the public domain. In the great policy debates on privatization, as well as in all the drama surrounding settlement itself, public revenue derived directly from land sales was a minor issue. Indirectly, the rapid settlement of a continent – spurred on, of course, by liberal land-sale and immigration policies – raised property values, and therefore property tax revenues, for state and local governments, just as it contributed to the income growth that generated increased customs and excise collections by the federal government.

The capital market, as intended by Hamilton, was another source of funds for the federal government. It was used primarily to finance wars, and secondarily to finance additions to territory, for example, the Louisiana Purchase of 1803. In big wars (that of 1812 and that with Mexico), the federal debt roughly tripled; in the biggest war of all, the Civil War, it grew some fortyfold. Between wars the debt was reduced, even eliminated altogether in the 1830s, because the dominant American opinion during the nineteenth century was that national debt should be paid down whenever it was feasible to do so. This was before the era of big government in the twentieth century, when the national debt seemed only to grow, in war and peace. The capital market, which had its origins in the federal debt, thrived when the debt rose. But it also thrived when the debt, especially that owned by Americans, was paid down, as it could then recycle surplus federal revenues into other American securities. Such recycling occurred when holders of retired federal debt reinvested the proceeds in securities issued by state and local governments and by private-sector corporations.

A CHRONOLOGY OF THE FEDERAL
SYSTEM IN ACTION

The Federalist Era, 1789–1801

The Constitution as such was mere words on paper. The great achievement of the Federalists after they assumed the reins of government in 1789 was breathing life into those words. They established the federal government as a going concern, its authority, its revenue, and its credit. In this, Treasury Secretary Hamilton, with the constant support of President Washington, was the key figure. In the realm of intellect, Hamilton was an economic, financial, and political thinker of the first order; in the realm of affairs and action, he was a skilled and energetic soldier, lawyer, financier, public administrator, and statesman. He was, according to Jefferson, a host within himself. These qualities dazzled his supporters and flummoxed his political enemies, who quickly organized themselves to oppose the man and his measures. His chief flaw, it seems, was to rise to their bait and become ever more involved in the nitty-gritty of politics, which eventually led to his untimely death at age forty-seven in an 1804 duel with a political rival, Aaron Burr. But Hamilton's vision of what the United States might become persisted, and, whether one likes or dislikes it, seems two centuries later to have prevailed.

Realizing that U.S. involvement in foreign wars or lesser entanglements might drastically reduce the flow of customs duties, thereby threatening the new financial system and government by weakening its base, Hamilton and other Federalist leaders pushed Congress hard to provide internal revenues. The resulting taxes were proved highly unpopular. The first, the whiskey excise of 1791, provoked an insurrection in 1794, the so-called Whiskey Rebellion, that was put down with a show of federal military power. Other excise taxes followed, but none – even the whiskey tax – produced much revenue. When war with France threatened toward the end of the 1790s (and actually broke out at sea, though never formally declared), the federal government imposed for the first time a direct tax on property. It led to another, relatively minor, taxpayers' revolt, Fries's Rebellion, in Pennsylvania, which again was put down. After the Federalists yielded to the Jeffersonians in 1801, in part over tax issues, the internal taxes, indirect and direct, were repealed.

The states of the 1790s, flush with federal securities from the funding program, reduced or eliminated property taxes and became investors.

Federal securities were sold via the capital market, often to European investors, and the proceeds were reinvested in banks and other corporations, which the states eagerly chartered at the behest of entrepreneurs. These corporate enterprises oiled the engine of commerce with credit as well as transportation improvements, though on a small scale compared to later ventures. Another popular method of state finance was the granting of lotteries to groups of citizens desiring to improve specific capital facilities, for example, roads, buildings, schools, water and sewer systems, and fire-fighting equipment. Quasi-public organizations such as churches and colleges also benefited from lottery finance. Lotteries satisfied, even encouraged, the public's gambling bent while at the same time raising the level of public developmental aid without requiring tax or debt finance. These starts on state assistance for economic development were promising, but their continuance required strong federal leadership and peace. Neither followed.

Jeffersonian Democracy, 1801–1825

Jefferson was a cleverer politician than Hamilton, but weaker in statecraft and economic insight. He and his followers were possessed by an idealistic vision of the U.S. economy becoming an ever expanding aggregation of small farms, the growing surpluses of which would be traded to the rest of the world. The United States was in a strong position internationally, the Jeffersonians thought, because the world needed American agricultural exports more than the United States needed the world's goods, which Americans could just as easily make for themselves. Proper federal policy therefore involved expanding the U.S. farm sector and insuring that its surplus products could move to American ports and be exported to world markets. The Louisiana Purchase of 1803 is easily understandable in such a framework. So too is the 1808 report of Albert Gallatin, Jefferson's treasury secretary, calling for a massive federal program to build interstate roads and canals. The effort had to be federal, Gallatin argued, because its benefits would be widely diffused and its financing in any case was beyond the capabilities of state and local governments and the private sector. Nonetheless, the Jeffersonians gutted the federal internal revenue system; because it was unpopular, it was deemed unnecessary. Import duties were growing and would suffice. The best use of surplus federal revenues, it was thought (at least before the transportation improvement plan came along), was to reduce the federal debt. And that is how the Jeffersonians used them. Hamilton's Bank of the United States, though it had proved useful to the government since 1791, was expendable. To the Jeffersonians, it remained of dubious constitutionality, and many state-chartered banks in the Jeffersonian fold resented the federal bank's competition and control. These smaller, more "republican" institutions could take up any slack its absence might create. The army and the navy could be downsized to save money because a world that needed America more than America needed it would not dare threaten. If the world failed to get this message, an embargo closing down America's ports would drive it home.

Most of the Jeffersonian vision, based as it was on a misreading of U.S. interests, capabilities, and prospects, proved to be illusory. As implemented, it led to a period of weakness and drift in U.S. public affairs. The Louisiana Purchase, its one real achievement, had no immediate economic impact, but did have longer-run benefits. Gallatin's grand federal transportation plan quickly was eviscerated by politics. Although many politicians agreed that something like it was necessary, why should they approve federal spending that would primarily benefit other states and localities? Such a position was all the easier to take when, at the time the plan was made public, federal revenues tumbled as a result of other policies such as the embargo and excise tax cuts. The end result was essentially no action on a plan that all agreed needed action. As politicians at the federal level were preventing action on major transportation improvements, others at the state level watched and waited to see if and when federal action on the plan, which was under discussion and had its supporters, would be taken.

Paying down the federal debt, which later in time would prove a good use of surplus revenues because it recycled them through the U.S. capital market, was in Jefferson's administration a dubious measure. The policy returned capital to Europe in a period of international turmoil not conducive to recycling the capital to America, which could use it better. Noting Gallatin's estimate that capital yielded at least 12 percent in America, an exasperated Samuel Blodget in 1806 wondered, *"Why are we now paying off 5½ percents, while 6 percents are under par? Why I repeat it, are we thus wastefully returning our money to Europe?"*[7] The answer is that Jefferson loathed debt, especially the federal debt that he associated with his 1790s antagonist, Hamilton.

---

[7] Samuel Blodget, Jr., *Economica – A Statistical Manual for the United States of America* (Washington, DC, 1806; reprint, New York, 1964), 200. The emphasis is Blodget's.

The old Bank of the United States came to be so sorely missed by the Jeffersonians after they allowed it to expire in 1811, that it was reincarnated in a new, larger Second Bank in 1816. (Two decades later, the Second Bank met the same fate as the First, when President Jackson vetoed Congress's bill to renew its charter.) Jefferson's embargo reduced federal customs revenues just as internal revenues were deliberately forgone. Its effects on the U.S. economy were disastrous; its effects on domestic politics were divisive to the point of serious secessionist talk. Gutting the military establishment was hardly good preparation for a war involving the United States that international events made more and more likely. History in the end is led to judge that Jefferson and Madison, his successor and erstwhile supporter, were fortunate to have established their reputations in the previous century, or perhaps for their handling of other than economic matters.

The War of 1812 exposed the essential weaknesses of the Jeffersonian policies of drift. Without the Bank to support it, and with a weakened public credit, the Madison administration was forced to print money, leading to inflation and suspension of specie payments in most of the country, and to borrow what it could on onerous terms. A federal direct tax was again imposed, but with memories of hostile reactions to that of 1798, it was billed as strictly an emergency measure to be undone after the war. States were offered a discount for paying their quotas of the tax directly from state coffers, which a number of them did to avoid the appearance of becoming federal tax collectors. Even so, the direct tax brought in little revenue until the war was nearly ended. States threatened by British armies and naval forces had to organize their own resistance because the federal government proved unable to defend them, which had, of course, been one of the main reasons for having a federal government. Charitably, the federal government later reimbursed these states for their expenses.

For Americans, one of the few good results of the war, which ended as a stalemate, was a paradoxical outburst of patriotism, particularly among westerners, that redounded to the federal government's long-term benefit. These hardy pioneers in newly established or establishing states developed their first loyalties to the United States rather than to their states. In this they differed from citizens of older states, whose state or regional loyalties, then and later, led to secessionist moves from a federal union that did not seem to serve their interests. As Americans became first Americans, and only secondarily and incidentally, say, New Englanders, South

Carolinians, or Southerners, the federal union and its government in Washington became stronger and stronger. Decades, even a century, passed before this transformation was more or less complete.

After the War of 1812, the politics of drift at the national level nonetheless continued. A new Bank of the United States came in 1816, but when John C. Calhoun proposed and Congress approved using the revenue it provided the federal government to fund internal improvements, Madison vetoed the bill. His successor Monroe, another Virginian and Jeffersonian, took similar actions. Henry Clay, a congressman every bit as ambitious as Calhoun, elevated federally sponsored improvement proposals to part of his "American System." Clay's slogan meant using higher federal tariffs to encourage domestic manufacturing, with the proceeds in federal revenues employed to finance internal improvement projects. Like Calhoun, Clay got nowhere. John Quincy Adams had a similar approach and actually got somewhere, making it to the presidency, 1825–1829. But his plans for greater federal involvement in the country's economic development were similarly shelved by Jeffersonian ideology and perceived state interests.

By the 1820s, many state leaders began to grasp some basic points about the federal system of their era, namely that while the federal Supreme Court could and did prevent states from interfering with interstate commerce and the rights of corporations, the rest of the federal government was politically incapable of advancing either in a proactive way. States themselves would have to act. An advantage of the U.S. federal system, one that likely would not have been present had the governmental system of the country been more monolithic and centralized while also as divided in outlook as it was, was that states could act on their own. And, in competition with one another, they did.

State Internal Improvements, 1820s–1840s

The politics of Jeffersonian drift at the federal level having failed to attack national economic problems, states embarked on their own programs of major transportation works and banking investments designed to aid them. New York was in the vanguard with the celebrated Erie Canal, built between 1817 and 1825. Approximately three-fourths of its $11 million cost was raised from the capital market, with many of the state-backed canal bonds being sold through it ultimately to European investors. The federal government's credit, despite its abuse at the hands of the

Jeffersonians, was restored after the War of 1812, and it rubbed off on the credit of the states. The Erie Canal's success was not fully anticipated, so New York prudently dedicated taxes and auction duties to servicing canal debts. Ohio shortly followed New York's example in its state-sponsored canal program. The taxes New York and Ohio dedicated to canal debts seemed to turn out to be unnecessary when canal toll collections were more than ample to service debts incurred, an example not lost on less prudent state governments. Looking at the successes of the Erie and Ohio canals, they decided that internal improvements would pay for themselves and perhaps even cover other costs of government. Hence, state taxes could be kept low or dispensed with altogether, and all the financing could be borrowed from the capital market.

With the successful early experiments in state-financed improvements in mind, some twenty states between 1820 and 1841 borrowed nearly $200 million for development investments, much of it from European investors. The total greatly exceeded what the federal government's debt had ever been up to that time, or indeed would be down to the Civil War. These state investments were but a small part of the economy's total capital formation, but the projects undertaken were of a nature that induced further investment from the private sector, so the states were leveraging the country's economic potential. More than a fourth of state debt issues were incurred to finance banks, mostly in western states, north and south, in which the newness of settlement had not given time to the private sector to develop banking facilities adequate to the great tasks envisioned. The rest of the state borrowings went largely to transportation improvements – canals, railroads, and roads. A third of the total came in the 1820s, and two-thirds during the 1830s, after Andrew Jackson demonstrated by vetoing both federal improvement aid and renewal of the Second Bank's charter that he would continue Jeffersonian policies in their original, pure form.

The federal government, however, fostered state improvement activities in ways other than eliciting them by its own inaction. Rapid economic growth after 1815 drew in imports, as Americans spent rising incomes on foreign as well as domestically produced goods. Increased tariff rates falling on the expanding imports filled the federal treasury with customs revenues. Since Calhoun, Clay, Adams, and other Whigs were not allowed by Jeffersonians and Jacksonians to spend this largesse on federally financed projects, the surplus revenues were used to extinguish the national debt. A federal debt of $127 million in 1816 went to zero by 1835, a unique event in the history of national debts. There is an element of truth in the notion that federal debt retirement paid for over half of the improvements financed by state borrowing, albeit indirectly as holders of redeemed federal debt reinvested the proceeds in state-issued securities.

The federal contribution rose further in 1837 when, its debt all gone and tariff revenues still rolling in, the federal government distributed $28 million of surplus revenue to the states. This early example of federal revenue sharing might have continued had not the financial Panic of 1837 slowed the economy's expansion and turned the federal surplus into a deficit. States used the money for a variety of purposes that included funding education and internal improvements. The whole experience of federal debt retirement and surplus revenue distribution illustrates an important strength of the federal system in practice. It would not allow the federal government to disengage itself from lower levels of government and the private sector, however much the ideology of its leadership recommended such a course.

Unfortunately, the improvement boom, borne along on rising tides of capital market credit, got ahead of itself. Eastern states and their port cities competed with one another to attract the trade of the growing west. Western states competed with each other to attract settlers and raise property values by providing the best transportation and banking facilities for moving agricultural commodities to eastern and gulf ports. Revenues sufficient to service the states' debts did not materialize from many of the projects. As a result, during the early 1840s nine states defaulted, and several more came close. Two older, eastern states that defaulted – Pennsylvania and Maryland – were sufficiently developed that they could have raised property and other taxes to avoid default, but so strong was the antipathy to taxation that they did not. A few years later, embarrassed and vilified by creditors, they finally raised taxes and met their obligations.

The other seven defaulting states – Illinois, Indiana, Michigan, Arkansas, Mississippi, Louisiana, and the Florida territory about to become a state – were frontier states with fewer options. Lacking the investment incomes and the business tax revenues of the older states, they already had levied substantial state property taxes on their citizens before the defaults occurred. To have raised taxes further, state leaders felt with some justification, would prove self-defeating. For then settlers might leave and prospective settlers might go to lower-tax states. These newer states recovered less rapidly from the default debacle, and a few – Arkansas,

Mississippi, and Florida – even repudiated portions of their debts. There is little doubt, nonetheless, that state-financed transportation improvements accelerated the pace of United States growth, even when state governments could not or chose not to tap into rising property values to avoid defaults. States that invested in banks, however, lost much of their investments without compensating benefits to their economic development.

European bankers and investors were furious with the defaulting states, and all American securities, even those of the federal government, came under suspicion. Pressures arose at home and abroad for the federal government to assume the state debts and restore American credit. Bills were introduced inviting Congress to take such action, which had precedent in the 1790 funding act. Congress, however, declined the invitation. The debts assumed in 1790 had been incurred in the common cause of independence, not in the particular cause of enhancing one state's competitive position relative to others.

But the federal government was not altogether passive during the 1840s. While not coming to the aid of debt-ridden states, it spent some $90 million, half of which was borrowed, to gain territory for future states. Some went to bring Texas into the Union. Considerably more was expended on the war with Mexico, 1846–1848, and a cash indemnity to that country that brought the Southwest, including California, into the United States. The government also settled boundary disputes in the Pacific Northwest by treaty with Britain, opening up the Oregon territory to American settlement. Some settlement, to be sure, had occurred before the treaty, which is why the issue arose.

In reaction to the debt debacle, many states rewrote their constitutions or passed laws to limit the ability of state government to incur debt. Eighteen took such actions between 1842 and 1857, and it became conventional to insert such limitations into later state constitutions when they were written or rewritten. Such limits, in context, may have had a paradoxical result. By making a state's ability to repay debt more certain, they likely increased its ability to borrow. That is one reason why the state debt crisis of the 1840s had minimal long-term effects on state credit.

Local Government Steps into the Breach, 1840s–1870s and Beyond

The federal system proved flexible and adaptable to experiments that sustained a proactive governmental role in economic development. Such flexibility and adaptability were never more evident than when government put limitations on itself. An early example was the states' loss of flexibility when the Constitution took away their long-exercised right to print paper money, without provision for the new federal government to replace it. What happened then is instructive. The states and the federal government chartered banks that provided money in the form of paper banknotes and deposit credits convertible into a monetary base of specie. A way was found around limitations of governmental authority that, however warranted on other grounds, might have interfered with economic expansion.

Another example came in the 1840s, when the federal government was disengaged from the economy and the states cut back on their borrowing and began to put strict limitations on future borrowing. These behaviors by themselves might have slowed the pace of transportation development and economic expansion. But they did not, in part because local government stepped into the breach. Local governmental or municipal debts, mostly those of cities, were some $25 million in 1840, far less than the approximate $200 million of state debts. In 1880, four decades later, state debts totaled only $275 million, the result of legal limitations, repayments, and – in the South (see next section) – repudiations of debts incurred during Reconstruction after the Civil War. Over the same period, local debt increased much more, to some $200 million by 1860, and to $821 million in 1880.

There were two main reasons for the rise of municipal debts. One was that as states in the 1840s curtailed their involvement with internal improvements, local governments – with state authorization – turned to the capital market to sustain the momentum of improvements aided by public funds. Just as states earlier had competed with one another to improve transportation facilities, counties, cities, and towns from the 1840s to the 1870s competed with one another for good railroad connections. If one of these local governments could come up with a few tens of thousands or hundreds of thousands of dollars to aid a railroad company, then the company would agree to locate its line to serve it. The capital market provided the funds, taking municipal bonds backed by the local tax base, and the local government turned the proceeds over to the railroad, taking stock or bonds or making outright grants-in-aid. This scenario was repeated over and over throughout the settled eastern half of the United States. It had a lot to do with the denseness of the late-nineteenth-century U.S. railroad network.

Local governmental aid to railroads came in bursts that, unsurprisingly, matched bursts in railroad construction. Two lesser bursts came during the mid-1840s and the early 1850s. The major one came after the Civil War, from 1865 to 1873, when the U.S. railroad network doubled in eight years from 35,000 to 70,000 miles of track. Local governments, like state governments earlier, had solid fiscal reasons for aiding internal improvements. A recent study concludes that "the increase in property values associated with railroad construction would, at typical levels of taxation, pay for a substantial share, if not all, of the construction costs solely on the basis of property tax revenues."[8]

Such historical hindsight helps us to understand why American governments became so involved in promoting infrastructure investments. But when the investments were actually made, the matching of revenues and debt service payments was not always so smooth. If 1865–1873 repeated at the local level the improvement boom of the 1830s at the state level, the remainder of the 1870s repeated the 1840s. The financial crisis of 1873 preceded a wider economic downturn. In it railroads failed to make payments to local governments (municipalities), and some of these governments then defaulted on, even repudiated, their railroad-aid bonds. In cases brought by aggrieved bondholders, the U.S. Supreme Court intervened to define municipalities as *public* corporations and creatures of their states that could not declare bankruptcy and repudiate debts, as *private* corporations might. In short, the Supreme Court protected the rights of municipal bondholders. Finally, the states, which were implicated in the mess by reason of their superior relationship to the municipalities, put limits on the capacity of local governments to incur debt, just as they had put debt limits on themselves after the 1840s debacle. Such state controls included limiting municipal debts to specified percentages of assessed property values and requiring that proposed bond issues be voted on by the electorate, and sometimes approved by supermajority (for example, two-thirds of the voters) rather than simple majority.

Urbanization was the other main reason for the rise of municipal debts from $25 to $821 million between 1840 and 1880. Cities had always spent more per capita than other governments in the U.S. federal system, and they were the first to incur local-governmental debt. But up to 1840 cities were few in number. Thereafter, their numbers and sizes increased rapidly, and they turned to the capital market to finance urban infrastructure

---

[8] Jac C. Heckelman and John Joseph Wallis, "Railroads and Property Taxes," *Explorations in Economic History* 34 (1997), 77.

investments. These included paved streets and sidewalks, bridges, street lighting, municipal buildings, waterworks and sewer systems, schools and hospitals, libraries and museums, parks and zoos, urban transit systems – just about every amenity of urban life that a municipal government could imagine.

Even the post-1870 borrowing limitations on municipal government imposed by states could not slow the growth of municipal debts. From $821 million in 1880, these debts – mostly those of cities – rose to $4 billion in 1913. Limiting debt to a percentage of assessed property values was no great barrier to absolute growth as long as urban property values grew, which they did. Beyond that, municipalities were creative in finding ways to circumvent state-imposed limits. One method exploited capital-market innovations, namely revenue and special-assessment bonds. If a city bumped up against a limit to its general-obligation borrowing authority based on assessed property values, it could use these new forms of security to borrow for, say, a waterworks and then service the debt with pledges of fees charged for water. Another method of circumventing debt limits was to create new forms of local government, special districts such as school, park, or water districts, that had their own authority to borrow and levy taxes. This was a way of making the same property do double, triple, or even more duty in financing local governmental investment and service provision. It was by means of such creatively financed urban growth that local government rose to its leading place, as noted in an earlier section, in the tripartite federal system by the early twentieth century.

THE CIVIL WAR AND THE REPUBLICAN ERA AFTER 1860

The Civil War of 1861–1865 remains by most relative and a few absolute measures the largest war in all of U.S. history. It was waged to preserve the Union and to end slavery. And it was won under the leadership of a new political party, the Republicans. Ideologically, the Republicans were the successors of the Whigs of the first half of the century, who in turn were the successors of the Federalists of the 1790s. Abraham Lincoln, the wartime Republican president, had been a Whig. His party would go on to hold the office and control the federal government during most of the period from 1861 to 1914. The Republican ascendancy brought a quantum enlargement of federal authority, new promotional and distributional initiatives from the government in Washington, and a pro-business slant to national policies. It marked a reversal of the Jeffersonian and Jacksonian emphases on states' rights, agrarianism, accommodation of slavery, and limited national government that had dominated decision making at the federal level during the decades after 1800. Lincoln after his assassination would become the Republicans' hero. But their political ideas and their economic and financial policies were Hamiltonian to the core.

Legacies of War Finance: Taxation

The Civil War was expensive, absorbing upwards of a fourth of national product at its peak. To finance such an unprecedented effort, the federal government set precedents that had consequences long after the conflict ended. They came in each of the three means by which government, any government, can gain control over resources, namely taxation, printing money, and borrowing.

Taxation covered about a fifth of the war's cost to the U.S. government, a proportion far larger than in previous wars. Tariffs, long the mainstay of the federal revenue system, were increased. Average tariff rates, measured by the ratio of customs duties to the value of the imports taxed, went from 20 percent before the war to nearly 50 percent by its end. Higher tariffs had been a component of the prewar agenda of the Republicans, as it long had been of their Whig predecessors. But the Democrats, reflecting the interests of the cotton-exporting South in freer trade and a small federal government, had thwarted moves for higher tariffs. Secession of Southern states led southern congressmen to leave Washington, making it easy for the Republicans to implement higher tariffs in 1861. Further increases came during the war years. The South's defeat in 1865 then solidified Republican dominance of Congress during postwar decades, and average tariff rates were continued at wartime levels. As noted earlier, customs duties furnished half or more of federal revenue in most years before 1914. Not until the collapse of world trade in the 1930s did the United States turn away from protectionist trade policies and begin to lead the world toward a freer trading order.

Internal taxation, which had been virtually eliminated at the federal level by the Jeffersonians and Jacksonians between 1800 and 1860, was revived with a fervor on the part of wartime Congresses that Hamilton himself would have liked but hardly anticipated. Excises were imposed on virtually all consumer goods and manufactured articles. License taxes were placed on many trades and occupations. Gross receipts taxes were levied on businesses producing services rather than selling goods. Stamp taxes were placed on many legal documents and a variety of commodities. Federal direct taxes on property, highly unpopular in the late 1790s and quickly eliminated after the War of 1812, were also revived. These were credited against state expenditures on troops and supplies, and therefore did not directly bring in much federal revenue.

Most of these taxes were regressive: lower-income persons paid a greater percentage of their means to the government than did those with higher incomes. To make the internal tax program more acceptable to citizens, Congress in 1861 therefore imposed the first federal income tax. It was a flat tax of 3 percent, but it achieved mild progressivity by exempting incomes under $800. By 1865, the exemption was reduced to $600, but progressivity was increased by taxing incomes up to $5,000 at 5 percent, and those over $5,000 at 10 percent. The income tax brought in 21 percent of federal tax revenues in 1865. Tariff revenues, while substantially higher than prewar, did not really begin to reflect the higher rates imposed by Republicans until the return of peace. In 1865, the tariff provided 29 percent of federal revenues. Customs duties and the income tax thus raised half of 1865 tax revenue. The other half came from the excise-type taxes.

The Civil War income tax established an important precedent in federal finance. Although it was reduced by postwar Congresses and phased out by 1872, along with most of the wartime excise taxes, its success in raising substantial revenues demonstrated the feasibility of a potentially fairer and less regressive tax than either customs duties or excises. For two decades after 1872, numerous attempts to reintroduce the income tax failed. In the 1892 elections, however, Democrats captured both houses of Congress and in 1894 they revived the income tax, with a larger exemption ($4,000) and a lower flat rate (2 percent). But in 1895, the Supreme Court found this income tax to be unconstitutional. Continued support for the income tax by 1909 resulted in the Sixteenth Amendment being submitted to the states. By 1913, the amendment was adopted by the requisite three-fourths of the states, and Congress immediately enacted a tax of 1 percent on incomes over $3,000, with graduated surtaxes on higher incomes (ranging from 1 percent on incomes over $20,000 to 6 percent on those over $500,000). Thus, by the end of the period surveyed here, the income-tax precedent established during the Civil War became a seemingly permanent component of federal taxation. It would subsequently prove to be a greatly expandable source of government revenue for every level of the federal system.

To administer its vast Civil War tax program, Congress created a Commissioner of Internal Revenue in the Treasury Department. Collection districts were formed throughout the country, staffed by a bureaucracy of deputies and agents. By the 1870s, most of the wartime taxes had been phased out, but the bureaucracy remained to collect the important alcohol and tobacco excises and a few lesser excises on luxury items. In recognition of its nature, the agency later was termed the Bureau of Internal Revenue. Still later, as if to deflect that recognition, it was renamed the Internal Revenue Service.

Legacies of War Finance: Money, Banking, and Debt

Civil War taxation, while establishing precedents for later U.S. public finance, raised only about a fifth of the war's cost to the federal government. The remainder came from fiat money issues (accounting for about 10 percent of war expenses) and, most important of all, from issuing interest-bearing debt (about 70 percent). Three issues of fiat United States Notes or "greenbacks" totaling $450 million came in 1862 and 1863, after banks in the North at the end of 1861 had been forced by Treasury demands and specie shortages to suspend specie convertibility of bank notes. The greenbacks were essentially acts of fiscal desperation on the part of Congress, as the war persisted and became bloodier than anyone had imagined possible.

Greenbacks were made legal tender for all payments except customs duties and interest on the federal debt, which continued to be in hard money. Their issue contributed to the 2½-fold increase in the general price level from 1860 to 1864, although given the effort to tax, which was greatly increased, the same resource diversion to warfare would have produced equivalent inflation by other means had the greenbacks not been issued. Then, presumably, the Treasury would have issued more bonds, and banks would have monetized the additional debt by means of banknote and deposit expansion, with equivalent inflationary effects. That is what happened in twentieth-century wars.

As with the income tax, the longer-term significance of the greenbacks was in the precedent they established. In 1787, the Constitution had taken away the right of states to issue fiat currency, but it had been silent on the federal government's authority to do so. Nonetheless, most assumed that the Framers of the Constitution had not intended to confer such a power on the federal government, and the strict-constructionist thinking that dominated federal affairs from 1800 to 1860 honored that assumption. After the Civil War the issue was tested in the courts. In 1869, the Supreme Court, with Chief Justice Chase (who as Treasury Secretary had issued the greenbacks on Congress's authorization during the War) writing the majority opinion, found that the greenbacks were unconstitutional. A differently composed Supreme Court reversed that decision in 1872, when it held that Congress had the power to issue fiat money in wartime. Later, in 1884, another decision broadened Congress's monetary powers to include fiat money issues in times of peace. By that time, the Treasury stood ready to convert greenbacks, most of which still remained in the United States money stock, into specie at prewar rates. Postwar deflation made possible the resumption of such convertibility in 1879.

After 1879, the U.S. dollar remained convertible into hard money through the first third of the twentieth century. In the middle third it was gradually detached from any semblance of convertibility, and by the last third all dollar notes were fiat legal tenders with, appropriately, green backs. As a result of the Civil War experience, Congress's long-doubted power under the Constitution to create fiat money finally had become undoubted.

By far the greatest part of Civil War financing came from debt issues. This was a tribute to the strength of public credit and the capital-market institutions that developed in the country after the Federalist financial revolution of the 1790s. In 1860 the interest-bearing debt of the federal government stood at $65 million, roughly half of what it had been at its previous peak of $127 million in 1816, in the wake of the War of 1812. In between, the federal debt had been fully discharged, if briefly, in the mid-1830s. By 1866 the bonded debt had soared to a new order of magnitude, $2,322 million. Five decades later, on the eve of World War I, the debt stood at $970 million, less than half of the 1866 level. In between, it had gone even lower, to $585 million in 1892. In reducing war-swollen public debts after the return of peace, the Republican era after 1860 was not so different from the Democratic era that preceded it.

Two innovations facilitated the unprecedented level of wartime borrowing. One was the mass marketing of securities perfected by Jay Cooke, a private banker who sold more than $1,000 million of government debt under contracts with the Treasury from 1862 to 1865. Cooke placed patriotic advertisements in numerous newspapers and distributed leaflets instructing ordinary Americans who had never before invested in securities on why they should do so. He also employed thousands of subagents throughout the country to sell government bonds in denominations as low as $50.

Cooke's bond marketing campaigns were aided by a second innovation, the National Banking System established by congressional acts in 1863 and 1864. Because a more detailed discussion of this system, which has lasted in modified form to the present day, is contained elsewhere in this volume, that here can be brief (see Rockoff, Chap. 14). At the time, the objectives of the banking legislation were twofold. Most pressing was the need to sell bonds to finance the war. National banks were federally chartered financial institutions, the first since the two ill-fated Banks of the United States chartered in 1791 and 1816. They were required to invest at least a third of their capital in U.S. bonds and deposit the bonds with a new Treasury official, the Comptroller of the Currency. In return for depositing this collateral, national banks received from the Comptroller banknote currency, uniform except for a stamp with the individual bank's name, equal to 90 (later 100) percent of the lower of par or market value of the bonds. The banks could then lend out this currency at interest, in addition to receiving interest on the federal bonds that backed the currency. In most respects, the legislation was essentially the New York state free banking act of 1838 applied to the entire United States.

Besides aiding bond sales, the act's second objective was providing the country with a uniform banknote currency to replace the variegated issues of some 1600 state chartered banks, which Congress thought would give up their state charters and join the new national system. It did not work out that way, even after Congress in 1865 placed a prohibitive tax on state banknotes, but most state banks did join the national system. Others kept state charters and banked on deposits while forsaking note issue.

The longer-term significance of the National Banking System, besides the greater uniformity it gave to the country's paper currency, was in restoring the federal government's authority and control in banking. This had disappeared in 1811 and again in 1836, when the First and Second Banks of the United States were not rechartered. The National Banking System was a far cry from those two institutions. It did not in any way embody the concept of a central bank. It was simply a system for chartering banks that in most respects were just like the banks chartered by the states. But it was under federal authority, and some of its features, in particular its reserve system, acted in time to make the large national banks of New York City something like a collective holder of the country's central banking reserves, that is, something like a central bank. The restoration of federal authority and the centralization of reserves that developed under the National Banking System paved the way for the "Third Bank of the United States" to appear as a full-fledged central bank in 1913, in the form of the Federal Reserve System. Alexander Hamilton no doubt would have been pleased by this vindication of the financial architecture he put in place more than a century earlier.

The Federalist leader of the 1790s would have been just as pleased with post–Civil War debt management, for making provision to redeem public debts had been an essential component of his plan to strengthen public credit. During the late nineteenth century, despite expanded federal spending initiatives (discussed below), tariff and excise tax collections generated substantial surplus revenues. The federal budget was in surplus every year from 1866 through 1893, and, as already noted, surplus revenues were used to redeem interest-bearing debt, which was reduced in these years from $2.3 to $0.6 billion. Since taxes were mainly on consumption and since the capital market recycled surplus federal revenues into corporate securities and state and local governmental issues that financed infrastructure, federal debt management added to America's savings and capital formation. Unsurprisingly, overall economic growth in these years was at some of the highest rates in U.S. history, which sustained the Republicans in power even though the distributional aspects of their policies were increasingly questioned.

There was so much capital sloshing through financial markets by the end of the century that interest rates fell to extremely low levels. To give one example, shortly after 1900 the federal government borrowed a third of the money required to build the Panama Canal by issuing bonds, in a period of moderate inflation, at 2 percent interest. The other two-thirds came from ordinary revenue. There was a certain irony in this. A federal government that was not allowed by executive and congressional proponents of states' rights to build canals and other infrastructure within the United States in the early nineteenth century could, by the early twentieth, borrow without serious challenge to build a canal in another country. Both the nation and perceptions of the national interest had certainly changed, and that, too, likely was a legacy of changes wrought by the Civil War.

Other Republican Wartime Initiatives

Besides higher tariffs, the Republicans' prewar agenda included federal aid for building transcontinental railroads and making land free to homesteaders. Both items had been stymied by states' rights, limited-government Democrats. When southern Democrats withdrew from Congress after secession, both became possible. In 1862, the Pacific Railway Act chartered two corporations, the Union Pacific and the Central Pacific railroads, which were granted public lands along their rights of way and federal bond subsidies per mile of track constructed. In 1864, additional lands were granted to the two companies, and new grants were made to a third, the Northern Pacific. By 1871, when the land-grant program ended, partly in response to scandals, Congress had given away 200 million acres of public land, although a third of it reverted to the United States when railroads failed to complete their construction on schedule. Still, the first transcontinental railway was completed in 1869, and others soon followed.

The Homestead Act also came in 1862. To that point, the federal government had always charged for land, although so much was offered that what it collected, apart from a few years when sales soared, did little more than cover the costs of surveying and selling it. Still, the Democrats in power prized land sales as a source of federal revenue that mitigated calls by their opponents for higher tariffs. The Homestead Act granted title to 160 acres of land for nothing, provided a homesteader settled on it for five years. Despite its political popularity, the act was less effective than it might have been in other circumstances. A tract of 160 acres was not as viable for farming in the arid West as in the Middle West and East. Land grants gave western railroads large quantities of land and an incentive to dispose of it unconstrained by the Homestead Act's limits. Moreover, another piece of 1862 legislation, the Morrill Act, granted states large tracts – 30,000 acres for each member of Congress – to endow "land-grant" colleges that would specialize in agricultural and mechanical instruction. The Act created still more sellers of land who were not constrained by Homestead Act provisions. In the end, the railroads and the states sold much more land to settlers than was homesteaded.

The Homestead Act, with its "free" land, was nonetheless symbolic as the ultimate liberalization of public-domain privatization. Its Republican sponsors gained politically by implementing it while at the same time spending federal land and money from the national budget to promote infrastructure investments and educational initiatives in ways not allowed by pre-1860 regimes in Washington. Defense considerations were used to justify both the Pacific Railway and Morrill acts – the Far West had to be defended, and the land-grant colleges would offer military training. In the long run, however, both acts, like much of the wartime financial legislation, were more important in setting precedents for a higher level of federal involvement in the nation's economy.

Postbellum Federal Transfer Programs

Modern government features extensive transfer programs, the expenditure of public funds not to purchase resources for public uses, but for the purpose of transferring purchasing power from taxpayers to other citizens. Large-scale federal transfer programs may be said to have begun in the decades after the Civil War. There were two such programs in these years, and each was related to the scale of that conflict. One was the payment of interest and principal on the national debt. Reductions of principal through budget surpluses channeled into debt retirement were discussed earlier. It should also be noted that from the end of the Civil War to 1880, roughly 40 percent of the federal budget went to pay interest on the debt. Interest and principal payments transferred money from taxpayers to bondholders. Since bondholders had bought their securities with cheap dollars during the Civil War inflation, and since most taxes were regressive consumption taxes, this transfer program favored investors at the expense of consumers. At the time, it was a high-investment, growth-promoting policy.

The other large transfer program involved payments to Union veterans and their widows and orphans. The confederacy's veterans were excluded, although southern state governments instituted programs of their own. Like debt-related expenditures, the federal program was not new. Payments to veterans had been a component of every federal budget since 1789. But before the Civil War such cash payments (there were also land grants to veterans) in most years had been a small part of a budget that itself was small – seldom more than $100 thousand before 1815, and then typically $1 to $3 million down to 1860. The amount leapt to $25 to $30 million per year during the late 1860s and 1870s, even though veterans pensions were paid only to those disabled in the line of duty. This restriction irritated veterans organizations who wanted pensions for service or, if that were not possible, for the disabled from the time of their service, and not just for service-connected disability from the time an application was approved. But little action was taken on the veterans' demands because the government's main financial concerns throughout the 1870s were resumption of specie payments and debt management.

By 1879 resumption was achieved, and debt management concerns were gone. Yet budget surpluses continued. In that year, lobbying groups for veterans persuaded Congress to pass a so-called Pension Arrears Act, with payments calculated from the time of a veteran's discharge from service. This generosity led to a large increase in pensioners (from 26,000 in 1879 to 345,000 in 1885) and in pension payments (veterans payments doubled between 1878 and 1885, making up some 20 percent of federal spending in the latter year). As usually is the case when entitlement programs are put in or enhanced, the magnitude of the response was underestimated. Since there were budget surpluses, the underestimation did not cause fiscal strains. A century later the United States would not be quite so fortunate with its much larger entitlement programs.

In 1890, while budget surpluses continued, pensions were further liberalized. Any veteran with 90 days of military service and a disability of any kind, war-related or not, became eligible, as did unremarried widows of veterans. The number of military-related pensioners soared to nearly a million by 1893, and pension payments rose to 40 percent of federal spending. The growth of pension spending slowed from then to 1914, when its budget share was around 25 percent. But the principle was firmly established that the federal government had a responsibility to provide large-scale transfer payments to Americans whom Congress deemed worthy of such support. The Civil War veterans entitlement program thus provided a preview of big government in the twentieth century.

State Governments: Debt Repudiation in the South

The southern confederacy's defeat ended slavery and rendered valueless its currency and debts. Debts of the southern states, $90 million in 1860, had increased through arrears of interest to $112 million in 1865. During the period called Presidential Reconstruction, 1865–1868, renewed borrowing for public works by Tennessee, Louisiana, and Georgia, plus accumulating interest arrears raised the southern-state debt total to $146 million.

Then came Congressional Reconstruction, with its "carpetbagger" governments cited then and later for corrupt practices. From 1868 to 1874, southern state debts increased through measures of questionable legality by somewhat more than $100 million, much of which disappeared into private pockets and failed ventures, serving little useful public purpose. With the end of Reconstruction in the mid-1870s, so-called "redeemer" Democrat control was established in southern state capitals. The new state governments proceeded to repudiate virtually all of the Reconstruction-era debts, and then some. Some $62 million was repudiated outright, and an additional $41 was repudiated through scaling down the principal of other debts. Adding interest not paid on scaled-down debt, the total repudiation came to $116 million.

Given the doubtful legality surrounding the debt-increasing measures of the "carpetbagger" governments, and the documented corruption involved, some – perhaps many – of the repudiations could be justified. That was less the case with some pre-Reconstruction and even prewar debts that were also repudiated. Even after the repudiations, because states outside the South reduced their debts while those in the South did not, the southern states, with incomes by then well below the national average, were left with substantially higher per capita debt burdens. The experience, along with the state debt defaults of the early 1840s, was one of the saddest in the annals of American government and public finance.

State Governments: New Responsibilities

The United States, already a rich country before the Civil War, became an even richer one after it, apart from the defeated South. Except in cities, many of which were new and required large public investments in order to function as cities, the role of government in developing basic economic infrastructures was largely completed by the 1870s – at least until the automobile created demands for better public roads after 1900. In a rich and maturing industrial economy most investment came to be planned privately and financed by private banking and capital market institutions.

Industrialization, however, created new demands for government action, demands that were less in the realm of helping to plan and finance infrastructure and more in the realm of ameliorating economic development's rougher edges and doing more to regulate it. As state, local, and federal promotional activities wound down in the 1870s, the winding down was accompanied by growing cries to regulate large transportation enterprises governmental policies had helped create. At the same time, the nationwide market area opened up by rail transportation summoned forth equally large and impersonal manufacturing firms and utility companies. These big businesses exploited new production and distribution technologies. It seemed to many Americans that they exploited their employees, customers, and communities as well. The result was a persistent demand for regulatory and other social interventions on the part of governments at every level of the federal system.

Many of these demands arose first at the state level because, as Woodrow Wilson noted in the passage quoted in an earlier section, under the U.S. federal system state legislation set most of the rules of economic life. Shortly after the Civil War, the New York state legislature established a state Board of Charities, a number of teachers colleges, and enacted housing regulations. The example of New York, then the largest and wealthiest state, is further instructive in showing how the initiatives of a leading state's government reached into more and more new areas, foreshadowing developments in other states and, later, at the federal level:

In 1860, New York State spent only $50,000 for regulative services other than public health, by 1880 it spent $300,000, and by 1900, $900,000. It established a railroad commission for the regulation of rates in 1882, a Bureau of Labor Statistics in the same year, and a Board of Mediation and Arbitration and a Board of Factory Inspectors four years later; mine inspection in 1890; and sweatshop and bakery inspection in 1892 to 1895. A state board of health was established in 1880 with powers to collect vital statistics, enforce pure food laws, and investigate disease. State expenditures for the mentally ill and for social welfare increased from $263,000 in 1860 to $1,230,000 in 1880 and to $6,500,000 in 1900. A state agricultural experiment station was established in 1880 and a Department of Agriculture, inaugurating cattle inspection and eradication of bovine tuberculosis and plant and nursery diseases, in 1893. Conservation of state resources started in 1868 with the creation of Commissioners of Fisheries, and a Forest Reserve Commission was established in 1885.[9]

Modern forms of state economic regulation were minimal before 1870. By 1887, when the federal Interstate Commerce Commission came in, twenty nine states already had state railroad commissions. By World War I, 44 of 48 states had such commissions. In 1914, twenty three states regulated most public utilities, and thirty five regulated telephone companies. Milk inspection was practiced by forty six states.

When the federal Sherman Antitrust Act was enacted in 1890, twenty one states already had legislated antitrust laws. By the time of World War I, thirty five states had such laws. Many states also regulated banks and insurance companies.

In the area of general labor law, twenty eight states limited child factory labor by 1900, and thirty nine limited women's hours of work by 1917.

[9] Paul Studenski and Herman E. Krooss, *Financial History of the United States* (2nd ed. New York, 1963), 193n.

Worker accident compensation measures were on the books of thirty one states by 1916. Particular occupations were covered by state licensing laws. By 1914, for example, every state licensed dentists and pharmacists, and many licensed architects. All the states by World War I had compulsory education laws, and all provided free textbooks.

These manifold public-sector innovations usually started in one or a few states and then diffused among the others as they proved to serve some important interests, if not always that of the general public. Occupational licensing, for example, could help to assure consumers that providers of goods and services met certain standards of training and experience. But it also could be used to restrict entry (including entry by minorities) into licensed occupations, thereby raising prices paid by consumers and the incomes of those licensed. Rent seeking, the economist's new name for what earlier generations called corruption, often was involved in government actions at all levels of the federal system. Like poverty, rent seeking is often lamented and yet never seems to go away.

Public assistance programs also grew. Local governments even in colonial times had always made some provisions for the poor in their midsts, and the state and federal governments from the first years of the republic had provided some aid to veterans. Industrial society expanded the list of those deemed worthy of similar assistance to include the aged, the incapacitated, and the unemployed. During the late nineteenth century, responsibility for helping people falling into one or another of these categories shifted from local communities to states, and from private charities to state institutions. Inexorably, there would be demands that the federal government take a greater role in such programs, but apart from veterans' entitlements, they would not be very effective until the 1930s.

A New Federalism

The twentieth century would witness still more centralization of regulatory and social welfare activities. But the trend toward centralization became evident even earlier in several areas. Woodrow Wilson, a keen observer of the political trends of the late nineteenth century, pointed to an important reason why the centralizing trend emerged:

The plan of leaving to the states the regulation of all that portion of the law which most nearly touches our daily interests, and which in effect determines the whole structure of our society, the whole organic action of industry and business, has some serious disadvantages: disadvantages which make themselves more and more emphatically felt as modern tendencies of social and political development more and more prevail over the old conservative forces. . . . State divisions, it turns out, are not natural economic divisions; they practically constitute no barriers at all to any distinctly marked industrial regions. Variety and conflict of laws, consequently, have brought not a little friction and confusion into our social and business arrangements.[10]

There were, in short, conflicts between, on the one hand, multiple and differing state regulations and, on the other, the requirements of a fully integrated national economic development. The experience of railroads, the dominant enterprises of the nineteenth century, illustrates the conflict that emerged. Federal regulation of railroads came with the Interstate Commerce Commission (ICC) in 1887, but only after the Supreme Court had first sanctioned railroad regulation by states in the 1870s, and then in the 1880s found it unconstitutional when states tried to extend their regulatory authority to interstate rail shipments. The railroad was not naturally confined within state boundaries. Neither was the large manufacturing corporation. Therefore, federal antitrust laws, following state precedents much as did railroad regulation, appeared in 1890. That pro-business Republican legislators endorsed (and even sponsored) such centralizing regulatory laws indicates that they were as much the product of business's frustrations with arbitrary and conflicting state regulations as of consumer frustrations with big business.

The so-called Progressive Era of the early twentieth century followed enactment of these initial federal regulatory and antitrust acts. It brought further centralization of regulatory, social welfare, and resource conservation functions at the federal level. During the administration of Republican president Theodore Roosevelt from 1901 to 1909, in the regulatory area the ICC was given stronger powers to set maximum railroad rates, the Pure Food and Drug Act came in, the federal Department of Agriculture was empowered to inspect meats shipped in interstate commerce, a Bureau of Corporations with investigative powers was established, and a National Monetary Commission began deliberations that culminated in 1913 in the act creating the Federal Reserve System.

In the areas of social welfare and services, Roosevelt and William Howard Taft, his Republican successor in the White House (1909–1913), initiated federal disaster relief programs and established a federal Public

---

[10] Wilson, *The State*, 478.

Health Service. In conservation, during the Roosevelt administration came the Reclamation (Newlands) Act of 1902 establishing federal dam and irrigation programs of great benefit to agriculture. Roosevelt and Taft reserved vast quantities of the remaining public domain for national forests. By 1910 these forests contained nearly 200 million acres, as much as had been granted to railroads in the land-grant programs of 1862–1871.

Many of the federal initiatives of the Progressive Era were carried out with the cooperation of business interests that often were thought to be adamantly opposed to such intrusions of big government. These "corporate liberal" interests had been frustrated by the chaos of parochial state regulatory and other measures as they expanded the scope of their operations nationwide. They wanted to bring more order to what was then a predominantly industrial society. Hence, they preferred, and worked with political leaders to bring about, orderly national solutions to national problems. Such solutions served corporate liberal interests better than the conflicting and often contradictory solutions reached through the deliberations and actions of forty eight independent state legislatures.

At the time of the Progressive Era, American financiers and industrialists were thinking internationally as well as nationally. Here, too, their Republican allies in Washington were helpful. By the end of his second administration in 1909, Theodore Roosevelt had quadrupled spending on the U.S. Navy compared to what it had been before the brief Spanish-American War of 1898. He also launched the Panama Canal project, which, when the canal opened in 1914, enhanced both world commerce and American prestige and naval power. In concrete and rather expensive ways, the federal government became an instrument for extending the reach of American business throughout the world.

Thus, the American federal system, which had introduced big government under the leadership of Washington, Hamilton, and other Federalists in the 1790s, and then backed off from it during the eras of Jefferson and Jackson prior to the Civil War, gradually came back to it in the decades before the outbreak of World War I in 1914. There was, of course, a major difference. The Federalists of the 1790s did their work in the context of a small, agricultural country on the periphery of a Euro-centered world economy. By 1914 the United States had become the world's largest and technologically most advanced economy. The intervening changes had broadened the range of the country's interests and given its governments more options and resources. The remainder of the twentieth century would witness an extrapolation of the centralizing trends re-established during and after the Civil War. It would usher in a new age of Federalism, presided over by both Republicans and Democrats, and perhaps not so different from what the Federalists of the nation's first years had in mind, even though the position of the United States among the world's nations was vastly different from what it had been in the 1790s.

13

INTERNAL TRANSPORTATION IN THE NINETEENTH AND EARLY TWENTIETH CENTURIES

ALBERT FISHLOW

INTRODUCTION

The United States was the first country of continental proportions to develop in the nineteenth century. This result was largely the consequence of the development of internal transportation. Through a combination of a massive investment in the transport sector and the initiation of newer and more efficient transport modes, the original coastal settlement on the Atlantic reached out to an ever-wider hinterland. The rich interior, with its better soils, was integrated into a regionally specialized whole. Without the allocation of resources to transportation on a large scale and the succession of nineteenth-century transport innovations in canals and railroads, the contours of the American economy would have been far different.

In this chapter I examine how the interplay of American market conditions and social intervention functioned to evoke transport investment in great abundance; how these facilities both lowered the costs of movement and widened the market; and how the benefits were distributed to the rest of the economy.

I begin by discussing some of the theoretical effects of transport investment. The second section then treats the motives, magnitudes, and financing of the succession of transport innovations undertaken in the nineteenth and early twentieth centuries. It also deals with their success in lowering transport rates and attracting traffic. The third and fourth sections examine the variety of economic effects attributable to the nineteenth- and twentieth-century transportation revolutions. The final section briefly reviews that entire experience to see what conclusions may be drawn from it.

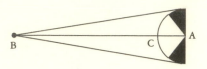

Figure 13.1.

THE EFFECTS OF TRANSPORT
INVESTMENT

As background for the discussion that follows, it will be helpful to consider the effects of transport investment, many of which can be illustrated
with the aid of a simple diagram.[1] Consider an area of uniform agricultural fertility, as shown in Figure 13.1, producing a single product for
which there is a perfectly elastic demand. Prior to construction of a railroad from the coastal city A to B, the extent of economic settlement is
limited to the semicircle around A. At the border of the semicircle the
cost of transport plus the cost of production exactly equals the price in A.
Hence the land earns zero rent and is at the margin of cultivation. At all
points within the area of cultivation, and proportional to the proximity to
market, positive locational rents are earned.

The construction of the railroad, by reducing transport costs, immediately widens the area of profitable cultivation, as shown. Now along the
margins of the triangle, and at B itself, the sum of the lower transport
costs and constant production costs equals the former revenue. Moreover,
within the previous boundary, at all points outside the shaded segment, it
is now cheaper to use a combination of railroad and overland transport.
Rents will rise in this new zone, reflecting the new lower supply costs and
the profits potentially earned on land brought closer to the market. Those
located at C are especially favored. Previously on the margin of cultivation, and therefore with the largest ton-mile shipments, such settlers
receive the greatest benefits from the railroad. These manifest themselves
in increased rents, which are nothing more than the annual value of the
direct benefits of the transport investment.

Obviously the creation of new economical production sites within the
compass of the market will encourage settlement in the area and lead to

---

[1] For a fuller treatment see A. A. Walters, *The Economics of Road User Charges*, World Bank Staff Occasional Paper no. 5 (Baltimore, 1968), chap. 5.

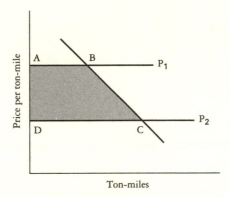

Figure 13.2.

increased output. Aggregate real income will rise by the amount of the additional cultivation. But since much of the increase is due to the influx of more labor and capital, productivity increases more modestly. Its growth is determined by the savings in transport costs on goods shipped to market. These lower charges have their analogue in reduced factor inputs, thereby releasing some inputs previously engaged in transportation to other productive activities. Figure 13.2 illustrates the direct benefits that can be ascribed to the road as area ABCD. The area represents the difference between what persons would have been willing to pay in transportation charges and what they actually paid. Since their willingness to pay is based on the exact equality of the sum of transport charges and costs of production with revenues, this difference is exactly the same as the locational rent discussed above. Note that we do not evaluate the differential cost of the total traffic DC after the road has opened, because that figure overstates its benefits; it is necessary also to take into account how the transport demand, and thus the resources potentially freed, depend on the rate charged.

This theoretical case can be extended to more complicated, and more realistic, alternatives without much alteration. For example, if settlement had already occurred between A and B and limited production for subsistence were already present, a much larger consequence would have to be ascribed to the investment. This is because the same aggregate real income increase could occur with a much smaller addition of new factors. Similarly, given a larger market area, if it is now feasible for A to specialize in manufactures at a lower production cost than the costs of previous imports or home manufacture, there is a further gain to the community. It is also easy to accommodate the cases of differential fertility or of less than perfectly elastic demand.

Perhaps the most important modification is to introduce explicitly the capital costs of constructing the improvement. The price line P_2 in Figure 13.2 will in general include only the variable costs of operation, for once the facility is constructed that is the relevant measure of the resource input. The decision to construct or not must depend upon the size and time profile of the benefits relative to the capital costs. Or if we wish to interpret the price as including some normal return on the capital, we must compare the sum of net revenues (receipts minus operating costs) and benefits (measured on a price rather than cost basis). If the innovation is costly, then although it will have a favorable effect on real income, it still may not be economical. It may be better to invest in improved techniques of cultivation, for example, and to lower the costs of production, rather than to reduce the costs of transportation.

In making such calculations, we emphasize the necessity of taking into account the totality of benefits, not merely the private profits. An essential attribute of transport investment, particularly when embodied in a more advanced technology (as when the canal superseded the turnpike or the railroad the canal), is that its social returns tend to be large. This is typically the case because transport serves as intermediate input into a variety of final outputs, and because of its spatial fixity. These characteristics lend to transportation routes a quality of essentiality. When the railroad is initially opened from A to B, it does not matter that there may already be a whole series of prior investments linking other cities. They are of no value to the immediate area because their capacity cannot be utilized there. When investment proceeds to the point where duplication of facilities occurs, the indirect benefits drop off quickly. The same is true when the technical characteristics of successive innovations leave little basis for choosing between them.

The indivisibility of transportation facilities in their early phase thus makes for quantum jumps in traffic carried, and large benefits. It also simultaneously poses a problem to private investors. They cannot recapture through their charges all of the benefits conferred by the road. Any single tariff will lead to smaller private revenues than benefits, since the latter represent the maximum that could be obtained through a set of perfectly discriminated prices (charging each potential user a different price based on his personal advantage, thereby absorbing all of the locational rent). This problem does not arise with the usual investment because it typically involves small enough changes in output to allow the private revenues obtained to approximate the social benefits. Indivisibility also operates on the cost side to increase the capital that must be mobilized to construct the road. As larger sums are required, the risk increases and finance becomes less readily available.

To these effects creating a divergence between social and private rates of return we may add still others. The durability of the typical transport investment makes it necessary to take into account a flow of revenues far into the future. Reduction in transport costs will set in motion ancillary investments – agricultural settlement in the example in Figure 13.1 – and these will affect the profitability of the original transport facility. If the private investor is myopic, he will understate the true, dynamic outcome and will focus upon the more limited current traffic. These *forward linkages*, as they have been termed, reflect themselves at least in traffic increases and thereby in revenues. (Of course, for reasons of indivisibility it may be impossible to capture all the benefits by charges.) The *backward linkages*, or effects upon suppliers to the transport sector, do not impinge upon the investor in the same way. The ultimate technological or scale impact of, say, the number of rails ordered upon the iron industry will only partially register itself through the indirect route of iron price reductions. Very rarely will such considerations enter into the individual investment decision. To the extent that the original transport investment sets in motion a unique sequence of further investment and technological change, the uncoordinated action of the market does not reward that initial investment sufficiently. Consequently, some socially desirable investments may not be undertaken.

Even if the private sector responds appropriately in constructing the right facilities, there may still be a problem of price determination. Transport investments, particularly in their early phases, confer natural monopolies upon their owners and operators. Users typically have no option among alternative routings. While optimal social policy requires that price be equal to marginal costs, the profit-maximizing monopolist will equate marginal revenue to marginal cost and produce less. Hence there will be insufficient utilization of the carrying capacity of the facility if market power is not restrained. This problem is further complicated by the existence of economies of scale that make any pricing rule based upon marginal cost privately nonviable: only a subsidy to compensate for intramarginal losses can make it feasible.

It is no surprise, in light of the above noted defects of market signals, that the history of internal improvements has been intimately tied up with government policy. Whether because of the desire to stimulate transport investment for its wide-ranging indirect effects, or because of the necessity for regulation, the public interest has asserted its presence even when the price system has ruled supreme in the rest of the economy. Yet compared to other international cases, the role of the private sector in the United States was surprisingly vigorous.

THE NATURE OF NINETEENTH-CENTURY TRANSPORT EXPANSION

The Turnpike Era, 1800–1820

The earliest expression of post-colonial demand for internal improvement was in the construction of better overland facilities. In the process the precedent was created of a strong reliance upon private enterprise and initiative. This emphasis was to characterize much of the subsequent investment in transportation. It was not that the public or common road was unknown: In 1800, before there was any sizable turnpike mileage, post roads already aggregated more than 20,000 miles. Rather, reliance upon independent local construction and repair, financed largely by required labor services, seemed unable to evoke a system of anything approaching adequate quality. And small wonder. Since passage on the roads was not limited to local residents, some part of the benefits devolved on others without compensating payment. Moreover, in the context of a seasonal agriculture, the additional costs in time and effort of inadequate transportation to market did not much conflict with productive labor. It seemed preferable to give up leisure after the harvest than be subject to the cash levies required for a more efficient road network.

Improvement in the road system therefore took the form of private turnpike construction rather than investment in public thoroughfares. Beginning with the prosperity engendered by the surge of commercial activity in the 1790s and ending with the rise of canals and railways, somewhat more than 11,000 miles of turnpikes were constructed in the northern

Table 13.1. *Cumulative turnpike construction in the New England and Middle Atlantic states (costs in thousands of dollars)*

	1810		1820		1830	
	Mileage	Cost	Mileage	Cost	Mileage	Cost
Maine	35	35	35	35	35	35
New Hampshire	455	455	527	527	527	527
Vermont	341	341	410	410	455	455
Massachusetts	767	1,851	843	1,966	964	2,086
Rhode Island	78	78	133	133	172	172
Connecticut	1,148	1,148	1,302	1,302	1,459	1,459
New York	1,100	2,000	4,000	8,000	4,500	9,000
New Jersey	200	600	500	1,000	550	1,100
Pennsylvania	500	1,500	1,800	6,400	2,500	8,800
Maryland	60	300	250	1,200	300	1,500
National road	—	—	130	1,561	200[a]	2,689
Total	4,684	8,308	9,930	22,534	11,662	27,823

[a] In process of construction; approximately 200 miles completed.

Source: **New England:** Frederick J. Wood, *The Turnpikes of New England and Evolution of the Same Through England, Virginia and Maryland* (Boston, 1919); Albert Gallatin, "Report on Roads and Canals," document no. 250, 10th Congress, 1st Session. Vol. 1 in *American State Papers: Miscellaneous* (1810). **Middle Atlantic:** Joseph A. Durrenberger, *Turnpikes: A Study of the Toll Road Movement in the Middle Atlantic States and Maryland* (Valdosta, GA, 1931); J. L. Ringwalt, *Development of Transportation Systems in the United States* (Philadelphia, 1888); George H. Evans, Jr., *Bussiness Incorporations in the United States, 1800–1943* (New York, 1948). **National road:** Thomas B. Searight, *The Old Pike* (Uniontown, PA, 1894).

states before 1830. The majority were completed by 1820, and in New England even earlier. All indications point to modest southern turnpike construction, despite Virginia's claim to the first road in 1785; nor was much done in the West until the era of plank roads. Thus the New England figures probably require an adjustment of only 10–20 percent to reflect the national picture.

Table 13.1 provides rough estimates of the magnitude, location, and timing of the investment. Since it is derived from the combination of literary accounts of individual New England turnpikes, various state reports, fragmentary additional references, as well as the annual distribution of cumulative totals indicated by reports of incorporation, the tabulation is inexact. Nonetheless, the general contours are probably valid enough.

The data reflect the early and rather complete system of roads radiating from commercial and political centers such as Boston, Concord, New Haven, Hartford, Albany, New York, Philadelphia, and Baltimore. Subsequent construction in the Middle Atlantic states extended already completed trunk lines westward and interlaced their larger territories. The more expensive and serious character of the Philadelphia and Baltimore links to the Ohio Valley, well surfaced according to the McAdam design, show up in the much higher costs per mile registered in Pennsylvania and Maryland. The total investment required to finance the construction of turnpikes, conservatively estimated at about $30 million by 1830, represented some 60 percent of the expenditure for all canals during this period.

This substantial sum, unlike the outlays for canals, was secured predominantly from private coffers. Apart from federal finance for the National Road, substantial state assistance was limited to Virginia, Ohio, and Pennsylvania during the period in question. (Kentucky, Indiana, and Illinois later became involved in the 1830s.) Only the Keystone State, attentive to regional interests, completed an extensive system, and there the proportionate contribution of the state came close to 30 percent. Taken as a whole, about $25 million was raised privately, an amount that was twice the private commitment to canals.

Such a feat was made possible by the decentralized character of the turnpike corporations. The average turnpike size in Massachusetts was less than 20 miles, and it was smaller still in Connecticut. The route between Philadelphia and Pittsburgh was operated by eight turnpike and three bridge companies. Few exceeded $100,000 in capitalization, and all relied quite heavily upon local contributions that were widely distributed within the participating communities. State charters frequently placed a maximum upon the number of votes a shareholder might cast and required immediate cash deposits upon subscription. The motivation for the investment seemingly was not the direct financial return but the indirect advantages accruing to those with access to better roads. Whatever the expectations, however, little direct profit was actually realized.

Even the Philadelphia and Lancaster Road, well constructed in a region already experiencing vigorous trade, and originally oversubscribed, could not remunerate its proprietors satisfactorily. Gallatin reports a net income of $12,000 upon a total cost of $465,000 for a return of less than 3 percent;

and profits did not exceed 4 percent even in later years, after the successful extension to Pittsburgh. The detailed accounts of the Massachusetts turnpikes likewise chronicle financial disappointment. The Salem Turnpike was well situated and excellently constructed; yet its average returns on cost were below 5 percent. The high cost of construction, $15,000 per mile, cannot be blamed. Less-expensive turnpikes in western Massachusetts fared little better, and more frequently worse. For New England as a whole, only 5 or 6 out of 230 turnpikes have been identified as profitable.[2] In light of these experiences, the Gallatin Report's attribution of an 11 percent return to the Connecticut roads in the first decade of the nineteenth century has to seem exaggerated.

What explains this lack of profitability, surprising because of both the continuing flow of private investment and the widespread eagerness for transport improvement? Among the reasons given are high overhead expenses, avoidance of tolls through the device of shunpikes, and construction in sparsely settled regions incapable of generating sufficient traffic. The most important factors, however, were the limitations of the available technology and the marginal advantage over common roads the turnpike represented. The only innovative feature of the turnpike was its better surface, which reduced friction. This gain in carrying capacity was calculated at 125 percent over that possible on ordinary roads in an 1831 Pennsylvania Canal Commissioners' report. Translated into transport costs, it converts to a 50 percent reduction. Whether such technical characteristics reflected themselves exactly in market prices is difficult to ascertain. The apparent decline in wagon rates during the turnpike era is in the right direction. Nevertheless tariffs remained high. The rates most frequently quoted were between 12 and 17 cents per ton-mile, and sometimes higher. At such prices, long-distance hauling of all but the highest-valued commodities continued to be excluded. Over this range of price reduction, the demand for long hauls was not very elastic. For shorter hauls, the disadvantages of a lighter load and lengthier elapsed time on common roads seemed to be less than the toll charges. These were determined by the type of vehicle rather than the load carried. For maximum load, the typical toll was 2 cents per ton-mile, but upon smaller shipments it became proportionately higher. This increased cost could become a significant deterrent where population density was limited and shipments small. The reports of the Pennsylvania and New York Turnpikes confirm that "long distance

---

[2] George R. Taylor, *The Transportation Revolution* (New York, 1951), 27.

traffic was the chief source of revenue on all turnpikes except a few situated near the larger centers of population."[3]

Two final points should be kept in mind. First, the turnpike corporation was limited to toll receipts without any possible additional profit on the transportation services themselves. A similar handicap was to harass canals, but their much lower charges frequently evoked a traffic large enough to compensate. Under such circumstances, the companies were able to appropriate to themselves only a part of the total transport savings. The increased profits accrued to stage operators and teamsters upon their investments in equipment. Second, as we have seen in the discussion of Figure 13.1, no charge could have recaptured the total benefits, because of the externalities present.

Ultimately, the unsatisfactory private financial outcome determined the turnpike's fate. Even before the competition of canals and railways had made itself felt, many turnpikes had fallen into disrepair, unable to repay even variable costs. The technology could not justify the cost. Peak mileage was reached about 1830, although the investment rate had been greatest some 15 years previously. The turnpike was to be partially responsible for far greater transport consequences, however. Completion of the Pittsburgh Pike and National Road, however inadequate, had given Philadelphia and Baltimore advantages in the western trade vis-à-vis New York. Out of that confrontation emerged the Erie Canal and, in reflex, the Baltimore and Ohio Railroad. We now turn to these other central innovations of the nineteenth century.

The Age of Canal Expansion, 1815–1843

Water as an internal transport medium retained the disadvantage of slowness but compensated with sharply reduced friction. Large loads could be carried cheaply with a minimal expenditure of energy. This principle had been applied since ancient times. Yet natural waterways were not always adequate or ideally located. The Duke of Bridgewater's success with his canal, begun in 1759 in England, set off a wave of imitation that involved an expenditure of some £13 million in Great Britain in the last 40 years of the eighteenth century.[4] The response in the United States was longer in coming, but ultimately more ambitious.

---

[3] Joseph A. Durrenberger, *Turnpikes: A Study of the Toll Road Movement in the Middle Atlantic States and Maryland* (Valdosta, GA, 1931), 118.

[4] T. S. Ashton, *An Economic History of England: The Eighteenth Century* (London, 1955), 75.

The delay in American response until the 1790s is easily explained by the Revolutionary War and the unsettled decade immediately following. Thereafter economic factors played a more decisive role in inhibiting canal construction. The large average size of most planned ventures, and the substantial costs per mile, made total capital requirements a significant deterrent. Moreover, there were no immediately paying propositions, such as the coal-carrying canals of England represented; the poor financial results of the pioneering Middlesex and Santee Companies reinforced such skepticism. It took the Erie Canal to undermine that view.

It was an epic undertaking, 364 miles in length, linking the Hudson to Lake Erie, begun in 1817 and completed in 1825.[5] The roots extend much earlier. An initial step was taken in 1792 when the Western Inland Lock Navigation Company was authorized to connect the Hudson River to Lake Ontario and Seneca Lake. Harassed by shortages of funds, compensated only partially by state assistance, the canal could not be completed to either of its termini. Nor was river improvement, which constituted the bulk of what was in fact done, efficient enough to compete successfully with neighboring turnpikes. The expenditure of $400,000 yielded little or no return. Yet that failure ultimately had the following consequences: (a) It established a precedent for the necessity of state intervention rather than reliance on private initiative; (b) it was the basis for later consideration of an all-canal alternative, constructed in a more technically satisfactory fashion; and (c) it also meant a more sympathetic hearing for an alternative route to the Great Lakes, via Lake Erie.

For many years, no such beneficial effects were apparent. Not until the Gallatin Report of 1808 included a proposal for the federal government to construct a canal from the Mohawk River to Lake Ontario did a significant revival of the earlier scheme take place. In 1810 one of the directors of the Western Company suggested that the legislature appoint a commission to examine the possibilities of further westward expansion by that enterprise. A resolution emerged empowering a commission to explore the entire route and to propose a program to the next session. Finally, in 1811, an expanded board was voted with additional financial support. By this time it was clear that private enterprise was not sufficient to the task. Federal funds were sought to fulfill the original Gallatin scheme. But that report, solicited in the commercial euphoria of 1807 and

---

[5] We have drawn extensively, in this and succeeding paragraphs, upon Julius Rubin, "An Innovating Public Improvement: The Erie Canal," in Carter Goodrich, ed. *Canals and American Economic Development* (New York, 1961).

concluded after the Embargo Act, was not about to receive implementation in the less satisfactory economic and political climate of 1810 and thereafter. New York State itself would have to shoulder the burden, now estimated at $6 million. The legislature cautiously followed its commission, authorizing in 1812 the borrowing of $5 million for the project, but retaining for itself the final decision to proceed.

Presages of early success proved false. The War of 1812 intervened to eliminate the possibility of a European loan and to diminish the enthusiasm of the legislature. Only an extensive campaign led by DeWitt Clinton, abetted by the postwar recovery and the rapidly increasing population of western New York, revived and consummated the proposal in April 1817. In addition to the Erie route, a canal was authorized linking the Hudson River to Lake Champlain, a plan which had been the unrealized intent of the earlier private Northern Company.

THE ERIE AND ITS IMITATORS

Few public investments were so well rewarded or so immediate in their impact. Prior to completion to its full length, the Erie Canal had collected almost $1 million in revenues. The annual *net* gain on the Erie and Champlain Canals over their first decade of operations, 1826–1835, amounted to almost 8 percent of the cost. Emulation did not await the ultimate confirmation of the success of the venture. Old projects were revived; new ones cogitated; and above all, large quantities of capital began to be expended.

Not the least of the reactions occurred in New York State itself. A general canal law was passed in 1825 providing for extensions through much of the state, many of which did not justify the expenditure. The Erie itself was an object of interest, as the legislature voted for enlargement of the main canal, thereby commencing a stream of expenditures that continued until the Civil War. By 1860 the original $9 million cost for the Erie and Champlain Canals had increased to almost $55 million.

The second-largest contributor to the canal boom was the state of Pennsylvania. For Philadelphia, the challenge of New York City's route to the West could only evoke immediate response. Already in ascent after the War of 1812, New York now threatened a death blow from which Philadelphia commercial interests would never recover. The inadequacy of the Pittsburgh Pike as a competitor to the Erie Canal was never in doubt. Neither was the willingness of the state to stand behind its premier city.

A tradition of state financial support had already been established in the turnpike era, and was not the subject of extensive debate.

The choice of technology, rather, was the crucial question. Nature had not treated Pennsylvania as kindly as New York. Only 655 feet of lockage was required to surmount the Appalachian barrier by the Erie route. A Pennsylvania canal implied 3,358 feet of lockage and a 4-mile tunnel. Under such adverse circumstances, the railroad alternative, although still visionary, was not excluded. The successful application of locomotive power on the Stockton and Darlington Lines in England in September 1825 intensified an already keen interest in the new form of transport. In March, an emissary of the Pennsylvania Society for the Promotion of Internal Improvement, William Strickland, had been dispatched to England to prepare a firsthand report on the subject. His favorable disposition to railways set off a brief but bitter debate between railroad and canal supporters that culminated in victory for the latter. Construction of the canal began on July 4, 1826.

Reality compelled substantial modification of the original scheme. A portage railroad substituted for the projected tunnel in the mountains, but not until 1831 did its construction begin. At its easternmost end, the narrow Union Canal was forsaken as the principal link from Philadelphia to the Susquehanna, and another railroad was authorized, the Philadelphia and Columbia. Its 81 miles were begun in 1828 and completed in 1834. The entire Mainline became operative in the same year. The final result, a hybrid of canal and railroad, replete with inclined planes, has been much maligned. Its cost of $12 million for the 395 miles was never adequately compensated by traffic over it. Whereas the annual profits on the Erie were 8 percent of cost in its first decade, those on the Mainline were not a fourth as large.[6] Nor did finances improve considerably thereafter.

More relevant from the standpoint of its motivation, through tonnage on the route both early and late compared even less favorably to the Erie results. This performance is still poorer considering that the Ohio Valley was at that time a more important source of surplus than the Great Lakes region served by the Erie Canal. The Mainline could not divert agricultural exports from their southward course over the Mississippi nor generate enough return transport in manufactures to make its existence worthwhile. Such a result is readily explained: Handicapped by multiple

<hr />

[6] A. L. Bishop. "The State Works of Pennsylvania," *Transactions of the Connecticut Academy of Arts and Sciences*, 13 (1907), 238–39, 278–80.

transshipments, a system in which the state provided only motive power and not freight cars on the Philadelphia and Columbia Lines, and less favorable grades of shipments, the Mainline always exceeded the Erie Canal in transport costs by a goodly margin.

Nonetheless, it is both unfair and inaccurate to criticize the decision to proceed with the venture too harshly.[7] In 1826 a delay of four or five years to verify the possibilities of railroads was not a feasible solution to Philadelphia's rapidly deteriorating commercial position. Apart from the completion of the Erie Canal, there was already underway construction of a system of Ohio canals designed to link the Ohio Valley to it. Immediate response or acceptance of secondary status were the options.

With full hindsight, the latter is recognized as the inevitable outcome. Choice of a railroad technology would not have been a successful strategy. Costs at that early date were still prohibitive. None of the great trunk lines succeeded in their objectives. When they did, it was with a better technology that could compete successfully with the alternatives afforded by the Erie Canal and the Mississippi River. The decision for the canal, moreover, was more ample in scope than construction of the Mainline alone. It encompassed a state *system* of canals, whose feeders cost an additional $6.5 million, as a price for state support of the commercial aspirations of Philadelphia. A through railroad, because it did not lend itself to similar extensions, had no guarantee of equivalent funding. The Pennsylvania Railroad was built in the 1850s under private auspices with only limited government support, primarily from Philadelphia and Pittsburgh. Parts of the statewide system did function reasonably well in serving local interests, moreover. The Delaware Division turned a net profit of $2.5 million from 1830 until its sale in 1858 for $1.8 million; its rate of return was about 5 percent over this interval; the Eastern Division of the Mainline did about as well.[8]

Overall, however, the public works were clearly a financial failure, even a disaster.[9] The total investment in construction was over $33 million. The sale value was only $11 million, augmented by cumulated net revenues of an additional $8 million. More impressive still was the constant drain on the public treasury – $43.5 million in interest was disbursed from initiation to sale. Much of the state loss originated in ventures which were begun

[7] For a view less sympathetic to the Pennsylvania decision, see Julius Rubin, "Canal or Railroad?" *Transactions of the American Philosophical Society*, 1, (1961).

[8] Bishop, "State Works," 278, 281.

[9] Bishop, "State Works," 228–29.

but not completed ($10 million plus interest thereon), and in failure to undertake until a very late date technical improvements that could have rendered the results more palatable. This experience is hardly an impressive argument for public investment.

Another response to the Erie, equally unsatisfactory, was the Chesapeake and Ohio Canal.[10] This was the successor of the Potomac Company, formed in the 1780s under the presidency of George Washington, which had successfully bypassed the rapids north of Georgetown, but had done little more. The idea of an extension to Cumberland and thence to the Ohio River was revived in the 1820s by the power of example. What made the Chesapeake and Ohio unique was the extent of national sponsorship. Congress subscribed $1 million in May, 1828 toward a projected expenditure of $4.5 million for a canal to be completed to Cumberland; Maryland contributed an additional $500,000, as did Alexandria and Georgetown, the termini; Washington allocated $1 million in addition. All told, only $606,400 was forthcoming from private sources.

This auspicious financial reserve was counteracted by mounting costs as construction began. Federal support was not an unmixed blessing, since it imposed standards far above those of the original plans or of other works under way. It required five years to reach Harper's Ferry, 65 miles distant, and the original capital was already exhausted. Andrew Jackson was not as favorably disposed to national assistance as his predecessor, and refused further involvement. Maryland alone was forced to rescue the project by a direct subscription totaling $5 million in 1839, as well as an additional loan of $2 million. Work continued until 135 miles were completed in 1840; the additional 50 miles to Cumberland were bridged a decade later and only after further debt had been contracted.

By that time, the canal faced the competition of the Baltimore and Ohio Railroad for transport of general merchandise. It was a losing struggle. The shipment of coal generated the largest part of its revenue, that commodity amounting to some two-thirds of tonnage in the 1850s. Some such specialized canals in the anthracite region of Pennsylvania did well; the Chesapeake and Oho did not. Net receipts were actually negative during the 1850s, and while the canal continued to be used into the twentieth century, its financial status never significantly altered for the better.

---

[10] See Walter S. Sanderlin, *The Great National Project: A History of the Chesapeake and Ohio Canal* (Baltimore, 1946).

The Erie excited not only emulative response from the commercial empires of the Middle Atlantic states seeking to extend their hinterlands westward, but also from the interior. The first and largest system was that of Ohio.[11] Begun in 1825, its objective was to connect Lake Erie to the Ohio River in both the eastern and western portions of the state. The eastern link was completed in 1833; the western was delayed by the economic decline of the late 1830s and not consummated until 1845. The cost for the 731-mile system, plus 91 miles of slack-water navigation, was almost $16 million. As in New York and Pennsylvania, no small part of this total was due to the uneconomical feeders constructed to the main lines. Revenues from the canals never succeeded in returning costs before their eventual demise due to the railroad.

Although the eastern segment was by far the more remunerative, its annual net revenues did not exceed 4 percent of cost, and only did that for 15 years. This was insufficient to pay the current interest on the debt, let alone amortize the investment. The canal did continue in operation into the twentieth century on a lease arrangement initiated in 1861. But in the absence of continuing improvements, its competitive position steadily worsened.

Despite this unfortunate denouement, the early success of the Ohio canals found ready imitators. There was no room in the calculations for eventual displacement by the railroad, and thus for sharply truncated earnings. Present benefits counted more than future payments on state debt. It was in such a spirit that Indiana and Illinois undertook their contributions to the wave of canal construction.[12] For Indiana, the vehicle was the Wabash and Erie Canal, supported in part by a federal land grant in 1827. Construction proceeded slowly, but in the gradually accelerating inflation of values and expectations of the 1830s – which had seen New York, Pennsylvania, and Ohio greatly expand their commitments – Indiana did not balk at initiating branch extension simultaneously. When depression descended in 1839, much was in process, but precious little was completed. Not until 1843 did the Wabash and Erie reach Lake Erie at Toledo, and not until ten more years had passed was it terminated at Evansville on the Ohio River. Its 450 miles made it the longest single canal in the

---

[11] For a factual treatment of the Ohio Canal, see C. P. McClelland and C. C. Huntington, *History of the Ohio Canals* (Columbus, 1905). For a more analytic study emphasizing public policy, see Harry Scheiber, *Ohio Canal Era* (Athens, OH, 1969).

[12] The two standard histories are those by Elbert J. Benton, *The Wabash Trade Route in the Development of the Old Northwest* (Baltimore, 1903); and James W. Putnam, *The Illinois and Michigan Canal* (Chicago, 1918).

United States, constructed at a cost of over $6.5 million. Completion to the full extent antedated abandonment of the southern section by less than a decade, and total net operating revenues of $1.3 million made the canal's financial performance among the least satisfactory of all antebellum ventures.

Illinois, too, received a grant of federal lands in 1827 to finance the Illinois and Michigan Canal, the missing link between Chicago and the Mississippi River. Construction began in 1836, along with an elaborate railroad network intended to bisect the state, and encountered the same depression-caused limitation of capital common to other projects. The canal was completed under new management and on a more modest scale in 1848. The construction cost was $6.5 million, augmented by continuing interest charges during the period of dormancy. The characteristically checkered early history augured the characteristic result: financial disaster. After 1879 expenditures for repairs and maintenance exceeded tolls. Only rental revenues from land holdings prevented the situation from deteriorating more. Peak traffic on the canal was realized in 1882, and the more adequate Chicago Sanitary and Ship Canal largely replaced it in the twentieth century.

Thus far we have described great interregional works undertaken with extensive state aid. These made up the majority, both in mileage and investment, of the canals constructed before the railroad. A second group of canals, smaller in extent, largely attached to coal interests like the original English model, and privately funded, also inherited the enthusiasm engendered by the Erie. They were to be found almost exclusively in the anthracite region of eastern Pennsylvania, from which they descended to serve the markets of New York and Philadelphia. In many instances canals were owned by the coal-mining enterprises themselves. In this category, the Delaware and Hudson, Lehigh, Schuylkill Navigation, and Morris were the most prominent. All were undertaken in the 1820s, completed shortly thereafter, and, with the exception of the last, became almost immediate financial successes. The Lehigh and the Schuylkill Navigation both underwent difficult periods in the 1840s, but recovered again in the 1850s to continue effectively for some time. The Schuylkill bowed to railroad competition sooner, helped along by a disastrous 1869 flood, while the Lehigh continued to operate, albeit in diminishing proportions and under railroad direction. The Delaware and Hudson remained one of the most attractive investments both before and after the Civil War. Its peak traffic was reached in 1872, and thereafter the coal tonnage diminished as

Table 13.2. *Canal investment (millions of dollars)*

Period	Total	Public
1815–1834	$58.6	$41.2
1834–1844	72.2	57.3
1844–1860	57.4	38.0

Source: Adapted from Harvey Segal, "Cycles of Canal Construction," in Carter Goodrich (ed.), *Canals and American Economic Development* (New York, 1961), 215.

railroad transportation, likewise owned by the company, replaced it. The Morris became a dividend payer in the 1850s and 1860s, but its useful life was likewise brought to an end by railroad purchase.

THE THREE INVESTMENT CYCLES

Table 13.2 summarizes the investment undertaken in the canal expansion just described. The first period, through 1834, includes the construction of the Erie Canal, the Pennsylvania Mainline, the commencement of the Chesapeake and Ohio, the completion of the Ohio and Erie, and the private eastern canals. In all, more than 2,000 miles were constructed at this time, with the large state-financed systems making the most important contribution. Two-thirds of the capital emanated from public sources.

The character of the second cycle, covering the later 1830s, is different. Apart from the ventures in Indiana and Illinois, its major components were the continuation of works already under way – the Chesapeake and Ohio and the west branch of the Ohio system, for example – and the construction of feeders to supplement the already-opened trunk lines. Governmental participation actually rose slightly in this period due to the earlier completion of the private anthracite canals. This is not the only difference between the two periods. Whereas foreign investment accounted for one-fourth of the finance in the earlier cycle, 60 percent originated in Europe during the second. Much of this amount entered after 1836, when a number of states passed legislation enlarging upon their original aspirations. This dependence on foreign funds created a vulnerability to financial conditions that was to prove disastrous. As the flow halted, investment declined from a peak outlay of $14.2 million in 1840 to $1 million in

1843.[13] Little mileage was brought to completion because the larger ventures did not construct consecutively.

The final investment cycle, the recovery from this trough, was surprisingly large due to the completion of many projects cut short previously. Continuation of work on the Erie enlargement and completion of two extensions to the New York canals account for almost half the total amount. The rest was expended on the completion of canals in Indiana and Illinois and the termination of the Chesapeake and Ohio. Less than 900 new miles were added after 1844, a measure of both the intensive character of the expenditure and the absence of new ventures as the railroad emerged as an alternative.

CANAL TRANSPORT SERVICES

The almost $200 million in canal investment created a substantial potential supply of transport services. Table 13.3 presents estimates of the actual ton-mileage carried by canals at two points during the antebellum period and at a third later date approximating their peak utilization. Note the independence of the construction cycle and the growth of ton-mileage. Although new mileage built after 1844 was limited, traffic increased quite rapidly until 1859, and beyond. Only with the later abandonment and decreased demand provoked by more intense railroad competition did the absolute ton-mileage diminish. In not a few instances railroad ownership was responsible for a premature demise: "In nearly every case where a canal had passed under the influence of a railroad the volume of canal traffic has decreased. In some cases it is apparent that railroads deliberately endeavored to kill off traffic by water route."[14] Railroads by 1909 owned 90 percent of the 632 active miles of private canals: in all, in 1909, there were almost 2,000 miles still in operation, but at utilization rates well below the 1870–1880 peaks.

The singular and extraordinary success enjoyed by the Erie Canal, the principal component of the New York state system, also stands out in Table 13.3. It alone among the canals operating in 1880 substantially exceeded its pre–Civil War performance, despite the parallel line of the New York Central and the competition of the Erie Railroad. The performance was

---

[13] Harvey Segal, "Cycles of Canal Construction," in Goodrich, ed., *Canals and American Economic Development*, 188, 192.

[14] *Report of the Commissioner of Corporations on Transportation by Water in the United States*, vol. 4 (Washington, DC, 1909–1913), 64.

Table 13.3. *Canal transportation services (millions of ton-miles)*

	Annual Average		
	1837–1846	1859	1880
New York system	227.5	544.3	1,223.6
Chesapeake and Ohio	9.6	58.8	104.8
Mainline	49.0	65.8	51.7
Pennsylvania Lateral Canals	23.0	172.8	—
Delaware	17.4	88.1	119.6
Lehigh Navigation	13.8	104.6	43.1
Schuylkill	23.4	169.9	50.4
Morris	4.6	51.0	42.2
Delaware and Raritan	11.2	75.0	67.4
Union	7.2	18.2	2.1
Chesapeake and Delaware	2.9	6.9	13.4
Susquehanna	11.1	29.1	10.9
Ohio system	79.5	70.4	83.7
Wabash and Erie	13.2	13.0	—
Illinois and Michigan	—	25.7	52.6

Source: 1837–1846: Segal, "Canals and Economic Development," 242; New York system calculated by multiplying average tonnage by 1856–1859 average haul, 145 miles; Morris Canal calculated by using 1845 tonnage only; Chesapeake and Ohio calculated by applying 1851 tolls per ton-mile to 1837–1846 tolls; Susquehanna calculated by averaging receipts from 1840 to 1846 and applying a 7 mill ton-mile rate; Ohio system based upon receipts and a 6 mill ton-mile rate; Wabash and Erie, 1846 receipts and an 8 mill charge; Pennsylvania Lateral Canals, receipts and an 8 mill toll. 1859: Albert Fishlow, *American Railroads and the Transformation of the Antebellum Economy* (Cambridge, MA, 1965), 21. 1880: U.S. Bureau of the Census, *Census of Population: 1880*, vol. 4, *Transportation* (Washington, DC, 1883); *Annual Report of the Auditor of the Canal Department for the Year 1881*, New York State Assembly Document no. 38, vol. 3 (1882), 41.

not effortless, however. Progressively lower tolls made revenues fall off quite rapidly after 1870, until the legislature abolished tolls altogether in 1882. Such sacrifice only delayed the inevitable. Continuing advances in railroad technology and rate discrimination made possible charges as low as those on the waterway. The course of the decline may be seen in the means of arrival of western grains at tidewater shown in Table 13.4.[15]

This is the most favorable comparison possible, focusing upon the trade

[15] U.S. Congress, Senate, *Preliminary Report of the Inland Waterways Commission*, Senate Document no. 325, 60th Congress, 1st Session (1908), 235.

Table 13.4. *Shipment of western grains (thousands of bushels)*

Year	Canal	Total	Canal percentage
1868	44,012	45,788	96.1
1880	69,346	143,856	48.2
1890	30,185	94,970	31.8
1898	19,407	161,115	12.0

in which the canal system remained most competitive. Of total ton-miles transported in New York State, the canal share shrank from 86 percent in 1853 to 5 percent in 1898.[16] Nonetheless, that early period of superiority was sufficient to establish the Erie's financial profitability. During the period of toll collection before 1822, the surplus earned after operating expenses was $92.2 million. This figure implies a rate of return on cost in excess of 10 percent, without assigning a value to the canal's facilities at that date. This unique record of private profitability, however, was not sufficient to offset the $4.2 million loss of the branch canals on an investment of equal magnitude. Thus, even the New York State system as a whole did not satisfy an accounting criterion of success: earnings sufficient to amortize the canal debt and to pay the accumulated interest.

The Erie Canal both ushered in the age of canal construction and also terminated the era of canal utilization. In the intervening half-century an irrevocable change in transport rates had occurred. Ton-mile charges, even on the best turnpikes, remained over 10 cents, and closer to 20, prior to the canal. The canal introduced rates on the order of 2.3 cents per mile, including tolls. By the 1850s the average costs for bulk commodities verged upon 1 cent per ton-mile, and even less in the case of the anthracite canals.[17]

Increased cargo capacity was the prime factor in increased canal efficiency; between 1835 and 1859, tonnage per vessel nearly quadrupled, from 38 to 143.[18] Thereafter technical gains were more modest. The principal contributor to reduced transport costs came to be reductions in tolls as canals struggled unsuccessfully to maintain their share of the transport

[16] Ibid., 228–29.
[17] Taylor, *Transportation Revolution*, 133–38.
[18] U.S. Auditor for the Treasury Department, *Report for 1881* (Washington, DC, 1881), 38.

market. Charges on Erie Canal tonnage in the early 1880s were less than 0.5 cents, but the gain was modest relative to the 7 mills already attained in the late 1850s. Attempts to introduce steam power on canals to lower costs of carriage further were unsuccessful.

Unlike the turnpike, the canal left an indelible mark on nineteenth-century transportation rates. The water technology was incomparably superior to the horse-and-wagon alternative even given well-surfaced roads. Its principal deficiency was geographic inflexibility: Not all areas were equally well suited to canal construction. One important nineteenth-century innovation utilizing steam power, the steamboat, compensated by making transportation on the naturally abundant navigable rivers and streams much more efficient.

The Exploitation of the River and Lake System, 1815–1900

Canal construction, for all its advantages, was of limited extension. The system of naturally navigable waters – rivers, lakes, and the coastal perimeter – possessed by the United States was many times larger. Rivers alone totaled more than six times the 4,000 accumulated miles of canals that the canal era had seen through to completion. Nor did exploitation of the water routes await the nineteenth century. From the beginning all manner of vessels were employed for commerce – sailing ships, flatboats, barges, keelboats. Economic activity was concentrated along bodies of water wherever possible.

ANTEBELLUM DIFFUSION

Development of the steamboat in the early nineteenth century extended the importance of water commerce, particularly upon the western rivers.[19] Not until considerably later would steam navigation become the preferred form for all water transport, both internal and international. The interest in the West, however, was immediate. Little time elapsed between Fulton's successful demonstration on the Hudson in 1807 and the first trip of the *New Orleans* from Pittsburgh to its namesake (1811). The feasibility of downstream navigation thus proved, four more years elapsed until the

---

[19] This section has depended heavily upon Louis C. Hunter, *Steamboats on the Western Rivers* (Cambridge, MA, 1949).

Table 13.5. *National and western steamboat tonnage,*
1820–1860

Year	United States	Western
1820	—	13,890
1830	62,409	29,481
1840	182,925	83,592
1845	261,034	98,246
1850	371,819	141,834
1855	559,508	173,068
1860	640,906	162,735

Source: Adapted from Louis C. Hunter, *Steamboats on the Western Rivers* (Cambridge, MA, 1949), 33. The national tonnage has been adjusted by the difference between Hunter's series of tonnage on western rivers and the official one.

Enterprise negotiated the more difficult return trip against the current. It was the unique capacity of the steamboat to master the upstream voyage that led to its rapid acceptance. In fact, however, downriver commerce always dominated, and by the time the West had developed to the point that return imports might have been significant, there were direct links to the East.

The early growth of steamboat tonnage on western rivers is documented in Table 13.5. Until 1840, western steamboats represented half the national tonnage; after that date, the geographic domain of steam expanded. The steamboat's position on western rivers, moreover, was dominant. Keelboats and barges outfitted for upstream travel were the first to be dislodged by the competition of the steamboat, although the keelboat lingered longer, particularly on the upper Ohio. Flatboats, on the other hand, showed a much greater vigor. They were used only for downstream transportation, and given the opportunity to sell the lumber from which they were made in New Orleans, the crew could return inexpensively and reasonably rapidly by steamboat. Thus the two transport forms were partially complementary. Not until 1846–1847 did flatboat arrivals at New Orleans reach their peak, a level five times their pre-steamboat rate. Yet relatively, they had long before begun to recede in importance. As early as 1830, the volume of freight carried by steamboats probably exceeded that by all other craft. Not until after the Civil War would the flatboat emerge reincarnated as a complement to steam power in the towing system.

The western steamboat not only made upstream commerce feasible, but also, as it evolved technologically, meant substantially lower rates and greater speed as well. The earliest trips from New Orleans to Louisville by steamboat required 30 to 35 days; by 1833 the duration had been reduced to 7 days and 6 hours, gradually declining thereafter to regular runs of 5½ to 6 days in the 1850s. This meant an average speed of 10 miles an hour; traveling south, the speed was closer to 15. Smaller boats, 200 to 300 tons, went perhaps half as fast. By contrast, keelboats and barges had required 3 to 4 months for the same upriver voyage.

Rates followed a corresponding tendency. The steamboat rate in 1816 was originally 4 to 5 cents per pound for delivery from New Orleans to Louisville. Gerstner in the late 1830s reported an average rate for freight of all kinds of 0.625 cents. Adjusting for the difference in price levels, the reduction is still more than fourfold. By the 1840s and 1850s, in part due to the imbalance caused by significantly larger downstream shipments, the upriver rate converged with the lower downriver charge. This meant a further reduction to perhaps half the previous amount by 1860. Per ton-mile (railroad distance) rates in the 1840s and thereafter for a variety of shorter routes averaged about 4 cents; for the longer hauls they were much less than 1 cent. On the eve of the Civil War, in short, the steamboat had cheapened upriver transportation by a factor of ten, and downstream trips by a ratio of between three and four.[20]

One important element in this downward trend was the widespread competition in the industry. This was particularly noticeable in the 1820s as tonnage rapidly mounted. The very nature of the innovation ideally fitted the competitive model. Unlike turnpikes and canals, which consti-tuted a capital-intensive and geographically fixed medium over which private conveyances might travel for a toll, the innovation of the steam-boat required little direct investment and yielded early returns. Steam-boats cost between $75 and $100 a ton.[21] A medium-sized boat by the standards of the 1850s could be constructed for a total investment of $30,000. Returns were immediate, although they varied considerably due to the hazards of navigation. Insurance was only partial in its coverage. To those with enough good fortune and good management to keep their ships

[20] Hunter, *Steamboats*, 374–77, 658–59; Thomas S. Berry, *Western Prices Before 1861* (Cambridge, MA, 1943), 42–70.

[21] Hunter, *Steamboats*, 110–11.

afloat longer than the four-year average, the gains were especially generous. It is difficult to generalize about the average rate of return because of
the dispersed and individual character of the enterprises, and also because
complaints about lack of profit were rife, biasing the limited reports available. The competitive character of the industry, along with a possible tendency among owner-captains to overestimate their own capacity for good
fortune should have made for a relatively modest return. Because of the
small units of investment, that private return probably approximated the
social gains more satisfactorily than those of other indivisible, capital-
intensive innovations. The market could and did work without public
intervention.

The usual form of ownership was the partnership: About half of the pre-
1860 tonnage was owned by groups of two to four, with another 20–25
percent being held by individuals.[22] Divided ownership with representation in different river cities was common. This arrangement assured direct
access to the supply of capital in those larger commercial centers that had
a direct interest in improved transportation. It thereby eased the possibility of entry. Such widespread ownership also assured that boats would
compete directly for the same traffic.

Competition and the rapid rate of depreciation assured the rapid diffusion of technological advance. Such technical progress was the ultimate
determinant of the trend in charges. Improvement expressed itself in two
complementary forms – evolution of the structure of the boat and refinement of the power source. Length and breadth increased as depth was
reduced to enhance maneuverability under the low-water conditions of
western rivers. The high-pressure engine was favored for its lesser bulk,
and its consequent expansion in power led to a ratio of horsepower to
tonnage that went from $1:3$ to the opposite $3:1$. Both developments
together made for larger boats and a more than proportional increase in
capacity. Cargo capacity which had stood in a $1:1$ ratio to measured
tonnage (actually a cubic foot measurement) had by the 1850s exceeded
it by 50 to 75 percent. The additional speed, moreover, meant the possibility of more intensive utilization of the boat and decreased capital costs
per individual trip.

Despite the low rates that were thereby made possible, particularly in
the Ohio-Mississippi system, the steamboat fell victim to railroad competition, as had the canal, and for the same reasons of directness, conve-

[22] Ibid., 311.

Table 13.6. *National and western steamboat tonnage,*
1868–1889 (yearly average)

Period	United States	Western rivers
1868–1869	1,012,056	332,279
1870–1874	931,402	265,269
1875–1879	983,665	231,584
1880–1884	1,169,999	246,184
1884–1889	1,392,347	217,014

Source: Adapted from Hunter, *Steamboats*, 565. These measurements are in the new-measure tonnage for western rivers established in 1865: for comparison with the tonnage on western
rivers given in Table 13.5, it is necessary to reduce them by
about 45 percent.

nience, and speed. Insurance costs, too, represented a financial burden that
could add as much as a third to steamboat charges that were superficially
lower. Relevant as well was the uncertainty of the river depth; in the
crucial decade of the 1850s, during the height of the railroad struggle, the
Ohio remained consistently low until quite late in the year. As soon as
the Pennsylvania and Baltimore and Ohio Railroads directly linked the
eastern ports to the Ohio Valley, steamboat arrivals went into decline at
Pittsburgh and Cincinnati; in the former, the 3,000 entries in 1848 dwindled to less than 600 in 1858. Total tonnage on western rivers was smaller
in 1860 than in 1855. On the southern reaches of the Mississippi, due to
a slower pace of railroad construction in the South and to the greater ease
of river shipment, the steamboat maintained its dominion and thereby
offset the rapidly declining arrivals at New Orleans from the West.
Increasingly, cotton replaced western foodstuffs in the commerce of the
Crescent City.

POST–CIVIL WAR DECLINE

After the Civil War, the pattern of decline continued and extended to the
South. Steam tonnage on western rivers recorded an unbroken decline, as
shown in Table 13.6. The statistics of the major river ports are equally
dolorous, St. Louis in 1891–1895 received and shipped by water only 62

percent of the 1871–1875 level; in the first decade of the twentieth century there was a further reduction. By 1890 St. Louis trade by rail amounted to eight times its river commerce.[23] As in the 1850s, the lower river traffic was more resistant to diversion, but no longer fully so. Arrivals in New Orleans were 29 percent fewer in 1880 than in 1860. However, almost two-thirds of the cotton continued to come by river. By 1890, the proportion was 20 percent, and the steamboat had become a minor factor even in New Orleans commerce.[24] This occurred despite efforts to stem the tide. Barge towing substituted for individual steamboats, each with its own cargo. Although this practice had been tried in the coal trade from Pittsburgh in 1860, it was applied much more widely thereafter. The same principle was adapted to the grain and lumber trade from the northern Mississippi southward. The innovation reduced capital costs by a factor of as much as four.[25] In 1889 more than two-thirds of all shipments were handled in this way, although general merchandise and upriver freight continued to be transported in the more conventional fashion. Accordingly, a large part of the post–Civil War steam tonnage on the western rivers consisted of towboats. In 1880 the ratio was 1:4; in 1890, 1:3.[26] Still, such methods did not alter the increasing superiority of the railroad, because their success depended on very large scale. The entire Mississippi system transported less than 4 billion ton-miles in 1890, or no more than the Pennsylvania Railroad alone.

The western steamboat represented the most dramatic, but not exclusive, application of steam power. Eventually steam power on the lakes and in the coastal trade – not to mention in international commerce – came to supersede its importance in the West. By the post–Civil War period the western steam tonnage represented only 15 percent of the national total. On the other hand, sailing vessels persisted much longer in these other trades. Steam did not power a majority of shipping in the lake trade until 1884; in the coastal trade, until the later 1890s; and in international trade, until the twentieth century. The gradual rise of the participation of the steamboat in its diverse uses is indicated in Table 13.7.

Sailing vessels dominated until much later in nonriver use for a variety of reasons. Long-distance routes afforded a problem of fuel storage, adding to the space already taken up by bulky machinery; on the river this was

[23] Frank H. Dixon, *Traffic History of the Mississippi River System* (Washington, DC, 1909), 53.
[24] Ibid., 59.
[25] Hunter, *Steamboats*, 567–75.
[26] Ibid., 638.

Table 13.7. *Tonnage, by trade and by type, 1851, 1870, and 1890 (thousands of tons)*

	1851	1870	1890
Foreign[a]			
Total	1,726	1,517	947
Steam	62	193	197
Coastal			
Total	1,548	1,647	2,120
Steam	150	478	804
Barges and canal boats	—	397	285
Northern lakes			
Total	216	685	1,063
Steam	77	143	653
Barges and canal boats	—	277	81
Western rivers			
Total	136	398	294
Steam	136	262	205
Barges and canal boats	—	133	89

[a] Includes whale fisheries.

Source: **1851**: U. S. Senate, Executive Document no. 42, 32nd Congress, 1st Session, 1853. *Foreign* total and steam from Commerce and Navigation Reports. *Coastal* total equal to total tonnage employed in internal trade (from Commerce and Navigation Reports) minus lake and river totals. Steam: total equal to Senate Executive Document no. 42 total for coastal minus registered steam tonnage as given in Commerce and Navigation Reports. *Northern lakes* total and steam tonnage taken from Israel Andrews, *Report on Trade and Commerce*, Senate Executive Document no. 112, 32nd Congress, 1st Session, 1853. *Western rivers*: Tonnage assumed to be all steam. **1870 and 1890**: Commerce and Navigation Reports.

no problem, since wood and later cheap coal were readily available at any number of places. Moreover, the costs of construction of sailing vessels were quite low due to the abundance of wood, and this fact give an edge to sailing vessels in initial capital requirements. Technical advances such as the iron hull for greater buoyancy; the screw propeller, which provided more efficient drive than the paddle wheel; and progress in the construction of the engine and boilers themselves later combined to make the steamship more economical. Almost from the earliest, propellers were applied to lake steamboats: half the 1860 fleet was so equipped. Nevertheless, the United States, which boasted an initial lead in the application of steam propulsion on the western rivers, lagged badly in its generalization to the ocean-going merchant marine. The success of the clipper ship, the satisfactory performance of wooden sailing vessels in general, and the lesser role of foreign trade made for this curious lapse of innovative energies.

INVESTMENT IN DOMESTIC SHIPPING

The expenditure generated by steamboat construction may be crudely calculated by applying a price of $100 a ton to construction prior to 1860; for the year 1880 and thereafter, we have direct census data. Until the Civil War, the gross cumulative outlay may thus be estimated at $150 million, an amount quite closely comparable to the total cost of canals over the same period. Much of this sum, however, went toward replacement rather than adding to the effective capital stock. As a consequence, the value of the accumulated 1860 capital was much smaller than that of canals and was worth probably no more than $33 million.

Inclusion of all vessels engaged in domestic commerce, including sailing ships and canal boats, increases construction outlays by $190 million and the 1860 capital stock by some $65 million.[27] The net 1860 value of $100 million for *all* vessels does not match the canal interest. Post–Civil War comparisons, on both a gross and net basis, concede to steamboats and other craft even less relative importance. In 1880 some 6,000 miles of railway were completed at a cost in excess of $210 million; steamboat construction consumed about $10 million in resources. Census valuation in

---

[27] The 1860 value of steamboats is calculated as 0.6 times the investment in the tonnage existing in that year. This recognizes that part of the capital stock had already undergone depreciation. The implicit rate employed is about 10 percent. Such an estimate corresponds closely to the observed 0.7 ratio between investment and value reported in the 1880 census.

For other vessels engaged in domestic commerce an average cost per gross ton of $50 was employed (cf. John G. B. Hutchins, *The American Maritime Industries and Public Policy, 1789–1914* [Cambridge, MA, 1941], 280–81). The number of vessels destined for the domestic trade was estimated at one-third the total number constructed from 1800 to 1815, and one-half thereafter. A ratio of 0.7 was applied to the cumulated investment in nonsteam tonnage engaged in domestic commerce to obtain the 1860 value.

For construction series of both sailboats and steamboats and tonnage engaged in domestic commerce, see U.S. Bureau of the Census, *Historical Statistics of the United States, Colonial Times to 1957*, (Washington, DC, 1960), Series Q-180, 181, and 166.

the same year was $80.2 million for steamboats; $5.2 billion for railways.[28] If we were to consider all ships, including vessels engaged in foreign trade, the annual flow and stock valuation would have to be adjusted by a factor of less than two.

Yet if the cost was small, this fact makes the services of internal water commerce that much more impressive. Only canal ton-mileage statistics are available before 1889. At that late date, a total of 35.9 billion ton-miles was transported by water – excluding canals – or nearly half the comparable railroad total.[29] Specialization on long hauls of coal and iron ore, where water enjoyed a competitive advantage, accounts for this good showing. Earlier estimates are quite precarious because of data limitations. Extrapolation back on the tonnage engaged in coastwise and internal trade would suggest an 1860 total of 20 million ton-miles. The information in the 1853 Andrews Report justifies assuming such a high level of activity. Thus, extraordinarily enough, even though railroad diversion had steadily eaten into the canal and Mississippi River system traffic during the 1850s, the total volume of waterborne domestic commerce continued to exceed railroad ton-mileage by a factor perhaps as high as eight or ten. The important, and largely ignored, role of the coastwise fleet is central to this result. Not until the unparalleled railway extension of the 1870s and 1880s would the natural and inexpensive routes of ocean and internal waterways yield their position.

The Ascendancy of the Railroad, 1830–1860

The canal and steamboat marked important steps in the solution of the American transport problem.[30] Between them, they afforded access to markets for large parts of the interior. Yet neither was to prevail as the nineteenth century unfolded. The torch instead passed to the railroad, the first rapid and efficient overland transport innovation. The basic principles underlying the railway were simple enough: a smooth surface, consisting of rails, to reduce as far as possible the friction of wheels passing over it, and efficient application of steam, by means of the locomotive, to expand carrying capacity. The first serious experiments in England in the 1820s

---

[28] U.S. Bureau of the Census, *Census of Population: 1880*, vol. 4, *Transportation* (Washington, DC, 1883), 5, 702.

[29] Harold Barger, *The Transportation Industries, 1889–1946* (New York, 1951), 254.

[30] For a more complete treatment of the 1830–1860 period, see Albert Fishlow, *American Railroads and the Transformation of the Ante-Bellum Economy* (Cambridge, MA, 1965).

rapidly proved the merits of the technology, and the United States there-after became its leading practitioner.

The proximate impetus, as in the rise of canal construction, was the Erie Canal. Baltimore, dissatisfied with the projected Chesapeake and Ohio Canal because its terminus would favor Alexandria, determined instead to construct a railroad of over 200 miles. The decision, even from this vantage point, was one of heroic folly. How else can one label an enterprise of that magnitude undertaken before steam locomotion had fully proven itself and when the few existing railroads in the world were modest ventures to exploit the coal trade? Impelled by the same competitive urgency as Philadelphia, Baltimore in the end wound up little better. The railroad was completed to Wheeling, its Ohio River terminus, only in 1853, well after the issue of western trade had been decided. The projected cost of $5 million became a realized investment in excess of $20 million.

Once under way, the Baltimore and Ohio served as a powerful incentive to imitators, and for very good reason: Few locations were so well favored that water transport could fully satisfy their needs, or better, their aspirations. The railroad also held out the prospect of more rapid and convenient passage, a not irrelevant consideration in the already densely populated coastal region. When its technical properties were proven, future financial problems could no longer diminish enthusiasm. Charleston business leaders, dissatisfied with their attempted canal solution to the problem of Savannah's competition, read and responded to reports issuing from Baltimore. In 1833 they completed what was then the longest railway in the world, 136 miles to Hamburg in the interior. Pennsylvania adopted the technology for parts of its route to Pittsburgh where canals were not feasible. Boston interests watched developments in Baltimore carefully before initiating their modest challenge to New York. More in the original English tradition, feeder roads, often relying upon horse power and limited in mileage, were built to canals in the coal regions. Commercial men in various population centers along the fall line saw an opportunity to capitalize upon the demands of a traveling public, from which emerged such projects as the Boston and Providence, the Camden and Amboy in New Jersey, and the Richmond and Petersburg, among others.

Railroad mileage increased rapidly in the 1830s, fed on the one hand by buoyant economic conditions and a relative abundance of capital, and on the other by glowing expectations. The expansion was a learning process. English methods were rapidly discarded. Iron rails were replaced by wood with iron bars; tunnels were avoided; great tolerance was exhibited for curvatures and gradients found in the terrain. In general, costs of construction were compressed as far as possible. More than substitution economies emerged, as American ingenuity was applied to the adaptation of both locomotive and rail design. American locomotives designed with a flexible truck to adapt to curves rapidly replaced imports. Experimentation with rails to support maximum weight with minimum iron input led to a prototype of the soon to be universal "T"-rail.

By the end of 1839, more than 3,000 miles of railway were in operation. A potential system of sorts was emerging. One axis lay east–west, the intent of the original Baltimore and Ohio. The Western Railroad in Massachusetts, the ill-fated Erie Railroad of New York, the individual ventures later to be consolidated in the New York Central, and the two Pennsylvania lines auxiliary to the canal completed this interregional category. A second axis was north–south, comprehending the roads paralleling the coast and oriented to the passenger traffic. In terms of completed mileage, these constituted the largest part of the emerging rail network. A third group of enterprises was in the western interior and was constructed under state auspices to feed into the great natural water courses serving the region. A final miscellaneous category includes the many coal roads in Pennsylvania and what Chevalier termed "the railroads which, starting from the great cities as centers, radiate from them in all directions."[31]

The depression lasting from the end of 1839 until 1843 played havoc with two important elements of this design. The east–west roads were forced to halt far short of their goal, with the exception of the Western, which struggled through with state aid, and the earlier completed and predominantly canal Pennsylvania Mainline. The interior western roads were affected more adversely. States, unable to borrow abroad after 1839, could not maintain construction out of their limited revenues. Abandonment of roads was not infrequent, resulting in additions to public debt without corresponding assets. The same dependence upon public assistance marked many southern ventures and with similar consequences. In general, the less

---

[31] Michel Chevalier, *Society, Manners, and Politics in the United States* (Garden City, NY, 1961, first published 1839), 260.

ambitious the undertaking, and the greater its private finance, the better it emerged after 1839.

This setback did not diminish enthusiasm for the innovation or alter conviction in its substantial benefits. It merely reflected the problem of finance. For this reason, the locus of construction was in New England and the East in the 1840s, while the South and West gradually recovered. Capital was more readily available in the settled regions and was independent of the foreign investment that had permitted public ventures to multiply in the interior. Appeals for funds were couched in terms of indirect gains as well as pecuniary rewards. Investment was concentrated in local railroads in the form of equity, partially in the hope of securing advantages to one community or another. This aim was most obvious in the 600 miles of railroad making up an alternative Boston route to the Great Lakes, which promised a more successful New England performance in the western trade.

At the end of the decade, despite the sluggish start, total railroad mileage had doubled to more than 7,500. Massachusetts, Connecticut, and New Hampshire possessed roughly half the mileage they would have a century later. In the 1840s, the east–west lines also began to emerge from their dormancy. The Baltimore and Ohio pushed on; the Pennsylvania Railroad was initiated to give that state an all-rail connection to the West; the group of independent New York railroads in the Mohawk Valley was completed from Buffalo to Albany – although these were useful primarily for passenger traffic; and the Erie Railroad reorganized in 1845 and completed over 200 miles toward the lake thereafter.

EXTENSION TO THE WEST AND SOUTH

The full-blown emergence of the railroad awaited the 1850s. In ten years the network more than quadrupled to 30,000 miles, making it possible to speak meaningfully of rail shipment and travel throughout the nation. It was possible to travel from New York to Dubuque, Iowa entirely by train. Hogs could be shipped from the Illinois prairie to slaughterhouses in Boston; manufactures could be delivered from Philadelphia to Holly Springs, Mississippi. Serious problems of articulation remained, however. There were few bridges over major rivers; a variety of gauges impeded continuous shipment; schedules were chaotic in the absence of time zones. Still, the tendency toward integration was clear.

The West and East had been joined overland, not once, but at least four times. The principal trunk lines – the New York Central, the Erie, the Pennsylvania, and the Baltimore and Ohio – each extended from tidewater to western termini by 1853. Festivities were widespread celebrating the joining of the areas, not to mention the realization of profits on a through traffic for the first time.

The western interior was the principal arena of new construction. Feeders not only linked the waterways of the regions but, more important, directly connected with the trunk lines as they were completed. Chicago emerged as a rail center second to none, the node for ten different railroad lines that, with branches and extensions, totaled more than 4,000 miles. Ohio possessed on the eve of the Civil War almost 3,000 miles of railroad, closely followed by Illinois with more than 2,700, and Indiana with over 2,000. The Mississippi had been bridged, and the railhead verged on the Missouri; Wisconsin and Iowa, admitted as states a few years earlier, together could claim 1,500 miles of track. In all, 10,000 miles were constructed in the West during the 1850s, more than the national total at the beginning of the decade.

This accomplishment was not the product of a unique American willingness to build ahead of demand, as Schumpeter and others have argued. It was rooted in the more prosaic, but frequently more effective, profit motive. The large majority of these western railroads in fact earned net revenues from the beginning; they were built through areas of previous and abundant settlement and successfully attracted private funds. These points merit brief elaboration.

The relationship with settlement shows up strikingly in the regular progression of construction over time from more to less densely settled areas. Ohio, the most settled area, by 1852 already possessed one-third of the mileage it was to acquire by the end of the decade; at the opposite extreme, Wisconsin and Iowa at that time had practically none. The same searching out of favorable opportunities exhibits itself at the regional level. Of the total number of miles of railroad built in Illinois by the end of 1853, over 60 percent can be found in the eleven leading wheat counties and the eight largest corn counties, both as measured by the census of 1850. The disproportion of railroad density – these counties represented only 25 percent of the land area – is clearly due to the existing level of settlement and economic activity. Wisconsin illustrates the point even more dramatically. There 10 percent of area accounted for over half the mileage at the end of 1860 and three-fourths at the end of 1856.

These early railroads, directed to immediate sources of demand, were rewarded by high profits. For the West as a whole, net earnings in 1855–1856 reached 7.2 percent of the cost of construction, exceeding the corresponding returns in New England and the Middle Atlantic states. Receipts per mile were smaller, but so were costs. The western railroads adapted their construction practices to the initially lower absolute demands in the region.

Such aggregate results do not accurately convey the varied fortunes of individual roads. Many railroads in older parts of the region, in Ohio and Indiana, did poorly over time because of excess competition. Railroad rivalry, induced by high fixed costs, produced an excess of feeder roads; commercial rivalry, responding to the high costs of inadequate transport facilities, abetted such a tendency by guaranteeing local subsidies. The consequence of overbuilding was lower profits in 1855–1856 in the established railroad states than in the newer ones.

The receptivity to western railroad securities in eastern money markets affords another clue to the worthiness of the early projects. Bonds were negotiated with relative ease until the tightness commencing in late 1854, as the market shared the view that "western roads are to be our best paying lines, and the great success that has followed the opening of the few roads in that section has done much to confirm this opinion."[32]

Access to capital markets was crucial due to the predominantly private character of the investment.[33] The unhappy experiment of the 1830s left a legacy in the West of constitutional prohibitions against state aid to internal improvements. Federal aid was sought and ultimately obtained in the form of land grants, but it came too late to influence the course of events prior to the Civil War. Local funds were sought, and successfully, but not in amounts sufficient to alter the dominant role of private profit motivation. Indiana communities contributed no more than 4 percent of total construction costs. In Illinois the ratio was not much greater. Significantly, Chicago gave nothing: it was the lesser towns that paid their tribute, hoping for a place in the sun that they only infrequently gained. Even in states farther west such as Wisconsin and Iowa, where the undertakings might seem more risky, local support probably did not much exceed 10 percent of the investment. In fact, as much was expended by Ohio communities as by those in Indiana, Illinois, and Wisconsin together.

---

[32] *American Railroad Journal*, 25 (1852), 121.
[33] Carter Goodrich, *Government Promotion of American Canals and Railroads, 1800–1890* (New York, 1960), presents the fullest accounting of governmental assistance and stresses its importance more than is done here.

Their contributions were defensive, designed to assure that they would not be bypassed by the new era. The benefits realized were always less than anticipated because all areas acted similarly; but the potential costs of a refusal to contribute made the behavior explicable, if not globally efficient. To be sure, local assistance could on occasion be catalytic and even crucial to obtaining other subscriptions. But it is well to contrast the passive character of this municipal assistance – sought *after* the railroad was decided upon by the initiative of others – and the state aid of the 1830s, which was clearly directive and in advance of demand.

Not only in the West, but also in the South, the sharp decline in activity in the 1840s was compensated by a robust rebound in the 1850s. The reaction was longer in coming and less a private response to potential profits than was true in the West. The natural river access enjoyed by the South had facilitated a cotton-based commercial agriculture well before western expansion, and rivers remained as a powerful competitor to railroad interests. The traumatic experience of the late 1830s was possibly even more influential in reducing enthusiasm for railroad investment. By the late 1850s, however, the debacle of earlier public assistance had diminished as a deterrent, and aid was once more forthcoming. The success of the railroads apparent elsewhere was an important incentive. States financed the competition of their ports for the commerce of the interior: The same motivation had spurred the beginning of the railroad era thirty years previously. New Orleans, Mobile, Memphis, Savannah, Charleston, Norfolk, and Wilmington, North Carolina, were the major participants. Louisville also was actively involved in seeking to divert the trade of the Ohio Valley southward. While aid was liberally given at both state and local levels, private investment was also encouraged by the favorable operating experiences of the southern roads completed earlier: Dividends commonly were being paid in 1855 in the seaboard states. Once under way, the commercial contest led to rapidly accelerating construction, with much mileage being brought to fruition only on the eve of the war. While western investment perceptibly peaked in 1854, investment in the South and Southwest halted only slightly in response to economic conditions and continued upward until 1859.

THE MAGNITUDE OF THE INVESTMENT

Table 13.8 recapitulates the cycles of antebellum investment. The concentration of expenditure in the East in the 1840s and the subsequent

Table 13.8. *Antebellum railway investment (millions of dollars)*

Period	New England	Middle Atlantic[a]	West[b]	South	Total
1828–1843	29.7	64.9	9.7	33.0	137.1[c]
1844–1850	79.5	52.8	20.2	19.7	172.3[c]
1851–1860	40.5	126.4	370.3	199.4	737.3[d]

[a] Includes Maryland and Delaware.
[b] Includes Missouri.
[c] May not add due to rounding.
[d] Includes $.7 million investment in California.
Source: Adapted from Fishlow, *American Railroads*, 53.

boom in the West and South are patent. So too is the extraordinary magnitude of investment. Already by the early 1850s, more resources had been
devoted to the railroad than to canal, steamboat, and turnpike construction together before the war. And as we shall later see, this margin accelerated for the remainder of the century.

To the more than $1 billion capital stock at the end of 1860, public
treasuries had contributed about 25 percent. The role of public subsidy
was largest in the South, where it amounted to more than 50 percent
over the period, and convincingly contradicted the image of uninvolved
laissez-faire. The greatest influence of public aid came during the first
upward surge, when it exceeded one-third of the total investment. It
was at its smallest in the 1840s, when privately financed construction in
New England dominated. In absolute terms aid reached its largest level
in the 1850s as publicly financed southern involvement rapidly increased.
Exact proportions are difficult to calculate due to uncertain factual bases
and conceptual problems. State guarantees of bonds, for example, are
included in some calculations, although they represent no transfer of
resources. Nor for that matter do state loans that are repaid, except to the
extent of an interest rate differential favoring the sale of state securities
over private instruments. For the purpose of determining the share of
immediate financial contribution, however, loans are a present transfer
even if they are subsequently amortized. It is this broader concept that is
applied here.

Public assistance to railroads differed from aid to canals in its form and
its relative importance. Canal construction was underwritten to the extent

Table 13.9. *Railroad output (millions of miles and dollars)*

Year	Passenger receipts	Passenger miles	Freight receipts	Ton-miles
1839	$4.5	90.1	$2.5	32.8
1849	13.6	468.1	14.1	347.0
1859	45.8	1,879.6	66.5	2,577.7

Source: Data from Fishlow, *American Railroads*, app. A.

of nearly three-fourths its total antebellum cost. Almost universally, the political unit from which assistance flowed was the state; and equally commonly, the form it took was direct ownership and operation. Railroads received a relatively smaller financial incentive and were operated as private corporations even when they received a capital subsidy. This difference derives in part from the technological characteristics of the innovations – state control was much easier when tolls alone were involved – and in part from their historical sequence. Railroads came later, when private sources of capital were more abundant. Moreover, the ability of railroads to draw upon private savings was enhanced because they were constructed in response to present demands.

RAILROAD TRAFFIC AND PRODUCTIVITY

Table 13.9 measures the results in transportation services of the $1 billion prewar investment. Of interest is the substantial initial dependence of railroads upon personal travel for their revenues. Not until 1849 do freight receipts exceed the income from passengers. Although canal freight service at that time continued to exceed railroad ton-mileage, the newer innovation had already monopolized the movement of persons. By the end of the following decade, the railroad succeeded in edging out the canals in freight, although total water commerce in all its forms bulked much larger, as we have seen. Rapid railroad growth presaged ultimate victory in that contest as well, and not too far in the future.

Acceptance of the new technology cut short the profits on canals and led to the abandonment of many; it also generated quite respectable net revenues for the railroad owners. Table 13.10 presents net earnings corrected for depreciation as a proportion of the capital stock for various benchmark years. These data, indicating rising profitability through the mid-1850s, help explain the continuing interest in railroad investment.

Table 13.10. *Adjusted net earnings relative to net capital stock (percentages)*

Year	Including expenditures on failed enterprises	Excluding expenditures on failed enterprises
1839	% 3.0	% 3.7
1849	4.5	4.8
1855–1856	5.9	6.0
1859	4.7	4.7

Note: Adjusted net earnings are net receipts minus depreciation not charged to current account; the latter is calculated as the difference between total capital consumption and replacement of equipment, ties, and rails.
Source: Data from Fishlow, *American Railroads*, apps. A and B.

Such ratios are not the equivalent of rates of return, which take into account the future stream of earnings over the lifetime of the enterprise. The latter are more impressive, since much of the capital was newly placed in 1855–1856 and 1859, and thus was not yet fully utilized and held prospects of a rapidly growing revenue flow. For example, a conservative annual net receipts growth of only 2 percent for thirty years from 1859 implies an average *private* return of some 6 percent. This is not a bonanza gain by any means, but it stands out in a sector in which private investors had previously been singularly unfortunate. That such a return was capable of evoking the private investment it did testifies to the appeal of indirect benefit in attracting local finance, and to the optimistic expectations which magnified the real possibilities.

Railroads earned profits because they overtook the canals in the volume of traffic carried. They successfully competed because they reduced the initial rate differential in favor of canals to such a degree that it was relevant only in the immediate vicinity of waterways. During the 1830s railroad rates per ton-mile were about 7½ cents; passenger fares were only 5 cents per mile. By 1859 the absolute level had been drastically reduced. Passenger rates stood at 2.44 cents, and ton-mile charges at 2.58 cents. Even at the earlier tariffs, and with the relative – although by no means absolute – comfort of railroad travel, the railroad easily gained a virtual monopoly in the movement of persons. For freight, canal charges continued to be significantly lower, but as the total differential narrowed

Table 13.11. *Productivity change in the railroad sector, 1839–1859*
(1910 = 100)

Year	Output	Labor	Capital	Fuel	Total input	Total factor productivity
1839	0.08	0.3	0.8	0.07	0.5	16.0
1849	0.46	1.1	2.2	0.20	1.4	32.8
1859	2.21	5.0	10.1	1.50	6.6	33.5

Source: Adapted from Albert Fishlow, "Productivity and Technological Change in the Railroad Sector, 1840–1910," in Dorothy S. Brady (ed.), *Output, Employment, and Productivity in the United States after 1800*, Studies in Income and Wealth, vol. 30 (New York, 1966), 626. Output is changed from this original version, being now based on 1910 weights and thereby altering the total factor productivity index.

on competing routes from 3 cents in 1849 to much less than 2 cents in 1859, the qualitative advantages of the railroad made the difference. Greater speed, all-season utilization, less transshipment, and concentrated responsibility succeeded in capturing the trade not only in highly valued merchandise, but also in the less bulky agricultural commodities: Flour and livestock, in particular, began increasingly to utilize the railroad, leaving the transport of grains and coal as the greatest source of the canals' demand.

Such a reduction in railroad rates was made possible by increased factor productivity, as Table 13.11 indicates. Between 1839 and 1859, productivity slightly more than doubled; that is, input requirements were halved. An appropriately weighted rate index correspondingly declined by 42 percent. The contributing factors to the productivity growth undoubtedly include some technological advance even in that experimental period. The average tractive force of locomotives considerably more than doubled between 1839 and 1859; eight-wheel freight cars began to be introduced and were by far the most common type in 1859, except in the carriage of coal, where they were introduced more slowly; rails had been improved from simple bars of iron on wooden stringers to edge rails of 50 to 60 pounds per yard. Yet during these first decades, what is most impressive is the effect of increasing utilization of the stock of capital. The capital–output ratio declined quite markedly after 1839 as traffic increased and the indivisible capital stock could be more fully employed. Such increased utilization, taking 1859 as a base, explains more than half of the rise in productivity observed before 1860. The constancy of the productivity index between 1849 and 1859 results from the absence of further reductions in the capital–output ratio. The rapid extension of the railway system during the 1850s caused capital accumulation to match the growth of output. In this sense of incompletely utilized potential capital services, it is quite legitimate to speak of construction being ahead of demand before 1860. In so doing, however, one must note that the imbalance between capital and output was considerably greater in 1839 than in 1859, that the 1859 capital–output ratio was actually somewhat smaller than in 1849, and that in 1859 output was artificially low due to cyclical influences. Taken together, these facts still do not add up to *increasing* excess capacity in the 1850s.

The ascendancy of the railroad before the Civil War marked a virtual end to the diffusion of the other transport innovations of the period. Not until the twentieth century, and the era of the automobile, would a new challenge arise. Further advance in the nineteenth century depended upon continued railroad extension and increasingly efficient transport capacity. Let us now examine the post–Civil War experience.

The Reign of the Railroad, 1860–1910

Impressive as were the first three decades of American railroads – the 30,000-mile network existing in 1860 represented half the world total – more epic still were the decades to follow. Whether the measure be quantitative, such as construction activity or output, or qualitative, such as the speculative performances of the great railroad entrepreneurs, the post–Civil War decades make the earlier epoch pale by comparison. By 1890 an additional 140,000 miles of railway were in place, and the extent was destined to reach over 250,000 miles by 1916. The 2.6 billion tonmiles of 1859 escalated to 80 billion by 1890, and trebled again by 1910. And what casual student is unaware of the exploits of Vanderbilt, Cooke, Gould, Morgan, and others who stood out among the rising robber barons?

LATE NINETEENTH-CENTURY EXPANSION:
THE POSTWAR SURGE

Like the earlier growth, the expansion after 1860 was not a smooth one, temporally or geographically. Table 13.12 portrays the three great waves

Table 13.12. *Railroad mileage constructed, by areas*

Area	1868–1873	1879–1883	1886–1892
New England	1,376	358	605
Middle states	3,833	2,873	2,557
Central North	3,847	7,539	6,839
Western North	3,749	9,036	9,396
South Atlantic	1,937	2,881	6,639
Gulf	2,041	2,323	4,409
Western South	5,709	10,343	11,754
Pacific	2,097	4,200	4,619
Total	29,589	39,553	46,818

Note: Differences of total mileage in operation between the specified years. New England: Me., N.H., Vt., Mass., Conn., R.I.; Middle States: N.Y., N.J., Pa., Md., D.C.; Central North: Ohio, Mich., Ind., Ill., Wis.; Western North: Iowa, Minn., Neb., N.D., S.D., Wyo., Mont.; South Atlantic: Va., W.Va., N.C., S.C., Ga., Fla.; Gulf: Ala., Miss., Tenn., Ky., La.; Western South: Mo., Ark., Tex., Kan., Col., N. Mex., Okla.; Pacific: Wash., Ore., Cal., Nev., Id., Ariz., Utah.
Source: Data from *Poor's Manual of the Railroads of the United States* (New York, 1869–1893).

of later nineteenth-century expansion in the periods 1868–1873, 1879–1883, and 1886–1892. Mileage continued to be constructed after these dates, but in lesser annual increments. The first acceleration occurred in the wake of the virtual cessation of investment during the Civil War. Railroads emerged from that conflict in excellent financial condition, since rapid output increases were absorbed without the necessity of substantial additional investment. For 1867, when *Poor's* tabulations effectively begin, a ratio of net earnings to capital account of 9 percent is shown.[34] Supply ultimately responded to this rising demand in the first three regions enumerated in Table 13.12. These areas were precisely those which previous construction had exploited and that afterward were even more intensively served. In 1873 the number of miles of railroad per square mile in these regions was 0.092; in the rest of the country it was 0.015.[35] In economically more meaningful terms, the Northeast per dollar of income had 60

[34] Bureau of the Census, *Historical Statistics*, 428, based on *Poor's Manual of the Railroads of the United States* (New York, 1884).
[35] Calculated from *Poor's Manual* (1873).

percent as much mileage as the rest of the country. Such potential demand provided an important and continuing impulse to the ongoing investment in this region.

A second factor was the land grants conceded by Congress, both prior to 1860 and in support of transcontinental extension thereafter. Of the trackage brought to completion in 1868–1873, some 10,000 to 12,000 miles arose from this source. They were located largely in the Pacific region, and in the states of the Western North and South. The single most dramatic event in the course of this federally supported construction was the junction of the Central Pacific and Union Pacific at Ogden, Utah, in 1869; only later would the allure of that accomplishment be tarnished by reflection upon the large profits accruing to private enterprises undertaking such large and risky ventures.

Noteworthy as the completion of the first transcontinental line was, the total mileage completed in the least settled areas by it and similar projects was limited. Kansas, Nebraska, Minnesota, and Texas ended up with more than twice the mileage of Colorado, Utah, Nevada, Wyoming, and the Dakotas. Even in an era of federally subsidized construction ahead of demand, designed to bind the Pacific states to the East, the attraction of a ready market was not altogether forgotten or uninfluential. Indeed, the Union Pacific yielded a price-adjusted ratio of net returns to construction cost of 6.7 percent by 1871, only two years after completion; for the first decade of operation, the ratio was 11.6.[36] This favorable operating performance resulted from an adjustment process similar to that of the 1850s. The railroads constructed to less populated regions charged proportionately higher rates for their services to compensate for the smaller demand.

What was relevant for the financial solvency of the new enterprises was current net earnings relative to capitalization, not the ratio of real profits to investment. Many fewer projects, whether in the East or the West, passed this test. In fact, average net earnings for all railroads during the 1870s did not exceed 5 percent on capital.[37] Of total railroad mileage, 18 percent was in the hands of receivers at the beginning of 1877, and probably a still larger proportion of railroad bonds had been in default.[38] The reason for such a poor showing was threefold: (a) the desire for immediate

---

[36] Robert W. Fogel, *The Union Pacific Railroad: A Case Study in Premature Enterprise* (Baltimore, 1960), 95, 102.

[37] Bureau of the Census, *Historical Statistics*, 428.

[38] Henry H. Swain, "Economic Aspects of Railroad Receiverships," *American Economic Association Economic Studies*, 3 (1898), 70.

profits during construction and discount below par on securities sold, which led to excessive capitalization; (b) a declining price level that increased real interest payments on the substantial funded debt previously issued; and (c) a cyclical decline in the 1870s that owed its origins largely to the deceleration in railroad investment. Construction ahead of demand was secondary in the poor financial showing during the decade.

Excessive capitalization was a consequence of paying contractors with securities rather than cash. Stocks and bonds were accepted only at a substantial discount, at prices which were frequently even lower than what was justified by risk. Construction companies charging high prices were frequently formed by the railroad promoters in order to gain an immediate return. With knowledge of this situation, potential bondholders could be cajoled into holding debt only under the most favorable terms. Sales at prices below par were the common mechanism of adjustment, rather than high interest rates. Issuers gained the advantage of postponing some part of the interest burden by this mechanism. Part of the discount on bonds has a place in construction costs, since it reflects the higher interest costs that must be paid during the period of construction. Typically, however, the entire discount was included, thereby greatly exaggerating the cost. Likewise, all shares issued were counted at par. This watered stock, without corresponding assets, became the basis for dividend payments and aroused a continuing controversy over what railroads claimed was an inadequate return and what users claimed were excessive profits. It was estimated in 1884 in *Poor's Manual* that the true investment in railroads did not exceed the sum total of the floating or funded debt, implying an excess capitalization of 50 percent.[39]

As net earnings in current dollars began to increase less rapidly because of the general price decline, annual interest payments, which remained fixed, became an increasing real burden. Market interest rates at the time of construction did not reflect an expected decline in prices. Later roads built at lower nominal cost could compete favorably, since their interest rates were not dissimilar and applied to a smaller debt. The reorganization of railroads during the 1870s, which affected especially those newly built, resulted less from sheer overbuilding in ignorance of returns than from an insupportable burden of debt. In most cases, the capital structure was altered to permit the roads to pay lower effective real rates of interest.

[39] *Poor's Manual* (1884), iii.

The final factor in the disappointing financial performance of the railways in the 1870s was the cyclical crisis that broke, ironically enough, with the failure of the Northern Pacific and Jay Cooke and Company in 1873. Railroad output, which had increased by 115 percent between 1868 and 1873, expanded in the next five years by little more than a third. Net earnings were less sensitive owing to the curtailed operating costs that were unsuccessfully resisted in the famed railroad strike of 1877. These lower costs explain the capacity of the older and better established lines to maintain their dividends through the crisis.

THE BOOM OF THE 1880S AND ITS AFTERMATH

Less rapidly but as inexorably as the storm had broken in 1873, it gradually cleared, and railroad construction resumed at a brisk rate in 1878. The course of this investment was largely the less developed regions, the states in the Western South and Western North accounting for some 50 percent of the total, as Table 13.12 illustrates. These efforts represented, most often, a continuation of projects already begun in 1873. Two of the original transcontinental lines, the Southern Pacific and the Northern Pacific, were completed, while the conclusion of the Atchison, Topeka, and Santa Fe permitted an alternative route from St. Louis to the Pacific Coast. The large amount of additional mileage in the southwestern states was a measure of the rising importance of Kansas City and the cattle trade. It also reflected construction of links to the Gulf ports, particularly Galveston, in the hope of funneling grain exports in that direction. In the North Central area, the various lines tributary to Chicago began a series of extensions to the then rapidly settling Dakotas and Nebraska, not to mention further construction in Iowa.

The extent of the construction so far surpassed previous efforts – an annual average of 8,000 miles was constructed during the five years 1879–1883 – that subsequent characterizations have stressed the speculative and exuberant features of the expansion. *Poor's Manual* retrospectively referred to the surge of investment as a delusion, not once but in almost every phase:

From 1877 to near the close of 1883 a most singular delusion rested upon the public . . . and this delusion was taken advantage of on a vast scale by able and unscrupulous adventurers. Whatever was manufactured and put afloat was seized with avidity by an eager and uninformed public. The delusion was increased and prolonged by payments on a very large scale of interest and dividends from capital.

In this delusion, the most loud-mouthed and unscrupulous promoters usually had the greatest success.[40]

Such a judgment, harsh as it was, correctly emphasized the role of abundant capital supply in permitting the boom to go forward. Railroad common-stock prices doubled between 1877 and 1881, and in such a setting it was quite easy for construction companies to sell their shares profitably. Bond yields declined during the expansion, not to reverse themselves until 1883 and then only insignificantly. Price deflation influenced this downward trend, but so too did the rapid decline of the federal debt, which liberated capital.

The question is whether these favorable evaluations had any basis in fact. Superficially, it might seem that all was overbuilding. In 1878 the average net earnings relative to the costs of construction in the newer western states were less than elsewhere. The instances of parallel construction – such as the Nickel Plate and West Shore ventures, which were designed primarily for sale at favorable prices to potential competitors – seem only to reinforce the speculative image. However, all was not quite so socially irrational. Most construction was undertaken by extant systems, either to complete previously demarcated through routes, or to extend into the newer areas whose potential contribution to traffic seemed favorable. This meant that returns could be paid out from older portions of line even while construction was under way. Completion and extension frequently resulted in more than proportional additions to earning capacity. This was natural when the areas between termini were meager sources of traffic. The Atchison approximately doubled its net earnings per mile after doubling its extent; the same advantage, albeit less pronounced, was enjoyed by the Southern Pacific and the Northern Pacific. The three most expansion-minded systems were perhaps the Chicago and Northwestern; the Chicago, Milwaukee, and St. Paul; and the Burlington. All experienced an initial increase in net revenue per mile, followed by a falling off; gross output per mile unambiguously increased. Net earnings performed less well due to deteriorating rate conditions that developed from the increasing competition for traffic.

Total demand, however, expanded quite rapidly in the newer states since settlement and commercialization occurred more synchronously than in the pre–Civil War period. An important fillip was added by the great increase in European demand for cereals and meat beginning in 1879.

---

[40] Ibid., iii.

Wheat exports in 1877 of 40 million bushels worth $47 million expanded in 1881 to 151 million bushels worth $168 million, later subsiding. States with significant railroad construction such as Iowa, Nebraska, Minnesota, the Dakotas, and Kansas contributed almost half of the 200,000-bushel increment in the output of wheat between 1874 and 1884.[41] This was the era of bonanza farms. Even where settlement and agricultural growth were not large in scale, there were other sources of demand, such as the silver-mining boom in Colorado. The Denver and Rio Grande did extraordinarily well – to the point of paying dividends – until an ambitious extension to Salt Lake City proved more costly than profitable. It and the Texas and St. Louis were the only significant western lines to pass into receivership after the check to construction in 1884.

Thus, despite the unprecedented magnitude of investment and the great increase in mileage, the boom was more than a delusion. Individual projects could anticipate favorable demand conditions, although admittedly, when the expansion plans of all were taken together, there were instances of excess construction. The rapid resumption of investment in 1886 and its continuation until 1893 in the very same areas previously exploited suggest that such instances were not numerous, and that previous investors were not completely deluded.

This last surge was much like its predecessor in motivation: Its aims were completion of an additional transcontinental line to the Northwest, as well as amplification of facilities serving that area; construction of tactical extensions by the large systems to compete for long-haul traffic in newer areas; and investment in trackage to provide direct and separate entrances for the major systems into the principal railroad centers, East and West. An additional stimulus was provided by a resurgence of construction in the southern and Gulf states. A combination of renewed economic activity and the passage of time since the debacle of public assistance during Reconstruction contributed to the resumption; the mechanism – expansion by established or newly formed extended systems – was the same as previously.

With the depression of 1893, extensive railway construction came largely to an end. Although an additional 80,000 miles was constructed in the next 25 years, the laying of secondary and yard track and the acquisition of equipment made the larger contribution to investment. Table

---

[41] Calculated from U.S. Department of Agriculture, *Report of the Commissioner of Agriculture for 1874*, 30, and *Report of the Commissioner of Agriculture for 1885* (Washington, DC, 1875, 1886), 361. All production in 1874 shown for territories was credited to the Dakotas.

Table 13.13. *Gross investment in construction and equipment (millions of 1909 dollars)*

Period	Track	Equipment	Total
1828–1838	85.3	4.0	89.3
1839–1848	158.5	13.7	172.2
1849–1858	854.3	72.6	926.9
1859–1869	793.1	126.8	919.9
1870–1879	1,677.7	332.7	2,010.4
1880–1889	3,413.4	681.1	4,094.6
1890–1899	1,755.8	742.8	2,498.6
1900–1909	3,023.4	1,922.4	4,945.8

Source: Adapted from Fishlow, "Productivity," 611.

13.13 restates gross investment in 1909 dollars from the inception of the railroad era until that year and clearly demonstrates the rapid rise of purchases of rolling stock after 1890. Construction of track other than mainlines accounted for approximately $900 million in 1900–1909 and $500 million in the preceding decade. Thus the sum of equipment purchases and intensive track construction equaled extension outlays in 1890–1899 and went on to exceed it by 50 percent in the next decade.

THE EXTENT OF THE INVESTMENT AND ITS SOURCES

The rapid growth of railroad investment in the 1870s and 1880s stands out in Table 13.13. Within twenty years real expenditures quadrupled, for an annual average rate of over 7 percent for two decades. This expansion retained for railroads its 1860 position as the leading nonagricultural activity in the country, even given the rising manufacturing sector. Railroad capital of $10 billion represented perhaps a sixth of the nation's reproducible wealth in the early 1900s; individual railroad enterprises were numbered among the corporate giants of the time.

In current prices between 1860 and 1910, the gross investment flow into the railway sector was between $9.1 and $15.9 billion, the correct total depending upon the degree of overcapitalization of share capital. The private sector was the principal source of finance. Apart from the land grants authorized in 1862–1871 and a federal loan (later repaid with interest) of nearly $65 million to the Central Pacific–Union Pacific project, state and local governments added only $275 million, about the same as their antebellum contribution.[42] Valuation of the land grants is difficult: As a lower bound the price per acre can be set equal to the value at the time of the grant, or less than $1; an approximate upper limit is the average value of sales, or $3.38 an acre. (This accounting is exclusive of the additional 22 million acres granted by states to railroads in the 1850s). Although it includes appreciation due to completion of the railroad and does not discount for the interval until sale, the higher price probably reflects better the real transfer of resources – that is, the present value of federal lands contributed. There was also a quid pro quo involved: reduced rates on transportation of federal property and troops.

For present purposes we can accept an estimate of $400 million for the 131 million acres bestowed by the federal government and the 27 million acres in the states of Texas. Overall, public aid was thus absolutely greater after the Civil War, but it still provided less than 10 percent of needed resources. In the first postwar surge, 1868–1873, especially in the land-grant incentive to undertake large-scale projects, government aid was much more crucial. Indeed, within this single interval, the gross financial assistance was comparable to the relative subsidy granted in the 1830s. Both were experimental periods: the first in the introduction of the innovation, the second for transcontinental systems. After the crisis of 1873, there was a parallel wave of revulsion, constitutional prohibition of aid, and dependence upon private finance.

Land grants were the principal component of assistance after 1860. There was abundant unsettled land in the West, and the grants seemed a costless way to subsidize construction. Since the government retained alternate sections along the right-of-way that could be sold at a higher price, its receipts would not decline and yet construction could be accelerated. In fact, since government sales were not made at higher prices, a financial opportunity cost was involved.[43] More fundamentally, however, the efficacy of the subsidy was diluted by the underlying contradiction of the grants, which impinged differentially upon the railway's construction, land, and transportation interests. The former required that the lands be converted immediately to a liquid asset. Immediate sale did not satisfy

---

[42] Goodrich, *Government Promotion*, chaps. 5–7.
[43] Paul. W. Gates, "The Railroad Land Grant Legend," *Journal of Economic History*, 19 (1954), 143–46.

this objective, since current prices were low. Rather, the grants secured bond issues, frequently sold at discount in any event, and could thus have been substituted by government guarantees. By withholding lands as they thus frequently did, and by further procrastinating in preempting lands in the wider indemnity zone to compensate for acreage along the right-of-way that had already been settled, the railroads succeeded in causing their value to appreciate. This procedure conflicted with the early development of traffic that the railroad might serve, as well as with the social advantage of earlier settlement. Land grants were therefore not an unambiguously optimal solution.

More important than public subsidy after the Civil War was foreign investment. Estimates suggest that as much as $2.5 billion of American securities found their way into European portfolios between the end of the war and the beginning of the twentieth century. Indeed, until the reversal that began in 1893, the net inflow totaled more than $3 billion.[44] The foreign contribution was two-thirds in bonds and only one-third in shares, a fact which made its role the more significant, since the former were sold at a lesser discount. Between 1865 and 1893, almost half the funded debt issued by railroads was absorbed abroad, and one-fourth of the stock, or more than a third of total capital.[45] Foreign investment and public subsidy responded inversely. European participation was perhaps greatest in the last surge of investment in the 1880s and least between 1878 and 1884. The fate of the foreign investors was not always happy. Their extensive finance of the Erie Railroad was always a source of grief, its failure being a regular feature of the American business cycle. On average, financial outcomes were undoubtedly better, however. Bonds of the leading railroads were favored objects of investment, sold at a premium in London in the late 1880s, and yielded a return of between 4 and 5.5 percent. Indeed, it was argued that they were undervalued, inasmuch as South American and Balkan railways, albeit government guaranteed, were quoted similarly.[46] English investors were accustomed to much lower returns than American, and the higher yield of the American railroad securities in London adequately compensated for the greater risk, while still securing to railroad promoters an abundant and cheap source of capital.

---

[44] Matthew Simon, "The United States Balance of Payments, 1861–1900," in William N. Parker, ed., *Trends in the American Economy in the Nineteenth Century*, Studies in Income and Wealth, vol. 24 (Princeton, 1960), 698–707.

[45] William Z. Ripley, *Railroads: Finance and Organization* (London, 1915), 5–8; Cleona Lewis, *America's Stake in International Investments* (Washington, DC, 1938), chap. 8.

[46] S. F. Van Oss, *American Railroads as Investments* (New York, 1893), 178–79.

Despite the size of the foreign interest, the major burden of the investment fell upon the Americans. How could such substantial finance have occurred with average returns on capital rarely in excess of 5 percent, frequent receiverships emanating from defaults of interest, and large quantities of stock not paying dividends? The answer lies partially in the already-cited exaggeration of capitalization and in the attraction of capital gains. The first factor meant that returns to investors were always greater than those to the enterprise; the second provided expectations for still-larger individual profits. Securities acquired at discount were increased in value by the completion and operation of the project, if only because its survival was then assured. This capital gain, a compensation for the risk involved, was sufficient to evoke the crucial inflow of domestic capital necessary to undertake construction. Unfortunately, the magnitude and variation over time of such returns is not easily assessed. Security prices rose and fell. Yet there seems to have been ample scope for capital gains. In the decade 1889–1899, an index of share prices fluctuated around a mean value of approximately 67 percent of par; in 1900, the index stood at 80; and in 1901, after a series of good years, it was above par.[47] If, as has been asserted, real investment was only half the nominal capitalization, the capital gains element must have varied between 34 and 100 percent. This was an addition to a higher current yield, based upon an original purchase price rather than reckoned against par capitalization.

In addition to such influences upon the investor's expected return, another mechanism was operating at the end of the century to assure abundant capital supply. This was the reinvestment of internally generated funds as part of the expansive strategy of existent or nascent consolidated systems. The return on such funds from the viewpoint of the enterprise was quite high, even though it was socially low and, even in realized terms, quite modest. Not to engage in feeder construction and other competitive investment might mean losses on previously sunk capital, even though the actual recorded gains from such investment were small.

In sum, construction was not undertaken for altruistic reasons, nor did investment go without reward. The success of individual financiers such as Drew, Gould, Cooke, Vanderbilt, and others exaggerate the average returns, but serve as a vivid reminder that profits were sought and earned.

---

[47] U.S. Industrial Commission, *Reports*, 19 (Washington, DC, 1902), 270–71.

Table 13.14. *Productivity in the railroad sector, 1870–1910 (1910 = 100)*

Year	Output	Labor	Capital	Fuel	Total input	Total factor productivity
1870	6.57	13.5	16.6	5.4	13.9	47.3
1880	13.87	24.5	31.5	11.7	25.9	53.6
1890	32.82	44.1	61.9	28.7	49.3	66.6
1900	54.84	59.9	72.3	45.9	63.2	86.7
1910	100.00	100.0	100.0	100.0	100.0	100.0

Source: Adapted from Fishlow, "Productivity," 626.

TRANSPORT SERVICES AND TECHNOLOGICAL CHANGE

Yet, impressive as its record of physical expansion and mobilization of financial resources was, the output and productivity performance of the railroad sector were no less spectacular.[48] Ton-mileage grew almost a hundredfold between 1859 and 1910; passenger miles, more than 16 times. As shown in Table 13.14, weighted output increased 7 percent per year from 1870 to 1910, a figure well in excess of such aggregates as national income or total commodity production, and more than that of any other single major sector. The most important factor in the increase was the sheer physical extension of mileage. Intensified demand, more tonnage originating per mile, accounts for only half as much of the change.

Productivity in the railroad sector likewise exceeded that in the economy as a whole by a goodly margin. The average annual rate of advance from 1870 to 1910 was 2 percent; for the national economy it was approximately 1.5 percent. This aggregate measure encapsulates the consequences of extensive organizational and technical changes introduced by railroads in the post–Civil War period. Bridges successfully vaulted natural gaps and the manmade obstacles of gauge differences, and confused time changes were overcome in the 1880s. The appearance of fast-freight lines after the Civil War eliminated the inconvenience of breaking bulk at each junction of independent roads, not an inconsiderable bother prior to

[48] For a more thorough treatment of this question, see Albert Fishlow, "Productivity and Technological Change in the Railroad Sector, 1840–1910", in Dorothy S. Brady, ed., *Output, Employment, and Productivity in the United States After 1800*, Studies in Income and Wealth, v. 30 (New York, 1966).

widespread consolidation. Participating railroads contributed cars in proportion to their share of the traffic, in a precursor of later rental arrangements. Some forty separate lines were formed and rapidly won the bulk of the through business. Less dramatic was the steady advance in the weight and quality of rails. The Pennsylvania Railroad was the first to introduce steel rails during the Civil War, motivated by the frequency of rail replacement under conditions of dense traffic. By 1880, almost 30 percent of national trackage was laid with steel rails; by 1890, 80 percent was so equipped. Rail weights increased from approximately 50 pounds per yard to a standard 70 pounds at the beginning of the century. On this heavier track, more numerous and more powerful locomotives pulled larger and more efficient freight cars. Tractive force increased by more than 100 percent between 1870 and 1910. Freight-car capacity more than trebled, but without proportional increases in dead weight, altering the ratio of capacity to weight from 1 : 1 to 2 : 1. Finally, block signaling devices, automatic couplers, and air brakes made important contributions to the expeditious movement of larger trains.

However, the most important, albeit prosaic, cost-saving change occurred in train size and composition. More powerful locomotives and more efficient freight cars together created a reduction in 1910 operating costs of $749 million, 40 percent over what the 1870 technology could have produced. Because of their increased longevity, steel rails represented a direct saving of another $200 million; and because of their greater strength – which permitted locomotive size to increase – another $279 million was saved. Automatic couplers and air brakes were of significantly less importance. The increased speed and safety they facilitated were translated into much smaller economies of $50 million. Therein lies an explanation for the long delay in their adoption by railroads. Although couplers and brakes both were experimented with as early as the 1870s, national legislation was necessary to secure their installation. Congress acted in 1893 and was forced to extend the period of adoption to 1900 because of the railroads' recalcitrance. The rapid diffusion of steel rails and the continuing and unheralded progress of locomotives and rolling stock, on the other hand, required no legislative enforcement: The market sufficed.

Economies of scale also continued to operate in the post–Civil War period as they had earlier. The capital–output ratio declined by 60 percent between 1870 and 1910. If capital services were proportional to output, economies of scale explain about half the observed productivity advance between these dates. The four innovations examined above – train size and composition, steel rails, automatic couplers, and air brakes – account for the largest part of the remaining half, and in that order.

This productivity gain was translated into lower railroad tariffs. Passenger rates of 2.8 cents in 1870 fell almost one-third to a 1910 value of 1.9 cents; average ton-mile costs decreased more sharply, from 2.2 cents to only 0.75 cents. While some part of the decline in the average is due to a rising share of low-rate commodities, especially coal, the reduction on various identical commodities was only slightly less impressive. Both reductions exceeded the 25 percent fall in the general price level over the same period. Yet during these years railroads and their pricing policies became the object of considerable complaint, publicity, agitation, and ultimately regulation.

These objections centered on the level of rates and discrimination in their application. Such discrimination could be personal, as in the case of rebates to large shippers, or locational, as in the controversy over the relative charges for long or short hauls. The first of these criticisms found national expression in 1874 in a senatorial report, *Transportation Routes to the Seaboard*, and would be repeated locally many times over. The region west of the Missouri River, in particular, complained of rates much higher than those in the trunk-line territory between Chicago and the seaboard. Discrimination did not lack for attention. Farmers especially complained of the advantages bestowed upon larger shippers, which gave to elevator operators a favored position in monopolizing the trade. Yet it was in the oil trade, and the rise of the Standard Oil monopoly, that perhaps the most audacious personal discrimination was found. Finally, the vexing and complicated problem of asymmetry between distance and transport charges could not fail to attract notice. Local rates, which were generally noncompetitive, were set considerably higher than through rates. It was not uncommon for localities lying close to a shipping point to be charged more for transportation than a competitive terminal at the far end of the same line.

In reply to such charges, railroads pointed to their low rates of return and to what their managers considered fair charges. James J. Hill of the Great Northern offered to accept state regulation if it would "guarantee the roads six percent on their actual cost and a fund for maintenance, renewal, and other necessary expenditures." President Dillon of the Union Pacific phrased the issue in a less conciliatory and also less relevant manner: "What would it cost for a man to carry a ton of wheat one mile? What would it cost for a horse to do the same? The railway does it at a cost of less than a cent."[49]

Central to the controversy was the inapplicability of the competitive model to the railroad industry. Competition in other sectors might be relied upon to drive prices down to cost; where there were excessive profits, new firms would enter, and where profits were insufficient, some would exit. But railroads did not lend themselves to such a self-regulating mechanism. Entry was costly and irreversible, and frequently predicated upon a profitability later eroded by overconstruction. Individual localities could not have uniform access to the supply of rail services because some were better situated than others. Nor was water competition evenly distributed. A railroad faced differential elasticities of demand at different points along its line. Thus profit maximization required locational discrimination. Economies of scale due to large fixed costs also conflicted with purely competitive behavior, although fostering rivalry. They encouraged personal discrimination and favorable differentials on marginal traffic. They also contributed to excessive construction of feeders, and ultimately to consolidation.

The post–Civil War period saw a playing out of the tendencies inherent in the structure of the industry. Rate wars were frequent, as were cartel arrangements to avoid them. Wars were usually initiated by the railroad most needing increased revenue, and without fear of the ultimate penalty of being forced from the market: Large, capital-intensive enterprises are permanent. To farmers, the instability and uncertainty resulting from such wars more than offset the benefits of the often absurdly low rate levels. Discrimination was inevitable. Areas with alternative forms of transportation received better service and lower rates. So did high-income regions generating substantial traffic. Individuals guaranteeing large shipments were always assured favorable treatment. Not surprisingly, because their own situations were not identical, many railroads were eager, by whatever means, to stabilize the potentially disruptive operation of this model. The pools that arose to divide traffic were one manifestation of this desire; the formation of large consolidated systems of railroads was another.

The grievances against the railroad gave little brief to such technically conditioned responses. On more than one occasion, the demands ignored even more obvious facts. North Dakota farmers farther from the market could not expect to receive the same price for wheat as those in Illinois.

---

[49] Quoted in John D. Hicks, *The Populist Revolt* (Lincoln, NB, 1961), 62.

Prairie farmers benefiting from long hauls gained as much as those disadvantaged by short hauls lost to others. Overproduction of agricultural crops and falling prices on world markets could not be compensated proportionally by lower transport costs, which were determined by altogether different considerations. Construction to serve areas generating little traffic could justify itself only by high rates. Seasonal traffic logically also had to bear the expense of additional investment in rolling stock not efficiently utilized. These higher charges did not imply high profits: High-rate railroads west of the Missouri were not singularly profitable. Indeed, the many comparisons of average receipts per ton-mile ignored all differences in the composition of freight and length of average haul; two railroads with identical rate structures could have far different averages if lower-cost transport dominated on one.

This is not to deny that some railroads did ungraciously accumulate profits at the expense of others. It is simply to point out that on average the industry did not grow fat. The degree of competition assured that. Even if overcapitalization had been as large as 100 percent, the average direct return to direct cost would not have exceeded 10 percent in the 1870s, 1880s, and 1890s. And of course, some part of overcapitalization was a real cost of securing the needed capital. Enterprises in other sectors could not have earned significantly less. The results shown earlier in Table 13.14 are again relevant. Real railroad rates, which could have been expected to decline commensurably with the 0.5 percent differential between national and sectoral productivity growth, fell even more rapidly. This situation implies that the rate of increase of factor returns in the railroad sector was less than in the rest of the economy, or more simply, that consumers of rail services benefited at the expense of owners of railroad inputs. The fact that railroads were unionized and facing a competitive labor market suggests that the incidence of the differential was borne by investors. The return on *real* investment, without regard to nominal capitalization, probably declined relative to profits in other sectors between 1870 and 1910.

As a further example of the inexorable realities involved, the various efforts at regulation, made in response to the complaints of shippers, did not much alter matters over the period. Despite the decision by the Supreme Court in 1877 in *Munn v. Illinois*, which upheld the rights of states to institute regulatory legislation, the Granger Laws setting rail rates were invariably softened, if not repealed. National regulation followed soon thereafter, hastened by another judicial decision in the *Wabash, St.*

Louis, and Pacific Railway Co. case that states could not regulate rates on interstate commerce. The passage of the Interstate Commerce Act of 1887, with the commission it created, was not the punitive action it has sometimes been made out to be. Railroads were by no means completely opposed to regulation as a means of achieving greater stability in the industry – the Iowa Pool had finally dissolved in 1885, and other traffic associations were little more effective. Despite the language in the act outlawing pools, its consequences were in fact contrary. Regulation worked initially to the advantage of the trunk lines by increasing through rates to the detriment of long-distance shippers.[50] However, the less discriminatory rate structure and the relative decline of short-haul rates imposed by regulation did work to benefit many localities.

Court decisions in the early 1890s, culminating in the Maximum Rate case (*Interstate Commerce Commission v. Cincinnati, New Orleans and Texas Pacific Railway Company*) in 1897 – which eliminated the authority of the Interstate Commerce Commission (ICC) to establish rates – set off new wars. The case of *Interstate Commerce Commission v. Alabama Midland Railway Company* in the same year also questioned the commission's authority to reduce short-haul rates; the Court insisted upon consideration of competitive conditions as well as the principle of non-discrimination. This judicial emasculation of the original act was remedied by the Hepburn Act of 1906 and later by the Mann-Elkins Act. Neither altered the fact that decisions of the regulatory agency tended to be strongly influenced by the industry itself, however.

Nor did either reverse the consolidation that had by that time concentrated about two-thirds of the extant mileage and 85 percent of earnings in the hands of seven groups. The Vanderbilt roads monopolized movement between New York and Chicago; the Pennsylvania interest dominated the lines running westward from Pennsylvania and Maryland; Morgan controlled the Southeast; Gould interests and the Rock Island group were paramount in the Mississippi Valley; Hill railroads functioned in the Northwest; and Harriman's lines were made up largely of the southern and central transcontinental routes. Moreover, these seven were in reality only four, since Morgan was associated with the Pennsylvania, Vanderbilt, and Hill groups, and assured a commonality of interest. Constructed out of the wreckage of the depression of 1893, and given

---

[50] For a statistical test of the effect of regulation upon through rates, see Paul W. MacAvoy, *The Economic Effects of Regulation* (Cambridge, MA, 1965); for a more general, revisionist view of the origins of regulation, see Gabriel Kolko, *Railroads and Regulation, 1877–1916* (Princeton, 1965).

impetus by favorable financial conditions after 1898 that yielded large capital gains to their investment-banker organizers, these consolidated units marked an end to the earlier rivalry. In part they represented a natural evolution of the underlying economic realities of the industry, although the concentration went well beyond such rationalization. Consolidation did not resolve the problems of the industry, however. The return on capital, which had reached almost 6 percent in 1907, receded to as little as 4 percent in 1914 and 1915, partially as a result of the reluctance of the ICC to grant petitioned rate increases – in spite of a rising price level. For the remainder of the twentieth century, the situation of the railroads was to get little better and frequently worse.

THE EFFECTS OF NINETEENTH-CENTURY TRANSPORT INNOVATION

Transport innovation profoundly altered existing production relationships in nineteenth-century America in three ways. First, it reduced direct resource requirements for producing a given amount of transport services. The lower cost of total input per unit of output led to a correspondingly lower real price for transport services.

Second, this lower price influenced the decisions of consumers of transport services. It made their current level of activity more profitable by virtue of the lower costs of inputs. The reaction to this change varied by sector, depending upon the importance of shipment expense in total costs and the response of consumers of the final product to lower price. The chief beneficiary was agriculture. Not only did transport charges loom large in the total costs of bulk commodities, but the export market was one of elastic demand. In addition, the lower costs of transportation made the abundant land accessible. This development illustrates the unique locational consequences of transport innovation. Other innovations typically lower costs at given sites, and do not carry with them the impetus to geographic extension and specialization. But accelerated settlement and increased marketable surplus were directly associated with the succession of internal improvements.

A third sequence of reactions followed from the demands generated by the transport sector. As canals or steamboats or railroads were introduced, they required engineering talents, marine engines, iron rails, and so on in their construction phase and, as their output expanded, inputs of labor and material inputs. This development occasioned a reallocation of resources. Investment in transportation represented a large share of capital formation throughout the nineteenth century. Moreover, when it declined relatively, the rapid growth of transport services substituted current for capital requirements. Together, they made the sector a potent force.

Note that these backward linkages, because of their technological origins, were more specific than either direct resource savings or forward effects. Canals or railroads could lead to identical price reductions and direct benefits without being substitutable in their impact on other sectors.

This gamut of effects did not go unnoticed. Contemporaries evaluated transport projects with unbridled optimism. Later commentators have not stinted their praise of what transportation innovation meant for nineteenth-century American economic development. While railroads have received the lion's share of the commendation, canals and steamboats, too, have had their partisans. Let us assess such contentions.

We shall do so from the perspective of the individual innovations, rather than in terms of the entire range of transportation advance. The cumulative contribution made by the transition from the common road through to the railroad is so large and so obvious as to defy accurate calculation. Without the canal, steamboat, or railroad, the contours of development in the United States would have been so different and less satisfactory that we need go no farther. David Wells already resolved the issue in 1889:

The railway freight service of the United States for 1887 was . . . equivalent to carrying a thousand tons one mile for every person, or every ton a thousand miles. The average cost of this service was about $10 per annum for every person. But if it had been entirely performed by horsepower, even under the most favorable of old-time conditions, its costs . . . would represent an expenditure greater than the entire value of the then annual product.[51]

The interesting question, rather, is the relative contribution of the various technological innovations, and their social rate of return, given the actual historical sequence. In this context, the question of indispensability is of little interest. Without the railroad, say, but with canals, automobiles, and airplanes, the transportation situation would not have totally impeded progress. Indeed, in a complex economy, the range of potential substitution is so great that no single innovation can be regarded as completely necessary. This is not the same as saying that individual advances

[51] David Wells, *Recent Economic Changes* (New York, 1890), 41–42.

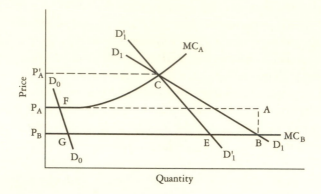

Figure 13.3.

were unimportant or insignificant. The assessment of importance depends upon the specific benefits of the change and the costs of its introduction. In measuring its effects, we shall consider the situation with and without the innovation, all else remaining the same. We shall not inquire into the possible alternatives that could have reduced, or altered, the perceived historical consequences. Nor shall we venture so far beyond the margin of observable adjustments that our analysis becomes vitiated in the process.[52]

Let us now turn to the consequences of the diverse transport innovations in terms of their direct benefits, their backward linkages, and the expansion they created in the using sectors.

Direct Benefits

To estimate resource savings, the following types of information are necessary: (a) the cost of carriage by the new mode, (b) the alternative cost by the existing facilities, and (c) the elasticity of demand. Then it is possible to estimate the consumers' surplus associated with price reduction, or the maximum value that could have been exacted by a discriminating monopolist leaving no gain for users.

This principle is illustrated in Figure 13.3, which is an expanded version of Figure 13.2. Our initial situation in period 0 is defined by the demand curve D_0 and the price P_A. The quantity of transport services $P_A F$ is uti-

[52] A considerable controversy has sprung up concerning the abiity to reach causal conclusions in general, and the importance of transport innovation specifically. For a statement explicitly differentiating historical necessity and sufficiency, see Albert Fishlow and Robert W. Fogel, "Quantitative Economic History: An Interim Evaluation," *Journal of Economic History*, 31 (1971), 15–42.

lized. By period 1, a more efficient means of transport has been introduced, and the charge is now a lower P_B. The demand curve is now D_1, shifted outward due to changing total income, and more elastic because of the use of a more transport-intensive technology in response to lower rates. Our objective is to measure the direct benefits. In the first instance, we must replace D_1 by the less elastic demand curve D'_1 appropriate to the older technology at the same level of income. (We assume that the change is sufficiently small not to have affected the total income substantially.) The correct area is $P_A FCEP_B$, since the older technology was subject to increasing costs and there is a gain in not extending it further.

In fact, we can easily calculate the sum $P_A ABP_B$ in which we ignore rising costs and apply the price differential $(P_A - P_B)$ to the quantity of transport output observed in period 1. This figure will always overstate benefits if $P_A = P'_A$ because the elasticity adjustment reducing quantity from B to E is ignored. But if costs are rising, a corresponding underevaluation is introduced whose effect may more than balance this positive bias. In particular, if the new technology is efficient at handling large volumes and the old is not, capacity constraints may make the relevant price P'_A much higher than P_A. Some allowance for rising costs and adjustment for demand elasticities can be introduced in practice to indicate the range within which the benefits can be expected to fall.

Criticism of the method has often ignored its approximative objective. The relevant question is not whether there was any violation of the assumption that price corresponded to marginal cost due to monopoly elements, or whether costs may have been increasing; it is rather the numerical implication of such violations. Evidence already presented concerning rates of return suggests that the monopoly problem was not a serious one. Rising costs have not been adequately shown to be serious enough to vitiate most applications; indeed, one purported demonstration of increased Erie Canal charges during the Civil War actually proves the opposite. The inherent merits of this quantification of benefits stand, and justify its continued use.[53]

---

[53] For a different view, see Peter McClelland, "Railroads, American Growth, and the New Economic History: A Critique," *Journal of Economic History*, 28 (1968), 102–23. Suffice it to say in rebuttal that most of McClelland's objections, while theoretically sound, are recognized in the works in question. See Fishlow, *American Railroads*, and Robert W. Fogel, *Railroads and American Economic Growth: Essays in Econometric History* (Baltimore, 1964). McClelland's one factual consideration, that Erie Canal rates in the early 1860s increased sharply under increased demand, thereby negating the availability of a low-cost water alternative to through rail shipment, is hardly so damning as he makes out. His own data show that a doubling of canal traffic between 1859 and 1863 left real canal freight rates virtually unchanged! Over the interim, they had temporarily risen owing to adjustment problems, to be sure, but that is totally irrelevant to the long-run question under consideration.

TURNPIKES

Estimation of the social benefits generated by the introduction of turn-pikes is hampered by the absence of traffic statistics. For two of the largest ones, the Pennsylvania Turnpike and the National Road, unverified reports cite annual shipments of 30,000 and 10,000 tons respectively around 1820.[54] In addition, a fair amount of livestock was driven to market over them. These magnitudes, and a cost differential in favor of turnpikes of 50 percent, imply an annual benefit of about $1 million. These roads cost some $4.5 million, yielding a social profit ratio of 22 percent. However, such a static view exaggerates the roads' true profitability. This reported volume of shipments was not an average annual flow over the life of the investment, but rather a maximum level that occurred after the rapid growth of settlement in the Ohio Valley subsequent to the War of 1812. Nor would it be continued indefinitely after the definitive success of the Erie Canal. Correction to incorporate a rising trend, with a time horizon of 1830, yields an internal rate of return of about 15 percent.

Moreover, this rate cannot be extrapolated to the remainder of turnpike investment. The National Road and the Pennsylvania were among the most densely traveled roads in the country. The private companies along the Pennsylvania route managed to obtain a net return on capital. Even in densely populated Massachusetts, the average financial experience was less favorable. Since total investment in turnpikes exceeded $27 million, of which less than a fifth occurred in these particularly successful projects, the overall results were by necessity much less encouraging. It is doubt-ful whether any but a handful of projects had a clearly favorable impact. Neither in the absolute magnitude of their benefits nor in their relative return did turnpikes distinguish themselves. This verdict is consistent with the general disinterest Americans subsequently manifested toward nonrail overland transportation until the late nineteenth century.

CANALS

Canals were another matter. Their introduction brought a palpable and dramatic reduction in rates. Equally clear are the rapid tonnage increases and the profitable returns on the Erie. That many of the enterprises con-structed in emulation of the New York canal later came to grief due to

[54] J. L. Ringwalt, *Development of Transportation Systems in the United States* (Philadelphia, 1888).

railroad competition does not necessarily negate their important interim contribution. One student of the subject has approximated their direct benefits prior to the railroad age and concludes that these social gains alone justified the total investment, including the investment in failures: "Canals seem clearly to have conferred upon the antebellum economy direct benefits that exceeded their cost by a substantial margin."[55]

This judgment is based upon the average 1837–1846 traffic on ten heavily utilized canals, and upon a cost differential of 23 cents per ton-mile between canals and overland transport. The calculation denies the feasibility of alternative shipment by water for any part of the total. This assumption appears reasonable in view of the localization of much of the canal business in areas not developed earlier because of lack of access to markets. Less plausible is the assumption of constancy of benefits over the fifty-year life span of the investment. For decision makers, *ex ante*, such a horizon and stream of benefits may have been appropriate; for subsequent measurement of the realized average rate of return, it is not. For in fact, within two decades, despite a threefold expansion in canal output, the relevant differential was no longer between canals and roads, but between canals and railroads. This change greatly altered the magnitude of the resources liberated by the relative efficiency of canals. Nor is it entirely appropriate to neglect those canals whose results, even prior to the production of the railroad, were less favorable.

Careful recalculation of the returns upon canal investment is beyond our present scope, but an approximation is possible. Setting the initial returns and cumulative investment both in 1830 to obviate adjustment for present values, substituting a more reasonable rate differential of 17 cents per ton-mile until 1846 and 2 cents thereafter, and using the observed output trend, the average internal rate of return for all canals well exceeds 50 percent. The reason for this impressive figure is simple. At such a large rate differential, the initial capital cost is immediately repaid. This result is admittedly upwardly biased due to the overstatement of benefits calculated on the basis of observed quantities. If the large terminal bias that is found to obtain on the Ohio canals by comparison of increased rents and direct benefit calculations is applied, the results change somewhat.[56] Such

[55] Segal, "Canals and Economic Development", in Goodrich, ed., *Canals and American Development*, 247.
[56] See also Roger Ransom, "Canals and Development: A Discussion of the Issues," *American Economic Review, Papers and Proceedings*, 54 (1964), 373, in which the terminal bias is shown to be a factor of six. Such a large magnitude seems unlikely, however, since it implies an extraordinary high elasticity of transport demand.

an adjustment reduces the rate of return to the neighborhood of 15 percent. The basic conclusion remains the same, however. Even this lower figure is impressive considering the short period in which the canal dominated the transport scene. In the years 1837–1846 in particular, the annual benefits may have represented as much as 2 percent of national product.

This favorable evaluation reflects the singular success of the Erie Canal, itself responsible for almost a third of ton-mileage, but representing only 10 percent of investment. One study suggests as much as 85 percent of government construction may not have yielded a socially profitable rate, largely because of lack of foresight concerning the imminence of the railroad alternative.[57] Projects like the Wabash and Erie barely opened in time to close much of their route, and the high-cost feeders in New York consistently produced deficits. Yet the record of deficits is itself not sufficient to establish lack of social profitability. Development-minded state agencies fixed tolls at modest levels, well below what the traffic might have borne. In any event, there was no way of fully recouping the transport benefits short of a discriminating tariff. Private coal canals did better, either paying dividends or merging transport gains with the profits of extraction.

As a technology, therefore, the canal represented a highly desirable investment solely from the standpoint of its reduced transport charges. More careful planning might have avoided much needless expenditure, to everyone's benefit. Yet even the failures should not be judged too harshly; beyond the direct benefits, there were other indirect consequences that may have tipped the balance favorably in some cases.

STEAMBOATS

The positive case for steamboats is, if anything, more certain. This is true despite the steamboat's smaller relative advantage compared to canals. Flatboats, keelboats, and barges, while more expensive, were more satisfactory alternatives than the horse and wagon, which competed with the canal. The steamboat's special advantage in upstream travel, moreover, was diluted by the considerably smaller traffic in that direction. What made the innovation socially profitable was the limited investment involved. The existence of private returns assures us of its social success. For direct social benefits are the *sum* of net revenues and noncaptured gains. Where

---

[57] Ibid.

the former already justify the investment, there can be no instance of social unprofitability, unless negative externalities are involved.

It is instructive, nonetheless, to attempt to gauge the approximate size of the rents earned by shippers. Ton-mileage has been estimated from arrivals at New Orleans, with a generous conversion to allow for the extensive tributary commerce that never reached that terminus. Given a rate advantage over nonsteam craft of 2 cents per ton-mile downstream and 8 cents upstream, the total annual gains come to $1 million in the 1820s, rising to $6.3 million in the 1840s. This takes no account of the passenger receipts and the gains in time afforded to travelers. But the results are already clear. These flows exceed the corresponding net investment in steamboats by a factor of between 0.5 and 1.5, being greater in the earlier period. As rail diversion began in the 1850s, less favorable results may have been realized.

The evident implication, regardless of later traffic erosion, is of enormous social returns to the steamboat in western waters. Yet the absolute levels also are informative, for, compared to canals, the steamboat was much less important. In other words, it was extraordinarily advantageous to adopt steam power, but the investment was not a large enough commitment of resources to influence profoundly the economy as a whole. The slower diffusion of steam power to lake and coastal shipping suggests that its advantage there was less marked. This only reinforces the conclusion of a limited impact.

RAILROADS

The canal achieved its social profitability from the large initial difference between overland and water rates. The steamboat exhibited extraordinary rates of return on a limited capital input. By contrast, the railroad depended for its importance upon a modest reduction of rates applied to an unparalleled extension of output. For this reason its impact awaited a considerable accumulation of mileage. Railroad benefits began to approach canal resource saving in absolute terms only in the later 1840s. Not until the late 1850s, when the railroads' proportion of GNP amounted to some 4 percent, did they surpass the earlier contribution of canals. The time path of benefits, corrected for much of the bias of terminal measurement, is given in Table 13.15. Despite this delayed fruition, a result of the modest pace of railroad construction until the feverish 1850s, the antebellum benefits still represented an average internal rate of return of 15

Table 13.15. *Social return of direct benefits to railroad investment (millions of 1860 dollars)*

Annual averages	Net capital formation	Noncaptured benefits	Net earnings	Gross direct benefits	Gross direct benefits less net capital formation
1828–1835	4.5	0.3	0.2	0.5	−4.0
1836–1840	14.0	3.9	2.0	5.8	−8.2
1841–1845	7.0	14.5	7.1	21.6	14.6
1846–1850	27.9	31.4	15.9	46.2	18.3
1851–1855	72.1	78.7	31.2	109.9	38.8
1856–1860	48.1	155.7	48.5	204.2	156.1

Source: Adapted from Fishlow, *American Railroads*, 53.

percent on all investment. That is, even without allowance for the continuing earning capacity of the system after 1860, it already had established its profitability. If our calculations are extended to 1890, the rate increases to 18 percent, as the flow of later investment continued to produce significant benefits.

Railroad technology, despite its expense, was thus a wise investment and justified its utilization vis-à-vis the alternative already in use. The same excessive enthusiasm that had marked governmental promotion of canals was not lacking in private prosecution of railroads. Excess construction was undertaken in response to competitive pressures. The areas into which duplicate facilities penetrated obviously gained a relative advantage, but at a cost in excess of the additional income generated. To put it another way, had some of this investment been reallocated to areas not served by railroads, or perhaps not undertaken at all, there would have been better use of resources. Yet, as with canals, the total assessment remains affirmative.

The favorable rate of return is only one aspect of the railroad's contribution; the absolute size of the benefits is another. These were large, owing to the sheer magnitude of the railroad interest and its continued dominance throughout the nineteenth century. By 1890, resource saving must have exceeded its 1859 dimensions relative to gross product, since the sector's output and productivity growth was more rapid than that of the economy as a whole. This view differs from other findings that suggest 5 percent as the maximum possible proportion for 1890.[58] This latter conclusion is based upon partial results for interregional and intrarregional agricultural shipments. Apart from the problem of extrapolation from a unrepresentative base, there is a more fundamental methodological problem: that of assessing the alternative costs of shipping 80 million ton-miles long after shipments and rates on water alternatives ceased to have the same significance they possessed before 1860. This difficulty makes the calculation distinctly nonmarginal and uncertain, and almost surely implies an understatement of gains arising from capacity constraints on other overland modes of transport.

Therefore, the 1890 gains probably exceeded 10 percent of national income rather than lying well below 5 percent. Such a performance constituted a significant contribution. In absolute terms, however, there is no useful criterion of what is large and what is small, and individual assessments will differ. The virtue of the rate of return is that it definitively resolves the question in favor of the social profitability of an investment of unprecedented size and duration.

All these transport innovations, then, with the possible exception of the turnpike, earned a social rate of return in excess of current interest rates due to the reductions in cost they introduced. Such direct benefits are but one aspect, albeit the most easily quantifiable, of the consequences of the nineteenth-century transport revolution. A second path of influence was that of backward linkages.

Backward Linkages

The derived demands of transport improvement, and especially those of railroads, have received special attention in recent years due to the role that they play in Walt Rostow's *Stages of Economic Growth*: "Perhaps most important for the take-off itself, the development of railways has led on to the development of modern coal, iron, and engineering industries. In many countries the growth of modern basic industrial sectors can be traced in the most direct way to the requirements for building and, especially, for maintaining substantial railway systems."[59] Nineteenth-century observers, particularly at the beginning of the railroad age, were less impressed; they were more concerned with the high costs and the limited

---

[58] Fogel, *Railroads*, 223. For a different view concerning these issues see Robert W. Fogel, "Notes on the Social Savings Controversy," *Journal of Economic History*, 39 (1974), 154.

[59] Walt W. Rostow, *The Stages of Economic Growth* (New York, 1960), 55.

domestic supplies of needed industrial inputs. Ultimately, as special supply interests developed, attitudes altered and the role of the transport system as a consumer was lauded, though never as enthusiastically as its reduced rates and its role as an inducement to geographic expansion.[60]

One reason for the early reserve was the limited reorientation of demand effected by turnpike and canal construction. Total investment during the turnpike era and in the first wave of canal construction until 1834 neither pressed upon total resources significantly nor was much impeded by capital shortage. Equally relevant, the structure of demand represented no sharp break with past patterns. The principal requirement was skilled labor and locally available building materials; engineering was scarce, but a handful of persons sufficed to direct the major projects, most commonly in sequential order.

The coming of the railroad altered matters in both respects. A large magnitude of investment in the new transport form rapidly made it evident to all that a powerful new element had emerged. In their initial decade of development, railroads surpassed canals in the volume of capital expenditure in less than five years. They remained in the lead, despite the large amount of aid for canals granted by the western states in the later 1830s. At that early date, railroads already absorbed almost 10 percent of all resources committed to capital formation. Moreover, railroads represented a break with the past in requiring relatively large quantities of iron and complicated capital equipment such as locomotives.

This said, it is necessary to put the technological discontinuity into perspective. The predominant demands in railroad construction remained the ones already familiar from the turnpike and, to a still greater degree, the canal. Expenditures for preparing the right-of-way, which involved the employment of unskilled labor with picks and shovels, always exceeded the more sophisticated industrial demands by a substantial margin, even in the post–Civil War period. In the first decade of construction, expenditures for iron rails and equipment came to perhaps 20 percent of outlays, rising to a third in the next two decades, and thereafter remaining stable until the era of intensive investment that began after 1893. It was as much the magnitude of the railroad impetus as its particular form that led it to consume an increasing share of industrial output.

The divergence of early American technique from the British experi-

---

[60] See Fishlow, *American Railroads*, chap. 3; and Fogel, *Railroads*, chaps. 4 and 5 for a more detailed exposition.

ence is marked in this respect. Railroad iron demands per mile stood at only one-fourth the British level before the Civil War, a reflection of the higher price of iron in the United States and the consequent substitution of less durable but cheaper construction practices. Equipment requirements were similarly modified to correspond to the less intense utilization of American railroads. In other features as well, American technology reflected American conditions. Rails were repaired rather than replaced. Locomotives burned wood rather than coal; as late as 1859, outlays for the former were ten times the purchases of mineral fuel.

Later, as the economy and the railways prospered, changes did occur. Use of coal became more common on the well-traveled roads, although wood consumption continued to be reported in the South as late as 1880. Iron rails became heavier, and eventually steel found a natural and economical application in the manufacture of standardized types. Equipment became more sophisticated; railway shops followed suit as maintenance requirements became more industrial in character. Still, by 1880 only about a fifth of all railroad workers were employed in shops, and a fourth of these were carpenters.

IRON AND STEEL

As technology altered, there was a corresponding magnification of the role of railroad demand in the industries most closely affected. In the first decade of railroad expansion, its demands for iron had virtually no influence on domestic producers. The tariff of 1830 permitted a drawback reducing the tax on imports of iron to 25 percent *ad valorem* (rather than the 75 percent represented by the specific duty of $37); two years later, a policy of free imports was instituted, which remained in force for 10 years. In the 1840s, because of tariff protection and because English supply was being diverted to rapidly rising English demands, local iron production to satisfy railway demands did begin. Lower tariffs in 1846 and a large reduction in British prices after the collapse of their railway boom combined to direct purchases abroad in the 1850s. Not until the end of the decade did gradually increasing domestic production of rails exceed imports. American production took firm hold only after new construction had passed its peak, and then only because of the specialized character of supply. The willingness of British suppliers to accept payment in securities was a powerful incentive for new roads to import their initial requirements. However, the American practice of rerolling used rail favored production for replacement. By the end of the 1850s, extension of mileage was reduced in importance relative to maintenance demands.

Several studies have examined the aggregate iron demands of the railroad for rails, equipment, and maintenance. These calculations confirm the small role of railroads until the 1850s. In 1840–1850, total railroad consumption constituted 7 percent of domestic pig iron production; despite extensive rail importation in 1851–1855, the proportion rose to almost a fifth; and by 1856–1860, it was greater still. The comparative incremental results are more informative: Changes in railroad demand absorbed 17 percent of the increased supply of the 1840s and over 100 percent in the 1850s. By 1860, rails constituted in volume more than 40 percent of all rolled iron. Rail mills were the largest mills in the country and functioned as technological leaders; five of the six integrated iron works in the country in 1854 were rail producers.

The antebellum experience was only a precursor to the later effort, however. From 1867 until 1891, rails comprised more than 50 percent of annual Bessemer steel output; until 1880, the average ratio exceeded 80 percent.[61] Mills were specialized to serve the rail demand. Requirements for equipment and its maintenance likewise grew more rapidly than output, broadening the influence of railroads upon the iron industry. An estimate for 1889 would allocate 29 percent of rolled iron and steel production to rails alone.[62] Thereafter, with the reduced rate of railroad investment, the growth in installed iron and steel capacity began to be led by other sources, ultimately by another transportation development, the passenger car. Railroad backward linkages to the iron industry thus became progressively more important during the later nineteenth century until the innovation finally yielded its preeminence to more diversified demands. However, this record cannot be extrapolated backward to the 1840s nor indiscriminately to other branches of industry.

MACHINERY

The experience of the machinery industry is a case in point. Quite contrary to the gradual initiation of rail production, domestic producers quickly met rolling-stock demands. Of the 450 locomotives in the United States at the end of 1839, only 117 were imported from England, and

---

[61] James M. Swank, *History of the Manufacture of Iron in All Ages* (Philadelphia, 1892).
[62] Peter Temin, *Iron and Steel in Nineteenth Century America* (Cambridge, MA, 1964) 276.

of these 78 arrived before 1836. This performance has led some to exaggerate the role of the railway in promoting the expansion of the machinery industry. Locomotive demand did not originate machine production. Rather, locomotive supply expanded rapidly because of the prior existence of general firms that converted to the new specialty. The first American locomotive was built by a producer of marine engines. Locomotive shops typically originated either in the production of cotton textile machinery – for example, Rogers, Ketchum and Grosvenor, the Taunton works, Manchester, and Locks and Canal Company – or in general machine work, such as Baldwin, Hinkley, Grant, and others. Many firms continued their former line of output until the new demand proved sufficiently large and stable to warrant total conversion. Later entrants, particularly in the West, sometimes proved less cautious. On the basis of the demand engendered by rapid extension of trackage, western producers mushroomed in the early 1850s only to disappear once investment decelerated.

Horsepower comparisons have also been suggested to measure the importance of railroad demands for machinery. Citing estimates that railroads accounted for 435,000 horsepower, or 35 percent of the total, in 1849 and 60 percent a decade later, Rostow concludes that the American engineering industry was a product of the growth of the railroad. More careful calculations lead to horsepower values for railroads that are about half as great. Indeed, they suggest that the steamboat may have been a more important source of demand for engines. Western steamboats developed two and a half times more horsepower than locomotives in 1850, an advantage lost only in the 1850s when the rapid rise of the railroad was coupled with the decline of the steamboat on western rivers. But if the tonnage on the lakes, in coastal trade, and in foreign commerce are considered as well, the total horsepower developed by steamboats was probably close to three-fourths of the 1860 railroad total.

Such a static comparison does not allow for the greater annual purchase of marine steam engines relative to stock, owing to the fact that they depreciated more rapidly than locomotives. The construction of marine engines between 1851 and 1860 exceeded the extant 1860 total by a wide margin; whereas the cumulative 1860 stock of locomotives exceeded recent purchases. Comparison of engine production in 1859 confirms this impression. One account lists sixty-eight machine shops, employing between 4,800 and 4,900 men, manufacturing machinery to be used on the western rivers alone; in the same year, locomotive producers employed 4,174. From the standpoint of antebellum engine demands, therefore, railroads were secondary to the steamboat.

In a more fundamental sense, railroad-derived demand could not be as crucial in the engineering industry as in iron and steel, due to the inherent diversity of machine output. The machinery industry catered to many users, often in a custom manner. The variety of products increased over time as the techniques embodied in industry progressed in their requirements for exactness. In 1859 locomotive production was valued at $4,866,900; the census accorded to cotton and woolen machinery a barely larger value of $4,902,704. Thus railroads were as important in their demands as the leading manufacturing interest of the country. Total production of the machine sector, however, came to more than $52 million, implying a railroad share of less than 10 percent. In the next census railroad participation rose modestly only to decline thereafter as the variety of producers' goods increased. At the end of the nineteenth century and the beginning of the twentieth, despite significantly larger railroad equipment purchases, the relative magnitude was smaller than in 1869.

Railroads had much greater influence through their development of elaborate repair facilities. They served as a powerful force for geographic dissemination of skills, even as the western steamboat had done for the growing river centers of Pittsburgh, Cincinnati, Louisville, and St. Louis. Railroads, of course, were not confined to watercourses and thus cast their influence more widely. Although the South supported only limited locomotive production, the larger railroads in the region all had extensive shops for the reworking of old metal, renewals of locomotives, and even manufacture of rolling stock. In any discussion of western machine firms, the repair shops of railroads are prominently featured, as well they should be. In Detroit, Cleveland, and other cities, they were among the best-equipped and largest enterprises. The repair function was extended with railroad trackage itself. Chicago became an important center, not to mention lesser cities along the expanding routes, which became "railroad towns" whose fate was tied to the giant enterprises. In 1870 railroad repairing and manufacture of locomotives and cars came to 20 percent of the output of the machinery sector, with establishments in 29 states.[63] Research facilities were established on the largest roads, standardization of

---

[63] Bureau of the Census, *Census of Population: 1870*, vol. 3, *Statistics of Wealth and Industry* (Washington, DC, 1872), 455.

equipment was imposed, and an industrial mentality was emphasized in the apprentice programs.

The railroad's influence on the engineering industry was thus related more to maintenance than to new equipment purchases. It was particularly important in the geographic dissemination of industrial skills. More machinists in many different states were probably directly employed by railroads than by locomotive works in 1860. Although, as we have seen, railroads and steamboats were an important source of demand for engines, steamboats were more important because of their temporal precedence and their continuing stream of demands.

COAL

A third sector alleged to have been profoundly influenced by rail demand was the coal industry. Neither canals nor turnpikes required fuel, nor did steamboats utilize coal in large amounts. Wood was preferred by the latter because of its relative cheapness – the low cost explains the wasteful inefficiency of western engines. In the East, where wood was no longer abundant, the low-pressure steamboat engines had been almost wholly converted to anthracite by the 1840s. Cheap bituminous found near the Ohio River began to be admixed on western boats during the 1850s, a practice that continued due to the better adaptation of boilers to wood. This factor, plus the decline in steamboating, led to coal consumption by western steam craft of less than a million tons in 1880, not even 2 percent of bituminous production. For all steamboats together, the share of total coal output was not much greater.

Railroad impact before the Civil War was little different, as has already been noted. By the century's end, it was another matter. Beginning in 1880, locomotives consumed close to a fifth of total production, a ratio they maintained until 1910. Yet the larger questions are how railroads influenced the expansion of mining, and why development of a coal industry was crucial to national progress. On both counts, the significance of the backward linkages are diluted. There has been no suggestion that railroad demand altered mining technology or otherwise influenced the structure of the coal industry. Likewise, it is possible to exaggerate the influence of mineral fuel as a source of energy. As late as 1860, coal provided less than 20 percent of total energy consumed in the United States. This fact did not impede the rise of a substantial industrial sector by that date. The coal tonnage carried was probably more significant as a source of revenue to the railroad than the consumption of coal was to mining interests.

A real difference existed between the railroad and its predecessors in the pattern of their specific demands. Larger industrial effects emanated from railroad construction and operation even before 1860. However, such linkages were less significant for both coal and the engineering industry than has been suggested. Not until the 1850s, moreover, were demand effects upon iron production perceptible. After the war, railroad demands exerted a greater influence. What made them more important were technological considerations – the use of coal instead of cordwood, the substitution of iron rails by steel – and, especially, the rapidly growing size of the industry. In 1860, 1 percent of the labor force was employed by railroads; in 1900, the figure was 5 percent. Twice as many were employed by railroads as in iron and steel production before the Civil War; eight times as many in 1900. Gross capital formation by railroads, even at its peak in the 1850s, reached only 15 percent of investment; in the 1880s, it increased to 18 percent. These are shares exceeded only by residential construction and far in excess of the claims on savings by other industries. Such magnitudes not only influenced derived demands but obviously reflected increasing utilization of railroads as well.

Forward Linkages

Reductions in transport rates facilitated significant response by present and potential shippers. The locational advantages bestowed by the various internal transport improvements led to marked regional realignments, sometimes temporary, sometimes permanent in character.[64]

With the best and earliest turnpikes, Philadelphia and Baltimore experienced rapid growth in the first two decades of the nineteenth century. It was not an advantage that withstood the construction of the Erie Canal. Steamboats upon the Ohio and Mississippi Rivers brought better access to market to the southern part of the Northwest and that area flourished after the War of 1812. Yet that region, too, fell under competition of the Erie Canal. Locations north of the National Road were no longer disadvantaged and the 1830s saw migration into those areas. Finally, the railroad rein-

---

[64] See Fishlow, *American Railroads*, chaps. 4–7, for an extended treatment of these questions in the antebellum period.

forced the advantages of existing and nascent centers such as Chicago and created others west of the Mississippi in Kansas City, Omaha, and elsewhere as trackage after 1860 penetrated into areas not previously settled.

These dramatic effects do not find equivalents in correspondingly large advantages bestowed upon the aggregate economy. These last depend upon relative efficiencies of production in one location versus another. These are typically small, since the range of possible alternatives is likely to be large. As always, what counts are the opportunity costs. The improvements in the regional terms of trade due to lower transport costs have already been credited in the direct benefits measured earlier, as have the increases in land value due to greater economic proximity to market. Each measures the distribution of the total gains between sectors and between regions.

Yet there are more than static locational effects involved in transport cost reduction. There is also the flow of immigration to the developing interior. There are the farmers encouraged to save and invest more in response to the new conditions of profitability. There are the technological changes, such as the reaper, whose dissemination was facilitated by larger scales of output that permitted their utilization. There are the internal economies made possible by the larger demand following upon lower transport costs, not to mention the impact of the wider market upon the division of labor.

These changes in the rate of supply of factors, and in the efficiency of their combination, are only partially and indirectly reflected in the demand curve for transportation, and hence are not subsumed in the direct benefits. These latter measure the difference in the efficiency of transportation, not the full difference in resource use set in motion by transport innovation. Thus the consequences of induced immigration show up in the direct benefits only to the extent of the savings realized on the additional goods shipped to market; while its contribution to income, in fact, is the value of the total increment in production. The magnitude of such indirect effects is virtually impossible to calculate in a dynamic process in which transport innovation was but one important element. Nevertheless, they should not be forgotten.

Our effort to examine forward linkages will proceed on a more modest level. In the first instance, we shall consider the effects upon the economy of westward settlement. Second, we shall touch on the differential response

Table 13.16. *Labor requirements as affected by interregional shifts (man-hours per bushel)*

	Wheat	Oats	Corn
Actual 1839	3.17	1.45	3.50
Actual 1910	0.76	0.40	0.96
Alternative 1910 without regional redistribution	2.90	1.18	2.70

Source: William N. Parker and Judith L. V. Klein, "Productivity Growth in Grain Production in the U.S., 1840–1860," in Brady (ed.), *Output, Employment, and Productivity in the United States After 1800.*

of manufactures and agriculture to lower transport rates. And finally, we shall explore the way in which the succession of transport innovations altered the traditional patterns of commerce.

REGIONAL REDISTRIBUTION

The question we must ask about the new settlement pattern evoked by better transportation is how much more productive was labor upon the newly cultivated areas than it would have been in the older region. Stories abound of a veritable surplus for the taking in the interior, implying a large forward effect of transportation. Estimates of regional productivity differentials provide a more sober but accurate account. Table 13.16 presents a measure of the efficiency differentials between 1839 and 1910 in wheat, oats, and corn arising solely from regional redistribution of output. The alternative output for 1910 is a reconstruction of production utilizing 1910 technology with the 1839 geographic distribution of acreage. As can be seen, the proportion of the total change explained by differing regional yields is not particularly great. A more sophisticated partition of the regional effect, including its interaction with changes in yields and mechanization, does not alter the general impression. These results allocate to regional effects 17 percent of the increased labor productivity in wheat, 29 percent in oats, and 21 percent in corn. This outcome, although inferior to the influence of mechanization, is not to be underestimated. The gain to the economy in monetary terms for these three crops alone amounted to $521 million, or an addition to the earned private profits of railways of more than 60 percent. Nor is this a fully accurate accounting. No allowance has been made for the declining marginal productivity in the East that would have resulted from a geographically limited and intensive agriculture. Other similar calculations relate to the redistributive consequences of westward movement in the 1850s. They are consistent in finding that the regional effect is only a partial explanation of the total productivity change. But again, the monetary amount was not totally negligible: a tenth of the railroad's total direct benefits, a fourth of the resource savings in rail transportation of agricultural products. That this single measurable external economy should be so important would seem to justify more than passing attention to the wider gamut of forward linkages.

THE PRINCIPAL BENEFICIARY: THE PRIMARY SECTOR

The sector in which the total range of forward linkages had greater and more immediate influence was undoubtedly agriculture, as this regional effect suggests. Regional differentialism in costs of production did not exist in manufactures. The relationship between the expansion of manufactures in Massachusetts and the rise of the railway network in that state does not run from the latter to the former. One does not find a great reduction in costs following upon the completion of a region's internal communication system or its better national articulation. Indeed, the period of peak dollar profits for the sizable textile industry preceded railroad investment noticeably and was an important source of capital for it.

Transport costs of raw materials and final products represented a small proportion of the total costs of manufactures. The 1859 estimates of railroad resource saving confirm this observation. Total estimated transport cost savings for nonagricultural commodities excluding coal amounted to 5 percent of value added in manufacturing, and half as much of total value. If all the cost reduction had been passed along in lower prices, the cumulative increment in total industrial demand, presuming an elasticity as great as two, would have been limited to 5 percent of the observed 1859 level. This is too small to have counted much.

This finding holds for the succession of other transport innovations. The steamboat never succeeded in shipping much merchandise upriver from

New Orleans because manufactures could bear the high overland rates to the West. To be sure, the Erie Canal created much better access and replaced the turnpike, but the manufacturer was less affected by it than agriculture. New England's industrial revolution of the 1820s preceded the existence of a cheap water route. It did so because industry could survive very well under primitive conditions of transport. Wagon shipment to and from Boston of all the inputs and outputs of Lowell at 1845 prices and levels of production would have occasioned no more than a 4 percent difference in costs. Cotton came by sailing ship, and its leading markets remained along the seaboard for many years.

Manufactures were not immune to the beneficent internal market created by an agricultural income much more sensitive to transport cost reduction. The introduction of the Erie Canal immediately led in adjacent counties to replacement of home production by factory-produced goods. People turned exclusively to agricultural production for the market, as increases in improved acreage clearly demonstrate. The principal effect of the canal, for many years, was the agricultural surplus it evoked in the western canal counties.

Transport cost reduction invariably brought with it higher relative prices for agricultural products in the regions farther from the market. This improvement in the terms of trade did not occur at the expense of consumers but was the consequence of lowering the artificial tariff of distance. The distribution of the total savings in transportation expense depended upon the nature of consumer demand: the more elastic it was, the larger the real income benefit derived by producers. Historically, transport expansion was concentrated in periods of buoyant agricultural demand and directed to areas of immediate supply response. This was true of the expansion of the Erie in New York State, of the railroads in the Midwest in the 1850s, and of the trans-Missouri construction of the 1880s. Foreign export was frequently a key factor in supporting agricultural prices. As a result, farmers retained a goodly share of the transport reductions through favorable terms of trade and higher real income. The decadal pattern of farmland price rises, capitalizing this gain, seems to confirm such an interpretation. The agricultural sector was not exploited as a source of savings for industrial growth or to maintain lower nominal wages in the cities. It was allowed to keep its advantageous terms of trade, which became a strength rather than a liability of subsequent aggregate development.

Another relationship between manufactures and the much more transport sensitive primary sector was in the rise of the agricultural processing industries. These are frequently given little attention in discussions of the process of industrialization; they are undramatic and uninteresting. One English visitor at the time of the Civil War refused to consider them as legitimate manufactures. Yet these activities were in fact more capital-intensive than the average. Virtually a fourth of industrial horsepower was developed by the milling industry in 1870, much of it by steam engines at interior sites that fed local machine demand.

The United States from 1850 to 1890 showed an increasing share of employment in processing activities. They migrated westward with agriculture itself to be close to the weight-losing material inputs. There evolved a sequential and repetitive natural process of transition from agriculture to processing to a broader industrial base. Milling, meat packing, and tanning contributed to the formation of such urban, and later industrial, nuclei as Cincinnati, Chicago, St. Louis, Minneapolis–St. Paul, Omaha, and Kansas City. They provided a mechanism by which high agricultural profitability could contribute directly to industrialization within the American context.

THE FLOW OF COMMERCE AND TRANSPORT INNOVATIONS

Our third line of indirect transport effects, the modification of trade relationships due to altered relative costs, is a recapitulation of the competition between steamboat, railroad, and canal for the trade of the West. Exports from that region at the beginning of the nineteenth century could go only by river through New Orleans – a situation that created an important pressure for the Louisiana Purchase. The emergence of the steamboat as a substitute, or more accurately, supplement for flatboats, made that route more attractive. Western foodstuffs arrived at New Orleans in ever-rising amounts, much more than doubling in every decade from the 1810s to the 1850s. Yet even as this advance occurred, an important and irreversible change in the pattern of trade had entered with the canal. Table 13.17 portrays the relative reduction in western exports via New Orleans after 1835 owing to the much-increased tonnage of western exports reaching tidewater via the Erie Canal. The lower growth in southerly shipments through 1849 is not to be attributed to direct competition between river and canal as much as to the accelerated development of the region tributary to the Great Lakes. This new era increased western exports and

Table 13.17. *Proportion of western exports shipped via New Orleans (percent)*

	1835	1839	1844	1849	1853	1857	1860
Flour	70	53	30	31	27	34	22
Meat products	—	51	63	50	38	28	24
Corn	98	98	90	39	37	32	19
Whiskey	95	96	95	67	53	48	40
Total foodstuffs[a]	—	49	44	40	31	27	17

[a] weighted by current prices.
Source: 1835: Albert L. Kohlmeier, *The Old Northwest* (Bloomington, IN, 1938), 20. 1839–1860: Fishlow, *American Railroads*, 284.

directed them almost exclusively eastward. The surplus of the Ohio Valley continued to travel southward. Production of wheat in the northern parts of Ohio, Indiana, and Illinois more than doubled between 1839 and 1849 and increased the surplus available for export by an even larger proportion; the area adjacent to the Ohio River experienced a substantial decline in marketable surplus over the same interval, suggesting that New Orleans may have diverted some of the flow from the area tributary to the canal. In 1849, "about a million bushels each from Iowa, from the Illinois River and Rock River in northern Illinois, and from the Middle Wabash River in northern Indiana found its way to the southern gateway."[65] In the same year, however, the newly completed Illinois and Michigan and Wabash and Erie Canals forecast the future pattern by siphoning off corn that had previously moved by river southward.

Between 1849 and 1860, absolute decline in shipments to New Orleans set in, and this time the explanation must be sought in altered market boundaries. The larger wheat surplus of the Ohio Valley was now definitively captured by the railways completed from Baltimore and Philadelphia. The entire decline in flour exports via New Orleans can be explained by increases in the flow to these two cities. The proportion of flour shipped upstream from Cincinnati, or dispatched directly eastward by railway or canal, was 90 percent in 1860; only a decade earlier, the downriver proportion had been 97 percent. A similar, if less drastic decline occurred in provisions, with the larger part following a direct rail course eastward.

[65] Albert L. Kohlmeier, *The Old Northwest* (Bloomington, IN, 1938), 84.

With the introduction of the railway, moreover, export of livestock became a much more attractive alternative and reduced the supply of processed meat for which the river route might compete.

During the 1850s, another and equally important development was occurring: the decline in re-export from New Orleans to the East and abroad. As the total volume of western receipts fell, New Orleans redistributed larger and larger amounts to other parts of the South and lost its function in interregional commerce. The decade marked the conversion of the river route from the West to the more limited role of supplier of the limited southern consumption of western products. After the Civil War, there was only further deterioration.

Did this diversion of trade have profound economic consequences, as has sometimes been claimed? Victor Clark, for one, argued that until New Orleans was supplanted, there was a continuing danger of imported manufactures flowing upriver to replace the domestic product. Such a view has little basis. New Orleans, despite the steamboat and its drastically reduced upriver rates, never succeeded in developing an import trade. The principal commodities delivered upriver were salt, coffee, and sugar. But bonds of commerce can have more subtle implications as well, for credit relationships and for diffusion of information about markets and prices. A more direct link was to the mutual advantage of the East and West, as much as it was to the detriment of New Orleans as a commercial center, and possibly to southern development.

THE TWENTIETH CENTURY

The nineteenth century marked the high point of the contribution of transportation to American economic growth. Never again – not even in the heyday of the bus and truck – would investment in transport facilities amount to more than 15 percent of capital formation, as it did in the 1870s. Nor would there be repeated the epic expansion of the United States to its continental limits, made possible by the more than 200,000 miles of railway in operation by the beginning of the twentieth century. Finally, the rate of transport growth, as a whole and not only for railroads, failed to maintain its earlier pace, which was substantially in excess of national product. That, in conjunction with the failure to develop further innovations, meant that the resource savings of transportation became less significant.

Despite the inability to replicate its earlier dominating role, the transport sector was not unimportant after 1900. Patterns of land use changed drastically with the introduction of the automobile and the development of the suburb. The motor vehicle industry, with by far the largest part of its production destined for consumption, advanced from seventeenth rank in value added in 1909 to first in 1925. Derived demands for gasoline and rubber sparked equally vigorous expansion of those activities. Schumpeter, in his classic work *Business Cycles*, found in the automobile the same dynamic force for the earlier twentieth century that the railroad had represented for the mid-nineteenth.

Few in 1900 were so visionary as to foresee the eventual decline of the railroad in favor of motor transport. It was at that time the largest single industrial interest in the country and the principal source of securities traded on the burgeoning New York Stock Exchange. The railroad stood at its moment of triumph. Indeed, its most pressing challenger was not the automobile, but another innovation, the interurban trolley. This substitute promised to compete away much of the short-haul passenger traffic which had been a railroad monopoly since the decline of the stagecoach. Or at least so its promoters thought. Their subsequent disillusionment sheds some light on the operation of market processes.

Interurban Railways

The electric streetcar, the basic technology of the interurban system, owed its development to urban needs at the end of the nineteenth century. The horsecar on public streets presented greater inadequacies with each passing year, the foremost of which was the increasing relative cost of operation. Rapid advances in technology were occurring all around while the basic characteristics of urban transport remained unchanged. Frank Sprague's successful installation of an electric system in Richmond in 1888 marked the beginning of a wave of investment that by 1901 had produced 15,000 miles of electric railway, almost exclusively urban. Whereas in 1890, 70 percent of street railway mileage had still been animal powered, 12 years later, electric cars operated over 97 percent of the trackage.[66]

Extension of the technology to intercity and rural service appeared the

---

[66] We have drawn primarily upon George Hilton and John Due, *The Electric Interurban Railways in America* (Stanford, 1960), in this and subsequent paragraphs in this section.

next logical step. Its great appeal vis-à-vis railroad passenger service was the much greater frequency of its service, its much larger number of stops, and lower cost. Beginning in the recovery from the collapse of 1893, and especially between 1901 and 1908, more than 11,000 miles of interurban railways were constructed. The apogee was attained in 1916, when the system extended over 15,000 miles. Some $1 billion had been spent. During 1901–1908, the outlays equaled the contemporaneous expenditures on roads and represented as much as 15 percent of the total investment in railroads.

Most of the construction was in the Midwest. Ohio alone possessed a quarter of the national mileage; no town of 10,000 was without service. Indiana, Illinois, Michigan, and Ohio together contained almost half of the national total. A dense rural population and the existence of many small urban centers were especially favorable conditions for construction, and they were abundant in the rich heartland of the Midwest as well as in such states as Pennsylvania and New York. Although it was never possible to go directly from New York to Chicago via interurban connections – there being two small breaks in the line in New York State – a true enthusiast could make his way continuously for more than a 1,000 miles from Elkhart Lake, Wisconsin, to Oneonta, New York.

The decline of the industry was only slightly less rapid than its rise. Between 1921 and 1939, three-fourths of the mileage fell into disuse under the pressure of automobile and bus competition. Even at its best, the performance of the interurbans could be described as disappointing. Average return on investment was no better than 3 percent in 1909, and perhaps slightly higher if over-capitalization is taken into account. By that time saner expectations had begun to prevail in the capital market, and the expansion in facilities began to peter out. As returns declined still further, falling below 1 percent in the late 1920s, stagnation gave way to accelerating abandonment.

The interurban episode illustrates both how badly and how well market processes work. Given extensive financial support on the basis of the urban streetcar's success, the interurbans repaid the faith of their backers most uncharitably. Even before the age of the automobile, they were an obvious error, as reflected by the diminished stream of investment after 1908. The market ultimately gave its correct signal, but it was too late for many. The mistake turned into an unmitigated disaster as motor cars and buses flowed off assembly lines.

The Rise of Surfaced Highways

The discussion of surfaced highways properly begins with yet another, but most unlikely, innovation, the rubber-tired bicycle. For it is to the League of American Wheelmen, organized in 1880, that the movement for surfaced roads owes its origins.[67] The good roads movement gathered enough momentum by the 1890s, prior to the automobile age, to secure legislation providing for state aid for road construction in New Jersey, Massachusetts, California, Connecticut, Maryland, Vermont, and New York. The federal government acted as well, establishing in 1893 an Office of Road Inquiry. Its informational function was a significant factor in augmenting the support for good roads, as well as in shaping legislation in the various states. The introduction and rapid dissemination of the automobile substantially intensified the pressures for surfaced highways by creation of a direct client interest. By 1913, all but six states had programs of highway construction, and all but ten had state highway departments. Annual state and local expenditures on construction by that time were running in excess of $200 million and absorbing increasing shares of revenue. Ultimately, in 1916, the largess of the national treasury was tapped; the first of what was to become a series of federal grants for construction was authorized by Congress.

Worthy of note in the good roads movement is the limited role played by agricultural interests until rather late in its history. Farmers, rather than seeking better outlets to market as might have been expected, had to be persuaded of the movement's advantages before joining. Indeed, that persuasion was one of the principal triumphs of the Office of the Road Inquiry. Not until 1907 did the National Grange declare itself affirmatively. The reluctance of farmers to involve themselves is explained by their fear of being disproportionately saddled with the cost through revenues obtained by property taxes. There were also doubts concerning the real advantages to be obtained. Farmers would be trading increased cash payments for increased leisure, because they themselves did most of the local hauling at very little direct financial expense. Proponents of legislation indicated both the substantial benefits to be derived – an annual saving of $600 million was promised on an investment not to exceed $2.4 billion – and of the possibility of diverting urban revenues to rural roads through state and federal aid.

[67] See also Charles L. Dearing, *American Highway Policy* (Washington, DC, 1942), app. A.

Railroads, however, were quite vocal in favoring better roads. They were viewed as complements rather than substitutes for the existing rail network. Feeder roads could only increase rail traffic, not reduce it. Few envisioned them as capable of long-distance service. By 1910, after the formation of the American Automobile Association, however, the divergent position of the railroad and automotive interests became clear. The latter favored federal construction of 50,000 miles of interstate highways on an integrated basis, leaving to states and their subdivisions the responsibilities for lesser arteries. The railroads, "at the risk of seeming to be actuated by [their] interest," asserted that "if the greatest good is to be done to the greatest numbers, the farmer is more interested in the improvement of the roads of the second class . . . those radiating from a market town or shipping station."[68]

This fundamental issue was not resolved in the 1916 Federal Aid Road Act. It appropriated $75 million in grants on a matching basis to be spent over a five-year period and distributed through state highway departments. The selection of routes to be supported was left, however, to the discretion of the Secretary of Agriculture. By 1921, with over 9 million automobiles and 1 million trucks in use, the direction of the future became clear. The application of federal funds was limited to a designated federal road system, composed of not more than 7 percent of the total nonurban mileage in each state. This not only defined a trunk network, but did away with the 1916 state allocation formula based upon the area's population and the extent of its post roads. Thereafter, at federal, state, and local levels, the rapidly growing automotive interest remained the principal pressure group shaping the extent and type of highway construction.

MAGNITUDE OF TRANSPORT INVESTMENT

From its modest origins in the propaganda of the League of American Wheelmen, highway construction grew to mammoth proportions. Table 13.18 presents estimates of road expenditures by quinquennia from 1902 to 1961, along with corresponding railroad investment and total investment data. A number of observations may be made. First, there is the rapid growth in highway expenditures expanded in constant dollars at an annual rate of 5.5 percent. The advance was not even – the Depression's effects

---

[68] W. W. Finley, President of the Southern Railway, quoted in Dearing, *American Highway Policy*, 260–61.

Table 13.18. *Twentieth-century gross investment in highways and railroads (annual averages in millions)*

Year	Highways Current Dollars	Highways 1929[b] Dollars	Railroads Current Dollars	Railroads 1929[c] Dollars	Total Gross Capital Formation[a] Current Dollars	Total Gross Capital Formation[a] 1929[d] Dollars
1902–1906	109	190	532	980	5,290	10,800
1907–1911	173	272	574	981	6,350	11,700
1912–1916	260	374	465	754	8,050	13,100
1917–1921	511	424	547	507	16,700	15,200
1922–1926	963	815	854	832	18,000	18,000
1927–1931	1,330	1,375	715	728	16,800	17,400
1932–1936	1,002	1,160	191	228	4,120	4,930
1937–1941	1,279	1,431	314	457	11,720	11,750
1941–1946	541	429	580	471	12,760	9,640
1947–1951	1,902	1,449	1,223	715	45,820	24,040
1952–1956	3,536	2,411	1,160	579	58,720	26,580
1957–1961	5,506	3,603	1,243	527	70,120	27,690

[a] Until 1932, private and public capital formation; thereafter, only private.

[b] For 1915 and thereafter, 1947–1949 base shifted to 1929 = 100; 1902–1914 based upon adjusted total construction deflator.

[c] For 1902–1914, 1914 base shifted to 1929 = 100.

[d] For 1932 and thereafter, base shifted to 1929 = 100 from 1958 dollars; earlier in 1929 dollars.

Sources: **Highways**: Robert E. Lipsey and Doris Preston, *Source Book of Statistics Relating to Construction* (New York, 1960), Series C20, C51, C52, 39–40. **Railroads**: *1902–1914*: Larry Neal, "Investment Behavior by American Railroads: 1897–1914," *Review of Economics and Statistics*, 51 (1969), 131–132. *1915–1950*: Melville Ulmer, *Capital in Transportation, Communications, and Public Utilities* (New York, 1960), 256–257. *1951–1961*: Interstate Commerce Commission, *Transportation Statistics in the United States* and for the deflator *Schedule of Annual Indices for Carriers by Railroad, 1914–1964*, mimeographed. **Total**: *1902–1931*: U.S. Bureau of the Census, *Historical Statistics of the United States, Colonial Times to 1957* (Washington, DC, 1960), 143–144. *1932–1961*: U.S. Department of Commerce, *National Income and Product Accounts of the United States. 1929–1965*: supplement to *Survey of Current Business* (Washington, DC, 1966).

are visible, and the war's even more so – but it was much more stable than other forms of investment. Massive infusions of relief funds by the federal government to provide employment were responsible for the favorable record in the 1930s. In 1936–1940, more than a third of total construction was financed by this means.

Prewar investment had already converted American roads from haphazard mud trails to reliable, all-season conduits for transportation. It was this change, rather than the geographic extension of the network, that was the principal accomplishment. In 1904, of little more than 2 million miles of nonurban roads, only 7 percent was surfaced, and these usually utilized gravel. There was more railroad mileage than improved highway in the country. Surpassing the railway network in 1914, the progression of surfaced mileage continued until in 1940 such roads extended more than 1,300,000 miles or almost half of all highway mileage. Thus, while total road mileage increased by only 50 percent between 1904 and 1940, improved mileage multiplied by a factor of eight! Moreover, high-quality surfaces such as concrete and asphalt had appeared with increasing frequency after federal standards went into effect. Some 150,000 miles of superior roads could be found in 1940.[69]

Even this accounting understates the extent of the change that had occurred. Since traffic is concentrated upon the highly improved portion of the road network, about 50 percent of the motor vehicle mileage had access to modern highways by 1940. At the other extreme, only 10 percent of the vehicle miles were dependent upon unimproved roads, although these were ten times greater in length.[70] By World War II, the more than 30 million registered motor vehicles were increasingly adequately provided for.

Thereafter, as the stock of vehicles trebled, the tendency toward intensive development accelerated. Through the toll road initially, and subsequently under the auspices of the Federal Interstate Highway Act of 1956, a system of nationwide superhighways emerged. These multiple-lane, limited-access roadways were designed for high-speed, nonstop driving. Initially, they more than redressed the technical imbalance caused by the evolution of bigger and more powerful vehicles and longer-distance traffic. But under the pressure of increasing utilization in high-density areas, even such advanced highway design could not eliminate congestion. Nor could

[69] Bureau of the Census, *Historical Statistics*, 458.
[70] Dearing, *American Highway Policy*, 120–21.

improved physical facilities alter the increasingly persuasive arguments against the social costs of vehicle emissions. Yet as attention rightly turns to rapid transit schemes, rehabilitation of railways in densely populated urban corridors, and devices to render the automobile less noxious, the extent and positive aspects of American highway development should not be lost sight of. There are now more than 2 million miles of surfaced highway in the United States, of which a substantial proportion are first class. Mass mobility and an end to rural America have been their irreversible consequences.

The rapid increase in highway construction emerges even more strikingly in contrast with the performance of railroad investment. Maintained at the beginning of the twentieth century by intensive investment in electrification, freight yards, line improvement, and equipment, railroad gross capital formation flagged after 1916. Extension of mileage had reached its natural limit, and the slowing rate of output growth made investment in further improvement less attractive. The Transportation Act of 1920, had it been implemented, might have helped. It was designed to promote increased efficiency through consolidation, while retaining competition. The inconsistent charges and divergent interests of weak and strong lines, long- and short-distance shippers, and poorly and well-served regions, made the task of the ICC an impossible one. Thus unassisted, the railroads entered into precarious maturity during the decade of the 1920s. Rates of return never reached the prescribed 6 percent "fair" return. Passenger output declined by 30 percent between 1920 and 1929 under the pressure of motor-car competition, and freight increases compensated only to the extent of maintaining total output at a constant level.

The 1930s, as the investment data attest, saw an outright decline of railroads. Gross investment became minimal and did not even succeed in offsetting depreciation for many years. The simple replacement of capital required from the 1920s on an annual outlay of $500 million in 1929 prices. While highway extension and surfacing continued apace, the rail network was diminishing in both physical and financial dimensions. The net value of the capital stock was less in 1939 than in 1929, and 14,000 miles of track were abandoned. Railroads were beset simultaneously by an unprecedented reduction in the demand for transport services as a whole resulting from the depression and increasingly effective competition resulting from the much larger stock of vehicles accumulated during the 1920s. For the first time trucks became a serious factor in intercity traffic. Although federal legislation could assist in the reorganization process that followed upon widespread railroad failure, like the earlier 1920 act, it did not secure consolidation of the industry. Whether even consolidation would have been enough to arrest the railroad decline is open to considerable doubt. The underlying technological efficiency of motor vehicles for short-haul and high-valued merchandise, the unprogressive cast of railway management, and the rail freight rate structure, stand out as persistent problems.

Nor, after the wartime surge in traffic and a brief rise in capital formation, did a more positive tendency assert itself. Despite complete reequipment with diesels, piggy-back transport of truck cargoes, and modern yard handling controls, among other innovations, the postwar investment data as a whole chronicle the continuing decline of the industry. A continuing inability to compete for high-valued, profitable traffic made average profits a dismally low proportion of capital as we shall see. Coupled with a large fixed debt from the past, these profits left precious little room for maneuver. It is not obvious whether merger and consolidation will be able to reverse the decline.

The contrast between the declining fortunes of railways and the ascendancy of the highway is summarized in the rise of road construction expenditures as a fraction of total investment. By the 1920s, road improvement and extension had come to represent almost a tenth of capital formation. During the 1930s, the proportion rose sharply due to decline in private investment. (This increase is somewhat overstated by the fact that aggregate gross investment does not include public construction.) Conversely, the emergency circumstances of the war restricted further expansion and reduced the ratio. By the beginning of the 1960s, which saw accelerated construction due to the stimulus of federal grants, highway construction had returned to its 1920s importance. Investment in highways over the postwar period proceeded far more rapidly than total capital formation, and this figure does not include considerable additional expenditure for maintenance and administration. The road system, amounting to more than 3 million miles in 1940, absorbed by that time half as much in the form of recurrent expenditures as was being spent for net extension. Maintenance requirements continued to grow, although their proportion declined to about a third of total capital outlays in the beginning of the 1960s, as investment returned to high levels. By any standard, still another form of transportation had established itself as a voracious consumer of resources.

Yet, construction and maintenance together are far from exhausting the tally. Highway transportation was unlike previous innovations, in which the fixed capital always greatly surpassed the investment in rolling stock.

Purchases of automobiles and trucks exceeded in value the expenditures on construction by a factor of at least two in *every* year from 1912 through 1940.[71] The largest part of this expenditure was for consumption purposes. Under this impetus, the automobile industry rose from seventeenth in value added in 1909 to first in 1925. Americans bought more than 4 million cars and 800,000 trucks in 1929, and these levels were not greatly exceeded in the 1950s. Few innovations were so eagerly seized upon. The campaign slogan of Herbert Hoover in 1928 is revealing: "Two cars in every garage, a chicken in every pot." Demand for cars was sustained by increasing incomes, lower relative prices, and – possibly more important – the introduction of credit sales. Installment purchases accounted for more than two-thirds of all sales in 1925.[72] The method itself was to be extended to all other consumer durables, and represented an essential element in creating a widespread market for initially costly, but durable items consumed over a number of years.

Aside from its direct production of 12.7 percent of the value of total manufactures in 1929, the automobile industry and vehicle operation contributed substantially to the industrial prosperity of the 1920s. They accounted for 20 percent of steel output and were the single largest source of demand for petroleum, rubber, plate glass, machine tools, nickel, and lead. In some instances, the linkages were nearly one for one: 90 percent of petroleum production was consumed, largely in the form of gasoline; 80 percent of the rubber; 75 percent of the plate glass.[73] During the 1920s automobiles and the complex activities related to them were the dynamic factor in economic expansion.

Abetting these effects was the stimulus afforded to construction. Although the suburb did not originate with the automobile – it was rather the creation of rail lines entering urban areas – its rapid growth in the 1920s and thereafter was the product of and completely dependent upon a motor-car civilization. This may be seen by the startling disclosure in 1940 that 13 million persons, or virtually a tenth of the population, lived in suburbs without access to any public transportation.[74] Although the residential construction boom gave way to the Depression of the 1930s – having peaked earlier in 1925 – the tendency toward suburbanization continued unchecked. Federal Housing Authority finance permitted addi-

---

[71] Bureau of the Census, *Historical Statistics*, 462.
[72] George Soule, *Prosperity Decade* (New York, 1947), 165.
[73] Ibid., 164–65; and John B. Rae, *The American Automobile* (Chicago, 1965), 88.
[74] Rae, *American Automobile*, 220.

tional new community development prior to World War II, and afterward, as residential construction recovered, such housing became the symbol of middle-class affluence.

The automobile industry regained its earlier influence in the years immediately following the end of the war. One of the major reasons the oft-predicted postwar recession did not materialize was the boom in consumer durables. Between 1946 and 1950, such expenditures increased from a tenth of total personal consumption outlays to 15 percent. Purchases of automobiles and parts grew even more rapidly, from little more than 2 percent of consumption to 7 percent. The entire sector, including purchases of gasoline and oil, repairs, and so on, amounted by 1950 to more than 10 percent of consumption, and to almost as much of the economy as a whole.

After this surge, the sector did not retain its dynamic properties. Purchases of cars and parts stabilized to a level between 3 and 4 percent of total product annually throughout the 1950s and 1960s. Individual years showed variation around this level, but without serious cyclical implications. Total expenditures, because they were in part dependent upon the stock of vehicles, which continued to grow, were slightly more buoyant. By the end of the 1960s, they had expanded to 13 percent of consumption and 8 percent of all economic activity.[75] With a total of 90 million cars registered, or almost one for every two persons, the most favorable prognosis seems to be continued proportional advance based upon replacement of existing vehicles and population growth. The growth cycle of the industry has brought it to maturity.

THE OUTPUT RECORD

The preceding sections have pointed up the dramatic realignment of transport activity in the twentieth century. Table 13.19 chronicles the matter still more directly. From virtually unchallenged supremacy before World War I – coastwise and lake shipments being the exception – the railroad proportion of total freight movement had by the 1960s shrunk to less than 40 percent. More notable still, since 1948, railroad and water shipments have hardly increased while pipelines and intercity trucking have expanded at annual rates in excess of 5 and 8 percent, respectively. Even the total

[75] U.S. Department of Commerce, *National Income and Product Accounts of the United States, 1929–1965*, supplement to *Survey of Current Business* (Washington, DC, 1966).

Albert Fishlow

Table 13.19. *Transport output*

Year	Railroad	Inland Waterway (Great Lakes included)	Pipeline	Intercity Truck[a]	Weighted Index 1939 = 100
Panel A. *Freight Traffic (billions of ton-miles)*[b]					
1899	126	n.a.	n.a.	—	22
1909	219	n.a.	n.a.	—	38
1919	367	78[c]	7[c]	1	65
1929	450	98	31	10	87
1937	363	103	45	35	91
1948	641	16	120	116	200
1953	609	202	170	217	268
1963	644	234	253	336	361

Year	Railroad	Intercity Bus	Local Transit[d]	Domestic Airlines	Passenger Total[e]	Automobile Intercity
Panel B. *Passenger Traffic (billions of passenger miles)*						
1899	15	—	10	—	—	—
1909	29	—	20	—	—	—
1919	47	1	30	—	90	—
1929	31	7	38	—	409	—
1937	25	10	31	—	559	—
1948	41	33	46	6	801	—
1953	32	28	29	15	1,088	576
1963	19	22	23	40	1,638	766

[a] Includes private as well as common carriers.

[b] Ton-miles weighted by 1939 revenues per ton-mile.

[c] 1920.

[d] Revenue passengers assumed to travel an average of three miles, based upon 1939 revenue per passenger.

[e] Passenger motor vehicle miles multiplied by 25, estimated average number of passengers based upon Barger.

Sources: Data from Harold Barger, *The Transportation Industries, 1899–1946* (New York, 1951); Bureau of the Census, *Historical Statistics*; and U.S. Bureau of the Census, *Statistical Abstract of the United States, 1967* (Washington, DC, 1967).

does not behave as it once did. Whereas through the beginning of the twentieth century, freight shipments grew much more rapidly than commodity output, they no longer did so in the 1950s and 1960s. Equality now seems to be the rule.

The passenger segment of the market exhibits even more rapid deterioration of the original modes. Railroads for intercity movement and electric railways for urban transit held undisputed sway in 1900. Soon after the introduction of the automobile in 1919, approximate parity between commercial and private passenger travel was established. Thereafter, the record was one of complete domination by the automobile. The railroad has not been alone in its demise. Intercity bus travel has shown little growth; indeed, it has declined in recent years, and the fate of local transit facilities has been equally pronounced.

These physical statistics clearly understate the emergence of motor trucking as a competitive factor. Since the revenue received per mile is greater by road than by rail, the shares in receipts give another dimension of the contest. By the mid-1960s, although railroads continued to transport twice as many ton-miles, the revenues of motor carriers and railroads were approximately the same.[76] On the passenger side, the outlays confirm the automobile's advantage. Consumers spent in 1969 more than $73 billion to purchase and nourish their private automobiles. They expended less than $3 billion on purchases of all other forms of land transportation, local and intercity combined. An additional $2 billion went for air travel, a mode of conveyance which has been an increasing factor in passenger transportation.[77] By the 1960s, airlines had become responsible for more than 5 percent of total intercity movement.

The decline of the railroad at the hands of the motor vehicle repeats many of the features of its own previous triumph at the expense of the canal. Passenger carriage was the first to be eroded in both instances; the freight diversion was more differentiated, high-valued manufactures moving to the newer mode, bulk commodities being retained by the older. The logical consequence of such market changes was rapidly increased investment in the new mode, as we have seen, and net decline in the old. However, the historical pattern differs in one important respect from the current context. Whereas the canal was in unequivocal decline within 50 years of the introduction of the railway – only a few specialized waterways

[76] Bureau of the Census, *Statistical Abstract of the United States, 1967* (Washington, DC, 1967), 552.
[77] *Survey of Current Business*, 50 (July, 1970), 28.

continuing in operation – the railroad remains, and is likely to remain, a general-purpose transporter. During the 1960s the share of rail freight traffic has stabilized and revenues have fallen at much slower rates.

Central to this result has been the fact that the technology of the truck does not dominate railroads in the same way that railroads surpassed canals. The same advantages of speed and flexibility of the newer mode exist, but their significance is much reduced. There are almost 200,000 miles of rail line covering the most important commercial routes; whereas canals were much more limited in extent when railroads were introduced. Moreover, the all-season capacity of rail versus water transport is not relevant in comparing road and rail alternatives.

The fact that railroads experienced competition from trucks only after reaching their full geographic extension has other implications. On the positive side, it has meant the capacity to utilize the resources generated by depreciation to introduce more modern equipment. Negatively, it has created problems of adjustment from a previous growth pattern to a situation in which output has not increased. Specifically, "featherbedding" requirements come to mind. On balance, the industry has managed surprisingly well over time to reduce its labor inputs and to improve the quality of its capital stock. Productivity in the sector has substantially and continuously increased between 1950 and 1970. Output per man-hour – capital stock had not changed much – has gone up at an annual rate of 6 percent, compared to a total for the private economy of only half as much.[78] Real freight rates have correspondingly declined. This is hardly the profile of a moribund sector, which has exhausted its technical capacities.

Why, then, have railroads lost out to the truck? Spokesmen for the industry as early as the 1930s cited unfair competition as the principal cause.[79] Their complaints have been lodged against the implicit subsidy received by motor carriers: The railroad has provided its roadbed at private expense and must pay taxes upon it; the trucker receives the road at public expense and thereby obtains the advantages of reduced capital cost and general taxation financing. There is some merit to these assertions, but their general import is much exaggerated. State construction yields lower capital cost only to the extent that the state can obtain credit on a more favorable basis than private firms. (This is the same advantage the railroads themselves enjoyed during the period of public assistance in the 1830s.) But since highways were constructed largely on a pay-as-you-go basis until the

---

[78] Bureau of the Census, *Statistical Abstract*, 1967, 237.
[79] See Dearing, *American Highway Policy*, 191–98, for a statement of the arguments.

1950s, the practical significance of the objection diminishes. The same is true of the property tax exemption, which is not a major matter.

Nor can the argument that trucks do not pay their own share of the capital costs be fully substantiated. The successful financial innovation that made highway construction proceed as rapidly as it did was the institution of user levies, principally in the form of gasoline taxes. The predominant share of capital expenditure was underwritten in this manner. Indeed, the early concern was that user revenues, because of their rapid growth, might be diverted to other purposes. Many states enacted constitutional amendments to prohibit such a possibility. Provided that fuel taxes, registrations, and other excises accurately measure capital consumption for different classes of vehicles, commercial truckers are accorded no advantage.

Studies based upon incremental costs seem to confirm that these excises do accurately reflect costs, the one exception being large diesel units. In these studies, the cost of facilities adequate for the lightest vehicles was first allocated evenly among all classes. Increments of cost – capital and current – were then charged against the appropriate type of larger truck. This method yielded implicit costs in 1964 of $31 per automobile, $462 per three-axle truck of 45,000 pound gross weight, and $1,369 per five-axle diesel-powered unit of 66,000 pound gross weight. Actual taxes paid were $30, $466, and $923.[80] The advantages enjoyed by diesels stem from their relative fuel economy over gasoline engines and the fact that the principal revenues derive from fuel taxes. That there should be such correspondence in the other classes, despite the fact that fuel consumption is not a fully satisfactory proxy for either capital or maintenance costs, is both surprising and encouraging. But it should not deter efforts to find more appropriate taxes that better correspond to the relevant consumption of facilities. Such taxes could be based upon the distribution of weight, speed, and other factors that determine highway costs.

Thus user payments do roughly approximate costs except for long-haul shipments. These studies also reveal the inherent economies of scale that truckers legitimately obtain. Because highways are joint facilities shared by private automobiles and commercial truckers, some part of the overhead is paid by the former. Because the railroad right-of-way is exclusively utilized by the rail companies, full and incremental cost are identical. From the standpoint of efficient social policy, what is relevant is not total but incremental resource utilization. It is better that trucks utilize a highway principally paid for by pleasure vehicles, if their user taxes cover the

---

[80] Cited in John B. Lansing, *Transportation and Economic Policy* (New York, 1966), 252.

additional wear and tear, than that traffic be diverted to railroads requiring larger inputs of resources for shipments. It is exactly such joint use that has made the technology of the motor vehicle efficient and that permits it to compete effectively against the railroad.

Although no large artificial advantage has been created in favor of trucks, this does not mean that the division of traffic reflects the operation of market forces in an ideal manner. There is little doubt that substitution of motor vehicles has gone too far due to ICC regulation and administration of the present railroad rate structure.[81] This set of rates is based not upon relative costs, but upon discrimination according to the elasticity of demand. Low-valued, bulky commodities receive low rates because they cannot bear higher tariff; manufactures, on the other hand, can afford to pay more – even if the service received is identical. This value-of-service rate-making process was perfectly rational as long as railroads were effectively monopolists in supplying that service; indeed, by increasing private profits, it accelerated the process of construction and the attendant social gains. But it is more difficult to defend now, particularly since motor carriers after 1935 adopted a similar structure – enabling them to meet exactly the price of the competition in the one part of the market in which they were interested.

Price discrimination is effective in maximizing the utilization of resources within the transport sector if the charge is greater than marginal cost and if commodities otherwise would not be shipped. But neither of these conditions is fulfilled in the case of some products for which railroad rates are kept artificially low. Moreover, what may be good for transportation may not be good in general. Departing from the rule that prices should reflect the costs of resource inputs means that distortions will occur in the rest of the economy. Too much of the subsidized, low-rate goods will be produced relative to high-value ones. A discriminatory rate structure is equivalent to an excise tax imposed upon the consumers of manufactures to cover transportation overhead expenses. The difference from an ordinary tax situation is that there is no equity or use principle to justify it. Moreover, given the lack of profitability of many rail carriers, the apparent justification of discrimination has probably been partially responsible for the poor financial health of the sector.

A clear consequence of the higher railroad rates imposed upon manu-

---

[81] John Meyer, M. Peck, W. Stenison, and C. Zwick, *The Economics of Competition in the Transportation Industries* (Cambridge, MA, 1959), chaps. 7 and 8.

factures has been large-scale erosion of the traffic by trucks through the 1950s. Truck costs and rates would be more efficient only within a range of about 100 miles, were they confronted with true rail costs.[82] This calculation takes into account considerations of time in transit and size of shipment. In fact, however, the *average* haul of common carrier truck cargoes in 1963 was 255 miles, because at equal rates longer-distance motor shipment is preferable to rail.[83] Thus we have an inefficient allocation of resources and responsibilities, and an explanation of the extensive diversion that has occurred.

In recent years, the rate differentials have narrowed, and with this change the position of railroads has ceased to deteriorate as rapidly as it did between 1945 and 1960. This is true even in the face of the continuing greater growth of manufactures, which favor highway delivery. In 1961, railroad carload revenues from the shipment of manufactures were 1.48 times out-of-pocket costs; for agricultural products they were 1.18; and for mineral products, only 1.06. Here we see clearly the value of the service rate structure. Compared to the 1952 differentials, however, these figures represent a distinct improvement. At the earlier date, the respective ratios are 1.85, 1.37, and 1.25.[84] While all revenues have thus declined relative to costs, those of manufactures have fallen more than those of either agricultural or mineral products.

This change has been associated with more permissive legislation governing ICC administration of the sector. The Transportation Act of 1958 directed that rates *not* be set to protect traffic from other modes, leaving open the possibility of greater competitiveness in future rate decisions. While the clear principle of traffic allocation according to efficiency seems to be accepted by all, the procedure of case-by-case analysis, the imprecision of accounting rather than the economic cost concepts, and the necessity of taking into account the "objective of national transportation policy" leave the matter less clearly resolved than it should be.

SUMMARY

The themes of almost two centuries of transport expansion in the United States are few and bold. The basic force stimulating nineteenth-century

---

[82] Ibid., 190.

[83] *Commodity Transportation Survey*, Vol. 3 in *Census of Transportation: 1963* (Washington, DC, 1966), Part III, 13.

[84] Lansing, *Transportation*, 227.

investment in canals, railroads, and steamboats was that of geographic extension and specialization. In 1800, economic activity in the United States was concentrated east of the Appalachians, and there it was limited to margins of water access. A century later, a national market existed, the frontier had closed, and long-distance transportation of commodities from the site of production to that of consumption was common. This process of extension featured early competition among the diverse transport modes and the ultimate triumph of the railroad – a victory won by a flexibility of location and capacity that permitted it to supply the exponential growth of demand for facilities. The nineteenth century was well served by the choice. Rapid advances in technology permitted railroad productivity to increase at rates greater than those for other sectors, and real transport rates to decline correspondingly. Moreover, the initial provision of efficient access to market brought with it a large and calculable saving of resources. Through the nineteenth century, the social rate of return upon railroad investment from this source alone was of the order of 15 percent.

Yet the railroads themselves earned much less. Indeed, the returns in the 1870s and thereafter had reached such modest levels that every cyclical swing brought with it extensive receiverships and reorganizations. Despite these impressive results, it was under predominantly private auspices that the rail network was created. Only in the breaching of the Appalachian barrier, in the infancy of the technology in the 1830s, had public support been prominent – and even then, the canal was the more significant instrument of state transport policy.

Such an apparently mysterious operation of the market is explicable. In the first instance, during the period of rapid extension prior to the Civil War, the private profitability of investment was better than thereafter and served to encourage private investors. Equally relevant the results after 1865 understate the gain achieved by investors as well as by individual enterprises. The distinction between the two entities is essential. Investors could and did purchase securities at discounts below par: Their expectation and objective were large capital gains after the completion of new projects and actual operation. While such investment was risky, the returns were high to compensate. Such risk showed up in overcapitalization of the enterprises and made the calculated profits relative to investment too small, perhaps by as much as a factor of a half. The effect of this private pursuit of gain was to get the job done, but probably at a higher cost to consumers of rail services, who had to pay the risk premium in their rates.

Governmental guarantees might have been more efficient, but they have their negative consequences as well.

In addition to this mechanism for eliciting funds, another continuing characteristic of the American scene made for large-scale private interest in transportation improvement. That was the capacity to internalize the social gains derived from lower transport costs. Internalization occurred in a variety of ways. The most direct example was the instance of private investors in railroads who were simultaneously shippers of commodities and thereby realized additional profits in their diverse enterprises. For them the return on railroad investment was the sum of their shares of the railroad plus their incremental profits in their own undertakings. Another instance of internalization was the optimism so characteristic of most promotions that permitted them to reckon, frequently rashly, the gains from the additional traffic a project would engender. There is no historical counterpart to the simplistic investor of static economic theory who fails to reckon the chain of consequences set in motion by his actions. Both factors operated to assure abundant construction of facilities in the period of expanding demand before the Civil War. Afterward, particularly toward the end of the century, as corporate direction of the investment decision and internal financing became more prominent, the expansion of systems was motivated in parallel manner. For each railroad it was rational to expect increasing returns from extension, since each firm was typically operating with excess capacity and falling costs. When all expanded, the expected gain was diluted and the final results were less profitable than anticipated. While tendencies toward overconstruction thus existed, they were more modest than is often claimed.

This competition among the giant firms had the effect of continuing a process by which private initiative satisfied the need for facilities and occasionally, wastefully, satiated it. Other consequences of competition were rate wars and periodic attempts at pooling and other means of cooperation. None were very successful over long periods. Stability came only after regulation by the ICC, a situation which illustrates how administrative control frequently operated to the benefit of the administered, and not necessarily and unequivocally in the public interest.

The challenge of the past was to maximize investment in transport facilities to serve the continental requirements of the United States. It was met by an unprecedented large commitment of resources. Rails spanned the nation at the beginning of the twentieth century, and it was accomplished by private capital market. Public regulation has been less prominent in its allocation achievements. Obviously, in the presence of natural monopoly or even the ruinous competition of giants, the unfettered market will not function perfectly. But it is interesting to observe that at the end of the twentieth century, the role of markets, rather than regulation, has again begun to dominate.

14

BANKING AND FINANCE, 1789–1914

HUGH ROCKOFF

At the beginning of the nineteenth century a substantial proportion of monetary transactions in the United States were conducted with specie (gold or silver coins), in particular the Spanish peso. Merchants used bills of exchange and other financial instruments, and several private banks and the First Bank of the United States had been established, but commercial banking was in its infancy. By 1914 the United States had become one of the world's leading financial powers; it possessed a well-developed banking system and a broad array of non-bank financial intermediaries. Watching over all stood the newly created Federal Reserve System. The development of the financial system in the interim had followed an erratic path. Wars, financial crises, changes in governments, changes in ideologies, and chance events often had produced substantial changes in the financial order in short periods of time. And it had been an unpredictable path. Often a very different path might have been followed were it not for the arguments laid out by a single individual or a single vote cast on an important bill. There was a tendency, moreover, to pass legislation that would have prevented the last crisis, only to discover that the next crisis presented entirely new features. Politicians, like generals, tended to fight the last war. Only by immersing oneself in the actual course of American financial history can one understand how the financial system evolved from its colonial roots to the complex system of specialized financial institutions that existed on the eve of World War I.

THE DEVELOPMENT OF THE BANKING
AND CURRENCY SYSTEMS

The U.S. Constitution imposed several fundamental constraints on the monetary system. Article 1, section 8 declares that "Congress shall have the power to coin Money, regulate the Value thereof, and of foreign Coin," and section 10 declares that no state shall "coin Money; emit Bills of Credit; or make any Thing but gold and silver Coin a Tender in Payment of Debts." Behind these provisions lay inflations produced by the issue of paper money (bills of credit) that had unbalanced debtor–creditor relations in a number of former colonies between the end of the Revolution and the Constitutional Convention. The states, in other words, had misused the power to issue paper money, so money was to be a federal responsibility.

These provisions, however, left important questions open. The federal government had the power to mint coins, but did it have the power to issue paper money? And did it have the power to control the private issues of tokens, banknotes (paper money issued by banks and intended to circulate from hand to hand), and deposits that were close substitutes for coins, and that on modern definitions would be considered money? Here the Constitution was silent.[1]

The Early National Period

It was left mainly to one man, Alexander Hamilton, the first Secretary of the Treasury, to supply the answers to many of the questions left open by the Constitution. In a series of famous reports Hamilton laid out the framework for the fiscal, commercial, and monetary and banking systems of the new nation. The mint was established in 1792 along the lines laid out by Hamilton in his *Report on the Establishment of a Mint*. Hamilton's starting point was the existing coinage system. The most common coins in circulation were the Spanish peso and its divisions, so Hamilton argued that minting a United States dollar weighing about the same as the peso would be the simplest way of introducing a national currency. He agreed with Jefferson and others, however, that the divisions of the dollar should follow

---

[1] The reference to regulating the value of foreign coins may seem surprising. But foreign coins circulated in the colonies, which minted few coins of their own. And it was a common practice even in independent nations to permit the circulation of foreign coins. Indeed substantial amounts of foreign coins remained in circulation in the United States until 1857, and it was up to Congress to determine their value for legal tender purposes.

the decimal system, based on ease of computation, rather than the Spanish system of division by eighths, for ease of physical division.[2] On the basis of assays of Spanish coins Hamilton argued that the United States dollar should contain 321.25 grains of silver. He also called for gold coins. Since the market price of gold by weight was then about 15 times as high as for silver, the gold dollar would contain 24.75 grains of gold. The services of the mint were to be available to all, and free of charge.

Thus the United States was launched on a bimetallic standard, a controversial subject throughout the nineteenth century. The advantage of a bimetallic standard is its diversification of the monetary base. Suppose that new silver mines are discovered. Under a pure silver system the money supply and the price level would rise. But under a bimetallic system the rise in the price level would stimulate the export of gold, or its melting for non-monetary purposes, dampening the impact of the new silver mines. Eventually, if all of the gold coins had been driven from circulation further increases of silver would affect the price level as under a pure silver standard. But even then bimetallism would provide standby protection. Suppose further that the new silver mines were eventually exhausted and the price level began to fall. At some point gold would reenter the money supply, again stabilizing the price level.

The disadvantage of a bimetallic system consists of precisely these swings from one metal to the other. If silver is driven from circulation there is a shortage of small-denomination coins; if gold is driven from circulation it is harder to make large transactions, since gold is best suited for high-denomination coins. The psychological effects of a change in the monetary metal, moreover, might be important, especially when the change is from gold to silver, for this change might produce fears of inflation, economic decline, and so on.

A change from gold to silver was more than a theoretical curiosity. Soon after the establishment of the coinage on the basis of 15 : 1, abundant supplies of silver lifted the world market ratio. By 1805 it had reached 15.79 : 1. This meant that as coin 24.75 grains of gold could be exchanged for 371.25 grains of silver; but as bullion 24.75 grains of gold could exchange for 390.81 grains of silver: it was profitable to export gold and import silver. Clearly by 1830, and probably earlier, gold had ceased to circulate as money in the United States.

---

[2] It was a common practice to cut a peso into 8 pieces known as bits, each worth 12.5 cents, to use for change when small coins were not available. The use of the phrase "two bits" in place of a quarter derives from this practice.

Hamilton's *Report on a National Bank* argued that the federal government should charter and partially fund a national bank, similar to the Bank of England. Hamilton had already helped organize one of the earliest private commercial banks, the Bank of New York, in 1784. But he felt that a large bank sponsored by the federal government bank was necessary to promote private commerce and to facilitate government financial dealings. The debate in Congress over establishing a national bank was bitter. Opponents of a Bank argued that a large semi-private monopoly was inconsistent with the functioning of a democracy and that a national bank was unconstitutional because the Constitution was silent on banking. But supporters of a national bank argued that it would aid the Treasury in obtaining loans and generally encourage savings, investment, and trade, especially foreign trade. President Washington was uncertain about whether he should sign the bill, and he asked for written opinions from his cabinet. Thomas Jefferson, the Secretary of State, submitted an adverse opinion, but Hamilton's defense of a national bank convinced Washington to sign.

The First Bank of the United States, which began operations in 1791, was a large organization by the standards of the day. Its capital was set at $10 million (the expenditures of the federal government in 1792 were $5.1 million), one-fifth to be provided by the government and the rest by the private sector. This structure partly fulfilled one of Hamilton's most cherished political goals: uniting the fortunes of the fledgling republic with those of the richest businessmen. Voting rights were not distributed on a one-share-one-vote basis; only residents of the United States were permitted to vote, and no one was permitted more than thirty votes. The Bank was authorized to establish branches throughout the country.

The government's subscription was to be paid with funds borrowed from the Bank; the public's subscription was to be paid one-fourth in specie and three-fourths in government stock (in those days the term stock was used for bonds as well as equities). The Bank thus provided a boost to the government's credit. The notes of the Bank were limited to the amount of capital and were receivable for taxes. The business the Bank could do was circumscribed; it could buy bills of exchange and deal in bullion, but it could only deal in real property taken as collateral when loans were defaulted. Loans to the government could not exceed $100,000 unless authorized by Congress. The maximum interest the Bank could charge was 6 percent. These restrictions reflected the so-called real bills doctrine, which held (as laid down by its most famous expositor, Adam

Smith) that banks could invest safely only in self-liquidating, short-term instruments; anything else left a bank open to illiquidity and failure. The interest rate restriction, in Smith's view, reinforced the real bills restriction by discouraging banks from making loans to speculators.

The Bank quickly became a source of loans to the government, and when the government had trouble repaying, it sold its shares, the last going in 1802. The Bank's policy of returning the notes of state-chartered banks for redemption in specie has been credited with helping to eliminate unsound banking. But a natural rivalry with the state banks developed. State banks felt that their note issue had been restrained, that it was unfair for the First Bank to absorb the largest proportion of the government's deposits, and that it was unfair for the First Bank to compete in local loan markets.

But the First Bank might be with us still were it not for an important limitation in its charter: the life of the charter was set at twenty years. When the charter came up for renewal in 1811, opposition was strong. The congressional debate centered on the constitutionality of the Bank, and the renewal bills lost by narrow margins: one vote in the House, and the Vice President's tie-breaker in the Senate. The lapsing of the charter could not have happened at a worse time, for the War of 1812 soon created a financial emergency for the federal government.

The number of banks increased rapidly during the war and immediate postwar years; according to Davis Rich Dewey's estimate from 117 to 232 between 1811 and 1816. These banks were chartered by state governments, and the increase in their number has been ascribed, in part, to a mania that overtook legislators and bankers. It seems likely, however, that the suspension of specie payments during the war, and the growth in legal tender demand notes to be discussed below, which served as an alternative form of bank reserves, had much to do with the growth of banking.

The Second Bank of the United States

The financial embarrassments of the federal government during the War of 1812 – Secretary of State James Monroe had to pledge his personal fortune to raise the funds to transfer Andrew Jackson's forces to New Orleans – led to calls for a Second Bank of the United States. Although no action was taken during the war, soon afterwards the disorganized state of the currency (without specie redemption, the price of banknotes varied from place to place) produced widespread support for a federal bank to manage the resumption of specie payments.

The bill establishing the Second Bank of the United States was signed by the president on April 10, 1816. The capital was set at $35 million, one-fifth to be supplied by the federal government. The bank could establish branches at its discretion and issue bank notes, redeemable in specie and receivable for taxes, in denominations of $5 and up. The maximum note issue was limited to the bank's capital. Three-quarters of the stock to be subscribed by the public was to be paid for with federal bonds. The government also benefited from a direct payment of $1.5 million to be made by the bank for its charter. The charter of the Second Bank, like the charter of the First, required renewal after twenty years.

The Second Bank opened in January 1817, and specie payments were resumed soon after. The bank did not get off to a good start. Although general economic conditions were unfavorable, there seems little doubt that the bank was badly managed under its first president, William Jones. There were allegations of speculation in the bank's stock financed with loans from the bank, and the western and southern branches of the bank appear to have been too free in issuing notes. The requirement that the notes of one branch be honored by all was abandoned in 1818, but considerable damage had been done already: the Baltimore branch was closed in January 1819 with a loss of $3 million.

Jones was replaced by Langdon Cheeves in 1819. Under Cheeves's conservative management, but owing more to policies already in place when he took over, the Bank enjoyed a resurgence. Nevertheless, in the West and South, where the Bank was most active, local banks chafed again at the policy of returning notes for redemption. During the depression year of 1820, moreover, Cheeves's stress on high reserves prevented a useful expansion of the stock of money. In 1823 Cheeves was replaced by Nicholas Biddle, who was destined to fight the "Bank War" with Andrew Jackson and become one of the most famous figures in the history of American finance. Biddle was appointed with the understanding that he would follow an aggressive policy of expansion, and he did. Borrowing and lending were increased, the bank moved into foreign exchange operations, and earnings increased.

President Jackson's attack on the Bank continues to be debated by historians. Jackson was determined to rid the nation of a "monster," and Biddle was equally determined to preserve the power and independence of the Bank. Jackson opened hostilities in his first annual message to Congress in

1829. He questioned the constitutionality of the Bank, and its success in creating a uniform national currency. He suggested that it be replaced by an agency of the Treasury that would issue notes and take deposits, but not make loans to the general public. The last recommendation may have been prompted by allegations that the Bank had favored anti-Jackson men in granting loans. Historians have not given much credence to these allegations, but the potential for political favoritism is not hard to see, and a cynical public would naturally take such allegations seriously.

Despite the attack by a popular president, Biddle was convinced that the public supported the Bank, and he launched an effort to renew the charter well before its scheduled expiration in 1836. The bill passed both houses of Congress but was vetoed by Jackson in July 1832. The accompanying message, full of anger and confusion, has been a focal point of historical debate. Biddle believed that the veto would doom Jackson's reelection campaign, but Jackson won an overwhelming victory, thus sealing the fate of the Bank. After the election Jackson allowed federal deposits in the Bank to run down, moving them to selected state banks – pet banks, as they were known to Jackson's critics. After its federal charter expired, the Bank obtained a charter from Pennsylvania, and Biddle remained President until 1839. In 1841 the Bank failed, a victim of depression and its own speculations.

How important was the Bank War to the election? Stuart Bruchey has argued that despite Jackson's vigorous language the public was only mildly interested. The Bank enjoyed wide support – after all, the bill to recharter did pass both houses of Congress – but Jackson was enormously popular. His overwhelming reelection was largely a personal triumph, and the Bank War may have received as much attention from the press as it did because it was a safe political issue.

But in any case, what was the source of Jackson's opposition, and what should we make of the arguments in the veto message? Some authorities see Jackson's fervor as the product of a frontiersman's lack of financial sophistication combined with personal experience – Jackson had lost a large sum of money in a bank failure. The veto message denounces the Bank as a monopoly, and lists various ill effects on the economy, some of which are hard to understand. These sections suggest that Jackson was opposed to any form of central banking. But another section simply points out that if Congress thought a Bank was needed, the government could allow competitors to bid for the Bank's charter, a position that modern economists might well find attractive.

The Free Banking Era

After 1836 the regulation of banking was left to the states. The resulting range of regulatory experiments was remarkable, and numerous economic historians have used this period as a laboratory in which to test theories about bank regulation. Some states (Texas and Arkansas, among them) prohibited all forms of banking. Some (Indiana and Missouri among them) organized state banks reminiscent of the Bank of the United States. Some (including the New England states) chartered banks one by one in the legislature. Some permitted branch banking, and some prohibited it. Ohio tried several different kinds of banking. The best-known experiment, and the one that gives its name to the period, was free banking.

It is important to be clear about what free banking really meant. Free banking laws, first adopted in Michigan in 1837 and New York in 1838, provided that anyone who could raise a certain minimum of capital, and fulfill certain other requirements, could start a bank; the legislature did not charter banks individually. Political connections, in other words, were not required to obtain a charter. This was the sense in which banking was free. But there was an important sense in which banking was not free. Any notes issued by a free bank had to be backed by government bonds, generally but not always bonds issued by the state where the bank was located. Notes could not be issued on the general assets of the bank.

The experience under free banking varied widely. In some states, when the bond security was inadequate (Indiana in the early 1850s for example) free banking produced wildcat banking. Numerous banks were set up in remote areas (where the wildcats roamed?) with the idea of forestalling redemption and making some quick profits. But these episodes were relatively infrequent, and easily corrected by increasing the bond backing for the notes. In many states, New York in particular, free banking encouraged the rapid expansion of the system while adequately protecting note holders.

Of the other systems, we should take note of the Suffolk system of New England. The Suffolk Bank of Boston first entered the note redemption business in 1818. Over time a well-defined redemption system evolved. New England country banknotes tended to flow toward Boston, where they were redeemed at par by the Suffolk, which acted as an agent for the city banks. In return, country banks were required to keep deposits at the Suffolk. The result was that banknotes circulated at par throughout New England, a result much appreciated by the public and much praised by historians. The amount of deposits that the country banks were forced to keep at the Suffolk, however, was substantial. As a result the Suffolk, whose stock was widely held by other banks in Boston, was regularly the most profitable in the city. The country banks chafed at this arrangement but for a long time were unable to do anything about it. Refusal to keep deposits at the Suffolk might mean a sudden, hard-to-meet demand for the redemption of a large block of notes accumulated by the Suffolk. Finally, in 1857, the country banks set up their own bank, The Bank of Mutual Redemption, to compete with the Suffolk in the redemption business. Because the Civil War and the end of state bank notes followed in a few years, it is hard to decide what the outcome of this rivalry would have been in the long run.

While the result of the Suffolk system, a uniform currency, has been widely applauded, divergent lessons have been drawn. Some writers have stressed the private nature of the system and argued that this bodes well for a privately issued currency, while others have stressed the hierarchical structure and argued that this implies that some form of regulation is necessary.

The National Banking Act

The Civil War brought a major reorganization of the banking system. Soon after taking up his post, Secretary of the Treasury Salmon Chase proposed a national banking law modeled on the free banking law (Chase had been governor of Ohio, a free banking state) but providing for federal charters and requiring the deposit of federal bonds as collateral for notes. Chase expected several advantages from a national system. During the war the system would provide a market for government bonds, and so strengthen the financial position of the government.

But the main argument had little to do with the immediate problems of the Treasury. Even as governor of Ohio, Chase had complained about the confusion caused by having large numbers of state banknotes circulating at varying discounts. It has been shown by Gary Gorton that this market was surprisingly efficient, so one can doubt that the costs of a heterogeneous currency were as high as was thought. But Chase's belief that establishing a uniform currency was an important reform was widely shared. Events soon added urgency to the case for reform: several western states had issued large amounts of notes secured by southern state bonds, and these systems were now riddled with closed and bankrupt banks. And even more important, the North had resorted to the issue of paper money, the famous greenbacks. "Lincoln green" provided a uniform currency and was popular in many parts of the country and with radical Republicans. But Chase and other more conservative Republicans worried that a permanent system of fiat money would be a dangerous temptation to inflation. A national banking system, in other words, was seen as a conservative alternative to a radical reform, a pure fiat currency.

If large deficits were run under the national banking system, one might expect banks to absorb the additional bonds and issue notes on them, with effects on the stock of money similar to the direct issue of fiat money. But whatever the validity of this argument, it seems not to have been considered at the time.

The National Currency Act was passed in 1863, and it was hoped that most state banks would quickly become national banks. But the early results were disappointing. A revised act, the National Banking Act, was passed in 1864. It corrected a number of flaws in the 1863 version – for example it corrected a provision that imposed a low uniform maximum on the interest banks could charge – and entry into the system accelerated, but the results were still disappointing to those who hoped that the new system would completely supplant the old.

The Revival of State Banking

In 1865 a prohibitive tax was levied on notes issued by state banks, and it was expected that this, finally, would force most banks into the National Banking System. Many did convert, but a core of state banks remained, and it expanded over the remainder of the century. Deposit banking was becoming steadily more important, so state banks that issued no notes could tap a growing source of funds. State banking laws, moreover, often made it more profitable to do business under a state charter. The result was that the state banks continued to constitute an important component of the American banking system. In 1870 state banks held only 9 percent of all commercial bank deposits; by 1890 the figure was 57 percent. Legislation based on an outmoded assumption, the primacy of notes, had produced an unintended result: the dual banking system.

The National Banking System has been blamed for the persistently high interest rates (relative to the North and Midwest) that characterized the rural areas of the South and West after the Civil War. The minimum capital requirement limited the number of national banks that could be supported in the small towns of these regions, and the prohibitive tax on state banknotes made it hard to start state banks. The few banks that did secure a foothold enjoyed local monopolies and pushed up interest rates. Gradually, however, the spread of deposit banking and the revival of free banking (easy entry) at the state level undermined local monopolies. By the turn of the century, regional interest rate differentials had narrowed considerably.

National banks apparently did not take full advantage of their monopoly of the note issue. Profit calculations, first performed by Phillip Cagan, and later highlighted by Milton Friedman and Anna J. Schwartz, showed that the rate of return to issuing notes was extremely high during long segments of the national banking period. Or to put it somewhat differently, one might have expected the price of the bonds eligible to back notes to be bid up until banks were earning only normal profits on their note-issuing operations. But this did not happen. Several explanations for the puzzle have been offered, but the most authoritative recent study finds that national banks may have rejected a profitable opportunity simply because they considered their primary business to be making loans rather than holding bonds.

TRENDS AND CYCLES IN MONEY AND PRICES

Figure 14.1, which shows a wholesale price index (1860 = 100) and an index of money per unit of output (1860 = 100) over the period 1800–1879, reveals that prices generally fell until the 1850s. This trend can be explained, in the first instance, by the relatively slow growth of money per unit of output in the United States, that is by the supply of money relative to the demand for it. Ultimately, however, the trend of prices in the United States was determined by the trend of prices in the rest of the world. Because the United States was linked by fixed exchange rates to other countries, its price level could not diverge from the price level in its major trading partners for long periods of time. If U.S. prices had diverged, the result would have been a balance of payments deficit and a loss of its monetary base. So the ultimate determinant of the U.S. trend in the U.S. price level was slow growth of the world stock of monetary metals relative to world output, a trend accelerated by Britain's return to the gold standard after the Napoleonic Wars, which increased the demand

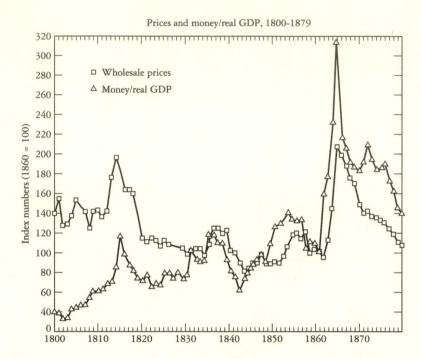

Prices and money/real GDP, 1800-1879

Figure 14.1. Prices and the ratio of money to real gross domestic product, 1800–1879. Sources and methods: see the data section of the bibliography.

for the monetary metals. This was true, of course, only over the long run. For substantial periods, differences between the price level in the United States and the price level in its trading partners could persist because of capital flows, and other offsetting forces. The trend in money per unit of output in the United States was, it should be noted, slightly upward, indicating an upward trend (although at a relatively moderate rate) in the demand for money. The fall in prices was interrupted by a sharp surge in the War of 1812; prices rose 45 percent between 1811 and 1814.

The War of 1812

The War of 1812 was financed mainly by borrowing rather than by taxation. Long-term loans, however, became hard to place, even after taxes were raised to provide for interest and eventual repayment. Short-term treasury notes, receivable for taxes, were issued as a stopgap. Table 14.1 shows the amount outstanding toward the end of each year. The first issues paid

Table 14.1. *Money and prices in the War of 1812 ($ million)*

	Government currency issues	Banknotes	Wholesale prices (1811 = 100)
1811	0.0	32.5	100
1812	2.8	36.8	104
1813	4.9	41.2	129
1814	10.6	45.5	145
1815	17.6	68.0	135
1816	3.4	62.6	120
1817	0.0	56.4	120

Source: See the data section of the bibliography.

interest and had fairly large face values; the last issue included small, non-interest-bearing notes. But in some measure they were all substitutes for cash: the large denominations served as bank reserves and for business transactions, and the small denominations served as hand-to-hand currency. The banks expanded their note issues concurrently, and they suspended specie payments in August 1814, when the British attacked Washington, D.C.

It is clear that the inflation was fueled primarily by the expansion of liquid assets. But prices undoubtedly responded to many forces besides the number of dollars currently in circulation. Expectations of future government deficits, of future increases in the money supply, and of future inflation, all conditioned on expectations about the course of the war, must have influenced how people decided between buying goods and holding money. The war also disrupted normal patterns of trade and commerce, further exacerbating inflation.

After the war the treasury notes were funded into long-term debt. But the currency remained disordered for some time. The federal government had to keep track of four separate instruments used to make payments: local banknotes at par, local banknotes below par, treasury notes bearing interest, and treasury notes bearing no interest. The money supply had declined due to the withdrawal of short-term treasury notes, and the reduction of banknotes through bank failures and reduction of outstanding issues by surviving banks. But the price level remained high. As shown in Table 14.1, the wholesale price index stood at 120 in 1816 compared with 100 in 1811, so resumption might have been further delayed. Congress pressed the banks to resume with a resolution that provided that only the notes of banks redeeming in specie would be receivable for taxes after February 1817, and partly for this reason resumption was accomplished in the early months of that year.

The Jacksonian Inflation

Prices fell from the wartime peak throughout the 1820s and early 1830s, but this trend was interrupted by a sharp inflation during the second Jackson administration. For many years the standard explanation was that Jackson's attack on the Second Bank had encouraged banks to overissue paper money because they no longer had to worry as much about their notes being returned for redemption. The president had deregulated the banking system and chaos had followed, a still familiar refrain.

But as George Macesich and Peter Temin pointed out, the traditional theory assumes that banks created additional notes on the basis of a given stock of specie. Instead, it appears that the supply of specie increased substantially, and that the banks were no more aggressive in issuing banknotes during the inflation than before the Bank War. The increase in the stock of specie was the result of an increase in the traditional inflow of silver from Mexico and a decrease in the traditional outflow to China.

Mexico was in the throes of a revolution, and considerable amounts of copper money were being issued to finance government expenditures producing a combination of capital flight and inflation-driven exports of silver. The reduction in the outflow of silver to China can be traced, somewhat surprisingly, to the rise of opium addiction. China had traditionally run balance of trade surpluses, but they shrank as imports of opium ate up more and more of China's export earnings. Ships from the United States could use long dated bills on London rather than chests filled with silver pesos to pay for China's exports.

The inflation of the 1830s came to an end with the Panic of 1837, to be described below. The specie flow was not reversed, but the public and the banks decided to hold larger reserves of specie. This kept money and prices below the levels of the 1830s throughout the 1840s, as can be seen in Figure 14.1. The decision to hold larger reserves imposed a cost on the economy in the sense that if the extra specie held in bank vaults or private hoards had been replaced with banknotes or fiat money, the specie could have been used to finance imports.

Gold and Greenbacks

The final price movement of the antebellum period was the sharp inflation in the first half of the 1850s. The new gold fields of California and
Australia vastly increased the world's gold supply, one of the crucial
levers of the world's money. Money per unit of real output in the
United States rose 36 percent between 1848 and 1855 and prices increased
29 percent. These were prosperous years, one of the longest peacetime
expansions before the twentieth century. And the surge in aggregate
demand produced by the influx of gold probably deserves much of the
credit.

As shown clearly in Figure 14.1, however, the inflation during the
1850s was dwarfed by the inflation during the Civil War. Prices in the
loyal states rose by a factor of 2.1 between 1860 and 1864, and the money
supply rose by a factor of 2.4. Ultimately, this inflation, like the inflation
during the War of 1812, derived from the government's fiscal policy.
Lincoln's first Secretary of the Treasury, Salmon Chase, whom we have
already met, initially anticipated a short war, the common expectation of
the day both North and South. He proposed a modest increase in tariff
revenues, and a loan of $150 million. Chase insisted that the banks pay
the proceeds of the loan to the Treasury in specie, perhaps hastening the
suspension that occurred in December 1861.

But suspension would have come eventually because the government's
reliance on inflationary finance made the price level in the United States
relative to the rest of the world inconsistent with the maintenance of specie
payments. Only by adopting a policy of financing the war completely
through taxation and borrowing from the public would it have been possible to maintain specie payments. But forgoing the tax on cash balances
implicit in issuing paper money was hard for a government desperately
seeking every source of revenue.

The first issue of legal-tender notes, the famous greenbacks, was authorized in April 1862: $150 million, although $50 million replaced outstanding demand notes. The argument for issuing paper money that
carried the day was simple necessity. The army was in the field waiting to
be paid, and no other expedient, except borrowing at very high interest
rates, was at hand. And if the troops were to be forced to take the notes,
then everyone should be forced to take them – they should be legal-tender
notes. In the end, however, their legal-tender status was limited: the

Table 14.2. *Money and prices in the Civil War ($ million)*

	Greenbacks	Other government currency	Total stock of money	Wholesale prices (1860 = 100)
1860	0	0	554	100
1861	0	0	603	96
1862	96.6	53.3	705	112
1863	387.6	23.6	965	143
1864	447.6	192.2	1,351	208
1865	431.1	216.6	1,385	199
1866	400.8	189.8	1,337	187

Source and methods: See the data section of the bibliography.

customs duties and the interest on government loans were to be paid in gold, to maintain the credit of the government, particularly with foreign borrowers.

Further issues followed: $150 million in July 1862 and $150 million in March 1863. Table 14.2 shows the amount outstanding in June of each year. Greenbacks were not the only form of money issued by the federal government. There were also small-denomination notes to replace the small change driven out of circulation, and small-denomination interest-bearing notes that served as bank reserves and may have enjoyed some hand-to-hand circulation. Table 14.2 gives the amount of these issues and an estimate of the total stock of money, which includes specie and bank notes and deposits. Given the flood of money, and given the disruptions and uncertainties of the war, it is not surprising that prices in the North rose dramatically, and even more in the South.

The link between the rapid increase in the stock of money and the rapid increase in the price level was well understood by the administration and by Congress. Strenuous efforts were made to raise additional tax revenues and long-term borrowing was resorted to on a massive scale. Northern victories in the summer of 1863 helped. And Jay Cooke, an investment banker, was hired to help sell the government's debt. Cooke put together a network of salesmen that sold bonds to middle-class investors many of whom had not previously bought financial assets. This not only kept rates on government debt down during the war, but it also helped to broaden and deepen the market for securities, thus paving the way for the postwar investment boom.

Prices in the loyal states and conquered areas of the South were quoted in greenback dollars, except on the Pacific coast, where the gold dollar remained the standard. The persistence of gold on the Pacific coast is an interesting phenomenon. There the use of greenbacks was beaten back through concerted social pressures – debtors attempting to pay with greenbacks were denounced as "greenbackers" – and the system settled into one in which gold was money and greenbacks were "foreign" exchange. But in the rest of the country payments were made with greenbacks or with banknotes and deposits convertible into greenbacks. Gold, however, held on to a subsidiary role: it was used to pay customs duties and interest and principal on the public debt, to make remittances to other countries, and to diversify portfolios. The price of gold varied from day to day, much like the prices of stocks or bonds, and there was considerable speculation. When the war news was exciting, the action at the gold exchange reached a fever pitch; sometimes the "bears," who were selling greenbacks and buying gold, would sing "Dixie" and the "bulls" would try to drown them out with a chorus of "John Brown."

Major movements in the gold value of the greenback were related to financial and political developments, and most of all to victories and defeats on the battlefield, which determined expectations about how long the war would last. The gold value of the greenback declined as the full dimensions of the war were realized, reaching a low of 58 cents in February of 1863. A rally followed, and the greenback reached a temporary peak of 82 cents in August 1863 after Vicksburg and Gettysburg. A reaction then set in when it was realized that Lee had retreated successfully; the low of 35 cents was reached in June 1864. The greenback then recovered, reaching a peak of 78 cents in May 1865.

Prices rose faster than wages in the North, substantially reducing the real wages of working men and women. The pay of an army private provides a poignant example: it rose from $11 per month at the start of the war to $16 at the war's end, a 37 percent increase, but in the meantime prices were rising 69 percent. The result was a substantial loss in purchasing power, although the loss was mitigated by the provision of food and clothing by the army and by the bonuses paid for enlisting. An index constructed by Wesley C. Mitchell for the real wage of over 5,000 wage earners fell from 100 in July 1860 to 67 in January 1865; it then recovered to 97 in July 1865. The rapid recovery was the result of a substantial deflation combined with stable wages. Mitchell went on to argue that although direct evidence is scanty, the lag in wages reflected the lack of labor's bargaining power, and that as a result real profits must have risen substantially because interest and other costs of production also failed to rise as fast as prices.

Why wages lagged by so much for so long when labor markets were tight due to the mobilization is something of a mystery. Mitchell's conclusion was challenged by Reuben Kessel and Armen Alchian, who argued that the depreciation of the dollar (the increase in the dollar price of foreign currencies) and the increase in excise taxes drove a wedge between prices and wages that had nothing to do with increased profits. But their argument was challenged, in turn, by Stephen DeCanio and Joel Mokyr, whose econometric study showed that even when real factors are allowed for, a substantial part of the fall in real wages is left to be explained by a wage lag.

Inflation was far worse in the South. The South's productive capacity was severely damaged by ground fighting and the naval blockade, and the South relied, even more than did the North, on the issue of paper money. In January 1861 the stock of banknotes and deposits was $95 million; by January 1864 it was $268 million, and the stock of Confederate government notes outstanding was $827 million. So the circulating medium, defined to include both, had risen by a factor of 11.6; prices over the same period, in the eastern Confederacy, rose even more, by a factor of 27.7. Part of the difference between the price rise and the money rise may be explained by a phenomenon common to periods of very high inflation: people see the value of their money declining rapidly, so they try to spend it as quickly as possible, putting further upward pressure on prices.

A currency reform in February 1864 seemed to do some good. It provided that Confederate dollars could be converted into bonds at par until April 1864; afterwards they had to be exchanged for new issues of paper money at the rate of three old dollars for two new ones. Attempts to dispose of the notes before the April exchange produced an increase in prices of almost 34 percent between February and March. Prices then remained relatively stable for the remainder of the year, but renewed issues of currency and military reverses reignited the inflation. By April 1865, when resistance ended, the price level in the eastern Confederacy was 91 times the level of January 1861.

The Resumption of Specie Payments

The end of the war did not mean a quick return to specie payments. The price level was still far above the level of 1862. Since the gold value of greenbacks was the exchange rate (foreign currencies, such as the pound, were convertible into gold), a rate of one dollar in gold for only one dollar in greenbacks would have made United States exports expensive and imports cheap, producing an unsustainable loss of gold. Devaluing the gold dollar (lowering its gold content) was a possibility, but it was not seriously considered by postwar administrations, because devaluation would have weakened the credit of both the government and private borrowers with foreign lenders.

To accomplish resumption without devaluation it was necessary to reduce the price level in the United States relative to foreign price levels. Hugh McCulloch, the first Secretary of the Treasury to deal with resumption, adopted a policy in the latter part of 1865 of retiring greenbacks out of surplus revenues made available by cutbacks in military expenditures. But Congress, responding to complaints about hard times, halted further retirement of the greenbacks in 1868. The result was a policy of allowing the country to "grow up to the currency." The stock of legal tender currency and national banknotes was held approximately constant, the total stock of money grew slowly, and rapid economic growth gradually lowered the ratio of money per unit output, and as can be seen in Figure 14.1) the price level.

Debtors and other advocates of soft money criticized the deflation, and some historians have been sympathetic to their claims. But it could be argued that the restoration of public and private credit, and the flow of foreign lending, helped finance the rapid economic expansion that took place after the war. In 1875 an act was passed that set a date for resumption (January 1, 1879) and authorized the secretary of the Treasury to build up a specie reserve so that government notes could be redeemed after that date. When the resumption act was passed the gold value of the greenback was about 89 cents, and the ratio of U.S. to British prices was about 27 percent above the level of 1862. By 1878, the gold value of the greenback was close to $1, the ratio of U.S. to British prices was about the same as it was in 1862. Resumption was achieved smoothly.

The Battle of the Standards

As shown in Figure 14.2, which plots prices and money per unit of real output from 1880 to 1914, prices continued downward for about fifteen years following resumption. This was true throughout the bloc of countries that adhered to the gold standard.[3] The root cause was that the world

---

[3] Countries on the silver standard, such as China, experienced a rising price level.

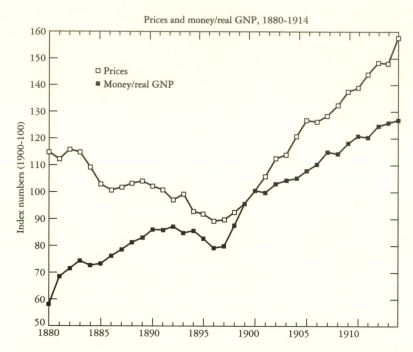

Figure 14.2. Prices and the ratio of money to real gross national product, 1880–1914. Sources and methods: see the data section of the bibliography.

gold supply, the base of the money stock, was not growing rapidly enough to provide for the growth in the demand for money at an unchanged price level. The demand for gold was compounded from several things: the adoption of the gold standard by more and more countries (Germany, which adopted the gold standard after the Franco-Prussian War, was the most important), the growth in real income, and, particularly in the United States, the increasing monetization of the economy. As Figure 14.2 shows, money per unit of output in the United States did rise during these years, but not at a rate sufficient to maintain a stable price level.

For much of the economy deflation was probably not burdensome. Economic growth was rapid, perhaps unprecedented. Giant new industries were emerging, immigration and natural increase were adding to the labor force, and agricultural output was expanding. A falling price level, moreover, spread the benefits of economic expansion widely: even the clergyman who was reluctant to ask his poor congregation for a raise saw his real income rise when the prices he paid for goods and services fell.

But debtors were angry; farmers, in particular, believed that deflation was raising the real cost of repaying their mortgages.[4] So political support for inflation remained strong throughout the 1880s and gained ground during the depression of the 1890s, when further declines in the price level were experienced. Initially, political support for inflation centered on proposals for more greenbacks, but during the 1890s the free coinage of silver took center stage. In part, the switch from greenbacks to silver reflected the search for a mechanism that would retain some of the safety provided by a commodity standard. But silver also had greater practical political chances because the industry, although a minor one in terms of total sales, was important in a number of western states, and could count on a good deal of support in the Senate.

The demonetization of silver had occurred in 1873 as a result of legislation that attracted little attention at the time, but subsequently became famous (to the inflationists) as the "Crime of 1873." The legislation simply listed the coins to be minted, the crime being the omission of the silver dollar. At the time the market price of silver was above $1 per 371.25 grains (the traditional content), so the omission was of little moment. Subsequently, the price of silver fell due to the opening of new mines, European conversions to the gold standard, and the falling price level. Silver producers awoke to the absence of a government floor under the price of silver, and inflationists awoke to the absence of a mechanism that would have expanded the money supply.

It appears that the demonetization of silver was deliberate: a number of key Republican officials believed that large discoveries of silver were eminent, and that if nothing were done resumption would take place on the basis of silver rather than gold. This they desperately wanted to avoid because it threatened inflation and the creation of a barrier between the United States and the world capital market centered in London. No basis, however, has been found for wilder claims, for example, that Congress had been bribed by European bankers.

The political agitation for silver reached a peak in the presidential campaign of 1896. The Democratic convention was deadlocked when William Jennings Bryan, a young congressman from Nebraska, gave one of the most famous speeches in American history. Bryan attacked the Republicans for

---

[4] The farmers's political spokesmen rarely framed the issue this narrowly. They often conflated the decline in general prices, a condition that was treatable with monetary remedies, with the decline in farm prices relative to prices paid by farmers, a problem that could be addressed only by acreage controls, price support subsidies, and the like.

supporting the gold standard, and ended his speech by declaring that "You shall not press down upon the brow of labor this crown of thorns, you shall not crucify mankind upon a cross of gold." The speech won Bryan the nomination. Bryan crisscrossed the country during the campaign, exhorting the public to support the Democrats and the free coinage of silver at 16:1. He lost the election, however, to William McKinley, who campaigned for "sound money." McKinley, however, did pledge to sponsor an international conference on bimetallism, a pledge he kept.

Historians have often belittled Bryan's understanding of monetary economics, but he was on sound ground in arguing that free coinage of silver would have created inflation by attracting silver to the mint and increasing the monetary base. Indeed, Milton Friedman has recently shown that had the "Crime of 1873" never been committed, resumption would have occurred on the basis of silver, and the price level in 1896 would have been considerably above the level actually achieved in 1896. In his view, the demonetization was indeed a serious error. It is less certain, however, that embarking on inflation in the early nineties would have relieved debtors or pulled the economy out of the depression. Inflation might have stimulated profits and employment, as it had on other occasions, but it is conceivable that investment might have been discouraged by the tinkering with the standard.

The degree of debt relief is also problematical. Farm mortgages were typically due in five years or less. As they came due they would have been renegotiated at higher interest rates that reflected the anticipated inflation. Indeed, the tendency of interest rates to rise during inflation is often known as the Fisher effect, because a paper published by Irving Fisher in 1896, an outgrowth of the controversy, convinced economists of the importance of the idea. Fisher actually found that interest rates typically had responded slowly to changes in the rate of price change. This suggested that debtors would have experienced some relief, although expectations might have coalesced more quickly when the source of inflation was a deliberate change in monetary policy.

The Heyday of the Classical Gold Standard

The free silver issue soon faded, however, for reasons that neither Bryan nor anyone else foresaw in 1896. The world supply of gold began to expand due to mining discoveries in South Africa, Western Australia, and elsewhere and the discovery of the cyanide process for extracting gold from ore, a process that was crucial in South Africa and useful in a number of other places. As can be seen in Figure 14.2, money per unit of real output grew at a higher rate after 1897, and the economy experienced a mild inflation (about 2 percent per year) until World War I. For agriculture it was a golden age of high production and high prices.

Thus the gold standard produced the inflation that Bryan and his supporters had wanted to produce through a deliberate change in policy. Bryan then argued, with some justice, that the inflation confirmed his faith in a monetary remedy for deflation. The gold standard had been saved by a totally unexpected increase in the supply of gold. The increase in the gold supply, it is true, was not entirely accidental – the high real price of gold had stimulated prospecting and the search for new extraction techniques. But not all searches are rewarded, an element of luck was involved.

The period after 1897 was the heyday of the gold standard, and the success of the system during this period is often pointed to by advocates of a gold standard or similar reforms of the monetary system. In certain respects things went well. Exchange rates were fixed, encouraging the free flow of capital across international borders, and the long-run price trend was satisfactory. But short-run output and price fluctuations may have been greater than under the post–World War II regime. The performance of the gold standard during its heyday, moreover, was in some measure accidental: new supplies of gold were sufficient to lubricate the world's financial system without causing excessive inflation.

BANKING CRISES AND THE FEDERAL RESERVE

The nineteenth-century trends in financial development, money, and prices were frequently punctuated by financial crises that affected the economy as a whole, and created long-term changes in the structure of financial regulations. Five of the major crises – 1837, 1857, 1873, 1893, and 1907 – are discussed below, along with what was intended to be the solution to the problem of financial crises, the Federal Reserve System.

The Panic of 1837

Although there had been previous crises (a crisis in 1819 brought the post–War of 1812 expansion to an end), the Panic of 1837 was by far the most severe before the Civil War. As would be typical of subsequent panics, one can point, in retrospect, to excessive speculation in banks, land, and so on, and the subsequent bursting of the bubble as the underlying story. This explanation has been argued repeatedly by economic historians. It satisfies our desire for a moral economic order, and is consistent with this and other crises. But why some bubbles burst leaving scarcely a trace and others have severe consequences is still an open question. One answer, and it seems to apply here, is that crashes in the stock market, or other speculative markets, damage the real economy only when they spread to the banking system.

A number of specific precipitants of the Panic of 1837 have been identified. The older literature stresses several government measures, in particular the Specie Circular issued in July 1836. The Circular was intended to curb land speculation by requiring that purchases of federal land be made with specie rather than bank notes. This measure allegedly raised doubts about the soundness of western banks and drained them of specie. The role of domestic policies such as the Specie Circular, has been questioned, however, by Peter Temin, who instead blamed the tight-money policy introduced by the Bank of England because of the worrisome amount of credit extended by British firms engaged in financing trade with America.

Interest rates soared in New York, and business and bank failures mounted. In May 1837 the New York City banks suspended specie payments. Business began to revive, and the banks resumed early in 1838; but a second collapse followed in 1839. Suspension by the Bank of the United States of Pennsylvania as a result of speculation in cotton markets, and the spread of the suspension to the south and west, although not to New York and New England, were the most prominent features of the second collapse. This time the economy failed to revive, and a long contraction, Van Buren's depression, followed. The recovery is usually dated as beginning in 1843.

Historical accounts are replete with anecdotes about the severity of the depression. But Peter Temin, although not denying the reality of depression, argues forcefully that it was much less severe than the depression of the 1930s, with which it is often compared. According to the estimates he reports, real GNP actually rose by 16 percent between 1839 and 1843, while prices fell 42 percent. The greater flexibility of prices and the prominent role of agriculture (where employment is less sensitive to short-run changes in demand) may account for the comparatively strong performance of the economy during Van Buren's depression.

The Crisis of 1857

Although not as severe as the Panic of 1837, the crisis of 1857, nonetheless, brought the great boom of the 1850s to an end and ushered in a severe recession, especially in the North. Most explanations stress the failure of the Ohio Life Insurance and Trust Company on August 24. The Ohio Life was a well-respected firm doing a banking business in Ohio and New York. Its failure was unexpected, and it led to a vicious cycle of forced liquidations as lenders scrambled for cash.

Concerted action by the New York banks, perhaps through their Clearinghouse established in 1853, might have staved off suspension. Instead, the New York banks ran for cover by reducing credit. Although this policy helped build reserves for a time, it soon failed because the public continued to withdraw specie. Suspension of specie payments was not, of course, the end of the world. People continued to make payments by using bank notes and checks. Confidence returned quickly, and specie payments were resumed in December, but the effects on the economy were substantial. The stock of money fell 18.5 percent between 1856 and 1857; in 1859 the stock of money was still about 1.5 percent below the level of 1856.

Prices and output also fell. National unemployment rates were probably not high by modern standards, but the distress in northern cities was acute. At one point the New York state militia was called out because a mob became threatening when it learned that promised relief would not be forthcoming. In the South the crisis was less severe, in part because the price of cotton did not fall as much as other farm prices, and in part because the banks in New Orleans were well stocked with specie. The crisis was not a major cause of the Civil War, but as James Huston has shown, Republicans in the North and secessionists in the South made skillful political use of the crisis.

The advent of the National Banking System did not reduce the frequency of panics. The bond-security provision did assure people that their notes were ultimately safe, but deposits were backed only by fractional reserves and the loan portfolios of the banks.

The Crisis of 1873

The banks as a whole were strong in 1873; the overall ratio of specie and legal-tender notes to deposit liabilities seemed reasonably high, about 23 percent. But a potentially dangerous situation had developed. Banks throughout the country when pressed for cash had come to rely on deposits that they maintained in a handful of New York City banks. Reliance on New York was natural, since country banks often used New York banks as correspondents when completing interregional or international transactions. But reliance on New York had been intensified by provisions of the National Banking Act, which allowed country banks to count deposits in New York as legal reserves. The New York banks typically invested the surplus deposits of country banks in the New York call loan market. Call loans were short-term loans, payable on demand (when called), and secured by investments in stocks. Thus, a small pressure spread over a wide swath of country banks would be magnified in New York. New York banks would be forced to scramble for funds, and call-loan rates would rise, possibly sending stock prices into a tailspin. It was, moreover, a two-way street. A stock market crash could perturb the call-loan market and the New York banks.

This system was normally subject to strong seasonal fluctuations. In the fall, money would flow from New York to the interior to pay for crops, and then return over the rest of the year, and particularly in the spring, as farmers spent their earnings. In 1872 the fall stringency was severe, and the Treasury came to the aid of the banks by selling gold, thus partly replenishing the reserves of legal tenders that had been drained to the West. But worse was to come in 1873.

During the late summer of 1873 the experts who read the tea leaves found a number of reasons for believing that the fall crop-moving stringency would be surmounted as usual. Even unusually large withdrawals of legal tenders from New York City in the first two weeks of September were interpreted favorably: the crop-moving season would be extended over a longer period of time. But in the third week the crisis broke. It was precipitated by commercial and bank failures. The most damaging was the failure due to a large loan to the Northern Pacific Railroad of Jay Cooke and Co., the firm run by the famous financier of the Civil War. The stock market was closed for a time, and panic spread to the banking system – two trust companies and a national bank closed – and the New York banks experienced a rapid withdrawal of cash by correspondent banks.

For a time the New York City banks tried to meet all demands placed on them, but they soon ran short of reserves. The Clearinghouse then stepped in, issuing Clearinghouse loan certificates. A bank obtained them by depositing securities with the Clearinghouse, and used them in lieu of greenbacks to pay their debts to the Clearinghouse. The Clearinghouse banks also adopted a policy of pooling reserves.[5] Reserves, however, continued to decline. On September 24 the Clearinghouse banks adopted a policy of stamping checks with the words "payable through the clearing house." Thus, the Clearinghouse took charge of the paying out of reserves. Some withdrawals were now denied, although some depositors, particularly banks, could still get cash when they needed it. Partial suspension, which was quickly emulated in other parts of the country, seems to have worked fairly well. By November, the banking crisis had abated, and full payment in greenbacks was resumed.

The crisis did not leave a strong impression on the aggregate economic statistics. The money stock did not decline on an annual basis, although there was a decline of 0.6 percent between the third and fourth quarters of 1873. Christina Romer's estimates of real GNP show an increase of about 1.4 percent between 1873 and 1874, although Nathan Balke and Robert Gordon's show a decline of about 0.6 percent, and both series show increases in the following years. The National Bureau of Economic Research, however, dates a long recession from October 1873 to March 1879, and qualitative evidence suggests that railroads and some other industries experienced problems.

The crisis of 1873 produced considerable discussion in Congress about how to reform the banking system, but the results were meager, and they did nothing to prevent a recurrence. The main change was the establishment of a central agency in Washington for redeeming national banknotes (in practice the Treasury redeemed them in other cities as well). This encouraged banks to forward notes to the redemption agency, rather than pay them out again or send them directly to the issuing bank. Centralized redemption made national banknotes an even closer substitute for greenbacks. It also gave banks an incentive to remove worn notes from circulation – in the end the most important effect literally may have been cosmetic.

The Crisis of 1893

There was a minor panic in 1884, and a financial "stringency" in 1890, but the Panic of 1893 was severe. Again, unexpected bankruptcies sparked the crisis. The failures of the Philadelphia and Reading Railroad in February and the National Cordage Company early in May cast a pall over

---

[5] Both Clearinghouse loan certificates and pooling reserves had been used in 1860 and 1861.

the stock market, which collapsed on May 4. Bank closings in the West and Southwest mounted leading to withdrawals from New York City where Clearinghouse loan certificates were issued. The New York banks continued to pay out specie for a time, but declines in reserves led to a partial suspension of specie payments in August, with the rest of the banking system following suit in short order.

The suspension brought the crisis home to the public by creating a shortage of cash for completing small transactions. Various substitutes were pressed into service: Clearinghouse certificates issued in small denominations, cashiers checks, and pay checks. But the suspension also had a salutary effect when compared with the situation that had immediately preceded it. The continual withdrawal of reserves had forced the banks to contract loans. Suspension halted this process.

The depth of Treasury's commitment to maintain gold payments was an important element determining confidence in the banking system. The threat was silver. In 1878 Congress had passed the Bland-Allison Act requiring the Treasury to purchase and coin between $2 and $4 million worth of silver per month. In 1890 it had passed the Sherman Silver Purchase Act, requiring the purchase of 4.5 million ounces per month, about twice the amount purchased under the Bland-Allison Act, to be paid for with legal-tender notes, known afterwards as the Treasury Notes of 1890. This was a compromise measure, designed to "do something for silver" without going all the way to free and unlimited coinage. But it created fears that the silver forces were growing stronger. Speculators bought gold or gold-denominated assets, and foreign investors viewed the United States with suspicion.

In April 1893 the gold reserve fell below what was deemed to be the magic figure of $100 million.[6] Although the extent to which this development affected the course of the crisis is debatable, it was widely believed at the time that fears about the Treasury's ability to maintain gold payments were a cause of the distrust of the financial system. So President Cleveland pushed for repeal of the Sherman Act. There was a hard fight in the Senate, and it was not until October 1893 that repeal was finally achieved. The attention of the Congress had focused entirely on the Silver

---

[6] When the United States returned to the gold standard in 1879, Treasury Secretary John Sherman suggested that a minimum gold reserve of $100 million would be adequate to maintain continuous redemption of outstanding Treasury obligations. Over time this figure became a symbol of the Treasury's ability to maintain gold convertibility.

Purchase Act, so no other legislation attempting to minimize the likelihood of future panics was forthcoming.

The suspension lasted throughout the month of August and into the first days of September. But while the banking panic ended quickly, the bad times lingered. There was a contraction from January 1893 to June 1894, followed by a weak recovery from June 1894 to December 1895, and then a further contraction from December 1895 to June 1897. Part of the problem was the continuing pressure on the gold reserve and the resulting fear of suspension. The Treasury was forced repeatedly to sell bonds to replenish the reserve. In one instance the Treasury sold $62,000,000 to a syndicate headed by J. P. Morgan and August Belmont, who pledged in return not to withdraw gold for six months. This transaction may have saved the gold standard, but it proved a major political embarrassment.

Unlike the downturn following the crisis of 1873, this one left a strong mark on aggregate economic statistics. The stock of money declined about 4 percent between 1892 and 1893, grew at a rate sufficient to make up this loss by 1895, and then declined 2 percent, leaving the stock of money lower in 1896 than it had been four years earlier. Bank suspensions were high; the worst year was 1893, when 496 suspended. Both Romer's and Balke and Gordon's real GNP series show declines from 1892 to 1893 and from 1893 to 1894. Both series rise in 1895, but then they diverge, Romer's showing an increase in 1896, and Balke and Gordon's, a fall. Unemployment was high throughout the "Great Depression" of the 1890s, and in certain industries and rural areas the distress was acute. Real factors may have played a role in causing the depression of the 1890s. But it is hard to believe that the depression would have been as severe as it was had the decline in money and credit been avoided.

More controversial is whether the distress in the banking system made itself felt primarily through its effect on the allocation of credit or through its effect on the stock of money. Charles Calomiris and Glenn Hubbard have argued that financial crises were important because they damaged the ability of the banks to allocate credit efficiently. Bank policies regarding collateral made it difficult for some borrowers to get loans, even when there were good reasons for thinking their projects would succeed. Michael Bordo, Peter Rappoport, and Anna J. Schwartz, on the other hand, have concluded that the decline in the stock of money (or its rate of growth) was the key factor. They show that business loans, as distinct from stock market loans, remained remarkably stable over the course of the business cycle.

The continuing agitation for silver also may have intensified the depression by creating uncertainty over the price level, as shown recently by Colleen Callahan, and inhibiting long-term investment, particularly by foreign investors. Indeed, Friedman and Schwartz concluded that "either acceptance of the silver standard at an early stage or an early commitment to gold would have been preferable to the uneasy compromise that was maintained."[7]

The Crisis of 1907

The direct effects of the crisis of 1907 on prices and output were limited compared with the crisis of 1893, but the effects on the legislative framework far exceeded those of 1893 or earlier crises. The collapse was precipitated by several events. In March 1907 there was a tremendous crash on Wall Street, known as the "Rich Man's Panic." Early in October problems in several New York trust companies came to light. On October 22 the Knickerbocker Trust, the second-largest trust company in the United States, was forced to suspend, spreading fear throughout the country, and producing substantial cash withdrawals from New York City. The Treasury stepped in by depositing $25 million in the New York banks, and J. P. Morgan organized a pool of $10 million. But these efforts proved insufficient. On October 26 the Clearinghouse issued loan certificates, and the New York banks partially suspended, an action that was quickly adopted in the rest of the country. Suspension lasted longer than during previous crises; it was not until early January 1908, and after considerable imports of gold, that specie payments were fully resumed. As in previous crises, various substitutes for cash – clearinghouse loan certificates in convenient denominations, special cashier's checks, pay checks, and so on – were pressed into service. The cash shortage undoubtedly disrupted business, but suspension also prevented further contraction of money and credit and bought time to accumulate gold.

The economic contraction from May 1907 to June 1908 might well have occurred in any case, but it was probably intensified by the banking crisis. The stock of money fell 6.8 percent from the second quarter of 1907 to the first quarter of 1908. Romer's estimate of real GNP falls 4.3 percent

---

[7] Friedman and Schwartz, *A Monetary History of the United States, 1867–1960* (Princeton, 1963), 134.

from 1907 to 1908, and Balke and Gordon's estimate falls 5.6 percent. The recession created considerable pressure for reform of the financial system. One reason for its greater legislative impact, paradoxically, was that the gold standard seemed to be in good working order when the crisis began. It was clear that the problem lay with the banking system rather than the monetary standard.

The Federal Reserve System

Various proposals for monetary reform had been circulating for some time, but which one to adopt was far from clear. In May 1908 the Aldrich-Vreeland Act was approved. The act permitted groups of banks acting in concert during emergencies to issue non-redeemable currency, subject to the requirement (enforced by taxes) that the issues be withdrawn rapidly once the emergency had passed. In essence, the law legalized and regulated what had happened spontaneously during the crisis of 1907. As has been emphasized recently by Richard Timberlake, and Gary Gorton and Donald Mullineaux, clearinghouses, originally established to provide a convenient place to settle accounts among banks, had begun to take on some of the functions of a central bank, including lender of last resort. During panics clearinghouses, as we have seen, issued loan certificates to member banks (in exchange for selected assets) that were used in place of specie to cover adverse clearing balances. During the crisis of 1907 smaller denomination clearinghouse certificates had been given to the public in place of legal tender. How far this evolution toward a private lender of last resort might have gone cannot be known. But in its one trial at the outbreak of World War I the Aldrich-Vreeland currency, the hybrid public-private version of the system, worked well.

In terms of its long-run impact on the financial system, however, it was not the provision for an emergency currency but another section of the Aldrich-Vreeland Act that was to prove the most important. This section provided for a National Monetary Commission to investigate the monetary system and make recommendations for reform. The output of the commission was impressive: some twenty three studies by the leading students of money and banking reviewing the monetary institutions and history of the United States and many foreign countries, and a final volume of recommendations. The historical and comparative studies wisely avoided precise prescriptions for policy. But a common theme ran through them: the need for a lender of last resort. Oliver M. W. Sprague, the author of the now classic *History of Crises under the National Banking System*, for example, concluded that "Somewhere in the banking system of a country there should be a reserve of lending power, and it should be found in its central money market."[8]

The final volume, however, described a precise plan for legislative action. The Commission submitted its report in 1912. On December 23, 1913, Congress passed the Federal Reserve Act very much along the lines laid out by the Commission.

The act addressed banking panics by creating a new form of currency, Federal Reserve Notes, that could be issued rapidly to meet a sudden demand for cash. Federal Reserve Notes would be created when the Federal Reserve made loans to banks secured by various forms of bank assets. The list of "eligible securities," although it included a majority of bank assets, excluded speculative investments, such as call loans, in order to encourage banks to invest in the short-term, self-liquidating assets approved by the real bills doctrine. Federal Reserve Notes could also be created when the Federal Reserve acquired gold. Indeed, the law required that Federal Reserve Notes be backed 40 percent by gold. Thus, the act took for granted the continuation of the gold standard, which was then at the height of its prestige.

It was possible for the Federal Reserve to carry out its lender-of-last-resort function, despite the 40 percent gold-reserve requirement, by maintaining a sufficiently large excess reserve of gold, or by relying on its ability to attract additional gold during a crisis. But it was conceivable that a panic would be so intense, and so prolonged, that the Federal Reserve would be unable to supply all of the currency demanded without violating the gold requirement.

The Federal Reserve Act also provided that Federal Reserve Notes could be created when the Federal Reserve acquired government bonds in the open market. At the time this was probably not expected to be a major vehicle for the expansion of the note issue. The Federal Reserve Act established a banker's bank; it was prohibited from making loans to businesses, other than banks, or to private individuals, thus insulating it from the charge of political favoritism that had plagued the Second Bank. Perhaps even more important, there was no termination date in its charter. The organization of the Federal Reserve differed in another important way from the First and Second Banks, and from European models. The nation was

[8] O. M. W. Sprague, *History of Crises Under the National Banking System* (Washington, DC, 1910), 318.

divided into twelve federal reserve districts, and member banks held their reserves in their district banks; a board of governors exercised overall supervision. The struggle between the board of governors and the district banks, particularly the Federal Reserve Bank of New York, which initially exercised considerable independent authority, would bedevil the system in years to come.

The Federal Reserve was also given supervisory powers, to see that banks were in compliance with reserve requirements and other regulations. Characteristically, the new bureaucratic structure was added on top of the old. Member banks were also regulated by either the Comptroller of the Currency if they were national banks, which were required to join, or by state banking authorities if they were state banks, which could join if they chose.

The Federal Reserve was based on a number of potentially conflicting ideas. Maintenance of the gold standard implied reducing money and credit when economic expansions produced balance of payments deficits. The real bills doctrine implied, on the other hand, increasing money and credit when economic expansions increased the demand for credit. And performing the role of lender of last resort implied, at times, expanding money and credit when Federal Reserve and bank gold reserves had been depleted. But so long as the gold standard reigned supreme, maintenance of convertibility provided an overriding goal. No sooner had the act been passed, however, than World War I made the crucial underlying assumption irrelevant by undermining the gold standard. The battles to be fought in the years to come would take place on battlefields for which the Federal Reserve was totally unprepared.

GROWING FINANCIAL SOPHISTICATION

Although the banking system was still the heart of the financial system in 1914, rival institutions had developed to cope with new demands and to escape from regulatory constraints. One important demand was for institutions that issued long-term deposits and invested in long-term assets such as mortgages on real property or bonds issued by governments or corporations, enabling these institutions to pay a higher rate of interest on the deposits. Commercial banks found it difficult to meet this demand because they had to invest a considerable portion of their assets in short-term assets to match their short-term liabilities, and to satisfy legislation flowing from the real bills doctrine. This demand was met by the rapid development of the savings banks and trust companies.

Savings Banks

Mutual savings banks, modeled after the British "friendly" society, were initially intended to be charitable institutions, to be run by a group of eminent trustees for the benefit of working poor. The first were established in Boston and Philadelphia in 1816. The success of the early mutuals in attracting deposits soon led to the establishment of savings banks for business purposes. In their early years many invested heavily in bank stocks (one of the few widely traded securities), but after the crisis of 1837 and the large number of bank failures that followed, this was prohibited.

The mutuals were concentrated in the Northeast. In the West and South the building and loan society gradually came to fill the same role. Initially, these were mutual societies to which shareholders contributed with the understanding that they could later borrow money for building a home. But as part of the so-called Dayton (Ohio) plan they began accepting deposits and resembling the mutual savings banks of the Northeast. From 1887 to 1897 a new version of the building and loan appeared, the Nationals. As the name suggests, these institutions sought investors and made loans nationwide. They do not appear, however, to have been soundly managed. Expenses for selling shares were heavy, and many of the loans taken had been rejected by local institutions. The failure of the Southern Building and Loan Association in Knoxville led to a run on the Nationals, and by 1897 most of them had been driven from the scene. Predictably, state supervision of building and loan associations was intensified after the fall of the Nationals, and the formation of the United States League of Building and Loan Associations, an important lobbying group, was hastened.

Provision was usually made in savings banks for a delay, at the option of the bank, in the payment of withdrawals. In normal times this was generally not invoked, and savings deposits could be withdrawn on demand. But in financial crises savings banks did exercise their option to require a delay, and in the late-nineteenth-century financial crises this saved them from getting caught in the maelstrom. From their small charitable beginnings in New England and the Middle Atlantic states, the savings banks grew into an important financial intermediary. In the latter part of the nineteenth century savings bank deposits typically averaged perhaps a third of all bank deposits.

Trust Companies

Trust companies were sometimes said to be savings banks for the rich, investing in long-term assets, and paying higher interest rates on deposits, than did commercial or savings banks. The growth of the trust business was relatively slow before the Civil War. The first trust company, according to one source, was the Farmer's Fire Insurance and Loan Co., established in 1822. The first company without "insurance" in its name was the United Trust Company established in 1853. Incorporations seem to have increased in the wake of the Civil War, perhaps because war debt created an important investment vehicle.

But it was not until the 1890s that trusts really began to hold substantial amounts of assets, and growth was even more rapid after 1900. In 1897 there were 390 trust companies, in 1900 there were 518, and in 1909, when growth seems to have leveled off, there were 1,504. In the latter year the capital of the trust companies amounted to 27 percent of the combined capital of state and national commercial banks; in the eastern states including New York and Pennsylvannia, 55 percent. The growth of the trust companies reflected, in part, regulatory constraints: they were a way around the restrictions placed on the investments of commercial and savings banks. But states had been willing to charter trust companies throughout the nineteenth century. The most important cause of their explosive growth at the turn of the century lay in their close association with the great investment houses and the marketing of industrial securities, which will be discussed below. First, however, let us look at a third intermediary coming into its own at the turn of the century.

Insurance Companies

Although the main function of insurance companies is protection against risk, insurance companies must also be financial intermediaries because premiums must be accumulated and invested before claims can be paid. When the century began marine and fire insurance were the main forms, and the industries supplying them were small. But as the century progressed the range of insured risks expanded, and the assets of insurance companies became a significant item on the national balance sheet. The history of the industry reflected the same interaction of innovation and regulation, the latter often the result of crises, that describes the evolution of commercial, savings, and trust banking.

Marine insurance developed rapidly with the expansion of the merchant fleet between the end of the Napoleonic Wars and the Civil War. The Civil War, however, led to a substantial setback from which recovery was slow; vessels were destroyed by Confederate privateers or transferred to foreign registry. Fire insurance also grew rapidly during the nineteenth century. Initially, many states prohibited companies chartered in other states from writing policies, but this changed abruptly in 1835 when a fire swept through the business district in New York City, forcing many local insurance companies into bankruptcy. Additional weaknesses were revealed by the great Chicago fire of 1871, and laws regulating fire insurance companies rose from the ashes.

Only a small number of life insurance policies were in existence in 1800, many of them issued by individuals, even though the no-doubt aptly named Corporation for the Relief of Poor and Distressed Presbyterian Ministers and Distressed Widows and Children of Presbyterian Ministers, had been organized in Philadelphia in 1759. Between 1800 and 1840 a number of well-capitalized stock insurance companies were founded. Then between 1840 and 1850 a number of mutual companies (owned by the policyholders) entered the field. The mutuals specialized in life insurance and marketed policies aggressively. The typical policy also changed. Earlier in the century, premiums had risen with age, now level premiums became the norm.

In 1868 the Equitable Life Assurance Society of the United States introduced tontine insurance. In addition to death benefits these policies provided for part of the premium to be invested in a pool that was divided among the surviving policyholders after a period of, typically, twenty years. In 1875 the Prudential Insurance Company of America introduced industrial life insurance – small policies for industrial workers with the premiums collected by company agents. Both tontine policies and industrial insurance proved popular, and the industry expanded rapidly. In 1854 life insurance companies held assets worth $11.4 million, less than 1 percent of commercial bank assets; by 1914 life insurance companies held 4.9 billion, about 18 percent of commercial bank assets.

Critics of the industry, however, alleged many abuses, including excessive spending by managements. In 1905 the Armstrong Commission investigation in New York led to increased regulation of the industry and the elimination of the tontine policy. Recent research by Roger Ransom and Richard Sutch, however, suggests that this may have been a case of muckraking gone amok.

The Stock and Bond Markets

The New York Stock Exchange is sometimes said to have originated with an agreement signed by a number of New York brokers in 1792. This document, however, established something closer to a guild than to a modern exchange. It was mostly concerned with maintaining fees and limiting access to the business; first things first. The number of securities available to be traded at that time, in any case, was limited mostly to government bonds and the stocks of a few private banks and the Bank of the United States. Slowly, however, the list of traded securities grew, with marine, fire, and life insurance companies taking a prominent place. In 1817 the New Yorkers adopted a set of trading rules, creating a true exchange, the New York Stock and Exchange Board.

In the early years of the century Philadelphia was the more important financial center; in fact, the New York exchange was modeled on the Philadelphia exchange. But in the following decades New York City emerged as the nation's financial center. Numerous factors have been cited to explain New York's dominant role, including the opening of the Erie Canal in 1825, which made New York a major center of the world's grain trade; the adoption of free banking in New York in 1838, which permitted a rapid expansion of its banking system; and the development of telegraphy in 1844, which undermined the regional stock markets and increased public interest in the market.

Throughout the antebellum period the new nation invested heavily in its infrastructure, and this was reflected in the stock market: canals, dock companies, gas companies, railroads, and mines in the 1850s made up an increasing fraction of listed securities. But the stocks of many industrial firms, the New England textile companies for example, were still tightly held. Industrial firms often turned to their own shareholders, informal networks of wealthy individuals, or private bankers to market shares.

The Civil War gave a major fillip to the stock market. Trading in government bonds, stocks, and gold took place at a fevered pitch. Numerous exchanges specializing in particular assets, or filling other niches, were started. One, the Open Board of Stock Brokers, adopted an important trading innovation. Traditionally stocks had been auctioned one by one, but on the Open Board trading was continuous. Brokers sought out specialists who remained in one spot on the floor of the exchange and made continuous markets in their chosen stocks. A merger between the Open

Board and the older exchange established the modern New York Stock
Exchange in 1869.

Perhaps more important in the long run, although less visible, was the
broadening and deepening of the market for securities produced by Jay
Cooke's effort to sell Civil War bonds. Cooke went beyond the traditional
networks of wealthy investors and sought out the middle class, which until
that time had invested mostly in their own businesses, in land, or in cash.
The habit of investing in financial assets remained after the war.

The power, prestige, and financial resources of the New York Stock
Exchange, and several lesser exchanges, continued to grow in the postbellum era. Again technological advances – the Atlantic cable in 1866, the
stock ticker in 1867, and the telephone in 1878 – increased interest in the
market, and increased the advantage of Wall Street over regional markets.
In the 1870s and 1880s attention centered on railroads, but in the 1890s
attention shifted to industrial securities. It was now possible for industrial
corporations to raise capital on an unprecedented scale. Giant firms in oil,
steel, and numerous other industries arose that could take advantage of
economies of scale.

But two developments associated with the growth of the stock market,
the linking of the stock exchanges and the banking system through the
call loan market and the imposition of demanding requirements for listing
a stock on the New York Stock Exchange, have troubled economic historians. The danger created by reliance on call loans has already been mentioned in the discussions of financial panics. Call loans were liquid in the
sense that if any one bank separately wanted to turn its loan into cash it
could do so quickly. But once a large fraction of banks and the brokers
became dependent on this market, disturbances in one market could be
quickly transmitted to the other, increasing the probability of a paralyz-
ing financial panic.

As the prestige of the New York Stock Exchange (and the value of a
seat on it) grew, it increasingly excluded the stocks and bonds of smaller
companies. These stocks had to be traded on other exchanges or on the
curb, thus fragmenting the market, and offsetting in some degree the benefits of new communication technologies. The exclusion of smaller companies, moreover, may have encouraged otherwise uneconomic mergers:
the stock of the combined firm might qualify for trading on the New York
Stock Exchange. But the selectivity of the exchange might have been
useful to investors who could look upon qualification for the New York
Stock Exchange as a seal of approval.

Investment Banking

The development of the stock and bond market went hand in hand with a growing role for the firms that specialized in marketing securities, the investment banks. Before the Civil War a number of important firms emerged that specialized in selling securities issued by canals, railroads, and state governments to European investors. Some were American firms with close ties to European bankers such as Prime, Ward and King that worked closely with Baring Brothers in London; some were branches of European firms, such as N. M. Rothschild and Sons. Their prime function was effecting the transfer of European capital to the United States, and they had little influence on the organization of the industries they served.

After the Civil War the role of investment bankers changed: increasingly they took an active role in the management of firms and concentrated on marketing securities in the United States. Indeed, by the end of the century foreigners were coming to Wall Street in search of capital. Jay Cooke and Co. was the transitional firm. After the War his firm underwrote railroads, and in particular the Northern Pacific. Initially, Cooke was successful in marketing its securities both at home, often to individuals who had invested in war bonds, and in Europe. But deflation undermined the value of Northern Pacific's securities, and its difficulties were the cause of the failure of Jay Cooke and Co. in 1873. In the ensuing depression many European investors were forced to liquidate and were reluctant to reenter the market for some time, furthering the reliance of American investment bankers on the American market.

In the 1880s and 1890s a number of firms that practiced aggressive, domestically oriented, investment banking rose to prominence, such as Kidder Peabody and Co., which was the first to underwrite American Telephone and Telegraph. But eventually two great financial empires tied to investment banking houses overshadowed the others: the "Standard Oil Crowd," an important component of which was the investment banking firm of Kuhn Loeb and Co., and standing at the summit of American finance, J. P. Morgan and Co.

J. Pierpont Morgan learned investment banking in part from his father, Julius Spencer Morgan, also a distinguished investment banker. The younger Morgan opened his own firm on Wall Street in 1862, and combined with a Philadelphia firm in 1871 to form Drexel, Morgan and Co. The firm became widely known for its reorganization of railroads, including that of the Baltimore and Ohio, the Chesapeake and Ohio, and the Erie. A combination of falling prices, hard times, and overbuilding had left many railroads bankrupt or on the verge of bankruptcy. Morgan offered quarreling holders of debt and equity a way out. Typically, bondholders accepted equity for part of their holdings and were assessed, along with the original shareholders, to raise working capital. But in exchange, bondholders saw Morgan's men placed on the board of directors, an assurance that the interests of bondholders would be protected from unscrupulous managers, and ruinous fare wars with their erstwhile competing railroads that were also undergoing reorganization. Shareholders saw their equity diluted, and they were forced for a time to give up their voting rights to a Morgan-appointed committee, but in exchange they avoided bankruptcy. Morgan's firm gained large commissions and enhanced power and prestige. "Morganization" of competing rail lines was thus a success for all parties except, perhaps, for the consumers of rail services who might have benefited, at least in the short run, from a continuation of the fare wars.

In the 1890s, as head of J. P. Morgan and Co., Morgan reached an unprecedented level of national prominence by refinancing railroads hard hit by the depression and underwriting the new industries and mergers of existing firms that were coming to dominate the economic landscape. He created a network of New York banks, insurance companies, and trust companies, and with these resources he was able to raise capital on a scale that dwarfed anything that had gone before. Edison Electric, International Harvester, Allis-Chalmers Co., and United Shoe Machinery Co. were among the firms that owed their existence to J. P. Morgan. His most spectacular deal was the formation of United States Steel Corporation, the first billion-dollar corporation, in 1901 (when a billion dollars still meant something).

But Morgan's power did not go unchallenged. The Standard Oil Crowd was Morgan's main rival. Combining the financial resources of the Standard Oil Company under John D. Rockefeller, the National City Bank under James Stillman, and the investment banking talents of Kuhn, Loeb and Company under Jacob Schiff, this group also financed mergers and brought a large number of industries within its domain. In an epic battle for control of the Northern Pacific Railroad in 1901 it fought Morgan to a draw. For a time it even seemed that Morgan might go under. In 1903 Morgan and Co. got caught with a large mass of securities in a falling market, but Morgan rode out the storm. And in the ensuing decade rivalry among the investment bankers gave way to cooperation; each firm carved out a niche with which it was content. But it was cooperation that left Morgan the preeminent American financier.

Why did finance capitalism, and men like Morgan and Schiff, play such a dominant role during this era? One factor, as pointed out by Lance Davis, was the American system of bank regulation: banks were barred from owning equities, and from branching across state lines. These regulations prevented them from playing the dominant role in corporate finance played by their less restricted European counterparts. The financial networks developed by Morgan, Schiff, and others, allowed them to bypass these constraints. Perhaps even more important, as Davis also notes, were new production technologies that created economies of scale that could be fully realized only by giant firms producing for a national and sometimes international market, and requiring unparalleled amounts of capital.

Historians continue to debate the net impact of the investment banking houses. Some see them as sources of monopoly that undermined competition and exploited the consumer to make great fortunes for the "robber barons" who ran them. Others see them as beneficent agencies that brought financial resources and institutional efficiencies to industries that would otherwise have suffered from "ruinous competition" (Morgan's phrase). Public criticism of the investment banks increased during the great merger wave of 1898 to 1902 and increased again after the crisis of 1907. A searching and critical investigation of the "money trust" by a congressional committee headed by Arsene Pujo in 1912 revealed the extent of interlocking directorates among American industrial firms and the investment banking houses. The investigation may have helped pave the way for the passage of the Federal Reserve Act, but it did not lead to regulation of the investment banks. For one thing, the findings of the committee were inconclusive; the extent to which having Morgan's men on the boards of competing companies actually affected industrial policy was not determined. And the death of Morgan shortly after the committee issued its report deprived the play of its chief villain.

THE FINANCIAL SYSTEM ON THE EVE OF WORLD WAR I

One could be forgiven in 1914 for being optimistic about the future of the financial system. The Federal Reserve, established after one of the most thorough and learned investigations in our history, stood ready to guide the growth of the system and serve as a lender of last resort. New York City rivaled London for dominance as a financial center. A complex system of bank regulation, it is true, fragmented the commercial banking system and reduced its flexibility. But investment bankers such as J. P. Morgan, nevertheless, had found the means to finance some of the world's leading industrial corporations. And Americans held more financial assets, of a more diverse type, than ever before. Such optimism, as will be seen, however, proved to be unjustified.

15

U.S. FOREIGN TRADE AND THE BALANCE OF PAYMENTS, 1800–1913

ROBERT E. LIPSEY

U.S. TRADE AROUND 1800

Trade was on the minds of the entrepreneurs who financed the first settlements in the Americas. They dreamed of riches – the kind that could come only from exploiting the natural resources of areas newly opened to European settlement and exporting the products. They did not envisage financing subsistence farmers or artisans or manufacturing settlements serving local markets.

As it turned out, the American colonies were, in their early days, heavily involved in exporting. They probably exported something like a quarter of their production in the early years of the eighteenth century (Gallman, and Lipsey, both in Davis, Easterlin, Parker, et al., 1972). By the end of the eighteenth century that export propensity had been cut in half. Thus, around 1800, something like 10 to 15 percent of U.S. output was exported (ibid., and Shepherd and Walton 1972, 44). To some extent, that decline in the export propensity could be attributed simply to population growth – larger countries tend to trade less in proportion to their output than smaller countries – but the decline in exporting was too large for much of it to be attributed to that cause.

Exports of domestic merchandise by the United States at the beginning of the nineteenth century were about 3 percent of world exports and 5 percent of Europe's exports at a time when the population of the United States was only about 0.5 percent of the world's population and 2.5 percent of Europe's (Bairoch, 1976a, 18). Thus in terms of exports of its own products per capita, excluding re-exports of products made by others, the United States was twice as trade-oriented as Europe, and more than five times as export-oriented as the world as a whole. The United States was also engaged as an intermediary in a variety of indirect "triangular" trades, especially with the nearby European colonies. If we measured the trade propensity by total exports, including re-exports, the U.S. ratios would be about twice as high.

American exports in the early 1800s were almost all natural resource products. More than three-quarters were the output of agriculture in 1803–07 and almost another fifth the output of forests and of the sea. Less than 5 percent were the product of manufacturing industries (U.S. Congress, 1884, table 3). The industry origin of American exports in these years was similar to that of thirty-five years earlier.

This almost total concentration of exports on natural resource products at the beginning of the nineteenth century, and the fact that it almost duplicated the export trade pattern of the mid-eighteenth century, contrasts with indications that the structure of production had already started to shift away from primary products. If Bairoch's (1982) very rough estimates are to be believed, the United States (or the area that was to become the United States) had a level of per capita industrial output far below the average world level, and below that of even China and India, in 1750. By 1800 it had reached a level above the average of developed countries and of Europe as a whole, behind only the United Kingdom, by a large margin, and Belgium and Switzerland by narrow margins. Thus, the structure of production seemed to be changing faster than that of other countries without altering the comparative advantage of the United States.

Most of the exports from the United States were destined for Europe (over 60 percent), about a quarter to Great Britain and Ireland. Those shares represented a considerable decline from the period around 1770 (over 70 percent to Europe, 57 percent to Great Britain and Northern Ireland alone). Almost all the exports not bound for Europe were destined for the West Indies (29 percent in 1768–72). New England's exports were largely to the West Indies, as were half the exports of the middle colonies, while exports from the southern colonies, the producers of rice and tobacco, went overwhelmingly to Great Britain. The southern colonies dominated exports to Great Britain in 1768–72 (almost 90 percent), the middle colonies, exports to Southern Europe (over half), and New England and the middle colonies, exports to the West Indies (three-quarters) (U.S. Bureau of the Census, 1975, Shepherd and Walton 1972, 94–95).

The southern colonies were the most dependent on exporting before the American Revolution. Their exports per capita were roughly twice as high as those of New England and the middle colonies. Imports per capita were much more similar among the regions, almost identical between New England and the middle colonies on the one hand, and the southern colonies on the other (Shepherd and Walton, 1972, 113).

A distinctive feature of U.S. trade at the turn of the century was the exceptionally high share of re-exports in total exports. Over half of exports consisted of re-exports, as opposed to exports of U.S. merchandise, in almost every year from 1796 through 1808, until the Embargo (U.S. Bureau of the Census, 1975, Series 190–192). This enormous re-exporting activity was a consequence of the European wars following the early 1790s, in which Great Britain and France each attempted to block the other's trade with its colonies. The effect "was to throw into our hands the greater part of the colonial carrying trade of the world – an economic prize for which European nations had been fiercely struggling for nearly two centuries" (Callender, Introduction to chapter 6).

The valuable articles of colonial produce, such as sugar, coffee, spirits, cocoa, indigo, pepper, and spices of all kind, were carried by them, either directly to Europe, or brought to the United States, and from thence exported in American vessels. . . . The manufactures of Europe, and particularly those of Great Britain, as well as the manufactures and produce of the East Indies and China, were, also, imported, and again exported in large quantities, to the West Indies, South America and elsewhere. (Pitkin, as quoted in Callender, 240–41)

The United States not only accounted for a disproportionate share of merchandise trade but also was heavily involved in the export of shipping services. Earnings on ocean freight were about 30 percent of export earnings during the five years around 1800. The revenue from shipping was larger than from exports of any commodity.

Imports of merchandise almost always exceeded exports at the beginning of the nineteenth century. The negative trade balance was more than offset by large freight earnings, but the United States had negative net balances on account of other services, such as insurance and interest. The interest item reflected the accumulated net current account deficit of earlier years, although during the quinquennium around 1800, there was a small net outflow of capital from the United States (North, 1960).

Wilkins (1989, 48, 646) estimated that America's long-term foreign obligations in 1803 were $65–70 million or more. These included foreign holdings of federal debt (almost $5 million) plus over $15 million in holdings of corporate stock, particularly stock in the Bank of the United States.

If Wilkins is correct that North had underestimated the foreign debt of the United States, the estimates of interest payments and the current account deficit mentioned above are also too low.

THE GROWTH OF TOTAL U.S. TRADE

The U.S. Share of World Trade

As the nineteenth century began, U.S. trade was a minor part of world trade. Over the course of the century, that part grew until, in 1900, U.S. exports were 15 percent of world exports (see Table 15.1). Some of that increase simply reflected the growth of the U.S. population from about a half percent of that of the world in 1800 to around 5 percent in 1900 and 1910.

The share of American domestic exports in the total of world export trade was far above the U.S. population share and probably well above the U.S. share in world output throughout the nineteenth century. In other words, the United States was more export-oriented than the average country. The export share relative to the world rose throughout the nineteenth century and then receded a bit before World War I.

Table 15.1. *United States as percentage of world exports and population*

	Exports	Population
1800	3.2	0.5
1860	9.8	2.5
1870	7.9	
1880	13.2	3.6
1900	15.0	4.8
1910	12.3	5.3
1913	12.9	

Sources: U.S. Bureau of the Census, *Historical Statistics of the United States, Colonial Times to 1970* (Washington, DC, 1975); Paul Bairoch, *Commerce Extérieur et Développement Economique de l'Europe au XIX Siècle* (Paris, 1976); Angus Maddison, "Growth and Fluctuations in the World Economy," *Banca Nazionale del Lavoro Quarterly Review*, 15 (1962).

The disparity between the U.S. share of world exports and its population share was steadily reduced over the 110 years. Relative to Europe, the disparity was much smaller, but it, too, fell through the nineteenth century, until it disappeared in 1910, with the United States at about 20 percent of Europe's exports and population. Thus by that time there was no difference from Europe with respect to the degree of orientation toward exports.

The comparison of U.S. trade with world trade can be made also for total trade measured by the sum of exports and imports (see Table 15.2). Since U.S. imports were not rising as fast as U.S. exports, as the U.S. reduced its foreign borrowing relative to its trade, the combined share leveled off earlier, before the end of the century. At its peak, the U.S. trade share was something around twice the U.S. share of the world's population.

Whatever the measure used, the trend of U.S. trade during the nineteenth century was one of increasing importance in the world market, particularly for U.S. exports. That growth in importance in trade reflected in large part the rising size of the United States in terms of population and

Table 15.2. *United States as percentage of world exports and imports*

1800	5.3
1820	6.5
1830	5.8
1840	7.2
1850	7.8
1860	9.7
1870	8.2
1880	10.7
1889	9.7

Note: U.S. domestic exports plus imports for consumption (imports passing through customs directly from abroad plus imports passing through customs from bond). For years when imports for consumption are not available, we use general imports minus exports of foreign merchandise (re-exports) as a substitute, assuming no change in inventories in bond.
Source: Walt W. Rostow, *The World Economy: History and Prospect* (1978), table B-1, with data in £ multiplied by 4.495, and Bureau of the Census, *Historical Statistics*, Series U191 through U194.

production, particularly the latter as U.S. growth in output per capita outpaced that of the rest of the world.

Total Trade and Output

The proportion of U.S. output that was destined for foreign markets went through some wide annual swings before the European peace settlement in 1815. However, aside from a few years of embargo and war, the main trend in the ratio of exports to aggregate U.S. output in current prices was a decline from the 10–15 percent of the 1790s and the much higher levels of the end of the colonial period (see Table 15.3). For the 100 years following the Napoleonic Wars the average decade ratios ranged only from about 5.5 to 7 percent. The lowest export proportions were around 1830 and in the 1850s and the highest, after the early period, were in the twenty years after 1890. The ratios for 1793 to 1860 are lower than those of the colonial period not only because trade declined in importance but also because these national output measures in the denominator include more non-market output – farm improvements and home manufacturing – than earlier and later output measures. By their nature, these forms of output are not likely to be exported. They declined from 15–20 percent to 7 or 8 percent of conventionally measured output between 1800 and 1860. Thus a conventional output measure would show some continued decline in the trade share in the early 1800s.

The ratio of exports to GNP in constant dollars tells something of the same story of lower dependence on export markets in the nineteenth century than earlier. In any case, the greatest dependence on export markets for the U.S. economy as a whole had ended before the nineteenth century began, and certainly before the 1820s.

The U.S. dependence on imports was even greater than on exports in the period around 1770, perhaps a third of the colonies' production or consumption. During the first half of the nineteenth century the import ratio was above the export ratio, especially in the early years, but imports fell below exports after the 1870s as the United States turned from capital importer to capital exporter.

In real terms, imports fell even more than exports relative to the GNP, but they followed the same path of decline to 1829–38 and then a recovery. The highest dependence on imports, in real terms, was just before the Civil War, after which the ratio fell by about a third.

One way to interpret the trade–output ratios is to think of growth in

Table 15.3. *U.S. merchandise exports and imports as percentage of GNP*

	Current dollars		1860 Prices	
	Exports	Imports	Exports	Imports
Early years				
1770	15–20	NA	NA	NA
1790–1800	10–15	15–20	NA	NA
1793–1860[a]				
1793	NA	NA	9.0	
1800	6.8	8.4	6.0	6.4
1810	4.9	5.6	6.1	4.5
1820	6.3	8.0	4.5	4.6
1830	5.3	6.1	5.4	4.9
1840	5.9	6.1	6.0	5.8
1850	5.8	6.6	6.3	7.5
1860	6.3	6.7	6.1	6.7
1834–1913[b]				
1834–1843	6.2	6.7	6.3	6.4
1839–1848	5.9	5.8	6.7	5.8
1849–1858	5.6	6.6	6.3	7.7
1869–1878	6.2	6.3	6.8	7.0
1879–1888	6.7	5.7	5.7	5.8
1889–1898	6.9	5.7	6.5	5.6
1899–1908	6.8	4.5	6.4	5.0
1899–1908	6.7	4.6	5.2	4.0
1904–1913	6.3	4.7	4.8	4.3

Note: [a] GDP data are the "broad concept" from an unpublished work by Thomas Weiss. Trade data are 5-year averages around the reported year, except for 1810, which is a 3-year average (1809–1811), and 1860, which is a 3-year average (1858–1860).

[b] Gallman GNP data, 1834–1908, and Kuznets GNP data, 1899–1913. GNP estimates from Romer, *Journal of Political Economy*, 97 (1989) and Balke and Gordon, *Journal of Political Economy*, 97 (1989) do not alter these trends substantially.

Source: Trade data are from the Bureau of the Census, *Historical Statistics*, Series U191, 192, 193, and 194, and Robert E. Lipsey, "Foreign Trade," in Lance E. Davis, Richard A. Easterlin, William N. Parker et al., *American Economic Growth: An Economist's History of the United States* (New York, 1972). Data are for exports of domestic merchandise and imports for consumption. For 1790–1820, imports for consumption are estimated as general imports minus re-exports. National output data are from: Robert E. Gallman, "Gross National Product in the United States, 1834–1909," in Dorothy S. Brady (ed.), *Output, Employment, and Productivity in the United States after 1800*, Studies on Income and Wealth, vol. 30 (New York, 1966); Robert E. Lipsey, *Price and Quantity Trends in the Foreign Trade of the United States* (Princeton, 1963), for Kuznets data; and Thomas Weiss, "U.S. Labor Force Estimates and Economic Growth, 1800–1860," in Robert E. Gallman and John Joseph Wallis (eds.), *American Economic Growth and Living Standards Before the Civil War* (Chicago, 1992) and unpublished estimates.

trade that is no faster than growth in output as representing "passive" trade behavior. Growth in trade more rapid than that in output, leading to a rise in the trade–output ratio, can be thought of as "active" or even "aggressive" trade behavior. Most of the period appears to be characterized by passive trade behavior in this sense, but there was a fairly long stretch of years, from the 1850s through the 1890s when American exporting became more aggressive, and each decade saw some rise in the export ratio. However, no such trend appears in the constant price series; the trend in the current price ratios reflects a rise in export prices relative to domestic prices in these decades.

THE U.S. BALANCE OF PAYMENTS AND CAPITAL FLOWS

For most of the period from the inauguration of George Washington to the end of the nineteenth century, the United States imported more merchandise than it exported. Only in the last three decades of the century did exports exceed imports, and that export surplus continued into the twentieth century (see Table 15.4).

Until the Civil War, the deficit on merchandise trade was roughly offset by a surplus on shipping earnings, as the U.S. merchant fleet earned much more than the United States paid to foreigners for freight shipments. That source of income dwindled during and after the Civil War, and by the 1880s, the United States had become a net importer of shipping services.

Even while freight earnings were offsetting the deficit in the merchandise trade account, the other main current account item, interest, was always in deficit. The United States began its existence as a net debtor and all through the nineteenth century and up to World War I it paid out more in interest on its debts than it earned on its foreign assets.

The obverse of this excess of current account payments was the import of capital into the United States. Until an abrupt turn to capital exporting at the end of the century, the United States was a net borrower from foreign countries throughout the nineteenth century (see Table 15.5).

The cumulation of borrowing year after year meant that the United States was a net debtor throughout these years. Even at the beginning of World War I, despite fifteen or twenty years in which the United States was a net foreign lender most of the time, the country was still a net debtor to the rest of the world (Table 15.6).

Table 15.4. *Balance of merchandise trade and international freight and interest payments of the United States (annual averages: millions of dollars)*

	Merchandise	Freight	Interest
1790–1798	−11.1	13.3	−4.7
1799–1808	−18.8	27.9	−4.8
1809–1818	−21.2	21.2	−4.9
1819–1828	−5.7	10.0	−5.0
1829–1838	−20.8	8.2	−6.5
1839–1848	−1.9	11.4	−9.5
1849–1858	−10.6	11.8	−16.3
1859–1868	−9.5	6.3	−38.8
1869–1878	52.7	2.7	−87.7
1879–1888	132.4	−6.0	−89.2
1889–1899	240.8	−8.0	−127.6
1900[a]	640.0	−7.0	−114.0
1900[b]	754.0	−36.0	−99.0
1901–1913	570.2	−39.2	−71.5

[a] Comparable with earlier years. [b] Comparable with later years.
Source: Bureau of the Census *Historical Statistics*, Series U2, 3, 5, 9, 10, 13.

Table 15.5. *Net flow of capital to the United States (annual averages, millions of dollars, current prices)*

1790–1798	0.4
1799–1808	0.8
1809–1818	0.7
1819–1828	1.1
1829–1838	15.8
1839–1848	−2.8
1849–1858	16.7
1859–1868	61.8
1869–1878	73.8
1879–1888	78.4
1889–1899	27.2
1900[a]	−296
1900[b]	−218
1901–1913	5.5

[a] Comparable with earlier years. [b] Comparable with later years.
Source: Bureau of the Census *Historical Statistics*, Series U18-23.

Table 15.6. *Net liabilities (−) of the United States,
1789–1914 (unit: $ million)*

	From cumulation of net capital flows	From compilations of assets & liabilities
1789	−60	
1800	−83	
1803	−77	
1815	−80	
1820	−88[a]	
1830	−75	
1840	−261	
1843	−217[b]	−225
1850	−217[b]	
1853	−295	
1860	−377	
1869	−1,152	−1,540
1870	−1,252	
1876	−1,933	
1880	−1,584	
1890	−2,894	
1895	−3,288	
1897	−3,305	−2,710
1900	−2,501	
1908	−2,060	−3,875
1914	−2,086	−3,686

[a] After defaults of $50 million in 1816–19.
[b] After defaults of $12 million in 1841 and 1842.
Sources: Cleona Lewis, *America's State in International Investments*
(Washington, DC, 1938), 445, 560; Bureau of the Census *Historical Statistics*, Series U40, taken from North and Simon,
extended by cumulating Series U18 to U23. Estimates by Mira
Wilkins *The History of Foreign Investment in the United States to
1914* (Cambridge MA, 1989), table 3.1 (50–52) and 5.4 (147–
150) suggest somewhat larger net liabilities in 1803, by
perhaps $15 million, and in 1914 by about $340 million.

These figures on net U.S. liabilities say that foreigners had some net
claim on part of the wealth of the United States throughout the nineteenth
century. That is, foreigners' claims on U.S. wealth were larger than U.S.
claims on foreign wealth. One comparison of foreign claims with reproducible wealth suggests that the net foreign claims amounted to almost

Table 15.7. *Net foreign claims as percentage of value of domestic capital in current and 1860 prices, 1774–1900*

	Current Prices	1860 Prices
1774	12.9	12.8
1799	9.2	7.5
1805	5.7	4.1
1815	3.1	2.7
1840	6.2	5.5
1850	1.3	1.3
1860	1.2	1.2
1870	6.9	6.0
1880	5.3	5.4
1890	4.8	5.2
1900	1.6	1.6

Source: Robert E. Gallman, "American Economic Growth Before the Civil War: The Testimony of the Capital Stock Estimates," in Gallman and Wallis (eds.), *American Economic Growth*, tables 2.1, 2.2, and 2.4.

14 percent of wealth at the beginning of the century. That share fell to about 7 percent by 1850, 4 percent by 1900, and only 2 percent on the eve of World War I (Davis, 1972, table 8.12). More recent calculations by Gallman (1992) that raise the estimated value of reproducible wealth, but put a rather low figure on foreign claims in comparison to Lewis (1938) and Wilkins (1989), are summarized in Table 15.7. They describe a fall in the foreign claims from 13 percent of domestic capital, excluding land, in 1774 to 9 percent at the end of the eighteenth century, and then some sharp fluctuations through the nineteenth century. These reflect not only inflows and outflows of capital and the rate of U.S. capital formation, but also the effects of U.S. inflation, which tended at times to reduce the ratio by raising the nominal value of U.S. capital.

There are several ways to view the role of these flows of financial capital in American development. One is as a source of financing for aggregate capital formation, permitting faster accumulation of capital than would have taken place if only domestic financing had been available. On this basis, it is hard to suppose that imports of capital had a great influence on the rate of development during most of the nineteenth century. The capital

Table 15.8. *Changes in international claims on the United States and net inflows of capital as percentage of changes in domestic capital stock and gross domestic capital formation*

	Change in international claims as percent of change in domestic capital stock (Gallman)		Net inflow of capital as percent of gross domestic capital formation (Edelstein)
	Current Prices	1860 prices	1860 prices
1774–1799	8.0	4.8	
1799–1805	−1.9	−4.3	
1805–1815	−0.6	−2.7	
1815–1840	11.7	7.2	
1834–1843			6.2
1839–1848			−2.8
1840–1850	−6.5	−6.0	
1844–1853			3.1
1849–1858			3.4
1850–1860	1.2	1.1	
1860–1870	16.0	23.3	
1869–1878			4.9
1870–1880	1.0	4.3	
1874–1883			−0.5
1879–1888			3.5
1880–1890	4.2	5.1	
1884–1893			5.6
1889–1898			1.8
1890–1900	−7.9	−6.9	
1894–1903			−3.1
1899–1908			−1.8

Sources: Gallman, "American Economic Growth," tables 2.1, 2.2, and 2.4; Michael Edelstein, *Overseas Investment in the Age of High Imperialism* (New York, 1982), table 10.1, cols. 1 and 3.

inflows or changes in net foreign obligations were rarely more than 6 percent of gross capital formation or of changes in the domestic capital stock of the United States (see Table 15.8). The major exceptions were 1815 to 1840 and the period including the Civil War, 1860 to 1870, when the main foreign investment was in federal government bonds. Edelstein has suggested that U.S. borrowing from foreign countries rose when U.S. capital formation surged; borrowing tapered off as U.S. saving, rising more gradually and steadily, caught up with capital formation. Thus, investment from abroad accommodated the large spurts in the demand for capital that characterized the rapidly growing economy.

There may have been other roles for borrowing from abroad. One might have been to supply funds for particularly risky forms of capital formation at a lower interest rate than would have been required by domestic lenders. Another might have been to supply funds when, in the face of heavy demands by rapidly growing sectors, U.S. domestic lenders' needs for diversification of risks made them reluctant to offer sufficient financing to these sectors. Another interpretation is that U.S. railway and government securities, relatively safe and requiring less local knowledge than investment in smaller-scale enterprises in agriculture, mining, and manufacturing, tended to be sold overseas, while domestic suppliers of capital invested in the riskier, but more profitable, sectors (Edelstein 1982, 237–38).

The bulk of foreign investment in the United States was portfolio investment rather than direct investment. That is, it consisted of purchases of bonds or, to a small extent, equities, that did not involve control over the enterprise receiving the capital. Just before World War I, about 80 percent of the stock of long-term foreign investment in the United States was portfolio investment; the same had been true for the flow over a long period (Edelstein 1982, 36 and 37). Governments and railways were the chief borrowers, and most of the financing was in the form of bonds rather than equities.

In 1789 it was public debt that was the main channel for foreign capital, and Wilkins (1989, table 2.1, 32), estimates that almost 30 percent was held abroad, mainly in France and Holland. That was clearly infrastructure financing, since it supported the establishment of the United States as an independent country. In 1803 foreigners also held a third of corporate stock, mainly of banks (Wilkins, 1989, table 2.3, 37). The Louisiana Purchase in 1803 added about $11 million to the total federal debt and the same amount to the federal debt held by foreigners, so that we can particularly describe this important jump in the size of the U.S. economy as having been financed from abroad.

Throughout the first half of the nineteenth century, almost all foreign financing went to governments, first the federal government and later, state governments, and to banks (Wilkins 1989, table 3.1, 50–51). Only after that did railroads become a major field for foreign capital, but federal borrowing during the Civil War far exceeded the total of other borrowing through the 1870s. We know more about British capital than about that of other countries, but that is not a great handicap because the British role was so large, over three-quarters of long-term foreign investment in the United States at the end of the nineteenth century and still 60 percent in 1914 (Wilkins 1989, table 58, 159).

Most of the foreign investment, whether for government or private companies, went to large, lumpy, social overhead capital projects, such as canals, railways, electrical utilities, and telephone and telegraph systems (Edelstein 1982, 39–41). Manufacturing enterprises were probably almost all too small to seek foreign financing by floating stock or bond issues, or in most cases, by any type of public financing, even from domestic sources.

After 1865 relatively little of the flow of new foreign financing went into government securities. From 1865 through 1914 over 60 percent of British portfolio investment flowed into transportation, almost entirely railroads. Manufacturing, utilities, mining, and finance and real estate each accounted for 6 to 7 percent, as did all levels of government (Wilkins 1989, table 5.9, 164). In 1910, 85 percent of British investment was in railroads, according to one estimate.

The likelihood that foreign investment was much more important in the flow of capital to the railroad sector than in U.S. fixed investment as a whole is suggested by the fact that the value of foreign investment in U.S. railroads in 1914 was about a quarter of the book value of railroad road and equipment (Wilkins 1989, table 6.1, 194, and Bureau of the Census, Series Q356). British investment alone was 16 percent of the book value in 1914 (Idem). Foreign holdings were estimated by Jenks to range from 20 percent to a third of the nominal value of U.S. railroad securities between 1873 and 1914 (Wilkins 1989, table 6.4, 198).

Since the United States was inferior to European countries in technology in a number of industries during the nineteenth century, it may seem surprising that there was so little inflow of direct investment, a natural channel for the exploitation of technological advantages. There were many instances of manufacturing enterprises set up by foreign craftsmen or entrepreneurs with special knowledge or skills. However, transportation and communication were so slow, by modern standards, that it was almost impossible to control a subsidiary enterprise from across an ocean. Under those circumstances, the transfer of technology and skills took somewhat different forms, particularly the migration of key personnel, often the owners, their children, or other relatives, to establish subsidiary enterprises or to manage them once they were acquired. The enterprises were frequently what Mira Wilkins (1989) referred to as "free-standing" enterprises, in the sense that while they were owned by foreigners, they were not subsidiaries of foreign companies. Such enterprises were likely over time to evolve into independent, domestic U.S. firms through the migration of their owners to the United States and their adaptation to American circumstances. The flow of financial capital was intertwined with a possibly more important flow of human capital.

Immigration is often thought of as a movement of labor, but it is also a flow of human capital. Movements of human capital are not tradition-ally included in balance of payments accounts, since no monetary payment is involved, at least when there is no slavery. However, the flow of human capital may have been more important to U.S. development than the flows of financial capital. In terms of numbers, immigration into the United States in each decade from the 1830s through the beginning of World War I ranged from about 5 percent to 10 percent of the number already in the country (Bureau of the Census, 1975, Series A 6, and C 89). Furthermore, most of the immigrants (a 50 percent larger proportion than in the pop-ulation as a whole) were between fifteen and forty-four years of age (Bureau of the Census, 1975, Series C 119, C 122–27, C 138, and C 141). They came to the United States with most of their rearing costs already incurred in their home countries and with a large part of their working lives still ahead of them.

CHANGES IN THE COMPOSITION OF U.S. TRADE AND THE COMPARATIVE ADVANTAGE OF THE U.S.

The Composition of Trade

The composition of American exports in the late eighteenth century and the beginning of the nineteenth century reflected the fact that American comparative advantage was based on the exploitation of abundant natural resources. The largest part of exports consisted of agricultural products, but products of the forest and of the sea were also important: 19 percent of the total in 1803–1810, already a large decline from the 28 percent of British continental colonies in 1770 (Bureau of the Census, 1975, Series Z294). Thus, the first great shift in export composition, as population moved away from the coast and as forest land was cleared for farming, was, within resource products, away from forest and ocean products toward those from agriculture. In the decades before the Civil War around 80 percent of U.S. exports were of agricultural products.

An indication of the shifts in importance of the sectors from which exports originated is given by Table 15.9. One of the trends is the shift away from forestry and fishing, responsible for almost 20 percent of exports in the first decade, already down from 27 percent in 1770, but for less than 7 percent before the Civil War.

There was some rise in the importance of manufacturing as a source of U.S. exports before the Civil War, but American exports were dominated throughout the period by agriculture. A more surprising fact is that despite the rise of manufacturing industry in the United States, discussed below, agricultural products were over 70 percent of total U.S. exports throughout the nineteenth century and a majority of exports up to World War I.

Within agriculture, the first half of the century saw the decline of tobacco, the great colonial staple, and its replacement by cotton, which alone accounted for half or more of exports from the 1830s to the beginning of the Civil War. Cotton remained important for the rest of the century, and in the years up to World War I, was still around a quarter of the value of all exports.

A different view of changes in the composition of trade is provided by broad economic classes of goods. Before the Civil War, the United States was mainly an exporter of raw materials and foods. Raw materials alone were 60 percent or more of exports, food exports were about 20–25 percent, and semi-manufactures and finished manufactures accounted for the rest, with the finished goods rising in importance and the semi-manufactures declining (see Table 15.10).

The period after the Civil War saw very different trends. The share of raw materials fell to around 30 percent and food exports increased to replace them, reaching a peak importance of over 40–45 percent in the last two decades of the nineteenth century and then declining to about a quarter just before World War I. Thus raw materials and foods together remained overwhelmingly predominant in exports almost until the eve of World War I, at 80 percent or close to it through the 1880s, and three-quarters of the total through 1908. The changing comparative advantage of the United States can be described by a comparison of the role of resource products in exports as compared with imports. By Vanek's (1963) definition of resource products (crude materials and crude foods) the share of these products in exports fell from four times that in imports to less

Table 15.9. *Composition of U.S. exports, by broad commodity categories, 1770 and 1803–1913* (percentages)

| | | Products of | | | | | | | |
| | | Agriculture | | | | The forest | The sea | Manufacturing | Unknown or unclassified |
	Total	Animal products	Vegetable foods	Tobacco	Cotton				
1770	69.5	4.8	32.0	27.3	0	12.4	15.8	0.2	2.3[a]
1803–10	75.3	8.2	25.4	13.0	24.4	12.4	6.6	4.7	1.0
1811–20	83.2	4.4	35.4	10.9	31.6	9.1	2.8	3.5	1.4
1821–30	79.4	5.0	18.0	10.6	47.6	7.8	3.0	8.0	1.8
1831–40	81.4	3.4	10.2	8.3	58.0	5.8	2.9	8.6	1.3
1841–50	80.4	6.9	16.1	7.4	49.8	5.4	2.8	9.3	2.0
1851–60	80.4	NA	NA	6.1	53.2	5.0	1.5	12.1	
1869–78	81.5	13.1[b]	16.6[c]	4.9	40.2	4.0	NA	15.8	
1879–88	78.0	14.1	30.9	2.7	28.9	3.4	NA	13.7	
1889–98	72.5	16.8	27.6	2.5	24.6	3.9	NA	16.2	
1899–1908	59.7	14.4	20.0	2.0	23.2	4.8	NA	23.3	
1904–13	52.9	11.5	14.4	2.0	25.5	5.3	NA	27.3	

[a] Mainly products of mines. [b] Meats and meat products only. The corresponding figure for 1879–1888 is 20.4 percent.
[c] Wheat and wheat flour only. The corresponding figure for 1879–88 is 10.0 percent.

Source: 1770: Bureau of the Census, *Historical Statistics*, Series Z 294. Data refer to British Continental Colonies. 1803–1850: U.S. Congress, House of Representatives (1884), Table 2. 1851–1860: U.S. Treasury Department (1860), Table 25, p. 401. 1869–1913: Lipsey, *Price and Quantity Trends*, tables A-6, A-7, B-5, and C-5. Meats are Intermediate Class 106; animal products, 107 plus 114; vegetable foods, 104 plus 113 minus 107. Tobacco is minor class 025. Bureau of the Census, *Historical Statistics*, Series U 274–294. Meats and meat products are series U 285; wheat and wheat flour is series U 281, products of the forest are series U 286, U 288, and U 289.

Table 15.10. Composition of U.S. exports and imports by economic classes

Year	Total	Crude materials	Foods Crude	Foods Manufactured	Semi-manufactures	Finished manufactures
				Exports		
1820	100.0	59.6	3.8	19.2	9.6	5.8
1830	100.0	62.7	5.1	16.9	6.8	8.5
1840	100.0	67.9	4.5	14.3	4.5	9.8
1850	100.0	62.2	5.9	14.8	4.4	12.6
1850–58	100.0	60.3	7.0	16.1	4.1	12.6
1859–68	100.0	41.3	14.0	23.8	5.3	15.7
1869–78	100.0	44.1	15.2	20.0	4.7	15.9
1879–88	100.0	34.2	20.9	25.0	4.8	15.1
1889–98	100.0	32.9	17.1	25.9	7.0	17.1
1899–1908	100.0	29.2	12.7	21.7	11.9	24.6
1904–1913	100.0	32.3	7.7	16.8	14.8	28.3
				Imports		
1821	100.0	5.5	10.9	20.0	7.3	56.4
1830	100.0	7.9	11.1	15.9	7.9	57.1
1840	100.0	12.2	15.3	15.3	11.2	44.9
1850	100.0	7.5	10.3	12.1	14.9	54.6
1850–58	100.0	8.7	11.2	14.4	13.2	52.5
1859–68	100.0	13.0	13.9	17.7	13.1	42.3
1869–78	100.0	15.7	15.5	21.4	12.8	34.6
1879–88	100.0	20.6	15.4	18.5	14.5	30.9
1889–98	100.0	24.7	17.7	17.0	13.9	26.7
1899–1908	100.0	33.0	12.4	13.0	16.6	25.0
1904–1913	100.0	34.6	11.9	11.8	17.7	24.1

Source: Bureau of the Census, *Historical Statistics,* Series II-274–301.

than that in imports between 1820 and 1904–13, with the sharpest drop coming between the beginning and end of the Civil War. By a broader definition of resource products that includes manufactured foods such as flour and meat, the decline in the resource share was only about half as large, and the Civil War played less of a role. Since the value added in manufacturing is relatively small in these industries, the broader definition seems more appropriate. Nevertheless, the shift away from U.S. comparative advantage in resource products is very substantial, from an export share over twice the share in imports to virtual equality.

All this is not to say that manufactured goods other than foods played no role in exports. The share of finished manufactures started very low: a little over 5 percent in 1820 and still less than 10 percent in 1840, but reached over a quarter in the first two periods of the twentieth century, over 40 percent for finished manufactures and semimanufactures together. Their steady growth in importance was interrupted in the period from the Civil War through the 1880s as crude food exports pushed them aside for a time.

On the import side, the United States began its existence as an importer of finished manufactures, more than half the total at first. As these products grew in importance among exports, they declined among imports. By the beginning of the twentieth century the United States was no longer a net importer of finished manufactures from the rest of the world. The manufactures share in exports grew from a tenth of that in imports in 1820–21 to more than the share in imports by 1904–13.

The Industry Distribution of Trade Relative to Output and Employment

The share of agriculture in American exports throughout the nineteenth century did not reflect the transformation that was taking place more generally in the American economy. In the economy as a whole, agriculture was shrinking in importance throughout the nineteenth century. The share of agricultural output in conventionally defined GDP fell from almost half in 1800 to a third in 1860 (Weiss 1993). If farm improvement is included in agricultural output, and farm improvement and home manufacturing are included in GDP, the decline appears more gradual and concentrated in the period from 1840 to 1860. The general story of the period, strongly influenced by the assumptions made in calculating GDP, is that agriculture was already much more dependent on exports than other sectors of the U.S.

economy and that this dependence, as measured by the ratio of exports to output, increased substantially up to the beginning of the Civil War.

After the Civil War, farm gross product in current prices fell from 40 percent or so of GNP in 1869 to 20 percent in 1900 and only a little over 15 percent in 1913, when the agricultural share in American exports was still over half.

Estimates of the industrial distribution of the U.S. labor force also show the shift out of agriculture, particularly after 1810 or 1820. The contrast between the stability of agriculture's share in exports and the decline in agriculture's share of the labor force is not quite as strong in Weiss' (1992) estimates – the agricultural share fell from 74 percent in 1800 to 56 percent in 1860 – as in those of Lebergott (1966) and David (1967) – 83 percent to 53 percent over the same period. All tell a similar story, however, of a large rise in the ratio of exports per worker in agriculture relative to other sectors. Agriculture's share of the labor force continued to fall in the second half of the century, from a little over half at the beginning of the Civil War to 40 percent in 1900 and a little over 30 percent by 1910, according to Lebergott (1966). Rapid as the decline in the agricultural share of the U.S. labor force was from before the Civil War to the beginning of World War I, the fall was even steeper in some other countries. For example, in Great Britain, the largest market by far for U.S. exports, the share of the labor force in agriculture, forestry, and fishing fell by more than half between 1861 and 1911 (Mitchell, 1978, 61), and the share of agriculture alone fell by 60 percent from 1841 to 1901, after a decline of a third in the previous forty years (Kuznets, 1966, table 3.2).

The combination of the falling importance of agriculture in production and the labor force with its stubbornly high share in exports meant that American agriculture was becoming increasingly dependent on exporting. Agricultural exports were about a tenth of agricultural gross income in the early 1800s, reached more than a fifth and at times almost a quarter in the late nineteenth century, and were still close to a fifth through the beginning of World War I (see Table 15.11).

Thus the export dependence (exports divided by output) of the agricultural sector, always high relative to that of the country as a whole, went from being twice as high in the early nineteenth century to three and a half times as high during the late nineteenth and early twentieth centuries.

The United States retained much of its comparative advantage in trade in agricultural products far into the period of industrialization and far into the era when the United States was becoming a major industrial power.

Table 15.11. *Export dependence (exports/output) of the United States and U.S.
agriculture*

	Agriculture	U.S. total	Agriculture relative to U.S. total
1810	9.8	4.9	2.0
1820	14.2	6.3	2.3
1830	10.6	5.3	2.0
1840	12.3	5.9	2.1
1850	14.7	5.8	2.5
1860	15.3	6.3	2.4
1869–78	18	6.2	2.9
1879–88	21	6.7	3.1
1889–98	24	6.9	3.5
1899–1908	22	6.7	3.3
1904–1913	19	6.3	3.0

Source: 1810–1860: Table 15.3 and sources cited there and 15.9. 1869–1913: Lipsey,
"Foreign Trade", tables 14.1 and 14.2. All these ratios are overstated because the denominators are gross product originating, net of purchases of inputs from other industries, but
the numerators are export values with no deductions for purchased inputs.

One reason for this was that, in contrast to European countries, the United
States was increasing its land area even as its population, labor force, and
capital stock were growing. Between 1790 and 1850, the end of the period
of growth in area, the land area of the United States more than tripled.
The population grew more than twice as fast, but the enormous increase
in acreage kept the population–land ratio to less than a doubling. Over
some periods, such as 1800 to 1810 or 1820, or 1840 to 1850, the ratio
declined (Bureau of the Census, 1975, Series A-1 to A-5). From 1800 to
1850 the population–land ratio in the United States rose less than that of
Europe and Asiatic Russia, despite the far more rapid population growth
rate in the United States.

Despite the declining importance of agriculture, the second half of the
nineteenth century represented a climax in the development of American
agriculture and the agricultural export trade. Farm productivity and
output per capita grew more rapidly in the second half of the century than
in the first half, and the per capita output of agricultural products reached
levels never again attained in later years.

This rapid growth of farm output involved large expansions in the
farming area of the United States, even after the land area of the United

States itself stopped growing; the land added to farms in the fifty years after 1850 was almost twice the 1850 acreage. Many of the great increases in farm production were associated with the migration of production to new areas. In the first half of the century, cotton production migrated from Georgia and South Carolina to Mississippi, Louisiana, Texas, and Arkansas. After 1850 the main shift was the migration of grain and meat production from the Atlantic states and the Ohio Valley to the states west of the Mississippi.

These additions to farm acreage involved increases in the U.S. supply of agricultural products. At the same time, the supply of North American agricultural products, as seen from Europe, was increased further by a rapid decline in freight rates both within the United States and on shipments across the Atlantic.

Rapidly increasing U.S. production and falling prices, combined with the decline of transport costs, enabled American products to drive continental suppliers out of the British market for grains and meat during the years after the Civil War. Eventually the same transport-cost developments, as well as increases in U.S. domestic demand and the development of still newer producing areas such as Canada, Australia, and Argentina brought about the dethronement of the United States as the major supplier of agricultural products to Europe.

One of the countries that felt the impact of U.S. grain exports was Sweden. As Swedish grain exports declined in the face of American competition, many Swedish farmers gave up their less productive Swedish land resources and moved to the United States, especially to Minnesota and Illinois. There they combined their human capital acquired in Sweden, their farming skills, with the more productive American land and climate, and thus added to the U.S. grain supply still further (Blomström, Lipsey, and Ohlsson, 1988).

The significance of the foreign market was greatest during periods of rapid expansions in agricultural output. For example, although post–Civil War agricultural exports ranged between 20 and 25 percent of output, the increase in agricultural exports was about one-third of the increase in output from 1870–1874 to the peak in 1895–1899. Exports absorbed large proportions of increases in agricultural output when agricultural output was growing most rapidly. They sustained agricultural prices, which might otherwise have dropped sharply, given the relatively low domestic elasticity of demand for most agricultural products. In that way, exports encouraged the flow of resources (both land and settlers) into new agricultural production. The flow might otherwise have been cut off at an earlier point if large price declines had made new settlement unattractive.

The histories of individual commodities contain illustrations of two somewhat different roles for export markets. One is to supply the initial impetus for the settlement of new lands and for production of a commodity. The other is to provide a wider market and a higher demand elasticity, and in some cases a more efficient scale of production, for goods that are initially made for local, or domestic, markets. Several products fall into the first of the categories mentioned – those initially oriented toward the export market and always mainly dependent on it. Tobacco, for example, was produced largely for export from an early stage in its development. Over two-thirds of the crop was exported in 1800 and about three-quarters in 1810. Cotton was the epitome of an export crop. Eighty percent of the output was exported in the 1830s, when it first reached major importance. Even in the second half of the nineteenth century, when cotton and tobacco had long since declined in significance as parts of American agriculture, the proportion of the crops exported remained over 50 percent.

Important as cotton and tobacco were, they accounted for only about a sixth of agricultural output in 1860, and were responsible for less than a fifth of the growth of agricultural exports between 1860 and 1890, although they had provided more than 80 percent of the growth in U.S. agricultural exports between 1800 and 1860. Many of the other agricultural products – even those that were export items – fell into the second class described above. They began as essentially domestic products but became export goods as American production developed and became more efficient and as transportation costs fell. The export market was not the main impetus in the early stages of development. The course of the trade–output ratios of some of these other products, such as grains, was very different from those of cotton and tobacco. At no time did the grain export ratio reach 50 percent – domestic consumption was always the main destination of grain output. However, the export market did, at times, take a large fraction of increases in the output of grains; in the case of wheat, for example, almost 50 percent of the increase in output from 1869–1873 to 1894–1898 went into exports.

For some products, the export–output ratios are deceptive, because the output is sold to another domestic industry and processed before exporting. Exports of live animals were almost always a small fraction of farm output, but the export of meat products accounted for considerable proportions of the farm sales. In the case of pork products, for example, the rise in exports was at times over 50 percent of the addition to farm income from hogs, although exports never accounted for a high proportion of any year's output. Exports of the animals themselves were negligible.

Thus the situation for grains and meat products differed from that of cotton and tobacco, to judge from the lower export–output ratios and the wider fluctuations in these ratios. There was, probably, a steady increase in domestic demand with the growth of population and urbanization. Domestic demand was, however, inelastic. That is, a decline in price would not have produced a great increase in domestic food consumption; an increase in output, all thrown on the domestic market, would have caused severe price declines. Foreign demand, at least in markets in which there were other suppliers, to replace, was much more elastic. The United States could increase its sales abroad by replacing other foreign suppliers, and the American agricultural sector did not have to rely on raising the domestic consumption of foods by lowering prices.

Changes in supply were irregular, as in the case of cotton, and also involved large population movements to new farming areas. These population movements were, however, partly autonomous – that is, they were not simply a response to rising prices. If there had been no foreign market, but only the domestic market with its inelastic demand, a period of rising supply from new land settlement, if it would have taken place, would have brought severe price declines. Thus, the existence of the foreign markets and their openness to U.S. exports may have been an essential precondition for rapid agricultural expansion.

Aside from agriculture, primary industries that were important in exports at the beginning of the nineteenth century, and even more in the eighteenth century, were forestry and fisheries. Both were declining as export industries during the first half of the nineteenth century, and the fisheries had already declined considerably in the final years of the eighteenth. Products of the sea fell from 16 percent of exports in 1770 to 7 percent in 1803–1810 and 2 percent in 1851–1860; and forest products, which accounted for 12 percent of the value of exports in 1770 and 1803–1810, declined to 5 percent in 1851–1860.

The export–output ratio for forestry was probably above 15 percent in the early 1800s. In the case of fishing, exports in the 10 or 15 years before the Civil War appeared to be well over a quarter of the total value of output, and the ratio must have been higher in earlier years. It might well have been a third or more, especially for the whale fisheries, in the 1770s. The importance of export markets thus seems to have been great in a wide range of primary products, including those derived from forestry and fishing as well as farming.

Even in 1869, before the peak in farm exports, the export ratio for agriculture was more than twice as great as the ratio for manufacturing. The few manufactured products that were exported reflected the richness of American resources, rather than American capabilities in processing them. The export ratio was inflated by the figure for food products, mainly grain and meat products, in which a high fraction of the value entering the final cost, over 80 percent, had been added in agriculture rather than in manufacturing.

The petroleum and coal products group, also highly dependent on a resource base, was the only manufacturing industry in which exports played a large role in the early stages of development. Exports accounted for more than half of output in 1869 and 1879, and the share remained above one-quarter through 1914. In no other manufacturing industry, even those such as foods which were close to the primary production stage, did the ratios ever go above 15 percent. In 1869, 14 out of 18 manufacturing industries showed export ratios below 4 percent, and 10 out of 18 ratios were below 2 percent.

The dominance of export trade as a factor in U.S. growth was confined to agriculture and other primary industries. Within agriculture, exports played a major role in two different ways. In some products, particularly in the early decades, the foreign market was the main outlet and the main stimulus to the flow of resources and the growth of production. In others, especially in the second half of the nineteenth century, the foreign market eased the path of rapid growth in output by cushioning the effect of increased supply on price, an effect which we might expect to have been large in view of the presumably low price elasticities of domestic demand for agricultural products.

Another indicator of the trend in American comparative advantage is provided by sectoral export–output ratios, available only from 1869 on. While the trends are not very strong, they do differ in direction. The export ratio in agriculture reached a peak in 1879 and then mainly declined (see Table 15.12). The ratio in resource-oriented manufacturing also reached its peak in 1879, while for other manufactured goods the export ratio showed an upward trend, if any. Thus, in both agriculture and

Table 15.12. *Export–output ratios (percentage) for agriculture and manufacturing*

	1869	1879	1889	1899	1904	1909
Agriculture	9.8	18.3	13.2	13.2	11.0	10.5
Resource-oriented manufacturing[a]	8.2	12.1	9.8	11.3	9.4	7.3
Other manufacturing	1.6	3.3	1.9	4.3	4.6	4.2

[a] Food products, tobacco products, petroleum and coal products, and forest products.
Source: Unpublished compilations by Phyllis A. Wallace. See National Bureau of Economic Research, *Thirty-third Annual Report*, 1953 (New York, 1953). These ratios are lower than those of Table 15.11 because no deductions have been made here in the denominators for the purchase of inputs from other industries.

Table 15.13. *Export–output ratios (percentage)*

	1869	1909
Iron and steel products	1.7	4.2
Nonferrous metal products	1.7	9.3
Machinery	3.2	7.7
Transportation equipment	0.8	3.2

resource-oriented manufacturing industries, for which export trade was relatively important – over 10 percent of production at times – the importance of export markets was declining. Resources were becoming less of a basis for American exports. In other manufacturing industries, on the other hand, for which the resource base was less important, exports rose as a percentage of production. That was particularly notable in metal products, machinery, and transport equipment (see Table 15.13).

On the import side, the opposite changes were taking place. The shares of imports in domestic consumption were declining sharply for manufacturing as a whole and for almost every manufacturing group, the main exception being forest products (see Table 15.14).

The import share of goods consumed generally increased for the resource industries, agriculture, fishing, and mining. In manufacturing, imports provided sharply decreasing shares of most products. Thus the import data

Table 15.14. *Import–Consumption ratios (percentage)*

	1869	1909
Agriculture	5.8	8.3
Fishing	1.1	4.8
Mining	2.1	7.3
Manufacturing	14.0	5.9
Foods	19.8	9.5
Textile products	20.8	8.6
Chemical products	26.8	11.8
Forest products	3.6	3.6
Iron and steel products	12.0	1.4
Nonferrous metal products	20.1	9.2

give clear indications of the shift in American comparative advantage toward manufacturing and away from natural resource products.

The Commodity Composition of U.S. Trade in Relation to World Trade

The changes in U.S. comparative advantage after the Civil War can be illustrated by the comparison of the composition of U.S. exports with that of world exports. The U.S. share of world exports of primary products fluctuated over a fairly narrow range from the 1870s through the first years of the twentieth century and only fell somewhat in the decade or so before World War I (Table 15.15). The U.S. share of world manufactured exports remained at about 4 percent through the 1880s and then rose rapidly. Thus the shift in comparative advantage on the export side took place only at the end of the century despite the large shifts in U.S. production and employment mentioned above.

Another way of seeing this change is by comparing the composition of U.S. exports with that of world exports. The world ratio of manufactured product to primary product exports was quite stable at around 60 percent from the late 1870s through 1913. The U.S. ratio was far lower, reflecting the U.S. comparative advantage as a primary product exporter, remaining at about 16 to 18 percent from the 1870s through the early 1890s. Then, in the next twenty years, it rose to 40 percent, as the shift in production and employment from primary products to manufacturing finally began to be reflected in the composition of U.S. exports.

Table 15.15. *U.S. and world exports of primary products and manufactures*

	U.S. exports as percent of world exports		Manufactures exports as percent of primary exports	
	Primary products	Manufactures	World	U.S.
1871–75	NA	NA	NA	16.8
1876–80	15.4	4.0	61.6	16.1
1881–85	16.0	4.2	62.5	16.2
1886–90	14.4	4.1	63.4	18.0
1891–95	16.1	4.7	58.5	17.0
1896–1900	16.7	7.0	59.2	24.7
1901–05	16.0	8.0	57.7	28.9
1906–10	14.7	8.2	60.5	33.7
1911–13	13.8	9.2	60.7	40.5

Source: League of Nations *Industrialization and Foreign Trade* (Geneva, 1945), tables 7, 8, 9, and 13.

THE DIRECTION OF U.S. TRADE

Changes in the Destination of Exports and the Origin of Imports

American exports were directed mainly to Europe from the country's earliest days, and almost all that did not go to Europe were shipped to European colonies in the West Indies (see Table 15.16). Since much of the trade pattern in these years reflected the effects of the Napoleonic Wars and the British blockade of Europe, some of the West Indies trade may have been disguised trade with Europe or a temporary substitute for European trade.

The concentration of American exports on Europe increased over most of the nineteenth century, despite the growth of the industrial economy of the United States. That growth was presumably giving the United States the capability of being more of a competitor to Europe in manufacturing, and less of a supplier of raw materials and foods, but the increasing focus on Europe as a market lasted through the 1880s and was only sharply reversed after the 1890s. The same was true for the role of the United Kingdom, which grew as a destination of U.S. exports from less than a quarter at the beginning of the eighteenth century, despite the ties of lan-

Table 15.16. *Distribution of U.S. exports (including re-exports), by destination, 1790–1913 (percentages)*

	Total	Europe			America	
	Total	Total	UK	Germany	Total	Canada
1790–98	100	62	21	16	38[a]	NA
1799–1808	100	62	22	8	38[a]	NA
1809–18	100	69	28	3	31[a]	NA
1819–28	100	64	34	4	34[b]	3[c]
1829–38	100	71	43	—	27	3
1839–48	100	73	47	—	24	5
1849–58	100	73	48	—	23	8
1860	100	75	51	4	21	7
1869–78	100	81	54	9	17	6
1879–88	100	81	52	8	14	5
1889–98	100	79	48	11	16	6
1899–1908	100	72	36	14	19	8
1904–1913	100	66	30	14	25	12

Note: — = less than 0.5 percent.
[a] Total minus Europe.
[b] Total minus Europe, 36 percent; Asia; 2 percent.
[c] 1821–28.
Source: Bureau of the Census, *Historical Statistics*, Series U 317–334. According to Timothy Pitkin, *A Statistical View of the United States* (New York, 1816), 215–17, almost all the exports to "America" in 1795–1802 (36 percent of the total, excluding exports to "Florida and Louisiana") were to the West Indies.

guage and tradition, to over half in the 1870s and 1880s before falling back rather steeply after 1900. Some of the former U.K. share went to Germany in the late nineteenth century, and some of it went to the Western Hemisphere, as U.S. exports began shifting to less-developed areas of the world.

Europe was about as important as a source of imports as it was as a destination for exports in the early decades of the nineteenth century (see Table 15.17). However, for imports the trend in the European share was steadily downward, from two-thirds or so to about half before World War I. The decline in the British share, and also in the French share, was steeper, while the German share of U.S. imports doubled. The other areas increasing in importance as sources of imports were Canada and Asia.

Table 15.17. *Distribution of U.S. general imports, by origin, 1795–1913*

		Europe				America				Asia
	Total	Total	UK	France	Germany	Total	Canada	Cuba	Brazil	Total
1795–1801	100	52	35	2	5	38ª	0	NA	NA	9
1821–28	100	63	40	10	3	26	<1	9	2	11
1829–38	100	64	37	15	3	22	1	8	4	8
1839–48	100	67	38	19	3	25	1	8	5	8
1849–58	100	66	42	14	5	26	4	8	6	7
1860	100	61	39	12	5	29	7	9	6	8
1869–78	100	54	33	9	7	35	6	13	7	10
1879–88	100	55	26	11	9	32	6	9	7	11
1889–98	100	52	21	9	12	33	5	7	10	11
1899–1908	100	51	17	9	11	30	5	6	7	16
1904–1913	100	50	17	8	11	32	6	7	7	15

ªOf which 1 from "Florida and Louisiana" and 37 from the West Indies.

Source: Bureau of the Census, *Historical Statistics*, Series U335–352, and Pitkin, *Statistical View*, 212–14.

The underlying causes of these shifts were changes in foreign supply and demand, arising from the growth of population and production in other countries, and changes in American supply and demand arising from U.S. growth and the changing structure of production.

The share of American exports going to Europe was not very different from the share of Europe's own exports other than to North America, going to Europe (intra-European trade) during much of the nineteenth century, despite the extra cost of ocean transport for shipping goods from the United States (see Table 15.18). The similarity in export destinations, despite the differences in the stage of development between Europe and the United States, suggests that these shares were determined mainly by the weight of Europe as a market.

On the import side, the story was different; Europe remained the source of close to three-quarters of Europe's imports other than those from North America throughout the century, but Europe declined as a source of U.S. imports after the mid-century. Either the weight of Europe as a producer was falling or U.S. demand was shifting away from the mix of products suited to Europe's comparative advantage as American manufacturing industries developed and their products supplanted imported manufactures in the U.S. market. The stability of Europe's share of U.S. exports, at least until the 1890s or later, is linked to the stability of agriculture's

Table 15.18. *Share of Europe as a destination for exports to or origin of imports from*

	Europe		U.S.	
	Exports to	Imports from	Exports to	Imports from
	(except to and from North America)			
1800	84	NA	58	NA
1830	82	70	67	63
1840	76	NA	74	63
1850	77	72	76	71
1860	74	71	75	61
1870	78	76	81	55
1880	79	77	86	56
1890	76	76	80	57
1900	76	74	75	52
1910	73	70	65	52

Source: Bairoch, *Commerce Extérieur*, tables 21 and 22, and Bureau of the Census, *Historical Statistics*, Series U317, U324, U335, and U342.

share of U.S. exports, up to the 1880s or 1990s. Both reflect the decline of European agriculture and the continued American comparative advantage in agricultural products. The decline in Europe's share of U.S. imports is linked with the falling share of finished manufactures in U.S. imports, discussed earlier.

One way to judge the closeness of trade relations is to take account of the sizes of destination countries, by population, for example. Canada, which never accounted for a noticeable share of total U.S. exports, can be seen from the U.S. exports per capita to be much more closely tied to the U.S. by trade than many larger countries (see Table 15.19). By this criterion of trade "intensity," both income per capita in the importing country and a common language appears to be important positive influences, to judge by the high trade intensity with distant Australia and the intensity of trade with the United Kingdom relative to Germany and France.

On the import side, the intensity of trade, as measured now by U.S. imports per capita of origin country population (with United Kingdom = 100), was especially high with Canada, to a much greater degree than for exports (see Table 15.20). Mexico, Brazil, and Germany all exported more to the United States per person in the source country than did Australia,

Robert E. Lipsey

Table 15.19. *U.S. exports relative to population in importing country (UK = 100)*

	1870	1913
Canada	78	114
United Kingdom	100	100
Australia	36	80
Germany	20	58
France	14	25
Mexico	7.6	26
Brazil	7.2	13
Japan	0.4	8
China	0.1	0.4

Table 15.20. *U.S. imports relative to population in exporting countries (UK = 100)*

	1820	1870	1913
Canada	NA	186	230
United Kingdom	100	100	100
Australia	NA	24	51
Germany	5	21	67
France	11	22	47
Mexico	NA	6	75
Brazil	NA	49	73
Japan	NA	2	26
China	1	1	1

despite the common language. Propinquity, for Mexico and Canada, and the nature of each country's comparative advantage seemed to be more important in determining the sources of imports than were language or per capita income.

TRENDS IN THE U.S. TERMS OF TRADE

Aggregate National Terms of Trade

The ratio of export to import prices, or terms of trade of a country (sometimes referred to as the "net barter terms of trade") measures changes in the purchasing power of exports: the quantity of imports purchased by each unit of export production. A rise in the terms of trade is often viewed as a favorable development for a country, and referred to as an "improvement" in the terms of trade, although that interpretation is questionable at times. If a rise is the consequence of increasing demands for the country's export products, the effect on real income is favorable. However, if it is the consequence of a rise in costs relative to other countries, it is an unfavorable development, representing a decline in the country's ability to compete in international markets. That is true whether the rise in costs is the result of inflation or of productivity growth that is slower than in other countries.

It is widely believed that countries depending on primary products for export revenue tend to suffer declining terms of trade in the long run. Several reasons have been suggested as to why such a decline is to be expected. One is that price elasticities of demand for agricultural products are low. Increases in world production are not easily absorbed by gains in consumption and therefore result in relatively large price declines. Furthermore, income elasticities of demand for food are low; a rise in income leads to a less than proportional rise in food consumption. Food prices therefore are not lifted by increases in world income. In addition, it is said that agricultural products are sold in competitive markets and there is little opportunity for producers to exercise monopoly power to raise prices. In contrast, manufactured products are said to be subject to higher demand and income elasticities and to the raising of their prices through monopolistic market practices.

Data on the terms of trade of the United States span a period of over 100 years, covering the metamorphosis from a primitive economy exporting almost entirely primary products to an industrial power with one of the world's highest income levels. On the whole, the picture is one of long-term improvement in the terms of trade – perhaps an increase of two-thirds from the founding of the country to World War I (see Table 15.21). The greatest gains took place before the Civil War, when the United States was almost entirely an exporter of primary – largely agricultural – products. These remained predominant through the end of the nineteenth century, as a gradual rise in the terms of trade continued. After the 1880s, the terms of trade improved little, if at all. Within the nineteenth-century history of the United States, therefore, there is no evidence that being an agricultural exporter led to an unfavorable evolution of the net barter terms of trade.

Table 15.21. *Terms of trade of the United States*[a]
(1913 = 100)

Period	Terms of trade index
1789–1798	58
1799–1808	66
1809–1818	60
1819–1828	65
1829–1838	79
1834–1843	83
1839–1848	77
1849–1858	90
1859–1868	80
1869–1878	87
1879–1888	97
1889–1898	90
1899–1908	97
1904–1913	99

[a] Export price index ÷ import price index.
Source: Lipsey, "Foreign Trade", table 14.3.

Sectoral Price Trends

Classical economic thought contained strong predictions about the long-term trends of the relative prices of agricultural and other primary products relative to manufactured goods. The classical view, starting at least as far back as Robert Torrens, continued by John Stuart Mill, and reinforced by Jevons's alarm at the exhaustion of British coal resources, was that "the exchange value of manufactured articles, compared with the products of agriculture and of mines, have, as population and industry advance, a certain and decided tendency to fall."[1] The opposite view was suggested from a reading of the factual record by Hilgerdt in a 1945 League of Nations report and was later promoted in a series of United Nations documents and articles, particularly by Raúl Prebisch and Hans Singer. That view was that primary goods prices had been declining secularly, and the decline was attributed to low price and income elasticities for food, declining demand arising from the replacement of natural raw materials by synthetic materials, and monopolistic or oligopolistic pricing practices of

[1] John Stuart Mill (1909), Vol. II, Book IV, Chapter 2, 282.

Tabel 15.22. *Relation between U.S. manufactured and agricultural product export prices and total factor productivity 1815–1860, 1879–1913*

	Export price indexes	Productivity
	Manufacturing/Agriculture	Agriculture/Manufacturing
1815–20	97	
1821–30	113	
1831–40	102	
1839–40	100	128
1841–50	110	123
1849–50	98	119
1851–60	106	109
1859–60	100	100
1879–88	142	137
1889–98	138	121
1899–1908	127	123
1904–13	110	118

Note: 1859–60 = 100 for 1815–1860; 1913 = 100 for 1879–1913.
Source: Gallman, "Commodity Output," 43; Stanley Lebergott, *Manpower in Economic Growth* (New York, 1964), 510; Lipsey "Foreign Trade", 575.

manufacturing firms in developed countries that prevented buyers of manufactured exports from reaping the gains from productivity improvements in manufacturing.

The United States in the nineteenth century was a good laboratory in which to test these theories because the record of the aggregate terms of trade goes back to the period when agriculture was predominant and extends through the transformation to an industrial economy, and the record of agricultural and manufacturing prices and productivity also reaches to earlier stages of development than for most other countries.

Within U.S. exports, the price index for agricultural products, dominated by exports of cotton, was so volatile that it is hard to see a trend, but there were clearly large declines in prices of both agricultural and manufactured products between 1815–20 and 1830 or the 1830s as a whole. Since the export prices of manufactures did not fall as fast as agricultural export prices, the relative export prices of manufactures increased (see Table 15.22). From the 1830s to the 1850s changes in relative prices were fairly small, not surprisingly in view of the fact that cotton and tobacco were very heavily weighted in the agricultural export price index, and cotton and tobacco manufactures accounted for 70 to 80 percent of the weight in the manufactured goods price index. After 1879 there was a considerable decline in the price of manufactured exports relative to prices of agricultural exports, a movement that accorded with the classical expectations and contradicted the Prebisch-Singer view.

The basis for the classical belief that manufactured goods prices would fall in the long run was the conviction that productivity would grow more rapidly in manufacturing than in agriculture. That part of the prediction seems to have been correct, both before and after the Civil War. From 1879 to the beginning of World War I, manufacturing productivity rose more rapidly than agricultural productivity, and manufactured goods export prices fell relative to agricultural export prices. The relative productivity change accounted for about 60 percent of the relative export price change.

In the twenty years before the Civil War, a similar relative growth in manufacturing productivity did not have any counterpart in export price developments; the export price ratio for manufactured goods relative to agricultural products was quite stable. In the earlier period also, from 1815–20 to 1839–40 there was little change in the export price ratio. In this earlier period too, a comparison of Sokoloff's (1986) productivity measures for selected manufacturing industries with the Towne and Rasmussen (1960) productivity measures for agriculture suggests that manufacturing productivity was growing much faster than agricultural productivity.

There are several possible reasons why the productivity and price ratios do not match before 1860. After 1830, North's (1961, appendix 2, table 4) export price index is dominated by cotton manufactures and to a much smaller extent, tobacco manufactures, both of which enjoyed productivity growth more rapid than that in agriculture (tobacco manufactures only after 1850, according to Sokoloff). However, both industries' outputs included large elements of agricultural input, and that may explain why North's manufactures price index rises by an amount identical to that of the raw material price index, dominated by cotton and tobacco.

Before 1830 the products in North's manufactures price index do not match Sokoloff's list well, the largest item in the price index being soap, not included by Sokoloff, and the second being tobacco manufactures, which not only include a large agricultural input content but also did not enjoy rapid productivity gains before 1850.

The price and productivity movements of the post–Civil War period reveal the changes in the rewards to the factors of production in the two

Table 15.23. *Agricultural and manufactured export price indexes and purchasing power of agricultural and manufactured products (1913 = 100)*

| | Price Indexes | | | |
	Agricultural	Agricultural as percent of manufactured	Agricultural productivity index	Agricultural factors' purchasing power over manufactured exports
1879–88	83.6	70.4	93.7	66.0
1889–98	67.8	72.4	95.6	69.2
1899–1908	77.0	78.9	106.6	84.1
1904–1913	89.8	90.6	106.3	96.3
1913	100.0	100.0	100.0	100.0

	Manufacturing	Manufactured as percent of agricultural	Manufacturing productivity index	Manufacturing factors' purchasing power over agricultural exports
1879–88	118.5	142.1	69.1	98.2
1889–98	93.1	138.2	78.7	108.8
1899–1908	97.0	126.8	86.8	110.1
1904–1913	98.2	110.4	90.0	99.4
1913	100.0	100.0	100.0	100.0

Source: Lipsey, *Price and Quantity Trends*, Appendix tables A-1 and A-3.

sectors. Just as the agricultural export price indicates the money return per unit of agricultural commodities sold, the ratio of the agricultural to the manufacturing price is one measure of the purchasing power of these agricultural commodities, assuming that manufactured exports are representative of U.S. manufacturing production in general. The product of the relative price and the agricultural productivity index indicates the course of returns to factors of production, or inputs, in agriculture: the purchasing power over manufactures of an hour of agricultural labor or a unit of capital employed in agriculture.

Agricultural factors of production did very well indeed after the 1890s, by this measure (see Table 15.23). Productivity in manufacturing increased much faster than in agriculture. Agricultural export prices rose rapidly, much faster than prices of manufactured goods. The purchasing power of agricultural factors over manufactured goods grew at a fast pace, while the purchasing power of manufacturing factors of production over agricultural products actually fell. The gains from growing productivity in manufacturing went largely to agricultural factors of production and, of course to foreign purchasers of U.S. manufacturing exports.

THE EFFECTS OF WARS AND OF TRADE POLICIES

The Navigation Acts

Most of what we have described here as the development of American trade in the nineteenth century could be thought of as being outside the realms of both chance events or conscious policy. We have attributed trade developments mainly to income levels, productivity changes, factor endowments and changes in endowments. One possible exception to the unimportance of government policies is the influence of the Navigation Acts on the trade pattern of the American colonies, the pattern with which the country began its existence.

The British government in the colonial period was no believer in leaving trade to the operation of the invisible hand. As Adam Smith described the exemptions from the Navigation Laws, their purpose was to exploit the incentives provided by access to foreign markets to encourage the cultivation of grain, the clearing and use of forests, and the raising of cattle beyond what would otherwise be feasible in "a thinly populated country." The key to the success of the policy was the fact that access to "extensive markets" would cause the prices of these products to be high, as they would not be in a country cut off from trade. These high prices would encourage the extension of cultivation and improvement of the breed of cattle.

The other side of the Navigation Acts, and their main purpose, was to give home (British) purchasers of some colonial raw materials a monopoly on the output of the colonies, to keep prices low, and to severely restrict the growth in the colonies of manufacturing industries that might compete with British sellers.

The initial pattern of colonial trade fit well with these plans, since the exports were so largely crude materials and foods and imports were mainly manufactured products. However, the same pattern could be explained by the factor proportions and technological backwardness of the colonies. The fact that the evolution of the pattern of trade after independence was gradual, and the fact that the United States moved toward greater concentration on trade with the United Kingdom after independence, when the earlier restrictions were absent, suggest that economic forces rather than the Navigation Acts were the main determinants of both the commodity and country patterns of U.S. trade.

A similar conclusion, minimizing the effects of British imperial policy on the welfare of the colonies and on the nature of their economies, was arrived at by North (1974). He dismissed restrictions on manufacturing as inconsequential, given the colonies' factor proportions, which did not point to any comparative advantage in that field. There was a burden placed on American producers of tobacco, particularly, as measured by the difference between prices received and those available outside the United Kingdom. And there were also burdens on consumers in the colonies from the artificially inflated prices of goods imported from other European countries. However, they were counterbalanced, to a considerable degree, by the advantages of British military protection.

North's analysis, treating 1785–1793 as the norm representing the situation without British restrictions, implies that if there were any effects from the restrictions they were short-lived and did not deflect the United States from its long-term growth path.

The Napoleonic Wars and the Trade Embargo

There is no doubt that the Napoleonic Wars and the accompanying trade embargo before the War of 1812 provided both great opportunities for trade and shipping, as is described in the earlier quotation from Callender, and also large negative shocks to the young U.S. economy. It is harder to say whether any of the effects were permanent, in the sense that the United States gained new industries that survived successfully after the period, or gained or lost footholds in world markets.

Most of the analyses of this period have focused on the immediate advantages of American neutrality at a time when almost all potential rivals were swept from the trade scene. North describes the years 1793 through 1807 as "extraordinarily prosperous ones," a characterization confirmed by "numerous literary descriptions" (1974, 69). The prosperity came from shipping earnings (which on net balance grew from $5–$8 billion to $38–$40 billion), and from increases in export prices and terms of trade.

Once the Embargo on trade began in 1808, and especially with the entry of the United States into the war in 1812, these gains were reversed. Shipping earnings and exports fell drastically, and the terms of trade turned against the United States. The Embargo did have some effect in promoting manufacturing in the United States, but the path of development did not match American comparative advantage at the time, according to North, and the artificially induced industrialization quickly withered under postwar competition. Thus the net balance of the war period, despite the prosperity of its early stages, does not seem to have propelled American economic development in any substantial way.

A later review of even the prosperous part of the Napoleonic War period by Goldin and Lewis (1980) attempted to deflate the "legendary importance" of the neutrality period by estimating effects on the rate of growth of per capita income. The estimated gains, while perhaps not of legendary dimensions, were substantial – increases in the annual growth rate of per capita income of something between 30 and 40 percent. Although the authors refer to these income gains as not dramatic they do suggest that there were more permanent gains to development – the growth of port cities and inland towns, additions to shipping tonnage, and the spread of banking and of commercialization in general.

The Civil War

The Civil War was the bloodiest of American history, was fought entirely on American soil, and divided the country on economic lines to a large extent. Despite these factors, there has always been some belief that the northern states experienced economic gains from the war. However, North (1966, 149) judged that the war "was not a major impetus to accelerated industrial growth" and presumably was not a major setback either. The basis for the statement was that the acceleration of industrial growth and the development of manufacturing had taken place before the war. Gallman (1972) pointed to the heavy manpower losses during the war, the decrease in immigration, and the smallness of the industrial requirements of the military forces in that period. What the Civil War did do was to alter the relation between the northern and southern states, greatly reducing the per capita income level of the South, and widening the income differential between the South and other areas. There was also a major shift in the balance of political power that was relevant to trade policy, since the southern states, more dependent on exports and more oriented to free trade, lost to the northern states, which were more import dependent and more favorable to protectionist legislation.

The negative effects of the war on the United States as a whole are reflected in the earlier description of U.S. shares in world trade, which fell between 1860 and 1870 in an unusual interruption of the long-term upward trend. The net indebtedness of the United States tripled between the beginning of the war and the end.

The distribution of exports did not change in a way that would suggest that the war violently altered the American industrial structure. The share of finished manufactures grew, but not to a degree that suggested a major break in the upward trend. The share of cotton exports declined, but no faster than it did between the 1830s and 1840s, and less than from the 1870s to the 1880s. On the whole, the Civil War appears more as an interruption to the changes in the composition of production and exports that were taking place than as a spur to them.

Effects of Tariff Policy

The extent to which protectionist legislation promoted manufacturing industry by restricting foreign competition in the U.S. market has been a perennial subject for dispute. The era after the Civil War is sometimes cited as a period in which the United States used high tariffs successfully to encourage infant industries that eventually became giants. In 1869 imports were 14 percent of the consumption of manufactured goods, and by 1909 that ratio had fallen to 6 percent. In every manufacturing industry in which the import share was 10 percent or more in 1869, that share fell to half or less in 1909. The iron and steel industry was an extreme case, with imports falling from 12 to about 1.5 percent. These declines suggest that some of the rapid growth in U.S. manufacturing involved import substitution: the replacement of imports by domestic production. That was obviously the case for shares of the market, but there were also a couple of examples of import substitution in the absolute sense, with declines in the amount of imports in an industry.

Two cases of import substitution in this absolute sense stand out in the nineteenth century, and both involve industries in which protection was increased. One was the large fall in imports of textiles before the Civil War and the other was the iron and steel industry in the 1880s and 1890s. In the textile case, the domestic industry had expanded under the embargo, which was, in effect, a prohibitive tariff, although it was never put in those terms. Taussig (1931) concluded that the embargo itself, rather than the tariffs adopted to preserve the industry, provided the main impetus to growth. North (1966) mentioned the possibility that the Tariff Acts of 1816, 1824, and 1828 helped revive some parts of the textile industry after the 1808 embargo and the War of 1812 severely damaged the industry, but suggested that by 1830 the industry, having become a net exporter, had no need for continued protection.

In later years, an array of econometric analyses, theories of policies to correct factor market distortions, theories of learning-by-doing, and formal production function fitting were combined with detailed studies of the industry, individual firms, and groups of firms to reopen the debate. An early, wide-ranging analysis by David (1970) that went beyond the effects of protection on the size of the industry, ended not too far from Taussig's earlier conclusions about the welfare effects of post-1820s protection. A more skeptical view of the cotton textile industry's viability without tariff protection in the 1830s, and therefore a view giving more credit to protection for the growth of the industry, was suggested in several later analyses by Bils (1984), Temin (1988), and Harley (1992). All challenged Taussig's conclusion that "by 1832, the industry . . . was able to meet foreign competition on equal terms" (Taussig 1931, 136). All these authors pointed to the relative U.S. advantage in coarse, as compared with fine cloth, but Bils came to the strongest conclusion about the necessity of tariff protection, to the effect that "removing protection would have eliminated the vast majority of value added in the cotton textile industry" (Bils, 1984, 1045). Harley, using different evidence, also concluded that the American industry, despite substantial exports that were typically over 10 percent of output during the 1850s, "Without protection . . . could have attained no more than a fraction of its actual size" (Harley 1992, 580).

North (1966) suggested that the U.S. iron industry, so regulated by the British Navigation Laws as Adam Smith had pointed out, was protected to some extent by the high transport cost of its products.[2] Imports of iron and steel fell between 1879 and 1899, as imports of textiles had declined earlier, in a period when domestic consumption of iron and steel products more than doubled. Since the decline in imports was insignificant relative to the growth of production, it cannot have been the main impetus to such growth. Most appraisals of the history of the industry have concluded that, while protection and the decline of imports may have hastened the growth

---

[2] "While Great Britain encourages in America the manufacture of pig and bar iron, by exempting them from duties . . . she imposes an absolute prohibition upon the erection of steel furnaces and slit-mills in any of her American plantations." Smith (1776), Book 4, Chapter 7.

of some elements of the industry, they were not the major influence in the long run for the industry as a whole (Taussig 1931; Temin 1964).

A study of the tariff on pig iron (Baack and Ray 1974) concluded that the tariff on that product did raise the level of domestic production. Part of that effect was through the impact on the quality of imports. Since the tariff on pig iron was a specific duty, framed in terms of dollars per ton, it weighed much more heavily on cheap grades of pig iron than on expensive grades. The result was a decline in imports of low-quality pig iron, and encouragement to domestic production at the low end of the quality scale.

An example of a strong effect of a tariff on output of an important product was that of the tariff on steel rails from 1866 to 1913. Head (1994) concluded that the tariff, combined with declining input (pig iron) prices resulting from technological progress "had an enormous impact on the performance of the domestic steel industry" (160). Much of the gain was attributed to large productivity increases from "learning-by-doing." Welfare improvements from the tariff were small, however, because the tariff cut off imports too quickly, causing high costs to rail buyers in the 1880s, and because the tariff was removed too late.

In general, the historical studies of protection have attempted to learn whether protection was successful, in the sense of encouraging the production of the protected item. Recent studies have moved toward a more frequently positive answer to this question. They usually have not, however, answered the more important policy question as to whether the growth and welfare of the country was enhanced, rather than only that of the protected industries and the factors of production employed in them. David (1970) and Head (1994) were exceptions in this respect, taking broader, national welfare issues into consideration.

TRADE AND U.S. ECONOMIC GROWTH

The United States, through much of its history, has been pointed to as a country for which international trade was unimportant. One reason was the relatively low and, at times declining ratio of U.S. trade to U.S. output described earlier.

These low ratios have affected the recurrent debate about the importance of trade for U.S. economic growth, particularly growth in the nineteenth century. A relatively modest role for international trade was assigned by Kravis (1972), partly on the argument that trade was too unimportant, in terms of its share of total output, to account for much of the growth in GNP or GNP per capita. A view of the economy as governed by some type of economy-wide production function in which inputs of factors of production lead to predictable outputs of product tends to find little room for any influence of trade. Output growth is assigned as far as possible to growth in the amounts of inputs or in their quality, to technological progress, and often to some unexplainable residual. What is missing from these analyses is the question of why the inputs of resources grew at the rate they did, and the role played not only by the actual exports and imports, but also by the broader trading circumstances – the existence of markets and the ability of producers and traders to have access to them.

The view that assigns a more crucial level to trade, and to the growth of foreign demand, has been associated with the work of Douglass North on U.S. economic growth. North described the role of growth in foreign demand for cotton in leading to the westward expansion of cotton farming and, in its wake, more general expansions in settlement and cultivation.

A more recent review of these controversies by Jeffrey Williamson (1980) shifted the emphasis to a more general influence of trade: the existence of foreign demand, rather than its growth, and the likelihood, or almost certainty, that the price elasticity of demand in foreign markets was higher than that in the domestic market – probably much higher. That high elasticity meant that rapid expansions of production, such as from the spread of cultivation to new areas, could take place without causing drastic reductions in the prices received by producers. Without the highly elastic demand of the foreign market, expansions of production would quickly face the effects of the low domestic demand elasticities, prices would fall quickly, and the expansion would be cut off. It is not implied that the elasticity of foreign demand for a product as a whole was necessarily different from that in the United States. The higher foreign elasticity of demand for an American export arose from the fact that it was, typically, a much smaller element of foreign supply than of American supply. Therefore the American export could substitute for foreign exports or local production of the same product. If there were efficiencies to be gained from concentrating an expansion in production in a short period, they might well be lost if trade were cut off or reduced.

A corollary of this effect of the international market is that the ratio of exports to production should increase when production grows most rapidly. As described earlier, that was the case for cotton production in the United States, and it was also true of the surges in middle-western grain and meat production in the second half of the nineteenth century. Thus the existence of a high-elasticity market, in combination with the factors that initiated the surges in production, may have been crucial to the westward expansion of the country.

On a more speculative note, one might consider that the advice now being given to most developing countries urges policies that are outward- rather than inward-oriented, and favor neutrality or export promotion over import substitution. Since many currently developing countries are much smaller than the United States was during the early stages of its industrialization, the trade orientation may be more necessary than it was for a large, continental, developing country such as the United States already was during most of the century. On the other hand, an outward-oriented trade policy that encourages trade may have ramifications for many other aspects of government policy. It may affect investment, competition, monetary, and fiscal policies. It may affect the choice of industries by investors, and the productivity of domestic producers. These broader influences could go far beyond what is suggested by the amounts of goods actually traded.

REFERENCES

Baack, Bennett D., and Edward John Ray. "Tariff Policy and Comparative Advantage in the Iron and Steel Industry: 1870–1929," *Explorations in Economic History*, 11 (1974), 103–21.

Bairoch, Paul. "European Foreign Trade in the XIX Century: The Development of the Value and Volume of Exports (Preliminary Results)." *Journal of European Economic History*, 2 (1973), 5–36.

Commerce Extérieur et Développement Économique de l'Europe au XIXe Siècle (Paris, 1976).

"Europe's Gross National Product: 1800–1975," *Journal of European Economic History*, 5 (1976), 273–340.

"International Industrialization Levels from 1750 to 1980," *Journal of European Economic History*, 11 (1982), 269–353.

Balke, Nathan S., and Robert J. Gordon. "The Estimation of Prewar Gross National Product," *Journal of Political Economy*, 97 (1989), 38–92.

Berry, Thomas Senior. *Revised Annual Estimates of American Gross National Product: Preliminary Annual Estimates of Four Major Components of Demand, 1789–1889* (Richmond, VA 1978).

Bils, Mark. "Tariff Protection and Production in the Early U.S. Cotton Textile Industry," *Journal of Economic History*, 44 (1984), 1033–45.

Bjork, Gordon C. "Stagnation and Growth in the American Economy, 1784–1792," University of Washington Ph.D. Dissertation, 1963 (Ann Arbor, University Microfilms.)

"The Weaning of the American Economy: Independence, Market Changes, and Economic Development," *Journal of Economic History*, 24 (1964), 541–60.

Blomström, Magnus, Robert E. Lipsey, and Lennart Ohlsson. *Economic Relations Between the United States and Sweden* (Stockholm, 1988).

Bogart, Ernest Ludlow. *The Economic History of the United States*. 3rd Ed. (New York, 1920).

Bogart, Ernest Ludlow, and Charles Manfred Thompson. *Readings in the Economic History of the United States* (New York, 1919).

Callender, Guy Stevens. *Selections from the Economic History of the United States, 1765–1860*, with introductory essays (Boston, 1909).

David, Paul. "The Growth of Real Product in the United States before 1840: New Evidence, Controlled Conjectures," *Journal of Economic History*, 27 (1967), 151–97.

"Learning by Doing and Tariff Protection: A Reconsideration of the Case of the Antebellum United States Cotton Textile Industry," *Journal of Economic History*, 30 (1970), 521–601.

Davis, Lance E. "Capital and Growth," Chapter 8 in Davis, Easterlin, Parker, et al., 280–310.

Davis, Lance E., Richard A. Easterlin, William N. Parker, et al., *American Economic Growth: An Economist's History of the United States* (New York, 1972).

Davis, Lance E., and Jonathan R. T. Hughes. "A Dollar-Sterling Exchange, 1803–95," *Economic History Review*, 32 (1960), 52–78.

Deane, Phyllis, and Cole A. W. *British Economic Growth, 1688–1959*, 2nd Ed. (Cambridge, 1969).

Edelstein, Michael. *Overseas Investment in the Age of High Imperialism: The United Kingdom, 1850–1914* (New York, 1982).

Gallman, Robert E. "Commodity Output, 1839–1899," in William N. Parker (ed.), *Trends in the American Economy in the Nineteenth Century*, Studies in Income and Wealth, vol. 24 (Princeton, 1960), 13–67.

"Gross National Product in the United States: 1834–1909," in Dorothy S. Brady (ed.), *Output, Employment, and Productivity in the United States After 1800*, Studies in Income and Wealth, vol. 30 (New York, 1966), 3–76.

"The Pace and Pattern of American Economic Growth," in Davis, Easterlin, Parker, et al., 15–60.

"American Economic Growth before the Civil War: The Testimony of the Capital Stock Estimates," in Robert E. Gallman and John Joseph Wallis, eds., *American Economic Growth and Standards of Living Before The Civil War* (Chicago, 1992), 79–120.

Goldin, Claudia D., and Frank D. Lewis. "The Role of Exports in American Economic Growth during the Napoleonic Wars, 1793 to 1807," *Explorations in Economic History*, 17 (1980), 6–25.

Harley, C. Knick. "International Competitiveness of the Antebellum American Cotton Textile Industry," *Journal of Economic History*, 52 (1992), 559–84.

Head, Keith. "Infant Industry Protection in the Steel Rail Industry," *Journal of International Economics*, 37 (1994), 141–65.

Kravis, Irving B. "Trade as a Handmaiden of Growth: Similarities Between the 19th and 20th Centuries," *Economic Journal*, 80 (1970), 850–72.

"The Role of Exports in Nineteenth-Century United States Growth," *Economic Development and Cultural Change*, 20 (1972), 387–405.

Kuznets, Simon. *Modern Economic Growth: Rate, Structure, and Spread* (New Haven, 1966).

League of Nations. *Industrialization and Foreign Trade* (by Folke Hilgerdt) (Geneva, 1945).

Lebergott, Stanley, *Manpower in Economic Growth* (New York, 1964).

Lebergott, Stanley. "Labor Force and Employment, 1800–1960," in Brady (ed.), *Output, Employment, and Productivity in the United States After 1800* (1966), 117–204.

Lewis, Cleona. *America's Stake in International Investments* (Washington, DC, 1938).

Lipsey, Robert E. *Price and Quantity Trends in the Foreign Trade of the United States* (Princeton, 1963).

"Foreign Trade," in Davis, Easterlin, Parker, et al., 548–81.

Maddison, Angus. "Growth and Fluctuations in the World Economy, 1870–1960," *Banca Nazionale del Lavoro Quarterly Review*, 61 (1962), 127–95.

Phases of Capitalist Development (Oxford, 1982).

Mill, John Stuart. *Principles of Political Economy*, 5th London Ed. (New York, 1909).

Mitchell, B. R. *European Historical Statistics, 1750–1970*, Abridged Ed. (New York, 1978).

North, Douglass C. "The United States Balance of Payments, 1790–1860," in Parker (ed.), *Trends in the American Economy in the Nineteenth Century*, 573–627.

The Economic Growth of the United States, 1790 to 1960 (Englewood Cliffs, 1961).

Growth and Welfare in the American Past (Englewood Cliffs, 1966).

Growth and Welfare in the American Past, 2nd ed. (Englewood Cliffs, 1974).

Pitkin, Timothy. *A Statistical View of the Commerce of the United States* (New York, 1816; reprinted New York, 1967).

Romer, Christina. "The Prewar Business Cycle Reconsidered: New Estimates of Gross National Product, 1869–1908," *Journal of Political Economy*, 97 (1989), 1–37.

Rostow, Walt W. *The World Economy: History and Prospect* (Austin, 1978).

Shepherd, James F., and Gary M. Walton. *Shipping, Maritime Trade, and the Economic Development of Colonial North America* (Cambridge, 1972).

Simon, Matthew. "The United States Balance of Payments, 1861–1900," in Parker (ed.), *Trends in the American Economy in the Nineteenth Century*, 629–711.

Smith, Adam. *An Inquiry Into the Nature and Causes of the Wealth of Nations* (New York, 1937, first printed 1776).

Smith, Walter Buckingham, and Arthur Harrison Cole. *Fluctuations in American Business, 1790–1860* (Cambridge, MA, 1935).

Sokoloff, Kenneth. "Productivity Growth in Manufacturing During Early Industrialization: Evidence From the American Northeast: 1820–1860," in Stanley L. Engerman and Robert E. Gallman, eds., *Long-Term Factors in American Economic Growth*, Studies in Income and Wealth, vol. 51 (Chicago, 1986), 679–736.

Taussig, Frank W. *The Tariff History of the United States*, 8th rev. ed. (New York, 1931).

Temin, Peter. *Iron and Steel in Nineteenth Century America* (Cambridge, MA, 1964).

"Product Quality and Vertical Integration in the Early U.S. Cotton Textile Industry," *Journal of Economic History*, 48 (1988), 891–907.

Towne, Marvin W. and Wayne D. Rasmussen. "Farm Gross Product and Gross Investment in the Nineteenth Century," in Parker (ed.), *Trends in the American Economy in the Nineteenth Century*, 255–312.

U.S. Bureau of the Census. *Historical Statistics of the United States, Colonial Times to 1970* (Washington, DC, 1975).

U.S. Congress, House of Representatives. *Domestic Exports, 1789–1883*, House Miscellaneous Document No. 2236, 48th Congress, 1st Session (1883–84), compiled by C. H. Evans (Washington, DC, 1884).

Vanek, Jaroslav. *The Natural Resource Content of United States Foreign Trade, 1870–1955* (Cambridge, MA, 1963).

Weiss, Thomas. "U.S. Labor Force Estimates and Economic Growth, 1800–1860," in Gallman and Wallis, eds., *American Economic Growth and Standards of Living Before the Civil War*, 19–75.

Weiss, Thomas. "Estimates of Gross Domestic Output for the United States, 1800 to 1860," Mimeo (University of Kansas, 1993).

Wilkins, Mira. *The History of Foreign Investment in the United States to 1914* (Cambridge, MA, 1989).

Williamson, Jeffrey. *American Growth and the Balance of Payments, 1820–1913* (Chapel Hill, 1964).

Williamson, Jeffrey G. "Greasing the Wheels of Sputtering Export Engines: Midwestern Grain and American Economic Growth," *Explorations in Economic History*, 17 (1980), 189–217.

16

INTERNATIONAL CAPITAL MOVEMENTS, DOMESTIC CAPITAL MARKETS, AND AMERICAN ECONOMIC GROWTH, 1820–1914

LANCE E. DAVIS AND ROBERT J. CULL

INTRODUCTION

For almost three-quarters of a century, from the end of World War I until the early 1980s,[1] the United States was the world's largest capital exporter. In the last decade of the previous century, Americans had begun to finance economic activity in Canada and Mexico; until recently these transfers grew and their geographic focus broadened. Over the past decade, however, the world's largest creditor has become its largest debtor.

Before 1914, however, it was Europe who acted as the world's banker; and within that continent, it was Britain who was the senior partner. Moreover, over the course of the nineteenth century, it was the United States that received the lion's share of Europe's foreign investment. Unlike their great grandchildren, nineteenth-century Americans displayed a high propensity to save. Although the evidence for the early years is sketchy, the share of net capital formation in net national product appears to have averaged about 6.5 percent in the years between 1805 and 1840

[1] This chapter draws heavily on five sources: in fact, it could not have been written without them. The quantitative estimates of capital flows are rooted in the pioneering work of Charles L. Bullock, John H. Williams, and Rufus S. Tucker, but the estimates owe even more to the careful work of Douglass C. North and Matthew Simon. Both the quantitative estimate of the sources of foreign capital and the industrial distribution of both foreign capital and American overseas investment as well as a substantial part of the institutional detail is drawn from the monumental work of Cleona Lewis. Finally much of the institutional detail is based on Mira Wilkins's excellent, carefully researched and far-reaching study of foreign investment in the United States.

Financially, this work has been supported by the National Science Foundation Grant No. SES-9122436, the Sloan Foundation, and the Division of Humanities and Social Sciences of the California Institute of Technology. Because of space limitations, this paper is relatively brief. For a more extensive analysis, see Lance E. Davis and Robert J. Cull, *International Capital Markets and American Economic Growth, 1820–1914* (Cambridge, 1994).

and to have risen to almost 20 percent by the end of the century; and most of the resources that were diverted from consumption were domestic not foreign.[2]

Between 1799 and 1900, net foreign investment accounted for less than 5 percent of the almost $60 billion increase in the nation's capital stock.[3] Because of the apparent minimal contribution, many modern economic historians have been quick to accept Kuznets's conclusion that foreign capital played a relatively insignificant role in American development.[4] Although the magnitudes that Kuznets cites are certainly correct, it is difficult to reconcile his conclusion with the emphasis that traditional economic historians have placed on the role of foreign capital in American development; Jeffrey Williamson and Raymond Goldsmith have demonstrated that the relatively small quantitative role played by foreign investment is not an adequate measure of its importance to American development.[5] Although, in the aggregate, the transfers do not loom large, for some periods the infusions represented a much larger share of total investment; and during those decades they appear to have played an important role in shaping American growth (see Table 16.1). In the years 1832 through 1839, foreign investment accounted for more than 15 percent of net capital formation; in the immediate post–Civil War decade, perhaps three-quarters of that amount, and, even in the 1880s, more than 7 percent. As late as the years 1906 to 1913, years when long-term American capital exports totaled almost a billion dollars, long term foreign investment in the United States exceeded $1.5 billion.

---

[2] Lance Davis and Robert Gallman, "Savings, Investment, and Economic Growth: The United States in the Nineteenth Century," in John James and Marks Thomas (eds.), *Capitalism in Context* (Chicago, 1994), table 2.

[3] Douglass North, "The Balance of Payments of the United States, 1790–1860," and Matthew Simon, "The Balance of Payments of the United States, 1861–1900," both of which were published in William N. Parker (ed.), *Trends in the American Economy in the Nineteenth Century*, Studies in Income and Wealth, vol. 24 (Princeton, 1960) and are used as cited in the U.S. Bureau of the Census, *Historical Statistics of the United States, Colonial Times to 1970* (Washington, DC, 1975), 858–61 and 864–67. The capital stock figures for 1840 to 1900 are from Robert E. Gallman, "The United States Capital Stock in the Nineteenth Century," Stanley L. Engerman and Robert E. Gallman (eds.), *Long Term Factors in Economic Growth*, Studies in Income and Wealth, vol. 51 (Chicago, 1986). The figures for 1799–1840 are from Robert E. Gallman, *The Capital Stock of the United States*, mss. Chapter 5, Table 5.1.

[4] Simon Kuznets, "Foreign Economic Relations of the United States and Their Impact upon the Domestic Economy: A Review of Long Term Trends," *Proceedings of the American Philosophical Society*, 92 (1948), 233.

[5] Jeffrey G. Williamson, *American Growth and the Balance of Payments, 1820–1913: A Study of the Long Swing* (Chapel Hill, 1964), 3–5. Raymond W. Goldsmith, "The Growth of Reproducible Wealth of the United States of America," in Simon Kuznets (ed.), *Income and Wealth of the United States: Trends and Structures*, Income and Wealth, Series II (Cambridge, 1952), 284–86.

Table 16.1. *Relative importance of net capital imports in new capital formation, 1799–1900*

Years	Net Foreign Capital Imports/Net Domestic Capital Formation (Gallman)	Net Foreign Capital Imports/Net National Capital Formation (Gallman)	Net Foreign Capital Imports/Net Capital Formation (Williamson)
1799–1805	−0.012	−0.013	
1806–1815	0.005	0.005	
1816–1840	0.220	0.199	
1841–1850	−0.008	−0.009	
1851–1860	0.027	0.026	
1861–1870	0.158	0.136	
1871–1880	0.055	0.055	0.045
1881–1890	0.086	0.082	0.102
1891–1900	−0.028	−0.030	−0.020
1799–1900	0.049	0.048	
1871–1900	0.038	0.036	0.042

Source: For columns (1) and (2) new capital imports are from *Historical Statistics*, Series U 18–25 and the capital stock series are from Robert E. Gallman, *The Capital Stock of the United States*, mss. chap. 5; and Robert E. Gallman, "American Economic Growth before the Civil War: The Testimony of the Capital Stock Estimates," in Robert E. Gallman and John Joseph Wallis (eds.), *American Economic Growth and Standards of Living Before the Civil War* (Chicago, 1992). Column (3) is from Jeffrey G. Williamson, *American Growth and the Balance of Payments 1820–1913; A Study of the Long Swing* (Chapel Hill, 1964), 142.

Moreover, given the initially primitive and only gradually developing state of the American capital markets, foreign capital, directed by more mature European markets, provided finance for projects that were unserved by the nation's embryonic financial institutions. As Goldsmith concluded, "If the United States had been limited to domestic saving, the growth of wealth would certainly have been slower until near the end of the nineteenth century . . . because these imports were concentrated in crucial areas of growth, and particularly because without them the development of the American railroad system, probably the main economic achievement of the second half of the nineteenth century, would have been slowed down considerably."[6]

Because of its potentially important contribution in some times and some places – the 1830s and 1880s were decades of rapid industrial and

[6] Goldsmith, "Reproducible Wealth," 285.

spatial transformation – and because of the problem raised by the difficulty of mobilizing domestic capital across geographic and industrial boundaries, the subject of foreign investment is important to an understanding of the process of this nation's growth in the years before 1900. Moreover, between 1896 and 1914 the United States became a major exporter of foreign capital, particularly to Canada and Latin America; and it is in these turn-of-the-century decades that the charges of Yankee economic imperialism are rooted.

This study describes and analyzes the history of foreign investment in the United States, and it details the beginnings of American capital exports. The first section sketches the time path of the net flows of capital. The second section provides quantitative estimates of the geographic source and industrial structure of foreign investment in the U.S.; and the third section adduces additional qualitative evidence of the extent, industrial and spatial distribution, and importance of those flows. The fourth section examines the nature of the capital mobilized through the New York and London stock exchanges; and the fifth section analyzes the nature of the institutional structure of the American capital market that led to the important role that foreign, in particular British, capital played in American development. The final two sections examine the export of American capital, particularly over the two and a half decades prior to the outbreak of World War I, and, finally, report some tentative conclusions.

THE NET FLOWS OF CAPITAL:
AN OVERVIEW

The data reported in Table 16.2 are indirect estimates obtained as a residual from the calculation of the balance of payments.[7] There have been three major quantitative studies of the history of the American balance of payments; and, while their focus and conclusions are somewhat

---

[7] The estimates of net flows are from North, "Balance of Payments" and from Simon, "Balance of Payments" as revised by the United States Office of Business Economics. The gross estimates for the years 1900 to 1918 are based on the work of Paul D. Dickens, "The Transitional Period in International Finance: 1897–1914," unpublished Ph.D. dissertation, George Washington University, 1933; C. J. Bullock, John H. Williams, and Rufus S. Tucker, "The Balance of Trade of the United States," *Review of Economic Statistics* 1 (1919), 215–54; and of the Department of Commerce's *Monthly Summary of Foreign Commerce* as revised by Raymond Goldsmith, *A Study of Savings in the United States*, 3 vols. (Princeton, 1955), Vol. I, 1078, 1080, 1084, and 1086.

Table 16.2. *Net international capital movements: capital inflow into the U.S. minus outflow (millions of dollars)*

Year	Net inflow	Year	Net inflow	Year	Net inflow	Long-term only
1790	1	1832	7	1874	82	
1791	8	1833	14	1875	87	
1792	8	1834	19	1876	2	
1793	−2	1835	30	1877	−57	
1794	−9	1836	59	1878	−162	
1795	13	1837	22	1879	−160	
1796	4	1838	3	1880	30	
1797	11	1839	49	1881	−41	
1798	2	1840	−31	1882	110	
1799	−15	1841	8	1883	51	
1800	2	1842	−6	1884	105	
1801	−2	1843	−22	1885	34	
1802	−7	1844	−4	1886	137	
1803	3	1845	−4	1887	231	
1804	−12	1846	−1	1888	287	
1805	10	1847	−19	1889	202	
1806	7	1848	2	1890	194	
1807	5	1849	−3	1891	136	
1808	17	1850	29	1892	41	
1809	−12	1851	6	1893	146	
1810	−7	1852	16	1894	−66	
1811	−35	1853	56	1895	137	
1812	21	1854	42	1896	40	
1813	−15	1855	15	1897	−23	
1814	9	1856	12	1898	−279	
1815	15	1857	17	1899	−229	
1816	58	1858	−23	1900[a]	−296	
1817	11	1859	26	1900[b]	−321	−218
1818	25	1860	−7	1901	−273	−245
1819	15	1861	103	1902	−82	−135
1820	−1	1862	0	1903	−154	−21
1821	−5	1863	13	1904	−117	−10
1822	8	1864	111	1905	−94	−83
1823	−2	1865	59	1906	22	68
1824	−1	1866	95	1907	35	71
1825	−7	1867	145	1908	−187	−46
1826	3	1868	73	1909	143	59
1827	−10	1869	176	1910	229	255
1828	11	1870	100	1911	40	48
1829	−2	1871	101	1912	36	23
1830	−8	1872	242	1913	−142	87
1831	−14	1873	167	1914	−72	−72

[a]Comparable to earlier years. [b]Comparable to later years. *Source*: U.S. Bureau of the Census, *Historical Statistics of the United States, Colonial Times to 1970* (Washington, DC, 1975), Series U 18–25.

different, their reports on the timing and magnitude of net capital imports are similar.[8] All three agree that, between 1790 and 1813, net capital movements fluctuated around zero. The figures indicate that there were thirteen years of net capital imports and ten of net exports; and, taken together, they suggest a very modest net capital inflow of $125,000 a year.

That flow was greatly magnified over the next six years. The new capital was primarily employed in financing the federal government, the Second Bank of the United States, and the nation's external trade. The following twelve years (1820–1831), however, saw a return to the pattern established in the years before 1814 – small annual flows fluctuating around zero – but, this time yielding, on average, a net outflow of about $1.3 million per year.

The 1830s were a period of very substantial foreign investment in the United States. Between 1832 and 1839 the nation received, net, no less than $189 million in foreign capital – more than $12 for every man, woman, and child in the country. Williamson approvingly cites North's conclusion that "relative to the size of the economy it was probably the most significant inflow of capital during the nineteenth century." All three studies agree that the lion's share of the inflow was contracted by state governments and that it was largely directed toward expanding the commercial banking and the transportation sectors.[9] Between 1830 and 1838 the states borrowed almost $150 million.

Although banks were established and the transport network built, financial panic and economic depression made it difficult for the borrowing states to meet their financial obligations; and many states went into default. Because of foreign reaction to those dishonored debts Americans encountered difficulties borrowing abroad.[10] In only two of the ten years 1840 through 1849 do the net figures show an inflow of capital;

---

[8] Chronologically, the first was Bullock et al., "The Balance of Trade." The second were the North and Simon pieces, and the last was Williamson's, *American Growth*. The discussion in this section is cast in terms of nominal dollars, since that is the measure used in the three studies. It should, however, be noted that, because of price changes, the pattern of real transfers differs somewhat from the standard scenario.

[9] Williamson, citing Bogart, reports that of the total of $170,356,187 in bonds issued by 18 states, 31 percent went to banks, 64 percent to transport (35 percent to canals, 25 percent to railroads, and 4 percent to roads), and the remaining 5 percent to various miscellaneous activities. Williamson, *American Growth*, table 19, 102.

[10] The OBE adjustments to North's capital estimates, for example, include $24 million in defaults in 1841 and 1842. Williamson, citing Imlah, argues that of Jenks' estimate of a total of $174 million of American debt held in England in 1838, "almost the whole was in default or repudiated by 1842." Williamson, *American Growth*, 106.

and, for the entire decade, capital exports exceeded imports by $60 million.

The next episode in the history of the American balance of payments encompassed the years 1850 through 1876. In twenty-five of those twenty-seven years the net capital flows were positive, in one year it was close to zero, and in only one year was there a measurable outflow of funds. Overall, net capital imports exceeded $1.7 billion.

The flow in the 1850s was about equal what it had been two decades before; however, it included a greater portion of portfolio transfers; and, within that portfolio, there appears to have been a greater proportion of private – mostly railroad – issues. Cleona Lewis argues that, in 1853, the total for all indebtedness was probably about $375 million; and by 1860 the investments in securities alone were thought to have been about $400 million.[11]

The next decade saw capital imports of unprecedented proportions; from 1860 through 1869, the net inflow totaled $761 million – more than $21 per capita. The federal government incurred interest-bearing debt of $2.4 billion, and state and local indebtedness had increased by some $500 million.

By 1868, according to *Hunt's Merchants' Magazine*, $700,000,000 of United States bonds were held abroad, and they had not netted American sellers more than 57½ percent. Secretary McCulloch estimated the foreign investments, excluding railway stocks, at $850,000,000. Altogether the amount of American securities held abroad was estimated at $938,000,000.[12]

Cleona Lewis, basing her calculations on David Wells' enumerations, estimates total U.S. indebtedness in 1869 at "a little above 1.5 billion."[13] Simon takes exception with this figure. He notes, "although sizable quantities of government bonds were sold at a discount in European markets, my estimates suggest that Wells's 1869 estimate is clearly extravagant"; and he suggests an alternative figure of $1.2 billion – a figure that can be reached by adding the balancing items in the OBE's revisions of the North

[11] See Bullock et al., "The Balance of Trade," 223 and Cleona Lewis assisted by Karl T. Shottenbeck, *America's Stake in International Investment* (Washington, DC, 1938), 521–22.
    The source of both Bullock et al. and Lewis's estimate is *Hunt's Merchants' Magazine* for October 1868, but the former attributes the assessment to the secretary of the Treasury, the latter to "currently accepted opinion."

[12] Bullock et al., The Balance of Trade," 223.

[13] Lewis, *America's Stake*, 522–23. Wells was Special Commissioner of Revenue. David A. Wells, *Report of the Special Commissioner of Revenue, 1869*, 41st Congress, House of Representatives, Executive Document No. 27, December 29, 1869, xxvi.

and Simon series.[14] Nor did 1869 see the end of the inflow. The years 1870 to 1876 added an additional $781 million.

Bullock delimits the next episode at 1874 and 1895, while Williamson, demarks it at 1879 and 1900. The net flows suggest that there may have been two distinct episodes. The first, spanning the years 1877 through 1881, was marked by four years of capital outflow; and, as a result, a reduction of American net foreign liabilities of $390 million.[15]

The second "era" stretches from 1882 through 1896. In fourteen of those fifteen years, capital flowed into the country; and the inflows equaled the $1.7 billion transferred between 1850 and 1876. Although there was a preponderance of railway securities in the total, those years also saw foreign funds flowing into western mining, agriculture, and land development. In the years 1890–1896 the net flow estimates show a decline over the totals of the previous decade; but even including the 1894 outflow, they indicate a continued capital importation of just less than $90 million a year.

The long-term increase of foreign investment was dramatically reversed in the nine years 1897–1905. Unfortunately, because of problems with the data, it is difficult to provide a precise estimate on the total size of the outflow. The net capital series indicate that, by Simon's calculations, net exports totaled $827 million between the beginning of 1897 and the end of 1900, and by Goldsmith's long term estimates, $712 million for the years 1900 through 1905.[16] The United States had become a major capital exporter. Between 1897 and 1908 American direct investments abroad rose from $635 to $1,639 million; portfolio investments increased from $50 to $886 million; and, taken together, all foreign holdings rose from $685 to $2,525 million.[17]

The last nine years before the outbreak of World War I, however, witnessed a return to the era of heavy American borrowing. In only two years was the nation a net exporter of capital, and in 1910 the import was $255 million. Overall, despite a more than 40 percent increase in American direct and portfolio investment abroad, between January 1906

[14] Simon, "Balance of Payments," 706. The $1.152 figure is from *Historical Statistics*, series U 40, 869. It may be possible to resolve the difference, if one notes that 43 percent of $700 million is about $300 million and that the difference between $1.5 and $1.2 billion is also about $300 million.

[15] According to Bullock et al., those transfers reflected a delayed European response to the fears engendered by the effects of the Panic of 1873. They report that $300 million of foreign-held securities were repatriated between 1876 and 1878, with half of that figure withdrawn in 1878 alone. Bullock, et al., "The Balance of Trade," 225.

[16] An estimate based on the extension of the Simon residual series suggests the outflow may have totaled something more than $1.4 billion, while using the average value for 1901 suggests the figure was in excess of $1.5 billion.

[17] Lewis, *America's Stake*, 605.

Table 16.3. *Industrial distribution of foreign investments in the United States*

Years	Total gov.	U.S. gov.	State & local gov.	Railroads	Other private securities	Direct inv.	Short-Term inv.	Total Foreign inv.
				Millions of dollars				
1843	150	0	150	0	53	small	28	231
1853	159	27	132	52	8	5	150	374
1869	1,108	1,000	108	243	15	25	153	1,544
1914	213	nd	nd	3,934	1,607	1,210	450	7,414
				Percentages				
1843	65	0	65	0	23	0	12	100
1853	43	7	36	14	2	1	40	100
1869	72	64	7	16	1	2	10	100
1914	3	nd	nd	53	22	16	6	100

Source: Cleona Lewis, *America's Stake in International Investment* (Washington, DC, 1938), 519–57.
Note: nd = no data.

and December 1914, long term capital imports exceeded exports by $493 million.[18] By that latter date, the country's net indebtedness again almost certainly exceeded $2.5 billion.

CROSS-SECTIONAL EVIDENCE ON THE INDUSTRIAL STRUCTURE OF FOREIGN INVESTMENT AND OF THE SOURCES OF THAT INVESTMENT: ESTIMATES OF THE GROSS FLOWS

Table 16.3 displays estimates of the distribution of both long and short term finance in 1843, 1853, 1869, and 1914. Table 16.4 reports the distribution of long-term investments at six dates between 1803 and 1880.[19] The 1803 total reflects the fact that 56 percent of all federal debt was also foreign held – the highest proportion of federal debt ever lodged in foreign hands. In

[18] Between 1908 and 1914 American direct investment abroad increased from $1,639 to $2,652 million, although portfolio investment declined by $25 million. Lewis, *America's Stake*, 605.
[19] One note: while there may be some question about the size of the total level of foreign investment on the dates in question, there is no reason to believe that the estimates of the sectoral composition of those investments should be badly distorted.

Table 16.4. *Industrial distribution of long-term foreign investments in the United States*

Years	Federal government	State & local	1st & 2nd U.S. & other banks	Turnpikes & canals	Railroads	Unidentified & Miscellaneous	Total Long-Term Foreign Investment
			Millions of dollars				
1803	48.7	0.0	15.2	0.2	0.0	3.4	67.5
1838	0.0	66.5	24.8	2.0	0.0	16.7	110.0
1838*	0.0	3.3	45.3	28.0	16.7	16.7	110.0
1853	27.0	132.5	6.7	2.5	52.1	1.3	222.1
1856	15.0	132.5	6.7	2.5	82.9	1.4	241.0
1869	1,000.0	107.5	(a)	5.0	243.0	35.0	1,390.5
1880	249.0	97.0	(a)	0.0	899.0	4.0	1,249.0
			Percentages				
1803	72.1	0.0	22.5	0.3	0.0	5.0	100.0
1838	0.0	60.5	22.5	1.8	0.0	15.2	100.0
1838*	0.0	3.0	41.2	25.5	15.2	15.2	100.0
1853	12.2	59.7	3.0	1.1	23.5	0.6	100.0
1856	6.2	55.0	2.8	1.0	34.4	0.6	100.0
1869	71.9	7.7	0.0	0.4	17.5	2.5	100.0
1880	19.9	7.8	0.0	0.0	72.0	0.3	100.0

*Distributes government loans on the basis of their announced purposes.
(a) Included in unidentified and miscellaneous.
Source: Mira Wilkins, *The History of Foreign Investment in the United States to 1914* (Cambridge, MA, 1989), 50, 91, and 147.

addition, it captures the issues of the First Bank of the United States ($6.2 million) and another $9 million of "other" bank issues.

While the federal debt had burgeoned to almost $120 million by the end of the War of 1812, only a quarter was held overseas; and by 1835 that entire debt (including the estimated one-third held in Europe) had been repaid. Increases in state borrowing had, however, more than offset that reduction; and perhaps as much as 40 percent of those funds were raised abroad.[20] Bonds of the State of New York were quoted in London

[20] McGrane's examination of the holders of the Pennsylvania loan of 1842 – a loan that may not be typical – indicates that, of the total of $34 million, $23.717 million, or about 70 percent, was held abroad. Reginald C. McGrane, *Foreign Bondholders and American State Debts* (New York, 1935), 71.

as early as 1817, and even the issues of American cities began to appear in Europe after 1830.[21] By 1838 eighteen states had borrowed $170 million; four years later the number of debtor states had risen to twenty and their total borrowings to $198 million.[22]

Although the states and cities acted as guarantors, it was the nation's financial and transportation infrastructure that received the bulk of the foreign funds. About 41 percent of the 1838 total was directed towards the nation's banks, 25 percent toward its canals, 15 percent towards its railroads, and 4 percent toward its roads. Thus, if the state and local government loans are reallocated on the basis of their announced purpose (see Table 16.4 entry for 1838), something more than $45 million was invested in banking, $28 million in canals and turnpikes, and $17 million in railroads. If the same exercise is repeated with the loans outstanding in 1842, foreign support for railroad investment appears to have been somewhere in the neighborhood of $38 million.[23]

The effects of the financial debacle of the early 1840s are still visible on the distribution of foreign investments in 1853. Although the total net indebtedness changed little between the 1830s and 1850s, the proportion of short-term debt rose from 12 percent in 1843 to 40 percent a decade later, and the relative share of government debt fell from 65 to 43 percent, despite a $27 million increase in the amount of federal debt held abroad. Clearly state and local governments had reduced – partially by default to be sure – their debts from the peak levels of the early 1840s. At the same time, the bankruptcy of the Second Bank of the United States reduced the share of banking investments on the nation's international balance sheet.[24] Thus, the proportion of government and bank issues in the total of long-term foreign investment declined from more than four-fifths in 1838 to two-thirds eighteen years later.

Wilkins cites Representative James Garland, who told the House that of all state securities outstanding, at least $65 million were held abroad, principally in England. She comments that this figure represents about 38 percent of state securities outstanding. See Mira Wilkins, *The History of Foreign Investment in the United States to 1914* (Cambridge, MA, 1989), 59.

[21] Leland Jenks, *The Migration of British Capital to 1875* (London, 1963), 360–61.

[22] Williamson, *American Growth*, table 19, 102; and Lewis, *America's Stake*, 21. The 1843 figures do not make adjustment for bonds in default.

[23] The distributions are made on the basis of the enumerations of state obligations in E. L. Bogart, *The Economic History of the United States,* 2nd edition (New York, 1913), 195.

[24] Lewis thinks that foreigners held as much as $20 million of the Bank's stock and had loaned the Bank another $12 million, and that these were probably included in the total for 1843. Lewis, *America's Stake*, 520. Wilkins's data for 1838 include $20 million of Second Bank stock in the total $24.8 million in bank securities. Her figure for "other" banks in 1853 is $6.7 million, an increase over 1838 of about 40 percent. Wilkins, *Foreign Investment*, 76.

In addition to the increasing proportion of short-term credit, the declines in banking and government investments were offset by an increasing commitment to privately financed railroads. Those railroads had attracted little foreign finance in 1838, but by 1853 they accounted for almost one-quarter of long-term and one-seventh of all foreign investment. In 1853 the Secretary of the Treasury noted that 76 of the 244 railroads that he had canvassed reported that they had attracted some foreign investors, and he put total foreign investment in American railroad securities at $52.1 million.[25]

The 1869 enumeration captures the Federal government's massive borrowing during the Civil War. Those obligations totaled $1.0 billion – 72 percent of long-term and 64 percent of all foreign investment. It also reflects the continued contraction of state and local borrowing, the fact that short-term investment remained constant in absolute terms but fell sharply in relative ones, and that railroad investment increased at an average rate that exceeded 35 percent a year.

The estimates for 1880 underscore two new trends in the pattern of foreign investment. Between 1869 and 1880 there was a dramatic reduction in the role of federal debt, and the vast majority of new investment was directed toward American railroads. Although the rate of increase declined somewhat, foreign investment in that sector continued to increase at almost 25 percent a year.

The 1914 enumerations provide a clear picture of the sectoral distribution of foreign investment on the eve of World War I (see Table 16.3). As American capital markets matured, the fraction of finance channeled to government continued to decline, as did the relative role of short-term credit. Although foreign holdings of American rails had more than tripled between 1880 and 1914, they constituted a far smaller share of those investors' total American commitments. In terms of their relative importance, it was the "other securities" and "direct investments" that increased most rapidly – from less than 1 to almost 40 percent of all foreign investment; and, by 1914, they represented some $2.8 billion dollars. By the outbreak of the World War I, foreign investment had penetrated almost every aspect of American life (see Table 16.5).

Who were the foreigners willing to invest their savings in the United States? Cleona Lewis begins her landmark study with the observation that "the American colonies were founded and developed by the aid of European capital; largely from Great Britain, but with funds from other coun-

---

[25] Wilkins, *Foreign Investment*, 78–80. D. C. M. Platt, *Foreign Finance in Continental Europe and the USA, 1815–1870: Quantities, Origins, Functions, and Distribution* (London, 1984), 157 and 163.

Table 16.5. *Estimated industrial distribution of long-term foreign investments in the United States, 1914*

Railroads	Government	Banks	Breweries & distilleries	Commercial & industrial	Agricultural & land related	Public utilities	Oil & mining
			Millions of dollars				
3,934	213	32	355	508	972	222	517
			Percentages				
58.3	3.2	0.5	5.3	7.5	14.4	3.3	7.7

Source: Underlying data are from Lewis, *America's Stake*, 529–57.

tries also participating – particularly from Holland, France and Spain."[26] The debts arising from the Revolutionary War and the Louisiana Purchase were initially funded by the French and the Dutch; but, within only a few years a substantial fraction of those claims had been transferred across the English Channel to be absorbed by the British investing public – the same investors who were to make large loans to the Second Bank of the United States within three years of the signing of the Treaty of Ghent.[27] Wilkins estimates that in 1818 the British held 48 percent of the foreign-held federal debt and the Dutch, 43 percent; a decade later the figures were 74 percent and 7 percent.[28] Similarly, the "greater part" of the New York State bonds issued to finance the Erie Canal was "bought up by English investors."[29]

British dominance continued into the "frenzied thirties"; but every major European financial center had private banking houses that dealt in state and local securities; and there is evidence that, after 1838, continental investors became more heavily involved in American finance.[30] By the 1850s, however, as European capital again began to flow to the United States in large quantities, it was the British who again played the leading role. Jenks places that nation's investment in the United States in 1854 at $240 to $290 million; and Hobson concludes that those investments rose from about $300 million in 1852 to about $500 million in 1857.[31]

By mid-century the Dutch, although still important, played a much less

---

[26] Lewis, *America's Stake*, 7.   [27] Jenks, *The Migration of British Capital*, 65–66.
[28] Wilkins, *Foreign Investment*, 53–54.
[29] Lewis, *America's Stake*, 17. The bonds were issued between 1817 and 1825.
[30] Wilkins, *Foreign Investment*, 70.
[31] Jenks, *The Migration of British Capital*, 413. C. K. Hobson, *The Export of Capital* (New York, 1914), 128.

significant role than they had five decades earlier. The German stake in American railroads had increased; there was a somewhat lesser amount of French investment; some "Swiss monies entered"; and other nationalities were also present.[32] During the postbellum era, both German and Dutch investment became more important. In the German case, the increase rested in large part on the close personal ties between emigrant Germans and the banking community at home. In the case of the Netherlands, to minimize risk to individual investors, Dutch bankers organized formal trusts or holding companies to invest in American securities, particularly in railroad issues.[33]

Lewis notes that the Dutch made substantial investments in railroads in the Mississippi Valley and the West – in the process, they were burned at least twice – and that, for a few years at least, the Germans were "the largest buyers" and held the title of "the chief center of European investments in our bonds."[34] Herbert Feis concluded that the securities of American railways had "long enjoyed an active market on the German stock exchanges," that German capital had built branch factories to utilize that nation's chemical and metallurgical patents, and that they had established numerous trading concerns.[35] More recently, Richard Tilly, citing both the close personal connections that existed between German and American bankers and Feis's quantitative study, concluded that "the United States was the largest single recipient of German foreign investment in the late 19th century," although "that weight declined after around 1900 – at least for portfolio investment."[36]

The British were, however, the major investors. Even as the Germans were being trumpeted as "the largest buyers," British holdings were seven times as large.[37] At the beginning of the 1860s, Britain may well have accounted for nine dollars of every ten of foreign investment in the United

---

[32] Wilkins, *Foreign Investment*, 89. Augustus J. Veenendaal, Jr., "The Kansas City Southern Railway and the Dutch Connection," *Business History Review*, 61 (1987), 292.

[33] Wilkins, *Foreign Investment*, 109 and 120.

[34] Lewis, *America's Stake*, 45. The quotations are from the *American Railroad Journal*, 1853, 370 and the *Commercial and Financial Chronicle*, July 16, 1870, 77.

[35] Herbert Feis, *Europe the World's Banker, 1870–1914: An Account of European Foreign Investment and the Connection of World Finance with Diplomacy before 1914* (New Haven, 1930), 76.

[36] Richard Tilly, "International Aspects of the Development of German Banking. In Rondo Cameron and V. I. Bovykin (eds.), *International Banking, 1870–1914* (New York, 1991), 90–112, and "Some Comments on German Foreign Portfolio Investment, 1870–1914," paper delivered in São Paolo, July 1989. His data suggest that North America received about 29 percent of German foreign portfolio investment in the years 1897 to 1906 and about 12 percent between 1907 and 1914. "International Aspects," table 3, 16.

[37] Lewis, *America's Stake*, 45.

Table 16.6. *Precentage of British investment in all foreign investment in the United States, 1861–1913*

Year	Percent
1861	90.0
1865	88.0
1870	85.5
1875	83.0
1880	80.5
1885	79.5
1890	77.0
1895	74.5
1900	71.0
1905	66.0
1910	61.0
1913	59.0

Source: John H. Dunning, *Studies in International Investment* (London, 1970).

States. Thereafter, although the United Kingdom's relative position had begun to erode – it had fallen to about three in every four by the mids-1890s, and it was probably less than three in five by 1913 – Britain retained its role as senior partner (see Table 16.6).[38] The studies of Nathaniel Bacon (1899) and George Paish (1908) capture the increased geographic scope of the sources of foreign investment: and Mira Wilkins's extensions of Cleona Lewis's estimates for 1914 confirm the spread of the capital base across Europe as well as a significant flow from north of the U.S. border (see Tables 16.7 and 16.8).

THE INDUSTRIAL DISPOSITION OF FOREIGN CAPITAL: MICRO EVIDENCE

1803–1840

Europeans held a substantial portion of federal debt in the early years of the nineteenth century; there is evidence of investment in land and financial institutions; and they also invested heavily in the Second Bank

[38] John H. Dunning, *Studies in International Investment* (London, 1970).

Table 16.7. *Sources of foreign investment in the*
United States by country

Country	1899	1908	1914
	Millions of dollars		
Great Britain	2,500	3,500	4,046
Germany	200	1,000	904
Netherlands	240	750	605
France	50	500	390
Other European	110	250	143
Canada	nd	na	263
Other	45	na	400
Total	3,145	6,000	6,751
	Percentages		
Great Britain	80	58	60
Germany	6	17	13
Netherlands	8	13	9
France	2	8	6
Other European	3	4	2
Canada	nd	na	4
Other	1	na	6
Total	100	100	100

Source: Lewis, *America's Stake*, 524, 530, and 546.

of the United States. Their holdings of Second Bank stock grew from $3
million in 1820 to $20 million in 1838, when they represented 57 percent
of the Bank's stock then in private hands.[39]

The majority of capital transfers between 1803 and the early 1830s,
however, took the form of short-term commercial credit channeled through
independent nonspecialized urban merchants. Those firms were sometimes
of American origin, but often they had been established by British manufacturers to facilitate the distribution of British goods to the very diffused
and diverse American market.[40] Even after widespread mercantile bankruptcies in the mid-1820s, British houses – houses such as Brown Brothers
and Barings – were able to continue to dominate American overseas trade.[41]

[39] Jenks, *The Migration of British Capital*, 66. Wilkins, *Foreign Investment*, 61–62.
[40] John H. Dunning, "British Investment in U.S. Industry," in *Moorgate and Wall Street* (1961), 5–23.
[41] Jenks, *The Migration of British Capital*, 68–69.

Table 16.8. *Estimates of long-term foreign investments in the United States by nationality of investor*

Nationality	1899	1907	1908	1914a	1914b	1914c
	Millions of dollars					
British	2,500	4,000	3,500	4,000	4,250	4,250
French	50	300	630	1,000	410	480
German	200	1,000	1,000	1,250	950	1,100
Dutch	240	600	750	650	635	650
Swiss	75	100	(a)	(b)	(b)	70
Belgian	20	0	(a)	(b)	(b)	30
Other Europeans	15	0	130	(b)	150	180
Canadian	(b)	0	0	(b)	275	225
Japanese	(b)	0	0	(b)	(b)	25
All Others	45	0	0	100	420	30
Toal	3,145	6,000	6,010	7,000	7,090	7,090
	Percentages					
British	79	67	58	57	60	60
French	2	5	10	14	6	7
German	6	17	17	18	13	16
Dutch	8	10	12	9	9	9
Swiss	2	2				1
Belgian	1	0				0
Other Europeans	0	0	2		2	3
Canadian		0	0		4	4
Japanese		0	0			0
All others	1	0	0	1	6	0
Total	100	100	100	100	100	100

(a) included in "Other Europeans".
(b) included in "All others."
Source: **1899**: Nathaniel Bacon, "American International Indebtedness" *Yale Review* 9 (1900) 268–279. **1907**: Charles F. Speare, "Selling American Bonds in Europe" *Annals of the American Academy of Political and Social Sciences*, 30 (1907), 269–293. **1908** U.S. Senate, National Monetary Commission, *Trade Balances in 1908 of the United States* (by George Paish), 61st. Cong., 2nd Sess., 1910, S. Doc. 579, 174–175. Publicly issued securities only. No figures given for any countries outside Europe. **1914a** Harvey E. Fisk, *The Inter Ally Debt* (New York, 1924), 312. **1914b**: Lewis, *American Stake*, 546. **1914c**: Wilkins, *Foreign Investment*, 159 all listed in Wilkins, *Foreign Investment*, 159.

In addition, the British short-term capital market "provided banks with funds to carry inventories of gold or securities, it supplied exchange dealers with the sterling bills to reduce fluctuation in the value of the dollar, and it advanced the funds that enabled American railways to continue building while they mobilized longer-term support at home." More than a quarter of all American imports were financed in London, and by 1836 the credit extended to Americans on commercial account totaled £20 million.[42]

State and local government borrowing dominated the 1830s, but there were also private placements. In 1830, for example, the promoters of the Camden and Amboy Railroad sold one-half of the initial capital stock offerings in the United Kingdom; and, in 1838, the C&A became the first American railroad to be included on the London Stock Exchange's "Official List." Before the decade was over, five other private American railroads had raised capital in London.

Both the Rothschilds and the Barings were included in the group of British investors who purchased the capital issues of at least ten banks located in five states, and Dutch capitalists invested in five other banks in New York, Louisiana, and Florida. An 1837 Louisiana state report indicated that foreigners had invested in twelve of the state's sixteen banks and that they held 52 percent of the state's banking capital. Moreover, although three-quarters of that investment was backed by state guarantees, almost $6 million was not.

The North American Trust, the New York Life Insurance and Trust, the American Life Insurance and Trust, the Ohio Life Insurance and Trust, and the New York Farmers Loan and Trust all raised capital abroad. Farther west, George Smith tapped Scottish investors for more than $1.8 million for the Wisconsin Marine and Fire Insurance Company and his four other land and investment companies.[43]

1840–1914: Railroads

From the late 1860s until World War I, railroads received far more attention from foreign investors than any other sector of the American economy;

---

[42] Lewis, citing G. S. Callender, puts the figure at £17.5 million and Jenks, citing the *Morning Chronicle* (London) places the figure at £20.5 million. Lewis, *America's Stake*, 13. Jenks, *The Migration of British Capital*, 87. Platt, *Foreign Finance*, Appendix IV, 195. Quote is from 144. Wilkins, *Foreign Investment*, 59–60.

[43] The discussion of private investments in the 1830s is drawn from Lewis, *America's Stake*, 20–22, Wilkins, *Foreign Investment*, 61–66.

and, if Civil War finance is excluded, that conclusion holds from the 1840s. Despite frequent bankruptcies, reorganizations, and skipped dividends, the United States was the beneficiary of some combination of "enlarged preferences for risky assets and a relatively sparse source of those assets originating elsewhere." Moreover, although certainly risky, those American rails paid substantially higher returns than their U.K. counterparts in the early years and still somewhat more after 1900, when they appear to have become substantially less risky.[44] Whether the inducement was a desire to hold risky assets, high expected returns, substantial risk-adjusted returns, or the dulcet voices of the likes of Jay Cooke, James McHenry, and Henry Villard, the British in particular, and northern Europeans in general, displayed an amazing affinity for the issues of American railroads.

It is estimated that, as early as mid-century, Europeans were absorbing between $30 and $40 million in American railroad securities annually.[45] By the early 1850s, a British wine grower and merchant had become the largest single investor in the New York Central; European investors held 60 percent of the Illinois Central's equity and an additional $12 million of its bonds; and the British holdings of the Philadelphia and Reading were so large that its president was selected from the firm's London bankers.[46] In 1856 the first American railroad was listed on the Amsterdam exchange; by 1860, the number listed in London had risen to seven.[47]

Four years later three-quarters of the Illinois Central's stock was in European hands; and the railroad continued to be "largely owned by English and Continental Investors until the turn of the century."[48] In 1872, when British investors forced Jay Gould's resignation as president of the Erie, foreign holdings of that railroad's stock increased from 60 to almost 100 percent.[49] Between 1865 and 1914 total railroad flotations in London

---

[44] It is estimated that in 1876, for example 65 percent of all European-held American railroad securities were in default. *Banker's Magazine*, 30 (1876), 846. Quote is from Michael Edelstein, *Overseas Investment in the Age of High Imperialism: The United Kingdom, 1850–1914* (New York, 1982), 93–101.

[45] Frederick A. Cleveland and Fred Wilbur Powell, *Railroad Promotion and Capitalization in the United States* (New York, 1909), 37–38; cited in Lewis, *America's Stake*, 30.

[46] Wilkins, *Foreign Investment*, 94–97. Lewis, *America's Stake*, 39. Salomon F. Van Oss, *America's Railroads as Investments* (New York, 1977), 315.

[47] The Illinois Central was the first American railroad listed in Amsterdam. Wilkins, *Foreign Investment*, 97–98. Veenendaal, "The Kansas City Southern Railway," 293.

[48] Wilkins, *Foreign Investment*, 105. Lewis, *America's Stake*, 105. Paul W. Gates, *The Illinois Central and Its Colonization Work* (Cambridge, MA, 1934), 76.

[49] Wilkins, *Foreign Investment*, 114.

Table 16.9A. *U.S. capital called London Stock Exchange (thousands of dollars) all years 1865–1914*

Industry	Total calls	Average calls per year	Percentage of total calls
Transport	2,841,739	56,835	54.4
Government	1,603,793	32,076	30.7
Manufacturing & commerce	233,635	4,673	4.5
Agricultural & extractive	256,786	5,161	4.9
Mining	(103,227)	(2,054)	(2.0)
Agricultural	(30,941)	(619)	(0.6)
Petroleum & chemical	(22,751)	(455)	(0.4)
Financial land & mort.	(99,868)	(2,023)	(1.9)
Finance	79,217	1,584	1.5
Public utilities	207,417	4,148	4.0
Total calls	5,222,586	104,476	100.0

exceeded $2.775 billion. In no year did they tally less than $3.2 million, and in 1902 they reached almost one hundred times that amount.[50] A summary of the capital called series on which those estimates are based is presented in Tables 16.9A, 16.9B, and 16.9C.

Railroad construction proceeded in a series of waves with peaks in 1872,

[50] These creations and calls are frequently referred to as London calls, but they include some from the provincial market. See A. R. Hall, "A Note on the English Capital Market as a Source for Home Investment Before 1914," *Economica*, 24 (1957), 59–66. The British data are taken from a series reported in Lance Davis and Robert Huttenback, *Mammon and the Pursuit of Empire: The Political Economy of British Imperialism, 1860–1912* (Cambridge, 1986), chap. 2. Unlike current practice, in the nineteenth-century issues were sometimes sold on "on time." That is, a £1,000 equity might be sold to an investor on the initial payment of £100 and his agreement to pay for the remainder as the issuing firm demanded. The term "call" was used to describe the announcements of the "periodic installments that were to be paid by the subscribers to the new issue." For purposes of simplicity, in this work, the term "capital called" is used to describe both capital created and capital called. Harvey H. Segal, and Matthew Simon, "British Foreign Capital Issues, 1865–1914," *Journal of Economic History*, 21 (1961). The reader should also bear in mind that this series represents an enumeration of new issues and it does not include American securities that British investors may have purchased or that may have been traded on the London Exchange and, thus, been available for British investment, unless they were initially floated in London.

Although limited to the British contribution, the series is useful because it can be disaggregated by industry and, to some extent, by region. The series does not reflect repatriations, and, therefore, mirrors the demand for finance at any moment in time.

Finally, as Segal and Simon noted, "one can never be sure that a foreign capital issue floated in the British market actually resulted in a foreign capital transfer." Segal and Simon, "British Foreign Capital Issues." There is no way to directly estimate the fraction of funds "called" that remained in Britain or that were directed to yet a third country, but a sampling of firms for which other records exist, suggest that the proportion was, in most cases, not large.

Table 16.9B. *U.S. capital called London Stock Exchange (thousands of dollars)*

Year	Mfg., comm. & misc.	Finance	Government	Agric. & extractive	Transport	Public utils.	Total cap call
1865–69	156	3,847	3,615	1,636	49,994	8,961	68,209
1870–74	16,207	4,869	518,972	27,233	275,338	8,369	850,988
1875–79	329	331	1,009,952	3,662	93,587	11,285	1,119,146
1880–84	4,927	21,322	0	31,084	289,908	1,269	348,510
1885–89	46,816	10,520	39	34,093	190,420	9,145	291,032
1890–94	51,578	12,791	3,931	45,205	269,022	158	382,686
1895–99	34,871	3,754	65,006	13,534	89,398	2,196	208,760
1900–04	6,517	7,549	0	13,765	476,267	2,620	506,718
1905–09	19,146	3,987	0	28,140	572,260	71,891	695,424
1910–14	53,087	10,245	2,280	58,433	535,546	91,522	751,114
Total	233,635	79,217	1,603,793	256,785	2,841,739	207,417	5,222,585

Percentages of total U.S. calls

Year	Mfg., comm. & misc.	Finance	Government	Agric. & extractive	Transport	Public utils.	Total cap call
1865–69	0.2	5.6	5.3	2.4	73.3	13.1	100.0
1870–74	1.9	0.6	61.0	3.2	32.4	1.0	100.0
1875–79	0.0	0.0	90.2	0.3	8.4	1.0	100.0
1880–84	1.4	6.1	0.0	8.9	83.2	0.4	100.0
1885–89	16.1	3.6	0.0	11.7	65.4	3.1	100.0
1890–94	13.5	3.3	1.0	11.8	70.3	0.0	100.0
1895–99	16.7	1.8	31.1	6.5	42.8	1.1	100.0
1900–04	1.3	1.5	0.0	2.7	94.0	0.5	100.0
1905–09	2.8	0.6	0.0	4.0	82.3	10.3	100.0
1910–14	7.1	1.5	0.3	7.8	71.3	12.2	100.0
Total	4.5	1.5	30.7	4.9	54.4	4.0	100.0

Table 16.9C. *U.S. capital calls, agricultural and extractive industry (thousands of dollars)*

Years	Total	Mining	Agriculture	Petroleum & chemical	FLD[a]
1865–69	1,636	1,636	0	0	0
1870–74	27,233	20,259	670	110	6,195
1875–79	3,662	650	146	0	2,866
1880–84	31,084	12,455	9,936	0	8,694
1885–89	34,093	14,549	8,115	317	11,112
1890–94	45,205	3,922	5,161	82	36,041
1895–99	13,534	7,765	354	73	5,342
1900–04	13,765	3,636	292	6,887	2,960
1905–09	28,140	13,631	326	5,834	8,348
1910–14	58,433	24,723	5,941	9,459	18,310
Total	256,785	103,226	30,941	22,751	99,868

Percentages of total U.S. calls

Years	Total	Mining	Agriculture	Petroleum & chemical	FLD[a]
1865–69	2.4	2.4	0.0	0.0	0.0
1870–74	3.2	2.4	0.1	0.0	0.7
1875–79	0.3	0.1	0.0	0.0	0.3
1880–84	8.9	3.6	2.9	0.0	2.5
1885–89	11.7	5.0	2.8	0.1	3.8
1890–94	11.8	1.0	1.3	0.0	9.4
1895–99	6.5	3.7	0.2	0.0	2.6
1900–04	2.7	0.7	0.1	1.4	0.6
1905–09	4.0	2.0	0.0	0.8	1.2
1910–14	7.8	3.3	0.8	1.3	2.4

[a] Financial, land and development.

Source: Lance E. Davis and Robert Huttenback, *Mammon and the Pursuit of Empire: The Political Economy of British Imperialism, 1860–1912* (Cambridge, 1986).

1879, 1890, 1902, and 1906; the financial data track that pattern closely but lag it slightly.[51] "Calls" on the British market reached $80 million in 1873, $79 million in 1881, $89 million in 1890, $291 million in 1902, and $210 million in 1907. British investments in U.S. rails are estimated

We note also that we are not dealing with the ultimate ownership, but with the funds that went through the London markets (that is, with "the first foreign parent").

[51] *Historical Statistics*, 732. The temporal lags strongly suggest that construction – construction undertaken either by the railroad itself or, like the Union Pacific, (the Crédit Mobilier) and the Central Pacific, through separate companies – was initially financed, in the case of land grant railroads, by government bonds, or by infusions of short-term finance. It appears that it was only after con-

to have risen from $486 million in 1876, to $1.7 billion in 1898, and to $3.0 billion in 1913; and the nominal value of American railroad securities quoted on the London Stock Exchange rose from £82.7 million in 1873, to £1,107.5 million in 1903, to £1,729.6 million in 1913.[52]

In 1874 foreign holdings of American railroads were estimated to be $390 million.[53] In the early 1890s, foreign investors held between 50 and 75 percent of the equity of the Pennsy, the Louisville and Nashville, the Illinois Central, the New York, Ontario, and Western, the Philadelphia and Reading, and more than one-fifth of the Great Northern's, the Baltimore and Ohio's, and the Chicago, Milwaukee, and St Paul's.[54]

Among those European investors, the majority lived in the United Kingdom. Robert Fleming, the entrepreneurial force behind three Scottish American Investment Trusts, believed that "Scottish capital made possible the building of the American rail network many years earlier than would otherwise have been possible"; and while he probably overstated his case, British and Scottish investments were very important.[55]

The first postbellum wave of finance – the wave that peaked in 1873 – was primarily associated with the expansion and near completion of the networks in the East and Midwest. Most of the major lines were represented; but the London exchange provided the funding mechanism that permitted a number of very small lines to raise capital as well. For example, the bonds of the Perkiomen railroad – a Pennsylvania line connecting Perkiomen and Emaus junctions, a distance of 38.5 miles – found their way onto that distant market.

The geographic focus of the second wave – a wave that peaked in 1880 – was focused on the West and, to a lesser extent, the South. By 1890 the national network was largely in place; but the railroads needed funds to upgrade their facilities. At the same time, integration and consolidation

struction was completed that the railroads began to search for permanent finance. Kent T. Healy, "Development of the National Transportation System," in Harold F. Williamson (ed.), *The Growth of the American Economy* (New York, 1951), 376.

[52] Dorothy Adler, *British Investment in American Railroads, 1834–1898* (Charlottesville, VA, 1970), 166–68. George Paish, "Great Britain's Capital Investments in Individual, Colonial and Foreign Countries," *Journal of the Royal Statistical Society*, 74, Part II (1911), 167–201 and "The Export of Capital and the Cost of Living," *Statist Supplement*, 79 (1914), i–viii. E. Victor Morgan and W. A. Thomas, *The Stock Exchange: Its History and Functions* (London, 1962), 280–81.

[53] Jenks, *The Migration of British Capital*, 426.

[54] William Z. Ripley, *Railroads: Finance and Organization* (New York, 1915), 5.

[55] W. Turrentine Jackson, *The Enterprising Scot: Investors in the American West after 1873* (Edinburgh, 1968), 71.

Mira Wilkins makes the more reasonable point that "it is doubtful that without the foreign capital [mainly British, German, Dutch, French, and Canadian], the U.S. railroad network could have been completed as swiftly or as effectively." Wilkins, *Foreign Investment*, 226.

had dramatically reduced the number of roads competing for funds. Between 1905 and 1909 calls on the London market totaled $572 million, but only twenty-five railroads were involved. By 1914, British investors owned between $1 and $60 million in the shares of at least sixteen American railroads, and their investments in bonds were estimated to be two and a half times as large as their equity holdings.[56]

If the standard is the level of investment in 1914, the Germans made the second-greatest foreign contribution to the American railroad network. After the Civil War, German investors became interested in the land grant railroads in the West; and, while the suspensions that followed the Panic of 1873 briefly dimmed their ardor, the reorganizations of the early 1880s calmed their fears. By the end of the century they had invested a total of more than $100 million in eighteen American railroads – most in the West or Middle West; and by 1914, their holdings were three or more times the end-of-the-century figure.[57]

The Dutch were the third-largest group of investors in American rails. Soon after Appomattox they began to purchase the issues of American railroads in the Mississippi Valley and the West.[58] Despite their treatment at the hands of James McHenry and James J. Hill, they maintained their interest.[59] A 1909 Interstate Commerce Commission report placed Dutch equity holdings in thirteen railroads at $70 million.[60]

1840–1914: Government Securities

By 1853 the burden of foreign-held state debt had been reduced by repudiation and repayment to about $127 million; and most of the states had resumed payments of principal and interest. Hardly more than a decade later, however, the southern states' need to finance the Civil War and reconstruction again led them to the European capital markets. The federal government also turned to those markets for some military loans and, in the 1870s, to refinance its war swollen debt. Finally, the costs of

---

[56] *Report of the American Dollar Securities Committee*, cited in Lewis, *America's Stake*, 41.
[57] Lewis, *America's Stake*, 45–49.
[58] Robert E. Riegel, *The Story of the Western Railroads* (Lincoln, NE, 1926), 139.
[59] The Panic of 1873, for example, triggered the suspension of thirty-six railroad issues listed on the Amsterdam exchange. The Dutch investors held $129 million of those issues. Veenendaal, "The Kansas City Southern Railway," 245–96. In the case of McHenry, his Atlantic and Great Western railroad, already in default in 1867, is said, "during the years 1869–80," to have broken "the record for defaults and reorganizations." Van Oss, *American Railroads*, 412.
[60] Wilkins, *Foreign Investment*, fn. 58, 730. Lewis, *America's Stake*, 44–45.

urbanization were partly underwritten by foreign capital. Taken together, between 1865 and 1914 the British market alone absorbed $1.6 billion in American public issues, but the vast majority of the transfers occurred before 1880.

By the early 1870s, the total debts of the southern states had ballooned to more than $200 million; and nine states proved unwilling or unable to service their obligations.[61] On paper, in addition to passed interest payments, repudiation produced losses to lenders of between $70 and $80 million; and negotiations between the states and their foreign creditors produced an additional reduction of about $55 million of principal. Since many of these loans had been heavily discounted at the time of issue, the extent of actual losses suffered by foreign lenders may not have been great.[62] Given the reputation of the American states, the new legal restrictions placed on their fiscal commitments, and the improvements in the domestic capital markets, there is little evidence of further foreign borrowing after 1880. In fact, in 1915 the American Dollar Securities found evidence of only a single foreign-held state loan still outstanding – $37,000 of a New York State issue of 1897.[63]

Although the federal government needed funds to prosecute the Civil War, initially Europe did not appear to be a possible source. Public opinion in the United Kingdom made it impossible to raise funds there; and continental markets were only slightly more open. By 1865, however, the government had been able to raise more than $300 million in continental Europe; and, within a very short time, British attitudes also changed. During the 1870s, the six refunding operations were conducted largely in London, since, by then, British investors were in possession of most (about $1 billion) of the foreign-held U.S. government bonds.[64] Thereafter, only once again, in 1895, did the Treasury turn to Europe; but by then foreign participation was hardly necessary. The American market had developed sufficiently that this country's half of the $62 million issue was oversubscribed six times.[65]

---

[61] There were actually eleven states in default. They included nine from the South (Alabama, Arkansas, Florida, Georgia, Louisiana, North Carolina, South Carolina, Tennessee, and Virginia), Minnesota, and West Virginia (the latter for debt incurred before it was separated from Virginia). The Minnesota debt had been in default since 1859.

[62] For example, the bonds issued by North Carolina in 1868 sold in Europe at prices ranging from 10 to 30 cents on the dollar.

[63] Lewis, *America's Stake*, 57–63.

[64] Lewis, *America's Stake*, 53–56. L. Jenks, *The Migration of British Capital*, 280.

[65] Lewis, *America's Stake*, 66–67. The British portion was oversubscribed ten times. For a more detailed discussion see Frederick Lewis Allen, *The Great Pierpont Morgan* (New York, 1949), 99–125.

Although state and federal governments found it less necessary to turn to foreign markets, the same was not true of local government – foreign funds were needed to finance the infrastructure of the nation's cities. Faced by demands for street improvements, water systems, sewers, urban transport, and ultimately electrification, cities such as Boston, Providence, St. Louis, and New York turned to Europe and particularly to London. Although the total was small in comparison to the figures for federal or state loans, New York City alone repaid more than $80 million due in Paris and London in the last four months of 1914.[66] Despite local borrowing, although government issues had accounted for almost seven-tenths of all London issues in the 1860s and 1870s, they constituted less than 0.1 percent in the first years of the present century. In this dimension, at least, the domestic American capital market showed evidence of rapid maturation.

In other dimensions, however, development was slower. Americans proved willing to invest in railroads, but not at a rate sufficient to underwrite the expansion of the national network at the pace that did occur. By the 1880s they were also willing to meet the financial demands of the federal and state governments, but they were far less willing to invest their savings in other economic sectors, especially in non-traditional endeavors located outside New England and the Middle Atlantic states. Foreign capitalists proved more amenable. Between 1865 and 1914 the British capital market channeled almost 15 percent of the flows destined for America toward the agriculture and extractive industries, manufacturing and commerce, finance, and public utilities. Although the fraction for the 1860s and 1870s was less than 5 percent, the total reached almost one dollar in four in the 1880s and 1890s – two decades of rapid structural transformation; and it was still almost that large in the last decade, 1905 to 1914. These were, of course, sectors not well served by the formal domestic capital markets, at least not the New York Stock Exchange.

1840–1914: Land-Related Investments

Between the late 1860s and the First World War, there were foreign investments in financial land and development companies, in firms launched to farm or raise cattle in the South and West, in investment trusts

---

[66] Lewis, *America's Stake*, 63–66.

that held portfolios of American land and mortgages, in western mines, and in oil exploration and production.[67]

The history of foreign investment in American lands can be traced back to the eighteenth century, when Robert Morris sold more than a million acres in New York to an investment group headed by Sir William Pulteney and another five million to an association of Dutch investors.[68] Large-scale foreign entry into the American land market was, however, delayed until after the Civil War. The sector accounted for less than 2 percent of British capital calls in the 1860s and 1870s, but it drew more than 10 percent between 1882 and 1896 and almost three-fourths of that amount over the fifteen years before the Great War.

In 1869 a British promoter organized the purchase of the Maxwell land grant – "2,000,000 acres of land more or less" – in New Mexico and, despite questions about the validity of their title, incorporated the Maxwell Land Grant and Railway Company, and sold bonds in Britain and Holland.[69] At about the same time, a second British promoter organized the sale of the land covered by the Sangre de Cristo grant – land located in New Mexico and Colorado – to investors in Europe. He incorporated the Colorado Freehold Land and Emigration Company in London to purchase the northern half and the Dutch-financed United States Land and Freehold Company to develop the southern portion.[70]

The major foreign boom in American lands was, however, delayed until the next decade. Beginning in 1879 with the organization of firms like the Missouri Land Company of Scotland, foreign capital – particularly British funds – poured into American lands.[71] Lewis reports that twenty-nine foreign land companies with aggregate capital of \$52 million were registered in the United States between 1879 and 1911, and other sources suggest the number may have been twice as large.[72] The best estimates

---

[67] The typical form of those investments involved the organization of a "free standing company." See Mira Wilkins, "The Free-Standing Company, 1870–1914: An Important Type of British Foreign Direct Investment," *Economic History Review*, 2nd Series, 41 (1988), 259–82.

[68] See A. M. Sakolski, *The Great American Land Bubble* (New York, 1932), 31–86; Shaw Livermore, *Early American Land Companies* (New York, 1939), 162 and 203; and Paul D. Evans, *The Holland Land Company* (Buffalo, 1924), passim.

[69] The original company itself went bankrupt in 1875; but in 1879 the Secretary of the Interior issued the company a patent for 1,714,764 acres; and the reorganized Maxwell Land Grant Company (a Dutch corporation) opened for business. Wilkins, *Foreign Investment*, 122–24 and 232–33.

[70] Wilkins, *Foreign Investment*, 124.

[71] Lewis, *America's Stake*, 84; Wilkins, *Foreign Investment*, 234. Between 1865 and 1914 financial land and development calls on the London market totaled \$101 million.

[72] Lewis, *America's Stake*, 85; *Philadelphia Bulletin* (December 6, 1909), 11.

indicate that foreign firms controlled between 30 and 35 million acres of mostly western lands.[73]

Land speculation was one major area of foreign investment; direct investment in agricultural activities was a second. By far the greatest number of those foreign farming ventures were in western cattle ranching – an activity that reached a peak in the mid-1880s. "In 1880 there were 800,000 range cattle in Texas and 250,000 in Wyoming; by 1883 there were 5 million in Texas and 1 million in Wyoming. . . . Foreign investors were in large part responsible."[74] Between 1879 and 1889 no fewer than forty foreign cattle companies – firms capitalized at more than £7.8 million and controlling more than twenty-one million acres in ten states and territories – were organized.[75] The first experiments were moderately successful, but falling cattle prices, severe weather, and outbreaks of disease spelled disaster in the middle years of the decade. Some firms such as the Prairie Cattle Company and the Matador Land and Cattle Company survived and ultimately proved profitable.[76] The financial future for the other firms proved less rosy; between 1884 and 1900 British investors lost more than $18 million.[77] Foreign agricultural investment was not limited to cattle. British investors also financed rice plantations in Louisiana, cotton farms in Louisiana and Mississippi, orange groves in California, and timber companies in states as far apart as California and the Carolinas.[78]

Given the level of interest in American lands, it is not surprising that these direct capital transfers were complemented by indirect transfers routed through European mortgage companies and investment trusts. Such indirect foreign investment – investment made primarily by the Scots and English but also supported by the Dutch and Germans – appears

---

[73] Although they were not all channeled through investment companies, studies indicate that foreign-held farm mortgages represented 3.8 percent of all farm loans in Nebraska, 3.7 percent in Minnesota, 9.6 percent in North Dakota, 14.5 percent in South Dakota, 1 percent in Iowa, and 2 percent in Kansas. Larry A. McFarlane, "British Investment and the Land: Nebraska 1877–1946," *Business History Review* 57 (1983), 258–92; "British Investment in Minnesota Farm Mortgages and Land, 1875–1900" (unpublished mss); "British Agricultural Investment in the Dakotas, 1877–1953," in Paul Uselding (ed.), *Business and Economic History*, 5 (1976), 112–26 and 196–98, and "British Investment in Midwestern Farm Mortgages and Land, 1875–1900, A Comparison of Iowa and Kansas," *Agricultural History*, 48 (1974), 179–98.

[74] Wilkins, *Foreign Investment*, 300.

[75] Lewis, *America's Stake*, 87; Wilkins. *Foreign Investment*, 304–305.

[76] The history of British investment in the American range is drawn from Jackson, *The Enterprising Scot*, 73–100 and 114–38; Peter J. Buckley and Brian R. Roberts, *European Direct Investment in the USA before World War I* (New York, 1982), 59–63; and Lewis, *America's Stake*, 87–88.

[77] Jackson, *The Enterprising Scot*, 137.

[78] Wilkins, *Foreign Investments*, 234. Buckley and Roberts, *European Direct Investments*, 60.

to have begun in the late 1870s, surged in the 1880s, and diminished somewhat between 1890 and 1914.

Although there are no reliable estimates of the total amount of the capital routed through the trusts, when combined with the direct flows to agriculture and the indirect transfers underwritten by the financial land and development companies, it was sufficient to produce major political repercussions. "Foreign bashing" became common, and two-thirds of the states passed laws prohibiting aliens or alien corporations from owning land.

While the Scots and English were the largest contributors, the Dutch and the Germans also invested in the 1880s, and there were French and Swiss investors two decades later. American mortgages proved an attractive alternative for European investors. Taking all countries and both institutional and private investors together, Lewis put the total foreign holding of American real estate mortgages in 1914 at "more than $200–250 million." Wilkins' estimate is somewhat more conservative, but she still places the figure at between $200 and $250 million.[79]

The number of American mines that benefited from foreign capital is unknown, but the magnitude of mining investment was substantial. Clark Spence has estimated that between 1860 and 1914 there were at least 584 mining and milling firms – corporations with a nominal capitalization of £81,185,000 – chartered in Britain in the "inter-mountain West and Southwest."[80] Edward Ashmead, identified 659 British firms with a nominal capital of £99,568,738 that were registered between 1880 and 1904 to conduct mining operations in the United States; and between 1865 and 1914 no less than $103 million was transferred through the British capital market.[81] Wilkins argues that British investment represented more than one-half of all foreign investment in mining; and she estimates that between 1815 and 1914 foreign capital financed 1,500 to 2,000 mining and mineral-related companies.[82]

The investments were, however, not particularly rewarding, at least to the foreign investors. Spence reports that no more than one in ten of the British firms ever paid a dividend; and Lewis concludes that among forty

[79] Lewis, *America's Stake*, 86–87; Wilkins, *Foreign Investment*, 502–12.

[80] Clark C. Spence, "British Investment and the American Mining Frontier, 1860–1914," *New Mexico Historical Review*, 36 (1961), 121. In his previous and better known *British Investments and the American Mining Frontier, 1860–1901* (Ithaca, NY, 1958), 241–60, he lists only 518. Spence's data exclude firms operating in the Pacific coast states, the Southeast, and Alaska.

[81] Edward Ashmead, *Twenty-five Years of Mining, 1880–1904* (London, 1909), 81–90.

[82] Wilkins, *Foreign Investment*, 241.

mining companies organized between 1870 and 1895, twenty were gone
by 1903 and the remaining twenty had disappeared by 1914.[83] Among
the most spectacular failures were the notorious Emma, whose Scottish
owners were finally forced to sue both its American and British promoters for fraud; and Cassels Gold Extracting Company, about which a
London financial journal reported that the British investors had fallen
victim to "gold extraction with a vengeance."[84] The editors of the *Economist* reported that "there is a pretty general belief that the profits were
never honestly made; that, as a matter of fact, the ore bodies which yielded
the dividends were planted by human hands and not by nature."[85] Despite
the less-than-satisfactory performance, for four decades after 1875,
"German, French, Belgian, and Dutch as well as British investors were
. . . excited by every announcement of U.S. mineral discoveries, and
investors remained dreamers about 'fabulous returns'."[86]

While it was the natural endowments of coal and iron that underwrote
American industrialization, it was the lure of silver and gold that initially
excited European investors. During the 1860's and 1870s Europeans
invested in gold mines in Arizona, California, Colorado, Montana, Nevada,
Utah, and Wyoming. In the 1880s, although gold and silver continued to
dominate the list, six copper mines received British funds; the securities
of the Montana Copper Company were sold abroad in 1880; and the
Scottish-owned Arizona Copper Company was organized two years later.
During the 1890's, the distribution – biased toward gold and silver (there
is evidence of the Alaskan gold rush) but including a number of copper
mines – looks much like the pattern of the previous decade. In 1895 the
Rothschilds purchased a one-quarter interest in the Anaconda Copper
Company; and four years later one-fourth of all U.S. copper output was
foreign controlled. Mining calls totaled $34 million between 1905 and
1912, and more than three-fifths of the total was directed to copper mining
firms. Overall, there was a significant level of British, French, German,
and Dutch investment in the traditional nonferrous metals – copper, lead,
and zinc – as well as in aluminum, phosphate, salt, and borax.[87]

---

[83] Spence, *British Investments*, 127. Lewis, *America's Stake*, 89.
[84] Spence, "British Investment," 84.
[85] Jackson, *The Enterprising Scot*, 142. The quotation is from *The Economist*, "The Speculation in Mining Shares," 28 January 1888, 105–6.
[86] Wilkins, *Foreign Investment*, 239.
[87] Lewis, *America's Stake*, 93–94. Wilkins, *Foreign Investment*, 264–83. For a comprehensive examination of the structure of the international copper industry see Christopher Schmitz, "The Rise of Big Business in the World Copper Industry 1870–1930," *Economic History Review*, 2nd series, 39 (1986) 301–310.

Oil was discovered in Titusville, Pennsylvania in 1859, but foreign investors did not move quickly to exploit that opportunity. Although the English Petroleum and Mining Company was organized in 1865 to buy oil lands in Pennsylvania, it disappeared with hardly a trace; and further foreign investment awaited the market expansion touched off by the innovation of the automobile. When foreign capital did begin to flow, British investors were initially the most important; they contributed to the exploitation of fields in California, Oklahoma, and Texas.

For example, the British investment firm of Balfour, Williamson, and Company launched the California Oilfields Ltd. with initial capital of more than $1 million in 1901; and, with some aid from the Dutch, that enterprise was followed by the organization of six other oil-producing firms.[88] By 1914, however, the Royal Dutch Shell group had become the most important foreign player in the American market. The Shell Transport and Trading Company began to buy American oil properties soon after the turn of the century. In 1905 Royal Dutch and Shell merged, and the new organization continued to expand into the American market. Thus, by the outbreak of the First World War, Royal Dutch had the "greatest direct investment of any single foreign industrial enterprise in the United States." Lewis estimates that the group controlled at least $17.7 million of the total foreign investment in American petroleum of about $35 million.[89]

1840–1914: Commerce and Manufacturing

Over the five decades between 1865 and 1914, $234 million of manufacturing and commercial calls passed through the British market. Almost $10 million was in transferred in 1874 – and that peak was associated with the issues of the United States Rolling Stock Company and those of several firms in the nation's infant iron and steel industry.[90] Between 1882 and 1898 the sector received almost 12 percent of all American funds passing through the British market ($41 million in 1889); and brewing received the major share.

Taken together, American breweries represented more than $38.5 million in British calls. Between 1888 and 1891 twenty-four British

---

[88] Lewis, *America's Stake*, 94–98. Wilkins, *Foreign Investment*, 285–92. Of the six, two were in California, two in Oklahoma, and two in Texas.

[89] Lewis, *America's Stake*, 94–98. Wilkins, *Foreign Investment*, 285–92. The quotation is from Wilkins, 292.

[90] For a more detailed description of the United States Rolling Stock Company, see Wilkins, *Foreign Investment*, 837.

"syndicates" purchased and reorganized some eighty American breweries. Although the largest were the St. Louis Breweries (capitalization £2.85 million) and the Milwaukee and Chicago Breweries Ltd. (capitalization £2.271 million), the movement toward merger was a national one; the twenty-four were spread from coast to coast. Amounting, at its peak in 1891, to somewhere in the neighborhood of $90 million, total British investment in American brewing was greater than all foreign investment in cattle ranches, meat packing, granaries, grain elevators, and flour mills. Although foreign investment in brewing declined somewhat from its peak in the early 1890s, Lewis put the total at $75 million in 1889 and at $58 million in 1914.[91] In addition to the British investment, at the latter date German investors held about $4.7 million of the securities of seven other American breweries.[92]

Although the British had invested $1.5 million in the Mount Savage Ironworks in 1844, most studies have tended to overlook the role of foreign investment in iron and steel.[93] While the totals were modest in comparison with the size of the American industry, there had been foreign investment – particularly in the South – at least as early as the British organized Southern States Iron and Coal Company in 1875. By 1914 British, Dutch, German, French, Swiss, and Canadian investors held $122.4 million of the common and $27.5 million of the preferred shares of the United States Steel Company; and they had substantial holdings in both Bethlehem and Otis Steel as well.[94]

In addition to breweries and iron and steel, manufacturing tied to land-related activities and to the exploding consumer market also benefited from foreign investment. In the 1890s the British directed funds into milling and meat packing. In 1889, for example, the British purchased Pillsbury mills, the nation's principal flour producer, and launched Pillsbury-Washburn with a capital stock of £1 million and debentures of £635,000.[95] In addition, within a few years they helped finance General Electric, Eastman's, Pullman, and Edison Photographic.

By 1900 almost every major manufacturer of sewing thread in the United States was British owned.[96] Lever Brothers began to manufacture

[91] Wilkins, *Foreign Investment*, 325. Lewis, *America's Stake*, 89.
[92] Wilkins, *Foreign Investment*, 325. Lewis, *America's Stake*, 99.
[93] Lewis, *America's Stake*, 100.
[94] Wilkins, *Foreign Investment*, 247, 252, and 263. Lewis, *America's Stake*, 101.
[95] Lewis, *America's Stake*, 101. Wilkins, *Foreign Investment*, 320.
[96] Wilkins, *Foreign Investment*, 361–68. Lewis, *America's Stake*, 100–101.

soap in the United States in 1889; and a decade later they operated three factories. American rayon production was a British preserve after Samuel Courtauld & Company (later Courtauld's Ltd.) opened its American subsidiary in 1909; and, in addition a number of more traditional British and German textile firms made direct investments in the United States. The surge into the manufacturing and commercial sector was particularly marked in the years after 1905, and capital calls from Britain exceeded $50 million over the five years 1910–1914. The list included both the Indianapolis and the St. Louis breweries: but it also included an additional $7 million in General Electric calls as well as more than $20 million of British-American Tobacco's, $8 million of Bethlehem Steel's, and even $50,000 of Quaker Oats.[97]

THE LONDON AND NEW YORK STOCK EXCHANGES IN THE LATE NINETEENTH CENTURY

Over the course of the four decades before World War I, the domestic capital market was gradually maturing; but the process was slow; and, even at the end of the period, certain sectors were unable to attract sufficient finance from domestic sources. Table 16.10 compares American equity issues traded in December on the London Stock Exchange with those traded on the premier domestic securities market – the New York Stock Exchange – in 1870, 1880, 1890, 1900, and 1910 and provides some evidence on the level of development of the American market.[98] It also provides a very broad industrial classification of those issues.

Among the American firms whose shares were traded in London in December, 1870, there were five railroads, one mining company, and one bank. The sixty-one equity issues of forty-three firms traded in New York contained forty-five rails, and, included among the sixteen issues of thirteen other firms, were two coal companies and two mines, three express companies, Western Union, the Boston Water Power Company, and the Pacific Mail steamship line. Only four stock issues, the shares of the

---

[97] Lewis, *America's Stake*, 101–2, Wilkins, *Foreign Investment*, 340, 352–56, 369, 374, 375, and 390.

[98] The listing of American firms on the London exchange is taken from the end of the year report of the *Investor's Monthly Manual*; the New York issues are those reported in the *New York Times* during the entire month of December of each year.

Table 16.10. *U.S. equity issues traded in December, various years*

	NYSE				LSE			
	Rails		Non-Rails		Rails		Non-Rails	
	Firms	# of Issues	Firms	# of Issues	Firms	# of Issues	Firms	# of Issues
1870	30	45	13	16	5	6	2	2
1880	63	81	30	31	14	19	20	25
1890	91	129	38	44	33	48	59	90
1900	80	133	65	96	31	53	61	92
1910	67	105	84	128	31	48	62	99

Sources: NYSE data comes from the *New York Times*, LSE data from the *Investor's Monthly Manual*.

Notes: Foreign (non-U.S.) firms that were traded on the New York Stock Exchange are excluded from NYSE totals.

In some cases, it was not possible to identify a firm as rail or non-rail based on the information provided in the *Times*. These firms are excluded from the NYSE totals. In no year did unidentified firms account for more than 4 percent of total firms.

The *Times* data have been cross-referenced with Listings Statements New York Stock Exchange. In a small percentage of cases, firms which appear in the *Times* listings were not found in New York Exchange Printing Company, various years. These firms are, however, included in the NYSE totals above.

Railroads that provided urban transportation services are included under rail issues.

Included among the equity issues for New York are all securities mentioned in the *Times* listings except those listed in a section reserved for bonds. Equity issues include all types of preferred shares, tradable rights, and tradable certificates.

The equity issues of investment companies that bought only railroad securities were counted as rail issues.

New York City bank stocks appeared frequently in the 1870 *Times* listings, but in subsequent years appeared rarely if at all. To facilitate consistent comparisons between 1870 and other years, we have chosen not to include bank stocks in the NYSE totals.

New York Central Railroad, the Illinois Central, and two issues of the Erie Railroad were traded on both exchanges.

The increase in American stock listings from 1870 to 1880 suggests rapid American economic expansion, and it is obvious that the financial demands engendered by that expansion placed a severe strain on the nation's adolescent capital market. The number of firms whose shares traded in December on the New York exchange more than doubled, while the number of American firms listed on the London exchange almost quintupled. The thirty-four issues traded in London included fourteen railroads, but it was the non-railroad issues that increased most rapidly. In 1870, only two nonrailroad firms were traded in London; the 1880 listings included those of one telegraph company, one canal, two banks, five investment trusts, three financial land and mortgage companies, one wagon and railway carriage company, and seven mines.

Although the 1880 listings on the New York exchange indicate some institutional response to the increased demand for finance in the nonrailroad sectors, more than two-thirds of the companies listed were railroads. The number of nonrailroad firms whose shares were traded more than doubled between 1870 and 1880, while New York's appetite for railroad shares was also increasing – the number of firms increased from thirty to sixty-three. In 1870 the New York rail total had been almost six times that of London, by 1880, it was more than four times as large. Although much of the expansion of the New York exchange can be traced to an increasing focus on railroad securities, the number of nonrailroad firms listed also increased. In 1880 the list included telephone and telegraph companies, mines, express companies, and a water and power company. In 1870 nonrail firms quoted in New York outnumbered their London counterparts by almost seven to one. A decade later, although the New York count had risen from thirteen to thirty, there were no fewer than twenty such firms listed on the British exchange.

In 1890 the total number of American firms whose equity issues were traded in London in December was now nearly three-quarters of the number traded in New York; however, if the focus of attention is turned to the nonrailroad sector, the London market was servicing over one and a half times the number of firms supported by the New York exchange. While railroads still accounted for more than one-third of the American firms traded on the London market, the listings included fifty-nine other American firms drawn from at least nine different industries. There was still one canal; one telephone and telegraph company; three banks; six cattle ranches; seventeen land, mortgage, and financial firms; eight trusts; four mines; and eleven breweries. In addition, there were eight other enterprises, including the Chicago and Northwestern Granaries, Eastman's, J&P Coats, and the Pillsbury-Washburn Flour Mills.

Over the previous two decades, the number of American firms traded on the New York Stock Exchange had tripled; over the same period the number traded on the London Stock Exchange increased thirteenfold.

Table 16.11. *U.S. equity issues traded in December,*
various years, rails as share of total issues

	New York Stock Exchange	London Stock Exchange
1870	0.75	0.75
1880	0.72	0.43
1890	0.75	0.35
1900	0.58	0.37
1910	0.45	0.33

Source: See Table 16.10.

The financial demands required to support the rapid pace of economic growth was clearly straining the newer nation's domestic financial network.

The degree of that strain is reflected in a comparison of the ratio of American railroad equity issues to all issues listed on the two exchanges (see Table 16.11). In 1870 the ratio tilted heavily toward rail issues, standing at 0.75 on both exchanges. A decade later the results were very different. As the demand for finance for new industries — industries often located in the South and West — grew, the British exchange reacted quickly, the New York Stock Exchange much more slowly. The proportion of nonrails on the London market had more than doubled, while the fraction in New York remained roughly at its former level. Nor was the trend reversed over the next decade. The British nonrail figure continued to increase (to almost two-thirds of the total), but the American proportion held constant at one in four.

Despite the overall expansion of the New York exchange, the number of nonrailroad firms whose issues traded increased by only eight between 1880 and 1890. The thirty-eight firms that were traded at the latter date included those of six of the firms that had been included two decades previously and an additional five companies that the *Times* referred to as "unlisted but traded." One new express company was traded; the list of iron, coal, and steel firms traded had increased by seven; the shares of three gas companies and three mines were traded, as were those of some nineteen miscellaneous firms — the latter included Edison-General Electric, the National Lead Trust, the National Linseed Oil Company, and the Pullman Palace Car Company.

Table 16.12. *U.S. firms with equity issues traded in London, fraction of total firms with no equities traded concurrently in New York*

Year	All firms	Railroads	Non-rails	Total firms
1870	0.57	0.40	1.00	7
1880	0.68	0.36	0.90	34
1890	0.75	0.33	0.98	92
1900	0.73	0.23	0.98	92
1910	0.65	0.13	0.90	93

Source: See Table 16.10.

Of the thirty-three American railroads whose equities were traded in London in 1890, twenty-two had equities that were also traded concurrently in New York; however, shares of only one "non-railroad" firm traded on both exchanges. Jointly traded railroad issues became more commonplace but among non-rails, joint trading remained rare (see Table 16.12). There had been significant overlap in rail issues in 1870; and, the fraction of rails whose equities traded concurrently in New York increased through the turn of the century, reaching almost nine-tenths in 1910. Though the data for rails provide some evidence of increasing market integration, the figures for nonrail firms clearly indicate that the London market supplied capital to firms still incapable of attracting finance on the New York exchange – the fraction of nonrails whose equities traded only in London never dipped below 0.90.

By 1900, however, New York had begun to respond to the "non-railroad" demands of American enterprise. Over the last decade of the nineteenth century, total American firms listed on the London exchange remained constant, and the share of "non-rail" enterprises increased very slightly. On the other side of the ocean, the number of firms traded on the New York Stock Exchange rose about an eighth; but the proportion of "non-rails" increased from 0.29 to 0.45. The New York trend away from rails continued – albeit slightly more slowly – over the first decade of the present century; and in 1910, for the first time, rails made up less than one-half of the total firm listings. The American market was maturing rapidly.

The 1900 "non-rail" enumeration for London of companies with substantial American investments had an eclectic flair. The list included nine breweries, twenty-one land, mortgage, and investment companies, one telephone and telegraph company, ten investment trusts, eight mines, three banks, and nine firms listed under "other companies." The extent to which the New York Stock Exchange (NYSE) had emerged as a conduit for capital to the previously neglected sectors of the American economy is captured in an enumeration of just some of the listings that begin with the word *American*. The list includes American Beet Sugar, American Car and Foundry, American Coal, American Cotton Oil, American District Telegraph, American Express, American Ice, American Linseed, American Malting, American Smelting and Refining, American Spirits Manufacturing, American Steel Hoop, American Telegraph and Cable, American Tin Plate, American Tobacco, and, finally, American Woolen.

By 1910 the NYSE was certainly teen-aged, if not yet adult. While London traded the issues of 93 American firms (62 "non-rails") in December, 151 were traded on Wall Street; and, of that number, 84 were from sectors other than rails. American commercial and industrial firms; iron, coal, and steel firms; investment trusts; and land, mortgage, and financial firms were still listed in London, but such firms also appeared on the New York exchange. Despite the obvious movement toward maturity, however, among nonrails the same firms were seldom listed on both exchanges. What joint listings there were, were dominated by rails; the only "non-rail" equity issues traded on both exchanges were of the United States Steel Company, AT&T, Anaconda Copper, Amalgamated Copper, International Merchant Marine, and General Electric.

One recent addition to the New York listings might have provided a glimpse into the future for those investors with foresight. The 1910 list included a British firm – the Underground Electric Railways of London. On the Big Board it joined the shares of the Canadian Pacific Railroad, the Cuban-American Sugar Company, and the National Railways of Mexico. In that year the Board also listed bond issues of the governments of Argentina, Japan, and Panama. Wall Street had begun to dip its toes into the waters of international finance.

Moreover, as far as domestic finance was concerned, the New York list began to resemble the lists we know today. The 128 "non-rail" listings ranged alphabetically from Adams Express to Westinghouse. In addition, since 1890 the exchange had expanded to include the offerings of a set of firms that are still household names today: Allis Chalmers, American Tobacco, Bethlehem Steel, International Harvester, National Biscuit, Republic Steel, Sears Roebuck, United States Rubber, and United States

Steel. The New York Stock Exchange was in the process of becoming a truly national capital market.

THE AMERICAN DOMESTIC CAPITAL MARKET AND THE DEMAND FOR FOREIGN CAPITAL

Given the size and the composition of the flows from savers in Britain to capital using firms in the United States, the question remains: why did those American firms look abroad for financial support when domestic help was so much closer at hand? The answer to that question is not simple – it has at least three different but not entirely unrelated components. First, while the American savings rate was high, it was probably not high enough to have underwritten the short-term surges in investment demand that marked this nation's development. Second, British savers were probably more sophisticated than their American counterparts. That is, while there may have been clusters of American savers who were willing to risk their accumulations in enterprises far removed from their everyday experience, most were not. Third, the institutional structure of the New York exchange was different than that of its London counterpart. That is to say, the New York market was constrained by an institutional structure and a set of operating rules that, although designed to reassure investors, made it somewhat difficult to adjust to rapidly changing demand considerations.

The evidence for the first component is relatively straightforward. The surges of foreign finance were temporally correlated with the Civil War and with periods of most rapid American growth and structural transformation: 1814–1819, 1832–1839, 1867–1875, and 1882–1896. Although there is substantial literature on the question of the relationship between American investment demand and the foreign supply of capital, the most convincing analysis can be found in Edelstein's study of *Overseas Investment in the Age of High Imperialism*. The author shows that over the four overlapping quinquennia between 1834 and 1858 and the five between 1869 and 1898 there was a strong positive relationship between the ratio of American gross domestic capital formation to gross national product and the ratio of net foreign investment to gross national product. Thus, he concludes that it was the American demand rather than the foreign supply of capital that was the engine that powered the transfer of finance from Europe to the United States. He also finds, however, that, in the last two overlapping quinquennia (1894–1903 and 1899–1908), the positive relationship no longer held. "Crudely, U.S. real domestic capital formation rates rose more rapidly than the U.S. real domestic saving, owing to explosive investment demand and/or slower moving savings desires, and the gap was filled by net foreign borrowing. Once the slower moving savings desires reached their long-run target, net foreign borrowing disappeared."[99]

Most scholars agree that both the second and third components contributed to the problem; but, to some extent, they disagree about the relative weights to be assigned to each. As early as the mid-1930s, M. M. Postan had become intrigued by questions about the evolution and integration of both national and international markets; and his concerns have led to a steady flow of work that focuses on questions of institutional innovation and capital market evolution.[100] More recently, Robert Zevin and Larry Neal have examined the question of the degree of integration of international capital markets. Zevin concludes that the international markets were well integrated by *at least* the end of the last century and probably before.[101] In a similar vein, Neal argues that, while international markets were reasonably well integrated in the eighteenth century, the international market disintegrated in the early nineteenth century and was only gradually reintegrated over the course of that century.[102]

Postan concluded that pre-modern capital transfers were usually not founded on market exchanges between unrelated savers and investors but on direct transactions based on personal relations. Before a modern capital market could develop, it was necessary to educate savers: to prove to them that investment in depersonalized "symbolic capital" (capital that was mobile and divisible – that is, liquid paper claims on assets rather than the assets themselves) was as safe as direct ownership of the physical asset itself. In the case of Britain, Postan argued that this

[99] Edelstein, *Overseas Investment*, 233–37.

[100] M. M. Postan, "Some Recent Problems in the Accumulation of Capital," *Economic History Review*, 6 (1935). See also Postan, an unpublished series of lectures given at The Johns Hopkins University, 1954–55.

[101] Robert B. Zevin, "Are World Financial Markets More Open? If So Why and With What Effects?" in Tariq Banuri and Juliet B. Schor (eds.), *Financial Openness and National Autonomy* (New York, 1992).

[102] Larry Neal, "The Disintegration and Reintegration of International Capital Markets in the 19th Century," mss. February 29, 1992. Craig and Fisher, however, have recently suggested that the American market may have been less well integrated than the British, French, and German. Lee A. Craig and Douglas Fisher, "Integration of the European Business Cycle: 1871–1910," *Explorations in Economic History*, 29 (1992), 144–68.

educational process began with the sleeping partnerships of the sixteenth century, but it was not completed until savers had first come to recognize the profitability of investments in government bonds issued during Napoleonic Wars and then had discovered the ultimate safety of investments in railroad securities during the "height of unsafety," the early 1840s.[103] Postan then went on to draw parallels in the histories of Russia, Germany, and France.

In the case of the United States, it has been argued that, because of the greater geographical distances between savers in the East and investors in the South and West and because of the marked disparity between the new expanding industries that required finance and the older traditional activities that were the source of savings, the problem was even more complex. The educational process in the United States was, however, similar, to that experienced on the other side of the water – similar, at least, as far as the North and West were concerned; but in the United States the process was delayed by at least half a century. Thus, Yankee and Midwestern savers' experience with the 5–20s (5 percent 20 year bonds) during the Civil War provided the same lessons as the British Napoleonic War debt; and, during the 1870s, 1880s, and 1890s, their experience with U.S. railroad bonds duplicated the lessons of the Hudson years in Britain.[104] In the South, however, investment in Confederate bonds did not have the same effect on the Southern saver's education. Despite the Southern experience, to the North, the educational process had proceeded far enough by the early twentieth century to lead Frank A. Vanderlip, a prominent New York banker, to argue that "the whole great Mississippi Valley gives promise that in some day distant perhaps it will be another New England for investments. There is developing a bond market there which is of constant astonishment to eastern dealers."[105]

---

[103] Somewhat later Alexander Gerschenkron made a similar case for Germany and Russia. See his *Economic Backwardness in Historical Perspective* (Cambridge, MA, 1962).

[104] Lance E. Davis, "Capital Immobilities and Finance Capitalism: A Study of Economic Evolution in the United States, 1820–1920," *Explorations in Entrepreneurial History*, 2nd Series, 1, (1963), 88–105. Recently Kerry Odell has found similar evidence for gradual integration *within* the Pacific Coast States even before that region was integrated into the national capital market. Kerry A. Odell, "The Integration of Regional and Interregional Capital Markets: Evidence from the Pacific Coast, 1883–1913," *Journal of Economic History*, 49 (1989), 297–310.

[105] Frank A. Vanderlip was vice president of the National City Bank. He made the statement in a speech in 1905. He is quoted in G. Edwards, *The Evolution of Finance Capitalism* (New York, 1908), 185.

There were, of course, a set of institutional developments that aided the process of interregional integration. Davis has argued for the role of life insurance companies and the expansion of the commercial paper market, Sylla has looked at changes in the national banking laws, and James at changes

That day was, however, in the twentieth century. Earlier, the situation was markedly different. Naomi Lamoreaux, in a study of New England commercial banking, has shown just how personalized capital remained despite the existence of an apparently depersonalizing institutional structure.[106] From her examination of the records of a number of nineteenth-century New England banks, she concludes that it was not market forces but kinship connections that structured the loans made by those institutions.

Drawing on a different body of evidence and making a distinct, but parallel, argument, Kenneth Snowden has demonstrated that as late as 1890, after the effects of risk have been netted out, there still remained significant inter-regional differences in mortgage interest charges.

> Mortgage rates were substantially higher for borrowers in the South and West [2 to 3 percent] and represented a tangible financial burden. . . . I conclude that home as well as farm borrowers paid high rates in the West and South because of the direct costs of moving funds between regions and uneven diffusion of financial innovation.[107]

Yet a third avenue of support for the immobility argument can be found in an examination of the monopoly profits earned by those few American financial capitalists who were able to exploit their personal ability to mobilize capital. The list includes, for example, Jay Cooke, John D. Rockefeller,

made by the states in the legal framework of banking. More recently, and perhaps more appropriately in the light of this paper, Clark and Turner have underscored the role played by the nation's real current account trade balance as an independent factor. Lance E. Davis, "The Investment Market, 1870–1914: The Evolution of a National Market," *Journal of Economic History*, 25 (1965), 355–93; Richard Sylla, "Federal Policy, Banking Market Structure, and Capital Mobilization in the United States, 1863–1913, *Journal of Economic History*, 29 (1969), 657–86; John James, "The Development of the National Money Market, 1893–1911," *Journal of Economic History*, 36 (1976), 878–97; William Clark and Charlie Turner, "International Trade and the Evolution of the American Capital Market, 1888–1911," *Journal of Economic History*, 45 (1985), 405–10.

[106] Naomi Lamoreaux, "Banks, Kinship, and Economic Development: The New England Case," *Journal of Economic History*, 46 (1986), 647–67 and *Insider Lending: Banks, Personal Connections, and Economic Development in Industrial New England* (Cambridge, 1994).

[107] Kenneth A. Snowden, "Mortgage Rates and American Capital Market Development in the Late Nineteenth Century," *Journal of Economic History*, 47 (1987), 671–92.

Recently Hugh Rockoff and Howard Bodenhorn have shown that there was little difference between short-term rates in the North and the Old South in the antebellum era. Despite the lack of correlation in the movements, there is evidence of an integrated market between those two sectors; and given the dependence of southern cotton factors on northern financial markets, that result is not surprising. They make a similar argument for the Midwest; however, their evidence is much less compelling; and they find no evidence for any significant integration between the Pacific Coast and any other region. Howard Bodenhorn and Hugh Rockoff, "Regional Interest Rates in Ante Bellum America," in Claudia Goldin and Hugh Rockoff (eds.), *Strategic Factors in Nineteenth Century American Economic History: A Volume to Honor Robert W. Fogel* (Chicago, 1992), 159–87.

and, of course, J. P. Morgan. As late as 1912, Morgan was able to control more than two billion dollars of the savings of Americans willing to put their funds into enterprises that he certified, even though they were still unwilling to trust the formal depersonalized financial markets.[108] Moreover, recent work by Bradford DeLong indicates that, given the existing structure of the financial markets, those savers were almost certainly correct.[109]

It seems safe to conclude that, until the end of the nineteenth century at the very least, the London capital market served a far more sophisticated group of savers than its New York competitor.[110] Obviously the two markets did not exist in isolation, but it appears that a substantial fraction of the American securities traded in London were not even imperfect substitutes for many of the stocks and bonds traded in New York. That is to say, while the British contribution to American capital formation was never large, the financial flows were not trivial; and, more importantly, they were often targeted at economic activities that lay outside the scope of the still embryonic American financial market. Moreover, they were particularly important during the 1830s and during the years 1880 to 1896, when the American economy was undergoing a very rapid structural transformation.

While a part of the relatively slow development of the New York market may merely reflect the preferences of the savers with which the market dealt, a part at least, can be traced to the institutional differences between the New York and London exchanges. The New York Stock Exchange was organized (and owned) by a collective to engage in the creation and maintenance of a securities market. While the London Stock Exchange was organized for ostensibly the same purposes, it was not owned solely by traders:

[When the LSE] decided to build its own exchange in 1801 it did so by issuing shares which could be purchased by anyone. Consequently, there was a divorce between those who used the building for the conduct of their business – the members – and those who controlled the building and saw it as a business – the owners. In 1878, for example, there were 2,009 members of the London Stock Exchange but only 508 shareholders, a number of whom were non-members.[111]

---

[108] See Davis, "Finance Capitalism," 588–90; Edwards, *The Evolution of Finance Capitalism.*

[109] Bradford DeLong, "Did Morgan's Men Create Value?" in Peter Temin (ed.), *Inside the Business Enterprise: Historical Perspectives on the Use of Information* (Chicago, 1991), 205–50.

[110] For a more extensive development of this point see Lance Davis, "The Capital Markets and Industrial Concentration: The U.S. and U.K., A Comparative Study," *Economic History Review*, 2nd Series, 19 (1966), 255–72.

[111] Ranald C. Michie, *The London and New York Stock Exchanges, 1850–1914* (London, 1987), 250.

The New York Stock Exchange building, constructed in 1868, was fully financed by its membership. Thus, the wedge between owners and members that marked the London market was absent in New York – there, the sets of owners and of members were identical.

In London the cleavage between owners and members was clearly reflected in the exchange's governing structure. Two committees – the Committee of Trustees and Managers and the Committee for General Purposes – were jointly vested with ultimate control over exchange matters. As their names suggest, however, the committees represented different interests: the Trustees and Managers Committee represented exchange owners and the General Purposes Committee represented members. Inevitably, their interests collided.[112] The identity between owners and managers of the NYSE meant that there would be no infighting between the two groups. A single committee, the Governing Committee, was final arbiter on all issues affecting the exchange, although it delegated much of its authority to subcommittees. As a collectively owned firm, the NYSE adopted policies typical of collectives in general; and those policies were quite different from the policies of the shareholder-owned London exchange.[113]

On the one hand, the evidence suggests that the rewards associated with organizing as an efficient cartel were high, relative to the costs. On the other hand, the cartel carefully screened potential issues and implemented rules that, while providing a valuable service to some, made trading on the NYSE more expensive than on other competing exchanges. Firms willing and able to sustain these costs were, in effect, buying a signal – a signal that assuaged the doubts of skeptical investors – and thus, those firms were able to attract a fairly wide range of relatively unsophisticated investors and build a national market for their securities. Of course, some investors felt no need to rely on NYSE certification to gauge the attractiveness of uncertain investment opportunities; and some firms were unable or unwilling to bear the additional costs.

The more sophisticated investors refused to bear the high NYSE transaction costs if they didn't have to, they often took their business to rival

---

[112] See Michie, *London and New York*, 250–53 on conflicts of interest. Generally, traders were eager to adopt any technological advance that could facilitate increased market activity. Owners resisted many innovations – for instance, ticker tape machines – fearing that their introduction made exchange price quotes readily available to outsiders, thus creating a disincentive for non-members to pay fees to join the exchange.

[113] See Lee Benham and Phillip Keefer, "Voting in Firms: The Roles of Agenda Control, Size and Voter Homogeneity," *Economic Inquiry*, 39 (1991) on actions taken by collectives.

Table 16.13. *U.S. securities markets, sales in 1910*

Market	Stocks		Bonds	
	Number	Proportion	Par Value	Proportion
New York Stock Exchange	164,150,061	68.5%	$635.0 m	90.6%
Consolidated Stock Exchange	32,238,773	13.4%	—	—
New York Curb Market	18,671,438	7.8%	$10.8 m	1.5%
New York: Total	215,060,272	89.7%	$645.8 m	92.1%
Boston Stock Exchange	15,503,336	6.5%	$32.7 m	4.7%
Philadelphia Stock Exchange	8,341,599	3.5%	$14.6 m	2.1%
Chicago Stock Exchange	894,362	0.4%	$7.4 m	1.1%
Total	239,799,569	100.1%	$700.5 m	100.0%

Source: Reprinted from Ranald C. Michie, *The London and New York Stock Exchanges, 1850–1914* (London, 1987), 170. NYSE: New York Stock Exchange, Special Committee on Commissions, Memorandum, 1924; Consolidated: Consolidated Stock Exchange, Annual Report, year ending 31 May 1910; Curb: Jones & Baker, *Profits and Dividends on America's Second Largest Stock Market* (New York, 1919); Boston: J. G. Martin, *Stock Fluctuations* (Boston, 1911); Philadelphia: A. W. Barnes (ed.), *History of the Philadelphia Stock Exchange, Banks and Banking Interests* (Philadelphia, 1911); Chicago: F. M. Huston and A. Russell, *Financing an Empire – History of Banking in Illinois* (Chicago, 1926), vol. I.

exchanges. It is clear that this group was small relative to the number of unsophisticated investors – the NYSE handled the lion's share of transactions in domestic securities (see Table 16.13). Because the numbers of sophisticated investors were small, the rival domestic exchanges were unable to mobilize sufficient capital to meet the demands of all the myriad of firms whose growth reflected the transformation of the industrial profile of the United States. Thus, British entrepreneurs were given an opportunity to purchase American enterprises, reorganize them as "free standing companies," and, through the aegis of the London exchange, raise capital from relatively more sophisticated British investors. At the same time, some American firms began to utilize the services of the London market themselves. From the point of view of the Governors of the New York Exchange, however, given the relative numbers of the two groups, the decision to forego the business of sophisticated investors in an attempt to attract the business of larger blocks of relatively unsophisticated investors appears to have been a sound one.

The minimum commission rule provides perhaps the clearest example of the exchange's desire to impose a single pattern of behavior on its membership – a pattern of behavior that would guarantee efficient cartel operation. NYSE members were permitted to charge no less than one-eighth percent on every transaction they handled for nonmembers. The minimum NYSE rate was high; and members of rival domestic exchanges, in an attempt to divert business to themselves, frequently undercut NYSE commissions; but, because of their relatively small size, they failed to provide effective competition. Traders on two rival New York exchanges – the Consolidated and the Curb market – and those on the Philadelphia Stock Exchange typically charged half the NYSE commission rate; but when, in 1875, twenty NYSE brokers petitioned the Governors to charge one-sixteenth percent commission on large volume trades for nonmembers, their request was flatly refused. The importance attached to the minimum commission rule was most clearly stated by the Governing Committee in 1894; "The Commission Law is the fundamental principle of the Exchange, and on its strict adherence hangs the financial welfare and the life of the Institution itself."[114] While such language may seem overly melodramatic, it is nevertheless apparent that NYSE rulemakers sought to eliminate any commission competition between its members – differences in commission rates would not be tolerated.

The Governing Committee also attempted to secure higher individual profits for members by strictly limiting membership. In the wake of its 1869 merger with the "Open Board," the committee placed a 1,060 cap on membership. Between then and 1914 that limit was increased just once (to 1,100). As business on the exchange grew – 1879 stock sales were $73 million as compared with a pre–World War I high of $262 million in 1906; and bond sales had grown from $571 million in 1879 to a $1,314 million peak in 1909 – the price of seats rose. Michie notes, "Reflecting the fact that membership was restricted, and did not meet demand, was the fact that the cost of purchasing a place rose [from] between $14,000 and $26,000 in 1880 to between $65,000 and $94,000 in 1910, or approximately fourfold."[115] Restricting membership, a tool employed by

---

[114] NYSE: Governing Committee, April 13, 1894; Constitution of the New York Stock Exchange Board, February 21, 1820, Article 10, quoted in Michie, *London and New York*. There was no minimum commission rule of the London Stock Exchange until 1912.

[115] Michie, *London and New York*, 194–196; Peter Wyckofff, *Wall Street and the Stock Markets: A Chronology (1644–1971)*, 1st Edition (Philadelphia, 1982), 150–51; Edmund C. Stedman, *The New York Stock Exchange: Its History, Its Contribution to National Prosperity, and its Relation to American Finance at the Outset of the Twentieth Century* (New York, 1969 [copyright 1905]), 473–74.

many collectives, kept numbers manageable; and, as seats became increasingly expensive, it guaranteed that only the relatively wealthy could join the fold.[116]

Because it was organized as a traders' cartel, the NYSE was able to pursue a collective strategy designed not only to maximize short-run profits but also to foster rapid growth in the volume of transactions. In the mid- to late nineteenth century, the typical American saver was relatively unsophisticated and, therefore, plagued by high levels of uncertainly about domestic investment opportunities.[117] The informational asymmetry faced by potential investors was great; and, in an effort to attract large national markets for its listed securities, the NYSE devised a set of procedures and trading rules that were designed to reduce the level of uncertainty. In such an environment, potentially viable firms faced what is still a standard problem in their attempts to attract capital:

Higher quality parties are usually adversely affected by the presence of lower quality parties; either the higher quality parties, are pooled with the lower quality parties, to their detriment, or they must invest in signals beyond the point that they would if there were no informational asymmetry to distinguish themselves from their low-quality peers.[118]

Market screening undertaken by the NYSE allowed certain firms to invest in costly signals to separate their securities from those of competing ventures.[119] An NYSE listing itself became a signal to American investors of the "quality" of an investment opportunity.

The most obvious of the NYSE's screening policies was its stringent vetting procedure – a procedure that required potential listings to meet high minimum standards in terms of, "size of capital, number of

[116] See Benham and Keefer, "Voting in Firms," 708–710 on restricting membership in collectives.

[117] The term uncertainty is used in the "Knightian" sense. That is, there was a lack of knowledge about the distribution of expected returns.

[118] David M. Kreps, *A Course in Microeconomic Theory* (Princeton, 1990), Chapter 17, "Adverse Selection and Market Signaling," 625–60. The term "quality" appears somewhat pejorative, but in this case it should be taken as a synonym for *either* unable or unwilling (i.e., could find alternative capital sources to signal).

[119] Kreps defines market screening as a situation in which the party to a contract without information proposes a menu of contracts from which the informed party selects. In this context, the NYSE, as the representative of unsophisticated investors, was the party to the contract at an informational disadvantage because the firms attempting to list their securities were better informed about the distribution of potential returns. The institutional rules imposed costs on those firms. These firms willing and able to absorb these costs separated themselves from other ventures.

For a treatment of how promoters of one notorious mining venture, the Emma, used their informational advantage to manipulate investors, see Spence, "British Investments," 84. Of course, this firm was listed on the London Stock Exchange; there, screening was far more lax than on the NYSE.

shareholders, and proven track record."[120] The Exchange made a deliberate effort to attract large, widely held and, price wise, relatively stable issues. The rules also imposed additional costs on securities whose prices dipped below par value, and they made it virtually impossible to trade a security that did not generate the required high level of trade volume in sufficiently large trade blocks. Moreover, an addendum to the commission rules mandated that commissions would be based not on the market price of the security but on a minimum $100 par value. Thus, the rule dictated that members demand at least 12.5 cents on every share traded on behalf of non-members, even if the share price was well below $100. The importance of par values as a signal to relatively unsophisticated investors is emphasized in one study of capital market development:

> A prerequisite for anonymous public markets was the development of mechanisms to enable outside investors to better estimate the value of businesses; this has been a very slow and arduous process, which even today appears far from complete. A rudimentary step, when most available accounting data was entirely unreliable, was the use of par value as a benchmark.[121]

Similarly, the Exchange imposed a minimum size requirement for a single transaction. Although in the 1890s the rules were relaxed to permit members to deal in "odd lots," until then members had been prohibited from dealing in quantities less than the "normal" lot of one hundred stocks or bonds.[122] In short, a firm that passed the admittance tests and continued to demonstrate that the market for its issues was active and stable had purchased an expensive signal about the probable quality of those issues.

The "par value rule" discriminated not only against $100 securities trading at less than that amount but also against "low-denomination" securities issued at values well below $100. Low-denomination securities were most often offered by companies with small capital bases; and there were many such firms in the industrial, in the land, mortgage, and

---

[120] Michie, *London and New York*, 198.

[121] Jonathan Barron Baskin, "The Development of Corporate Financial Markets in Britain and the United States, 1600–1914: Overcoming Asymmetric Information," *Business History Review*, 62 (1988), 225.

[122] Since most stocks and bonds listed on the NYSE traded near a par value of $100, the value of the smallest allowable transactions was about $10,000, a sum far too large for the typical investor of the day. Michie reports that, of the 131 million shares sold on the exchange in 1912, less than 19 percent were priced at under $50, while 43 percent were over $100. Michie, *London and New York*, 199. NYSE: Special Committee on Commissions, 1924; Governing Committee, May 11, 1886, April 13, 1887, November, 1902, May 27, 1903, March 16, 1910, March 30, 1910; Special Joint Committee on Copper Stocks, May 18, 1903.

financial, and in the mining industries. Even if investors were willing to trade in normal lots, and it is likely that the small investor preferred odd lots, the par value rule made purchases or sales very expensive. It is therefore not surprising that most of these securities were listed on exchanges with more liberal trading rules.

Institutional rules are, however, not set in stone; and changing conditions led to changes in institutional structure. The NYSE did not, for example, turn away business because of an irrational prejudice against certain types of securities – it was, in fact, interested in any security that passed its "signal" test and, equally importantly, could attract investors from all regions and all walks of life. As long as a security was of interest to only a small or to a geographically concentrated group of investors, there were few benefits to be gained from a listing on the "Big Board," and neither the issuing firms nor the investors themselves were willing to pay the price of admission. By the mid-1880s, however, the continued viability of certain industrial, land-mortgage-finance, and mining shares on rival exchanges led the Governing Committee to conclude that those issues were beginning to attract a broad range of investors. As a result, in order to permit its members to share in those potential profits while not diluting the Exchange "quality" signal, the Board of Governors created the "unlisted department" – a division designed to permit members to trade in certain securities without granting those issues an official quotation.

The institutional innovation did not include a weakening of the Exchange's trade rules, that is, commission and trade block regulations; and by the turn of the century, the majority of these "unlisted but traded" issues had still not managed to attract a truly national clientele. The attractiveness of the new market was obviously limited. Although the unlisted department struggled along until 1910, few of its issues generated any significant trading volume. In 1895, for example, of the surprisingly large number of industrial stocks (435) covered by the department, the securities of just three firms – American Sugar Refining, National Lead, and U.S. Leather – generated 94 percent of the department's $13.6 million sales total.[123]

In part, at least, as a result of the Exchange's trading rules, many firms were not listed on the NYSE; and, they turned to other American (the Boston, the Philadelphia, or perhaps, the Consolidated), or to foreign

---

[123] Michie, *London and New York*, 198–9; Sereno S. Pratt, *The Work of Wall Street* (New York, 1903), 86, 153.

(particularly the London) exchanges. Because potential American investors in these enterprises often tended to be geographically concentrated, some mining and land, mortgage, and financial firms were adequately served by other, more local American exchanges. The San Francisco and the Boston Exchanges and the Curb Market in New York listed a wide array of mine shares throughout the years 1880–1914. Before the turn of the century, land companies and investment trusts were also often listed on the Boston Exchange.[124] Other firms – those whose capital requirements could not be met by domestic savers – turned to the more broadly based British market. It was not that all mining and land ventures could not find homes for their securities in the United States; many could and did, but that home was not the New York Stock Exchange.

In general, as long as rival exchanges steered clear of transactions in NYSE issues, peaceful coexistence was possible. For example, the Curb Market appears to have served as a proving grounds for securities unable to measure up to the rigorous standards required for an NYSE listing. NYSE brokers, moreover, recognized that there were small pockets of investors willing to channel savings into securities that did not pass the exchange's screening procedures:

> The Curb existed in uneasy harmony with the New York Stock Exchange, never officially recognized but extensively utilized by its membership to fill orders for clients throughout the country. . . . An estimated 85 percent of the Curb's total business was on behalf of members of the NYSE, with whom constant contact was maintained through the use of messenger boys, signaling from upper office windows, and conveniently sited telephones at ground-floor window level.[125]

Interestingly, this quote not only underscores the tacitly accepted division in function between the two exchanges, but it also suggests that Curb listings enjoyed something more than local or regional interest.

The continued existence and viability of regional exchanges indicates that there was also a fragmentation between investors in different regions of the country. If there were gains to be had from consolidation of trade activity in national issues, at some point in the period, one would have expected the smaller American exchanges to handle only regional listings as national issues gradually gravitated to New York. Through at least 1910, however, the Boston Stock Exchange, for example, listed land,

---

[124] Robert J. Cull, "Capital Market Failure and Institutional Innovation," Ph.D. Dissertation, California Institute of Technology, 1992. Michie, *London and New York*, 211–12. Joseph G. Martin, *A Century of Finance, Martin's History of the Boston Stock and Money Markets* (Boston, 1898), 196–223.

[125] Michie, *London and New York*, 206–7.

mortgage, and financial firms and mining concerns located throughout the country. At least one market observer, Charles Head, a member of both the New York and Boston Exchanges, noted the regional fragmentation between investors:

> We do a pretty large business in Boston which does not come to this city [New York] at all – where the customers are Boston men, and the business is done there. We do large business in these Boston stocks – in all the copper stocks.[126]

The persistence of trade activity unique to a single exchange – the Boston (and to a lesser extent the Philadelphia) – suggests that the exchange served a group of relatively sophisticated investors who did not rely solely on the New York Stock Exchange's "certification" to reduce their uncertainty. Arthur Johnson and Barry Supple argue that Boston investors' early experience in the China trade made them particularly suited to investment in the American West. Those investors were a "close-knit group, accustomed to managing far-flung enterprises, they appeared on the domestic scene at a time when the West offered great opportunities to capital and entrepreneurial talent."[127] In sum, it is quite apparent that not all American savers were equal in their abilities to evaluate uncertain investment opportunities; and, even at the turn of the century, the majority, even of those willing to hold paper securities at all, still demanded "official certification."

The combination of rapid increases in the demand for capital, relatively unsophisticated investors, and restrictive trade rules meant that firms in certain sectors of the American economy, particularly corporations located in the South and West, went unserviced by the New York market; they were, however, often able to attract capital on the British market. Certainly by the end of the period the New York market had begun to display evidence of approaching maturity – that is, its traders and specialists had begun to serve a wider array of enterprises; however, it lagged its London counterpart by at least two decades. Domestic land, finance, and investment companies as well as mining, agricultural, and other land-based firms were forced to retain their British connections until well into the present century.

In the final analysis, except perhaps in the short run, it was not lack of American savings that led American firms to the London capital market.

---

[126] NYSE: Special Investigation Committee, Continuous Quotations, January 27, 1903; cited in Michie, *London and New York*, 210.

[127] Arthur M. Johnson and Barry E. Supple, *Boston Capitalists and Western Railroads* (Cambridge, MA, 1967), 19.

While there may still remain questions of the level of American savings in the antebellum decades, there is little doubt that the gross savings rate averaged almost 25 (and the net rate more than 18) percent from about 1870 to at least 1908; and these rates were far higher than those observed in Britain.[128] Instead, it was a combination of the organizational structure of the New York exchange and the perceptions of the majority of American savers – savers who were unwilling to risk their accumulations in enterprises far removed from their usual experience. As those savers became more sophisticated, the potential economies of scope from a more broadly based exchange increased; and ultimately, it paid those who governed the New York exchange to increase their listings – at least somewhat.

Despite the very high rate of domestic savings, the New York exchange failed to mobilize sufficient savings to provide finance for the entire range of investment opportunities then available in the United States. That problem became particularly acute in the decades following the Civil War as the rapid transformation of the American economy generated a substantial demand for finance in sectors of the economy that were well outside the normal experience of American savers. At the same time, European, and particularly British, savers possessed sufficient resources and demonstrated a willingness to fill at least a part of the gap; but they appear to have been more comfortable dealing with their local brokers and a known market than with strangers and strange institutions located thousands of miles away.

AMERICAN INVESTMENTS ABROAD

Introduction

For more than a century after the ratification of the Constitution, the United States was the world's largest international debtor; but, while World War I triggered what appears to have been a revolutionary regime change, there was evidence two decades earlier that the flows through the international financial network had begun to reverse. Between 1790 and the end of 1896, the net capital import totaled $3.4 billion; over the last eighteen years of the prewar period, and despite massive foreign investments in the United States, the net capital *outflow* totaled about $1.4 billion. Similarly, the ratio of long-term U.S. investment abroad to long-

---

[128] Davis and Gallman, "Savings, Investment, and Economic Growth," passim.

term foreign investment in the United States rose from 0.22 in 1899 to 0.42 in 1908 and to 0.50 in 1914.[129]

The Early Years: 1797 to 1896

Bullock and his co-authors conclude that, "American investments abroad were insignificant until the late nineties," and in a similar vein, Cleona Lewis wrote, "Until the closing decade of the nineteenth century, the outward flow of capital . . . was of negligible proportions."[130] While there were American trading companies in Canada since the early eighteenth century, in China since 1783, in Argentina since 1801, in Mexico and Brazil since the 1820s, and in Japan since the 1850s, there is no evidence of extensive American investment.[131] Similarly, although two Americans established a paper mill in Quebec in 1804, Samuel Colt opened the first foreign branch of an American manufacturing firm in Britain in 1852, and three Baltimoreans were apparently "extensively engaged in building locomotives, cars, casting of cannon, and making a variety of machinery for government" near St. Petersburg in 1857, there is no evidence of significant American investment in foreign manufacturing until the 1860s, when the Pullman Company, R. Hoe and Company, and the Singer Sewing Machine Company all built plants in the United Kingdom.[132]

Nor did foreign railroads draw substantial amounts of American capital. In 1849, American investors contributed to the construction of the Great Western Railroad in Canada; and they invested $8 million in the Panama Railroad; but those forays did not lead to further commitments.[133] In the 1870s American capital supported the extension of the nation's railroad network into Canada, and construction of the Boston-financed Sonora railroad in Mexico began.[134]

[129] See Lewis, *America's Stake*, 546 and 606; Nathaniel T. Bacon, "American International Indebtedness," *Yale Review*, 9 (1900), 159; and George Paish, "Trade Balances of the United States," U.S. Senate, *National Monetary Commission*, 61st Congress, 2nd session, Senate Document 579 (Washington, DC, 1910).

[130] Bullock et al., "The Balance of Trade," 229; Lewis, *America's Stake*, 173.

[131] Lewis, *America's Stake*, 175–80. Carl F. Remer, *American Investments in China* (Honolulu, 1929), 21–24.

[132] Lewis, *America's Stake*, 293; John H. Dunning, *American Investment in British Manufacturing* (London, 1958), 18–19. Charles T. Haven and Frank A. Belden, *A History of the Colt Revolver and Other Arms Made by Colt's Patent Fire Arms Manufacturing Company from 1836 to 1940* (New York, 1940), 86–89.

[133] Peter Baskerville, "Americans in Britain's Backyard: The Railway Era in Upper Canada, 1850–1880," *Business History Review*, 55 (1981), 317.

[134] Lewis, *America's Stake*, 313–17. Fred Wilbur Powell, *The Railroads of Mexico* (Boston, 1912), 123–24.

Despite the fact that there was little American foreign investment before the late 1890s, the industrial profile of investment established in those early years set the pattern for American transfers as investment surged in the years between the turn of the century and the Depression of the 1930s. Aside from the capital needed to underwrite the export of the products of American technology or of the country's natural resources – and the specialized knowledge inherent in domestic production often led, in the long run, to American investment in foreign production – the bulk of American investment was in activities that can best be viewed as extensions of the American domestic market (see Tables 16.14, 16.15, and 16.16).[135]

In 1897 American financial commitments in Mexico and Canada represented just less than 60 percent of all American long-term foreign investment, and Cuba, the West Indies, and Central and South America accounted for an additional 15 percent. By 1914 the pattern was similar, and as late as 1935 the Western Hemisphere still accounted for almost 65 percent of all American long-term commitments.

The major exceptions to the "home market" scenario were American firms that had found a European market for their products. Firms such as Singer, Westinghouse, and Edison–General Electric exploited their new technical developments; and Standard Oil, when faced with potential Russian competition, moved quickly into international distribution and, ultimately, into production.[136]

Both foreign electric and telephone companies also received infusions of American capital. By the early 1890s Edison (later General Electric) had invested in Deutsche Edison Gesellschaft, in Edison Swan Electric Company Ltd. (Britain), in the Canadian General Electric Company Ltd., and had bought Thomson-Houston International – a firm that developed an extensive sales network in South America, Egypt, Russia, and Spain and soon began manufacturing in France.[137] Bell Telephone opened a manufacturing subsidiary in Antwerp in 1882; and between 1910 and 1915 its successor (AT&T) expanded into France, Britain, Italy, Spain, and Norway.[138]

---

[135] Fred W. Field, *Capital Investment in Canada: Some Facts and Figures Respecting One of the Most Attractive Investment Fields in the World* (Montreal, 1914), 21. Alfred D. Chander, "The Growth of the Transnational Industrial Firm in the United States and the United Kingdom: A Comparative Analysis," *Economic History Review*, 2nd series, 33 (1980), 396–410.

[136] Dunning, *American Investment*, 22.

[137] The Edison companies were the predecessors of General Electric. Dunning, *American Investment*, 23. John Winthrop Hammond, *Men and Volts, The Story of General Electric* (New York, 1941), 91. Lewis. *America's Stake*, 294. Frank A. Southard Jr., *American Industry in Europe: Origins and Development of the Multinational Corporation* (Boston, 1931: reissued New York, 1976), 23.

[138] Southard, *American Industry in Europe*, 43.

Table 16.14. *American investments abroad by geographical area (millions of dollars)*

Region	1897	1908	1914
Direct investments			
Europe	131.0	369.3	573.3
Canada	159.7	405.4	618.4
Cuba & other West Indies	49.0	195.5	281.3
Mexico	200.2	416.4	587.1
Central America	21.2	37.9	89.6
South America	37.9	104.3	323.1
Africa	1.0	5.0	13.0
Asia	23.0	74.7	119.5
Oceana	1.5	10.0	17.0
International Banking	10.0	20.0	30.0
Total direct	634.5	1,638.5	2,652.3
Portfolio investments			
Europe	20.0	119.9	118.5
Canada	30.0	291.9	248.8
Cuba & other West Indies	0.0	30.0	55.0
Mexico	0.0	255.6	266.4
Central America	0.0	3.1	3.6
South America	0.0	25.4	42.6
Africa	0.0	0.0	0.2
Asia	0.0	160.5	126.4
Oceana	0.0	0.0	0.0
International banking	0.0	0.0	0.0
Total portfolio	50.0	886.3	861.5
Direct and portfolio investments			
Europe	151.0	489.2	691.8
Canada	189.7	697.2	867.2
Cuba & other West Indies	49.0	225.5	336.3
Mexico	200.2	672.0	853.5
Central America	21.2	41.0	93.2
South America	37.9	129.7	365.7
Africa	1.0	5.0	13.2
Asia	23.0	235.2	245.9
Oceana	1.5	10.0	17.0
International banking	10.0	20.0	30.0
Total direct & portfolio	684.5	2,524.8	3,513.8

Source: Lewis, *America's Stake*, 606.

Table 16.15. *American investments abroad by geographical area (percentages)*

Region	1897	1908	1914
Direct investments			
Europe	20.6	22.5	21.6
Canada	25.2	24.7	23.3
Cuba & other West Indies	7.7	11.9	10.6
Mexico	31.6	25.4	22.1
Central America	3.3	2.3	3.4
South America	6.0	6.4	12.2
Africa	0.2	0.3	0.5
Asia	3.6	4.6	4.5
Oceana	0.2	0.6	0.6
International banking	1.6	1.2	1.1
Total direct	100.0	100.0	100.0
Portfolio investments			
Europe	40.0	13.5	13.8
Canada	60.0	32.9	28.9
Cuba & other West Indies	0.0	3.4	6.4
Mexico	0.0	28.8	30.9
Central America	0.0	0.3	0.4
South America	0.0	2.9	4.9
Africa	0.0	0.0	0.0
Asia	0.0	18.1	14.7
Oceana	0.0	0.0	0.0
International banking	0.0	0.0	0.0
Total portfolio	100.0	100.0	100.0
Direct and portfolio investments			
Europe	22.1	19.4	19.7
Canada	27.7	27.6	24.7
Cuba & other West Indies	7.2	8.9	9.6
Mexico	29.2	26.6	24.3
Central America	3.1	1.6	2.7
South America	5.5	5.1	10.4
Africa	0.1	0.2	0.4
Asia	3.4	9.3	7.0
Oceana	0.2	0.4	0.5
International banking	1.5	0.8	0.9
Total direct & portfolio	100.0	100.0	100.0

Source: Lewis, *America's Stake*, 578–604.

In 1879 Standard Oil began to invest in foreign distribution facilities, and the company's distribution network soon spanned most of the world.[139] The company opened its first foreign refinery in Galicia in 1879; and within a few years it controlled refineries in Cuba, Mexico, Canada, France, and Germany. Investment in foreign production, however, was delayed until 1905.[140]

It was, however, the extension of the American market into Canada and Mexico that drew the majority of American foreign investment in the years before 1897. In the case of Mexico, the largest single recipient of American long-term investments, it was the extension of the American railroad network and the expansion of the western mining frontier that accounted for almost 90 percent of the total. Between 1877 and 1897 Mexico's railroad network grew from 400 to more than 7,000 miles; and, although there were infusions of British, French, Dutch, and German capital, much of the growth – growth that included the promotion and construction of the Mexican Central, the Mexican National, and the Southern Pacific of Mexico – was American financed.[141]

Railroads accounted for 55 percent of American investment, but mining ventures contributed another 34 percent. There had been American mines in Mexico as early as the 1820s, but it was not until Diaz imposed "order and stability" and guaranteed property rights that capital began to flow in substantial proportions. In the early years it was gold and silver that attracted American interest – in 1886 there are estimated to have been forty American companies mining gold and silver in Mexico.[142]

Gradually, however, the focus shifted toward industrial minerals, and by 1897 precious metals accounted for less than three-quarters of the total. For example, the Guggenheims received government concessions that permitted them to build three smelters; they organized the Compaña de la Gran Fundiciòn Nacional Mexicana, built a smelter in Monterrey, and they leased or purchased a number of iron, lead, and copper mines.

---

[139] As late as 1882 Standard still commanded almost 100 percent of the foreign market for kerosene; but by 1888 the Russians had managed to capture about 22 percent, and by 1891 their share was nearly 30 percent. Ralph W. Hidy and Muriel E. Hidy, *History of the Standard Oil Company (New Jersey), Pioneering in Big Business, 1882–1911* (New York, 1955), 132 and 153; Southard, *American Industry in Europe*, 49–50.

[140] Hidy and Hidy, *Standard Oil*, 42, 128, 256, and 497.

[141] Lewis, *America's Stake*, 316–17. J. Fred Rippy, *The United States and Mexico* (New York, 1931), 312.

[142] The estimate on the number of American mines is from David A. Wells, *A Study of Mexico* (New York, 1887), 161. Isaac Marcosson, *Metal Magic, The Story of the American Smelting and Refining Company* (New York, 1949), 210–11.

Table 16.16 America's direct foreign investments, 1897–1914 by geographic region and class of investment

Millions of Dollars

	Total			Sales			Mines			Oil			Agriculture		
	1897	1908	1914	1897	1908	1914	1897	1908	1914	1897	1908	1914	1897	1908	1914
Europe	131.0	369.3	573.3	80.0	125.0	215.0	0.0	3.0	5.0	0.0	3.5	8.0	0.0	0.0	0.0
Canada	159.7	405.4	618.4	10.0	15.0	27.0	55.0	136.0	159.0	6.0	15.0	25.0	18.0	25.0	101.0
Cuba & other West Indies	49.0	195.5	281.3	5.0	8.0	12.0	3.0	6.0	15.2	1.0	2.0	3.0	24.0	92.3	144.3
Mexico	200.2	416.4	587.1	1.5	2.0	4.0	68.0	234.0	302.0	1.5	50.0	85.0	12.0	40.0	37.0
Central America	21.2	37.9	89.6	0.0	0.5	0.5	2.0	9.6	11.2	0.0	0.0	0.0	3.5	18.2	36.5
South America	37.9	104.3	323.1	13.0	26.0	40.0	6.0	53.0	220.8	2.0	5.0	22.0	9.0	11.0	25.0
Africa	1.0	5.0	13.0	1.0	3.0	9.0	0.0	2.0	4.0	0.0	0.0	0.0	0.0	0.0	0.0
Asia	23.0	74.7	119.5	20.0	48.0	55.0	0.0	1.0	2.5	0.0	0.0	0.0	0.0	0.0	12.0
Oceana	1.5	10.0	17.0	1.0	4.0	7.0	0.0	0.0	0.0	0.0	0.0	0.0	0.0	0.0	0.0
International banking	10.0	20.0	30.0												
Total	634.5	1,638.5	2,652.3	131.5	231.5	369.5	134.0	444.6	719.7	10.5	75.5	143.0	76.5	186.5	355.8

Percentages

	Total			Sales			Mines			Oil			Agriculture		
	1897	1908	1914	1897	1908	1914	1897	1908	1914	1897	1908	1914	1897	1908	1914
Europe	20.6	22.5	21.6	12.6	7.6	8.1	0.0	0.2	0.2	0.0	0.2	0.3	0.0	0.0	0.0
Canada	25.2	24.7	23.3	1.6	0.9	1.0	8.7	8.3	6.0	0.9	0.9	0.9	2.8	1.5	3.8
Cuba & other West Indies	7.7	11.9	10.6	0.8	0.5	0.5	0.5	0.4	0.6	0.2	0.1	0.1	3.8	5.6	5.4
Mexico	31.6	25.4	22.1	0.2	0.1	0.2	10.7	14.3	11.4	0.2	3.1	3.2	1.9	2.4	1.4
Central America	3.3	2.3	3.4	0.0	0.0	0.0	0.3	0.6	0.4	0.0	0.0	0.0	0.6	1.1	1.4
South America	6.0	6.4	12.2	2.0	1.6	1.5	0.9	3.2	8.3	0.3	0.3	0.8	1.4	0.7	0.9
Africa	0.2	0.3	0.5	0.2	0.2	0.3	0.0	0.1	0.2	0.0	0.0	0.0	0.0	0.0	0.0
Asia	3.6	4.6	4.5	3.2	2.9	2.1	0.0	0.1	0.1	0.0	0.0	0.0	0.0	0.0	0.5
Oceana	0.2	0.6	0.6	0.2	0.2	0.3	0.0	0.0	0.0	0.0	0.0	0.0	0.0	0.0	0.0
International banking	1.6	1.2	1.1	0.0	0.0	0.0	0.0	0.0	0.0	0.0	0.0	0.0	0.0	0.0	0.0
Total	100.0	100.0	100.0	20.7	14.1	13.9	21.1	27.1	27.1	1.7	4.6	5.4	12.1	11.4	13.4

Millions of Dollars

	Manufacturing			Railroads			Public utilities			Miscellaneous		
	1897	1908	1914	1897	1908	1914	1897	1908	1914	1897	1908	1914
Europe	35.0	100.0	200.0	0.0	0.0	0.0	10.0	12.8	10.8	6.0	125.0	134.5
Canada	55.0	155.0	221.0	12.7	51.4	68.9	2.0	5.0	8.0	1.0	3.0	8.5
Cuba & other West Indies	3.0	18.0	20.0	2.0	43.2	23.8	0.0	24.0	58.0	1.0	2.0	5.0
Mexico	0.0	10.0	10.0	110.6	56.8	110.4	5.6	21.6	33.2	1.0	2.0	5.5
Central America	0.0	0.0	0.0	15.7	9.0	37.9	0.0	0.6	3.5	0.0	-0.0	-0.0
South America	0.0	2.0	7.0	2.4	1.0	3.6	4.5	5.3	3.7	1.0	1.0	1.0
Africa	0.0	0.0	0.0	0.0	0.0	0.0	0.0	0.0	0.0	0.0	0.0	0.0
Asia	0.0	5.0	10.0	0.0	0.0	10.5	0.0	15.7	16.0	3.0	5.0	13.5
Oceana	0.5	6.0	10.0	0.0	0.0	0.0	0.0	0.0	0.0	0.0	0.0	0.0
International banking										10.0	20.0	30.0
Total	93.5	296.0	478.0	143.4	161.4	255.1	22.1	85.0	133.2	23.0	158.0	198.0

Percentages

	Manufacturing			Railroads			Public utilities			Miscellaneous		
	1897	1908	1914	1897	1908	1914	1897	1908	1914	1897	1908	1914
Europe	5.5	6.1	7.5	0.0	0.0	0.0	1.6	0.8	0.4	0.9	7.6	5.1
Canada	8.7	9.5	8.3	2.0	3.1	2.6	0.3	0.3	0.3	0.2	0.2	0.3
Cuba & other West Indies	0.5	1.1	0.8	0.3	2.6	0.9	0.0	1.5	2.2	0.2	0.1	0.2
Mexico	0.0	0.6	0.4	17.4	3.5	4.2	0.9	1.3	1.3	0.2	0.1	0.2
Central America	0.0	0.0	0.0	2.5	0.5	1.4	0.0	0.0	0.1	0.0	-0.0	-0.0
South America	0.0	0.1	0.3	0.4	0.1	0.1	0.7	0.3	0.1	0.2	0.1	0.0
Africa	0.0	0.0	0.0	0.0	0.0	0.0	0.0	0.0	0.0	0.0	0.0	0.0
Asia	0.0	0.3	0.4	0.0	0.0	0.4	0.0	1.0	0.6	0.5	0.3	0.5
Oceana	0.1	0.4	0.4	0.0	0.0	0.0	0.0	0.0	0.0	0.0	0.0	0.0
International banking	0.0	0.0	0.0	0.0	0.0	0.0	0.0	0.0	0.0	1.6	1.2	1.1
Total	14.7	18.1	18.0	22.6	9.9	9.6	3.5	5.2	5.0	3.6	9.6	7.5

Source: Lewis, *America's Stake*, Appendix D, 575–606.

Table 16.17. *Rationalization of summed capital flows with stocks of foreign investment in U.S. and U.S. investment abroad (millions of dollars)*

	Stock 1 foreign in U.S. (measured)	Summed flows	Stock 2a U.S. in foreign (estimated)	Stock 2b U.S. in foreign (measured)	Residual
1843a[1]	225	300	−75	(small)	−75
1843b[2]	253	276	−23	(small)	−23
1853a[3]	377	378	−1	(small)	−1
1853b[4]	381	378	+3	(small)	+3
1869a[5]	1,546	1,235	+311	75	+236
1869b[6]	1,116	1,235	−119	75	−194
1869c[7]	1,246	1,235	+11	75	−64
1897a[8]	3,395	3,388	+8	685	−677
1899a[9]	3,400	2,880	+520	+500	+20
1914a[10]	7,540	3,109	+4,431	3,514	+917
1914b[11]	6,623	3,109	+3,514	3,514	0

Note and Source: See text discussion on p. 807, this volume.

[1] Lewis, *America's Stake*, 519–21.

[2] 1843a adjusted for 24 million defaulted state bonds and with short-term capital assumed equal to $56 million.

[3] Lewis, *America's Stake*, 521–22. Secretary of the Treasury's estimate for foreign long-term investment plus an 1857 estimate of short-term investment ($222 million + $155 million).

[4] Stock 1 adjusted for $4 million defaulted Florida loan.

[5] Lewis, *America's Stake*, 522–23. Commissioner Wills's estimates of foreign long- and short-term investment in the United States adjusted for an additional $80 million in short-term investment. U.S. investment abroad from Lewis, 442.

[6] Stock 1 adjusted for sale of U.S. bonds at a 43 percent discount.

[7] Stock 1 adjusted for sale of U.S. bonds at a 30 percent discount.

[8] Lewis, *America's Stake*, 442.

[9] Lewis, *America's Stake*, 529. Lewis' adjustment of Bacon's estimates.

[10] Stock 1 = Lewis and Wilkins $7,090 million long-term plus $450 million short term. Stock 2 = Lewis, *America's Stake*, 606. Sum flows includes estimated increases in short-term of $200 million between 1897 and 1914.

[11] Stock 1 assumes common stocks were issued at the 1914 market prices rather than at par *and* that one-fourth of railroad bonds and preferred shares were issued before 1890 at 67 percent of par. See Lewis, *America's Stake*, 554.

The experiment proved so profitable that they soon expanded their operations.[143]

While American investment in Mexico was concentrated in transport and mining, the investment pattern in Canada was much more diversified. In 1897 the fraction of total American long-term capital invested in mining was almost as large as the proportion of mines in the Mexican total, but manufacturing drew an equal proportion. Moreover, investment in railroads accounted for less than 10 percent of the total Canadian investment; and sales agencies, oil production and distribution, and agriculture received substantially larger fractions than their Mexican counterparts. American investors appear to have viewed Canada much like they viewed states like Michigan or California – as a potential market and a source of raw materials.

In 1877, when Boston capitalists were investing in Michigan copper, they also invested in the Orford Nickel and Copper Company – a firm organized to mine ore in Quebec and process it in New Jersey. By 1886 Americans had interests in antimony and manganese mines in New Brunswick and in gold and copper mines in Quebec; New York and St. Paul investors had organized five firms to mine for gold, iron ore, and mica on the prairies; and an Ohio carriage builder and railroad entrepreneur had incorporated both the Canada Copper Company and the Anglo American Iron Company. During the 1880s American investors financed one-half of all Canadian mining capital. Note, however, that these were direct investments, not funds routed through the New York Stock Exchange.[144]

While the American Screw Company may have been the first American manufacturing firm to build a plant in Canada, between 1875 and 1887 some fifty American firms located branches in that country.[145] American insurance firms began selling policies in Canada at an early date; and those sales ultimately meant the investment of their reserves in a wide range of enterprises.[146] Finally, American portfolio investors did begin to add a few Canadian securities to their holdings.[147]

---

[143] Marcosson, *Metal Magic*, 50, 52–53. Gattenby Williams (a pseudonym for William Guggenheim) in collaboration with Charles Monroe Heath, *William Guggenheim* (New York, 1934), 70, 84, 93, 95, and 100. Lewis, *America's Stake*, 201–2 and 249–50. Thomas E. O'Brien, "Rich Boy and the Dreams of Avarice: the Guggenheims in Chile," *Business History Review*, 63 (1989) 126.

[144] Field, *Canada*, 24. Lewis, *America's Stake*, 207–8 and 251. Herbert Marshall, Frank A. Southard Jr. and Kenneth W. Taylor, *Canadian-American Industry, A Study in International Investment* (New Haven, 1936), 10. E. S. Moore, *American Influences on Canadian Mining* (Toronto, 1941), 16–20, 27–30.

[145] Lewis, *America's Stake*, 229, 294. Wilkins, *Multinational Enterprise*, 46, 60.

[146] Wilkins, *Multinational Enterprise*, 64–5.

[147] Lewis, *America's Stake*, 335–36. Marshall, Southard and Taylor, *Canadian-American Industry*, 16, 114, and 194.

At least two decades before the Platt Amendment turned Cuba into a de facto American colony, businessmen had, on a very small scale, begun to draw Cuba and the rest of the Caribbean region into the American domestic market.[148] While Mexico contributed minerals and Canada minerals, lumber, and wheat, the Caribbean supplied sugar and fruit to the American market. Even as late as 1897, however, Cuba, the West Indies, and Central America accounted for little more than 10 percent of total American long-term investment abroad. Moreover, if railroads are excluded, almost 90 percent of the $49 million total of American direct investment in the Caribbean was in Cuba, and 65 percent was in Cuban agriculture.

American merchants had long financed Cuban sugar growers; but, in the wake of war-induced defaults, those merchants found themselves in control of a number of operating plantations. In 1883 the Boston-based E. Atkins & Company took over one of the Sarria family's agricultural estates and made the first major American investment in the sugar industry. Other Americans followed. Changes in market conditions induced the management of the more progressive of these American plantations to expand into milling as well as production; and, although "such mills represented large capital expenditures . . . they were tremendously efficient and greatly reduced the unit costs of production." In time these grower-refiners became the center of the production distribution network – they financed the small growers, contracted for their output, processed the product, and used their own railways to ship the refined sugar to the seacoast.[149]

The initial investments in bananas can be traced at least as far back as 1870, when Captain Lorenzo Dow Baker began to ship fruit from Jamaica. The initial experiment was so successful that, a decade and a half later, he was able to persuade his Boston agent and nine other partners to organize the Boston Fruit Company (the predecessor of United Fruit).[150]

The years before the mid-1890s also set the boundary conditions for the political-economic model of future American involvement in the Caribbean. As early as 1853, marines were landed in Nicaragua to prevent

---

[148] So close was the relationship between the American and Cuban governments that in the late 1920s the distinguished economic historian Leland Jenks entitled his study of Cuba, *Our Cuban Colony*. Leland Hamilton Jenks, *Our Cuban Colony: A Study of Sugar* (New York, 1928).

[149] Lewis, *America's Stake*, 265–66. Jenks, *Our Cuban Colony*, 35.

[150] Stacy May and Galo Plaza, *The United Fruit Company in Latin America*, Seventh Case Study in a National Planning Association series on United States Business Performance Abroad (Washington, DC, 1958), 4.

"any depredations of the property of the Accessory Transit Company"; and two years later the company underwrote a revolution that overthrew the nation's government. Forty years later marines were again lan█, this time to make certain that the Maritime Canal Company's concession was not canceled; and in 1895 marines landed to protect American merchants and banana planters in Panama.[151] In each instance the sums involved were trivial. Total investment in the Accessory Transit Company did not exceed $4 million, and only a tiny fraction was ever threatened. Construction of the Maritime Canal across Nicaragua was never begun, and total American agricultural investment in *all* of Colombia was only about $3 million.

Towards Maturity: 1897–1914

Between 1897 and 1905 American long-term foreign investment surged, and despite a return to borrowing in the last decade, by 1914 direct investments had increased more than fourfold, portfolio investment more than seventeen times, and the total from less than $700 million to more than $3.5 billion; however, while the geographic pattern of investment was largely unchanged, the industrial profile was altered substantially (see Tables 16.14, 16.15 and 16.16). The fraction of total capital invested in railways fell by more than half while the proportion directed toward manufacturing and mining – particularly the mining of industrial minerals – increased.

Outside of the "extensions of the home market," American direct investments continued to reflect the areas of American technological leadership and the nation's long-held dominant position in petroleum production. Between 1897 and 1914 direct investments in the American sales network increased almost three times, those in manufacturing more than five times, and those in oil production and distribution more than thirteen times.

By 1911 Standard Oil had twenty-two foreign subsidiaries that represented a combined investment of at least $150 million; and the firm controlled at least sixty-seven foreign enterprises. Most were marketing companies, but there were also transport and refining firms as well as two firms engaged in oil production.[152] Moreover, Standard's domination of the overseas market for American oil was at least partially undercut by the

---

[151] Wilkins, *Multinational Enterprise*, 25–26 and 153.
[152] Hidy and Hidy, *Standard Oil*, 514 and 524–25.

entry of the Pure Oil Company in the 1890s and the Texas Company (Texaco) in 1905.[153]

Aside from oil, while firms like Singer continued to expand their foreign marketing and manufacturing activities, new entrants from the rapidly expanding domestic manufacturing sector began to make their presence felt. For example, the Pittsburgh Wire Company began to employ its own foreign sales force in 1893, and that investment proved so profitable that it was soon copied by its competitors. By 1900 the Deering Harvester Company had begun to manufacture abroad; and, by 1911, its successor had plants in Canada, Sweden, France, Germany, and Russia that together accounted for more than 40 percent of the company's total sales. Similarly, by 1901 the American Tobacco Company was operating four manufacturing plants in Australia as well as single plants in Canada, Japan, Germany, and the United Kingdom. U.S. Rubber began manufacturing in Canada in 1907, and B. F. Goodrich established a French plant three years later.[154]

Finally, American portfolio investment in foreign enterprises – particularly in government bonds – increased from $50 to $862 million; and Europe and Asia accounted for one-fourth of that increase. Between 1900 and 1903 alone, the American market absorbed $263 million in new portfolio issues.[155] So rapid was the increase that, in 1902, the Secretary of State, John Hay, was moved to say:

The "debtor nation" has become the chief creditor nation. The financial center of the world, which required thousands of years to journey from the Euphrates to the Thames and Seine, seems passing to the Hudson between daybreak and dark.[156]

Nor had the surge ended. In just six months of 1904, $535 million of Japanese government loans were floated in American and European markets; and it appears that as much as half were carried by American financial houses.[157] In all, between 1901 and 1905 the influx of foreign

---

[153] Lewis, *America's Stake*, 182–84. Wilkins, *Multinational Enterprise*, 83 and 86. Harold F. Williamson and Arnold R. Daum, *The American Petroleum Industry: The Age of Illumination* (Evanston, 1955), 660. Marquis James, *The Texaco Story, the First Fifty Years* (Houston, 1953), 31 and 102.

[154] Lewis, *America's Stake*, 184, Wilkins, *Multinational Enterprise*, 91 and 103. M. J. French, "The Emergence of a U.S. Multinational Enterprise: The Goodyear Tire and Rubber Company, 1910–1939," *Economic History Review*, 2nd series, 40 (1987), 69 and 72.

[155] Bullock et al., "Balance of Trade," 229–30.

[156] 57th Congress, 1 Session, *Congressional Record* (Washington, DC, 1902), 2201.

[157] Robert W. Dunn, *American Foreign Investments* (New York, 1926), 2. The data are from a New York weekly, the *Annalist*, 16, 452.

bonds reached $460 million; and between 1906 and 1914 the American investors absorbed an additional $442 million. Of the $902 million total, $596 million represented European and Asian loans – including $17 million for the London underground.[158]

Despite the attraction of European securities, it was the Western Hemisphere that drew most of the attention of American investors in the years between 1897 and 1914. Although the proportion of long-term investment flowing to both Canada and Mexico had declined some-what and the former had overtaken the latter in terms of total American investment, the two were still by far the largest recipients of American capital.

In the case of Mexico, nationalization of the Mexican Central and the Mexican National railways initially reduced the level of direct American investment in railroads; but that decline was more than offset by the increase in portfolio holdings of the securities of the two roads.[159] Overall, despite the fact that the railroads' share of the U.S. total had fallen from 55 to about 45 percent, American investment in Mexican railroads had increased from $111 to *at least* $387 million.[160]

Over the same period, the fraction of investment flowing to mining increased from 1897 to 1908 and then declined slightly; however, the distribution between precious and industrial metals changed dramatically. Gold and silver had accounted for almost three-quarters of the total in 1897; but, despite the fact that Mexico had become the world's leading silver producer, in 1914 precious metals represented less than half of the mining total.[161]

In 1902 there were an estimated 294 American-financed mining ventures in Mexico, in 1908 the Mexican government announced that American investors controlled 840 of the 1,000 foreign owned mines, and two years later those same officials argued that Americans controlled half of all mines in Mexico and that those mines represented 70 percent of all

---

[158] Lewis, *America's Stake*, 338–45. In 1914, for example, the list of foreign capital issues publicly offered in the United States included $11 million in loans to European governments (Greece, Norway, and Sweden), $6 million to cities and provinces in Canada, $10 million to the government of Cuba, $1.5 million to the government of Panama, $6 million to the National Railways of Mexico, and $8 million in corporate issues. The latter were all to Canadian firms (the Central Railway of Canada, the Northern Electric Manufacturing Company Ltd., the Dominion Power and Transmission Company (Ltd.), the Northern Navigation Company, and the Toronto Railway). Ralph A. Young, *Handbook of American Underwriting of Foreign Securities*, U.S. Department of Commerce, Trade Promotion Series # 104 (Washington, DC, 1930), 58–59.

[159] The $180 million in direct investment was converted into $197 million in bonds and preferred stock.

[160] Lewis, *America's Stake*, 316–17 and 346.

[161] Mexico had passed the United States in silver production in 1902.

mineral output. In that latter year American investment in Mexican mining and smelting was placed at $125 million.[162]

The Revolution of 1911 changed the economic environment, but until then there is little question that American investors took a very rosy view of the potential profitability of Mexican mines.[163] In 1895 Phelps-Dodge bought the Guggenheims' copper mines near Nacozari and incorporated the newly acquired property as the Moctezuma Copper Company. Between 1895 and 1914, Moctezuma paid its parent dividends totaling $9.7 million. In 1898, a western cattleman found traces of copper at Cananea Mountain, and he was able to obtain sufficient funding from New York financiers to organize the Greene Consolidated Copper Company. When in 1906 the copper mines were taken over by the Amalgamated Copper Company, the reorganized firm was capitalized at $50 million.[164] In 1903 the Guggenheims took over the American Smelting and Refining Company and merged its properties with their existing holdings.[165] With sixty-four mining properties scattered over Mexico, the enlarged ASARCO became the largest single foreign investor in that country.[166] Nor was the copper rush over. Between 1900 and 1902 Americans organized at least seven other companies with a total capitalization of almost $25 million.[167]

While oil had been discovered in 1876, there was no commercial development until 1900, when Edward Doheny organized the Mexican Petroleum Company of California; in 1914 its holdings were valued at $57.9 million. By 1911 Mexico had become the world's third-largest producer of petroleum; and half of its production was controlled by American-owned companies.[168]

---

[162] John R. Southworth and Percy C. Homs, *El Directo Oficial Minero de Mexico*, 9 (Mexico, 1908), 17. John R. Southworth, *El Directo Oficial Minero de Mexico*, 11 (Mexico, 1910), 6.

[163] Lewis, *America's Stake*, 202–3. Wilkins, *Multinational Enterprise*, 116 and 120.

[164] Ira B. Joralemon, *Romantic Copper, Its Lure and Lore* (New York, 1936), 136–65. Harold Underwood Faulkner, *The Decline of Laissez Faire, 1897–1917* (New York, 1951), 76. David M. Pletcher, *Rails, Mines, and Progress: Seven American Promoters in Mexico, 1867–1911* (Ithaca, NY, 1958), 222–25.

[165] ASARCO had been organized "to combine all the principal smelting works in the United States with the exception of the Guggenheim's"; but without the cooperation of the brothers, its position was very fragile. Marcosson, *Metal Magic*, 62.

[166] Marcosson, *Metal Magic*, 57–83. John Moody, *The Truth About the Trusts* (New York, 1904), 42–48. Henry O'Connor, *The Guggenheims: The Making of an American Dynasty* (New York, 1976), 104 and 117.

For a discussion of the Guggenheims' ability to take over ASARCO, see O'Brien. "The Guggenheims in Chile," 126–27. As earlier noted, for a general discussion of the organization of the world copper industry, see Schmitz, "The World Copper Industry," 392–410.

[167] Lewis. *America's Stake*, 234–37.

[168] Lewis, *America's Stake*, 220. Wilkins, *Multinational Enterprise*, 123–24.

In the case of Canada, the four and a half fold increase in American investment was partially fueled by an increase of $220 million in portfolio investment; but American direct investment in agriculture, manufacturing, and mining also increased dramatically. Investment in the agricultural sector went largely into timberlands (in 1909 it was estimated that 90 percent of the available timber in British Columbia was controlled by Americans or American companies), but there was some investment in western farms, and there were large speculative holdings of land in British Columbia and the prairie provinces.[169]

In the manufacturing sector, the first decade of the twentieth century saw a number of large American corporations – firms such as General Electric and Westinghouse – move part of their production north. American millers and other food processors opened plants, International Harvester began to manufacture farm machinery, Ford and Buick cars, and U.S. Rubber and Goodyear rubber products.[170] In part, at least, these shifts were induced by Canadian tariffs that gave a substantial subsidy to "domestic" enterprise. In part they reflected nothing more than an attempt to exploit a growing market.

Americans continued to establish and finance Canadian firms. There were, for example, multi-million-dollar investments in the Canadian Steel and Coal Company, the Federal Sugar Refining Company, and the Northern Cereal Company as well as smaller placements in a variety of other firms.[171] The largest American investments in Canadian manufacturing were, however, reserved for the pulp and paper industry. By 1914, investments in pulp and paper mills represented more than a third of the $221 million American investment in manufacturing.[172]

Investment in mining continued. The twentieth century saw the Canadian Copper Company and the Anglo American Iron Company merge to form the International Nickel Company, a firm that was the world's largest producer of nickel. In 1910, Johns Manville began to mine asbestos

[169] In the words of a contemporary observer, "These [American investments] are principally mining, and lumbering, and timber, with some colonization propositions." Field, *Canada*, 21. Lewis, *America's Stake*, 288. Wilkins, *Multinational Enterprise*, 138.

[170] Faulkner, *Laissez Faire*, 75. French, "The Emergence of a U.S. Multinational Enterprise," 69 and 71.

[171] Lewis, *America's Stake*, 596–97.

[172] Lewis, *America's Stake*, 595. Wilkins, *Multinational Enterprise*, 138–39. Faulkner, *Laissez Faire*, 75. For a complete analysis of the American and Canadian newsprint markets, see Constance Southworth, "The American-Canadian Newsprint Paper Industry and the Tariff," *Journal of Political Economy*, 30 (1922), 681–97.

in Quebec; and Field's 1913 enumeration of American investments in Canada included $60 million in British Columbian mining.[173]

Altogether, Field placed American investments in Canada at $279 million in 1909, $417 million in 1911, and $637 million in 1913. The 1913 total was broken down into $135 million invested in 450 Canadian branches of American firms, $124 million of government, municipal, and corporate bonds, $71 million of British Columbia mills and timber lands, $68 million of investments by American life insurance companies, $62 million in British Columbia mines, $60 million in speculative land holdings in that province and $41 million in similar investments in the prairie provinces, $20 million in city and town property, and the remainder in a series of miscellaneous activities that included $3.5 million in theatrical enterprises and $1 million in fox farms on Prince Edward Island.[174]

Given the market opportunities presented by the Spanish-American War and the political environment created by the Platt Amendment, it is not surprising that the fraction of American investment directed toward Cuba and, to a lesser extent, the West Indies rose from just more than 7 percent in 1897 to something less than 10 percent in 1914. By that latter date, long-term American investment in the region totaled more than $335 million. Although agriculture's share of total investment declined from just less than half to 36 percent, the bulk of the new funds ($120.3 million) were directed towards that sector. In addition, however, there were substantial commitments to public utilities ($58 million) and additions to the portfolios of American investors ($55 million).

About three-quarters of the agricultural investment was in sugar; and, of that amount, more than 80 percent was invested in Cuba. It is estimated that by 1905 there were some twenty-one American-owned mills processing about a fifth of the island's crop, and that proportion had doubled by 1909.[175] Once the island became independent, investment in Cuban utilities, particularly in electrification, began to lure American investors. The Havana Electric Railway, Light and Power Company, for example, was purchased with American capital and successfully operated by American management.[176] Finally, except for the American bankers' 20

---

[173] Lewis, *America's Stake*, 208 and 596. Wilkins, *Multinational Enterprise*, 136–37. E. S. Moore, *American Influence on Canadian Mining* (Toronto, 1941), 71–72.

[174] Field, *Canada*, 25.

[175] Jenks, *Our Cuban Colony*, 35 and 131–32. Lewis, *America's Stake*, 267–68. Wilkins, *Multinational Enterprise*, 155.

[176] Jenks, *Our Cuban Colony*, 171–72. Scott Nearing and Joseph Freeman, *Dollar Diplomacy* (New York, 1925), 180.

percent holding of the National Bank of the Republic of Haiti (value $400,000) and Kuhn Loeb's $13.5 million refunding of the $20 million Santo Domingo debt, most of the reported portfolio investment was in Cuban securities. About $35 million were in government and about $11.4 million in private issues.[177]

In 1911 the American consul general placed American investment in Cuba at $205 million. Of that sum, he estimated that $50 million was invested in sugar, $15 million in other lands, $10 million in other agriculture, $25 million in railway equity, and an equal amount in mines, mercantile activity, and manufacturing taken together, $5 million each in shipping and banking, $20 million in mortgages and credit, $20 million in public utilities, and $30 million in the island nation's public debt.[178]

While the proportion of American long-term investment directed toward Central America declined slightly between 1897 and 1914, the fraction flowing to South America almost doubled. Taken together, the Latin American commitment increased from just less than $60 to almost $460 million. More than half of that total was directed toward mining, but railroads and agriculture together represented another $100 million, and portfolio investment, an item that had been absent in 1897, added an additional $46 million.

Although there were minor American mining investments in Costa Rica, Honduras, Nicaragua, Salvador, Bolivia, Brazil, Colombia, and Ecuador, by 1914 the largest financial commitments were to copper mines in Peru and Chile. In the case of the former, lack of transport and the technical difficulties associated with production at altitudes up to 14,000 feet proved a major barrier even for the combination of American finance (J. P. Morgan) and technological know-how (the Hearst-Haggin group). Although organized in 1902, it was 1912, and even then only after receiving substantial additional capital infusions, before the Cerro de Pasco Mining Company was able to produce any copper – and it was 1917 before the company began to pay dividends.[179]

By far the largest mining investments were in Chile, but American penetration did not begin until 1904, when William Braden incorporated

[177] Lewis, *America's Stake*, 325, 344 and 347. Faulkner, *Laissez Faire*, 71.
[178] Jenks, *Our Cuban Colony*, 164–65.
[179] H. Foster Bain and Read Thomas Thornton, *Ores and Industry in South America* (New York, 1934), 282–83 and 296. Joralemon, *Romantic Copper*, 234–38. Lewis, *America's Stake*, 237–38.

the Braden Copper Company and began to exploit the low-grade ores in the Andean region southeast of Santiago. Reorganized in 1909 as the Braden Copper Mines Company, it was recapitalized at $14 million in 1911, and output reached sixteen million pounds in 1913.[180]

Braden's success convinced the Guggenheims of the profit potential of the porphyr ores, and by 1912 they had bought a number of "exhausted" mines in Chuqicamata and organized the Chile Exploration Company. The initial investment of $1 million revealed the existence of 154 million tons of 2.5 percent ore, but the sum proved woefully inadequate to underwrite production. It required an additional $11 million to reach even the most easily accessible deposits; and, ultimately, it required the organization of a new and heavily financed firm (the Chile Copper Company). Even then, however, "100 million dollars was poured into the desert before Chile Copper was a success."[181]

While it was sugar that dominated American agricultural investment in Cuba and the West Indies, it was tropical fruit in general, and bananas in particular, that drew the bulk of such investment to Central and South America. Although sugar production in Colombia and Peru absorbed about $8 million of American capital in 1914, tropical fruit accounted for all of the $36.5 million invested in Central and $8 of the $25 million invested in South American agriculture.

Much of that investment was channeled through the United Fruit Company, a firm chartered in New Jersey in 1899 to operate sales agencies in five American cities, and plantations in Cuba, Jamaica, Santo Domingo, Cost Rica, Colombia, and Nicaragua. The Company initially owned 212,394 acres of land, eleven steamships, and 112 miles of railroad; and in its first year it exported fifteen million stems of bananas to the United States. Within a very few years, the firm expanded into Guatamala and Honduras and increased its holdings in Nicaragua, Jamaica, and Colombia. Between 1900 and 1910 United Fruit accounted for well over three-quarters of the total number of banana stems imported into the combined North American and European markets. Despite some competition, United Fruit maintained its near monopoly position until the outbreak of

[180] O'Brien dates the Braden Copper Company in 1908, and he puts the initial capitalization at $23 million. O'Brien, "The Guggenheims in Chile," 130. O'Brien's dating probably refers to the date that the Guggenheims took over the Braden Copper Company. They initially retained the original name. Wilkins, *Multinational Enterprise*, 178–81.

[181] Bain and Thornton, *Ores and Industry in South America*, 221–22. Joralemon, *Romantic Copper*, 238–47. Lewis, *America's Stake*, 238–40. O'Connor, *The Guggenheims*, 346–49.

World War I. In 1913 it owned or leased more than 850,000 acres, of which 221,837 were under cultivation.[182]

Railroad investment was never substantial, and what there was largely confined to Guatemala. That country received about 80 percent of the region's $37.9 million total. Of the remaining $7.3 million, $1.5 million represented two American banks' (Brown & Co. and J. & W. Seligman) 50 percent share of the Pacific Railway of Nicaragua, and the remaining $5.8 million was invested in the Salvadorian system.[183]

In terms of portfolio investment, the United States appears to have absorbed something more than $64 million of Central and South American issues; and, of that total, some $46 million were still outstanding in 1914. While funds were directed to the governments of nine countries, the major recipients were Argentina (40 percent), Brazil (32 percent), and Bolivia (12 percent). In the case of Argentina, the $25 million advanced had not been repaid by 1914, and at that time it represented more than one-half of American investment in the region's portfolio issues.[184]

By 1914 the relative share of American investments in Cuba, the West Indies, and in Central America had increased somewhat, but the level of American political interference in the region's political affairs had risen dramatically. Even if this country's overt and covert support for the Panamanian "revolution" is ignored – that support was almost certainly not engendered by a desire to protect American investments in the region but by far more global military and economic concerns – there appears to have been a near exponential increase in direct intervention.[185]

The Treaty of Paris, which ended the Spanish-American War, permitted the direct annexation of Puerto Rico; and, indirectly, it produced the Platt Amendment to the Cuban constitution. That amendment prohibited Cuba from concluding any treaty with a foreign power "which will impair or tend to impair the independence of Cuba," and from incurring any foreign debt where interest and payments to the sinking fund could not be met with "the

[182] Charles David Kepner and Henry Soothill Jay, *The Banana Empire: A Case Study of Economic Imperialism* (New York, 1935), 35–36, 34, 70, and 101. May and Plaza, *United Fruit*, 6–7, 13, and 15–16. Charles Morrow Wilson, *Empire in Gold and Green: The Story of the American Banana Trade* (New York, 1947), 91, 107–10, and 118.

[183] May and Plaza, *United Fruit*, 10–11. Lewis, *America's Stake*, 280 and 602. Wilkins, *Multinational Enterprise*, 159.

[184] Lewis, *America's Stake*, 343 and 347. Benjamin H. Williams, *Economic Foreign Policy of the United States* (New York, 1929), 400–2.

[185] Howard C. Hill, *Roosevelt and the Caribbean* (Chicago, 1927), 44 and 68. Nearing and Freeman, *Dollar Diplomacy*, 83.

ordinary revenues of the Island of Cuba." It also granted the United States military bases in Cuba, required that the Cubans invest in sanitation to protect the people and commerce of Cuba, and permitted the United States to intervene militarily for the "protection of life, property, and individual liberty, and for discharging the obligations with respect to Cuba imposed by the treaty of Paris, now to be assumed and undertaken by the government of Cuba."[186] Not only did the American government successfully object to attempts by the Cuban government to borrow funds; but American troops intervened directly in 1906, 1912, and 1917.[187] It was not, however, the American investor who was the chief beneficiary of this country's involvement in Cuban affairs. Although American investment had increased, in 1914 European capital was still predominant.[188]

An executive agreement concluded in 1904 and modified and ratified as a treaty in 1907 gave the United States the right to collect the customs of Santo Domingo and to distribute 55 percent of the funds collected to foreign creditors until such time as that nation's foreign debts had been repaid. In 1904 the Santo Domingan custom houses were taken over to guarantee the payments on an American-held loan; and American control of Santo Domingan customs continued for another three decades. Control of the island's customs was, however, not the limit of American involvement. In 1912, the American government forced the resignation of the Dominican president; it supervised Santo Domingan elections in 1913 and in 1914; and, two years later, the country was invaded by American marines.[189]

The basis of American political penetration of Haiti can be traced at least as far back as 1910, when New York bankers purchased one-fifth of the shares of the National Bank of Haiti – a purchase that was largely the result of pressure applied by the American secretary of state.[190] Direct military intervention, however, did not occur until half a decade later; but, at that time, the resulting treaty reduced the island republic to the status of an American protectorate – a status that continued for almost two decades.

---

[186] William M. Malloy (ed.), *Treaties, Conventions, International Acts, Protocols and Agreements between the United States and Other Powers*, 4 vols. (Washington, DC, 1910–1938), vol. I., 362–64.

[187] Williams, *Economic Foreign Policy*, 202–3. Nearing and Freeman, *Dollar Diplomacy*, 180.

[188] Robert F. Smith, "The United States and Cuba," in Marvin Bernstein (ed.), *Foreign Investment in Latin America: Cases and Attitudes* (New York, 1966), 147–48.

[189] Melvin M. Knight, *The Americans in Santo Domingo* (New York, 1928), 18–23. Nearing and Freeman, *Dollar Diplomacy* 125–28.

[190] U.S. Government, Select Committee on an Inquiry into the Occupation and Administration of Haiti and Santo Domingo, *Hearings*, 67th Congress, 1st and 2nd sessions, (Washington, DC, 1922), 2 vols., 105. Cited in Nearing and Freeman, *Dollar Diplomacy*, 133–35.

Nicaragua had seen marines land to protect American investments in the 1890s, but those incursions were merely the opening guns of a much larger campaign. In 1909 and 1910, the United States provided direct and indirect support for a revolution against the governments of both José Zelaya and his successor, José Madriz. The next year the American bankers, Brown Brothers and J. & W. Seligman, negotiated a loan secured by a lien on customs – the customs to be collected by an American chosen by the banks and approved by the State Department. Other similar loans followed and, perhaps not surprisingly, the marines landed in 1912; with only a brief interruption, they remained until 1933.[191]

Clearly the political and military interference in the lives of the residents of Cuba, Santo Domingo, Haiti, and Nicaragua laid the foundation for seven decades of anti-American feelings; but it is difficult to rationalize the level of intervention with the size of this country's investment stake in those countries. In 1914 the total amount of American investment in all of Cuba, the West Indies, and Central America did not exceed $430 million. Granted Cuba was somewhat important; but investment in the other countries that witnessed direct American intervention was trifling. The total for Nicaragua did not exceed $2.5 million; the figure for Panama (outside the Canal Zone) was probably not more than $4 million; for Haiti it could hardly have been more than $11 million; and the Santo Domingan total was no more than $16 million – a grand total of less than $33 million, a third of the amount invested in Canadian agriculture.

While direct military intervention is guaranteed to raise hackles, the level of rhetoric raised against "Yankee" economic imperialism is much more difficult to explain. Not only was the level of American investment in Latin America not large, but the evidence suggests the level of profits was hardly exploitative. Very early Leland Jenks concluded that American involvement in Cuba was more beneficial to the Cubans than to the Americans. More recently, Vasquez and Meyer have come to a similar conclusion about Mexico; and William Schell in his study of American investment in tropical Mexico also concludes, that "the prevailing flow of wealth was from north to south."[192]

[191] Faulkner, *Laissez Faire*, 70–73. Lewis, *America's Stake*, 343–44. Nearing and Freeman, *Dollar Diplomacy*, 151–52.
[192] Jenks, *Our Cuban Colony*. Josefina Zaraida Vasquez and Lorenzo Meyer, *The United States and Mexico* (Chicago, 1985), 91. Schell, "American Investment in Tropical Mexico," 252.

Stanley Lebergott, in his more general study of U.S. imperialism, reached much the same conclusion.

In summary, American imperialism after the Spanish American War worked systematic effects on interest groups in Latin America. (a) It increased the income of workers and peasants because it expanded the demand for labor . . . (b) Workers' real wages often increased more than their money wages . . . (c) Imperialist investment increased the value of land held by landlords . . . (d) American imperialism injured the vested interests of the existing native business group by destroying monopoly profits . . .

In his last conclusion, Lebergott may have discovered the root of the anti-American rhetoric. In his words, "The heart of the anti-imperialist struggle, then, may prove to be a squabble between two capitalist groups, one native and the other foreign, fighting over the spoils of progress."[193]

CONCLUSIONS

It is difficult to summarize more than one hundred years of international transfers, but three issues stand out. The first deals with the reliability and comparability of the data, the second with the role of foreign capital in American development, and the third with the relationship between capital exports, "dollar diplomacy," and the origins of the belief in "Yankee economic imperialism."

The data in this chapter are drawn from two quite different sources: the net flow estimates are derived from an analysis of the nation's balance of payments; the estimates of the stocks of foreign investment in the United States and of American investment abroad are the product of enumerations – censuses, if you like – of the nation's debit and credit balances. In theory, of course, the two are closely related; but, like many empirical exercises, the two are more closely linked in theory than the data often suggest.[194]

---

[193] Stanley Lebergott, "The Returns to U.S. Imperialism, 1890–1929," *Journal of Economic History*, 40 (1980), 229–52. The quotations are from 249.

[194] Using stock estimates to estimate net flows is, however, made more complex because, among a myriad of problems: (1) the portfolio components of the stock estimates are included at par; but, if the issues are sold at a discount, the flow figure captures only the discounted value; and (2) repudiated debt is subtracted from the stock estimates but there is no offsetting adjustment to the flows. These problems are discussed in great detail in Mira Wilkins's unpublished paper, "Flows Do Not Stock Make: Guidelines for Determining the Level of Long Term Foreign Investments in the United States – Methodological Quandaries in Handling Pre-1914 Data," Florida International University, 1986.

Table 16.17 (see p. 792) displays the estimated stocks and the sum of the net flows for a number of years in the nineteenth and early twentieth centuries.[195] Although there appears to be a substantial discrepancy in the 1843 figures, closer examination reveals that the residuals, while still substantial, are not that large. Clearly, an estimate of a negative $75 million of American investment abroad is absurd; however, it should be kept in mind that the summed net flow figures do not capture the state debts that went permanently into default or that were substantially written down between 1839 and 1843.[196] In addition, Lewis acknowledges that her estimate of short-term indebtedness is low. Thus, if the net flow figure is reduced by $24 million to account for the defaults and the short-term component of the stock figure is doubled, the resulting residual (–$23 million) represents a believable statistical discrepancy.

Despite North's concern, it is not difficult to rationalize the two sets of 1853 estimates.[197] The Lewis estimate of the stock is $377 and the flows sum to $378 million leaving a small negative residual of $1 million – a figure that appears to be well within normal bounds, particularly given the fact that the estimate of the flow includes "errors and omissions" and the fact that the $4 million repudiated Florida debt is not included in the stock estimate.

The 1869 figure for foreign investment in the United States, on the other hand, is, as Simon has suggested, quite difficult to accept.[198] If Wells's estimate is correct, it implies that American investments abroad were an astounding $311 million – more than four times the generally accepted figure. If, however, Wells's figures are adjusted downward to reflect the international market's discount on the $1 billion in U.S. government obligations, the adjusted figure of $1,116 million turns the +$236 million residual into a –$194 million figure.[199] Moreover, if the discount had been only 30 percent, as Cleona Lewis suggests, the two sets of estimates are relatively close.[200]

---

[195] The estimate of the sum of the net capital flows assumes that there was $19 million dollars in foreign investment in the United States and no American investment abroad in 1790. That figure is based on the known foreign-held U.S. debt of $12.1 million and an estimated $6.9 million of short-term credit.

[196] Office of Business Economics puts those reductions at $24 million in 1841 and 1842 alone, and some sources suggest it may have been more.

[197] North's concern centers on Lewis's use of an 1857 estimate of the balance of short-term capital. He feels the 1857 figure is too high, but any reduction makes the two sets of estimates even more difficult to rationalize. North, "Balance of Payments," 626.

[198] Simon, "Balance of Payments," 706.

[199] The 43 percent discount is from *Hunt's Merchants' Magazine*, 59 (1868), 241–48.

[200] Lewis, *America's Stake*, 158.

Some of the later estimates, however, are much more difficult to ratio-nalize. As Simon noted, Cleona Lewis's estimates for 1897 ($3,395 million in foreign investments in the U.S. and $685 million in American invest-ments abroad) would imply a sum of capital flows of $2,710 million; but the figure from the North-Simon data is $3,388 million, a discrepancy of $677 million.[201] Moreover, since a substantial fraction of the American securities had been issued at not insignificant discounts, the actual dis-crepancy is almost certainly much larger.[202] The inability to rationalize the 1897 estimates is particularly troubling, since the two stock figures are not the estimates of a contemporary such as Wells or Bacon, but are based on Lewis's own extensive research. This problem clearly deserves further academic attention.[203]

Nathaniel Bacon's 1899 estimate – an estimate that Simon applauds but that Lewis deplores – seems reasonable. Bacon's figure for foreign invest-ment in the United States ($3,400 million) when coupled with the summed flow projection implies a level of American foreign investment of $520 million – a total close to Bacon's own $500 million but still well below Lewis's $685 million for 1897.

Finally, even the well-documented stock figures for 1914 are not easily squared with the net flow series. If one accepts Wilkins's and Lewis's esti-mate of $7,540 million in foreign investment in the United States, Lewis' $3,514 million estimate of American investment abroad, and a flow figure that captures the gradual run-up of foreign short-term investment, the residual is a very large, and positive, $917 million.[204] In this case, however, there do appear to be adequate explanations of the discrepancy. Lewis, herself, believes that "many direct investments are probably omitted" from the estimate of American investment abroad.[205] There is also no allowance for any short-term American investment abroad, although that omission is probably not great.[206] Most importantly, however, the portfolio

---

[201] Simon, "Balance of Payments," 707.

[202] Lewis, for example, puts the average discount on railroad bonds issued before 1890 at 33 percent and the discount on railroad equities at 90 percent. Lewis, *America's Stake*, 160.

[203] The problem could, of course, be solved, if some of the capital outflow that Simon places in the years 1898 to 1901 had actually taken place in earlier years.

[204] The stock estimates are all for July 1914; and, since most of the large capital repatriation that occurred in that year happened after the outbreak of the war in August, the summed flow figures used in these calculations are those for the end of 1913, not for 1914. The summed flow figures are, for the years after 1900, Goldsmith's long-term estimates adjusted for the increase in short-term from Lewis' $250 million figure in 1897 to the "official" $450 million figure in 1914.

[205] Lewis, *America's Stake*, 606.

[206] It averaged only $79 million for the first three years that data are available, and those years (1923–1925) followed a decade of very large American investments abroad.

investment is included at par; and some, perhaps a substantial amount, of those securities were sold at significant discounts. If, for example, common stocks are included at their 1914 market prices and if as little as one-fourth of the railroad bonds and preferred shares were issued prior to 1890 when discounts averaged a third of par value, it is possible to account for the entire discrepancy.

What is it possible to conclude about the contribution of foreign capital to American growth? Clearly, in the aggregate, foreign capital cannot have played a major role; and, in fact, the flows of financial capital were almost certainly less significant than the flows of human capital that moved across the Atlantic with the nation's voluntary and involuntary immigrants.[207] Overall, between 1790 and 1900 the ratio of foreign capital imports to net national capital formation was almost 5 percent, and over the last three decades of the century, it was about four-fifths of that amount.

Despite the small overall relative magnitude, between 1790 and the beginning of 1914 there was a net inflow of some $3.1 billion; and in some times and in some places those transfers were very important. Thus, between 1816 and 1840 capital imports accounted for 22 percent of net capital formation. For the years 1861 to 1870 the figure was almost 16 percent, and between 1880 and 1890 almost 9 percent. It should, of course, be remembered that the first of these periods saw the rapid development of the nation's first interstate transportation system; the second encompasses the years of the Civil War and reconstruction as well as the completion of the first inter-continental railroad link; and the third captures the rapid development of the American West and its integration into the national economy.

In the 1830s, the 1860s, and the 1880s foreign capital was important. In 1838, for example, it is estimated that no less than 40 percent of foreign long-term capital (almost $45 million) had been directed toward the construction of canals, railroads, and turnpikes. Without those funds it would have taken much longer to develop integrated markets in the East and Upper Midwest. In 1869, the record indicates that foreigners had invested very substantial sums in the issues of the federal government and smaller but still significant amounts in the bonds of the states; and those funds

---

[207] For example, Neal and Uselding find that in 1912, *at minimum*, 13 "percent of the capital stock of the American economy could be attributed to the social savings arising from immigration" (their maximum estimate was 42 percent). Larry Neal and Paul Uselding, "Immigration, a Neglected Source of American Economic Growth: 1790 to 1912," *Oxford Economic Papers*, 24 (1972).

had been used to relieve the short-run pressures engendered by the War and reconstruction. At the same time European investors had made more than $100 million dollars available to the nation's railroads.[208] In the 1880s, while railroads continued to draw the bulk of foreign capital – and the railroad network could not have been completed as quickly without those infusions – there were also major transfers to land and land-related industries (mines, agriculture, and financial, land, and development companies). These investments played a major role in opening the American West and, taken together with the resources poured into railroad construction, in integrating that sector into the developing eastern industrial economy.

A breakdown of foreign investment in 1914 shows that, although the railroads still commanded almost three in every five dollars of foreign investment, the land-related industries drew more than 14 percent, the commercial and industrial sector (including breweries and distilleries) received nearly 13 percent, and oil and mining ventures almost 8 percent of the total. As late as 1900, although Americans had demonstrated a willingness to place their accumulations in government and transport issues, they were still hesitant to risk their savings in less familiar enterprises. Nor was the mobilization problem made easier by the managers of the nation's premier securities market – in their attempts to provide signals for the relatively unsophisticated American investors, they had largely ruled out the issues of these new and emerging sectors. As a result, foreign capital played an important role not only during periods of rapid economic growth but also during periods of rapid industrial transformation.

It is hardly a surprise that it was the British saver who proved most willing to risk his resources in the new world. The country had been the first to industrialize; and, although U.K. savings rates had never been high, the period over which they had been accumulating was long. As a result, the potential pool of investible funds was large; and even as late as 1914, British investments represented the bulk of the foreign commitment to the United States. What is perhaps more surprising is the erosion of the British position over the postbellum decades and the increase in importance of the savings of citizens of countries that had only begun to commercialize and industrialize. Thus, by 1914, although about 60 percent of foreign long-term investment was British, 16 percent was German, 9

---

[208] Wells' estimates puts the holdings of federal government issues at $1 billion and those of states at one-tenth that amount. He also places the increase in railroad issues at just less that $200 million. Those figures are, however, par values; the actual transfers were almost certainly less.

percent Dutch, 7 percent French, 4 percent came from the rest of Europe, and an equal amount from our neighbor to the north.

Finally, although in 1914 the United States remained a substantial net debtor, it had also become a major creditor. American investments abroad, trivial before the 1890s, had reached almost $700 million in 1897 and stood at an estimated $3.5 billion seventeen years later.[209] While there were American investments scattered across the globe, about a fifth of the total was in Europe, a quarter in Canada, and something more than a third in Mexico, Central America, Cuba, and the West Indies. To a large extent, the European commitments reflected the export of the nation's technology and its long-held but no longer dominant position in petroleum production. The questions raised by Canadian, Mexican, Caribbean, and Central American transfers are more interesting.

In the first place, an examination of those investments suggests that the Americans viewed the regions to the north and south as natural extensions of the domestic market – a source of food for its citizens, raw materials for its industrial sector, and a market for its products. No region can, however, be economically integrated until transport links are established. While the British provided the investment needed to integrate the Canadian market, it was largely American capital that financed the railroads that opened the Mexican economy.

It might be easy to conclude that the Americans treated the British dominion to the north differently from the ex-Spanish colonies to the south. Forty percent of American nonrailroad direct investment in Canada went to support that nation's manufacturing sector, while less than a tenth of that fraction supported the industrial sector to the south. A closer scrutiny, however, indicates that the conclusion is almost certainly false. American manufacturing capital flowed into the developed and urbanized sectors of Ontario and Quebec. It did not go into British Columbia, the Prairies, the Maritimes, or even rural Ontario and Quebec. Those regions, like Mexico, Central America, and the Caribbean – and like the American West – were certainly the recipients of direct investment from the American East; but it was capital directed toward mining and other land-related industries. The economic role assigned to all three "western" regions, whether in Canada, the United States, or in the ex-Spanish colonies to the south, was the production of primary products

---

[209] Since the bulk of the investment was direct, not portfolio (over 90 percent in 1897 and still more than 75 percent in 1914), the question of discounted issues is much less important than it was for foreign investment in the United States.

– foodstuffs, timber, and minerals – for the rapidly urbanizing and industrializing East.

In the second place, this study raises serious questions about the basis for the charges of "Yankee economic imperialism" and the relevance of the term "Dollar Diplomacy." It is clear that the American government continually interfered – both politically and militarily – in the life of Central America, Cuba, and the other Caribbean nations. It is equally clear that vocal objections were raised to American investment in those regions. It is, however, not clear that there was a close correlation between political interference and the level of American investment; and it is clear that the lot of the average native was much improved by the entrance of American investment into those otherwise largely closed markets.

American investment in Cuba was significant, but, even there, it was not as large as the European component; and in the rest of the Caribbean and in Central America it was trifling. Studies of both Cuba and Mexico have underscored the benefits of American investments to both workers and landlords; and there is no reason to believe the same cannot be said for workers on banana plantations in Costa Rica and the native owners of sugar plantations in Cuba.

Stanley Lebergott has concluded that it was the politically amplified voice of a few native businessmen – businessmen angry when forced to confront foreign competition in what had been their own nearly monopolistic markets – that was responsible for the anti-American rhetoric. Perhaps, then, it was the politically amplified voice of a few native American businessmen who pushed the government into political action to "protect American investments" even when there were, for all intents and purposes, no American investments to protect. That question, however, is best left to the new generation of political economists.

Although almost certainly of less importance than the movement of European and African immigrants across the Atlantic, the pace of growth and the evolution of the structure of the American economy were influenced by the availability of foreign capital. In a similar fashion, the pace of growth and the evolution of the structure – to say nothing of the political climate – of the Canadian, Mexican, Central American and Caribbean economies were influenced by the availability of American capital. As Karl Marx and Boris Yeltsin have shown themselves to be fully aware, foreign capital can make a difference.

17

THE SOCIAL IMPLICATIONS OF U.S. ECONOMIC DEVELOPMENT

STUART M. BLUMIN

The preceding chapters of this volume have elaborated upon two interrelated themes defined by Robert Gallman in Chapter 1; the persistent if occasionally interrupted long-term growth of the American economy, and the structural reorganization of economic institutions, practices, and norms that compel us to characterize the growing economy in certain ways – as, say, industrializing, or centralizing, or, to use terms with greater ideological resonance, as moving toward a system of free enterprise or toward capitalism. This final chapter, while referring frequently to both economic growth and structural change in economic affairs, will explore some of the most significant interrelations between these two phenomena and the more purely *social* relations of Americans during the "long nineteenth century." Put in slightly different terms, it asks: how shall we understand the ways in which economic development influenced and was influenced by changes in nineteenth-century American society?

This distinction between the "economic" and the "social" is arbitrary to the degree that it represents divisions within modern social thought (and the departmental structure of modern universities) rather than in the day-to-day lives of ordinary people, and we will see that it is more useful and convincing in some settings than in others. The search for all of the "social implications" of economic development, moreover, is an impossibly large task, and the qualifier "most significant" leaves an assignment that is daunting enough, even if one were to presume to know exactly where the "economic" ends and the "social" begins. In this chapter the various answers offered to the question asked in the previous paragraph will be based on a degree of indeterminacy in the relation between the economic and the social. Moreover, they will fall within three categories of inquiry that are large and significant, but that do not presume to contain all of the questions that can be raised about the people who experienced, and whose daily lives expressed, the economic transformations of the nineteenth century.

The social geography of productive and market relations is the first of these categories. With this single phrase I refer mainly to two sets of different, and very nearly opposing phenomena, one concentrating and centralizing, the other dispersing and diffusing. The first consists of the movement of people from the countryside into cities and towns, and of urban-based institutions (including capitalist institutions) outward into closer contact with the persisting rural population; in other words, of urbanization, understood not only as the concentration of populations, but also as the expanding sphere of urban influence, and as the emergence of cities and city-systems as engines of growth and carriers of capitalism. The second set consists of the mostly westward expansion of European-American and African-American populations into areas more distant from established urban centers and market systems. Frontier history has a longer pedigree than the history of urbanization, but it can be, and recently has been, freshly examined from a geographic perspective that includes both the rural frontier and the city – the forces of diffusion and of concentration – in a larger model of expanding market relations.

While American economic development generated regularized systems of exchange across increasingly wide geographical spaces, it also generated increasingly clear distinctions among the people who inhabited and made their livings within those spaces. Hence, a second category of inquiry recognizes that the system of exchange that developed in the nineteenth century was also a system for articulating economic roles and distributing economic rewards, and that these two processes underlay a broader social phenomenon that contemporary historians are inclined to designate "class formation." The applicability of the concept of class to nineteenth-century American society is not yet a settled issue among historians; nor will my suggestion that it ought to refer to an array of social experiences rooted in but stretching well away from relations within the workplace necessarily sit well with those who are most insistent upon its explanatory power. Nonetheless, I will use the terms "class" and "class formation" to help describe and explain fundamental changes in American society, and a variety of new experiences and new social identities flowing as much from the distribution of the monetary rewards of a growing economy as from the capitalist reorganization of work and workplace relations.

The third category is more properly "cultural" than "social," but seems indispensable to any consideration of how American society was organized and reorganized in conjunction with economic growth, new modes of production, and the ever-more-pervasive market. I refer to those values and norms guiding behavior toward profitable enterprise, self-satisfying and socially expressive forms of consumption, and, a little less obviously, schemes of organized benevolence and social improvement that also characterize this era of "expectant" and developing capitalism. But I refer also to those values and norms, often expressed as traditions and traditionally understood rights, that underlay *resistance* to all these innovative and improving things. Not all Americans embraced the free and expanding market, or technological improvements in transportation and production, or banks and grain exchanges, or even the material benefits of economic growth. Some people (craft workers facing the introduction of de-skilling machinery into their trades, small farmers facing the rate discriminations of powerful railroads, to cite two well-known examples) opposed them vigorously because they perceived change as threats to their own interests and well-being. Others, including many we would count among the winners in the competitive marketplace, accepted them nervously, or perceived ambiguities, costs, and contradictions in the march of economic progress. It ought to be understood, indeed, that the march itself did not bring all Americans to the same destination with equal speed and in lock-step order. Implicit in all the categories I have described – in the geography and social structure of developing America as well as in its culture – there is a story of persistence as well as one of change, of a transformation that affected nearly everyone in some way, but that left behind it more than a mere trace of older ways of life and thought. The march, moreover, was sometimes a halting one, a fact I have emphasized by organizing much of the following discussion into two half-century-long historical periods that turn upon one of the deepest economic crises in American history.

1790–1840

It is a commonplace among historians to observe that the United States at the time of the first national census was overwhelmingly rural – that only 5 percent of the population lived in the two dozen or so communities that reasonably could be called cities or towns; that only five of these urban places contained as many as 10,000 inhabitants; and that the largest among them, Philadelphia, was home to no more than 42,000 Americans, barely one of every hundred of the nearly four million who populated the new nation. These are striking statistics, immediately suggestive of a world very different from our own. Yet, they only begin to convey the actual social geography of the United States in 1790 – the thinness of human occupation of the land, the relative isolation of communities and households, the attenuating effects of the vast wilderness into which numerous American households were moving year after year. Less well-known statistics of rural population density help somewhat, especially when they are set against equivalent statistics pertaining to the mother country. Thus, while the English countryside supported a population of more than 100 persons per square mile at the end of the eighteenth century, the average rural density of the United States in 1790 was only 9 persons per square mile, and only 15 on the coastal plain and piedmont east and south of the Appalachian frontier. In both countries rural densities varied from place to place, but nowhere in America, not even in heavily populated southern New England, did they approach the ordinary levels of habitation in the English countryside. English *urban* statistics reinforce the American emptiness: 30 percent of the population in cities and towns, nearly fifty cities larger than 10,000, market towns along every country road, and a metropolis of 900,000 containing not one in a hundred, but one in ten of the national population. If we consider both the striking difference in rural population densities, and the much more significant presence of cities and towns on the English landscape, we can begin to understand differences in economic and social life that underscore the peripheral and underdeveloped character of the fledgling nation on the western edge of the Atlantic world.

Historians sometimes place against this image of a thinly settled, profoundly rural society, which carries with it a further sense of localized, "pre-capitalist" economic exchange and a corresponding social insularity, a contrary image; that is, of a coastal and riverine society, whose farmers were well positioned to engage in a fairly active waterborne (and to a lesser extent overland) commerce with port towns in their immediate region, or, in the case of the Chesapeake, with the major cities of Britain itself. This contrary image is valuable, but is best understood as a qualification to the more important pattern of population dispersal. American rural folk did locate first and most plentifully along the rivers and bays that enhanced their access to the docks of Boston, Philadelphia, London, or Glasgow. But what is most striking is how quickly they spread their settlements inland, away from the avenues of trade, eschewing by choice or necessity more costly land along the trade routes in favor of cheaper land that reduced their access to the world outside. Dispersal was most evident in the South, including Virginia, where the gradient of population density decline from tidewater to piedmont, and more locally from riverfront to backland, was very gradual, and in some areas (most notably the vast Southside stetching back from the York River) all but disappeared as the population spread nearly evenly toward the distant mountains. But dispersal was also characteristic of town-centered New England. In Worcester County, covering most of the central portion of Massachusetts, the average population density of 40 persons per square mile was much higher than that of the Virginia piedmont, and was particularly high along the Boston Post Road crossing the center of the county, and along several small rivers providing a modest outlet to the Connecticut and Merrimack Rivers and to Narragansett Bay (see Figure 17.1). But, as in Virginia, the dominant pattern was the spread of population, not its concentration. Two-thirds of the towns in Worcester County had more than 30 and fewer than 50 persons per square mile, and about half of the towns outside that narrow range – the more recently settled and remotely situated towns of the northwestern corner of the county – were rapidly approaching it.

Americans of all regions, the Middle Atlantic states no less than Virginia and New England, did not cling to the rivers and roads but spread themselves across the land in a manner captured by James Madison when he observed that population seeks "those places where it least abounds, and always has the same tendency to equalize itself."[1] Madison was referring to broad movements of people from the settled east to the unsettled west, but his point applied to local patterns as well, and for essentially the same reason. Westward migration and local diffusion both expressed the primacy of the land itself, and of production upon the land, in the economic lives of the vast majority of Americans. This is not to say that most American farmers were isolated from commercial markets in an endless round of self-sufficient family production. Quite to the contrary, farmers in all regions relied heavily on local systems of exchange in labor, equipment, and commodities, and the smaller the farm – the closer the family to mere subsistence levels of production – the more enmeshed its occupants were likely to be in a complicated network of local exchange. Nor

---

[1] Quoted in Drew McCoy, "James Madison and Visions of American Nationality in the Confederation Period," in Richard Beeman, Stephen Botein, and Edward C. Carter II, eds., *Beyond Confederation: Origins of the Constitution and American National Identity*, (Chapel Hill, 1987), 228.

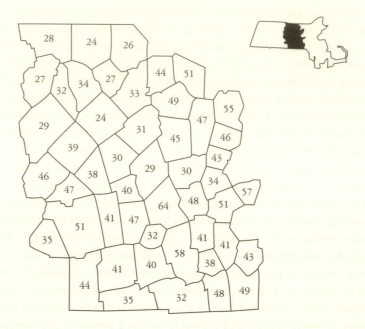

Figure 17.1. Estimated number of inhabitants per square mile, by town, Worcester County, Massachusetts, 1790. Note: County population density = 40 persons per square mile.

were farmers, whatever their location, entirely removed from or indifferent to more distant markets. Even those who were not in a position to help meet the rapidly growing European demand for American grain, or to participate actively in older forms of long-distance trade, supplemented subsistence and community-oriented production with goods intended for distant markets. In the Virginia Southside small planters rolled individual hogsheads of tobacco down rough country roads, while backland farmers of less commercialized regions in New England drove cattle overland to urban markets, and loaded cider, potash, salted meat, skins, and other rural produce on flatboats and even on canoes to be floated, portaged, and floated again to wherever the shallow and uncertain upland rivers led. But for all American farmers, and for these smaller, more dispersed farmers in particular, the carrying of goods to market was an intermittent activity, an occasional adjunct to the much more continuous activity of production itself – the clearing of land, the growing and preparing of crops, the care of animals, the construction and repair of buildings, fences, and tools. This, finally, the primacy of production and the distinctly secondary nature of exchange beyond the local community, is why the American rural population of the late eighteenth century was so dispersed – why it was the land and not the avenues of trade that focused the ambitions of ordinary rural people and sent them off to subdue so many "wildernesses," driving native peoples and landscapes before them.

The communities they formed, and the lives they lived within these communities, were more insular than they were later to become, in part because of the day-to-day preoccupations of household-oriented production, and in part because the embryonic network of cities and towns provided so few points of contact, and so few of the institutions and media of extralocal exchange. For example, fewer than a hundred newspapers, and a mere handful of magazines, were published in the United States in 1790. Most of the newspapers appeared but once per week, and in the course of the year the number of individual newspapers that were lifted off the presses of America (they did not yet roll off) was no larger than the population itself. Newspaper publication was concentrated in, but was by no means restricted to, the largest towns, and issues of city papers circulated to some extent through the countryside. (In Pennyslvania, twelve of twenty newspapers, including all four of the state's dailies, were published in Philadelphia, while weekly papers were published in Germantown, Lancaster, Harrisburg, Carlisle, Chambersburg, Reading, York, and Pittsburgh.) But the closest recent analysis of information diffusion in early America suggests that newspapers were not read regularly by large numbers of ordinary rural people, who more characteristically sought word-of-mouth news of the world from post riders and other travelers, and from clergymen and other local notables who maintained a regular correspondence beyond the community. Middling and poor rural folk did not themselves write or receive many letters, and the nation as a whole was served in 1790 by only seventy-five post offices and 1,875 miles of post roads. In general the roads of America were very poor, and unmechanized transportation on both the land and the water was slow and uncertain. In the depth of winter not only many northern and western rural communities but also some of the nation's busiest port cities were very nearly cut off from the world by rivers and harbors that filled with ice, and roads that disappeared beneath the snow. And finally, just as the new nation lacked a dense network of cities and towns, it also lacked a network of cosmopolitan institutions – political parties, regional and national reform societies, translocal fraternal associations, and the like – capable of lifting personal horizons beyond the affairs of the household, neighborhood, and community.

The relative insularity and small size of most eighteenth-century American communities made them excellent milieux for the perpetuation of deferential social and political relations. Hierarchies of wealth, prestige, and influence were fundamental to the way American society functioned, and suffused not only the central institutions of power, but also the local institutions that enclosed the daily lives of most Americans — the family, the church, and the community. There were no lords in these communities, but there were patriarchs within local families who commanded the obedience of wives, children, and servants, long-settled ministers who spoke powerfully on spiritual and secular matters to entire communities, and local political leaders drawn from limited numbers of families to serve repeatedly in positions of political authority. Perhaps more importantly, in both rural and urban communities there were generally recognized differences between social superiors and inferiors, and a more or less pervasive set of understood codes regulating day-to-day relations between the two. Especially in smaller communities — but recall that even the port towns were not very large — these differences and relations were highly personal and particular, taking shape as they did in the daily routines of a small, face-to-face social world; hence, it would be more misleading than helpful to characterize them in the language of social class. The culture of deference implies a society of individually understood ranks, rather than of categorically understood classes, and it was this kind of culture and society that characterized the Atlantic world of the eighteenth century.

It did not, of course, characterize both sides of the Atlantic with equal force. The very process of transatlantic migration loosened the bonds of traditional society, and the continuing process of migration beyond the original coastal communities to the piedmont and mountain valleys loosened them still further. Independent freeholding was extensive in many American communities, and even where tenancy was common it did not usually create as thick a web of patronage and clientage as it did in Europe. The larger towns, for their part, lacked the guilds and guild-based municipal governments that, despite many changes, continued to invest European urban life with a customary and ritualized hierarchical order. Finally, specific events such as the Great Awakening and the Revolution challenged the culture of deference by altering the conditions, the practice, and even the underlying rationale of local authority. And yet, traditional forms of authority were modified in this era rather than destroyed. Indeed, a general increase in the levels of wealth and income among the better sort, made visible after 1750 in a more genteel style of living, underscored traditional differences between the few and the many, and buttressed deference just when it was most seriously challenged by contention and new ideas in religion and politics.

Living standards were actually rising for most Americans during the eighteenth century, but the differing pace and character of consumption among wealthy and middling families were more notable than the general improvement. The diverging patterns of material life, moreover, help illuminate not only the perpetuation of local systems of authority, but also the differing relations of large and small producers to profit-yielding extralocal markets. It was in these markets that wealthy Americans acquired the means to fill larger and more elegant city and country houses with fine furniture, rugs and draperies, expensive tableware, family portraits, and other purchased artifacts expressive of gentility and high social position. Improvements in the material conditions of middling people were much more contained, and are not suggestive of a pattern of living or aspiration to which we might attach the label "consumerism." To be sure, many ordinary Americans during these years acquired greater numbers of bedsteads and chairs, replaced wooden tableware with coarse earthenware, bought a few books, and filled their cellars with preserved foods to get them through what once had been months of scarcity in the late winter and spring. But these were moderate gains, many of which were achieved entirely within the realms of the producing household and the local network of exchange. It is worth noting, too, that the houses in which these goods were placed remained small and plain. The typical Worcester County farmhouse was a wooden, single-story or story-and-a-half dwelling of 700 to 1,000 square feet, while the vast majority of farmers living in the Virginia piedmont county of Halifax occupied log or frame houses of only 400 square feet. Even at the very end of the century, the buildings that housed both the homes and the stores of Philadelphia's retail storekeepers averaged 900 square feet, while the city's artisans lived and worked in only 600 or 700 square feet of space. Within these small spaces large families accommodated to each other and to the tools and tasks of the workshop, the store, or the ordinary farm's round of domestic production. In both their size and character, they were not spaces that encouraged a significant attachment to the marketplace of status-defining consumer goods.

In the first edition of his *American Geography*, published in 1789, Jedidiah Morse provides a suggestive glimpse of the interaction between local hierarchy and the relative detachment of ordinary Americans from the marketplace. Surveying the prospects of each state in the new nation, Morse applauds a spirit of agricultural improvement among the "gentlemen of fortune" in Federalist Massachusetts. Of smaller producers, however, even in this most advanced of states, Morse is more dismissive. "The common husbandmen in the country," he writes, "generally choose to continue in the old track of their forefathers."[2] Morse does not trouble himself to describe this "old track," but recent historians have identified a series of traditional norms governing the determination of prices, the carrying and collection of debt, the exchange of labor and equipment, the occasional pooling of labor in barn raisings and husking bees, the settlement of disputes, and other activities constituting the essentially local economies in which "common husbandmen" participated, in Massachusetts and elsewhere. These norms were communal, and in many ways constrained the enterprise of individuals, who were expected, for example, not to charge interest on the small credits gained in day-to-day exchange among neighbors, or to press for payment until after a considerable period of time, or to sue for payment in court. Historians disagree as to whether these constraints, and others like them, reflect a "pre-capitalist" culture among ordinary farmers, or whether they suggest only the limited opportunities open to small producers in an underdeveloped economy. Untangling the interplay of circumstances and culture in the perpetuation of the "old track" may well prove impossible; indeed, to attempt to separate the two is to ignore the ways in which expectations, values, and systems of belief are shaped by long-standing material circumstances into a merging of the desirable and the possible. Thus, the limitations of the relatively insular economies and relatively plain material lives of the majority of Americans did not necessarily discourage hard work or a desire for gain, but rather channeled ambitions along lines that only later generations would consider quaintly modest: the achievement and maintenance of a reliable sufficiency, or competency, in the sustaining goods of day-to-day living, and possession of the means eventually to settle one's children on the land, or in trades, or in marriages, that would provide them with a way of life roughly equal to that of their parents. This was not the absence of ambition, but its realistic expression within the constraints of the only

---

[2] Jedidiah Morse, *The American Geography; or, a View of the Present Situation of the United States of America* (Elizabethtown, 1789), 182.

world ordinary Americans of the late eighteenth century could know; yet, it expressed too the *norm* of respectable restraint, the proper limits of personal ambition in a still largely communal local world. Both circumstances and values, therefore, to cite the recent conclusion of one historian, tied enterprise to "the limited human needs of individual families" rather than to "the logic of endless accumulation."[3]

The "old track" perpetuated by the "common husbandmen" of the late eighteenth century did not always double back upon itself in an unchanging cycle of local life. If ordinary rural Americans did not participate actively in extralocal markets and other recurring systems of exchange beyond their local communities, they did leave their communities from time to time to fight in imperial wars. They also received and responded to letters from Revolutionary committees of correspondence, elected delegates to constitutional conventions and new state legislatures, and marched with and against their neighbors to participate in or put down rebellions against debt-enforcing county courts. The quarter-century preceding the 1790 census was unusually rife with these kinds of events, each of which countered in some degree the parochializing forces of rural life. From the 1790s forward, however, the world would impose itself on local communities less crucially in the form of wars, revolutions, and other crises, and more crucially in the form of new technologies of transportation and new modes of production, more intensive and regularized patterns of trade, new institutions, vastly expanded communications media, and an increasingly complex network of growing cities and towns. Crises of all sorts would continue to occur, needless to say, but the social geography of the new nation would henceforth belong less to the realm of events and more to the realm of structural developments in the economy, in society, and even in politics. So, too, would changes in local social structures and in the personal aspirations and social ideals of ordinary Americans.

Many of these structural developments have been described elsewhere in this volume. What merits discussion here is the increasing presence of cities and towns, as well as the changing role of communications media and other institutions, in the intensification of extralocal exchange. To be sure, some of the most dramatic changes of the half-century or so following the first American census – the turnpikes and other new roads, the

---

[3] Daniel Vickers, "Competency and Competition: Economic Culture in Early America," *William and Mary Quarterly*, 3d. ser., 47 (1990), 12.

steamboats, the bridges and harbor improvements, and especially the 3,000-mile network of canals, all combining to form the first important phase of what is rightly called the "Transportation Revolution" – would seem to have as much to do with the continuing diffusion of the American population as with its concentration, and it is certainly the case that European- and African-Americans conquered and settled a great deal of space during this period. The total land area of the United States more than doubled between 1790 and 1840, and, perhaps more importantly, the area settled at densities exceeding 2 persons per square mile more than tripled, as Americans pushed well beyond the Appalachians, into and along the Great Lakes plain, down the Ohio River valley, along the Gulf coast, and into and beyond the Mississippi River valley. But James Madison's model no longer described the dynamics of this process, for the same transportation systems that stimulated westward migration simultaneously stimulated a much greater flow of commodities between rural and urban places, setting off in turn the first stages of the nineteenth-century urban revolution. The age when the population would tend to "equalize itself" in space was over; henceforth, it would seek those places where it *most* abounds.

In the crudest quantitative terms, the urbanization of the American population during the period 1790–1840 was not all that impressive; the proportion of the population living in cities and towns rose from 5 percent to a little less than 11 percent over the half-century. But in a country that was growing by a third every ten years, this modest shift suggests a rapid growth of individual towns, and a significant expansion of the array of urban places across the countryside. And in fact the numbers are a good deal more impressive when looked at in this way. New York City increased more than ninefold from 33,000 to a population of more than 300,000, while Baltimore grew from a town of 13,000 to a major city of more than 100,000. Philadelphia, best known for having been overtaken by New York as the nation's largest city, nonetheless increased fivefold to nearly a quarter of a million inhabitants. Albany, located some 150 miles inland along New York's major transportation artery, grew slightly *faster* than the new metropolis to almost exactly the size New York had been in 1790, and in several inland regions cities were appearing and growing to sizes that rivaled those of the largest ports of the preceding half-century – Cincinnati numbered 46,000, Rochester, Pittsburgh, and Louisville all exceeded 20,000. The old French and Spanish Gulf port of New Orleans was now an American city of more than 100,000. Much smaller places, old and new, were crossing the census-defined urban threshold of 2,500 inhabitants, and the array of urban places, as defined by the census, increased more than fivefold to include 131 cities and towns.

That this expanding array might also be forming itself into a city-system, connecting farms and villages to the largest urban centers through a number of more dispersed, smaller, intervening centers, is suggested by some of the more detailed patterns of urban growth. First, some of the most impressive growth rates were achieved by Eastern inland towns that were emerging as secondary collection and distribution points for the shippers and wholesalers of the major ports. During the first decade of the nineteenth century, when the four major Eastern ports were growing by 58 percent, eleven Eastern inland towns were growing by 51 percent, and there were a number of other emerging inland centers (whose populations at the start of the decade cannot be separated out from the immediately surrounding countryside) that appear to have been growing even more rapidly. During the next decade, when international trade was disrupted by the Napoleonic Wars and their aftermath (crisis still having its role to play), and when the urban system and the largest port towns actually grew slightly more slowly than the national population, the growth of Eastern inland towns slowed commensurately, suggesting something of the relation between the ports and the towns of their hinterlands. And in the following two decades, as the major ports renewed their rapid growth, so too did the Eastern inland towns. Second, the major ports were not only growing rapidly, but were growing from larger baseline populations into imposing, institutionally complex, and powerful cities, while distinct (and as it turns out, enduring) primary centers were emerging in virtually every developing inland region. And finally, the only kinds of towns that did *not* grow impressively were precisely those that might have impeded the articulation of urban regions around specific large centers. Smaller "outports" such as Salem, Newburyport, and Marblehead in Massachusetts, Providence and Newport in Rhode Island, and Norfolk and Annapolis on the Chesapeake Bay, grew consistently at much slower rates than the larger ports with which they competed, or than the inland towns that lay along the new transportation routes leading so decisively to each region's largest city. Thus, while Boston was increasing in population by more than 500 percent over the half-century, Salem failed to double in size; Newburyport increased by only 50 percent; Newport, once one of the largest and most active ports in North America, grew by less than 25 percent; and Marblehead actually declined slightly. In the Chesapeake Bay, Baltimore grew twice as rapidly as Norfolk, while Annapolis remained a small town of fewer than 3,000 inhabitants, forgoing entirely its role as a regional port. Most of these smaller ports, indeed, were in varying degrees losing their independent role as importers and exporters, and were becoming subservient to the major ports in a manner similar to that of the growing inland towns. Such growth as they had probably derived from their secondary role in an increasingly metropolitan-centered region.

Much more needs to be learned about the relations between larger and smaller cities, and between smaller cities and the countryside, before we can conclude that the city-system was developing as impressively as the individual urban places within it. Indeed, at present it is reasonable to conclude that some significant portion of the growth of smaller cities and towns was the product of the continuing development of *local* systems of exchange, and that these inland centers, and the rural hinterlands they served, were not yet extensively connected with their regional centers in a complex and hierarchical flow of commodities, credits, information, and influence. On the other hand, extralocal lines of contact of this sort – etching a deepening path from countryside to town and from town to city – were surely multiplying. And there were other connections, tracing only part of this path, or perhaps leaving it altogether, that did no less to add a cosmopolitan dimension to local life. Political parties, for example, became highly significant institutions linking local officials and electorates with party influentials, programs, and campaign strategies and symbols on the state and even on the national level. A start in this direction was made around the turn of the century, and if this was a false start – if the "first party system" was really not a system at all – then the era of the "second party system" must be regarded as all the more remarkable for the depth and breadth of its political institutional development. The content of partisan discourse was itself a cosmopolitan force, for it was centered on the question of how the state should oversee the development of the interregional capitalist economy, the Whigs (and before them the National Republicans) proposing, and the Democrats reacting against, a federally integrated program of high tariffs, centralized banking, and "internal improvements." But party institutions considerably magnified the force of these issues. By 1840, when even the more reluctant Whigs had embraced the techniques of mass political mobilization, a durable, hierarchical system of political organization was to be found in every corner of the nation, directing the attention of the most parochial of citizens to the issues and symbols of national political life.

Moreover, the development of a wide variety of voluntary associations, organized like the political parties into extralocal networks of community-based institutions, was one of the prominent new features of this half-century, and one of the most significant forces contributing to a new social geography. The excitements of the Revolutionary and Confederation decades had demanded a good deal of cooperative effort at various geographical levels, but the generalization holds true that before 1790 most Americans participated in few institutions beyond the essentially local and locally interlocking triad of family, church, and community. In the 1790s, however, and at a quickening pace through each following decade until the economic crisis of the latter 1830s, voluntary associations were formed to promote good morals and the keeping of the sabbath, to perpetuate the right kind of Christianity on the western frontier, to eliminate slavery from part of the nation and alcoholic drink from all of it, to provide and to regulate the rituals and fellowship of fraternal lodges, to protect the interests of wage earners, and for a host of other purposes. Increasingly, these associations organized themselves into statewide, regional, and inter-regional networks. As early as 1816 the American Bible Society and the American Education Society promoted by their very names a view of themselves as national organizations, and they were followed by a series of others, including the American Colonization Society (1817), the American Sunday School Union (1824), the American Tract Society (1825), and the American Home Missionary Society (1826). In 1833 The New England Anti-Slavery Society combined forces with New Yorkers and others to form the American Anti-Slavery Society, which eventually incorporated some 2,000 constituent local organizations representing 200,000 members. The American Society for the Promotion of Temperance, founded in 1826, coordinated 4,000 constituent organizations representing 500,000 members by 1833, and in 1836 became part of an even more complex organization with the formation of the American Temperance Union. These and a variety of other voluntary associations were organized at least partly along central-place pathways, at least in the sense that the proliferating towns were the usual loci of organization at the local level, and the coordinating headquarters were often found in larger cities. But even where associations followed other paths, organizing, say, according to township and county boundaries, and pyramiding upward to a central office located in the state capital rather than in the regional metropolis, the effect was the same. Each, according to the tempo of its own activities and the intensity of its demands, connected significant numbers of the inhabitants of local communities with a wider world.

Cosmopolitanism was fostered also by a greatly intensified flow of written words across the growing nation. A portion of the expansion of periodical publication in the United States between 1790 and 1840 was an adjunct to the development of voluntary associations, most of which communicated with their members, recruited new members, and advanced their programs through newspapers, magazines, and other publications. But newspapers, and to a lesser extent magazines, were expanding as institutions in their own right. From fewer than 100 in 1790, the numbers of newspapers increased to some 235 by 1800, to more than 500 twenty years later, and to more than 1,400 by 1840, a rate of growth three and a half times that of the population. Newspapers were also issued in larger editions, with big-city papers in particular being written not only for much larger numbers of local readers but also for a wider circulation in the countryside. Where only one newspaper copy was published per capita in 1790, eleven were published in 1840. Country and small-town people obviously were reading more, and as they did they connected themselves in yet another way with the emerging urban system, even if they read only the papers of their local community. For these papers were informally connected with a larger network of city and town papers, from which they routinely copied and reprinted news. Magazines, which were published almost exclusively in cities, provided a more direct link between city and country, and so did books, whose publication was becoming increasingly concentrated in New York, Philadelphia, and Boston.

Less obviously reflective of the influence of urban development was a striking increase in the pace of personal and business correspondence. Again, the upswing is evident as early as the 1790s, when the number of post offices was increased from 75 to more than 900 in order to handle mail producing a more than sevenfold increase in postal revenues over the course of the decade. By 1840, there were more than 13,000 post offices in the United States, and postal revenues were 120 times higher than they were in 1790 – twenty seven times higher in per capita terms. Improved postal services no doubt created as well as answered demand, but we must first understand this remarkable increase in the pace of correspondence in terms of the expansion of extralocal markets and the growing urban network. Postal revenues were concentrated in cities in every region of the country, with the important regional cities producing four, five, or even ten times as much mail as they would have if mail had been evenly distributed across the population. But the expansion of extralocal correspondence was simply too great to be accounted for solely by the businesses, or even the private individuals, of cities and towns. Country people, to an extent that has not yet been estimated, were also participating in a privately generated flow of words across American space.

All of these phenomena, even the upsurge in personal correspondence, were linked in the most crucial way to economic development, if only because of the routes along which written exchanges traveled. The new transportation systems, and the cities and towns to which they led, were primarily artifacts of a developing economy, the most notable feature of which was the increasing penetration of extralocal markets into the affairs of people otherwise caught up in the production of goods in local farms and workshops, and in the private use or exchange of goods, labor, and credit in local market systems. Put another way, temperance societies and Odd Fellows' lodges, newspapers and novels, and not least the cities and towns that nurtured them, came within the horizons of ordinary country and village people as parts of a larger process of integration across space – a process in which the flow of commodities from farm to city and city to farm, within and increasingly between regions, was the driving force.

The changing social geography of the new nation was integral to changes in its social structure, and only in part because a significant number of the commodities moving across large spaces flowed from new kinds of workplaces – mechanized textile factories, unmechanized but specialized and task-divided small workshops in a variety of trades, and the homes of domestic outworkers in such industries as shoes, brooms, palm-leaf hats, and ready-to-wear clothing. New modes of production were beginning to redefine relations between industrial employers and employees, and in the larger cities especially were already causing many of the latter to identify themselves as an exploited working class. But for larger numbers of people in this early industrial era a more vital connection between social geography and social structure resided not so much in the production as in the extralocal movement of goods, which, by contributing to the widening of local horizons, contributed also to a relocation of authority within the community, and to a redefinition of social relations.

During the early decades of the nineteenth century, the spreading pattern of religious voluntarism was joined by secular voluntarism in the marketplace of both consumer goods and institutions, with the result that *choice* became an important element of life within the community. In addition to choosing one's own church and minister in communities where, say, a Baptist church had destroyed the Anglican or Congregationalist hegemony, increasing numbers of ordinary Americans could choose to buy and sell greater numbers of material goods outside local networks of exchange. They could more readily get information from newspapers, magazines, books, and their own personal correspondence; that is, in a more private manner, no longer mediated by face-to-face transmission, which in the past had often flowed from local elites to ordinary people who did not maintain regular correspondence or read newspapers. ("The professional, merchant, and landed elites," writes the historian Richard D. Brown, "were no longer the information gatekeepers for their neighbors.")[4] They could join voluntary societies organized elsewhere by leaders quite different from and possibly even antagonistic to local leaders who might, for example, oppose the abolition of slavery, or fail to join a fraternal lodge. And as the enduring system of political parties took shape during the first four decades of the new century, they found a new mechanism, as well as a new source of legitimization, for choosing between those who would presume to public authority. Changes with similar implications could also come from the opposite direction, in the form of new choices available to those at the top of local society. For example, in the investment portfolios of the wealthier property owners of Middlesex County, Massachusetts, there was a decisive shift after 1780 or so away from the holding of local debt and toward the ownership of stocks and bonds – abstract instruments of an emerging capitalist economy, carrying with them none of the face-to-face authority and dependency relations that accompanied traditional rural debt. This sudden increase in the "liquidity of rural portfolios," concludes the author of this study of changing capital markets, "must henceforth loom large in whatever is meant by the coming of capitalism to the New England village economy."[5]

The "coming of capitalism" to the rural community, in sum, altered local patterns of authority and local relations of personal dependency, even where it did not introduce new modes of production. And in the form of increased numbers of consumer goods it promoted a more commodified type of social awareness, one more nearly derived from styles of living than

---

[4] Richard D. Brown, *Knowledge is Power: The Diffusion of Information in Early America, 1700–1865* (New York, 1989), 294.
[5] Winifred Rothenberg, "The Emergence of a Capital Market in Rural Massachusetts, 1730–1838," *Journal of Economic History*, 45 (1985), 806.

from personal and particular hierarchical relations; hence, an awareness of one's position in society that is more suggestive of class than of rank. For middling Americans in particular, living standards improved dramatically during the nineteenth century, to the point where historians have identified a commodified "cult of domesticity" as the very core of an emerging middle-class social life and culture. The efforts of historians have thus far been focused mainly on the decades immediately preceding and following the Civil War, but it is evident that this was a longer process, and that significant changes were underway well before the depression that began in the late 1830s. In the rapidly growing cities, larger and more stylish houses were being built for middle-income families in the 1820s and 1830s, and, by 1830 at least, the more general diffusion of the ideal of the commodious and comfortable home was suggested by the appearance of reader-submitted farmhouse plans in progressive agricultural magazines.[6] More important in these decades, however, was the proliferation and declining prices of portable goods, both of which resulted from much cheaper transportation and various changes in modes of production, including the mechanized factory production of textiles. The long and steady price decline that characterized the post-Napoleonic era was essential to the rising living standards and more intense consumerism of middling folk, in the villages and on farms as well as in the larger cities.

Empowered by rising personal incomes and falling prices, middling Americans responded to both the greater array of consumer goods on storekeepers' shelves and the social instruction becoming available in etiquette books and fashion magazines (*Godey's Lady's Book*, the most influential of the new fashion magazines, first appeared in 1830) to construct a more comfortable and genteel way of life. Living that life contributed in turn to a new sense of the foundations of status and appropriate demeanor. Personal relations of a hierarchical nature were by no means eliminated from the small social world of the local community, but they were less frequently suffused with the deferential traditions of the eighteenth century. The nature of social hierarchy was changing, partly in response to ascending republican political ideas, but in response also to new social identities formed in a world of commodities, information, and institutions that imposed themselves, from outside, on the face-to-face community.

[6] Sally Ann McMurry, *Families and Farmhouses in Nineteenth-Century America: Vernacular Design and Social Change* (New York, 1988).

The consumption gains of the 1820s and 1830s had their most significant effects upon the social identities of middling people. The wealthy had already reached a high level of material life, and would consolidate their upper-class identity during the nineteenth century as much by creating exclusive clubs and circles of sociability as by elevating still further their standard of living. At the other end of the scale, wage-earning workers experienced no sustained increase in real incomes during these years, and if some workers improved their living standards it was in only modest ways that did little to offset much stronger feelings of exclusion and exploitation deriving from their experience with new modes of production. The most powerful sense of a new, class-based social structure was felt by workers in the most rapidly changing trades, who began to form trades' associations limited to wage earners very early in the century, and who began to refer to themselves as the "working classes" by the 1820s. Clearly, it was change at the workplace, not in the marketplace, that was fueling this new identity. But the growing disparity between middling and working-class living standards was becoming significant by the 1830s, and would soon grow more significant in the clarification of both middle-class and working-class social identities.

It is important to emphasize that these emerging identities, growing out of city-directed trade networks and shaped in less impersonal ways in city-based publishing houses, were persuasive in the country, even beyond the borders of villages well connected with the arteries of trade. Richard Bushman has written of the "opening of the countryside" not only to improved methods of farming, but also "to influences from the city — to urbanity, refinement, and middle-class values." More forcefully put, farmers adopted more productive agricultural practices *because* these practices "enabled them to furnish parlors, dress their daughters in fashionable gowns, and send their children to school." The "spreading standards of vernacular gentility," to use Bushman's excellent phrase, redefined the terms of social worth in rural America, dumping "the burden of rural shame" on those who were unable to shed their rusticity by competing successfully in the intensifying marketplaces of production and consumption.[7] Increasingly, in this new age, those who continued in the "old track" were pushed from the middle to the bottom of the social order. It is but a slight extension of Bushman's argument to add that

[7] Richard L. Bushman, "Opening the American Countryside," in James A. Henretta, Michael Kammen, and Stanley N. Katz, eds., *The Transformation of Early American History: Society, Authority, and Ideology* (New York, 1991), 255–56.

they were pushed as well from the core to the margin of rural American culture.

To what extent was a long-standing "logic of sufficiency" superceded during the Jacksonian era by a more persuasive "logic of accumulation"? Bushman refers to winners and losers in the competitive marketplace among free, mostly European-American farmers, but we should be careful not to lose sight of the nearly two and a half million African-American rural workers, fully 15 percent of the American population in 1840, whose enslavement prevented them even from expressing the desire to compete. And among those free farmers who did not prosper, there remains the question of how many were not so much unable as *unwilling* to compete according to the new standards of "vernacular gentility." Whether or not the entirely rustic farmers and husbandmen of the Southern uplands constituted a brawling, hard-drinking, work-eschewing "Celtic fringe," whose subsistence way of life was a point of pride rather than of shame, there were certainly large numbers of rural folk in all regions who resisted or ignored new forms of production and consumption. Communal constraints, even among entrepreneurial farmers, did not suddenly or entirely disappear. They continued to set the rules of local exchange well into the era of expanding extralocal trade, and were especially visible as expressions of "moral economy" during crises that ordinary people construed as illegitimate incursions by external, elite-led forces on the interests and methods of the local community. To all this, we should note, there was an urban analogue in the responses of journeymen and other workers to threats to the continuing availability of inexpensive food, and to skill- and income-threatening innovations within particular trades. And yet, according to both contemporaries and historians, this was not an age to be characterized by faithful adherence to the "old track." For many if not for most Americans, it was an era of "expectant capitalism," and of "the self-made man"; it was a "go-ahead" age, when men "saw opportunities where before they had seen obstacles."[8] I will argue in the next section that this emerging entrepreneurialism is a complex subject, even apart from the hostility or ambivalence of some Americans to its precepts. Here I will note only that the quickening of competitive values in the Jacksonian era was the intangible, cultural effect of a quite tangible constellation of changes – the sudden appearance of steamboats that turned rivers into two-way

---

[8] Lee Benson, *The Concept of Jacksonian Democracy: New York as a Test Case* (Princeton, 1961), 13.

highways of trade, of canals that linked the Great Lakes plain to Atlantic
seaports, of magically productive textile machines and mills, of cities
growing to the size of European capitals, of presses that could print 4,000
sheets of newspaper per hour and bring news of all these developments to
nearly everyone's attention. All of this impressed large numbers of ordinary Americans with the general sense of an energized nation undergoing
rapid and fundamental change. But the effects were felt as well, and
perhaps more consequentially, on a personal level in the form of reduced
transportation costs, cheaper and more varied goods on local storekeepers'
shelves, and magazine articles that defined the terms of the new "vernacular gentility." The ascendancy of entrepreneurial values in the age of
"expectant capitalism" was above all a response to the changing opportunities and circumstances of day-to-day life.

1840–1890

These opportunities and circumstances did not, from the Jacksonian period
forward, always change for the better. Indeed, the half-century following
the recording of the 1840 census was a period of recurring crisis. Starting
in the mid-point of a severe six-year economic depression, it included at
least two shorter but sharp economic downturns (in the late 1850s and
mid-1880s), a six-year depression in the 1870s noted for some of the most
extensive and violent labor–capital confrontations in all of American
history, and, most tragically of all, a Civil War of breathtaking destruc-
tiveness. And yet, it was at the same time a period of massive and multi-
faceted national development: of economic growth, industrialization,
territorial expansion, urbanization, and both public and private sector
institutional centralization. If one looks at some of the statistics of the era
– at say, the numbers of miles of railroad operated in each year of the half-
century – one sees the recurring crises in the smaller numbers of miles
added to the national rail system during the years of depression and war.
But one also sees that the system grew at least modestly in *every* year, and
that it grew rapidly in most, the cumulative effect being a dramatic
quantitative expansion of the sort that Americans have long since come
to equate with the larger pattern of their nation's history. In 1840 a
fragmented set of short rail lines and embryonic intra-regional systems
totalling fewer than 3,000 miles of track had, by 1860, grown into an
inter-regional rail system of more than 30,000 miles. By the time of the

1877 national rail strike this system reached from the Atlantic to the Pacific, and totalled nearly 80,000 miles of track. By 1890 it had filled out in every region to more than 160,000 miles, to which one can add yard track and sidings that totaled more miles than the entire national rail network at the start of the Civil War. In railroad building as in so many other things, the great "go-ahead" engine of American development was occasionally slowed, but it was never stopped.

Railroads were not merely a metaphor of American development, but a crucial participant in, among other things, the nation's rapidly shifting social geography. They were certainly a part of the massive expansion of the territory of the United States, an event whose magnitude, character, and outcome – the creation of a vast nation stretching "from sea to shining sea" – constitutes one of the central events and defining myths of American history. This was the half-century during which pioneer Americans trekked the Oregon Trail to the Pacific Northwest, rushed to pan and dig for gold in California and in the Rocky Mountains, and created, successively, the long cattle trails and the horizon-to-horizon wheat fields of the Great Plains. Most of these fabled episodes in American history not only began but ended during the half-century, as did the imagining of a distinct frontier line marking the advance of Americans across the continent. It was the 1890 census that printed a decade-by-decade series of population density maps, the last of which dissolved this line, so clearly plotted on all the others, into a series of amoeba-like blotches of partially settled plains and mountain valleys extending all the way to the more densely populated Pacific rim. And it was this last map that inspired (or rather dismayed) the historian Frederick Jackson Turner to declare the "closing" of the American frontier; even more, the ending thereby of "the first period of American history," in an 1893 address that itself has become part of the frontier myth.

One can challenge in a number of ways not only the significance that Turner attached to the frontier, but also the statement that the frontier had "closed" by 1890. One can, for example, point to the fact that most of the free federal lands offered to settlers under the terms of the Homestead Act of 1862 were taken up and transferred *after* the turn of the twentieth century. One can argue also that the American settlement of California and Oregon in the 1840s, the scattering of settlements within the Rocky Mountain chain in the succeeding decades, and the completion of various transcontinental railroads in and after 1869 nullified the significance of the advancing mass of continuous settlement. Perhaps most importantly, one can object that the cartographic convention of drawing a line on a map where population densities fell below two persons per square mile does not represent the way the land was experienced and perceived by those who moved across and lived upon it. This being said, it cannot be denied that the magnitude of territorial expansion and population movement was very great during these years, or that the experience of settling the trans-Mississippi west was a significant and in many respects a unique chapter in American history. To descend for a moment from myth to statistics, the territory inhabited by Americans at densities exceeding two persons per square mile increased nearly two and a half times between 1840 and 1890, and by the latter date it did extend, though by no means continuously, from sea to sea. In 1840 fewer than a million Americans, one in twenty of the national population, lived west of the Mississippi River. By 1890 the number of trans-Mississippi westerners approached seventeen million, and accounted for more than one of every four Americans. Thirty-five percent of the nation's population increase during the half-century occurred west of the great river. In 1840 only three states had been formed in this region, and large areas of what was to become the American West were not yet in American hands. By 1890 all of the state boundaries in the continental United States had been established, and lacked only the transformation of Oklahoma, New Mexico, and Arizona from territories into states to complete the continental federal system.

Turner's argument was focused not upon the magnitude or pace of westward migration but upon the character and influence of the frontier experience. We do not have to accept the specific connections he made between frontier life and the defining attributes of American society and culture to agree that the continuing expansion of American settlement into aboriginal lands was a significant and often problematic dimension of national development, even apart from the issues posed by the existence and frequent resistance of native populations, and, before 1861, by the potential incorporation of a vast, institutionally unformed region into a nation already "divided against itself" over the future of chattel slavery. That both of these issues were resolved militarily and with much bloodshed should not distract us from the somewhat more mundane problems and circumstances accompanying the day-to-day taking up of the land by families and communities of settlers. The frontier *was* different, even within the familiarly forested and well-watered eastern half of the continent, and especially upon the treeless, semi-arid plains that European-Americans at first comprehended as a "Great American Desert" and only gradually learned how to utilize for stock raising and agriculture. To Easterners especially concerned with the maintenance of a stable and Christian social order, the west was always "wild," both in the ways it seemed to attract disproportionate numbers of society's outcasts and misfits, and in the primitive conditions that loosened constraints even among the most respectable migrants. Writing of a late-eighteenth-century frontier no farther from the seaboard than central Pennsylvania, Jedidiah Morse described the typical pioneer as "a man who has outlived his credit or fortune in the cultivated parts of the state," and who, living in close proximity to Indians, "soon acquires a strong tincture of their manners." The frontiersman lives, according to Morse, in rags in a wilderness hut, works violently but sporadically, allows his cattle to forage, spends much of his time hunting, fishing, and drinking, and moves on to new frontiers when others begin to move in, expressing thereby an increasing preference to remain outside of society.[9] This would soon become a quite standard image, and would follow the pioneer to more distant frontiers.

Eastern fears of regression to primitivism among western settlers, which were strong enough to stimulate missions, the formation of Bible and tract societies, and other efforts to reclaim the migrants for a decent Christian order, were obviously exaggerated and to no small extent self-serving. But they were reasonably based on the perception that rapid westward expansion did attenuate both formal and informal means of social control, and presented peaceable and God-fearing pioneers with the problem of how to construct a stable social order in the wilderness. The problem was easiest to solve where neighbors and kin moved and settled together in locations not terribly distant from older regions, and was most acute where young men on the make (or on the lam) collected in a remote land to trap, prospect for gold, or drive cattle. For some years before and after the Civil War the trans-Mississippi west was the particular locale of such collections of young men, a simple demographic fact that does much to explain why the "wild west" reached its apogee in its mining camps, ranches, and cattle trails, and in the predominantly male cities and towns that sprouted in the gold regions and at the cattle trail rail-heads. To be sure, the forty-niners and other prospectors quickly created rules among themselves for staking claims and arbitrating disputes, while Texas ranchers recognized each other's brands in the sorting out of free-grazing herds. But crime and vio-

[9] Morse, *American Geography*, 313–14.

lence were endemic to these societies, and the extra-legal means created to punish claim jumpers, cattle rustlers, and other criminals were often more violent than the crimes themselves. Vigilante justice was also common within the gold and cattle towns, which in their earliest years were as vio-lence-ridden, and, according to some residents with a large stake in the social order, as poorly served by the legal institutions of justice as the mining camps and cattle ranges. At various times during the 1850s, the booming new city of San Francisco was virtually ruled by vigilante committees organized by some of the city's wealthiest businessmen. These committees arrested, tried, hanged, and deported criminals even after the city was declared by California's governor to be in a state of insurrection.

Farmers who crossed the river and pushed on to the plains did not nec-essarily create a more peaceable and closely knit social order. The slavery issue destabilized much of the southern plains before the Civil War, and the war itself was fought by guerrilla bands as well as by official armies in the western theater on both sides of the Mississippi. Farmers and ranch-ers clashed repeatedly over rights to the previously unfenced and unculti-vated range, an historic battle resolved in the farmers' favor only after the railroad could replace the cattle trail and the cattle car could perform the job of the cowboy. When this occurred, when rail systems crossed the west at all latitudes, and when barbed-wire fencing, wind-driven deep-well water pumps, and an array of new farm machines and techniques made farming feasible on the plains, farmers could finally domesticate the "wild west." But the form of the domesticated agricultural landscape was a new one, shaped by monoculture and the necessarily large scale of individual farms. Bonanza wheat farms, of which there were some three thousand on the northern plains by 1880, could encompass as many as thirty or forty thousand acres (they averaged seven thousand), and were organized much like factories, with dozens or even hundreds of male farm hands respond-ing to the orders of professional supervisors and managers. Family farms, too, were larger than they were back east, and this meant that neighbors were always fewer and farther between. Communities were formed and maintained with difficulty outside the scattered railroad and river towns. Emptiness and loneliness, not community, are the dominant themes of the literature of the Great Plains, from Hamlin Garland and Ole Rolvaag to Willa Cather.

Turner's frontier thesis, formed primarily with reference to earlier fron-tiers in the wooded eastern half of the continent, was easily accommodated to the greater challenges of the trans-Mississippi west, if not to Garland's or Rolvaag's tales of misery and defeat. Here was yet another crucible for the forging of a distinctly American individualism, and a peculiarly American democracy – including, perhaps, even the violent "democracy" of vigilantism. But if the experience of this and earlier frontiers "explain American development" (Turner did not qualify the word "explain" in his 1893 essay), it was an experience that must have been powerful indeed, for there were regions of American society from which the frontier was distant in both time and space, and in which there were contrary forces that would seem to have explanatory power quite apart from any inherited or geographically transmitted influences from man's primal contact with the wilderness. Behind the frontier, and long before its "closing" – indeed, *on* the frontier of big cattle ranches, bonanza wheat farms, mining companies, and railroads – America was developing a capitalist system of integrated markets and productive, commercial, and financial institutions. This system was an important force driving and shaping territorial expansion itself, but its primary geographic expression was centralizing rather than diffusing. During this classic age of westward expansion, when the Euro- and Afro-American population of the trans-Mississippi west was increasing by sixteen million, more than twenty million people (including four million who lived west of the Mississippi) were added to the nation's cities and towns.

Urbanization in all its dimensions was significant throughout this half-century. During the twenty years preceding the Civil War (perhaps more accurately the sixteen or seventeen years following the economic recovery of the early 1840s) the urban population of the United States increased from under two million to more than six million, the urban proportion of the national population nearly doubled to 20 percent, and the numbers of officially recognized cities and towns increased from 131 to nearly 400. These were the largest proportionate increases in all of American history, before or since, and reflect the quickening pace of city-centered industrial activity, the continuing integration of market-oriented farms into nearby and distant urban markets, and a dramatic upsurge of foreign immigration, consisting mostly of Irish and German refugees from famine, economic dislocation, and revolution. To a much greater extent than the less alien, less desperate, and less numerous immigrants of earlier periods, these "new" immigrants of the 1840s and 1850s (the Irish more than the Germans) were compelled to find work in America's industrializing cities, and they swelled the populations of inland canal and railroad towns as well as ports of entry. The tendency of both foreign and native-born rural-urban population flows was primarily toward the larger cities, which, despite the proliferation of small cities and towns, captured the lion's share of this period's urban growth. New York added a half-million residents during these two decades, and, amazingly, the recently rustic town of Brooklyn just across the East River had become the nation's third-largest city. Between them, the two cities constituted an increasingly integrated metropolis of more than a million inhabitants.

Urban growth continued during the Civil War decade, and perhaps during the war itself, and by 1870 25 percent of the American population lived in 663 cities and towns. Despite wartime devastation, Richmond's population grew by more than a third between 1860 and 1870, and Atlanta's more than doubled. By striking at the industrial core of urban economies, the depression of the 1870s probably did more than the war to slow the pace of urbanization. But by 1890, after a generally prosperous decade and another upsurge in city-focused foreign immigration, the urban population constituted 35 percent of the national total, and the number of cities and towns exceeded 1,300 – a tenfold increase since 1840.

These national statistics mask considerable variations by region. Not surprisingly, urbanization was most advanced in the Northeast, and in the band of Midwestern states extending from Ohio to Wisconsin. Between 1840 and 1890 the proportion of city and town dwellers in New England, New York, New Jersey, and Pennsylvania rose from nearly 20 percent (already much higher than any other region) to a clear majority of 60 percent of the region's population. Midwestern urban dwellers increased from only 4 percent in 1840, when a portion of the region was still a frontier, to 38 percent in 1890. But cities and towns were developing even in the least urban regions. The trans-Mississippi west, as I have already suggested, was at once a region of vast spaces and booming cities. There were fewer towns in the west, and few indeed that went back more than a generation, but by 1890 eight of the twenty-eight American cities larger than 100,000 were west of the Mississippi. One of every four westerners was a city or town dweller in 1890, and one in ten lived in one of these eight large cities. The Southeast, below the Potomac and east of the Mississippi, was the least urbanized American region, with only 3.5 percent of its 1840 population, and less than 13 percent of its 1890 population, living in cities and towns. However, cities such as Baltimore, Washington, Cincinnati,

St. Louis, and New Orleans all reached into this region in various ways, providing portions of it with an urban presence greater than these numbers suggest. The statistics of urban growth beyond the immediate reach of these cities, moreover, indicate that even within this most rural of American regions cities and towns were growing faster than the rural population.

The meaning of all these statistics is probably best understood by considering again the ways in which growing cities and proliferating towns contributed to the reshaping of routines of production, exchange, and daily social life in both town and country. Can we speak more forcefully of a city-system (or an array of such systems) in this era, and, therefore, of a more substantially urbanized *society*? It is clear that cities, towns, commercial farms, and other rural extractive industries were cohering in new ways, especially in the more heavily urbanizing northeast and midwest, but to what extent can we identify the main lines of social change in nineteenth-century America with the thickening network of population clusters and central-place pathways? Urbanization brought large numbers of rural Americans and immigrants into big cities to live and caused numerous towns and cities to grow larger around many people who did not need to move to experience the force of a new urban environment. How did urban development affect these people, and how did it affect the lives of the majority of Americans who continued to live in the smaller communities of rural America?

Let us first take a closer look at the human landscape of an urbanizing region, choosing as a brief case study an eleven-county section of west-central Ohio, located at approximately the geographic center of that broad set of northern regions in which urbanization was most pervasive, and displaying in 1890 an overall urban population profile almost exactly the same as the nation as a whole (see Figure 17.2). The eleven counties form an irregular rectangle of midwestern cornland, extending some 80 to 85 miles across its east–west axis and approximately 65 miles from north to south. Within this small area in 1890 were thirteen localities that the census counted as urban places: a medium-sized city of 60,000 (Dayton), a second city of 30,000 (Springfield), four small cities with populations ranging from 5,000 to 10,000 (Piqua, Xenia, Urbana, and Greenville, in size order), and seven large villages (one was chartered as a city) that exceeded the census-defined urban threshold of 2,500. The census lists sixteen other villages with more than 1,000 inhabitants, and no fewer than fifty-seven with less than 1,000. There were unincorporated villages as

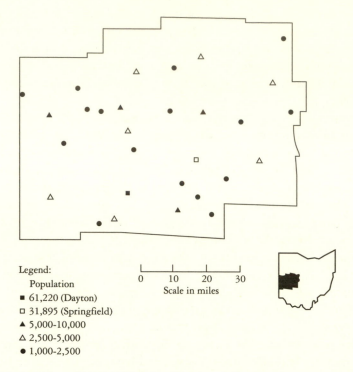

Legend:
 Population
 ■ 61,220 (Dayton)
 □ 31,895 (Springfield)
 ▲ 5,000–10,000
 △ 2,500–5,000
 ● 1,000–2,500

0   10   20   30
Scale in miles

Figure 17.2. Cities and larger villages (population exceeding 1,000), 11 counties of west-central Ohio, 1890.

well, all very small but numbering in the dozens, that the census did not isolate from their township populations.

This was a landscape fairly sprinkled with clustered communities of various sizes, surprisingly, one might say, given the custom of rural dispersal brought to the region by its Virginia- and Pennsylvania-born settlers. The distances between the six largest urban centers ranged from 15 to 38 miles, and averaged only about 24 miles. In the intervening spaces were smaller centers that shortened still further the distance between towns, and between town and country, while distance itself had taken on new meaning with the interconnection of all the region's cities, towns, and larger villages, and even many of its smaller villages, by at least a dozen different railroad lines. Villages and hamlets that were not on the railroad were connected to larger places by turnpikes and local roads, which crossed virtually every section of every township. No small hamlet, and no individual farm, was remote in such a landscape of towns and routes. And it was a human landscape, finally, that was steadily growing more concentrated. Between 1880 and 1890 population growth in the eleven counties correlated perfectly with locality size. Dayton, the largest city, grew by 58 percent, Springfield, the second largest, grew by 54 percent, the four next largest urban centers increased by an average of 24 percent, and the six smallest averaged 23 percent. Among the villages identified on the 1890 census, those containing between 1,000 and 2,500 inhabitants grew during the decade by 10 percent, while smaller villages grew by 9 percent. The remaining population, consisting of those who lived in unincorporated hamlets and on individual farms, actually declined by 5 percent.

The cities and towns of regions such as this one were "central places" in an increasing variety of ways. Geographers and historians who analyze central-place development focus primarily on the role medium-sized and small cities played in the shipping of crops, the wholesaling and retailing of consumer goods, and the inter-regional transfer of bank credits. During the second half of the nineteenth century these economic roles were expanded and routinized, as ordinary farmers participated increasingly in extralocal systems of exchange. Thus, the small urban centers of Ohio and elsewhere were above all the sites of rail depots, shipping agencies, banks, and retail stores, while the medium-sized centers served a somewhat wider region with wholesalers, insurance offices, and larger banks. But the towns were political and social centers as well, and in the late nineteenth century offered to both townspeople and nearby rural residents an array of institutions and experiences that, among other things, added a more cosmopolitan dimension to local life. Many of these were already characteristic of towns at the beginning of this period, although some, such as the fraternal lodges (and now the women's auxiliaries of these lodges), had expanded enormously during the half-century. What had changed most of all was the proximity of lodges and other institutions of this sort to rural people as one consequence of the sprinkling of towns across the land. Urbana, which had two dozen or more lodges, temperance societies, social clubs, and the like, was a town of 6,500 inhabitants in 1890, connected by less than 30 miles of rail and turnpike to the somewhat larger town of Piqua. Between them, about 10 miles from Urbana on both the railroad and the pike, lay the curiously named village of St. Paris (population 1,145), which contained at least four lodges, a Y.M.C.A., and two newspaper offices. Local roads shot off in all directions from Urbana, Piqua, and even from St. Paris, bringing all of the intervening countryside into close orbit around these local centers.

The clustering of rail depots, stores, banks, newspaper offices, lodges, and other institutions into proliferating cities and towns accounts for the use of the term "urbanization" to describe the increasing availability of these institutions to rural people and the growing impact of external markets and other cosmopolitan forces on country life. But because the local centers that mediated between farmers, townspeople, and the world outside were themselves small and relatively rustic in character, and because the land was only very gradually drained of those who worked it, "urbanization" also overstates the result. Rural and small-town life behind the frontier may be more accurately characterized as a more richly and complexly organized but still distinctly rural array of activities and relationships, a more densely ordered country world of developed farms and well-worn country roads, of villages and towns well-rooted in local ways, of known neighbors and nearby kin – a social world contrasting well enough with the less well settled and more socially attenuated western frontier, but still more rural than urban in character. "Rural concentration" may be a better term to describe this part of the larger process of what is rightly called "urbanization."

Geographers and urban historians have sensed the rustic quality of small-scale urbanization within regions such as the one I have been describing, and have contrasted locally-rooted central-place systems with much more cosmopolitan networks of large cities that are nourished as much by their contact with each other as by their relations with the smaller cities and towns of their own hinterlands. This wider network helps explain why big cities are characteristically located at the edge rather than the center of their hinterlands, why they are usually founded early rather than late in their region's history, and why they grow so much more rapidly and become so much larger than the cities beneath them in the urban hierarchy. Big cities do reach out to their hinterlands, connecting them to wider markets and influences, but when they do it is from a greater distance and across a greater divide than that which separates smaller centers from the countryside.

It is in these big cities, therefore, that we find not simply the clearest, but also a rather different expression of the power of the nineteenth-century urban revolution. Only three American cities (New York, Chicago, and Philadelphia) topped a million inhabitants in 1890, but there were a number of somewhat smaller places – St. Louis, Boston, New

Orleans, San Francisco, Washington, among others – that were clearly more than regional centers. These were the cities that controlled the flow of products, currency, credits, equities, and even ideas in national and international markets, and whose presence shaped vast regions into specialized zones of dairy farming, pork raising, or commercial forestry. They were centers of manufacturing, that bred specialized satellite industrial towns such as Lowell, Lynn, Paterson, and Passaic. Moreover, these big cities, and in most respects their industrial satellites too, were as impressive in their physical appearance as they were powerful in their external relations. Their downtowns, industrial zones, and suburbs were distinctive environments, to which office buildings, department stores, theaters, art museums, suspension bridges, and even "rustic" parks and "rural" cemeteries contributed the unmistakable feeling – perhaps even a new popular definition – of urbanity. Dayton, the largest central place in the eleven Ohio counties discussed here as an urbanizing region, did not convey this kind of urbanity. But Cincinnati, some 50 miles to the south, did, to large if unspecifiable numbers of people who lived in Dayton, Urbana, St. Paris, and on the farms of surrounding townships. And so too did distant New York, whose emergence as an international capital was more powerfully emblematic than any cattle trail or bonanza wheat farm of the main lines of national development during the "first period of American history."

The complexity of the big-city environment was paralleled by (and even bound up with) a social complexity that makes the city the fruitful starting place for considering the relationship between economic development and further changes in the social structure during this half-century. Even before this period urban workers were responding to the first stages of industrial reorganization by forming separate and increasingly militant journeymen's trades associations, and by characterizing themselves as "producers," the "producing classes," the "working classes," and even the "working class" in the debate with "bosses" and "capitalists." It may be argued that this was at first little more than a political language, used mainly by radical editors and organizers, and energized by the very novelty and seeming reversibility of changes in the workshops. As industrial change became more pervasive, however, and the role and status of wage-earning workers became rather more settled within industrial capitalism, terms such as "working class" and "capitalists" did not recede. Rather, they came to express the widening perception of manual workers as a distinct social class within a society more clearly divided along class lines.

The division, de-skilling, and eventual mechanization of labor, the corruption of apprenticeship, the migration of work from the artisan household to separate manufactories and sweatshops, the abandonment of old trade rituals and the creation of new work rhythms and rules, the severing of commonalities and sympathies between master and journeyman, the shift in power in the determining of both the conditions and the material rewards of labor, and the shrinking opportunity for journeymen to rise within their trades to become employers themselves – these, in various ways and in various trades, were the industrial changes that bred and nourished the perception that wage-earning producers had become a working class. But there were other changes beyond the workplace that significantly reinforced this perception. Most importantly, when production left the household, as it did in many trades in the middle half of the nineteenth century, workers left it too, relocating their own homes in increasingly distinct working-class neighborhoods within the expanding city.

Physically separate neighborhoods bred separate neighborhood institutions, most of which acquired a distinctive working-class flavor. The cheap furniture stores and second-hand clothing shops that came to line the principal streets of working-class neighborhoods were new institutions, but saloons, theaters, and volunteer fire companies were old institutions transformed into class-segregated centers of a specifically working-class style of city living. Fire companies and saloons were the most important vehicles for the creation and maintenance of a social world of male conviviality, and often of physical violence, the latter organized to some degree into recurring brawls between rival fire companies and into illegal boxing matches arranged, promoted, and presided over by working-class saloon keepers. Men and women attended theaters that once had catered to all the strata of the city, but that now portrayed the boisterous heroism of Mose the Bowery B'hoy to audiences made up almost entirely of working people. As early as the 1840s, according to an acute contemporary observer of New York life, the Bowery Theater itself had become "representative of that immense and important class of our population, inhabiting the Sahara of the East, and living – somehow – from day to day and week to week – upon the labor of their hands."[10]

[10] George G. Foster, *New York by Gas-Light: With Here and There a Streak of Sunshine* (New York, 1850), 87.

At the moment those words were being written, the exotic "Sahara" of New York's East Side, and the working-class neighborhoods of most other American cities as well, were being transformed by the immigration of large numbers of Irish and German immigrants. By providing a bountiful supply of cheap labor these migrants greatly facilitated the continuing reorganization of American workshops, and by the 1850s the manual workforces of many American cities were predominantly foreign-born. This complicated working-class identities by creating sharp divisions within the institutions and in the daily life of the poorer neighborhoods, and, for native-born workers at least, by cross-cutting the lines of conflict between capital and labor with new, perpendicular lines separating Protestant native from Catholic immigrant. But the very character of the conflict within the politics of plebeian wards, between rival fire companies, between the pugilistic champions of American or Irish honor, and in a host of other local arenas, only sharpened the separation between the working-class neighborhoods and the rest of the city and reinforced even the native working-men's sense of belonging to a social world increasingly distinct from that of the bourgeois middle and upper classes. For immigrants, the vast majority of whom were manual workers of some sort, the boundary was even clearer. In Roy Rosenzweig's words, "to assert an ethnic identity was also to assert a working-class identity,"[11] even during the immediate post–Civil War decades when an upsurge in migration from Sweden and other Protestant countries brought workers into this country who shared religious and other values with the middle-class Anglo-Saxon majority. Swedes and other Protestant immigrants were more likely to join in middle-class crusades against excessive drinking or against overly boisterous celebrations of the Fourth of July, but those who worked in factories were also likely to join labor unions, and even as temperance advocates often expressed an explicitly working-class point of view.

Ethnic identities, indeed, intersected class identities in a variety of ways, and the relation would grow still more complicated after 1880, when another "new immigration" infused large numbers of Eastern and Southern European Catholics, Jews, and Orthodox Christians into an already diverse working class. Most of these new groups were more "ghettoized" than the antebellum Irish and Germans had been, and were less likely to relate, even through combat, with native-born workers in the perpetuation or re-creation of a common working-class culture. But again, cultural

[11] Roy Rosenzweig, *Eight Hours for What We Will: Workers and Leisure in an Industrial City, 1870–1920* (Cambridge, 1983), 86.

diffusion and animosity, even of the sort that kept "Hunkies" out of steelworkers' unions, or channeled activist Jews or Italians into their own
unions or locals, did not preclude a working-class identity that overarched
all these groups. Native-born steelworkers (including second-generation
Irish and Germans!) reviled the "Hunkies," but in the years just before the
Homestead strike they understood well enough their own relation to the
American class structure. Ethnic diversity, in sum, complicated, but it did
not destroy, working-class identity.

One reason it did not is that workers of all ethnic backgrounds found
themselves in fairly similar economic circumstances. Throughout the nineteenth century, and unlike the twentieth, the annual incomes of nearly all
manual workers were distinctly lower than the incomes of those who
worked in what would later be called the "white-collar sector." To be sure,
some of the better-paid skilled workers in industries and trades where work
was most regular earned more than most junior clerks, and some of the
larger department stores were beginning to hire (mostly female) sales
clerks, who were paid low wages and given no real opportunity to rise to
higher positions. But until late in the century clerking was for the most
part still a form of business apprenticeship, and the junior clerks who
learned their trade rapidly advanced to higher salaries and to their own
business proprietorships. Industrial workers who learned their trade
remained where they were, unless they left the shop floor to open saloons,
groceries, or other small stores in their own working-class neighborhoods
– the only "white-collar" enterprises that ordinarily did not generate
significantly more income than industrial work itself. Industrial wage
levels varied, of course, by skill level, industry, and region, but few urban
manual workers in nineteenth-century America made more than $1,000
in a year of steady employment, and most made far less. In Philadelphia,
where wages were higher than they were in most places, skilled workers
averaged less than $600 in 1880, and unskilled workers averaged only
$375. Male store and office clerks with three or four years of experience
were paid salaries that usually exceeded $1,000, while accountants, sales-
men, downtown retailers, and other small businessmen generally made
significantly more than that. If $1,000 per year was a ceiling for the aspi-
rations of most manual workers, it was no more than a floor for those men
who worked in or owned offices and stores.

This consistent disparity of incomes provided a material basis for the
recognition of a "working class." Americans who wished to deny the
significance of class distinctions were correct to point out that American

workers were paid better, and lived better, than their European counterparts. American workers did enjoy a more diverse and plentiful diet, dressed better, and lived in larger and more adequately furnished homes. But the latter, in particular, were humble by American urban standards, consisting usually of three or four rooms of a city tenement or shared house, furnished with rag carpets and factory-made furniture purchased from the cheap neighborhood stores. Often, these modest quarters, no larger on average than the artisans' and laborers' homes of the late eighteenth century, were shared with one or more boarders, a fact that underscores an important aspect of working-class material life – that it was usually paid for by more than one income. Only a minority of industrial workers received enough in wages to support an average-sized family in what was considered a decent working-class style of living. In most working-class families, therefore, incomes contributed by wives and children were crucial. Wives contributed most often by caring for rent-paying boarders, but children left school when necessary to become wage earners, filling a shortfall that rose and fell in response to both the family life-cycle and, outside the home, the larger cycles of available employment.

The higher incomes of professionals, businessmen, and senior clerical employees purchased a way of life that reinforced the social meaning of nonmanual work, and helped to define what was increasingly called the "middle class." Earlier in the century Americans employed this term, and others like it ("middling class," "middle classes") with imprecision and reluctance, sometimes including and sometimes excluding master craftsmen and even journeymen in trades not yet transformed by industrialization, and often qualifying it with some sort of disclaimer (e.g., "the 'middle class,' if we may so call it"). During the middle half of the century, however, the term was used with increasing frequency, precision, and boldness to refer almost entirely to those families who, while lacking great wealth or long-established social prominence, gained comfortable livings from nonmanual occupations. The occupations themselves were significant as class credentials, as were the clothes worn on the job, and even the location and ambience of stores and offices as places contrasting with industrial workshops in ways that underscored the social meaning of the distinction between "headwork" and "handwork." But important too was the further elaboration of a distinctly middle-class domestic life, located, as were the domestic lives of manual workers, in increasingly class-segregated neighborhoods within the city. From about the 1870s, moreover, significant numbers of middle-class families relocated their neighborhoods beyond the city in "streetcar suburbs," where larger homes in semi-rustic settings fostered the continuing elaboration of parlors and other domestic spaces as the well-furnished settings of respectable sociability.

In the city as well as the suburbs middle-class homes were growing larger, and the cost of furnishing their parlors with Brussels carpets, horse-hair sofas, pianos, and assorted Victorian bric-a-brac was not inconsiderable. Yet, a hallmark of middle-class life was the meeting of this and other costs by means of only one income, and the consequent differentiation in the roles and expectations of middle-class wives and children from those of their working-class counterparts. These differences can be exaggerated. Middle-class women did sometimes take in boarders (though usually within homes large enough to establish a significant spatial separation between the boarder and the family), just as some working-class wives looked after only their own families. Nearly all working-class children did attend school for a half-dozen years or more. But the differences were great enough to sharpen, and even to serve to some extent as the emblems of, class division. Middle-class children, whose earning power was not needed when their fathers brought home three or four thousand dollars each year, stayed in school to acquire the skills that would help keep them in the middle class as they formed families of their own. Their mothers devoted themselves to the children's nurturance and socialization, and to the tasks of furnishing and managing the home. This kind and conception of "women's work," so carefully separated from the income-producing marketplace, confined many women to roles they would not otherwise have chosen, and consistently and deliberately devalued their labor. But this very devaluation lay at the core of nineteenth-century middle-class formation, which consisted not merely of changes in work, workplace authority, and income distribution, but also of a largely female-directed, intensely domestic style of living that contrasted with the largely male-directed working-class life of the saloon, the union hall, and the fire house.

The social and spatial complexities of the city also nourished a distinction between the middle and upper classes. Types of work and work milieux were less decisive at this level of social differentiation, as, investment bankers aside, the professional and business activities of the rich differed from those of the middle class as much in the scale of their operations and profits as in the nature of their activities. To be sure, some of the very wealthy had retired to live as *rentiers* upon investments in real estate, while others differed from more ordinary *bourgeois* by participating in a wide empire of enterprises rather than in a single business. But the categorical quality of the urban upper class derived not so much from these workday distinctions as from the process of mutual recognition, expressed through acceptance into a small number of elite clubs, invitations to a particular circle of dinner parties and balls, and service on the boards of the city's most important cultural and philanthropic organizations. Recognition was imperfectly correlated with great wealth at any given moment, for there were upstarts with newly acquired fortunes who were not yet quite ready for Society, and the patriciate was itself divided in some cities between studiously dignified "nobs" of long-established social prominence and fashionable "swells" of more recent (and often greater) wealth. But if the rapid ascent of the "swells" suggests that the urban upper class was something less than a closed and unified caste, exclusivity was its essence, and there was more continuity than flux in the membership of any of its "sets." Nor did the divisions at the top of urban society seem as important to those below it, who, nonetheless, accorded considerable celebrity to the upper class as a whole. Ward McAllister found himself banished from fashionable society when he actually compiled and published a list of the "Four Hundred" New York families that Mrs. William Backhouse Astor offhandedly estimated to be the outer limits of the set she dominated (McAllister's list actually amounted to 273). But ordinary New Yorkers who did not already know most of these names, or the exact length of the list, did immediately understand the meaning of McAllister's "Four Hundred," and this widespread knowledge of so carefully bounded and guarded an upper class contributed significantly to their awareness of the hierarchical structure of urban society as a whole.

This social structure, so crucially shaped by the complexities of the big city, could not have existed in the same form and degree in the smaller communities in which most Americans lived. And yet, much more than an echo of the urban social structure can be found outside the big cities. Even fairly small cities were commercial and industrial centers with rather diverse populations. They may have lacked the scale, the ambience, and the most impressive institutions of great cities, but they did replicate most of the ordinary institutions that helped give structure to a distinctly urban society. Their class-segregated neighborhoods, too, went beyond the simple distinction (significant in the smallest towns and villages) between the "right side" and the "wrong side" of the tracks. Cities the size of Terre Haute (1890 population, 30,000) developed impressive neighborhoods of large houses built in the fashionable styles of the day – Italianate, Queen Anne, Romanesque – and that constituted instantly recognizable zones of affluence and social worth.[12] Still smaller cities and towns did the same on a scale commensurate with the size of their affluent classes. None of these smaller urban communities had an upper class large or affluent enough to separate itself from the rest of local society in the manner of New York's Old Guard or Four Hundred, or Boston's Brahmins (though in many towns there were one or more families who were "known" in urban polite society), and it may be more accurate to think of those who lived in the Elm Street mansions of small cities as leaders of the local middle class rather than as a class unto themselves. The self-awareness of this middle class, however, seems to have been hardly less intense, and its separation from the working class hardly less complete, than it was in the larger cities. Thus, in a somewhat truncated form that preserved the distinction between the middle and working classes, the social structure of middle-sized and small cities may be said to have resembled that of the great urban centers.

Rural hierarchies were also brought more closely into alignment with those of larger places by the proliferation of small cities, towns, and villages across the rural landscape, and the much closer integration of rural populations into local societies in which town- and village-dwelling professionals, businessmen, clerks, and other non-agricultural folk played prominent roles. Here, though, we require a stronger qualification. Rural and small-town society was not simply urban society on a smaller scale. More personalized networks of kinship and community, and the widespread feeling that city ways ought to be resisted by good country people, continued to moderate "urbanization" into "rural concentration." Still, those city ways were increasingly influential in the countryside, not only because of the physical proximity of cities and towns to the countryside, but also because of the ever-increasing flow of words across the American landscape. Most of the twelve thousand weekly newspapers published in 1890 were issued from villages and towns no larger than St. Paris, Ohio (which published two), but these local papers still routinely passed along items gleaned from the big-city newspapers. The latter were expanding, too (there were sixteen hundred city dailies published in the United States in 1890), and were circulating more widely in their hinterlands. Mail-order catalogues, a new form of publication, were sent from city-based merchandisers to countless rural homes, and surely some significant

---

[12] Robert W. Bastian, "Architecture and Class Segregation in Late Nineteenth-Century Terre Haute, Indiana," *Geographical Review*, 65 (1975), 166–79.

portion of the four *billion* pieces of mail handled by the U.S. post office in 1890 consisted of letters sent "back home" from rural-urban migrants, whose personal descriptions of urban experience were perhaps the most important textbooks in city life for those who remained behind. Hardly less important for some types of rural folk were mass-circulation magazines such as *The Ladies' Home Companion*, which combined various forms of personal instruction with advertising more alluring, and more oriented to contemporary urban fashion, than that of the mail-order catalogues. It is perhaps impossible to assess the impact of all these media on the social identities of country people, but it is clear that one effect was a shortening of the cultural distance between city and country. Ironically, social distinction was an important part of this increasingly common culture.

Underlying this divisive commonality was the spread of capitalism, which integrated vast numbers of urban and rural folk into organized extralocal markets at the same time that it reshaped the economic roles and rewards around which new social distinctions cohered. Even as Americans spread themselves from sea to sea, and in particular as they concentrated within cities and in the regions around cities, they engaged more and more crucially in the types of exchanges that tended to undermine the old rules that once governed a more localized market economy. This shifting of the rules of the marketplace signified a deeper shift of values and expectations, as increasing numbers of Americans became profit-seekers as well as producers, competitors as well as neighbors. The legitimization of entrepreneurial values across widening areas of the American landscape was a long-term process, but we cannot expect to map its progress as though attitudes towards personal gain, or communal obligation, or the proper relations between debtor and creditor were like so many miles of railroad built in a given year through a given length and width of terrain. Values are obviously more complex, more elusive of definition, and a good deal more resistant to counting up, than lengths of rail. And if an advancing culture of capitalism is to be mapped in some way, it must be on a complex "relief map" reflective of the varying slopes and altitudes of social terrain.

Earlier, following the historian Daniel Vickers, I identified the advancing entrepreneurialism of the Jacksonian era with the "logic of endless accumulation," an alluring phrase that ought to signify not only a more positive attitude toward individual gain but also a somewhat wider constellation of perceptions, values, and beliefs. For example, there were important collective aspects of what Christopher Lasch has called "Adam Smith's rehabilitation of desire" – the belief that, quoting Smith, the "uniform, constant, and uninterrupted effort of every man to better his condition" was the "principle from which public and national, as well as private opulence is originally derived."[13] Private striving may have appeared to be corrupting and crassly selfish to those most comfortable with traditional ideals and practices, but liberals insisted that it was the very foundation of national growth, and that all but the *least* virtuous would gain, not only from their own efforts, but from the wealth-creating efforts of others. Endless accumulation was in this manner translated into a collective, national property, and, as Lasch points out, into the very core of an ascending ideal of national progress. In this increasingly persuasive progressivism, entrepreneurialism enhanced the well-being of the community in the very process of destroying its constraining traditions.

Second, liberals (and less reflective profit-seekers) insisted that there was little ground for compromise between progress and tradition in a marketplace that must become openly competitive. Striving could not be merged with older communal practices regulating the pursuit of personal interest and could not assume new communal forms. There were numerous attempts at the latter by separatist religious and secular communities, as well as by trades unionists and other workers who sought to channel the capitalist market into cooperative institutions of production and exchange. But these efforts, which tended to appear and to disappear relatively early in this era of capitalist expansion (mostly in the 1840s), were dismissed by the majority of Americans, who believed that the family farm and the individually owned business would remain the basic units of the competitive market. And, third, if "free enterprise" would become the normative expression of the unrestrained market, "equality of opportunity" and "the open society" would become normative expressions of that market's social correlate. Success in a truly competitive marketplace was a better and surer foundation of social worth, and in the merging of economic success and social ascendancy Americans found their favorite argument for the superiority of American republican institutions over those of aristocratic Europe. "No exclusive privileges of birth, no entailment of estates, no civil or political disqualifications," stands in the way of the

---

[13] Christopher Lasch, *The True and Only Heaven: Progress and Its Critics* (New York, 1991), 52–53.

American entrepreneur, argued the Whig publicist Calvin Colton in 1844. "This is a country of *self-made men*, than which nothing better could be said of any state of society."[14]

Americans frequently expressed the gratifying fluidity of their competitive society by invoking the image of a "wheel of fortune." The apparent fatalism of this metaphor – its suggestion that rewards were distributed randomly, without regard for individual effort or worth – would seem to indicate a degree of anxiety among even the most enthusiastic apologists of the free market and the open society. That anxiety was no doubt real, and Americans could address it only by denying that the turning of the wheel was random. This they did with considerable frequency. Thus, a fourth element of the "logic of endless accumulation" was an insistence on the essential fairness of economic and social reward. Americans who wrote on such matters consistently associated worldly success with a generally agreed-upon list of personal virtues. Industriousness, ingenuity, honesty, reliability, punctuality, and other merits in the conduct of business affairs were joined to general qualities of personal character to identify what would and would not result in individual success. To be sure, the rise of Horatio Alger's young heroes (in the one hundred novels for boys that historians continue to regard as the quintessential "success manuals" of the second half of the nineteenth century) seems always to have depended on the lucky opportunity to rescue some rich man's child from accidental death. But in all of Alger's influential tales the wheel of fortune turned not randomly but on traits of character. His readers were told at the outset of each book, long before the daring rescue that would confirm the hero's ascent from poverty, that this was a boy who possessed those personal qualities that made success the most natural of outcomes. Even as a poor bootblack, for example, Ragged Dick "was above doing anything mean or dishonorable. He would not steal, or cheat, or impose upon younger boys, but was frank and straight-forward, manly and self-reliant. His nature was a noble one, and had saved him from mean faults."[15] This was, in short, the right boy to save the rich merchant's drowning child, and to rise in the world. On the mean streets of the nation's real cities, and on the Main Streets of its villages, success may well have been associated with a different mix of personal qualities than those offered by Alger and other moralists. But even those who respected a less scrupulous ambition tended, in most cases, to believe that the wheel of fortune was turned by human hands.

[14] [Calvin Colton], *The Junius Tracts*, no. 7 (New York, 1844), 15.
[15] Horatio Alger, Jr., *Ragged Dick and Struggling Upward*, Carl Bode, ed., (New York, 1985), 7.

This list of entrepreneurial perceptions, values, and beliefs could no doubt be further extended, or connected to such closely related matters as domestic privatism and normative definitions of true womanhood, or attitudes toward the proper functioning of the democratic state. However long the list of components or correlates, the essential point is that a complex "logic of endless accumulation" could appeal to or repel different groups of people in different ways. Hence, the mapping of cultural change over an extensive and uneven social terrain consists of more than a simple summing up of the extent to which a received package of values was accepted or rejected by different social classes, ethnic groups, and geographical regions on the relief map of American society. The package was itself opened and repacked from place to place on this map with different terms and even with different understandings of similar terms, such that some of the most significant cultural divergences resided within the meanings attached to "self-interest," "community," "common good," and other terms that nearly everyone appeared to accept or defend in some way. There is an observable if not a consistent class difference, for example, on the very face of the argument over whether and how the pursuit of private gain ought to be moderated on behalf of the common good, for most workers and small farmers were slower than most businessmen and large farmers to accept the idea that self-interest was the very source of that good. But the difference ran deeper than that. Middle-class liberals tended to conceive of the common good in terms of abstract principles (not unlike those that ruled the marketplace itself) that took into account new forces and institutional arrangements, but that at the same time resisted significant changes in the structure of power and prestige in society. Bourgeois virtues were to them moral universals that both embraced and contained progress. Workers and small farmers who feared the effects of an unbridled pursuit of self-interest tended to conceive of a common good grounded in the particular traditions guiding relations within communities of equals, and in particular rights and guarantees of rights negotiated over long periods of time between the more and less powerful. Theirs was a plebeian conception – at bottom a clinging to hard-won gains by those who generally gained little – that at once promoted and imparted a deeply traditional cast to radical expressions of industrial and agrarian grievance. Both groups, in sum, promoted and resisted the liberal marketplace in defense of the common good. But the commonalities they defended – a commonwealth of principles and power on the one hand, one of particularities and rights on the other – were, perhaps ironically, the deepest difference between them.

This is not to suggest that understandings of the terms of debate were fixed, or that they aligned perfectly with social class divisions in all times and places. Historians have found local businessmen who supported striking workers in their protests against the practices of externally owned corporations, and have made it clear that there were workers and small farmers who embraced in varying degrees the entrepreneurial values we most easily associate with the middle class. Perhaps more importantly, the debate and its underlying assumptions shifted with the advance of capitalist markets, even for some of those who had the best reasons to contest the ways those markets worked. The small farmers of the Georgia upcountry that Steven Hahn has studied so effectively lived, before the Civil War, according to the traditional rights and understandings that we would expect to find in a relatively isolated local market economy. In the decades after the war, as these farmers turned increasingly to commercial cotton growing in the contexts of declining world cotton prices and mounting debt to the local organizers of external markets, they developed a protest movement based on "sensibilities at odds with the tenets of bourgeois individualism and the free market." Populists, Hahn argues, "did not wish to unfetter the 'invisible hand' of the marketplace; they wished to protect a 'liberty tree' rooted in petty ownership of productive resources."[16] But the upcountry Populist response was not entirely traditional, and not entirely hostile to the capitalist marketplace. The extralocal market, linked up by all those miles of rail, was now the given condition on which all the contests over principles and rights ultimately rested, and it did reshape the "liberty tree" of producers' rights to some extent. Small producers of the Georgia upcountry may not have been bourgeois individualists, but their daily efforts were increasingly directed toward, and routinized within, an individualizing capitalist market. As one historian has recently written, "Populists could only have escaped the influence of capitalism if they had lived in another age, another society, and another political culture."[17]

If the expansion of extralocal markets gradually shifted the ground under the feet of those who did not readily embrace entrepreneurial values, then the late nineteenth century's rapid centralization of capitalist institutions was an earthquake that shook the ground on which nearly all Americans stood. The integration of rail systems before and after the Civil

[16] Steven Hahn, *The Roots of Southern Populism: Yeoman Farmers and the Transformation of the Georgia Upcountry, 1850–1890* (New York, 1983), 282.
[17] Norman Pollack, *The Humane Economy: Populism, Capitalism, and Democracy* (New Brunswick, NJ, 1990), 58.

War, and the more sudden appearance of large industrial companies and combinations after the depression of the 1870s, made it clear that the capitalist market would not develop only as a diffuse array of relatively small, freely competing, units. There had always been inequalities of size and power in the American economy, but none that threatened to restructure the very nature of competition in the way that the Standard Oil Trust and other new giants portended. Was oligopoly, or perhaps even monopoly, where the "logic of endless accumulation" really led? This is not what free-market liberals intended, and the consolidations of the 1880s began to undermine the liberal faith. The popularity among middle-class readers of Edward Bellamy's socialist solution to ever-increasing centralization in his best-selling utopian novel *Looking Backward: 2000–1887* (in which Bellamy made socialism more palatable by calling it Nationalism, and by surrounding it with all the decorum of middle-class Victorian family life and romance) may be taken as one measure of this growing unease. But few middle-class Americans became enduring socialists, and the liberal faith was accommodated to and largely preserved within an increasingly corporate economy. This would not be done easily; indeed, achieving the corporate-liberal accommodation was one of the central cultural and political tasks of the generation to come.

POSTSCRIPT: 1890–1914

"The modern city marks an epoch in our civilization," wrote the reformer Frederic C. Howe in 1905. "Through it, a new society has been created. Life in all its relations has been altered."[18] To write this in 1905 was to recite a very common belief that the big city, the polyglot cultures that resided there, and powerful new institutions that were in varying degrees associated with urban development, were overwhelming an American society and culture deeply rooted in the life of the farm and the small town. In a real sense it was to fulfill Frederick Jackson Turner's warning, issued a dozen years earlier, that a new type of society was to follow upon the closing of the frontier. Howe was a little more sensitive than Turner to the difficulty of drawing such precise boundaries between rural and urban historical regimes. But in his turn-of-the-century description of the urban revolution it is the recent statistics that dominate, and that preach

---

[18] Frederic C. Howe, *The City: The Hope of Democracy* (New York, 1905), 9.

to the converted of a radically new social, economic, and political order, urgently in need of attention.

To set the trends of the new century in a longer perspective is not necessarily to dispel that urgency. Reasonable people could have read the short-term statistics of the era with a sense that America was reaching critical thresholds of urban development. Between 1890 and 1910, for example, the urban population increased from 35 percent to 45 percent of the national total, a trend that pointed clearly to an imminent urban majority. In New England and the Middle Atlantic states an already established urban majority now exceeded 70 percent. The number of cities exceeding 100,000 inhabitants increased over these years from twenty-eight to fifty. The nation's largest city was now a vast metropolis of more than 4.7 million inhabitants. These kinds of developments, which were visible even to those who did not read the census, established in people's minds the urban character of the American present and future, and no doubt encouraged an underestimation of the role of cities in the nation's more rural past. Equally important were perceived changes in the sources of urban growth, and in the character of cities as unsettling forces in American life. Native-born white Protestants did not have to read statistics to understand that cities were the collecting points of a growing ethnic diversity. That the numbers of foreign immigrants were steadily increasing – from fewer than a half-million per year around the turn of the century to an average of more than a million per year between 1905 and the outbreak of the war in Europe – could be seen in the crowded ghettos of every big city. Some could also see the emergence of significant black urban neighborhoods, as increasing numbers of African-Americans, driven by declining cotton prices and proliferating Jim Crow laws, left the rural south for the urban North. Both of these migrations, and the urban sub-communities they produced, deepened the sense of fundamental change centered in the nation's cities.

Howe placed the city at the center of the "new society," but others would have emphasized instead the power of the new corporate combinations. Though based in cities and clearly expressive of the growing role of city-centered manufacturing, commerce, and finance, the great corporations and trusts seemed also to transcend any specific place – to be centered nowhere in the process of being everywhere. Perhaps more accurately, they were themselves centers, exercising a new kind of power independent of the urban nodality even while they drew upon the city's resources and reshaped its skyline. Corporate combinations had developed, too, with a more frightening rapidity. The first of them had appeared in the 1880s and, as Martin J. Sklar has emphasized, the real "avalanche of corporate reorganization" occurred even more recently, during a brief six-year period beginning in 1898. By 1904 there had been some three hundred industrial consolidations representing about $7 billion in capital. More than three-quarters of these, capitalized at $6 billion, had occurred since 1898. About half of this capital was consolidated in only two years, 1899 and 1900.[19]

How was this rapid concentration of populations and power to be reconciled with the old liberalism of dispersal and open competition? For some Americans – those, for example, who found and then lost a political voice in the People's Party in the mid-1890s – such a reconciliation was difficult, if not impossible, and we must recognize some uncountable segment of the population who greeted the age of big cities and corporate capitalism with various combinations of rejection and denial. There remained considerable resources to support a seemingly traditional way of life in rural and small-town America. Family farms and Main Street stores relied upon the values and practices of proprietary enterprise no less than upon centralized capitalist markets and corporate suppliers and advertisers. Automobiles, telephones, and other new consumer goods influenced, but did not destroy, the patterns of small-town sociability. Still, to recognize only the traditional elements of local life increasingly required a parochialism that threatened well-being in direct proportion to its denial of the forces that did impinge on the economy and society of the countryside. At stake was the understanding of the very bases of economic survival, and of an evolving society that would, among other things, instruct one's children in the contemptible inadequacies of rural life. In his autobiography the city-born patrician Henry Adams identified himself, at once ruefully and smugly, as a "child of the seventeenth and eighteenth centuries" who was "required to play the game of the twentieth."[20] Ordinary folk who felt no less out of phase with modern times had also, in some measure, to "play the game" of the twentieth century.

Those who were less resistant to change were quick to point out how the rules of that game had changed. In the same year that Frederic Howe published his book on the new urban age, Simon Patten told an audience of social workers (and two years later a wide readership) that some of the

---

[19] Martin J. Sklar, *The Corporate Reconstruction of American Capitalism, 1890–1916: The Market, the Law, and Politics* (Cambridge, 1988), 45–46.
[20] Henry Adams, *The Education of Henry Adams* ([1907], Boston, 1971), 4.

most fundamental assumptions and values of the nineteenth century were now obsolete. Traditionally, production and saving were valued over consumption, and future abundance was predicated on present restraint. The "logic of endless accumulation," as we have seen, was tied to the practice of an array of bourgeois virtues, at the core of which was a surplus-yielding combination of industriousness and thrift. Patten argued that old virtues of this sort were now a drag on prosperity, not its source, and were a barrier to the extension of the benefits of prosperity to workers and the poor. They constituted an obsolete morality, which prevented us from seeing that in an economy of vast productive resources the real problem was underconsumption – not too little thrift, but too much. "The new morality," he argued, "does not consist in saving, but in expanding consumption; . . . not in the process of hardening, but in extending the period of recreation and leisure." What we have lacked, he continued, is the "courage to live joyous lives, not remorse, sacrifice, and renunciation." The poor, in particular, must be encouraged to consume, for "men need restraint only after poverty disappears."[21] This was an extraordinary reversal of economic principles and moral values, truly a "new basis of civilization." And though it did not inspire a wholesale abandonment of bourgeois virtues, it did underscore the need to create new truths for an age that seemed to differ fundamentally from what had gone before.

Patten's new truths were bold for the lecture platform, but in some respects they were anticipated in the responsiveness of millions of Americans to a host of new recreational institutions and consumer goods. The term "recreation" betrays an older moral stance toward the purpose and benefit of leisure-time activities, but in the "gay nineties" and beyond many Americans were learning how to pursue a good time without bothering to justify themselves in terms of moral or physical regeneration. Leisure time was itself expanding as the work day shortened (for factory workers, from an average of sixty hours per week in 1890 to fifty-five in 1914) and as the practice of taking regular vacations spread within the middle class. Middling Americans used their vacations to travel to seaside and mountain resorts and to national parks. On vacation and at home they amused themselves with Kodak cameras, Columbia bicycles, and other new leisure-time products. Industrial workers were generally not given vacations during this era, and could afford few of these new consumer goods, but they were able to join in the throngs that daily attended the

---

[21] Simon N. Patten, *The New Basis of Civilization* (New York, 1907), 215.

vaudeville shows, nickelodeons, and amusement parks that multiplied in and around the nation's cities. This unapologetic pursuit of amusement was most evident in cities, but the ascendance of a pleasure-oriented conception of the good life was more than an urban phenomenon. Symptomatic of the larger pattern of change was the booster literature directed toward rural and small-town Midwesterners by the Chamber of Commerce of the booming city of Los Angeles. At first, this literature emphasized traditional themes of agricultural, industrial, and commercial opportunity. After the turn of the century, however, it shifted decisively to new themes centered on leisure in a pleasant climate. Los Angeles was now the place to enjoy the new American good life – a life of pleasure, lived in the sun.

While Simon Patten and the Los Angeles Chamber of Commerce challenged the work-centered virtues of the previous age, others challenged long-standing fears of centralized institutions. The "promise of American life," argued Herbert Croly in 1909, lay not in the restoration of a Jeffersonian world of small, dispersed, competing units of production and exchange. That world was "essentially transient," and "contained within itself the seeds of its own dissolution and transformation." Competitive enterprise, that is, led naturally to the growth of the most creative and efficient businesses, whose increasing size and increasingly complex organization permitted still more impressive advances. To break up trusts and limit the market power of large corporations on behalf of an outdated ideal of small-scale competitive capitalism was, therefore, as foolish as it was futile. Croly was aware of the real and potential abuses of great power that the trusts and great corporations permitted, but where others saw only the danger of powerful men Croly saw also the promise of powerful institutions. "The new organization of American industry has created an economic mechanism which is capable of being wonderfully and indefinitely serviceable to the American people."[22]

Croly's book must be placed in the context of a wide-ranging debate over trusts, corporations, unions, and the state's role in regulating all of these centralizing institutions, that for some years had occupied the very center of American politics. This debate was more intense and more closely applied to fundamental principles than it was or has been in any other generation before or since. It was addressed, as Sklar writes, to the basic question, "could corporate capitalism and the American liberal tradition

---

[22] Herbert Croly, *The Promise of American Life* (New York, 1909), 104, 115.

be adapted the one to the other?"[23] Croly's book, which appeared relatively late in the debate, suggests that this issue was not yet settled, for large numbers of Americans still needed instruction in the ways in which modern institutions fulfilled the progressive aspects of the liberal dream. But it is also symptomatic of the enduring political resolution that would appear by 1914 in the Wilsonian version of what Sklar has called corporate liberalism, the acceptance of a state-regulated, but not state-directed, corporate capitalism. Was it symptomatic as well of a broad popular accommodation to the massive organizations that, after all, produced the harvesting machine that sat out behind the barn, and the uniform white flour that sat on the kitchen counter? In the same year as the Federal Trade Commission and Clayton Antitrust acts, a young Walter Lippmann looked back at William Jennings Bryan's campaign of 1896. "What Bryan was really defending," wrote Lippmann, "was the old and simple life of America, a life that was doomed by the great organization that had come into the world. He thought he was fighting the plutocracy: as a matter of fact he was fighting something much deeper than that; he was fighting the larger scale of human life."[24] What Croly and Lippmann both sensed was that Americans already did accept, in their daily experience and in their expectations for the future, the "larger scale of human life."

[23] Sklar, *Corporate Reconstruction*, 34.
[24] Walter Lippmann, *Drift and Mastery* ([1914], Englewood Cliffs, 1961), 80–81.

BIBLIOGRAPHIC ESSAYS

CHAPTER 1 (GALLMAN)

Notable contemporary efforts to measure the scale and performance of the U.S. economy were made in the nineteenth century. (See Robert E. Gallman, "Estimates of American National Product Made Before the Civil War," in *Economic Development and Cultural Change*, 9 [1961, supplement 397–412]). The best of this work was by Ezra Champion Seaman, *Essays on the Progress of Nations* (New York, 1846, Supplement I, 1847, Supplement II, 1848, 2nd ed. 1852, 3rd ed. 1865); see also, *The American System of Government* (New York, 1870). Seamen invented a conceptual system very like modern national accounts and made excellent estimates for 1840, 1850, 1860, and 1869. He also derived the size distribution of income in the late 1860s, on the basis of income tax data.

In the early twentieth century Willford Isbell King and Robert F. Martin (the latter on behalf of the National Industrial Conference Board) prepared national product figures for various dates in the nineteenth century: King, *The Wealth and Income of the People of the United States* (New York, 1919) and Martin, *National Income in the United States, 1799–1938* (New York, 1939). The Martin estimates for the antebellum years were subject to a devastating critique by Simon Kuznets ("Long-Term Changes in the National Income of the United States of America since 1870," in Simon Kuznets [ed.] *Income and Wealth in the United States, Trends and Structure*, Income and Wealth, Series II [Cambridge, 1952], 221–41, and "National Income Estimates for the United States prior to 1870," *Journal of Economic History*, 12 [1952], 115–30). Modern efforts to measure the large nineteenth-century aggregates were initiated by William Howard

Shaw, *Value of Commodity Output since 1869* (New York, 1947), who modified and extended backward from 1919 to 1889 Simon Kuznets's annual series of the value of commodity output, consisting of final output flows, in producers' prices. Shaw also added estimates for the two census years, 1869 and 1879. His book is an important achievement.

On the basis of Shaw's work, Kuznets built up GNP series covering the period 1869–1919, by deriving inventory changes, the cost of distribution, and final expenditures on services, and adding these data to Shaw's commodity flow series. Kuznets also produced annual figures for 1870–78 and 1880–88, although he never published them, except as elements of decade averages: Simon Kuznets, *National Product since 1869* (New York, 1946); *Capital in the American Economy, Its Formation and Financing* (Princeton, 1961); "Long-Term Changes in the National Income of the United States of America since 1870." Kuznets's final series consist of three variants (*Capital in the American Economy*), differing in concept and in the methods by which the annual estimates were derived. So far as trends are concerned, the three tell roughly the same story. See also, John W. Kendrick, *Productivity Trends in the United States* (Princeton, 1961), for a comprehensive analysis of productivity changes between 1889 and 1957.

Robert Gallman next proposed changes to the Shaw and Kuznets series, involving the value of perishables, the value of distribution, and the value of services. He also made use of new deflators (base 1860), that had been prepared by Dorothy S. Brady, based on true retail prices. Finally, he extended the series into the antebellum years, 1834–1859. The work of Brady and Gallman appeared in Volume 30 of Studies in Income and Wealth: Brady, "Price Deflators for Final Product Estimates," and Gallman, "Gross National Product in the United States, 1834–1909," both in Dorothy S. Brady (ed.), *Output, Employment, and Productivity in the United States After 1800*, Studies in Income and Wealth, vol. 30 (New York, 1966), 3–115. See also, Brady's fine essay on price index numbers, 'Relative Prices in the Nineteenth Century," *Journal of Economic History* 25 (1964), 145–203. Earlier, Gallman had prepared estimates of value added by the commodity-producing sectors of the economy, and subsequently, with Thomas J. Weiss, he published estimates of value added by the tertiary industries: Gallman, "Commodity Output, 1839–1899," in William N. Parker (ed.), *Trends in the American Economy in the Nineteenth Century*, Studies in Income and Wealth, vol. 24 (Princeton, 1960), 13–67; and Gallman and Weiss, "The Service Industries in the Nineteenth Century," in Victor R. Fuchs (ed.), *Production and Productivity in the Service Industries*, Studies in Income and Wealth, vol. 34 (New York, 1969), 287–365. The series in these two volumes, taken together, provide approximations to GNP, measured from the sectoral income side, to complement the volume 30 estimates, which are measured from the final flow side.

The Gallman final flow GNP series were in turn revised by Christina D. Romer and by Nathan S. Balke and Robert J. Gordon. The revised series were published in the form of annual estimates: Balke and Gordon; "The Estimation of Prewar Gross National Product: Methodology and New Evidence," and Romer, "The Prewar Business Cycle Reconsidered: New Estimates of Gross National Product, 1869–1908," both in *Journal of Political Economy*, 97 (1989), 1–92. Balke and Gordon introduced new evidence on transportation and communications, and both Balke/Gordon and Romer devised new techniques for estimating the annual fluctuations in GNP. Neither new series altered markedly the long-term patterns of growth exhibited by the series they were designed to replace, but they did yield different patterns of fluctuation – different from those of the earlier series, and from each other.

Many efforts have been made to describe the growth of aggregate output before 1834. The work along these lines up to the early 1980s is reviewed by Stanley L. Engerman and Robert E. Gallman, "U.S. Economic Growth, 1783–1860," in *Research in Economic History*, 8 (1983), 1–46, which contains a comprehensive bibliography. In the years since then, Thomas J. Weiss has provided new labor force estimates, which have served as the bases for new real GDP estimates for the years 1774, 1793, 1800, 1807, 1810, 1820, 1830, 1840, 1850, and 1860. The text of this chapter depends upon the Weiss figures. See "U.S. Labor Force Estimates and Economic Growth, 1800–1860," in Robert E. Gallman and John Joseph Wallis (eds.), *American Economic Growth and Standards of Living Before the Civil War* (Chicago, 1992), 19–75, which draws together and extends his earlier work. Thomas Senior Berry has prepared annual estimates beginning in 1789 and linking with the work of John Kendrick and Simon Kuznets late in the nineteenth century, a revision of a series reviewed by Engerman and Gallman: *Production and Population since 1789, Revised GNP Series in Constant Dollars*, Bostwick Paper No. 6 (Richmond, VA, 1988).

Notable discussions of the concept of national product are contained in Simon Kuznets, *Economic Change* (New York, 1953), chaps. 6 and 7; Kuznets, *National Income, A Summary of Findings* (New York, 1946); *A*

Critique of the United States Income and Product Accounts, Studies in Income and Wealth, vol. 22 (Princeton, 1958), especially the essays by George Jaszi, Raymond Bowman, and Richard Easterlin as well as the exchange between Easterlin and Jaszi; Milton Moss (ed.), *The Measurement of Economic and Social Performance*, Studies in Income and Wealth, vol. 38 (New York, 1973); and Dan Usher, *Rich and Poor Countries, A Study in Problems of Comparisons of Real Income* (Hereford, 1966).

An interpretation of long-term American economic growth is contained in the work of Moses Abramovitz and Paul A. David: "Economic Growth in America: Historical Parables and Realities," *De Economist*, 121 (1973), 251–72; "Reinterpreting Economic Growth: Parables and Realities of the American Experience," *American Economic Review, Papers and Proceedings* 63 (1973), 428–39 (a short version of the *De Economist* paper); Abramovitz alone: "The Search for the Sources of Growth," *Journal of Economic History*, 53 (1993), 217–43; David alone: "Invention and Accumulation in American Economic Growth: A Nineteenth Century Parable," in K. Brunner and A. Meltzer, (eds.), *International Organization, National Policies and Economic Development* (Amsterdam, 1977); David with John L. Scadding, "Private Savings: Ultrarationality, Aggregation, and 'Denison's Law'," *Journal of Political Economy*, 82 (1974), 225–49. See also, Jeffrey G. Williamson, *Late Nineteenth-Century American Development: A General Equilibrium History* (Cambridge, 1974).

The very extensive debate over the causes of the rise in the U.S. savings and investment rates is reviewed in Lance E. Davis and Robert E. Gallman, "Savings, Investment, and Economic Growth: The United States in the Nineteenth Century," in John A. James and Mark Thomas (eds.), *Capitalism in Context* (Chicago, 1994), 202–29. This paper contains a comprehensive bibliography. (It should be said that Davis and Gallman have been active participants in the debate and hold a position not universally assented to.) For a dissenting view with regard to the convergence of regional interest rates, see Howard Bodenhorn and Hugh Rockoff, "Regional Interest Rates in Antebellum America," in Claudia Goldin and Hugh Rockoff (eds.), *Strategic Factors in Nineteenth-Century Economic History: A Volume to Honor Robert W. Fogel* (Chicago, 1992), 159–88.

Measurements of the capital stock and interpretations of its growth are contained in: Kuznets, *National Product since 1869*; Raymond Goldsmith, "The Growth of Reproducible Wealth of the United States of America from 1805 to 1950," in Kuznets (ed.), *Income and Wealth of the United States,*

Trends and Structure, 245–328; Robert E. Gallman, "The United States Capital Stock in the Nineteenth Century," in Stanley L. Engerman and Robert E. Gallman (eds.), *Long-Term Factors in American Economic Growth*, Studies in Income and Wealth, vol. 51 (Chicago, 1986), 165–206; Robert E. Gallman, "Investment Flows and Capital Stocks: U.S. Experience in the Nineteenth Century," in Peter Kilby (ed.), *Quantity and Quiddity, Essays in U.S. Economic History* (Middletown, 1987), 214–54; Robert E. Gallman, "American Economic Growth before the Civil War: The Testimony of the Capital Stock Estimates," in Gallman and Wallis (eds.), *American Economic Growth and Standards of Living Before the Civil War*, 79–115.

As to alternative indexes of well-being, see Clayne Pope, "Adult Mortality in America before 1900: A View from Family Histories," in Goldin and Rockoff (eds.), *Strategic Factors in American Economic History, A Volume to Honor Robert W. Fogel* (Chicago, 1992), 267–96, and the essay by Michael Haines, Chap. 4 in this volume. The work on anthropometric measures is extensive. See in particular, Robert William Fogel, "Nutrition and the Decline in Mortality since 1700: Some Preliminary Findings," in Engerman and Gallman, (eds.), *Long-Term Factors in American Economic Growth*, 439–527; Richard H. Steckel, "Stature and Living Standards in the United States," in Gallman and Wallis (eds.), *American Economic Growth and Standards of Living before the Civil War*, 265–308. Both of these pieces contain extensive bibliographies. Steckel's paper for the *Journal of Economic Literature*, "Stature and the Standard of Living," *JEL*, 33 (1995), 1903–40, treats the subject very fully and also has an excellent bibliography. On the relationship between economic growth and human happiness, see Richard A. Easterlin, "Does Economic Growth Improve the Human Lot?" in Paul A. David and Melvin W. Reder (eds.), *Nations and Households in Economic Growth: Essays in Honor of Moses Abramovitz* (New York, 1974), 89–125, and *Growth Triumphant, The Twenty-first Century in Historical Perspective* (Ann Arbor, 1996).

On consumption, see Lorena S. Walsh, "Consumer Behavior, Diet, and the Standard of Living in Late Colonial and Early Antebellum America, 1770–1840," in Gallman and Wallis (eds.), *American Economic Growth and Standards of Living before the Civil War*, 217–61. The essay contains an extensive bibliography. See also, Dorothy S. Brady, "Consumption and the Style of Life," in Lance E. Davis, Richard A. Easterlin, William N. Parker, et al., *American Economic Growth, An Economist's History of the United States* (New York, 1972), 61–89. The entire volume remains a useful treatment of long-term American economic growth, with emphasis on quantitative aspects of growth.

Two essays by Richard A. Easterlin provide an excellent view of regional economic development: "Interregional Differences in Per Capita Income, Population, and Total Income, 1840–1950," in Parker (ed.), *Trends in the American Economy in the Nineteenth Century*, 73–140; "Regional Income Trends, 1840–1950," in Seymour E. Harris (ed.), *American Economic History* (New York, 1961), 525–47.

For the economic consequences of the Civil War, see Stanley L. Engerman, "The Economic Impact of the Civil War," *Explorations in Entrepreneurial History*, Second Series, 3 (1966), 176–99, Claudia Goldin and Frank Lewis, "The Economic Cost of the American Civil War: Estimates and Implications," *Journal of Economic History*, 35 (1975), 299–326, and Stanley L. Engerman and J. Matthew Gallman, "The Civil War Economy: A Modern View," in Stig Förster and Jörg Nagler, *On the Road to Total War: The American Civil War and the German Wars of Unification* (Cambridge, 1996), 217–47. The long swing is treated in Simon Kuznets, "Long Swings in the Growth of Population and Related Economic Variables," in *Proceedings of the American Philosophical Society*, 102 (1958), 25–52, reprinted in Kuznets, *Economic Growth and Structure: Selected Essays* (New York, 1965), 328–78. See also, two essays in *Economic Development and Cultural Change*, 9 (1961) supplement: Moses Abramovitz, "The Nature and Significance of Kuznets Cycles," 225–48, and Richard A. Easterlin, "Influences in European Overseas Emigration Before World War I," 331–51. Easterlin's book, *Population, Labor Force, and Long Swings in Economic Growth* (New York, 1968) analyzes the long swing in the nineteenth and twentieth centuries. Moses Abramovitz considers the same topic in "The Passing of the Kuznets Cycle," *Economica*, New Series, 35 (1968), 349–67. This paper and "The Nature and Significance of Kuznets Cycles" are reprinted in Abramovitz, *Thinking About Growth* (Cambridge, 1989), 245–97. Abramovitz treats the relations among the balance of payments, the money stock, and long swings in "The Monetary Side of Long Swings in U.S. Economic Growth," Center for Economic Policy Research, Publication No. 471 (Stanford, 1973). Douglass C. North's treatment of the subject is in *The Economic Growth of the United States, 1790–1860* (Englewood Cliffs, 1961), and Brinley Thomas's in *Migration and Economic Growth* (Cambridge, 1954). For the role of the balance of payments, see Jeffrey G. Williamson, *American Growth and the Balance of Payments, 1820–1913* (Chapel Hill, 1964). J. D. Gould critically reviewed the literature in "European Inter-Continental Emigration 1815–1914: Patterns and Causes," *Journal of European Economic History*, 8 (1979), 593–680.

CHAPTER 2 (MCINNIS)

Canada has not been abundantly served with comprehensive economic histories. Until recently there was little to choose from, but in the past fifteen years several new texts have appeared. The most up to date is the second edition of Kenneth Norrie and Douglas Owram, *A History of the Canadian Economy* (Toronto, 1996). The revised second edition of Richard Pomfret, *The Economic Development of Canada* (Toronto, 1993) offers a compressed, if rather superficial, overview. Graham Taylor and Peter Baskerville, *A Concise History of Business in Canada* (Toronto, 1994) is as much a general economic history as a business history and offers a fresh perspective on many topics. William Marr and Donald Paterson, *Canada: An Economic History* (Toronto, 1980), while the first of the new generation of textbooks, is rather uneven and now somewhat dated.

The tone and general outline of what became, and to a considerable extent continues to be, the dominant interpretation of Canadian economic development was set by Oscar Skelton, *General Economic History of the Dominion, 1867–1912* (Toronto, 1913), perhaps more readily found as a lengthy chapter in the multi-volume history *Canada and Its Provinces*. This "staples" interpretation reached its most extended treatment in W. T. Easterbrook and Hugh Aitken, *Canadian Economic History* (Toronto, 1956), a text that for a very long time remained the standard. It still provides more detailed treatment of many topics than its more up-to-date alternatives. Two recently published anthologies that are useful are Douglas McCalla and Michael Huberman (eds.), *Perspectives on Canadian Economic History*, 2nd ed. (Toronto, 1994) and M. T. Watkins and H. M. Grant (eds.), *Canadian Economic History: Classic and Contemporary Approaches* (Ottawa, 1993).

The pioneer quantitative study of Canadian economic development, O. J. Firestone, *Canada's Economic Development, 1867–1953* (London, 1958) has now largely been superseded by M. C. Urquhart et al., *Gross National Product, Canada, 1870–1926: The Derivation of the Estimates* (Kingston, 1993). The latter is now the authoritative source of Canadian historical national income statistics and their components. Much useful material on nineteenth-century Canada is also to be found in Louis Gentilcore (ed.),

Historical Atlas of Canada: Volume II, The Land Transformed, 1800–1891 (Toronto, 1993).

The numerous regional general histories tend to be sketchy on economic issues, and the economic histories of the individual regions focus on limited time periods. An exception is Robert Armstrong, *Structure and Change: An Economic History of Quebec* (Toronto, 1984). Fernand Ouellet, *Economic and Social History of Quebec, 1760–1850* (Toronto, 1980) provides an abundance of material on the earlier period and offers an interpretation that has been quite controversial. For Ontario a superb account of the pre-Confederation period is to be found in Douglas McCalla, *Planting the Province: The Economic History of Upper Canada, 1784–1870* (Toronto, 1993). Its companion piece by Ian Drummond, *Progress Without Planning: The Economic History of Ontario from Confederation to the Second World War* (Toronto, 1987) is somewhat uneven but provides a lot of quantitative evidence. S. A. Saunders, *The Economic History of the Maritime Provinces* (Ottawa, 1939) was originally written for a Canadian Royal Commission but has been reprinted (Fredericton, 1984). There has been no comparable comprehensive economic history of the western regions.

The Loyalist influx is covered by Christopher Moore, *The Loyalists: Revolution, Exile, Settlement* (Toronto, 1984). On settlement and early agriculture in the Maritime colonies see A. R. MacNeil, "Early American Communities in the Fundy: A Case Study of Annapolis and Amherst Townships, 1767–1827," *Agricultural History*, 62 (1989), 101–19; the same author's "The Acadian Legacy and Agricultural Development in Nova Scotia, 1760–1861," in Kris Inwood (ed.), *Farm, Factory and Fortune: New Studies in the Economic History of the Maritime Provinces* (Fredericton, 1993); and Graeme Wynn, "Late Eighteenth-Century Agriculture in the Bay of Fundy Marshlands," in Phillip Buckner and David Frank (eds.), *Atlantic Canada Before Confederation* (Fredericton, 1985); also Andrew Hill Clark, *Three Centuries and the Island: A Historical Geography of Settlement and Agriculture in Prince Edward Island, Canada* (Toronto, 1959). The agricultural economy of early central Canada and the role of wheat as a "staple" export is the subject of John McCallum, *Unequal Beginnings: Agriculture and Economic Development in Quebec and Ontario until 1870* (Toronto, 1980). A critical view of that approach is found in Marvin McInnis, *Perspectives on Ontario Agriculture* (Gananoque, 1992). The most thorough and up-to-date account is given by Douglas McCalla, *Planting the Province*. Early immigration and settlement is thoroughly examined by Norman MacDonald, *Canada, 1763–1841: Immigration and Settlement*

(London, 1939), but the authoritative source on immigration is Helen Cowan, *British Emigration to British North America: The First Hundred Years*, rev. ed. (Toronto, 1961). On the disposition of land in Upper Canada see Lillian Gates, *Land Policies of Upper Canada* (Toronto, 1968). The Canada Land Company deserves more thorough study but Clarence Karr, *The Canada Land Company: The Early Years* (Toronto, 1974) makes a start. Other aspects of early agriculture in Canada are treated by Peter Russell, "Forest Into Farmland: Upper Canadian Clearing Rates, 1822–1839," *Agricultural History*, 57 (1983), 326–39 and the same author's "Upper Canada: A Poor Man's Country? Some Statistical Evidence," *Canadian Papers in Rural History*, 3 (1978), 129–47. See also two papers by Marvin McInnis – "Marketable Surpluses in Ontario Farming, 1860," *Social Science History*, 8 (1984), 395–424; and "The Size Structure of Farming, Canada West, 1861," *Research in Economic History*, supplement 5 (1989), 313–29.

The state of agriculture in French Canada in the early nineteenth century has been a topic of great and heated debate that is reviewed in R. M. McInnis, "A Reconsideration of the State of Agriculture in Lower Canada in the First Half of the Nineteenth Century," *Canadian Papers in Rural History*, 3 (1982), 9–49. See also Serge Courville and Normand Seguin, *Rural Life in 19th Century Quebec* (Ottawa, 1989). A quantitative assessment is provided by Frank Lewis and Marvin McInnis, "Agricultural Output and Efficiency in Lower Canada, 1851," *Research in Economic History*, 9 (1984), 45–87.

The classic work on the timber and lumber trade was done by A. R. M. Lower. See his *Settlement and the Forest Frontier in Eastern Canada* (Toronto, 1936); *The North American Assault on the Canadian Forest* (Toronto, 1938); and *Great Britain's Woodyard: British America and the Timber Trade* (Montreal, 1974). Refer also to Graeme Wynn, *Timber Colony: A Historical Geography of Early Nineteenth Century New Brunswick* (Toronto, 1981). The effects of termination of colonial protection by Great Britain are surveyed by Gilbert Tucker, *The Canadian Commercial Revolution, 1845–1851* (Ottawa, 1970). On the Canada–U.S. Reciprocity Treaty of 1854 see Robert Ankli, "The Reciprocity Treaty of 1854," *Canadian Journal of Economics*, 4 (1971), 1–20 and Lawrence Officer and Lawrence Smith, "The Canadian American Reciprocity Treaty of 1855 to 1866," *Journal of Economic History*, 28 (1968), 598–623. On an early Canadian move towards protectionism see D. F. Barnett, "The Galt Tariff: Incidental or Effective Protection?" *Canadian Journal of Economics*, 9 (1976), 389–407, and A. A.

Den Otter, "Alexander Galt, the 1859 Tariff and Canadian Economic Nationalism," *Canadian Historical Review*, 58 (1982), 151–78.

An early, comprehensive history of transport in Canada is G. P. de T. Glazebrook, *A History of Transportation in Canada* (Toronto, 1938). An even earlier classic on canal development is T. C. Keefer, *The Canals of Canada* (Montreal, 1894). There is no cliometric study of Canadian canals but see also Hugh Aitken, *The Welland Canal Company: A Study in Canadian Enterprise* (Cambridge, MA, 1954) and Thomas McIlwraith, "Freight Capacity and Utilization of the Erie and Great Lakes Canals before 1850," *Journal of Economic History*, 36 (1976), 852–75. In addition to the general works that give a lot of attention to transport development generally and to railways in particular, early railway development is covered by A. W. Currie, *The Grand Trunk Railway of Canada* (Toronto, 1957), G. R. Stevens, *The Canadian National Railways*, vol. 1 (Toronto, 1962); T. C. Keefer, *Philosophy of Railroads* (orig. published 1850, revised edition with introduction by H. V. Nelles, Toronto, 1972); and Ann Carlos and Frank Lewis, "The Profitability of Early Canadian Railroads," in Claudia Goldin and Hugh Rockoff, eds., *Strategic Factors in Nineteenth Century American Economic Growth: A Volume to Honor Robert W. Fogel* (Chicago, 1992).

The literature on early industrialization in Canada is limited and under-developed but see Peter Goheen, *Victorian Toronto 1850 to 1900* (Chicago, 1970); Gerald Tulchinsky, *The River Barons: Montreal Businessmen and the Growth of Industry and Transportation, 1837–53* (Kingston, 1978); J. M. Gilmour, *Spatial Evolution of Manufacturing: Southern Ontario, 1851–1891* (Toronto, 1972); and Jacob Spelt, *Urban Development in South-Central Ontario* (Toronto, 1972). The lagging state of the Maritime provinces is considered by Kris Inwood, "Maritime Industrialization from 1870 to 1910: A Review of the Evidence and its Interpretation," in Inwood (ed.), *Farm, Factory and Fortune: New Studies in the Economic History of the Maritime Provinces* (Fredericton, 1993).

On the Confederation arrangements see Donald Creighton, *British North America at Confederation: A Study Prepared for the Royal Commission on Dominion-Provincial Relations* (Ottawa, 1939); Ged Martin (ed.), *The Causes of Canadian Confederation* (Fredericton, 1990); W. L. Morton, *Canada, 1857–1873: The Critical Years* (Toronto, 1964), and Phillip Buckner, "The Maritimes and Confederation," *Canadian Historical Review*, 71 (1990), 1–45. Confederation, railway building, western settlement, and tariff protection as an integrated development strategy is a well-developed standby of Canadian history. Among the better and more prominent treatments are W. A. Mackintosh, *The Economic Background of Dominion-Provincial Relations* (Ottawa, 1939) and V. C. Fowke, *The National Policy and the Wheat Economy* (Toronto, 1957). A critical assessment is offered by John Dales, "Some Historical and Theoretical Comments on Canada's National Policies," *Queen's Quarterly*, 71 (1964), 297–316. Also consult Doug Owram, *Promise of Eden: The Canadian Expansionist Movement and the Idea of the North West, 1856–1900* (Toronto, 1992).

The conventional view of the post-Confederation period as one of slow and halting growth is well represented by Skelton (1913), Mackintosh (1939), and Easterbrook and Aitken (1956). It was challenged by Firestone (1958) and by Gordon Bertram, "Economic Growth in Canadian Industry, 1870–1914: The Staple Model and the Take-Off Hypothesis," *Canadian Journal of Economics and Political Science*, 29 (1963), 159–84. See also Gordon Bertram, "Historical Statistics on Growth and Structure of Manufacturing in Canada, 1870–1957," in J. Henripin and A. Asimakopoulos (eds.), *Conference on Statistics, 1962 and 1963* (Toronto, 1964); Duncan McDougall, "Canadian Manufactured Commodity Output, 1870–1915," *Canadian Journal of Economics*, 4 (1971), 21–36; and E. Vickery, "Exports and North American Economic Growth, 'Structuralist' and 'Staplist' Models in Historical Perspective," *Canadian Journal of Economics*, 7 (1974), 189–206. M. Altman, "A Revision of Canadian Economic Growth 1870–1910 A Challenge to the Gradualist Interpretation," *Canadian Journal of Economics*, 20 (1987), 86–107, points to a return to a more pessimistic interpretation.

The building of the Canadian Pacific Railway has been the topic of much attention. Classic studies range from the scholarly Harold Innis, *A History of the Canadian Pacific Railway* (Toronto, 1930) to the popular and racy Pierre Berton, *The National Dream: The Great Railway, 1874–1881* (Toronto, 1970). Estimates of "excess subsidy" to the Canadian Pacific Railway are made by Peter George, "Rates of Return to Railway Investment in Canada," *Canadian Journal of Economics*, 1 (1968), 740–62 and Lloyd Mercer, "Rates of Return and Government Subsidization of the Canadian Pacific Railway," *Canadian Journal of Economics*, 6 (1973), 428–37.

CHAPTER 3 (POPE)

The most comprehensive sample of nineteenth-century wealth may be found in Lee Soltow, *Men and Wealth in the United States, 1850–1870*

(New Haven, 1975). The results of Soltow's national samples may be usefully compared with wealth estimates in Alice Hanson Jones, *Wealth of a Nation to Be* (New York, 1980) and Lee Soltow, *Distribution of Wealth and Income in the United States in 1798* (Pittsburgh, 1989). Both Jeffrey Williamson and Peter Lindert, *American Inequality: A Macroeconomic History* (New York, 1980) and their "Three Centuries of American Inequality," *Research in Economic History*, 1 (1976), 69–123 draw on disparate sources to offer an interpretation of the trends in inequality of wealth and wages. They, like many others, consider Kuznets's hypothesis about the relationship of inequality to economic growth, which was first articulated in Simon Kuznets, "Economic Growth and Income Inequality," *American Economic Review*, 45 (1955), 1–27. Kuznets reviews more quantitative evidence in "Quantitative Aspects of the Economic Growth of Nations: Distribution of Income by Size," in *Economic Development and Cultural Change*, 11 (1963), 1–80. Jeremy Atack and Fred Bateman, *To Their Own Soil: Agriculture in the Antebellum North* (Ames, IA, 1987) is based on a large sample of Northern farmers for 1860. Robert Gallman, "Trends in the Size Distribution of Wealth in the Nineteenth Century," in Lee Soltow (ed.), *Six Papers on the Size Distribution of Wealth and Income*, Studies in Income and Wealth, vol. 33 (New York, 1969) uses the demographic trends and structural shifts of the nineteenth century to examine the trend in inequality. Joseph Ferrie, *Yankeys Now: Immigrants in the Antebellum United States, 1840–1860* (New York, 1999), examines the fortunes of mid-nineteenth-century immigrants and their adjustment to the opportunities available to them.

Comparisons of European inequality to that of the United States may be done with Y. S. Brenner, Harmut Kaelble, and Mark Thomas (eds.), *Income Distribution in Historical Perspective* (Cambridge, 1991); P. H. Lindert and J. G. Williamson, "Reinterpreting Britain's Social Tables, 1688–1913," *Explorations in Economic History*, 20 (1976), 94–109; and Soltow, *Distribution of Wealth and Income in the United States in 1798*, chap. 6.

The best summary of nineteenth-century occupational mobility in the United States is found in Stephan Thernstrom, *The Other Bostonians* (Cambridge, MA, 1973), especially chap. 9. Other important studies of urban mobility include Stephan Thernstrom, *Poverty and Progress* (Cambridge, MA, 1964), Clyde and Sally Griffen, *Natives and Newcomers* (Cambridge, MA, 1978), and Michael B. Katz, *The People of Hamilton, Canada West* (Cambridge, MA, 1975) for a Canadian perspective. Richard

Steckel, "Poverty and Prosperity: A Longitudinal Study of Wealth Accumulation, 1850--1860," *Review of Economics and Statistics*, 72 (1990), 275–85 examines movement of households within the distributions of real estate wealth in 1850 and 1860.

A number of studies of wealth and its covariates have substantially expanded the knowledge of wealth distributions for certain locales. Before reviewing those studies, it might be well to look at Timothy G. Conley and David W. Galenson, "Quantile Regression Analysis of Censored Wealth Data," *Historical Methods*, 27 (1994), 149–65, which raises serious methodological issues about the use of conventional regression techniques with mid-nineteenth-century wealth data. Place-specific studies include Trempeauleau County, Wisconsin, found in Merle Curti et al., *The Making of an American Community* (Stanford, 1959); and in Lee Soltow, *Wealthholding in Wisconsin* (Madison, 1971); Chicago, found in David W. Galenson, "Economic Opportunity on the Urban Frontier," *Journal of Economic History* 51 (1991), 581–601; rural Missouri, found in Mary Gregson, "Wealth Accumulation and Distribution in the Midwest in the Late Nineteenth Century," *Explorations in Economic History* 33 (1996), 524–38; Boston, found in Steven Herscovici, "The Distribution of Wealth in Nineteenth Century Boston: Inequality among Natives and Immigrants, 1860," *Explorations in Economic History* 30 (1993), 321–35; Appanoose County, Iowa, found in David W. Galenson and Clayne Pope, "Economic and Geographic Mobility on the Farming Frontier: Evidence from Appanoose County, Iowa, 1850–1870," *Journal of Economic History*, 49 (1989), 635–56; Texas, in Randolph B. Campbell and Richard G. Lowe, *Wealth and Power in Antebellum Texas* (College Station, TX, 1977) and in Donald Schaefer, "A Model of Migration and Wealth Accumulations: Farmers at the Antebellum Southern Frontier," *Explorations in Economic History*, 24 (1987), 130–57. Livio Di Matteo and Peter George, "Canadian Wealth Inequality in the Late Nineteenth Century: A Study of Wentworth County, Ontario, 1872–1902," *Canadian Historical Review*, 73 (1992), 453–83; Livio Di Matteo, "The Wealth of the Irish in Nineteenth-Century Ontario," *Social Science History*, 20 (1996), 209–33; and Gordon Darroch and Lee Soltow, *Property and Inequality in Victorian Ontario: Structural Patterns and Cultural Communities in the 1871 Census* (Toronto, 1994) give examples of local Canadian inequality for comparison purposes.

The unusual data resources of Utah have been extensively used to consider many dimensions of wealth and income distributions, starting with J. R. Kearl, Clayne L. Pope, and Larry T. Wimmer, "The Distribution of Wealth in a Settlement Economy: Utah 1850–1870," *Journal of Economic History*, 40 (1980), 477–96. A summary of most of this work may be found in Clayne Pope, "Households on the American Frontier: the Distribution of Income and Wealth in Utah, 1850–1900," in David W. Galenson (ed.), *Markets in History: Economics Studies of the Past* (Cambridge, 1989). J. R. Kearl and Clayne Pope, "Choices, Rents, and Luck: Economic Mobility of Nineteenth Century Utah Households," in Stanley L. Engerman and Robert E. Gallman (eds.) *Long-Term Factors in American Economic Growth*, Studies in Income and Wealth, vol. 51, (Chicago, 1986) examines occupational mobility in Utah, while Kearl and Pope, "Wealth Mobility: The Missing Element," *Journal of Interdisciplinary History*, 13 (1983), 461–88 summarizes wealth and income mobility. Kearl and Pope, "Unobservable Family and Individual Contributions to the Distributions of Income and Wealth," *Journal of Labor Economics*, 4 (1986), 548–79 measures the influences of family background on income and wealth.

CHAPTER 4 (HAINES)

There exist a number of comprehensive monographs and papers on the American population. Among the classic works, see Warren S. Thompson and P. K. Whelpton, *Population Trends in the United States* (New York, 1933); Conrad Taeuber and Irene B. Taeuber, *The Changing Population of the United States* (New York, 1958); and Wilson H. Grabill, Clyde Kiser, and Pascal K. Whelpton, *The Fertility of American Women* (New York, 1958). Among more recent works, the reader is directed to Richard A. Easterlin, "The American Population," in Lance E. Davis, Richard A. Easterlin, William N. Parker, et al., *American Economic Growth: An Economist's History of the United States* (New York, 1972), 121–83; "Population Issues in American Economic History: A Survey and Critique," in Robert Gallman (ed.), *Recent Developments in the Study of Business and Economic History: Essays in Honor of Herman E. Krooss* (Greenwich, CT, 1977), 131–58; and Robert V. Wells, *Uncle Sam's Family: Issues in and Perspectives on American Demographic History* (Albany, 1985). An overview of more recent population information is found in Donald J. Bogue, *The Population of the United States: Historical Trends and Future Projections* (New York, 1985). An excellent collection of articles up to the late 1970s is furnished in Maris A. Vinovskis (ed.), *Studies in American Historical Demography* (New York, 1979). The best compilation of statistical information remains U.S. Bureau of the Census, *Historical Statistics of the United States, Colonial Times to 1970* (Washington, DC, 1975), chaps. A–D. The best straight-forward coverage of demographic methods with a good discussion of the statistics of the United States is Henry S. Shryock, Jacob S. Siegel, and associates, *The Methods and Materials of Demography* (Washington, DC, 1971). The published federal census volumes have now been reprinted up through 1880, and the published state and territorial censuses have been reprinted in a microfiche collection. An up-to-date discussion of mortality in nineteenth-century America may be found in Samuel H. Preston and Michael R. Haines, *Fatal Years: Child Mortality in Late Nineteenth Century America* (Princeton, 1991). A recent synthetic work on immigration is John Bodnar, *The Transplanted: A History of Immigrants in Urban America* (Bloomington, 1985). Other references are in the footnotes to Chapter 4.

CHAPTER 5 (MARGO)

Basic statistics on the nineteenth-century labor force may be found in U.S. Bureau of the Census, *Historical Statistics of the United States, Colonial Times to 1970* (Washington, DC, 1975). Many of these were first presented in Stanley Lebergott, *Manpower in Economic Growth: The American Record Since 1800* (New York, 1964). Revisions to Lebergott's pre-1870 estimates of the total labor force, on which Tables 5.1 and 5.2 and the discussion in the text are based, are reported in a number of published and unpublished papers by Thomas Weiss. A convenient published source is his "U.S. Labor Force Estimates and Economic Growth, 1800–1860," in Robert Gallman and John Wallis (eds.), *American Economic Growth and Standards of Living Before the Civil War* (Chicago, 1992). A fine discussion of the difficulties of interpreting statistics on gainful workers is Jon Moen, "From Gainful Employment to Labor Force: Definitions and a New Estimate of Work Rates of American Males, 1860–1980," *Historical Methods*, 21 (1988), 149–59. The decline in labor force participation among southern blacks after the Civil War is discussed by Roger Ransom and Richard Sutch, *One Kind of Freedom: The Economic Consequences of Emancipation* (New York, 1977). For a detailed discussion of female labor force participation throughout American history, see Claudia Goldin, *Understanding the*

Gender Gap: An Economic History of American Women (New York, 1990). Evidence on and discussion of the occupations of slaves can be found in Robert W. Fogel, *Without Consent or Contract* (New York, 1989). Data from the 1880 public use sample are taken from the "preliminary release" version described in Steven Ruggles, 1880 Public Use Sample: User's Guide (Social History Research Laboratory, Department of History, University of Minnesota, October, 1990). For information on the public use sample of the 1900 census, see Center for Studies in Demography and Ecology, *United States Census Data, 1900: Public Use Sample* (Ann Arbor, 1990). The public use samples of the 1880 and 1900 censuses are available from the Inter-University Consortium for Political and Social Research at the University of Michigan. Retirement in the late nineteenth is examined by Roger Ransom and Richard Sutch, "The Labor of Older Americans: Retirement of Men On and Off the Job," *Journal of Economic History*, 46 (1986), 1–30; and Jon Moen, "The Labor of Older Americans: Comment," *Journal of Economic History*, 47 (1987), 761–67. Analyses of ethnic and racial differences in occupations may be found in Robert Higgs, "Race, Skills, and Earnings: American Immigrants in 1909," *Journal of Economic History*, 31 (1971), 420–28; Peter Hill, "Relative Skills and Income Levels of Native and Foreign-Born Workers in the United States," *Explorations in Economic History*, 21 (1975), 47–60; Joan Hannon, "Ethnic Discrimination in a Nineteenth-Century Mining District: Michigan Copper Mines, 1888," *Explorations in Economic History*, 19 (1982), 28–50; Roger Ransom and Richard Sutch, *One Kind of Freedom*; Gavin Wright, *Old South, New South* (New York, 1986) and Robert A. Margo, *Race and Schooling in the South, 1880–1950: An Economic History* (Chicago, 1990).

The literature on nominal and real wages in the nineteenth century is voluminous. Substantial amounts of primary data are reported in Lebergott's book and *Historical Statistics*. Classic articles on nineteenth-century wages are Edith Abbott, "The Wages of Unskilled Labor in the United States, 1850–1900," *Journal of Political Economy*, 13 (1905), 321–67; Alvin Hansen, "Factors Affecting the Trend in Real Wages," *American Economic Review*, 15 (1925), 27–42; and Walter B. Smith, "Wage Rates on the Erie Canal," *Journal of Economic History*, 23 (1963), 298–311. The study by Wesley Clair Mitchell referred to in the chapter is *Gold, Prices, and Wages During the Greenback Era* (Berkeley, 1908). For a survey of research on wages before the Civil War, see Robert A. Margo, "Wages and Prices During the Antebellum Period: A Survey and New Evidence," in Gallman and Wallis, eds. *American Economic Growth and Standards of Living Before the Civil War.* For a comprehensive study of the army wage data discussed here, see Robert A. Margo, *Wages and Labor Markets in the United States, 1820–1860* (Chicago, 2000). The real wages of manufacturing workers during the antebellum period are discussed in Kenneth Sokoloff and Georgia Villaflor, "The Market for Manufacturing Workers During Early Industrialization: The American Northeast, 1820 to 1860," in Claudia Goldin and Hugh Rockoff (eds.), *Strategic Factors in Nineteenth-Century American Economic Development: Essays in Honor of Robert W. Fogel* (Chicago, 1992). Wage gaps between farm and non-farm workers are examined in Jeffrey G. Williamson and Peter H. Lindert, *American Inequality: A Macroeconomic History* (New York, 1980); Margo, *Wages and Labor Markets*; and Timothy Hatton and Jeffrey G. Williamson, "Wage Gaps Between Farm and City: Michigan in the 1890s," *Explorations in Economic History* 28 (1991), 381–408.

Aggregate wage movements during the postbellum period are covered in two important monographs: Clarence Long, *Wages and Earnings in the United States, 1860–1890* (Princeton, 1960); and Albert Rees, *Real Wages in Manufacturing, 1890–1914* (Princeton, 1961); and in Christopher Hanes, "Comparable Indices of Wholesale Prices and Manufacturing Wage Rates in the United States 1865–1914," *Research in Economic History*, 14 (1992), 269–92.

Data and analysis of geographic wage differentials can be found in Lebergott; Sokoloff and Villaflor, "The Market for Manufacturing Workers"; Margo, "Wages and Prices"; Margo, *Wages and Labor Markets*; Winifred B. Rothenberg, "The Emergence of Farm Labor Markets and the Transformation of the Rural Economy: Massachusetts, 1770–1855," *Journal of Economic History*, 48 (1988), 537–66; Philip R. P. Coehlo and James F. Shephard, "Regional Differences in Real Wages: The United States 1851–1880," *Explorations in Economic History*, 13 (1976), 203–30; Joshua Rosenbloom, "One Market or Many? Labor Market Integration in the Late Nineteenth Century," *Journal of Economic History*, 50 (1990), 85–107; and Rosenbloom, "The Extent of the Labor Market in the United States, 1850–1914," *Social Science History*, 22 (1998), 287–318; Gavin Wright, *Old South, New South*; and Robert A. Margo, "Regional Wage Gaps and the Settlement of the Midwest," *Explorations in Economic History*, 36 (1999), 128–43. On the recruitment of workers, particularly immigrants, to labor-scarce regions, see Rosenbloom and William Sundstrom, "Responding to Labor Scarcity: The Development of American Labor

Markets: From the Civil War to World War I," unpublished paper, Department of Economics, University of Kansas, 1992; and Rosenbloom, "Employer Recruitment and the Integration of Industrial Labor Markets, 1870–1914," National Bureau of Economic Research Working Paper Series on Historical Factors in Long Run Growth, Working Paper No. 53 (Cambridge, MA, 1994).

Various long-term series of occupational wage differentials are conveniently summarized in Williamson and Lindert, *American Inequality*, 305–12. Williamson and Lindert's conclusion that a significant increase in the relative wage of skilled artisans took place before the Civil War is challenged by Robert A. Margo and Georgia C. Villaflor, "The Growth of Wages in Antebellum America: New Evidence," *Journal of Economic History*, 47 (1987), 873–95. Evidence on wages of clerks may be found in Claudia Goldin and Robert A. Margo, "Wages, Prices, and Labor Markets Before the Civil War," in Goldin and Rockoff (eds.), *Strategic Factors in Nineteenth Century American Economic Development*, and in Margo *Wages and Labor Markets*, Econometric evidence on capital–skill complementarity in nineteenth-century American manufacturing is presented in John James and Jonathan Skinner, "The Resolution of the Labor Scarcity Paradox," *Journal of Economic History*, 45 (1985), 513–40. For Habakkuk's argument about international differences in skilled–unskilled wage ratios, see his *American and British Technology in the Nineteenth Century: The Search for Labor-Saving Inventions* (New York, 1962).

Additional evidence on wage differentials along various dimensions may be found in Goldin, *Understanding the Gender Gap*; Robert Higgs, *Competition and Coercion* (Cambridge, 1977); Wright, *Old South, New South*; Margo, "Wages and Prices" and his *Wages and Labor Markets*; Susan B. Carter and Elizabeth Savoca, "Gender Differences in Earning and Learning in Nineteenth Century America: The Role of Expected Job and Career Attachment," *Explorations in Economic History*, 28 (1991), 323–43; Barry J. Eichengreen, "Experience and the Male-Female Earnings Gap in the 1890s," *Journal of Economic History*, 44 (1984), 822–34; Joan Hannon, "City Size and Ethnic Discrimination: Michigan Agricultural Implements and Iron Working Industries, 1890," *Journal of Economic History*, 42 (1982), 825–45; Christopher Hanes, "Immigrants' Relative Rate of Wage Growth in the Late Nineteenth Century," *Explorations in Economic History*, 33 (1996), 35–64; and Timothy, Hatton, "The Immigrant Assimilation Puzzle in Late Nineteenth Century American," *Journal of Economic History*, 57 (1997), 34–62.

Macroeconomic influences on wages are examined by Peter Temin, *The Jacksonian Economy* (New York, 1969); Goldin and Margo, "Wages, Prices, and Labor Markets Before the Civil War"; Stephen DeCanio and Joel Mokyr, "Inflation and the Wage Lag During the American Civil War," *Explorations in Economic History*, 14 (1977), 311–36; and Christopher Hanes, "Explaining a Decrease in Cyclical Wage Flexibility in the Late Nineteenth Century," unpublished paper, Department of Economics, University of Pennsylvania, 1990. International wage comparisons may be found in Jeffrey G. Williamson, "The Evolution of Global Labor Markets Since 1830: Background Evidence and Hypotheses," *Explorations in Economic History*, 32 (1995), 141–96.

An excellent source of data and discussion of the shorter hours movement in the United States is Robert Whaples, "The Shortening of the American Work Week: An Economic and Historical Analysis of Its Context, Causes, and Consequences" (doctoral dissertation, Department of Economics, University of Pennsylvania, 1990). Jeremy Atack and Fred Bateman, "How Long Was the Workday in 1880?" *Journal of Economic History*, 52 (1992), 129–60, investigate variations in daily hours across industries in 1880. Additional evidence on the determinants of variations in hours in the late nineteenth century may be found in Joshua Rosenbloom and William Sundstrom, "The Decline in Hours of Work in U.S. Labour Markets, 1890–1903," in G. Grantham and M. MacKinnon (eds.), *Labour Market Evolution: The Economic History of Market Integration, Wage Flexibility, and the Employment Relation* (London, 1994), 161–84. For evidence on the motivation behind maximum hours laws and the potential impact of shorter hours on productivity and worker health, see Atack and Bateman, "Whom Did Protectionist Legislation Protect? Evidence from 1880," National Bureau of Economic Research Working Paper Series on Historical Factors in Long Run Growth, Working Paper No. 33 (Cambridge, MA, 1991); and Atack and Bateman, "The Effects of Long Hours of Work on Productivity and Health: Some Evidence," unpublished paper, Department of Economics, University of Illinois, 1992.

The economic effects of the displacement of the artisanal shop by the factory is the subject of Kenneth Sokoloff, "Was the Transition from the Artisanal Shop to the Nonmechanized Factory Associated with Gains in Efficiency? Evidence from the U.S. Manufacturing Censuses of 1820 and 1850," *Explorations in Economic History*, 21 (1984), 351–82. The role of women and children in early industrialization is explored by Claudia Goldin and Kenneth Sokoloff, "Women, Children, and Industrialization in the Early Republic: Evidence from the Manufacturing Censuses," *Journal of Economic History*, 42 (1982), 741–74. On outwork, sweated labor, and the antebellum labor movement, see Sean Wilentz, *Chants Democratic: New York City and the Rise of the Working Class, 1788–1850* (New York, 1984).

The academic discipline of labor history focuses on the history of the American labor movement, government policy towards labor, and the complex interweaving of economic development, politics, and culture. The classic work is John R. Commons, et al., *History of Labor in the United States* (New York, 1918, 4 vols.). New labor history is written largely in response to the work of Commons and his associates. A compact synthesis of new labor history is Bruce Laurie, *Artisans into Workers: Labor in Nineteenth-Century America* (New York, 1989). The sections of the chapter on the transition to factory work and on unions draw heavily on Laurie's excellent monograph and on Gary M. Walton and Hugh Rockoff, *History of the American Economy*, 6th ed. (New York, 1990), 197–200, 223–34, 370–91. The econometric analysis of strike outcomes referred to in the text is David Card and Craig Olson, "Bargaining Power, Strike Durations, and Wage Outcomes: An Analysis of Strikes in the 1880s," *Journal of Labor Economics* 13 (1995), 32–61. The importance of geographic mobility in answering Sombart's question is stressed by Stephan Thernstrom, *The Other Bostonians* (Cambridge, MA, 1973). The role of labor violence and big-city construction unions is discussed in two excellent papers by Gerald Friedman, "Worker Militancy and Its Consequences: Political Responses to Labor Unrest in the United States, 1877–1914," *International Labor and Working Class History*, 40 (1991), 5–17; and "Dividing Labor: Urban Politics and Big-City Construction in Late Nineteenth-Century America," in Goldin and Rockoff (eds.), *Strategic Factors in Nineteenth-Century American Economic History*.

Elizabeth Brandeis, "Labor Legislation," in Commons, et al., *History of Labor*, vol. 4, is the classic discussion of early attempts by government to regulate labor markets through protectionist legislation. On the effects of compulsory schooling and child labor laws, see William M. Landes and Lewis C. Solmon, "Compulsory Schooling Legislation: An Economic Analysis of Law and Social Change in the Nineteenth Century," *Journal of Economic History*, 32 (1972), 54–91; Robert A. Margo and T. Aldrich Finegan, "Compulsory Schooling Legislation and School Attendance in Turn-of-the-Century America: A 'Natural Experiment' Approach,"

Economics Letters, 53 (1996), 103–10; and Carolyn M. Moehling, "State Child Labor Laws and the Decline of Child Labor," *Explorations in Economic History*, 36 (1999), 72–106. The importance of enforcement to the effectiveness of maximum hours laws is stressed by Atack and Bateman, "Whom Did Protectionist Legislation Protect?"

The nature and development of American labor markets from the Civil War to World War I has received considerable attention in recent years. Two books by labor historians containing useful background information and (somewhat contradictory) analyses are Daniel Nelson, *Managers and Workers: Origins of the New Factory System in the United States, 1880–1915* (Madison, WI, 1975) and David Montgomery, *The Fall of the House of Labor: The Workplace, the State, and the American Labor Movement, 1865–1925* (New York, 1987). Two important papers on the "spot market" paradigm are William Sundstrom, "Internal Labor Markets before World War I: On-the-Job Training and Employee Promotion," *Explorations in Economic History*, 25 (1988), 424–45; and Susan Carter and Elizabeth Savoca, "Labor Mobility and Lengthy Jobs in Nineteenth Century America," *Journal of Economic History*, 50 (1990), 1–16. For a critique of Carter and Savoca's contention that lengthy jobs were more prevalent in the late nineteenth century than previously believed, see Sanford M. Jacoby and Sunil Sharma, "Employment Duration and Industrial Labor Mobility in the United States, 1880–1980," *Journal of Economic History*, 52 (1992), 161–79. Additional evidence on job tenure can be found in John James, "Job Tenure in the Gilded Age," in Grantham and MacKinnon (eds.), *Labour Market Evolution*, 185–204.

Analyses of unemployment data from the late nineteenth century are contained in a pioneering book by Alexander Keyssar, *Out of Work: The First Century of Unemployment in Massachusetts* (New York, 1986). For estimates of the probabilities of entering and leaving unemployment, see Robert A. Margo, "The Incidence and Duration of Unemployment: Some Long-Term Comparisons," *Economics Letters*, 32 (1990), 217–20. Seasonality of employment is examined in Stanley Engerman and Claudia Goldin, "Seasonality in Nineteenth-Century Labor Markets," in Thomas Weiss and Donald Schaefer (eds.), *American Economic Development in Historical Perspective* (Stanford, 1994). The frequency of industrial suspensions is discussed in Susan B. Carter and Richard Sutch, "Sticky Wages, Short Weeks, and 'Fairness': The Response of Connecticut Manufacturing Firms to the Depression of 1893–1894," unpublished paper, Department of Economics, University of California–Berkeley, 1991. The effect of unemployment on wages is econometrically assessed by Timothy Hatton and Jeffrey Williamson, "Unemployment, Employment Contracts, and Compensating Wage Differentials: Michigan in the 1890s," *Journal of Economic History*, 51 (1991), 605–32; and Price Fishback and Sean Kantor, " 'Square Deal' or Raw Deal? Market Compensation for Workplace Disamenities, 1884–1903," *Journal of Economic History*, 52 (1992), 826–48.

CHAPTER 6 (ATACK, BATEMAN, AND PARKER)

As the northern agricultural economy spread westward and land settlement progressed, farmers' attention shifted increasingly toward market participation. Not inclined to follow the Jeffersonian self-sufficiency model, the yeoman farmers began to trade the "marketable surpluses" from their productive farms. Through this linkage, farming evolved into a business activity supplementing its traditional character as "a way of life."

International and Interregional Trade and Marketing

Westward settlement, eastern urbanization, and the extension of the transportation system in nineteenth-century America created new market opportunities that tempted farmers increasingly into commercial production. The historic significance has been matched by scholarly interest. One of the most important continuing debates during the past two decades has centered on economic specialization and regional trade in the nineteenth century. The controversy extended beyond the usual bounds of agricultural history into the broader area of economic development. At the center of the academic exchange are questions of surplus, self-sufficiency, and interregional trade patterns. The belief in an emerging system of regional specialization is an old one, in which the Northeast was seen as the major manufacturing zone, the Middle West as the food production center, and the South as the area where agricultural staples were produced for international export. This is the subject of much of Mary Eschelbach Gregson's work, including her 1993 doctoral disertation. Mary Eschelbach Gregson, "Strategies for Commercialization: Missouri Agriculture, 1860–1880," Ph.D dissertation, University of Illinois at Urbana-Champaign, 1993; "Specialization in Late-Nineteenth-

Century Midwestern Agriculture: Missouri as a Test Case," *Agricultural History* 67 (1993), 16–35; and "Agricultural Specialization in the United States: Some Preliminary Results," *Agricultural History* 70 (1996), 90–101.

There have been studies concerned more directly with northern agriculture. Franklin Fisher and Peter Temin's paper on wheat supplies reflect upon aspects of regional specialization after the Civil War, as does John G. Clark's book on the western grain trade. More recently, Colleen Callahan and William Hutchinson examined interregional trade from the western perspective, finding an East–West food exchange link but, like most others, no notable southern demand for western agricultural commodities. See Franklin M. Fisher and Peter Temin, "Regional Specialization and the Supply of Wheat in the United States, 1867–1914," *Review of Economics and Statistics*, 52 (1970), 134–49; John G. Clark, *The Grain Trade in the Old Northwest*, (Urbana, 1966), and "The Antebellum Grain Trade of New Orleans: Changing Patterns in the Relations of New Orleans with the Old Northwest," *Agricultural History* 38 (1964), 131–42; Colleen Callahan and William K. Hutchinson, "Antebellum Interregional Trade in Agricultural Goods: Preliminary Results," *Journal of Economic History* 40 (1980), 25–31. Those interested in trade patterns within a smaller area should see James Mak, "Interregional Trade in the Antebellum West: Ohio, A Case Study," *Agricultural History* 46 (1972), 489–97. For a measurement of the potential surplus and revenue in northern dairying, see Fred Bateman, "The 'Marketable Surplus' in Northern Dairy Farming: New Evidence by Size of Farm in 1860," *Agricultural History* 52 (1978), 345–63, which indicates a reasonably large potential for surplus sales in the East, but relatively little in midwestern states in 1860.

Despite the strong American comparative advantage in agriculture that has existed historically and endures today, surprising little attention has been directed recently toward northern agricultural participation in international markets. Morton Rothstein fortunately has continued his interest in American export of agricultural goods, particularly with reference to trade relationships between Great Britain and the United States during the last half of the nineteenth century. His research provides an extremely useful perspective on this important aspect of America's foreign trade in agricultural goods during this period of national development. William David Zimmerman's study of the export trade in livestock between these two countries complements this work, as does Harry D. Fornari's historical survey pieces on American grain exports. Western agricultural trade on the Erie Canal link that played a major role in the Northeast-Midwest trade is discussed well in Robert Shaw's *Erie Water West* (Lexington, 1966). More recently William Cronon's *Nature's Metropolis* (New York, 1991) examines Chicago's rise resulting from the growth of her hinterland.

As the magnitude of commercial agricultural production and trade grew, so did the need for improved marketing mechanisms. Rothstein's article on wheat and cotton exports compares marketing arrangements for these crops; Thomas Odle has reviewed the evolving co-operative efforts among grain merchants in the Great Lakes region as they struggled to deal with the marketing of that product during the last century; Norman Crockett has investigated wool marketing procedures, and William Ferris has written about the grain trade of the Chicago Board of Trade. Although most such studies concern nineteenth-century practices, John Schlebecker's investigation of agricultural marketing in the 1774–77 period provides some clues to an earlier time. Among individual farm products, dairying continues to concern writers with an interest in marketing, such as H. E. Erdman, in his examination of the "associated dairies" of New York, H. S. Irwin, who investigated butter marketing in Chicago, and Roy Ashmen, who studied butter price determination by the Elgin, New York, Board of Trade. See Morton Rothstein, "Antebellum Wheat and Cotton Exports: A Contrast in Marketing Organization and Economic Development," *Agricultural History* 40 (1966), 91–100; Thomas Odle, "Entrepreneurial Cooperation on the Great Lakes: The Origin of the Methods of American Grain Marketing," *Business History Review* 38 (1964), 439–55; Norman Crockett, "The Marketing of Wool in the Nineteenth Century: The Case of the Middle West," *Agricultural History* 42 (1964), 315–26; John Schlebecker, "Agricultural Markets and Marketing in the North, 1774–1777," *Agricultural History* 50 (1976), 21–36; H. E. Erdman, "The 'Associated Dairies' of New York as Precursors of American Agricultural Cooperation," *Agricultural History* 36 (1962), 82–90; H. S. Irwin, "Some Early Chicago Butter Marketing Practices," *Agricultural History* 35 (1961), 82–84; Roy Ashmen, "Price Discrimination in the Butter Market: The Elgin Board of Trade, 1872–1917," *Agricultural History* 35 (1961), 156–62. On related topics, see Stuart Bruchey, "The Business Economy of Marketing Change, 1790–1840: A Study of Sources of Efficiency," *Agricultural History* 46 (1972), 211–26, and Dale E. Trevelen, "Railroads, Elevators and Grain Dealers: The Genesis of Antimonopolism in Milwaukee," *Wisconsin Magazine of History* 52

(1969), 205–22. Morton Rothstein, "America in the International Rivalry for the British Wheat Market, 1860–1914," *Mississippi Valley Historical Review* 47 (1960), 401–18; "The American West and Foreign Markets, 1850–1900," in David M. Ellis (ed.), *The Frontier in American Development* (Ithaca, 1969), 381–406, and "Antebellum Wheat and Cotton Exports: Contrast in Marketing Organization and Economic Development," *Agricultural History* 40 (1966), 91–100. William David Zimmerman, "Live Cattle Export Trade Between the United States and Great Britain, 1868–1885," *Agricultural History* 36 (1962), 46–52; and "U.S. Grain Exports: A Bicentennial Overview," *Agricultural History* 50 (1976), 137–50.

Other Issues in Northern Agriculture

The most comprehensive survey of the extension system is presented in Roy V. Scott's *The Reluctant Farmer: The Rise of Agricultural Extension to 1914* (Urbana, 1971). In it he discusses the stimulative effects of the era of agricultural discontent on farmer education, the emergence of the institute movement, demonstration work, and the role of the county agent. The volume contains a through bibliography including references to Scott's other work on agricultural education in Missouri, Minnesota, and Illinois. More recently, the Department of Agriculture historian Wayne Rasmussen addressed the issue in *Taking the University to the People* (Ames, IA, 1989). Allied with the experiment station activity, the colleges of agriculture and their related institutions of higher learning, the land-grant colleges, also payed a major role in agricultural research and teaching. Indeed, the 1890 "separate-but-equal" land grant colleges were the subject of a special Agricultural History Society symposium. Several studies place this topic within a broad context, among them Paul E. Waggoner's overview of American agricultural education and research, Wilson Smith's review of education's social history, and Mary Jean Bowman's economic analysis of the land-grant colleges' contribution to developing human resources. State or regional variations in the pursuit and development of formal agricultural education can be seen in research on such states as New York, Minnesota, Maryland, and Illinois. See Paul E. Waggoner, "Research and Education in American Agriculture," *Agricultural History* 50 (1976), 230–47; Wilson Smith, "'Cow College' Mythology and Social History: A View of Some Centennial

Literature," *Agricultural History* 44 (1970), 299–310; Mary Jean Bowman, "The Land-Grant College and Universities in Human Resource Development," *Journal of Economic History* 22 (1962), 523–46. For work on individual states, see Donald B. Marti, "The Purposes of Agricultural Education: Ideas and Projects in New York State, 1819–1865," *Agricultural History* 45 (1971), 271–84; Roy V. Scott, "Early Agricultural Education in Minnesota: The Institute Phase," *Agricultural History* 37 (1963), 21–34; Vivian Wiser, "Maryland in the Early Land-Grant College Movement," *Agricultural History* 36 (1962), 194–99; Gould P. Colman, "Pioneering in Agricultural Education: Cornell University, 1867–1890," *Agricultural History* 36 (1962), 200–206.

Beyond issues of education, there have been several studies of labor in northern agriculture, although not to an extent approaching that for southern workers. David E. Schob's *Hired Hands and Plowboys: Farm Labor in the Midwest, 1815–1860* (Urbana, 1975) provides a wide-ranging survey of labor on northern farms. On specific tasks such as land-clearing or capital-building, the works of Martin Primack and of Schob are useful; on the aggregate level research on the rural and urban labor force by Thomas Weiss, and by Weiss and Ermisch, are revealing of broad trends. Edith Lang, Theodore Soloutos, and Frank Lewis have provided new insights into migration and mobility in the agricultural sector. And, within the past few years, increased attention has been paid to the long-neglected study of the role of women and children in the farm labor supply and in farm operations generally. Lee Craig's *To Sow One More Acre* (Baltimore, 1993) is a recent contribution. Post-Columbian Native Indian practices are discussed by Wishart, who portrays a relatively sophisticated and productive Cherokee agriculture in the southern Piedmont prior to removal by President Jackson. There are as yet no other recent published studies of nineteenth-century agricultural practices by indigenous people. See D. Schob, "Sodbusting on the Upper Midwestern Frontier, 1820–1860," *Agricultural History* 47 (1973), 47–56; Martin L. Primack, "Farm Fencing in the Nineteenth Century," *Journal of Economic History* 29 (1969), 287–91. Thomas Weiss, "The Industrial Distribution of the Urban and Rural Workforces: Estimates for the United States, 1870–1910," *Journal of Economic History* 32 (1972), 919–37; and John Ermisch and Thomas Weiss, "The Impact of the Rural Market on the Growth of the Urban Workforce, U.S., 1870–1900," *Explorations in Economic History* 2 (1973), 137–53; Edith Lang, "The Effects of Net

Interregional Migration on Agricultural Income Growth: The United States, 1850–1860," *Journal of Economic History* 32 (1972), 393–5; Theodore Saloutos, "The Immigrant Contribution to American Agriculture," *Agricultural History* 50 (1976), 45–67; Frank Lewis, "Exploring Rural Emigration in the United States: 1869–1899; Partial and General Equilibrium, Approaches to Determining the Impact of Productivity Change on the Direction of Labor Migration," MSSB Workshop Paper, Madison, Wisconsin, 1972. On the contribution of women to the agricultural enterprise, see Mary W. M. Hargreaves, "Women in the Agricultural Settlement of the Northern Plains"; Gladys L. Baker, "Women in the United States Department of Agriculture," Minnie Miller Brown, "Black Women in American Agriculture," all in *Agricultural History* 50 (1976), 179–89, 190–201 and 202–12, respectively; Donald B. Marti, "Women's Work in the Grange: Mary Ann Mayo of Michigan, 1882–1903," *Agricultural History* 56 (1982), 439–52; Lee A. Craig, "The Value of Household Labor in Antebellum Northern Agriculture," *Journal of Economic History* 51 (1991), 67–82. Also see David M. Wishart, "Evidence of Surplus Production in the Cherokee Nation Prior to Removal," *Journal of Economic History*, 55 (1995), 120–138.

Another area of continuing research among agricultural historians has been livestock husbandry and, to a lesser extent, plant cultivation. Among the books devoted to livestock are Eric Lampard's *The Rise of the Dairy Industry in Wisconsin* (Madison, WI, 1963) and Paul Henlein's *The Cattle Kingdom in the Ohio Valley, 1783–1860* (Lexington, 1959). There have also been articles on sheep husbandry, dairy agriculture, and animal science that extend our understanding of this branch of the agricultural enterprise as it grew in importance through the nineteenth century and into the twentieth. John Stover, "Early Sheep Husbandry in Ohio, *Agricultural History* 36 (1962), 101–7; T. C. Byerly, "Changes in Animal Science," *Agricultural History* 50 (1976), 259–74.

CHAPTER 7 (ATACK, BATEMAN, AND PARKER)

In 1916, Louis B. Schmidt, a pioneer of agricultural history in the United States, urged historians to direct more attention to American agriculture and its role in national economic development. (See Louis B. Schmidt,

"The Economic History of American Agriculture as a Field of Study," *Mississippi Valley Historical Review*, 3 (1916), 39–40. See also Louis B. Schmidt, "The History of American Agriculture as a Field of Research," *Agricultural History*, 14 (1949), 117–26.) His call has been repeated regularly ever since. Indeed Harold Woodman, writing in the 1970s on the state of research, felt that "What has been most lacking in a good deal of previous work and what is now needed in agricultural history is a synthesis, a conceptual framework." (Harold D. Woodman, "The State of Agricultural History," in Herbert J. Bass (ed.), *The State of American History* [Chicago, 1970], 223.) Similarly, Harry Scheiber has complained that "More than perhaps any other major subfield of American economic history, research on agriculture has gone forward without much sense of a unifying broad design or 'leading hypothesis.'" (Harry N. Scheiber, "Poetry, Prosaism, and Analysis in American Agricultural History," *Journal of Economic History*, 36 (1976), 919.) These comments are still as true today.

The major topics discussed in this essay as in the preceding bibliographic essay are those receiving the most attention in the periodical and monographic literature. The volume of existing research precludes the citation of every pertinent work on these subjects or inclusion of other topics. Our selections are thus representative rather than exhaustive on each topic and of the field as a whole. Some useful collections of essays on agricultural history have recently appeared – several of them germane to this study – notably Louis Ferleger (ed.), *Agriculture and National Development: Views on the 19th Century* (Ames, IA, 1990); Morton Rothstein and Daniel Field (eds.), *Quantitative Studies in Agriculture History* (Ames, IA, 1993); Frederick V. Carstensen, Morton Rothstein, Joseph Swanson (eds.) *Outstanding In His Field* (eds.) (Ames, IA, 1993); George Grantham and Carol S. Leonard (eds.), *Agricultural Organization in the Century of Industrialization* (Ames, IA, 1989).

Readers seeking additional bibliographical sources are referred to the following; Douglas E. Bowers, *A List of References for the History of Agriculture in the Midwest, 1840–1900*, (Davis, CA, 1973); Henry C. Dethloff and Worth Robert Miller, *A List of References for the History of Farmers Alliance and the Populist Party* (Davis, CA, 1973, revised 1989); John T. Schlebecker, *Bibliography of Books and Pamphlets on the History of Agriculture in the United States, 1607–1967* (Santa Barbara, 1969); and Dennis S. Nordin, "Graduate Studies in American Agricultural History", *Agricultural History* 41 (1967), 275–312.

The Northern Farm Economy: an Overview

In the methodological shift that began to transform research in American economic history during the late 1950s, scholars using the new techniques largely neglected the study of northern farming. More conventionally inclined historians, however, sustained and even strengthened their interest in northern agriculture. Consequently, several books published since 1960 have provided a fresh overview of agrarian development in that region. None does so more comprehensively than Clarence Danhof's *Change in Agriculture: The Northern United States, 1820–1870* (Cambridge, MA, 1969). Covering almost every aspect of the farm enterprise, this book has become one of the most commonly cited works on this subject, as a result of its fresh perspective and accessibility. Three other books also present an overview (albeit with a more national orientation) strengthening our historical understanding of the American farmer: Paul Gates's *The Farmer's Age* (New York, 1960), Gilbert Fite's *The Farmers' Frontier* (New York, 1960), and John Schlebecker's *Whereby We Thrive* (Ames, IA, 1975). Each provides detailed, careful literary accounts of broad aspects of agricultural change.

Complementing these volumes are various collections of articles published in book form or as special issues of journals. *Agricultural History* sponsored symposia in 1969, 1972, 1974–77, 1979, 1980, 1982, and 1990. Several appeared as separate volumes, among them D. P. Kelsey (ed.), *Farming in the New Nation: Interpreting American Agriculture, 1790–1840* (Washington, DC, 1972) and James W. Whitaker (ed.), *Farming in the Midwest, 1840–1900* (Washington, DC, 1974). Dealing with a more limited topical or geographic coverage are Earl Hayter's *The Troubled Farmer, 1850–1900: Rural Adjustment to Industrialization* (De Kalb, IL, 1969), Allan Bogue's *From Prairie to Corn Belt* (Chicago, 1963), Paul Gates's *Agriculture and the Civil War* (New York, 1965), Gilbert Fite's *American Farmers: The New Minority* (Bloomington, 1983), and Merle Curti, et al., *The Making of an American Community* (Stanford, 1959). Among the newer works are Donald H. Parkerson, *The Agricultural Transition in New York State* (Ames, IA, 1995) and Winifred Rothenberg's *From Market – Places to a Market Economy* (Chicago, 1992), (which focuses upon Massachusetts agriculture before the Civil War). Both are underpinned by cliometrics but appear more conventionally literary and historical. These may be supplemented by Wayne Rasmussen's *Readings in the History of American Agriculture* (Urbana, 1960) as well as by his four-volume set, *Agriculture in the United States, A Documentary History* (New York, 1975).

To Their Own Soil (Ames, IA, 1987) by Jeremy Atack and Fred Bateman, remains one of just two unabashedly cliometric studies on this topic. The other study is Sue E. Headlee, *The Political Economy of the Family Farm*, (New York, 1991).

Land Policy, Settlement, and the Westward Expansion

The contribution by Paul Gates and by his students to this subject is unmatched. Among his list of publications since 1960 are these books: *History of Public Land Law Development* (Washington, DC, 1978), *Pressure Groups and Recent American Land Policies* (Ithaca, 1980), and *Landlords and Tenants on the Prarie Frontier: Studies in American Land Policy* (Ithaca, 1973). Among his articles is "Research in the History of Public Lands," *Agricultural History* 48 (1974), 31–50.

These are complemented by Vernon Carstensen's collection of articles, *The Public Lands: Studies in the History of the Public Domain* (Madison, 1963), Howard B. Ottoson's *Land Use Policy and Problems in the United States*, (Lincoln, NB, 1963) and David M. Ellis's (ed.) *The Frontier in American Development: Essays in Honor of Paul Wallace Gates* (Ithaca, 1969). The volumes by Malcolm Rohrbough, *The Land Office Business: The Settlement and Administration of American Public Lands, 1789–1837* (New York, 1986) and Marion Clawson, *The Land System of the United States* (Lincoln, 1986), further supplement these collections, as does James Oberly's 1990 analysis of miltary land warrants, *Sixty Million Acres* (Kent, OH, 1990)

The westward movement on a broader scale that this land policy helped stimulate continues to interest historians, as reflected in the publication of the fourth edition of Ray Billington's *Westward Expansion: A History of the American Frontier* (New York, 1974), his *The Westward Movement in the United States* (Princeton, 1959), and his second edition of *The American Frontier* (Washington, DC.) produced in 1965. A second edition of Thomas Clark's *Frontier America: The Story of the Westward Movement* (New York) appeared in 1969.

The bicentennial celebrating for the nation as well as specific legislative events such as the Northwest Ordinances further renewed interest. In a special symposium observing the American national bicentennial, both

Paul Gates and Gilbert Fite contributed survey pieces on land policy and the pioneer farmer; while in an earlier issue of *Agricultural History* Gates had reviewed research on public land history. Geographers have also revealed a strengthening interest in this subject as well. Readers desiring a more complete historiographical review should see Robert Swierenga's very thorough article in the *Western Historical Quarterly* in 1977. Paul W. Gates, "An Overview of American Land Policy," in Vivian Wiser (ed.), "Bicentennial Symposium: Two Centuries of American Agriculture," *Agricultural History* 50 (1976), 213–29; Gilbert C. Fite, "The Pioneer Farmer: A View Over Three Centuries,' *Agricultural History* 50 (1976), 275–89. For examples of the geographer's work, see Andrew H. Clark, "Suggestions for the Geographical Study of Agricultural Change in the United States, 1790–1840," *Agricultural History* 46 (1972) 155–72; Hildegard Binder Johnson, "A Historical Perspective on Form and Function in Upper Midwest Rural Settlement," *Agricultural History* 48 (1974), 11–25; and P. J. Perry, "Agricultural History: A Geographer's Critique," *Agricultural History* 46 (1972), 259–67; Robert P. Swierenga, "Land Speculation and its Impact on American Economic Growth and Welfare: A Historiographical Review," *Western Historical Quarterly* 8 (1977), 283–302.

The impact of this federal land policy is discussed in a variety of works. At a theoretical level, Robert Fogel and Jack Rutner concluded that the efficiency effects of land policy and sale, including those resulting from speculative activity, were relatively minor. Their conclusions were challenged by R. Taylor Dennen, whose dynamic model suggested a more significant influence on efficiency. Moreover, Peter Passell and Maria Schmundt, who analyzed the relationship between land disposal policy and industrial development, found that combining cheap land with high tariffs encouraged rather than inhibited manufacturing growth in nineteenth-century America. Robert Swierenga's work on Iowa land speculation, both in articles and in his book *Pioneers and Profit*, reveals comparatively little distortive effect from speculation in that state. Robert P. Swierenga, *Pioneers and Profits: Land Speculation on the Iowa Frontier*, (Ames, IA, 1968). Also see his "The Tax Buyer as a Frontier Investor Type," *Explorations in Economic History* 7 (1970), 257–92, and "Land Speculator 'Profits' Reconsidered: Central Iowa as a Test Case," *Journal of Economic History* 26 (1966), 1–28. The economics of land policy is discussed by Robert Fogel and Jack Rutner, "The Efficiency Effects of Federal Land Policy, 1850–1900: A Report on Some Provisional Findings," in William O. Aydelotte, et al.

(eds.), *The Dimensions of Quantitative Research in History*, (Princeton 1972), 390–418; Dennen's comments are in R. Taylor Dennen, "Some Efficiency Effects of Nineteenth-Century Federal Land Policy: A Dynamic Analysis" *Agricultural History* 51 (1977), 718–36. For another economic examination of land policy and speculation, see Edward H. Rastatter, "Nineteenth Century Public Land Policy: The Case for the Speculator," in David Klingaman and Richard Vedder (eds.), *Essays in Nineteenth Century Economic History: The Old Northwest*, (Athens, OH, 1975), 118–32; Thomas De Luc offers an historian's comment on this issue in his "Public Policy, Private Investment, and Land Use in American Agriculture, 1825–1875," *Agricultural History* 37 (1963), 3–9. On the issues of land scarcity and its relationship to other economic variables, see Peter Passell and Maria Schmundt, "Pre–Civil War Land Policy and the Growth of Manufacturing," *Explorations in Economic History* 9 (1971), 35–48; Peter Temin, "Land Scarcity and American Economic Growth," *Journal of Economic History* 26 (1966), 277–98; Peter Lindert, "Land Scarcity and American Economic Growth," *Journal of Economic History* 34 (1974), 851–84. For complementary studies on these issues, see Theodore Saloutos, "Land Policy and its Relationship to Agricultural Production and Distribution, 1862–1933," *Journal of Economic History* 22 (1962), 445–60, and Folke Dovring's interesting report on contemporary reactions to U.S. policy in his "European Reactions to the Homestead Act," *Journal of Economic History* 22 (1962), 461–72. C. Knick Harley, "Western Settlement and the Price of Wheat, 1872–1913," *Journal of Economic History* 38 (1978), 865–78 offers an explanation of land expansion and settlement as a response to market prices in an interesting economic approach to the issue.

Frederick Jackson Turner's notion that the West offered a "safety-valve" outlet for eastern labor has continued to attract interest, particularly among economists. Ellen Von Nardhoff's "The American Frontier as a Safety Valve – The Life, Death, and Reincarnation and Justification of a Theory," published in *Agricultural History* in 1962, offered both an economist's critique and a summary review of the literature. More recent quantitative estimates by Ankli and by Atack place the cost of establishing a viable farm operation by someone already resident in newly settled areas at substantially less than estimated by Clarence Danhof in his classic 1941 article on this subject, breathing some renewed life into the debate over who could afford what. Ellen Von Nardroff, "The American Frontier as a Safety Valve – The Life, Death and Reincarnation and Justification of a Theory," *Agricultural History* 36 (1962), 123–42; William M. Tuttle, Jr., "Forerunners of Frederick Jackson Turner: Nineteenth Century British Conservatives and the Frontier Thesis," *Agricultural History* 41 (1967), 219–27; Robert E. Ankli, "Farm-Making Costs in the 1850s," *Agricultural History* 48 (1974), 51–70 (see also Judith L. V. Klein's comments on Ankli's paper in the same issue on 71–74); Jeremy Atack, "Farm and Farm-Making Costs Revisited," *Agricultural History* 56 (1982), 663–76. Danhof's piece appeared as "Farm-Making Costs and the 'Safety Valve': 1850–1860," *Journal of Political Economy* 49 (1941), 317–59.

Once in the West, individuals who had migrated started establishing their farm and beginning a family. Martin Primack's work on clearing, fencing, and capital formation provides quantitative evidence on this aspect of western agricultural development. Combining demographic with economic analyses, Richard Easterlin generated new interpretations of farm families, fertility change, and settlement centered around notions of land scarcity in a world where farmers had notions of target bequests for their offspring. Lee Craig's estimates of the relative values of women and children on farms in different parts of the country provide additional insights into farm fertility decisions. Like Easterlin's, Richard Peet's analyses of the spatial expansion of agriculture, which applies von Thünen locational theory, both complements more traditional studies and points a ways for further interdisciplinary investigation of agricultural development. Many of these ideas were subsequently explored by Mary Eschelbach Gregson in her dissertation, "Strategies for Commercialization: Missouri Agriculture, 1860–1880," completed in 1993. Richard Easterlin, George Alter, and Gretchen A. Congran, "Farms and Farm Families in Old and New Areas: The Northern States in 1860," in Tamara Hareven and Maris A. Vinovskis (eds.), *Family and Population in Nineteenth Century America* (Princeton, 1978), 22–84; Richard Easterlin, "Population Change and Farm Settlement in the Northern United States," *Journal of Economic History* 36 (1976), 47–75; and his "Factors in the Decline of Farm Fertility in the American North," *Journal of American History* 62 (1976), 600–614. Also on this subject, also see Don R. Leet, "Human Fertility and Agricultural Opportunities in Ohio Counties: From Frontier to Maturity, 1820–60," in Klingaman and Vedder (eds.) *Essays in Nineteenth Century Economic History*, 138–58, in which the author analyses the relationship between land availability and the fertility pattern. Richard Peet, "The Spatial Dynamics of Commercial Agriculture in the Nineteenth

Century: A Von Thünen Interpretation," *Economic Geography* 45 (1969), 283–301, and "Von Thünen Theory and the Dynamics of Agricultural Expansion," *Explorations in Economic History* 8 (1970/71), 181–201. These works are based on his dissertation, "The Spatial Expansion of Commercial Agriculture in the Nineteenth Century: A Theoretical Analysis of British Import Zones and the Movement of Farming into the Interior United States," Ph.D. dissertation, University of California, Berkeley, 1968. Lee A. Craig, *To Sow One More Acre* (Baltimore, 1993); Mary Eschelbach Gregson, "Strategies for Commercialization: Missouri Agriculture, 1860–1880," Ph.D. dissertation, University of Illinois at Urbana-Champaign, 1993.

Technological Change, Scientific Farming, and Productivity Growth

Technological improvement closely interacted with westward expansion and with a new attitude – a more scientific one – among American farmers. In "The Mechanization of Reaping in the Ante-Bellum Midwest," Paul David developed a model involving farm size and relative factor prices to account for the slow acceptance of the mechanical reaper by American farmers. David's calculations of the threshold farm size required to justify adoption placed this major issue into a more quantitative, rigorous context, but some of his assumptions have been questioned. Alan Olmstead, for example, who proposed a generally more dynamic explanation, suggests that equipment-sharing among farmers could alter minimum farm size requirements for an individual producer, and Robert Ankli stresses the importance of machine reliability improvements and non-wage influences to reaper adoption. The threshold controversy finally seems laid to rest with Olmstead and Rhode's "Beyond the Threshold: An Analysis of the Characteristics and Behavior of Early Reaper Adopters," in the *Journal of Economic History* 55 (1995), 27–57. Paul A. David, "The Mechanization of Reaping in the Ante-Bellum Midwest," in Henry Rosovsky (ed.), *Industrialization in Two Systems: Essays in Honor of Alexander Gerschenkron*, (New York, 1966); Alan L. Olmstead, "The Mechanization of Mowing and Reaping in American Agriculture, 1833–1870," *Journal of Economic History* 35 (1975), 327–52; Robert Ankli, "The Coming of the Reaper," in Paul Uselding, (ed.) *Business and Economic History* (1976), 1–24. Those interested in the related issue of motive power in the Midwest should see Ankli's "Horses vs. Tractors on the Corn Belt,"

Agricultural History 54 (1980), 134–48, and Olmstead and Rhode, "Beyond the Threshold."

Articles by Rasmussen, Lave, Schlebecker, Drache, and Feller explore the ramifications of technological change in a broader context than those considering a single innovation such as the reaper. Each reveals the comparative ease with which Americans in the northern states accepted and utilized new technology. Similarly, in pieces dealing with New York, Gould P. Colman and Richard A. Wines investigate technological adoption by farmers in that state, both finding relatively ready acceptance of new machinery by producers. Wayne D. Rasmussen surveys a century of technological development in "The Impact of Technological Change on American Agriculture, 1862–1962," *Journal of Economic History* 22 (1962), 578–91; Lester B. Lave, "Empirical Estimates of Technological Change in United States Agriculture, 1850–1958," *Journal of Farm Economics* 44 (1962), 941–52; John T. Schlebecker, "Farmers and Bureaucrats: Reflections on Technological Innovation," *Agricultural History* 51 (1977), 641–55; Irwin Feller focuses on innovation and patent activity in "Inventive Activity in Agriculture, 1837–1890," *Journal of Economic History* 22 (1962), 560–77; Hiram Drache investigates the influence of technological change on midwestern agriculture in the recent past in "Midwest Agriculture: Changing with Technology," *Agricultural History* 50 (1976), 290–302; E. L. Jones surveys long-term influences on agricultural evolution in "Creative Disruptions in American Agriculture, 1620–1820," *Agricultural History* 48 (1974), 510–28; Richard K. Vedder examines technological development from the implement manufacturers' perspective in "Some Evidence on the Scale of the Antebellum Farm Implement Industry," in Uselding, (ed.) *Business and Economic History* (1976), 25–35. Gould P. Colman, "Innovation and Diffusion in Agriculture," *Agricultural History* 42 (1968), 173–87; Richard A. Wines, "The Nineteenth-Century Agricultural Transition in an Eastern Long Island Community," *Agricultural History* 55 (1981), 50–63.

Scientific farming, being a less tangible and somewhat later development, has received less study over the past twenty years by agricultural historians than has technological change. Margaret Rossiter's *The Emergence of Agricultural Science* (New Haven, 1975) explores the development and application of agricultural chemistry with reference to Justus Liebig, the agricultural chemist. Zvi Griliches's econometric studies of the diffusion of hybrid corn demonstrates the substantial effect that this innovation had on corn yields in the United States, especially since the Second World

War. Although many writers stress the importance of biological and chemical advances and, in a broader sense, the significance of a "scientific outlook" among American farmers, the area remains largely unexplored. Zvi Griliches, "Hybrid Corn: An Exploration in the Economics of Technological Change," *Econometrica* 25 (1957), 501–22; "Research Costs and Social Returns: Hybrid Corn and Related Innovation," *Journal of Political Economy* 66 (1958), 419–31; "Hybrid Corn and the Economics of Innovation," *Science* 132 (1960), 275–80.

In 1961 the Department of Agriculture published as a Technical Bulletin 1238, Ralph A. Barton and Glen T. Loomis' *Productivity of Agriculture, 1870–1958*, thus providing a new long-term continuous measure of change in agriculture; the following year, estimates for this same period were published by Charles Meiburg and Karl Brandt. On a more analytical level, the effects of technological advance, innovational diffusion, scientific methods, and western settlement on productivity growth also were investigated. In 1966, William Parker, working with Judith L. V. Klein, published what is generally accepted as the first "new economic history" piece devoted to northern agricultural history. The article, "Productivity Growth in Grain Production in the United States, 1840–60 and 1900–10," appeared in *Output, Employment and Productivity Growth in the United States*, Studies in Income and Wealth, vol. 30, (New York, 1966). As with an earlier book in this series, the articles in the collection had been presented originally at a conference jointly sponsored by the Economic History Association and the National Bureau of Economic Research in which methods of economics were applied to historical issues. Parker and Klein moved a step beyond earlier work by attempting to assess the individual contribution of a complex of historical forces, notably the westward movement, technological change, and scientific improvement, to measured productivity change. After this piece, Parker and others continued to expand the literature on related topics and for other farm products. Charles O. Meiburg and Karl Brandt, "Agricultural Productivity in the United States: 1870–1960," *Stanford Research Institute Studies* 3 (1962), 63–85. William N. Parker and Judith L. V. Klein, "Productivity Growth in Grain Production in the United States, 1840–1860 and 1900–1910," in Dorothy S. Brady (ed.), *Output, Employment and Productivity in the United States After 1800*, 523–82. See, for example, Fred Bateman, "Improvement in American Dairy Farming, 1850–1910," *Journal of Economic History* 27 (1968), 255–73, and "Labor Inputs and Productivity in American

Dairy Agriculture, 1850–1910," *Journal of Economic History* 29 (1969), 206–29.

Parker, whose interests and skills led him to become a major link between the old and the new economic history as well as between economics and history, had been working on his agricultural studies since the late 1950s. In a recent re-examination of the Parker-Klein analysis, Atack and Bateman, using a different data source for the nineteenth-century figures, calculated new yield and labor productivity estimates that were used to isolate the sources of measured change in an exercise modeled on the original one. The conclusions indicate a larger growth in labor productivity in the 1860–90 period in wheat, oats, and corn production, and enhanced the role of yield improvement relative to the original results.

Parker and Klein's study, while path-breaking, nevertheless measured only partial productivity. The next obvious step was to measure total factor productivity, a step taken by Robert Gallman in papers published in 1972 and 1975. His estimates reveal a sustained and substantial expansion of productivity growth through the nineteenth century. These two carefully crafted pieces quickly became standard references on this subject. The analysis of wheat supply and productivity by Franklin Fisher and Peter Temin, and the responses it elicited from Robert Higgs and Walter Page, although more limited in scope, provide a similarly interesting exchange on an issue that merits attention from a wide range of scholars. William N. Parker, "Productivity Growth in American Grain Farming: An Analysis of its 19th-Century Sources," in Robert W. Fogel and Stanley L. Engerman (eds.), *The Reinterpretation of American Economic History* (New York, 1971), 175–86; "Sources of Agricultural Productivity in the Nineteenth Century," *Journal of Farm Economics* 49 (1967), 1455–68; "On a Certain Parallelism in Form Between Two Historical Processes of Productivity Growth," *Agricultural History* 50 (1976), 101–16; and William N. Parker and Stephen J. DeCanio, "Two Hidden Sources of Productivity Growth in American Agriculture, 1860–1930," *Agricultural History* 56 (1982), 648–62. See also Parker's "The Magic of Property," *Agricultural History* 54 (1980), 447–89; Jeremy Atack and Fred Bateman, "Mid-Nineteenth Century Crop Yields and Labor Productivity Growth in American Agriculture: A New Look at Parker and Klein," in Gavin Wright and Gary Saxenhouse (eds.) *Technique, Spirit, and Form in the Making of Modern Economies: Essays in Honor of William N. Parker* (Greenwich, CT, 1984); Robert Gallman, "Changes in Total U.S. Agriculture Factor Productivity in the Nineteenth Century," *Agricultural History* 46 (1972), 191–210, and "The Agricultural Sector and the Pace of Economic Growth: U.S. Experience in the Nineteenth Century," in Klingaman and Vedder (eds.), *Essays in Nineteenth-Century Economic History*, 35–76; Robert Fogel and Stanley Engerman, "The Relative Efficiency of Slavery: Reply," *American Economic Review* 70 (1980), 672–90; Thomas L. Haskell, "Explaining the Relative Efficiency of Slave Agriculture in the Antebellum South: A Reply to Fogel and Engerman," *American Economic Review* 69 (1979), 206–7; Donald F. Schaeffer and Mark D. Schmitz, "The Relative Efficiency of Slave Agriculture: A Comment," *American Economic Review* 69 (1979), 208–12; Paul A. David and Peter Temin, "Examining the Relative Efficiency of Slavery: Comment," *American Economic Review* 69 (1979), 213–18; Gavin Wright, "The Efficiency of Slavery: Another Interpretation," *American Economic Review* 69 (1979), 219–26; Franklin M. Fisher and Peter Temin, "Regional Specialization and the Supply of Wheat in the United States, 1867–1914," *Review of Economics and Statistics* 52 (1970), 134–49; Robert Higgs, "Regional Specialization and the Supply of Wheat in the United States, 1867–1914: A Comment," *Review of Economics and Statistics* 53 (1971), 101–2; Peter Temin, "Regional Specialization and the Supply of Wheat in the United States, 1867–1914: A Reply," *Review of Economics and Statistics* 52 (1971), 102–3. On the subject of productivity before the nineteenth century, see Duane E. Ball and Gary M. Walton, "Agricultural Productivity Change in Eighteenth Century Pennsylvania," *Journal of Economic History* 36 (1976), 102–17.

Agrarian Discontent, Railroads, and Populism

Farmer discontent over economic conditions and the resultant political agitation that occured after the Civil War has continued to interest historians. On these complicated historical questions, many leading historians accepted the position that the discontent expressed by farmers was justified. This view is represented in John Hicks's *The Populist Revolt* (Lincoln, NE, 1961), originally published in 1931. While this subject involves an admittedly complex amalgam of economic and non-economic elements, farmers' complaints ultimately rested on their perception of economic sacrifice and discrimination. Thus several purely economic issues are fundamental, most notably, the level and trend in railroad rates for agricultural commodities, the course of income distributional changes between farm and non-farm sectors, domestic terms of trade in the agricultural sector, allegedly discriminatory interest or mortgage rates, and the presumed monopoly power exercised against farmers by the middlemen with whom they had to deal.

Since World War II, two parallel re-evaluations of late-nineteenth-century agrarian unrest and the political response it engendered were emerging, one dominated by historians and the other by economists. In his presidential address before the Agricultural History Society in 1966, Theodore Saloutos reviewed the long history of academic debate over populism, focusing on the changing perceptions of that political movement. Among those who had been engaged in this re-examination were Richard Hofstadter, David Shannon, Walter T. K. Nugent, Oscar Handlin, and Norman Pollack. Historians, usually displaying a broader interest than the purely political one, produced several books on this enduring topic in U.S. history, including such studies as Pollack's *The Populist Response to Industrial America* (Cambridge, MA, 1962), Nugent's the *The Tolerant Populists* (Chicago, 1963), the collection of essays edited by Vernon Carstensen, *Farmer Discontent, 1865–1900* (New York, 1974), and Lawrence Goodwyn's *Democratic Promise: The Populist Movement in America* (New York, 1976).

While historians debated the political implications of populism and the unrest from which it arose, economists were focusing more specifically on the economic questions. In his *Growth and Welfare in the American Past*, (Englewood Cliffs; first published 1966) Douglass North joined the debate by abstracting from the wider social and political context to examine railroad rates, agricultural terms of trade, and mortgage charges. Using aggregated and long-term data series, he found little to support the protestors' economic complaints. Among historians more concerned with what actually happened than with what justifiably should have, North's seemingly attenuated analysis was received skeptically. But even fellow economists sympathetic to his methodological approach questioned North's conclusions. On the level and trend of railroad rates, for example, North's data, like that of Robert William Fogel in his *Railroads and American Economic Growth* (Baltimore, 1964), indicated that generally rates had fallen over the decades of the "agrarian unrest." Robert Higgs, in *The Transformation of the American Economy, 1865–1914* (New York, 1971), failed to find any clear trend in farmers' terms of trade with the railways. Indeed his calculations showed real terms of trade improving for farmers during the periods of most intense farmer agitation, a finding consistent with the traditional interpretation. His series also reveal years when, despite complaints to the contrary, rates paid to ship agricultural products were declining, and terms of trade shifting toward farmers. More recently, Mark Aldrich has challenged even Higgs's somewhat guarded conclusion that economic conditions at least during some periods justified farmer dissatisfaction, presenting a stronger economic case in favor of farmer political protest. Theodore Saloutos, "The Professors and the Populist," *Agricultural History* 40 (1966), 235–54; Richard Hofstadter, "The Folklore of Populism," in *The Age of Reform* (New York, 1955); David Shannon, "Was McCarthy a Political Heir of LaFollette?" *Wisconsin Magazine of History* 45 (1961), 3–9; Walter T. K. Nugent, "Some Parameters of Populism," *Agricultural History* 39 (1965), 68–74; Norman Pollack, "Fear of Man: Populism, Authoritarianism, and the Historian," *Agricultural History* 39 (1965), 59–67; Mark Aldrich, "A Note on Railroad Rates and the Populist Uprising," *Agricultural History* 54 (1980), 424–32.

On a related economic issue, John Bowman had analyzed midwestern land values in his dissertation and in subsequent published work. In 1974, working with Richard Keehn, he entered the debate regarding agricultural terms of trade during the last three decades of the nineteenth century. Bowman and Keehn found no support for believing that farmers in the states of Illinois, Indiana, Iowa, and Wisconsin suffered from deteriorating terms of trade over that period (1870–1900) as a whole. Actually, their analysis indicated a secular improvement in farmer's real purchasing power in those four states. On the other hand, like Higgs, they found substantial year-to-year fluctuations, and a close correspondence between them and variations in the strength of farmer protest. To some extent, Anne Mayhew attempted to bridge the seemingly contradictory gap between the nineteenth-century farmers' protestations and the positions of North, Fogel, and Bowman and Keehn by arguing that the agrarian outcries were in large measure a response to the commercialization of American agriculture, a development that, through price and market behavior, introduced the farmer to the unfamiliar, sometimes intimidating, world of business. John D. Bowman, "An Economic Analysis of Midwestern Farm Land Values and Farm Land Income, 1860 to 1910," *Yale Economic Essays* 5 (1965), 317–62; John D. Bowman and Richard Keehn, "Agricultural Terms of Trade in Four Midwestern States, 1870–1900," *Journal of Economic History* 34 (1974), 592–609; Anne Mayhew, "A Reappraisal of the Causes of Farm Protest in the United States, 1870–1900," *Journal of Eco-*

nomic History 32 (1972), 464–75. See also Robert Klepper, "The Economic Bases for Agrarian Protest in the United States, 1870–1900" (paper prepared for the University of Chicago Workshop in Economic History, April 1970), and Jeffrey C. Williams, "Economics and Politics: Voting Behavior in Kansas During the Populist Decade," *Explorations in Economic History* 18 (1981), 233–56.

CHAPTER 8 (ENGERMAN)

There are few, if any, topics in American or even world history that have been more extensively written about than U.S. slavery, so this bibliographic essay can only scratch the surface of the existing literature. To approach the study of U.S. slavery, the two best bibliographic reference works are John David Smith's 2-volume *Black Slavery in the Americas: An Interdisciplinary Bibliography, 1865–1980* (Westport, 1982) and Randall M. Miller and John D. Smith (eds.), *Dictionary of Afro-American Slavery* (New York, 1988). A useful bibliographic guide to slavery in the United States and elsewhere is Joseph C. Miller, *Slavery and Slaving in World History: A Bibliography*, 2 vols. (Armonk, 1999), which is annually updated by Miller in the journal *Slavery and Abolition*. Other useful bibliographies are found in various recent books or collections of essays on slavery; see, for example, John Hope Franklin and Alfred A. Moss, Jr., *From Slavery to Freedom: A History of Negro Americans*, 7th ed. (New York, 1994); Peter Kolchin, *American Slavery, 1619–1877* (New York, 1993); Lawrence B. Goodheart, Richard D. Brown, and Stephen G. Rabe (eds.), *Slavery in American Society*, 3rd ed. (Lexington, 1993); and Mark Smith, *Debating Slavery: Economy and Society in the Antebellum American South* (Cambridge, 1998). The literature on the postbellum South is extensive, but not so much as that on the antebellum period. Useful bibliographies on the Reconstruction period can be found in Eric Foner, *Reconstruction: American's Unfinished Revolution* (New York, 1988); Howard Rabinowitz, *The First New South, 1865–1920* (Arlington Heights, 1992); and James M. McPherson, *Ordeal by Fire: The Civil War and Reconstruction*, 2nd ed. (New York, 1992).

For comparisons of slavery in the United States with slavery elsewhere in the Americas, see Herbert S. Klein, *African Slavery in Latin America and the Caribbean* (New York, 1986), and Barry Higman, *Slave Populations of the British Caribbean, 1807–1834* (Baltimore, 1984). For broad comparisons with slavery elsewhere in time and place, see M. I. Finley, *Ancient Slavery and Modern Ideology* (New York, 1980); Orlando Patterson, *Slavery and Social Death* (Cambridge, MA, 1982); David Brion Davis, *Slavery and Human Progress* (New York, 1984); and Paul E. Lovejoy, *Transformations in Slavery: A History of Slavery in Africa* (Cambridge, 1983). See also Seymour Drescher and Stanley Engerman (eds.), *A Historical Guide to World Slavery* (New York, 1998).

Three important general works on U.S. slavery, each reflecting the time in which it was written, are: Ulrich B. Phillips, *American Negro Slavery: A Survey of the Supply, Employment and Control of Negro Labor as Determined by the Plantation Regime* (New York, 1918); Kenneth M. Stampp, *The Peculiar Institution: Slavery in the Antebellum South* (New York, 1956), and Eugene D. Genovese, *Roll, Jordan, Roll: The World the Slaves Made* (New York, 1974). These all contain sections dealing with economic issues. For a survey of these, and other works see Peter J. Parish, *Slavery: History and Historiography* (New York, 1989).

For basic discussions of the southern slave economy and of the overall southern economy, the major starting point remains Lewis Cecil Gray, *History of Agriculture in the Southern United States to 1860*, 2 volumes (Washington, DC, 1933). A more recent debate was triggered by the classic article of Alfred H. Conrad and John R. Meyer, "The Economics of Slavery in the Antebellum South," *Journal of Political Economy*, 66 (1958), 95–130, while another set of debates was opened by Robert W. Fogel and Stanley L. Engerman, *Time on the Cross*, 2 vols. (Boston, 1974). This analysis drew upon the pioneering work of large-scale data collection from the manuscript census schedules of population and agriculture for the "Cotton South" in 1860, undertaken under the direction of William N. Parker and Robert E. Gallman, which was expanded upon by several of their students to include other crops and regions.

Central to the analysis of the southern economy in response to *Time on the Cross* were Paul A. David, et al., *Reckoning with Slavery: A Critical Study in the Quantitative History of American Negro Slavery* (New York, 1976); Gavin Wright, *The Political Economy of the Cotton South: Households, Markets, and Wealth in the Nineteenth Century* (New York, 1978); and the subsequent volume by Robert W. Fogel, *Without Consent or Contract: The Rise and Fall of American Slavery* (New York, 1989), with its accompanying three volumes of essays and analysis; Robert W. Fogel, Ralph Galantane, and Richard L. Manning (eds.), *Evidence and Methods* (New York, 1992), and Robert W. Fogel and Stanley L. Engerman (eds.), *Technical Papers*, 2 vols.

(New York, 1992). For an earlier and still influential interpretation of the southern economy, see Eugene D. Genovese, *The Political Economy of Slavery: Studies in the Economy and Societies of the Slave South* (New York, 1965). On these (and related) issues, see also the essays in Elizabeth Fox-Genovese and Eugene D. Genovese, *Fruits of Merchant Capital: Slavery and Bourgeois Property in the Rise and Expansion of Capitalism* (New York, 1983). A major examination of the economic role of the antebellum South in the national economy is in Douglass C. North, *The Economic Growth of the United States, 1790–1860* (Englewood Cliffs, 1961).

Central for understanding the early period of slavery in the British West Indian and mainland colonies are: Richard S. Dunn, *Sugar and Slaves: The Rise of the Planter Class in the English West Indies, 1624–1713* (Chapel Hill, 1972); Allan Kulikoff, *Tobacco and Slaves: The Development of Southern Cultures in the Chesapeake, 1680–1800* (Chapel Hill, 1982); and John J. McCusker and Russell R. Menard, *The Economy of British America, 1607–1789*, revised edition (Chapel Hill, 1991).

The discussions of slave demography begin with works on the slave trade and international migration more generally. The work that initiated the ongoing measurement of the magnitude of the slave trade was Philip D. Curtin, *The Atlantic Slave Trade: A Census* (Madison, WI, 1969). Some of the implications for the settling of the Americas are presented in David Eltis, "Free and Coerced Transatlantic Migrations: Some Comparisons," *American Historical Review*, 88 (1983), 251–80. The nature of indentured servitude and the shift from servants to slaves are discussed in David Galenson, *White Servitude in Colonial America* (Cambridge, 1981).

Key material on slave fertility and mortality patterns are found in Fogel, *Without Consent or Contract*, and articles by Richard Steckel and by others in Fogel and Engerman (eds.), *Without Consent or Contract: Technical Papers, Volume II*. On fertility patterns, see also Steckel, *The Economics of U.S. Slave and Southern White Fertility* (New York, 1985), while the question of slave diseases and health is examined in Kenneth F. Kiple and Virginia H. King, *Another Dimension to the Black Diaspora: Diet, Disease, and Racism* (Cambridge, 1981).

There are numerous studies of the specific aspects of the southern economy and society of which those that are most useful include Fred Bateman and Thomas Weiss, *A Deplorable Scarcity: The Failure of Industrialization in the Slave Economy* (Chapel Hill, 1981) and Robert S. Starobin, *Industrial Slavery in the Old South* (New York, 1970) on manufacturing; Claudia D. Goldin, *Urban Slavery in the American South, 1820–1860: A*

Quantitative History (Chicago, 1976) on urbanization; Michael Tadman, *Speculators and Slaves: Masters, Traders and Slaves in the Old South* (Madison, WI, 1989) on the internal slave trade; Harold D. Woodman, *King Cotton and his Retainers* (Lexington, 1968) on the cotton factors; Larry Schweikert, *Banking in the American South from the Age of Jackson to Reconstruction* (Baton Rouge, 1987) on banking; and William K. Scarborough, *The Overseer: Plantation Management in the Old South* (Baton Rouge, 1966) on agricultural management. For other issues related to the social and economic history of the South, see Bruce Collins, *White Society in the Antebellum South* (London, 1985) on the white population, poor and otherwise; Herbert Aptheker, *American Negro Slave Revolts* (New York, 1943) and Eugene D. Genovese, *From Rebellion to Revolution: Afro-American Slave Revolts in the Making of Modern World* (Baton Rouge, 1979) on slave resistance and rebellions; Herbert G. Gutman, *The Black Family in Slavery and Freedom, 1750–1925* (New York, 1976) on the slave family; Roderick A. McDonald, *The Economy and Material Culture of Slaves: Goods and Chattels on the Sugar Plantations of Jamaica and Louisiana* (Baton Rouge, 1993) on the slaves' "internal economy"; and Ira Berlin, *Slaves without Masters: The Free Negro in the Antebellum South* (New York, 1974) on the free black in the South.

The literature on the coming and the fighting of the Civil War is also extensive. For works with useful bibliographies see McPherson, *Ordeal by Fire*; Emory Thomas, *The Confederate Nation, 1861–1865* (New York, 1979), and Phillip S. Paludan, *A People's Contest: The Union and Civil War, 1861–1865* (New York, 1988). For descriptions of the role of blacks in the Civil War, see the documents and introductions in the series edited by Ira Berlin and others, *Freedom*, 4 vols. (Cambridge, 1982, 1985, 1990, 1993). Several of the essays in Frank McGlynn and Seymour Drescher (eds.), *The Meaning of Freedom: Economics, Politics, and Culture After Slavery* (Pittsburgh, 1992) help to place the adjustments to slave emancipation in the United States in comparative perspective.

The important works dealing with the economy of the postbellum South include: Robert Higgs, *Competition and Coercion: Blacks in the American Economy, 1865–1914* (Cambridge, 1977); Gavin Wright, *Old South, New South: Revolutions in the Southern Economy since the Civil War* (New York, 1986); Roger L. Ransom and Richard Sutch, *One Kind of Freedom: The Economic Consequences of Emancipation* (Cambridge, 1977); Jay R. Mandle, *Not Slave, Not Free: The African American Experience since the Civil War* (Durham, NC, 1992); Gerald D. Jaynes, *Branches Without Roots: The*

Genesis of the Black Working Class in the American South, 1862–1882 (New York, 1986), and a wide-ranging essay by William N. Parker, "The South in the National Economy, 1865–1970," *Southern Economic Journal*, 46 (1980), 1019–48. For broader comparisons of sectional economic change, see Harvey S. Perloff (and others), *Regions, Resources and Economic Growth* (Baltimore, 1960), and the work by Richard A. Easterlin and others, summarized most usefully in his "Regional Income Trends, 1840–1950," in Seymour Harris (ed.), *American Economic History* (New York, 1961), 525–47. C. Vann Woodward, *Origin of the New South, 1877–1913* (Baton Rouge, 1951), presents much information and interpretation dealing with economic and other issues.

For discussions of related social and economic issues, regarding blacks and the postbellum South, see William Cohen, *At Freedom's Edge: Black Mobility and the Southern White Quest for Racial Control, 1861–1915* (Baton Rouge, 1991) on black migration within and outside the South; J. Morgan Kousser, *The Shaping of Southern Politics: Suffrage Restriction and the Establishment of the One-Party South, 1880–1910* (New Haven, 1974) on southern voting; Howard N. Rabinowitz, *Race Relations in the Urban South* (New York, 1978) and Joel Williamson, *The Crucible of Race: Black-White Relations in the American South since Emancipation* (New York, 1984) on the patterns of race relations after slavery; Robert A. Margo, *Race and Schooling in the South, 1880–1950: An Economic History* (Chicago, 1990) on changing expenditures on black and white education; and Reynolds Farley, *Growth of the Black Population: A Study of Demographic Trends* (Chicago, 1970) on demographic matters.

CHAPTER 9
(ENGERMAN AND SOKOLOFF)

Economic development is often equated with the process of industrialization of the economy. For this reason there is a considerable body of historical literature dealing with the growth of the manufacturing sector, and this is particularly the case with the nineteenth-century American economy. Thus a considerable number of useful studies must remain uncited here, although the reader will profit greatly from referring to the bibliographies and references in the works mentioned below.

The classic work on manufacturing in the nineteenth century remains the three volumes by Victor S. Clark, *History of Manufactures in the United*

States (1929 ed. 3 vols; Washington, DC, 1929). A mid-nineteenth-century work still of some interest is James L. Bishop, *A History of American Manufactures from 1608 to 1860*, 3 vols. (Philadelphia, 1868). Recent surveys of manufacturing development covering at least some of this period are Peter Temin, "Manufacturing," in Lance E. Davis, Richard A. Easterlin, William N. Parker, et al., *American Economic Growth: An Economist's History of the United States* (New York, 1972); Thomas C. Cochran, *Frontiers of Change: Early Industrialization in America* (New York, 1981); and Glenn Porter, *The Rise of Big Business, 1860–1910*, 2nd ed. (Arlington Heights, 1992). A very useful set of bibliographic essays on American industries is in David O. Whitten (ed.), *Manufacturing: A Historiographic and Bibliographic Guide* (New York, 1990).

For a general background to economic changes in this period, see two essays by Robert Gallman, "Gross National Product in the United States, 1834–1909," in Dorothy S. Brady (ed.), *Output, Employment, and Productivity in the United States after 1800*, Studies in Income and Wealth, vol. 30 (New York, 1966), 3–76, and Robert E. Gallman "Commodity Output, 1839–1899," in William N. Parker (ed.), *Trends in the American Economy in the Nineteenth Century*, Studies in Income and Wealth, vol. 24, (Princeton, 1960), 13–71. For examinations of the role of institutions and institutional change, see Lance E. Davis and Douglass C. North, *Institutional Change and American Economic Growth* (Cambridge, 1971); and Douglass C. North, *Institutions, Institutional Change, and Economic Performance* (Cambridge, 1990).

There are numerous sources of data for the study of manufacturing development, including business organizations, government reports, and newspaper and magazine articles, but most important for the nineteenth century are the data collected as part of the federal census and published by the Burean of the Census. For the nineteenth century, moreover, the firm-level data underlying the aggregate published data are still available in the manuscript schedules, and these have been used by a number of economic historians in various studies. Manufacturing data were collected as part of the general census for 1810, 1820, and 1840–1890, and published with industrial and geographic breakdowns. Since the census of 1830 did not include data on manufacturing, the secretary of the Treasury, Louis McLane, collected information for some regions for 1832, and the McLane Report remains an important source of manufacturing data. At the end of the nineteenth century it was decided to take a separate manufacturing census, and this was done every five years during the rest of the period, with data collected for years 1899, 1904, 1909, 1914, and 1919. There are summary presentations of these censuses in United States, Bureau of the Census, *Historical Statistics of the United States, Colonial Times to 1790* (Washington, DC, 1975). Useful compilations and analysis of manufacturing information at the end of this period are in Solomon Fabricant, *Employment in Manufacturing, 1899–1939: An Analysis of its Relation to the Volume of Production* (New York, 1944); Solomon Fabricant, *The Output of Manufacturing Industries in the United States, 1899–1937* (New York, 1940); and Daniel Creamer, Sergei Dobrovolsky, and Israel Borenstein, *Capital in Manufacturing and Mining: Its Formation and Financing* (Princeton, 1960).

The basic studies of manufacturing productivity used in this chapter are Kenneth L. Sokoloff, "Productivity Growth in Manufacturing during Early Industrialization: Evidence from the American Northeast, 1820–1860" in Stanley L. Engerman and Robert E. Gallman (eds.), *Long-Term Factors in American Economic Growth*, Studies in Income and Wealth, vol. 51 (Chicago, 1986), 679–736; and John W. Kendrick, *Productivity Trends in the United States* (Princeton, 1961). There are useful data for comparative examination in S. N. Broadberry, *The Productivity Race: British Manufacturing in International Perspective, 1850–1990* (Cambridge, 1997). Studies of changing scale, productivity, and economic growth include: Kenneth L. Sokoloff, "Was the Transition from the Artisanal Shop to the Nonmechanized Factory Associated with Gains in Efficiency? Evidence from the United States Manufacturing Censuses of 1820 and 1850," *Explorations in Economic History*, 21 (1984), 351–82; Alfred D. Chandler, Jr., *The Visible Hand: The Managerical Revolution in American Business* (Cambridge, MA, 1977); Jeremy Atack, "Firm Size and Industrial Structure in the United States during the Nineteenth Century," *Journal of Economic History*, 46 (1986), 463–75; Jeremy Atack, "Economies of Scale and Efficiency Gains in the Rise of the Factory in America, 1820–1890," in Peter Kilby (ed.), *Quantity and Quiddity: Essays in United States Economic History* (Middletown, CT, 1987), 286–335; David Hounshell, *From the American System to Mass Production, 1800–1932* (Baltimore, 1984); and Anthony Patrick O'Brien, "Factory Size, Economies of Scale, and the Great Merger Wave of 1898–1902," *Journal of Economic History*, 48 (1988), 639–49. Useful examinations of the impact of changing power sources include Allen H. Fenichel, "Growth and Diffusion of Power in Manufacturing, 1838–1919," in Brady (ed.), *Output*, 443–78; Richard Duboff, "The Introduction of Electric Power in American Manufacturing," *Economic History*

Review, 20 (1967), 509–18; and Louis C. Hunter, *A History of Industrial Power in the United States, 1780–1830*, 3 vols. (Charlottesville, 1979, 1985; Cambridge, MA, 1991). Important studies of the causes and consequences of technical change in manufacturing include Nathan Rosenberg (ed.), *The American System of Manufactures* (Edinburgh, 1969); Nathan Rosenberg, *Technology and American Economic Growth* (New York, 1972); and Paul A. David, *Technical Choice, Innovation and Economic Growth* (Cambridge, 1975). For a rather negative view of technology in this period, see David F. Noble, *America by Design: Science, Technology and the Rise of Corporate Capitalism* (Oxford, 1977). The debate on labor scarcity and its impact on the nature of technical change in manufacturing has been considered by, among others, H. J. Habakkuk, *American and British Technology in the Nineteenth Century: The Search for Labor Saving Invention* (Cambridge, 1962); Peter Temin, "Labor Scarcity and the Problem of American Industrial Efficency in the 1850s," *Journal of Economic History*, 26 (1966), 277–98; and John A. James and Jonathan S. Skinner, "The Resolution of the Labor-Scarcity Paradox" *Journal of Economic History*, 45 (1985), 513–540. The role of a favorable natural resource base has recently been studied by Gavin Wright, "The Origins of American Industrial Success, 1879–1940," *American Economic Review*, 80 (1990), 651–68.

There are numerous studies of individual industries, to which Whitten (ed.) *Manufacturing* is a useful guide. Of particular interest are, for cotton textiles; Caroline F. Ware, *The Early New England Cotton Manufacture: A Study in Industrial Beginnings* (Boston, 1931); Paul F. McGouldrick, *New England Textiles in the Nineteenth Century: Profits and Investments* (Cambridge, MA, 1968); and Lance E. Davis and H. Louis Stettler III, "The New England Textile Industry, 1825–60: Trends and Fluctuations: in Brady (ed.) *Output*, 213–42; Robert Brooke Zevin, *The Growth of Manufacturing in Early Nineteenth-Century New England* (New York, 1975); Philip Scranton, *Proprietary Capitalism: The Textile Manufacture at Philadelphia, 1800–1883* (Cambridge, 1983), and on industrial borrowings in this sector, see Lance E. Davis, "The New England Textile Mills and the Capital Markets: A Study of Industrial Borrowing, 1840–1860," *Journal of Economic History*, 20 (1960), 1–30; on woolen manufactures see Arthur H. Cole, *The American Wool Manufacture* (Cambridge, MA, 1926); on iron and steel, see Peter Temin, *Iron and Steel in Nineteenth-Century America: An Economic Inquiry* (Cambridge, MA, 1964), and Robert W. Fogel and Stanley L. Engerman, "A Model for the Explanation of Industrial Expansion during the Nineteenth Century: With an Application to the American

Iron Industry," *Journal of Political Economy*, 77 (1969), 306–28; for food and livestock products see Rudolf Alexander Clemen, *The American Livestock and Meat Industry* (New York, 1923) and Margaret Walsh, *The Rise of the Midwestern Meat Packing Industry* (Lexington, 1982); and for machine tools, Nathan Rosenberg, "Technological Change in the Machine Tool Industry, 1840–1910," *Journal of Economic History*, 23 (1963), 414–46. For regional studies, see Margaret Walsh, *The Manufacturing Frontier: Pioneer Industry in Antebellum Wisconsin, 1830–1800* (Madison, WI, 1972), and Fred Bateman and Thomas Weiss, *A Deplorable Scarcity: The Failure of Industrialization in the Slave Economy* (Chapel Hill, 1981). Still the leading study of the decline of household manufactures is Rolla M. Tryon, *Household Manufactures in the United States, 1840–1860: A Study in Industrial History* (Chicago, 1917). Amidst the attention to large-scale plants at the end of the century, Philip Scranton, *Endless Novelty: Specialty Production and American Industrialization, 1865–1925* (Princeton, 1997) describes the important role of smaller, more flexible firms.

Data on the labor force in manufacturing is in Stanley Lebergott, *Manpower in Economic Growth: The American Record since 1800* (New York, 1964). An analysis of the reasons why women and children formed an important part of the factory labor force is presented in two articles by Claudia Goldin and Kenneth Sokoloff, "Women, Children, and Industrialization in the Early Republic: Evidence from the Manufacturing Censuses," *Journal of Economic History*, 42 (1982), 741–74 and "The Relative Productivity Hypothesis of Industrialization: The American Case, 1820 to 1850," *Quarterly Journal of Economics*, 99 (1984), 461–87.

The merger movement has been counted and analyzed in Ralph L. Nelson, *Merger Movements in American Industry 1895–1956* (Princeton, 1959); and Naomi R. Lamoreaux, *The Great Merger Movement in American Business, 1895–1904* (Cambridge, 1985). The wealth that was created during the late nineteenth century, and the presumed great inequality that it provided the so-called Robber Barons, has been discussed by Matthew Josephson, *The Robber Barons: The Great American Capitalists, 1861–1901* (New York, 1934) and Gustavus Myers, *History of the Great American Fortunes*, 3 vols. (Chicago, 1910). For somewhat different interpretations of the changing patterns of wealth and its distribution, see Edward Kirkland, *Industry Comes of Age: Business, Labor, and Public Policy, 1860–1897* (New York, 1961) and Alfred D. Chandler, Jr., *Scale and Scope: The Dynamics of Industrial Capitalism* (Cambridge, MA, 1990), particularly 47–233.

Detailed examinations of one important institution influencing manufacturing growth, the patent system, are provided by Fritz Machlup, *An
Economic Review of the Patent System* (Washington, DC, 1958), and Zvi
Griliches, *R & D and Productivity: The Econometric Evidence* (Chicago, 1998),
particularly "Patent Statistics as Economic Indicators: A Survey,"
287–343. Studies presenting information on the relation between patents
and economic growth include Jacob Schmookler, *Invention and Economic
Growth* (Cambridge, MA, 1966); Kenneth L. Sokoloff, "Inventive
Activity in Early Industrial America: Evidence from the Patent Records,
1790–1846," *Journal of Economic History*, 48 (1988), 813–50; Kenneth L.
Sokoloff and B. Zorina Khan, "The Democratization of Invention during
Early Industrialization: Evidence from the United States, 1790–1846,"
Journal of Economic History, 50 (1990), 363–78; and Naomi R. Lamoreaux
and Kenneth L. Sokoloff, "Inventors, Firms, and the Market for Tech-
nology: United States Manufacturing in the Late Nineteenth and Early
Twentieth Centuries," in Naomi R. Lamoreaux, Dan M. G. Raff, and Peter
Temin (eds.), *Learning by Doing in Markets, Firms, and Countries* (Chicago,
1999).

Studies of the tariff and industrialization start with Hamilton's *Report
on Manufactures*. Taussig has two studies: Frank W. Taussig, *The Tariff
History of the United States*, 8th rev. ed. (New York, 1931) and *Some Aspects
of the Tariff Question*, 3rd ed. (Cambridge, MA, 1931), which remain the
most systematic overviews of changing laws and their effects on firms and
industries. More recently, J. J. Pincus, *Pressure Groups and Politics in Antebellum Tariffs* (New York, 1977) studied the legislative debate in 1824,
while Mark Bils, "Tariff Protection and Production in the Early United
States Cotton Textile Industry," *Journal of Economic History*, 44 (1984),
1033–46, and C. Knick Harley, "The Antebellum American Tariff: Food
Exports and Manufacturing," *Explorations in Economic History*, 29 (1992),
375–400, re-examine the consequences of tariff protection. Data on the
tariff and foreign trade in manufactures is provided in *Historical Statistics*
and in Robert E. Lipsey, "U.S. Foreign Trade and the Balance of Payment,
1800–1913," Chapter 15 in this volume.

CHAPTER 10 (LAMOREAUX)

Gary M. Walton and James F. Shepherd offer a concise overview of
colonial economic development in *The Economic Rise of Early America*

(New York, 1979). See also Edwin J. Perkins, *The Economy of Colonial America* 2nd ed. (New York, 1988). Thomas M. Doerflinger has detailed the economic activities of merchants in late-eighteenth-century Philadelphia in *A Vigorous Spirit of Enterprise: Merchants and Economic Development in Revolutionary Philadelphia* (Chapel Hill, 1986). The history of one prominent merchant family can be followed in *The Browns of Providence Plantations*, 2 vols. by James B. Hedges (Providence, 1968). The first volume traces the family's activities in the colonial period; the second explores its increasing involvement in manufacturing during the nineteenth century.

In *Merchants and Manufacturers: Studies in the Changing Structure of Nineteenth-Century Marketing* (Baltimore, 1971), Glenn Porter and Harold C. Livesay document the important role that merchants played in financing early industrial development. Many of the examples in this essay come from their book. For merchants' role in the development of the putting-out system in shoes, see Mary H. Blewett, *Men, Women, and Work: Class, Gender, and Protest in the New England Shoe Industry, 1780–1910* (Urbana, 1988); and Alan Dawley, *Class and Community: The Industrial Revolution in Lynn* (Cambridge, MA, 1976). On textiles, see Robert F. Dalzell, Jr., *Enterprising Elite: The Boston Associates and the World They Made* (Cambridge, MA, 1987); Paul F. McGouldrick, *New England Textiles in the Nineteenth Century: Profits and Investment* (Cambridge, MA, 1968); Barbara M. Tucker, *Samuel Slater and the Origins of the American Textile Industry, 1790–1860* (Ithaca, 1984); Anthony F. C. Wallace, *Rockdale: The Growth of an American Village in the Early Industrial Revolution* (New York, 1972); and Robert Brooke Zevin, *The Growth of Manufacturing in Early Nineteenth Century New England* (New York, 1975).

Other valuable industry studies that I have tapped for this essay include John N. Ingham, *Making Iron and Steel: Independent Mills, 1820–1920* (Columbus, OH, 1991); Amos J. Loveday, Jr., *The Rise and Decline of the American Cut Nail Industry: A Study of the Interrelationships of Technology, Business Organization, and Management Techniques* (Westport, CT, 1983); Judith A. McGaw, *Most Wonderful Machine: Mechanization and Social Change in Berkshire Paper Making, 1801–1885* (Princeton, 1987); Paul F. Paskoff, *Industrial Evolution: Organization, Structure, and Growth of the Pennsylvania Iron Industry, 1750–1860* (Baltimore, 1983); and Joseph E. Walker, *Hopewell Village: A Social and Economic History of an Iron-Making Community* (Philadelphia, 1966). For general treatments of early economic development, see Thomas C. Cochran, *Frontiers of Change: Early Industrialism in*

America (New York, 1981); and Douglass C. North, *The Economic Growth of the United States, 1790–1860* (Englewood Cliffs, 1961). See also such classic industry-by-industry accounts as J. Leander Bishop, *A History of American Manufacturers from 1608 to 1860*, 3 vols. (Philadelphia, 1868); and Victor S. Clark, *History of Manufacturers in the United States*, 3 vols. (Washington, DC, 1929).

In *Relevance Lost: The Rise and Fall of Management Accounting* (Boston, 1987), H. Thomas Johnson and Robert S. Kaplan describe merchants' accounting practices and the ways in which they were modified to suit industrial needs. On the legal history and use of the corporate form of organization, see Oscar Handlin and Mary Flug Handlin, *Commonwealth: A Study of the Role of Government in the American Economy: Massachusetts, 1774–1861* (New York, 1947); Louis Hartz, *Economic Policy and Democratic Thought: Pennsylvania, 1776–1860* (Cambridge, MA, 1948); Herbert Hovenkamp, *Enterprise and American Law, 1836–1937* (Cambridge, MA, 1991); and James Willard Hurst, *The Legitimacy of the Business Corporation in the Law of the United States, 1780–1970* (Charlottesville, 1970). Joseph A. Pratt has documented some of the restrictive implications of state regulation of corporations in "The Petroleum Industry in Transition: Antitrust and the Decline of Monopoly Control in Oil," *Journal of Economic History*, 40 (1980), 815–37. Naomi R. Lamoreaux has shown how banks can provide partnerships with many of the advantages of the corporate form (see "Banks, Kinship, and Economic Development: The New England Case," *Journal of Economic History*, 46 (1986), 647–67, and *Insider Lending: Banks, Personal Connections, and Economic Development in Industrial New England* (New York, 1994)). For a quantitative analysis of the spread of corporations, see George Herberton Evans, Jr., *Business Incorporation in the United States, 1800–1943* (New York, 1948).

Joseph A. Schumpeter's theory of entrepreneurial innovation is most clearly spelled out in *The Theory of Economic Development: An Inquiry into Profits, Capital, Credit, Interest, and the Business Cycle* (Cambridge, MA, 1934). Patterns of patenting activity are analyzed in Kenneth L. Sokoloff, "Inventive Activity in Early Industrial America: Evidence from Patent Records, 1790–1846," *Journal of Economic History*, 48 (1988), 813–50; and Sokoloff and B. Zorina Khan, "The Democratization of Invention during Early Industrialization: Evidence from the United States, 1790–1846," *Journal of Economic History*, 50 (1990), 363–78. Additional information on patent law can be found in B. Zorina Khan, "Property Rights and Patent Litigation in Early Nineteenth-Century America," *Journal of Economic*

History, 55 (1995), 58–97; and Floyd L. Vaughan, *The United States Patent System: Legal and Economic Conflicts in American Patent History* (Norman, OK, 1956). For information on early technological innovations, see Carolyn C. Cooper, *Shaping Invention: Thomas Blanchard's Machinery and Patent Management in Nineteenth-Century America* (New York, 1991); Donald R. Hoke, *Ingenious Yankees: The Rise of the American System of Manufactures in the Private Sector* (New York, 1990); and David A. Hounshell, *From the American System to Mass Production, 1800–1932: The Development of Manufacturing Technology in the United States* (Baltimore, 1984). For insight into the voluntary and involuntary sharing of technical information, see Robert C. Allen, "Collective Invention," *Journal of Economic Behavior and Organization*, 4 (1983), 1–24; and Ross Thomson, "Firms and U.S. Lathe Development, 1790–1919: Explorations in the Dynamics of a Technological Center," unpublished paper. As William N. Parker has observed, farmers exchanged information in similar ways. See Lance E. Davis, Richard A. Easterlin, William N. Parker et al., *American Economic Growth: An Economist's History of the United States* (New York, 1972), 379–402.

General studies of nineteenth-century transportation innovations include George Rogers Taylor, *The Transportation Revolution, 1815–1860* (New York, 1951); Albert Fishlow, *American Railroads and the Transformation of the Antebellum Economy* (Cambridge, MA, 1966); and Robert W. Fogel, *Railroads and American Economic Growth: Essays in Econometric History* (Baltimore, 1964). Alfred D. Chandler, Jr. argued that railroads were the nation's first big business in *The Visible Hand: The Managerial Revolution in American Business* (Cambridge, MA, 1977). For the development of modern management in railroads, see also Thomas C. Cochran, *Railroad Leaders, 1845–1890: The Business Mind in Action* (Cambridge, MA, 1953). Studies probing the effectiveness of the railroad cartels include Paul W. MacAvoy, *The Economic Effects of Regulation: The Trunk-Line Railroad Cartels and the Interstate Commerce Commission before 1900* (Cambridge, MA, 1965); Robert H. Porter, "A Study of Cartel Stability: The Joint Executive Committee, 1880–1886," *Bell Journal of Economics*, 14 (1983), 301–14; Thomas S. Ulen, "The Market for Regulation: The ICC from 1887 to 1920," *American Economic Review, Papers and Proceedings*, 70 (1980), 306–10. Albro Martin has argued that the Interstate Commerce Commission kept railroad rates below the level needed to sustain investment spending during the early twentieth century. See his *Enterprise Denied: Origins of the Decline of American Railroads, 1897–1917* (New York, 1971).

Chandler's *Visible Hand* provides an invaluable account of the rise of large-scale organizations in distribution and manufacturing, as well as in the railroad sector. For additional information on individual cases, see Glenn D. Babcock, *History of the United States Rubber Company: A Case Study in Corporation Management* (Bloomington, IN, 1966); Harold C. Livesay, *Andrew Carnegie and the Rise of Big Business* (Boston, 1975); Joseph M. McFadden, "From Invention to Monopoly: The History of the Consolidation of the Barbed Wire Industry, 1873–1899," unpublished Ph.D. dissertation, Northern Illinois University, 1968; McFadden, "Monopoly in Barbed Wire: The Formation of the American Steel and Wire Company," *Business History Review*, 52 (1978), 465–89; Daniel M. G. Raff and Peter Temin, "Business History and Recent Economic Theory: Imperfect Information, Incentives, and the Internal Organization of Firms," in Temin, ed., *Inside the Business Enterprise: Historical Perspectives on the Use of Information* (Chicago, 1991), 7–35; David C. Smith, *History of Papermaking in the United States, 1691–1969* (New York, 1970); and Mary Yeager, *Competition and Regulation: The Development of Oligopoly in the Meat Packing Industry* (Greenwich, CT, 1981).

Most large firms were created by mergers. Naomi R. Lamoreaux has analyzed the giant merger wave that occurred at the turn of the century and traced the effect of the new consolidations on competitive behavior during the early twentieth century. See *The Great Merger Movement in American Business, 1895–1904* (New York, 1985). On the behavior of dominant firms and their attempts to erect entry barriers, see also Joe S. Bain, *Barriers to New Competition: Their Character and Consequences in Manufacturing Industries* (Cambridge, MA, 1956); Richard E. Caves, Michael Fortunato, and Pankaj Ghemawat, "The Decline of Dominant Firms, 1905–1929," *Quarterly Journal of Economics*, 99 (1984), 523–46; David F. Noble, *America by Design: Science, Technology, and the Rise of Corporate Capitalism* (New York, 1977); Leonard S. Reich, *The Making of American Industrial Research: Science and Business at GE and Bell, 1876–1926* (New York, 1985); Reich, "Research, Patents, and the Struggle to Control Radio: A Study of Big Business and the Uses of Industrial Research," *Business History Review*, 51 (1977), 208–35; F. M. Scherer, *Industrial Market Structure and Economic Performance*, 2nd ed. (Chicago, 1980); and Gertrude G. Schroeder, *The Growth of Major Steel Companies, 1900–1950* (Baltimore, 1953). Mira Wilkins demonstrated that large firms developed a new interest in protecting their brands in "The Neglected Intangible Asset: The Influence of the Trade Mark on the Rise of the Modern Corporation,"

Business History, 34 (1992), 66–75. Shaw Livermore measured the performance of consolidations formed during the Great Merger Movement in "The Success of Industrial Mergers," *Quarterly Journal of Economics*, 50 (1935), 68–96; and G. Warren Nutter explored their effect on industrial concentration in Nutter and Henry Adler Einhorn, *Enterprise Monopoly in the United States, 1899–1958* (New York, 1969). For an analysis of the continuing role of bankers in the management of consolidations, see J. Bradford DeLong, "Did J. P. Morgan's Men Add Value? A Historical Perspective on Financial Capitalism," in Temin, ed., *Inside the Business Enterprise*, 205–36. For information on the changes in state law that made large consolidations possible, see Christopher Grandy, "New Jersey Corporate Chartermongering, 1875–1929," *Journal of Economic History*, 49 (1989), 677–92. Thomas R. Navin and Marian V. Sears have traced the effect of the merger movement on the stock market in "The Rise of a Market for Industrial Securities, 1887–1902," *Business History Review*, 29 (1955), 105–38. On antitrust policy in a comparative context, see Tony Freyer, *Regulating Big Business: Antitrust in Great Britain and America, 1880–1990* (Cambridge, 1992).

For an exploration of the idea that the United States economy in the twentieth century was divided into center and peripheral sectors, see Robert T. Averitt, *The Dual Economy: The Dynamics of American Industry Structure* (New York, 1968). Chandler expanded on his notion that managerial capitalism brought gains in efficiency in *Scale and Scope: The Dynamics of Industrial Capitalism* (Cambridge, MA, 1990). For a similar argument, see William Lazonick, *Business Organization and the Myth of the Market Economy* (New York, 1991). Oliver Williamson argued that large firms emerged because they economized on transactions costs in "The Modern Corporation: Origins, Evolution, Attributes," *Journal of Economic Literature* 19 (1981), 1537–68; and *The Economic Institutions of Capitalism: Firms, Markets, Relational Contracting* (New York, 1985). In *An Evolutionary Theory of Economic Change* (Cambridge, MA, 1982), Richard R. Nelson and Sidney G. Winter shifted Williamson's analysis to a dynamic framework, arguing that large firms developed organizational capabilities that were responsible for their longevity and success. Other scholars, however, have emphasized the dangers of managerial capitalism. See Michael C. Jensen, "Eclipse of the Public Corporation," *Harvard Business Review*, 67 (1989), 61–74; and Harvey H. Segal, *Corporate Makeover: How American Business is Reshaping for the Future* (New York, 1989).

CHAPTER 11 (FREYER)

James Willard Hurst's *Law and the Conditions of Freedom in the Nineteenth-Century United States* (Madison, WI, 1956) demonstrates how law facilitated economic growth and in so doing influenced the interaction between business law and the economy from the making of the Constitution to the early twentieth century. His *Law and Social Order in the United States* (Ithaca, 1977) and *Law and Markets in the United States: Different Modes of Bargaining Among Interests* (Madison, WI, 1982) are particularly useful for the study of the interaction between formal legal and market institutions as a working system. For insights into the methodological and ideological origins of Hurst's work, see Hendrik Hartog, "Snakes in Ireland: A Conversation with Willard Hurst," *Law and History Review*, 12 (1994), 370–90. While acknowledging Hurst's enormous influence, the present essay blends the insights of Douglass C. North in *Institutions, Institutional Change, and Economic Performance* (Cambridge, 1990) and Clifford D. Shearing, "A Constitutive Conception of Regulation," in Peter Grobosky and John Braithwaite (eds.), *Business Regulation in Australia's Future* (Canberra, 1993), to suggest a constitutive view of American business law and economic history.

The leading survey of substantive law during the long nineteenth century is Lawrence M. Friedman, *A History of American Law* (New York, 1985). Although Friedman often refers to English doctrinal developments, a comprehensive survey that employs a similar contextualist analysis, is W. R. Cornish and G. de N. Clark, *Law and Society in England: 1750–1950* (London, 1989). A classic treatment of the English legal developments that influenced America is P. S. Atiyah, *The Rise and Fall of Freedom of Contract* (Oxford, 1979). See also companion works by Morton J. Horwitz, *The Transformation of American Law, 1780–1860* (Cambridge, MA, 1977) and *The Transformation of American Law, 1970–1960: The Crisis of Legal Orthodoxy* (New York, 1992); and William E. Nelson, *Americanization of the Common Law: The Impact of Legal Change on Massachusetts Society, 1760–1830* (Cambridge, MA, 1975). Another useful survey, including a discussion of business law developments, is Kermit L. Hall, *The Magic Mirror: Law in American History* (New York, 1989).

Invaluable for an understanding of the era of the making of the Constitution, especially the influence of mercantilism, is Forrest McDonald, *Novus Ordo Seclorum: The Intellectual Origins of the Constitution* (Lawrence, KS, 1985). An innovative revisionist treatment of mercantilism during the last third of the eighteenth century is John E. Crowley, *The Privileges of Independence: Neomercantilism and the American Revolution* (Baltimore, 1993). See also Drew R. McCoy, *The Elusive Republic: Political Economy in Jeffersonian America* (Chapel Hill, 1980). The significance of federalism as a profoundly new polity shaping the interplay of legal rules and market behavior in light of pervasive institutional fragmentation is explored by Harry N. Scheiber's "Federalism and the American Economic Order, 1789–1910," *Law and Society Review*, 10 (1975), 57–118; and his "Property Law, Expropriation, and Resource Allocation by Government, 1789–1910," *Journal of Economic History*, 33 (1973), 232–51. For the influence of the federal courts within the evolving federal system see Tony A. Freyer, *Forums of Order: The Federal Courts and Business in American History* (Greenwich, CT, 1979).

The institutional development of the constitutional order and the corresponding multiplicity of rules during America's formative antebellum era are considered in Tony A. Freyer, *Producers versus Capitalists: Constitutional Conflict in Antebellum America* (Charlottesville, 1994). An insightful study of the institutions and ideology shaping the Supreme Court and constitutional law under John Marshall is G. Edward White, *The Marshall Court and Cultural Change, 1815–1835* (New York, 1991); a useful overview of the Court's role during Roger B. Taney's tenure and his successors is Harold H. Hyman and William M. Wiecek, *Equal Justice Under Law: Constitutional Development, 1835–1875* (New York, 1982). A good overview of American constitutional development from the earliest times to the 1990s is Michael Les Benedict, *Blessings of Liberty* (New York, 1996).

Three case studies of leading contract and commerce clause decisions within an economic context are: Maurice G. Baxter, *The Steamboat Monopoly: Gibbons v. Ogden, 1824* (New York, 1972); Stanley I. Kutler, *Privilege and Creative Destruction: The Charles River Bridge Case* (Baltimore, 1990); and Francis N. Stites, *Private Interest & Public Gain: The Dartmouth College Case, 1819* (Amherst, 1972). F. Thornton Miller's *Juries and Judges versus the Law, Virginia's Provincial Legal Perspective, 1783–1828* (Charlottesville, 1994) is a good study of the local institutional culture shaping rules and market relations during the early antebellum period. A study that explores how the local courtroom culture influenced the development of federal judicial independence in one state is Tony A. Freyer and Timothy Dixon, *Democracy and Judicial Independence, The Federal District Courts in Alabama, 1820–1994* (Brooklyn, 1995).

Although there are numerous studies of slavery and Jim Crow as the sources of southern distinctiveness, works focusing on legal institutions and the economy are less common. On the overall issue of institutional and economic distinctiveness see Lawrence M. Friedman, "The Law Between the States: Some Thoughts on Southern Legal History;" Tony A. Freyer, "Law and The Antebellum Southern Economy: An Interpretation"; Harry N. Scheiber, "Federalism, the Southern Regional Economy, and Public Policy Since 1865"; and Thomas D. Morris, "'Society Is Not Marked by Punctuality in the Payment of Debts': The Chattel Mortgages of Slaves," all in James W. Ely, Jr. and David J. Bodenhamer (eds.), *Ambivalent Legacy: A Legal History of the South* (Jackson, MS, 1984). The economic role of slave property supported by formal rules, and the collapse of the system, are discussed in Richard Holcombe Kilbourne, Jr.'s *Debt, Investment, Slaves, Credit Relations in East Feliciana Parrish Louisiana, 1825–1885* (Tuscaloosa, 1995). More general works, which nonetheless provide a law-oriented perspective, are Gavin Wright, *Old South, New South: Revolutions in the Southern Economy since the Civil War* (New York, 1986); and C. Vann Woodard, *The Strange Career of Jim Crow*, 2nd rev. ed. (New York, 1966). For a different view see: Harold D. Woodman, "Post–Civil War Southern Agriculture and the Law," *Agricultural History*, 53 (1979), 319–37; and Robert W. Fogel, *Without Consent or Contract: The Rise and Fall of American Slavery* (New York, 1989).

Morton Keller shows how interest-group struggle contributed to a diffusion of rule-making authority across fields of law in *Affairs of State: Public Life in Late Nineteenth-Century America* (Cambridge, MA, 1977); his *Regulating a New Economy: Public Policy and Economic Change in America, 1900–1933* (Cambridge, MA, 1990) applies the same analysis to the Progressive era. Thomas K. McCraw's *Prophets of Regulation: Charles Francis Adams, Louis D. Brandeis, James M. Landis, Alfred E. Kahn* (Cambridge, MA, 1984) has much to say about business–government relations, bureaucracy, interest groups, and administrative policy that is invaluable in explaining the working realities of the American political economy during the late nineteenth and early twentieth centuries. On these same themes see also Samuel P. Hays, "Political Choice in Regulatory Administration," in Thomas K. McCraw (ed.) *Regulation in Perspective: Historical Essays* (Cambridge, MA, 1981). An insightful interpretation of law, the economy, and economic theory during the same period is Herbert Hovenkamp, *Enterprise and American Law, 1836–1937* (Cambridge, MA, 1991). Walter T. K. Nugent's *From Centennial to World War: American Society, 1876–1917* (Indianapolis, 1977) is a useful overview of institutions, popular values, and politics; it is particularly good on the diversity among the Progressives. Two works that show how strong were state lawmakers' defense of a "public interest," are: Peter Karsten, *Heart versus Head: Judge-Made Law in Nineteenth-Century America* (Chapel Hill, 1997); and William J. Novak, *The People's Welfare: Law and Regulation in Nineteenth-Century America* (Chapel Hill, 1996).

The centrality of antitrust to the turn-of-the-century political economy is explored in Martin J. Sklar, *The Corporate Reconstruction of American Capitalism, 1890–1916: The Market, the Law and Politics* (Cambridge, 1988); a comparative study of the same theme that reaches somewhat different conclusions is Tony A. Freyer, *Regulating Big Business: Antitrust in Great Britain and America 1880–1990* (Cambridge, 1990). Two studies of the railroads as progenitors of the regulatory state that present opposing interpretations are Gerald Berk, *Alternative Tracks: The Constitution of American Industrial Order, 1865–1917* (Baltimore, 1994) and Albro Martin, *Enterprise Denied: Origins of the Decline of American Railroads, 1897–1917* (New York, 1971). On the contrasting origin and outcome of local versus national railroad regulatory policy compare Mark T. Kanazawa and Roger G. Noll, "The Origins of State Railroad Regulation: The Illinois Constitution of 1870"; and Keith T. Poole and Howard Rosenthal, "Congress and Railroad Regulation: 1874 to 1887," both in Claudia Goldin and Gary D. Libecap (eds.), *The Regulated Economy: A Historical Approach to Political Economy* (Chicago, 1994). For the impact of federalism on railroad regulation see William R. Doezema, "Railroad Management and the Interplay of Federal and State Regulation," 1885–1916, *Business History Review*, 50 (1976), 153–78.

All of the above works have much to say about the law and structure of the American business corporation. A classic treatment is James Willard Hurst, *The Legitimacy of the Business Corporation in the Law of the United States, 1780–1970* (Charlottesville, 1970). Alfred D. Chandler, Jr.'s *The Visible Hand: The Managerial Revolution in American Business* (Cambridge, MA, 1977); and *Scale and Scope: The Dynamics of Industrial Capitalism* (Cambridge, MA, 1990), considered in the framework developed above, clarifies how the rise of the large-scale, diversified, corporate industrial firm was the outcome of a distinctive American institutional environment. An excellent study of the relation between corporate organization and the turn of the century merger wave is Naomi R. Lamoreaux, *The Great Merger Movement in American Business, 1895–1904* (Cambridge, 1985); an incisive study suggesting the comparative distinctiveness of American versus British managerial corporate structures is Leslie Hannah, "Visible and Invisible Hands in Great Britain," in Alfred D. Chandler, Jr. and Herman Daems (eds.), *Managerial Hierarchies: Comparative Perspectives on the Rise of the Modern Industrial Enterprise* (Cambridge, MA, 1980), 41–76. Neil Fligstein's *The Transformation of Corporate Control* (Cambridge, MA, 1990) is especially good on the corporate organizational significance of antitrust during the turn of the century. Allen D. Boyer, "Activist Shareholders, Corporate Directors, and Institutional Investment: Some Lessons from the Robber Barons," *Washington and Lee Law Review*, 50 (1993), 977–1042 is useful for legal issues of corporate governance and the separation of owners and management.

The institutional impact of multiple sources of rulemaking in the federal system during the period 1870–1920 is creatively explored in Edward A. Purcell, Jr., *Litigation and Inequality: Federal Diversity Jurisdiction in Industrial America, 1870–1958* (New York, 1992). For the importance of the *Swift* doctrine see Tony A. Freyer, *Harmony and Dissonance: The Swift and Erie Cases in American Federalism* (New York, 1981). Peter J. Coleman's *Debtors and Creditors in America: Insolvency, Imprisonment for Debt and Bankruptcy, 1607–1900* (Madison, WI, 1974), examines the changing role of the law governing debtor–creditor relations. Gary T. Schwartz, "Tort Law and the Economy in Nineteenth-Century America: A Reinterpretation," *Yale Law Journal*, 90 (1981), 1717–75 critiques the subsidy theory of tort; Robert J. Kaczorowski, "The Common Law Background of Nineteenth-Century Tort Law," *Ohio State Law Journal*, 51 (1990), 1127–99 emphasizes the primary significance of ideological moralism. But see also Randolph E. Bergstrom's, *Courting Danger: Injury and Law in New York City, 1870–1910* (Ithaca, 1992). For business law issues involving women see Joan Hoff, *Law, Gender, and Justice: A Legal History of U.S. Women* (New York, 1991). For the origins of labor law as it bears upon the themes discussed above, Christopher L. Tomlins' *Law, Labor, and Ideology in the Early American Republic* (Cambridge, 1993) is helpful.

CHAPTER 12 (SYLLA)

Comprehensive accounts of many of the issues treated in this essay can be found in several general studies of historical public finance. The most valuable of these is Paul Studenski and Herman E. Krooss, *Financial History of the United States: Fiscal, Monetary, Banking, and Tariff, including Financial Administration and State and Local Finance*, 2nd ed. (New York, 1963). Among many other things, it gives excellent coverage to the finances of wars. Less comprehensive but with more material on private as well as public finance is Margaret G. Myers, *A Financial History of the United States* (New York, 1970). An older book of a similar nature that focuses almost exclusively on the federal government is Davis Rich Dewey, *Financial History of the United States* (New York, 1931). These volumes, especially Studenski and Krooss, and Dewey, contain a lot of data on government finances, but for a comprehensive look at the data on public finances throughout the period 1789–1914, consult U.S. Bureau of the Census, *Historical Statistics of the United States, Colonial Times to 1970* (Washington, DC, 1975), Chapter Y; unfortunately, only data for the federal government extend over the whole period, with comprehensive data on state and local finances available only after 1900. For an engaging overview of federal taxation over two centuries, see W. Elliott Brownlee, *Federal Taxation in America: A Short History* (Cambridge, 1996); however, the period covered here is treated only in the first of Brownlee's four chapters.

A recent and useful study of how the American financial system, public and private, evolved down to the end of the War of 1812 is Edwin Perkins, *American Public Finance and Financial Services, 1700–1815* (Columbus, OH, 1994); among other things, it provides a detailed account of Hamilton's financial program and the ways in which the Jeffersonians attacked it before and after they came to power in 1801. For a narrower treatment of how government financed itself during the Confederation period, see E. James Ferguson, *The Power of the Purse: A History of American Public Finance, 1776–1790* (Chapel Hill, 1961). Closely related is Mary M. Schweitzer, "State-Issued Currency and the Ratification of the U.S. Constitution," *Journal of Economic History*, 49 (1989), 311–22. For a detailed study of how the Revolution affected taxation as colonies became states, see Robert A. Becker, *Revolution, Reform, and the Politics of American Taxation, 1763–1783* (Baton Rouge, 1980).

A full account of Federalist policies, including Hamilton's financial program, during the three Federalist administrations is given by Stanley Elkins and Eric McKitrick, *The Age of Federalism: The Early American Republic, 1788–1800* (New York, 1993). For a similar treatment of Jefferson's economic policies, one that brings out their contradictions, see Drew R. McCoy, *The Elusive Republic: Political Economy in Jeffersonian America* (Chapel Hill, 1980). Further insights into Jefferson's complex character and contradictory policy stances are contained in Joseph J. Ellis, *American Sphinx: The Character of Thomas Jefferson* (New York, 1997). On Jefferson's loathing of debts, his own and those of the United States, see Herbert Sloan, *Principle and Interest* (New York, 1994).

On government and the augmentation of the factors of production, the classic study of land privatization is still Benjamin H. Hibbard, *A History of Public Land Policies* (New York, 1924); also useful is Malcolm J. Rohrbaugh, *The Land Office Business: The Settlement and Administration of American Public Lands, 1789–1837* (New York, 1968), and Paul W. Gates, "The Homestead Law in an Incongruous Land System," *American Historical Review*, 41 (1936), 652–81. A comprehensive treatment of immigration from the colonial period to the twentieth century is Maldwyn A. Jones, *American Immigration* (Chicago, 1960). The broad elements involved in the formation of the capital market are treated by Edwin Perkins in the volume cited above.

Banking in the United States was intimately tied to government and government finances from its inception. The banking sector is treated in Hugh Rockoff's chapter (Chap. 14) in this volume, which should be consulted. The general topic of the bank–government nexus is covered in two classic works, Fritz Redlich, *The Molding of American Banking: Men and Ideas* 2 vols. (New York, 1947, 1950; one volume reprint, 1968); and especially with sensitivity to the politics of banking in Bray Hammond, *Banks and Politics in America, From the Revolution to the Civil War* (Princeton, 1957; reprint 1991). The early growth of state-chartered banking is detailed in J. Van Fenstermaker, *The Development of American Commercial Banking: 1782–1837* (Kent, OH, 1965). Right and wrong ways for states to involve themselves with banking are the subject of a study of southern states by Larry Schweikart, *Banking in the American South from the Age of Jackson to Reconstruction* (Baton Rouge, 1987). The connection of state banks and state public finance is the subject of Richard Sylla, John B. Legler, and John J. Wallis, "Banks and State Public Finance in the New Republic: The United States, 1790–1860," *Journal of Economic History*, 47 (1987), 391–404. The same authors also study how the ways in which states raised revenue from banks affected the ways they regulated them; see Wallis, Sylla, and Legler, "The Interaction of Taxation and Regulation in Nineteenth-Century U.S. Banking," in Claudia Goldin and Gary D. Libecap (eds.), *The Regulated Economy: A Historical Approach to Political Economy* (Chicago, 1994), 121–44. Free banking, an innovation of the 1830s that spread, as noted in the chapter, to many states and then the federal government, was important for public finance because it usually backed bank notes with government bonds, thereby linking banks, state finances, and the capital market; see the full set of references to free banking in the bibliography to the chapter on banking by Hugh Rockoff (Chap. 14), in this volume. Linkages of federal finance, the banking system, and the capital market during and after and Civil War are studied in Richard Sylla, "Federal Policy, Banking Market Structure, and Capital Mobilization in the United States, 1863–1913," *Journal of Economic History*, 29 (1969), 657–86, and Sylla, *The American Capital Market, 1846–1914: A Study of the Effects of Public Policy on Economic Development* (New York, 1975).

Chartering and regulating corporations was an important activity of American states from the first years of the republic. The early development and extent of this activity are treated in two old classics, Joseph S. Davis, *Essays in the Earlier History of American Corporations*, 2 vols. (Cambridge, MA, 1917); and G. Heberton Evans, Jr., *Business Incorporations in the United States, 1800–1943* (New York, 1948). Ronald E. Seavoy, *The Origins of the American Business Corporation, 1784–1855* (Westport, CT, 1982) discusses how the corporation developed under the auspices of New York State, while Richard Sylla in "Early American Banking: The Significance of the Corporate Form," *Business and Economic History*, 14 (1985), 105–23, traces the modern, private, competitive corporation's origins to the U.S. banking sector and shows that as the corporate form spread through the liberalization of state chartering, banks became safer by attracting more capital.

The economic share of government and its components in the period covered in the essay is the subject of several works. Lance Davis and John B. Legler, "The Government in the American Economy, 1815–1902: A Quantitative Study," *Journal of Economic History*, 26 (1966), 514–52, made an early pass at estimating total and component shares for the most of the nineteenth century. That work was extended and revised by John B. Legler, Richard Sylla, and John J. Wallis, "U.S. City Finances and the Growth of Government, 1850–1902," *Journal of Economic History*, 48 (1988), 347–56. In the interim, Charles Frank Holt, *The Role of State Government in the Nineteenth Century American Economy, 1820–1902: A Quantitative Study* (New York, 1977), produced fairly comprehensive estimates of state revenues and spending and compared them with similar measures for the federal government. A detailed study of similar issues in the context of one state is Richard Sylla, "Long-Term Trends in State and Local Finance: Sources and Uses of Funds in North Carolina, 1800–1977," in Stanley L.

Engerman and Robert E. Gallman (eds.), *Long-Term Factors in American Economic Growth* (Chicago, 1986), 819–68.

Studies of the role of state governments in the era of internal improvements are voluminous and have a long the distinguished history of their own. A seminal article is Guy S. Callender, "The Early Transportation and Banking enterprises of the States in Relation to the Growth of Corporations," *Quarterly Journal of Economics*, 17 (1902), 111–62. During the middle decades of this century, many studies focused on individual states before, during, and after the improvement era. They include Oscar Handlin and Mary Flug Handlin, *Commonwealth, A Study of the Role of Government in the American Economy – Massachusetts: 1776–1861* (New York, 1947; revised edition, Cambridge, MA, 1969); Louis Hartz, *Economic Policy and Democratic Thought: Pennsylvania, 1776* (Cambridge, MA, 1948); Milton S. Heath, *Constructive Liberalism: The Role of the State in Economic Development in Georgia to 1860* (Cambridge, MA, 1954); James N. Primm, *Economic Policy in the Development of a Western State: Missouri, 1820–1860* (Cambridge, MA, 1954); Nathan Miller, *The Enterprise of a Free People: Aspects of Economic Development of New York during the Canal Period, 1792–1838* (Ithaca, 1962); and Harry N. Scheiber, *Ohio Canal Era: A Case Study of Government and the Economy, 1820–1861* (Athens, OH, 1969). In the middle of this outpouring came an influential article contending that the studies toppled the notion that Americans had ever practiced laissez faire, however much they may have believed in it in theory: Robert Lively, "The American System: A Review Article," *Business History Review*, 29 (1955), 81–96. More recent studies of particular states are Peter Wallenstein, *From Slave South to New South: Public Policy in Nineteenth Century Georgia* (Chapel Hill, 1987) and L. Ray Gunn, *The Decline of Authority: Public Economic Policy and Political Development in New York State, 1800–1860* (Ithaca, 1988). Related to all this literature is a study of California, which of course was not involved in the early internal improvement era: Gerald D. Nash, *State Government and Economic Development: A History of Administrative Policies in California, 1849–1933* (Berkeley, 1964).

Less state-focused studies of the era of state improvements include George Rogers Taylor, *The Transportation Revolution, 1815–1860* (New York, 1951); Carter Goodrich, *Government Promotion of Canals and Railroads, 1800–1890* (New York, 1960); and Carter Goodrich (ed.), *Canals and American Economic Development* (New York, 1961). A recent study of a state that built, owned, and operated a railroad is Allen W. Trelease, *The*

North Carolina Railroad, 1849–1871, and the Modernization of North Carolina (Chapel Hill, 1991).

The debt problems of states in the wake of the improvement boom are treated specifically in Reginald C. McGrane, *Foreign Bondholders and American State Debts* (New York, 1935); in a wider historical context, by B. U. Ratchford, *American State Debts* (Durham, 1941); and with new twists in Richard Sylla and John J. Wallis, "The Anatomy of Sovereign Debt Crises: Lessons from the American State Defaults of the 1840s," *Japan and the World Economy*, 10 (1998), 267–93.

Although it covers only one state's experience, the most detailed study of how local governments became deeply involved in providing governmental aid to railroad improvements during and especially after the states themselves retreated to the sideline, is Harry H. Pierce, *Railroads of New York: A Study of Government Aid, 1826–1875* (Cambridge, MA, 1953). For a summary of a comparative micro-level study of two counties' involvement with improvements, see John Majewski, "Commerce and Community: Internal Improvements in Virginia and Pennsylvania, 1790–1860," *Journal of Economic History*, 56 (1996), 467–69. Jac C. Heckelman and John Joseph Wallis, "Railroads and Property Taxes," *Explorations in Economic History*, 34 (1997), 77–99, document the fiscal rationale for the heavy involvement of American governments in aid to internal improvements.

Studies of important forms of taxation in the period covered by the essay include, besides the Robert Becker book referred to above, Sidney Ratner, *The Tariff in American History* (New York, 1972); Ratner, *Taxation and Democracy in America* (New York, 1967); and Glenn W. Fisher, *The Worst Tax? A History of the Property Tax in America* (Lawrence, KS, 1996).

Financial connections between the federal and state governments are treated by Paul B. Trescott, "Federal-State Financial Relations, 1790–1860," *Journal of Economic History*, 15 (1955), 227–45. Post–Civil War debt policies are the subject of Robert T. Patterson, *Federal Debt-Management Policies, 1865–1897* (Durham, 1954); their impacts on the capital markets are discussed in Sylla, *The American Capital Market*, cited above. Legal and constitutional limits placed on state debts starting in the 1840s are discussed by A. James Heins, *Constitutional Restrictions Against State Debts* (Madison, WI, 1963). Later limitations that states placed on the ability of municipalities to incur debt are treated in Lane Lancaster, *State Supervision of Municipal Indebtedness* (Philadelphia, 1923).

The growing importance of city governments is studied in quantitative terms in Legler, Sylla, and Wallis, "U.S. City Finances," cited earlier. Two books providing much more narrative detail about city growth and city government functions are Eric H. Monkkonen, *America Becomes Urban: The Development of U.S. Cities and Towns, 1780–1980* (Berkeley, 1988), and Jon C. Teaford, *The Unheralded Triumph: City Government in America, 1870–1900* (Baltimore, 1984).

The expansion of state regulatory and social welfare functions in response to industrialization and the rise of big business in the late nineteenth century are discussed by William R. Brock, *Investigation and Responsibility: Public Responsibility in the United States, 1865–1900* (Cambridge, 1984), and Ballard C. Campbell, "Federalism, State Action, and 'Critical Episodes' in the Growth of American Government," *Social Science History*, 16 (1992), 561–77. How these state initiatives prompted the federal government to do the same is developed in Richard Sylla, "The Progressive Era and the Political Economy of Big Government," *Critical Review*, 5 (1992), 531–57. A review of other treatments of the rise of modern regulation is given by Thomas K. McCraw, "Regulation in America: A Review Article," *Business History Review*, 49 (1975), 164–71.

CHAPTER 13 (FISHLOW: BIBLIOGRAPHY ESSAY BY JOHN MAJEWSKI)

Historians have long recognized the crucial importance of transportation improvements to nineteenth-century development. George Rogers Taylor's aptly titled *The Transportation Revolution, 1815–1860* (New York, 1951) puts transportation improvements front and center stage of antebellum economic development. W. W. Rostow imbued railroads with even more significance, arguing that the iron horse propelled America into "sustained economic growth." See especially "Leading Sectors and Take-Off," in Rostow (ed.), *The Economics of Take-Off into Sustained Growth* (New York, 1963) and *Stages of Economic Growth: A Non-Communist Manifesto* (New York, 1960).

Rostow's claims, in part, motivated several economists to estimate the "social savings" of railroads. The two most well-known works in this tradition – Albert Fishlow, *American Railroads and the Transformation of the Antebellum Economy* (Cambridge, MA, 1965), and Robert William Fogel, *Railroads and American Economic Growth: Essays in Econometric History* (Baltimore, 1964) – did much to disprove Rostow's leading sector hypothesis. Fogel's conclusion that railroads made a relatively modest contribution to GNP as late as 1890, however, set off a storm of controversy. Among the many critiques are Paul A. David, "Transportation Innovations and Economic Growth: Professor Fogel On and Off the Rails," *Economic History Review*, 22 (1969), 506–25; Jeffrey G. Williamson, *Late Nineteenth-Century American Development: A General Equilibrium Model* (New York, 1974); and Peter McClelland, "Railroads, American Growth and the New Economic History," *Journal of Economic History*, 28 (1968), 102–23. Fogel replies to these critics at length in "Notes on the Social Saving Controversy," *Journal of Economic History*, 39 (1979), 1–50.

A large business history literature documents the impact of railroads on management strategies, capital markets, and other economic institutions. The defining work of this tradition has been Alfred D. Chandler, Jr., *The Visible Hand: The Managerial Revolution in American Business* (Cambridge, MA, 1977). Among the numerous studies of individual railroads and entrepreneurs, the best include James A. Ward, *J. Edgar Thomson: Master of the Pennsylvania* (Westport, CT, 1980); Mary Yeager, *Competition and Regulation: The Development of Oligopoly in the Meat Packing Industry* (Greenwich, CT, 1981); John Lauritz Larson, *Bonds of Enterprise: John Murray Forbes and Western Development of America's Railway Age* (Cambridge, MA, 1984); and Allen W. Trelease, *The North Carolina Railroad, 1849–1871, and the Modernization of North Carolina* (Chapel Hill, 1991).

Canals have generated less debate than railroads, but a number of scholars have carefully considered the timing and financing of the canal boom. Some of the most important studies include Harry N. Scheiber, *Ohio Canal Era: A Case Study of Government and the Economy* (Athens, OH, 1969); Ralph D. Gray, *The National Waterway: A History of the Chesapeake and Delaware Canal, 1769–1985* (Chicago, 1989); Ronald E. Shaw, *Erie Water West: A History of the Erie Canal, 1792–1854* (Lexington, 1966); and the essays in Carter Goodrich (ed.), *Canals and American Economic Development* (New York, 1961). Ronald Shaw synthesizes these studies in *Canals for a Nation: The Canal Era in the United States, 1790–1860* (Lexington, 1990). For an application of the social savings model to canals, see Roger Ransom, "Canals and Development: A Discussion of the Issues," *American Economic Review, Papers and Proceedings*, 54 (1964), 365–89.

Until very recently, historians have given relatively little attention to turnpikes. The standard works on turnpikes include Frederick J. Wood, *The Turnpikes of New England and the Evolution of the Same Through England, Virginia, and Maryland* (Boston, 1919), and Joseph A. Durrenberger, *Turnpikes: A Study of the Toll Road Movement in the Middle Atlantic States and*

Maryland (Valdosta, GA, 1931). More recent work documents the ability of private investors to fund turnpike construction in the face of poor direct profitability. See Daniel B. Klein, "The Voluntary Provision of Public Goods? The Turnpike Companies of Early America," *Economic Inquiry*, 28 (1990), 788–812; Daniel B. Klein and John Majewski, "Economy, Community, and Law: The Turnpike Movement in New York, 1797–1845," *Law and Society Review*, 26 (1992), 469–512; and John Majewski, Christopher Baer, and Daniel B. Klein, "Responding to Relative Decline: The Plank Road Boom in Antebellum New York," *Journal of Economic History*, 53 (1993), 106–22.

Another distinct literature documents extensive government investment in turnpikes, canals, and railroads. Important state-level studies in the "Commonwealth School" include Oscar and Mary Flug Handlin, *Commonwealth: A Study of the Role of Government in the American Economy, Massachusetts, 1774–1861* (New York, 1947; revised edition, Cambridge, MA, 1969); Louis Hartz, *Economic Policy and Democratic Thought: Pennsylvania, 1776–1860* (Cambridge, MA, 1948); Milton S. Heath, *Constructive Liberalism: The Role of the State in Economic Development in Georgia to 1860* (Cambridge, MA, 1954); and Harry H. Pierce, *Railroads of New York: A Study of Government Aid, 1826–1875* (Cambridge, MA, 1953). For a general survey of transportation and public policy, see Carter Goodrich, *Government Promotion of American Canals and Railroads, 1800–1890* (New York, 1960), as well as Robert A. Lively's excellent review article "The American System," *Business History Review*, 29 (1955), 81–96. Douglass C. North, *Growth and Welfare in the American Past: A New Economic History* (Englewood Cliffs, 1966), 98–107, provides a more skeptical assessment of government investment to economic growth.

The relationship between transportation and public policy continues to draw the attention of scholars. For the cultural and ideological impact of transportation improvements, see Carol Sheriff, *The Artificial River: The Erie Canal and the Paradox of Progress, 1817–1862* (New York, 1996), and William Deverell, *Railroad Crossing: California and the Railroads, 1850–1910* (Berkeley, 1994). John Majewski compares state investment in Virginia and Pennsylvania in "The Political Impact of Great Commercial Cities: State Investment in Antebellum Pennsylvania and Virginia," *Journal of Interdisciplinary History*, 28 (1997), 1–26, while Colleen A. Dunlavy puts U.S. railroad policy in an international context in *Politics and Industrialization: Early Railroads in the United States and Prussia* (Princeton, 1994).

CHAPTER 14 (ROCKOFF)

This bibliography essay is divided into two parts. The first, "Sources of Data," describes sources of quantitative data and explains how the tables and the numbers underlying the figures were constructed. The second, "Institutions and Interpretations," surveys the major interpretations. It is intended merely to get the reader started on particular topics, and is by no means exhaustive.

Sources of Data

Data on money, prices, and related variables are important for understanding the development of the financial system. From about 1870 on the estimates are fairly reliable, but for the antebellum period, and particularly before 1840, they are subject to a wide margin of error. Walter Buckingham Smith and Arthur Harrison Cole, *Fluctuations in American Business, 1790–1860* (Cambridge, MA, 1935) is the classic source for data on prices and related variables before the Civil War. Wesley C. Mitchell, *A History of the Greenbacks* (Chicago, 1903; reprinted 1968) has numerous tables concerning money, prices, wages, and interest rates during the Civil War era. A subsequent volume, *Gold, Prices, and Wages Under the Greenback Standard* (Berkeley, 1908), presented data on the years between the end of the war and the resumption of specie payments. The business cycle chronology developed by the National Bureau of Economic Research is generally accepted as authoritative. See Geoffrey H. Moore, "Business Cycles, Panics, and Depressions," in Glenn Porter, ed., *Encyclopedia of American Economic History: Studies of the Principal Movements and Ideas* (New York, 1980). The most comprehensive compilation of historical data is U.S. Bureau of the Census, *Historical Statistics of the United States, Colonial Times to 1970*, 2 vols., (Washington, DC, 1975).

Figures 14.1 and 14.2 employ money divided by output to show the degree of inflationary or deflationary pressure in the economy. Figure 14.1 employs some relatively crude estimates of the money supply for the period 1800–1820. I took estimates for 1799, 1809, and 1819 made by Clark Warburton, as reported in Milton Friedman and Anna J. Schwartz, *Monetary Statistics of the United States: Estimates, Sources, Methods* (New York, 1970), 231–32, and then used more frequent estimates of government currency issues and bank notes, also reported by Friedman and Schwartz, to interpolate between Warburton's estimates. For the period 1820 to 1832 Figure 14.1 employs Peter Temin's estimates from *The Jacksonian Economy* (New York, 1969), 71. Temin's estimates are based in part on the banking data collected by J. Van Fenstermaker, *The Development of American Commercial Banking, 1782–1837* (Kent, OH, 1965). For the period 1833 to 1859, Figure 14.1 employs George Macesich's estimates, as reported in Friedman and Schwartz. The Temin and Macesich estimates differ slightly in years of overlap, partly because Temin includes balances held by the Treasury in the stock of money, although Macesich excludes them. For the years 1860 to 1866 Figure 14.1 and Table 14.2 employ estimates based on Milton Friedman and Anna J. Schwartz, *Monetary Trends in the United States and the United Kingdom: Their Relation to Income, Prices, and Interest Rates, 1867–1975* (Chicago, 1982), 224–25. For 1867 to 1914 Figures 14.1 and 14.2 employ estimates from Friedman and Schwartz, *Monetary Trends*, 122–23.

Figure 14.1 also employs a measure of the trend level of real gross domestic product. I started with the estimates for 1800, 1807, 1810, 1820, 1830, 1840, 1850, and 1860 recently computed by Thomas Weiss: "Labor Force Estimates and Economic Growth 1800–1860," in Robert Gallman and John Wallis (eds.), *American Economic Growth and Standards of Living Before the Civil War* (Chicago, 1992). I then interpolated the intervening estimates assuming a constant rate of growth. For the period 1869 to 1914 I relied on estimates made by Christina Romer, "The Prewar Business Cycle Reconsidered: New Estimates of Gross National Product, 1869–1908," *Journal of Political Economy*, 97 (1989), 22–23. Alternative estimates are given in Nathan S. Balke and Robert J. Gordon, "The Estimation of Prewar Gross National Product: Methodology and New Evidence," *Journal of Political Economy*, 97 (1989), 84. To get figures for the Civil War decade I employed a log linear interpolation between Weiss's estimate of gross domestic product in 1860 and Romer's estimate of gross national product for 1869, without making an allowance for the difference in definition. For the period 1861 to 1864 I deducted one-third of the 1860 estimate to account for the loss of the South.

The prices shown in the tables and figures are wholesale prices up to 1869 and the GNP deflator thereafter. The wholesale price index was originally developed by George Warren and Frank Pearson. The most convenient source for it is Bureau of the Census, *Historical Statistics*, vol. 1, 201–2, series E52. The GNP deflator shown in the graphs is Romer's.

Institutions and Interpretations

There are several good general financial histories that cover the nineteenth century. Four that I have relied upon are Davis Rich Dewey, *Financial History of the United States* (New York, 1931) which is especially good for federal government finance; Margaret G. Myers, *A Financial History of the United States* (New York, 1970); William J. Shultz and M. R. Caine, *Financial Development of the United States* (New York, 1937); and Paul Studenski and Herman Krooss, *Financial History of the United States*, 2nd ed. (New York, 1963). Milton Friedman and Anna J. Schwartz, *A Monetary History of the United States* (Princeton, 1963) is indispensable for the period after 1867. The classic study of the political economy of banking before the Civil War is Bray Hammond, *Banks and Politics in America, from the Revolution to the Civil War* (Princeton, 1957, reprinted 1991). Hammond carries the story through the Civil War in *Sovereignty and the Empty Purse: Banks and Politics in the Civil War* (Princeton, 1970). The classic study of bankers and their ideas is Fritz Redlich, *The Molding of American Banking: Men and Ideas*, 2 vols. (New York, 1947, 1951; 1 vol. reprint, 1968). For southern banking see Larry Schweikart, *Banking in the American South from the Age of Jackson to Reconstruction* (Baton Rouge, 1987). There are many histories of individual banks that are useful. Harold Van B. Cleveland and Thomas Huertas, *Citibank, 1812–1970* (Cambridge MA, 1985), is an outstanding recent example, although it concentrates on the post-1914 period. Richard Sylla, "Monetary Innovation in America," *Journal of Economic History*, 42 (1982), 21–30, and Eugene N. White, "The Political Economy of Banking Regulation, 1864–1933," *Journal of Economic History*, 42 (1982), 33–42, develop some theoretical insights useful for understanding the evolution of the financial system. Lloyd Mints, *A History of Banking Theory In Great Britain and the United States* (Chicago, 1945) is the classic attack on the real bills doctrine. Thomas J. Sargent and Neil Wallace, "The Real Bills Doctrine versus the Quantity Theory: A Reconsideration" *Journal of Political Economy*, 90 (1982), 1212–36, defends it.

The pre-Constitutional, revolutionary, and early national periods provide fascinating experiments for monetary historians to ponder, many still unexplored. An overview and synthesis of considerable material is provided in Edwin J. Perkins, *American Public Finance and Financial Services, 1700–1815* (Columbus, OH, 1994). The surprising connections between banking and public finance are described in Richard Sylla, John B. Legler, and John J. Wallis, "Banks and State Public Finance in the New Republic: The United States, 1790–1860," *Journal of Economic History*, 47 (1987), 391–404. Monetary issues are discussed in Charles W. Calomiris, "Institutional Failure, Monetary Scarcity, and Depreciation of the Continental," *Journal of Economic History*, 48 (1988), 47–68; Mary M. Schweitzer, "State-Issued Currency and the Ratification of the U.S. Constitution," *Journal of Economic History*, 49 (1989), 311–22; J. Van Fenstermaker and John E. Filer, "The U.S. Embargo Act of 1807: Its Impact on New England Money, Banking, and Economic Activity," *Economic Inquiry*, 28 (1990), 163–84; and Arthur J. Rolnick, Bruce D. Smith, and Warren E. Weber, "In Order to Form a More Perfect Union," *Federal Reserve Bank of Minneapolis Quarterly Review*, 17 (1993), 2–13. An important reconstruction of the data is carried out in J. Van Fenstermaker, John E. Filer, and Robert S. Herren, "Monetary Statistics of New England, 1785–1837," *Journal of Economic History*, 44 (1984), 441–54.

The literature on the Second Bank and the Bank War is extensive. Edwin J. Perkins, "Langdon Cheeves and the Panic of 1819: A Reassessment," *Journal of Economic History*, 44 (1984) 455–61 criticizes Cheeve's administration. Some of the effects of the Second Bank are described in Arthur Fraas, "The Second Bank of the United States: An Instrument for an Inter-regional Monetary Union" *Journal of Economic History*, 34 (1974), 447–67. Monetary aspects are discussed in George Macesich, "Sources of Monetary Disturbances in the U.S., 1834–1845," *Journal of Economic History*, 20 (1960), 407–34; Temin, *The Jacksonian Economy*; and J. Van Fenstermaker and John E. Filer, "Impact of the First and Second Banks of the United States and the Suffolk System on New England Money: 1791–1837," *Journal of Money, Credit, and Banking*, 18 (1986), 28–40. The consequences of the Bank War for the economy as a whole are discussed in Stanley L. Engerman, "A Note on the Economic Consequences of the Second Bank of the United States," *Journal of Political Economy*, 78 (1970), 725–28. An important alternative interpretation is provided in Richard A. Highfield, Maureen O'Hara, and Bruce D. Smith, "Do Open Market Operations Matter? Theory and Evidence from the Second Bank of the United States," *Journal of Economic Dynamics and Control*, 20 (1996), 479–519. Stuart Bruchey, *Enterprise: The Dynamic Economy of a Free People* (Cambridge, MA, 1990), discusses the link between political and economic events during the Bank War.

The free banking era has been the subject of much recent research because of the implications that this experiment might have for contemporary regulatory policy. Useful studies include Hugh Rockoff, "The Free

Banking Era: A Re-Examination," *Journal of Money, Credit, and Banking*, 6 (1974), 141–73, and three papers by Arthur J. Rolnick and Warren E. Weber: "New Evidence on the Free Banking Era," *American Economic Review*, 73 (1983), 1080–91; "The Causes of Free Bank Failures: A Detailed Examination of the Evidence," *Journal of Monetary Economics*, 14 (1984), 267–91; and "Explaining the Demand for Free Bank Notes," *Journal of Monetary Economics*, 21 (1988), 47–71. The benign picture of free banking that emerges from these studies was challenged by James A. Kahn, "Another Look at Free Banking in the United States," *American Economic Review*, 75 (1985), 881–85. Kenneth Ng, "Free Banking Laws and Barriers to Entry in Banking, 1838–1860," *Journal of Economic History*, 48 (1988), 877–89, is skeptical of claims that free banking encouraged entry. Richard Sylla, "Early American Banking: The Significance of the Corporate Form," *Business and Economic History*, 14 (1985), 105–23, points out that the free banking law represented an important legal innovation. Andrew J. Economopoulos provides useful case studies in the "Illinois Free Banking Experience," *Journal of Money, Credit, and Banking*, 20 (1988), 249–64, "Free Bank Failures in New York and Wisconsin: A Portfolio Analysis," *Explorations in Economic History*, 27 (1990), 421–41, as does Robert G. King, "On the Economics of Private Money," *Journal of Monetary Economics*, 12 (1983), 127–58. Gary Gorton, "Reputation Formation in Early Bank Note Markets," *Journal of Political Economy* 104, (1996) 346–97, uses data on the notes of individual banks to explore the efficiency of the bank note market. George Green, *Finance and Economic Development in the Old South: Louisiana Banking, 1804–1861* (Stanford, 1972) covers a banking system that had elements of free banking, but was in many ways unique. Charles Calomiris, "Is Deposit Insurance Necessary? A Historical Perspective," *Journal of Economic History*, 50 (1990), 283–95, discusses some early experiments with deposit insurance and branch banking.

The Suffolk system is discussed in D. R. Whitney, *The Suffolk Bank and Its Redemption System* (Boston, 1881); S. Wilfred Lake, "The End of the Suffolk System," *Journal of Economic History*, 7 (1947), 183–207; J. Clayburn La Force, "Gresham's Law and the Suffolk System: A Misapplied Epigram," *Business History Review*, 40 (1966), 149–66; George Trivoli, *The Suffolk Bank: A Study of a Free-Enterprise Clearing System* (London, 1979); Donald J. Mullineaux, "Competitive Monies and the Suffolk Bank System: A Contractural Perspective," *Southern Economic Journal*, 53 (1987), 884–98; George A. Selgin and Lawrence H. White, "Competitive Monies and the

Suffolk Bank System: Comment," *Southern Economic Journal*, 55 (1988), 215–19; Donald J. Mullineaux, "Competitive Monies and the Suffolk Bank System: Reply," *Southern Economic Journal*, 55 (1988), 220–23; and Charles W. Calomiris and Charles M. Kahn, "The Efficiency of Self-Regulated Payments Systems: Learning from the Suffolk System," *Journal of Money, Credit, and Banking*, 28 (1996), 766–97.

The formation of the National Banking System is discussed in Andrew McFarland Davis, *The Origin of the National Banking System* (Washington, DC, 1910), and its performance is evaluated in Phillip Cagan, "The First Fifty Years of the National Banking System – An Historical Appraisal," in Deane Carson (ed.), *Banking and Monetary Studies* (Homewood, IL, 1963). Helen Hill Updike, *The National Banks and American Economic Development, 1870–1900* (New York, 1987) is a more recent evaluation. Note redemption is discussed in George A. Selgin and Lawrence H. White, "Monetary Reform and the Redemption of National Bank Notes, 1863–1913," *Business History Review*, 68 (1994), 205–43.

A substantial literature on regional interest rate differentials in the postbellum period has evolved from Lance Davis's pioneering paper, "The Investment Market, 1870–1914: Evolution of a National Market," *Journal of Economic History*, 25 (1965), 355–99. Major subsequent contributions include Richard Sylla, "Federal Policy, Banking Market Structure, and Capital Mobilization in the United States, 1863–1913," *Journal of Economic History*, 29 (1969), 657–86; Gene Smiley, "Interest Rate Movements in the United States, 1888–1913," *Journal of Economic History*, 35 (1975), 591–62; John James, "The Development of the National Money Market," *Journal of Economic History*, 36 (1976), 878–97; Jeffrey G. Williamson, *Late-Nineteenth-Century American Development: A General Equilibrium History* (New York, 1974), 119–45; and Marie Elizabeth Sushka and Brian W. Barrett, "Banking Structure and the National Capital Market, 1869–1914," *Journal of Economic History*, 44 (1984), 463–77. John J. Binder and David T. Brown, "Bank Rates of Return and Entry Restrictions, 1869–1914," *Journal of Economic History*, 51 (1991), 47–66, tests a number of the existing hypotheses.

Several studies investigate capital market integration at the state and regional level: Richard Keehn, "Market Power and Bank Lending: Some Evidence from Wisconsin, 1870–1900," *Journal of Economic History*, 35 (1975), 591–620; James T. Campen and Anne Mayhew, "The National Banking System and Southern Economic Growth: Evidence from One Southern City, 1870–1900," *Journal of Economic History*, 48 (1988),

127–37; and Kerry A. Odell, "The Integration of Regional and Interregional Capital Markets: Evidence from the Pacific Coast States, 1883–1913," *Journal of Economic History*, 49 (1989), 297–310.

Mortgage rates are explored in Barry Eichengreen, "Mortgage Interest Rates in the Populist Era," *American Economic Review*, 74 (1984), 995–1015; and Kenneth Snowden, "Mortgage Rages and Capital Market Development in the Late Nineteenth Century," *Journal of Economic History*, 47 (1987), 671–92. Antebellum bank rates are explored in Howard Bodenhorn and Hugh Rockoff, "Regional Interest Rates in Antebellum America," in Claudia Goldin and Hugh Rockoff (eds.), *Strategic Factors in Nineteenth Century American Economic History: A Volume to Honor Robert W. Fogel* (Chicago, 1992).

Neglected aspects of banking, such as the relationship between banking and entrepreneurial activity, have been explored recently by Naomi Lamoreaux: "Banks, Kinship, and Economic Development: The New England Case," *Journal of Economic History*, 46 (1986), 647–67; "Bank Mergers in Late-Nineteenth-Century New England," *Journal of Economic History*, 51 (1991), 537–58; and *Insider Lending: Banks, Personal Connections, and Economic Development in Industrial New England* (Cambridge, 1994).

The national bank note puzzle was first uncovered by Phillip Cagan, *Determinants and Effects of Changes in the Quantity of Money 1875–1960* (Princeton, 1965), 86–95. Subsequent contributions include Charles A. E. Goodhart, "Profit on National Bank Notes, 1900–1913," *Journal of Political Economy*, 73 (1965), 516–22; John A. James, "The Conundrum of the Low Issues of National Bank Notes," *Journal of Political Economy*, 84 (1976), 362–67; Phillip Cagan and Anna J. Schwartz, "The National Bank Note Puzzle Reinterpreted," *Journal of Money, Credit, and Banking*, 23 (1991), 293–307; and Bruce Champ, Neil Wallace, and Warren E. Weber, "Resolving the National Bank Note Paradox," *Federal Reserve Bank of Minneapolis Quarterly Review*, 16 (1992), 13–21. The assumption that the nonbank public treated notes and other currencies as perfect substitutes is challenged in Bruce Champ, Neil Wallace, and Warren E. Weber, "Interest Rates Under the U.S. National Banking System," *Journal of Monetary Economics*, 34 (1994), 343–58.

The classic of inflation during the Civil War in the North is Wesley C. Mitchell, *A History of the Greenbacks* (Chicago, 1903; reprinted 1968). More recent interpretations are Reuben Kessel and Armen Alchian, "Real Wages in the North During the Civil War: Mitchell's Data Reinterpreted," *Journal of Law and Economics*, 2 (1959), 95–113; and Stephen DeCanio and Joel

Mokyr, "Inflation and Wage Lag During the American Civil War," *Explorations in Economic History*, 14 (1977), 311–36. Specie resumption is discussed from a monetarist perspective in James Kindahl, "Economic Factors in Specie Resumption: The United States, 1865–1879," *Journal of Political Economy*, 69 (1961), 31–48. The role of news about the government's fiscal policy is emphasized in Richard Roll, "Interest Rates and Price Expectations during the Civil War," *Journal of Economic History*, 32 (1972), 476–98; Charles W. Calomiris, "Price and Exchange Rate Determination During the Greenback Suspension," *Oxford Economic Papers*, 40 (1988), 719–50; and Kristen L. Willard, Timothy W. Guinnane, and Harvey S. Rosen, "Turning Points in the Civil War: Views from the Greenback Market," *American Economic Review*, 86 (1996), 1001–18. The survival of a gold-based monetary system in California during the Greenback era is discussed in Robert L. Greenfield and Hugh Rockoff, "Yellowbacks Out West, and Greenbacks Back East: Social Choice Dimensions of Monetary Reform," *Southern Economic Journal*, 62 (1996), 902–15.

Money and prices in the Confederacy are discussed in Eugene Lerner, "Inflation in the Confederacy" in Milton Friedman (ed.), *Studies in the Quantity Theory of Money* (Chicago, 1956); and Gary M. Pecquet, "Money in the Trans-Mississippi Confederacy and the Confederate Currency Reform Act of 1864," *Explorations in Economic History*, 24 (1987), 218–43. George K. Davis and Gary M. Pecquet, "Interest Rates in the Civil War South," *Journal of Economic History*, 50 (1990), 133–48, resolves the paradox of stable interest rates in the South.

The classic history of bimetallism is J. Lawrence Laughlin, *The History of Bimetallism in the United States*, (New York, 1892). It was skeptical of the claims for bimetallism. Recent interpretations, however, have been more sympathetic. See Milton Friedman, "Bimetallism Revisited," *Journal of Economic Perspectives*, 4 (1990), 85–104; Milton Friedman, "The Crime of 1873," *Journal of Political Economy*, 98 (1990), 1159–94; and Hugh Rockoff, "The Wizard of Oz as a Monetary Allegory," *Journal of Political Economy*, 98 (1990), 739–60. William P. Yohe's appendix, "An Economic Appraisal of the Sub-Treasury Plan," to Lawrence Goodwyn, *Democratic Promise: The Populist Moment in America* (New York, 1976), explores one of the radical populist proposals. Peter M. Garber, "Nominal Contracts in a Bimetallic Standard," *American Economic Review*, 76 (1986), 1012–30; and Colleen Callahan, "The 19th Century Silver Movement and Aggregate Price Uncertainty," in Thomas Weiss and Donald Schaefer (eds.), *American Economic Development in Historical Perspective* (Stanford, 1994), examine the effects of the bimetallism controversy on interest rates and price level uncertainty, respectively.

The notion that "bad money drives out good," Gresham's law, explains flows of metal under the bimetallic standard has been challenged in Arthur J. Rolnick and Warren E. Weber, "Gresham's Law or Gresham's Fallacy?" *Journal of Political Economy*, 94 (1986), 185–99. But their evidence was challenged in turn by Robert L. Greenfield and Hugh Rockoff, "Gresham's Law in Nineteenth Century America," *Journal of Money, Credit, and Banking*, 27 (1995), 1086–98.

The debate over how well the gold standard worked has not been resolved. Michael D. Bordo, "The Classical Gold Standard: Some Lessons for Today" *Federal Reserve Bank of St. Louis, Review*, 63 (1981), 1–17; and "The Gold Standard, Bretton Woods and Other Monetary Regimes: A Historical Appraisal," *Federal Reserve Bank of St. Louis, Review*, 75 (1993), 123–91, compare the gold standard with subsequent regimes. Michael D. Bordo and Finn E. Kydland, "The Gold Standard as a Rule: An Essay in Exploration," *Explorations in Economic History*, 32 (1995), 423–64, compares the gold standard in different countries and provides a theoretical framework for understanding the gold standard. Michael D. Bordo and Anna J. Schwartz (eds.), *A Retrospective on the Classical Gold Standard, 1821–1931* (Chicago, 1984) contains fifteen thoughtful essays. Donald N. McCloskey and J. Richard Zecher, "How the Gold Standard Worked, 1880–1913," in Jacob A. Frenkel and Harry G. Johnson (eds.), *The Monetary Approach to the Balance of Payments* (Toronto, 1976) is an influential statement of a nontraditional approach. John A. James, "The Stability of the 19th-century Phillips Curve Relationship," *Explorations in Economic History*, 26 (1989), 117–34, looks at the effects of changing standards on the output-inflation trade-off.

Lawrence H. Officer has written a number of influential papers and a book on the efficiency of exchange-rate arbitrage under the gold standard: "Dollar-Sterling Mint Parity and Exchange Rates, 1791–1834," *Journal of Economic History*, 43 (1983), 579–616; "Integration in the American Foreign-Exchange Market, 1791–1900," *Journal of Economic History*, 45 (1985), 557–585; "The Efficiency of the Dollar-Sterling Gold Standard, 1890–1908," *Journal of Political Economy*, 94 (1986), 1038–73; "The Remarkable Efficiency of the Dollar-Sterling Gold Standard, 1890–1906," *Journal of Economic History*, 49 (1989), 1–41; and *Between the Dollar-Sterling Gold Points: Exchange Rates, Parity, and Market Behavior* (Cambridge, 1996). Some of Officer's results are confirmed in Pablo T. Spiller and Robert O.

Wood, "Arbitrage during the Dollar-Sterling Gold Standard, 1899–1908: An Econometric Approach," *Journal of Political Economy*, 96 (1988), 882–92.

Charles P. Kindleberger, *Manias, Panics, and Crashes* (New York, 1978; 2nd ed., 1989) provides a general explanation of panics, emphasizing the causative role of speculation and the need for lenders of last resort. Oliver M. W. Sprague, *History of Crises Under the National Banking Act* (Washington, DC, 1910; reprinted 1977) is still indispensable. Frederic S. Mishkin, "Asymmetric Information and Financial Crises: A Historical Perspective" in R. Glenn Hubbard (ed.), *Financial Markets and Financial Crises* (Chicago, 1990) surveys the history banking crises in the United States, concluding that a breakdown in the ability of lenders to control risks was an important feature. Charles W. Calomiris and Gary Gorton, "The Origins of Banking Panics: Models, Facts, and Bank Regulation," in the same volume also surveys the history of panics, concluding that Wall Street crashes were crucial precipitant of banking panics. Michael D. Bordo, "Financial Crises, Banking Crises, Stock Market Crashes, and the Money Supply: Some International Evidence, 1870–1933," in Forest Capie and Geoffrey E. Wood (eds.), *Financial Crises and the World Banking System* (London, 1986) reaches a similar conclusion. Charles Calomiris and Glenn Hubbard, "Price Flexibility, Credit Availability, and Economic Fluctuations: Evidence from the United States, 1894–1909," *Quarterly Journal of Economics*, 104 (1989), 429–52, argue that credit rather than money was the key variable in crises. But Michael D. Bordo, Peter Rappoport, and Anna J. Schwartz, "Money Versus Credit Rationing: Evidence for the National Banking Era, 1880–1914," in Goldin and Rockoff (eds.), *Strategic Factors*, argue the opposite.

On the panic of 1837 see Temin, *The Jacksonian Economy*, 113–47. On the panic of 1857 see Peter Temin, "The Panic of 1857," *Intermountain Economic Review*, 6 (1975), 1–12; James L. Huston, *The Panic of 1857 and the Coming of the Civil War* (Baton Rouge, 1987); and Charles Calomiris and Larry Schweikart, "The Panic of 1857: Origins, Transmission, and Containment," *Journal of Economic History*, 51 (1991), 807–34. J. S. Gibbons, *The Banks of New York, Their Dealers, the Clearing House, and the Panic of 1857* (New York, 1859) is still worth reading. Peter Garber and Vittorio Grilli, "The Belmont-Morgan Syndicate as an Optimal Investment Banking Contract," *European Economic Review*, 30 (1986), 649–72 discusses an important event in the crisis of the 1890s. Ellis W. Tallman and Jon R. Moen, "Lessons from the Panic of 1907," *Federal*

Reserve Bank of Atlanta Economic Review, 75 (1990), 2–13, focuses on the trust companies.

The role of the clearinghouse in postbellum crises has received attention recently because it was a private institution acting as a lender of last resort. See Richard H. Timberlake, Jr., "The Central Banking Role of Clearinghouse Associations," *Journal of Money, Credit, and Banking*, 16 (1984), 1–15; Gary Gorton, "Clearinghouses and the Origins of Central Banking in the U.S," *Journal of Economic History*, 45 (1985), 277–283; and Gary Gorton and Donald J. Mullineaux, "The Joint Production of Confidence: Endogenous Regulation and 19th Century Commercial Bank Clearinghouses," *Journal of Money, Credit, and Banking*, 19 (1987), 457–68.

The origins of the Federal Reserve system are explored in Robert Craig West, *Banking Reform and the Federal Reserve, 1863–1923* (Ithaca, 1974); Richard H. Timberlake, Jr., *The Origins of Central Banking in the United States* (Cambridge, MA, 1978); Richard H. Timberlake, Jr., *Monetary Policy in the United States: An Intellectual and Institutional History* (Chicago, 1993); James Livingston, *Origins of the Federal Reserve System: Money, Class, and Corporate Capitalism, 1890–1913* (Ithaca, 1986); and Steven G. Horwitz, "Competitive Currencies, Legal Restrictions, and the Origins of the Federal Reserve: Some Evidence From the Panic of 1907," *Southern Economic Journal*, 56 (1990), 639–49. Charles A. E. Goodhart, *The Evolution of Central Banks* (Cambridge, MA, 1988) adds an international perspective.

Securities markets and non-bank financial intermediaries in the nineteenth century have received less attention than commercial banks. On savings banks Emerson W. Keyes, *A History of the Savings Banks of the United States from their Inception in 1816 down to 1874*, 2 vols. (New York, 1876–78) is still standard. More recent are Peter L. Payne and Lance E. Davis, *The Savings Bank of Baltimore, 1818–1866* (Baltimore, 1963); Weldon Welfling, *Mutual Savings Banks: Evolution of a Financial Intermediary* (Cleveland, 1968); and Alan L. Olmstead, *New York City Mutual Savings Banks, 1819–1861* (Chapel Hill, 1976). Henry Morton Bodfish (ed.), *History of Building and Loan Societies in the United States* (Chicago, 1931) has a considerable amount of descriptive material, including a discussion of the Nationals. George E. Barnett, *State Banks and Trust Companies since the Passage of the National-Bank Act* (Washington, DC, 1911) provides data on the trust companies. Larry Neal, "Trust Companies and Financial Innovation, 1897–1914," *Business History Review*, 45 (1971), 35–51, explains their growth at the turn of the century. Henrietta Larson, *Jay Cooke, Private Banker* (Cambridge, MA, 1936) includes a good deal of economic analysis.

Robert Sobel, *The Big Board: A History of the New York Stock Market* (New York, 1965) is a highly readable account. Ranald C. Michie, "The London and New York Stock Exchanges, 1850–1914," *Journal of Economic History*, 46 (1986), 171–87; and Jonathan Barron Baskin, "The Development of Corporate Financial Markets in Britain and the United States, 1600–1914: Overcoming Asymmetric Information," *Business History Review*, 62 (1988), 199–237, discuss the economic effects of securities markets. Kenneth Snowden, "American Stock Market Development and Performance, 1871–1929," *Explorations in Economic History*, 24 (1987), 327–53 tests the efficiency of the market. Long-term rates of return are developed in Kenneth Snowden, "Historical Returns and Security Market Development, 1872–1925," *Explorations in Economic History*, 27 (1990), 381–420; G. William Schwert, "Indexes of U.S. Stock Prices from 1802 to 1987," *Journal of Business*, 63 (1990), 399–426; and Jack Wilson, Richard Sylla, and Charles P. Jones, "Financial Market Volatility, Panics Under the National Banking System Before 1914, and Volatility in the Long Run, 1930–1988," in Eugene N. White (ed.), *Crashes and Panics: A Historical Perspective* (Homewood, IL 1990). Sidney Homer and Richard Sylla, *A History of Interest Rates* (New Brunswick, 1991) is the standard compilation. The history of the insurance industry is recounted in Harold F. Williamson, "Insurance," in Glenn Porter (ed.), *Encyclopedia of American Economic History* (New York, 1980). Roger L. Ransom and Richard Sutch, "Tontine Insurance and the Armstrong Investigation: A Case of Stifled Innovation, 1868–1905," *Journal of Economic History*, 48 (1987), 379–90 analyzes the prohibition of tontine policies.

Vincent P. Carosso is the dean of American historians of investment banking. See *Investment Banking in America, A History* (Cambridge, MA, 1970); *More than a Century of Investment Banking, the Kidder, Peabody Co.* (New York, 1979); and *The Morgans: Private International Bankers, 1854–1913* (Cambridge, MA, 1987). Lance E. Davis, "Capital Immobilities and Finance Capitalism: A Study of Economic Evolution in the United States," *Explorations in Entrepreneurial History*, 1 (1963), 88–105, relates the rise of investment banking to the fragmentation of commercial banking and the growth of big business; but J. Bradford De Long, "Did J. P. Morgan's Men Add Value? A Historical Perspective on Financial Capitalism," in Peter Temin (ed.), *Inside the Business Enterprise* (Chicago, 1991) complements Davis's analysis while ascribing a more positive role to the investment bankers.

CHAPTER 15 (LIPSEY)

The basic detailed data on values and physical quantities in U.S. exports and imports were published in various issues of monthly, quarterly, and annual publications issued by the Bureau of Statistics of the U.S. Treasury Department and later the Bureau of Statistics of the U.S. Departments of Commerce and Labor and the Bureau of Foreign and Domestic Commerce of the U.S. Department of Commerce. A fuller listing of the original sources is provided in U.S. Bureau of the Census, *Historical Statistics of the United States, Colonial Times to 1970*, Part 2 (Washington, DC, 1975). Many of the same detailed statistical data are also reported in the *Statistical Abstract of the United States* and in various issues of the annual *Report of the Secretary of the Treasury on The State of the Finances.*

The trade data in summary form and by various broad classifications were published in *Historical Statistics*, which also includes a collection of data on trade of the American colonies before 1790. The colonial trade data, particularly for 1768–1772, are exhibited and discussed extensively in James F. Shepherd and Gary M. Walton, *Shipping, Maritime Trade, and the Economic Development of Colonial North America* (Cambridge, 1972). There are also extensive colonial and early nineteenth-century trade data collected in Timothy Pitkin, *A Statistical View of the Commerce of the United States*, (New York, 1816; reprinted New York, 1967).

Information on prices and quantities in U.S. trade is from Douglass North, *The Economic Growth of the United States, 1790–1860* (Englewood Cliffs, 1961) for 1790 to 1860, and from Robert E. Lipsey, *Price and Quantity Trends in the Foreign Trade of the United States* (Princeton, 1963) for 1879 to 1913. These price indexes were combined, with the use of other data, to form a continuous time series in Robert E. Lipsey, "Foreign Trade," in Lance E. Davis, Richard A. Easterlin, William N. Parker et al., *American Economic Growth: An Economist's History of the United States* (New York, 1972), 548–81.

Balance of payments estimates rely mainly on two papers, one by Douglass C. North, "The United States Balance of Payments, 1790 to 1860," and one by Matthew Simon, "The United States Balance of Payments, 1861–1900," in William N. Parker (ed.), *Trends in the*

American Economy in the Nineteenth Century, Studies in Income and Wealth, vol. 24 (Princeton, 1960), 573–627 and 629–711 respectively. The role of foreign investment is discussed in Michael Edelstein, *Overseas Investment in the Age of High Imperialism: The United Kingdom, 1850–1914* (New York, 1982).

Data on the stock of investment are from Cleona Lewis, *America's Stake in International Investment* (Washington, DC, 1938), with some revisions from Mira Wilkins, *The History of Foreign Investment in the United States to 1914* (Cambridge, MA, 1989) which contains not only some revisions of the earlier data, but also hundreds of descriptions of individual foreign direct investments in the United States and their evolution.

World trade and population, for comparisons with the United States, have been estimated in several articles and books by Angus Maddison and Paul Bairoch. Maddison's estimates appear in "Growth and Fluctuations in the World Economy, 1870–1960," *Banca Nazionale del Lavoro Quarterly Review*, 15 (1962), 127–195 and in *Phases of Capitalist Development* (Oxford, 1982). Bairoch's are in "European Foreign Trade in the XIX Century: The Development of the Value and Volume of Exports (Preliminary Results)," *Journal of European Economic History*, 2 (1973), 5–36; in *Commerce Extérieur et Développement Économique de l'Europe au XIXe Siècle* (Paris, 1976); and *Structure par Produits des Exportations du Tiers-Monde, 1830–1937* (Geneva, 1985). Estimates of developing country trade, and comparisons with developed countries, are published also in John R. Hanson II, *Trade in Transition: Exports from the Third World, 1840–1900* (New York, 1980). Estimates of world exports and imports were made in Walt W. Rostow, *The World Economy: History and Prospect* (Austin, 1978).

U.S. national output estimates, especially for the period before 1860 but also for the late nineteenth century, have been the subject of a good deal of recent scrutiny and proposals for revision. The earliest estimates used here are discussed in Lipsey, "Foreign Trade," and pre–Civil War U.S. economic growth was reviewed in Stanley L. Engerman and Robert E. Gallman, "U.S. Economic Growth: 1783–1860," *Research in Economic History*, 8 (1983), 1–46. The later estimates used here, up to the Civil War, are new measures of a broad concept of income, including farm improvements and home manufacturing, from Thomas Weiss, "U.S. Labor Force Estimates and Economic Growth, 1800–1860," in Robert E. Gallman and John Joseph Wallis (eds.), editors, *American Economic Growth and Standards of Living Before the Civil War* (Chicago, 1992), 19–75. Overlapping decade data for periods after 1834 used here are from Robert E. Gallman, "Gross

National Product in the United States: 1834–1909," in Dorothy S. Brady (ed.), *Output, Employment, and Productivity in the United States after 1800*, Studies in Income and Wealth, vol. 30 (New York, 1966), 3–76, and from Simon Kuznets' data underlying *Capital in the American Economy: Its Formation and Financing* (Princeton, 1961) as summarized in Lipsey, *Price and Quantity Trends*. Some alternatives to the Kuznets estimates have been provided by Nathan S. Balke and Robert J. Gordon, in "The Estimation of Prewar Gross National Product: Methodology and New Evidence," *Journal of Political Economy*, 97 (1989), 38–92, and by Christina Romer in "The Prewar Business Cycle Reconsidered: New Estimates of Gross National Product, 1869–1908," *Journal of Political Economy*, 97 (1989), 1–37. Data on numbers and ages of immigrants are summarized in *Historical Statistics*, and estimates of the inflow of resources embodied in immigration are given in Larry Neal and Paul Uselding, "Immigration, A Neglected Source of American Economic Growth: 1790–1912," *Oxford Economic Papers*, 24 (1972), 68–88.

The composition of U.S. trade by the distinction among products of the sea, the forest, agriculture, and manufacturing is given for the British North American colonies in 1770 in *Historical Statistics* and for later years in U.S. Congress, House of Representatives, *Domestic Exports, 1789–1883* (House Miscellaneous Document No. 2236, 48th Congress, 1st Session, 1883–84), compiled by C. H. Evans and referred to as the Evans Report. The same breakdown is given in various issues of the U.S. Treasury Department, *Annual Report of the Secretary of the Treasury on the State of the Finances*. Data on exports and imports by degree of processing and by some individual commodity classes are given in *Historical Statistics*, and a more detailed breakdown for periods after 1879 is provided in Appendix A of Lipsey, *Price and Quantity Trends*. The natural resource content of U.S. trade is examined in Jaroslav Vanek, *The Natural Resource Content of United States Foreign Trade, 1870–1955* (Cambridge, MA, 1963).

The industrial distribution of the American labor force was extensively analyzed by Stanley Lebergott in "Labor Force and Employment, 1800–1960," in Brady (ed.), *Output, Employment, and Productivity*, 117–204, and some alternative estimates have been offered by Paul David, in "The Growth of Real Product in the United States before 1840: New Evidence, Controlled Conjectures," *Journal of Economic History*, 27 (1967), 151–97, and by Thomas Weiss, in "U.S. Labor Force Estimates." Labor force distributions for other countries can be found in Simon Kuznets, *Modern Economic Growth: Rate, Structure, and Spread* (New Haven, 1966), and in B. R. Mitchell, *European Historical Statistics, 1750–1970*, abridged edition (New York, 1978).

Export–output ratios for U.S. industries during the nineteenth century are difficult to calculate. We have made use here of unpublished compilations by Phyllis A. Wallace, some of which were published and discussed in National Bureau of Economic Research, *Thirty Third Annual Report* (New York, 1953). For the world as a whole, compilations of trade divided between manufactures and primary products were constructed by Folke Hilgerdt in League of Nations, *Industrialization and Foreign Trade* (Geneva, 1945). Some information on the geographical distribution of exports and imports is in *Historical Statistics* and details for early years are from Pitkin, *A Statistical View*. Comparisons with European trade draw on some of the work of Paul Bairoch, particularly "European Foreign Trade" and *Commerce Extérieur et Développement Economique*.

The long-term development of the terms of trade of the United States is summarized in Lipsey, "Foreign Trade," drawing mainly on North's *Economic Growth* and Lipsey's *Price and Quantity Trends*. Productivity data for agriculture and manufacturing for years after the Civil War, including both labor productivity and total factor productivity, are discussed in Lipsey, "Foreign Trade" and *Price and Quantity Trends*, and are taken mainly from John W. Kendrick, *Productivity Trends in the United States* (Princeton, 1961) and *Postwar Productivity Trends in the United States, 1948–1969* (New York, 1973). For earlier years, sectoral productivity can be roughly estimated from output data in Robert Gallman's "Commodity Output, 1839–1899," in Parker (ed.), *Trends in the American Economy*, 13–67, and labor force and employment data in Stanley Lebergott, *Manpower in Economic Growth* (New York, 1964). A longer-term perspective on agricultural productivity is provided in Marvin W. Towne and Wayne D. Rasmussen, "Farm Gross Product and Gross Investment in the Nineteenth Century," in Parker (ed.), *Trends in the American Economy*, 255–312, and early productivity developments in manufacturing are analyzed in Kenneth Sokoloff, "Productivity in Manufacturing During Early Industrialization: Evidence from the American Northeast: 1820–1860," in Stanley L. Engerman and Robert E. Gallman (eds.), *Long-Term Factors in American Economic Growth*, Studies in Income and Wealth, vol. 51 (Chicago, 1986), 679–736.

The effects of British imperial policy on the pattern of trade in the colonial period and the long-term impact of the expansion during the Napoleonic Wars were discussed by Douglass C. North, in *Growth and*

Welfare in the American Past, 2nd ed. (Englewood Cliffs, 1974). The latter period was later analyzed in a more formal fashion by Claudia Goldin and Frank D. Lewis, "The Role of Exports in American Economic Growth during the Napoleonic Wars, 1793 to 1807," *Explorations in Economic History*, 17 (1980), 6–25. North also assessed the impact of the Civil War, a subject also commented on by Robert Gallman in the chapter on "The Pace and Pattern of American Economic Growth," in Davis, Easterlin, Parker, et al., *American Economic Growth*, 15–60.

The long-term effects of American tariff policy in general on economic growth are assessed by North and later by North, Anderson, and Hill in various editions of *Growth and Welfare*. There have also been many studies of effects on particular industries, including those of Frank W. Taussig in *The Tariff History of the United States* (New York, 1931, first published in 1888) and *Some Aspects of the Tariff Question* (Cambridge, MA, 1934, first published in 1915).

Taussig's conclusions regarding the role of tariff protection in the development of the cotton textile industry and the date at which protection became redundant were challenged in a later series of studies making use of econometric tests, formal production functions, and measures of learning-by-doing. An early and influential entry was Paul David's "Learning by Doing and Tariff Protection: A Reconsideration of the Case of the Antebellum United States Cotton Textile Industry," *Journal of Economic History*, 30 (1970), 521–601. Later examinations of the issue have included Mark Bils, "Tariff Protection and Production in the Early U.S. Cotton Textile Industry," *Journal of Economic History*, 44 (1984), 1033–1045; Peter Temin, "Product Quality and Vertical Integration in the Early Cotton Textile Industry," *Journal of Economic History*, 48 (1988), 891–907; and C. Knick Harley, "International Competitiveness of the Antebellum American Cotton Textile Industry," *Journal of Economic History*, 52 (1992), 559–84. The effects of tariffs on the American iron and steel industry have been studied by Peter Temin, in *Iron and Steel in Nineteenth-Century America* (Cambridge, MA, 1964); V. Sundararajan, "The Impact of the Tariff on Some Selected Products of the U.S. Iron and Steel Industry," *Quarterly Journal of Economics*, 74 (1970), 590–610; Bennett D. Baack and Edward John Ray, "Tariff Policy and Comparative Advantage in the Iron and Steel Industry: 1870–1929," *Explorations in Economic History*, 11 (1974), 103–21; and by Keith Head, in "Infant Industry Protection in the Steel Rail Industry," *Journal of International Economics*, 37 (1994), 141–165.

Skeptical views on the role of trade in U.S. economic growth or economic growth of countries in general were expressed by Irving B. Kravis in "Trade as a Handmaiden of Growth: Similarities Between the 19th and 20th Centuries," *Economic Journal*, 80 (1970), 850–872, and "The Role of Exports in Nineteenth-Century United States Growth," *Economic Development and Cultural Change*, 20 (1972), 387–405. Somewhat different assessments appear in Lipsey "Foreign Trade," and in Jeffrey G. Williamson, "Greasing the Wheels of Sputtering Export Engines: Midwestern Grains and American Growth," *Explorations in Economic History*, 17 (1980), 189–217. Both the Williamson paper and the one by Goldin and Lewis mentioned earlier were part of a collection of essays on "Exports and Economic Growth" edited by Richard E. Caves, Douglass C. North, and Jacob M. Price and published in *Explorations in Economic History*. The issue of effects of trade on growth was also explored by Richard Cooper in "Growth and Trade: Some Hypotheses About Long-Term Trends," *Journal of Economic History*, 24 (1964), 609–28.

CHAPTER 16 (DAVIS AND CULL)

Adler, Dorothy. *British Investment in American Railways, 1834–1898*. Charlottesville, 1970.

Aitken, Hugh G. J. *American Capital and Canadian Resources*. Cambridge, MA, 1961.

Allen, Frederick Lewis. *The Great Pierpont Morgan*. New York, 1949.

Ashmead, Edward. *Twenty-five Years of Mining, 1880–1904*. London, 1909.

Bacon, Nathaniel T. "American International Indebtedness." *Yale Review*, 9 (1900).

Bain, H. Foster, and Thornton, Read Thomas. *Ores and Industry in South America*. New York, 1934.

Baskerville, Peter. "Americans in Britain's Backyard: The Railway Era in Upper Canada, 1850–1880." *Business History Review*, 55 (1981).

Baskin, Jonathan Barron. "The Development of Corporate Financial Markets in Britain and the United States, 1600–1914: Overcoming Asymmetric Information." *Business History Review*, 62 (1988).

Blodget, Samuel. *Economica: A Statistical Manual for the United States of America*. New York, 1964, first published, 1806.

Bodenhorn, Howard and Rockoff, Hugh. "Regional Interest Rates in

Antebellum America." In Claudia Goldin and Hugh Rockoff (eds.), *Strategic Factors in Nineteenth-Century American Economic History: A Volume to Honor Robert W. Fogel*, Chicago, 1992.

Bogart, E. L. *The Economic History of the United States*, 2nd ed. New York, 1913.

Buckley, Peter J., and Roberts, Brian R. *European Direct Investment in the USA before World War I*. New York, 1982.

Bullock, Charles L., Williams, John H., and Tucker, Rufus S. "The Balance of Trade of the United States." *Review of Economic Statistics*, 1 (1919).

Cairncross, Alexander. *Home and Foreign Investment 1870–1910*. Cambridge, 1953.

Chandler, Alfred D. "The Growth of the Transnational Industrial Firm in the United States and the United Kingdom: A Comparative Analysis." *Economic History Review*, second series, 33 (1980).

The Railroads: The Nation's First Big Business. New York, 1965.

Clark, William, and Turner, Charlie. "International Trade and the Evolution of the American Capital Market, 1888–1911." *Journal of Economic History*, 65 (1985).

Clements, Roger V. "British Controlled Enterprise in the West Between 1870 and 1890, and Some Agrarian Response," *Agricultural History*, 27 (1955).

"British Investment and American Legislative Restrictions in the Trans-Mississippi West, 1880–1900." *Mississippi Valley Historical Review*, 42 (1955).

"The Farmers' Attitude Toward British Investment in American Industry." *Journal of Economic History*, 15 (1955).

Cleveland, Frederick A., and Powell, Fred W. *Railroad Promotion and Capitalization in the United States*. New York, 1909.

Cockcroft, James D. *Mexico: Class Formation, Capital Accumulation, and the State*. New York, 1983.

Craig, Lee A., and Fisher, Douglas. "Integration of the European Business Cycle: 1871–1910." *Explorations in Economic History*, 29 (1992).

Crapol, Edward P. *America for Americans: Economic Nationalism and Anglophobia in the Late Nineteenth Century*. Westport, CT, 1973.

Cull, Robert J. "A Comparative Study of Capital Market Failure and Institutional Innovation." Ph.D. dissertation, California Institute of Technology, 1992.

Cull, Robert J., and Davis, Lance E. "Un, Deux, Trois, Quatre Marchés?

L'Intégration du Marché du Étas-Unis et Grande-Bretagne, 1865–1913." *Annales: Économies Sociétiés Civilisations*, 47 (1992).

Curle, John Herbert. *Gold Mines of the World*. London, 1896.

Davis, Clarence B. "Financing Imperialism: British and American Bankers as Vectors of Imperial Expansion in China, 1908–1920." *Business History Review*, 56 (1982).

Davis, Lance E. "The Capital Markets and Industrial Concentration: The U.S. and U.K., A Comparative Study." *Economic History Review*, Second Series, 19 (1966).

"Capital Immobilities and Finance Capitalism: A Study of Economic Evolution in the United States, 1820–1920." *Explorations in Entrepreneurial History*, Second Series, 1 (1963).

"The Investment Market, 1870–1914: The Evolution of a National Market." *Journal of Economic History*, 25 (1965).

Davis, Lance E., and Gallman, Robert E. "Savings, Investment, and Economic Growth: The United States in the Nineteenth Century." In John James and Mark Thomas (eds.), *Capitalism in Context*. Chicago, 1993.

Davis, Lance E., and Huttenback, Robert. *Mammon and the Pursuit of Empire: The Political Economy of British Imperialism, 1860–1912*. Cambridge, 1986.

DeLong, Bradford. "Did J. P. Morgan's Men Add Value? A Historical Perspective on Financial Capitalism." In Peter Temin (ed.), *Inside the Business Enterprise: Historical Perspectives on the Use of Information*. Chicago, 1991.

Dickens, Paul D. "The Transitional Period in American International Financing: 1897–1914." Ph.D. dissertation, George Washington University, 1933.

Dunning, John H. *Studies in International Investment*. London, 1970.

"British Investment in U.S. Industry." In *Moorgate and Wall Street*, Autumn (1961).

American Investment in British Manufacturing. London, 1958.

Edelstein, Michael. *Overseas Investment in the Age of High Imperialism: The United Kingdom, 1850–1914*. New York, 1982.

Edwards, G. *The Evolution of Finance Capitalism*. New York, 1908.

Evans, Paul D. *The Holland Land Company*. Buffalo, 1924.

Faulkner, Harold U. *The Decline of Laissez Faire, 1897–1917*. New York, 1951.

Feinstein, Charles. "Britain's Overseas Investments in 1913." *Economic History Review*, 2nd Series, 43 (1990).

Feis, Herbert. *Europe the World's Banker, 1870–1914: An Account of European Foreign Investment and the Connection of World Finance with Diplomacy before 1914.* New Haven, 1930.

Field, Fred W. *Capital Investment in Canada: Some Facts and Figures Respecting One of the Most Attractive Investment Fields in the World.* Montreal, 1914.

French, M. J. "The Emergence of a U.S. Multinational Enterprise: The Goodyear Tire and Rubber Company, 1910–1939." *Economic History Review,* 2nd series, 40 (1987).

Gallman, Robert E. "The United States Capital Stock in the Nineteenth Century." In Stanley Engerman and Robert Gallman (eds.), *Long-Term Factors in American Economic Growth.* Studies in Income and Wealth. vol. 51, Princeton, 1986.

Gates, Paul W. *The Illinois Central and Its Colonization Work.* Cambridge, MA, 1934.

Gerschenkron, Alexander. *Economic Backwardness in Historical Perspective.* Cambridge, MA, 1962.

Goldsmith, Raymond W. *A Study of Savings in the United States.* 3 vols. Princeton, 1955.
"The Growth of Reproducible Wealth of the United States of America." In Simon Kuznets (ed.), *Income and Wealth of the United States: Trends and Structures,* International Association for Research in Income and Wealth, Series II. Cambridge, 1952.

Hall, A. R. "A Note on the English Capital Market as a Source of Funds for Home Investment Before 1914." *Economica,* 24 (1957).

Hammond, John Winthrop. *Men and Volts, The Story of General Electric.* New York, 1941.

Hansen, Roger D. *The Politics of Mexican Development.* Baltimore, 1971.

Haven, Charles T., and Belden, Frank A. *A History of the Colt Revolver and Other Arms Made by Colt's Patent Fire Arms Manufacturing Company from 1836–1940.* New York, 1940.

Healy, Kent T. "Transportation." In Harold F. Williamson (ed.), *The Growth of the American Economy.* New York, 1951.

Hidy, Ralph W., and Hidy, Muriel E. *History of the Standard Oil Company (New Jersey), Pioneering in Big Business, 1882–1911.* New York, 1955.

Hill, Howard C. *Roosevelt and the Caribbean.* Chicago, 1927.

Hobson, C. K. *The Export of Capital.* New York, 1914.

Hughlett, Lloyd J. *Industrialization in Latin America.* New York, 1946.

Imlah, A. H. *Economic Elements of the Pax Britannica.* Cambridge, MA, 1958.

Jackson, W. Turrentine. *The Enterprising Scot: Investors in the American West after 1873*. Edinburgh, 1968.

James, John. "The Development of the National Money Market, 1893–1911." *Journal of Economic History*, 36 (1976).

James, Marquis. *The Texaco Story, the First Fifty Years*. Houston, 1953.

Jenks, Leland H. *The Migration of British Capital to 1875*. London, 1963. *Our Cuban Colony: A Study of Sugar*. New York, 1928.

Johnson, Arthur M., and Supple, Barry E. *Boston Capitalists and Western Railroads*. Cambridge, MA, 1967.

Joralemon, Ira B. *Romantic Copper, Its Lure and Lore*. New York, 1936.

Kennedy, William P. *Industrial Structure, Capital Markets, and the Origin of British Economic Decline*. Cambridge, 1987.

Kepner, Charles David, and Jay, Henry Soothill. *The Banana Empire: A Case Study of Economic Imperialism*. New York, 1935.

Knight, Melvin M. *The Americans in Santo Domingo*. New York, 1928.

Kuhlman, Charles B. *Development of the Flour Mill Industry in the United States*. Boston, 1929.

Kuznets, Simon. "Foreign Economic Relations of the United States and their Impact upon the Domestic Economy: A Review of Long Term Trends." In *Proceedings of the American Philosophical Society*, 92 (1948).

Lamoreaux, Naomi. *Insider Lending: Banks, Personal Connections, and Economic Development in Industrial New England*. New York, 1994. "Banks, Kinship, and Economic Development: The New England Case." *Journal of Economic History*, 46 (1986).

Lebergott, Stanley. "The Returns to U.S. Imperialism, 1890–1929." *Journal of Economic History*, 40 (1980).

Lewis, Cleona (assisted by Karl T. Schottenbeck). *America's Stake in International Investment*. Washington, DC, 1938.

Levitt, Kari. *Silent Surrender: The American Economic Empire in Canada*. New York, 1970.

Livermore, Shaw. *Early American Land Companies*. New York, 1939.

Madden, John J. *British Investment in the United States, 1860–1880*. (New York: 1985); Ph.D. dissertation, University of Cambridge, 1958.

Malloy, William M. (ed.). *Treaties, Conventions, International Acts, Protocols and Agreements between the United States and Other Powers*. Washington, DC, 4 vols., 1910–1938.

Marcosson, Isaac. *Metal Magic, The Story of the American Smelting and Refining Company*. New York, 1949.

Marsh, Margaret A. *The Bankers in Bolivia: A Study of American Foreign Investment*. New York, 1928.

Marshall, Herbert, Southard, Frank A., and Taylor, Kenneth W. *Canadian-American Industry, A Study in International Investment*. New Haven, 1936.

Martin, Joseph G. *A Century of Finance, Martin's History of the Boston Stock and Money Markets*. Boston, 1898.

May, Stacy, and Plaza, Galo. *The United Fruit Company in Latin America*. Seventh Case Study in a National Planning Association series on United States Business Performance Abroad, Washington, DC, 1958.

McFarlane, Larry A. "British Investment and the Land: Nebraska 1877–1946." *Business History Review*, 57 (1983).

"British Agricultural Investment in the Dakotas, 1877–1953." *Business and Economic History*, 5 (1976).

"British Investment in Midwestern Farm Mortgages and Land, 1875–1900, A Comparison of Iowa and Kansas." *Agricultural History*, 48 (1974).

"British Investment in Minnesota Farm Mortgages and Land, 1875–1900." Mimeographed.

McGrane, Reginald C. *Foreign Bondholders and American State Debts*. New York, 1935.

Michie, Ranald C. *The London and New York Stock Exchanges, 1850–1914*. London, 1987.

Moody, John. *The Truth About the Trusts*. New York, 1904.

Moore, E. S. *American Influences on Canadian Mining*. Toronto, 1941.

Morgan, Victor E. and Thomas, W. A. *The Stock Exchange: Its History and Functions*. London, 1962.

Navin, T. and Sears, M. "The Rise of a Market for Industrial Securities." *Business History Review*, 29 (1955).

Neal, Larry. "The Disintegration and Reintegration of International Capital Markets in the 19th Century." Mimeographed, 1992.

Neal, Larry, and Uselding, Paul. "Immigration, a Neglected Source of American Economic Growth: 1790 to 1912." *Oxford Economic Papers*, 24 (1972).

Nearing, Scott, and Freeman, Joseph. *Dollar Diplomacy*. New York, 1925.

North, Douglass C. "The Balance of Payments of the United States, 1790–1860." In William N. Parker (ed.), *Trends in the American Economy in the Nineteenth Century*, Studies in Income and Wealth, vol. 24. Princeton, 1960.

Norrie, K. H. "Tariffs and the Distribution of Prairie Incomes." *Canadian Journal of Economics*, 7 (1974).

O'Brien, Thomas E. "Rich Boy and the Dreams of Avarice: The Guggenheims in Chile." *Business History Review*, 63 (1989).

O'Connor, Henry. *The Guggenheims: The Making of an American Dynasty*. New York, 1976.

Odell, Kerry A. "The Integration of Regional and Interregional Capital Markets: Evidence from the Pacific Coast, 1883–1913." *Journal of Economic History*, 49 (1989).

Paish, George. "The Export of Capital and the Cost of Living," *Statist Supplement*, 79 (1914).

"Great Britain's Capital Investments in Individual, Colonial and Foreign Countries." *Journal of the Royal Statistical Society*, 74 (1911).

"Trade Balances of the United States." U.S. Senate, *National Monetary Commission*, 61st Cong., 2nd sess., 1910, Senate Document 579.

"Our New Investments in 1908," *Statist*, 63 (1909).

"Great Britain's Capital Investment in Other Lands." *Journal of the Royal Statistical Society*, 72 (1909).

Platt, D. C. M. *Foreign Finance in Continental Europe and the United States 1815–1870: Quantities, Origins, Functions and Distributions*. London, 1984.

"British Portfolio Investment Overseas Before 1870: Some Doubts," *Economic History Review*. 2nd Series, 33 (1980).

Pletcher, David M. *Rails, Mines, and Progress: Seven American Promoters in Mexico, 1867–1911*. Ithaca, 1958.

Postan, M. M. "Some Recent Problems in the Accumulation of Capital." *Economic History Review*, 6 (1935).

Powell, Fred Wilbur. *The Railroads of Mexico*. Boston, 1912.

Pratt, Sereno S. *The Work of Wall Street*. New York, 1903.

Proust, Henry G. *A Life of George Westinghouse*. New York, 1921.

Ratchford, B. U. *American State Debts*. Durham, 1941.

Remer, Carl F. *American Investments in China*. Honolulu, 1929.

Reynolds, Clark W. *The Mexican Economy: Twentieth Century Structure and Growth*. New Haven, 1970.

Riegel, Robert E. *The Story of the Western Railroads*. Lincoln, NE, 1926.

Ripley, William Z. *Railroads: Finance and Organization*. New York, 1915.

Rippy, J. Fred. *British Investments in Latin America, 1822–1949: A Case*

Study of the Operations of Private Enterprise in Retarded Regions. Minneapolis, 1959.

The United States and Mexico. New York, 1931.

Sakolski, A. M. *The Great American Land Bubble.* New York, 1932.

Schell, William Jr. "American Investment in Tropical Mexico: Rubber Plantations, Fraud, and Dollar Diplomacy, 1897–1913." *Business History Review,* 64 (1990).

Schmitz, Christopher. "The Rise of Big Business in the World Copper Industry 1870–1930." *Economic History Review,* 2nd series, 39 (1986).

Segal, Harvey H. and Simon, Matthew. "British Foreign Capital Issues, 1865–1914." *Journal of Economic History,* 21 (1961).

Simon, Matthew. "The Balance of Payments of the United States, 1861–1900." In William N. Parker (ed.), *Trends in the American Economy in the Nineteenth Century,* Studies in Income and Wealth, vol. 24. Princeton, 1960.

Smith, Robert F. "The United States and Cuba." In Marvin Bernstein (ed.), *Foreign Investment in Latin America: Cases and Attitudes.* New York, 1966.

Snowden, Kenneth A. "Mortgage Rates and American Capital Market Development in the Nineteenth Century." *Journal of Economic History,* 47 (1987).

Solberg, Carl H. *The Prairies and the Pampas: Agrarian Policy in Canada and Argentina, 1880–1930.* Stanford, 1987.

Southard, Frank A., Jr. *American Industry in Europe: Origins and Development of the Multinational Corporation.* Boston, 1931.

"American Industry in Europe." Ph.D dissertation, Univ. of California, Berkeley, 1930.

Southworth, Constance. "The American-Canadian Newsprint Paper Industry and the Tariff." *Journal of Political Economy,* 30 (1922).

Southworth, John R. *El Directo Oficial Minero de Mexico.* Vol. 11, Mexico D. F., 1910.

Southworth, John R., and Homs, Percy C. *El Directo Oficial Minero de Mexico.* Vol. 9, Mexico D. F., 1908.

Spence, Clark C. "British Investment and the American Mining Frontier, 1860–1914." *New Mexico Historical Review,* 36 (1961).

British Investment and the American Mining Frontier, 1860–1901. Ithaca, 1958.

Stedman, Edmund C. *The New York Stock Exchange: Its History, its Contribution to National Prosperity, and its Relation to American Finance at the Outset of the Twentieth Century*. New York, 1969; copyright 1905.

Sylla, Richard. "Federal Policy, Banking Market Structure, and Capital Mobilization in the United States, 1863–1913." *Journal of Economic History*, 29 (1969).

Thompson, Robert Luther. *Wiring a Continent: The History of the Telegraph in the United States, 1832–1866*. Princeton, 1947.

Tilly, Richard. "International Aspects of the Development of German Banking," In Rondo Cameron and V. I. Bovykin (eds.), *International Banking, 1870–1914* (New York, 1991).
"Some Comments on German Foreign Portfolio Investment, 1870–1914." Paper delivered in São Paolo, 1989.

Urquhart, M. C. "Canadian Economic Growth 1870–1980." Queens University, Department of Economics, Discussion Paper 734, 1988.

Urquhart, M. C. (ed.). *Historical Statistics of Canada*. Cambridge, 1965.

U.S., Census Office. *Report on Valuation, Taxation, and Public Indebtedness of the United States Tenth Census*. Washington, DC, 1884.

U.S., Congress. House, 27th Cong., 3rd sess., 1843, H. Document 296.

U.S., Congress. Senate, 33rd Cong., I sess., Secretary of the Treasury report to the United States Senate, Executive Document 42, March 2, 1854.

U.S., Congress. Senate, 50th Cong., 2nd sess., 1889, S. Document 2690.2.

U.S., Congress. Senate, 61st Cong., 2nd sess., 1910, S. Document 579.

U.S., Bureau of the Census. *Historical Statistics of the United States, Colonial Times to 1970*, 2 volumes, Washington, DC, 1975.

U.S., Bureau of the Census. *Statistical Abstract of the United States, 1990*. Washington, DC, 1990.

U.S., Department of Labor. *News*. Washington, DC, 1989.

U.S. Government, Select Committee on an Inquiry into the Occupation and Administration of Haiti and Santo Domingo, *Hearings*, 67th Cong., 1st and 2nd sessions, 2 vols. Washington, DC, 1922.

Van Oss, Salomon F. *Railroads as Investments*. New York, 1977.

Vasquez, Josefina Zaraida, and Meyer, Lorenzo. *The United States and Mexico*. Chicago, 1985.

Veenendaal, Augustus J. Jr. "The Kansas City Southern Railway and the Dutch Connection," *Business History Review*, 61 (1987).

Viner, Jacob. *Canada's Balance of International Indebtedness, 1900–1913*. Cambridge, MA, 1924.

Wells, David A. *Report of the Special Commissioner of Revenue, 1869.* 41st Congress, House of Representative, Executive Document 27, 1869.
  A Study of Mexico. New York, 1887.

Wilkins, Mira. *The History of Foreign Investment in the United States to 1914.* Cambridge, MA, 1989.
  "The Free-Standing Company, 1870–1914: An Important Type of British Foreign Direct Investment." *Economic History Review*, 2nd Series, 41 (1988).
  The Emergence of Multinational Enterprise: American Business Abroad from the Colonial Era to 1914. Cambridge, MA, 1970.

Williams, Benjamin. *Economic Foreign Policy of the United States.* New York, 1929.

Williams, Gattenby [William Guggenheim], and Heath, Charles Monroe. *William Guggenheim.* New York, 1934.

Williamson, Harold F., and Daum, Arnold R. *The American Petroleum Industry: The Age of Illumination.* Evanston, 1955.

Williamson, Jeffrey G. *American Growth and the Balance of Payments, 1820–1913: A Study of the Long Swing.* Chapel Hill, 1964.

Wilson, Charles Morrow. *Empire in Gold and Green: The Story of the American Banana Trade.* New York, 1947.

Wyckoff, Peter. *Wall Street and the Stock Markets: A Chronology (1644–1971).* Philadelphia, 1982.

Young, Ralph A. *Handbook of American Underwriting of Foreign Securities.* U.S. Department of Commerce, Trade Promotion Series # 104, 1930.

Zevin, Robert B. "Are World Financial Markets More Open? If So Why and With What Effects." In Tariq Banuri and Juliet B. Schor (eds.), *Financial Openness and National Autonomy.* New York, 1992.

CHAPTER 17 (BLUMIN)

The broad scope of this chapter precludes a listing of all major works, but I have tried to identify a sufficient number of representative texts through which the reader can explore each area of American society and culture I have discussed. Prior to these, however, I would mention several general social histories that focus on or include the "long nineteenth century," each written from a point of view that is well worth engaging, James A. Henretta, *The Evolution of American Society, 1700–1815: An Interdisciplinary Analysis* (Lexington, MA, 1973), and an updated and expanded version with Gregory H. Nobles entitled *Evolution and Revolution: American Society, 1600–1820* (Lexington, MA, 1987), include syntheses of the early national period. Robert H. Wiebe, *The Opening of American Society: From the Adoption of the Constitution to the Eve of Disunion* (New York, 1984), carries the story of American expansion and development through the antebellum era and can be compared to Charles Sellers, *The Market Revolution: Jacksonian America, 1815–1846* (New York, 1991). Wiebe's *The Search for Order, 1877–1920* (New York, 1967) is a notable interpretation of the post-Reconstruction era.

Many different kinds of studies inform what I have called "the social geography of productive and market relations." The continuing European settlement of America in the era immediately preceding the one I have examined is thoroughly analyzed in Bernard Bailyn, *Voyagers to the West: A Passage in the Peopling of America on the Eve of the Revolution* (New York, 1986), while the more general geographic development of the American continent can be examined in the three remarkable volumes of D. W. Meinig, *The Shaping of America: A Geographic Perspective on 500 Years of History* (New Haven, 1986, 1993, 1998). The standard study of general patterns of urbanization is still Adna Ferrin Weber, *The Growth of Cities in the Nineteenth Century: A Study in Statistics* (New York, 1899), but a rather more recent and quite adequate survey is Blake McKelvey, *American Urbanization: A Comparative History* (Glenview, IL, 1973). A good survey of frontier history is Richard A. Bartlett, *The New Country: A Social History of the American Frontier, 1776–1890* (New York, 1974). These overviews should be supplemented by fleshed-out studies of individual regions and communities. Among the many fine local studies, rural and urban, are: Richard R. Beeman, *The Evolution of the Southern Backcountry: A Case Study of Lunenburg County, Virginia, 1746–1832* (Philadelphia, 1984); John L. Brooke, *The Heart of the Commonwealth: Society and Political Culture in Worcester County, Massachusetts, 1713–1861* (Cambridge, 1989); Robert A. Gross, *The Minutemen and Their World* (New York, 1976); Joan M. Jensen, *Loosening the Bonds: Mid-Atlantic Farm Women, 1750–1850* (New Haven, 1986); John Mack Faragher, *Sugar Creek: Life on the Illinois Prairie* (New Haven, 1986); Don Harrison Doyle, *The Social Order of a Frontier Community: Jacksonville, Illinois, 1825–70* (Urbana, 1978); Timothy R. Mahoney, *River Towns in the Great West: The Structure of Provincial Urbanization in the American Midwest, 1820–1870* (Cambridge, 1990); Robert R. Dykstra, *The Cattle Towns* (New York, 1968); Gunther Barth, *Instant Cities: Urbaniza-*

tion and the Rise of San Francisco and Denver (New York, 1975); and William Cronon, *Nature's Metropolis: Chicago and the Great West* (New York, 1991). Essential texts for the examination of extralocal exchange are Richard D. Brown, *Knowledge Is Power: The Diffusion of Information in Early America, 1700–1865* (New York, 1989) and two books by Allen R. Pred, *Urban Growth and the Circulation of Information: The United States System of Cities, 1790–1840* (Cambridge, MA, 1973) and *Urban Growth and City-System Development in the United States, 1840–1860* (Cambridge, MA, 1980). Exchange involved institutional development in politics and in other areas of American life. I will mention only four items to represent a vast historical literature tracing various aspects of institutional development in nineteenth-century America: Joel H. Silbey, *The American Political Nation, 1838–1893* (Stanford, 1991); Peter Dobkin Hall, *The Organization of American Culture, 1700–1900: Private Institutions, Elites, and the Origins of American Nationality* (New York, 1982); Lawrence A. Cremin, *American Education: The National Experience, 1783–1876* (New York, 1980); and Ian R. Tyrrell, *Sobering Up: From Temperance to Prohibition in Antebellum America, 1800–1860* (Westport, CT, 1979).

Class and class formation are most often examined by focusing upon a specific social stratum in a specific local context. Two recent texts make more general statements about American society and about changing social relations in the eighteenth and nineteenth centuries in quite powerful (and quite different) ways: Richard L. Bushman, *The Refinement of America: Persons, Houses, Cities* (New York, 1992); and Gordon S. Wood, *The Radicalism of the American Revolution* (New York, 1992). The majority of more specific studies focus on the nineteenth-century working class, and often on the workers of a single community (and sometimes a single industry). Among them are Sean Wilentz, *Chants Democratic: New York City and the Rise of the American Working Class, 1788–1850* (New York, 1984); Paul Faler, *Mechanics and Manufacturers in the Early Industrial Revolution: Lynn, Massachusetts, 1780–1860* (Albany, 1981); Mary H. Blewett, *Men, Women, and Work: Class, Gender, and Protest in the New England Shoe Industry, 1780–1910* (Urbana, 1988); Richard B. Stott, *Workers in the Metropolis: Class, Ethnicity, and Youth in Antebellum New York City* (Ithaca, 1990); Steven J. Ross, *Workers on the Edge: Work, Leisure, and Politics in Industrializing Cincinnati, 1788–1890* (New York, 1985); Roy Rosenzweig, *Eight Hours for What We Will: Workers and Leisure in an Industrial City, 1870–1920* (Cambridge, 1983); and Francis G. Couvares, *The Remaking of*

Pittsburgh: Class and Culture in an Industrializing City, 1877–1919 (Albany, 1984). Bruce Laurie, *Artisans into Workers: Labor in Nineteenth-Century America* (New York, 1989) synthesizes these and many other studies of this type. Studies of the middle class are fewer and form a less settled genre. They include: Stuart M. Blumin, *The Emergence of the Middle Class: Social Experience in the American City, 1760–1900* (Cambridge, 1989); Mary P. Ryan, *Cradle of the Middle Class: The Family in Oneida County, New York, 1790–1865* (Cambridge, 1981); Burton J. Bledstein, *The Culture of Professionalism: The Middle Class and the Development of Higher Education in America* (New York, 1976); Karen Halttunen, *Confidence Men and Painted Women: A Study of Middle-Class Culture in America, 1830–1870* (New Haven, 1982); and John S. Gilkeson, Jr., *Middle-Class Providence, 1820–1940* (Princeton, 1986). The most comprehensive study of upper-class America is Frederic Cople Jaher, *The Urban Establishment: Upper Strata in Boston, New York, Charleston, Chicago, and Los Angeles* (Urbana, 1982). Other useful studies include E. Digby Baltzell, *Philadelphia Gentlemen: The Making of a National Upper Class* (New York, 1958); Edward Pessen, *Riches, Class, and Power Before the Civil War* (Lexington, MA, 1973); and Ronald Story, *The Forging of an Aristocracy: Harvard and the Boston Upper Class, 1800–1870* (Middletown, 1980).

There are many thematic studies of American values relating to work, ambition, and material well-being, and to capitalism as a system in which these things are carried out in daily life. Work and success are explored as cultural themes in Daniel T. Rodgers, *The Work Ethic in Industrial America, 1850–1920* (Chicago, 1978) and Rex Burns, *Success in America: The Yeoman Dream and the Industrial Revolution* (Amherst, 1976). Cultural meanings of consumption and material abundance are examined in David E. Shi, *The Simple Life: Plain Living and High Thinking in American Culture* (New York, 1985) and Daniel Horowitz, *The Morality of Spending: Attitudes Toward the Consumer Society in America, 1875–1940* (Baltimore, 1985). These issues and others are seen as problems of capitalist development in Ann Douglas, *The Feminization of American Culture* (New York, 1977); T. J. Jackson Lears, *No Place of Grace: Antimodernism and the Transformation of American Culture, 1880–1920* (New York, 1981); and Christopher Lasch, *The True and Only Heaven: Progress and Its Critics* (New York, 1991). And again there are local studies, examining the local and extralocal market relations of specific populations and the social and cultural responses to the "coming of capitalism" to American communities. The ones through which the liveliest debates are carried out focus upon rural America. They include:

Winifred Barr Rothenberg, *From Market-Places to a Market Economy: The Transformation of Rural Massachusetts, 1750–1850* (Chicago, 1992); Christopher Clark, *The Roots of Rural Capitalism: Western Massachusetts, 1780–1860* (Ithaca, 1990); Wilma A. Dunaway, *The First American Frontier: Transition to Capitalism in Southern Appalachia, 1700–1860* (Chapel Hill, 1996); Allan Kulikoff, *The Agrarian Origins of American Capitalism* (Charlottesville, 1992); and Steven Hahn, *The Roots of Southern Populism: Yeomen Farmers and the Transformation of the Georgia Upcountry, 1850–1890* (New York, 1983).

INDEX